The SAGE
Handbook of
Film Studies

International Editorial Board

The SAGE
Handbook of
Film Studies

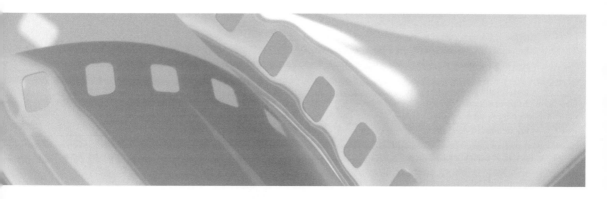

Edited by
James Donald and
Michael Renov

Los Angeles • London • New Delhi • Singapore

SAGE Publications Ltd
1 Oliver's Yard
55 City Road
London EC1Y 1SP

SAGE Publications Inc.
2455 Teller Road
Thousand Oaks, California 91320

SAGE Publications India Pvt Ltd
B 1/I 1 Mohan Cooperative Industrial Area
Mathura Road
New Delhi 110 044

SAGE Publications Asia-Pacific Pte Ltd
33 Pekin Street #02-01
Far East Square
Singapore 048763

Library of Congress Control Number: 2007933315

British Library Cataloguing in Publication data

A catalogue record for this book is available from
the British Library

ISBN 978-0-7619-4326-6

Typeset by CEPHA Imaging Pvt. Ltd., Bangalore, India
Printed in Great Britain by The Cromwell Press Ltd., Trowbridge, Wiltshire
Printed on paper from sustainable resources

Contents

Notes on Contributors

Ian Aitken is Associate Professor in Film Studies at Hong Kong Baptist University and Senior Research Fellow at De Montfort University. He is the author of *Film and Reform* (Routledge, 1990), *The Documentary Film Movement: An Anthology* (Edinburgh University Press, 1998), *Alberto Cavalcanti* (Flicks Books, 2001), *European Film Theory and Cinema* (Edinburgh University Press, 2001), and *Realist Film Theory and Cinema* (Manchester University Press, 2006), and editor of *The Encyclopedia of the Documentary Film* (Routledge, 2006).

Philip Brophy is a filmmaker, sound designer, composer, performer, and writer. His published books include *100 Modern Soundtracks* (2004) and *100 Anime* (2005) for the British Film Institute, London. He instigated the Cinesonic International Conference on Film Scores and Sound Design (1998–2001), and has edited three volumes from the conferences, published by the Australian Film Television and Radio School (AFTRS), Sydney. He currently writes occasionally on film sound/music for the journals *The Wire* (London) and *Film Comment* (New York), and manages his own website: http://www.philipbrophy.com.

Warren Buckland, Senior Lecturer in Film Studies at Oxford University. He is the author of six books: *The Film Spectator* (ed., Amsterdam University Press, 1995); *The Cognitive Semiotics of Film* (Cambridge University Press, 2000); *Studying Contemporary American Film* (with Thomas Elsaesser, Arnold, 2002); *Film Studies* (McGraw-Hill, 2003); *Directed by Steven Spielberg* (Continuum, 2006); and *Puzzle Films: Complex Storytelling in Contemporary Cinema* (ed., Blackwell, 2008). He also edits the *New Review of Film and Television Studies*. He has been a British Academy Post-Doctoral Fellow and has received funding from the Leverhulme Trust.

Alison Butler teaches Film Studies in the Department of Film, Theatre and Television at the University of Reading, UK. She is the author of *Women's Cinema: The Contested Screen* (Wallflower, 2002). She has published essays on women's cinema, feminist Film Studies and experimental film in books and journals including *Camera Obscura* and *Screen*. She is a member of the Editorial Advisory Board of *Screen*.

John Caughie is Professor of Film and Television Studies at the University of Glasgow. His publications include *Theories of Authorship* (Routledge and Kegan Paul/BFI), which he edited in 1982, and *British Television Drama: Realism, Modernism and British Culture* (Oxford University Press, 2001). He is an editor of *Screen*, and was co-editor with Charlotte Brunsdon of the series, *Oxford Television Studies*.

Angela Dalle Vacche is Associate Professor of Film Studies at the Georgia Institute of Technology in Atlanta and the founding director of Italian Film Studies (IFS), a summer documentary filmmaking school with the University of Udine-Gorizia. She is the author of

The Body in the Mirror: Shapes of History in Italian Cinema (Princeton University Press, 1992); *Cinema and Painting: How Art History is Used in Film* (University of Texas Press, 1996); *The Visual Turn: Classical Film Theory and Art History* (Rutgers University Press, 2002); *Color: The Film Reader* (Routledge, 2006) and *Diva: Early Cinema, Stardom, Italian Women 1900–1922* (University of Texas Press, 2008).

James Donald is Professor of Film Studies and Dean of the Faculty of Arts and Social Sciences at the University of New South Wales, Australia, having worked previously at the Open University, Sussex University and Curtin University of Technology, Western Australia. He edited *Screen Education* in the late 1970s and was founding editor of *New Formations*. He is the author of *Imagining the Modern City* (Athlone Press/University of Minnesota Press, 1999) and *Sentimental Education: Schooling, Popular Culture and the Regulation of Liberty* (Verso, 1992), co-author of *The Penguin Atlas of Media and Information* (Penguin, 2001), and editor of a dozen volumes including *Fantasy and the Cinema* (BFI Publishing, 1989), *Psychoanalysis and Cultural Theory: Thresholds* (Macmillan, 1991), and *Close Up, 1927–1933: Cinema and Modernism* (Cassell, 1998). His main research at present looks at the impact of Josephine Baker and Paul Robeson on inter-war European culture.

Hamish Ford is a Sydney-based film scholar. In addition to the Film Studies-Continental European philosophy nexus, his areas of research and teaching specialization include the formal, conceptual, and aesthetic relationship of film to time and negativity; European modernist cinema (in particular Antonioni, Resnais, and Bergman); German, French, and Italian cinema; contemporary Iranian (notably Abbas Kiarostami), East Asian, and Australian cinema; and documentary. He is a regular contributor to *Senses of Cinema* and *RealTime*.

Patrick Fuery is Professor of Media and Cultural Studies at the University of Newcastle, Australia. He has previously held Chairs at the University of Sussex and University of East London. He is the author of eight books, including most recently *Madness and Cinema: Psychoanalysis, Spectatorship and Culture* (Palgrave Macmillan, 2003). His forthcoming book is on the ethics of the sublime.

Jane Gaines is Professor of Literature and English at Duke University where she founded the Program in Film/Video/Digital. She is the author of two award-winning books, *Contested Culture: The Image, the Voice, and the Law* (University of North Carolina Press, 1991) and *Fire and Desire: Mixed Race Movies in the Silent Era* (University of Chicago Press, 2001). She now directs the Perspectives on Marxism and Society Program at Duke and is working on a book on women in the international film industry in the silent era.

Faye Ginsburg is Director of the Center for Media, Culture and History at New York University, where she is also the David B. Kriser Professor of Anthropology, and the Co-Director of the Center for Religion and Media. Her films and books have focused on cultural activism, from her multiple-award-winning book, *Contested Lives: The Abortion Debate in an American Community* (University of California Press, 1995), to her edited collection (with Lila AbuLughod and Brian Larkin), *Media Worlds: Anthropology on New Terrain* (University of California Press, 2002). Recipient of many awards and grants, including Guggenheim and MacArthur awards, she is currently completing a book entitled *Mediating Culture: Indigenous Identity in the Digital Age*.

Jostein Gripsrud is Professor of Media Studies and Head of the Department of Information Science and Media Studies at the University of Bergen. He has published extensively in several languages on theatre, popular literature, film history, television, journalism, popular music, media and cultural policy, and relevant social and cultural theory for all of these media, genres and cultural forms. He has also been involved in cultural policy work (for UNESCO) and was active in the media policy field (1996–9) as Chair of the government-appointed but independent Public Service Broadcasting Council. He has had a regular column in a national daily newspaper since 1998 and wrote, hosted, and partly produced a six-part TV series on *Cultural Disorder* which ran in prime time on both the national public service (NRK) channels in the spring of 2003.

Carlos A. Gutiérrez is co-founding director of Cinema Tropical, a non-profit media arts organization dedicated to the distribution, programming, and promotion of Latin American cinema in the United States. Created in 2001, Cinema Tropical has become one of the leading purveyors of Latin American films in the US. He has been a guest lecturer at various universities throughout the country and serves as a contributing editor to *BOMB Magazine*.

Stephanie Hemelryk Donald is Professor of International Studies in the Centre for Research in Social and Cultural Change in China at the University of Technology, Sydney. Her books include *Public Secrets Public Spaces: Cinema and Civility in China* (Rowman and Littlefield, 2000); *Little Friends: Children's Film Culture in China* (Rowman and Littlefield, 2005); *The State of China Atlas* (University of California Press, 2005); *Branding Cities on the West Pacific Rim: Film, Tourism and Urban Identity* (Ashgate, 2007). She is currently working on the emerging taste structures of the 'middle class' and new rich class in China.

Matt Hills is Senior Lecturer in Media and Cultural Studies at Cardiff University. He is the author of *Fan Cultures* (Routledge, 2002), *The Pleasures of Horror* (Continuum, 2005) and *How to do Things with Cultural Theory* (Hodder-Arnold, 2005). Amongst other things, he is currently working on *Triumph of a Time Lord: Regenerating Doctor Who in the 21st Century* for I.B. Tauris, and a textbook called *Key Concepts in Cultural Studies* for Sage.

Noel King is Senior Lecturer in the Department of Media at Macquarie University, Sydney. He co-edited a collection of ficto-critical writing called *No Substitute* (Fremantle Arts Centre Press, 1990), and co-edited *The Last Great American Picture Show: New Hollywood Cinema in the 1970s* (Amsterdam University Press, 2004). He has chapters in *The Last Great American Picture Show*, the *Oxford Guide to Film Studies* (Oxford University Press, 1998), and the *Cinema Book* (BFI, 2007). He has published in journals such as *Screen, Critical Quarterly, Framework, Cinema Journal, Continuum, Metro* and *Southern Review*.

George Kouvaros is Associate Professor in Film in the School of English, Media and Performing Arts, University of New South Wales, Sydney. He is the author of *Where Does it Happen? John Cassavetes and Cinema at the Breaking Point* (University of Minnesota Press, 2004) and *The Films of Paul Schrader* (University of Illinois Press, 2008). He is currently working on a study of photography and post-war American acting.

Erlend Lavik is Research Fellow in the Department of Information Science and Media Studies at the University of Bergen. He is currently writing his dissertation on the relationship between classical and post-classical Hollywood cinema.

Scott McQuire teaches in the Media and Communication Program in the School of Culture and Communication at the University of Melbourne. His most recent books are *The Media City* (Sage, 2007), and *Empires, Ruins + Networks: The Transcultural Agenda in Art* (Rivers Oram Press) which he co-edited in 2005.

Vijay Mishra is Professor of English Literature at Murdoch University, Australia. Among his major publications are: *Dark Side of the Dream: Australian Literature and the Postcolonial Mind* (with Bob Hodge, Allen and Unwin, 1991); *The Gothic Sublime* (State University of New York Press, 1994); *Devotional Poetics and the Indian Sublime* (State University of New York Press, 1998); *Bollywood Cinema: Temples of Desire* (Routledge, 2002); and *The Literature of the Indian Diaspora: Theorizing the Diasporic Imaginary* (Routledge, 2007).

Julian Murphet is Professor in Modern Film and Literature in the School of English, Media and Performing Arts at the University of New South Wales, Sydney. His publications include the books *Literature and Race in Los Angeles* (Cambridge University Press, 2001), *Bret Easton Ellis'* American Psycho (Continuum, 2002), *Literature and Visual Technologies* (co-edited with Lydia Rainford, Palgrave Macmillan, 2003), *Narrative and Media* (with Anne Dunne, Helen Fulton and Rosemary Huisman, Cambridge University Press, 2005) as well as various articles and book chapters on postmodernism, film, race, literature and theory.

Tom O'Regan is Head of the School of English, Media Studies and Art History at the University of Queensland. He is the author of *Australian Television Culture* (Allen and Unwin, 1992), *Australian National Cinema* (Routledge, 1996) and co-author with Ben Goldsmith of *The Film Studio: Film Production in the Global Economy* (Rowman and Littlefield, 2005).

Michael O'Pray is Professor of Film in the School of Architecture and the Visual Arts, University of East London. His publications include *Derek Jarman: Dreams of England* (BFI, 1996), *Avant-Garde Film: Themes, Forms and Passions* (Wallflower Press, 2003), and as editor *Andy Warhol Film Factory* (BFI, 1989) and *The British Avant-Garde Film 1926–1995: An Anthology of Writings* (University of Luton Press, 1996).

David Oubiña is Researcher of the Conicet and teaches Cinema and Literature at the University of Buenos Aires, and Scriptwriting at the Universidad del Cine. He is a member of the Editorial Board of the journals *Las ranas (arte, ensayo, traducción)* and *Otrocampo (estudios sobre cine)*. He is the author of several books including, most recently, *Filmología. Ensayos con el cine* (Manantial, 2000); *El cine de Hugo Santiago* (Festival de cine de Buenos Aires, 2002); *Jean-Luc Godard: el pensamiento del cine* (Paidós, 2003); and *El silencio y sus bordes: Discursos extremos en la literatura y el cine argentinos, entre los 60 y los 70* (Siglo XXI, forthcoming).

Dana Polan is Professor of Cinema Studies at New York University. He is the author of seven books in film and cultural study including, most recently, *Scenes of Instruction: The Beginnings of the U. S. Study of Film* (University of California Press, 2007) and the forthcoming *The French Chef*, on Julia Child's classic TV cooking show.

Michael Renov is Professor of Critical Studies and Associate Dean of Academic Affairs at the School of Cinema Arts, University of Southern California. He is the author of *The Subject of Documentary* (University of Minnesota Press, 2004) and *Hollywood's Wartime Woman: Representation and Ideology* (UMI Research Press, 1988), editor of *Theorizing Documentary* (Routledge, 1993), *Collecting Visible Evidence* (University of Minnesota Press, 1999), and *Resolutions: Contemporary Video Practices* (University of Minnesota Press, 1996), and series editor of the *Visible Evidence* (University of Minnesota Press) book series. His main research interests include documentary theory, autobiography in film and video, video art and activism, and representations of the Holocaust. He has curated documentary programs around the world and has served as a jury member at documentary festivals including Sundance, Silverdocs, and Brazil's It's All True.

Bhaskar Sarkar is Associate Professor of Film and Media Studies at the University of California, Santa Barbara. He is the author of *Mourning the Nation: Indian Cinema in the Wake of Partition* (Duke University Press, 2008), and co-editor of an anthology of essays, *The Subaltern and the Popular* (Routledge, forthcoming). He has also published essays in several anthologies and in journals such as *Quarterly Review of Film and Video*, *Rethinking History: Theory and Practice*, and *Journal of Commonwealth and Postcolonial Studies*. His research interests include globalization and culture, uncertainty and speculation, trauma and history, and postcolonial cultural studies.

Vanessa R. Schwartz is Professor of History at the University of Southern California, where she directs the Visual Studies Graduate Certificate. The author of *Spectacular Realities: Early Mass Culture in fin-de-siècle Paris* (University of California Press, 1998) and *It's So French! Hollywood, Paris and the Making of Cosmopolitan Film Culture* (University of Chicago Press, 2007), she is now working on the French reception of Pop Art and the work of Jacques Demy. She has also co-edited two volumes, *Cinema and the Invention of Modern Life* (University of California Press, 1995) and *The Nineteenth-Century Visual Culture Reader* (Routledge, 2004), and co-edited a special issue of *Urban History* in 2006 called 'Urban Icons' which includes a multi-media companion.

Brian Shoesmith has a long-standing interest in Indian cinema. He was a founding editor of *Continuum: Journal of Media and Cultural Studies* and has edited several collections on film history. He is currently working on a text on global media with Mark Balnaves (Edith Cowan University, Australia) and Stephanie Hemelryk Donald (University of Technology, Sydney). He now lives and works in Dhaka, where he is Director and Professor of Media Studies and Journalism at the University of Liberal Arts, Bangladesh (ULAB).

Murray Smith is Professor and Head of Film Studies at the University of Kent, UK, where he has taught since 1992. Since 1995 he has been an advisory board member of the Centre for Cognitive Studies of the Moving Image. His research interests include the psychology of film viewing, and especially the place of emotion in film reception; the philosophy of film, and of art more generally; music and sound design in film; and popular music. He is currently working on the implications of evolutionary theory for film culture. His publications include *Engaging Characters: Fiction, Emotion, and the Cinema* (Clarendon, 1995), *Film Theory and Philosophy* (co-edited with Richard Allen, Clarendon, 1998), *Contemporary Hollywood Cinema* (co-edited with Steve Neale, Routledge, 1998), *Trainspotting* (British Film Institute, 2002), and *Thinking through Cinema* (co-edited with Tom Wartenberg, Blackwell, 2006).

Lynn Spigel is the Frances E. Willard Professor of Screen Cultures at Northwestern University. She is the author of *Make Room for TV: Television and the Family Ideal in Postwar America* (University of Chicago Press, 1992) and *Welcome to the Dreamhouse: Popular Media and Postwar Suburbs* (Duke University Press, 2001). Her book *TV by Design: Modern Art and the Rise of Network Television* is forthcoming from the University of Chicago Press. She has edited numerous anthologies including *Television after TV: Essays on a Medium in Transition* (Duke University Press, 2004).

Graeme Turner is an Australian Research Council Federation Fellow and Director of the Centre for Critical and Cultural Studies at the University of Queensland. His work has crossed Media Studies, Film Studies and Cultural Studies; his cultural studies inflected introduction to film, *Film As Social Practice* (Routledge) has gone into four editions (the most recent in 2006). *The Film Cultures Reader* (Routledge, 2002) introduces and contextualizes key examples of cultural studies approaches to popular film. Other recent publications include *The Media and Communications in Australia* (co-edited with Stuart Cunningham, Allen and Unwin, 2006); *Ending the Affair: The Decline of Television Current Affairs in Australia* (UNSW Press, 2005); and *Understanding Celebrity* (Sage, 2004).

Ruth Vasey is Senior Lecturer in Screen Studies at Flinders University, South Australia, where she teaches topics on American cinema, television and global media. Her book, *The World According to Hollywood, 1918–1939* (University of Wisconsin Press, 1997), won the Kraszna-Krausz Moving Image Book Award in 1998, and her articles on American film industry history have been published in leading journals in the fields of Film Studies and American Studies. She lives in the Adelaide Hills with her partner Richard Maltby and their son Ben.

Constantine Verevis is Senior Lecturer in Film and Television Studies at Monash University, Melbourne. His articles have appeared in *Australian Studies, Bright Lights Film Journal, Film Criticism, Film Studies, Framework, Hitchcock Annual, Media International Australia, Senses of Cinema*, and other periodicals. He is the author of *Film Remakes* (Edinburgh University Press, 2006), and is at present working (with Noel King and Deane Williams) on an Australian Research Council-funded project-titled 'Australian Film Theory and Criticism'.

Paola Voci is a lecturer at the University of Otago, New Zealand. Her area of study combines East Asian Studies (specifically, Chinese language and culture), Film and Media Studies, and visual culture. In particular, her recent research has focused on documentary film/videomaking in contemporary China and the media of the Chinese diaspora. She has published in *Modern Chinese Literature and Culture* and *Senses of Cinema*, and has contributed to the *Encyclopedia of Chinese Film* (Routledge, 1998). Her work is also included in several edited collections of essays, such as *Lingyan xiangkan: haiwai xuezhe ping dangdai Zhongguo jilupian* (*A New Look at Contemporary Chinese Documentary*) (Shanghai Wenhui Publishing House, 2006), *Ombre Elettriche. Cento anni di cinema cinese 1905–2005* (*Electric Shadows: 100 Years of Chinese Cinema 1905–2005*) (Fondazione La Biennale di Venezia, 2005), and *Asia in the Making of New Zealand* (Auckland University Press, 2006). She is currently writing *China on Video*, a book that analyzes movies made and viewed on smaller screens (for example, the DV camera, the computer monitor – and, within it, the internet window – and the cellphone display).

Deane Williams is Head of Film and Television Studies at Monash University, Melbourne. He has written widely on Australian documentary film, is the author of *Mapping the Imaginary: Ross Gibson's Camera Natura* (AFI/ATOM, 1996) and *Michael Winterbottom* (with Brian McFarlane, Manchester University Press, forthcoming), editor of the journal *Studies in Documentary Film*, and is (with Noel King and Constantine Verevis) currently working on a large research project entitled 'Australian Film Theory and Criticism'.

Ismail Xavier teaches in the Department of Film and Television in the School of Communications and Arts, University of São Paulo. He has published extensively in journals such as *Screen, Sight and Sound* and *Review 73: Literature and Arts of the Ameritas*, and is the author of several books, including: *O Discurso Cinematográfico: a opacidade e a transparência* (Editora Paz e Terra, 1977), *Sertão Mar: Glauber Rocha e a estética da fome* (Editora Brasiliense, 1983), *Allegories of Underdevelopment: Aesthetics and Politics in Brazilian Modern Cinema* (University of Minnesota Press, 1997), and *O olhar e a cena: Melodrama, Hollywood, Cinema Novo, Nelson Rodrigues* (CosacNaify, 2003).

Introduction: Hooray for a Mickey Mouse Subject!

The sober but brave ambition of this volume, which for the editors turned out to be more hubristic than it sounds, is to offer a reasonably comprehensive overview of the state of Film Studies as an intellectual field towards the end of the first decade of the twenty-first century. Our focus on Film Studies itself, as a discipline with its own objects of study, conceptual boundaries and institutional histories, is what distinguishes this volume from the many existing, and often excellent, collections that offer multi-authored introductions to film history, world cinema or film theory. Although, in the end, the medium of film or the institution of cinema may be more compelling topics than a study of how they have been studied, we as editors have tried to respond imaginatively, argumentatively, and above all, usefully to the brief given to us by our publishers. In doing so, we hope that we have managed to capture the passion as well as the seriousness of our subject.

The scholarly purpose of Sage Handbooks is to offer a retrospective and prospective overview of the discipline or field under scrutiny by asking: What is the state of the art? Where is the discipline going? What are the key debates and issues that comprise the discipline? For us, then, the apparently simple question to which we were required to come up with an answer was this: What is Film Studies? Implicit in that question, of course,

are two others: How has Film Studies come to be the way it is? What future does the study of film have in universities and in what disciplinary configuration will it be studied? It is the last of these three questions that gives some urgency to the first two and makes the timing of the Handbook's appearance opportune.

As the various histories collected here indicate, the widespread introduction of Film Studies as a university subject was in part an institutional response, on the one hand, to the critique in the 1960s and 1970s of the perceived narrowness and anachronism of the Humanities in the US, the UK and elsewhere and, on the other hand, at the same time, to the curriculum opportunities opened up by the expansion of higher education. The publication of a book like this might therefore be read as a quiet celebration of the fact that Film Studies, a discipline often greeted with heavy-handed humour as a Mickey Mouse subject when its introduction is first mooted in a university or college, has now survived in continuing rude health for at least thirty years, and in some places for half a century and more. Sceptical cultural conservatives, as it turned out, had grounds to feel nervous. The claim that the study of film deserved to be taken seriously – seriously enough to become an established part of the university curriculum – represented part of a paradigm shift that was both iconoclastic and constructive, and film was indeed part of the avant-garde of that movement.

One aspect of the iconoclasm is best captured in Raymond Williams' famous observation that 'culture is ordinary'. This axiom marked an important shift in the centre of gravity in the Humanities away from the aesthetic and towards the anthropological. A deliberately narrow and exclusive Arnoldian understanding of culture as 'the best that has been thought and said in the world' was progressively displaced by a more inclusive and demotic conception of culture as the product of social activities and patterns of meaning and understanding that produce and sustain collective life situated in time and place – in Williams' terms, culture as 'a whole way of life' with its own particular 'structures of feeling'.

The constructive argument for the serious study of film and cinema was only in part that some films deserved by any standards to be taken seriously as works of art. The broader and more pressing case was that the study of the cinematic sounds and images that haunted the minds and shaped the desires of twentieth-century citizens could provide uniquely revealing insights into those cultural structures of feeling. Of course, it so happened that many of the people at the leading edge of this movement were also inspired by the rebellious political energy of 1968 and (in a way not exactly congenial to Williams' own tastes) by an iconoclastic, cosmopolitan culture projected onto an imagined 'America' conjured up from B-movies, hard-boiled detective fiction, Magnum photographs, jazz and rock music. And often, paradoxically or not, this 'American' populism went hand-in-hand with an enthusiasm for theoretical traditions of political and cultural explanation often disdained by the British academy as esoteric and irrelevant, and therefore for the most part inaccessible in English translation.

Another feature of the moment in which Film Studies really became established was the deliberate strategy of making such works available: the 'Western Marxism' of Georg Lukács, the Frankfurt School, Walter Benjamin, Antonio Gramsci, Jean-Paul Sartre, Lucien Goldmann, Louis Althusser and others systematically translated, introduced and put to work by the *New Left Review* in the 1970s and the bodies of primarily Soviet and French film theory espoused by *Screen* in the same period. (These were later 'acronymically and a little acrimoniously' caricatured by David Bordwell as SLAB theory: a *nouveau mélange* of tenets derived from Saussurean semiotics, Lacanian psychoanalysis, Althusserian Marxism and Barthesian textual theory.) What happened next could be recounted in a somewhat soapy narrative about ambitious academics, accusations of abstract and arcane scholasticism, and imperial designs on the study of film both by beleaguered departments of Literature and an expansionist and increasingly institutionalized Cultural Studies.

That story of institutional rivalries and turf wars is not the one we choose to tell here. With the benefit of hindsight, we prefer to take stock of the achievements of Film Studies and to reflect how the unholy mixture of low tastes and high theory did manage to redraw the map of university Humanities in ways that, so far, have resisted attempts to eradicate them. At the same time, looking somewhat anxiously forward – and here is another reason that now is an opportune moment for this Handbook to appear – it is equally evident that the future viability of Film Studies is being called into question not only as a result of developments within the field, but also because the world studied by the discipline is changing radically.

Put bluntly, the question is this: Can the systematic academic study of 'Film' or 'Cinema' be sustained and justified when its grounding objects of study – the medium of film and the institution of cinema – have ceased to exist in their classical unity, and when they have been changed almost out of recognition by emerging technological, market and demographic forces? Does it still make sense to study the protean, digital, multi-platform manifestations of what we still call 'films' (or more precisely audio-visual information and commodities) through the conceptual prism of 'Film Studies' or 'Cinema Studies'? To put that another way, does Film Studies as such have a future when the Society of Cinema Studies in the US has reinvented itself as the Society of Cinema and Media Studies, and when it seems that Film Studies might be absorbed into some other less narrowly bounded – or, depending on how you look at it, more amorphously inclusive – new disciplinary field such as Media Studies, Screen Studies or Visual Culture?

The editors' hope is that this volume will help readers to think through those questions, and to reach their own conclusions. In our transcontinental conversations, the two editors have not always agreed about whether the continued autonomy of Film Studies is either possible or desirable. But we are agreed that our job is more to praise Film Studies than to bury it. Let others write obituaries for Film Studies. We are happy that the clear-eyed self-reflection and the liveliness of thought demonstrated by our contributors more than make the case that Film Studies has a staying power even in a radically changed media landscape. And this was our original agenda. We set out wanting readers to come away from the Handbook with an appreciation of the quality of scholarship and analysis provoked by the study of film over the past half-century and more. More polemically, we wanted to show that Film Studies as a discipline has been defined not only by its object of study, but as a field that has produced characteristic ways of thinking that have always drawn on a variety of disciplines, perspectives and methods that are applicable beyond their narrowly defined original objects of study. Whatever the academic rubric turns out to be, we hope to persuade you that it is those ways of thinking that still have the power to illuminate new audio-visual media, new media audiences and users and emerging media cultures.

AUDIENCES

In our collective editorial mind, the implied reader targeted first and foremost by the Handbook has always been a clever, ambitious and reasonably well-informed postgraduate student embarking on a research degree in Film Studies, but who would not necessarily have an extensive grounding in the genealogy of the discipline. When commissioning contributions, at any rate, this was the ideal addressee we asked authors to bear in mind. If the goal of such students is to make an original contribution to their field of study, we have seen it as our responsibility to give them a reliable map of that field, along with some explanation of how the landscape got to be the way it is. Like all maps, of course, this one represents a particular perspective that will make some features of the landscape appear more prominent than they perhaps should be, and will at the same time make other features diminish or even disappear. Although we have tried to achieve a genuinely international breadth of topics and approaches, we have been conscious that the primary audience of the Handbook will be researchers and scholars in the English-speaking world, and therefore we have particularly addressed their concerns.

Each of the Handbook's three sections projects a different version of Film Studies. The first is both historical and geographical, showing how pre-histories and traditions of film culture, film scholarship and cultural studies have led to these different iterations of Film Studies in various parts of the world. The second section is epistemological, but historically so. That is, rather than trying to define Film Studies in terms of the ontology of its object and the uniqueness of its methodology, the contributions record how Film Studies is loosely and always provisionally defined by a series of negotiations or conversations with a range of contributory and contiguous disciplines. The third section is primarily conceptual or paradigmatic: it records the contribution to the field of certain key concepts, issues and debates, and assesses their continuing relevance.

Although we want the Handbook to provide a scrupulous guide for that imagined Film student as he/she sets off on the adventure of a first research project, we would of course be disappointed if this were our only readership. The book should prove of equal value to the apparently increasing number of research students working on film and cinema topics in other disciplines, and also to those scholars across the Humanities and Social Sciences who, for whatever reason, need or want to gain a reliable overview and understanding of Film Studies. We also want the Handbook to prompt those who practise the craft of Film scholarship, research and teaching, whether as veterans or apprentices, to reflect on the conceptual infrastructure of the field, on its historical emergence as a discipline, and on its likely and possible futures. And it goes almost without saying that if any general readers interested in film and cinema are sufficiently fascinated to turn to this volume as a guide to the ways in which these subjects have been studied, then we are confident in offering them accounts that are stimulating, authoritative and trustworthy without imagining that they could ever be or have the last word on their topic.

A handbook is by definition made for use, and we have stressed that aspect of the work. The volume might equally well have been named a companion and we hope that it also captures the less utilitarian connotations of that term. In other words, the book should appeal to a variety of different readers because it can be read in a variety of different ways: for interest and pleasure, we hope, and not just for work.

VOICES AND SILENCES

Even though it has a comparatively short history, Film Studies contains within it many perspectives and certainly its early development was marked by often passionate and even bitter disagreements and disputes. Even if these days the waters seem to be calmer, it is important to acknowledge a continuing diversity of perspectives and methods. We hope that something of this dissonance and range is captured in the contributions to this volume. Although all reflect scholarly expertise in their survey of different parts of the field, we have encouraged authors to speak in their own distinctive voice and the result

has been often passionate, argumentative and even opinionated. The result is a lively conversation rather than a disinterested catalogue. There is no pretence that there is unanimity of position or consistency in approach or tone. Nor would we wish there to have been, not least because such unanimity and consistency would misrepresent the reality of the field. Instead, authors who represent competing views, as well as different generations and a reasonably international spread, were deliberately invited to participate.

We do not pretend that the book is exhaustively universal or altogether comprehensive in its coverage, whether in terms of topics or regions or opinions, and that is partly due, no doubt, to the nature of our own interests and perspectives and to the reach of our scholarly networks. It will come as no surprise that the incompleteness and partiality of the book also reflects the reality of working in universities at the beginning of the twenty-first century. We referred at the outset to a sense of hubris in trying to take on a major research and editorial project like this Handbook at the same time as meeting our other professional responsibilities. This over-ambition has manifested itself in the length of time it has taken to complete it and our inevitably spasmodic communication with equally busy contributors scattered around the globe. As a result, a number of planned or potential contributors understandably found it impossible to fulfil their commissions, and in one or two cases this has left some holes or blanks on the map that should really have been filled in. But research, including research into the history of disciplines, is always a work in progress, and we hope that others will address those gaps (and our partialities) whether through critical responses or as new contributors to possible future editions of the Handbook.

DEBTS

The Handbook of Film Studies has its origins in a conversation over a dinner during the 2002 Society of Cinema Studies annual conference in Denver between James Donald and the Sage editor Julia Hall. She was obviously persuasive in the beginning and she has remained supportive, and remarkably, patient ever since. She therefore deserves special thanks. Pleasure at bringing the project to a conclusion is tinged with sadness at writing this introduction in the week that Julia is leaving Sage for a position with a different publisher. But so it goes.

We are grateful to all the contributors included here. They too have been more patient and cooperative than any harried, and sometimes, no doubt, peremptory editor has a right to expect when making sudden demands and then remaining silent for months on end. We are grateful to our distinguished editorial board, whose members have generously (but not uncritically) provided comment and guidance both on the design of the project and on drafts of individual contributions. Above all, we are grateful to Effie Rassos for her Herculean labours in handling and editing the manuscript. A fine film scholar in her own right, who was awarded her doctorate during the production process, she has brought precision, insight and good humour to a lengthy and complex task.

Mapping Traditions

The concept of national cinemas is a familiar, if not uncontentious, one in the academic study of film. It represents the proposition that certain bodies of film can speak for, as well as to, a national population and so help to invent that population as a nation, to articulate an identity for a mass of people that is always in fact extraordinarily diverse and more often than not characterized by internal tensions and antagonisms.

The chapters in this section of the Handbook address a related but less explored set of issues. One is simply to ask whether the history of the emergence of Film Studies as a distinct academic discipline, an intellectual field or at least a familiar title in university timetables is similar in all geographical and cultural circumstances. Without giving the story away, we can say that it is not. This then leads to the question of what socially and historically specific factors have shaped the development of cinema cultures, systematic thinking about film as an aesthetic form and cinema as an economic and cultural institution (commonly known as 'film theory') and the formal study of film through research and teaching. What emerges is not only an indication of the intriguing differences between the various national and regional traditions surveyed here but also a sense of the very different ways in which – and the reasons why – the phenomenon of cinema has been taken seriously.

Our sense is that these various reflections on where we as Film scholars came from and how we got to where we are pick up on a broader consensus that Film Studies has reached a stage of maturity in its development that makes such reflective institutional histories timely, not least to ensure the knowledge and memories of those involved in them at first hand are available for future generations of researchers.

It is important to be quite clear about two points.

First, and to repeat, this section offers not an overview of national or regional cinemas, but rather a synoptic survey of different histories of Film Studies and of the traditions of thinking about cinema from which they emerged. The question of whether there are any hypotheses to be proposed or conclusions to be drawn about possible links between the ethos, orientation and style of national cinemas, national film cultures and the emergence of formal Film Studies in national educational systems is left open for speculation and further research.

Second, these case-studies in the genealogy of Film Studies are intended to be indicative rather than comprehensive. As the chapters presented here represent – so far as we know – the first attempt at this kind of mapping, it will be no surprise if some readers feel that the cases included may not be the right ones in terms of global significance or personal interest, that some cases not included may be sufficiently compelling to merit inclusion, or that in some instances we may have drawn the boundaries too broadly, too narrowly, or simply in the wrong place. As the bodies of work addressed in Bhaskar Sarkar's contribution imply, borders are always in question and subject to dispute. In that spirit, if we have helped to initiate a continuing conversation about such topics, we shall be content that the section has served its purpose.

North America

Dana Polan

In outlining the trajectories of American Film Studies, it can be productive to approach the object of our history in particularly literal terms. That is, it is useful to consider what in such Film Studies is specifically American insofar as it invokes and enacts particular national preoccupations. To what extent does the development of twentieth – and now twenty-first – century inquiry into moving images projected on a screen serve in its own way as an articulation of US self-definition (and perhaps self-critique), especially in the area of culture? Does a field of study which at times has become intensely specialized nonetheless reflect – in however mediated a fashion – the concerns of the nation as it confronts modernity and offers symbolic responses to it in the form of aesthetic representation? Is there something specifically American about American film study?

Such questions can seem surprising since it is not customary to think of a body of disciplinary knowledge – especially for one so specific, small and specialized within the larger academic context, let alone within the social context – as somehow reflective of a national identity. Instead, the tendency is to imagine that the individual contributions by this or that thinker to the particular field somehow have their identity as moments of a specific and internally constituted tradition in which each critical work influences the next and all of them form an ideal and coherent whole – a discipline, precisely. And, it must be said, this image of disciplinary history is not entirely false: disciplines do proceed at their own historical pace and do form internally coherent traditions that only indirectly could be related to the social moment. But the question of any field of study is also the question of how its object of study gained legitimacy as an object of study and that specifically is a question about the larger academic context and about the cultural context in which certain areas are felt to be amenable to critical thought – and others aren't. In its own way, for instance, Film Studies plays out pressing questions that the American university faced as it moved into the twentieth century: the necessity or not of higher education for the masses, rather than a privileged elite; the extent to which modern education should devote itself to vocationalism and/or professionalization, rather than to the inculcation of general values (perhaps to be found in a canon of great works of Western culture); the degree to which humanistic inquiry still could offer valuable lessons in an age geared to an increasingly instrumental reason that might seem better addressed by social sciences than by the looser culturalist interpretations of the Humanities.

Note: in all that follows, I use 'American' as a short-hand for 'United States' in large part because the former is easier to use in adjectival form – it seems more euphonious – and because it has become a conventionalized way of speaking about the nation. Clearly, though, the term 'American' is a fraught one in its projection from one nation to an entire continent. The question itself of a discipline's 'Americanness' might seem to beg some important questions of its own. What does it mean, for instance, when there is the slippage from reference specifically to the United States to the imperial gesture in which the condition of that one country is assumed to apply to the whole of North America? To take just one example, it is worth suggesting some of the difference of some Canadian film scholarship from equivalent work in the United States. For instance, one could argue the context-specific critical force of the Toronto-based journal, *CineAction*, and the writers around it, such as Robin Wood, in articulating a complex analysis of the complicated ideological operations of Hollywood cinema: there is awareness here of the hegemonic status of mainstream Hollywood cinema, but interest also in finding those works, Hollywood and otherwise, that offer sites of resistance to dominant Hollywood and US ideology. Likewise, it has been a strong concern of a number of Canadian scholars to theorize imperial relations of Canada and the United States through the articulation of a political economy approach to North American mass media, including film. And it might not even be pushing things too far to note how a group of scholars in Montréal especially have been instrumental in articulating a theory of early cinema as a mode of representation not reducible to the narrative forms that would come later to characterize dominant, US-based feature filmmaking.

One aspect of this theorization, most evident in the 1980s and subsequent to André Gaudreault's work studying editing patterns in pre-feature cinema, has centred on formalistic elaboration of structural patternings and stylistic regularities in earliest film. At the same time, just as central to the work of the Québecois scholars of early cinema has been attention to local exhibition practices in the early period. It is more than tempting to understand such research as a form of regionalism in which the broad impositions of cinematic ideology on the public are tempered by local viewing practices and regionally differential practices of spectatorship.

In this respect, the pointed decision by the authors of *Global Hollywood* to use '*yanqui*' (Miller et al., 2001) as their term to describe the nation is tempting in its recognition of the imperial nature of US politics and culture. But insofar as 'American' reiterates the nation's own grand design and ambition at self-definition, I will use the term here.

CAVEATS IN THE STUDY OF AMERICAN FILM STUDIES

But to offer the history of 'American' film study as somehow inextricably linked to the nation's own history requires several caveats. First of all, there needs to be a certain modesty to the enterprise. From within a field of study, it is tempting for the discipline's practitioners to imagine that the stakes and resonances of their work are high – that what they are doing has consequences beyond the boundaries of the discipline in the society at large. Certainly, indeed, there have been moments in film study in which its proponents have claimed ambitiously that their efforts have greater cultural and social ambition. Certainly, too, it is possible that efforts in pedagogy and in writing beyond the coterie of academic practitioners can mean that the concerns of the discipline have extended beyond its scholarly borders. The cinema obviously has been a resonant force of popular culture, and it would seem inevitable that the concerted articulation of insights about it by scholars would thereby have some larger impact. For example, there are now several generations of cultural workers in the film industry who have come to it from film schools and bring to their creative efforts an awareness of film history and film theory. To take just one case, it is likely – although the exact lineage would be hard to trace – that the fundamental insight in Laura Mulvey's breakthrough essay from 1975, 'Visual Pleasure and Narrative Cinema', that in popular film the gaze of the camera comes to centre on the image of woman, fetishized as object, is an insight that has impacted on everyday understanding of filmic meaning. When, for instance, Brian de Palma's 1981 thriller *Blow Out* (US) begins with a long-take shot from the first-person point-of-view of a psycho killer moving through a sorority house and then reveals the scene to be a sequence from a horror film being worked on by the film's protagonist, a sound editor, it is easy to imagine that de Palma's work is responding to a concept that is in the air – that began from rigorous theoretical elaboration (Mulvey indicates that her argument was first presented in the French department at Northwestern University in the US) and then spread to become general currency.

Nonetheless, we shouldn't overestimate the importance of any particular scholarly field. To the extent that any discipline can be tied back to a social and even national context, film study has no special privilege in this respect. (Even the hard sciences have their cultural belonging, as the meta-discipline known as 'social studies of science' reminds us.) And this connects to a second caveat: even as fields of study have a cultural standing and participate in the world at large, it is necessary to realize that they do so in their own way, at their own momentum and according to their own rules. There is a temporality to disciplinary practices that is not directly mappable onto the flow of social history. Disciplines bear what we might, following a concept elaborated by the Marxist philosopher Louis Althusser for the analysis of human practices, term a 'relative autonomy' in which they move at their own rate and are shaped by their own internal laws even as they also mediate the deeper laws of the society they derive from.

A final caveat brings us closer to the specific object at hand. To the extent that we wish to trace the history of American film study, we need not only to know what we mean by 'American' but also by 'study'. If the hard sciences often seem very disciplinary in their confinement of knowledge to the laboratory, the research institute, the specialized journals and colloquia, it seems clear that film study is much more porous as a discipline, much messier in terms of its boundaries. On the one hand, the porosity of the field means also the work that did – and does still today – go on in academia under the name of film study is itself often belletristic, impressionistic, and lacking in the rigor and distance that we might expect in a scholarly field. That films are a source of personal affect and pleasure has sometimes meant that so-called scholarly work has actually been a disguised form of guilty-pleasure confessionalism in which the cinematic delights that one holds dear are hidden beneath the rationalizations of critical discourse: in recent years, such blurring of academic analysis and personal taste – which is not necessarily a bad thing – has been reinforced by emergent topics for study like stars, fandom, and cult and exploitation cinema.

On the other hand, for much of its history, serious analysis of film took place outside academia (for instance, in the work of cultural commentators or critics who had ambitions to go beyond mere judgment of individual films, such as Andrew Sarris who through the 1950s and 1960s set out to elaborate a theory and classification of directors as the veritable auteurs of films). Even as late as the 1960s, Film Studies found its useful literature not in the efforts of film scholars (one of the rare published books on film by a university instructor of the art was 1960's *Motion Pictures: The Development of an Art from Silent Films to the Age of Television* by Purdue professor Albert Fulton) but in works of criticism (for example, the writings of Pauline Kael or Sarris [who later would go on to have an academic career]) or in scholarly writings by people in other fields (for example, Erwin Panofsky who gave the first keynote talks for the newly-founded Society of Cinematologists at the end of the 1950s).

Film has been a cultural practice so engrained in everyday life that many people can feel they have important opinions about it, and there is a strong and consequent discourse – some of it quite learned in appearance – on the movies that occurs quite outside the borders of an established discipline. To take just one example, the discourse of cinephilia – of extreme lovers of movies, of what we call the film 'buffs' – has often had its own degree of studiousness in the lists, the filmographies, the rigorous acts of collecting and so on that surround intense devotion to the art form. With etymology reminding us that the notion of the 'amateur' has its origins in love ('amour'), we can note how sometimes the critical distance supposedly necessary for study falls back into a closeness in which one's love for the object is proudly displayed. In some cases, then, cinephilia has tipped over into academic practice as when certain cinephiles have come to have university careers in which they can enthuse over their filmic passion with their students. (One classic example: at New York University, William K. Everson turned a lifetime of film collecting, often centred on very obscure titles, into a pedagogy closely focused on the movies he had lovingly amassed.) In looking at film study, then, we need as much to note its continuity with non-academic approaches to the art as its separation from them.

POROUS BOUNDARIES IN THE HISTORY OF ACADEMIC ATTENTION TO FILM

No doubt cinema's assumed status as an object of popular taste about which everyone has opinions has meant that much of the available writing on film has been non-scholarly, but it is still striking to encounter an important field of critical attention where, for so much of its history, the respected discourse on the object has been offered by figures other than those who actually study the object academically. It is noteworthy that one of the very first consequential works on film aesthetics, 1915's *The Photoplay: A Psychological Study* (Münsterberg, 1916) (a work still cited favorably in the critical literature on cinema), was written by an academic, Harvard professor Hugo Münsterberg, but that Münsterberg engaged in his theorization of film outside of his primary academic research and pedagogy and clearly saw it as something that didn't bear important connection to his scholarship. It is perhaps equally noteworthy that the first university press book on film – *Motion Picture Continuities*, published in 1929 by Columbia University Press, and edited by Columbia University adult-education instructor Frances Taylor Patterson – is an anthology of film scripts, not an authored critical study, again showing that the study of film, and the recording of that study in books and articles, was generally slow to find a place within the specifically academic context.

Motion Picture Continuities is revealing in another way. Frances Taylor Patterson put the volume together to offer exemplars of the finest work in screen art so that the reader, imagined logically as a consumer of films, might both witness the sort of uplifting quality works he/she should demand at local theaters and, as a potential maker of films him/herself, might have models to emulate in the quest for Hollywood success. Patterson was the second-ever teacher of film in a university setting, having taken over an adult-education course, Photoplay Composition, from its first instructor, Victor Freeburg, who taught it at Columbia from 1915 to 1917 before going into the army at the outbreak of World War One and retiring from academic life upon his return home. Both Patterson and Freeburg intended the term 'composition' in the title of their course to imply several things. Most ambitiously, it suggested a parallel or even assimilation of the new art of cinema to established arts – especially, music and painting – in which there would be an emphasis on films as achievements of rhythm, pattern, tonality, balance and so on (not for nothing was one of Freeburg's books on film entitled *Pictorial Beauty on the Screen* [1923]). As the feature film was gaining in cultural legitimation in the mid-teens, comparison to the fine arts became a way of promoting the newer art's artistic potentials, and in this respect both Freeburg and Patterson took strong inspiration from poet Vachel Lindsay's well-known book on film aesthetics, *The Art of the Moving Picture* (1915), which equated each genre of film with a different high art. Interestingly, though, where Lindsay saw the 'composer' of film images and stories as most likely being the film's director, both Freeburg and Patterson tended to focus on the photoplaywright, whom they saw as the veritable author of a film's narrative and of its visual style.

But there was also a more specific meaning to the notion of 'composition'. For Freeburg and, even more so, Patterson, an education in film was not only to be cultural – to improve appreciation at the point of consumption by teaching the ways in which film was like the (other) fine arts – but also practical: composition here referred to the nuts-and-bolts hands-on work of actually crafting photoplays that students might eventually submit to studios as the first steps in lucrative careers. Even as they imagined a necessary feedback loop between consumption and production – wherein a training in appreciation would lead spectators to demand better films and thereby, consequently, to have a salutary impact on film producers – Patterson and Freeburg held out the possibility that through training their students could become producers and cinematic composers, too.

In other words, from the start, film study as aesthetic appreciation was mixed with practical instruction in filmmaking. The teaching of film has always been caught, in variable and fraught ways, between critical study of the art and professional training in it. If in the best of moments – as in Freeburg's and Patterson's notion of the feedback loop – the ideal has been held out of a necessary relationship between studying films and making them,

there have also been sometimes legendary cases of non-communication or even rivalry and conflict between filmmaking instructors and cinema scholars. Indeed, Patterson's own desire to hold the two sides of the equation together in a productive relationship may itself have seemed a problem to those who wanted to maintain boundaries: when in 1926–27, Columbia undertook to create a fully-fledged degree-granting professional program in film production, Patterson's concern to maintain a place for film appreciation and aesthetics within a photoplay composition course could only seem too belletristic and she was not included in any discussions of the new program (which, for what it's worth, never got off the ground).

PROGRESSIVISM AND THE RISE OF ACADEMIC FILM STUDY

In fact, if Freeburg and Patterson included a strong hands-on component in their course, to the extent of writing aesthetics of film that were also veritable manuals rich in practical advice, this was due in large part to the cultural context in which they operated, one in which humanistic learning in skills of art appreciation and manual training in skills of craft and practical application were seen as overlapping forms for cultivation of the whole human being.

Freeburg and Patterson can be seen as part of the moment of Progressive reform in which intellectuals and professionals attempted to deal with new conditions of modernity – especially, the influx of immigrant populations who then come into contact with potentially corruptive influences ranging from contagion via alcoholism to the immoralities of popular entertainment – not so much by condemnation as by the ameliorative wish to find moments of uplift and aesthetic goodness within the very heart of popular culture and everyday life. The Progressive reformers realized, at the very least, that mass culture could not be wished away and, at the very best, that it might be turned to effective and positive ends. In this respect, filmmaking instruction ceased, in the case of Freeburg and Patterson, to be imagined as mere technical training. In the context of Progressivism's valorization of human acts of making (especially of art marking), film making came to be seen instead as a demonstration of human achievement and accomplishment. Throughout the age of Progressive reform, there was a constant ode to craftsmanship as the idea that in the act of making things, human beings would make themselves better. Not for nothing was Patterson's first book of photoplay composition entitled *Cinema Craftsmanship* (1920) ('craftsmanship' and its allied 'workmanship' were keywords of the Progressivist belief in skilled acts of doing as personal amelioration). Patterson outlined there how aesthetic appreciation of the finer films along with refined training in the best aspects of high-class photoplay-making were both superior exercises of human creativity. Interestingly, Patterson also spoke of human creative potential as a form of 'industry', and she sometimes pointedly contrasted that personalized sense of industriousness to the large-scale and fairly anonymous operations of the film 'industry' which she saw as not always giving sufficient space to individual and personal creativity and allowing it to flourish. If, from the start, film study was caught in a tension between appreciation and hands-on practical instruction, it also had to navigate the tensions between art and commerce.

FROM HUMANIST APPRECIATION TO PROFESSIONAL TRAINING

I have noted, however, that in 1926–27, when Columbia University administrators came to envision a program in practical training in film, their vision was so dominated by notions of professionalism that Patterson's earlier humanistic mediation of art and craft could only seem irrelevant to them. In fact, the administrators set out to create a cinema production curriculum at the behest of the film industry itself, and Columbia University was actually only one such venue in which the industry's own administrators sought to outsource the training of their own workings by calling upon the world of academia. Here, the date of the enterprise explains a lot: 1926–27 was the moment of the coming of sound, a technological development of portentous implication, but one that also consolidated ongoing trends in the business and craft of film toward rationalization, laboratory research, regularization of production, articulation of industry standards and practices, and so on. All of this required rigorous, intensely applied training in occupations and professional aspects of industry-based filmmaking. It was also at this time, in 1926–27, that the Academy of Motion Picture Arts and Sciences (AMPAS) was founded, geared to combating labour unrest by liberalist adjudication among branches of the industry and by also professionally inscribing workers into the Hollywood system in ways that would make them team-players rather than resistant labour activists. Additionally, this was a time in which the Hays Office, the censorship and public relations service for the film industry, was actively attempting to improve the film industry's image by presenting it as a well-run and salutary business that was good for America. Will Hays himself saw industry association with academia as providing both rationalized professionalization and an aura of respectability and profundity of purpose that he felt could only benefit the film business.

Consequently, these years reveal a series of initiatives between academic institutions and the film industry to create fully professional programs of film training. Early on, then, not merely do we have film study linked to filmmaking, but caught up in sponsorship by Hollywood forces, the implications of which major film programs on both coasts of the US still grapple with today.

I have already mentioned Columbia University. Here in 1926–27, Will Hays negotiated with administrators (such as his Republican Party friend, Nicholas Murray Butler, President of the University) for a three-track curriculum in practical work in film (the tracks were cinematography, screenwriting, and set design and staging) to be based initially on existing courses at the university (for instance, cinematography could start from physics department courses on optics) but to then expand into offerings expressly created for the curriculum. The Columbia initiative seems to have fallen apart simply because the university administrators realized that film industry leaders were hoping not to put money into the endeavour and were instead counting on the university itself to come up with the resources. Interestingly, a virtually identical three-track curriculum was also floated as an idea at the University of Southern California (USC) whose president, Rufus Von KleinSmid, was a fencing partner of AMPAS's first president, Douglas Fairbanks, and got to talking with the actor about industry-academia cooperation. In the event, however, USC's plans for a multi-track major that would have required lots of support (both financial and material) from the film industry foundered and the initial idea was scaled back into one general course, Introduction to Photoplay, where professors and industry representatives talked about the art and industry of Hollywood cinema.

Meanwhile, Will Hays was also instrumental in another professional venture: with financier Joseph P. Kennedy, he arranged for the Harvard School of Business to run a Business Policy course on the film industry that centred around lectures given by luminaries from the industry (for example, Marcus Loew, William Fox, Harry Warner, Adolph Zukor and Hays himself). Where the Columbia and USC initiatives focused on on-set aspects of the filmmaking process, the Harvard course concentrated, as befitted a professional program of business training, on financing, distribution, marketing, and so on. The hope was that this first course would lead to regularly offered instruction in the business of film, but soon Kennedy withdrew his financial support as he left the film industry and turned to other areas of investment. The course idea died.

Even though none of these initiatives in professional training went according to plan, they are revealing of an interest at the end of the 1920s in developing a film pedagogy geared toward practical ends. (In any case, it is worth noting that the professional initiatives were not all completely without consequence: although it had to be scaled back, the USC idea of a film production program endured, and in the 1930s it gradually expanded into a curriculum that constituted the first degree-granting major in film in the country.) Industry support and practical intent did not mean, however, that attention to film's cultural or humanistic status dropped away completely. In fact, to the extent that the initiatives in film professionalization had to do in no small part with public relations efforts to make the industry of film seem rational, ethical and reasonable, it was important for curricula of hands-on training in filmmaking to also acknowledge the special value of the 'thing' made, the films themselves. Cinema might be a business like any other – for example, Harvard's Business Policy course concentrated each year on a model industry and followed its typical item of manufacture from production to distribution to consumption – but it was essential to also suggest that its exemplary productions were ones that radiated cultural and aesthetic value and had a core of humanistic uplift. Thus, Harvard's business course was directly conjoined to an effort in Fine Arts to set up an annual award for artistic excellence in film production, while at USC, the head of the film curriculum, Boris Morkovin, offered courses both on the fundamentals of motion picture production and on the great directors who, in his view, made film a fundamental force for aesthetic cultivation.

THE 1930s AND THE RESURGENCE OF CULTURAL APPROACHES TO FILM APPRECIATION

The need to justify film culturally actually strengthened in the 1930s even as there was a drive toward the professional needs of the film curricula, and the period can be seen as one in which there was a propitious (if sometimes calculated and tactical) alliance of industry and academia around cinema as a vital form of American cultural life. One rallying point ironically was the research project of a number of social scientists funded by the Payne Fund, a religiously-inspired foundation that worried about the seemingly deleterious impact of popular culture on ordinary citizens. As the authors of a history of the Payne Fund efforts in the area of cinema clarify (Jowett et al., 1996), the religious leaders behind the research project realized that mere moral condemnation of the movies would not seem rigorous enough and they turned to the social scientists for experiments and analyses that they hoped would confirm their sentiment as to the danger of films. Despite the fact that many of the efforts of the Payne Fund researchers relied on dubious procedures and that, in any case, many of their conclusions were not in unambiguous support of the religious leaders' assertion of the movies' capacity for evil, the Payne Fund Studies still matter as the first concerted attempt by the social sciences to deal with cinema, and the initiative is still cited for its precedence in the critical literature on the history of mass media research. At the time both supporters and detractors took the implications of these studies very seriously. In particular, for our purposes, the findings encouraged strong response from humanists who either were disdainful of those specific moments when the Payne Fund researchers did criticize the movies or were doubtful more generally about the wisdom of letting social scientists think that their work could say anything useful about a popular cultural form like the cinema.

Two cases in which the humanities response was to reaffirm cinema's transcendence of mere social or sociological influence so as to constitute a vital form of cultural uplift and aesthetic refinement are particularly noteworthy. At New York University, sociologist Frederick Thrasher had in fact been commissioned by the Payne Fund sponsors to work on a project volume on the impact of movies on delinquency. Thrasher, who had published a book on gangs with a chapter on the impact of movies on delinquent behaviour, seemed a logical candidate for the Payne

Fund proponents. Soon, however, he came to realize that he liked the movies – liked them for himself (by the 1940s, he would edit a coffee-table celebration of Warner Bros. talking pictures, *Okay for Sound* [1946]) but also liked them for their potential cultural value vis-à-vis the general public, both young and old, who he imagined could find in the movies a form of 'informal education' that could compensate for failings in the official educational system. Having begun his efforts at film pedagogy with a Payne Fund-inspired course on worrisome media effects of the movies, Thrasher now began teaching a course on film appreciation little different from the ones currently taught in so many humanities programs and film study departments.

The other important humanities reclamation of the movies came from within the heart of Payne Fund research territory. At the University of Chicago, from which a number of Payne Fund social scientists had been recruited, philosopher Mortimer Adler had engaged in a vicious battle to reclaim knowledge of realms of human achievement away from the social sciences and for the humanities. Adler took to task his social scientist colleagues – especially those who conducted research for the Payne Fund – for what he saw as their category error in assuming that the realm of culture could be accessible to the positivist modes of knowledge of the sciences. A convert to Catholicism but also a fervent defender of the Western philosophical tradition starting with the Greeks, Adler imagined a hierarchy of humans in their relation to ultimate truth. Catholics were closest to pure spirit through their inner and intuitively felt possession of grace, below them were the philosophers (the models here were Plato and Aristotle) who could achieve spirit through the dialectic work of reason. Below them were, in descending order, the artists who transcended the crass materiality of the world through creativity (but not through philosophers' reason); those citizens with enough time and talent to understand (or to be taught) the insights of philosophy and to intuit the deepest accomplishments of the fine arts; and, at the bottom of the hierarchy, the mass consumers for mass art, the public, who could participate vicariously in the imaginative creations of popular artists and who by means of catharsis would purge themselves of earthy and earthly inclinations. Strikingly, even if it assumed gradations of mind, intellect and taste, Adler's hierarchy also assumed that for each population in the society, there were corresponding works of human creation that spoke trenchantly and appropriately to the group. Philosophers had philosophy to raise them up; ordinary audiences had popular culture. While Adler became an intense propagandist for the so-called Great Books of the Western World – those seeming pinnacles of complex philosophy and elevated literature that seemed ready-made for philosophers and elite taste communities – he also militated strongly for a rich popular culture that he felt would provide the mass public with a vital art at its own level of appreciation and to its own benefit and uplift. For Adler, there was no conflict between high and low culture since each met needs of its particular audience that the other couldn't.

In the mid-1930s Adler was commissioned by the Hays Office to defend the popular art of cinema against detractors like the proponents of the Payne Fund and, for that purpose, he produced a massive (over 600 pages) aesthetics of cinema, *Art and Prudence* (1937). Certainly, the fact that Adler was paid to write a philosophical defense of the movies might imply that his interest in that art wasn't pure, but the very extent to which he devoted himself to the assignment, reading a vast number of works on the art of film and fashioning such a big book of patiently argued points suggests conversely that he was quite caught up in his project. Indeed, in *Philosopher at Large* (1977), his autobiography, Adler spoke of his great love of the movies, and it is clear that *Art and Prudence* represented more than a professional assignment that devolved to him from the film industry. His book was one of the most concerted attempts up until that time to argue for the worthiness of cinema as a popular art.

As a follower of the ideas of Saint Thomas, Adler took an Aristotlean approach to art, seeing film as a poetic form that diverged imaginatively from everyday reality thereby to arouse emotions but in a purely fictive and controlled fashion that enabled their ultimate purgation. Hence, film raised its viewers from the purely carnal realm of appetite and desire to give them a glimpse of the finer potentialities the human mind was capable of. Quite strikingly, Adler's ode to cinema as the ultimate democratic art – the art most readily resonant with the demos – would inspire his philosopher friend, Scott Buchanan, another fervent defender of the Great Books, to see film study as a logical companion to – and indeed culmination of – a curriculum fully based on Great Books study that he was proposing for the newly revamped St. John's College in Maryland. (St. John's still functions as an institution of higher education in which students spend their four years reading the Great Books in chronological order from the Greeks to more recent dead, white males – with a few token women now thrown in.)

THE MUSEUM OF MODERN ART AS A DIVIDING LINE IN THE HISTORY OF SERIOUS ATTENTION TO FILM

Interestingly, the increasing concern of a cohort of intellectuals such as Adler, Buchanan, along with their friends Robert Maynard Hutchins (president of the University of Chicago) and critic-poet Mark Van Doren, among others, to militate for the Great Books canon overlapped temporally with a 1930s canonization of a singular, and supposedly great, tradition in cinema. In 1935, New York's Museum of Modern Art (MoMA) opened its film section which, among other activities, put into circulation a collection of high-points of cinema history, organized chronologically but also thematically. The MoMA films were, at first, rentable only as series (not as individual titles) and came with program notes and introductory explanatory titles that inscribed each film within a larger seemingly authoritative history. The history that the MoMA collection of films told seems an eminently logical and predictable one but only because the MoMA series became so popular that it was rented widely and basically established the basic story of film history for years to come. The story it told was, for instance, that of crude single-take actualities hovering in a pre-artistic state until individual geniuses like Georges Méliès or Edwin Porter discovered the creative powers of editing and transcended the single image for complex narratives.

As cinema scholar Haidee Wasson (2005) has chronicled in a recent account of the MoMA Film Library, virtually overnight the US study of film changed. Teachers of film art now had easy access to a set of exemplary works whose arrangement in thematic and chronological series did much of their curricular planning for them. In consequence, film appreciation and film history courses sprouted up at an explosive pace. To give just one example, until the mid-1930s, Stanford University had been offering a half-hearted course on Photoplay Appreciation based on the AMPAS-sponsored lecture series at USC. When AMPAS indicated a desire to make the content of the USC course available to other universities, the USC Dean of Arts and Sciences, Karl Waugh, who was additionally the convener of the Introduction to Photoplay course, had contacted the chair of Stanford's Psychology Department since that was Waugh's field and the two were friends. A junior professor of applied and experimental psychology was assigned to teach the class but he had no enthusiasm for it and it died quickly. However, when MoMA announced the availability of its circulating library of films – which clearly framed cinema as cultural form and aesthetic achievement – it became easier for Stanford to entertain the idea of a film appreciation class and one came into existence in Fine Arts, where it would remain until at least the 1950s.

Just as Frederick Thrasher at NYU's School of Education had found his admiration for the movies leading him away in the early 1930s from a more strictly social science concern with the sociological effects of film to an humanistic interest in studying film as an art that in its best moments transcended mere social effect, so too did the re-location at Stanford of the cinema from Psychology to Fine Arts appear to signal an increasing annexation of the movies to the province of the humanities insofar as they now would be defined as higher forms of cultural value. MoMA's Film Library had an increasingly important role to play in this shift. Indeed, if Thrasher had initially had to learn the history of film on his own (amusingly, he wrote to the National Board of Review, the film uplift organization that sponsored his class, to ask them about *Potemkin* [Sergei Eisenstein, USSR, 1925] which it had been recommended he show in class but which he had never heard of), MoMA did much of the preparatory homework for budding film pedagogues from the moment of the mid-1930s on. Thus, another NYU professor, Robert Gessner in English, who had been teaching film within the rubric of a course on literary adaptation, now started in the mid-1930s to offer classes on classic traditions in motion-picture art, directly facilitated by MoMA rentals. Soon, Gessner was ambitiously conceiving an NYU degree program in Cinema, one that, unlike USC's more filmmaking track, would emphasize the cultural study of movies rather than their production.

But the dream of a curriculum of film as canonic fine art – and the larger dream of cinema taking up an appropriate, respected place in the humanities – would be deferred. Advertisements for Gessner's program appeared in 1940 and it is (now) evident that this was not a propitious moment for the leisurely study of a newly discovered branch of culture: with the looming threat of war and mobilization, new curricula in the humanities would have to be placed on hold (especially as they required new budget lines). Not until the end of the 1950s would Gessner come back to the idea of a critical studies film degree at NYU.

WORLD WAR TWO PUTS FILM APPRECIATION CURRICULA ON HOLD

Much of what passed for an education in film during the Second World War was training in filmmaking for military purposes: for example, with strong sponsorship from the Signal Corps, USC's program – already geared to a practical pedagogy in hands-on production rather than cultural appreciation of cinema – became a veritable branch of the state. (This was an alliance that would continue into the post-war period with the enlistment of documentary in the battles of the Cold War. Not for nothing did the USC film school win its first Oscar for the documentary, *The Face of Lincoln* [Edward Freed, US, 1956], in which a USC sculptor bit by bit shapes the face of the president. The film has its own filmic documentation of the sculpting process coincide with the sculptor's demonstration of that process so that film and sculpture alike are seen to participate in a Cold War celebration of great American statesmen.)

The coming of war had signalled that the very idea of treating film favourably as a humanistic democratic art above the fray of combat and politics would come under challenge. To a certain degree, the Payne Fund Studies had served earlier as the last gasp of a religious-inspired condemnation of mass art for its supposedly deleterious impact on morals: in this respect, Adler's *Art and Prudence* easily demolished the Payne Fund's fuddy-duddy conservativism and showed just how antiquarian its moralism was. But there was a newer critique of mass culture coming into play in the late 1930s on into the war period and its impact was more consequential. Here, the suspicion of the impact of the popular arts was not so much a moral one coming from religious custodians worried about culture's impact on ethical standards as a more trenchant and seemingly grounded fear about mass culture's role in the formation of political attitudes, especially in times of social upheaval and global threat. In fact, if the Payne Fund Studies are the last gasp of religious moralism, they also hint at a growing

concern through the decade of the 1930s with mass communication as a form of political persuasion, a concern that other detractors of cinema would engage in but without the bothersome remnants of religious outrage. Whether it be the threat of Fascist/Nazi propaganda all too clearly conveyed by mass communication organs such as radio, or the more home-grown revelation of similar public vulnerability to media in the case of Orson Welles' 1938 *War of the Worlds* broadcast, the late 1930s were run through by a concern from intellectuals and academics about the potentially worrisome effects of communicational forms. Most revealingly, Mortimer Adler himself ended the decade with a best-selling volume, *How to Read a Book* (1940), which, despite the seeming general purview of its title, was actually a privileging of the reading of Great Books particularly and now came to see time spent on lesser forms of culture (such as cinema) as a waste, if not an impropriety, at a time of world crisis. Specifically citing the movies as one of the wasteful forms of mass leisure, Adler asserted that the coming of war required that American citizens had to defend Western civilization and that the 'great dialogue' across time that he felt was contained in the Great Books offered the strongest cultural tool in that battle. Not only was popular culture a distraction, but it was itself a potential enemy in its propagandistic tendencies to speak loudly and seductively and thereby overwhelm public opinion.

THE IMPACT OF THE INTELLECTUAL CRITIQUE OF THE AMERICAN MASS ARTS

As the 1930s drew to an end, the alliance between American intellectuals and demo-cratic popular culture, including film, began to fall apart. One strong symptom was the (in)famous 1939 essay by budding art critic Clement Greenberg, 'Avant-Garde and Kitsch'. Greenberg argued that popular culture betrayed formal qualities of art to wallow in contents rife with sentimentalism, formula and cliché, pre-governed simplicity of response and so on. Likewise, the threat of fascism brought to the United States a slew of refugee intellectuals, a number of whom both lamented what they saw as fascism's destruction in Europe of the vital high culture they had grown up with and now confronted an American popular culture that they saw as no less destructive of reason and refinement in its crassness, its omnivorous omnipresence, its surrender to ideology and so on. In the most famous – or, depending on one's view, infamous-example, Theodor Adorno and Max Horkheimer sought to continue, once they managed to escape to the United States, the work of critical theory they had been elaborating under the guise of the Frankfurt Institute for Social Research. After a sojourn in New York, where they honed their analysis of popular culture through conjoined studies of Fascist ideology and of mass media as conveyor of standardized, popular thought, Adorno and Horkheimer moved west to, as it were, the belly of the beast – Los Angeles, centre of what they came to term the 'culture industry'. Here, they wrote a sharp, even curmudgeonly, critique of what they took to be the deadening acceptance of mass reason in the Western tradition, of which they argued the most recent avatar was American mass culture. Just at the end of the Second World War, Adorno and Horkheimer's 'The Culture Industry: Enlightenment as Mass Deception' (1972), published as part of their *Dialectic of Enlightenment*, virtually established the fundamental terms by which post-war intellectuals in the US would look at the popular culture of the nation.

Indeed, as world war was superseded by Cold War, it became ideologically useful to many such intellectuals to single out mass culture as an especially noxious form of social ill. Whether Cold Warriors like Robert Warshow – who wrote an intensely nasty critique of the letters of the condemned, alleged atomic-bomb spies Julius and Ethel Rosenberg on the grounds that even in their most seemingly intimate and heartfelt moments their missives exemplified the unthinking internalization by *hoi polloi* of the dead and empty formulae of popular thought – or former Communist fellow-travellers like Dwight MacDonald – who wrote virulently against the middlebrow nature of much mass-produced American arts – the intellectuals needed to affirm a faith in the American way of politics even as they recoiled in their heart of hearts from what they took to be the vulgarity of its media. (To be fair, Warshow could admit the possibility of an authentic American folk culture, traces of which survived in artificially produced mass culture. Warshow famously wrote two important essays on the movies, 'The Westerner' and 'The Gangster as Tragic Hero', but these served as odes to indigenous art against the kind of formulaic ersatz culture he felt the Rosenbergs revelled in. In any case, Warshow's career was cut short by early demise, and full assessment of his attitudes toward popular culture remains difficult.)

The critique of mass culture served the Cold War intellectuals' needs perfectly: by so overwhelming but exclusively assailing a superstructural aspect of American society, they could insist that they were in no way impugning the deeper infrastructure of American economics and social value itself. Indeed, by delving in detail into the intricacies of the culture industry, such critics could reiterate that theirs was a quite specific object of disapprobation that could in no way be generalized to the rest of the society. For instance, when at the beginning of the 1950s, anthropologist Hortense Powdermaker (1950) undertook a sojourn in Hollywood, so that she could try out the possibilities for an ethnography of a modern community, her ultimate conclusion was that Hollywood was such an artificial, empty, mind-numbing locale that she hoped never to return.

In like fashion, within the ideological space of the Cold War, more reactionary intellectuals than the liberal Powdermaker could still maintain a critical edge – by virtual definition, intellectuals have to be dissatisfied with some aspect of the status quo! – while parading their loyalty to the US political system. As American studies scholar Andrew Ross trenchantly argues in his renowned

No Respect: Intellectuals and Popular Culture (1989), the 1950s became the period of, in his term, a 'failure' of encounter between American intellectuals and the popular culture of the day.

1950s AND 1960s INTIMATIONS OF MODERN FILM STUDY

And yet, the period was also one in which the broken lineage of serious study of film was being mended and would eventually be re-established in ways that more directly set the terms for the film study we still know today in much of US higher education. Beneath the blanket condemnation of mass culture, there were rumblings and rumours of a somewhat surreptitious cult valorization of an often cheesy popular culture that would encourage new writing – and new appreciations – of a vernacular American tradition in lowbrow arts. In his book on the emergent affirmative film study of the 1950s, *Artists in the Audience* (1999), film historian Greg Taylor treats the new glimmerings of film criticism as a veritable underground culture which he ties to the parallel groping for new means of expression by experimental and bohemian artists of the time (thus, Taylor's title intends to treat critics as virtual creators themselves, evolving a discourse that allowed a new appreciation of film to be constructed).

Manny Farber, who also honed a career as an abstract expressionist painter, and Parker Tyler, who worked as a poet, were part of the new generation of film writers who found in American film an energy and a rawness that they could appreciate and admire, in contrast to the Cold Warrior naysayers. Taylor goes so far as to argue that the affirmative critics were in the process of refining a camp aesthetic – in which low culture is valorized precisely because it gains no respect in the dominant taste hierarchy. Thus, although Andrew Sarris exhibited less of the precise attention to details of *mise en scène* that were so masterfully on display in Manny Farber's close analysis of the look and feel of the films of '50s action directors, there

is also a lineage around auteurism in which Sarris became the prime 1960s typologizer of directors according to their perfection of crafts of Hollywood story-telling. Sarris' voracious mastery of American cinema – he seemed to have seen everything, both big-studio extravaganza and B-movie alike – had its own camp dimensions. He could wax eloquently about the kitsch *oeuvre* of an Edgar G. Ulmer or a H. Bruce Humberstone – names that even sounded cheesy. But this omnivorous quality also brought an aura of rigor, and therefore scholarly respectability, in the form of cataloguing and classification, careful evaluation, and unification of expressive style and expressed themes.

Likewise, it is indeed easy to see a lineage from Tyler and Farber in the 1950s to an influential 1960s figure such as Susan Sontag, whose 1964 'Notes on Camp' (1966) became a veritable manifesto for a new rethinking of all categories of high and low in the arts. In contrast to Sarris, Sontag was no mere apologist for a kitsch culture of the vernacular. She was a true cosmopolitan who regarded it as part of her intellectual mission to introduce Americans to recent developments in European experimentation; she wrote revered essays on such topics as Jean-Luc Godard, or Ingmar Bergman's *Persona* (Sweden, 1966), for example. In doing so, she was typical, after her own fashion, of another glimmering set of forces that through the 1950s and on into the 1960s would encourage affirmative attention to film as an object worthy of serious study. Here, the decisive factor was a growing interest among urban professionals in new European (and to a lesser degree, Japanese) art cinema. Where the works of the American auteurs for the most part had to be discovered from within a Hollywood past that was pretty much over – and to this extent, later auteurism is not fully an example of Taylor's argument about a temporal overlap between the creative work of critics and that of cutting-edge artists contemporane-ous to them – the *oeuvre* of Godard, Bergman, Michelangelo Antonioni, François Truffaut, Andrzej Wajda, Akira Kurosawa, and others were fully of their moment and resonated a creativity, a richness of theme and self-reflexive style that energized young intellectuals.

The find-yourself/express-yourself bent of the 1960s also nourished a growing culture of cinema in which both artists and audiences turned intensely to the art form as a site for cutting-edge experimentation and up-to-date relevance. This was the period, for instance, in which the film schools really took off as bold visionaries – from George Lucas at USC to Francis Ford Coppola at UCLA to Martin Scorsese at NYU – began to use practical coursework to give the technical know-how that personal vision could be based upon. And ironically, it was also a moment in which some of the old Hollywood auteurs realized that there were advantages to being flattered as rediscovered artists who stood out from Hollywood regularity. For example, Alfred Hitchcock began to retool himself, as Robert Kapsis (1992) chronicles in a sociological study of the changing fate of Hitchcock's own image as artist, as a sort of European creator whose seemingly visceral efforts in suspense and fright actually were but the mere surface for deeper reflections on art and the human condition. As Kapsis shows, Hitchcock specifically tried to make and then promote his 1963 film, *The Birds* (US), as a European art film with scenes of alienation *à la* Antonioni, an ending that resisted closure (the characters drive off into a horizon filled with birds and there is pointedly, according to Hitchcock's wishes, no title that indicates 'The End'), and a premiere at the Museum of Modern Art. Hitchcock's apotheosis came in 1967 with a book-length interview conducted with him by French critic and film director François Truffaut. Quickly translated into English, *Hitchcock* by François Truffaut (1967) became a widely read – and reread – volume for budding analysts of the art of film, a veritable bible for anyone interested in the creative potentials of cinema.

Truffaut's vastly influential volume would soon be complemented by others. Quite consequential, for instance, was Jerome Agel's *The Making of Kubrick's 2001* (1970) which came out three years after Truffaut's tome and which more than suggested that a single film could merit the sort of close interpretive attention that previously had been reserved for the established narrative arts such as literature. Significantly, there had been several serious books on single films in previous decades – 1952's *Picture*, Lillian Ross' study of the making of John Huston's *The Red Badge of Courage*, (US 1951) is probably the most famous example – but none set out to examine the meanings, influences, critical reception and metaphysics of a film in the way that Agel did. Despite its title, *The Making of Kubrick's 2001* was fully a critical analysis which, for the most part, eschewed technical details of the film's production and opted instead for deep interpretation and hermeneutic commentary, which Agel assembled from essays and long letters that fans had written about the film. Like Truffaut's book, Agel's would be much pored over by budding cinephiles and it suggested to them that film appreciation was a rigorous, serious activity marked by patient and close attention to the particularities of film style and structure.

To the extent that we can define the concretization of a discipline by such signs as the rise of professional societies, the legitimation of some critical practices and a concomitant de-legitimation of others, deemed to be less scholarly, rigorous, or scientific, the regularization of practices of credentialization such as the granting of degrees and diplomas, the garnering of academic respect through the publication of books that become standard points of reference, the crystallization of networks of dialogue and interchange among credentialed practitioners through such forums as conferences, the perfection of channels for the dissemination of disciplinary research in the form of scholarly journals, and so on, then the 1960s are indeed the period when Film Studies as an academic field did begin to take on disciplinary solidity and regularity. The year 1960, for example, would see the inaugural meeting of the newly-founded Society for

Cinematologists, at which Society president Robert Gessner would welcome guest speaker Erwin Panofsky, the art historian, who gave film analysis more than a patina of disciplinary respectability.

EUROPEAN INFLECTIONS OF AMERICAN FILM STUDY

But the very extent to which 1960s film, 1960s film culture and film study alike were invested in an understanding of the creative potentials of the language of cinema opened them up to a forceful influence that would change them in dramatic fashion. Specifically, the 1960s were also the great moment of the discovery of French Theory, particularly in the area of the analysis of the signs, including cultural signs, of contemporary society. To take just one example, in 1964, French film theorist Christian Metz published a long critique of metaphoric references to cinema as language that ignored the growing literature in semiology and linguistics that might make the reference to film language quite literal (Metz, 1990).

The decisive introduction of English-language readers to Theory came in 1969 with the publication of Peter Wollen's *Signs and Meaning in the Cinema*. Wollen's book included not only an outline of the semiology of cinema (which he argued had its specifically artistic complement in the cinema work of Godard on the signs of cinema) but also a rethinking of auteur theory away from directors as expressive figures to structures of meaning to be extracted from works and assigned, in a *posteriori* fashion, to the director seen now as little more than a convenient fiction to describe structural regularities. Wollen's volume had tremendous impact as a manifesto for a new analytic rigor in film study (even if it didn't always match its call for anti-impressionistic precision with an objective exactitude of its own: when, for instance, Wollen asserted that John Ford rendered the conventions of the Western complex in ways that Howard Hawks didn't, it is hard not to see that what is claimed

as a structural point – there is more variety in structure in Ford – is also an old-style example of personal judgement). But for our purposes, what is most significant is that Wollen was a Britisher writing from the UK both to re-evaluate American cinema and to call for European derived theories in the elaboration of that re-evaluation. Wollen was one of the figures who in the 1970s would be associated with the decisive English-language journal of film theory, *Screen*, and much of the inspiration for US Film Studies would now, for at least a decade, be continental in nature, even if UK inflected.

No doubt, there would still be indigenous forms of American study of film – the last decades, for instance, have been marked by an immensely rich rethinking of the history and historiography of US cinema by US scholars – but it can also be argued that from the 1970s on, US Film Studies becomes cosmopolitan in ways that make the study of it as a 'national' tradition less appropriate. Not for nothing does the present volume begin with a 'Mapping of Traditions' that is then succeeded by sections whose contributions are far from inevitably national in orientation. Perhaps the most tempting way to map the US tradition of film study is not only to outline its formation but also suggest its dissolution – a dissolution of geographical preoccupations that parallels perhaps the dissolution of the object of cinema itself in a new age of the audio-visual.

REFERENCES

Adler, Mortimer J. (1937) *Art and Prudence: A Study in Practical Philosophy*. New York: Longmans, Green and Co.

Adler, Mortimer J. (1940) *How to Read a Book: The Art of Getting a Liberal Education*. New York: Simon & Schuster.

Adler, Mortimer J. (1977) *Philosopher at Large*. New York: Macmillan.

Adorno, Theodor and Horkheimer, Max (1972) 'The Culture Industry: Enlightenment as Mass Deception', in *Dialectic of Enlightenment*. Tr. John Cumming. New York: Herder & Herder. pp. 120–67.

Agel, Jerome (1970) *The Making of Kubrick's 2001*. New York: New American Library.

Freeburg, Victor (1923) *Pictorial Beauty on the Screen.* New York: Macmillan.

Fulton, A.R. (1960) *Motion Pictures: The Development of an Art from Silent Films to the Age of Television.* Norman, OK: University of Oklahoma Press.

Greenberg, Clement (1986) 'Avant-Garde and Kitsch', in John O'Brian (ed.), *Clement Greenberg, The Collected Essays and Criticism Vol.1.* Chicago: University of Chicago Press. pp. 5–22.

Jowett, Garth S., Jarvie, Ian C. and Fuller, Kathryn H. (1996) *Children and the Movies: Media Influence and the Payne Fund Controversy.* New York: Cambridge University Press.

Kapsis, Robert (1992) *Hitchcock: The Making of a Reputation.* Chicago: University of Chicago Press.

Lindsay, Vachel (1915) *The Art of the Moving Picture.* New York: Macmillan.

Metz, Christian (1990) 'The Cinema: Language or Language System', in *Film Language: A Semiotics of the Cinema.* Tr. Michael Taylor. Chicago: University of Chicago Press. pp. 31–91.

Miller, Toby, Govil, Nitin, McMurria, John and Maxwell, Rick (2001) *Global Hollywood.* London: BFI.

Mulvey, Laura (1975) 'Visual Pleasure and Narrative Cinema', *Screen*, 16(3): 6–18.

Münsterberg, Hugo (1916) *The Photoplay: A Psychological Study.* New York: Dover.

Patterson, Frances Taylor (1920) *Cinema Craftsmanship.* New York: Harcourt, Brace and Howe.

Patterson, Frances Taylor (ed.) (1929) *Motion Picture Continuities.* New York: Columbia University Press.

Powdermaker, Hortense (1950) *Hollywood: The Dream Factory.* Boston: Little Brown.

Ross, Andrew (1989) *No Respect: Intellectuals and Popular Culture.* New York: Routledge.

Ross, Lillian (1952) *Picture.* New York: Rinehart.

Sontag, Susan (1966) 'Notes on Camp', in *Against Interpretation, and Other Essays.* New York: Dell Publishing. pp. 13–23.

Taylor, Greg (1999) *Artists in the Audience: Cults, Camp, and American Film Criticism.* Princeton, NJ: Princeton University Press.

Thrasher, Frederick (1946) *Okay for Sound: How the Screen Found Its Voice.* New York: Duell, Sloan and Pearce.

Truffaut, François (1967) *Hitchcock.* New York: Simon & Schuster.

Wasson, Haidee (2005) *Museum Movies: The Museum of Modern Art and the Birth of Art Cinema.* Berkeley: University of California Press.

Wollen, Peter (1969) *Signs and Meaning in the Cinema.* Bloomington: Indiana University Press.

2

European Film Scholarship

Ian Aitken

The European experience of Film Studies and film scholarship is a particularly diverse one, and inherently difficult to encapsulate within a circumscribed review such as this. Given so, the approach adopted here will be aimed at managing this difficulty through a partition of that experience into six major categories: 'nineteenth century realist, naturalist and classical Marxist'; 'intuitionist realist'; 'intuitionist modernist'; 'auteurist'; 'Saussurian' and 'postmodern post-structuralist/pragmatist'. Such a partition may be reductive in effect but any similar approach to such a subject would, necessarily, be forced into equivalent diminutions. It will be argued that the ancestries of the European engagement with film scholarship are to be found, not just in twentieth-century schools of film theory, but also in much older European intellectual and cultural legacies, and that it is imperative to recognize the origins of these historical traditions, and their influence upon European film scholarship. Such an approach, inevitably, shapes the overall orientation of this assessment. The first five sections of this study will be concerned largely with film theory, rather than with scholarship in the broader sense, because the

European engagement with theory has been so central to the evolving course of European Film Studies. Scholarship, and, in particular, historical scholarship, will be addressed in the final section of the chapter, which explores the broad spectrum withdrawal from high theory which occurred from the mid-1980s, to more or less the present.

THE NINETEENTH CENTURY REALIST, NATURALIST AND CLASSICAL MARXIST TRADITION

One of the principal sources of early traditions of film scholarship in Europe was nineteenth-century realist and naturalist thought. Naturalism, in particular, exercised a considerable influence upon early film scholarship in France, Italy, Spain, Scandinavia and elsewhere. Although naturalism had lost much of its intellectual pre-eminence by the time the cinema came into being, that appearance revived interest in the ideas of figures such as Emile Zola. It was the modern, technological and 'scientific' character of the cinematograph, in conjunction with the inherent potential which the machine possessed for generating photographic accounts of reality, which led scholars back to the naturalist premises espoused by Zola in the foreword to *Thérèse Raquin* (1867). Examples of such a sanction of cinematic naturalism can be found in the writings of a number of critics active during the period, including Ricciotto Canudo, Louis Haugmard, André Antoine, Jean Epstein, André Sauvage, Hubert Revol and others (Abel, 1988). Even though 1920s French cinematic impressionist film theory, embodied in works such as Louis Delluc's book *Photogénie* (1920) and Léon Moussinac's theoretical manifesto *Naissance du cinéma* (1925), arose, to some extent, in opposition to this naturalist legacy, aspects of naturalism still coursed powerfully through cinematic impressionist discourse, and continued to influence European film theory throughout the silent period.

After 1930, this realist and naturalist tradition of film scholarship was challenged by the emergence of the sound film, an occurrence which posed complications for models of film theory which had been founded upon the primacy of the image. In response to such difficulties an array of critical debates and positions began to emerge within Europe over how to respond to a conceptual environment which had now been irretrievably transformed. French critics such as René Clair, Marcel L'Herbier, Epstein and Benjamin Fondane initially reacted with suspicion and apprehension to the emergence of the sound film, whilst others, such as Moussinac, were more positive in their response. As Europe drew closer to war again in the late 1930s, and critical debate returned to the questions of realism and national cinema which had first been aired around the ideas of Zola in the 1902–14 period, leftist critics such as Moussinac and Claude Vermorel began to argue once more for the development of a cinema which could build on the combination of popular appeal, realistic description, and depiction of large-scale social and political forces which characterized the novels of Zola. Thus, Vermorel, argued for a version of *L'Argent* (1891) which would directly refer to the Stavisky scandal, then

a matter of topical concern, and regretted the untime death of Jean Vigo, who had been planning a version of *Germinal* (1885) (Andrew, 1995: 199).

Between 1934 and 1939, the quest to construct an effective cinema of popular national political impact, and one which drew upon the realist and naturalist legacy, became an important political objective for film scholars on the European left. In France, intellectual groupings such as the Groupe Octobre, an eclectic congregation of left-wing intellectuals founded in 1932 by the surrealist poet Jacques Prévert, became active in attempting to cultivate film theories and strategies informed by the legacy of Zola, nineteenth-century realism, Marxism and other sources. In addition to France, the same line of attack was adopted amongst film scholars in other European countries. For example, in Italy, a version of nineteenth-century naturalism, known as 'verism', which, like the later novels of Zola, combined a poetic humanist sensibility with a concern for detailed empirical description of landscape and community, was to influence the development of Italian neorealism, and critics such as Cesare Zavattini drew explicitly upon this legacy in his 'Some Ideas on the Cinema: Neorealism' (1953). Naturalism provided the foundation for the two increasingly oppositional film journals which developed in fascist Italy during the late 1930s: *Bianco e Nero*, and *Cinema*; and also influenced debate over film culture then taking place within the newly established national film school, the Centro Sperimentale. Elsewhere in Europe during the 1930s, it was Marxism, rather than naturalism, which was to influence critics such as Ivor Montagu in Britain, Joris Ivens in Holland and Bertolt Brecht in Germany. However, as will be argued, the links between nineteenth-century realism and naturalism and early-twentieth-century Marxist and communist thought are close and convoluted.

After 1945, naturalism ceased to be debated overmuch as a theoretical position within European film scholarship. In Italy, critics such as Guido Aristarco, and the journal

Cinema nuovo, adopted a more 'socialist realist' position, and denounced the naturalism of films such as Roberto Rossellini's *Viaggio in Italia* (Italy/France, 1953). Nevertheless, naturalism remained an important trope within Italian cinema from the 1950s until more recent times, in films such as Michelangelo Antonioni's *Il Grido* (Italy/US, 1959) and Francesco Rosi's *Cristo si è fermato a Eboli* (France/Italy, 1979). A type of theoretical naturalism is also evident in the ideas of Pier Paolo Pasolini, and particularly in his notion of 'mythic realism', which combines naturalism with archaic symbolism. However, Pasolini's notion of 'technical sacracity' was to later evolve into a model of 'semiotic realism', in which he combined elements of naturalism with others derived from post-structuralist and Brechtian theory. In France, naturalism largely ceased to be discussed at the theoretical level within film scholarship, although it could be argued that the influence of the new history movement in the 1970s led to the re-introduction of a naturalist sensibility in films such as *Lacombe Lucien* (Louis Malle, France/West Germany/Italy, 1974), and in the writings of critics and filmmakers such as Louis Malle and Bertrand Tavernier. In Spain, after 1945, naturalism provided an oppositional vehicle for film theorists opposed to the fascist dictatorship. In 1955, the Spanish film journal *Objectivo* helped to organize a First National Film Congress, at which Italian neorealism was extensively debated; and this eventually led to the appearance of Spanish neorealist films such as Juan Antonio Bardem's *Calle Mayor* (Spain/France, 1956). As in France and Italy, no general theoretical re-articulation of the naturalist legacy was to emerge in the 1950s, although naturalism is clearly evident in the work of filmmakers such as Victor Erice, Carlos Saura, José Luis Borau and Ricardo Franco. In Scandinavia, realist cinema drew heavily on the nineteenth-century naturalist and realist traditions, particularly as in the theatre of Henrik Ibsen and August Strindberg, and these influenced filmmakers such as Ingmar Bergman and Carl Theodor Dreyer. Although, once more, no theoretical re-articulation of naturalist theory

emerged within Scandinavian film culture, it is possible to argue that the naturalist spirit remains palpable in the semi-theorized notion of 'dogma' cinema that emerged in the 1990s with the 'Dogma 95' manifesto and the films of Lars von Trier. Even here, a naturalist emphasis on improvisation and avoidance of the 'artistic' is mixed with a more ironic, postmodern sensibility which sets the Dogma movement apart from the central currents of the naturalist tradition.

Although nineteenth-century naturalism exercised a considerable influence upon some early schools of European film scholarship, that influence was condemned as a reactionary one by other parties, and particularly by film scholars influenced by classical Marxist-Leninist thought. The position on naturalism adopted within the Soviet Union from the mid-1920s onwards stemmed from a distinction which Fredrich Engels had initially drawn between realism and naturalism in the 1880s. Engels had argued that, whereas naturalism (and also, as we will see, modernism) merely provided a fragmentary and superficial account of social reality, 'realism', as in the work of Honoré de Balzac, afforded a more profound account, by connecting the atomized particular to the unifying general. Following Engels' distinction, this elevation of Balzacian realism over Zolaesque naturalism was adopted as official policy within the Soviet Union, and, in 1934, evolved under Alexander Zhdanov, and in conjunction with other imperatives, into the more or less obligatory doctrine of Soviet socialist realism.

It could be argued, however, that Soviet socialist realism did not embody the more critical spirit of Engels' 1888 formulation. Whereas Engels had argued that realism should not be tendentious but should aspire towards the creation of an 'impartial', 'chronicle-fashion' interpretation of the social and historical environment (1977: 270), Soviet socialist realism and its giddier offspring, revolutionary romanticism, demanded a much more affirmative and steadfast approach to the portrayal of 'correct' values than he had initially envisioned.

Nevertheless, even if Engels' position is to be preferred to that of Zhdanov, the interpretation of Zolaesque naturalism in both positions remains incongruous. It is one of the stranger quirks of modern European cultural history that a committed and principled democratic activist such as Zola should be pilloried by avowed socialists, whilst a right-wing monarchist such as Balzac is held up for the higher esteem.

The doctrine of Soviet socialist realism, a doctrine which relentlessly returned to the nineteenth-century realist novels of Balzac, Leo Tolstoy and other such for legitimation, became entrenched within the Soviet Union from the mid-1920s onwards, and, after 1945, within the Soviet Bloc countries of eastern Europe. In these countries, film scholars strove diligently to develop 'dialectical materialist' approaches to film form and analysis which were based on the nineteenth-century realist model. Much of this work was of variable quality, pedestrian and doctrinaire, and tended to discount the phenomenon of modernized 'western Marxism' in order to focus as entirely as feasible upon the canonical texts of Engels, V.I. Lenin, Joseph Stalin, Zhdanov and, occasionally, Karl Marx. For all its limitations, this tradition did have one pre-eminent though highly controversial adherent: the Hungarian literary and political theorist Georg Lukács.

Like Engels, Lukács adopted a categorical distinction between realism on the one hand, and naturalism and modernism on the other; and, as with Engels, Lukács believed that the emergence of naturalism and modernism in the arts, and the attendant decline of realism, could be traced to a disheartening epochal turn of events: the defeat of the Paris Commune in 1848. Following this defeat, the incremental entrenchment of a prevailing bourgeois consciousness 'destroyed the subjective conditions which made a great realism possible' (Lukács, 1977: 282). As realism declined, and the undertaking to portray society as a whole became unsustainable against the context of accelerating class inequality, modernism and naturalism emerged as unfortunate and despairing responses to the unfolding historical catastrophe: responses which deposited the utopian ideals of the Enlightenment ever deeper within the stone-dead sarcophagus of modernity.

Although Lukács was a literary, rather than film theorist, he did write on the cinema in the Hungarian journal *Filmkultúra* in the 1950s, and devoted a chapter of his *The Specificity of the Aesthetic* (1965) to film. In addition to this fairly limited contribution, Lukács' writings on literary theory and history were influential in both eastern and western European film scholarship from the 1930s onwards. In the east, Lukács' ideas provided the foundation for the development of an enlightened realist film aesthetic which aspired to distinguish itself from the doctrinaire orthodoxy of the official communist schools of thought. This became particularly important after 1950, when the theory and practice of Italian neorealism, which went on to inspire leftist filmmakers and theorists around the world between 1950 and 1980, was condemned as an expression of bourgeois naturalism by the commissars of the Soviet bloc.

Such repudiation effectively left Lukácsian critical realism as the only enlightened alternative to Zhdanovist socialist realism. The model went on to influence both film scholars and directors such as Andrzej Wajda and Miklós Jancsó in Poland, and Sergei Bondarchuk, Andrei Konchalovsky, Andrei Tarkovsky and Mikhail Kalatozov in Russia. It also provided the intellectual underpinning for courses of Film Studies established in Lodz (1945), Budapest (1945), Belgrade (1946), Prague (1947), Bucharest (1950) and Potsdam (1954). Of course, Lukács was not the only influence on the eastern European and Soviet forms of moderate film scholarship which appeared and disappeared periodically between 1950 and 1989. Neorealism was often slipped surreptitiously back into the equation. Films such as Antonioni's *Il Grido*, Pasolini's *Il Vangelo secondo Matteo* and Rosi's *Cristo si è fermato a Eboli* – inheritors of the seditious, naturalist lens of 1940s classics such as Rossellini's *Germania anno zero* – were simply too compelling to be excommunicated.

In general, one can characterize the film scholarship of the Soviet bloc during this period, in an admittedly simplified manner, as dividing into two tendencies. One was the dominant Zhdanovist school of socialist realism. The other embraced a series of attempts to stretch the permissible boundaries of the hegemonic formula through recourse to Lukács, neorealism, and the European art cinema of Bergman, Antonioni and others. Such attempts became more pronounced during the various de-Stalinization 'thaw' periods during the 1950s in Czechoslovakia, Hungary, Poland and the Soviet Union (and, of course, in the 'Prague Spring' period around 1968), but continued to appear from time to time throughout the 1960–89 period. After the fall of the Soviet bloc in 1989, Zhdanovist socialist realism almost entirely disappeared from eastern European film scholarship. One side-effect of this welcome collapse of a doctrinaire aesthetic theory was the rapid decline of a critical film scholarship culture in eastern Europe, as previously State-subsidized institutions came under the full onslaught of a triumphal, globalizing Hollywood machine.

Whilst in eastern Europe the influence of Lukács waxed and waned over the 1950–89 period, in western Europe Lukácsian critical realism provided a less intermittent, if subsidiary, source of inspiration for leftist film scholars and filmmakers. Such scholars were particularly influenced by Lukács' distinction between realism and naturalism as embodied in his essay 'Narrate or Describe' (1970), an essay which became the standard Lukács text to be delivered to students across the western European academic scene. Although some Marxist film scholars were able to accept Lukács' criticism of naturalism as set out in 'Narrate or Describe', they were considerably less inclined to accept his concomitant repudiation of modernism. Eventually, even Lukács' disciples in eastern Europe, such as Agnes Heller, Ferenc Fehér, György Marcus and Mihály Vajda, abandoned him on this issue (Heller, 1983: 130).

During the 1970–2000 period, Lukács' ideas on realism were increasingly rejected in favour of Brechtian models of anti-realism and models of ideology and representation derived from post-structuralism, from the writings on culture by Antonio Gramsci, and from the sociology of Pierre Bourdieu. During the seventies and eighties, when anti-realist film theory dominated much of the critical agenda, this anti-Lukácsian tendency was extended to the entire nineteenth-century realist/classical Marxist tradition, which was habitually regarded with misgivings by those intent on the development of a progressive, critical film practice. And yet, behind blanket denunciations, there often lurked a profound misunderstanding of the critical legacy embedded within a nineteenth-century realist and naturalist tradition which had, in point of fact, emerged in opposition to bourgeois capitalist hegemony. Similarly, few in the West who denounced Lukács during the 1970s and 1980s, or who simply ignored his work, had read his writings on the cinema, or understood the extent to which he had struggled against Zdhanovism and Stalinism throughout his career.

INTUITIONIST REALISM

In addition to this nineteenth-century Lukácsian, classical Marxist and realist tradition, another important identifiable tradition of European realist film scholarship emerged from an arrangement of influences, including those of nineteenth-century realism and naturalism, but encompassing romanticism, existentialism, classical German philosophy and phenomenology. This tradition, which will be described here as 'intuitionist realist', comprises the work of John Grierson, Siegfried Kracauer and André Bazin, and is centrally concerned with the relationship between cinema and modernity. This intuitionist tradition is, therefore, characteristically 'epochal' in its anticipations for film theory, and sees film as offering a prospective cure for the problems inherent in the edifice of modernity. Grierson, for example, believed that film could play a crucial role in contemporary society by providing an effective medium of communication between the state and the public, and one which would stem the collapse of the institutional, democratic public sphere – a collapse which, during the 1930s, appeared greatly probable. For Grierson, influenced by neo-Hegelian philosophy as he was, the existing institutional structures of the state were the invaluable consequence of the historical evolution of human society across the centuries, and the most important repository of the human aspiration towards that harmony and unity which Grierson believed to be embodied within the Hegelian notion of the Absolute. It was these institutions, and their commitment to the common good over private profligacy (including, in particular, *laissez-faire* capitalist profligacy) that was one of the great altruistic achievements of mankind in its struggle over a base egocentrism set deep within human nature.

Under Grierson's tutelage, therefore, film was to be a medium of altruistic social engagement, placed at the service of the state in opposing that individualism which threatened the progressing advancement of society towards societal integrity, at one level, and the likeness of the absolute at another. Such a role could never by its very extravagant and amorphous nature be sharply defined, and this, in conjunction with the level of abstraction implicit within philosophical idealism, provided Grierson's theory of film with a necessarily intuitionist, rather than rationalist character. This disposition was reinforced by Grierson's belief, inherited from American 'mass society' theory and scientific naturalism, that modern mass society had become so multifaceted that traditional models of social communication fashioned upon rationalist premises were no longer practicable, and that, as a consequence, film had no option but to instil a general and intuitive, rather than conceptual, understanding of things within the public psyche. This intuitionist perspective led Grierson to argue that film should attempt to symbolize the interdependence and evolution of social relations through the application of all the formative potential at its disposal.

Although this formulation emphasized modernist, formative editing technique, the actual content of the documentary image remained an important factor for Grierson, as is made clear by a philosophical idealist distinction which he drew between the 'real' and the 'actual'. Writing about his own film *Drifters* (UK, 1929), for example, Grierson argued that the empirical content (the actual) of its documentary images was organized so as to express general truths (the real) which existed at a level of abstraction beyond the empirical, but which could only be portrayed through the empirical (Aitken, 2001: 166). Such a formulation makes it clear that Grierson's early theory of intuitionist cinematic realism, like the other theories of intuitionist realism to be discussed here, placed great emphasis on the empirical qualities of the medium, and the ability of those qualities to disclose more general truths concerning the nature of the human condition within modernity.

Like Grierson, Kracauer's theory of cinematic realism was centrally concerned with the relationship between film and modernity (Kracauer, 1974; 1995; 1997). Like Grierson, Kracauer was influenced by the classical German philosophical critique of the Enlightenment, and the impact of capitalism on social structures. Whereas for Grierson, though, it was G.W.F. Hegel who was the pre-eminent influence, for Kracauer it was Immanuel Kant, and, in particular, Kant's contention that, within modernity, the spheres of ethics and aesthetics had become subordinated to the dominion of technical reason. This notion of the impoverishment of the human experience within modernity was reinforced in Kracauer's thinking by the influence of Max Weber's concepts of disenchantment and instrumental rationality, and, in the 1920s, by the Frankfurt School's approach to the rise of German fascism and the instrumental, ideological impact of the culture industry. All of this led Kracauer to a particularly negative conception of the state of the human subject within modernity.

This position led Kracauer to argue that the true value of film lay in its potential to re-direct the spectator's attention to the texture of life which had been lost beneath the abstract, ideological discourses which now regulated experience (1997: 298). In developing this aspect of his thought, Kracauer was influenced by two particular concepts: Edmund Husserl's concept of the *Lebenswelt* ('Lifeworld'), or the phenomenological world of immediate experience; and Kant's idea of *Naturschöne* ('natural beauty'). Kracauer believed that film was a privileged medium, generated by the condition of modernity in order to 'redeem' the *Lebenswelt* for the modern subject. Such deliverance would take place through the adoption of an orientation associated with that of *Naturschöne*, where the eye gazes freely across the visual panoplies of the natural world (and human *Lebenswelt*) in order to formulate self-governing sense. Kracauer's theory of cinematic realism is, then, best described as a form of phenomenological, idealist realism which, like the Kantian aesthetics and Husserlian phenomenology from which it is derived, seeks a basis for knowledge and representation through close observation of the material world. Again, as with Grierson, we see the same intuitionist, materialist approach, directly linked to the disclosure of more abstract realities.

Like Kracauer and Grierson, Bazin's theory of cinematic realism was influenced by the idea that something had gone fundamentally wrong with the human condition within modernity. Bazin derived this conviction from forms of French Catholic existentialism espoused by figures such as Charles du Bos, Albert Béguin, Emmanuel Mounier and Marcel Legaut. Legaut, for example, was a Christian activist, committed to the re-introduction of religious values and debate into the secular French educational system; and Bazin was particularly influenced by Legaut's call for a revolution in conscious-ness, premised on the need to build a new spiritual community suffused by moral and social values. Similarly, Mounier was associated with the personalist movement, a Christian existentialist movement opposed to what its members considered to be the

widespread 'depersonalisation' of existence within contemporary society (Gray, 1972: 2–4). Following these influences, and like both Grierson and Kracauer, Bazin argued that the modern world suffered from a loss of spirituality, and that the modern individual was oppressed by dehumanizing, instrumental systems and by ideologies. Bazin's theory of cinematic realism was based on the need to counter this dehumanization by returning greater autonomy to the spectator, and his theory of realist spectatorship is grounded in the idea that, when the spec-tator gazes upon the realistic film image, they are able to achieve a degree of self-realization founded on free thought and action.

None of the three theories of intuitionist realism considered here can be regarded as 'naive realist'. These theories are 'realist' in contending that film corresponds to certain aspects of reality. But, such correspondence is a homological one, and not affected by naive realist assumptions about film's relationship to perceptual reality. Nevertheless, cinema's relationship, rather than correspondence, to perceptual, empirical reality is a crucial component of all three theories. All these theories link intuitionist models of knowledge to an empirical foundation able to disclose higher, more abstract forms of knowledge. These forms of knowledge are also premised on the overriding imperative of freedom. It is argued that the dense, empirical richness of the realistic image allows film to transcend ideological indoctrination; and this, in turn, makes it clear that these theories of cinematic realism emerged in response to what was perceived to be an overarching context of instrumental socialisation and loss of indi-vidual freedom within the modern situation. Intuition is preferred to reason, as the foremost means of effecting emancipation and insight in all three of the theories of cinematic realism considered here, and this, in turn, reflects their origins both in idealist philosophy and phenomenology, and in the historical context from which they emerged.

That context, one of suspicion concerning the darker uses to which reason had been put, is summed up in Kracauer's apocalyptic notion of the '*go-for-broke game* of history' (Hansen, 1997: xii). Kracauer argues that the gathering forces of modernity are fast approaching the verge of a catastrophic impasse, in which the innermost and most negative tendencies of modernity – those of fragmentation, disenchantment and alienation – would, if left to course freely, eventually reach such a point of critical mass that some cataclysmic implosion might occur. At that point, modernity would either plunge further into abstraction, or turn backwards, towards meaning and value (Frisby, 1986: 121). As he was writing in the 1920s and 1930s, Kracauer believed this point of no return was fast approaching its conclusion, with the growth of Nazism, and the inevitable slide into world-wide conflagration. For him, the events of the larger 1914–45 period always amounted to much more than a struggle between right-wing totalitarianism and democracy, and were, he believed, associated with an even more historically important struggle for the existential condition of humanity within a modernity which would either become comprehensively inscribed with the spirit of instrumental rationality, or, more optimistically, the liberating energy of the *Lebenswelt* (Hansen, 1997: xiii). The same approach to the historical context can be found in the ideas of Grierson and Bazin. Grierson developed his ideas in opposition to the havoc wrought by unfettered capitalism in his native Scotland, and what he took to be the impending collapse of democracy into totalitarianism or unbridled capitalism; whilst Bazin inherited a humanist insistence upon the imperative of individual freedom which arose in renunciation of the mass slaughter of the 1914–18 and 1939–45 periods. All of this makes it clear that this tradition of European film scholarship is associated with a distinctively European philosophical critique of modernity, and with particularly overwhelming historical events. As one critic has put it, this body of film theory developed in the face of the 'full blast of modernity' (Branston, 2000: 29).

INTUITIONIST MODERNISM

Another important area to be considered is that of intuitionist modernism. As the name suggests, intuitionist modernism shares similar influences and themes with intuitionist realism. At the heart of intuitionist modernism is the conviction, shared by intuitionist realism, that intuition, rather than reason should be the structuring principle underlying a revitalized film aesthetic. Once again, the main influences here are Kant's theory of aesthetic experience, and Husserlian phenomenology. According to Kant, during aesthetic experience the mind freely seeks patterns of meaning in the object of aesthetic contemplation, which should possess the potential to generate a profusion of meaning in the mind of the perceiving spectator. This means that the aesthetic judgement is essentially intuitive and impressionistic in character. This Kantian model of the aesthetic judgement is reinforced, within intuitionist modernism, by Husserl's emphasis upon the detailed exploration of phenomenal immediate experience. Both these influences can be found expressed within film theory in the Russian formalist tradition, and particularly in Viktor Shklovsky's notion of *ostranenie*, or to 'make strange'. The concept of *ostranenie* is motivated by the proposal that, in an instrumental modern world, art should present an ambivalent image to the spectator, and Shklovsky's idea finds its most important manifestation in Soviet montage cinema in the writings and filmmaking of Dziga Vertov and Sergei Eisenstein. Eisenstein's late aesthetic, in particular, in its appropriation of nineteenth-century romantic and symbolist forms, and twentieth-century modernist forms, derived from the writings of James Joyce, and others, displays this tendency. As we shall see, Soviet montage theory also displayed a directive tendency which is at odds with such an insistence upon the ambivalent image.

Outside the Soviet Union, intuitionist-modernist film theory founded on German philosophical idealism and other influences can be found in Weimar film theory. One characteristic of Weimar film theory, for example, was a belief that the systematic structures which afflicted the individual within modernity were deeply inscribed in language, and that visual experience constituted a domain of potential freedom from linguistic determination (Hake, 1993: 131). The visual was regarded as embodying a primal and underlying mode of communication which pre-dated the rise of modernity and offered the possibility of a return to a more valid form of human experience. This overarching concern with the redemptive powers of the visual influenced many Weimar theorists at the time, including Kracauer, Rudolf Arnheim and Béla Balázs; and Balázs' contention that gestural expression could amount to a 'spiritual experience' rendered visible amounted to a strikingly visual and non-cognitive aesthetic (1924: 40). In both Russia and Germany, though, theorists attempted to link this intuitionist approach to the kind of modernist formalism implicit in the idea of *ostranenie*, and in films such as *Man with a Movie Camera* (Dziga Vertov, USSR, 1929) and *The Cabinet of Dr. Caligari* (Robert Wiene, Germany, 1920).

If an intuitionist-modernist approach can be associated with elements of the two most important early film movements in European cinema, those of German expressionism and Soviet montage cinema, then it can also be associated with the third most important, that of French cinematic impressionism. Here, intuitionist modernism is influenced by specifically three French nineteenth-century aesthetic traditions: those of symbolism, naturalism and impressionism. During the 1910s, France experienced the growth of the world's first genuine alternative film culture. A key figure here was Delluc, who was appointed editor of the journals *Le Film* and *Cinéma* in 1917 and 1920 respectively, and who published one of the key works of the impressionist movement, *Photogénie*, in 1920. An intellectual film culture soon began to grow in France, building on Delluc's contributions. So, for instance, in 1919 the journal *Littérature*, edited by

André Breton, Louis Aragon and Philippe Soupault, began to publish film criticism; whilst figures such as Epstein, Moussinac and Canudo contributed to this growth of French film scholarship by publishing key books, including Epstein's *Bonjour cinéma* (1921), and Moussinac's *Naissance du cinéma*. Like Weimar film theory, this school of film scholarship placed emphasis upon the evocation of subjective experience, the foregrounding of film technique, and the conveying of 'multiple and contradictory impressions' (Germaine Dulac, quoted in Williams, 1992: 101). The key concept of French cinematic impressionism, *photogénie*, can be associated with the intuitionist-modernist concern with ambiguous and indeterminate representation, and the related conviction that aesthetic experience was primarily non-rational in character. This is made evident, for example, in Delluc's assertion that 'explanations here are out of place' (quoted in Ray, 1998: 68) and in Epstein's claim that 'The cinema is essentially supernatural' (quoted in Ray, 1998: 74).

In recent times, more emphasis tends to have been placed on a study of the French surrealist and dada movements of the 1930s than on cinematic impressionism. Nevertheless, all three can be linked together, and placed alongside Weimar film theory and branches of Russian formalism, as forming an overall intuitionist-modernist tradition. That tradition, as we have seen, was influenced by a number of intellectual factors and also, like later intuitionist realism, by the context of history. Intuitionist modernism was informed, in the first place, by the critique of modernity stemming from Kant, Hegel, Weber, Husserl and others. The intuitionist-modernist film scholarship which emerged from France and Germany during the 1920s and 1930s was also deeply affected by the impact of the First World War, and the ways in which reason and rationality had been put to the service of the creation of engines of mass destruction. The culture of modernism turned to the irrational and intuitive one as a way of escaping from the dominion of such brutish instrumental rationality.

Two principal tendencies can be identified as emerging from the influence of Husserl and Russian formalism. One was the focus on the ambivalence and impressionistic nature of the aesthetic experience, and it is this which developed into the tradition of intuitionist modernism, in Russian, German and French film scholarship, and is embodied in concepts such as *ostranenie*, *photogénie* and Kracauer's idea of 'distraction'. It was the other tendency, largely derived from Husserl and emphasizing the search for deep structures of meaning and determination, that was to have the greater influence upon a linguistically-based, or 'language'-oriented, school of film theory which emerged during the 1920s. Instead of the indeterminacy and autonomy of *Naturschöne*, this school of theory sought to establish the determinate, and determining, underlying units and principles of the film medium. This early formalist tradition of film theory is summed up in Eisenstein's essay 'The Montage of Attractions' ([1923] 1968); and in a movement such as constructivism, with its emphasis on the art work as a rationally assembled artefact. Constructivism was also the product of a revolutionary consciousness predicated upon the need to totally re-create art in the image of a new Soviet era which would abandon pre-existing bourgeois norms. This approach is summed up in Grigori Kozintsev, Leonid Trauberg, Sergei Yutkevich and Georgi Kryzhitsky's article 'Eccentrism' ([1922] 1988), with its rejection of figurative art. Consequently, the engaged productivist tendency within constructivism embraced the scientific approach fully, and repudiated supposedly bourgeois aesthetic concepts such as genius, imagination, 'art' or vision – all concepts central to the intuitionist-modernist approach.

Despite the early eminence of constructivism, pre-revolutionary forms of aesthetic theory such as cubism and futurism remained evident within the new society of the 1920s, giving Russian formalism a diverse configuration. So, for example, whilst constructivist artists such as Vladimir Tatlin, Alexander Rodchenko and El Lissitsky sought to develop a rationalized, directive approach, others, such as Naum Gabo and Kasimir Malevich, sought to develop constructivist techniques for more aesthetic and symbolic ends. The formalist and constructivist legacy which was handed on to Soviet film theory and scholarship during the 1920s consisted therefore of an incongruous fusion. On the one hand there was an essentially reductive hunt to establish the deep structures, aesthetic specificity, and rationalized configurations of the medium in order to determine 'objectively' predictable forms of representation and spectatorial interpretation. On the other hand there still remained a tendency towards the de-familiarization of representation in order to create more ambivalent portrayals of reality. This dialectic is particularly present in the career of Eisenstein, which began with a 'constructivist' model of film form but ended with the adoption of an approach steeped in symbolist expressionism: an approach represented in his essay 'Synchronisation of Senses' in his *The Film Sense* ([1943] 1968). A similar dialectic between rationalism and intuitionism can be found in the ideas of a German 'formative' film theorist such as Arnheim. Arnheim fully shared the Russian and Soviet formalist desire to establish the subject-specificity of the film medium, and went to great lengths to elaborate on how the fundamental aesthetic concepts of film should lead to a form of film practice in which the 'special attributes of the medium should be clearly and cleanly laid bare' to the spectator (1933: 44–5). Arnheim, however, betrayed the influence of the intuitionist element of the formalist tradition in arguing that film should attempt to 'capture something universally significant in the particular' (1967: vi).

If the film theory of Arnheim and Eisenstein indicates the presence of a tension between the two strands of the formalist tradition referred to above, it also illustrates a dilemma which formalist film theory was forced to face over the question of realism. Whilst stressing the point that film should fore-ground the properties of its medium, Arnheim wished to stop short of a radical formalist approach which would lead to a pronounced anti-realism. Thus, he insisted that, whilst possessing a formative dimension, film must maintain a balance between representation and a display of the means of representation (1933: 46). Arnheim's approach here reflected a wider accommodation between modernism and realism which took place in both Germany and the Soviet Union during the 1930s. The concept of *ostranenie* elaborated by Shklovsky, Boris Tomasevsky and Osip Brik during the 1920s, was increasingly opposed by formalist theorists such as Jan Mukurovsky during the 1930s, because, such theorists argued, it encouraged excessive formalism. One outcome of this dispute was the emergence of a more realist film aesthetic in the Soviet Union during the 1930s – also, of course, influenced by the official doctrine of Soviet socialist realism. At the same time, in Germany, the period of *Neue Sachlichkeit* (new realism/objectivity) ushered in a new accommodation between modernism and realism.

During the 1930s, European formalist film theorists and filmmakers felt impelled to reconcile four different imperatives. One was a rationalized, purposive, even objectivist inclination, influenced both by a desire to render film scholarship more 'scientific', and by a felt requirement to provide the medium of film with a more pronounced social and political utility. A second imperative was a converse desire to lay emphasis on the use of indeterminate representation in order to counter the force of instrumental rationality, manipulation and the deadening hand of a utility that had become ubiquitous. The third imperative was a modernist penchant to foreground the means of aesthetic representation. And the fourth imperative was, as argued, an aspiration to accommodate the demands of realism. Despite the obvious importance of formalist and modernist concerns, European film theorists remained committed to the realistic or documentary base of the film medium. So, for example, although Soviet, Weimar and French film scholars were clearly preoccupied with the way that the empirical trace of external reality could be transformed by the techniques of the medium, that trace remained a vital one for theorists and scholars

as diverse as Eisenstein, Delluc, Vertov and Balázs.

There are a number of reasons why early European film scholarship retained an unbroken interest in the question of realism. It was widely held that the aesthetic specificity of the medium was based on visual realism. The influence of Kant and Husserl led to a focus on the importance of the empirical, which then became translated into a support for documentary realism. Suspicions concerning the instrumental role of rationality and language led to a desire to engage with visual realism. The influence of the nineteenth-century realist and naturalist tradition, as well as Marxism, fuelled the continuing engagement with realism. The subversive potential of film in bringing into the sphere of representation that which had previously been excluded for political reasons was a powerful influence on Russian formalism, Weimar film theory, the British documentary film movement, French realist and impressionist film theory, and the Italian neorealist movement. And finally, during the inter-war period, a general realist aesthetic emerged across Europe, in response to the deteriorating international situation, and this led filmmakers such as Jean Renoir in France, Grierson in Britain and G.W. Pabst in Germany to move from avant-garde to realist positions.

AUTEURISM

After 1930, European cinematic modernism in both its intuitionist and rationalist manifestations went into decline. As this occurred, intuitionist realism, and the ideas of Grierson, Bazin and Kracauer, became increasingly influential. Alongside intuitionist realism, another tendency, that of auteurism, became gradually more evident, particularly during the 1945–75 period. The auteurist tendency was based on entirely different notions of the aesthetic distinctiveness of film from those taken up within intuitionist modernism and realism. Whilst intuitionist modernism sought to locate the aesthetic specificity of film in formal aesthetic categories, and intuitionist realism attempted to locate such specificity in film's ability to portray 'reality', the auteurist tradition drew on romantic conceptions of art to affirm that the chief (as opposed to specific) aesthetic value associated with the medium lay in the creative role played by the film artist. Two key shifts of orientation are evident here: (a) from a focus on the art work and the representation of reality to the world-view and vision of the artist-filmmaker, and (b) from an emphasis on aesthetic specificity to an approach which focuses on the autonomous, manifold perspectives apparent in the range of such world-views and visions. Whilst auteurism retained the concern for underlying structures of meaning apparent in the formalist tradition, therefore, it also implied a degree of value pluralism which can be distinguished from intuitionist modernism, and looks forward to later post-structuralist and postmodern positions. Auteurism, in addition, implies a commitment to the inter-pretative role of the critic that distinguishes this approach from the more rigorous, or theoretical-foundational orientations assumed within intuitionist modernism and realism.

The idea of film as an original work of art created by a film artist, who uses the film as a vehicle through which both to express their own vision and coterminously to portray truths which exist in the world, has its source in cultural ideologies deeply entrenched within Western society since at least the Romantic period. Those cultural ideologies emerged largely in relation to forms of art that were the product of individual artistry, and this Romantic position on authorship does not apply particularly well to art which is collaboratively produced, or which is fashioned within the legislative confines of a school, studio, or craft workplace. This would, in turn, suggest that attempts to apply the Romantic conception of authorship to a collaborative, workplace-oriented medium such as film would likewise experience such difficulties.

Even so, during the 1940s and 1950s such attempts took place, and quickly came to dominate European film scholarship. This was the stance adopted by Roger Leenhardt and Bazin writing in the journal *La Revue du Cinéma* between 1946 and 1949. The same position was reiterated in Alexandre Astruc's influential 1948 essay, 'The birth of a new avant-garde: *La camera stylo*', in which Astruc argues that 'The filmmaker-author writes with his camera as a writer writes with his pen' (quoted in Bordwell, 1994: 493). In 1951 the first issue of *Cahiers du cinéma* was devoted to an auteurist study of the films of Rossellini and Robert Bresson, whilst, in 1954, François Truffaut's *Cahiers du cinéma* essay, 'Une certaine tendance du cinéma Français', further encapsulated the auteurist position. Thereafter, writers and critics such as Jacques Rivette, Eric Rohmer, Truffaut, Fereydoun Hoveyda, Luc Mollet and Claude Chabrol continued to advance what the British critic Richard Roud sceptically referred to as the 'French line' (1960): a 'line' perhaps summed up in Rivette's enthusiastic endorsement of *The Genius of Howard Hawks* in terms of 'a beauty which demonstrates existence by breathing and movement and walking. That which is, is' ([1953] 1985: 131). In Britain, critics such as Robin Wood, Ian Cameron and Victor Perkins carried out highly detailed authorship studies of filmmakers such as Max Ophuls, Howard Hawks and Alfred Hitchcock in the journal *Movie*. Wood's analysis of Ophuls' *Letter from an Unknown Woman* (US, 1948), which concludes with the assertion that Ophuls is 'one of the cinema's great romantics', is a particularly successful example of this approach (1976: 131). The approach adopted by critics writing in *Movie*, who tended to conceive of the film director as a kind of facilitating catalyst, analogous to the conductor of an orchestra, can nonetheless be distinguished from the French position, which emphasized the primary importance of the director as the source of all significant meaning in the film.

Although this Romantic conception of authorship found its clearest articulation in the '*politique des auteurs*' of *Cahiers du Cinéma*, it could be argued that this position did not succeed in becoming estab-lished as a major paradigm within European film scholarship. Clearly, a considerable amount of European film scholarship has focused on authorship studies, particularly since the emergence of an identifiable European 'art cinema'. Much of the work of *Movie* falls into this category, but the British journals *Sequence* and *Sight and Sound* also played an important role in publishing auteurist studies of European filmmakers such as Bergman, Federico Fellini and Antonioni. Such scholarship should be distinguished from the auteur 'theory' of the *Cahiers* critics, which espouses a particularly extreme conception of auteurism in the cinema. That conception must, in the end, be rejected as philosophically untenable, as the significant structures of meaning in a film cannot all be attributed to the coherent vision of the film director.

Having said this, a distinction has to be made between the auteur theory and the auteur method, which consists of examining a corpus of films for an underlying grouping of coherent themes, and which has led to some highly sophisticated film analysis. Such analysis has often been directed at Hollywood, rather than European cinema, as in Wood's *Howard Hawks* (1968) and Bazin's *Orson Welles* (1978), although Wood's *Claude Chabrol* (1970), Raymond Durgnat's *Luis Buñuel* (1967), Geoffrey Nowell-Smith's *Visconti* (1967) and Bazin's *Jean Renoir* (1973) are studies of major European filmmakers; whilst Bazin's *What is Cinema? Vol.1* (1967) and *What is Cinema? Vol.2* (1972) contain complex auteurist studies of filmmakers such as Bresson, Rossellini, Vittorio De Sica, Dreyer and others. Even here though, problems persist, as it is not always clear why any given corpus of films should be automatically related to a director, as opposed to scriptwriter, or even genre. Another major benefit of the auteur approach lay in the extent to which it became applied to popular, as well as art house cinema, leading to a focus of critical attention on films previously regarded as unworthy of such attention. Finally, perhaps the most significant role played by the auteur theory in the development of European film scholarship, although one which the original

French advocates of auteurism would, as we will see, come to regard with a considerable sense of *dégoût*, was in providing a gateway into film scholarship for the fifth major category of European film scholarship to be discussed here: the Saussurian paradigm.

THE SAUSSURIAN PARADIGM

The Saussurian paradigm, which, for the purposes of this chapter, is regarded as encompassing semiotics, structuralism and post-structuralism, can be traced back initially to developments in the disciplines of linguistics, philosophy and symbolic logic during the 1880s (Johnson-Laird, 1989: 45). Within linguistics the key change, as far as later film theorists were concerned, was from a historical and philological approach to the study of language, to one more concerned with the structural relations which existed within contemporary language systems. One of the most influential works in this developing field was the *Cours de linguistique générale* ([1916] 1922; 1959), which was posthumously compiled from the notes of the Swiss linguist, Ferdinand de Saussure. Although the *Cours* would go on to provide a model for the development of structural linguistics in Europe over the 1916–40 period, it is important to appreciate that Saussure was by no means the only European structural linguist of note during this period, and others, such as Roman Jacobson, Vladimir Propp, Nikolay Trubetskoy, Mukurovsky, and the important Prague, Geneva and Saint Petersburg schools, also made substantial contributions. Nor was Saussurian 'semiology' the only such model to emerge during the 1920s. The 'semiotic' theories of Charles Sanders Peirce, who was more or less contemporary with Saussure, would be another important influence on writers such as Peter Wollen. Nevertheless, it was the work of Saussure which was to have the predominant influence upon the development of European film scholarship during the period of what came to be called 'screen theory'.

Initially, the seemingly irresistible sway of Saussurian thought centred on Saussure's distinction between *langue* and *parole* – a distinction that informed the key premise that film scholars would derive from Saussure. This was that generative 'deep' structures ultimately determined the content of cultural artefacts such as films, and that the chief objective of 'structuralist' analysis was to reveal those structures and show how they shaped the text. Like its formalist predecessors of the 1910–30 period, structuralist analysis, when applied to Film Studies, was often endowed with the virtues of rigour and rationally applied modus operandi, and sometimes led to the production of detailed accounts of the structures of meaning thought to be present in films. Jim Kitses' *Horizons West* (1969) and Raymond Bellour's *L'Analyse du film* (1979) are cases in point here. As will be argued later, however, structuralist methodology was also pervaded by some doubtful characteristics.

Structuralist analysis first entered Film Studies as a revision of the *politique des auteurs*, and under the sobriquet of 'auteur-structuralism', a position elaborated in the work of writers such as Wollen, Nowell-Smith, Jean-Pierre Oudart, Stephen Heath, Ben Brewster, Kitses, Alan Lovell and others. Here, structuralist ideas derived from Roland Barthes and Claude Lévi-Strauss were applied in order to effect a crucial reconsideration of the conception of authorship stemming from the *la politique des auteurs*. That amendment consisted of an abandonment of the idea that the underlying structures within a film should be considered as a manifestation of the vision of the film author. Instead, those structures were to be considered as, in the main, manifestations of more overarching social and cultural ideologies. Thus, in his *Signs and Meaning in the Cinema*, Wollen argued that the central thematic oppositions within John Ford's *The Searchers* (US, 1956) were derived from cultural antinomies between 'garden' and 'wilderness' long established in American cultural history (1969: 102). This revision effectively undermined the auteurist position which had been endorsed by Truffaut, Rivette, Rohmer, Hoveyda, Moullet, Astruc

and others during the 1950s; and we move from the *politique des auteurs* to the idea of the 'death of the author' developed by Barthes during the 1960s (1977: 208–13). Ironically, though, Bazin himself may have unwittingly begun this process of radical disengagement from auteurism as early as 1957, with his qualification of *la politique* as a problematic method which consisted of selecting only 'the personal factor in artistic creation as a factor of reference' (1981: 45).

As we have seen, Bazin's position on authorship, based as it was on a conception of existential realism, certainly differed from the steadfast auteurism of a Rivette or Hoveyda. It must also be clearly distinguished from the positions held by Barthesian/Saussurian influenced writers such as Wollen, Oudart, Christian Metz, Jean-Louis Comolli, Jean Narboni and Heath, the latter of whom, writing in *Screen*, in 1973, argued that 'the author is constituted only in language and a language is by definition social, beyond any particular individuality' (Heath, 1981: 215). Here, though, we see one of the fundamental problems of the Saussurian paradigm as it came to be applied within Film Studies: the inherent difficulties which the paradigm displays when confronting questions of individual agency. This was not acknowledged as a difficulty by structuralist film theorists (as the quotation from Heath implies): they tended to regard such questions as the residue of a discredited 'humanist' discourse that was to be consigned to history. This is the position adopted, for example, in Rosalind Coward and John Ellis' *Language and Materialism* (1977).

Despite the value of its rigorous and systematic approach, which brought real improvements to a discourse of Film Studies which, within the auteurist tradition at least, was sometimes based upon subjective judgement, structuralism, both in general and as applied in film scholarship, was also characterized by a number of methodological problems. In prioritizing the description of deep structures over an exploration of the particularities of surface content, structuralist analysis was often excessively reductivist.

Structuralist analysis was often premised upon a deterministic conception of structure, where the deep structures involved were thought to shape all possibilities of expression at the level of content. Structural analysis also tended to bracket out consideration of contextual factors, because it was ill-equipped to deal with such factors. Despite being empirical in methodological inclination, structuralism tended to subordinate the empirical to *a priori* semi-theorized models, drawn from theorists such as Lévi-Strauss and Barthes, that were themselves not held up to sufficient critical assessment. Many auxiliary troubles stemmed from this.

Although structuralism initially emerged in Europe, and achieved something of a high point in terms of Film Studies in the highly scrupulous and painstaking character of Metz's *Essais sur la signification au cinéma* (1974), the empirical, objectivist orientation of structuralism, when combined with its employment of a relatively limited range of abstract theoretical categories, tended, at that time (and for whatever reason) to appeal more to North American rather than European theorists. Consequently, many more applications of structuralist methodology to particular films were to appear in America than Europe, in the work of writers such as Will Wright, Patricia Erens and John Fell. In both Europe and America, however, the inherent problems of structuralism led to its decline during the 1970s. This decline was also precipitated by the fact that some of the main advocates of the movement turned their back on structuralism during this period. In his *Structural Anthropology: Volume Two* (1973), Lévi-Strauss forthrightly criticized the formalist essentialism in Vladimir Propp's *Morphology of the Folk Tale* (1977), and, by implication, its structuralism per se. Under the influence of Jacques Lacan, Barthes and Jacques Derrida, Lévi-Strauss then went on to endorse the consequence of what was to become that central tenet of post-structuralism: polysemy (Aitken, 2001: 104–5). Following Lévi-Strauss, Metz too denounced his own attempt to develop a general structuralist model of film form as a mistake, and moved over to a 'post-structuralist' phase in his *Psychoanalysis and Cinema* (1983). In addition to these individual critical repudiations, one of the crucial reasons for the decline of structuralism was the finding, by Metz, André Martinet, Ellis, Bellour and others, that 'film language' did not really possess a distinct *langue* in the sense that linguistic language did. The essentialism which had initially inspired structuralism proved to be its undoing when the basis of that presumed essentialism turned out to be a delusion.

Despite these problems, structuralism had at least one overriding quality, already referred to: that is, its systematic stance and related reliance upon often highly refined linguistic categories. At its best, the structuralist method could be employed as a highly detailed form of measure, against which film texts could be understood in terms of their nuanced departures from that measure. The more problematic structuralist approaches from the 1960s and 1970s also evolved into the more rewarding French school of 'post-semiotics' of the late eighties and nineties, in the work of writers such as Jacques Aumont, Michel Marie, André Gaudreault, François Jost, Francis Vanoye, Marc Vernet and Michel Chion. Perhaps the most important work here, because it attempts a re-appraisal of a major figure within the Saussurian tradition, is Marie and Vernet's *Christian Metz et la théorie du cinéma* (1990). Within much of this work precise analyses of both image and narrative led to subtle as well as highly detailed analyses of film texts. Even here though, the central problems of structuralism still remained, most notably a tendency towards a scrutiny of the internal dynamics of the text which conferred a problematic degree of autonomy on the medium, and continued to bracket out context, as in Gaudreault and Jost's *Le Récit cinématographique* (1990). Structuralism, even of the post-semiotic variety, is a type of formalism, and, although formalism may sometimes be an indispensable component of textual analysis (though that is also debatable), its inability to deal well with context created problems for this body of work.

Structuralism evolved into post-structuralism in the late 1960s under the influence of French theorists such as Barthes, Lévi-Strauss, Lacan, Louis Althusser, Derrida and Michel Foucault. Although post-structuralism, as a movement, was far less coherent than structuralism had been, it emerged across a range of disciplines as part of a perceived need to oppose both dominant institutional and ideological structures of power and authority, and foundationalist, realist or humanist conceptions of the self, reason, intentionality and knowledge. Structuralism did not by any means evolve seamlessly into post-structuralism, nor did post-structuralists move *en masse* from essentialism into a philosophical position founded upon anti-essentialist premises. A further distinction must be drawn here between a post-structuralist position which is largely indistinguishable from so-called 'postmodernism', and a form of 'modernist' post-structuralism which still encapsulated what is often referred to as 'screen theory'. The former position, derived from the ideas of Derrida and the later Barthes, was largely taken up within the American deconstruction movement during the 1970s and 1980s, and emphasized the need to subvert authoritarian and normative values by focusing on the utopian polysemic potential of communication. The second position combined this same imperative to subvert dominant ideology with a project to formulate and advance alternative ideological tropes that sought to elaborate an explanation of the world. Another more pivotal philosophical distinction can be traced between these two positions. In the latter case, a modernist project based upon a synthesis of de-familiarization and analytical renovation is evident; whilst, in the former case, a 'postmodern' position, based upon de-familiarization and the repudiation of such renovations, takes precedence. The first of these positions remained foundationalist to a degree, in positing the possibility of a convergence between theory and reality, albeit one in which dominant 'naturalized' convergences were rejected; while the second

is fundamentally relativist, and radically anti-foundationalist in its rejection of the value, or possibility, of seeking any such convergence.

As with structuralism, both of these positions were founded upon forms of determinism premised upon the possibility, or in this case the dearth of possibility, for effectual agency. These forms of determinism were derived from Saussurian thought and were based on a conviction that the modern subject was shaped by systemic, institutionalized and language-based structures. For modernist post-structuralists such as Althusser the subject was inescapably 'overdetermined' by such structures. For postmodern post-structuralists, the subject was not so much seen as a potential agent at all in this sense. Instead, the postmodern subject was regarded as a complicit participant in a process of discursive engagement taking place within a reflexive, intertextual system. Agency here comes to be defined not in terms of autonomous will leading to accomplishment, as it is in most established philosophical definitions of the notion, but in terms of an only partly-mindful involvement in a dialectic of meaning consumption and production. A clear evolution can be traced, therefore, from structuralism (foundationalist, essentialist and determinist) to screen theory post-structuralism (partly-foundationalist, partly-relativist and determinist) to postmodern post-structuralism (anti-foundationalist, anti-essentialist, relativist, and based on a depleted, and rather unconventional notion of agency). This was a portentous course for Film Studies to take, one which commenced with determinist linguistic realism, but finished up with a form of *laissez-faire* utopian linguistic relativism. As will be argued below, Film Studies did not have to take this anomalous philosophical route between a determinist rock and a relativist hard place.

The first development from structuralism, that of post-structuralist screen theory, can, to some extent, be regarded as a Saussurian-inspired variant of 'Western Marxism': a term which came to designate the various schools of analysis which emerged in western Europe from the 1920s onwards, and which sought to revise a classical Marxism which had become disfigured by an unbending Stalinist and communist tenet. Western Marxism encompassed the work of a range of scholars of the highest calibre, including that of Lukács, Brecht, Bourdieu, Lucien Goldmann, Henri Lefebvre, Jean-Paul Sartre, Raymond Williams, Gramsci and members of the Frankfurt School. The model of Western Marxist thought which was to influence European film scholarship the most – that associated with the ideas of Althusser and Lacan – was probably the most determinist to emerge from this body of work. European post-structuralist film scholarship adopted this deterministic variant of Western Marxism because it was already committed to Saussurian thought, and, during the 1970s, Althusserian and Lacanian inspired ideas influenced French journals such as *Positif*, *Tel Quel*, *Cinétique*, *CinéAction*, and *Cahiers du Cinéma*; English journals such as *Framework* and *Screen*; and writers such as Heath, Colin MacCabe, Comolli, Oudart, Jacques-Alain Miller, Daniel Dayan and Narboni. The various attempts made by these journals and individuals during the 1970s to establish an alternative, post-structuralist counter-culture within film theory all eventually foundered on the rock of problematic conceptualization, and on an inadequate model of agency.

Western Marxist thought was premised upon a belief in the need to refocus attention upon the role of the ideological superstructure, rather than economic base of society in reproducing dominant relations of power within capitalism. This change of orientation from a more classical Marxist position was influenced by a need to understand why socialism had failed to achieve hegemony in the developed countries of western Europe – even though the overwrought condition of the economic base in those countries suggested (to Marxists) that such hegemony ought to occur – and a desire to theorize a more positive role for agency and progressive intellectual venture in the face of the mounting instrumentalization of intellectual enquiry within the Soviet bloc. Although the

Althusserian/Lacanian school was influenced by the first of these imperatives, it tended to theorize the role of ideology in such a way that notions of active, effectual agency were conceived of mainly as the residue of a false and disingenuous bourgeois humanist discourse which must be repudiated. So, just as Althusser argued that the subject was 'positioned', and so 'misrecognized' what it took to be its own 'free' self, Althusserian (and Lacanian) inspired film scholars such as Jean-Louis Baudry, Comolli, Metz and Narboni argued, in papers such as 'Cinéma, idéologie, critique' (Comolli and Narboni, 1969), that dominant cinema too participated in a process of subject-positioning in relation to the interests of the dominant order. Yet, had post-structuralist film theory taken a different course during this crucial period, say in order to embrace some more salient blend of the ideas of a Williams, Gramsci or Bourdieu, rather than of Althusser and Lacan, things may have worked out quite differently for the development of the discipline.

It was in the pages of the journal *Screen*, in particular, that a systematic attempt was made, by critics such as Heath, MacCabe, Ellis, Laura Mulvey and others to develop an overarching theory of modernist post-structuralist cinematic representation, based on the influence of Althusser, Saussure and Lacan, and on the 'encounter of Marxism and psychoanalysis on the terrain of semiotics' (Easthope, 1991: 35). What has become known as 'screen theory' was constituted from an amalgam of influences, including those of French structuralism and post-structuralism, Western Marxism, Brecht, early formalism, Soviet montage cinema, feminism and other influences. Screen theory was undoubtedly motivated by high ideals. The objective was to utilize film and film theory in an effort to challenge the dominant capitalist or patriarchal order, and establish a 'counter cinema' within an intellectual 'counter-culture'. Although the committed idealism of screen theory cannot be faulted, the conceptual foundations upon which it relied can.

The problems of screen theory have been well documented elsewhere, but can be summarized for present purposes as follows: (a) The screen theory tradition contained an implicit commitment to determinism, and preoccupation with the determining influence of 'deep', or 'innate', or 'self-regulating' internal structures. (b) This orientation led to depleted conceptions of agency. (c) These lesser conceptions of agency, whilst problematic in themselves, also negated the overall objectives of the screen theory project, because such an account of agency implied that the attempt to develop a counter-culture must be predestined to fail. (d) The idea that realism, in the shape of the 'classic realist text' hypothesized by Colin MacCabe (MacCabe, 1974), was intrinsically politically reactionary at the level of form, led to a counter-productive rejection of an aesthetic form consumed by spectators over the world. The advocacy of anti-realist filmmaking thus ensured that an effective oppositional cinema would never become commonplace. (e) Screen theory often employed unhistoricized accounts of subjectivity, determination, representation and agency. (f) Whilst screen theory (in structuralist mode) was often able to describe representational relationships in great detail – because it was based on a relational theory of signification – it was often unable to explain what such representations meant in a more conceptual and wide-ranging sense.

Despite such objections, important work was carried out within the parameters of screen theory. The critique of romantic conceptions of authorship was a major step forward, as was work on feminist and gender theory by Mulvey, Claire Johnston, Elizabeth Cowie and others. Mulvey's paper 'Visual Pleasure and Narrative Cinema' (1975) has been particularly influential. Other achievements included the critical reassessment of Brecht, political modernism and Soviet montage theory in works such as the special *Screen* edition on Brecht which appeared in 1974, MacCabe's *Godard: Images, Sounds, Politics* (1980), Martin Walsh's *The Brechtian Aspect of Radical Cinema* (1981) and Sylvia Harvey's *May '68 and Film Culture* (1980). The screen

theory concern with ideology and subjectivity also led to the appearance of influential work by Heath, MacCabe and others. Heath's 'Narrative Space' (1976) was a significant intervention in this respect. Finally, work on narrative by Heath, Bellour and others looks forward to later work on film narratology by David Bordwell, Edward Branigan and others. From the 1980s onwards, *Screen* abandoned the attempt to establish a unified theory of film, based on psychoanalytic, Marxist and semiotic/structuralist theory, and, instead, pioneered a number of influential debates in areas such as postmodernism, gay and lesbian spectatorship, and postcolonial/post-national/alternative cinemas.

As previously argued, the modernist post-structuralist screen theory position can be distinguished from a more 'postmodern' post-structuralist philosophical orientation within European film scholarship. That latter orientation drew on the ideas of Foucault and Derrida, as well as theorists more evidently categorized as 'postmodern' such as Jean-François Lyotard and Jean Baudrillard. Although there are differences between, say, Derrida and Lyotard, such dissimilarities are not as great as the similarities that bind them together. In many respects, the term 'post-structuralism' actually seems more helpful in representing a school of thought concerned with a radical position on the relativity and plurality of meaning, than does the term 'postmodern', given that the 'modern' encompasses deconstructive tendencies, and the sorts of philosophical positions on relativity which are putatively the preserve of the postmodern. Modernist post-structuralism marks one stage along the road towards relativism, whilst post-structuralism proper marks not just one further point along that route, but something approaching a full-blown relativist point of reference. Frankly, although it might be more helpful to refer to a distinction between 'political modernism' and 'post-structuralism', to abandon the term 'postmodern' in favour of 'post-structuralism' would probably lead to confusion, given the current state of understanding of what is meant by that term. In what follows, therefore, and in order to maintain the earlier distinction from modernist post-structuralism, the term 'postmodern post-structuralism' will be substituted for both 'post-structuralism' and 'postmodernism'.

POSTMODERN POST-STRUCTURALISM/PRAGMATISM

The problems engendered by screen theory led to the emergence of the latest period of European film theory and scholarship, which stretches from the 1980s to the present. Although the various movements and schools of thought which make up this period are quite disparate, many of them are related, to varying degrees, in their shared refutation of the high-theoretical, totalizing ambitions of screen theory and modernist post-structuralism (or high political-modernism), and, by implication, in their subsequent commitment to a more circumscribed stance towards the theorization of film in relation to particular aesthetic, social, cultural and political questions. It is because of this loosely shared affiliation, and for the sake of expediency, that this period in film scholarship will be referred to here as that of 'postmodern post-structuralism/pragmatism'.

One school of European film scholarship which developed during the 1980s carried on the psychoanalytic tradition inherited from Lacan and Julia Kristeva. It is particularly difficult to distinguish clearly between post-structuralist modernist and post-structuralist postmodern psychoanalytic modalities here, and more appropriate to delineate a continuity which encompasses the work of thinkers such as Derrida, Kristeva, Lacan, Baudrillard and Lyotard; and film scholars such as Mulvey, Jacqueline Rose, Baudry, Metz, Oudart, Heath, Cowie and Juliet Mitchell. This work relies on an associated range of psychoanalytic concepts, including those of the 'imaginary/symbolic/real', 'phallocentrism', 'identification', 'the gaze', 'masochism', the 'mirror stage' and 'scopophilia'; as well as on less specifically psychoanalytic notions,

such as those of 'discourse', 'intertextuality', 'deconstruction', 'pleasure', 'subjectivity', 'patriarchy', and the centrality of power relations. In fact, there is not much to choose, in the end, between a post-structuralist screen theory reading of Lacan from the mid-1970s, and Lyotard's notions of the *Dispositif* and 'libidinal', or Baudrillard's writing on seduction, masculinity and femininity in *Seduction* (1990). Such lack of distinction apart, it should be pointed out that this area of scholarship has been particularly influential within the feminist theory of French writers such as Hélène Cixous, Luce Irigaray and others. Cixous, for example, advances a 'counter-writing' strategy of feminist writing – *écriture féminine*, derived from Lacan and Derrida – whilst the same approach is evident in Irigaray's notion of *parler femme* (Fuery, 2000: 47). Although both these writers were largely concerned with literature rather than film, their ideas have been developed within European Film Studies by some of the film scholars previously referred to, and in critical studies such as *Contemporary Film Theory* (Easthope, 1993), *New Developments in Film Theory* (Fuery, 2000) and *Film Theory: An Introduction* (Lapsley and Westlake, 2006).

Outside of psychoanalysis, postmodern post-structuralism also tends to reject 'meta-discourse', essentialism and 'grand narratives', in order to emphasize the pluralism and relativity of discourse, the value of creativity and intertextuality, and the more definable practical 'micro' purposes (including, in some cases, political purposes) to which theory should be put. Definitions of postmodern film vary, but, in general, such definitions tend to emphasize the prioritization of spectacle over narrative, the intertextuality of reference, the effacement of the difference between past and present, the use of pastiche, visual and visceral excess, parody, the fluidity of identity, the fictionality of cause and effect, and the establishment of a sense of the perpetual present. Different views prevail concerning the significance of such films. Critics such as Alan Williams take the view that 'postmodern' films such as *Les Amants du Pont-Neuf* (Léos Carax, France, 1991) both reveal the 'postmodern condition' in terms of a 'profound nihilism' and celebrate pluralism and difference (1992: 401). On the other hand, other critics take the view that such films merely reinforce the commodification of culture which is unremittingly taking place within 'late capitalism'. Fredric Jameson argues for the latter in the case of the films of Brian de Palma, but attempts to steer a more discriminating line elsewhere in arguing that, whilst some postmodern films (and post-modern aspects of other films) do reinforce the commodification of culture within late capitalism, a film such as *Diva* (Jean-Jacques Beineix, France, 1982) employs postmodern stylistics in order to critique aspects of the postmodern condition (1992: 62).

Many writers on postmodernism and film, including Linda Hutcheon, Jameson, Laura Kipnis and others, tend to focus on Hollywood films because of postmodernist theory's general orientation towards popular culture, although they often centre on atypical Hollywood films, such as David Lynch's *Blue Velvet* (US, 1986). Some scholars, including Robert Stam, Ella Shohat and Hal Foster turn towards forms of critical postmodern cinema evident in Third World cinema. Others such as Phil Powrie and Susan Hayward engage with postmodern European cinema, and follow Jameson's endorsement of *Diva*, by similarly sanctioning the postmodern style employed within the *cinéma du look* of Beineix, Luc Besson and Carax. Jim Collins argues for the effective critical postmodernism of a film such as Hans-Jürgen Syberberg's *Parsifal* (France/West Germany, 1984), whilst Kobena Mercer argues that the work of black British filmmakers in the 1980s, as in a work such as *Handsworth Songs* (John Akomfrah/ Black Audio Film Collective, UK, 1986), constitutes a kind of postmodern practice of collage-like filmmaking, which reworks and deconstructs existing and dominant representations of black Britain (1988: 11). Within a perspective of feminist theory, Annette Kuhn has argued that a collage-like postmodern approach to filmmaking may be particularly appropriate for a female spectator who may be simultaneously experiencing

a number of different and shifting identities (1994: 202).

Within postmodern film theory in general, both European and other, a division can be found between those who adhere more to the position that a postmodern film culture should eschew analysis (grand narratives) altogether, and those who argue that some kind of theoretical foundationalism must be retained, in the interests of realizing political or other objectives. Philosophically, at the centre of the postmodern approach we find the contention that the aspiration to procurement of insight through analytic critique is to be given up in favour of a contrary aspiration to engender a free space of semantic manufacture and consumption. Perhaps it does not particularly matter, in the end, that these two approaches appear to be philosophically incompatible, so long as some provisional, 'practical' incorporation of the two is able to intervene to effect within specific areas of social/cultural contest, as Cultural Studies-based scholars such as Stuart Hall have argued (see below). For such critics it is more important that theory is able to effect change than be endowed with internal lucidity. On the other hand, even if such conceptual incongruity does manage to deliver some dividends on the ground as a consequence of activist commitment, it might eventually lead to the refutation of the postmodern post-structuralist edifice within Film Studies. In addition, the adoption of a postmodern position based on extreme relativism is inevitably problematic. An approach, for example, based on a study of the film 'text' as vehicle of contradiction and aporia, such as that endorsed by the French scholar Marie-Claire Ropars-Wuilleumier in her *Le Texte divisé* (1981), is clearly of value in avoiding naive interpretations of films – and, also, possibly, in averting the regressive positioning of the spectator (a prime objective of Ropars-Wuilleumier's method). At the level of epistemology, it has to be questioned whether an approach premised upon the need to avoid explanation per se is actually sustainable, and not ultimately counterproductive. Within a feminist perspective, this is the question raised by scholars such as Linda Nicholson and Nancy Fraser in their anthology *Feminism/Postmodernism* (1988: 34).

As with post-structuralism in both its modern and postmodern phases, the notion that society was composed of dominant and subordinate power and interest groups, and competing ideological discourses, influenced a school of English-language popular Cultural Studies. Cultural Studies drew on a wide range of intellectual frameworks, including various strands of Western Marxism, sociological theory, psychoanalysis, the Frankfurt School, empirical methodology, communications theory, reception studies, policy studies, feminism, gender theory, classical Marxism, the post-structuralist theory of Lacan, Althusser and Foucault, theories of colonialism, post-colonialism and postmodernism. Despite such an array of theoretical positions, this school can be collectively distinguished by two principal features: first, a rejection of the determinism implicit within much Saussurian thought; and, second, a related sanction of popular cultural forms as valuable and authentic modes of social expression. Such endorsement has a particularly lengthy lineage within British Cultural Studies, and includes work carried out on working-class history and culture by E.P. Thompson, Richard Hoggart and Raymond Williams during the 1950s and 1960s. Central to this body of work, in studies such as *The Uses of Literacy* (Hoggart, 1957), *Culture and Society, 1780–1950* (Williams, 1958) and *The Making of the English Working Class* (Thompson, 1968), was a desire to explore the means by which a culture of moral resistance could survive within working-class life, against the background of a debilitating and stifling capitalist hegemony.

The work of Thompson, Hoggart and Williams generally conceived of popular cultural forms as valid expressions of such resistance. However, during the period in which Althusserian-based screen theory was dominant, this conception of popular culture tended to be replaced by one in which such forms were seen as overdetermined by the dominant institutions of society. In reaction to this, later work within British Cultural

Studies, by Hall, Graeme Turner, Martin Barker, Tony Bennett, Dick Hebdige, Judith Williamson and others, explored previously uncharted areas of popular culture, including popular cinema, in an attempt to illuminate the complex relationships which existed between popular culture, a climate of resistance, and the audience.

Study of the audience from a Cultural Studies perspective became particularly influential during the 1980s. Much of the emphasis here tended to be on television rather than film, though, amongst others, studies were carried out by Janet Woollacott on the James Bond films, and by Philip Corrigan on the development of the British film audience. Bennett, Woollacott, Tony Mercer and Susan Boyd-Bowman also co-edited the influential *Popular Television and Film* in 1981. In some cases, the focus on the idea of popular culture as a form of subcultural resistance within this body of work led to an undue valorization of texts which might not necessarily always be as 'authentic' or oppositional as proponents of the Cultural Studies approach imagined them to be. This point was made by Barker and Anne Beezer in *Reading into Cultural Studies* (1992). Disproportionate attention paid to texts made it more likely that such texts would become estranged from their various contexts, and particularly from their historical contexts; a point made by Raymond Williams in his *The Politics of Modernism: Against the New Conformists* (1989), when he called upon Cultural Studies to relate such texts more to both the social formations and aesthetic history from which they had emerged. The wide range of theoretical approaches brought to bear within Cultural Studies meant that, although the discipline displayed a pluralist, postmodern sensibility, it possessed few cohesive intellectual parameters, and was, as Raymond Williams himself put it, something of a 'baggy monster' (quoted in Barker and Beezer, 1992: 9). Some Cultural Studies practitioners did not necessarily see this as a bad thing.

Another response to the exigencies of grand theory and the problems of screen theory, and one which emerged more or less completely outside the Saussurian tradition, was the rise of empirically-based film historiography from the late 1970s onwards. Initially, such work emerged out of the history departments of universities and concentrated on the propaganda, newsreel and fiction film as a form of documentation of historical events. Work in this category includes *Politics, Propaganda and Film, 1918–1945* (Pronay and Spring, 1982) and *Feature Films as History* (Short, 1981). Although such work had the advantage of bringing academic historiographical method to bear upon the study of film, it usually failed to engage sufficiently well with existing and prior schools of film analysis, or with the aesthetic qualities of the medium. One very positive outcome of this development, however, was the formation of the *Historical Journal of Film, Radio and Television*, which went on to publish high-quality historical research into film throughout the 1980s and up until the present.

Outside of traditional university history departments, another body of historical work on film, influenced by the earlier tradition of Cultural Studies, attempted to base a new popular film historiography upon premises derived from Thompson and Williams, and, also, from Western Marxist theoreticians such as Gramsci, Eric Hobsbawm, Lukács, Bourdieu, Walter Benjamin, the Frankfurt School and others. The work of Stuart Hood, Vincent Porter, Kuhn, Sue Harper, Michael Chanan and others falls into this area, whose spirit is, to some extent, encapsulated in James Curran and Vincent Porter's edited anthology *British Cinema History* (1983). This theoretical turn proved difficult to sustain, given the problems of elaborating a unified theoretical model of film history based on Western Marxist and Cultural Studies approaches. One exception here is, perhaps, feminist-inspired scholarship, in the work of Harper, Christine Gledhill, Christine Geraghty, Cowie and others. Eventually, scholarship in this area became more directly engaged in primary research on filmmakers, film genres, production, distribution and exhibition practices and institutional issues;

under the conviction that an extensive terrain of materials urgently required attention. Although such work did not normally employ particularly rigorous theoretical models and was as a consequence sometimes criticized by proponents of the Saussurian paradigm, it was informed by various theoretical positions, including those drawn from feminism and Marxism; and did result in some of the most rigorous and productive scholarship to emerge within European Film Studies. In Britain, Charles Barr, Harper, Andrew Higson, Sarah Street, Tony Aldgate, Nicholas Pronay, Jeffrey Richards, Robert Murphy, John Hill and others carried out intensive studies of British film history; whilst Ian Aitken, Alan Burton, Harvey, Brian Winston and others wrote on the British documentary film. A journal – the *Journal of Popular British Cinema* (now the *Journal of British Cinema and Television*) – was established, whilst the *Encyclopedia of the Documentary Film* (Aitken, 2006) contained extensive sections on British and European documentary filmmaking, and *The Encyclopedia of British Film* (McFarlane, 2003) covered the area of British cinema in a comprehensive manner.

During the 1980s and 1990s, concepts such as national identity, national cinema, cultural identity, postcolonialism, regionalism, hybridity and globalization became increasingly important within European film scholarship, and a range of publications appeared dealing with such issues as they affected Europe as a whole. Examples here would be Duncan Petrie's *Screening Europe* (1992), Nowell-Smith and Stephen Ricci's *Hollywood and Europe: Economics, Culture and National Identity* (1998), and *National Identity and European Cinema* (Drummond et al., 1993). During the 1980s, the acceleration of globalization, privatization of public broadcasting, and development of a European-wide media policy supported by the European Union, led to an increase in scholarship which examined policy issues in relation to film. Work falling into this category included Richard Collins' *From Satellite to Single Market* (1998) and *Media and Identity in Contemporary Europe* (2002); and

Albert Moran's *Film Policy* (1996). Attention also tended to be paid here to the European 'co-production' as a creature of a European, as opposed to national, film market, as in Anne Jackel's *European Film Industries* (2003) and Mette Hjort and Scott MacKenzie's *Cinema and Nation* (2000).

In addition to dealing with Europe as a whole, much work appearing during this period dealt more directly with issues of particular national cinemas, and it is possible to argue that this eventually became established as one of the most important bodies of historical film scholarship to be produced during the 1990s and beyond. Writers on British cinema have already been referred to, but in addition to these, writers such as Ginette Vincendeau, Serge Daney, Aumont, Jill Forbes, Martin O'Shaugnessey, Antoine De Baerque, Guy Austin, Carrie Tarr, Phil Powrie, Hayward, Michèle Lagny, Pierre Sorlin, Marie and others explored various aspects of French cinema. Sorlin's *The Film in History* (1980) and *European Cinemas, European Societies* (1991), Lagny's *Senso* (1990) and Marie's *La Nouvelle Vague* (2001) can all be cited as good examples of such scholarship. The same phenomena was evident in relation to the Italian cinema, where Roy Armes, Georgio Bertellini, Pierre Leprohon. Mira Liehm, Gianni Volpi, James Hay, Sorlin and others produced important work. An example here would be, once again, Sorlin and his *Italian National Cinema* (1996). Outside of France and Italy, writers such as Dina Iordinova, Yuri Tsivian, Anna Lawton, Graham Petrie, Lynne Attwood, David Gillespie, Paul Coates, Richard Taylor, Anikó Imre and David Goulding wrote on Russian and central/eastern European cinemas. Imre's edited anthology, *East European Cinemas* (2005), is a good example of such scholarship, though Richard Taylor's extensive research on and translation of Eisenstein and the Soviet film scholarship of the 1920s and 1930s, including his and Ian Christie's edited collection *The Film Factory: Russian and Soviet Cinema in Documents 1896–1939* (1988) deserves special mention here. Peter von Bagh's work on Finnish cinema, and Tytti Soila's *Nordic National Cinemas* (1998) and *The Cinema of Scandinavia* (2005), dealt with issues of film and national identity in northern Europe; whilst writers such as Anton Kaes, Sabina Hake, Julian Knight, David Clarke, Gertrud Koch, Erwin Leiser, Terri Ginsberg, Patrice Petro, Eric Rentschler, Marc Silberman, Miriam Bratu Hansen, Richard Taylor, Eric Rentschler, Julian Petley, Thomas Elsaesser and others wrote on the German cinema (see, for example, Ginsberg and Thompson, 1996). Rob Stone, Barry Jordan, Alberto Mira and Peter William Evans' work on Spanish and Portuguese national cinema deserves mention, as do Maria Stassinopoulou (2006) on Greek cinema, Ruth Barton (2004) on Irish cinema, Robert Von Dassanowsky (2005) on Austrian cinema, and Paul Coates (2005) on Polish cinema. Many other examples could be given. Such work adds up to a particularly significant body of European film scholarship, supported by the emergence of new journals, such as *Studies in European Cinema*, which first appeared in 2003.

The school of popular cinema historiography referred to above could be labelled 'pragmatist' with a small 'p' in recognition of its turn from high theory to more empirical, observable and realizable forms of analysis. However, during the 1990s, a school of scholarship emerged, largely in America, which might be labelled 'Pragmatist' with a capital 'P'. Like postmodernism and historicist approaches, American Pragmatist-influenced film theory eschewed a concern for abstract theory, and turned, instead, to more restricted enquiries into empirical or intermediate categories of concept and material. It was impelled to do so, in part, by the conviction that such concepts and material would provide more useful, classifiable and testable results. However, whether consciously or unconsciously, this pragmatist practice tended to secrete a bracketing of high theory under the veil of an opposition to screen theory, and, in particular, the unifying imperative underlying screen theory. So, for example, Bordwell argues against the need for a 'Big Theory of Everything', by which he means screen theory, or any contemporary facsimile of screen theory (Bordwell and Carroll, 1996: 29–30). The problem is that what Bordwell calls 'middle-level' theorizing (Bordwell and Carroll, 1996: 29), and what Noël Carroll refers to as 'piecemeal generalisation' (Carroll, 1996: 332), does not just stand as an opposition to screen theory, or even to 'big' comprehensive theories, but also, as argued, as a general opposition to the predominant use of chiefly abstract theoretical categories within film research.

One consequence of this is an avoidance of the high 'culturalist' issues which fall too far outside the technical discursive territory of what Bordwell calls the 'middle-level research programme' (Bordwell and Carroll, 1996: 29). Another is an avoidance of engagement with the political. Although there is no necessary contradiction between a pragmatist approach and political engagement, in practice, the general orientation of the pragmatist approach is to bypass the political. This pragmatist school of Film Studies developed in the United States, was influenced by North American pragmatist philosophy, from William James to Richard Rorty, and is closely linked to the development of film scholarship based upon principles derived from cognitivist methodology and Anglo-American analytical philosophy. A pragmatist orientation towards theory fits less easily with the history of European film theory and scholarship, which has always been based on high theory, and on the engagement with the kinds of 'culturalist' categories which pragmatist film theorists would prefer to distance themselves from.

Some attempts have been made to introduce both analytical philosophy and cognitivist methodology into European scholarship, as (in the latter case) in Murray Smith's *Engaging Characters: Fiction, Emotion and the Cinema* (1995) and Torben Grodal's *Moving Pictures* (1997). As with Smith and Grodal's work, the value of applying cognitivist methods to the study of film lies in the degree of detail and close empirical analysis which can be generated. Another important intervention into the field of film

scholarship stemming from the analytical tradition is that offered by Stanley Cavell, and, in particular, by *The World Viewed: Reflections on the Ontology of Film* (1979). Whilst writing mainly on the American cinema, Cavell has written on some European films and filmmakers, including Jean-Luc Godard, Bergman and Rohmer. When discussing Godard's *Je vous salue, Marie* (France/Switzerland/UK, 1984), for example, Cavell invokes Ludwig Wittgenstein in order to explore notions of the 'soul', 'miracle', and the Christian idea of the relationship between soul and body, as he believes them to be portrayed in Godard's film (2005: 179–80). Although Cavell's work continues to spawn ongoing critical interpretations, most of this work, as in William Rothman's *Cavell on Film* (2005), tends to be carried out in North America, rather than Europe. In addition to Cavell, scholars such as Carroll and Cynthia A. Freedland, write on Film Studies from within the perspective of analytical philosophy. Finally, Terry Lovell's *Pictures of Reality* (1980) and Aitken's *Realist Film Theory and Cinema* (2006) attempt a critique of conventionalist, relativist, pragmatist and cognitivist positions from within a theoretical framework of 'philosophical realism': a branch of analytical philosophy associated with philosophers such as Roy Bhaskar, Roger Trigg, Rom Harré and others, and encapsulated in Trigg's *Reality at Risk: A Defense of Realism in Philosophy and the Sciences* (1989).

In addition to the Anglo-American analytical tradition, another relatively recent, though in this case 'continental', philosophical influence on European film scholarship, has been that of Gilles Deleuze, and particularly his *Cinema 1: The Movement-Image* (1986) and *Cinema 2: The Time-Image* (1989). In these two books, Deleuze attempts to develop an understanding of the aesthetic specificity of cinematic form based on conceptions of temporal experience which he derives from the philosophy of Henri Bergson. Bergson considered space and time to be aspects of '*durée*', or 'duration'. The universe (duration) is conceived of as a flow of matter-movement, which condenses into space, time and discrete objects. *Durée* is, therefore, a continuously changing manifold flow of succession, which constitutes an evolving totality (Bogue, 2003: 3). This notion of duration as fluctuating totality forms the basis of Deleuze's understanding of the cinema, within which he conceives of the film 'frame' as a slice of duration, 'montage' as a linked combination of such slices, and the 'shot' as the material basis of both frame and montage. The cinematic image is, therefore, a framed image-in-movement: what Deleuze refers to as the 'movement-image', because the image captures the movement occurring within a slice of *durée*. Deleuze argues that the 'movement-image' characterizes the cinema from its origins to the 1940s, after which it evolves into the 'time-image', which provides the aesthetic basis for later, more modern/modernist cinema. Deleuze's account of the progression from movement-image to time-image appears to suggest that such progression is both inevitable and benign, and, although Deleuze has claimed that he is not arguing that 'the modern cinema of the time-image is more "valuable" than the classical cinema of the movement-image', the thrust of his argument leads in that direction (Deleuze, 1986: x).

Deleuze argues that the film image is a material entity in itself before it is an image of something, and that, because of this, the expressive potential of the image should be allowed to transcend any representational imperative imposed upon it. At the same time, Deleuze also contends that, in the case of the 'movement-image', the primary expressive and substantial character of the film image is beset by such an imperative. Furthermore, that imperative is necessarily caught up within dominant, ideological representational systems of logic, language and rationality, because such macro-systems possess the power to determine the structure and function of all representational systems operating within and beneath them. The cinema of the movement-image is therefore problematic for a number of reasons. Above all, it subordinates expression to representation, and such representation necessarily serves to reproduce dominant ideologies. In addition, the movement-image is only able to encase a segment of duration, and is, as a consequence, unable to portray the extensive nature of *durée* directly: although the image is able to indicate the presence of the manifold as it spreads beyond the confines of the image, it is unable to portray that presence directly. Finally, the movement-image is unable to portray the movement of duration itself, because each shot constitutes only a fragment of duration. Despite the overall thrust of his argument, Deleuze does not abandon the belief that the movement-image remains of value, because of its ability to represent duration, albeit indirectly, and because it still holds onto some of its latent, expressive character.

For Deleuze, two principal factors explain the shift from the movement-image to the time-image around 1940. The first was the experience of the carnage and atrocities of the Second World War: an experience subsequently directed into a critique of the forms of naturalized rationalism and ideologically-driven logic which had provided legitimation for such carnage and atrocities. This critique found expression in the cinema in terms of a desire to free the medium from the overriding sway of its representational and normative functions: functions which worked to make manifest an 'effect of truth' that had now been brought into profound question (Deleuze, 1989: 142). In place of the naturalizing function of the movement-image, the time-image now emphasized the expressive and material character of the film image. In addition, the cinema of the time-image sought to establish 'unnatural' links between things, as part of a deconstructive 'modern' phase of the cinema, in which film mobilized the 'powers of the false' in repudiation of prevailing assumptions (Deleuze, 1989: 126). The second cause of the shift to the time-image lay in the inability of the movement-image to portray *durée* directly, as an open, evolving whole. Such incapacity made it imperative that a new means of portraying *durée* more directly be found. It was in the use of long-take deep-focus photography by Orson Welles, suggests Deleuze, that, perhaps for the first time in the cinema, the time-image came to correspond more directly to the actual character of duration as continuously changing totality.

Although preoccupied, at one level, with film's ability to represent space and time as he believes they exist within duration, it is clear that, at another level, Deleuze's film theory is driven by a contrary stipulation that film should not be regarded primarily as a representational medium. Such a stipulation has larger implications, which stretch well beyond the prospective significance of Deleuze's own theoretical system. His insistence that the deconstructive and 'expressive' aspects of the film medium must take precedence over any representational function ultimately derives from his more general understanding of the philosophical concept as an expressive 'force', rather than as something which is particularly commensurable, or representational; and this, in turn, places Deleuze's thought firmly within a greater body of postmodernist thought, one which has become increasingly influential within European film theory and scholarship since the 1980s. That postmodernist tradition possesses many attributes, including a predisposition for the deconstruction of naturalized ideology, the mobilization of an array of complex concepts drawn from a variety of disciplines, the ability to engage with the political, and a celebration of the values of polysemy and difference. It also draws upon important intellectual sources in European intellectual history, including figures such as Sören Kierkegaard, Friedrich Nietzsche and Martin Heidegger, and theoretical schemas such as those of psychoanalysis, linguistics and philosophy.

Although a great deal of highly productive European film scholarship continues to be carried out within this postmodernist tradition, it would be unfortunate if it were to become hegemonic at the expense of the other traditions of scholarship addressed in this chapter. The academy of European film scholarship needs to remain open and accessible. It should resist the temptation to close in on itself as it tended to during the period of screen theory, and as it could again. In addition to supporting postmodernist research, European film scholarship will flourish best if it adopts a reflective, and, in cases where it is warranted, revisionist stance, in order to engage with the heritage of European film, and European Film Studies, as they have developed from the beginning of the twentieth century to the present. This, in turn, will require the continued deployment of historiographical and related methodologies as part of a larger study of European film history. European film scholarship will also benefit from a continued engagement with both pre-twentieth century traditions of European thought, and the other traditions covered in this chapter, namely, those of nineteenth-century realism/classical Marxism, intuitionist realism and modernism, auteurism, Saussurian and postmodern post-structuralism/pragmatism.

REFERENCES

Abel, Richard (ed.) (1988) *French Film Theory and Criticism: A History/Anthology, 1907–1939*. Vol.2. Princeton, NJ: Princeton University Press.

Aitken, Ian (2001) *European Film Theory and Cinema*. Edinburgh: Edinburgh University Press.

Aitken, Ian (2006) *Realist Film Theory and Cinema*. Manchester: Manchester University Press.

Aitken, Ian (2006) *Encyclopaedia of the Documentary Film*. London: Routledge.

Andrew, Dudley (1995) *Mists of Regret: Culture and Sensibility in Classic French Film*. Princeton, NJ: Princeton University Press.

Arnheim, Rudolf (1933) *Film*. London: Faber & Faber.

Arnheim, Rudolf (1967) *Art and Visual Perception*. Berkeley: University of California Press.

Balázs, Béla (1924) *Der sichtbare Mensche öder Der Kultur des Films*. Vienna: Deutsch-Osterreichischer Verlag.

Barker, Martin and Beezer, Anne (eds) (1992) *Reading into Cultural Studies*. London: Routledge.

Barthes, Roland (1977) 'The Death of the Author', in John Caughie (ed.), *Theories of Authorship*. London: BFI/Routledge & Kegan Paul. pp. 208–13.

Barton, Ruth (2004) *Irish National Cinema*. London: Routledge.

Baudrillard, Jean (1990) *Seduction*. Tr. Brain Singer New York: St Martin's Press.

Bazin, André (1967) *What Is Cinema? Vol.1*. Ed. and tr. Hugh Gray. Berkeley: University of California Press.

Bazin, André (1972) *What is Cinema? Vol.2*. Ed. and tr. Hugh Gray. Berkeley: University of California Press.

Bazin, André (1973) *Jean Renoir*. Tr. W.W. Halsey and William H. Simon. New York: Simon & Schuster.

Bazin, André (1978) *Orson Welles: A Critical View*. Tr. Jonathan Rosenbaum. New York: Harper and Row.

Bazin, André (1981) 'La Politique des auteurs', in John Caughie (ed.), *Theories of Authorship*. London: BFI/Routledge & Kegan Paul. pp. 44–6.

Bellour, Raymond (1979) *L'Analyse du film*. Paris: Editions Albatros.

Bennett, Tony, Woollacott, Janet, Mercer, Tony and Boyd-Bowman, Susan (eds) (1981) *Popular Television and Film*. London: BFI.

Bogue, Ronald (2003) *Deleuze on Cinema*. New York: Routledge.

Bordwell, David and Carroll, Noël (eds) (1996) *Post-Theory: Reconstructing Film Studies*. Madison: University of Wisconsin Press.

Bordwell, David and Thompson, Kristin (1994) *Film History: An Introduction*. New York: McGraw-Hill.

Branston, Gill (2000) 'Why Theory?', in Christine Gledhill and Linda Williams (eds), *Reinventing Film Studies*. London: Arnold. pp.18–33.

Carroll, Noël (1996) *Theorizing the Moving Image*. Cambridge: Cambridge University Press.

Cavell, Stanley (1979) *The World Viewed: Reflections on the Ontology of Film*. Cambridge, MA: Harvard University Press.

Cavell, Stanley (2005) 'Prénom: Marie', in William Rothman (ed.), *Cavell on Film*. Albany: State University of New York Press. pp. 175–82.

Coates, Paul (2005) *The Red and the White: The Cinema of People's Poland*. London: Wallflower Press.

Collins, Richard (1998) *From Satellite to Single Market: The Europeanisation of Public Service Television*. London: Routledge.

Collins, Richard (2002) *Media and Identity in Contemporary Europe: Consequences of Global Convergence*. Bristol: Intellect Books.

Comolli, Jean-Louis and Narboni, Jean (1969) 'Cinéma, idéologie, critique', *Cahiers du cinéma*, 216: 11–15.

Coward, Rosalind and Ellis, John (1977) *Language and Materialism: Developments in Semiology and the Theory of the Subject*. London: Routledge & Kegan Paul.

Curran, James and Porter, Vincent (eds) (1983) *British Cinema History*. London: Weidenfeld and Nicolson.

Deleuze, Gilles (1986) *Cinema 1: The Movement-Image*. Tr. Hugh Tomlinson and Barbara Habber jam. Minneapolis: University of Minnesota Press.

Deleuze, Gilles (1989) *Cinema 2: The Time-Image*. Tr. Huge Tomlinson and Robert Galeta. Minneapolis: University of Minnesota Press.

Delluc, Louis (1920) *Photogénie*. Paris: Editions de Brunoff

Drummond, Philip, Paterson, Richard and Willis, Janet (1993) *National Identity and European Cinema: The Television Revolution*. London: BFI.

Durgnat, Raymond (1967) *Luis Buñuel*. London: Studio Vista.

Easthope, Antony (1991) *British Post-structuralism Since 1968*. London: Routledge.

Easthope, Antony (ed.) (1993) *Contemporary Film Theory*. London: Longman.

Eisenstein, Sergei [1923] (1968) 'The Montage of Attractions', in *The Film Sense*. Tr. Jay Leyda. London: Faber & Faber. pp. 181–3.

Eisenstein, Sergei [1943] (1968) 'Synchronisation of Senses', in *The Film Sense*. Tr. Jay Leyda. London: Faber & Faber. pp. 60–91.

Engels, Friedrich (1977) 'Letter to Margaret Harkness', in David Craig (ed.), *Marxists on Literature: An Anthology*. Harmondsworth: Penguin. pp. 269–71.

Epstein, Jean (1921) *Bonjour cinéma*. Paris: Editions de la Siréne.

Frisby, David (1986) *Fragments of Modernity*. Cambridge, MA: MIT Press.

Fuery, Patrick (2000) *New Developments in Film Theory*. New York: St. Martin's Press.

Gaudreault, André and Jost, François (1990) *Le Récit cinématographique*. Paris: Nathan.

Ginsberg, Terri and Thompson, Moana Kristen (eds) (1996) *Perspectives on German Cinema*. New York: G.K. Hall.

Gray, Hugh (1972) 'Translator Introduction', in André Bazin, *What is Cinema? Vol.2*. Ed. Tr. Hugh Gray. Berkeley: University of California Press. pp. 1–15.

Grodal, Torben (1997) *Moving Pictures: A New Theory of Film Genres, Feelings, and Cognition*. Oxford/New York: Clarendon Press/Oxford University Press.

Hake, Sabine (1993) *The Cinema's Third Machine: Writing on Film in Germany 1907–1933*. Lincoln, NE: University of Nebraska Press.

Hansen, Miriam Bratu (1997) 'Introduction', in Siegfried Kracauer, *Theory of Film: The Redemption of Physical Reality*. Princeton, NJ: Princeton University Press. pp. vii–xiv.

Harvey, Sylvia (1980) *May '68 and Film Culture*. London: BFI.

Heath, Stephen (1976) 'Narrative Space', *Screen*, 17(3): 68–112.

Heath, Stephen (1981) 'Comment on "The Idea of Authorship"', in John Caughie (ed.), *Theories of*

Authorship. London: BFI/Routledge & Kegan Paul. pp. 214–20.

Heller, Agnes (ed.) (1983) *Lukács Reappraised*. New York: Columbia University Press.

Hjort, Mette and MacKenzie (eds) (2000) *Cinema and Nation*. London: Routledge.

Hoggart, Richard (1957) *The Uses of Literacy*. London: Chatto and Windus.

Imre, Anikó (ed.) (2005) *East European Cinemas*. New York: Routledge.

Jackel, Anne (2003) *European Film Industries*. London: BFI.

Jameson, Fredric (1992) *Signatures of the Visible*. New York: Routledge.

Johnson-Laird, P.N. (1989) *The Computer and the Mind*. London: Fontana.

Kitses, Jim (1969) *Horizons West*. London: Thames & Hudson.

Kozintsev, Grigori, Trauberg, Leonid, Yutkevich Sergei and Kryzhitsky, Georgi [1922] (1988) 'Eccentrism', in Richard Taylor and Ian Christie (eds), *The Film Factory: Russian and Soviet Cinema in Documents, 1896–1939*. New York: Routledge. pp. 58–64.

Kracauer, Siegfried (1974) *From Caligari to Hitler: A Psychological History of the German Film*. Princeton, NJ: Princeton University Press.

Kracauer, Siegfried (1995) *The Mass Ornament: Weimar Essays*. Tr. Thomas Y. Levin. Cambridge, MA: Harvard University Press.

Kracauer, Siegfried (1997) *Theory of Film: The Redemption of Physical Reality*. Princeton, NJ: Princeton University Press.

Kuhn, Annette (1994) *Women's Pictures: Feminism and Cinema*. London: Verso.

Lagny, Michèle (1990) *Senso*. Paris: Nathan.

Lapsley, Robert and Westlake, Michael (2006) *Film Theory: An Introduction*. Rev. edn. Manchester: Manchester University Press.

Lévi-Strauss, Claude (1977) *Structural Anthropology: Vol. 2, Tr. Monique Layton*. Harmondsworth: Penguin.

Lovell, Terry (1980) *Pictures of Reality: Aesthetics, Politics, Pleasure*. London: BFI.

Lukács, Georg (1965) *The Specificity of the Aesthetic*. Budapest: Akademia.

Lukács, Georg (1970) 'Narrate or Describe', in Arthur Kahn (ed.), *Georg Lukács: Writer and Critic*. Tr. Arthur Kahn. London: Merlin. pp. 110–48.

Lukács, Georg (1977) 'Tolstoy and the Development of Realism', in David Craig (ed.), *Marxists on Literature: An Anthology*. Harmondsworth: Penguin. pp. 282–345.

MacCabe, Colin (1974) 'Realism and the Cinema: Notes on Some Brechtian Theses', *Screen*, 15(2): 7–27.

MacCabe, Colin (1980) *Godard: Images, Sounds, Politics*. London: Macmillan.

Marie, Michel (2001) *La Nouvelle Vague*. Paris: Nathan.

Marie, Michel and Vernet, Marc (1990) *Christian Metz et la théorie du cinéma*. Paris: Meridiens-Klincksieck.

McFarlane, Brian (2003) *The Encyclopedia of British Film*. London: Methuen.

Mercer, Kobena (ed.) (1988) *Black Film British Cinema*. London: ICA.

Metz, Christian (1974) *Essais sur la signification au cinéma*. Paris: Klincksieck.

Metz, Christian (1983) *Psychoanalysis and Cinema*. London: Macmillan.

Moran, Albert (ed.) (1996) *Film Policy: International, National and Regional Perspectives*. London: Routledge.

Moussinac, Léon (1925) *Naissance du cinéma*. Paris: J. Povolozky.

Mulvey, Laura (1975) 'Visual Pleasure and Narrative Cinema', *Screen*, 16(3): 6–18.

Nicholson, Linda and Fraser, Nancy (eds) (1988) *Feminism/Postmodernism*. London: Routledge.

Nowell-Smith, Geoffrey (1967) *Luchino Visconti*. London: Secker and Warburg/BFI.

Nowell-Smith, Geoffrey and Ricci, Stephen (eds) (1998) *Hollywood and Europe: Economics, Culture and National Identity*. London: BFI.

Petrie, Duncan (ed.) (1992) *Screening Europe: Image and Identity in Contemporary European Cinema*. London: BFI.

Pronay, Nicholas and Spring, D.W. (eds) (1982) *Politics, Propaganda and Film, 1918–1945*. London: Macmillan.

Propp, Vladimir (1977) *Morphology of the Folk Tale*. Austin: University of Texas Press.

Ray, Robert B. (1998) 'Impressionism, Surrealism and Film Theory', in John Hill and Pamela Church Gibson (eds), *Oxford Guide to Film Studies*. Oxford: Oxford University Press. pp. 67–76.

Rivette, Jacques [1953] (1985) 'The Genius of Howard Hawks', in Jim Hillier (ed.), *Cahiers du cinéma: The 1950s: Neo-Realism, Hollywood, New Wave*. London: BFI/Routledge & Kegan Paul. pp. 126–31.

Ropars-Wuilleumier, Marie-Claire (1981) *Le Texte divisé*. Paris: Presses Universitaires de France.

Rothman, William (ed.) (2005) *Cavell on Film*. Albany: State University of New York Press.

Roud, Richard (1960) 'The French Line', *Sight and Sound*, 29(4): 167–71.

Saussure, Ferdinand de [1916] (1922) *Cours de linguistique générale*. Paris: Payot.

Saussure, Ferdinand de (1959) *Course in General Linguistics*. Tr. Wade Baskin. New York: Philosophical Library.

Short, K.R.M. (ed.) (1981) *Feature Films as History*. Knoxville: University of Tennessee Press.

Smith, Murray (1995) *Engaging Characters: Fiction, Emotion and the Cinema.* Oxford/New York: Clarendon Press/Oxford University Press.

Soila, Tytti (1998) *Nordic National Cinemas.* London: Routledge.

Soila, Tytti (2005) *The Cinema of Scandinavia.* London: Wallflower Press.

Sorlin, Pierre (1980) *The Film in History: Restaging the Past.* Oxford: Blackwell.

Sorlin, Pierre (1991) European Cinemas, European Societies, 1939–1990. New York: Routledge.

Sorlin, Pierre (1996) *Italian National Cinema, 1896– 1996.* London: Routledge.

Stassinopoulou, Maria A. (2006) *Reality Bites: A Film History of Greece after WWII.* Vienna: LIT Verlag.

Taylor, Richard and Christie, Ian (eds) (1988) *The Film Factory: Russian and Soviet Cinema in Documents, 1896–1939.* New York: Routledge.

Thompson, E.P (1968) *The Making of the English Working Class.* Harmondsworth: Penguin.

Trigg, Roger (1989) *Reality at Risk: A Defense of Realism in Philosophy and the Sciences.* 2nd edn. New York: Harvester Wheatsheaf.

Truffaut, François (1954) 'Une certaine tendance du cinéma français', *Cahiers du cinéma,* 31: 15–29.

Von Dassanowsky, Robert (2005) *Austrian Cinema: A History.* Jefferson, NC: McFarland.

Walsh, Martin (1981) *The Brechtian Aspect of Radical Cinema.* London: BFI.

Williams, Alan (1992) *Republic of Images: A History of French Film-making.* Cambridge, MA: Harvard University Press.

Williams, Raymond (1958) *Culture and Society, 1780– 1950.* London: Chatto and Windus.

Williams, Raymond (1989) *The Politics of Modernism: Against the New Conformists.* London: Verso.

Wollen, Peter (1969) *Signs and Meaning in the Cinema.* London: BFI/Secker and Warburg.

Wood, Robin (1968) *Howard Hawks.* New York/London: Doubleday/BFI.

Wood, Robin (1970) *Claude Chabrol.* New York: Praeger.

Wood, Robin (1976) *Personal Views.* London: Gordon Fraser.

Zavattini, Cesare (1953) 'Some Ideas on the Cinema: Neorealism', *Sight and Sound,* 23(2): 64–9.

3

China: Cinema, Politics and Scholarship

Stephanie Hemelryk Donald and Paola Voci

In 2005, film scholars from inside and outside China came together at a conference to celebrate one hundred years of Chinese cinema under the rubric of 'National, Transnational, and International: Chinese Cinema and Asian Cinema in the Context of Globalization'.[1] This ambitious title implied a broad definition of 'Chinese cinema' that includes both Hong Kong and Taiwanese cinemas, whilst 'Asian cinema' was a gesture towards the rising star of Korean film. The terminology in part reflects a constraint of the Chinese language, in which the absence of plural markers does not allow the use of the English phrase 'Chinese cinemas'. (An emerging alternative is the phrase *huayu dianying* or 'Chinese language cinema', which is increasingly being used to acknowledge the different geopolitical and cultural contexts in which Chinese cinema has developed.)[2] In addition to its title, the location and the scope of the conference offer insights into Film Studies in the Chinese context. The conference took place in two venues, Beijing and Shanghai, and participants were expected to be present at both events. The split location reflected a commonly accepted, albeit oversimplified, view of these two cities and their roles in defining film production and discourse around cinema. The importance of place in shaping the subtleties of the Chinese tradition of film analysis is the first point in our story here.

Pre-liberation cinema – that is, films made before the foundation of the People's Republic of China (PRC) in 1949 – is generally identified with Shanghai studios. Film scholarship on the *Shanghai pai*, the Shanghai movement or trend of the 1930s and 1940s, has grown both in China and abroad especially since the mid- to late 1990s (Lee, 1999; Zhang Y., 1999). Beijing studios gained more importance after 1949, and informed discussion and scholarship on film has since developed mostly, although by no means exclusively, in the capital. For example, scholars based at the Beijing Film Academy and Beijing University in particular played a major role in the theoretical debate on new cinematic trends in the 1980s. According to this division, Chinese cinema's tension between the national and the transnational, mirrors the opposition between Beijing's political soul with its idealism and ideology, and Shanghai's cultural essence with its creativity and pragmatism. Whereas Beijing is the default setting for a cinema concerned with the nation, the choice of Shanghai as an additional location for the centennial celebration points to the importance of a more globally oriented cinema and also implicitly pays homage to Hong Kong filmic tradition (Fu, 2003).

Spatial contingencies and political movements define the histories of Chinese film analysis rather more accurately than would a narrative based on individual scholars and their influence. It may be a question of attitude within China studies in general or it may truly be a reflection of a different process in the formation of knowledge, but, whereas names define movements in Anglophone traditions, it is more usual in Chinese Film Studies for names to become attached to, or representative of, times, places and political events. That said, we shall, of course, cite those film scholars who have been particularly responsive to historical conditions, or especially alert to the key issues in film of their day.

The stated goal of the 2005 conference was 'to re-examine the role of cinema in the formation of *Chinese modernity*' (our italics). This is not surprising to scholars of any aspect of Chinese culture, society and politics. Chinese modernity sits at the centre of much discussion of how China has developed over the past four hundred years, and of how its particular trajectory both complements and contradicts patterns of development elsewhere in the world. In Chinese Film Studies the issue of Chinese modernity as a shaping discourse for the politics of culture over the past century has been a major inspiration for filmmakers and a preferred critical angle for cultural commentators. Western scholars writing about European film and the emergence of Hollywood have also associated cinema with technological revolution and, very early on in cinema's growth, viewed it as a modern medium which

could capture and possibly transform the new, fast-paced, changing reality of modern life. As such, the discussions were not far removed from Walter Benjamin's observation that the speed of film was almost necessitated by the pace of modern existence. In China, however, the introduction and development of cinema were not just apposite to modern times, it contributed to the revolutionary and radical character of the entire twentieth century. Studies of Chinese film theory should never omit this socio-political understanding.

The modernity in China was not new to the twentieth century. Modernity was emergent throughout the Manchu-Qing dynasty (1644–1911) in the eighteenth and nineteenth centuries.[3] However, cinema began as imperial China ended, with the revolution of 1912 which ushered in the first republic and a period of great uncertainty and multiple conflicts. From the start, the discourse on cinema found itself closely tied to the debate surrounding the rebuilding of a nation in a new international context. One hundred years later, after the refashioning of the old Communist regime and the explosion of consumerist culture in China, things seem to have come full circle. In the latest 'global age' of cinema, as film scholars are asked to reflect on the role of cinema in the formation of Chinese modernity, cinema still finds itself deeply linked to the *nation*, in a more or less tense relationship with the *state*, and central to the articulation of the *idea of China* through cinematic art, spectatorship and narrative.

We have begun this chapter with the brief tale of two cities in the 2005 centennial celebration of Chinese cinema in order to establish the premise that Film Studies in China has traditionally enjoyed very little autonomy, and most of the work that addresses issues of film culture and film theory relates them directly to the more prevalent discourse generated by national film history. For instance, Li Daoxin's in-depth survey of the century of Chinese film culture from 1905 to 2004, published in 2005, still frames the story as a sequence of stages in the creation of a national cinema. Film culture as it developed up until the late 1940s is related almost exclusively to film history and the discussion of representative films; film culture after the 1980s is presented through the discourse surrounding some of its most prominent auteurs. The first three sections of Li's history, covering the period up to 1979, present long lists of movies accompanied by in-depth analyses of films like *Yijiang chunshui xiangdong liu* (*Spring River Flows East,* Cai Chusheng, China, 1947) and *Wuya yu maque* (*Crows and Sparrows*, Zheng Junli, China, 1949). In the final section, which spans the period from 1979 to 2004 that Li defines as 'integrated cultural expansion' (2005: 351), the focus shifts to specific directors: whole chapters are dedicated to Xie Jin, Chen Kaige, Zhang Yimou as the leading auteurs in Mainland China; to Hou Hsiao-hsien, Edward Yang and Ang Li in Taiwan; and to John Woo and Tsui Hark in Hong Kong. As a result, notions of genre and film aesthetics are mostly derived from commentaries on specific film texts or filmmakers. The role of audiences in the creation of the film experience – that is, not just as consumers of films but also as producers of meaning – is not acknowledged. It is therefore history above all that drives forward the framing of Li's analytical approach.

Two other important factors further complicate the localization of film culture in China. The first is that film theory in China has traditionally been linked to film practice. Up until very recently, many Chinese film theorists and critics have worked outside universities. Even nowadays, although more Chinese film scholars are affiliated to tertiary institutions, many not only teach both theory and practice but they are also often involved in the film industry as screenwriters, consultants or producers. The blending of practitioner and critic is less usual in the Western context. Although one could argue that the film practice and writing of the ficto-documentarist Cui Zi'en (2001; 2003) is somewhat akin to the marriage of practice and theory attempted by someone like Laura Mulvey, the difference is that Cui is professionally both a writer and a filmmaker whilst most Western writers take up filmmaking as a secondary exploration of their theoretical ideas.

The second complicating factor is that up until the late 1970s, most Western film theory was not available in translation, and concepts such as cinematic ontology, auteur theory, or simply discussions about cinematic forms of expression and artistic techniques did not become part of the discourse on cinema until the early 1980s. It is important to remember that some Chinese film theoretical concepts, such as *minzu shi* (nation-style), emerged from problematics and philosophical traditions other than the imported ideas of more recent debates. For instance, in the 1980s, many film scholars distanced themselves from Western film theory and argued that in China film aesthetics were better approached by relying on earlier Chinese traditional arts (Chen Xihe et al., 2005: 13).

Now, however, Chinese Film Studies has moved decisively beyond the nation and into a global context, and film theory has become thoroughly internationalized in relation to the study of global Chinese cinema. Comparative studies and collaborative projects between Chinese scholars in China and other scholars, both Chinese and non-Chinese, living elsewhere in the world are becoming routine. There has been a shift away from the translation and adaptation model – a model that was characterized by periodic discoveries (and translations) of Western theories which were subsequently applied to the national context. Chinese scholars are now also translated into English (Dai, 1995; Dai, 1999; Dai, 2002; Lü, 2005; Ni, 2002), and Chinese cinema scholars are seeking publication in Chinese rather than exclusively in English-language publications (see Lu and Yeh, 2005; Marchetti, 2005; Voci, 2006; Zhang Y., 2005, 2006a and 2006b; Zhang Z., 2006). Conferences, like the one referred to at the beginning of the chapter, now discuss not only Chinese national cinema but also broader issues in film theory and aesthetics in specifically Chinese contexts (Chen Xihe et al., 2005).

Despite the increasing interaction between scholarly traditions, however, Chinese theory continues to depend on historical periodization to frame both its ideas and reflection on its own development as an intellectual field. In a collection on contemporary film theory, Chen Xihe (2005) discusses what he terms the three main stages in the development of Chinese film theory. This first is the 'red phase' (1949–79), in which film was seen as a vehicle for didacticism and revolutionary ideology. Second is the 'blue phase', characterized by the Chinese appropriation of ideas from main Western theorists like Nick Browne, Janet Staiger, Bill Nichols, Robert Rosen and Ann Kaplan. And third is the 'post-blue phase', referring to contemporary developments including discussion of new media. Chen argues that this latest phase has largely been shaped by globalization and transnational trends which, rather than leading theorists away from the focus on contingency, have revived questions of the national, although now in a more complex international and global situation (Chen Xihe et al., 2005: 10). According to Chen, a top-down approach was dominant in the earlier periods, with an emphasis on ideology in the red phase and on aesthetics and theory in the blue phase. In the post-blue phase of recent years, however, Chinese film scholars have begun to adopt a bottom-up perspective that pays greater attention to the film text, to films' cultural and social context, and also to data analyses reflecting the industrial context of production and distribution (Chen Xihe et al., 2005: 10). As many of China's concerns and debates likewise focus on this issue of regional, national and transnational influence, it is reasonable to infer that once again film theory is being true to its political and social time and space (Zhang, 2002).

Our central argument, then, is that the link between cinema and the nation has always been, and remains not only a crucial analytical framework in the analysis of Chinese cinema (Berry and Farquhar, 2006) but also in the development of Chinese film theory. This chapter therefore has two main objectives. The first is to provide a guide to some of the key moments and issues that have contributed to the film experience in China. Yet as we want to challenge any monolithic vision of Chinese Film Studies, our second objective is to show how, even within the 'nation' paradigm, the role of cinema has changed quite considerably – most notably through the impact of the diverse Chinese cinemas from within the Mainland and beyond. Although a chronological narrative of Chinese film history and the tensions which have characterized film culture in China structures the chapter, our final section switches the focus away from historical periods to three overarching issues that have helped to define Chinese Film Studies: realism, national style (*minzu shi*) and the opening of the national to other (non-Mainland) Chinese cinemas.

BEFORE 1949

In 2000, Ann Hu directed *Xi yang jing* (*Shadow Magic*, China/Germany/Taiwan/US), a romantic retelling of the beginning of Chinese cinema, inspired by the first historically documented Chinese film, *Ding Jun Shan* (*Dingjun Mountain*, RenOingtaé, China), which in 1905 captured the performance of the famous Beijing Opera actor Tan Xinpei (Ge, 2002).[4] In the film an English entrepreneur, Raymond Wallace (Jared Harris), arrives in Beijing in 1902 to start a new business: showing movies to the Chinese. Liu Jinglun (Xia Yu), a young photographer with a deep curiosity for novelties, becomes his partner and friend. Together they manage to attract the public to their screenings and also begin to shoot films locally. Liu's love for cinema, along with his passion for the woman of his dreams, causes a series of cultural misunderstandings and social conflicts that arise from the opposition between Chinese tradition and Western modernity. Despite oversimplifying both historical events and cultural issues, *Xi yang jing* thus dramatizes a couple of themes that have been at the core of critical work by film scholars inside and outside China. First, cinema started out as a *foreign* technological innovation. And secondly, cinema was viewed as a symbol of an imported modernity and, as such, became part of the larger debate concerning the West and its influence on Chinese culture and society.

The debate about form and content

By the early 1920s, cinema had gained significant popularity, mostly within the urban limits of Shanghai and Beijing. As film showings became more frequent and more accessible, movie stars began to appear on the pages of pictorial magazines and joined – without quite displacing – opera performers in the eye of public fascination (Voci, 2002).[5] Among the first to address theoretical issues were intellectuals coming from literary studies and the question of cinema was thereby mixed up, in the 1920s and arguably through to the 1950s, with a broader controversy concerning the respective values of socially and politically engaged literature and popular reading matter.

Cinema was thus seen not as an object to be appreciated or analyzed for its own sake, but as a medium to be struggled over and improved for the sake of the nation. Some of the intellectuals in the 1920s viewed cinema as a symbol of a more international or transnational modernity. For them, cinema was primarily a spectacle to be appreciated aesthetically, an icon of the new cosmopolitan urban culture most evident in Shanghai. They championed a 'soft cinema' (*ruanxing dianying*) that would emphasize form as well as content. Liu Na'ou, a writer who was part of the New Perceptionist literary movement, criticized the use of theatrical or literary strategies and advocated the use of a film language and visual grammar which reflected the medium's visual and technological nature.[6] In *Zhongguo dianying miaoxie de shendu wenti (Problems of depth in Chinese film representation),* Liu criticizes Chinese cinema for not being cinematic and for overemphasizing words (intertitles) over images: 'in our national cinema, words are many but images are few' ('*guochan dianying shi zi duo ying shao'*) (Liu, 1993: 260). Liu's support for a soft cinema was echoed by Huang Jiamo's critique in the same period of the low artistic quality of leftist cinema,

which he accused of being too concerned with content to pay attention to form (Voci, 2002: 74). Liu argued that form (*xingshi*) should be of equal importance at least to content (*neirong*) (Liu, 1993: 256–61).

Supporters of the May Fourth movement presented an opposing view of cinema. Taking its name from demonstrations on 4 May 1919 protesting against the treaties of Versailles, May Fourth intellectuals advocated cultural and political renewal through social responsibility. Cinema, like literature and art in general, was viewed as a modern tool for engineering social and political change. In opposition to the New Perceptionists, May Fourth adherents argued that cinema needed to serve the greater cause of rebuilding the Chinese nation. A 'hard cinema', or 'leftist cinema' (*zuoyi dianying*) as it was labelled later, should contribute to educating the people and inspiring revolution. In 'Qingsuan ruanxing dianying lun' ('A critique of soft cinema'), Tang Na attacked the softness of soft cinema explicitly, criticizing it for being too concerned with emotions (*ganqing*) and being simply entertaining (*yule*) (Tang, 1993: 269–80). He argued that films should convey ideas as their main goal and that form and technical concerns should be subordinate to content. For Tang, filmmakers' ideas (*sikao*) rather than their formal aesthetic choices should define a film (Tang, 1993: 274–78). Although after 1949 the needs of ideology increasingly determined which ideas were acceptable, up until then the debate about form and content remained relatively open. At the time, there were no clear winners. Even so, Mainland Chinese histories up until the late eighties conventionally, and conveniently, portrayed pre-liberation cinema as dominated by leftist filmmakers and theorists (Cheng, 1963).

Leftist cinema and Shanghai star culture

Although supporters of soft cinema remained visible both at the level of production and public response, they tended to be less vocal than their leftist counterparts. This may have been in part because they seldom fulfilled the dual role of filmmaker and film critic that was already a feature of film culture in China. People involved in leftist film productions, like the screenwriters Tian Han and Xia Yan, took an active and a high-profile role in political and theoretical discussions about cinema. And crucially, their writings appeared at a time of national emergency (Xia, 1982).[7] It is not surprising that those who saw themselves as creating the nation's future displayed more passion and more conviction when championing their vision of cinema's role in the new society than modernist intellectuals like the New Perceptionists. Furthermore, the foundation of the PRC in 1949 sanctioned the 'victory' of leftist cinema. This version of film history was further entrenched in 1963 with the publication of Cheng Jihua's *History of the Development of Chinese Cinema,* which became the authoritative point of reference in the field. Emphasizing the leftist tradition as the driving force in the development of both Chinese film production and film criticism, Cheng disregarded or denounced any alternatives. Even though pioneering histories by Western scholars like Jay Leyda (1972) and Paul Clark (1987) clearly diverged from Cheng's Communist party orthodoxy, they, like him, still emphasized political concerns over other critical perspectives and left unchallenged the view that socialist realist productions of the 1950s and 1960s were a natural development from the earlier leftist films.

A re-evaluation of non-leftist films from the 1930s and 1940s really got underway only in the 1980s when Fifth Generation directors like Zhang Yimou, Li Shaohong and Chen Kaige were attracting the attention of domestic critics and winning prizes at international festivals. At the same time as establishing new Chinese cinema's connections with Western cinema, to which the Fifth Generation directors had been the first to be exposed after many years of quasi-isolation, Chinese and Western film scholars started to rediscover pre-liberation Chinese cinema, seeking sources of inspiration outside

the leftist and socialist-realist tradition, and setting out to uncover a variety of previously unexplored issues related to both genre and production. In this vein, for example, Zhang Zhen has noted the self-referential approach to femininity and womanhood of films made in the 1930s (2001: 229).

The reassessment of the role of leftist cinema pointed to the existence of a less explicitly ideological and more escapist cinema which proved to be popular in the decades before 1949. The fact that Hong Kong-based scholars led this revisionist history may have had something to do with Hong Kong and Guangdong's part in film history being written out of the Communist orthodoxy (Fu, 2000; Li S., 2003 and 2005). Studies of early Hong Kong cinema and its development after 1949 highlighted the role played by the Hong Kong industry before it became internationally popular – first in the 1970s though the success of the martial arts genre and then again in the 1990s thanks to directors like John Woo, Stanley Kwan and Wong Kar-wai (Fu and Desser, 2000).

The new histories also noted that, even at their most dominant, leftist themes were often complicated or even distorted by cinematic genres and studios' economic priorities. Iconic leftist (*zuopai*) films like *Dalu* (*Big Road*, Sun Yu, China, 1934), *Shizi jietou* (*Crossroads*, Shen Xiling, China, 1937) or *Malu tianshi* (*Street Angels*, Yuan Muzhi, China, 1934) were revisited to reveal their neo-realist flavour and melodramatic *mise en scène,* or to uncover representational and narrative elements that belied the revolutionary tenor of the times (Berry, 1988a; Berry, 1988b; Feng, 1985; Ma, 1989; Pang, 2002; Pickowicz, 1993).

Many studies demonstrated that rather than being simply oppositional to leftist ideology, Hollywood-like star culture and fascination with certain film genres radically upset the political agenda. Christine Harris' 1997 analysis of *Xin nüxing* (*The New Woman*, Cai Chusheng, China, 1937) focuses on the intersection between film star culture and leftist cinema and reveals the connections between the film's narrative and iconography as well as its industrial and cultural contexts: publicity, production conditions and an audience reception mediated through the debate about 'new' or 'modern' women. Similarly, Yomi Braester's essay on Maxu Weibang's *Yeban gesheng* (*Singing at Midnight*, China, 1937) argues that the role of 'monstrosity' in the revolutionary rhetoric of 1930s cinema has been overlooked in analyses that privilege a binary opposition between ideological or political messages and commercial entertainment strategies. In *Yeban gesheng*, argues Braester, the horror genre reveals both a Hollywood-influenced pleasure in spectacle and an implicit political commentary on the Revolution's contradictions and unsolved problems (2000: 107).

Two films that exemplify the shift in critical discourse surrounding pre-liberation films and the reassessment of the role of the nation in filmmaking are *Shennü* (*Goddess*, Wu Yonggang, China, 1934) and *Dalu*. Both belong to the revolutionary tradition of left-wing filmmaking committed to patriotic and communist ideals, and were praised for their service to nation-building ideals in Cheng Jihua's standard history (1963). From the late 1980s on, however, both were critically re-evaluated, especially in light of theoretical work on performance and charisma in stardom studies (Berry, 1988b; Chow, 1995: 23–6; Mu, 1985). *Shennü*'s protagonist, a prostitute who fights her evil pimp to achieve a better life for her son, was played by Ruan Lingyu, a legendary actress who committed suicide at the age of 24.[8] Ruan Lingyu's intense close-ups and '*regard èn camera*' create a sensual atmosphere in which the political message is almost totally lost. A shot of her legs as she walks side by side with a client, for example, is a textbook example of fetishization. The narrative of *Dalu* concerns six young road workers who are constructing a strategic road for the Chinese army during the war of resistance against the Japanese invasion. The film's political message is complicated, however, by the presence of two female characters who befriend the workers – one of them played by the glamorous Li Lili, a sexual icon of her times (Berry, 1988b). The girls

experience a social and political awakening, but they are also protagonists in several scenes which clearly evoke romantic connections, intimacy and sexuality.

In the 1940s the urgent need to rescue the nation from both external and internal dangers – Japanese invasion and the corrupt Nationalist government – led to an even stronger push to homogenize and rectify film productions and scholarship in order to eliminate possible distractions from, or distortions of, the political message. In his *Yan'an Talks on Arts and Literature* (1942), Mao Zedong challenges artists to ensure that 'our literature and art are first for the workers, the class that leads the revolution' (1967: 78). He insisted that they should put 'the political criterion first and the artistic criterion second' (1967: 89). Such changes did not occur overnight, but it is fair to say that Chinese filmmakers' work became progressively constrained by Party critiques and the demand for self-critique. Similarly, the scope for critical analysis was increasingly limited by the demands of revolutionary Communist ideology.

CINEMA AND REVOLUTION: 1949–76

In Chinese Film Studies, the conventional view is that socialist realism dominated the period from 1949 to the early 1980s. That this politicized aesthetic was given a particular slant in China, with realism imbued with a unique sense of romanticism and revolutionary passion, became apparent in the critical revisionism of the late 1980s and the 1990s. In 1989 Esther Ching-mei Yau commented on the intensity of the central relationships in war films – an observation given further weight by Michael Berry's account of *Hongse nianzi jun* (*Red Detachment of Women*, Xie Jin, China, 1963), which cites the admission of the director Xie Jin that political interference spoilt the second half of the film by insisting that all sexual references be removed from the script (2000).[9] Likewise, Stephanie Hemelryk Donald (1997; 2005) observed the passionate kernel of the Party-state-people relationship in cinema drama and has more recently shown how children's films of the 1980s, many of them commissioned through the Children's Film Studio which was founded and directed by the older revolutionary film elites of the 1950s, continued to present human feeling (*ganqing*) as an emotional core of sociality rather than as interior individual feeling. Such approaches find, in other words, a degree of connection or convergence between the soft and leftist turns of thirty years earlier. At the time the films were made, however, few international film scholars were paying much attention to what was being screened in China.[10]

Just as the creation of a film industry dedicated to promoting the socialist romance of revolution was not achieved overnight, so the adoption of socialist realism failed to banish completely all traces of other styles – despite the often brutal imposition of censorship that reflected not just formal Party directives, but also, and less predictably, the state of play in factional infighting between hardliners and 'softer' forces in the power hierarchy.[11] Although often subordinated to revolutionary themes, romance remained evident in many comedies and dramas. Other genres with their origins in traditional Chinese opera, early Hollywood and popular entertainments of the 1920s – melodrama, family movies, war films and historical romances, for example – continued to be produced, and their formal conventions and cultural connotations led to moments of slippage, or even contradiction, within the orthodoxies of socialist realism. The 1959 drama *Lin jia puzi* (*Lin Family Shop*, Shui Hua, China), for example, tells the story of the self-interested but ultimately hopeless decisions of the shopkeeper Lin (Xie Tian) in response to the boycott of Japanese goods after the 1919 treaty. Finally bankrupted, Lin flees leaving poorer creditors behind him, and the voice-over reminds the audience that big fish eat little fish in a cruel, capitalist world. Against the grain of this heavy-handed extra-diegetic voice, the complexity of the film's narrative suggests that Lin's decisions are driven by multiple forces and confusions and, in the end, the character comes across as not entirely unsympathetic. Despite its socialist-realist style, then, *Lin jia puzi* could be seen ultimately as a bourgeois film – as it was a few years later during the Great Proletarian Cultural Revolution (1966–74). The lead actor, Xie Tian, was criticized for taking on the role of the shopkeeper. This was typical of incidents at the time. Key members of the film elite like Yu Lan and Tian Fang were thrown out of the studios and into labour camps. Jiang Qing, Mao's last wife and a former actress, used her factional power during the Cultural Revolution to punish more successful erstwhile colleagues from the film and theatre worlds of the 1940s. The denunciation of Xie Tian provides an unhappy example of film theory being used to undermine the film as a work of art and the actor as a professional performer for reasons of personal advantage in political factions.

AFTER MAO: 1976–89

The economic reforms following the death of Mao Zedong in 1976 are generally referred to as the 'New Era' – a term that is designed, as Zhang Xudong observes, 'to make discontinuity clear while leaving ambiguous room for continuity with the socialist past' (1997: 9). This 'ambiguous room' meant that during the New Era, albeit within certain limits, criticism was not just tolerated but actively encouraged. As a result, all aspects of both cultural production and critical discourse underwent major changes.

In Film Studies, debates during the 1980s focused on issues of modernization, tradition and innovation, and national cinema. Among the main critical voices during this time were Chen Xihe, Shao Mujun, Li Tuo, Yang Ni and Zhu Dake; and in the Chinese tradition of combining theory and practice, filmmakers such as Xie Fei, Zheng Dongtian, Wu Yigong and Zhang Nuanxin also took an active part in the conversation (Semsel et al., 1990; Semsel et al., 1993).

Many scholars complained about the overwhelming preponderance of literary adaptations and the continuing dominance of melodramatic *mise en scène* and narration. They objected to the theatrical acting, ethical preoccupations and excessive sentimentalism that characterized most Chinese cinema both before and after liberation in 1949. The film critic Bai Jingsheng called for the revival of a specifically cinematic language:

> It is time that we throw away the walking stick of drama that we have used for so long. We should let ourselves go and make great progress in our filmmaking … The key is not to construct film on the basis of dialogue, but rather on that of synthesis. Furthermore, filmmakers should deviate from their concept of drama and adopt montage, which combines sound and image. (1990: 6, 8)

This debate heated up even more when the Fifth Generation's new wave of films began to appear. Even though they did not have an immediate impact in Chinese movie theatres, the films' exploration of new styles and new genres fuelled the ongoing debate on how to renew Chinese cinema and generate a chain of changes in both film production and scholarship.

The complexity of these changes and their ramifications can be illustrated by the different fates of two ground-breaking Fifth Generation films: *Yige he bage* (*One and Eight*, Zhang Junzhao, China, 1984) and *Huang tudi* (*Yellow Earth*, Chen Kaige, China 1984). Both films relied on a very simple storyline, a very slow narrative pace, and the use of cinematography, depth of shot and frame composition to get across their political points. Both were labelled as 'art films' in China as well as overseas and neither became a blockbuster. Yet *Huang tudi* became an international phenomenon, whereas *Yige he bage* remained a domestic one.

Even though it was mostly limited to film festival circles and film scholars, the unprecedented international attention given to *Huang tudi* had a great impact within Chinese film culture as it marked a shift in the dominant paradigm of national cinema. While the West had previously been seen as a source from which to import and adapt new film theories and techniques (and to a lesser extent films), from the mid- to late 1980s on, filmmakers started to become aware of the potential Western audience.

Huang tudi's international achievement was followed by the even greater success of *Hong gaoliang* (*Red Sorghum*, Zhang Yimou, China, 1988). This film managed to perform well at the domestic box office as well as gaining some distribution on the European circuit. Initially, the commercial aspect was subordinate to the need for intellectual and artistic recognition. As Chinese directors won awards at Berlin, Cannes, Toronto and Venice, it became clear that some themes were more easily exportable than others. Zhang Yimou's narrative style and his portrayal of China as the land of 'primitive passions' fell within the broad appeal of orientalism and exoticism to Western audiences, and thus attracted the interest of Chinese film scholars and cultural critics working in Western paradigms but with a finely nuanced intra-cultural understanding which made strong and innovative critiques of these new wave phenomena: Rey Chow's *Primitive Passions* (1995), for example.

Starting in the mid-1980s, film scholarship on Chinese cinema exploded and articles on the Fifth Generation like Clark's 'Reinventing China' (1989) and Yau's 'Cultural and economic dislocations' (1989) were published in Europe and the US. In more recent years the Fifth Generation has continued to provide a focus of attention. In 2002, *Memoirs from the Beijing Film Academy*, a first-hand account of the 'genesis of China's Fifth Generation' by the screenwriter, historian and critic Ni Zhen appeared in English translation, while Clark's 1989 article grew into the 2005 monograph *Reinventing China: A Generation and its Films*.[12] At the same time, scholarship on Chinese cinema has expanded around and beyond the phenomenon of the Fifth Generation, continuing to embrace the central theme of modernity in Chinese cultural debate while bringing Chinese cultural scholarship to the forefront of new critical theory in the West.[13] For example, American-based cultural critics Chen Xiaomei and Jing Wang championed the work of Dai Jinhua, a leading Chinese intellectual, who has effectively raised the issue of women's cinema in terms of both production and representation through-out the 1990s. Their campaign successfully culminated in the publication of a collection of Dai's translated essays as *Cinema and Desire* (2002) and a number of visiting fellowships in the US.

As noted earlier, this period of scholarship has also seen 'soft' cinema re-evaluated for the first time since pre-1949, as Chinese cinema was analyzed from new critical angles beyond the national paradigm. In an influential article, 'Chinese classical painting and cinematographic signification' (1994), Ni Zhen points to the similarities between the Fifth Generation and the Taiwanese new wave director Hou Hsiao-hsien, whose *Beiqing chengshi* (*City of Sadness*, Hong Kong/Taiwan, 1989) won the Golden Lion at the Venice Film Festival in 1988, and relates their overlapping styles to traditional Chinese painting. In *China into Film* (1999), the Princeton art historian Jerome Silbergeld likewise underlines the importance of his disciplinary perspective for understanding the aesthetics of Chinese cinema, while in *Hitch-cock with a Chinese Face* (2004) he expands the method to include comparative cross-cultural analyses of image-making in films and other visual arts. This approach enables Silbergeld to demonstrate the influence of Chinese philosophical and artistic views as they are worked through in the presentation of cinematic space and time. He also pays heed to the impact of Western cinema, however, recognizing it as an unstable point of reference rather than a straightforward source of inspiration or appropriation. Rather like the 'translingual practices' in literature studied by Lydia Liu (1995), Silbergeld shows how Chinese filmmakers have translated and transformed foreign cinematic practices as well as traditional Chinese aesthetics into a distinctive cinematic visuality.

Ni Zhen's observation that the Taiwanese New Wave was coterminous with the Fifth Generation is important. Although Taiwanese cinema theory is beyond the scope of this chapter, some issues are so closely related to film in the PRC that they must be mentioned if only in passing. The government-sponsored

In Our Time project that started in 1982 fostered the careers of new filmmakers like Edward Yang and Wu Nien-jen as well as Hou Hsiao-hsien. The outcome was a self-consciously intellectual cinema that has attracted significant scholarship, much of it interested in the relationship between Taiwanese national (or quasi-national) identities and ethnicities, and its cinematic tendency to ask difficult questions about time, space and the evaluation of human suffering (Berry and Lu, 2004; Chen F., 2000; Yeh and Davis, 2005; Yip, 2004). The existence of the Taiwanese new wave, along with the increasing links between production houses in Hong Kong, Mainland China and Taiwan that cater to both PRC and 'greater China' Chinese-language audiences and also the interlinking of the star system in Asia, has helped to establish the themes of transnationalism and regionalism at the centre of contemporary debates.

NEW DIRECTIONS: 1990s AND 2000s

Urban cinema

The publication in 2006 of Paul Pickowicz and Yingjin Zhang's *From Underground to Independent*, a collection of essays examining and explaining alternative film culture in contemporary China, consolidated another step in the development of Chinese Film Studies. Building on a number of earlier, mostly Chinese-language, publications (Cui, 2001; Cui, 2003; Zhang X., 2004; Zhang Z., 2006), the volume represents a considered response to some new social, cultural and theoretical questions posed over the past fifteen or twenty years by the emergence of new styles of filmmaking.

One label for this new trend has been the 'Sixth Generation' – but the term has proved both controversial and misleading. Certainly, not all 'Sixth Generation' film-makers would see themselves as part of a single movement, let alone the same gener-ation (Dai, 2000; Teo, 2003; Zheng, 2003). They constitute a very broad and diverse grouping that embraces not only emerging filmmakers working in Mainland China, such as Jia Zhangke whose films include *Zhantai* (*Platform*, Hong Kong/China/Japan/France, 2000) and *Ren xiao yao* (*Unknown Pleasures*, South Korea/France/Japan/China, 2002), but also transnational talents like the German-based Li Yang, whose best, known work is *Mangjing* (*Blind Shaft*, China/Germany/Hong Kong, 2002). The two directors most often associated with the 'Sixth Generation' are Wang Xiaoshuai and Zhang Yuan, both of whom boast long filmographies. Wang's key films are *Dong Chun de rizi* (*The Days*, China, 1993), *Shiqi sui de danche* (*Beijing Bicycle*, France/Taiwan/China, 2001) and *Er Di* (*Drifters*, Taiwan/China, 2003). Zhang Yuan, who creates a breakthrough with almost every work, is best seen as an 'issues' director. Of his fourteen features, which include a number of documentaries, *Mama* (*Mom*, China, 1990) deals with disability and maternal emotion, *Beijing za zhong* (*Beijing Bastards*, China, 1992) ruminates eloquently on the post-Tiananmen atmosphere of Beijing bohemian life, *Fengkuang yingyu* (*Crazy English*, China, 1998) pursues the mad brilliance of a millionaire English teacher, and *Dong gong xi gong* (*East Palace West Palace*, China, 1996) paints a tense and erotic picture of the capital's gay and transgendered populations.

Film scholars have attempted to provide an alternative analytical framework to the overly loose 'Sixth Generation' label, which perpetuated the periodic or generational model established by Cheng Jihua's Party line history (Cheng, 1963). This had imposed a somewhat simplistic categorization that grouped directors on the basis of their affiliation with a particular historical moment. The impact of the Fifth Generation actually helped to undermine the model. That group of directors at least had in common the fact that they enrolled in the Beijing Film Academy just after the Cultural Revolution and graduated together in 1983. However, the categories of First and Second Generation are rarely used in relation to directors active before the 1980s as debates about earlier cinema are usually couched in terms of the opposition between 'leftist' or 'nationalist' cinemas.

Third Generation directors, including Xie Jin who is still working today, tend to be subsumed into discussions of socialist realist cinema. Since Cheng's day, the labels of Fourth Generation and Fifth Generation have been commonly applied to directors active after the Cultural Revolution period ended with the death of Mao in 1976. But the attempt to extend his approach and categorize directors who began their careers in the 1990s or after as Sixth or even Seventh Generation filmmakers, often simply on the basis of the date they graduated from the Beijing Film Academy, fails to take account of their differences or of the loss of a sense of historically-defined cohesion or shared concerns.

The search for alternative descriptions or explanations of the newer films has led some scholars to emphasize their urban location and inspiration – although, again, this does not apply to them all. Others use a paradigm of independent filmmaking (*duli dianying* or *duli zhipian*). Some of the more cynical talk rather of 'individualistic film' (*geren dianying*) and criticize some of the works as representative of a new 'me-me-ism' (*wowo zhuyi*) (Pickowicz and Zhang, 2006). This controversy is compounded by the notion that all new and interesting talent in Chinese film is necessarily believed to be 'underground'. The 'underground' quality appears in many cases to be a question of style rather than substance. Again, sceptics allege that some young filmmakers are not actually censored by the Film Bureau, but elect to bypass its official approval processes so that they can claim the status of being banned, dissident or underground and so enhance their recognition and credibility abroad. Selling a 'banned' film to a non-Chinese-speaking audience is easier than trying to persuade people that a mainstream film with subtitles might be educational and entertaining.

The emergence of this independent or underground movement has had the interesting consequence of prompting Chinese film scholars, both local and transnational, to focus more than previously on political-economic questions about production, distribution and viewership – to the extent that these discussions have sometimes overshadowed critical assessment of the films' formal innovations and narratives.

This debate has also pointed to the split between directors making films for Chinese audiences and those making films for the West or for the international festival circuit. There are no grounds for assuming that the more commercially successful and 'entertaining' side of urban cinema is of poor artistic quality, nor that it unquestioningly serves propagandistic government goals. *Xizao* (*Shower*, Yang Zhang, China, 2000) and *Shouji* (*Cellphone*, Feng Xiaogang, China, 2003) are two films of this type that have not yet received intensive critical attention because, despite their huge popularity at home, they are entertainment pieces which touch on modern issues (alienation, relocation, technology and marital discord) in ways which do not conform easily to 'independent' or 'underground' paradigms. Arguably, Zhang Yuan's *Guo nian hui jia* (*Seventeen Years,* Italy/China, 1999) – which tells how a prison officer gives up a precious holiday weekend to help a killer on day-release find her family – is much more actively supportive of the social order and the representatives of state paternalism than either of these light-hearted popular films.

It is noticeable how in the contemporary period the old critical distinction between 'soft' cinema and 'hard' films recurs – entertainment, aesthetics and commercial success versus ideology, plot and social message – even though it has become much more complicated and can no longer be easily reduced to a binary opposition.

Video documentary

Overlapping with the new urban, independent or underground cinema that helped to shape the discourse of what Chen Xihe calls the 'post-blue phase' (2005: 10) in Chinese film theory has been the work of a new wave of documentary film- and videomakers like Duan Jichuan, Du Haibin, Cui Zi'en, Jiang Yue, Li Hong and Wu Wenguang. Since the early 1990s they have gone a long way to reinventing the genre – incidentally shifting Chinese Film Studies away from its almost excusive concern with narrative feature films in the process. Since documentary film in China traditionally took the form of war reportage and political or educational propaganda, this new documentary has no official history. It certainly did not develop in a vacuum, however, and it needs to be understood in relation to the renewal of television, to the emergence of urban cinema, and to the world of avant-garde artists.

Reforms to Chinese television have been instrumental to the development of a less ideological approach to documentary. Although great emphasis is placed on the independence of the new documentarians, most of them have also worked for Chinese state television from time to time and some of the resulting productions have displayed typically 'independent' characteristics and concerns. They stress authenticity, minimize intervention (by eschewing or underplaying 'voice of God' commentary) and tend to focus on marginal communities, the poor and 'outsiders' (Voci, 2004).

This approach brings the new documentary close to urban cinema in terms of both subject matter (marginal worlds and anti-heroes) and style (fragmented and often minimalist narratives). Zhang Yuan and Jia Zhangke have directed both feature films and documentaries. Li Yu's *Jinnian xiatian* (*Fish and Elephant*, China, 2001) uses a documentary style to portray a lesbian couple (played by two actresses, but with many other characters in the film playing themselves). Both Zhang Yimou's *Qiuju da guansi* (*The Story of Qiuju*, China/Hong Kong, 1999) and Li Yang's *Mangjing* also mix professional and non-professional actors and were shot on location, often using hidden cameras to achieve a more 'authentic' outcome. As filmmakers work across genre boundaries, the very division between fiction and non-fiction has arguably become artificial and inadequate.

The discourse on film generated by the new documentary movement also overlaps with the underground and avant-garde scene in the visual arts. Some of these artists are the topic of Wu Wenguang's *Liulang Beijing: zuihou de mengxiangzhe* (*Bumming in Beijing: The Last Dreamers*, China, 1990). Zhao Liang's experimental videomaking blurs the boundaries of the real and the surreal, and his work includes art video as well as documentary – for example, his video on drug addicts in Beijing, *Zhi feiji* (*Paper Airplane,* China, 2001). The concerns, approaches and socio-economic spaces shared by the new documentarians, urban filmmakers and other underground or avant-garde artists are clearly chronicled and catalogued in events such as *The First Guangzhou Triennial Reinterpretation: A Decade of Experimental Chinese Art* (1990–2000) and its associated publications (Wu et al., 2002).

The scholarly debate about documentary remains quite specialized. Among those taking an active role in the discussions in China are, typically, filmmakers like Wu Wenguang (2001) along with scholars like Lü Xinyu (2003) and Wang Weici (2000; 2001) (see also Fang, 2003; Mei and Zhu, 2004). In the West, Chris Berry (1997; 2002) and Bérénice Reynaud (1996; 2003) have taken the lead in opening up the topic (see also Leary, 2003; Voci, 2004; Zhang Y., 2004). Increasingly, however, the two groups are involved in transnational conversations as both scholars and theory travel. In March 2006, for example, a Chinese-language volume on contemporary Chinese documentary edited by Ping Jie was published in Shanghai. The collection combines essays by Western and Chinese scholars, who are based overseas and who had previously published mostly in English. This format represents a challenge not only to the divide between domestic and international Chinese Film Studies, but also to the translation and adaptation model that assumes the flow of theory from the West to China (Ping, 2006). Fixed boundaries between Chinese and Western critical discourse are giving way to flows as scholars move in and out of China, publishing in both Chinese and English.

CRITICAL ISSUES

In this final section we review briefly a few enduring themes and topics that are likely to continue to set the agenda for Chinese Film Studies in the coming years, as they have done over its history.

A Chinese perspective on Film Studies

According to Hu Ke (Hu 1995; Hu et al., 2000), critical discourse on film in China has mostly focused on social politics, rather than art or, in fact, cinema per se. For most of its history, it had no autonomy from the unified system of film production and distribution, which in turn was subservient to political propaganda. It remained almost wholly isolated from international film culture: Western film theories were simply inaccessible.

Even though it underplays some of the earlier, pre-revolutionary debates about soft and hard cinema, Hu's overall assessment is in general terms accurate. Our chronological overview has also shown why 'serving the nation' has been the main concern of both film theorists and practitioners, and how cinema and nation can hardly be separated in the Chinese context. From the mid-1930s, the emphasis was on cinema's role in the building of the modern Chinese nation. When, following Mao's directives on the arts, cinema was asked to become a political tool for the promotion of ideology and education of the masses, the revolutionary ideology simply incorporated the nation into its rhetoric and claimed, in fact, that the two were the same. '*Meiyou gongchandang meiyou xin Zhongguo*' was the slogan: 'Without the Communist Party there is no new China'. In many ways, despite its claims of 'breaking with old ideas', socialist realism remained closely related to the earlier realism of leftist cinema: both essentially identified the primary responsibility of cinematic realism in a Confucian loyalty towards history, society and the Chinese nation.

Hou Yao, for example, a major filmmaker and one of the few film theorists of the early history of Chinese cinema, in 1926 defined cinema as a kind of drama and the film script as the soul of film. Identifying this principle of Hou Yao's as the normative thread running through the history of Chinese cinema, Chen Xihe (1990) argues that the focus on everyday life and society, which derives directly from the Confucian tradition, is the reason why Chinese cinema is concerned with narrative – and in particular narrative drama with educational goals – rather than cinematic techniques or formal experiments. Although this may be an overgeneralization, it is reasonable to maintain, as Chen does, that 'the social and instrumental values of film' (1990: 200) have been the main concern for the majority of directors. The realism that Chinese films strive to achieve has been conditioned most of the time by ideological and educational purposes which lie behind the faithful reproduction of reality. It was only after the debates of the 1980s that Soviet film theory was opened up to André Bazin's cinematic realism and Chinese scholars began to argue about film aesthetics, semiotics and spectatorship. Even though many of them called for a more autonomous discourse on cinema, the concern with the making of a modern nation remained the central overarching issue, even after social politics loosened its control over film culture (Semsel et al., 1990; Semsel et al., 1993).

The shift in perspective in the early 1980s was a major one, as translations were published of Bazin and Siegfried Kracauer, and then of Christian Metz, Dudley Andrew, Browne and Mulvey. While still within the boundaries of a national modernity, film scholars began to reflect not just on Chinese cinema but on broader ontological issues concerning cinema. Those first debates quite soon became available in the West, with the publication of two anthologies which included a number of articles by Chinese film scholars in English translation (Semsel et al., 1990; Semsel et al., 1993).[14] Although these anthologies potentially made Chinese Film Studies and Chinese perspectives on cinema accessible to Western film scholars they were, for the most part, read only by the circle of Chinese film scholars who had already been following the original debates in China. Twenty years on, however, the number of international conferences about Chinese film and collaborative research projects between Chinese and transnational scholars provide evidence of a belated response to those first exchanges.

National style and Chinese cinemas

Much of the analysis chronicled in this chapter has focused primarily, if not exclusively, on the relationship between politics and style on the Mainland. Nevertheless, we have also noted the work of writers and commentators who think about the formal properties of film art in China, and their work is particularly valuable in revealing the continuities in aesthetic production values and perspectives over many years, and across different media. Art historians, directors, cinematographers and designers are successfully claiming a national style (*minzu shi*) – which also encompasses 'consciousness' of national identity and cultural belonging – in the high points of Chinese filmmaking (Chu, 2002; Hu J., 2003; Lin, 1985; Silbergeld, 1999). Of course, such Chinese cultural consciousness is not homogeneous, nor is it limited to the PRC or to cinema created on the Mainland. The cinemas of Hong Kong, Taiwan, Singapore and Macao, possibly in that order, have contributed a great deal to the art and depth of Chinese film, defined through language and location. In the past few years, Mainland Chinese scholars have increasingly tended to include consideration of at least Taiwanese and Hong Kong cinemas in their work on aesthetics, theory or audience studies.[15] Whether in the Chinese context this indicates a new internationalism or an expansionist nationalism remains an open political question.

To conclude this survey of Chinese Film Studies, however, it is appropriate to note not only the growth of international interest in Chinese film over recent decades but also the broadening of that interest to include non-Mainland Chinese cinemas. The reasons for both developments are several. Global communications and distribution opportunities have made a wider range of Chinese films more freely available to Western audiences. The flowering of talent in a series of new 'waves' in Taiwan and Hong Kong as well as the PRC drew attention to the emerging regional cinemas in the first place. The theoretical work of Teshome Gabriel (1982; 1994) and Paul Willemen (1994) on Third Cinema offered young scholars new ways of thinking about 'other' cinemas – perspectives and approaches which they quickly adapted to specific films and film cultures. At the same time, a number of dedicated journalists as well as academic writers have helped to create the time and space for thinking about China on the world scene: people like Tony Rayns, Derek Elley, Chris Berry, Bérénice Reynaud and Mary Farquhar, who in turn built on the earlier work of Régis Bergeron (1983) and Joris Ivens. A broader debate about 'Chineseness' in the 1990s paved the way for the publication of Sheldon Lu's influential collection on transnational Chinese films in 1997 (Chun, 1996; Tu, 1994). The emergence of transnational and global China as a compelling analytical framework for studying Chinese film was no doubt due in part to the increasingly diasporic nature of Chinese film scholars. Many of the younger generation were born and raised in the PRC, Hong Kong or Taiwan, but have received their tertiary education in the US and gone on to achieve tenure in American universities.

Recent scholarship has begun to study the small but politically and socially interesting Singaporean and Macao industries in the context of 'global', transnational, or, most immediately, 'regional' Chinese cinemas (Khoo, 2006). At the same time, work on the major film centres has continued. Hong Kong has been a vital centre of Cantonese-language film since the 1950s, supplying the region with at least one cinema that was not obliged – at least not all the time – to produce films in standard Mandarin, and that has claimed a realm of authenticity, energy and local grounding for its genres, stars and fads. It now also boasts a number of locally-based scholars who are giving a lead to

international colleagues in analyzing Hong Kong cinema. The film historian Law Kar has published widely in Chinese on aspects of its style, genres and history, and acts as the advising historian to the Hong Kong Film Archive and Gallery. In 2004, he was the curator of an exhibition that programmed a retrospective season at the Archive to celebrate the contribution of Lai Manwai, the 'Father of Hong Kong cinema'. These events, along with a documentary Law Kar produced, not only remind cinema scholars of the relationship between Guangdong and Hong Kong in the development of early film, but they also suggest how it is possible to link location and place to film analysis. The exhibition was related to a series of 'trails' devised to take visitors around Hong Kong to see places and sites of note in film history. This approach exemplifies the sense that, despite the international take-up of theoretical adventures in Chinese film over the past two decades, the field is now returning home to its sources and origins. This is not to say that the field is shrinking back to a place 'outside' traditional centres of film scholarship in Europe and the US, but rather that film scholarship is becoming regionally and spatially coherent.[16]

NOTES

1 The Centennial Celebration of Chinese Cinema and the 2005 Annual Conference of ACSS, 'National, Transnational, International: Chinese Cinema and Asian Cinema in the Context of Globalization', was held in Beijing (5–7 June 2005) and Shanghai (9–10 June 2005).

2 *Huayu dianying* might more appropriately be translated as 'Chinese languages cinema', as a variety of Chinese languages have been used in Chinese cinema, with Mandarin and Cantonese being only the most recurrent ones.

3 As part of the broader debate over a more China-centred historiography (Cohen, 1984), many scholars studying such social and economic factors as literacy rates, urban development and commerce strategies have argued for the existence of an 'early modern China' that dates back to the late Ming Dynasty (1368–1644).

4 'The film *Dingjun Mountain* was made by Ren Qingtai (1850–1932), the owner of the Fengtai

Photography Studio, in Beijing in 1905. The cameraman was Liu Zhonglun, the best photographer in Ren's photo studio, while Ren Qingtai himself could be regarded as the first Chinese film director' (Ge, 2002).

5 'In the 1920s and 1930s, the popular press became increasingly more affordable (thanks to the introduction of copper plate first and photographic plate later) and more sophisticated (i.e., the development of combined prints). As a result, over twenty pictorials and magazines became available in cities like Beijing and Shanghai' (Voci, 2002: 101). While readership was restricted by the limited literacy of the urban population and the cost of the magazines, their content was often displayed on walls or on the site of news-stands (Voci, 2002: 102–103).

6 New Perceptionists (*xin ganjue pai*) are also referred to as '*xiandai pai*' (modernists), '*shuimo she*' (foam society) and '*xinli fenxi xiaoshuo pai*' (psychoanalytic novelists) (Chen B., 1993: 256–66; Voci, 2002: 72–90).

7 Besides writing for and about film, Tian Han was a well-established dramaturge who also wrote the lyrics of the PRC's national anthem.

8 Thousands of people attended Ruan Lingyu's funeral and her legend has not faded since. In 1992 Stanley Kwan directed a film based on her life, *Ruan Lingyu* (*Centre Stage*, a.k.a. *Actress*, Hong Kong).

9 The view of the present authors is that the tension was not removed but displaced.

10 Chinese cinema was never totally isolated. On 8 May 1955, for instance, André Bazin, Jacques Doniol-Valcroze and George Sadoul sponsored the Cannes premiere of *Liang Shangbo yu Zhu Yingtai* (*Liang Shangbo and Zhu Yingtai*, Sang Hu, Hong Kong, 1954).

11 Censorship has been the rough end of film's connection to the 'story' of the nation, or the national political agenda as a process of critique. Its variations in harshness and subtlety, and its ideological rationality or political arbitrariness, provide an important shadow history of Chinese cinema.

12 On the Fifth Generation, see also Zhang Xudong (1997: 233–56) and the analyses of *Huang tudi* and *Lan feng zheng* (*Blue Kite*, Tian Zhuangzhuang, Hong Kong, 1993) in Donald (2000: 57–61; 63–78; 48–55). In many edited volumes on Chinese cinema the Fifth Generation's novelty/revolution is the most discussed topic: see Berry (1991); Ehrlich and Desser (1994) and Browne et al. (1994).

13 For sample discussions of other aspects and periods of Chinese filmmaking, see Lu (1997) and Zhang (1999).

14 Some of the translations were not of a very high standard, it should be noted.

15 This trend should not be overemphasized. Whereas Wang Haizhou (2004) includes sections on Taiwanese and Hong Kong cinemas, Chen Xuguang (2004) still focuses exclusively on Mainland cinema. Conversely, most of the recent English-language publication on Chinese film or its most representative filmmakers include Taiwan and Hong Kong cinemas. See Browne et al., (1994); Berry M. (2005); Lu. (1997); Lu and Yeh (2005); Zhang Y. (2002).

16 This development is producing new names and a new paradigm of regional scholarship: Laikwan Pang and Siu-Leung Li are examples of young scholars trained in Hong Kong and the US now publishing in Chinese and English on an international stage (Li S., 2003; Li et al., 2005; Pang, 2002).

REFERENCES

Bai, Jingsheng (1990) 'Throwing Away the Walking Stick of Drama', in George Semsel, Xia Hong and Hou Jianping (eds), *Chinese Film Theory: A Guide to a New Era*. New York: Praeger. pp. 5–20.

Bergeron, Régis (1983) *Le Cinéma chinois: 1949–1983*. Paris: Harmattan.

Berry, Chris (1988a) 'Chinese Left Cinema in the 1930s: Poisonous Weeds or National Treasures?', *Jump Cut*, 34: 87–94.

Berry, Chris (1988b) 'The Sublimative Text: Sex and Revolution in *Big Road*', *East-West Film Journal*, 2(2): 66–86.

Berry, Chris (ed.) (1991) *Perspectives on Chinese Cinema*. London: BFI.

Berry, Chris (1997) 'On Top of the World: An Interview with Duan Jinchuan, Director of *16 Barkhor South Street*', *Film International*, 5(2): 60–2.

Berry, Chris (2002) 'Facing Reality: Chinese Documentary, Chinese Postsocialism', in Hung Wu, Huangsheng Wang and Boyi Feng (eds), *Reinterpretation: A Decade of Experimental Chinese Art, 1990–2000*. Guangzhou: Guangdong Museum of Art. pp. 121–31.

Berry, Chris and Farquhar, Mary Ann (2006) *China on Screen: Cinema and Nation*. New York: Columbia University Press.

Berry, Chris and Lu, Fei-I (eds) (2004) *Island on the Edge: Taiwan New Cinema and After*. Hong Kong: Hong Kong University Press.

Berry, Michael (2005) *Speaking in Images*. New York: Columbia University Press.

Braester, Yomi (2000) 'Revolution and Revulsion: Ideology, Monstrosity, and Phantasmagoria in Maxu Weibang's *Film Song at Midnight*', *MCLC*, 12(1): 81–114.

Browne, Nick, Pickowicz, Paul, Sobchack, Vivian and Yau, Esther (eds) (1994) *New Chinese Cinemas*. New York: Cambridge University Press.

Chen, Bo 陳播 (ed.) (1993) *Zhongguo zuoyi dianying yundong* 中國左翼電影運動 (The leftist film movement in China). Beijing: Zhongguo dianying chubanshe.

Chen, Feibao (2000) *Taiwan dianying daoyan yishu (Taiwan Cinema Directorial Act)*. Taipei: Yatai.

Chen, Xihe (1990) 'Shadowplay: Chinese Film Aesthetics and their Philosophical and Cultural Fundamentals', in George S. Semsel, Xia Hong and Hou Jianping (eds), *Chinese Film Theory: A Guide to a New Era*. New York: Praeger. pp. 192–203.

Chen, Xihe 陳犀禾, Shi, Chuan 石川, Nie, Wei 聶偉 (2005) *Dangdaidianying lilun xin zouxiang* 當代電影理論新走向 (New trends in contemporary film theory). Beijing: Wenhua yishu chubanshe.

Chen, Xuguang 陳旭光 (2004) *Dangdai Zhongguo yingshi wenhua yajiu* 當代中國影視文化研究 (Studying contemporary Chinese visual culture). Beijing: Beijing daxue chuban she.

Cheng, Jihua 程季華 (1963) Zhongguo dianying fazhan shi 中國電影發展史 (History of the development of Chinese cinema). 2 vols. Beijing: Zhongguo dianying chubanshe.

Chow, Rey (1995) *Primitive Passions: Visuality, Sexuality, Ethnography and Contemporary Chinese Cinema*. New York: Columbia University Press.

Chu, Yingchi (2002) *Hong Kong Cinema*. London: Routledge Curzon.

Chun, Allen (1996) 'Fuck Chineseness: On the Ambiguities of Ethnicity as Culture as Identity', *Boundary 2*, 23(2): 111–38.

Clark, Paul (1987) *Chinese Cinema: Culture and Politics Since 1949*. New York: Cambridge University Press.

Clark, Paul (1989) 'Reinventing China: The Fifth Generation of Filmmakers', *Modern Chinese Literature*, 5(1): 121–36.

Clark, Paul (2005) *Reinventing China: A Generation and its Films*. Hong Kong: The Chinese University Press.

Cohen, Paul (1984) *Discovering History in China: American Historical Writing on the Recent Chinese Past*. New York: Columbia University Press.

Cui, Zi'en 崔子恩 (2001) 'Dianying minjian sheng' '電影民間聲' ('Unofficial voices from film'), *Yinyue yu biaoyan* 音樂与表演 (Music and performance), 3: 32–8.

Cui, Zi'en 崔子恩 (2003) *Diyi guanzhong* 第一觀眾 (The first audience). Beijing: Xiandai chubanshe.

Dai, Jinhua (1999) 'Rewriting Chinese Women: Gender Production and Cultural Space in the Eighties and Nineties', in Mayfair Mei Hui Yang (ed.), *Spaces of Their Own: Women's Public Sphere in Transnational China*. Minneapolis: University of Minnesota Press. pp. 191–206.

Dai, Jinhua 戴錦華 (2000) *Wuzhong fengjing* 霧中風景 (A scene in the fog). Beijing: Beijing daxue chubanshe.

Dai, Jinhua (2002) *Cinema and Desire: Feminist Marxism and Cultural Politics in the Work of Dai Jinhua*. Eds. Jing Wang and Tani E. Barlow. London: Verso.

Donald, Stephanie (1997) 'Landscape and Agency: *Yellow Earth* and the demon lover', *Theory, Culture and Society*, 14: 97–112.

Donald, Stephanie (2000) *Public Secrets, Public Spaces: Cinema and Civility in China*. Lanham, MD: Rowman and Littlefield.

Donald, Stephanie Hemelryk (2005) *Little Friends: Children's Film and Media Culture in China*. Lanham, MD: Rowman and Littlefield.

Ehrlich, Linda C. and Desser, David (eds) (1994) *Cinematic Landscapes: Observations on the Visual Arts and Cinema of China and Japan*. Austin: University of Texas Press.

Fang, Fang 方方 (2003) *Zhongguo jilupian fazhan shi* 中國紀錄片發展史 (History of the development of Chinese documentary cinema). Beijing: Zhongguo xiju chubanshe.

Feng, Min 封敏 (1985) 'Malu tianshi yu xinxianshizhuyi' '馬路天使与新現實主義' ('Street Angels and Neorealism'), *Dangdai dianying* 當代電影, 5: 95–100.

Fu, Poshek (2000) 'Eileen Chang, Woman's Film, and Domestic Shanghai', *Asian Cinema*, 11: 97–113.

Fu, Poshek (2003) *Between Shanghai and Hong Kong: The Politics of Chinese Cinemas*. Stanford, CA: Stanford University Press.

Fu, Poshek and Desser, David (eds) (2000) *The Cinema of Hong Kong: History, Arts, Identity*. Cambridge: Cambridge University Press.

Gabriel, Teshome (1982) *Third Cinema in the Third World: An Aesthetic of Liberation*. Ann Arbor, MI: UMI Research Press.

Gabriel, Teshome (1994) 'Towards a Critical Theory of Third World Films', in Jim Pines and Paul Willemen (eds), *Questions of Third Cinema*. London: BFI. pp. 30–5.

Ge, Congmin (2002) 'Photography, Shadow Play, Beijing Opera and The First Chinese Film', *Eras*, 3. Available at: http://www.arts.monash.edu.au/eras/edition_3/ge.htm.

Harris, Christine (1997) 'The New Woman Incident: Cinema, Scandal and Spectacle in 1935 Shanghai', in Lu Sheldon Hsiao-Peng (ed.), *Transnational Chinese Cinemas: Identity, Nationhood, Gender*. Honolulu: University of Hawaii Press. pp. 277–302.

Hu, Jubin (2003) *Projecting a Nation: Chinese Cinema Before 1949*. Hong Kong: Hong Kong University Press.

Hu, Ke 胡克 [1995] (1998) 'Contemporary Film Theory in China' ('*Dangdai Zhongguo dianying lilun*'), *Screening the Past*, 3. Available at: http://www.latrobe.edu.au/screeningthepast/reruns/hkrr2b.html.

Hu, Ke 胡克, Zhang Jianyong 張建勇, Chen Mo 陳默 (eds) (2000) *Zhongguo dianying meixue: 1999* 中國電影美學：1999年 (Aesthetics of Chinese film: 1999). Beijing: Beijing Broadcasting Institute Press.

Khoo, Olivia (2006) 'Love in Ruins: Spectral Bodies in Wong Kar-wai's *In the Mood for Love*', in Fran Martin and Larissa Heinrich (eds), *Embodied Modernities: Corporeality, Representation, and Chinese Cultures*. Honolulu: University of Hawaii Press. pp. 235–52.

Leary, Charles (2003) 'Performing the Documentary, or Making it to the Other Bank', *Senses of Cinema*, 27. Available at: http://www.sensesofcinema.com/contents/03/27/performing_documentary.html.

Lee, Leo Ou-fan (1999) *Shanghai Modern: The Flowering of a New Urban Culture in Cjhina, 1930–1945*. Harvard: Harvard University Press.

Leyda, Jay (1972) *Dianying: An Account of Films and the Film Audience in China*. Cambridge, MA: MIT Press.

Li, Daoxin 李導新 (2005) *Zhongguo dianying wenhua shi* 中國電影文化史 (History of Chinese film culture). Beijing: Beijing daxue chubanshi.

Li, Siu-leung (2003) *Cross-Dressing in Chinese Opera*. Hong Kong: Hong Kong University Press.

Li, Siu-leung, Morris, Meaghan and Chan, Ching-kiu Stephen (2005) *Hong Kong Connections: Transnational Imagination in Action Cinema*. Hong Kong: Hong Kong University Press.

Lin, Niantong (1985) 'A Study of the Theories of Chinese Cinema in their Relationship to Classical Aesthetics', *Modern Chinese Literature*, 1(2): 185–200.

Liu, Lydia H. (1995) *Translingual Practices: Literature, National Culture, and Translated Modernity – China 1900–1937*. Stanford, CA: Stanford University Press.

Liu, Na'ou 劉吶鷗 (1993) 'Zhonguo dianying miaoxie de shendu wenti' '中國電影描寫的深度問題' ('Problems of depth in Chinese film representation'), in Chen Bo 陳播 (ed.), *Zhongguo zuoyi dianying yundong* 中國左翼電影運動 (The leftist film movement in China). Beijing: Zhongguo dianying chubanshe. pp. 256–61.

Lu, Sheldon Hsiao-peng (ed.) (1997) *Transnational Chinese Cinemas: Identity, Nationhood, Gender*. Honolulu: University of Hawaii Press.

Lu, Sheldon Hsiao-peng 魯曉鵬 and Yeh, Emily Yueh-yu 葉月瑜 (2005) 'Huayu dianying zhi gainian: yige lilun tansuo cengmianshang de yanjiu' '華語電影之概念：一個理論探索層面上的研究' ('Perspectives on Chinese-language film: an analysis of theoretical investigations'), in Chen Xihe 陳犀禾, Shi Chuan 石川, Nie Wei 聶偉 (eds), *Dangdai dianying lilun xin zouxiang* 當代電影理論新走向 (New trends in contemporary film theory). Beijing: Wenhua yishu chubanshe. pp. 191–200.

Lü, Xinyu 呂新雨 (2003) *Jilu Zhongguo: dangdai Zhonguo xin jilupian yundong* 紀錄中國：當代中國新紀錄片運動 (Recording China: Contemporary Chinese new documentary movement). Beijing: Sanlian shudian.

Lü, Xinyu (2005) 'Ruins of the Future: Class and History in Wang Bing's *Tiexi District*', *New Left Review*, 31: 125–36.

Ma, Ning (1989) 'The Textual and Critical Difference of Being Radical: Reconstructing Chinese Leftist Films of the 1930s', *Wide Angle*, 11(2): 28.

Mao Zedong (1967) 'Talks at the Yenan Forum on Literature and Art: May 1942', in *Selected Works of Mao Tse-tung*. Vol. 3. Beijing: Foreign Languages Press. pp. 69–98.

Marchetti, Gina (2005) 'Zhongguo dianying nuxing diangying xiang he chu qu?' '中国女性电影向何处去?' ('Where is Chinese women's cinema heading towards?'), in Chen Xihe 陳犀禾, Shi Chuan 石川, Nie Wei 聶偉 (eds), *Dang dai dian ying li lun xin zou xiang* 當代電影理論新走向 (New trends in contemporary film theory). Beijing: Wenhua yishu chubanshe. pp. 307–17.

Mei, Bing 梅冰 and Zhu Jingjiang 朱靖江 (2004) *Zhongguo duli jilu dang'an* 中國獨立紀錄片檔案 (Records of China's independent documentary). Xi'an: Shaanxi shifan daxue chubanshe.

Mu, Zi 木子 (1985) '*Shennü.* Woguo mopian de xianshizhuyi jiazuo' '《神女》我國默片的現實主義佳作' ('*Goddess*: A realist masterpiece of Chinese silent films'), *Dianying Yishu* 電影藝術 (Film art), 1: 53–7.

Ni, Zhen (1994) 'Classical Chinese Painting and Cinematographic Signification', in Linda Ehrlich and David Desser (eds), *Cinematic Landscapes: Observations on the Visual Arts and Cinema of China and Japan*. Austin: University of Texas Press. pp. 63–80.

Ni, Zhen (2002) *Memoirs from the Beijing Film Academy: The Genesis of China's Fifth Generation*. Tr. Chris Berry. Durham, NC: Duke University Press.

Pang, Laikwan (2002) *Building a New China in Cinema: The Chinese Left-Wing Cinema Movement, 1932–1937*. Lanham, MD: Rowman and Littlefield.

Pickowicz, Paul (1993) 'Melodramatic Representation and the "May Fourth" Tradition of Chinese Cinema', in Ellen Widmer and David Wang (eds), *From May Fourth to June Fourth: Fiction and Film in Twentieth-Century China*. Cambridge, MA: Harvard University Press. pp. 295–326.

Pickowicz, Paul and Zhang, Yingjin (eds) (2006) *From Underground to Independent: Alternative Film Culture in Contemporary China*. Lanham, MD: Rowman and Littlefield.

Ping, Jie 平杰 (ed.) (2006) *Lingyan xiangkan: haiwai xuezhe ping dangdai Zhongguo jilupian* 另眼相看:海外學者評當代中國紀錄 (REEL CHINA: A new look at Chinese documentary). Shanghai: Shanghai Wenhui Publishing House.

Reynaud, Bérénice (1996) 'New Visions/New Chinas: Video-Art, Documentation, and the Chinese Modernity in Question', in Michael Renov and Erika Suderburg (eds), *Resolutions: Contemporary Video Practices*. Minneapolis: University of Minnesota Press. pp. 229–57.

Reynaud, Bérénice (2003) 'Dancing with Myself, Drifting with My Camera: The Emotional Vagabonds of China's New Documentary', *Senses of Cinema*, 28. Available at: http://www.sensesofcinema.com/contents/03/28/chinas_new_documentary.html.

Semsel, George S., Chen, Xihe and Xia, Hong (eds) (1993) *Film in Contemporary China: Critical Debate, 1979–1989*. Westport, CT: Praeger.

Semsel, George S., Xia, Hong and Hou, Jianping (eds) (1990) *Chinese Film Theory: A Guide to a New Era*. New York: Praeger.

Silbergeld, Jerome (1999) *China into Film: Frames of Reference in Contemporary Chinese Cinema*. London: Reaktion Books.

Silbergeld, Jerome (2004) *Hitchcock with a Chinese Face: Cinematic Doubles, Oedipal Triangles, and China's Moral Voice*. Seattle: University of Washington Press.

Tang, Na 唐納 (1993) 'Qingsuan ruanxing dianying lun' '清算軟性電影論' ('A critique of soft cinema'), in Chen Bo 陳播 (ed.), *Zhongguo zuoyi dianying yundong* 中國左翼電影運動 (The leftist film movement in China). Beijing: Zhongguo dianying chubanshe. pp. 269–80.

Teo, Stephen (2003) '"There Is No Sixth Generation!": Director Li Yang on *Blind Shaft* and His Place in Chinese Cinema', *Senses of Cinema*, 27. Available at: http://www.sensesofcinema.com/contents/03/27/li_yang.html.

Tu, Wei-ming (1994) 'Cultural China: The Periphery as the Center', in Tu Wei-ming (ed.), *The Living Tree: The Changing Meaning of Being Chinese Today*. Stanford, CA: Stanford University Press. pp. 1–3.

Voci, Paola (2002) 'Visual Dissent in Twentieth-Century China: A Study of the Exhibitionist Mode of Representation in Cinema, Literature, and Media'. PhD dissertation, Indiana University.

Voci, Paola (2004) 'From the Center to the Periphery: Chinese Documentary's Visual Conjectures', *Modern Chinese Literature and Culture*, 16(1): 65–113.

Voci, Paola (2006) 'Zhongguo jilupian: yingxiang Zhongguo dianying wenhua' '中國紀錄片: 影響中國電影文化' ('Chinese Documentary: Changing Film Culture in China'), in Ping Jie 平杰 (ed.), *Lingyan xiangkan: haiwai xuezhe ping dangdai Zhongguo jilupian* 另眼相看: 海外學者評當代中國紀錄 (REEL CHINA: A new look at Chinese documentary). Shanghai: Shanghai Wenhui Publishing House. pp. 103–13.

Wang, Haizhou 王海洲 (ed.) (2004) *Zhongguo dianying: guannian yu guiji* 中國電影: 觀念与軌跡 (Chinese film: perspectives and directions). Beijing: Zhongguo dianying chubanshe.

Wang, Weici 王蔚慈 (2000) *Jilu yu tansuo: yu dalu jilupian gongzuozhe de shiji duihua* 紀錄與探索: 與大陸紀錄片工作者的世紀對話 (Recording and exploring: Conversations with documentarians from Mainland China). Taibei: Yuanliu.

Wang, Weici 王慰慈 (2001) *Jilu yu tansuo: 1990–2000 dalu jilupian de fazhan yu koushu jilu* 记录与探索: 1990–2000 大陆纪录片的发展与口述记录 (Documentation and exploration: the growth of documentary in mainland China and its related oral histories, 1990–2000). Taipei: Guojian dianying ziliao guan.

Willemen, Paul (1994) *Looks and Frictions: Essays in Cultural Studies and Film Theory*. Bloomington: Indiana University Press.

Wu, Hung, Huangsheng, Wang and Boyi, Feng (eds) (2002) *Reinterpretation: A Decade of Experimental Chinese Art: 1990–2000*. Guangzhou: Guangdong Museum of Art.

Wu, Wenguang 吳文光 (2001) *Jingtou xiang ziji de yanjing yiyang* 镜头像自己的眼睛－样 (The lens is the same as my eye). Shanghai: Shanghai yishu chubanshe.

Xia, Yan 夏衍 (1982) *Xie dianying juben de jige wenti* 寫電影劇本的幾個問題 (Film scenario writing problems). Beijing: Zhongguo dianying chubanshe.

Yau, Esther Ching-mei (1989) 'Cultural and Economic Dislocations: Filmic Phantasies of Chinese Women in the 1980s', *Wide Angle*, 11(2): 6–21.

Yeh, Emilie Yueh-yu and Davis, Darrell (2005) *Taiwan Film Directors: A Treasure Island*. New York: Columbia University Press.

Yip, June (2004) *Envisioning Taiwan: Fiction, Cinema and the Nation in the Cultural Imaginary*. Durham, NC: Duke University Press.

Zhang, Xianmin 張獻民 (2004) *Kanbujian de yingxiang* 看不見的電影 (Films banned from watching). Shanghai: Sanlian shudian.

Zhang, Xudong (1997) *Chinese Modernism in the Era of Reforms: Cultural Fever, Avant-garde Fiction, and the New Chinese Cinema.* London: Duke University Press.

Zhang, Yingjin (ed.) (1999) *Cinema and Urban Culture in Shanghai, 1922–1943.* Stanford, CA: Stanford University Press.

Zhang, Yingjin (2002) *Screening China: Critical Interventions, Cinematic Reconfigurations, and the Transnational Imaginary in Contemporary Chinese Cinemas.* Ann Arbor: Center for Chinese Studies, University of Michigan.

Zhang, Yingjin (2004) 'Styles, Subjects, and Special Points of View: A Study of Contemporary Chinese Documentary', *New Cinemas: A Journal of Contemporary Film,* 2(2): 119–35.

Zhang, Yingjin 張英進 (2005) 'Dianying lilun, xueshujizhi yu kuaxue yanjiu fangfa: zhenglun shijue wenhua' 電影理論, 學術机制与跨學科研究: 爭論視覺文' ('Film theory, academic apparatus and interdisciplinary studies methodologies: debating visual culture'), in Chen, Xihe 陳犀禾, Shi, Chuan 石川, Nie, Wei 聶偉 (2005) *Dangdai dianying lilun xin zouxiang* 當代電影理論新走向 (New trends in contemporary film theory). Beijing: Wenhua yishu chubanshe. pp. 72–85.

Zhang, Yingjin 張英進 (2006a) *Shenshi Zhongguo: cong xuekeshi de jiaodu guancha Zhongguo dianying yu wenxue yanjiu* 審視中國: 從學科使的角度觀察中國電影與文學研究 (A close look at China: examining Chinese cinema and literary studies from a disciplinary perspective). Nanjing shi: Nanjing daxue chubanshe.

Zhang, Yingjin 張英進 (2006b) 'Dangdai Zhongguo duli jilupian yanjiu' 當代中國獨立紀錄片研究' ('An analysis of contemporary independent Chinese documentary'), in Ping Jie 平杰 (ed.), *Lingyan xiangkan: haiwai xuezhe ping dangdai Zhongguo jilupian* 另眼相看: 海外學者評當代中國紀錄 (REEL CHINA: A new look at Chinese documentary). Shanghai: Shanghai Wenhui Publishing House. pp. 53–68.

Zhang, Zhen (2001) 'An Amorous History of the Silver Screen: The Actress as Vernacular Embodiment in Early Chinese Film Culture', *Camera Obscura,* 16(3): 229–63.

Zhang, Zhen (ed.) (2006) *The Urban Generation: Chinese Cinema and Society at the Turn of the Twenty-first Century.* Durham, NC: Duke University Press.

Zheng, Dongtian 鄭洞天 (2003) 'Diliudai dianying de wenhua yiyi' '第六代電影的文化意義' ('The cultural significance of the sixth generation film'), *Dianying yishu* 電影藝術 (Film art), 1: 42–3.

4

Our Films, Their Films: Some Speculations on Writing Indian Film History

Brian Shoesmith

When I first began writing about Indian cinema as an Australian film scholar in the 1970s, there was very little material available. There was, it seemed, Erik Barnouw and S. Krishnaswamy's *Indian Film* (1963; 1980), *A Pictorial History of Indian Cinema* (1979), a chronicle by Firoze Rangoonwalla, and Satyajit Ray's *Our Films, Their Films* (1976).[1] The major film journals carried very little – the odd review and comment about the size of the industry. On the few occasions that I was brave enough to present a paper at a conference I was greeted with incredulity. Australian colleagues were puzzled as to why I would want to talk about a cinema nobody knew anything about and probably never would, which was totally under-theorized and culturally inaccessible. Indian colleagues were puzzled about the reasons why I wanted to talk about what they regarded as 'rubbish', whilst they recounted in great detail the plot line of every individual film I put forward for discussion and corrected any error I made with

a command of detail that daunted me. In short, writing about Indian cinema for a foreigner, a *gora*, has always been problematic.

What are the problems? Here I wish to discuss two. First, what is Indian cinema? In a culture fragmented by community, language and regional difference it is difficult to be sure what constitutes our field of study. Convention has it that 'Bollywood' films, produced within an industry based in Bombay and following a set of narrative tropes of excess, are representative of India and therefore may be regarded as constituting Indian cinema. The metaphysics of this decision are dealt with elsewhere in this handbook (see Chapter 30), but in industrial terms Bollywood accounts for little more than 25 to 30 per cent of films produced within India in any one year, and yet the burgeoning discourse on Indian cinema focuses almost overwhelmingly on this one segment of film production. The reasons for this are not difficult to detect if you go back and look at the literature.

The Bombay industry engaged in remorseless self-promotion from the late 1920s on, proclaiming itself to be the national cinema for three basic reasons: it used Hindi as its primary language of dialogue, although many of the scripts in the National Film and Television Archives in Pune are written in Urdu; it had created national distribution chains throughout India, thereby ensuring a national audience for its productions; and the Bombay industry controlled the professional and industrial organizations that were designed to promote and represent the industry to largely unsympathetic governments, both British and Indian.[2] Organizations like the Motion Picture Society of India (MPSI), formed in 1932, the Indian Motion Picture Producers Association (IMPPA), founded in 1936, and the Indian Motion Picture Distributors Association (IMPDA) have consistently promoted the claims of Bombay to be the primary centre of film production in India in their publications with considerable success (see MPSI, 1939; Shah, 1950). The outcomes of this promotional activity have been twofold: first, to create a view, largely accepted by the critical establishment, that Bollywood is Indian cinema and second, to ensure that any history of the writing of Indian cinema is a history of absences rather than a 'cinema of interruption' (Gopalan, 2002).

This leads to my second problem: What is absent? I have yet to find a thorough analysis of the myriad of magazines that surround the industry in all its phases. In the 1930s there were over 68 magazines devoted exclusively to the cinema, including the excellent *Filmland*, a Calcutta journal that addressed industrial as well as cultural issues. There is no study of *Cineblitz*, an influential Bombay journal or the idiosyncratic *Filmindia* (later *Mother India*) edited, written and published by Baburao Patel in the 1940s and 1950s. This leads us to confront another significant absence – the lack of translation of significant accounts of the regional film industries from the regional Indian languages into English. The *Continuum* publication (O'Regan and Shoesmith, 1987) of Phalke's writing first published in *Kesari* (*The Lion*),

the major Marathi-language nationalist newspaper (which is published to this day even), in 1916 and subsequently translated by Narmada Shahane and published in mimeographed form by the Film and Television School in Pune, remains in demand.[3] There is no other source for this important body of work and the translation and publication of other local writings would greatly enrich our understanding of early cinema in India.

There are other absences too numerous to cover here, with two exceptions. It should be acknowledged that the regional cinemas have been largely ignored in comparison to Bollywood. Tamil cinema is best served through the work of Theodore Baskaran, M.S.S. Pandian, Sarah Dickey and recently Salvaraj Velayutham, and there is the work on Ray and the Bengali cinema but beyond that there is really very little. Telegu, Marathi and Malayali cinemas have, on the whole, been ignored in English-language accounts of the Indian cinema, although there is a considerable body of work in the local languages. Another serious absence is the lack of scholarly work on the studios that dominated the industry between the 1930s and 1950s. John Lent's essay, 'Heyday of the Indian studio system' (1983), remains an important work and has been augmented by my own work (see Shoesmith, 1987; forthcoming). Barnouw and Krishnaswamy discuss the studios, and an implicit recognition of the significance of the studios infuses Manjunath Pendulkar's *Indian Popular Cinema* (2003) but beyond that there is very little serious scholarship on Imperial Studios, Bombay Talkies or Ranjit Studios other than the occasional reference in the hagiographies of the stars that seem to dominate much of the writing about early Bollywood. A recent exception is Dorothee Wenner's excellent biography of Nadia, which hints at the riches yet to be uncovered (2005). Wenner uses the career of Nadia (Mary Evans) to investigate the importance of Wadia Movietone, a major studio from the 1930s on, the cultural perceptions of women as actors and the general economic status of studios in an economy that placed enormous emphasis on nation-building economic activity and paradoxically chose to ignore the cinema. Wenner demonstrates the rich veins that run through Bollywood and how mining the archives can produce a perceptive historical account of Indian film history, albeit in popular form.

With these qualifications in mind I shall develop a tentative historical schema of writing about Indian cinema since the 1920s under three headings. Cinema arrived in India towards the end of the *colonial era* and coincided in the 1920s and 1930s with increasing pressure for independence – this was the period in which the campaigns led by Mohandas Ghandi were developing widespread support. A *transitional period* began in effect with the start of the Second World War in 1939 and continued through the granting of independence and the partition of the country into India and Pakistan in 1947 and the nation-building led by Jawaharlal Nehru and the Congress Party during the 1950s and 1960s. The third period I identify is the *postcolonial era* that can be said to start some time in the 1970s. Each era will focus on: the recurring themes of control and censorship, incorporating the issues of imperialism and ideology; state support for the industry through subsidies and protection from foreign productions; the studio system that in its heyday produced the social genre that dealt with social issues of class and caste; the meretricious nature of the popular commercial films collectively known as *masala* films, and latterly Bollywood and the rise of the star system.

THE COLONIAL ERA

There are four major sources of information about the formative years of cinema in India. First, there are extensive files relating to cinematography in the National Archives of India, and to a lesser extent in the regional archives, the India Office and Library files now lodged at the British Library. Second, the Indian Cinematographic Committee of Inquiry, 1927–28 Report (ICC) (Government of India, 1928), supported by five volumes

of evidence amounts to over 2,000 pages of detailed enquiry, which is the most thorough review of an emerging film industry ever undertaken. The holdings of the various archives combined with the volumes of evidence published by the ICC provide a vast reservoir of data and information about the formative period of the Indian film industry that has yet to be fully explored. Third, there are also partial runs of film magazines and journals published in the major cities between 1920 and the Second World War and lodged in the National Film and Television Archives. Fourth, there are publications that emerged from professional organizations such as the MPSI and IMPPA in the 1930s and 1940s. These four sources collectively constitute the basis of all subsequent accounts of the formation of the film industry in India, such as Wenner (2005) and Priya Jaikumar's work on the ICC (2006). They are significant because they provide insight into the impact of film, as social imaginary or ideological resonators, outside the usual Hollywood-dominated view of film.

Indian film began to attract British attention when concerns were expressed to parliamentarians in London and to the Government of India about the impact the medium would have on the 'credulous minds of the childlike masses'. British residents in India felt deeply that cinema undermined the prestige of the European in Asia – a view that was shared by the Dutch in Indonesia. The files in archives such as the India Office in London and Indian National Archives in New Delhi are littered with complaints by such expatriates about film corrupting the masses, portraying European women in unseemly ways and showing 'lesser breeds' (a term used especially frequently between 1913 and 1920) rebelling against the power of Europe. The India Office in London demanded action against this perceived social evil that possessed the potential to disrupt a finely balanced social and political order. The Government of India prevaricated but introduced a Cinematographic Act in 1918 that was subsequently modified to conform to the new political realities in a post-war era. This failed to produce a decline in the level of complaints from Europeans or, it must be added, from socially conservative Indians who tended to see film in similar terms to the British residents. The outcome was the ICC, established in 1927.

Although Australia, England, France and Germany all conducted enquiries into their local film industries and their putative relationship to Hollywood at around the same time, none was as thorough as India. Every major Indian urban centre was visited, including Rangoon, then part of the Indian empire. All of the major participants in the industry, importers, producers, distributors, exhibitors and viewers were consulted and the evidence was collected and published in four volumes. A fifth volume of evidence included the Commissioners' responses to specific films viewed, along with the in-camera evidence made available to officials by members of the industry and deemed to be commercially sensitive, was also published for limited circulation within government circles. The ICC produced a remarkably balanced and comprehensive report that provided an in-depth look at an emerging cinema. The committee was united on all recommendations made except one: the introduction of quotas to encourage Indian film production. The division within the committee was along racial lines. The Indian members supported the idea and pointed to England where quotas for English-made films had been introduced. The European members rejected the idea, and in his minute of dissent John Coatman, who later became an important administrator at the BBC, argued that the introduction of synchronized sound would ensure sufficient protection for Indian cinema – an example of the right decision being made for the wrong reasons![4]

Once it was established, the ICC was given a tripartite brief: to investigate the workings of the established censorship system and make recommendations for its improvement; to investigate the possibility of introducing an empire film scheme, which in effect would guarantee a market for English-made films in India; and almost as an afterthought, to investigate the state of the local industry.

In one form or another, these themes have dominated the history of film writing in India ever since the ICC published its report. From a nationalist perspective the committee was formed to find ways of suppressing local production and capturing the Indian market for British-produced films. The British film industry certainly wished for this to happen but the members of the committee quickly dismissed any suggestion that it would take this path and concentrated on the issues of censorship and the emerging Indian film production. Censorship has attracted more attention than any other single issue relating to Indian film, both in the British period and post-Independent eras. The ICC found that, generally speaking, the devolved censorship system, comprised of censorship boards in the major cities of Bombay, Calcutta, Madras and later Rangoon and Lahore, worked effectively. What really fascinated the ICC was the emerging film industry, something the British governing apparatus knew very little about. The ICC documented the industry in great detail and went on to make a series of recommendations designed to encourage its growth. In all three areas – imperial preference for films, film censorship and state support for the Indian film industry – the ICC's recommendations proved contentious and in many respects are still contested. Since Independence there have been three government-sponsored enquiries into the state of the Indian film industry that traversed the same ground as the ICC.[5]

Other writing about Indian film during the British era in the 1920s and 1930s is thin. Apart from the ICC there are three main sources of information: the film journals that sprang up in Bombay and Calcutta in the 1930s; the industry propaganda issued by the professional film bodies such as the IMPPA; and Y.A. Fazalbhoy's *The Indian Film: A Review* (1939).

The All-India Film and Television Archives in Pune contain incomplete runs of a number of film journals such as *Filmland*, which was published in Calcutta in the 1930s. *Filmland* provides film analysis, industry news and commentary. Although the series is incomplete, the extant issues provide an interesting antidote to the Bombay-centric information contained in *Filmindia*, for example, which was published from about 1936 to 1958. We know that 68 film journals were published in 1938 and that they varied in focus and quality (Barucha, 1939: 301–18). Some were little more than gossip tabloids, what Vijay Mishra calls the 'fanzines' (2002: x–xi), inventing behaviour for stars (something that still occurs), but others were more serious in intent such as *Film India* and *Filmland* and at a later stage *Filmfare*, *Cinemaya: The Indian Film Quarterly* and *Cineblitz*, for example. The editors of *Filmland* were convinced that the professional organizations emerging in Bombay in the 1930s were designed to advance the interests of the Bombay industry at the expense of the other regions, despite claims to the contrary (see *Filmland*, 1933). *Filmindia*, on the other hand, made no attempt to disguise its bias towards the Bombay industry. In more recent times academic journals such as *Indian International Centre Quarterly*, *Journal of Arts and Ideas* (India), *Framework* edited by Paul Willemen (UK) (1986) and the *Quarterly Review of Film Television and Video* edited by Myra Reyms Binford (US) (1989) have published special issues devoted to Indian film. However, it is the local popular publications, the fanzines, which should become the focus of a major study.

Wenner uses *Filmindia* most effectively in her study of Nadia and Wadia Movietone studio. The Wadia brothers were key members of the Bombay film establishment. From the 1930s to the 1950s they turned Wadia Movietone into the most successful and most prosperous Bombay studio. J.B.H. and Homi Wadia were Parsi brothers who built a studio around stunt films that starred Nadia. Their studio was run something like an extended Indian family with a loyal group of actors and artisans working on all of their films. Further, they ploughed their profits back into their studio, which they had organized vertically and horizontally in order to have continuity of production. The Wadias were founding members of the MPSI and IMPPA. J.B.H. Wadia

was the industry representative on the Film Advisory Board, which allocated film stock to production houses during World War Two. They were Parsi intellectuals who recognized the importance of collective behaviour and along with Chandulal Shah, Nanbhai Desai and Chunilal Moti, all major figures in the Bombay industry who had appeared before the ICC, supported the formation of a number of interlocking industry organizations that made representations to both the regional and the central governments and published a number of souvenir programmes and reports that remain a rich source of information about this crucial period of Indian film history (see Film Federation of India, 1956).

The most important book to be published in this period was Y.A. Fazalbhoy's *Indian Film: A Review* (1939). It draws heavily on the publications of the IMPPA and its related organizations such as the MPSI and IMPDA, in particular the *Report of the Indian Film Congress* held in Bombay in 1939 (see MPSI, 1939). *Indian Film* provides considerable detail about the Bombay industry, its structure and organization, its aspirations and fears. Clearly the Bombay industry took Hollywood as its inspiration and it feared the independents that were beginning to emerge at this point. The independents or 'freelances' were filmmakers who sought to work outside of the studio system, funding production through innovative arrangements with the film distributors and the indigenous banking system. Together with B. Barucha's *Indian Cinematographic Yearbook, 1938* (1939), a compendium that provides information on film personnel and the studios, as well as advertisements for a variety of film technologies, processing and stock, *Indian Film* provides a clear picture of an industry on the cusp of change. As Fazalbhoy makes clear, the studios were under threat from the independent producers who were actively seeking ways to capture the stars and production personnel from the established studios. It was not just paranoia on the part of the heads of studios. However, reading between the lines of the book where the various aspects of the Indian industry are discussed in detail including distribution, exhibition as well as production, it is clear the studios were vulnerable. Few had invested as extensively in their infrastructure as the Wadias – they paid their staff, including the stars, miserable salaries and provided little security to their employees. Consequently, after 1942 when black money became freely available for investment in film the studios were ripe for the plucking.

THE TRANSITIONAL PERIOD

The declaration of war on Germany made by Lord Linlithgow in 1939 without reference to any of the Indian political parties saw the introduction of the Indian Defence of the Realm Act that superseded all civil legislation and had an enduring impact on the Indian film industry. 'At the beginning of the war the studios in Bombay, Calcutta and Madras were in a position' otherwise it sound as though studios declared war!! By its end in 1945 this had been undermined completely by a combination of factors including internal dissent amongst the major producers about where they stood in relation to the war effort and support for the British in a tense political situation, the burgeoning war economy and the influx of black money that supported the 'freelance' production at the expense of the studios, and the decision by the British to allocate as much scarce film stock to the independents as to the established studios.

The studios dominated production in Bombay, Calcutta, Madras and Poona from the 1930s to the 1950s for a number of reasons. The men and women attracted to the industry from the 1920s onwards admired Hollywood and sought to emulate it in India, which proved a continual struggle because of the insecure financial arrangements they operated under. Nevertheless, this period of film production is indelibly linked to the studios and their generic productions. Their dominance was achieved through relentless publicity and industry organization that sought to protect the economic interests of the studio heads and squeeze out any opposition. The underlying

theme of the 1930s and 1940s was the perennial struggle between the producers and the distributors, the established studios and the independent producers. By the 1950s the dominance of the studios had ceased and the fourth major theme of Indian film writing had emerged: what happened to the studios?

Between the 1940s and the 1970s there was very little serious writing about Indian film. The magazine industry continued to flourish, especially in Bombay, and compendia like those by B.V. Dharap and Firoze Rangoonwalla (1968) were produced and served a valuable function insofar as they provided production details of films and preserved photographs from the era.[6] There are, however, four exceptions, to this sweeping observation, namely Panna Shah's *Indian Film* (1953; 1981), Barnouw and Krishnawsamy's *Indian Film* (1963; 1980), Ray's *Our Films, Their Films* (1976) and Aruna Vasudev's *Liberty and Licence in the Indian Cinema* (1978).

Shah had impeccable connections within the industry and produced a fine book, based on her PhD, and sought to establish and analyze a taxonomy of film genres produced within the Bombay industry, thereby reflecting institutionalized links to the studios.[7] Shah goes into great detail about the generic conventions of Bombay cinema, especially the socials (films that dealt with explicit social issues that seemed to trouble the Indian middle classes, such as love across caste boundaries and widow remarriage), the historicals (films such a Sohab Modhi's *Sikander* [India, 1941]) and the adventure films such as *Hunterwali* (Homi Wadia, India, 1935) that starred Nadia. This work is of considerable value as she arrives, albeit implicitly, to the conclusion that the costume drama had become the dominant genre of studio production, and not the socials that many commentators seem to remember with great nostalgia (Lent, 1983). In emphasizing the costume drama Shah identifies the origins of the *masala* film, a style of film that seamlessly combines traits from all other generic types, that has dominated film production from the 1950s to the present. Shah acknowledges the influence of Hollywood on

Indian popular film production but sees the *masala* film as a specifically Indian style that synthesizes Indian cultural traditions with Hollywood stylistic tropes. By contrast, Mishra points out that this multigeneric film form has transformed itself into Bollywood, a quite distinctive form with transnational, even global, implications and is no longer particular to India (2002: x).

For many years Barnouw and Krishnaswamy's book was the standard text, indeed the only text on Indian film known in the West. As such it carried an impossible burden: it had to be all things to all people. Part history, part analysis, part film plot summaries and apologia, it is a much better book than it has any right to be and is still a useful guide to the early history of Indian film. This is due, in part, to Barnouw and his vast experience in writing about large topics (see also Barnouw 1966; 1968; 1970) and to the fact that Krishnaswamy was a child of the industry and provided openings that hitherto had been closed to Western writers.[8] In short, *Indian Film* remains an important book even if it's only to write against. The authors elaborate on the four main themes of Indian film scholarship – censorship; the impact of British government policy and actions on the fledgling industry; state support for the Indian cinema; and the decline of the studios – in an exemplary manner. It remains a great feat of synthesis.

In contrast to Barnouw and Krishnaswamy, Ray was an essayist and polymath. He wrote detective novels, the Faluda series, children's books as well as music for his films and wonderfully detailed story boards. Although he is venerated in Bengal and acknowledged as a master in the West, in much of India he is either unknown or seen as a regional filmmaker – and this despite his links to Tagore, Santiniketan and the Bengali intelligentsia, all important components in defining modern Indian identity. *Our Films, Their Films* reflects the cultural ambiguity that surrounds Ray. Whose films is he referring to? In truth it can be any number of possible combinations: Indian cinema versus the West; Indian aesthetic traditions versus Western

aesthetics which draw on entirely different ways of seeing the world; or even his films, which are heavily influenced by Western film techniques and aesthetics versus the mass-produced *masala* film, which Ray sees as highly formulaic and devoid of any artistic or cultural value. Ray's essays reproduce an aesthetic stance common among Indian intellectuals of the time. Ray is very much a product of elite Bengali culture with its long-standing literary and artistic traditions, which learnt to accommodate and then transcend the British influence long before other Indian cultures were presented with the problems of modernity. Ray's films are rooted in this culture. The imagery and symbolism are clearly Bengali but always, in the background, are the signs of modernity, the trains and cars and the slippage between the Bengali language and English by his characters. In his book Ray demonstrates his mastery of Bengali culture, his deep knowledge of film history and practice but at the same time betrays his prejudices. The essays in the book proclaim Ray as a modernist beyond doubt.

Vasudev has strong links to this position insofar as she disapproves of the commercial film production system, which she views as devoid of any artistic merit. Vasudev is a prolific author and successful activist taking the opportunity to promote Indian and Third Cinema at every opportunity. Her first book, *Liberty and Licence in the Indian Cinema* (of which there was precious little under either the British or their Indian successors), makes significant use of the vast collection of files pertaining to cinema in the National Archives in New Delhi and looks closely at the workings of film censorship in India under the British and subsequent Congress governments. Vasudev argues that the crass commercialism of the mainstream Indian cinema gives rise to the need for censorship and further that commercialism may be attributed to the British because of their refusal to subsidize the Indian film industry by not implementing the recommendations of the ICC, thereby leaving it open to commerce rather than art. Vasudev ploughs a strictly nationalistic furrow in her interpretation of events. In her account of the history of censorship and its affects on popular Indian film there are two villains. The British because they created an elaborate censorship system that, in her view, stifled the artistic growth of film. The other villain is the industry itself, which chose not to challenge the censorship regime but comply and go on to produce anodyne, formulaic films of little artistic merit. Vasudev slots neatly into the dichotomy set out by Mishra who argues that Indian film writers 'have divided Indian cinema into two almost irreconcilable parts'; the art house films for the transnational aesthetic elites and the commercial cinema for the masses (2002: xv). After a perfunctory survey of the British period – where she finds little evidence of actual censorship but clear evidence of the creation of an ethos in which it becomes an accepted part of the process of film production – Vasudev moves on to the more significant part of her history. This deals in much greater detail with censorship post-Independence, where she shows conclusively that censorship under Indian control was much more rigorous and limiting than under the British. Nevertheless the book marks a major transition in thinking about Indian film as Vasudev makes an important contribution to the ongoing debate on censorship and state support for the industry through her use of the archives that had hitherto been largely ignored.

THE POSTCOLONIAL ERA

In the 1970s a new paradigm of Indian film scholarship began to emerge that has given birth to a new discourse on and about Indian film that escapes the limitations of the nationalistic discourse. Young Indian scholars like Ashish Rajadhyaksha (1986) and Ashish Nandy (1980) could invoke Michel Foucault and psychoanalysis respectively without having to gesture towards the old nationalist shibboleths. There was a new confidence in the writing about the origins of Indian cinema and its contents that articulated a clearly defined sense of 'Indianness'. Rajadhyaksha subsequently collaborated with

Paul Willemen who had produced the BFI Dossier on Indian Film with Beroze Gandhi. Rajadhyaksha and Willemen went on to edit the highly influential and indispensable *Encyclopaedia of Indian Cinema* (1999) that has subsequently been emulated in a number of other encyclopaedic publications such as Tejaswimi Gauli's *Bollywood: A Guide to Popular Hindi Cinema* (2007). At the same time as Willemen and Rajadhyaksha were redefining approaches to Third Cinema in *Framework*, Rosie Thomas (1985) and Ravi Vasudevan (1989; 1990) were publishing in *Screen*. In short, not only was a new paradigm for thinking and talking about Indian film being forged but also a new audience for the films was being created. Interest in Indian cinema was no longer a marginal and eccentric activity but had moved to the mainstream, if not centre, of contemporary Film Studies. This shift was confirmed by the 2002 Victoria and Albert Museum exhibition in London devoted to Indian film and its associated publications (see Patel and Dwyer, 2002).

The underpinnings of this new paradigm can be found in the theoretically-informed historical work of people like Gyan Pandey (2001), Dipesh Chakravarty (1989; 2000) and the subaltern studies group led by Ranajit Guha, who rejected the old colonial historicist approach and reworked our understanding of nationalism by discovering the voice of the subaltern (see Guha and Spivak, 1988). Writing about Indian cinema now drew upon a variety of disciplines thereby dramatically expanding our understanding and appreciation of the form and breaking irrevocably the old distinction based on aesthetics. The diversity of approach can be found in the work of the likes of Rachel Dwyer with a background in linguistics; Vijay Mishra who comes from comparative literature; Manjunath Pendulkar who comes out of the industry and writes from political science and communication studies perspectives; and Ashish Nandy whose work draws heavily on psychoanalysis. Dwyer (2006) has a deep love of the lush melodramas of Yash Chopra but at the same time seeks to explore Indian film from a perspective deeply influenced by her knowledge of Indian cultural mores. Mishra also shows how Indian films draw heavily on existing cultural traits. It is the 'Indianness' of the films that attracts the attention and leads to the realization that we need to understand the films within that context rather than one manufactured out of lament that the films are not more like Hollywood, or better still European art house cinema.

The last of the major themes I wish to deal with, that of the star syndrome, also feeds back into this sense of 'Indianness'. Stars have always played a pivotal role in delineating the commercial Indian cinema. Initially they were paid employees of the studios, but by the 1940s they had begun to acquire such cultural capital that they became the agents that allowed the independents to undermine and ultimately destroy the established studios. Quite simply, the independents paid the stars such huge sums that they defected from the studios and, in effect, brought their fans with them (Shoesmith, 1987). Stars became the public's main reason for seeing films. In the 1940s and 1950s people like Dilip Kumar, Raj Kapoor, Dev Anand, Nargis, and Waheeda Rahman built up huge fan bases that were supported by a strong film press in the major cities. The apogee of stardom appeared in the form of Amitabh Bachchan who created a persona of the angry young man that captured the imagination of many Indians through his appearance in films like *Zanjeer* (Prakash Mehra, India, 1973), *Deewaar* (Yash Chopra, India, 1975) and *Sholay* (Ramesh Sippy, India, 1975) (see Dasgupta, 2006). The social capital of stars is immense and it has been translated into political power with regional stars like N.T. Rama Rao in Andrha Pradesh and M.G.R. (M.G. Ramachandran) and Jayalalitha in Tamilnadu forming governments in the respective states. At the same time, stars are perceived as role models with their every action, real or imagined, commented on and often emulated. It is therefore not surprising that an entire genre of publication devoted to stars has emerged. The more populist of these are little more than hagiographies but the work of B. Reuben (1994) in particular can be most useful when we want to understand

the role of the studios in the 1940s and 1950s. However, Mishra, Peter Jeffery and Brian Shoesmith's 'The Actor as Parallel Text in Bombay Cinema' (1989) showed that stars could be written about from a more scholarly point of view. Others have followed culminating in Susmita Dasgupta's biography of Amithab Bachchan (2006), which is based on her doctoral thesis undertaken at JNU in New Delhi. This publication more than any other sums up the crucial shift whereby Indian film is no longer an object of derision, marginalized and frequently ignored. It has moved squarely into the mainstream of Indian academia, which in itself is a narrative waiting to be written.

Two other aspects need to be commented on. First, the rise of academic interest in Indian film in the US university system that has become the engine for much of the most recent and interesting material on Indian cinema. The work of Sumita S. Chakravarty and Priya Jaikumar is notable here. These scholars are working in the South Asian film programmes at institutions like the University of Texas, Austin, where young scholars are slowly filling the absences identified above. They are also well served by such sympathetic publishers as Duke University Press (US) and BFI Publishing (UK) who produce as a matter of course, recent scholarship dealing with Indian and other non-European cinemas. The second is the emerging interest in regional Indian cinemas. The best served are Bengal and Tamil. Bengal because of the presence of Ray and other major figures such as Ritwik Ghatak, Mrinal Sen and, from an earlier period, Nitin Bose, P.D. Barua and B.N. Sircar. These figures are claimed and celebrated as important figures within Bengali culture by writers such as Chidananda Das Gupta and Gaston Roberge, a Jesuit who pioneered Film Studies with the creation of the Chitra Bani Centre at St Xavier's College, Calcutta.[9] Interestingly the work of Zakir Hossain Raju (2000), whose focus is Bangladeshi film, has expanded this interest and creates the possibility of talking about a greater Bengali cinema that incorporates Bengali and Bangladeshi cinema after 1971.[10]

The Tamil cinema is different as it is the political dimension that has attracted the most interest. First discussed by Robert Hardgraves (1973), the links between cinema, especially scriptwriting and Tamil politics, have long been the focus of scholarly attention, notably by Baskaran (1996), whose meticulous historical writing traces the evolution of Tamil cinema, and in Pandian's fine monograph on the career of M.G.R. (*The Image Trap*, 1992), the charismatic leader of Tamilnadu in the 1960s. Other aspects of Tamil cinema are explored in Dickey's anthropologically-based study of peoples' use of, and ideas about, cinema in rural India (1993), and in Salvaraj Velayuthan's edited collection, which covers virtually all areas of Tamil cinema (2007). In a sense, the fact that Tamil cinema is now being taken seriously may be seen as a tribute to its position as one of the three most important cinemas in India after Telegu and Hindi in terms of production and reach (a position it has long held). We can only hope that this interest will be extended to the other major regional cinemas like the Marathi, Telegu and Bengali film industries.

CONCLUSION

This chapter, like its topic, is marked by omission. The number of books published relating to Indian cinema has proliferated in the past decade. Books that I could have mentioned in this survey that have made significant contributions to the historiography must include the works of T.G. Vaidyanathan, Ravi Vasudevan, Madhava Prasad and Prem Chowdhury.[11] However, what I have tried to show in this highly selective and partial account of the writings about Indian cinema is two things. We have moved from a situation of drought, as it were, to a flood of publications. But, even though Indian cinema has moved into the mainstream and is no longer confined to a few paragraphs or a small section in surveys of world cinemas, nevertheless the range of themes discussed remains limited. These are, broadly speaking, confined to censorship and control, state subsidy for the cinema, the demise of the studios and the star system. It is also apparent that the writing about Indian cinema has become more theoretically informed and sophisticated. It is no longer possible to write simplistic and reductionist accounts of the film industry or film content based on aesthetics or taste. These are welcome developments. However, there is still a great deal to be done, hence my characterizing the writing about Indian cinema as a cinema of absences. There is still no history of the Indian cinema from an industry perspective in the manner of Tino Balio's analysis of Hollywood (1985). There is no comparative work that focuses on the differing cultural practices in filmmaking between Bombay, Calcutta and Madras. There is no major study of the trade unions involved in the industry at any stage of its history. There is no detailed, major study of Bombay Talkies, Imperial Film or Ranjit Studio – all major Bombay studios of the 1930s through to 1950s that were instrumental in creating an industry – not to mention New Theatres Ltd in Calcutta. The list could go on. What is encouraging, however, is that young scholars are emerging who can take on these tasks even though the above demands are unrealistic and the archives incomplete. But as Wenner demonstrates, it is possible to construct a more than adequate account of a major studio as well as an insightful portrait of a major star from the available materials. I look forward to the future with interest.

NOTES

I would like to thank Theodore Baskaran, author of the noted message bearers (1981), for his perceptive comments on an earlier draft of this paper.

1 I have consciously chosen to appropriate Ray's beautifully ambiguous term for this paper.

2 The colonial names for Indian cities have been retained for a variety of reasons, not least of which is the fact that they are used in the sources cited. Moreover, in many respects the modern names are not always adopted by Indian institutions, for example in Chennai we still have the University of Madras, the Madras Club and the Madras Film Society.

3 The special issue of *Continuum: The Australian Journal of Media and Cultural Studies* on Asian

Cinema edited by Tom O'Regan and Brian Shoesmith (1987) is now unfortunately long out of print.

4 John Coatman was a Punjabi policeman who was appointed to the ICC to ensure British interests were protected. He was, surprisingly, sympathetic to Indian aspirations in regard to the film industry, as his writings/musings, found in Volume 5 of the ICC Evidence show, with the exception of quotas. He wrote the rebuttal to the Indian members' support for quotas arguing that the introduction of sound was sufficient protection for the nascent Indian film industry. Events, I think, proved him right. Coatman finished his career as Comptroller of the Northern Area of the BBC during World War Two.

5 The other government enquiries into film in India are the Patil Committee Inquiry (1951), The Khosla Committee enquiry into film censorship (1963) and the 1971 enquiry into the establishment of the Film Finance Corporation.

6 Dharap, a Pune film theatre owner, compiled a series of books in the 1960s and 1970s that contained brief synopses and production details of all the films he could identify between 1913 and the 1970s. It is an invaluable source of information as is Rangoonwalla's (1968) *Film Indexes 1912 – 1967*.

7 As far as I can ascertain Shah's is the first doctoral thesis written about Indian film.

8 Barnouw is the author of the distinguished three-volume history of broadcasting in the US between 1966 and 1970; and Krishnaswamy was the son of one of the pioneers of Tamil cinema and went on to have a distinguished career as a documentary filmmaker in India.

9 Chidananda Das Gupta was a founding member of the Calcutta Film Society along with Ray and has written extensively on Bengali and Indian cinema. Gaston Roberge established Chitra Bani (Sight and Sound) as a study centre in the 1960s and introduced a Film Studies degree at St Xavier's College, University of Calcutta in the 1970s.

10 Zakir Hossain Raju lectures at the Independent University of Bangladesh in Dhaka, which ensures he takes a broader view of Bengali culture.

11 Among the most important texts not referred to elsewhere are Chakravarty (1993), Das Gupta (1981; 1991), Dissanayake (2004), Dwyer (2000; 2005), Joshi (2002), Nandy (1998), Nihalani, Chatterjee, and Gulzar (2003), Rajadhyaksha (1993; 1996), Rangoonwalla (1982), Roberge (2005), Vasudev (1986; 1987; 1995), Vasudev and Lenglet (1983) and Willemen and Gandhi (1982).

REFERENCES

Balio, Tino (1985) *The American Film Industry*. Rev. edn. Madison: University of Wisconsin Press.

Barnouw, Erik (1966) *Tower of Babel*. New York: Colombia University Press.

Barnouw, Erik (1968) *The Golden Web*. New York: Colombia University Press.

Barnouw, Erik (1970) *The Image Empire: A History of Broadcasting in America*. New York: Colombia University Press.

Barnouw, Erik and Krishnaswamy, S. (1963) *Indian Film*. New York: Columbia University Press.

Barnouw, Erik and Krishnaswamy, S. (1980) *Indian Film*. 2nd edn. New York: Columbia University Press.

Barucha, B. (1939) *Indian Cinematographic Yearbook, 1938*. Bombay: Motion Picture Society of India.

Baskaran, S. Theodore (1981) *The Message Bearers: Nationalist Politics and the Entertainment Media in South India, 1880-1945*. Madras: Cre-A.

Baskaran, S. Theodore (1996) *The Eye of the Serpent: An Introduction to Tamil Cinema*. Madras: East West Books.

Binford, Myra Reyms (ed.) (1989) 'Special Issue: Indian Cinema', *Quarterly Review of Film Studies*, 2.

Chakravarty, Dipesh (1989) *Rethinking Working-Class History: Bengal, 1890-1940*. Princeton, NJ: Princeton University Press.

Chakravarty, Dipesh (2000) *Provincializing Europe: Postcolonial Thought and Historical Difference*. Princeton, NJ: Princeton University Press.

Chakravarty, Sumita S. (1993) *National Identity in Indian Popular Film, 1947-1987*. Austin: University of Texas Press.

Chowdhury, Prem (2000) *Colonial India and the Making of Empire Cinema: Image, Ideology and Identity*. Manchester: Manchester University Press.

Das Gupta, Chidananda (1981) *Talking About Films*. Delhi: Orient Longmann.

Das Gupta, Chidananda (1991) *The Painted Face: Studies in India's Popular Cinema*. Delhi: Roli Books.

Dasgupta, Susmita (2006) *Amitabh: The Making of a Super Hero*. New Delhi: Penguin.

Dharap, B.V. (ed.) (1972–8) *Indian Film*. Pune: Alka Talkies.

Dickey, Sarah (1993) *Cinema and the Urban Poor in South India*. Cambridge: Cambridge University Press.

Dissanayake, Wimal (2004) *Indian Popular Cinema: A Narrative of Cultural Change*. London: Trentham Books.

Dwyer, Rachel (2000) *Yash Chopra*. London: BFI.

Dwyer, Rachel (2005) *100 Bollywood Films*. London: BFI.

Dwyer, Rachel (2006) *Filming the Gods: Religion and Indian Cinema*. London: Routledge.

Dwyer, Rachel and Patel, Divia (2002) *Cinema India: The Visual Culture of Hindi Film*. London: Reaktion Books.

Fazalbhoy, Y.A. (1939) *The Indian Film: A Review*. Bombay: Bombay Radio Press.

Film Federation of India (1956) *Indian Talkie 1931–56 Silver Jubilee Souvenir Program*. Bombay: Film Federation of India.

Filmland (1933) 4 (12–13).

Gauli, Tejaswimi (2007) *Bollywood: A Guide to Popular Hindi Cinema*. London: Routledge.

Gopalan, Lalitha (2002) *The Cinema of Interruptions: Action Genres in Contemporary Indian Cinema*. London: BFI.

Government of India (1928) *Report of the Indian Cinematograph Committee, 1927–1928*. 5 vols. Calcutta: Central Publication Branch.

Guha, Ranjit and Spivak, Gayatri Chakravorty (eds) (1988) *Selected Subaltern Studies*. New York: Oxford University Press.

Hardgraves, Robert L. (1973) 'Politics and the Film in Tamilnadu: The Stars and the DMK', *Asian Survey*, 13(3): 288–305.

Jaikumar, Priya (2006) *Cinema at the End of Empire: A Politics of Transition in Britain and India*. Durham, NC: Duke University Press.

Joshi, Lalit Mohan (2002) *Bollywood: Popular Indian Cinema*. London: Dakini Books.

Lent, John A. (1983) 'Heyday of the Indian studio system: the 1930s', *Asian Profile*, 11(5): 467–474.

Mishra, Vijay (2002) *Bollywood Cinema: Temples of Desire*. London: Routledge.

Mishra, Vijay, Jeffery, Peter and Shoesmith, Brian (1989) 'The Actor as Parallel Text in Bombay Cinema', *Quarterly Review of Film Studies*, 2: 49–67.

Motion Picture Society of India (MPSI) (1939) *Proceedings of the First Session of the Indian Motion Picture Congress and Other Sectional Conferences, 1939*. Bombay: Motion Picture Society of India.

Nandy, Ashish (1980) 'The Popular Indian Film: Ideology and First Principles', *India International Centre Quarterly*, 8(1): 89–96.

Nandy, Ashish (ed.) (1998) *The Secret Politics of Our Desires: Innocence, Culpability and Indian Popular Cinema*. London: Zed.

Nihalani, Govind, Chatterjee, Sahal and Gulzar (2003) *Encyclopaedia of Hindi Cinema*. Delhi: Popular Prakash.

O'Regan, Tom and Shoesmith, Brian (eds) (1987) 'Special Issue: Asian Cinema', *Continuum: The Australian Journal of Media and Cultural Studies*, 2(1).

Pandey, Gyandra (2001) *Remembering Partition: Violence, Nationalism and History in India*. Cambridge: Cambridge University Press.

Pendukar, Manjunath (2003) *Indian Popular Cinema*. Cresskill, NJ: Hampton Press.

Prasad, M. Madhava (1998) *Ideology of the Hindi Film: A Historical Reconstruction*. Delhi: Oxford University Press.

Rajadhyaksha, Ashish (1986) 'Neo-traditionalism: Film as Popular Art in India', *Framework*, 32–33: 20–67.

Rajadhyaksha, Ashish (1993) 'The Epic Melodrama: Themes of Nationality in Indian Cinema', *Journal of Arts and Ideas*, 25–6: 55–70.

Rajadhyaksha, Ashish (1996) 'Indian Cinema: Origins of Independence', in Geoffrey Nowell-Smith (ed.), *The Oxford History of World Cinema*. Oxford: Oxford University Press. pp.398–409.

Rajadhyaksha, Ashish and Willemen, Paul (1999) *Encyclopaedia of Indian Cinema*. 2nd rev. edn. London/Delhi: BFI Oxford University Press.

Raju, Zakir Hossain (2000) 'National cinema and the beginning of film history in/of Bangladesh', *Screening the Past*, 11. Available at: http://www.latrobe.edu.au/screeningthepast/firstrelease/fr1100/rzfr11d.htm.

Rangoonwalla, Firoze (1968) *Film Indexes 1912–1967*. Pune: National Film and Television Archives. Mimeographed compilation.

Rangoonwalla, Firoze (1979) *A Pictorial History of Indian Cinema*. London: Hamlyn.

Rangoonwalla, Firoze (1982) *Indian Cinema: Past and Present*. Delhi: Clarion.

Ray, Satyajit (1976) *Our Films, Their Films*. Delhi: Orient Longmann.

Roberge, Gaston (2005) *Another Cinema for Another Society*. Kolkata: Seagull Books.

Reuben, B. (1994) *The Life and Times of Nargis*. New Delhi: Indus/HarperCollins.

Shah, Panna (1950) *The Indian Cinema*. Bombay: Motion Picture Society of India.

Shah, Panna (1981) *The Indian Film*. Westport, CT: Greenwood.

Shoesmith, Brian (1987) 'From Monopoly to Commodity: The Bombay Studios in the 1930s', in Tom O'Regan and Brian Shoesmith (eds), *History on/and/in Film*. Perth: History and Film Association of Australia. pp.68–75.

Shoesmith, Brian (forthcoming) 'Changing the guard: The transition from studio-based film production to independent production in post-colonial India', in Kaushik Bhaumik and Leila Jordan (eds), *The Indian Cinema Book*. London: BFI.

Thomas, Rosie (1985) 'Indian Cinema: Pleasures and Popularity', *Screen*, 26(3–4): 116–31.

Vaidyanathan, T.G. (1996) *Hours in the Dark: Essays on Cinema*. Delhi: Oxford University Press.

Vasudev, Aruna (1978) *Liberty and License in the Indian Cinema*. Delhi: Vikas.

Vasudev, Aruna (1986) *The New Indian Cinema*. Delhi: Macmillan.

Vasudev, Aruna (ed.) (1987/1995) *Frames of Mind: Reflections on Indian Cinema*. Delhi: UBSPD.

Vasudev, Aruna and Lenglet, Phillipe (eds) (1983) *Indian Cinema Superbazaar*. Delhi: Vikas.

Vasudevan, Ravi (1989) 'The Melodramatic Mode and Commercial Hindi Cinema', *Screen*, 30(3): 29–50.

Vasudevan, Ravi (1990) 'Indian Commercial Cinema', *Screen*, 31(4): 446–53.

Vasudevan, Ravi (1993) 'Shifting codes, dissolving identities: The Hindi social film of the 1950s as popular culture', *Journal of Arts and Ideas*, 23–4: 51–79.

Vasudevan, Ravi (ed.) (2000) *Making Meaning in Indian Cinema*. Delhi: Oxford University Press.

Velayutham, Selvaraj (ed.) (2007) *Tamil Cinema: The Cultural Politics of India's Other Film Industry*. London: Routledge.

Wenner, Dorothee (2005) *Fearless Nadia: The True Story of Bollywood's Original Stunt Queen*. New Delhi: Penguin.

Willemen, Paul (ed.) (1986) 'Special Issue: Third Cinema', *Framework*, 32–3.

Willemen, Paul and Gandhi, Behroze (1982) *Indian Film Dossier No.5*. London: BFI.

5

Film Research in Argentina

David Oubiña

Throughout the twentieth century, Argentine audiences had an intense cinematographic experience. The first films arrived in the country a few months after Auguste and Louis Lumière's exhibition at the Grand Café on the Boulevard des Capucines. From as early as 1897, Eugenio Py and Max Glücksmann were using the new invention of the movie camera to record newsreels or documentaries, and in 1909, Mario Gallo made the first fiction film. However, from its very beginning, cinema was looked upon solely as a popular entertainment for the people. Cinema needed rather a long time before it acquired its own aesthetic entity and to shape itself into a cultural product worthy of attention.

The first film publications either targeted mass audiences, focusing on the world of stars and providing information about upcoming releases – magazines like *Film-Exelsior*, from 1914, and then *Imparcial film*, *Cinegraf*, *Sintonía*, *Cine popular*, *Cine argentino* and *Cine revista* – or were meant for exhibitors, and contained information about technical or industrial issues – trade journals which included, from 1914, *La película*, and then *Cine productor*, *Gaceta de los espectáculos* and the

most enduring, *Heraldo del cinematografista*, which circulated between 1931 and 1988. In none of the magazines mentioned did the film writing have any resemblance to the notion of film criticism as we understand it today. The articles had no pretensions to investigation or analysis: they attempted merely to be informative about the films and their social context, or about cinema as a business.

Certainly, some writers – such as Jorge Luis Borges, Roberto Arlt and Horacio Quiroga – did notice the new medium's potential and their path-breaking writings are precursors of systematic scholarly reflection on cinema in Argentina. For the most part, however, during the first half of the twentieth century the educated or academic elites seldom ventured into mass media. As a result, that territory was left open to newspapers and popular magazines. It was not until the 1950s and 1960s, with the emergence of ciné-clubs, archives and specialized magazines, that cinema started to be appreciated as a culturally respectable product worthy of serious consideration. And even then, it was only towards the end of the 1980s that cinema would become a field of study and a specific area of knowledge taught in university classrooms.

CINEPHILIA, AVANT-GARDE, MASS CULTURE AND MILITANCY

The *Historia del cine argentino* by Domingo Di Núbila was first published in 1959(1960). This work could be considered the first, reasonably systematic, historiographical attempt to account for the films made in the country. The book is dominated by a journalistic tone, it offers a level of analysis that would be deemed superficial by today's standards, and its conception of history amounts to an endless listing of film titles. Even so, it is equally evident that there is a willingness to regard film history research as an autonomous discipline structured by specific rules. It is significant that Di Núbila's history appeared alongside the emergence of ciné-clubs and novel filmmakers, that is, at a time when the films described by the critic started themselves to become historical objects. It is almost as if that summing up of the classical period had been a necessary closure before Argentine cinema entered modernity.

In fact, since the mid-1940s the decay of the industrial system and the dismantling of the studios left a margin for the development of ciné-clubs and film magazines that would accompany the emergence of the new cinema of the so-called 'Generación del 60'. Publications such as *Cuadernos de cine, Cinecrítica, Gente de cine,* and above all, *Tiempo de cine* were responsible for fashioning a type of critic and a type of reader knowledgeable about films and fully able to debate theoretical, aesthetic and historical questions.

Tiempo de cine, published between 1960 and 1968, was a product of the activities of the Cine Club Núcleo, and was modelled on publications such as *Cinema novo* and *Cahiers du cinéma*. The magazine encouraged the development of a number of young critics: Salvador Sammaritano, Víctor Iturralde, José Agustín Mahieu, Edgardo Cozarinsky, Homero Alsina

Thevenet, Emir Rodríguez Monegal and Jorge Couselo, among others. Some came from journalism, others had studied filmmaking in France or Italy, and a few had an academic background. The one thing they all shared was a cinephilic passion for ciné-clubs.

The key features of the *Tiempo de cine* style were rigorous research and methodological precision; an eagerness to intervene in the struggle against censorship and in debates on cinematographic policies; a certain flair for essay writing and an effort to process the new theories coming from Europe. Thus, as in a continuum, the magazine's pages contain comments about *Hiroshima mon amour* (Alain Resnais, France/Japan, 1959), *La Dolce Vita* (Federico Fellini, Italy/France, 1960), Ingmar Bergman, Vera Chytilová and Jerzy Skolimowski alongside articles and interviews with the young Argentine filmmakers of the time: Lautaro Murúa, Manuel Antín, José Martínez Suárez, David José Kohon and Leonardo Favio. Common to all the contributions is an enthusiasm for the notions of experimentation, rupture and auteur filmmaking typical of the new cinemas of the 1960s.

In this context we find *La obra de Ayala y Torre Nilsson en las estructuras del cine argentino* (1961) by Tomás Eloy Martínez, and the *Breve historia del cine nacional* (1974) by Mahieu.[1] In contrast to Di Núbila's two volumes, these texts are brief, marked by an essay tone, concerned with formal analysis and clearly interested in the innovations of modern Argentine cinema. Worthy of special mention is Cozarinsky's *Borges y el cine* (1974) which introduces an elaborate hypothesis about the influence of a certain cinema in the shaping of the writer's early works. At this time, when the basis of his poetry was being forged, Borges found, in the films by Joseph von Sternberg, Ernst Lubitsch and King Vidor, a resonant device to amplify his general ideas on narrative.

The decade of the 1960s was a time of profound political turmoil and of notable production in both film praxis and film theory.

On the one hand, there was Roland Barthes (1964), structuralism, semiotics and Jacques Lacan; and on the other, Franz Fanon, Jean-Paul Sartre and Marxism. In this context two names should not be overlooked: Oscar Masotta and Eliseo Verón. The former introduced Lacan's thinking to Argentina and the latter was an early translator of Claude Lévi-Strauss.[2] Through them, Marxism intersected with psychoanalysis, structuralism and semiology. In that intersection of several lines of thought, the films themselves were viewed as a reflection on their modes of producing meaning. As regards film theory, this allowed the inclusion of studies of mass culture into ideological discussions, and their use against the mechanisms of spectacle cinema. If the Marxism acknowledged a process of awareness and reflexivity, then the structuralism showed the functioning of the work as a system of variable relations.[3] For its part, the work of Christian Metz provided the basis for a film semiology that, in Argentina, would remain a productive model of scientific legitimization in academia well into the 1980s.[4]

During the 1960s and the beginning of the 1970s there was a boom in communication studies. Researchers with backgrounds in literature, philosophy and the social sciences began to take an interest in mass media and popular culture. Even so, it was still not possible to speak of a specific and distinctive study of the cinematographic phenomenon: films became part of research as yet another facet of a set that included radio, television, comic books and pop music. But certain works on social communication media from this period proved fundamental for later research on cinema as they clarified a field of study even though they did not specifically tackle films: *Literatura y cultura de masas* (1967) by Jaime Rest; *La historieta en el mundo moderno* (1970a) by Masotta; the writings of Aníbal Ford on popular culture; and the work of Héctor Schmucler on communication (mainly through his contributions to the magazine *Comunicación y cultura*).[5] The common thread in these works was a displacement from fine arts or highbrow literature towards unexplored zones of popular culture, and the use of analytic tools, until then restricted to conventionally prestigious objects, to the study of expressive media deemed marginal or of little interest.

As the debate on the ideology of form deepened, purely scientific concerns came more and more under siege from attempts to question the dominant model of representation in films. The view was that film analysis must be based on a process of generalized distancing and disassembling: a process learned from an intersection between Bertolt Brecht and structuralism and whose purpose (as Barthes puts it) is, precisely, 'reconstructing the "object", so that in this reconstruction the rules of functioning (the "functions") are manifested in the object' (1983: 257). Representation can and must become an ideological questioning of representation itself. In reaction against the dominant form of classical realist cinema, modernism should choose a critical model that would culminate in what Peter Wollen defined as 'counter-cinema' (1986: 126). This perspective entailed an interrogation of the codes of Hollywood narrative cinema: criticism of the narrative unity, linearity and closure that provide a false harmonious totality; questioning of the strategies of transparency that erase the film's materiality and its production conditions; and rejection of the codes of verisimilitude that foster a passive acceptance of the fictional world.

The paradigm for this critical alternative was, of course, Jean-Luc Godard's Vent d'est (France/Italy/West Germany, 1970) which reverses all the mechanisms employed by realist discourse to achieve its fluency. Using them against this very discourse, the filmmaker produces its 'disarticulation' and leaves in plain sight the devices that uphold it and ensure its continuity. Though the film was never well known in Argentina, Godard became, towards the end of the 1960s, the mandatory point of reference for any study dealing with political radicalization and aesthetic rupture. Godard and his anti-realist aesthetic were cited not only in film praxis from the artistic avant-garde of certain ciné-clubs to the militant films of the Grupo Cine Liberación, but also in critical publications such as *Cine & Medios* as well as in more academic research. The question was: how to denounce oppression without reproducing its means? How to pose revolutionary ideas without articulating a new language? Hence, Godard's option was interesting because it showed a dramatic distance from of Michelangelo Antonioni's model which just a few years earlier had characterized many of the choices of the Generación del 60. Certainly, although there was a marked change of style in Antonioni compared to previous cinema, it was Godard who introduced a radical rupture, as though cinema could start all over again, relying on new creative premises.

In the early 1970s, the aesthetic avant-garde fostered by the Instituto Di Tella and the political radicalism supported by militant cinema established a tense but productive space of friction and exchange among different cultural spheres. *La hora de los hornos* (Fernando Solanas, Argentina, 1968) is a key film because it was intended to be not so much an artwork as an audio-visual analysis of neo-colonialism. It soon became the focus of a debate about the diverse ways in which it might be possible to articulate an artistic avant-garde with a political avant-garde. The dilemma was this: is it more effective to intervene politically from the specificity of aesthetic praxis or to make political use of aesthetic mechanisms? That enriching tension would eventually lead to a violent confrontation between aesthetic reflection and political agitation. But what is left from that period is a notable consolidation of intellectual activity and several contributions that, even if not systematic, still offer an interesting reflection on cinema. These pioneers' purposes set the basis for what in the 1980s would become a more clearly defined field of research. After the brutal fracture imposed by the military dictatorship and its attempts to repress all kinds of research in the second half of the 1970s, cinema studies would continue from that point, which had come to a halt before the coup d'état, to explore the media.

NEW CRITICISM AFTER MILITARY DICTATORSHIP: CINEMA STUDIES AND FILM MAGAZINES

The coup d'état of 1976 put a stop to any possible developments in Film Studies and film scholarship. Apart from those who had been killed or who had 'disappeared', many researchers went into exile or were forced to work in grim conditions. With the exception of *Heraldo del cine*, all film magazines stopped circulation and most ciné-clubs closed down. Not being a securely established field, film research suffered the rupture caused by the military dictatorship in a more distressing manner than any other discipline within the social sciences or the liberal arts.

During this period, the most interesting works were written in exile. From very different perspectives, two filmmakers, Raúl Beceyro and Octavio Getino, endeavoured to reflect on cinema by intertwining history, theory and politics. Getino, one of the makers of *La hora de los hornos* (1968), outlines in *Cine y dependencia* (1990) a brief history of Argentine cinema along the lines of the critical analysis of neocolonialism staged by Fernando Solanas' film.[6] Even if Getino's historiographic scheme is partial and his selection of films may come across as biased, the value of his work lies in its dismissal of the supposedly innocent historicism of other similar works and its explicit declaration of its ideological viewpoint. Getino's great virtue is that he views Argentine cinema as a space, and a topic, for debate. In response, Beceyro in *Cine y política* (1976) criticizes the way that Getino and Solanas conceptualize the links between militancy and aesthetics. Borrowing from Theodor Adorno's theories, Beceyro defends aesthetic autonomy, and asserts that cinema's revolutionary character is not to be found in its capacity to be used for a concrete action but in its form's radical rupture.

In 1983, with the return of democracy, some small signs of research timidly started to surface. Co-ordinated by Couselo, *Historia del cine argentino* (1984) came to replace Di Núbila's old book. It is an informative work, almost a film catalogue, which does little more than update a descriptive panorama. Like the book by Di Núbila, perhaps its value lies in looking back and revisiting earlier cinema to put it in an historical perspective. It so happens that towards the end of the 1980s and the beginning of the 1990s, a series of simultaneous changes took place: the boom of film schools (headed by the Fundación Universidad del Cine, and the Centro de Experimentación y Realización Cinematográfica, the film school of the Instituto Nacional de Cinematografía), the emergence of several film magazines and of a new generation of filmmakers who brought in an alternative approach to cinema.

Film schools and technical progress have given filmmakers a different kind of education, and paved the way for new ways to make cinema. These young filmmakers have a background in making short films (not from the industry or the advertising arena) and in academia (and as such are well-versed in film history and film theory). The first trait suggests a parallel with the young filmmakers of the Generación del 60 and the second reveals a difference. In fact, in both groups the short film is a common origin, but whereas the directors of the 1960s discovered their influences in the ciné-clubs, the learning experience during the 1990s was found in the more institutional frame of film schools.

All this activity and innovation has been presaged and accompanied by new magazines, new critics and new ways of understanding cinema. Between 1984 and 1985 there was a debate on creating a university degree in 'Combined Arts' (which would include historical, critical and theoretical studies on cinema, theatre and dance) within the Arts School of the Facultad de Filosofía y Letras de la Universidad de Buenos Aires. In 1986 the first two courses of this program were introduced – 'Film Aesthetics' and 'Introduction to the Language of the Combined Arts' –

and later on 'Film Analysis and Criticism', 'History of Argentine and Latin American Cinema', 'History of Universal Cinema', and 'Cinema and Literature'. However, what is regarded as the common element that gathers studies on cinema, theatre and dance within the same academic program is their supposed common location in the field of the 'performing arts'. Unavoidably, this perspective has limited the manner in which films and film history are studied.

Even so, the program in 'combined arts' installed the systematic study of cinema within academia for good. If the works of Barthes and Metz were already present in cinema studies, now semiotics applied to film analysis expanded to embrace other authors. The writings of Yuri Lotman, Dudley Andrew and, above all, those of the critics from *Screen* were integrated with local readings of *Cahiers du cinéma*, which had traditionally taken centre stage.[7] Gradually, academic research brought together elements from studies on enunciation, narratology and reception. And with the works of Laura Mulvey, Teresa de Lauretis or Annette Kuhn, feminist theory and genre studies entered the field.[8] It must be noted that, in general, this was not a mere repetition of models. Instead, many researchers use and continue to use these concepts for the analysis of Argentine or Latin American films and even provide reformulations, confrontations, or local inflections.

Initially, the most influential figure was probably Noël Burch (1985) and his notion of the Institutional Mode of Representation, which flourished in numerous works of analysis during the 1980s. Then came the studies by Gilles Deleuze on the 'movement-image' (1983) and the 'time-image' (1985) and, in recent years, authors as diverse as Serge Daney or David Bordwell. The case of Bordwell is significant because the cognitivist approach does not obviously blend harmoniously into the perspective traditionally adopted by local cinema studies. Nevertheless, his works offer a model of academic research legitimating a novel field which in Argentine universities had to be developed in a short time. That perhaps also explains why these heterogeneous proposals have not always been engaged in a debate. Instead, they have often been combined in a single statement. In this sense, it must be said that the field of cinema studies in Argentina has been particularly receptive to the inclusion of new theories. For better or worse, Argentine Film Studies has developed through integration and assimilation rather than through confrontation.

In recent years, and in parallel with these academic studies, intense critical activity has been promoted through the film magazines *Film*, *Haciendo cine* and *Sin cortes*, as well as a number of other more short-lived publications. Above all, and especially in its early years, *El amante*, published continuously since 1991, has played an important role in the re-education of a critical gaze through its irreverent and passionate style and its consistent, sceptical questioning of the cinematic establishment. Broadly speaking, it is probably true to say that academic research and film magazine criticism embrace opposite viewpoints. University studies tend to take shelter in scientific rigor, analysis, objectivity and historicism. Magazines, in contrast, have favoured a strongly personal and subjective perspective, emphasising arbitrariness of opinion and the use of the first person. Reacting against an academic approach that aims to be classificatory and rigorous, magazines celebrate cinephilic passion and usually adopt an anti-intellectual stance. As regards Argentine cinema, this debate has had some positive effects. It has allowed different appraisals of the tradition and has recovered a polemic gaze on the role of films during the dictatorship, and about the relationship between cinema and society.

Some recent magazines such as *Kilómetro 111* and the web magazine *Otrocampo* have tried to cover the lack of academic publications and, with more or less success, have built some bridges between the contrasting perspectives of film magazine criticism and academic research. In this context, *Punto de vista*, which began its publication in 1978, amidst the military dictatorship, is a peculiar case. Though its writers are related to academia, the magazine is not institutional by any means. Its writing seeks to achieve analytical profundity and methodological rigor but to express them in the manner of an essay rather than a research paper. And although it is not a publication specializing in film, it has gathered an important corpus of writings (by Beceyro, Rafael Filippelli or Beatriz Sarlo, among others) that aims to reflect on the current state of cinema through the complex intertwining of politics, theory, history and society.

Even if it is still far from being an established discipline, film research can certainly be said to have acquired in recent years a certain methodological strength and to have recovered the polemical edge of a battlefield.

THE RESEARCH SCENARIO

In Argentina, there is no tradition of film research. The Fundación Cinemateca Argentina (founded in 1945) and the Museo del Cine (founded in 1971) have meagre and poorly preserved archives. Academic studies are still too young and the first graduate students in film completed their studies between 1990 and 1995 (there are very few doctoral theses in the field). However, it should be acknowledged that there has been a notable increase in filmmaking students and a growth in the exploration of alternative film poetics, as well as a scattered yet dynamic interest in ciné-clubs, festivals of independent cinema and magazines.

The research scenario is still in an early and disorderly condition, but it shows some promising signs for the future. Even though the few publishing houses that put out film books deal largely with translations or imported writings from Spain, works that study Argentine cinema from multiple directions are starting to surface. They offer critical re-appraisals of past cinema, director studies, dictionaries variously focused on films, filmmakers, actresses or magazines, and interpretations of the poetics of the new cinema. Argentine cinema is a territory still to be conquered. These filmographic maps confirm that its exploration is definitely under way.

NOTES

1 Mahieu's *Breve historia del cine nacional* (1974) revisits and expands his previous work in *Breve historia del cine argentino* (1966).

2 See, for example, Masotta's *Introducción a la lectura de Jacques Lacan* (1970b) and Verón's edited collection *Lenguaje y comunicación social* (1969).

3 Significantly, the notions of 'conscience' and of 'structure' are united in the same syntagma in the title of Masotta's book: *Conciencia y estructura* (1968). The same tense bond between Marx's ideas and those of Lévi-Strauss is noticeable in the book by Verón titled *Conducta, estructura y comunicación* (1968).

4 Metz's influence is perceptible mainly through his books *Essais sur la signification au cinéma* (1968; 1973); *Langage et cinéma* (1971) and *Le signifiant imaginaire* (1977).

5 See, for example, Schmucler's 'La investigación sobre comunicación masiva' (1975) and Ford's 'Literatura, crónica y periodismo' ([1972] 1985).

6 Getino began writing his book in 1976 and finished it in 1983. But it was not published until 1990.

7 The most influential works were Lotman's *Estética y semiótica del cine* (1979); *The Major Film Theories* (1976) and *Concepts in Film Theory* (1984) by Andrew; Wollen's *Signs and Meaning in Cinema* (1972); and Stephen Heath's *Questions of Cinema* (1981).

8 See Mulvey's *Visual and Other Pleasures* (1989), de Lauretis' *Alice Doesn't* (1984) and Kuhn's *Women's Pictures: Feminism and Cinema* (1982).

REFERENCES

Andrew, Dudley (1976) *The Major Film Theories.* New York: Oxford University Press.

Andrew, Dudley (1984) *Concepts in Film Theory.* New York: Oxford University Press.

Barthes, Roland (1964) *Essais critiques.* Paris: Éditions du Seuil.

Barthes, Roland (1983) 'La actividad estructuralista', in *Ensayos críticos.* Barcelona: Seix Barral. pp. 255–62.

Beceyro, Raúl (1976) *Cine y política.* Caracas: Dirección General de Cultura de la Gobernación del Distrito Federal.

Burch, Noël (1985) *La lucarne de l'infini.* Paris: Scolar Press.

Couselo, Jorge Miguel, Calistro, Mariano, España, Claudio, García Olivieri, Raúl, Insaurralde, Andrés, Landini, Carlos, Maranghello, César and Rosado, Miguel Angel (1984) *Historia del cine argentino.* Buenos Aires: CEAL.

Cozarinsky, Edgardo (1974) *Borges y el cine.* Buenos Aires: Sur.

de Lauretis, Teresa (1984) *Alice Doesn't: Feminism, Semiotics, Cinema.* Bloomington: Indiana University Press.

Deleuze, Gilles (1983) *L'image-mouvement: Cinéma I.* Paris: Éditions de Minuit.

Deleuze, Gilles (1985) *L'image-temps: Cinéma II.* Paris: Éditions de Minuit.

Di Núbila, Domingo (1960) *Historia del cine argentino.* 2 vols. Buenos Aires: Cruz de Malta.

Ford, Aníbal [1972] (1985) 'Literatura, crónica y periodismo', in Aníbal Ford, Jorge Rivera and Eduardo Romano, *Medios de comunicación y cultura popular.* Buenos Aires: Legasa. pp. 218–48.

Getino, Octavio (1990) *Cine y dependencia: El cine en la Argentina.* Buenos Aires: Puntosur.

Heath, Stephen (1981) *Questions of Cinema.* Bloomington: Indiana University Press.

Kuhn, Annette (1982) *Women's Pictures: Feminism and Cinema.* London: Routledge & Kegan Paul.

Lotman, Yuri (1979) *Estética y semiótica del cine.* Barcelona: Gustavo Gili.

Mahieu, José Agustín (1966) *Breve historia del cine argentino.* Buenos Aires: EUDEBA.

Mahieu, José Agustín (1974) *Breve historia del cine nacional.* Buenos Aires: Alzamor.

Martínez, Tomás Eloy (1961) *La obra de Ayala y Torre Nilsson en las estructuras del cine argentino.* Buenos Aires: Ediciones culturales argentines.

Masotta, Oscar (1968) *Conciencia y estructura.* Buenos Aires: Jorge Alvarez Editor.

Masotta, Oscar (1970a) *La historieta en el mundo moderno.* Buenos Aires: Paidós.

Masotta, Oscar (1970b) *Introducción a la lectura de Jacques Lacan.* Buenos Aires: Proteo.

Metz, Christian (1968) *Essais sur la signification au cinéma I.* Paris: Klincksieck.

Metz, Christian (1971) *Langage et cinéma.* Paris: Larousse.

Metz, Christian (1973) *Essais sur la signification au cinéma II.* Paris: Klincksieck.

Metz, Christian (1977) *Le signifiant imaginaire.* Paris: Union Générale d'Editions.

Mulvey, Laura (1989) *Visual and Other Pleasures.* Bloomington: Indiana University Press.

Rest, Jaime (1967) *Literatura y cultura de masas.* Buenos Aires: CEAL.

Schmucler, Héctor (1975) 'La investigación sobre comunicación masiva', *Comunicación y cultura*, 4: 3–14.

Verón, Eliseo (1968) *Conducta, estructura y comunicación*. Buenos Aires: Jorge Alvarez Editor.

Verón, Eliseo (ed.) (1969) *Lenguaje y comunicación social*. Buenos Aires: Nueva visión.

Wollen, Peter (1972) *Signs and Meaning in Cinema*. London: Secker and Warburg/BFI.

Wollen, Peter (1986) 'Godard and Counter-Cinema: *Vent d'est*', in Philip Rosen (ed.), *Narrative, Apparatus, Ideology: A Film Theory Reader*. New York: Columbia University Press. pp. 120–29.

6

Cinema Studies in Brazil

Ismail Xavier

In Brazil, academic research on film developed from the late 1960s on, initially inflected by a particular dialogue with the film culture produced by the tradition of ciné-clubs and the cinematheques in São Paulo and and Rio de Janeiro.

In its first stage, academic work engaged film critics who became concerned, during the 1950s, with film history, and especially with the national film tradition. After a short period in which research on film developed in close dialogue with literary and historical studies, the rise of the media as a privileged subject matter in the late 1960s made the recently created communication schools the place for cinema studies in universities. This was a time when linguistics and semiotics were establishing a new framework for film theory, and when the established work on film history was challenged to develop a new sense of rigor and method. During the 1970s and 1980s the academic circle gradually asserted its own style as the new generations of scholars, even if not in great numbers, consolidated the inscription of Film Studies within the normative codes of scientific research in the humanities (or media studies), while maintaining a close dialogue with people involved in film production in Brazil.

The first two film departments (Universidade de São Paulo [USP] and Universidade Federal Fluminense [UFF]) were structured to combine Film Studies (history, criticism and theory) and film production courses (practice): a fact that has favoured a continuous interaction between the university and the film milieu (filmmakers and critics), giving continuity to the spirit of the 1960s and its concern for the unity of theory and practice. This institutional arrangement has survived until now, at USP and UFF, thus obliging both universities to reconcile their twin missions of providing undergraduate (professional) and graduate (theory and research) courses. With the dissemination of Film Studies in the 1980s and 1990s, each new university that incorporated cinema in its curriculum had to find its own way to deal with that question, with most keeping only cinema studies as part of media studies programmes within communication schools, and leaving aside film production.

The concern for the interaction between theory and practice has been significant in Brazilian Film Studies because the shape of film production in the country – its instability and its subaltern status vis-à-vis foreign films that dominate the market – creates the sense that any institution related to film has to make its own contribution towards the development of Brazilian cinema. This is partially true even today, although the expansion of media studies and the variety of approaches to film in academia changed the entire picture concerning cinema studies. Younger scholars trained in graduate programmes in media studies and in comparative literature, from the 1990s onwards, have moved towards the diversification of research topics and theoretical sources.

THE LEGITIMATION OF CINEMA AS AN ACADEMIC FIELD

The spirit of the 'ciné-club' *à la française* manifested itself in Brazil early in the twentieth century. Since the classic period of silent film, it created a tradition of information and debate – the idea of 'public education for film aesthetics' – that combined the exaltation of cinema as a central value of modernity with the sense of a theoretical responsibility on the part of cinephiles. Cinema had to be praised as art, and the aesthetic discussion had to go beyond what was seen in the standard fare of film criticism found in newspapers and weekly magazines. It was not an accident that it was the Chaplin Club, founded by a group of young intellectuals in Rio de Janeiro, Octavio de Faria and Plínio Sussekind Rocha among them, that brought the first examples of a specific and rigorous discussion of film aesthetics in Brazil, in the essays found in *Fan* (the magazine they published between 1928 and 1931). For many years, the Chaplin Club leaders were very influential among more erudite cinephiles, including the poet Vinicius de Moraes who also worked as a film critic. Vinicius de Moraes expressed, in the early 1940s, ideas that resumed the Chaplin Club's arguments in a discussion about the superiority of silent film over the talkies. Before the 1960s, although ciné-clubs and professional criticism formed the two major sources of the conceptual debate on film, the universities too had their role in film culture. They sometimes provided the lively

cultural milieu within which ciné-clubs were created, producing an interesting intersection involving film and academic life. Literary modernism and its defenders in academia took part in the exaltation of cinema as an icon of modernity, and the ciné-clubs created by university students gave birth to a productive exchange of ideas among intellectuals of different aesthetic concerns. A ciné-club created by Paulo Emilio Salles Gomes in the early 1940s at USP, for example, can be seen as the first step towards the foundation, many years later, of the Brazilian Cinemateca (1954), followed by the creation of the Cinemateca of the Museum of Modern Art of Rio de Janeiro: two milestones in the expansion of a concern for archival memory that Brazilians took from Henri Langlois and the French Cinematheque.[1]

In the late 1960s, when public universities inaugurated their courses on cinema, the hegemonic film culture of the time, well represented by the Cinema Novo generation, fostered the convergence of three different traditions: (1) that of the cinephiles who congregated in ciné-clubs; (2) that of the modernist writers and artists who, although not engaged in film, favoured, since the 1920s, a cultural atmosphere inflected by the European historical avant-garde that had itself fostered and energized film theory; (3) that of the film critics engaged in historical analyses that discussed the conditions for the development of film production in Brazil.

Since the late 1950s and during the 1960s, a major task assumed by leftist critics and by Cinema Novo filmmakers was the critique of what was considered a 'colonial mentality' expressed in the writings of people who implied that Brazilians did not have a sense of cinema, and that the poor sections of Brazilian cities did not fit cinematographic standards.[2] That critique of social prejudices was connected with the dominant political debates in the country, and expressed a change in mentality that is worth mentioning here because it played a role in legitimating film as a topic in university courses.

The graduate programmes in media studies – cinema studies included – began during the 1970s (first in São Paulo, then in Rio de Janeiro, Brasilia and other States). However, film scholars with a doctoral degree in cinema studies were still rare in the 1980s, even if one considers those who had received their qualifications abroad (in the US or France). The expansion and the change in scale only came in the 1990s – the decade in which the large majority of those currently at work in the university system were hired. As a sign of that expansion, the more systematic exchange involving film scholars led to the creation of the Brazilian Society of Cinema Studies (SOCINE): a society that in its Annual Conference has reached, after the year 2000, an average of 150 panelists (about 100 scholars, with a considerable number of graduate students).

FILM HISTORY AS A FIELD OF RESEARCH

Memory, the national, and cinephilia. It was this combination that set the framework for the choice of film history as the hegemonic field when Film Studies emerged in universities around the 1960s. The academic context demanded scientific discipline and method, a demand which produced, in the first instance, the usual mutual estrangement and suspicion between amateur film researchers and academic scholars. In fact, this estrangement had become obvious even earlier: a first sign of it was Salles Gomes' harsh critical review of Alex Viany's *Introdução ao cinema brasileiro* (1959), a book that was, and still is, celebrated as the first classic on Brazilian film history, and a kind of synthesis of the many efforts expressed in books, articles and film retrospectives during the 1950s. And a second sign was the way the leaders of the Brazilian Cinematheque (Salles Gomes included) received Glauber Rocha's book *Revisão crítica do cinema brasileiro* (1963) as a welcome manifesto that brought a legitimate programme for a new cinema in Brazil even though it could not be seen as a consistent historical approach to Brazilian cinema (see Viany, 1959).[3]

The Cinemateca group demanded a sense of rigor that only came later when they started their work at USP from the late 1960s onwards. Something similar happened in Rio de Janeiro, where critics, intellectuals and filmmakers, who had been formed in the same spirit, were incorporated into the faculty of the film department at UFF. The scholars of my generation – that is, the first to be trained in film schools – were educated within the intellectual framework provided by the Cinematheques. Since that first period, the research on Brazilian film history – which is characterized by a great variety of topics and has been, and continues to be, one of the major sectors of the work carried out in the universities – is principally situated in São Paulo and Rio de Janeiro where the major archives are located. New directions of research also include foreign cinema, studies in early cinema from the 1980s onwards, and specific topics of different national cinemas.[4] In some circles, this research includes a debate on methods that reproduces the ongoing debates in France and the US. In its interaction with the new trends in film history, the investigation that focuses on Brazilian cinema has changed in purpose and scale but undoubtedly gives continuity to the original national concerns that marked the interest in history in the 1950s and 1960s.[5]

FILM THEORY AND SPECIFIC TOPICS OF FILM ANALYSIS

In terms of its directions and specific contents, the research carried out in Brazil – at each stage of its development since the 1970s – tends to reflect, with some delay, the conceptual framework and methods that the major centres of theory (France, US, England) have been producing in the last thirty years. Although restricted to a small group of institutions, the graduate programmes have steadily given impetus to a debate on film theory, fostering the incorporation of a body of work produced abroad (mainly in France until 1980) and gradually incorporating the Anglo-American theoretical references.

Initially, Brazilian scholars were more involved with structuralism and semiology, or C.S. Peirce's semiotics, and Film Studies followed the trends of literary theory and narratology, a framework that oriented a revision of classic film theory from the 1920s as well as the phenomenology implied in André Bazin's work and in the early theory of modern cinema produced by the *Cahiers du cinéma* culture, including the *politique des auteurs*.[6] As the academic work developed along those lines, Brazilian scholars had (and still have) to face problems that, before them, were dealt with by literary scholars: how to reconcile the incorporation of new theories and methods coming from abroad while offsetting the danger of precociously interrupting the immanent development of some productive lines of investigation which might be overshadowed by the hasty borrowing of new paradigms from Europe or the United States. How might one conduct a politics of exchange with the major centres, something indispensable but unfortunately also asymmetrical, without losing the sense of pertinence – after all, what really matters? – in terms of purposes and methods?

This is a question that persists, since the flow of concepts and of new theoretical fields, with very few exceptions, is hardly equal or bi-directional. Scholars linked to different theoretical traditions deal with – or decide not to deal with – those questions in different ways, making this 'geo-political' factor a sometimes significant aspect of the debate, apart from more general philosophical arguments.

Although a 'system' (taken as a metaphor) deeply involved with the digestion of concepts and methods coming from abroad, Brazilian scholarship on film has at the same time developed its own dynamics and shown its energy in its continuous struggle with scarce resources and, depending on the research topic, limited access to important sources. (That situation at least is radically changing nowadays with new information technologies

such as DVD, etc.). Such problems are typical in regard to any academic production within a huge country obliged to make major changes in its university system in order to cope with its basic needs.

As the conceptual systems become more and more diversified in the major centres, the work done in Brazil tends to reproduce that variety, even if inevitably on a minor scale. Nowadays, the shape of Film Studies is closely related to the concerns of a generation that was educated at the time in which the topics for debate in the US and Europe involved the impact of Gilles Deleuze's cinema books (translated into Portuguese in 1985 and 1987), the crisis of film theory as a unified conceptual field, the critique of psychoanalysis and of Grand Theory launched by cognitivism, the development of gender and race studies, the discussion around the 'death of the author', the renovation of genre studies (comedy, melodrama) and other forms of research combining history, anthropology and media theory to displace the emphasis from the analysis of form to the analysis of cinema (and television) as a social experience.

Up to the late 1970s, the theories linked to modernism formed the hegemonic paradigm – again linking academic work to the defence of a particular cinema (avant-garde and modern cinema). For my generation, the central question was – apart from the already established historical research – to incorporate different theoretical references to deal with the specificity of Film Studies strongly inflected by a concern with film aesthetics and what was called the critique of illusionism. (In this theoretical project Bertolt Brecht had a stronger hand than Theodor Adorno, although the notion of cultural industry also had its place). In recent years, the defence of modern cinema and the concern for style and the 'auteur theory' have changed their theoretical references, turning increasingly to philosophy and especially to Deleuze's work – a trend stronger in Rio de Janeiro and Minas Gerais, but hardly exclusive to them.[7] At the same time, the revision of pre-modern cinema in Brazil (the study of popular genres, for instance) and the work done on contemporary cinema have fostered the incorporation of a wide range of inter-disciplinary studies that, within the Anglo-American context, would be called cultural studies. (This tendency is especially strong in UFF, UFSC and UNISINOS-Rio Grande do Sul).[8]

Roughly speaking, the major topics of debate and the new proposals in Film Studies all have their place in Brazilian academic life today. Some research incorporates the new concern with Film Studies as a part of aesthetics, including the new insertion of film (and video) in the field of art history. Other work incorporates the new methodological discussion in film history and the recent studies on the representation of history in films. A number of analyses integrate the variety of approaches gathered under the trans-disciplinary umbrella of 'cultural studies', which include television and other media products in their scope. Various theorists also defend the primacy of a philosophy of cinema within an intellectual project that takes film criticism as a 'poetic genre' and positions the film critic as an author, while others still interrogate film theory and its so-called 'crisis' as an autonomous field (meaning its commitment to specificity). And finally, there is a 'boom' in the investigation focused on the question of the documentary as a modality of film practice and a general problem for film theory.

As this inventory suggests, Brazilian scholars, although small in number when compared with those in the major centres, in their context tend to make visible a great diversity of theoretical approaches. The pragmatic adjustment of concepts coming from different sources – something not exclusive to this country – forms a striking feature of their production, making Brazilian scholarship an example of a 'system' able to displace theories and adapt them to a national context. There is no hegemonic thought, and the particular ethos of Brazilian academic life favours what seems to be at present a significant trend on the international scene: the development of inter-disciplinary approaches in the study of film.

NOTES

1 To give some examples of the role played by the tradition of ciné-clubs, one can mention the case of Salvador Bahia, in which a ciné-club set up a frame for the work done by Walter da Silveira in the formation of young cinephiles. This played a significant role in the rise of Cinema Novo, since Glauber Rocha, a young student involved with theatre, was part of the audience for the screenings and debates. In Mina Gerais, there was an intense aesthetic debate among intellectuals around the Centro de Estudos Cinematográficos (CEC): a ciné-club founded by talented film critics that, on the pages of *Revista de Cinema*, built one of the most important contexts of film criticism in Brazil by aligning themselves with the European trends of the time (such as auteur politics, *mise en scène* analysis and the defence of 'art cinema'). In the mid-1960s, cinephiles linked to Catholic institutions created the first courses devoted to cinema in the context of higher education (Minas Gerais and São Paulo). A prime example of this is the University of Brasilia's commencement of a pioneering Film Studies programme (interrupted by political repression after the 1964 military coup d'état). These experiences did not last for long but were central because they came just before the creation of the schools of communication in public universities in the late 1960s, when cinema was consolidated as a new field of teaching and research.

2 These prejudices can be found in texts published in some of the film magazines of the first half of the twentieth century – *Cinearte, Selecta* and *Cinelândia*.

3 Salles Gomes' reviews were published in the newspaper *O Estado de São Paulo* on 30 January 1960 and 6 February 1960 (see Salles Gomes, 1982). For the 1963 responses to Rocha's *Revisão crítica do cinema brasileiro* (1963), see the Appendix in its recently revised edition (2002), which presents a collection of reviews including the short pieces by Salles Gomes, Jean-Claude Bernardet and Ruda de Andrade, from the Brazilian Cinematheque.

4 The research on Brazilian film history, after the major impulse given by Viany, Salles Gomes, Jean-Claude Bernardet, Maria Rita Galvão, José Inácio de Melo Souza, Carlos Roberto de Souza, José Tavares de Barros and Vicente de Paula Araújo, among others, has received new academic contributions brought by scholars like Roberto Moura, João Luiz Vieira, Arthur Autran, Mariarosaria Fabris, Afrânio Cattani, Eduardo Morettin, Luciana Corrêa de Araújo, Tunico Amâncio, Miguel Pereira, Sheila Schvarzman, Hernani Heffner, Glênio Póvoas, Maria do Socorro Carvalho e Hilda Machado. Academic studies on documentary features include work by Jean-Claude Bernardet, Consuelo Lins, Leandro Saraiva, Sílvio Da-Rin, Marcius Freire, Henri Gervaiseau, Francisco Elinaldo Teixeira, Maria Dora Mourão, Cláudia Mesquita, Ruben Caixeta de

Queiróz and Daniela Dumaresq. The focus on modern and contemporary film includes works published by Ivana Bentes, Rubens Machado Junior, Andrea França, Lucia Nagib, Ivonette Pinto, Alexandre Fiqueirôa, Bernardette Lyra, Mauro Pommer, Gelson Santana, Renato Pucci Junior, Mauro Batista, Josette Monzani and Maria Ester Maciel. Researchers such as Flávia Cesarino, João Luiz Vieira, José Inácio de Melo Souza and Máximo have focused on early cinema.

5 As a sign of these hegemonic concerns, one should mention the existence of the Brazilian Cinema Research Society (Centro dos Pesquisadores do Cinema Brasileiro) which, since the late 1960s, has been coordinated by Salles Gomes: a society that brought together film critics, cinephiles and young film scholars (after 1971) who performed studies on Brazilian film history. The Society continues to flourish through events such as its annual meetings. These days unlike the early years when it had a central role in the organization of the dispersed research work by 'amateurs' in different regions of the country, the society has become an integral aspect of enriching university and film culture developed by the scholars who deal with Brazilian cinema (and mentioned above in note 4).

6 For examples of more systematic work on film theory in Brazil – since the impact of structuralism and semiology in the late 1960s up to the controversy on postmodernism around 1980 – see Eduardo Peñuela Cañizal, Rogério Luz, Arlindo Machado, Fernão Ramos, André Parente, Stella Senra, Cláudio da Costa, Jorge Vasconcelos and César Guimarães.

7 From Rio de Janeiro, one can mention André Parente, Ivana Bentes, Andrea França and Jorge Vasconcelos; from Minas Gerais, César Guimarães and the group of scholars from *Devires* magazine.

8 Examples of inter-disciplinary studies come from the research done by Denílson Lopes, José Gatti Junior, Fernando Mascarello, Ângela Prysthon, José Mário Ortiz Ramos, Wilton Garcia, Anelise Corseuil, Tunico Amâncio, Regina Mota and João Luiz Vieira.

REFERENCES

Rocha, Glauber (1963) *Revisão crítica do cinema brasileiro*. Rio de Janeiro: Civilização Brasileira.

Rocha, Glauber (2002) *Revisão crítica do cinema brasileiro*. Rev. edn. São Paulo: CosacNaify.

Salles Gomes, Paulo Emilio (1982) Review of *Introduction to Brazilian Cinema* by Alex Viany, in *Crítica de cinema no Suplemento Literário de O Estado de São Paulo*. Vol.2. Rio de Janeiro: Editora Paz e Terra. pp. 145–55.

Viany, Alex (1959) *Introdução ao cinema brasileiro*. Rio de Janeiro: Instituto Nacional do Livro.

7

Y Tu Crítica También: The Development of Mexican Film Studies at Home and Abroad

Carlos A. Gutiérrez

Mexico has a remarkable audio-visual history. Once a country that boasted a vigorous film industry, Mexico has been a large and influential creator of cultural capital and a key player in transnational media flows. It has produced more than 5,000 films, equal to the combined production of all other Latin American countries (see Paranaguá, 1995: 12). Yet, despite the existence of a considerable literature that treats the subject of Mexican cinema both at home and abroad, its study remains largely entrapped in questions of 'the national' and 'the popular' as well as of 'national specificity'. Many other aspects of Mexican cinema remain overlooked or are practically ignored.

As is the case with comparable countries such as India, Mexican cinema shows the pressing need to create more accurate ways to study notions of 'national cinema', particularly those gathered under 'Third World' and postcolonial theories, since the traditional categories have proved themselves to be inadequate.[1] Many scholars still succumb to the theoretical temptation to postulate a unifying aesthetic for non-Euro-American cinema. In doing so, they only create more dead ends for the study of these nominally 'other' cinemas. In addition, the persistent Eurocentrism of Film Studies, paired in some cases with the ethnocentrism of film scholars in Mexico, has prevented a much needed dialogue concerning the position of the study of Mexican cinema within the larger context of world Film Studies. This, it could be argued, is evident from the limited role that Mexican film scholars and critics have played in the international arena.

This chapter tells the story of cinema studies in Mexico from the earliest reviewers to present-day trends in film criticism and theory. This history provides a context in which to address questions not only about the current study of Mexican cinema within Mexico, but also about how the particularity of Mexican cinema might be incorporated into larger debates about 'Third World' cinema in Film Studies internationally.

THE FIRST FILM REVIEWERS

The arrival of Thomas Edison's Kinetoscope and Vitascope in Mexico at the end of the nineteenth century, along with Auguste and Louis Lumière's 'cinématographe' projector, coincided with the hegemony of the French-influenced positivism in Mexico. President Porfirio Díaz's regime undertook an ambitious programme of modernization and industrial development that provided a sympathetic ideological context for the new invention. As in other parts of the world, many of the first writings on film in Mexico consisted of impressionistic accounts of the technological phenomenon or were mere reviews of the spectacle, which often included moral judgments.[2] The columnists borrowed terms from theatre and other visual arts to describe the film experience, even though they underestimated cinema as a form of artistic expression (Miquel, 1992: 23).

At the same time, some journalists and writers began to value the new invention for its scientific possibilities, which usually led them to prefer actuality over fiction film. Some years later, the armed insurrection against Díaz's dictatorship that turned into the Mexican Revolution provided fertile ground for the development and practice of documentary filmmaking, which some scholars have later argued was 'Mexico's principal contribution to world cinema' (de los Reyes, 1995: 71). Many writers at the time praised the Mexican Revolution and World War one documentaries for their informational, educational and even historical value. However, this trend was short-lived and by 1916 actuality films were seen as a propagandistic tool.

The first regular film columnists began to appear in local newspapers at around this time. In *El Nacional*, Jean Humblot was a passionate promoter of film as an art form (Miquel, 1992: 247). Hipólito Seijas, under the pseudonym of Rafael Pérez Taylor, and

Carlos Noriega Hope, alias Silvestre Bonnard, also wrote for *El Universal*. The Nicaraguan-born Francisco Zamora wrote for *Excélsior*. Whatever the claims of those writers, the poet and essayist Alfonso Reyes and the novelist Martín Luis Guzmán are generally considered to have been the first true film critics in Mexico. Both were members of the 'Ateneo de la Juventud', the cultural group that produced some of the leading intellectual figures in the country and that ultimately overthrew positivism as the dominant discourse in the country. Reyes and Guzmán shared the pseudonym 'Fósforo' in the weekly *España*, edited in Spain by José Ortega y Gasset, and they developed a serious yet engaging approach to cinema as an art form.

By the early 1920s, fiction once again dominated Mexican screens, under the hegemony of the North American industry.[3] This decade saw the rise of new film critics. Cube Bonifant, under the pen-name Luz de Alba, was one of the first women to write about film in Mexico and one of the first critics to pay serious attention to the filmmaker as an auteur; the film critic Jorge Ayala Blanco has called her 'the first solid antecedent of film criticism in Mexico' (quoted in Rivera, 1990: 12). The criticism of Jaime Torres Bodet, who twice served as Secretary of Education, was published under the name 'Celuloide' in the magazine *Revista de Revistas* and shows a cultural and literary rigor rare for the time.[4]

THE NATIONAL PROJECT AND THE FILM INDUSTRY

In the 1920s, Mexico was recovering from the devastating effects of the Revolution. The government of the day launched an ambitious national cultural campaign in which intellectuals, artists and filmmakers were to play an active role. The project was driven by a modernist quest to discover (or create) *mexicanidad*, an 'authentic' Mexican identity, through the cultivation of uniquely Mexican cultural and artistic values that would reconcile and blend the cultures of pre-Hispanic and modern day Mexico. This quest for an identity was to become a persistent legacy in the country for much of the twentieth century. Key academic figures in the movement were the anthropologist Manuel Gamio, architect of Mexican *indigenismo*[5]; the philosopher Samuel Ramos, who argued that in order to understand Mexican culture one had first to understand the Mexican mind and considered that the best tool for doing so was Adlerian psychology; and the educator José Vasconcelos, head of the National University of Mexico and Secretary of Education, who coined the concept of 'raza cósmica' with reference to *mestizo* culture. This national project, which permeated all of the country's disciplines, laid the ground for the creation of the Partido Revolucionario Institucional (PRI) – the political party that would rule the country for more than sixty years.

The advent of sound in film, and hence the need for films in the national language, created an opportunity for a Mexican industry to conquer its domestic market, as happened in a number of countries around the world. The determined attempt to create a local film industry was based on the idea of 'nationalizing' Hollywood – in other words, adapting the Hollywood model of infrastructure to Mexican conditions, which meant in part combining state and private production, distribution and exhibition (Monsiváis, 1995: 117). Many film critics and intellectuals would actively participate in this burgeoning Mexican film industry as screenwriters, and even as impresarios. Among them were Noriega Hope, the renowned poet and playwright Xavier Villaurrutia, who wrote about film in the magazines *Hoy* (1937–41) and *Así* (1941–43); the novelist and political activist José Revueltas who wrote for *Hoy* and decades later published the film theory book *El conocimiento cinematográfico y sus problemas* ([1965] 1981); and Juan Bustillo Oro, who directed some silent films and wrote in *El Universal* before returning to filmmaking.[6] In 1931, thanks to the initiative of the influential journal *Contemporáneos*, Mexico's first film society was created with an executive committee composed of well-known artists and intellectuals.[7]

The Mexican film industry demanded its own publications for the promotion of its stars, and this led to the birth of *Mundo cinematográfico*, *El cine gráfico*, *México cinema*, *Cinema reporter*, *Diario fílmico mexicano* and *Cine continental*. These magazines were mostly self-congratulatory and lacked any serious criticism of popular Mexican cinema. The 1940s and the 1950s witnessed international success for the industry. This was the 'Golden Era of Mexican cinema', a time when it became one of the strongest and most profitable industries in the country and when it was able to 'function imperialistically in most Spanish-speaking countries of the continent, which lacked a film industry of their own' (Ayala Blanco, quoted in de la Vega Alfaro, 1995: 86). The very success of the industry seemed to inhibit any serious critical study – with a few notable exceptions. Besides Villaurrutia, the poet Efraín Huerta, the Spanish-born Francisco Piña and Álvaro Custodio developed a consistent approach to cinema and were more critical of the Mexican film industry. For several years Huerta wrote about film for such publications as *Diario de México*, *El Fígaro*, *Cinema Reporter*, *México Cinema* and *Esto*. Piña wrote for *Novela semanal cinematográfica*, for the cherished cultural supplement 'Mexico en la cultura' of the newspaper *Novedades*, and for the magazine *Siempre!*; Custodio, who had already regularly written for publications in Belgium, France and Cuba, wrote for *Excelsior*.[8]

By the 1950s the Mexican film industry was showing many signs of decay. Bernal Méndez and Santos Mar's *El embrollo cinematográfico* (1953) and Miguel Contreras Torres' *El libro negro del cine mexicano* (1960) denounced industry excesses and warned of a looming crisis. At the same time, the country was showing encouraging signs of a new cinephilia, partly influenced by the emergence of the 'European art cinema', and partly because of the flourishing of new film societies such as the one at the National University and at the Instituto Francés de América Latina (IFAL). Also noteworthy was the creation of Reseña de Acapulco, a film festival that would contribute to the emerging film culture among the younger generations. And, in 1957, the magazine *Séptimo Arte*, edited by Francisco Zárate and published by Universidad Iberoamericana, showed the pressing need for an aesthetic approach to the study of film. Following in the footsteps of Villaurrutia and Huerta, the renowned Mexican intellectuals Carlos Fuentes and Octavio Paz would also write about film from time to time.

NUEVO CINE

Influential French auteur theories as well as notions of the 'New Latin American cinema' were championed by the group that created the magazine *Nuevo Cine* – among them Emilio García Riera, Jomí García Ascot, Manuel Michel, José de la Colina, Salvador Elizondo, Tomás Pérez Turrent, Carlos Monsiváis and Jorge Ayala Blanco. Although short-lived – it published only seven issues between 1961 and 1962 – the magazine had a tremendous impact on film criticism and Film Studies in Mexico.

Using fashionable concepts such as *mise en scène* and auteurism, this young generation of film critics and aspiring filmmakers looked again at Mexican cinema to study its 'alienating effects' (Pick, 1982: 230) and (sometimes influenced by foreign film critics such as George Sadoul) re-evaluated the work of local filmmakers – Luis Buñuel, Emilio 'El Indio' Fernández, Fernando de Fuentes and Alejandro Galindo. The *Nuevo Cine* group also made an incursion into filmmaking with the low-budget independent feature *En el balcón vacío* (1961). The burgeoning of film culture in Mexico was consolidated by the creation of the Filmoteca de la Universidad Nacional Autónoma de México (UNAM) in 1960, which was the first official film archive in the country, and the Centro Universitario de Estudios Cinematográficos (CUEC) also at the UNAM in 1963, the first film school in Mexico. Also influential was an experimental film competition organized by the trade union Sindicato de Trabajadores de

la Producción Cinematográfica. This aimed to 'renovate the artistic and technical structure of the national industry' (Pérez Turrent, 1995: 95) by offering young directors an opportunity to access the film industry. In these promising circumstances, the end of the 1960s saw the publication of two seminal works: García Riera's *Historia documental del cine mexicano* ([1969–78] 1992–97) and Ayala Blanco's *La aventura del cine mexicano* ([1968] 1979).

As has been widely acknowledged, 1968 marked a milestone in the political history of Mexico. Just ten days before the beginning of the Olympic Games in Mexico City, the government crushed a student rally and massacred several participants. This act of repression polarized the country. The incoming president, Luis Echeverría, saw the cracks in the political system and created an astute strategy for transforming the image of Mexico through cinema, presenting it both at home and abroad as a democratic and liberal state.

Between 1970 and 1976 the state not only became the major film producer but also largely controlled distribution and exhibition. It was no coincidence that the president named his brother, a well-known actor and president of the actor's guild, to serve as the head of the Banco Nacional Cinematográfico. In this apparently exciting new era, a double discourse reigned: those willing to join the system would benefit greatly, but those who opposed it would be completely marginalized. Many of the members of *Nuevo Cine* were incorporated in the state's film project along with many young filmmakers. Even the term 'Nuevo Cine' became part of the official discourse. García Riera would later reassess Echeverría's administration:

> In the final analysis, the new Mexican cinema has served the official ideology, and its supposedly militant character, the political commitment claimed for it, its revolution from within were never more that an imposture. It is more exact to give it the label that suits it: that of an auteur cinema. Not a stylistic revolution, a collective project, a group social commitment, nor even a movement ... (quoted in Lerner, 1999: 7)

Two important legacies of this time were the creation of the Cineteca Nacional in Mexico City in 1974, and the Centro de Capacitación Cinematográfica (CCC), the country's second film school. At the time, a dissident group known as the 'superocheros' who saw 8mm film as an effective means of breaking with industrial cinema and experimenting with new narrative forms, denounced filmmakers such as Felipe Cazals, Arturo Ripstein, Paul Leduc, Jaime Humberto Hermosillo, along with their 'spokespersons' García Riera and Pérez Turrent, for participating in the state's film project under the banner of an 'independent' cinema (Menéndez et al., [1972] 1999: 37). One of the members of this group, Sergio García, wrote the manifesto 'Towards a Fourth Cinema' (1999: 70). Eventually some filmmakers who were members of this group, such as Gabriel Retes and Alfredo Gurrola, went on to work with 35mm film, while García continued to teach film and to write in a number of publications.

THE RUPTURE

Inevitably, with the state being a major player in filmmaking, the Mexican film industry was profoundly influenced by political factors. Echeverría's successor as president dismantled much of his political project, and filmmaking suffered as a result. The residual structure of the national film industry was destroyed once and for all and independent producers who specialized in low-budget genre films exploited its remains. As an ominous sign of the times, in 1982 a fire destroyed the Cineteca National, and with it many invaluable film prints, negatives, documents and archives. Nevertheless the 1980s, the 'lost decade' as some have referred to it, saw the creation of the Mexican Film Institute (Instituto Mexicano de Cinematografía, IMCINE) as well as the leading academic centre for Film Studies in Mexico: the Centro de Investigación y Estudios Cinematográficos (CIEC) at the Universidad de Guadalajara. CIEC has maintained a close relationship with the

Guadalajara Film Festival which was created that same year and is still the only academic program in the country that offers a Masters degree in Film Studies.

At around this time a personal clash between Mexico's two foremost film historians and critics, García Riera and Ayala Blanco, divided the country's film community and would continue to polarize it through the coming decades. This feud also helped to establish two hegemonic lines of study that are still in place: one historiographical, the other semiotic and post-structuralist, the former more institutionalized and delineated than the latter.

García Riera founded the magazines *Imágenes* and *Dicine*. The latter, subsequently edited by Nelson Carro, Susana López Aranda and Leonardo García Tsao, was published bi-monthly between 1984 and 1997, and for some years it was the most consistent and important film magazine in Mexico. In addition to producing the six-volume *Mexico visto por el cine extranjero* (1987–90), a detailed account of Mexican references in world (and especially Hollywood) cinema from 1894 until 1986, García Riera also revised his *Historia documental del cine mexicano* (1992–97) and expanded it to 18 volumes. This massive work provides a thorough account of all Mexican film productions from 1929 to 1976. García Riera was also one of the founders of CIEC and remained its director until his death in 2002.

Ayala Blanco, for his part, completed *La búsqueda del cine mexicano* (1986a) and *La condición del cine mexicano* (1986b) as further instalments in his rigorous analysis of Mexican cinema. He also published with María Luisa Amador *Cartelera cinematográfica* (1985–99), a collection of historiographical books on film exhibition in Mexico. He has taught at CUEC, while writing as a film columnist for *Excélsior* and later for *El Financiero*. More recently, Ayala Blanco has published *La fugacidad del cine mexicano* (2001), *La grandeza del cine mexicano* (2004) and *La herejía del cine mexicano* (2006), which incorporate the work of some local video artists into his study of local cinema.

The 1980s saw the emergence of a new generation of often prolific film scholars, many of them related to CIEC, who specialized in the historiographical aspects of the emergence of Mexican filmmaking and its film industry – an emphasis possibly motivated by a kind of nostalgia for the extinct film industry and the lost Cineteca Nacional archives. Among these scholars are Aurelio de los Reyes (1983a; 1983b; 1995), Eduardo de la Vega (1995; 2001) Angel Miquel (1992), Margarita de Orellana, Federico Dávalos (1996) and Moisés Viñas (1992). In addition, scholars like Patricia Torres San Martín (2001) and Julia Tuñón (1998; 2000), also linked to CIEC, and more recently Márgara Millán (1999) at UNAM, have incorporated feminist perspectives and placed particular emphasis on the history of women filmmakers in Mexico. Also noteworthy is the work of Norma Iglesias (1991) for its take on the US-Mexico border in Mexican cinema.

Through his extensive research and publications, the cultural essayist and former Nuevo Cine member Carlos Monsiváis prepared the ground for the re-evaluation and recontextualization of Mexican popular cinema and helped to focus attention on some overlooked filmmakers and genres. Among the critics who have followed his example and extended it to include studies of film stars and audience reception are Carlos Bonfil (1994), Rafael Aviña (1997), José Felipe Coria (1997), Andrés de Luna (1985), and Gustavo García (1986) along with novelist and journalist Paco Ignacio Taibo I (1986; 1991).

MEXICAN FILM STUDIES NORTH OF THE BORDER

The 1970s saw the birth in the US and Europe of an academic interest in 'Third World' cinema, although it was primarily in terms of the ideological struggle that these films exemplified. Notions of 'Third Cinema' fuelled by the 'New Latin American Cinema' movement provided, in the words of Chon A. Noriega, 'a theoretical paradigm that in many ways restricted critical interest to the radical cinema

of the 1960s and 1970s' (2000: xii).[9] For many years, the terms 'Third World Cinema' and 'Third Cinema' would be erroneously interchangeable, thus leading to notions that all texts produced in these countries were 'necessarily allegorical' (Jameson, 1986: 69). Furthermore, the 'Third Cinema' movement, in order to justify its existence, scorned the popular cinema of the 'Third World' countries, thus reinforcing the prevailing academic underestimation of the popular cinema produced in these countries.[10] In this context, Mexico's peculiar case of an existent film industry and large-scale state participation meant that references to the country in the literature of 'New Latin American Cinema' at the time were mostly relegated to side notes and footnotes. It was at around this time, in 1974, that Mexican journalist Beatriz Reyes Nevares published *Trece directores del cine mexicano*; in its English translation two years later as *The Mexican Cinema: Interviews with Thirteen Directors* (1976), this was almost certainly the first book devoted to Mexican cinema to be published in the US.[11]

It was only in the 1980s that Mexican cinema became a point of reference in debates about 'Third World cinema'. This was due largely to film scholars working in the US and the UK, some of whom had previously written about 'New Latin American Cinema', such as Julianne Burton-Carvajal (1981; 1983; 1986; 2003), Michael Chanan (1983), John King (1990; 1993), and Chon A. Noriega (2000), along with a new wave of scholars such as Carl J. Mora (1989), Charles Ramírez Berg (1992) and Ana M. López (1993). These scholars have drawn on studies by their Mexican counterparts to provide historical context, but they have brought new and fresh approaches, including feminist, queer and cultural theories to Mexican cinema research and criticism.

A seminal book in English is *Mexican Cinema* (1995), edited by the Paris-based Brazilian film scholar Paulo Antonio Paranaguá, which features essays by some of the leading Mexican scholars.[12] The publication of an anthology offering such a broad overview has allowed the next generation of scholars, including David R. Maciel (1990), Joanne Herschfield (1996; 1999), Jesse Lerner (1999), Jeffrey M. Pilcher (2001), David William Foster (2002) and Andrea Noble (2005), to make more specific studies of Mexican cinema, such as Lerner's account of the 'superocheros' movement. Paradoxically, some of the more finely grained research into Mexican cinema has been done abroad, mainly in the US and the UK.

CURRENT CHALLENGES

The current prospects for Film Studies in Mexico are not promising. The 1990s saw the appearance – and disappearance – of the film journals *Intolerancia*, edited by Gustavo García, and *Nitrato de plata*, edited by José María Espinasa, and the apparently inexorable growth of American-style entertainment magazines such as *Cine Premier*, *24 x segundo* and *Cinemanía*. The only current film research and criticism publications in Mexico are *Estudios cinematográficos*, published quarterly by CUEC, and the online journal *www.elojoquepiensa.com*, edited by CIEC.

Cultural studies is just beginning to flourish in Mexican academia, but so far its limited connection with film criticism has produced a somewhat timid impact on the study of film. Special mention, however, should be made of the Argentinean-born scholar Néstor García Canclini, who has opened up new possibilities through his research into Mexican cultural industries and audience reception within the current context of 'globalization' (Canclini, 1994). What is also noticeable, despite some high-profile exceptions, is how few people are undertaking textual analysis. Serious research into Mexican cinema in Mexico is almost completely dominated by historiographical work.

Questions about 'East/West' and the 'postcolonial' that have had wide currency elsewhere have been of marginal relevance in Mexican academia: the terms of the debate have simply not resonated locally. The country

has considered itself, in Paz's words, a 'distinct version of western civilization' (1980: 402). Whereas the term 'postcolonial', as Robert Stam has pointed out, 'tends to be associated with Third World countries that gained independence after World War II' (Stam, 2000: 294), Mexico gained its independence from Spain in the nineteenth century. Another easily overlooked factor is that most of the pre-dominant literature in Film Studies is in English and has not been translated into Spanish; many film critics in Mexico are not fluent in English. In these circumstances, more consistent and more effective communication channels between film scholars at home and abroad are clearly desirable. A successful model was the conference held in Guadalajara in 1997 that gathered film scholars from different countries working on Mexican, Latin American and Chicano cinemas and that led to the publication of the anthology *Horizontes del segundo siglo: Investigación y pedagogía del cine mexicano, latinoamericano y chicano* (Burton-Carvajal et al., 1998).

In 2000, the long entrenched PRI lost the presidential elections. As a result, at the beginning of the twenty-first century Mexico has witnessed the emergence of new debates around old cultural issues, including questions about the viability of a new nationalist cultural project under the current hegemonic international order, the degree of participation of the state in cultural practices and the political role of intellectuals. These not-soon-to-be-concluded debates are pivotal to the future of film practice and Film Studies in the country. At the same time, Mexican cinema has been experiencing a comeback in the international arena. Some of its films have achieved great critical and box-office success and some Mexican filmmakers working abroad have won unprecedented recognition. A vibrant experimental video art scene in different parts of the country has allowed young artists to explore new ways of linking aesthetics to current political, social, sexual and national identity issues. Indigenous people in different regions of the country have been undertaking diverse media projects in order to represent themselves without intermediaries.

But if the landscape of film and video production is changing rapidly, the study of film in Mexico remains largely trapped within the paradigms of earlier decades. The international resurgence of Mexican films, along with Argentinean and Brazilian films, has been accompanied by critical responses trumpeting the birth of yet another 'New Latin American cinema'. That old impulse to lump all non-Hollywood and non-European films together in one restrictive 'Third World' category provides a poor guide to understanding the complexities of particular 'national' cinemas – including Mexican cinema. More relevant would be a study of particular modes of film production, distribution and exhibition in the context of today's global geopolitics. The study of Mexican cinema could benefit greatly from drawing comparisons, not just with the cinemas of Latin American countries like Brazil, but also with culturally dissimilar cinemas (India, Egypt, Turkey) that have nonetheless shared similar economic, industrial and political experiences.

Paul Willemen has asserted that

> it must be acknowledged that comparative studies in cinema do not yet exist. What is worse, given the current insufferably ethnocentric bias of film theory, it may well be a while before this urgently needed discipline of comparative studies displaces the kind of Film Studies currently being inflicted on university and college students. (1994: 207)

If we are to develop a deeper understanding of non-European cinemas and move beyond the impulse to place 'Third World' films into one oversimplified category, Willemen's statement should have been taken seriously into consideration more than a decade ago.

NOTES

Special thanks to Bob Stam, Ismail Xavier, Ana M. López, Naief Yehya, Alejandra Leal, Jessica Scarlata, Valeria Mogilevich and Nissa Perry for their precious input.

1 Ella Shohat and Robert Stam refer to 'Third World' countries as 'the colonized, neocolonized, or decolonized nations and "minorities" whose structural disadvantages have [been] shaped by the colonial process and by the unequal division of international labor. The term itself was formed against the backdrop of the patronizing vocabulary which posited these nations as "backward", "underdeveloped", and "primitive"' (1995: 25). For practical purposes I will use this definition for this essay.

2 According to Angel Miquel in his book *Los exaltados* (1992), at the time Mexican journalism had showbiz columnists, under the figures of Salvador Díaz Mirón, Luis G. Urbina, José Juan Tablada and Amado Nervo, among others, who were the first to write about film in newspapers.

3 It was during these years that the country saw the publishing of its first film magazines, which were vehicles for promoting Hollywood's burgeoning star system. That was the case of *Cinelandia*, which reportedly was merely a translated version of its American counterpart.

4 As a Mexican functionary, Torres Bodet was opposed to Luis Buñuel's *Los Olvidados* (Mexico, 1950) representing Mexico at the Cannes Film Festival arguing the film 'offered a distorted image of the country' (quoted in Ruy Sánchez, 1994: 96).

5 Gamio also directed some ethnographic films including *Danza de los indígenas de Teotihuacán y de las pirámides* (Mexico, 1920) and *La población del valle de Teotihuacán* (Mexico, 1923).

6 Noriega Hope was the screenwriter of the film *Santa* (Antonio Moreno, Mexico, 1929), the first sound film in Mexico, and directed the film *Los chicos de la prensa* (Mexico, 1921); Xavier Villaurrutia was the screenwriter for the films *Vámonos con Pancho Villa* (Fernando de Fuentes, Mexico, 1936) and *Distinto amanecer* (Julio Bracho, Mexico, 1943), among others; José Revueltas was the screenwriter for the films *La diosa arrodillada* (Roberto Gavaldón, Mexico, 1947), *La ilusión viaja en tranvía* (Luis Buñuel, Mexico, 1953), and *El apando* (Felipe Cazals, Mexico, 1967), among others; Juan Bustillo Oro directed *En tiempos de don Porfirio* (Mexico, 1939), *Ahí está el detalle* (Mexico, 1940), *El hombre sin rostro* (Mexico, 1950) and *Acá las tortas* (Mexico, 1951), among many others. Even Nobel Prize-winner Octavio Paz had a fleeting participation in film collaborating on the screenplay of *El rebelde* (Jaime Salvador, Mexico, 1943) where he wrote a song that was performed in the film by popular *charro cantor* Jorge Negrete (Ruy Sánchez, 1994).

7 The executive committee was constituted by photographers Manuel and Lola Álvarez Bravo, painters María Izquierdo and Carlos Mérida, and poet and scholar Bernardo Ortiz de Montellano.

8 He would also write the screenplays for *Aventurera* (Mexico, 1949), *Sensualidad* (Mexico, 1950) and *No niego mi pasado* (Mexico, 1951), all of them directed by Alberto Gout.

9 The term 'Third Cinema' was launched by Argentine filmmakers Fernando Solanas and Octavio

Getino, who defined it as 'the cinema that recognizes in (the anti-imperialist struggle in the Third World and its equivalents within the imperialist countries) … the most gigantic cultural, scientific and artistic manifestation of our time … in a word, the decolonization of a culture' (quoted in Shohat and Stam, 1995: 28).

10 In the particular case of Latin America, Ana López has written that 'vehemently criticized, the old (Latin American) cinema was rejected as imitative of Hollywood, unrealistic, alienating and sentimental, over the years, it became little else than a clichéd straw man in all arguments for cinematic and cultural renovation and change' (1993: 148).

11 The featured filmmakers are Emilio Fernández, Alejandro Galindo, Ismael Rodríguez, Luis Buñuel, Luis Alcoriza, Felipe Cazals, Salomón Laiter, Juan López Moctezuma, Jorge Fons, José Estrada, Sergio Olhovich, Arturo Ripstein and Alberto Isaac.

12 The English version, translated by Ana M. López from the original French text that appeared in 1992, was published by the British Film Institute in association with the Mexican Film Institute. The contributors include Carlos Monsiváis, Aurelio de los Reyes, Ariel Zúñiga, Tomás Pérez Turrent, Eduardo de la Vega Alfaro, Emilio García Riera and Andrés de Luna.

REFERENCES

Aviña, Rafael and Gustavo García (1997) *Época de oro del cine mexicano*. Mexico City: Editorial Clío.

Ayala Blanco, Jorge (1979) *La aventura del cine mexicano*. Mexico City: Ediciones Era.

Ayala Blanco, Jorge (1986a) *La búsqueda del cine mexicano*. Mexico City: Editorial Posada.

Ayala Blanco, Jorge (1986b) *La condición del cine mexicano*. Mexico City: Editorial Posada.

Ayala Blanco, Jorge (1991) *La disolvencia del cine mexicano: entre lo popular y lo exquisito*. Mexico City: Editorial Posada.

Ayala Blanco, Jorge (1996) *La eficacia del cine mexicano*. Mexico City: Editorial Grijalbo.

Ayala Blanco, Jorge (2001) *La fugacidad del cine mexicano*. Mexico City: Océano.

Ayala Blanco, Jorge (2004) *La grandeza del cine mexicano*. Mexico City: Océano.

Ayala Blanco, Jorge (2006) *La herejía del cine mexicano*. Mexico City: Océano.

Ayala Blanco, Jorge and Amador, María Luisa (1985–99) *Cartelera cinematográfica*. 7 vols. Mexico City: UNAM/Centro Universitario de Estudios Cinematográficos.

Bonfil, Carlos and Monsiváis, Carlos (1994) *A través del espejo: El cine mexicano y su público*. Mexico City: Intituto Mexicano de Cinematografia/Ediciones El Milagro.

Burton-Carvajal, Julianne (1981) *Film Artisans and Film Industries in Latin America, 1956–1980: Theoretical and Critical Implications of Variations in Modes of Filmic Production and Consumption*. Washington, DC: Wilson Center.

Burton-Carvajal, Julianne (ed.) (1983) *The New Latin American Cinema: An Annotated Bibliography of Sources in English, Spanish, and Portuguese, 1960–1980*. New York: Smyrna Press.

Burton-Carvajal, Julianne (ed.) (1986) *Cinema and Social Change in Latin America, Conversations with Filmmakers*. Austin: University of Texas Press.

Burton-Carvajal, Julianne (2002) *Matilde Landeta, hija de la Revolución*. Mexico City: Consejo Nacional para la Cultura y las Artes (CONACULTA)/Dirección General de Publicaciones e Instituto Mexicano de Cinematografía (IMCINE).

Burton-Carvajal, Julianne, San Martín, Patricia Torres and Miquel, Angel (eds) (1998) *Horizontes del segundo siglo: Investigación y pedagogía del cine mexicano, latinoamericano y chicano*. Guadalajara, Mexico: Universidad de Guadalajara/Instituto Mexicano de Cinematografía (IMCINE).

Chanan, Michael (ed.) (1983) *Twenty Five Years of the New Latin American Cinema*. London: BFI/Channel Four.

Contreras Torres, Miguel (1960) *El libro negro del cine mexicano*. Mexico City: Editora Hispano-Continental Films.

Coria, José Felipe and García, Gustavo (1997) *Nuevo cine mexicano*. Mexico City: Editorial Clío.

Dávalos Orozco, Federico (1996) *Los albores del cine mexicano*. Mexico City: Editorial Clío.

de la Vega Alfaro, Eduardo (1995) 'Origins, Development and Crisis of Sound Cinema (1929–64)', in Paulo Antonio Paranaguá (ed.), *Mexican Cinema*. Tr. Ana M. López. London: BFI/Instituto Mexicano de Cinematografía (IMCINE). pp. 79–93.

de la Vega Alfaro, Eduardo (ed.) (2001) *Microhistorias del cine en México*. Guadalajara, Mexico: Universidad de Guadalajara/Universidad Nacional Autónoma de México (UNAM)/Instituto Mexicano de Cinematografía (IMCINE)/Cineteca Nacional/Instituto Mora.

de los Reyes, Aurelio (1983a) *Cine y sociedad en México 1896–1930*. Mexico City: Instituto de Investigaciones Estétaticas de la Universidad Nacional Autónoma de México.

de los Reyes, Aurelio (1983b) *Los orígenes del cine en México (1896–1900)*. Mexico City: Fondo de Cultura Económica.

de los Reyes, Aurelio (1995) 'The Silent Cinema', in Paulo Antonio Paranaguá (ed.), *Mexican Cinema*.

Tr. Ana M. López. London: BFI/Instituto Mexicano de Cinematografía (IMCINE). pp. 63–78.

de Luna, Andrés (1985) *La batalla y su sombra: la Revolución en el cine mexicano*. Mexico City: Universidad Autónoma Metropolitana – Xochimilco.

de Orellana, Margarita (1991) *La mirada circular. el cine norteamericano de la Revolución, 1911–1917*. Mexico City: Joaquín Mortiz.

Foster, David William (2002) *Mexico City in Contemporary Mexican Cinema*. Austin: University of Texas Press.

García, Gustavo (1986) *La década perdida: imagen 24 x 1*. Mexico City: Universidad Autónoma Metropolitana – Azcapotzalco.

García, Sergio (1999) 'Towards a Fourth Cinema', *Wide Angle*, 21(3): 70–5.

García Canclini, Néstor (ed.) (1994) *Los nuevos espectadores: Cine, televisión y video en México*. Mexico City: Instituto Mexicano de Cinematografía (IMCINE).

García Riera, Emilio (1987–90) *Mexico visto por el cine extranjero*. 6 vols. Guadalajara, Mexico: Universidad de Guadalajara.

García Riera, Emilio (1992–7) *Historia documental del cine mexicano*. 18 vols. Guadalajara, Mexico: Universidad de Guadalajara.

Gutiérrez, Carlos A. (1996) 'La situación actual de la crítica cinematográfica en México'. BA dissertation, Universidad Iberoamericana, Mexico City.

Hershfield, Joanne (1996) *Mexican Cinema/Mexican Woman, 1940–1950*. Tucson: University of Arizona Press.

Hershfield, Joanne and Maciel, David (1999) *Mexico's Cinema: A Century of Film and Filmmakers*. Wilmington, DE: Scholarly Resources.

Jameson, Fredric (1986) 'Third World and Literature in the Era of Multinational Capitalism', *Social Text*, 15: 65–88.

King, John (1990) *Magical Reels, A History of Cinema in Latin America*. London: Verso.

King, John, López, Ana and Alvarado, Manuel (eds) (1993) *Mediating Two Worlds: Cinematic Encounters in the Americas*. London: BFI.

Iglesias, Norma (1991) Entre yerba, polvo y plomo: Lo fronterizo visto por el cine mexicano. 2 vols. Tijuana, Mexico: El Colegio de la Frontera Norte.

Lerner, Jesse (1999) 'Superocheros', *Wide Angle*, 21(3): 1–35.

López, Ana (1993) 'Tears and Desire: Women and Melodrama in the "Old" Mexican Cinema', in John King, Ana López, and Manuel Alvarado (eds), *Mediating Two Worlds: Cinematic Encounters in the Americas*. London: BFI. pp. 147–63.

López, Ana (2006) Interview by author. Telephone conversation. 2 March.

Maciel, David (1990) *El Norte: The U.S.-Mexican Border in Contemporary Cinema*. San Diego, CA: San Diego State University.

Méndez, Bernal and Mar, Santos (1953) *El embrollo cinematográfico*. Mexico City: Cooperación.

Menéndez, Óscar, Fosado, Víctor, Béjar, Sergio, Gámez, Rubén, Godoy, Jorge, Zayas, Armando, de la Cabada, Juan, Ayala, Leopoldo, Buñuel Luis, Rosete, Antonio, Fabila, René Avilés and Gurrola, Juan José [1972] (1999) 'Manifesto: 8 Millimeters Versus 8 Millions', *Wide Angle*, 21(3): 36–41.

Millán, Márgara (1999) *Derivas de un cine en femenino*. Mexico City: Universidad Nacional Autónoma de México/Miguel Angel Porrúa.

Miquel, Angel (1992) *Los exaltados*. Guadalajara, México: Universidad de Guadalajara.

Monsiváis, Carlos (1995) 'Mythologies', in Paulo Antonio Paranaguá (ed.), *Mexican Cinema*. Tr. Ana M. López. London: BFI/Instituto Mexicano de Cinematografía (IMCINE). pp. 117–27.

Mora, Carl J. (1989) *Mexican Cinema: Reflections of a Society: 1896–1980*. Berkeley: University of California Press.

Mora, Carl J. (2005) *Mexican Cinema: Reflections of a Society, 1896–2004*. Jefferson, NC: McFarland & Co.

Noble, Andrea (2005) *Mexican National Cinema*. New York: Routledge.

Noriega, Chon A. (ed.) (2000) *Visible Nations: Latin American Cinema and Video*. Minneapolis: University of Minnesota Press. pp. xi–xxv.

Paranaguá, Paulo Antonio (ed.) (1995) *Mexican Cinema*. Tr. Ana M. López. London: BFI/Instituto Mexicano de Cinematografía (IMCINE).

Paz, Octavio (1980) 'Reflections: Mexico and the United States', *The History Teacher*, 13(3): 401–15.

Pérez Turrent, Tomás (1995) 'Crisis and Renovations (1965–91)', in Paulo Antonio Paranaguá (ed.), *Mexican Cinema*. Tr. Ana M. López. London: BFI/Instituto Mexicano de Cinematografía (IMCINE). pp. 94–115.

Pick, Zuzana M. (1982) 'En búsqueda de una crítica del cine latinoamericano', in Ambrosio Fornet (ed.), *Cine, literatura, sociedad*. La Habana, Cuba: Editorial Letras Cubanas. pp. 230–41.

Pilcher, Jeffrey M. (2001) *Cantinflas and the Chaos of Mexican Modernity*. Wilmington, DE: Scholarly Resources.

Ramírez Berg, Charles (1992) *Cinema of Solitude: A Critical Study of Mexican Film, 1967–1983*. Austin: University of Texas Press.

Revueltas, José (1981) *El conocimiento cinematográfico y sus problemas*. Mexico City: Editorial Era.

Reyes Nevares, Beatriz (1974) *Trece directores del cine mexicano*. Mexico City: Secretaría de Educación Pública.

Reyes Nevares, Beatriz (1976) *The Mexican Cinema: Interviews with Thirteen Directors.* Alburquerque: University of New Mexico Press.

Rivera, Rosa Nidia (1990) *La revista Nuevo Cine.* BA dissertation, Universidad Nacional Autónoma de México (UNAM), Mexico City.

Ruy Sánchez, Alberto (1994) 'Jorge Negrete canta a Octavio Paz', *Artes de México*, 10: 96.

Shohat, Ella and Stam, Robert (1995) *Unthinking Eurocentrism: Multiculturalism and the Media.* New York: Routledge.

Stam, Robert (2000) *Film Theory: An Introduction.* Malden, MA: Blackwell.

Taibo, Paco Ignacio I (1986) *El Indio Fernández, el cine por mis pistolas.* Mexico City: Joaquín Mortiz/Planeta.

Taibo, Paco Ignacio I (1991) *La Doña.* Mexico City, Mexico: Editorial Planeta.

Torres San Martín, Patricia (2001) Cine y género: La representación social de lo femenino y lo masculino en el cine mexicano y venezolano. Guadalajara, Mexico: Universidad de Guadalajara.

Tuñón, Julia (1998) Mujeres de luz y sombra en el cine mexicano: La construcción de una imagen, 1939–1952. Mexico City: El Colegio de México y el Instituto Mexicano de Cinematografía (IMCINE).

Tuñón, Julia (2000) *Los rostros de un mito: Personajes femeninos en las películas de Emilio 'Indio' Fernández.* Mexico City: Consejo Nacional para la Cultura y las Artes (CONACULTA)/Dirección General de Publicaciones e Instituto Mexicano de Cinematografía (IMCINE).

Viñas, Moisés (1992) *Índice cronológico del cine mexicano (1896–1992).* Mexico City: Dirección General de Actividades Cinematográficas de la UNAM.

Willemen, Paul (1994) *Looks and Frictions: Essays in Cultural Studies and Film Theory.* London: BFI.

8

Australia

Noel King, Constantine Verevis and
Deane Williams

In Australia, Film Studies became firmly established as an institutionally recognized discipline in the decade from 1975 to 1985. Although this history in many ways reflected international trends, there are two aspects of the story that may be unique to the Australian case. One was the coincidence between the rise of Film Studies and the strategic revival of the Australian feature film industry in the early seventies with significant government funding and institutional support. The other was the coincidental emergence of a new style of film reviewing and criticism that acted as both a counterpoint and a complement to the new academic discipline.

In his book *Making Meaning* (1989), David Bordwell provides a history of the 'academicization' of film theory and criticism. Having noted various critical schools that developed after the Second World War in the US and Europe, mostly outside the universities, Bordwell identifies the appearance in the 1970s of professional associations and journals of film educators that contributed to this academicization at the same time as Film Studies was being introduced into university departments of drama, literature and art history that were already committed to the study of canonical cultural texts. Inspired by Bordwell, Barrett Hodsdon's *Straight Roads and Crossed Lines* attempts an equivalent history for Australia, 'charting and explicating a range of film culture activities' (2001: 59) from the 1960s, 1970s and 1980s that anticipate, intersect and occasionally conflict with the burgeoning realm of screen education. Hodsdon contrasts three spheres of 'unofficial' film culture – university-based film societies, the Sydney filmmakers co-operative and the Super-8 scene – against what he sees as examples of 'official' film cultural and educational institutions: the Australian Film Television and Radio School (AFTRS), Swinburne Film School, the National Film and Sound Archive (NFSA), and the growing number of higher education programmes in Film Studies.

Hodsdon identifies two defining characteristics of the 1950s university film societies, most prominently the Melbourne University Film Society and Sydney University Film Group, and the film festivals associated with them. First, they pursued the kind of left-wing political agenda advanced by the Realist

Film Group (2001: 62–3). Second, they developed, through the introduction of regular bulletins, a film appreciation framework that promoted the cultural status of the medium (2001: 64). These bulletins – *Melbourne University Film Society Annotations* (later, *Annotations on Film*), *The University Film Group Bulletin* (later *Melbourne Film Group Bulletin*), *Sydney University Film Group Bulletin* and others – moved from the provision of programme notes, short reviews and commentaries to more substantial critical and theoretical reflection. Hodsdon contrasts these 'authentic publications' to the 'academic overkill' and 'French intellectual fashion that overtook the academic scene of screen studies (as it "evolved" in the 1970s)' (2001: 68, 86). He suggests that academicized Film Studies, along with other factors such as weekly screenings from the National Film Theatre of Australia and double-features at inner city repertory cinemas, ultimately contributed to the demise of university film societies (2001: 82–3).

The second of Hodsdon's unofficial institutions, the Sydney Filmmakers Co-op (1970–85), arose out of Ubu Films, a distribution and exhibition operation headed by activists Albie Thoms and Aggy Read that focused on avant-garde and alternative films, mostly 16mm shorts, low budget features and documentaries. Thoms and Read envisaged the Co-op as a participatory organization that would encourage upcoming and marginal filmmakers to disseminate their work to local audiences at a time when Australian feature film production was at a nascent stage (Thoms, 1978; Hodsdon, 2001: 89). In 1972 the Co-op launched a monthly newsletter that ran until 1975 and then transformed in 1976 into the tabloid-format *Filmnews*. (Continuing publication until 1995, *Filmnews* ultimately outlasted the Co-op by a decade.) During the 1980s, under the editorship of Tina Kaufman, the journal became not just a house journal for the independent film community but also a forum for critical commentary on cultural policy and broader industry issues and an important cross-over vehicle into academic Film Studies (Collins, 1983; 1984).

Local academics such as Meaghan Morris, Tom O'Regan, Stuart Cunningham, Susan Dermody and Elizabeth Jacka published on aspects of Australian cinema, and UK-style screen theory was mediated through interviews with Paul Willemen and others.

The third institutional space described by Hodsdon is the Super-8 scene in Sydney and Melbourne in the 1980s and 1990s. The Sydney Super-8 Film Group started as a cell of activists and ended up, after several transformations, as the Sydney Intermedia Network (1990). The Melbourne group, formed in 1985, had antecedents in the TCH! TCH! TCH! Super-8 and video collective of the late 1970s and early 1980s, headed by Philip Brophy in association with Jayne Stevenson, Adrian Martin, Rolando Caputo and others. These Super-8 groups received extensive coverage in such publications as *Filmnews*, *On the Beach* (1983–87) and *Filmviews* (1986–88), including writings by some of the key participants – Martin, Mark Titmarsh and Michael Hutak, for example. The Super-8 filmmakers were sometimes also cinephile critics, and their intimate knowledge of film and television culture enabled them to recycle and rework movie images encountered on television. Putting these fragments into new contexts, they were able to open up original and unpredictable possibilities for critical reflection.

One lesson from these 'unofficial' Australian film movements, which Hodsdon addresses in the final section of *Straight Roads and Crossed Lines*, is the importance of reviewing and criticism in producing a local film culture. In the mid-1980s critics such as Morris (1983; 1985) and Martin (with Caputo) had questioned the practice of film reviewing and the rigid conformism imposed by film theory paradigms (Hodsdon, 2001: 155). In his book on *Australian National Cinema* (1996), Tom O'Regan took up the question of how film theory and criticism help to disseminate a particular understanding of what constitutes that cinema. Again drawing on Bordwell's *Making Meaning*, O'Regan distinguishes between explicatory and symptomatic criticism – between comprehension and interpretation – in order to explain how critics typically engage in a process of de-mythologizing and re-mythologizing film texts (1996: 333–41). To show how this process has worked in the Australian setting, O'Regan postulates three personae that represent three interconnected critical paradigms: the *cinephile*, the *critical intellectual* and the *film historian*. In order to give these ideal types historical substance, O'Regan notes the need to contextualise them in the appropriate institutional spaces and public arenas (1996: 341–6). His brief account of the three positions provides a point of departure for our attempt to map the institutional spaces, local personnel and critical positions of film theory and criticism that have shaped the particularity of Australian Film Studies.

INSTITUTIONS

The arrival of Film Studies in the Australian academy in the 1970s and 1980s was marked by the official opening of the AFTRS in 1975 (it had been in operation since 1973) and the proliferation of Film Studies courses in Australian upper-level secondary schools, in colleges of advanced education (CAES), in institutes of technology (WAIT, NSWIT, RMIT), in newer universities like Murdoch, Griffith and Deakin, and in critical disciplines (such as English and comparative literature, art history and communication studies) in some of the older universities. Although in places like Melbourne's La Trobe University and Sydney's University of New South Wales Film Studies was established as a discrete aesthetic field and discipline of inquiry, the emergence of cultural studies during the 1980s meant that it more often became part of a larger interdisciplinary formation.[1]

Of special importance during these formative years were a number of conferences, organizations and journals that helped to consolidate the position of Australian Film Studies by encouraging the local and international exchange of critical ideas and perspectives. Among them were the Australian Screen

Studies Association (ASSA) conferences and its antecedents (1978–84), the biennial conference of the Film and History Association of Australia and New Zealand and its precursors (1981–present), and the annual conferences of the Cultural Studies Association of Australia (1991–present).

The ASSA developed out of the *Australian Journal of Screen Theory*, a mid-1970s publication edited by Philip Bell, Colin Crisp, Stephen Crofts, Peter R. Gerdes, Neil McDonald, John Tulloch and others. Its manifesto, announced on the inside cover of its first issue, was to provide 'regular interdisciplinary reflection on the increasingly complex body of film theory at a level suited to the many film courses springing up at tertiary and senior secondary level'. Launched in 1981 at the second Australian Film Conference, held at Nedlands College of Advanced Education in Perth, Western Australia, the ASSA operated during its brief lifespan as an informal and perennially under-funded network across a number of universities and colleges. The first official Australian Screen Studies Conference was held at La Trobe University in December 1982. By the time of the second ASSA Conference at Griffith University in Brisbane in 1984, both the association and the journal were being wound up, citing declining interest in mid-1970s 'screen theory' in the face of increasingly well-established media and communications studies courses.

Despite their premature demise, the ASSA conferences and the *Australian Journal of Screen Theory* remain testament to a vibrant exchange of ideas at the borders of the new academy. The journal published not just conference papers, but also explications of new critical approaches such as semiotics and linguistic models, local scholars engaging with international debates around such topics as feminism and melodrama, critical approaches to Australian cinema and new work on television studies as well as new articles by overseas writers.[2] Conferences like the ASSA, as well as university departments and the Melbourne and Sydney film festivals, further enhanced the influence of international – and especially British – screen culture on the development of Australian Film Studies by sponsoring visits by overseas academics and filmmakers such as Isaac Julien, Annette Kuhn, Laura Mulvey, Mark Nash, Dana Polan, Pierre Sorlin, Paul Willemen and Peter Wollen.

Much editorial space in the *Australian Journal of Screen Theory* was devoted to a perceived need to create dialogue between screen theorists and a community of unfashionably 'atheoretical' film practitioners, historians and archivists alienated by the former group's 'esoteric-elitist thinking and use of almost unintelligible language' (Gerdes, 1978: 3). That a significant gap really did exist between the screen theory and film history positions was confirmed when the historians and archivists decided to set up a series of History and Film conferences to alternate with the ASSA conferences, the first of which was held at the National Library of Australia in 1981. History and Film had soon outlasted its rival and, having survived a hiatus in 1991, it was revived in 1993 at La Trobe University and renamed the Film and History Association of Australia and New Zealand (FHAANZ) conference at Australian National University in Canberra in 1995. With the shift in the 1990s to a more inclusive brand of Film Studies, the FHAANZ has gone to become 'by default the regular Australian conference for film academics of all persuasions' (Bertrand, 2005: 11).[3]

Apart from the *Australian Journal of Screen Theory* and *Filmnews*, significant journals since the 1960s have included the long-running *Metro*, the journal of the Australian Teachers of Media (ATOM) (1974–present) and the Melbourne-based *Cinema Papers*. *Cinema Papers* had several incarnations: first as a short-lived film society publication started by La Trobe University students Peter Beilby and Philippe Mora in 1967; then as a limited circulation tabloid (1969–70) which was resurrected by the then London-based filmmaker Mora during a visit to the 1973 Melbourne International Film Festival; then, with funding from the Film and Television Board, as a large-format

96-page quarterly (1973–79) and an 80-page bi-monthly (1979–89) before it merged with *Filmnews* in 1989 and eventually ceased publication in 2001 (see Murray, 1984). The editorial board of Mora, Beilby and Scott Murray wanted the magazine not only to document the growth of a local film culture, but also to provide a 'forum to stimulate the interchange between filmmakers, critics and educators' and so to act as 'an agent for investigation, criticism and innovation' (Murray, 1984: 41).

Significant journals not solely dedicated to film include *Media Information Australia* (from 1998, *Media International Australia*) and *Continuum*, a media and cultural studies journal originating in Perth (1987) under the general editorship of O'Regan (Murdoch), Brian Shoesmith (WA College of Advanced Education), Noel King (Curtin University) and Toby Miller (Murdoch). *Continuum* 'updated' the *Australian Journal of Screen Theory* and was later adopted as the official publication of the Cultural Studies Association of Australia. Other journals contributing to the intellectual culture that has supported the expansion of Australian Film Studies have included *Antithesis*, *Art & Text*, *Filmviews*, *Flesh*, *Intervention*, *Meanjin*, *On the Beach*, *Southern Review* and *Tension*. More recently a number of lively online journals have made an appearance: *Screening the Past* (founding editor: Ina Bertrand, 1997–present), *Senses of Cinema* (founding editor: Bill Mousoulis, 1999–present), and *Rouge* (editors: Helen Bandis, Adrian Martin and Grant McDonald, 2003–present).[4]

PERSONNEL

All the activity around Film Studies and film culture in the 1970s was paralleled by an upsurge of interest in the cinephile institutions of review journalism. This was embodied most notably in Colin Bennett's long tenure as film critic at Melbourne's the *Age* newspaper. He was later followed by Meaghan Morris at the *Sydney Morning Herald* and the *Australian Financial Review*,

Adrian Martin at the *Age*, Helen Garner at the *Australian's Review of Books*, Paul Byrne at the *Sydney Morning Herald* and Sandra Hall at the *Australian*.

As it took root within the academy from 1975 to 1985, however, Film Studies was dominated less by the figure of the *cinephile* than by the persona of the *critical intellectual*. International developments in film theory, in particular the politically progressive reflection on film language and practice developed in the pages of the UK journal *Screen*, were given an Australian inflection in the writings of David Boyd, Brophy, Creed, Crisp, Cunningham, Ross Gibson, Helen Grace, Ian Hunter, Laleen Jayamanne, King, Martin, Morris, O'Regan, Noel Purdon, Rohdie, Bill Routt, Stern, Graeme Turner and Dugald Williamson. Although a number of these writers became internationally recognized for a particular brand of cultural studies, it was arguably Film Studies that gave the Australian style its unique inflection. In the introduction to *Australian Cultural Studies: A Reader*, a 1993 anthology which includes essays by Cunningham, Gibson, Grace, Martin, Morris, O'Regan, Stern and Turner, the editors John Frow and Meaghan Morris make the point that

first encounters with a culture and society approach in the late 1960s came not from reading Raymond Williams but from attending WEA [Workers Education Association] summer schools on film run at Newport Beach in Sydney by John Flaus [who] (like Lawson) helped create a constituency for the project of cultural studies as well as to train a generation of film and media critics. (1993: xxv–xxvi)

At the same time, encouraged by the 1970s feature film revival and interest in Australian film histories, another discourse distinct from that of either the cinephile or the critical intellectual was becoming increasingly evident. This was the voice of the *film historian*, to be heard in the writings of people like Ina Bertrand, Diane Collins, Crisp, Lawson, Moran, Andrew Pike and Ross Cooper (1980), Graham Shirley and Brian Adams (1989) and Tulloch (1981; 1982). Although the mid-1980s may have been the high noon of high theory internationally, in Australia, at least, publications about film history were

on the rise. One reason may have been a shift in the focus of research provoked by the impact of cultural studies. Another was certainly a resurgence in nationalist sentiment that not only garnered government assistance for the film industry but also, as a spin-off, predisposed Australian publishers to favour any new writing about Australian history, including work in the area of film history. Both nationally and internationally, it is also possible to discern around 1985 a theoretical shift in Film Studies marked by post-structuralist currents, and in particular the influence of Michel Foucault's *The Archaeology of Knowledge* (1972). A 1980s 'crisis' in film theory and the proclaimed 'end of grand theory' were signalled by Bordwell's *Making Meaning*. This provoked a re-appraisal of concepts such as *mise en scène* and realism, a return to empirical investigation, and an attempt to negotiate the tension between theory and history via a non-totalizing concept of difference that could respect the heterogeneity of historical material.

In the late 1980s such contextual factors as government endorsement of democratic multi-culturalism and shifts in communication technologies and broadcasting regulations contributed to the breakdown of the imaginary 'identity' of Australian screen studies that had been dominant in 1975–85 and the emergence of a more inclusive brand of Film Studies. These changes prompted diversification into distinct specializations often associated with particular writers. Thus, with the publication of *Perspectives on Chinese Cinema* (1985), *A Bit on the Side: East-West Topographies of Desire* (1994) and *The Filmmaker and The Prostitute: Dennis O'Rourke's The Good Woman of Bangkok* (Berry et al., 1996), Chris Berry (initially) was seen to be responsible for Asian cinema studies in Australia. Jon Stratton and Ien Ang made the running on multi-cultural media studies, while in the 1990s Jennings, Michael Meadows, Felicity Collins and Therese Davis (2004) forged names for themselves in the study of Indigenous film and television.

In the mid to late 1980s, the arrival of UK television scholars John Fiske and John Hartley in Perth and cultural/media academics such as Tony Bennett, Colin Mercer and Gillian Swanson at Griffith University in Brisbane paved the way for a shift of emphasis towards television research. Local scholars like Cunningham and Miller, Jacka, Moran, O'Regan, David Rowe, Tulloch and Turner (1989) were especially active in the new field, many of them – most notably perhaps Cunningham and O'Regan – also taking a growing interest in media policy. More recently, the increase of investment in, and production at, international film studios on Australian shores has provoked research into 'Australian inter-national pictures' with O'Regan (again), Ben Goldsmith and Nick Herd making major contributions (Goldsmith and O'Regan, 2005; Herd, 2004). The professionalization of Film Studies has meanwhile continued to see Australian film researchers publishing internationally on film authors and genres.[5]

CRITICAL POSITIONS

Even if the first decade of Film Studies in Australia was dominated by the emblematic figure of the *critical intellectual*, and more specifically by that of a high theorist importing intellectual frameworks from Europe, we have attempted to show that this migration of ideas involved local adaptation and not just assimilation. It was this process of translation that shaped the 'particularity' of Australian Film Studies. The new discipline took on local inflections as the result of its location in specific educational institutions, its engagement with the parallel growth of historical research, and its responses to developments in the Australian film and television industries. These specifically Australian developments generated new positions that were soon being re-exported through the international exposure of scholars and critics like Creed, Cunningham, Gibson, Martin, Morris, O'Regan, Stern and Turner.

The period since 1985 has seen an increasing degree of intersection and cross-pollination

between the traditions of the critical intellectual, the film historian and the cinephile. An early engagement between critical intellectuals and film historians was initiated by the intervention of Albert Moran and Tom O'Regan in their 1983 essay 'Two Discourses of Australian Film' in the *Australian Journal of Screen Theory*. Their declared aim was 'to challenge the various histories of Australian film that already exist' and to 'call for a different account of Australian film'. For Moran and O'Regan, the problem with books like Eric Reade's *The Australian Screen* (1975), Andrew Pike and Ross Cooper's *Australian Films 1900–1977* (1980) or Ina Bertrand and Diane Collins's *Government and Film in Australia* (1981) was that they presented Australian film as 'a homogenous object' and offered merely 'an account of linear growth and development'. As critical intellectuals Moran and O'Regan proposed a Foucauldian alternative:

> Australian film is not a single unified object but a series of different objects, differently realised. Australian film can be thought of as a series of different discursive constructions, the discourses occupying a series of different institutional sites that variously allow or impede the issue of that discourse as a set of filmic texts.... There is no evolution or development across time. There is instead a series of different distinct constructions of Australian film having little or nothing in common with each other. (1983: 163)

Two years later, in 1985, Moran and O'Regan showed what this alternative would look like when they published *An Australian Film Reader*. Eschewing a 'definitive authorial voice', the book assembled 'a series of voices about Australian film' and juxtaposed documentary material with historical commentary in order 'to emphasise that issues around the film work of each period were never settled' (1985: 14).

Ina Bertrand is the doyenne of Australian film historians.[6] She has been an advocate for the historiography of Australian film since the 1970s (see for example Bertrand, 1978), and she has the distinction of having presented a paper on Charles Tait's 1906 film *The Story of the Kelly Gang* at the second Film Studies conference in 1981 and then returning to it twenty-five years later at the FHAANZ conference in 2006. Her 1981 book with Diane Collins, *Government and Film in Australia*, was one of those criticized by Moran and O'Regan. What is striking is Bertrand's response. Her monumental 1989 edited collection, *Cinema in Australia: A Documentary History*, avoids their charge of homogenization and teleology by republishing a host of written documents from different periods of Australian film history, giving voice to particular discourses as they arose at any given moment. In the book, discourses such as those around avant-garde cinema, censorship, women's film and exhibition practices form a mosaic of Australian cinema.

In the same year as Bertrand's collection appeared, Moran and O'Regan published a second edited volume, *The Australian Screen* (1989). This presented specialist essays on such topics as early cinema, Aborigines and film, women's film, film in the 1980s, television drama, institutional documentary and independent film and video. What emerges from the interchange between them and Bertrand thus appears to be less a consensus than a degree of convergence and at least a conversation between 'critical intellectual' and 'film historian' perspectives.

At around this time two 'critical intellectuals' rose to prominence who have in different but symptomatic ways engaged with the concerns and personae of both the film historian and the cinephile critics. In 1983, Ross Gibson's 'Camera Natura: Landscape in Australian Feature Films' appeared in *On the Beach*, a journal he had co-founded and edited. Meaghan Morris's 'Tooth and Claw: Tales of Survival, and *Crocodile Dundee'* was first published in *Art & Text* in 1987 and then included in *The Pirate's Fiancee* the following year.

Gibson's essay, revised and republished several times over subsequent years, is a reaction against the so-called 'AFC genre' of the 1970s feature-film Renaissance. Divining a shift in Australian film culture marked by the contrast between the colossal failure of *The Lighthorsemen* (Simon Wincer, 1987)

to connect with audiences and the popular success of George Miller's *Mad Max* films, in 1988 Gibson traced the Australian settler culture's fascination with the landscape back to the masculinist-nationalist impulse that was invoked when whites invaded the Great Southern Land. Drawing on his first book *The Diminishing Paradise* (1984), Gibson understands the landscape cinema of the 1970s and 1980s in relation to the larger history of imaging in writing, painting and photography performed by whites in Australia (see also Gibson, 1992).

In her equally influential essay on the Paul Hogan vehicle *Crocodile Dundee* (Peter Faiman, 1987), Morris invokes Deleuze in order to refute the binary two-industries 'commerce and culture' model of Australian film put forward by Dermody and Jacka (1987; 1988a; see also 1988b). In its place, Morris proposes 'positive unoriginality' as a strategy that sustains the survival of cultural specificity through 'the revision of American cultural codes by Australian [film] texts'. The cultural logic of positive unoriginality is scarcely concealed in a film such as *Crocodile Dundee*, declares Morris: the film's 'borrowings are as clearly displayed as Dundee's outback costume, with its comic mishmash of cowboy/western, bushman/jungle shreds – originating and imitating nothing but a late rural effort at vintage *Bow-wow-wow*' (1987: 43). In this essay, and in others from the period such as Cunningham's 'Hollywood Genres, Australian Movies' (1985) and O'Regan's '*The Man from Snowy River* and Australian Popular Culture' (1985), positive unoriginality – 'the art of combining economic pragmatism with cultural assertion' – somewhat unexpectedly 'acquires a nationalist aura' (1987: 46).[7]

Although both Gibson and Morris were to some degree co-opted by the new cultural studies moment, and their writings on film picked up in academic Film Studies under that rubric, in style their essays tend more towards that of the cinephile criticism being published in some of the more ephemeral film magazines and reviews of the time. Their work thus brings us back to those 'largely ephemeral sites with little or no institutional "standing"', which Adrian Martin described as keeping alive 'a collective dream of marginal criticism' outside the academy (1992b: 7). Across countless review articles and essays and, more recently, in several books, Martin has railed against those 1970s and 1980s accounts that reduce Australian film to purely *national* social and cultural agendas – a politics of representation – and ignore its international flows (initially, American and avant-garde film, but more recently World cinema) and the very form and style that animate both the film object and 'the act of criticism'. Imbuing Australian (inter-national) Film Studies with the vitality and originality of a cinephile-mentor such as Manny Farber, Martin's work demonstrates what is important in thinking and writing seriously about film. It is not so much one's critical agenda, whether that be theoretical or historical, depending on your position. Rather, it is 'the *action* of critical writing, what it can conjure, perform, circulate, transform'. Martin's conclusion can stand as a manifesto for Australian Film Studies: 'In writing as much as in film, we must come to close terms with what is "at once mysterious and materialistic" in matters of style' (1992a: 131).

NOTES

1 A full account of the appearance and development of Australian Film Studies would attend to the various educational contexts that have given Film Studies specific inflection as influenced by critical formations, regional locations and the migration of key personnel.

2 Papers from the 1977 Conference of the Tertiary Screen Education Association of Victoria (TSEA-V) and the First Australian Film Conference (University of New South Wales, 1978) appeared in numbers 4 and 5/6 respectively. Sylvia Lawson wrote on semiotics (no.3), Sam Rohdie on linguistic models (no.4), Barbara Creed and Lesley Stern on feminism and melodrama (no.4) and Tom O'Regan and Albert Moran on Australian cinema (no.15/16). Nos. 111/12 and 13/14 were the special issues on television studies. Overseas contributors included Geoffrey Nowell-Smith, Laura Mulvey, Raymond Bellour and Edward Buscombe.

3 In 1996, the conference moved to even years with a conference at the University of Waikato.

Subsequent events have been held in Brisbane (1998), Wellington (New Zealand Film Archive, 2000), Adelaide (Flinders University, 2002), Canberra (National Film and Sound Archive, 2004), Melbourne (Monash and RMIT Universities, 2006) and the University of Otago in New Zealand (2008).

4 A number of monograph series should be noted in this context. The Australian Film Institute and the Australian Teachers of Media along with Deakin University (Melbourne) initiated the Moving Image series, which included Karen Jennings' *Sites of Difference* (1993) and Felicity Collins' *The Films of Gillian Armstrong* (1999). The Australian Film Commission contracted Marcia Langton's '*Well I Heard it on the Radio and I Saw it on the Television*' (1993) and facilitated Hodsdon's *Straight Roads and Crossed Lines*. Currency Press published an Australian Screen Classics series, most notable in which is Martin's *The Mad Max Movies* (2003).

5 Examples include Lesley Stern's *The Scorsese Connection* (1995) and Sam Rohdie's *The Passion of Pier Paolo Pasolini* (1995) in Colin MacCabe and Paul Willemen's British Film Institute (BFI) Perspectives series; Adrian Martin's *Once Upon a Time in America* (1998) in the BFI Modern Classics series (see Morris, 1998: 688–702), his co-edited *Raul Rúiz: Images of Passage* (2004) with Helen Bandis and Grant McDonald for the Rotterdam Film Festival, and his studies of *Terrence Malick* (2008) in the BFI Filmmakers series and *Brian De Palma* in the Contemporary Film Directors series from University of Illinois Press (2008); George Kouvaros' *Where Does it Happen? John Cassavetes and Cinema at the Breaking Point* (2004) for University of Minnesota Press and *Paul Schrader* (2008) for the Illinois Contemporary Film Directors; Crisp's *The Classic French Cinema 1930–1960* (1997) and *Genre, Myth, and Convention in the French Cinema 1929–1939* (2002) for Indiana University Press; Brian McFarlane's *An Autobiography of British Cinema* (1997), his edited *Encyclopedia of British Film* (2003) and the Wallflower Press's *The Cinema of Britain and Ireland* (2005); Gabrielle Murray's *This Wounded Cinema, This Wounded Life: Violence and Utopia in the Films of Sam Peckinpah* (2004); Lorraine Mortimer's forewords for re-publications of Edgar Morin's *The Stars* (2005b) and *The Cinema, or The Imaginary Man* (2005a) and Meaghan Morris's *Hong Kong Connections: Transnational Imagination in Action Cinema* (edited with Sui Leung Li and Stephen Ching-Kui Chan) (2006).

6 Bertrand's publications such as *Film Censorship in Australia* (1978), *Government and Film in Australia* (Bertrand and Collins, 1981) and *Cinema in Australia: A Documentary History* (1989) have set benchmarks for film historical research. With Routt she has investigated local and international industrial flows and the establishment of the vertically integrated Australasian Films ahead of the First World War (Bertrand and Routt, 1989). Their monograph on

Tait's film – *'The Picture That Will Live Forever': The Story of the Kelly Gang* – accompanies the DVD of the National Film and Sound Archive's partial restoration of the film (2007).

7 The essays of Gibson and Morris also provide a link to contemporary essayistic film and video work by film scholars and intellectuals. Gibson's own 'Camera Natura' became the short film *Camera Natura* (Australia, 1985) with Gibson directing, and writing the shooting script with producer John Cruthers (see Williams, 1996). Helen Grace's *Serious Undertakings* (1983), Laleen Jayamanne's *A Song of Ceylon* (1985), Sarah Gibson and Susan Lambert's *Landslides* (1986), Tracey Moffatt's *Nice Coloured Girls* (1987) and Gillian Leahy's *My Life Without Steve* (1986) were all sponsored by the Australian Film Commission's Creative Development Fund and were associated with the Sydney Film-makers Co-Op. Other relevant films included Philip Brophy's *Salt, Saliva, Sperm and Sweat* (1988), Stuart Cunningham, Susan Charlton and Ross Harley's *One Block From Heaven* (1987), Susan Dermody's *Breathing Under Water* (1991), John Hughes' *Traps* (1985) and *All That Is Solid* (1988), and the Super-8 films of Brophy and Rolando Caputo.

REFERENCES

Bell, Philip (ed.) (1984) 'Special Issue: Papers from the Australian Screen Studies Conference 1984', *Australian Journal of Screen Theory*, 17–18.

Bell, Philip and Crofts, Stephen (eds) (1982) 'Special Issue: Television', *Australian Journal of Screen Theory*, 11–12.

Bell, Philip and Crofts, Stephen (eds) (1983) 'Special Issue: Television', *Australian Journal of Screen Theory*, 13–14.

Berry, Chris (ed.) (1985) *Perspectives on Chinese Cinema*. Ithaca, NY: Cornell University Press.

Berry, Chris (1994) *A Bit on the Side: East-West Topographies of Desire*. Sydney: EmPress Publications.

Berry, Chris, Hamilton, Annette and Jayamanne, Laleen (1996) *The Filmmaker and The Prostitute: Dennis O'Rourke's The Good Woman of Bangkok*. Sydney: Power Publications.

Bertrand, Ina (1978) *Film Censorship in Australia*. St Lucia: University of Queensland Press.

Bertrand, Ina (ed.) (1989) *Cinema in Australia: A Documentary History*. Kensington: University of New South Wales Press.

Bertrand, Ina (2005) ' "Wot's in a name?" and how did we get here from there?', in Marilyn Dooley (ed.), *Credits Rolling! Selected Papers from the 12th Biennial Conference of the Film & History Association of Australia and New Zealand*. Canberra: National Film and Sound Archive.

Bertrand, Ina and Collins, Diane (1981) *Government and Film in Australia*. Sydney: Currency Press.

Bertrand, Ina and Routt, Bill (1989) 'The Fairest Child of the Motherland: Colonialism and Family in Australian Films of the 1920s and 1930s', in Albert Moran and Tom O'Regan (eds), *The Australian Screen*. Melbourne: Penguin. pp. 28–52.

Bertrand, Ina and Routt, Bill (2007) *'The Picture That Will Live Forever': The Story of the Kelly Gang*. In *The Story of the Kelly Gang*. DVD. Canberra: National Film and Sound Archive.

Bordwell, David (1989) *Making Meaning: Inference and Rhetoric in the Interpretation of Cinema*. Cambridge, MA: Harvard University Press.

Collins, Felicity (1983) 'Following the AFI', *Filmnews*, 13(4–5): 4–7, 18.

Collins, Felicity (1984) 'We Aim to Please', *Filmnews*, 14(7): 12–17.

Collins, Felicity (1999) *The Films of Gillian Armstrong*. St Kilda, Victoria: Australian Teachers of Media.

Collins, Felicity and Davis, Therese (2004) *Australian Cinema after Mabo*. Port Melbourne: Cambridge University Press.

Crisp, Colin (1997) *The Classic French Cinema 1930–1960*. Bloomington: Indiana University Press.

Crisp, Colin (2002) *Genre, Myth, and Convention in the French Cinema 1929–1939*. Bloomington: Indiana University Press.

Cunningham, Stuart (1985) 'Hollywood Genres, Australian Movies', in Albert Moran and Tom O'Regan (eds), *An Australian Film Reader*. Sydney: Currency Press. pp. 235–41.

Dermody, Susan and Jacka, Elizabeth (1987) *The Screening of Australia: Anatomy of an Industry*. Sydney: Currency Press.

Dermody, Susan and Jacka, Elizabeth (1988a) *The Screening of Australia: Anatomy of a National Cinema*. Sydney: Currency Press.

Dermody, Susan and Jacka, Elizabeth (1988b) *The Imaginary Industry: Australian Film in the Late '80s*. Sydney: AFTRS.

Foucault, Michel (1972) *The Archaeology of Knowledge*. London: Tavistock.

Frow, John and Morris, Meaghan (eds) (1993) *Australian Cultural Studies: A Reader*. Sydney: Allen and Unwin.

Gerdes, Peter R. (ed.) (1978) 'Special Issue: Papers from the First Australian Film Conference 1978', *Australian Journal of Screen Theory*, 5–6.

Gibson, Ross (1983) 'Camera Natura: Landscape in Australian Feature Films', *On the Beach*, 1: 5–10.

Gibson, Ross (1984) *The Diminishing Paradise*. Sydney: Angus and Robertson.

Gibson, Ross (1988) 'Formative Landscapes', in Scott Murray (ed.), *Back of Beyond: Discovering Australian Film and Television*. Sydney: Australian Film Commission. pp. 20–32.

Gibson, Ross (1992) *South of the West: Postcolonialism and the Narrative Construction of Australia*. Bloomington: Indiana University Press.

Goldsmith, Ben and O'Regan, Tom (2005) *The Film Studio: Film Production in the Global Economy*. Lanham, MD: Rowman and Littlefield.

Herd, Nick (2004) *Chasing the Runaways: Foreign Film Production and Film Studio Development in Australia, 1988–2002*. Sydney: Currency Press.

Hodsdon, Barrett (2001) *Straight Roads and Crossed Lines: The Quest for Film Culture in Australia from the 1960s?* Shenton Park, Western Australia: Bernt Porridge Group.

Jennings, Karen (1993) *Sites of Difference: Cinematic Representations of Aboriginality and Gender*. Melbourne: Australian Teachers of Media/Australian Film Institute.

Kouvaros, George (2004) *Where Does it Happen? John Cassavetes and Cinema at the Breaking Point*. Minneapolis: University of Minnesota Press.

Kouvaros, George (2008) *Paul Schrader*. Urbana: University of Illinois Press.

Langton, Marcia (1993) *'Well I Heard it on the Radio and I Saw it on the Television': An Essay for the Australian Film Commission on the Politics and Aesthetics of Filmmaking by and about Aboriginal People and Things*. North Ryde, New South Wales: Australian Film Commission.

Martin, Adrian (1988) 'No Flowers for the Cinéphile: The Fates of Cultural Populism 1960–1988', in Paul Foss (ed.), *Island in the Stream: Myths of Place in Australian Culture*. Sydney: Pluto Press. pp. 117–38.

Martin, Adrian (1992a) '*Mise en scène* is Dead, or The Expressive, the Excessive, the Technical and the Stylish', *Continuum*, 5(2): 87–140.

Martin, Adrian (1992b) 'S.O.S', *Continuum*, 5(2): 6–14.

Martin, Adrian (1998) *Once Upon a Time in America*. London: BFI.

Martin, Adrian (2003) *The Mad Max Movies*. Sydney: Currency Press.

Martin, Adrian (2008) *Brian De Palma*. Urbana: University of Illinois Press.

Martin, Adrian (2008) *Terrence Malick*. London: BFI.

Martin, Adrian, Bandis, Helen and McDonald, Grant (eds) (2004) *Raul Rúiz: Images of Passage*. Melbourne: Rouge Press.

Martin, Adrian and Caputo, Rolando (1985) 'The State of Film Criticism in Australia', *Filmnews*, 15(1): n.p.

McFarlane, Brian (1997) *An Autobiography of British Cinema*. London: Methuen.

McFarlane, Brian (ed.) (2003) *The Encyclopedia of British Film*. London: Methuen.

McFarlane, Brian (ed.) (2005) *The Cinema of Britain and Ireland*. London: Wallflower Press.

Moran, Albert and O'Regan, Tom (1983) 'Two Discourses of Australian Film', *Australian Journal of Screen Theory*, 15–16: 163–73.

Moran, Albert and O'Regan, Tom (eds) (1985) *An Australian Film Reader*. Sydney: Currency Press.

Moran, Albert and O'Regan, Tom (eds) (1989) *The Australian Screen*. Melbourne: Penguin.

Morris, Meaghan (1983) 'The Practice of Reviewing', *Framework*, 22–3: 52–8.

Morris, Meaghan (1985) 'Fetish Busters in the Temple of Doom', *Filmnews*, 15(2): 5–6.

Morris, Meaghan (1987) 'Tooth and Claw: Tales of Survival, and *Crocodile Dundee*', *Art & Text*, 25: 36–68.

Morris, Meaghan (1988) *The Pirate's Fiancee: Feminism, Reading, Postmodernism*. London: Verso.

Morris, Meaghan (1998) 'On Going to Bed Early: *Once Upon a Time in America*', *Meanjin*, 4: 688–702.

Morris, Meaghan, Sui, Leung Li and Chan, Stephen Ching-Kui (eds) (2006) *Hong Kong Connections: Transnational Imagination in Action Cinema*. Durham, NC: Duke University Press.

Mortimer, Lorraine (2005a) 'Foreword', in Edgar Morin (ed.) *The Cinema, or The Imaginary Man*. Minneapolis: University of Minnesota Press.

Mortimer, Lorraine (2005b) 'Foreword', in Edgar Morin (ed.) *The Stars*. Minneapolis: University of Minnesota Press.

Murray, Gabrielle (2004) *This Wounded Cinema, This Wounded Life: Violence and Utopia in the Films of Sam Peckinpah*. Westport, CT: Praeger.

Murray, Scott (1984) 'A Personal History of *Cinema Papers*', *Cinema Papers*, pp. 41–8.

O'Regan, Tom (1985) '*The Man from Snowy River* and Australian Popular Culture', in Albert Moran and Tom O'Regan (eds), *An Australian Film Reader*. Sydney: Currency. pp. 242–51.

O'Regan, Tom (1996) *Australian National Cinema*. London: Routledge.

Pike, Andrew and Cooper, Ross (1980) *Australian Film 1900–1977: A Guide to Feature Film Production*. Melbourne: Oxford University Press.

Reade, Eric (1975) *The Australian Screen: A Pictorial History of Australian Filmmaking*. Melbourne: Lansdowne.

Rohdie, Sam (1995) *The Passion of Pier Paolo Pasolini*. London: BFI.

Shirley, Graham and Adams, Brian (1989) *Australian Cinema: The First Eighty Years*. Rev. edn. Sydney: Currency Press/Angus and Robertson.

Stern, Lesley (1995) *The Scorsese Connection.* London: BFI.

Thoms, Albie (1978) *Polemics for a New Cinema: Writings to Stimulate New Approaches to Film.* Sydney: Wild and Woolley.

Tulloch, John (1981) *Legends on the Screen: The Narrative Film in Australia 1919–1929.* Sydney: Currency Press.

Tulloch, John (1982) *Australian Cinema: Industry, Narrative and Meaning.* Sydney: Allen and Unwin.

Tulloch, John and Turner, Graeme (eds) (1989) *Australian Television: Programs, Pleasures and Politics.* Sydney: Allen and Unwin.

Williams, Deane (1996) *Mapping the Imaginary: Ross Gibson's Camera Natura.* The Moving Image, 4. Melbourne: ATOM.

9

Postcolonial and Transnational Perspectives

Bhaskar Sarkar

Taking Gayatri Chakravorty Spivak's evaluative statement, 'The best of postcolonialism is autocritical' (2000: xv), as a necessary injunction, this overview begins with an interrogation of its two principal terms, 'postcolonial' and 'transnational', and of the implications of their juxtaposition. Contrary to what this grouping might suggest, the terms – whether as analytical categories, ideological 'isms', or as historical experiences – are neither coeval, nor necessarily antithetical: one does not simply lead up to or negate the other. The postcolonial indexes lifeworlds, sections of which continue to be external to the transnational: to presume that the former is being completely subsumed by the transnational would be to erase these lifeworlds altogether. Such a supposition would take us back to a Hegelian epistemology, retooled for our times: if, in an earlier era, to be acknowledged as an agent of World History one had to possess national consciousness, now basic recognition requires the stamp of transnationality.

Much recent scholarship in Film Studies, awash in the oceanic promises of neoliberal globalization and an unmitigated techno-determinism, breathlessly proclaims the end of the postcolonial and the national, just as it engages in polemics about the death of cinema. In an increasingly unified intellectual endorsement of the core logic of capital – the endless production of novelty (new improved detergents, cereals, fashions, toys, technologies, models) – a large number of academics have called for new categories and paradigms, without always establishing convincingly, beyond the glibly evident, why we need such rethinking and re-articulation. The new assemblages surely demand innovative conceptualizations; but the problem is in a kind of academic new ageism that tends to dismiss earlier structures, processes and theories – as if the past is done with, and has no bearings on the present or the future. Meanwhile, the banal proliferation of the obsolete and the disposable – dead technologies, dead media forms, dead tastes, dead critical approaches – have produced a series of spectral doubles for film (and television [and video] and new [and digital {and wireless}] media) studies, leading to a disciplinary 'crisis'. This haunted cultural-epistemological field indexes, beyond all presumptions of a linear progression, the anachronistic interpenetrations of media forms and paradigms, experientialities and publics, and their uneven spatio-temporal distribution. The uneasy spectrality, an endemic condition of (colonial) modernity, intimates the problems presented by a celebratory transnationalism unhinged from a critical postcolonial optic, not the least of which is a global regime of knowledge production closely complicit with the imperialist moulding of a monolithic World History.

The present chapter proceeds from two deliberate choices. The first section of this Handbook, an admittedly partial inventory of national and regional cinemas and film cultures, has had to leave out certain cinematic 'traditions' (for instance, Japanese and Arab cinemas). The exclusion of African cinema, in particular, has ramifications for this overview. The gap evokes, wittingly or not, a particular Film Studies genealogy (resistance to colonialism ⇒ postcolonial nationalisms and cultures ⇒ Third Cinema as an oppositional movement arising in the global South) that subsumes all of African cinema under the sign of 'postcolonial resistance'; thus, in spite of the evidence of recent scholarship (Shafik, 2007; Ukadike, 2003), popular Egyptian and Maghrebi cinemas or Nigerian and Ghanaian video productions continue to be marginalized within our discipline. Such a genealogy might raise an expectation that this overview of postcolonial and transnational perspectives would 'cover' African cinema(s). This essay eschews such token coverage as it would only reproduce structures of thought that deny the continent of Africa, conceived in the modern era as a terrain of lack, the possibility of any consciousness or culture except as a horizon of radical alterity (Mudimbe, 1988). A facile inclusiveness would constitute, epistemologically speaking, a further erasure of Africa. Secondly, in what

follows, the focus is on cinema – but broadly construed to accommodate recent techno-economic and socio-political transformations commonly placed under the rubric of 'media convergence'.

FROM POSTCOLONIAL TO TRANSNATIONAL?

The postcolonial and the transnational are both spatio-temporal categories: each indexes an historical break marking a before and an after, and simultaneously conjures up a geopolitical topography. To situate the terms in relation to each other, one might begin with their embeddedness in the history of capitalist modernity. If imperialism refers to the gradual and relentless expansion of a capitalist system across the planet, then colonialism – the annexation of other people's territories by imperial powers for the commandeering of resources – is, like slavery, an early stage in that history. But even after territorial decolonization, widespread expropriation is sustained through international economic, political and legal systems. In the face of contemporary neocolonial exploitation, the two components of the 'postcolonial' imply both continuity and a beyond (Loomba, 2005). An anti-colonial project is still relevant to a global struggle against imperialism, against exclusionary hegemonies and against cultural colonization. Thus, the postcolonial is best understood as both an historical stage, and a generalized political stance.

The field of postcolonial studies is found to be vexing in many intellectual quarters. If the ideological Right is threatened by its anti-imperialist critical polemics, segments of the Left question its strong connections to Western academia, especially its debts to poststructuralist theory's radical anti-foundationalism (which makes it difficult to mobilize political community and action) and focus on textuality (which appears to place concrete reality under erasure). The field's dispersed institutional locations (from Australia to Mexico, from South Africa to the Netherlands) and disciplinary ties (anthropology and history, literary studies and art history), with divergent – even incommensurate – genealogies and research protocols, concerns and commitments, resist efficacious parsing or characterization. But this fuzziness, this porosity, is also a measure of postcolonialism's broad and ongoing relevance: the discourse enjoys strong resonances and productive intersections with critical race theory (JanMohamed and Lloyd, 1991), indigenous studies (Povinelli, 2002), feminism (Spivak, 1988), queer criticism (Arondekar, forthcoming), globalization studies (Slater, 2004) and an emergent ecocriticism (Guha and Martinez-Alier, 1997).

According to some critics, the oft-rehearsed debates between historical-materialist approaches and poststructuralist paradigms, between Western and non-Western sites of knowledge production, between social science and humanities methodologies – debates that once energized postcolonial studies – seem to have largely exhausted themselves. They suggest that translocal perspectives, in the flexibility they afford beyond limiting antinomies, might bring new vigour to critical discourse. But the local and wildly divergent invocations of 'global' or 'transnational' underscore the continuing necessity of attending to the geopolitics of intellectual labour. And the more recent disciplinary formation of globalization studies cannot supplant the critical acuity of postcolonial discourse: the former frequently celebrates neocolonialism, and the latter remains particularly adroit in challenging cultural colonization. That so many academics are intent on jettisoning postcolonialism may well be a mark of its continuing power to provoke, to put pressure on epistemological certitudes that shore up geopolitical hierarchies. Indeed, this intellectual antagonism accompanies privatization, deregulation, 'increased poverty and infrastructure failure' in the global South and 'huge transfers of wealth from the South to the North in the form of debt payment and repackaging' – shifts that Mark Driscoll describes as components of a 'reverse postcoloniality' (2004: 60).

A conflation of postcolonialism with decolonizing nationalisms produces the common perception of an adversarial relation between the postcolonial and the transnational. Yet others argue that colonial encounters and postcolonial dispersion and hybridization pave the way for transnational formations. In what sense can we relate, if not reconcile, these polar viewpoints? Nationalism provided the emotive and utopian basis for the bureaucratic modern state, which became necessary at an early stage of capitalism to enforce private property rights, maintain market institutions and uphold legal arrangements. In colonial contexts, the practical needs of the state came into conflict with the utopian promises of nationalism: decolonizing nationalisms were born of these contradictions. Over time, the ossification of unifying essentialisms, once crucial to a nascent collective consciousness, led to structures of oppression and marginalization. Totalitarian tendencies, endemic corruption and rent-seeking behaviour further attenuated the legitimacy of nationalism. Already in the late 1950s, in the heydays of decolonization, Frantz Fanon (1965) was deeply troubled by the power-mongering of the comprador bourgeoisie in the post-colonies, who were vitiating the goal of emancipation by merely replacing the departing colonial machinery with their own networks of exploitation. As Fanon (1967) saw it, the roots of this disillusionment lay in the acute depersonalization produced by the colonial negation of blackness and the simultaneous internalization or 'epidermalization' of a European consciousness by the black (for Fanon, male) subject who donned a 'white mask' over his 'black skin'. Subsequent interventions from neocolonial forces and international agencies undermined economic and political sovereignties from Argentina to Zaire, reducing postcolonial liberation to mere 'flag independence' in many cases. On the other hand, persistent global inequities and an intensifying international division of labour have set in motion trans-border flows and presented opportunities for translocal social movements. Thus, postcolonial thought has had to reckon with both domestic and external troubles, adopting positions ranging from the staunchly nationalist to the critically transnational.

Nationalism was discredited as parochial, and a cosmopolitan humanism upheld as the core of progressive values, precisely at a point when decolonizing movements were gathering force: hence the postcolonial suspicion of cosmopolitanism with its roots in post-Enlightenment idealism. Nationalism remains a potent force in our transnational era, and not only in a backward 'Third World': witness the constant rhetoric of German or US patriotism, and the unrestrained jingoism during the Olympics. Even for critics of the nation state, any alternative political community or organization is not self-evident. Can cosmopolitan realms of belonging, transnational justice movements and various institutions of a global civil society (such as non-governmental organizations and legal advocacy coalitions) adequately represent local or subaltern interests in an increasing unilateral world? These seem to be most effective when they are rooted in local concerns, and utilize local resources and passions in tandem with transnational networks and protocols. On the other hand, large masses of people do not enjoy the fruits of trans-border mobility, nor can they avail of global standards and institutions. Indeed, emerging global players such as China, South Korea or Brazil embrace a rootless cosmopolitan ideal, and assume a global chic, to attract foreign and expatriate capital and expertise: while elite groups attain stratospheric levels of income and luxury, the bulk of their populations have to bear the brunt of the costs of structural adjustments. As Masao Miyoshi (1993) claims, the transnational is qualitatively different from the international or the multinational, in that the former designates a situation in which huge corporations transcend their national roots and become dedicated, full-time engines of global capital. Fantasies of connectivity and oneness, encapsulated in the rhetoric of a 'global village', serve to mask this ground-level reality. Many nation states are still able to deflect the pressures of globalization, to substantially recalibrate planetary scripts and trends. Nevertheless, national regimes and institutions become increasingly more complicit with – even subservient to – global capital, bringing about their own partial erasure: a condition Pheng Cheah (1999) refers to as 'spectral nationality'.

Often used interchangeably with more established categories such as 'world' (as in 'world literature'), 'international' (as in 'international relations') and 'global' (as in 'global citizen'), the nomenclature 'transnational' is in need of clarification in order to muster any analytical potency: we need to identify what is new about it, not just in terms of its heightened reach or intensity, but also qualitatively speaking. In particular, it is necessary to track and interrogate emergent translocal institutions, flows, processes, subjectivities, affiliations and constellations of power. Arjun Appadurai's work, particularly his 1990 essay 'Disjuncture and Difference in the Global Cultural Economy', lays out an innovative approach to mapping these new formations, these transnational spatial imaginations, as 'scapes' of ethnic communities, financial systems, enclaves of ideas, technological networks and media circuits. His emphasis on 'imagination' as 'the key component of the new global order' has had great appeal for cultural theorists in general, and media scholars in particular, although he has been criticized for downplaying materiality (see Wayne, 2002: 123). However, Appadurai's initial polemic against a social scientific obsession with regularities and structures, in favour of a fluid conception of global flows and practices, does not preclude a situated, materialist approach. Faye Ginsburg, for instance, adopts the notion of mediascapes, Appadurai's term for 'the different kinds of global cultural flows created by new media technologies and the images created with them', to produce a 'situated analysis' of 'the interdependence' of Australian Aboriginal 'media practices with the local, national and transnational circumstances that surround them'. She demonstrates how this approach demarcates 'a more generative discursive space' for Aboriginal media production, allowing her to highlight 'the specific situatedness' of such cultural labour without 'the fetishizing of the local' (1994: 366).

More recently, the term 'global assemblages' has gained wide currency, especially among anthropologists of globalization. 'Assemblage', which conjures up a sense of the plastic, the networked and the novel, carries within it the sedimentation of an array of earlier attempts to capture nascent formations, including Raymond Williams' invocation of the 'emergent', Gilles Deleuze and Félix Guattari's notion of 'machinic assemblages', Ernesto Laclau and Chantal Mouffe's 'articulation' and Manuel Castells' 'network society'. The term might refer to the political promises and socio-cultural tribulations of 'flexible citizenship' within diasporic ethnic communities and mobile business and managerial classes (Aihwa, 1999); the translocal 'cultures of expertise' that are employed in the 'management of globalization', for instance in dealing with conditions of contingency and uncertainty when 'contradiction, exception, facts that are fugitive' cannot be apprehended by 'the reigning statistical mode of analysis' (Holmes and Marcus, 2006: 237); or to the global traffic of human organs and the emergence of a post-human ethics involving organ transplant and scarcity (Scheper-Hughes, 2006). Global assemblages include not simply hegemonic transnational regimes associated with the World Bank, the International Monetary Fund (IMF) or the World Trade Organization (WTO), but also subaltern mobilizations and 'transnationalism from below' embodied in the Green Movement and the World Social Forum.

FILM STUDIES AND THE POLITICS OF INTELLECTUAL LABOUR

A cursory look through our field's leading journals, books and conference panels reveals extensive references to postcolonial frameworks, but their implications have not been integrated enough to produce essential transformations. Many of the fundamental disciplinary shibboleths, questionable at best

when not outright offensive to a postcolonial sensibility, continue to inform our field. Thus, it remains necessary and instructive to rehash certain analytical gestures that congealed by the mid-1990s, and now appear to inspire, within postcolonial anthropology, literary studies, or history, all the excitement of dead-end homilies.

The mainstream of cinema studies continues to be enthralled with Hollywood. Most scholarship that deploys postcolonial and transnational frameworks retains Hollywood as a putative norm, reducing every other cinematic tradition to its satellite that emulates, aspires to or resists it. In this 'relational' world (to take a poststructuralist buzzword with great critical purchase), the relationality is, ultimately, in reference to a singular centre: only the margins are reserved for all parallel formations with their own aesthetic genealogies and local social concerns. Colonial representations and diasporic mediations garner an inordinate share of critical attention; when the focus is on other national cinemas, they are quickly consigned to the peripheries as quirky exceptions. Transnational film circuits that do not involve Hollywood continue to be ignored, unless they are framed as a cinema of resistance: Third Cinema remains a prime example (see Pines and Willemen, 1989). But this constant reiteration of Hollywood as the dominant film industry, even if true in terms of its business clout and cultural influence, becomes something of a cliché that forecloses investigations of other significant translocal cinematic channels and publics (say, Hong Kong cinema's hegemony in Asia, or Hindi cinema's popularity in the Arab world and in East Africa). So assured is the effective hold of this 'Hollywood over the rest' perspective on our field that it is impossible to use its categories and paradigms and be able to talk about 'other', 'alternative', 'non-Hollywood' cinemas without lapsing precisely into such marginalizing categories.

To harp on the centrality of Hollywood in Film Studies (either approvingly or critically) is to risk the reproduction of a certain essentialist polarity – a problem that marks much work on colonialist ideology and representation, including Edward Said's seminal book *Orientalism* (1979) on the discursive production of a reductive and stereotypical orient as the passive object of Western curiosity and mastery. Said's nuanced exegesis of imperial discourse produces the notion of a unified, self-same Europe; it thus constitutes a kind of critical Occidentalism that was, nonetheless, a polemical necessity at the time, and that staked out for such critique a central place within cultural theory. Drawing on Antonio Gramsci's theory of building consensus and hegemony through the institutions of civil and political societies, and adopting Michel Foucault's conception of discourse (as a knowledge set comprising what is articulated, what gets left out, and the institutions regulating these enunciations and erasures) and the equivalence he posited between the formation of knowledge and the generation of power, Said demonstrated the ways in which a colonial imaginary and its disciplinary bulwarks (colonial geography, colonial anthropology and so on) produced and maintained hierarchies and relations of power. Colonial knowledge, in its 'disinterested objectivity', legitimized imperialist interests and projects by purveying rationales for them (including the notorious 'white man's burden' thesis). He also revealed the constitutive, if latent, traces of an orientalist episteme in (post)colonial subjectivities and knowledge structures.

Said's contrapuntal readings, with their focus on discursive and textual formations and their trenchant attentiveness to the fear of, and fascination for, the Other, provided a powerful methodology for text-oriented disciplines such as literary studies, art history and Film Studies. Scholars such as Ella Shohat and Robert Stam (1994) and Fatimah Tobing-Rony (1996) have explored the cinematic production of a colonial worldview in which romance and desire consistently seep into objectivity: space is mapped out in terms of exotic fantasies about the New World and the Dark Continent, the sensuousness of the oriental harem and the savagery of the desert nomads; entire lifeworlds are compressed into modules of facts and artefacts and put on display in museums (Egyptology's mummies and Indology's sculptures being salient examples); ethnographic films produce spectacles of distant (non-European) populations as a panoply of racialized, gendered, sexualized and, ultimately, infantilized stereotypes. Recent scholarship has built on this work to engage pre-cinematic visual cultures and early mass cultural sites like exhibitions, world fairs, and science and technology expos (Griffith, 2001), and also colonial documentaries (travelogues and instructional films) related to automobile technology, hygiene and colonial landscapes (Bloom, 2008).

Historians of imperialism have explored the mutual constitution of the colonizer and the colonized, focusing on the mechanisms of exclusion and inclusion, myriad negotiations, and the gradual elaboration of a bourgeois order in both metropolitan and colonial societies (Cooper and Stoler, 1997). Continuing in this vein of interrogating colonial interpenetrations, and shifting the focus to the cusp of the colonial and the postcolonial, Priya Jaikumar (2006) examines the cultural endgames of empire when the British colonial project in South Asia had already lost its moral legitimacy and political efficacy. The interaction between film regulations and film aesthetics (involving markets, genres, censorship, realism and modernism) articulated the shifting imperial relations: from governmentality to redemption of empire, and finally to autonomy. These transformations defined the future contours of the British and Indian film industries, and their relations to Hollywood and to the British and Indian states. Thus, Jaikumar traces persistent colonial structures back to the discourses and to the inter-industry and state-industry relations of late empire.

With territorial decolonization, the postcolonies faced the task of dismantling the material and psychic structures of imperialism. In particular, cultural sectors had to take on the project of 'decolonizing the mind', a project that had already begun with nationalist liberation movements (Gabriel, 1982; Ngugi wa Thiong'o, 1986). Central to this project were questions of subject for-mation, nation-building and nationalist ped-agogy, aesthetic and political representation. The recovery of marginalized modes of sociality, of erased experiences and traditions, and of discounted modes of historiography was crucial to the exigency of countering the self-justificatory myths of Eurocentric (and, in the case of East Asia, Japanese) imperialism, including the inscription of its Others in perpetual lack, and the inexorable denouement of a universal History (Fanon, 1965; Landy, 1996). The mobilization of anti-imperialist political action, the consolidation of communities, and the continuing struggle for social justice became the preoccupations of postcolonial film cultures.

An agenda of politicized cultural inter-vention with an eye to social transforma-tion was most clearly articulated around Third Cinema (Solanas and Getino, 1976), envisioned as an innovative, robust and combative alternative to 'first' or commercial-industrial (consumerist) cinema and 'second' or art cinema of bourgeois interiority (effete aestheticism). Articulating a possibility of transnational cultural cooperation on behalf of the global South around a model of resistance, Third Cinema mobilized itself in terms of a series of polemical dichotomies: integrity versus selling out, challenging versus pandering, education versus entertainment, passive complicity versus active struggle. The very 'problems' besetting Third Cinema – poverty, scarcity, lack of resources and train-ing, urgency and rawness – were embraced as its strengths in the various rhetorics of 'imperfect cinema' (Julio García Espinosa), 'cinema of hunger' (Glauber Rocha), 'cinema of underdevelopment' (Fernando Birri), 'rev-olutionary cinema' (Jorge Sanjinés) (Pines and Willemen, 1989). These early mani-festos were elaborated into garbage cin-ema, guerilla cinema and cannibal-tropicalist cinema. Third Cinema's origins, objectives, accomplishments and entanglements have been widely documented and evaluated (Guneratne and Dissanayake, 2003; Oubiña, this volume; Pines and Willemen, 1989); however, a few salient points are worth

recounting. Third Cinema is best understood as a loose paradigm of counter cinema (or a cinema of negation) aiming not only to dis-mantle colonial legacies, but also to challenge neocolonial pressures and an exploitative centralization of power. This homogenizing emphasis on a combative alterity ultimately concedes a referential centrality to that which it is supposed to oppose. Meanwhile, Third Cinema's oppositional status is complicated in practice by the facts of institutional and financial assistance by the state (for example, in Cuba), and by ex-colonizers (French aid for the cinemas of Senegal and Tunisia, for instance). The relentlessly masculinist articulations of Third Cinema align it with a mainstream heteropatriarchy. Produced by well-meaning (usually middle class, educated, male) urban filmmakers obsessed with subaltern subjects, the films are often notoriously pedantic, an attribute that limits their audiences.

It is not possible to reduce Third Cinema to specific national contexts, marked as it is by significant globalist impulses: Fanon's call for a genuine form of political, mate-rial and psychic liberation; Marxist cultural theory (specifically a Brechtian aesthetics of estrangement); influence of socialist real-ism, and even of neorealism. FESPACO, the biennial international film festival in Burkina Faso, emerged as an important transnational forum for coalition building, and as an alternative channel for distri-bution and exhibition. In their inaugural manifesto, Fernando Solanas and Octavio Getino (1976) included certain filmmaking practices of the industrialized nations within the ambit of Third Cinema. Nevertheless, as Paul Willemen (1989) argued, Third Cinema was frequently grounded in local struggles (against Latin American dictator-ships, Filipino and Senegalese elite classes, Indian landlords and industrialists) of the postcolonies. Extrapolating from these two seemingly incongruous tendencies, it is pos-sible to situate Third Cinema as an instance of rooted cultural cosmopolitanism.

Largely because of its associations with familiar analytical and aesthetic canons, and its resonances with Western social movements of the 1960s, Third Cinema enjoyed critical currency within metropolitan cultural theories, and came to stand in for a far wider and more popular set of filmmaking practices all over the so-called 'third world', notwithstanding the former's disdain for, and outright hostility towards, commercially-oriented cinemas. This conflation was possible because, until the mid-1980s, popular cinemas from developing countries were either consigned to critical oblivion or misrecognized as cinemas of negation because of their formal difference from Western filmmaking traditions. This preoccupation with imputed counter cinemas from the 'third world' was shaped largely by Western fantasies about oppositional cultural politics springing forth from geopolitical peripheries. The US-based Third World Newsreel embodies this tendency in its singular focus on radical independent media dealing with social issues relating to people of colour in developing nations and diasporic communities. Such grafting together of Third Cinema and 'third world' or postcolonial cinemas is responsible for the marginalization of various popular cinemas. At the other extreme, the confusion leads to the occlusion of Third Cinema theory and praxis from many recent accounts of film theory and postcolonial film cultures: nowadays, filmmaking practices of the 'third world', diasporic and marginalized communities apparently subsume Third Cinema (Guneratne, 2003: 4).

More than a hint of this conflation (not to mention a projected fantasy of oppositionality) is present in Fredric Jameson's writings on third world literature and film (1986; 1992), his privileged figures being modernist and politicized auteurs such as Lu Xun, Ousmane Sembene, Kidlat Tahimik and Edward Yang. As Vilashini Cooppan points out (2004: 17–18), we notice in Jameson a homology of the antinomies first world/third world, global/national, bourgeois individualism/collectivism, and a simultaneous recognition of the embeddedness of third world national cultures in global processes – particularly, their 'life-and-death

struggle with first world cultural imperialism – a cultural struggle that is itself a reflexion of the economic situation of such areas in their penetration by various stages of capital' (Jameson, 1986: 68). Jameson sees this struggle mapped in the obsessively allegorical figurations of third world literature. Ultimately, his objective is to locate a 'geopolitical aesthetic' that produces a 'cognitive mapping' of a global totality, however fragmented and opaque (1992). Thus, in spite of its essentializing characterization of all third world literature as national allegories, Jameson's analysis is valuable for stressing the links between postcolonial nationalisms and global formations. His influence is evident in explorations of the cultural politics of an allegorical mode within various national contexts – from Brazilian cinema's 'allegories of underdevelopment' in which scarcity is productively transformed into a signifier (Xavier, 1997), to Chinese fifth generation filmmakers' allegories 'of the social landscape' in the wake of the Cultural revolution and economic liberalization (Zhang, 1997).

Not all postcolonial cinemas are primarily about resistance to global capital, Eurocentrism, or bourgeois paradigms of filmmaking: popular films involve far more modulated negotiations with these hegemonic structures. Even an allegorical mode may have to do less with a struggle against imperialism than with historically contingent local concerns: for instance, Indian popular cinema's flight to allegory in mediating the collective trauma of national partition (Sarkar, forthcoming). Nevertheless, to the extent that colonial modernity remains constitutive of the material and psychic structures in the postcolonies, fundamental schisms continue to animate the politics of cultural production. Thus, cinema's mediation of postcolonial projects of nationhood has had to contend with the interpenetrations of racist structures and class differences in Cuba or Mexico (Chanan, 2004; Paranagua, 1996; 2003); questions of cultural pedagogy, citizenship and subalternity in relation to the national-popular (tensions captured with respect to Indian cinema in Ashish Nandy's notion of popular cinema as a 'slum's eye view of politics' [1999], in Sumita Chakravarty's trope of cultural 'impersonation' [1994] and Madhav Prasad's identification of 'an aesthetics of mobilization' [2001]). Scholars examine the spectral jostling of incommensurate epistemologies and non-synchronous temporalities in recent Indian writing in English (Ghosh, 2004), and in Asian ghost films (Lim, 2001). Ackbar Abbas tracks the dislocations and disorientations wrought by the entanglements of imperialism and globalism in contemporary Hong Kong. Something about Hong Kong reality and subjectivity is always on the verge of getting lost, but its trace remains – like the bamboo scaffoldings on the construction sites of post-modern high-rise buildings. The city becomes a space of *dis*appearance: marked not by the absence of appearances, but by an *uneasy* appearance. 'History now goes through strange loops and becomes difficult to represent in terms of traditional realism... Hence the frequent excesses and exaggerations of the new Hong Kong cinema: they register a sense of the incredible as real' (Abbas, 1997: 16–17).

The category of national cinema became central to Film Studies with its institutionalization in North American universities in the late 1960s (following the popularity of Italian neorealism, French New Wave and Italian modernism – the golden age of 'foreign films' in the US). At that point, the national was not so much a structure as a descriptive and organizing term. Film historians presumed the unity of national character and culture: hence the cinema of a particular nation was supposed to reflect its collective sensibility, its spirit. The national emerged as a problematic within Film Studies in the late eighties, when mounting multiculturalist pressures in the US and Great Britain brought its problems to the fore. Poststructuralist difference and problems of immigration inspired more complicated models of 'national culture' that saw it not as having a stable referent, but as a culturally constructed and deeply contested field where notions of national patrimony, heritage, tradition, authentic identity and community were being constantly debated. In the 1990s, with

the rising tides of globalization, the sense of an inside clearly marked from an outside became difficult to sustain: the emphasis shifted to the transnational dimensions of the production, distribution and reception of any national cinema (Higson, 2000; Miller et al., 2005). Communications technologies from satellite television to the Internet conjured up new terrains of affiliation and identity beyond national borders and standard territorialities (Crang et al., 1999; Morley and Robins, 1989).

A shift from nationalism to transnationalism has multiple implications for cinema studies (and for media studies in general). At the very least, we need to distinguish between (a) globalizing the terms and paradigms of film theory and criticism, and (b) theorizing global formations.

Film theory, in its focus on medium specificity, built a supposedly general theory drawing on the evidence of Western national cinematic traditions. Other cinemas remained precisely that: marginalized alternatives to the global norm, curious exceptions that only proved the universal rule. How do we move beyond these limitations? Certain pointers have been in operation for quite some time now, in the guise of questions and controversies that have continued to vex film scholarship. One such concern involves the cross-cultural critical apprehension of cultural forms, including the legibility of various national cinemas in their encounter with Western models and methodologies, and their place in film theory and history. The anxiety regarding the application of Western theory (a master narrative) to non-Western cinemas (aberrant supplements), an anxiety that is rooted in the opposition Self/Other, was first articulated around the study of Japanese cinema. Mitsuhiro Yoshimoto (1991) provides a useful critical map of this debate. While Noël Burch idealizes Japanese cinema, following Roland Barthes into 'an empire of signs' dissociated from the materiality of social life, and thus coincident with universal theory, and David Bordwell seeks to appropriate Yasujiro Ozu as a modernist auteur on account of his 'defiance' of Classical Hollywood cinema principles, Peter Lehman criticizes such approaches for completely ignoring the relevance of Japanese aesthetic traditions to an assessment of Ozu's oeuvre. Lehman, in turn, proceeds from a Eurocentric and art historical understanding of modernism: as Yoshimoto argues, the question is not whether Ozu was a (European-style) modernist but, rather, what might be the contours of a specifically Japanese modernism (1991: 244). He also points out the operative binary general theory/ contingent history, which produces a further polarity between a film theory approach (privileging trans-cultural frameworks) and area studies model (stressing deep immersion in, and mastery of, cultural specificities). It is this opposition that comes into play in E. Ann Kaplan's reflexive essay on the problematic of studying Chinese cinema without erasing its specificities (1989). Kaplan suggests that the limitations from her lack of familiarity with the Chinese context are somewhat offset by the objectivity afforded by her distance. Thus, as Yoshimoto points out, she counterposes a distant and somewhat disengaged critical mastery to another form of scholarly expertise achieved through conscientious immersion in the local, conducting what Spivak describes as an arrogant production of the Other through the collection of information (1988). One might add that this second form of mastery is tied up with the primary impetus behind the inauguration of the area studies model: imperialist intelligence. In sum, as long as the anxious discourse about cross-cultural analysis is predicated on the Self/Other dichotomy, Film Studies cannot hope to move beyond its implicit orientalism.

Kaplan's intervention came at a point when, following China's 'opening up' to the forces of globalization, and the emergence of the 'fifth generation' filmmakers, anxieties about cross-cultural analysis were played out with respect to Chinese cinema. Rey Chow (1991) questioned the very notion of a radically other Chinese culture, claiming that 'Chinese' and 'Western' were dialectically interactive. She also argued in favour of moving beyond the binary opposition of 'Western theory' as subject and 'Chinese cinema' as object, so that the mutually constitutive relation between the two categories could be explored. Both she and Esther Yau (1987–88) stressed the mutability of film theory and practice. They also challenged the equation of China with tradition and the West with modernity, calling for a more complicated conceptualization of Chinese modernity that would capture its convolutions, and what Ernst Bloch (1977) might call its 'synchronicity of the non-synchronous' (see also Donald and Voci in this volume).

The Film Studies debate over China at that particular conjuncture (late 1980s–early 1990s), while advancing our understanding about the stakes of cross-cultural analysis, accompanies China's rise as a global economic power. In that sense, the debate presages current discourses around the global ascendancy of 'Bollywood' following India's economic liberalization, and paves the way for possibly more supple theorizations of translocal industrial, aesthetic and epistemological interpenetrations. The point here is that the production of intellectual discourse, the shifting paradigms, the fresh insights are all elements of a global system largely driven by the logic of capital: there is no pure critical 'there' outside of the space of capital. The shift to transnationalism, and frames of analysis that champion the hybrid and the plastic, are significant components of capitalist globalization.

Among postcolonial theorists, Homi Bhabha consistently nudges us beyond all kinds of binarisms – Self/Other, first world/ third world, theory/politics – and locates culture in the interstitial or 'third' spaces between competing structures, incommensurate experiences and polarized frameworks. Foregrounding migrancy and liminality, Bhabha (1989) explores subjectivities, positionalities and cultural formations that are in the continual process of becoming: resisting foreclosure and maintaining constant critical vigilance constitute his 'commitment to theory'. Grafting Lacanian psychoanalytic models and deconstructive methodologies to Fanon's psycho-Marxist take on colonial ambivalence, Bhabha examines the mechanisms of racial and cultural othering (in 'The Other Question' [1983], an essay first published in *Screen*), and the contradictions of a colonial civilizing mission paving the way for cultural performance and political negotiation (in 'Of Mimicry and Man' [1984]). But the analytic charge of Bhabha's work is reduced mainly to the notion of hybridity: his detractors criticize him for privileging psychic structures over material conditions (although most Marxists are liable of an inverted hierarchy), and for romanticizing the liminal subject whose ideal embodiment appears to be the cosmopolitan intellectual residing in the West (see Lazarus, 1993).

While Bhabha's writings have had a profound influence on Film Studies since the late 1980s, a focus on hybridity has to contend with the concrete specificity of the cinematic sign: in spite of the polysemic nature of representation, actual place trumps analytic 'third space'. This return of the real *qua* geophysical site raises questions about the locational politics of otherwise salutary interventions in Film Studies that proceed from hybridity and the fluid analytic possibilities presented by it: for instance, scholarship on (a) the constitutive presence of colonial experience in the contemporary identities and cultures of erstwhile colonial powers, (b) mediations of immigrant populations in host countries and (c) diasporic filmmakers. The thrust of all these approaches, which is to overcome the essentializing and homogenizing elements of both colonial and anti-colonial epistemologies, is, no doubt, a productive tendency. Thus, to point out the centrality of colonial Others to the self-constructions of French or British nationalisms is to destabilize the subjective autonomy and coherence of imperialist powers. Kristin Ross (1996) brilliantly interrogates the disavowal of the anguish of decolonization, and the spectral presence of Indochina and the Maghreb, in 1950s and 1960s French structuralist theory and mainstream cinema. More recent scholarship examines projections of the Balkans or Turkey in western European films (Diaconescu-Blumenfeld, 2003). Insightful studies about Beur cinema, Black British Cinema, films about Asian-Americans and Hispanic-Americans, African, Arab and Turkish populations in Germany have enriched our understanding of migrant subjectivities and experiences in relation to host societies. However, these approaches tenaciously bring the focus back to the US or to Europe.

Hamid Naficy (2001) provides one of the most materially grounded approaches to hybrid cultural forms and practices. He stresses the commonalities of films produced by displaced (exilic and diasporic) people and focuses on the 'interstitial and artisanal' mode of production of what he calls 'accented' cinemas. Following Deleuze and Guattari's formulation of a 'minor' literature (marked by 'the deterritorialization of language, the connection of the individual to a political immediacy, and the collective assemblage of enunciation'), Naficy characterizes 'accented' cinema as:

> driven by its own limitations, that is, by its smallness, imperfection, amateurishness, and lack of cinematic gloss (many of the films are low-tech shorts with extremely low budgets and small crew and casts). It is also driven, in the exemplars of the style, by the style's textual richness and narrative inventiveness (deterritorialized language). (2001: 45)

Themes of dislocation, looking for a new home, and yearning to return home mobilize a dialectic of wholeness and loss. The simultaneous precariousness *and* promises of liminal subjectivities are intimated through autobiographical gestures, authorial voice-overs, presence of filmmakers in front of the camera, and epistolary forms. Space and spatial tropes take centre stage to mediate deterritorialization; performative aspects (reflexivity, doubling, masquerade) initiate a politics of intersubjectivity and empathy.

The category of 'accented' cinema allows Naficy to circumvent the problems associated with 'Third Cinema', although the latter's impact (as well as the influence of Teshome Gabriel's work) remains palpable. What are the effects of such a shift in critical focus to 'exilic and diasporic' modes of filmmaking, besides the invaluable attention brought to bear upon in-between lifeworlds and their challenges to the tyranny of normalizing and homogenizing structures? As Guneratne points out, there is no reference to 'Third Cinema' theory or practice in a recent anthology on Mexican cinema that, nevertheless, examines in great detail Mexican-US cultural interaction in the 'border films' genre and Hollywood's constitutive role in the Mexican film industry (2003: 4). Note the tremendous critical attention paid to women filmmakers of the South Asian diaspora (Gurinder Chadda, Mira Nair, Pratibha Parmar) as opposed to South Asian women filmmakers (Aparna Sen, Sai Paranjpye) (see, for instance, Foster, 1997). It appears that displaced people, who now reside in the West, matter more than the underprivileged that remain in the postcolonies: the periphery matters mainly when it shows up in the centre. Likewise, while all border zones are interesting because of their liminality, on the evidence of Film Studies scholarship, some borders remain more riveting than others. The point here is not to advocate a return to archaic 'centre-periphery' type polarities, but to point out that habitual binaries endure underneath even while the sophisticated intellectual moves to problematize and dislodge them. At stake is the recognition of the persistence of colonial power/knowledge relations at the heart of contemporary intellectual labour.

While not the first book seeking to bring anti-imperialist filmmaking discourses and practices to the centre of mainstream Anglophone Film Studies (see Armes, 1987), Shohat and Stam's *Unthinking Eurocentrism* (1994) remains the most significant and far-ranging intervention with a clear pedagogical intent. Among their many contributions is the rethinking of difference – influenced, no doubt, by the Gramscian turn in cultural studies – not in terms of the structuralist centre/margin dichotomy, but as a polyvocal, contestatory and radically de-centred multiculturalism. The purchase of a multiculturalist model is certainly not limited to Australia, Canada, the UK or the US; *multiculturidad* is also important to Latin America (the primary focus of Stam's own research), where large populations of European settlers stayed on after decolonization and where extensive

genocides of indigenous populations were followed by great racial mixing to create *mestizo/mestiço/métis* nations. Population movements and both official and illegal exchanges in transnational regions such as the Amazon basin (including Brazil, Colombia and Peru) and the free trade zone known as Mercosur (Argentina, Brazil, Paraguay, Uruguay) produce domains of flux. Racially hybrid communities, while not altogether unknown, are not that common in Asia or Africa, although diasporic populations of immigrant workers are becoming more prevalent. At any rate, multiculturalism stands in for the policies of particular states aimed at managing social diversity by setting off a play between assimilationist policies and the reification of difference (Povinelli, 2002). So the question arises: what allows the imposition of a multiculturalist model on a global scale? After all, there are certain equivalences, however imperfect, of economic and legal institutions, political systems and cultural norms within a nation state: these structures diverge wildly across countries. An implicit assumption of simultaneity and equivalence, which ultimately helps co-opt difference and institutionalize hybridity, seems not that far removed from neoliberal celebrations of the levelling of global opportunities (of the 'world is flat' variety).

Shohat and Stam's location within Western academia and their objective of producing a groundbreaking textbook in postcolonial media studies for a North American audience inform the thrust of their larger argument about a de-centred multiculturalism on a global scale. Chow is one postcolonial critic who regularly engages cinema and whose work has been acutely sensitive to questions of cross-cultural translation, location and audience, research paradigms and methodologies, and modes of diffusion of intellectual frameworks. Writing in 2001 on the state of Film Studies in 'A Phantom Discipline', she warns against the presumed self-evident referentiality of cinematic representations (with politically retrograde implications), and the salvific politics of 'cultural difference' – of minority representations within national cultures and of national film traditions in the global arena. Chow seeks to disabuse us of such 'critical prerogatives', so that we accept images as artifice and explore the complex relations between economics, desire and identity. And yet, the contingency of her specific forum (a special issue of *PMLA* at the turn of the millennium) leads her to frame her essay in terms of identity politics, a move that she herself astutely contextualizes by pointing to the demands of a specific academic-discursive formation, including a socio-cultural particularism that 'generate[s] research agendas, competitions for institutional space and funding, and self-reproductive mechanisms such as publications, and the training and placing of students' (2001: 1391).

The location of critical labour also matters in terms of local exigencies, familiarity and ease with material, and access to archives. This is why a politics of disciplinary formation is crucial – a politics that comprises what we choose to study, what questions we ask, what genealogies we follow, whom we cite. To become fundamentally global, Film Studies must transcend the automatic and naturalized language barriers and engage with, and encourage translations of, works originating in various geographic sites. Translations of critical writing from the postcolonies – such as Chinese intellectual Dai Jinhua's *Cinema and Desire* (2002) and Néstor García Canclini's *Hybrid Cultures* (2005) – enrich our field, not because these present the thoughts of native informants, nor because they afford an axiomatic informational depth and immediacy, but because of their articulation of a wider range of perspectives in the service of a genuinely transnational discipline.

How can film scholars think globally, beyond the deeply entrenched binaries of an older planetary mapping? One persuasive direction is provided by the approach to cultural globality inaugurated by Appadurai's influential 1990 essay, and developed in the pages of the journal *Public Culture* throughout the 1990s. Thus, Ana López declares:

Rather than a face-off between Hollywood and its others, what we now seek to understand is a broader zone of cultural debate and economic relationships in which we can trace the tensions and contradictions between national sites and transnational processes. It is in this zone, after all, that the cinema is and has been 'lived' as a part of public culture. (2000: 435)

In a similar vein, Ravi Vasudevan charts a critical repositioning away from an endless global politics of difference based on 'national film cultures' and their 'patterns of distinction', highlighting:

particularity against hegemonic norms of narrative filmmaking associated with Hollywood cinema. Today, however, it is possible to pose another future for Screen Studies, one which might look to a more intricate cultural history of identity: to the web of exchanges, flows and translations that underlie cultural identity; to the negotiations of territoriality, in markets and geolinguistic spaces, that govern its changing terms. (2000: 119)

The shift to more thoughtful and sophisticated paradigms, with their premium on complexity, texture and nuance, is, without doubt, a productive development. However, such subtlety remains susceptible to misrecognition, even cynical appropriation – as in Catherine Grant and Annette Kuhn's estimation of Vasudevan's approach: 'while Vasudevan is clear about the critical-political issues at stake, there is no sense that the terrain has to be fought over' (2006: 6). The notion of unequivocal resistance, and the binaries that undergird such an idealist fantasy, do seem passé in our era of intricate interactions and negotiations. But when did the 'critical-political stakes' become merely a matter of refined reflection? From what vantage point is the 'fight' over? Who gets to enjoy this kinder, gentler, can-we-all-get-along 'terrain'? Even a cursory look at the Delhi-based *SARAI* project, which Vasudevan co-directs, reveals a bristling virtual public space that is deeply engaged with questions of representation, global knowledge formation, and quotidian, street-level struggles (including paradigms of development and urbanization, slum-dwellers' rights, media piracy and terrorism).[1] Depoliticizing generalizations such as Grant and Kuhn's assertion help secure an academic consensus about the 'uncontroversial' and ideologically neutral status of the categories that reproduce and sustain the hierarchies of global power/knowledge structures: they serve, in spite of themselves, to underscore the continuing necessity of critical vigilance.

A second imperative facing contemporary Film Studies is the mapping and theorization of global formations. These include new technologies of production, new production conglomerates (transnational financing, studio and post-production services), media convergence and the transnationalization of film culture (new channels of distribution and new audiences, including satellite television, in-flight exhibition, screenings in themed bars and restaurants, global niche markets for experimental works and political documentaries). National or regional cinemas are becoming globalized, not just in terms of financing and distribution, but also through the performance – ironically – of national distinction as exotic otherness for a global audience (for instance, the exaggerated, stereotypical Britishness of many a recent British film, not to mention much of the Chinese 'fifth generation' work). This last tendency is closely related to what Kuan Hsing Chen (2006) calls the 'global nativism' of Taiwan New Cinema. Meanwhile, certain Asian formations are emerging as the new hubs of transnational cinematic cultures and imaginations: most notably, the Indian 'musical' and the Hong Kong action genre (Morris et al., 2005). On the other hand, local reception contexts implement their own nationalizing function: thus French or Danish critics bring their own criteria and national outlooks to their readings of international blockbusters from Hollywood (Hedetoft, 2000). As Shujen Wang (2003) points out, multilateral treaties on copyright issues, such as the World Intellectual Property Organization (WIPO) and the WTO's Agreement on Trade-Related Aspects of Intellectual Property (TRIPS), continue to depend on state laws and local attitudes for enforcement and compliance. Some of this scholarship is beginning to undertake a role that Timothy Brennan (2005) wants postcolonial theory to

assume: pay closer attention to the 'economics of culture'.

A significant impetus for thinking in transnational terms comes from the formation of the EU. Thomas Elsaesser (2005) places European cinema within a global context that is dominated by Hollywood (purveying stars and spectacles) and Asian cinemas (providing colourful vitality and choreographed action). Tim Bergfelder (2000) counters the presentism of recent discourse: drawing on 1950s and 1960s European productions, he argues that cinema has always been a transnational medium. While the current salience of planetary imaginations is evident from the publication of so many recent volumes on world, global or transnational cinema, their precise invocations remain wildly divergent.

In their recent reader on transnational film, Elizabeth Ezra and Terry Rowden (2006) ascribe the rise of a transnational perspective in cinema studies to the global expansion of capital, the porosity of national borders, post-cold war geopolitical climate, new technologies and the global reach of Hollywood. They present a largely unilateral sense of Americanization (thus all action films are described as 'American-style'), their gestures towards Hollywood's own globalization remaining vague in spite of the detailed evidence presented by recent scholarship (Miller et al., 2005). Transnationalism itself is essentialized as a form of elitist cosmopolitanism: thus, in their estimation, transnational cinema addresses itself to publics 'who have expectations and types of cinematic literacy' that transcend parochial national values and affiliations, and is best represented by festival-circuit auteurs such as Pedro Almódovar, Krzysztof Kieslowski and Agnes Varda (Ezra and Rowden, 2006: 3). There is practically no acknowledgment of the popular (except for the hegemony of an entertainment-oriented Hollywood), or of the considerable transnational following of non-Western stars (Bollywood's Amitabh Bachchan in the UK and the Arab world, Chow Yun-fat in East and South-east Asia, Tamil star Rajnikant in Japan) and films (Hong Kong martial arts films in the B-circuit of the Indian province of Andhra Pradesh [Srinivas, 2003]). Postcolonialism is reduced either to the early stages of decolonizing nationalism with its stress on cultural authenticity (without recognizing that rhetoric of authenticity was a necessary bulwark against the deracination wrought by the colonial order), or to a more recent preoccupation with the 'deconstructive critique' of 'imperial or colonial pre-histories'. In contrast, transnationalism is lauded for its grasp of 'the impact of history on contemporary experience', because of its focus on 'immigration, exile, political asylum, tourism, terrorism and technology' – all transnational phenomena that apparently are 'straightforwardly readable in "real world" terms' (Ezra and Rowden, 2006: 5). The evidence of 'contemporary experience' returns with a vengeance, no longer mauled by 'deconstructive critique', and made immediate and immanent by its decoupling from all past links. As if this restitution of a wholesome ontology were not enough, the editors breathlessly proclaim this 'real world' to be 'defined not by its colonial past (or even its neocolonial present), but by its technological future': technology, it would appear, is neutral of power relations and past and present structures. They further claim, in a naïve techno-utopian vein, that 'previously disenfranchised people will gain ever greater access to the means of global representation' (Ezra and Rowden, 2006: 5), thus ignoring the well-documented complications to the erotics of new technologies (for example, William Mazzarella [2006] on e-governance and transparency in India, and Cristina Venegas [2004] on the introduction of the Internet in Cuba). Compare their techno-romance to Sean Cubitt's articulation of a critical responsibility in our engagement with new media constellations:

Millions homeless, millions starving, millions destroyed physically and mentally by sickness and poverty, millions without hope of a better or even a sustainable life on a planet increasingly poisoned by the industrial and consumer experiments of an uncontrolled economy. Any responsible account of cultural activity today must begin in the brutal exclusions of the contemporary world, even more

so when we single out for attention the cultural uses of networked communications and digital media. (1999: 3)

In contrast to Cubitt's trenchant attention to the enduring inequities of our neocolonial moment, Ezra and Rowden's brand of planetary consciousness, produced through a wilful erasure of history, resurrects the (now globalized) West as the locus of value and agency. They instantiate the neoliberal unconscious of contemporary knowledge production, also in play in historian Niall Ferguson's attempted recuperation of the positive legacies of the British empire ('Anglobalization') for the contingencies of today's world (2003).

In their editorial introduction to an anthology of essays culled from the premier journal *Screen*, Grant and Kuhn state that 'world cinema' is a non-contentious term (2006: 1). This stunning claim flatly ignores sustained critiques of 'world literature' or 'world music', not to mention challenges to the disciplinary project of comparative literature (Cooppan, 2004). David Byrne, who is widely credited with making 'world music' popular in the West, wrote in 1999:

The term is a catchall that commonly refers to non-Western music of any and all sorts, popular music, traditional music and even classical music. It's a marketing as well as a pseudomusical term – and a name for a bin in the record store signifying stuff that doesn't belong anywhere else in the store. (1999: AR1)

Stephanie Dennison and Song Hwee Lim astutely point out that the reasons for the global hegemony of Western culture industries, 'and the ghettoizing of world music (or cinema) are more numerous and complex than the use of a specific terminology', and that the 'mechanics of consumerism and identification are arguably more subtle than Byrne's account' (2006: 3). True, but terminology helps reproduce structures of thinking that assume and naturalize the hegemony of Western culture, and erase the multiple hegemonies (Indian or Egyptian cinema, Latin American telenovelas, Arab music) of global public culture, confining them under the sign of the Other. Dennison and Lim do begin with a clear articulation of the problematic status of the category itself, stating that 'in its situatedness, it is … the world as viewed from the West', and arguing that '[i]t is futile, if not hypocritical, to pretend' that such a 'loaded term … can be value free' (2006: 1). Then they go on to claim, against the evidence of new nationalisms, rabid xenophobic attitudes, not to mention terrorism and the war against it (the 'clash of civilizations' rhetoric), that 'distinctions between dichotomies such as Western and non-Western, self and other, although entrenched in the popular imagination, are beginning to dissolve' (2006: 4).

Dennison and Lim reprint a 2004 essay by Dudley Andrew, 'An Atlas of World Cinema' (2006), in which Andrew reiterates the dominant episteme of Film Studies with a gusto not that different from the triumphalist rhetoric of the 'end of History'. For Andrew, 'foreign films' – that is, non-Hollywood cinemas – constitute 'world cinema', which he describes as a 'freshly recognized' global phenomenon (2006: 19): but who is coming to this recognition finally? He does not offer a 'freshness' of perspective in thinking globally about global cinema; nor does he acknowledge, let alone examine, the power relations involved in upholding such an us/them paradigm of 'world cinema'. One is left with a very definite sense of one particular location taken as the fulcrum of a theoretical gaze. Even if we acknowledge Andrew's address of a North American pedagogical context, and his attempt to chart a set of methodological approaches, the unproblematic espousal of a 'parochial posing as cosmopolitan' taxonomy remains troubling. He adopts a conscientiously ethical approach to teaching world cinema, stressing the need to make the pedagogical situation unfamiliar for students. However, this ethical gesture functions mainly as a depoliticizing ruse for what is, at heart, a political move: effectively retaining Hollywood's hegemony by holding on to a self/other paradigm. A sincerely global approach to 'world cinema' would have to (a) dispense with the category altogether, or (b) include Hollywood and mainstream British and French cinemas in its orbit, in

which case the term loses its descriptive or explanatory relevance, or (c) dispense with an additive model of world cinema as the constellation of all national cinemas (a model operative in Linda Badley et al., 2006) and adopt lateral ways of approaching the topic, in terms of translocal cinematic movements, genres, institutions, circuits and publics (see Rosenbaum and Martin 2003).

Attempts to theorize translocal media assemblages encounter two sets of tensions: the first has to do with striking a balance between idealizing mutability, even uncertainty, and obsessing about determinate structures (as I suggested above); the second entails trade-offs between, on the one hand, a 'flora and fauna' approach and, on the other hand, a 'deep immersion' model. The former approach often devolves into a kind of academic tourism, conjoining interesting and seemingly homologous phenomena from various geographic locations to hypothesize about larger trends and formations, without paying enough attention to local conjunctural embeddedness. The latter, often associated with area studies and nationalism studies, is characteristically attentive to specificities of historical context at the cost of comparative insights and trans-border experientialities (Lutgendorf, 2003). Transversal approaches are better equipped to capture emergent global assemblages that, from their inception, transcend national boundaries; however, national policies remain important determinants (Parks, 2006). While innovative methodologies are needed to do justice to the new assemblages, the scholastic solipsism of postcolonial theory (endlessly fine-tuning existing models for past formations) impedes creativity. On the other hand, a need for a fresh perspective produces a demand for a decisive break with the past: as if the past is done with, has no ramifications for the present, and the future will be a level field of globally equal opportunities. Recent anthropological studies of media circuits and communities articulate the two models with some success (Ginsburg et al., 2002). However, as Lutgendorf (2003) warns, in sociological and anthropological works on cinema, the film texts and their specific representational strategies tend to disappear. Most translocal studies continue to restrict themselves to channels that involve the West: postcolonial/transnational Film Studies must pay attention to the multiplicity of global cultural circuits, not just the ones that are routed through America or Europe (see Larkin, 2003; Srinivas, 2003).

FUTURES: INTEGRATION AND TRANSFORMATION

At an earlier stage in its career, postcolonial studies had a profoundly transformative impact on disciplines such as anthropology and literary studies, two intellectual fields that had to come to terms with their role in the production of colonial knowledge structures and ideologies. Now, with global media's promotion to the role of the pre-eminent servant of neocolonialism, Film Studies must undertake similar reflection and renewal. If new technologies and transnational regimes are generating novel assemblages not beholden to any 'local', then a genuinely global model must account for the multifarious entanglements and their ambiguous ramifications, and the ways in which they recalibrate a universal techno-rationalist script of modernization. A truly global attitude must transcend all 'locals' and not protect the hegemony of one 'local masquerading as global'.

The critical interventions of poststructuralist and postcolonial theories have radically dislodged liberalist certitudes about the trajectory of World History (Chatterjee, 1986). Now we understand modernity not as a unidirectional process but, rather, as a series of encounters and exchanges producing effects that are devastating as often as they are salutary (Mignolo, 1995). Knowledge of differentiated experiences of modernity in different geographic locales (for instance, a Dutch modernity as distinct from a Nigerian modernity), and of earlier constellations before post-Enlightenment modernity (associated with, say, the T'ang dynasty of China, or the Persian empire) rend the linear coherence of master-narratives of Progress and History: now

we speak of multiple, parallel modernities instead of a teleological model according to which it all begins in Europe and then gradually spreads to the rest of the world, with the postcolonies forever consigned to the 'waiting room of history'. Even in the era of the so-called Washington Consensus (a unipolar and global hegemonic system consisting of free trade, liberalization of economic policies, and majoritarian democracy as the only acceptable political system), there are all kinds of challenges, detours and recalibrations by local imaginations and lifeworlds (Chakrabarty, 2000). Thus, in spite of anxieties about a homogenizing, unilateral 'global culture', ample space remains for negotiations and variations: the script of global capital cannot subsume every other impulse into its totalizing agenda.

Even as a postcolonial perspective dismantles Eurocentric master-narratives, how can we critically salvage the fecundity of their utopian vision to facilitate a more egalitarian global future? As James Ferguson (2005) has argued recently, without the promise of a golden history that is yet to come, could it be that Africans feel not less developed for now, but simply less? The challenge is to rearticulate transformative promises in ways that are fundamentally translocal and shorn of imperialist underpinnings. This might involve considerable adjustments in our thinking habits, including not dismissing terrorism as mad and misguided, but examining it as a radical form of historical consciousness emanating from prolonged experiences of disenfranchisement – a transnationalism from below.

Globalization studies does not render postcolonial studies obsolete; rather, each complements the other in terms of their relative strengths. While the former is adept at examining structural and material transformations, the latter is more capacious in engaging questions of imagination and meaning-making, mutuality and social justice. As the editors of *Postcolonial Studies and Beyond* ask:

[W]hat visions of a postcolonial world can we as humanists offer that will interrogate, perhaps even interrupt, the forms of globalization now dictated by politicians, military strategists, captains of finance and industry, fundamentalist preachers and theologians, terrorists of the body and the spirit, in short, by the masters of our contemporary universe? (Loomba et al., 2005: 13)

The neoliberal agenda and the resurgent imperialism that propel globalization also generate pressing imperatives for retooling postcolonial thought. It is less important to hold on to a putative discourse (which, like feminism, is not only an analytical framework but also a political stance) than to consider how its intellectual clarity and political efficacy can be extended to engage emergent realities. For instance, what are the effects on translocal subaltern populations when postcolonial states comply with trade and copyright regimes? When, say, the Indian government signs onto TRIPS, and the supply of Indian-produced generic HIV medicines to Africa is cut off? How do we come to grips with a post-9/11 world, in which new claims to rights and recognition arise simultaneously with brazen forms of sovereign power that jeopardize previously unassailable human rights? The agon of contemporary postcolonial and transnational criticism is embodied in the fact that some-times the very transformations that make possible new political emergences, such as ecofeminism or an incipient queer politics, also cause incalculable sufferings, such as the contradictions of the North American Free Trade Agreement (NAFTA) or the rampant suicides by Indian farmers in the wake of structural adjustments.

How can film (and media) studies transcend its neoliberal unconscious, and maintain a critical relationship to an imperial apparatus of global consensus building? What forms of media literacy must we, as media scholars, help develop and disseminate to our media-saturated, supposedly media-savvy, publics? In short, how do we move beyond the current blind spots of our discipline, and attempt to wrest for us a measure of relevance in the global public sphere? 'Post'-ing contemporary Film Studies will involve not only being attentive to trans-media forms

and practices, but also developing new cognitive frames. The following are a set of suggestions from a postcolonial-transnational position.

- Postcolonialism need not be limited to the national only, just as cultural studies approaches need not valorize only the local (as they did in the 1980s). Since metahistorical processes and metanarratives of transformation do have critical impacts on local outcomes, we have to consider the interactions of macro- and micro-level structures, including transnational media circuits and publics that largely bypass Hollywood.

- The binaries cultural texts versus structural conditions, discursivity versus empiricism, while in wide operation, do not make much analytic sense. Film Studies needs to combine textual, semiotic and discursive interrogation with economic, institutional-legal, policy analysis. As Toby Miller has suggested, we cannot simply continue to pose 'textual determinism' as an antidote to 'economic determinism' (2001: 308).

- Adopt transversal approaches to patents and copyrights – related not only to media, but also to medicines, biodiversity/biopiracy.

- Develop what Film Studies has to offer to other disciplines in terms of its attention to technology and society, indexicality and iconicity, plasticity, the popular, formations of media environments, media networks and media publics, and transformative politics. Establish significant intersections with cultural geography, cultural anthropology, sociology, political science, history and, now, science studies.

- Explore what the institution of cinema has to contribute to convergences and coalitions, and how it is entangled with networks of power. How does cinema bolster or challenge new forms of sovereignty? How does it engage questions of citizenship, state violence, terrorism, human rights and international law?

- Investigate what it means to be human: as we consider the new possibilities charted in contemporary media (interactive technologies, genomics, mutations of social institutions like family and labour), we must carefully analyze the shifting power equations, the production of new subalternities, new strategies of exploitation and the demarcation of a new global South.

- Study the planetary range of pre-cinematic forms of popular entertainment, such as shadow puppets, magic, opera, narrative painted scrolls, vaudeville, acrobatic shows and folk stage traditions. This might help in (a) situating the traces of various aesthetic traditions; (b) questioning, from a postcolonial perspective, standard notions of modern popular and mass culture, and the teleological history of cinema as a Western medium; (c) challenging the very construction of the enlightened modern era in relation to its other, the medieval 'dark ages', and the designation of barbarians, heretics and heathens and (d) tracking sedimented memories and representations (for example, in oral traditions) of historical experiences (hostilities and betrayals, triumphs and traumas) that continue to impel contemporary structures of difference.

- A strict, narrow facticity/empiricism will not do. We need to consider not just what happens, but also what might have happened, and what ought to happen. Resuscitate half-forgotten, unrealized visions of progressive transformation by reading cinematic and other types of documents against the grain. Deploy the power of speculation as a critical and imaginative force to project futures of subject formation, community life and political solidarities beyond the grammar and mappings of an imperialist consciousness.

- Pay attention to the protocols of institutionalizing Film (and Cultural) Studies: citational practices, pedagogical imperatives and long-term hiring policies. How do we re-imagine the curriculum, so that it reflects a genuinely global perspective? (Most US departments now offer US film history and International Film History or World Cinemas courses separately – as if the US is an extra-world, transnational entity, a higher dimension of pure normativity, knowledge and subjectivity.) What acquisitions principles are operative in our libraries? (While acquisitions at the University of California libraries have been affected in the 2000s by recent budget cuts, certain fields have been more affected than others. In spite of all the lip-service paid to the importance of the study of the Asia-Pacific to California, only two campuses subscribe to *Inter-Asia Cultural Studies* while the *Journal of Visual Culture*, another Taylor and Francis journal started around the same time, adorns the library shelves on all nine campuses.) What rationales inform the publishing agendas of academic presses? (Is one token Egyptian or Hong Kong industry book, which introduces yet another 'national cinema' to Western audiences, enough?)

At the risk of sounding prescriptive, this overview offers the above suggestions for integrating the lessons of critical postcolonial and transnational thinking within Film Studies – not as additive supplement, but with the objective of producing a revitalizing transformation of our field.

NOTES

1 Available at: http://www.sarai.net.

REFERENCES

Abbas, Ackbar (1997) 'The New Hong Kong Cinema and the *Déjà Disparu'*, in *Hong Kong: Culture and the Politics of Disappearance*. Minneapolis: University of Minnesota Press. pp. 16–47.

Andrew, Dudley (2006) 'An Atlas of World Cinema', in Stephanie Dennison and Song Hwee Lim (eds), *Remapping World Cinema*. New York: Columbia University Press. pp. 19–29.

Appadurai, Arjun (1990) 'Disjuncture and Difference in the Global Cultural Economy', *Public Culture*, 2(2): 1–24.

Armes, Roy (1987) *Third World Filmmaking and the West*. Berkeley: University of California Press.

Arondekar, Anjali (forthcoming) *For the Record: On Sexuality and the Colonial Archive in India*. Durham, NC: Duke University Press.

Badley, Linda, Palmer, R. Barton and Schneider, Steven Jay (eds) (2006) *Traditions in World Cinema*. New Brunswick, NJ: Rutgers University Press.

Bergfelder, Tim (2000) 'The Nation Vanishes: European Co-Productions and Popular Genre Formulae in the 1950s and 1960s', in Mette Hjort and Scott MacKenzie (eds), *Cinema and Nation*. New York: Routledge. pp. 139–52.

Bhabha, Homi (1983) 'The Other Question', *Screen*, 24(6):18–36.

Bhabha, Homi (1984) 'Of Mimicry and Man: The Ambivalence of Colonial Discourse', *October*, 28: 125–33.

Bhabha, Homi (1989) 'The Commitment to Theory', in Jim Pines and Paul Willemen (eds), *Questions of Third Cinema*. London: BFI. pp. 111–32.

Bloch, Ernst (1977) 'Nonsynchronism and the Obligation to its Dialectics', *New German Critique*, 4(2): 22–38.

Bloom, Peter (2008) *French Colonial Documentary: Mythologies, Archive, Humanitarianism*. Minneapolis: University of Minnesota Press.

Brennan, Timothy (2005) 'The Economic Image-Function of the Economy', in Ania Loomba, Suvir Kaul,

Matti Bunzl, Antoinette Burton and Jed Esty (eds), *Postcolonial Studies and Beyond*. Durham, NC: Duke University Press. pp. 101–22.

Byrne, David (1999) 'I Hate World Music', *New York Times*, 3 October: AR1, AR36.

Canclini, Néstor García (2005) *Hybrid Cultures*. Minneapolis: University of Minnesota Press.

Dipesh Chakrabarty (2000), *Provincializing Europe*. Princeton: Princeton University Press.

Chakravarty, Sumita (1994) *National Identity in Indian Popular Cinema, 1947–87*. Austin: University of Texas Press.

Chanan, Michael (2004) *Cuban Cinema*. Minneapolis: University of Minnesota Press.

Chatterjee, Partha (1986) *Nationalist Thought and the Colonial World: A Derivative Discourse?* Minneapolis: University of Minnesota Press.

Chen, Kuan Hsing (2006) 'Taiwan New Cinema, or a Global Nativism?', in Valentina Vitali and Paul Willemen (eds), *Theorising National Cinema*. London: BFI. pp. 138–47.

Chow, Rey (1991) 'Seeing Modern China: Toward a Theory of Ethnic Spectatorship', in *Women and Chinese Modernity*. Minneapolis: University of Minnesota Press. pp. 3–33.

Chow, Rey (2001) 'A Phantom Discipline', *PMLA*, 116(5): 1386–95.

Cooper, Frederick and Stoler, Ann Laura (eds) (1997) *Tensions of Empire: Colonial Cultures in a Bourgeois World*. Berkeley: University of California Press.

Cooppan, Vilashini (2004) 'Ghosts in the Disciplinary Machine: The Uncanny Life of World Literature', *Comparative Literature Studies*, 41(1): 10–36.

Crang, Mike, Crang, Phil and May, Jon (eds) (1999) *Virtual Geographies: Bodies, Space and Relations*. London: Routledge.

Cubitt, Sean (1999) 'Orbis Tertius', *Third Text*, 47: 3–10.

Dai, Jinhua (2002) *Cinema and Desire: Feminist Marxism and Cultural Politics in the Work of Dai, Jinhua*. Ed. Jing Wang and Tani Barlow. London: Verso.

Dennison, Stephanie and Song, Hwee Lim (eds) (2006) *Remapping World Cinema*. New York: Columbia University Press.

Diaconescu-Blumenfeld, Rodica (2003) 'Desire for the Other: Balkan Dystopia in Western European Cinema', in Eva Reuschman (ed.), *Moving Pictures, Migrating Identities*. Jackson: University Press of Mississippi. pp. 90–104.

Driscoll, Mark (2004) 'Reverse Postcoloniality', *Social Text*, 78: 59–84.

Elsaesser, Thomas (2005) *European Cinema: Face to Face with Hollywood*. Amsterdam: Amsterdam University Press.

Ezra, Elizabeth and Rowden, Terry (2006) *Transnational Cinema: The Film Reader*. London: Routledge.

Fanon, Frantz (1965) *The Wretched of the Earth*. New York: Grove Press.

Fanon, Frantz (1967) *Black Skin, White Masks*. New York: Grove Press.

Ferguson, James (2005) 'Decomposing Modernity: History and Hierarchy after Development', in Ania Loomba, Suvir Kaul, Matti Bunzl, Antoinette Burton and Jed Esty (eds), *Postcolonial Studies and Beyond*. Durham, NC: Duke University Press. pp. 166–81.

Ferguson, Niall (2003) 'The British Empire Revisited: The Costs and Benefits of "Anglobalization"', *Historically Speaking*, 4(4): 21–7.

Foster, Gwendolyn Audrey (1997) *Women Filmmakers of the African and Asian Diaspora*. Carbondale: Southern Illinois University Press.

Gabriel, Teshome (1982) *Third Cinema in the Third World: An Aesthetics of Revolution*. Ann Arbor, MI: UMI Research Press.

Garcia Canclini, Néstor (1995) *Hybrid Cultures: Strategies for Entering and Leaving Modernity*. Tr. Christopher Chiapper and Silvia L. López. Minneapolis: University of Minnesota Press.

Ghosh, Bishnupriya (2004) 'On Grafting the Vernacular: The Consequence of Postcolonial Spectrology', *boundary 2*, 31(2): 197–218.

Ginsburg, Faye (1994) 'Embedded Aesthetics: Creating a Discursive Space for Indigenous Media', *Cultural Anthropology*, 9(3): 365–82.

Ginsburg, Faye, Abu-Lughod, Lila and Larkin, Brian (eds) (2002) *Media Worlds*. Berkeley: University of California Press.

Grant, Catherine and Kuhn, Annette (eds) (2006) *Screening World Cinema*. London: Routledge.

Griffith, Alison (2001) *Wondrous Difference: Cinema, Anthropology, and Turn-of-the-Century Visual Culture*. New York: Columbia University Press.

Guha, Ramachandra and Martinez-Alier, Juan (1997) *Varieties of Environmentalism: Essays North And South*. London: Earthscan.

Guneratne, Anthony (2003) 'Introduction: Rethinking Third Cinema', in Anthony Guneratne and Wimal Dissanayake (eds), *Rethinking Third Cinema*. New York: Routledge. pp. 1–28.

Hedetoft, Ulf (2000) 'Contemporary Cinema: Between Cultural Globalisation and National Interpretation', in Mette Hjort and Scott MacKenzie (eds), *Cinema and Nation*. London: Routledge. pp. 278–97.

Higson, Andrew (2000) 'The Limiting Imagination of National Cinema', in Mette Hjort and Scott MacKenzie (eds), *Cinema and Nation*. London: Routledge. pp. 63–74.

Holmes, Douglas R. and Marcus, George E. (2006) 'Cultures of Expertise and the Management of Globalization: Toward the Re-Functioning of Ethnography', in Aihwa Ong and Stephen J. Collier (eds), *Global Assemblages*. Malden, MA: Blackwell. pp. 235–52.

Jaikumar, Priya (2006) *Cinema at the End of Empire*. Durham, NC: Duke University Press.

Jameson, Fredric (1986) 'Third World literature in the Era of Multinational Capitalism', *Social Text*, 15: 65–88.

Jameson, Fredric (1992) *The Geopolitical Aesthetic*. Bloomington: Indiana University Press.

JanMohamed, Abdul and Lloyd, David (eds) (1991) *The Nature and Context of Minority Discourse*. Oxford: Oxford University Press.

Kaplan, E. Ann (1989) 'Problematizing Cross-Cultural Analysis: The Case of Women in the Recent Chinese Cinema', *Wide Angle*, 11(2): 40–50.

Landy, Marcia (1996) 'Folklore, Memory and Postcoloniality in Ousmane Sembene's Films', in *Cinematic Uses of the Past*. Minneapolis: University of Minnesota Press. pp. 30–66.

Larkin, Brian (2003) 'Itineraries of Indian Cinema: African Videos, Bollywood and Global Media', in Ella Shohat and Robert Stam (eds), *Multiculturalism, Postcolonialism and Transnational Media*. New Brunswick, NJ: Rutgers University Press. pp. 170–92.

Lazarus, Neil (1993) 'Disavowing Decolonization: Fanon, Nationalism, and the Problematic of Representation in Current Postcolonial Theory', *Research in African Literatures*, 24(4): 69–98.

Lim, Felicidad (2001) 'Spectral Times: The Ghost Film as Historical Allegory', *Positions*, 9(2): 287–329.

Loomba, Ania (2005) *Colonialism/Postcolonialism*. New York: Routledge.

Loomba, Ania, Kaul, Suvir, Bunzl, Matti, Burton, Antoinette and Esty, Jed (eds) (2005) *Postcolonial Studies and Beyond*. Durham, NC: Duke University Press.

López, Ana (2000) 'Facing up to Hollywood', in Christine Gledhill and Linda Williams (eds), *Reinventing Film Studies*. New York: Hodder Arnold. pp. 419–37.

Lutgendorf, Philip (2003) '*Jai Santoshi Maa* Revisited: On Seeing a Hindu "Mythological" Film', in S. Brent Plate (ed.), *Representing Religion in World Cinema*. New York: Palgrave MacMillan. pp. 19–42.

Mazzarella, William (2006) 'Internet X-Ray: E-Governance, Transparency and the Politics of Immediation in India', *Public Culture*, 18(3): 473–505.

Miller, Toby (2001) 'Cinema Studies Doesn't Matter; or, I Know What You Did Last Summer', in Matthew Tinkcom and Amy Villarejo (eds), *Keyframes: Popular Cinema and Cultural Studies*. New York: Routledge. pp. 303–11.

Miller, Toby, Govil, Nitin, McMurria, John and Maxwell, Richard (2005) *Global Hollywood 2*. London: BFI.

Mignolo, Walter (1995) *The Darker Side of the Renaissance*. Ann Arbor: University of Michigan Press.

Miyoshi, Masao (1993) 'A Borderless World? From Colonialism to Transnationalism and the Decline of the Nation-State', *Critical Inquiry*, 19(4): 726–51.

Morley, David and Robins, Kevin (1989) 'Spaces of Identity: Communications Technologies and the Reconfiguration of Europe', *Screen*, 30(4): 10–34.

Morris, Meaghan, Li, Siu Leung and Chan, Stephen Ching-kiu (eds) (2005) *Hong Kong Connections*. Hong Kong: Hong Kong University Press.

Mudimbe, V.Y. (1988) *The Invention of Africa: Gnosis, Philosophy and the Order of Knowledge*. London: James Currey.

Naficy, Hamid (2001) *An Accented Cinema: Exilic and Diasporic Filmmaking*. Princeton, NJ: Princeton University Press.

Nandy, Ashish (ed.) (1999) *The Secret Politics of Our Desires: Innocence, Culpability and Indian Popular Cinema*. London: Zed Books.

Ngugi wa Thiong'o (1986) *Decolonizing the Mind*. London: James Currey.

Ong, Aihwa (1999) *Flexible Citizenship*. Durham, NC: Duke University Press.

Ong, Aihwa and Collier, Stephen J. (eds) (2006) *Global Assemblages*. Malden, MA: Blackwell.

Paranagua, Paulo Antonio (1996) *Mexican Cinema*. London: BFI.

Paranagua, Paulo Antonio (2003) *Tradicion ý Modernidad en el Cine de America Latina*. San Diego, CA: Fondo de Cultura Economica USA.

Parks, Lisa (2006) *Cultures in Orbit: Satellites and the Televisual*. Durham, NC: Duke University Press.

Pheng, Cheah (1999) 'Spectral Nationality: The Living On [sur-vie] of the Postcolonial Nation in Neocolonial Globalization', *boundary 2*, 26(3): 225–52.

Pines, Jim and Willemen, Paul (eds) (1989) *Questions of Third Cinema*. London: BFI.

Povinelli, Elizabeth (2002) *The Cunning of Recognition: Indigenous Alterities and the Making of Australian Multiculturalism*. Durham, NC: Duke University Press.

Prasad, M. Madhava (2001) *Ideology of the Hindi Film*. New Delhi: Oxford University Press.

Rosenbaum, Jonathan and Martin, Adrian (eds) (2003) *Movie Mutations: The Changing Face of World Cinephilia*. London: BFI.

Ross, Kristin (1996) *Fast Cars, Clean Bodies: Decolonization and the Reordering of French Culture*. Cambridge, MA: MIT Press.

Said, Edward (1979) *Orientalism*. New York: Vintage Books.

Sarkar, Bhaskar (forthcoming) *Mourning the Nation: Indian Cinema in the Wake of Partition*. Durham, NC: Duke University Press.

Scheper-Hughes, Nancy (2006) 'The Last Commodity: Post-Human Ethics and the Global Traffic in "Fresh" Organs', in Aihwa Ong and Stephen J. Collier (eds), *Global Assemblages*. Malden, MA: Blackwell. pp. 145–67.

Shafik, Viola (2007) *Popular Egyptian Cinema: Gender, Class and Nation*. Cairo: AUC Press.

Shohat, Ella and Stam, Robert (1994) *Unthinking Eurocentrism*. New York: Routledge.

Shujen, Wang (2003) 'Recontextualizing Copyright: Piracy, Hollywood, the State and Globalization', *Cinema Journal*, 43(1): 25–43.

Slater, David (2004) *Geopolitics and the Postcolonial: Rethinking North-South Relations*. Malden, MA: Blackwell.

Solanas, Fernando and Getino, Octavio (1976) 'Towards a Third Cinema', in Bill Nichols (ed.), *Movies and Methods, Vol.1*. Berkeley: University of California Press. pp. 44–64.

Spivak, Gayatri Chakravorty (1988) *In Other Worlds*. New York: Routledge.

Spivak, Gayatri Chakravorty (2000) 'Upon Reading the *Companion to Postcolonial Studies*', in Henry Schwarz and Sangeeta Ray (eds), *A Companion to Postcolonial Studies*. Malden, MA: Blackwell. pp. xv–xxii.

Srinivas, S.V. (2003) 'Hong Kong Action Film in the Indian B Circuit', *Inter-Asia Cultural Studies*, 4(1): 40–62.

Tobing-Rony, Fatimah (1996) *The Third Eye: Race, Cinema and Ethnographic Spectacle*. Durham, NC: Duke University Press.

Ukadike, Frank (2003) 'Video Booms and the Manifestations of "First" Cinema in Anglophone Africa', in Anthony Guneratne and Wimal Dissanayake (eds), *Rethinking Third Cinema*. New York: Routledge. pp. 126–43.

Vasudevan, Ravi (2000) 'National Pasts and Futures: Indian Cinema', *Screen*, 41(1): 119–25.

Venegas, Cristina (2004) 'Will the Internet Spoil Fidel Castro's Cuba?', in Henry Jenkins and David Thorburn (eds), *Democracy and New Media*. Cambridge, MA: MIT Press. pp. 179–202.

Wayne, Mike (2002) *The Politics of Contemporary European Cinemas: Histories, Borders, Diasporas*. Bristol: Intellect.

Willemen, Paul (1989) 'The Third Cinema Question: Notes and Reflections', in Jim Pines and Paul Willemen (eds), *Questions of Third Cinema*. London: BFI. pp. 1–30.

Yau, Esther (1987–8) '*Yellow Earth*: Western Analysis and a Non-Western Text', *Film Quarterly*, 41(2): 22–33.

Yoshimoto, Mitsuhiro (1991) 'The Difficulty of Being Radical: The Discipline of Film Studies and the Postcolonial World Order', *Boundary 2*, 18(3): 242–57.

Xavier, Ismail (1997) *Allegories of Underdevelopment: Aesthetics and Politics in Modern Brazilian Cinema*. Minneapolis: University of Minnesota Press.

Zhang, Xudong (1997) *Chinese Modernism in the Era of Reforms*. Durham, NC: Duke University Press.

SECTION II

Disciplinary Dialogues

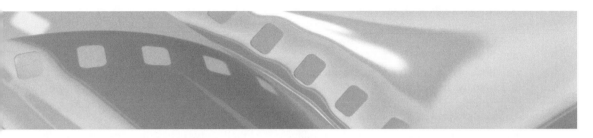

Section 2 of the Handbook addresses the nature and status of Film Studies as an academic discipline. That attempt of course presupposes the question of what an academic discipline is, and what criteria Film Studies would need to meet in order to claim the name.

One way of thinking about that question is through epistemology. In the case of Film Studies, this approach might start by asking whether it is possible to draw secure conceptual boundaries around the discipline's object of study. One obvious answer is that Film Studies is about the study of film, but it is equally apparent that Film Studies is not just about the study of films as examples of aesthetic form and as immaterial commodities. Film Studies is, or at least has been, equally concerned to understand the institution of cinema as it existed for the greater part of the twentieth century: that is, as both a cycle of meaning-making, spectatorial engagement and aesthetic evaluation and as an economy of production, distribution and theatrical exhibition.

If the discipline's defining object thus turns out to be both epistemologically insecure and historically transient, is it then possible to tie Film Studies down to a defining methodology or repertoire of methodologies? Although there are undoubtedly characteristic inflections and refinements to the way that methods of explanation, interpretation, analysis and evaluation are deployed in Film Studies, it might be difficult to make the case that the discipline has created any wholly new approach.

That would then leave the claim that Film Studies constitutes a discipline resting on its history. As the varied histories of when, where, how and why it came into being charted in Section 1 show, from this point of view Film Studies does look very like a discipline. They revealed how Film Studies has been embedded and embodied in university courses and departments and how it has spawned academic journals, organizations and conferences. It boasts the requisite competition between perspectives, traditions and coteries. And, like any true discipline, its history has been punctuated by memorable rows and scandals and its business has been oiled by anecdotes and gossip about retrospectively mythologized personalities.

The approach in this section takes as given the acknowledgement in the General Introduction that it is both difficult and quixotic to draw secure boundaries around our unstable object of study. Instead of worrying too much about the ontology of film, therefore, the contributions to this section accept the historical contingency of the emergence of Film Studies. Rather than approach its epistemological status through any a priori assumptions about criteria that have to be met or hoops that have to be jumped through, they take a more pragmatic approach.

They show how Film Studies has developed and been defined as a discipline through a series of conversations with other established and emergent disciplines or intellectual fields – conversations that have occasionally, it is true, erupted into border disputes, but which have often prompted a degree of self-reflection and adaptation in those disciplines.

We should acknowledge that there are two significant gaps in this series of conversations, gaps that reveal two polar forces that have undoubtedly helped to shape the field of Film Studies. One concerns the relationship between Film Studies and Literary Studies. There is nothing more likely to make scholars of Film Studies scratchy than for colleagues in Literature departments to breezily assert that as films are just another type of text, and as often as not narrative texts, then it is obvious that the analysis of film is part of 'what they do' and that Film Studies is little more than an uppity stepchild of 'English' or 'Literary Studies'. Perhaps the reason that it ultimately proved impossible to find a satisfactory way of addressing this relationship reflects its very intimacy, and a lack of resolution that suggests an incompletely worked through separation. The decision not to have a separate chapter on the relationship between Film Studies and Media Studies has a different impetus. It reflects our view that Film Studies is rightly seen as an inalienable component of any defensible Media Studies, even though in many places they have developed as discrete and sometimes mutually suspicious disciplines. That differentiation is here traced by the inclusion of the chapters addressing, on the one hand, Cultural Studies and, on the other, Political Economy – the two wings, one might say, of Media Studies as it has developed over recent decades.

Finally, two of the chapters in this section were not written specifically for this Handbook but for other occasions. That is why Faye Ginsburg's chapter on anthropology takes mass media rather than film as such as its interlocutor. Nonetheless, it raises many pertinent issues in this new context. So too does Lynn Spigel's review of a Television Studies conference, which was originally written as a contribution to a *Cinema Journal* symposium on the relationship between that discipline (or sub-discipline?) and Film Studies.

10

Film and Philosophy

Murray Smith

Squidward fulminates against the 'Krabby Patty' – the fast-food snack of choice at the Krusty Krab restaurant.

SpongeBob: But it doesn't make any sense – the Krabby Patty is an Absolute Good – nobody is immune to its tasty charms!

'Just One Bite', *SpongeBob SquarePants* (US, 2001)

Writing in 1890, William James expounded the idea that human subjective experience is characterized by a continuous 'stream of consciousness' via a striking metaphor (1950: 200). James likened the flow of conscious thought to the impression of continuous movement produced by that proto-cinematic device, the Zoetrope – a circular drum with a succession of pictures on its inner surface, the pictures representing successive, incremental changes in the movement of the figure depicted, viewed through narrow slots while the cylinder revolves. James' metaphor predated a similar and more famous one ventured by Henri Bergson in 1907, positing an analogy between the human experience of temporal continuity, or *durée*, and the cinema (Bergson, 1944: 272–370). James and Bergson were among the first to explore one kind of relationship between the modern art of the moving image and the ancient tradition of philosophy: the use of the moving image – whether as a technology, a type of film, or an individual film – as a suggestive analogue or model of a philosophical concept, or a phenomenon with philosophical significance. Over time, the development of cinema (and related moving image media) has given rise to another form of reflection on the relationship between philosophy and the moving image, one that moves in the opposite direction: the deployment of philosophical tools, old and new, to explore and unpack the questions thrown up by this juvenile art form, giving rise to film theory and what has recently been christened 'the philosophy of film' (Allen and Smith, 1997; Wartenberg and Curran, 2005; Smith and Wartenberg, 2006). In this overview, we consider a sampling of both lines of exploration.

FILM AS PHILOSOPHY

The contemporary incarnation of the practice of using films as models or metaphors of philosophical ideas has come to be known as 'film as philosophy'. The very idea of film as a vehicle of philosophy has been greeted with scepticism by some commentators, but there is a long established context within the philosophy of art for such claims – namely, debate around the epistemic dimension of art, that is, the question of whether art provides us with knowledge, and if so of what kind. In this sense, the 'film as philosophy' debate puts a new spin on an old question, but raises the stakes by posing the question in terms of the relationship between a modern, highly commercial medium, and what is traditionally regarded as the most elevated and 'pure' form of knowledge.

The idea of a relationship between philosophy and the arts is a very familiar one in other ways too. Critical discussion of films and other works of art commonly includes reference to the 'philosophy' or 'philosophies' embodied in such works, and allusion to philosophical ideas, and particular philosophers, as exemplified by the exchange from *SpongeBob*, is also widespread in the arts. Thus we have *The Simpsons and Philosophy* (Irwin et al., 2001), *The Matrix and Philosophy* (Irwin, 2002; see also Grau, 2005), *The Sopranos and Philosophy* (Greene and Vernezze, 2004) and so on – *SpongeBob SquarePants and Philosophy* cannot be far off – a whole new sub-industry devoted to sniffing out the philosophical assumptions embodied in popular culture and art (see also Falzon, 2002; Kupfer, 1999; Light, 2003; Litch, 2004; Wartenberg, 1999). But some philosophers of film, paralleling similar arguments in the philosophy of literature and the plastic arts (Danto, 1981; Diamond, 1991a; 1991b; Nussbaum, 1990), have pressed a more precise and thoroughgoing analogy between philosophy and at least some kinds of filmmaking. Indeed, on the strongest of these accounts, the relationship argued for is not one of analogy, but of membership or identity: certain kinds of film just *are* instances of philosophy. In the words of Stephen Mulhall, such films – and it is important to note here that Mulhall's primary examples are mainstream action films, like the

Alien and *Mission: Impossible* franchises[1] – constitute 'philosophy in action' (Mulhall, 2002; see also Mulhall, 2006). And it this stronger type of claim – characterized by Paisley Livingston (2006) as the 'bold thesis' that cinema may make a powerful and unique contribution to the philosophical enterprise – that has generated a lively debate about the scope and character of the relationship between film and philosophy.

Contemporary debate on this issue has been preceded by two sustained attempts to treat film as a form of philosophical expression, both reaching back more than thirty years. French philosopher Gilles Deleuze elaborated a distinctive view of the creative conceptual work embodied by films in his two-volume study *Cinema 1* (1986) and *Cinema 2* (1989), taking as his starting point Bergson's reflections on temporality and cinema (see Chapter 11). In the Anglo-American context, Stanley Cavell has developed an equally distinctive and ambitious view of the philosophical import of cinema. Beginning with *The World Viewed* (1979), and sustained and developed in later works focusing on the 'comedy of remarriage' (1981) and the 'melodrama of the unknown woman' (1990), Cavell has sought to reveal the ways in which certain genres of narrative filmmaking nurture and harvest an intrinsic philosophical potential in the medium of film. That potential bears in particular on the significance of *scepticism* – uncertainty in our knowledge of the world and other minds. Cavell conceives of scepticism not as a narrowly philosophical worry, but as a profound existential question, an aspect of the human condition felt more acutely than ever in the modern (secular and disenchanted) age. In this sense, Cavell's is a philosophy 'in the key of life'. In advancing this thesis, Cavell examines and interprets films in the context of some of the landmarks of philosophy, including, for example, Immanuel Kant in relation to the screwball comedy *It Happened One Night* (Frank Capra, US, 1934) (Cavell, 1981: 73–109). In his most recently published work on film, the emphasis falls on the notion of 'moral perfectionism' (Cavell, 2004) – the problem of the distance between our moral ideals and reality – considered first in relation to Ralph Waldo Emerson's essay 'Self-Reliance' (1993) and *The Philadelphia Story* (George Cukor, US, 1940), and then elaborated through the juxtaposition of kindred ideas in other philosophers and other films: John Locke in relation to *Adam's Rib* (George Cukor, US, 1949), Friedrich Nietzsche in relation to *Now, Voyager* (Irving Rapper, US, 1942), and John Rawls in relation to *Mr Deeds Goes to Town* (Frank Capra, US, 1936), to take three further examples. Impressive in its ability to illuminate the thematic and conceptual sophistication of these popular films, Cavell's work constitutes a major influence on contemporary philosophy of film, even as that body of debate has opened onto a wider range of questions and films (Mulhall, 2002 and 2003; see also Read and Goodenough, 2005).

Like many other philosophers working on this terrain, Cavell and Mulhall are eager to plunge into the detail of particular cases and tease out the philosophical implications of individual films. Where philosophers do pause to consider the idea of the 'film as philosophy' thesis itself, sooner or later the debate is driven onto the territory of 'metaphilosophy' – the philosophy of philosophy itself – as the participants appeal to what they take to be paradigms of philosophy in order to underline either the contrast or the continuity between such exemplary instances of philosophy and particular films, or types of filmmaking. Those with a narrow conception of philosophy, defining it in terms of the self-conscious pursuit of knowledge by means of argument, tend to be sceptical of the idea that films can act as vehicles of philosophy. Those with a broader and more expansive conception of philosophy, associating the reflexive pursuit of knowledge with an array of techniques in addition to those of formal argument, tend to be much more sympathetic to the idea of film as philosophy. These alternative techniques include the thought experiment and the counterexample (Carroll, 2002; Wartenberg, 2005), various methods inspired by the philosophy of Ludwig Wittgenstein

(Davis, 2006) and, most generally, artistic narration and depiction. We shall return to each of these techniques over the rest of this discussion.

Three problems: Narrative, fiction and depiction

Jerry Fodor gives blunt expression to the narrow conception of philosophy when he states, in the course of commenting on a book exploring the philosophical implications of Richard Wagner's *The Ring of the Nibelung* (1854-6) (Kitcher and Schacht, 2004), that the opera is not 'an enthymeme [an argument with a hidden premise], a paradox or a dilemma. It isn't any kind of argument at all' (2004: 8). The disanalogy between works of art and philosophy can be broken down into three more specific problems: of *narrative*, of *fiction*, and of *depiction*. The problem of narrative focuses on the fact that narratives and arguments are distinct forms, each with its own internal logic. Whereas a narrative presents a succession of causally related events, especially those events brought about intentionally by human agents, an argument proceeds by moving from one or more initial propositions to subsequent propositions on the basis of logical relations, whether of strict entailment or implicature. Narratives thus cannot *just* be treated as if they were arguments. Any kinship that might exist between the two forms needs to be spelt out. This is just what has been undertaken by a number of theorists and philosophers (Carroll, 1993; Chatman, 1990; Wartenberg, 2006b; for critical discussion of such proposals also see Russell, 2000; Smith, 2006a).

The terms 'narrative' and 'fiction' are widely used in an interchangeable fashion, perhaps for the simple reason that most fictions are narratives, and in the world of film the dominant form of filmmaking through most of the history of the moving image has been feature-length fictional narrative film. The terms nevertheless name distinct phenomena. A narrative relates a series of events causally and intentionally, but the events it represents may be real or imaginary (or some mix of the two). *Roger and Me* (Michael Moore, US, 1989) is, among other things, a narrative, but it is not a fiction – it purports to tell us about real events and people (and the effect of the actions of some of these people on others). And if and where it fails to inform us accurately about real events and people, it trades in falsehood rather than fiction: for a fiction is a representation of imaginary – though often plausible – events and persons, explicitly or implicitly represented as such.[2] Moreover, while the events and existents of a fiction are usually presented in narrative form, non-narrative fictions are possible: imagine a fictional equivalent to Andy Warhol's series of *Screen Tests* (US, 1964–66) – films which show us a diverse series of fictional portraits, of imaginary people or places, where no causal connections between these entities are indicated or suggested. So the problem of fiction points to a different impediment to the claim that films can act as vehicles of philosophy: don't, or shouldn't, philosophical texts make truth claims about the world (Baggini, 2003: 6), rather than positing imaginary worlds?

There are several responses to this concern. The first notes that, while fictions do not make direct truth claims about the world in the way that histories or documentaries do, there clearly is a sense in which fictions routinely make indirect claims about the world (Searle, 1975): claims about the human condition, or social reality, or history, or particular aspects of these. Edgar Reitz's *Heimat* follows its imagined characters living through Germany in the twentieth century, but it draws on a host of facts about that society in creating its fiction, and reciprocally it implies things about the real world which forms the deep background to its fictional entities. This remains true even for fictions not bound, to the degree that *Heimat* is, to the reality of history. If we dig deep enough, we will always reach a layer of assumptions drawn from reality, even in the most extravagantly fantastical or surreal fictions. A sliced eye is a shocking thing to behold in the deranged world of *Un chien andalou* (Luis Buñuel, France, 1929) because it is a shocking thing to behold or to

contemplate in the real world; and the visual incongruity of an armpit transplanted onto a face, in the same film, acquires its charge in large part from its violation of the constraints of reality.

The second response to the problem of fiction takes a different tack, pointing to the presence *in philosophy* of fictions, in the form of *thought experiments*. A thought experiment is an imagined scenario used by a philosopher to make a particular philosophical assumption or conundrum salient.[3] Plato's myth of the cave is an ancient example: a miniature fiction which aims to make salient our dependence on what is, for Plato, a dubious philosophical assumption about the 'reality' revealed by ordinary perception (Plato, 1991: Book VII). John Searle's 'Chinese Room' thought experiment provides a well-known contemporary example (1980): in order to stress the importance of conscious understanding to human mentality and its absence from the calculations of a computer, Searle concocts a scenario in which Chinese text is translated with human participation but without any understanding of the Chinese language. By drawing attention to the presence and role of such fictions in philosophy, the apparent gap between fictional and philosophical discourse is narrowed.

A third line of defence against the problem of fiction focuses on the fact that not all films with philosophical implications are fiction films. Many experimental and avant-garde films have been interpreted as conveying philosophical theses, or as provoking a kind of philosophical attention, with respect to the ontology or aesthetics of film. Jinhee Choi, for example, has argued that films such as Michael Snow's *Wavelength* (Canada/US, 1967) and Kurt Kren's *TV 15/67* (Austria, 1967) make a 'philosophical contribution' by suggesting 'new philosophical hypotheses regarding the film medium' (2006: 165; see also Carroll, 2006; Ponech, 2006). Other films, it has been argued, embody the filmic equivalent of the philosophical essay, as in the case of certain films by Jean-Luc Godard (*Letter to Jane* [Jean-Luc Godard/Jean-Pierre Gorin, France, 1972], *Histoire(s) du cinéma*

[France/Switzerland, 1988-98]) and Chris Marker (*Le joli mai* [Chris Marker/Pierre Lhomme, France, 1963], *Sans Soleil* [France, 1983]), and there is at least one case of a film which presents itself as a philosophical reflection on a classic philosophical text: Peter Forgács' *Wittgenstein Tractatus* (Hungary, 1992) (Davis, 2006).

Finally there is the problem of depiction, which identifies the primary difficulty for the 'film as philosophy' hypothesis in terms of the contrast between verbal and depictive representation. Of the three problems considered here, this is probably the one with the most ancient roots. Among the great systematic philosophers of the Enlightenment, G.W.F. Hegel probably accords the arts as much or more philosophical power than any other philosopher, treating art as the precursor to the fully self-conscious form of knowledge achieved with philosophy proper. But by the same token art, for Hegel, is still bound up with the 'picture-thinking' (*Vorstellen*) through which religion is primarily articulated, and to that extent precisely cannot obtain the epistemic status of philosophy (1977: 410–78). Within twentieth-century analytic philosophy, Monroe Beardsley argued that images cannot be analysed into propositions (1981: 369–76); and in his early writings, Christian Metz (1974) explored in detail the limits of the analogy between language and cinema fundamental to semiotics. These arguments are echoed in the dilemma that Livingston (2006) presents to proponents of the 'film as philosophy' thesis: if the moving image is verbally paraphrasable then much of the value of the idea of a filmic embodiment of philosophy seems to drain away; but if the moving image is not verbally paraphrasable, it is hard to see how it can make a contribution to the practice of philosophy, defined as it is and always has been by verbal interaction.

Imaginative reasoning

A very recent expression of the problem of depiction is to be found in John Carey's *What Good are the Arts?* (2005). Carey makes the familiar argument that literature possesses certain capacities lacked by other forms of art, but he does so with unusual candour and lucidity, and in the context of a broader argument which relinquishes or deflates many other traditional assumptions about the power of art. His argument moves in three stages. First, he argues that only literature is capable of *criticizing* other works of literature, where full-blooded 'criticism' is contrasted with actions like 'parody' and 'caricature', where a critical stance is implicit rather than explicitly articulated. The capacity of literature for such criticism, which includes the possibility of the 'total rejection' of literature itself, shows that in this respect literature is 'more powerful and self-aware than any other art' (2005: 174). The second stage in Carey's argument is crucial in bringing out the source of literature's special 'critical' power: 'Literature is not just the only art that can criticize itself, it is the only art … that can criticize anything, because it is the only art *capable of reasoning*' (2005: 177, my italics). And what gives literature the power of reason? In a word: words. Paintings are 'locked in inarticulacy', while '[o]peras and films can criticize, but only because they steal words from literature, which allow them to enter the rational world' (2005: 177).[4] In another passage, painting, music and dance are said to 'delight', while literature gets on not just with delighting but questioning 'everything including itself' (2005: 176). Thus, just as for Hegel 'picture thinking' is an inferior form of thinking to that exemplified by philosophy, so for Carey among the arts, literature is the most closely aligned with philosophy because of its capacity to reason: 'literature gives you ideas to think with. It stocks your mind. It does not indoctrinate, because diversity, counter-argument, reappraisal and qualification are its essence. But it supplies the materials for thought. Also, because it is the only art capable of criticism, it encourages questioning, and self-questioning' (2005: 208). Though Carey does not mention philosophy explicitly, if this is not a description of philosophy, what is?[5] Carey's third move is to claim that only literature can 'moralize', where moralization is understood as the explicit verbal articulation of a moral view. Literature is able to mobilize both oblique, implicit moral reflection, through narrative, as well as such explicit moralization.

Carey's argument is relevant to us here because most of his literary examples, through which he extols the special capacities he claims for literature, are instances of prose narrative fiction. It is thus the foundational role of language as the medium of literature that makes it significantly different from other media, like film, which also characteristically offer us narrative fictions. Carey's claim that literature alone is capable of criticizing and moralizing, and that a medium such as film can only do so by 'stealing words' from literature, reveals his dependence on a problematic understanding of how the arts relate and evolve historically, reminiscent of some classical film theorists, like Rudolf Arnheim. Alluding to the classic argument made by Gotthold Ephraim Lessing (1962) on the contrasts between painting and poetry, Arnheim (1958) argued that film and each of the traditional arts possessed essences, and that the 'talking picture' was a *hybrid* art form, mixing elements of literature and film (properly understood). And such hybrid forms were inherently unstable. Does the history of sound film bear this out? Perhaps it is too early to say; eighty years is not long in the history of art conceived on the grandest scale. But, if the history of sound film counts for anything, it shows that the 'hybrid' form has considerable stability, adaptability and durability. It also makes a bit of a nonsense of Carey's internecine vision of the arts: film – as we have it, as it has evolved, rather than as it was theorized – represents a synthesis of techniques drawn from literature, the stage, music, oral storytelling, and painting, along with the new resources unique to cinematography. While it is true that traditional literary forms are distinct in their wholesale dependence on language as their medium, language is no more the sole possession of literature than it is of film, or stage drama, or opera. And once we accept

this point, it looks as if film will possess the capacity to reason – critically and morally – and not merely in some 'stolen', second-hand sense. Nevertheless, this position would leave intact the problem of depiction, insofar as the capacity of film to 'reason' is being linked to its inclusion of language. Visual depiction, static or moving, still appears to suffer from shortcomings in relation to the goal of fully explicit critical thinking – which, once more, is the gold-standard by which we measure the degree to which something might be said to be truly 'philosophical'.[6]

Thus in the case of each problem, attempts have been made to win the argument more or less on the terms implicit in the statement of the problem – by showing, that is, how narratives can carry arguments, how fictions make truth claims about the world, and how depictive art forms like film may nevertheless 'reason' and articulate philosophical claims. Other philosophers have pursued a different tactic, circumventing these problems by arguing that these objections to film, or art more generally, conceived as philosophy miss the point. Perhaps the most forthright example of such an approach is due to Cora Diamond, focusing on the case of literature, in an essay tellingly entitled 'Anything but Argument?' (1991a). Prompted by philosophical debate on animal rights, Diamond considers the means available to us to engage in moral deliberation, and to effect change in the moral views of ourselves and of others. Reacting to what I have described here as the 'narrow' conception of philosophy, as it is adopted in the context of moral philosophy, Diamond's thesis is that 'argument is simply one way people approach moral questions, and there are other ways of trying to convince someone of one's view of animals or foetuses or slaves or children or whatever it may be' (1991a: 292). Consequently her approach contrasts strongly with one we have already considered, which accepts the centrality of argument to philosophical discourse and attempts to show how narratives may bear or embody arguments; Diamond rejects the idea that there is a simple choice to be made between the mere assertion of a view and argument for it.

What emerges as the alternative to argument is, broadly, the (literary) imagination: a capacity which may be even more important, in moral life, than argument. Diamond takes as one of her examples William Wordsworth's poem 'The Old Cumberland Beggar' (1798), noting that Wordsworth's stated intention in the *Lyrical Ballads* (1991) is 'to enlarge the reader's moral and emotional sensibilities' (1991a: 297). She notes that the poem includes an argument, in enthymematic form, but that even in such a case – where a literary work actually employs argument as a device – it would be risible to hold that the argument is doing the moral work. Rather 'the moral force of the poem is created by the way objects are described and feelings given in connection with each other' (1991a: 296) – by the way in which the poem expresses an attitude towards its subject matter.

What stands behind Diamond's case for the significance of the literary imagination to moral psychology is a view of morality as rooted in our emotions, in contrast to a narrowly rationalistic conception of morality – roughly speaking, a Humean rather than Kantian view of moral life. It follows that moral deliberation or reasoning must involve the emotions, rather than being detached from them: in the moral domain, 'thinking well involves thinking charged with appropriate feeling' (1991a: 298). We might conceive of such thinking as *imaginative reasoning*, a form of cognition that is, so to speak, the 'natural' possession of literature and the arts rather than philosophy traditionally, or at least narrowly, conceived. I say 'literature and the arts' because, although Diamond restricts her attention to literature, it would appear that the kind of imaginative 'enlargement' and refinement of the moral and emotional sensibilities of which Diamond writes, can be achieved as much through other representational arts, like depictive painting or narrative filmmaking, as through literature. Precisely because this power resides in the *'manner'* in which a situation is represented – what aspects of the situation are made salient to us, what sort of tone the work adopts towards the situation and its dramatis personae – rather

than in an implicit argument or explicit 'criticism' (in Carey's sense) contained in the work, all the representational arts may both possess and engender imaginative reasoning. It does, after all, seem odd to think of Pablo Picasso's *Guernica* (1937) or Sergei Eisenstein's *Battleship Potemkin* (USSR, 1925) as works 'locked in inarticulacy', on the grounds that they are depictive works, making little or no use of language. By definition neither work is verbally articulate, but it would be hard to deny the expressive and imaginative 'articulacy' of the painting or the film – the *way* in which they ask us to attend to, think about, feel about, war and its consequences, or the violence engendered by class conflict.[7]

WHAT IS THIS THING CALLED 'FILM THEORY'?

The exploration of the potential of film to act as a vehicle of philosophy looms large in contemporary debate, but it constitutes only one side of the equation in which we are interested. Of at least equal importance, historically and conceptually, is the theoretical or philosophical analysis *of* film, a form of enquiry the reaches back at least as far as Hugo Münsterberg's *The Photoplay: A Psychological Study* (1916), and extends through the work of such figures as Arnheim (1958), André Bazin (1967), Eisenstein (1988; 1991) and Metz (1974), to a host of contemporary theorists. But just what is 'film theory', in a general sense, and how does it relate to other branches of film study? What are its goals? What sorts of questions does it ask, and what methods are at its disposal in answering these questions? What other disciplines – within the Humanities, the Social or Natural Sciences – might it model itself upon?

Explanation and understanding

One answer to this cluster of questions is that film theory is in the business of offering *explanations*. As such, it might be thought of as a 'science' of some kind – a 'special science', to be sure, in Fodor's sense of a new explanatory domain (1974), possessed of certain distinctive, proprietary concepts and methods, irreducible to other sciences concerned with phenomena at lower levels (physics, chemistry, biology, psychology). Arguments and concepts from the philosophy of science might be profitably employed as a way of characterizing what film theory is (and has been) and what it might aspire to be. Overtly scientific approaches to the study of film have occasionally arisen, for example in the form of the 'Filmology' movement in France in the 1950s (Lowry, 1985). But the scientific status of film theory (and related research on narrative and the other arts) has more often been a vexed but vague issue, invoked by charges of 'scientism', but rarely examined. Over the past decade, however, a debate over this issue has emerged, prompted by Noël Carroll's circumspect proposal that 'what can be claimed for science may be claimed eventually for film theory' (1996b: 59) (and more generally by the emergence of *cognitive film theory* – of which more below). A scientific model of film theory makes sense when we think of questions like the following: when we watch a film – which is literally comprised of a succession of still frames or fields – why do we perceive motion? How does our perception of films differ from our perception of the world? How do films move us emotionally? Note how these questions differ from the questions posed by James and Bergson, discussed at the outset of this chapter. James and Bergson were concerned with characterizing the phenomenology of human consciousness, and drew on the Zoetrope and cinema as metaphors for aspects of this phenomenology. The questions here, by contrast, are explanatory rather than phenomenological, seeking explanations rather than perspicuous descriptions of aspects of our experience of cinema. For example, the question 'what *gives rise* to the impression of continuity, given the physically discrete composition of images on the film strip?' seeks an explanation for what is *assumed* in

the metaphorical appeal to the continuity of filmic preception.

These explanatory questions are primarily empirical questions. We can see how the empirical investigation of films and film viewing would lead us toward answers, whether we undertake original empirical research, or draw on existing research on perception and emotion to propose answers. We can also appreciate here the significance of *competition* among potentially rival explanatory accounts of perception and emotion (Carroll, 1996b: 56–61). Our perception of motion might be explained by the notion of persistence of vision, *or* via the phi phenomenon, *or* on the basis of other features and limitations of the human visual system (Anderson, 1996: 54–61). Our ability to be moved by films might be explained on the basis of illusion, *or* on the basis of imagination; and the form of these emotional responses might be held to be a matter of universal, innate responses, *or* of culturally specific ones. In each case, we can assess the power of the competing explanations according to their breadth (how comprehensively do they explain all the facts that we regard as pertinent to the question?) and their degree of coherence with other theories we might hold about related phenomena (for example, we might ask how well a given theory of perception coheres with assumptions we make about cognition and emotion). Much of the agenda of cognitive film theory has been driven by questions of this sort, and pursued in a broadly scientific spirit (see Anderson, 1996; Barratt and Frome, 2006; Bordwell, 1989a; 1989b; Currie, 1995; Plantinga and Smith, 1999; Smith, 1995).

This scientific conception of film theory has been challenged, however. Malcolm Turvey, for example, questions the logical aptness of the model. He argues that the causal investigations and explanations of the natural sciences are inappropriate tools given the object of film theory, namely, a human invention used in a variety of human practices and contexts (Turvey, 2005; see also Allen and Turvey, 2001; Turvey, 2006). Turvey advances his argument as a challenge to the rise of 'theory' more generally in the Humanities, and in defence of 'traditional humanistic methods – understanding the intentions of filmmakers, interpreting the meanings of their films, identifying the formal and stylistic conventions they are employing and the innovations, if any, they are introducing' (2005: 21). Causal investigation and explanation, Turvey warns us, may be a square peg to the round hole of the human *understanding* called for by a phenomenon like film (on the distinction between explanation and understanding, see von Wright, 1971).

Noting that film theorists rarely in fact engage in controlled, scientific experimentation, Turvey draws a distinction between *internal* and *external* knowledge of the domain of human thought and action in which film is situated. Internal knowledge of the game of tennis – to use Turvey's example of another human practice, analogous with filmmaking – involves a grasp of the various rules and norms which comprise the game: what a service is, how scoring proceeds, the zones of the court, as well as more implicit factors such as standards of fair play and propriety. By contrast, external knowledge pertains to all those facts about the natural world exploited by the game of tennis: everything from facts about the physiology and neurology of perception and motor control, to the properties of rubber, chalk, grass or clay or concrete, the effect of spin on the trajectory of a moving sphere and so on. While the facts at stake in such external knowledge are facts independent of human perception – clay has certain properties even if these properties aren't exploited by the invention of tennis – internal knowledge, by contrast, is *constituted* by human decisions and conventions: the concept and practice of a 'serve' in tennis is meaningless outside of the invented framework of the game. The implication of this distinction, for Turvey, is that our relationship to the kind of knowledge produced by the natural sciences and humanistic disciplines respectively is in marked contrast. While natural science aims to identify causal mechanisms which are typically 'invisible', or at least unknown to

us, the humanist works to clarify concepts which are, in some sense, *already known to us*. Thus, for example, neuroscience aims to identify which parts of the brain are involved in particular kinds of activity – a kind of knowledge about which we will be in ignorance until scientific investigation begins. But the enterprise of film theory seeks knowledge of things like montage, *mise en scène*, narrative form, distinctions between genres, the contrast between fiction and non-fiction – all matters about which we (the human community) must already have some knowledge, since without us none of these concepts and practices would exist at all. 'We do not need any knowledge of the way our own eyes work, least of all a *theory*, in order to watch a film' (Turvey, 2005: 27).

It is, then, no surprise that film theorists rarely engage in scientific experimentation, because, on Turvey's account, they are not primarily interested in causal knowledge of that bit of the world defined by film. Instead they pursue – or ought to pursue – what Wittgenstein (1958) characterized as the 'grammatical' investigation of our concepts. (Here we encounter a point of connection with the discussion of 'film as philosophy' in the first section of this chapter, for both the work of Cavell, in that context, and of Allen and Turvey, in the current context, are notably influenced by Wittgenstein.) Just as a grammarian examines the rules for sentence formation in specific languages, so the 'conceptual grammarian' examines, and tries to bring to light, the norms which govern a particular 'form of life' – that is, a distinctive domain of human activity, like filmmaking or film criticism. Thus it is important to stress that through such 'elucidation' the humanist does make an epistemic contribution, in spite of the fact that the object of their study is in one sense 'already known'. In clarifying the 'logic' of concepts used in a given domain, or providing a perspicuous 'overview' (*Übersicht*) of the way that they interrelate, the humanist is making explicit what was, for the most part, tacit and imperfectly registered knowledge (Wittgenstein, 1958; see also Cioffi, 1998).[8]

The 'know-how' of a skilled filmmaker is rendered explicit, the object of self-conscious knowledge-for-its-own-sake rather than the vehicle of a practical goal (that is, the making of a film).

Now it is certainly true that film theory encompasses a range of different kinds of question and method, and some of the questions it poses do not call out for causal investigations or answers. In asking the question, 'what is the medium of film?' – a central question for most early and classical film theorists, like Arnheim and Bazin, and one that is still debated (Carroll, 1996a; 2003; Danto, 1979; Gaut, 2002; Smith, 2006b; Walton, 1984; Wilson, 1986) – we are asking a definitional question, one that principally requires conceptual and logical analysis; that is, we might put forward an initial definition, and then consider the soundness of the definition in terms of the logical relations between its components. Similarly, the debates around the 'film as philosophy' thesis, discussed in the first part of this chapter, are primarily conceptual. However, it seems unlikely that we will be able to keep empirical matters entirely out of the frame in such cases; we will certainly have to make reference to and examine some films, even if this empirical work doesn't take the systematic, controlled form of a scientific experiment. Note also that several of Turvey's 'traditional humanistic methods' themselves require empirical – rather than conceptual – investigation of a certain sort: discovering intentions, examining patterns of style, assessing them in terms of their originality.

In addition, the burden of much of the philosophy of science over the past fifty years has been to reveal the conceptual dimension of scientific practice. Science does not simply accumulate facts independently of both the physical and conceptual tools – the technologies and theories – available to scientists. Any empirical question will make implicit conceptual assumptions – about the nature of the entities being studied – assumptions which may be more or less reasonable and well supported, but assumptions nonetheless. So, on the one hand, conceptual questions posed within the human sciences require attention to empirical matters; and on the other hand, the empirical questions standard in the natural sciences make conceptual assumptions and are thus susceptible to conceptual scrutiny. Once we take this into account, the lack of first-hand involvement of most film theorists in scientific experiment does not seem nearly as revealing of radically divergent underlying principles as Turvey suggests. For fifty years, philosophers and experimental scientists have been collaborating in the endeavour known as 'cognitive science': why should philosophers of film and film theorists not engage with experimental data on the cognition of film in the same spirit? If this is correct, then Turvey's sharp contrast between internal and external knowledge of human practices, and the equally strong contrast between the human and natural sciences on which the internal/external distinction depends, comes under renewed pressure. Is the domain of film theory quite as autonomous, and quite as distinct from causal enquiry, as Turvey contends?

Naturalism and the human sciences

Consider again Turvey's claims concerning knowledge. When it comes to humanly constituted phenomena – like games or art or entertainment – there is a sense in which we already have knowledge of such things, to the extent that we are able to participate in such practices. But, since Turvey clearly regards Wittgensteinian elucidation as capable of contributing to our fund of knowledge, the kind of knowledge it delivers must be qualitatively different from the ordinary knowledge we possess just by virtue of being competent participants in human institutions. This latter form of knowledge is *practical knowledge* – tacit knowledge which enables us to 'inhabit' human practices – quite different in form from the *propositional* knowledge that both the natural and human sciences deliver. Turvey argues that 'we do not need to know anything about gravity ... to play tennis' (2005: 27) (just as we have seen that he notes that we don't need to know anything about the neurophysiology of perception in order to watch films). But don't we need a kind of 'pre-theoretical', practical knowledge of rubber and gravity in order to play the game? If I lacked such intuitive know-how, how would I be able to hit the ball with the right amount of force? Consider a range of human activities: walking; swimming; bike-riding; speaking and writing; and watching fiction films. In every case we develop know-how with respect to these activities as we engage with them and eventually become participants in the 'worlds' opened up by them, ranging in skill from minimal competence to virtuoso mastery. *But the know-how appears to be as much tacit knowledge of the physical, causal world as it is of human concepts*: to use a language is to know, tacitly, certain things about sound, as much as it is to know, tacitly, certain rules about grammar. We know that raising our voice – speaking more loudly – projects our speech acts over greater distances. We know that speaking in a soft, lulling fashion is more likely to calm a child than loud, staccato utterances. At what point do we cross definitively from the natural world of causality to the human world of intention and invention? Can we disentangle internal from external knowledge in the way and to the degree that Turvey suggests?

If the two forms of knowledge are as sharply separated as Turvey suggests, then enhanced external knowledge of some domain ought to make no appreciable difference to our internal knowledge of that domain; all that is available to the student of human culture is the 'sharpening' of implicit internal knowledge through elucidation or 'grammatical' clarification. Let us consider this in relation to the contemporary scientific study of emotion. Turvey himself alludes to Antonio Damasio's research on the neurology of emotion and reasoning. Damasio (1994) discusses a particular type of brain damage (to the ventromedial prefrontal region of the frontal lobe) which profoundly disrupts, and in the most serious cases destroys altogether, the ability to plan for the future. Individuals with such brain damage suffer from 'flat affect'. It is not that

they lack knowledge about factors bearing on a decision, nor an ability to reason about these factors in certain ways. What they lack is an ability to respond emotionally to imagined possibilities, leaving them stranded among an array of equally (un-)attractive options.[9] This is but one instance of a larger analysis of the structure of the brain and its functions by which Damasio demonstrates the significance of emotions to human reasoning. It is no coincidence that Damasio chose to name the first of his books on this subject *Descartes' Error* (1994); his point is that the conceptual framework posited by René Descartes, concerning the nature of emotions and their relationship with thought, is a mistaken one. There's the rub: Damasio offers up a large body of neurological research that supports a picture of the human brain, and the mind that depends on it, which differs significantly from the picture of the mind we inherit from Descartes (along with many other earlier philosophers). To the extent that concepts related to the mind are part of our fund of *internal* knowledge, it is hard to see how Damasio's investigation into that bit of the causal world known as the human brain has *not* affected the conceptual landscape of our internal knowledge. It is not merely that our tacit understanding of the concepts of 'emotion' and 'reason' have been clarified or elucidated; they have been *revised* in the light of a more informed understanding of their physical, causal underpinnings. If we accept Damasio's findings, then in certain respects our understanding of – that is, our concepts of – emotion and reason will have changed.

As we have seen, the emphasis in the 'grammatical' approach is very much on the concepts we employ in an understanding of any given domain of human practice.[10] But – to continue with our example – though we obviously possess a host of concepts of emotion, *emotions are not merely concepts*. An emotion is a particular type of human response to the environment. The prototypical emotions – happiness, fear, sadness, anger and so forth – have deep evolutionary histories, and are thus ones which we share in some measure with many other animals. Such emotions are defined by characteristic triggers in the environment, by patterns of neural activity, bodily response, subjective feel and 'action tendencies'. Disgust, for example, is typically prompted by violations of physical, moral and social boundaries, expressed by distinctive signals (scrunching up the nose) and aversive withdrawal, associated with nausea-like feelings, all subtended by neural activity in the insula region of the brain (Plantinga, 2006; Rozin, 1993). Emotions are therefore, fundamentally, embodied psychological processes. The concepts we have collectively formed in order to think and communicate about emotions may feed back into the emotional process and affect the emotions that we experience (Robinson, 2005: 75–86). But neither our concepts, nor the words we use to express those concepts, consume and nullify our embodied experience of emotion. Like perception, emotional experience may be characterized by 'non-conceptual content', content which our concepts register only vaguely and imperfectly (Bermúdez, 2003). Our emotion concepts come into play relatively late in the day, not only in evolutionary terms but also in terms of the development of the individual and the aetiology of a particular emotional response. Even if we grant a major role to our concepts of emotion in the way we experience emotions – as seems warranted with respect to those aspects of emotional life in which we see notable cultural variation – it nevertheless remains the case that our emotion concepts are bound up with a complex psychophysical process, defined by our evolutionary history as well as our current cultural belief systems, by patterns of bodily change as much as by cognitive judgements (Griffiths, 1997; Prinz, 2004). In this context, the idea of a clean break between internal and external knowledge seems, once more, implausible.

Turvey acknowledges that concepts may change, but such change as does occur, or at least the way in which we track and come to know about this change, takes place only *within* the realm of internal knowledge. Conceptual change can only occur, as it were, horizontally, within the internal sphere. Consequently, when conceptual change of this sort is identified and clarified, there is no question of construing it as an *improvement* on previous concepts and conceptual distinctions. We have simply moved from one conceptual framework to another. Turvey thus rules out, or at least ignores, another kind of conceptual change: 'vertical' change, which results from the interaction between the internal and external knowledge of some domain. This is a kind of conceptual change that a more naturalistic framework would accept and even highlight (Griffiths, 1997). Recognizing conceptual change of this sort is premised on the idea that many of our concepts reflect or track aspects of the world, including our own being. They may do so imperfectly, but they can be improved, as in the case of emotion and reason. The concepts of phlogiston, the humours, miasma and persistence of vision have all yielded to what most of us take to be more plausible – though doubtless imperfect and still provisional – concepts, or conceptual frameworks, which articulate our knowledge of gas, human motivation, infection and the perception of motion.

What is the yield of this naturalistic perspective on the study of film, and the character of film theory? Turvey argues that 'when we make the decision to watch a film at the local multiplex … [w]e simply use our decision-making capacity' (2005: 26) – that is, we don't need to reflect on which bit of our brain is active in this process. It might as well be some other region of the brain, or for that matter the knee-bone or thigh-bone, as the ventromedial prefrontal region of the frontal lobe that does the work – the matter is so completely irrelevant to the execution of the task. This claim is parallel with the claim that we don't need to understand physical laws to play tennis, and the claim that we don't need a theory of perception in order to watch a film (2005: 27). But note how the ground has shifted in each of these cases. Here, we are talking about simply performing one of a range of actions (playing tennis, deciding to watch a movie, watching a movie); the pursuit of knowledge is not really at stake. In deciding whether or not to go to the cinema I am not seeking to enhance my knowledge of the nature of such decision-making. The moment we shift our focus from the practical to the *theoretical* dimension, however, things look different. Film theory is not merely about the execution of certain actions; it entails the search for knowledge about them. Let's say our question is: on what basis do movie-goers make their decisions about whether and when to go to movies? Many factors will surely come into play in answering this question, including, of course, various social phenomena. But we are more likely to gain an accurate grasp of the nature of such decision-making if we pay attention to what Damasio's evidence suggests, even if his evidence is only indirectly relevant, and only relevant as part of a wider array of different types of evidence. We will be able to see how the neuropsychology of decision-making bears on the particular context of movie-going – and how our understanding of such decision-making is affected by Damasio's model of mental activity and the brain on which it depends (as distinct from a more traditional 'rational choice' model of decision-making). The character and dynamics of decision-making, especially in relation to the role of emotion within the decision-making process, will look very different (for more on emotion and the cinema, see Carroll, 1990; Plantinga and Smith, 1999; Smith, 1995).

Not everything is in dispute between the two accounts of film theory that we have examined here; indeed, considerable common ground is shared between them. Advocates of film theory as conceptual analysis (like Turvey), along with those who defend the role of causal investigation in the domain of film theory (like Carroll) converge on the idea that film theory is a process of generalization about film in which conceptual analysis plays a central role. Both parties conceive of film theory as being properly driven by questions about a given phenomenon – film – rather than by particular doctrines (for example, psychoanalysis or existentialism). What is in dispute between the two perspectives is the

place of empirical study within film theory, especially the kind of controlled, systematic, and quantitative empirical methods associated with the hard sciences; the potential role of empirical discovery in driving conceptual change; and the possibility of progress with respect to certain questions in film theory.

The value of each of these two models to the enterprise of film theory – as science and as conceptual analysis – does not lie in their comprehensiveness: there are many strands of film theory which don't fit straightforwardly into either model. Carroll and Turvey are both well aware of this, and present their models as ideals of practice, ones to which film theory ought to aspire, currently met only here and there in reality. Given the actual diversity of questions asked within film theory, however, this may be a misplaced ambition. The questions we ask about film are of very different sorts – ontological, epistemological, ethical and aesthetic. Each of these perspectives will call upon different methods, indeed probably different *mixes* of method. We must cut our methodological cloth according to the shape of the question asked, and we are more likely to end up with a patchwork than a pure fabric. Film theory is a heterogeneous business. From this point of view, the primary value of the arguments of Carroll and Turvey on the nature of film theory is that they bring the issue itself into focus, and describe particular approaches which undoubtedly form important parts of the armoury of film theory, even if neither approach constitutes the whole of it.

Plato was famously suspicious of the seductive, irrational power of the arts, as exemplified by poetry, music, painting, and drama (Plato, 1991: Books II, X) – ancient artistic practices that are clearly fundamental to the form of mainstream narrative cinema, combining as it does visual depiction, dramatic structure and performance, and the musical underscoring of these elements. Plato might have frowned upon cinema, then, as the most dangerous art of them all, as in fact many philosophers and social commentators have done; certainly he would have been sceptical of those arguing for its value as a form of philosophical expression. Nevertheless, acknowledging its power, he would have recognized the importance of detailed investigation of and rigorous argument about film. In this way, the philosophy of film stakes its claim not only as an intervention in film theory, but also as the latest chapter in the long history of the philosophy of art.

NOTES

1 *Alien* (Ridley Scott, UK, 1979), *Alien 2* (James Cameron, US/UK, 1986), *Alien 3* (David Fincher, US, 1992) and *Alien 4* (Jean-Pierre Jeunet, US, 1997); and *Mission: Impossible* (Brian De Palma, US, 1996) and *Mission: Impossible 2* (John Woo, US/Germany, 2000).

2 For an analysis of the fiction/non-fiction distinction, see Plantinga (1997).

3 See Martin Cohen (2004), Roy A. Sorensen (1999), Wartenberg (2007) on *The Matrix* (Andy Wachowski/Larry Wachowski, US, 1999) and *Empire* (Andy Warhol, US, 1964) as thought experiments, and Smith (2006a) for criticism.

4 Carey's stance might be compared with Roger Scruton's argument that film and photography are wholly parasitic on other art forms: '[a] film is a photograph of a dramatic representation, and whatever representational properties belong to it belong by virtue of the representation that is effected in the dramatic action, that is, by virtue of the words and activities of the actors in the film' (1983: 122). One might have thought that this kind of view had been dispelled by 1925, with the already rich body of silent filmmaking and a growing literature of film theory, devoted mostly to demonstrating the artistic distinctiveness and value of film. But here it is again, in Carey's book, published in 2005.

5 Note also that Carey's first example of the capacity of literature to criticize other literature is really a work of philosophy (2005: 174–5), or at least a work by a philosopher: Jean-Paul Sartre's *What is Literature?* (1967).

6 Carroll (2006) attempts to crack this nut through an exploration of the philosophical implications of *Serene Velocity* (Ernie Gehr, US, 1970), a wordless avant-garde film.

7 Building on similar intuitions, Wartenberg (2006a) has recently argued that the visual illustration of a philosophical argument may make a genuine philosophical contribution to it, rather than merely acting as handmaiden to an essentially verbal affair. In its emphasis on the importance of the imagination for moral deliberation, Diamond's essay resonates with the perspective on film articulated by Cavell and Mulhall. Mulhall, for example, writes of an 'open

border' between the philosophical and the literary (quoted in Baggini, 2003), and his discussion of film is conducted in the same spirit. Diamond is more tentative on this point, noting that making arguments is 'what all [philosophers] do some or most of the time' (1991a: 293), and that different criteria are appropriate for judging the quality of imaginative as opposed to argumentative works, even as she insists that philosophical works that disdain argument for more imaginative approaches should nevertheless count as instances of philosophy (1991a: 294). (Diamond has in mind works like Stephen Clark's *The Moral Status of Animals* [1977], a critical review of which prompted 'Anything but Argument?'.) She seems more wary of appearing to collapse philosophy and literature ('… philosophy, as contrasted with literature [or at any rate with literature not itself steeped in philosophy] …') (1991a: 304). Note also the connection here with the idea, discussed above in relation to the problem of fiction, that films and literary works can be likened to philosophical *thought experiments*, as well as *counter-examples*. As with Diamond's argument on the importance of imagination as distinct from argument, this strategy involves sidestepping the centrality of argument to philosophy; the fiction-as-thought experiment strategy, however, places an emphasis on other features and techniques of philosophy which strongly resemble those of imaginative fiction.

8 Cioffi (1998) provides an illuminating discussion of the method of *Übersicht* – putting into order that which we already know – in Wittgenstein.

9 In a little more detail: the brains of individuals suffering from such damage fail to lay down 'somatic markers', or bodily feeling tones, which label or categorize situations in at least certain broad ways (as threatening, inviting, etc.). Experimental evidence shows that they retain an ability to make immediate rational judgements about their situation – but lack the ability to extend such rational planning into the future, because they benefit from no emotional guidance as they contemplate future possible outcomes.

10 Turvey's essay on the imagination and cinema is a good example, with its unwavering focus on the importance of a 'correct' understanding and use of the concept of imagination (2006).

REFERENCES

Allen, Richard and Smith, Murray (eds) (1997) *Film Theory and Philosophy*. Oxford: Clarendon Press.

Allen, Richard and Turvey, Malcolm (eds) (2001) *Wittgenstein, Culture, and the Arts*. London: Routledge.

Anderson, Joseph D. (1996) *The Reality of Illusion: An Ecological Approach to Cognitive Film Theory*. Carbondale: Southern Illinois University Press.

Arnheim, Rudolf (1958) *Film as Art*. London: Faber & Faber.

Baggini, Julian (2003) 'Alien Ways of Thinking: Mulhall's *On Film*', *Film-Philosophy*, 7(24). Available at: http://www.film-philosophy.com/vol7-2003/n24baggini.

Barratt, Daniel and Frome, Jonathan (eds) (2006) 'Special Issue: Film, Cognition and Emotion', *Film Studies: An International Review*, 8.

Bazin, André (1967) *What is Cinema? Vol.1*. Ed. and tr. Hugh Gray. Berkeley: University of California.

Beardsley, Monroe (1981) *Aesthetics: Problems in the Philosophy of Criticism*. 2nd edn. Indianapolis: Hackett.

Bergson, Henri (1944) *Creative Evolution*. Tr. Arthur Mitchell. New York: Modern Library.

Bermúdez, José (2003) 'Nonconceptual Mental Content', *Stanford Encyclopedia of Philosophy*. Available at: http://plato.stanford.edu/entries/content-nonconceptual/.

Bordwell, David (1989a) 'A Case for Cognitivism', *Iris*, 9: 11–41.

Bordwell, David (1989b) *Making Meaning: Inference and Rhetoric in the Interpretation of Cinema*. Cambridge, MA: Harvard University Press.

Carey, John (2005) *What Good are the Arts?* London: Faber & Faber.

Carroll, Noël (1990) *The Philosophy of Horror, or, Paradoxes of the Heart*. New York: Routledge.

Carroll, Noël (1993) 'Film, Rhetoric, and Ideology', in Salim Kemal and Ivan Gaskell (eds), *Explanation and Value in the Arts*. Cambridge: Cambridge University Press. pp. 215–37.

Carroll, Noël (1996a) *Theorizing the Moving Image*. New York: Cambridge University Press.

Carroll, Noël (1996b) 'Prospects for Film Theory: A Personal Assessment', in David Bordwell and Noël Carroll (eds), *Post-Theory: Reconstructing Film Studies*. Madison: University of Wisconsin Press. pp. 37–68.

Carroll, Noël (2002) 'The Wheel of Virtue: Art, Literature and Moral Knowledge', *Journal of Aesthetics and Art Criticism*, 60(1): 3–26.

Carroll, Noël (2003) *Engaging the Moving Image*. New Haven, CT: Yale University Press.

Carroll, Noël (2006) 'Philosophizing through the Moving Image: The Case of *Serene Velocity*', *The Journal of Aesthetics and Art Criticism*, 64(1): 173–186.

Cavell, Stanley (1979) *The World Viewed: Reflections on the Ontology of Film*. 2nd edn. Cambridge, MA: Harvard University Press.

Cavell, Stanley (1981) *Pursuits of Happiness: The Hollywood Comedy of Remarriage*. Cambridge, MA: Harvard University Press.

Cavell, Stanley (1990) *Contesting Tears: The Hollywood Melodrama of the Unknown Woman*. Chicago: University of Chicago Press.

Cavell, Stanley (2004) *Cities of Words: Pedagogical Letters on a Register of the Moral Life*. Cambridge: Belknap Press.

Chatman, Seymour (1990) *Coming to Terms: The Rhetoric of Narrative in Fiction and Film*. Ithaca, NY: Cornell University Press.

Choi, Jinhee (2006) 'Apperception on Display: Structural Films and Philosophy', *Journal of Aesthetics and Art Criticism*, 64(1): 165–72.

Cioffi, Frank (1998) *Wittgenstein on Freud and Frazer*. Cambridge: Cambridge University Press.

Clark, Stephen (1977) *The Moral Status of Animals*. Oxford: Clarendon Press.

Cohen, Martin (2004) *Wittgenstein's Beetle and Other Classic Thought Experiments*. Oxford: Blackwell.

Currie, Gregory (1995) *Image and Mind: Film, Philosophy, and Cognitive Science*. New York: Cambridge University Press.

Damasio, Antonio R. (1994) *Descartes' Error: Emotion, Reason and the Human Brain*. New York: Avon Books.

Danto, Arthur C. (1979) 'Moving Pictures', *Quarterly Review of Film Studies*, 4(1): 1–21.

Danto, Arthur C. (1981) *The Transfiguration of the Commonplace: A Philosophy of Art*. Cambridge, MA: Harvard University Press.

Davis, Whitney (2006) 'The World Rewound: Peter Forgács' Wittgenstein Tractatus', *Journal of Aesthetics and Art Criticism*, 64(1): 199–211.

Deleuze, Gilles (1986) *Cinema 1: The Movement-Image*. Tr. Hugh Tomlinson and Barbara Habberjam. Minneapolis: University of Minnesota Press.

Deleuze, Gilles (1989) *Cinema 2: The Time-Image*. Tr. Hugh Tomlinson and Robert Galeta. Minneapolis: University of Minnesota Press.

Diamond, Cora (1991a) 'Anything but Argument?', in *The Realistic Spirit: Wittgenstein, Philosophy, and the Mind*. Cambridge, MA: MIT Press. pp. 291–308.

Diamond, Cora (1991b) 'Missing the Adventure: Reply to Nussbaum', in *The Realistic Spirit: Wittgenstein, Philosophy, and the Mind*. Cambridge, MA: MIT Press. pp. 309–18.

Eisenstein, Sergei (1988) *Selected Works 1: Writings 1922–1934*. Ed. and tr. Richard Taylor. London: BFI.

Eisenstein, Sergei (1991) *Selected Works 2: Towards a Theory of Montage, 1937–40*. Eds Michael Glenny and Richard Taylor. Tr. Michael Glenny. London: BFI.

Emerson, Ralph Waldo (1993) 'Self-Reliance', in *Self-Reliance and Other Essays*. Mineola, NY: Dover.

Falzon, Christopher (2002) *Philosophy Goes to the Movies: An Introduction to Philosophy*. London: Routledge.

Fodor, Jerry (1974) 'Special sciences (or: the disunity of science as a working hypothesis)', *Synthèse*, 28: 97–115.

Fodor, Jerry (2004) 'What Wotan Wants', review of *Finding an Ending: Reflections on Wagner's 'Ring'* by Phillip Kitcher and Richard Schacht, *London Review of Books*, 5 August: 8–10.

Gaut, Berys (2002) 'Cinematic Art', *Journal of Aesthetics and Art Criticism*, (60)4: 299–312.

Grau, Christopher (ed.) (2005) *Philosophers Explore the Matrix*. New York: Oxford University Press.

Greene, Richard and Vernezze, Peter (eds) (2004) *The Sopranos and Philosophy: I Kill Therefore I Am*. Chicago: Open Court.

Griffiths, Paul E. (1997) *What Emotions Really Are: The Problem of Psychological Categories*. Chicago: University of Chicago Press.

Hegel, G.W.F. (1977) *The Phenomenology of Spirit*. Tr. A.V. Miller. Oxford: Oxford University Press.

Irwin, William (2002) *The Matrix and Philosophy: Welcome to the Desert of the Real*. Chicago: Open Court Press.

Irwin, William, Conrad, Mark T. and Skoble, Aeon (eds) (2001) *The Simpsons and Philosophy: The D'oh! of Homer*. Chicago: Open Court.

James, William (1950) *The Principles of Psychology, Volume I*. New York: Dover.

Kitcher, Philip and Schacht, Richard (2004) *Finding an Ending: Reflections on Wagner's 'Ring'*. New York: Oxford University Press.

Kupfer, Joseph (1999) *Visions of Virtue in Popular Film*. Boulder, CO: Westview.

Lessing, Gotthold Ephraim (1962) *Laocoön*. Tr. E.A. McCormick. Indianapolis: Bobbs-Merrill.

Light, Andrew (2003) *Reel Arguments: Film, Philosophy and Social Criticism*. Boulder, CO: Westview.

Litch, Mary (2004) *Philosophy through Film*. New York: Routledge.

Livingston, Paisley (2006) 'Theses on Cinema as Philosophy', *Journal of Aesthetics and Art Criticism*, 64(1): 11–18.

Lowry, Edward (1985) *The Filmology Movement and Film Study in France*. Ann Arbor, MI: UMI Research Press.

Metz, Christian (1974) *Film Language: A Semiotics of the Cinema*. Tr. M. Taylor. Chicago: University of Chicago Press.

Mulhall, Stephen (2002) *On Film*. London: Routledge.

Mulhall, Stephen (2003) 'Ways of Thinking: A Response to Andersen and Baggini', *Film-Philosophy*, 7(25). Available at: http://www.film-philosophy.com/vol7-2003/n25mulhall.

Mulhall, Stephen (2006) 'The Impersonation of Personality: Film as Philosophy in *Mission: Impossible*',

Journal of Aesthetics and Art Criticism, 64(1): 97–110.

Münsterberg, Hugo ([1916] 2002) *The Photoplay: A Psychological Study, and Other Writings*. Ed. Allan Langdale. New York: Routledge.

Nussbaum, Martha (1990) *Love's Knowledge*. New York: Oxford University Press.

Plantinga, Carl (1997) *Rhetoric and Representation in Nonfiction Film*. New York: Cambridge University Press.

Plantinga, Carl and Smith, Greg M. (eds) (1999) *Passionate Views: Film, Cognition, and Emotion*. Baltimore, MD: Johns Hopkins University Press.

Plantinga, Carl (2006) 'Disgusted at the Movies', *Film Studies: An International Review*, 8: 81–92.

Plato (1991) *The Republic*. 2nd edn. Tr. Allan Bloom. New York: Basic Books.

Ponech, Trevor (2006) 'The Substance of Cinema', *Journal of Aesthetics and Art Criticism*, 64(1): 187–98.

Prinz, Jesse J. (2004) *Gut Reactions: A Perceptual Theory of Emotion*. Oxford: Oxford University Press.

Read, Rupert and Goodenough, Jerry (eds) (2005) *Film as Philosophy: Essays on Cinema after Wittgenstein and Cavell*. New York: Palgrave.

Robinson, Jenefer (2005) *Deeper Than Reason: Emotion and its Role in Literature, Music, and Art*. Oxford: Clarendon Press.

Rozin, Paul (1993) 'Disgust', in Michael Lewis and Jeanette M. Haviland-Jones (eds), *Handbook of Emotion*. 2nd edn. New York: Guilford. pp. 575–94.

Russell, Bruce (2000) 'The Philosophical Limits of Film', *Film and Philosophy*, Special Interest Edition on the Films of Woody Allen: 163–67.

Sartre, Jean-Paul (1967) *What is Literature?*. Tr. Bernard Frechtman. London: Methuen.

Scruton, Roger (1983) 'Photography and Representation', in *The Aesthetic Understanding*. London: Methuen. pp. 102–26.

Searle, John R. (1975) 'The Logical Status of Fictional Discourse', *New Literary History*, 6(2): 319–32.

Searle, John R. (1980) 'Minds, Brains, and Programs', *The Behavioral and Brain Sciences*, 3(3): 417–24.

Smith, Murray (1995) *Engaging Characters: Fiction, Emotion, and the Cinema*. Oxford: Clarendon Press.

Smith, Murray (2006a) 'Film Art, Argument, and Ambiguity', *Journal of Aesthetics and Art Criticism*, 64(1): 33–42.

Smith, Murray and Wartenberg, Thomas (eds) (2006) 'Special issue: Film as Philosophy', *Journal of Aesthetics and Art Criticism*, 64(1); reprinted as Smith and Wartenberg (eds) (2006). *Thinking through Cinema: Film as Philosophy*. Malden, MA: Blackwell.

Smith, Murray and Wartenberg, Thomas (eds) (2006b) *Thinking through Cinema: Film as Philosophy.* Malden, MA: Blackwell.

Sorensen, Roy A. (1999) *Thought Experiments.* New York: Oxford University Press.

Turvey, Malcolm (2005) 'Can Scientific Models of Theorizing Help Film Theory?', in Thomas E. Wartenberg and Angela Curran (eds), *The Philosophy of Film: Introductory Text and Readings.* Oxford: Blackwell. pp. 21–32.

Turvey, Malcolm (2006) 'Imagination, Simulation, and Fiction', *Film Studies: An International Review,* 8: 116–25.

von Wright, Georg Henrik (1971) *Explanation and Understanding.* Ithaca, NY: Cornell University Press.

Walton, Kendall (1984) 'Transparent Pictures: On the Nature of Photographic Realism', *Critical Inquiry,* 11(2): 246–77.

Wartenberg, Thomas E. (1999) *Unlikely Couples: Movie Romance as Social Criticism.* Boulder, CO: Westview Press.

Wartenberg, Thomas E. (2005) 'Philosophy Screened: Experiencing *The Matrix*', in Thomas E. Wartenberg and Angela Curran (eds), *The Philosophy of Film: Introductory Text and Readings.* Oxford: Blackwell. pp. 270–83.

Wartenberg, Thomas E. (2006a) 'Beyond *Mere* Illustration: How Films Can Be Philosophy', *Journal of Aesthetics and Art Criticism,* 64(1): 19–32.

Wartenberg, Thomas E. (2006b) 'Film as Argument', *Film Studies: An International Review,* 8: 126–37.

Wartenberg, Thomas E. (2007) *Thinking on Screen: Film as Philosophy.* New York: Routledge.

Wartenberg, Thomas E. and Curran, Angela (eds) (2005) *The Philosophy of Film: Introductory Text and Readings.* Malden, MA: Blackwell.

Wilson, George M. (1986) *Narration in Light: Studies in Cinematic Point of View.* Baltimore, MD: The Johns Hopkins University Press.

Wittgenstein, Ludwig (1958) *Philosophical Investigations.* 2nd edn. Tr. G.E.M. Anscombe. Oxford: Basil Blackwell.

Wordsworth, William and Coleridge, Samuel Taylor (1991) *Lyrical Ballads.* Ed. R.L. Brett and A.R. Jones. London: Routledge.

11

Difficult Relations: Film Studies and Continental European Philosophy

Hamish Ford

This chapter looks at three central case-studies in the sometimes vexed relationship between European philosophy and the quintessentially, if ambivalent, modern institution of cinema. The aim is not only to address what European philosophy has had to say about cinema and film, but also to suggest some of the questions that cinema has posed to such philosophy and to show how, in doing so, cinema has impacted upon philosophy.

The case-studies considered are: the relationship between film writing and Frankfurt School philosophy; Merleau-ponty's phenomenology as a broadly influential strand of philosophy-related film scholarship; and, finally, an assessment of the most substantial study of the cinema by a major European philosopher, Gilles Deleuze, most notably his notion of the 'time-image'.

One other key intersection between European philosophy and Film Studies is missing from this list. That is the take-up by the discipline, as newly institutionalized

in the 1970s, of Lacanian psychoanalysis and Barthesian semiotics. That story is told elsewhere in this Handbook, particularly in Chapter 3 and Chapter 15.

RADICAL INVESTMENT AND CRITIQUE: THE FRANKFURT SCHOOL'S VISION OF CINEMA

The nexus between philosophy and film was substantially developed, even inaugurated to a large extent, by writers associated more or less officially with the Frankfurt School, in particular Siegfried Kracauer and Walter Benjamin. Very much thinkers of their time, their Weimar period writing in the mid- to late 1920s presciently warned about the susceptibility of Germany's emerging consumer culture to its exploitation by fascist politics. Within this context, and as part of a wider revival of interest in the problematic of 'modernity', it is their theoretical yet politically engaged responses to cinema understood as a key feature of modern urban life that led to a critical re-evaluation of Kracauer and Benjamin in the 1990s. (See Chapter 22 for an account of the Frankfurt School that places their thinking about film in the context of cinema, modernity and modernism.)

The work of scholars such as Heide Schlüpmann (1987), Gertrud Koch (1991; 2000) and particularly Miriam Hansen (1992; 1993; 1995; 1997) has helped to reclaim Kracauer from a reputation as a naïve realist, so that now he is acknowledged as a significant forerunner to later, more famous Frankfurt School analysts of consumer culture such as Theodor Adorno.[1] As Kracauer, along with Benjamin, is sometimes treated as a celebratory commentator on early popular culture at its now often romanticized 1920s apogee, it is important to remember the darker elements of his early writing. Rather than heralding the beginning of a new age, the Weimar essays often feature language describing a historical process of 'decay'. Metaphysical 'lack' and 'crisis' are exposed as the root of modern reality for the early Kracauer, in an extension of the sociologist Max Weber's influential early twentieth-century descriptions of modernity's 'iron cage' (1958: 181) and its prevailing 'disenchantment' (1946: 155). In his best known essay from this period, 1927's 'The Mass Ornament', Kracauer argues that it is the 'metaphysical suffering' caused by people's 'exile from the religious sphere' that makes them 'companions in misfortune' (1995: 129). Nonetheless, the Weimar era writing at least maintains some heavily qualified investment in modernity's consumer culture as one possible means of bringing about historical disruption and change, including a cautiously hopeful vision of cinema's role in this process.

At the centre of Kracauer's investment in cinema is his advocacy of a complex understanding of realism. This realism is radically different either from that of 'classical Hollywood' or the 'classic realist text', or from mainstream documentary realism (see also Chapter 23 and Chapter 24).

Kracauer's 'radical' cinematic realism has the potential to prompt perception that transcends teleological movement, whether the narrative of 'official' history or the coercion of institutional modernization. As he later argued in *Theory of Film,* first published in 1960, the camera's ability to record the minutiae of the physical world captures and displays multiple material fragments of contemporary life that escape the constraints of narrative. In doing so, a complex physical reality is 'redeemed' (1997). This 'redemption' undermines not only the narrative and political closure of classical realism, Hollywood or otherwise, but also the idea of psychological motivation – and, by extension, the possibility of 'centred' subjectivity. Kracauer saw film as seizing 'the human being with skin and hair', which is why '[t]he "ego" of the human being assigned to film is subject to permanent dissolution, is incessantly exploded by material phenomena' (quoted in Hansen, 1993: 458). The key to this displacement of the human ego is the rendering of the modern world in the form of objects that clutter it. While the Hollywood tradition is defined by the centrality and importance of people (characters) and their dramas, Kracauer emphasizes 'the tremendous importance of objects'. For him, 'the actor too is no more than a detail, a fragment of the matter of the world' who makes up 'real-life complexes which the conventional figure-ground patterns usually conceal from view' (1997: 252, 255). This refusal of distinctions between form and content, subject and object, figure and ground, exposes 'openings' that provide new, paradoxical focal points for the viewer, fissures of possibility (rather than lack) typically concealed in narrative-based filmmaking.

Bearing witness to, and 'democratically' rendering, all of modernity's physical elements – including its discarded objects and human beings – film challenges the viewer to engage with modernity's confronting materiality as liberated from rationalizing structures and regimes. Contemporary history can then be charted as indeterminacy and experience, rather than closure. This meant that Kracauer was able to differentiate what he saw as film's potential for liberatory distraction from reactionary distraction, or 'alienation'. His view was that not only teleological narratives but also the ritualistic spaces of cinema-going encouraged this reactionary distraction, seduced the proletariat into the rituals and mythologies of the social real that oppressed them, rather than allowing them a critical distance from it (Kracauer, 1987). At the same time, however, Kracauer also describes a radical distraction in response to film's democratic rendering of modernity's material surface, which allows the viewer a chance to recognize his or her alienation. Herein lies cinema's potential to generate an ethical response to mass culture via the rendering of its surface phenomena – an aesthetics in which the moving image, filled with the rich heterogeneity of material history, can be claimed for a potentially rethought and negotiated experiential sense of collective life. Kracauer's politics, aesthetics and philosophical investments come together in this idea of the liberated fragment-spaces of the image in engagement with the self-liberating viewer in concert with others.

The grounding of Kracauer's Weimar-era analysis of cinema in modernity's historical forms prefigures the emphasis on historical specificity, contingency, and difference in today's culturally engaged Film Studies – hence its appeal. The key to his philosophy is the impact of surface material reality as presented in the film image, not as a superficial skin to be penetrated in order to discover the 'truth' beneath it, but rather as the very stuff of modernity's real, embodying the marks of all its potentially enabling radical energy *and* its regressive re-mythologization – a reality intimately connected to the crisis-engendering energy of modern capitalism. For him, this ambivalent modernity, potentially radical but easily regressive, can be seen nowhere more clearly than in and through film.

Walter Benjamin also discerned radical transformative potential in film, in particular through the violence this technological art inflicted on pre-modern tradition and belief. His most famous essay, 'The Work of Art in the Age of Mechanical Reproduction', first published in 1935, assesses how photography, film and sound recording destroy the metaphysical originality and 'aura' of the work of art: 'for the first time in world history, mechanical reproduction emancipates the work of art from its parasitical dependence on ritual' (1992: 669). This loss of aura, the effective eviction of religion or the sacred from art, is another symptom of Weber's disenchanted modern world and yet also offers the possibility of emancipation. However, Benjamin notes how replacement mythologies and metaphysical investments re-emerge, the most obvious being through the iconic power of close-up images of movie stars. Art's auratic element is re-energized with 'modern' forms and mythology to match. Technology thus forces, and enables, the aura to take new, more popular forms that appear more 'democratic' at best, and offer frightening propagandistic potential at worst.

For Benjamin, the potentially regressive aspect of 'aura' lay in its seductive powers of reification and consumption. The alternative he hoped for was a new, 'radical' aura gleaned from the very heart of social reality, activating the contradictions or 'gaps' for creative and transformative potential and so creating an energized contemporary subjective experience. The commodity, says Benjamin, is always 'bathed in a profane glow' (1973: 105) – one easily pressed into the service of consumer desire but one which also has the potential to be harnessed for more revolutionary purposes. But a kind of double bind emerges when it comes to any possible 'content' for any such non-regressive aura. Although he welcomed its disappearance as a marker of privileged class access to art, Benjamin (1972) also lamented the destruction of a new aura's potential, such as the socialist possibilities of photography, by commercialization's 'use value'. Here Benjamin's idiosyncratic Marxism reveals itself, combining an intermittently materialist-historical approach with a 'Messianic' meta-physics, sometimes in the form of Jewish theology, concerning revolutionary (but non-prescriptive) change.[2] Benjamin's work is less philosophically 'consistent' than that of his contemporaries, and its lack of system stretched the limits of Frankfurt School interdisciplinarity. Yet his sometimes romantic celebration of fragmentary textual practice and thinking is one of the things that has attracted film scholars to Benjamin's work. An emphasis on experience in all its unpredictable and unknowable specificity is the key to a general commitment to subjectivity as a means of personal resistance and creative 'escape' from an oppressive social reality and the dictatorial elements of consumer culture.

Benjamin's emphasis on subjectivity, play and fragmentary experience meant that he was from the outset more sympathetic to the avant-garde than Kracauer. He aligned himself with the dadaists, expressionists and surrealists in searching for an aesthetic means of rendering and prompting the transformation of everyday experience as a mechanism of revolutionary change. Despite that difference, Benjamin did also share Kracauer's interest in cinema's ability to liberate and activate the 'rubbish' of history, and he believed that the best means to this end was *montage*. This became his ultimate textual principle irrespective of form, a method that allowed an articulation of the modern world in all its rupture and incoherence (Bronner, 1998). In effect, montage became both form and content: material and spiritual rupture, artistic and socio-political possibility. His unfinished *Arcades Project* (1999), the fragmented textual form of which suggests a mythic 'ur-history' of cultural modernism, is the quintessence of this in literary form (Bronner, 1998; for extended discussion, see Buck-Morss, 1991). This is where Benjamin's modernist utopianism resides: it is an always-in-process creative act with an unattainable material condition or end-point – an experience, conception and expression of lived history ripped from linearity and prescribed progress. The role of cinematic experience is then to draw out subversive socio-political powers that frequently lie dormant or suppressed in film's conventional formal presentation. Film's 'social significance', Benjamin writes,

'is inconceivable without its destructive, cathartic aspect, that is, the liquidation of the traditional value of the cultural heritage' (1992: 668).

Benjamin's advocacy of the cinematic experience rests ultimately on a hopeful, non-regressive metaphysics enabled by the sheer immediacy of film's affective impact, but that has the potential to bring about real-world changes. Central to this conceptualization of the medium is a capacity for perception uniquely engendered by the photographic arts – first, still photography (1972), and then cinema. As Benjamin puts it: 'The camera introduces us to unconscious optics' (1992: 677). This *unconscious optics* ties together Benjamin's conception of montage as generative fragmentation and the idea of reality's unfettered rendering on screen in all its gaps and unconsidered elements, and in doing so it opens up thus far unrealized potential not only for perception, but also for understanding and action. Much of the scholarship on the optical unconscious has treated it as the evocative genesis for a politically engaged avant-garde theory of cinematic – and 'modern' – experience that is agonistic vis-à-vis more 'official' narratives of modernism (see especially Krauss, 1994). This approach is framed in quasi-utopian terms. It implies that subjective effect can lead to socio-political outcomes by means of a virtual experience or event. In doing so, this understanding of 'unconscious optics' seems to assume that the individual subject's way of experiencing the world is shared by others, by means of both trans-individual psychic perception and social agreement as to desirable change.

The much-discussed core of this modern experience is 'shock', a term that encapsulates Benjamin's version of Bertolt Brecht's principle of the 'interruption' or 'alienation' effect (1964). Benjamin suggests that cinema can potentially bring about a shock of recognition on the part of an audience affected similarly, one made up of subjects able to recognize the conditions revealed to them on the screen. In Benjamin's idiosyncratic model, this occurs less through rational reflection than through unconscious or 'absent-minded' processes:

> Distraction as provided by art presents a covert control of the extent to which new tasks have become soluble by apperception. Since, moreover, individuals are tempted to avoid such tasks, art will tackle the most difficult and most important ones where it is able to mobilize the masses. Today it does so in the film ... The film with its shock effect meets this mode of reception halfway. The film makes the cult value recede into the background not only by putting the public in the position of the critic, but also by the fact that at the movies this position requires no attention. The public is an examiner, but an absent-minded one. (1992: 679)

This beguiling idea of *shock*, with its ambiguous yet potentially radical impact upon a mass of viewers on the unconscious level, perhaps shows most clearly Benjamin's hybrid of Marxist philosophy and mystical Messianic thought. It is at the heart of Benjamin's attempt to shape an aesthetics by which socio-political 'liberation' can be energized as well as a prefiguring of how such movement might subsequently come about.

The implications for film theory of Benjamin's thinking about the process of experiential montage and shock have only been worked through since his death. Because they presuppose an extraordinarily close relationship between the viewer and the very apparatus of cinema, they offer a distinct perspective on spectatorship and ideological complicity. In Benjamin's view, the audience really identifies less with the actor than with the camera (1992: 672). Rather than empathizing, temporarily, with one or other of the characters in a film, the idea of shock and reflexive alienation relies upon any such subjective alignment being short-circuited. This not only has the potential to 'liberate' the viewer in terms of subjectivity, their social real, and the possibility of political engagement; it also radically opens up long sustained assumptions about what constitutes films, filmmaking and cinema per se.

Kracauer and Benjamin remain foundational figures in the traffic between philosophy and film, offering both critique and potentially radical visions of twentieth-century modernity's quintessential medium,

and they are widely held in high regard within present-day Film Studies. By contrast, their Frankfurt School colleague Theodor Adorno has often been scorned, especially from a populist cultural studies perspective, for his 'elitist' view of the 'culture industry'. This critique was articulated most polemically with Max Horkheimer in their *Dialectic of Enlightenment* (1979), first published in 1944. Here the Frankfurt School's 'new Marxism' found its most influential (and controversial) account of the oppressive and homogenizing structures of mass consumer culture. Capitalist modernity, Adorno and Horkheimer argued, was reneging upon Enlightenment promises about individual freedom. It was re-enslaving workers through the mechanized industrial processes of Taylorism and Fordism, while offering the bourgeoisie a pseudo-individuality through consumption. The glamorous zenith of this delusory individuation was the movie star, they suggested, whose hairstyle was supposed to express her uniqueness. But Adorno and Horkheimer's critique of cinema went further than the conformist process of subjectification evident in Hollywood iconography. They also made something of a pre-emptive strike against auteurism in its original 1950s incarnation. When the new culture industry *cognoscenti* read the 'personal signature' of a film director as a marker of creative freedom, argued Adorno and Horkheimer, as often as not they were falling into the trap of misrecognizing a standardized, assembly-line product as a work of individual artistic expression (Andrae, 1979: 34).

Unlike Kracauer and Benjamin, Adorno and Horkheimer appeared to deny cinema any possible radical aesthetics, impact or outcome, let alone the 'vernacular modernism' later perceived by Hansen (1999). This is why they are frequently considered not to have 'understood' film at all, especially given the contrast between the sophistication of their analysis of other art forms and a passage like this:

> The sound film, far surpassing the theater illusion, leaves no room for imagination or action on the

part of the audience, who is to respond within the structure of the film yet deviate from its precise detail, without losing the thread of the story; hence the film forces its victims to equate it directly with reality ... Sustained thought is out of the question, if the spectator is not to miss the relentless rush of the facts. (1979: 126–7)

Film becomes an irredeemable mechanism of the enslaving culture industry in which 'the regression of enlightenment to ideology ... finds its typical expression in cinema and radio', fuelled by mass desire for a model of heavily delimited 'individuality' as prescribed by the ideological dictates of what they call 'the administered life' (1979: xvi).[3]

In its defence, it should be remembered that *Dialectic of Enlightenment* was written at a time when Hollywood and European fascism's domination of the moving image needed very much to be addressed, and when there seemed little hope for a more radical modernist vision of cinema. Benjamin's writing on film was itself equally coloured by its context: in particular, the often avant Soviet, German and French cinema of the 1920s. Although Benjamin did not survive to reconsider his thoughts on film during and after the war, Kracauer did, and his post-war work is highly pessimistic about the future development of cinema.

In 1966, Adorno published a late essay on film that appears to reflect both the influence of his friend, the filmmaker Alexander Kluge, and also the impact of recent modernist feature films like Antonioni's *La Notte* (Italy/France, 1961). With its more nuanced attitude towards cinema – and perhaps towards the culture industry as a whole (Hansen, 1981–82) – 'Transparencies on Film' (1991) provides Film Studies scholars with a useful point of entry into Adorno's monumental final work, *Aesthetic Theory* (1983), published in 1970 after his death. Such late writing has been the main focus of film scholarship's thus far limited and sporadic interest in his work, often in the context of assessing the philosophical importance of post-war European film modernism.[4] A new look at Adorno's relevance to Film Studies also allows a

deeper recognition of his work's relationship to Benjamin and Kracauer, as Hansen's meticulous re-evaluation of Frankfurt School scholarship has shown. Furthermore, it provides a clearer back-history to the arguments influencing many early critical theorists of postmodernism, such as Jean Baudrillard and Fredric Jameson.

Adorno's late work addresses artistic praxis and aesthetic experience as commentaries upon an alienated social real that, potentially, may move from commenting on that real to subverting it. Art, for Adorno, should not be an escapist discourse – or at least genuine, radical modern art. This means art that critically reflects alienation back upon its social conditions. *Reflexivity* is the key. Appropriating techniques and materials from a reality defined by the culture industry, radical works of art must draw attention to the marks or fractures resulting from the appropriation process, preserving traces of those elements that resist integration (Adorno, 1983: 10). Although this can enable means to transformative ends, the tone of such artworks is anything but affirmational. For Adorno, 'black is the ideal' as the means to both trenchant critique and possible newness (1983: 58). Modern art can provide sites through which radical, appropriation-resistant 'negativity' can partially be enacted. This is potentially achieved by the material work itself and by engaging the subject in confrontation with this challenging force (see his *Negative Dialectics* [1973], first published in 1966, for Adorno's ultimate philosophical exposition of negation.) The work of art's critical rendering of horrific social reality through its formally reflexive appropriation of materials provokes an affective 'tremor' in the subject (Adorno, 1983: 346). For this most pessimistic Frankfurt School thinker, only the reflexive and fragmentary rendering of a reified modernity can deliver art's promise of epistemological assault and ethical impact: 'art may be the only remaining medium of truth in an age of incomprehensible terror and suffering' (Adorno, 1983: 27). What it offers is the potential for an engaged capacity for creative fantasy, a potential space in which the un-free subject might experience and think anew.

Once the excesses of the culture industry thesis are contextually faced then put aside, Adorno's late aesthetic perspective suggests a challenging Frankfurt School account of cinema very different from those of Kracauer and Benjamin. It offers two valuable strains. On the one hand, it provides a way of engaging critically with all the psychic and philosophical dimensions of cinema's starring – or 'mirroring' – role within a sometimes ethically regressive socio-political reality. On the other hand, Adorno's philosophy suggests a framework within which it might be possible to explain film's more properly challenging incarnations, and to assess the extent of its potential for radical critique and disruption.

EMBODIED CINEMA: MERLEAU-PONTY'S PHENOMENOLOGICAL SENSE

The return to favour of some Frankfurt School contributions to Film Studies, along with André Bazin's concurrent resurgence, has often been achieved by re-framing earlier debates around realism, history and ontology – ideas out of fashion in some schools of film theory during the 1970s and 1980s (see Chapter 24). At the same time, and in relation to these revived debates, a different strand in European philosophy has also been taken up in contemporary Film Studies: the phenomenology of Maurice Merleau-Ponty and its legacy.

In her book *Address of the Eye* (1992), Vivian Sobchack demonstrates the potential usefulness of Merleau-Ponty's phenomenology by highlighting some of the blind spots in the theoretical underpinning of dominant film theory since the 1970s. Psychoanalysis and Marxism, she argues, have 'converged in a mutual recognition of the originary nature and productive function of language and discourse in constituting the libidinal "economy" of the "self" and the political "unconscious" of the social formation' (1992: xiii). The key impulse

in Sobchack's book – one increasingly evident across diverse Film Studies discourses, including some that don't engage with phenomenological language as well as those that do – is to address the *affective experience of embodied subjectivity*, conceived through non-psychoanalytic means. Adapting Merleau-Ponty's language, Sobchack describes this liberation of embodied experience from its repressed position beneath structuralist theory as the ' "fleshing out" of film' (1992: xviii).

A broadly phenomenological perspective has been a recurrent feature in European thinking about film. Both Kracauer and Bazin maintained a phenomenological emphasis on spatiality and the relationship between subjects and objects as rendered on screen, while also demonstrating a keen interest in the precise formal means of that rendering. Writing in the first half of the 1950s, Bazin proposed that the invention of sound and deep-focus lenses had allowed the viewer freedom to select focus from a hermeneutically open image (1967: 35). If cinema and physical reality are as intrinsically related as Italian neorealism famously persuaded Bazin they are, then the subject must also share in this technological-organic relationship. This broad principle makes for the opposite of a semiotically-informed vision of cinema, as pointed out by Peter Wollen in Bazin's emphasis on the organic nature-world the camera records (1976: 22). Yet the *kind* of material world Bazin describes, and the result of its being filmed, make for a loosely phenomenological film writing that can be read today as ultimately reinforcing neither the subject's nor the world's ontological status.

While phenomenological principles have, in largely non-explicit form, coloured much important film writing over the decades, in recent times there has been a more concerted theoretical attempt to harness a phenomenological approach. This is evident, most notably, in the reassessment of film spectatorship under the rubric of 'affect' theory. Here, however, the focus will be specifically on the usefulness of

Merleau-Ponty's phenomenology for Film Studies.

Although Merleau-Ponty's phenomenology is governed by existentialist principles, his existentialism model of the subject that emphasizes an embodied 'being-in-the-world' at the heart of all perception (1964c; 1989). Merleau-Ponty thus offers film theory philosophical tools to assess on-screen space, *mise en scène* and bodies, as well as the viewer's visual perception. In doing so, his philosophy offers an alternative to structuralist semiotics (or indeed Derridean textual theory) and psychoanalysis. Although perhaps 'universalizing' subjective experience along his own existentialist lines in the process, Merleau-Ponty's phenomenology is productive in seeking to encompass object and subject as part of the same spatio-temporal reality – embodied relationships shared among subject-'perceivers' and objects such as a film, without reducing these interrelations to the status of textual play or exemplary models of the psyche.

On the basis of common perceptual and material grounds of existence, the subject is constantly transforming itself through the fluid, always in-process mode of being-in-the-world. This idea can at first seem somewhat mystical, and it is true that the first page of Merleau-Ponty's philosophical treatise *The Phenomenology of Perception*, first published in 1945, describes phenomenology as a 'transcendental' philosophy that 'puts essences back into existence' (1989: vii). Nevertheless, it is then immediately emphasized that individual and socio-political transformations are linked via an inescapable starting point for all perceiving relations: the world, which is ' "already there" before reflection begins – as an inalienable presence' (Merleau-Ponty, 1989: vii). Such a seemingly self-evident yet epistemologically destabilizing axiom effectively sidelines both presumptions about the centrality of the subject and the idea of pure objectivity. The world can be 'known' by no other means than (inter)subjective experience. This axiom is illuminating for Film Studies as a way of addressing the experience of an on-screen 'reality' that is

resolutely *there* at least for the duration of the film – and longer in remembered, even more virtual form.

Also relevant to Film Studies in a more applied sense are Merleau-Ponty's writings on aesthetics, particularly his essays 'The Film and the New Psychology', first published in 1948, and the masterly 'Eye and Mind' from 1961 (Merleau-Ponty, 1964b; 1964a). Although the subject of the latter is Paul Cézanne's painting, the writing resonates with the perceptual and conceptual vertigo of film experience. 'Essence and existence, imaginary and real, visible and invisible – a painting mixes up all our categories in laying out its oneiric universe of carnal essences, of effective likenesses, of mute meanings' (Merleau-Ponty, 1964a: 169). But his philosophical project at large is inherently concerned with aesthetic experience. Marjorie Grene aptly describes this aspect of Merleau-Ponty's work when she observes that it 'shows how in our very distance from things we are near them, … [illuminating] our attachment through detachment, the very core of our way of being-in-a-world' (1994: 232). Merleau-Ponty's refusal to maintain a Hegelian subject/object dialectic means that he can describe the capacity for 'objectively observable behaviour' as a site for meaning or feeling to an extent no less than within the realm of subjective experience – provided, of course, that 'objectivity is not confused with what is measurable' (1964c: 24). When it comes to the leap of faith the film viewer enters into, so as to empathize with the figures on screen as subjects rather than merely as flattened shadows of human forms or spectral after-images of people that were presumably once in front of the camera, Merleau-Ponty reminds us of the object-status of on-screen bodies. But a different *kind* of subject is also thrust into play where we might not usually envisage it, allowing the traditionally sacred (even spiritual) prize of subjectivity to be spread across the aesthetic field – to the extent of characterizing the actual 'text' itself.[5] Object/subject and work/human distinctions thus break down in a move most relevant for present-day conceptions of human relations to technology and virtual experience.

In this way, films, the characters within them, and engaged viewer-perceivers can all be seen as making up and sharing a slippery 'ground' of relationships between embodied entities. This understanding can provide for a deceptively precise description of both the relationship on-screen bodies appear to have with their physical world (if it is a vaguely recognizable 'realistic' one) and the relationship the viewer has to that reality. The language in 'Eye and Mind' is both startlingly 'cinematic' and useful for conceptualizing the spectator's relationship to the individual image and the film frame, scrambling control and origin of the visual field in the process: 'In principle all my changes of place figure in a corner of my landscape; they are recorded on the map of the visible. Everything I see is in principle within my reach, at least within reach of my sight, and is marked upon the map of the "I can"' (1964a: 162). This suggests an understanding of the spectator's relationship to the image and vision per se, bereft of its Enlightenment powers of epistemological access and gain, and instead as the central machinery that enables an extraordinary virtual yet 'grounded', embodied experience.

When considering Merleau-Ponty's emphasis on the 'irrational' nature of experience, one needs to keep in mind his work's context within the atheist-existentialist response to Nietzsche's rejection of both religious and rationalist epistemologies. Merleau-Ponty's vision of subject and world dictates that at the centre of consciousness lies an 'emptiness' that is 'observable only at the moment when it is filled by experience. We do not ever see it, so to speak, except marginally. It is perceptible only on the ground of the world' (1964c: 41). He offers a very paradoxical possibility here in suggesting that somehow this 'emptiness' can be momentarily perceived by the seeking viewer within spatial reality as viewed, energized both by desire and the co-dependent relations of subjects, objects and world. The generative, creative nature of

this process in the context of cinema is such that the viewer-subject can feel they have perceived glimpses of a character's ('empty') interior consciousness, less perhaps through the classical form of close-ups and performed expressivity than through juxtapositions of bodies with places and things: a spatial configuration brought about intentionally, yet reaching beyond intentionality.

Motivated by the desire for meaning, generating such resonance and spectrality, the perceiving subject's act of vision fails to bring about mastery and knowledge as such yet at the same time produces much more than a 'simple' view of the world. In two much quoted passages from 'Eye and Mind', we read:

> [T]he real problem is to understand how it happens that our fleshly eyes are already much more than receptors for light rays colours and lines .... They are computers of the world, which give the gift of the visible as it was once said that the inspired man had the gift of the tongues .... Now perhaps we have a better sense of what is meant by that little verb 'to see'. (1964a: 165, 186)

For the film viewer, 'to see' encompasses communicative potential defined by radically *open* subjectivity – desires, beliefs and psychological position as being-in-the-world, but in a process that undermines epistemological regimes. This leads to a paradoxical realization. Although the viewer's subjectivity energizes the image, in the process that very subjectivity becomes displaced, not fully present to itself, so that in the process of film spectatorship we are partially 'absent' from ourselves as subjects. And through our 'absence' during engagement, we cannot ever affirm knowledge, mastery or proof of our experience.

For a theoretical account of cinematic spectatorship, Merleau-Ponty effectively contradicts the notion that film is made up of different textual/image layers to be deciphered by a subject at one remove from their embodied experience of that film/world. In 'The Film and the New Psychology', we read:

> [T]he movies are peculiarly suited to make manifest the union of mind and body, mind and world, and the expression of one in the other ... the

mingling of consciousness with the world, its involvement in a body, and its coexistence with others; and because this is movie material *par excellence*. (1964b: 58–9)

What emerges both from Merleau-Ponty's philosophical account of being-in-the-world and from the more concentrated writing on artistic experience is a distinctive aesthetics of perception. Wilful, fully conscious subjects may *try* to engage their rational powers to explain what they see, but their embedded, visual-sensual relation with the world remains beyond reason.

A phenomenological approach to cinema involves a correspondence between conscious thought, embodied affect and the technology of film, including the specific formal incarnation of the particular film in question. Together, all these factors enable a perceptual reality to be felt or engaged through the senses. Sobchack's work has been important in demonstrating how effectively phenomenological methods can be employed to address embodied film experience, the ramifications of which undermine established philosophical assumptions about cinema. She rejects theoretical accounts that see film as an object of vision, and the spectator either as allied with the ideological regime in play or as a victim trapped by foreclosed understandings of subjectivity and the cinematic apparatus. Such explanations ignore the material and cultural-historical situations of both the spectator and the film and, as a result, they universalize both power relations and ideological-linguistic regimes. A very different aesthetics and politics of the gaze result from a critical-theoretical project engaged with phenomenological philosophy. In fact, the rethink is quietly radical. Cinematic experience, in light of Merleau-Ponty's work, comes to be seen as encapsulating *two* viewing positions: the spectator and the film itself, each existing as both subject and object of vision. Film experience can thereby provide insight into the perceptual and signifying nature of embodied vision in a way that transcends individual subjectivity: a process that occurs in exaggerated form in the cinema. In Sobchack's explicitly

phenomenological film theory – and her later work on affect and 'cinesthesia' follows this dimension through more specifically – cinema becomes a 'sensuous' phenomenon indeed (2000). As engaged by the viewer's human perception, the experience of film is activated as a truly sensory and 'sense'-making event/object/subject.

'Sense' comes across in Sobchack's account as a corporeal conduit of affect and communication, comparable to Merleau-Ponty's 'ground of the world' (1964c: 41). 'Sense' is thus presented as being onto-logically more authentic or more real than any semiotic codes or textual-theoretical interpretations. Sobchack argues that a film offers 'wild meaning' before it is 'fragmented and dissected in critical and theoretical analyses', and that in the first instance a film's 'existence emerges *embodied and finitely situated*' (1992: 12). In the experience of cinema, in other words, film 'makes sense' to the viewer only for it to be destroyed or sullied by analysis. Such a statement seems to resonate with those elements in Merleau-Ponty's writing on aesthetics that invoke quasi-primordial, ahistorical 'being'. This affirms a 'truth' in the special encounter between film and subject, but one that can only be addressed through attempts to evoke in language the *a priori* – but already past – experience of embodied being-in-the-cinema/world.

PHILOSOPHY MEETS CINEMA: DELEUZE AND THE TIME-IMAGE

In *Cinema 1: The Movement-Image*, originally published in 1983, Gilles Deleuze makes some critical remarks about phenomenology for insufficiently addressing immanence and difference, and for offering an 'ancient' account of experience as framed by the existential privileging of subjectivity (Deleuze, 1986: 57–8, 60–1). Even so, there are some notable points of intersection in the way that Film Studies has appropriated and applied Merleau-Ponty and Deleuze. Perhaps most crucially, both philosophers strongly oppose epistemological systems that deny or overlook corporeality in the search for signifying networks and subjective models, and both are instead largely concerned with the perceptual and aesthetic dimensions of embodied experience.[6]

If 'big-T theory' has been in retreat for some time in Film Studies, Deleuze's cinema books stand out as offering a serious engagement with cinema from a genuinely philosophical position, while retaining a close relationship to the object of study via the discussion of particular films and filmmakers. Deleuze's historiography and his philosophical coverage of film history are both eccentric yet rich in bringing together, and making substantial contributions to, theoretical and critical ideas that have played out in various ways for many decades. One such connection, made at the start of *Cinema 2: The Time-Image* (1989), originally published in 1985, is with Bazin. For Bazin, the enhanced 'perceptual realism' that comes into play with deep-focus and quality sound reproduction has two consequences. Not only does it give the viewer much greater opportunity to work hermeneutically with a more ambiguous image, it also has the effect of 'bringing together real time, in which things exist, along with the duration of the action' (1967: 39). Radically expanding this idea, Deleuze charts both the historical and aesthetic extent of the process in coming to concentrate on films that take such a temporalized image to its apogee (particularly the post-1950s European modernism Bazin did not live to write about) and its philosophical significance.

The framing process for Deleuze's study is quite simple. *Cinema 1* philosophically demarcates pre-World War Two cinema by suggesting that classical Hollywood, French Impressionism and Soviet montage are all governed by images and on-screen subjectivities guided by perceptually and ethically confident action and movement. Towards the end of the book, and leading into *Cinema 2*, Deleuze records how the movement-image becomes disabled in some advanced Hollywood films that push the system to its limits, and is then superseded

more wholly by temporality in the post-war European cinema. He thus highlights the epistemological, moral and subjective challenges that emerge as soon as *movement* (which in its pre- and inter-war incarnation keeps time beneath the surface) itself becomes subverted or engulfed by *time*. This process he sees, like Bazin in his demarcation of the 'new' cinema, first in the 1940s work of Orson Welles and into the 1950s with Alfred Hitchcock, and then more importantly in Italian neorealism. Most of *Cinema 2* is then taken up with discussion of the time-image's most radical incarnation (according to Deleuze) in the films of directors such as Ozu Yasujiro, Alain Resnais, Michelangelo Antonioni, Jean-Luc Godard and Andrei Tarkovsky.

The change from hegemonic movement to foregrounded time in the cinematic image may represent an aesthetic, ethical and philosophical 'advance' for Deleuze, but it is also a process of violence. The disablement of productive movement brings negativity and doubt into play. In a formulation indebted to Nietzsche, Deleuze explains this subversion of movement's epistemological and moral content and motivation by arguing that the time-image is generated by (and reproduces) what he calls 'powers of the false' (1989: 126–55). These forces not only override movement, they also forge a new kind of parodic inversion of movement by conjuring up 'false' or 'aberrant' movements (1989: 39–41). In a key passage, Deleuze summarizes the aesthetic and epistemological ramifications of such temporally enforced falsity and suggests how it eats out movement from within:

> A purely optical and sound situation does not extend into action, any more than it is induced by an action. It makes us grasp, it is supposed to make us grasp, something intolerable and unbearable .... It is a matter of something too powerful, or too unjust, but sometimes also too beautiful, and which henceforth outstrips our sensory-motor capacities. (1989: 18)

That 'something' is the power of immense temporality, what Deleuze ambiguously calls 'the full, that is, the unalterable form filled by change' (1989: 17). It is this that disables the ability of characters, narrative logic, fictional world and film to engender morally confident action and direction in classical movement-image cinema – irrespective of its ideological content, be it D.W. Griffith in the USA or Sergei Eisenstein in the USSR. The time-image treats these mainstays of film content entropically:

> If normal movement subordinates the time of which it gives us an indirect representation, aberrant movement speaks up for an anteriority of time that it presents to us directly, on the basis of the disproportion of scales, the dissipation of centres and the false continuity of images themselves. (1989: 37)

The emphasis on a vertiginous foregrounding of time makes for a decentred, unreliable world that cannot be assumed beyond its rendering in the image. Deleuze describes reality in the time-image as being made up of spaces that are 'reduced to their own descriptions', through 'direct presentations of an oppressive, useless and unsummonable time which haunts the characters' (1989: 136).

In a quintessential Italian neorealist film such as *The Bicycle Thief* (Vittorio de Sica, Italy, 1948) Deleuze sees the process of the new time-image 'taking over', as the initially teleological narrative generated by the search for the stolen bicycle entropically opens out into an enlarged wandering and passive gazing upon the world brought about by temporal expansion. He describes this as forcing substantial change upon and within the subject:

> [T]he character has become a kind of viewer. He shifts, runs and becomes animated in vain, the situation he is in outstrips his motor capacities on all sides, and makes him see and hear what is no longer subject to the rules of a response or an action. He records rather than reacts. (Deleuze, 1989: 3)

This process in neorealism can still come across as classically humanist in its holistic asserting of subject, image and world (as Bazin often powerfully argued in relation to such films). European cinema would go on to increase more radically the prominence of falsity and 'unbelief'.

The common element Deleuze sees in epistemologically, perceptually and morally vertiginous time-image films is encapsulated in the concept of 'the crystal': that is, the dissolution of classical sensory-motor abilities and their accompanying epistemological description and understanding of the world in the face of achronological time. Dispersing spatial coordinates and melting away distinctions between inside and outside, subject and object, the crystal becomes:

> the most fundamental operation of time: since the past is constituted not after the present that it was but at the same time, time has split itself in two at each moment as present and past ... We see in the crystal the perpetual foundation of time, non-chronological time, Chronos and not Chronos. This is the powerful, non-organic Life which grips the world. (1989: 81)

This 'Life', which requires that we acknowledge the virtual and (only perhaps seemingly) 'non-organic' aspects of temporal experience, disrupts any conventional understanding of time's operation. D.N. Rodowick describes the dizzying implications of the dangerously *excessive* time produced by intermingling 'Chronos' with 'not Chronos' as 'an emptiness, a pure virtuality rendered by the incommensurability of perception ... This is the highest power of the false that cinema can express' (1997: 190).

For many scholars of Deleuze and the cinema books, the vertiginous impact of this difficult time-thought relation both enables and is partly mitigated by the philosophical notion of 'becoming', defined via Deleuze's particular take on Nietzsche's vision of auto-creating subjectivity and the idea of the 'eternal return'.[7] It is notable that Rodowick, for example, asserts any identity or notion of being as possibly 'affirmed in the principle of becoming' by means of 'the eternal return of difference' and the willed power of the false – all brought about by time 'forcing us to think' (1997: 133). The time-image creates the possibility of a certain kind of thought: that is, *difficult* thought. Played out simultaneously on screen and spectatorially, this process is marked by a dialectic of creativity and devastating ontological impotence. This is why Deleuze states:

> What cinema advances is not the power of thought but its 'impower', and thought has never had any other problem. It is precisely this which is much more important than the dream: this difficulty of being, this powerlessness at the heart of thought. (1989: 166)

In its creative potential, the virtual time-thought 'machine' is often the key to framing the time-image in a quasi-utopian light (Schwab, 2000: 162). In seeming contrast to Merleau-Ponty's phenomenology, and although Deleuze remains strongly anti-Cartesian, in *Cinema 1* and *2* the body seems to represent the price paid for the modern world's nihilism, its revolutions and its potential. The body takes on the form of a burdensome repository sluggishly holding subject and future world back. Using starkly oppositional language in describing Antonioni's cinema, Deleuze demarcates:

> the two aspects of the effect of the time-image: a cinema of the body, which pulls all the weight of the past into the body, all the tiredness of the world and modern neurosis; but also a cinema of the brain, which reveals the creativity of the world, its colours aroused by a new space-time, its powers multiplied by artificial brains. (1989: 205)

This is a sensitive response to what are still sometimes derided as purely depressing and hermetic films. And yet, in stressing the potential for new thinking forged from the ashes of ontological destruction, Deleuze's account of post-war European modernists such as Antonioni can tend towards a rather 'positive' or idealist reading. The risk here, then, is a conceptual blunting of time-image cinema's impact both in terms of affective experience and philosophical importance.

Theoretical accounts of the time-image can suggest a very different kind of cinema from that which is actually experienced when watching the post-war European films Deleuze discusses in *Cinema 2*. His analysis of time in these films does convey some sense of the destructive force that motivates the particular modern impulses and potential so important to his philosophy of the cinema.

But their more disturbing and destabilizing impact can be elided or underplayed.[8] In this way, the radical critique and challenging confrontations brought about by 'difficult thought' in Deleuze's account seem largely to commit violence against regressive elements of the Enlightenment subject and notions of 'being' without in turn potentially also undermining re-conceived, and favoured, understandings of subjectivity emphasized as 'becoming'.

For good or ill, Deleuze's cinema books and the scholarship around them appear to constitute the most notable discourse based on European philosophy in Film Studies over the last decade or so. Given the sceptical trend in the discipline away from such styles of thinking, this scholarship has been persistent and devoted rather than voluminous. It would be problematic, of course, if Deleuze's methodology and *a priori* assumptions were to become a new theoretical orthodoxy internalized by a generation of film scholars. If it did, then it would require breaking down for the same reasons as the paradigms of the 1970s. Although critique has so far been sporadic, the cinema books have been around long enough to provoke attacks on their methodology and on Deleuze's particular philosophical framing of time as read in the film image.

Sean Cubitt, for example, has argued that – like Hollywood, in fact – the post-war European cinema Deleuze celebrates ultimately lays claim to a sublime image outside of history, and that he therefore essentializes film *as* time with a problematic end point of pure stasis (2004: 338–9). This objection that time-image films have as their aim a pure stasis, because their settings and formal presentation feature temporal and spatial dislocation, may itself presuppose that cinema can only offer socio-historical resonance and critique when rendering recognizable milieux using a realist aesthetic. Although it is of course desirable that Deleuze's historiograph-ical agenda and methodology should be scrutinized and questioned, *Cinema 2* at its best – both as philosophy and as genuine film scholarship – discusses films in a way that actually subverts any idea of stasis and rest for the subject facing a cinema/world of such achronological *durée*, and whose engagement and thought are so central to the event of the time-image. It is, rather, pre- and inter-war cinema that is treated in Deleuze's analysis as typically allowing the subject and their social morality to assert confidence and ahistorical stability through the unproblematic forging and engagement of movement. When it comes to time-image cinema, subjectivity and the world are reconfigured away from all such sureties – even if for Deleuze utopianist possibility is also enabled by such breakdown.

Explaining why he sees Deleuze's contribution to Film Studies as so productive and fresh, Gregory Flaxman addresses the waning of highly theoretical writing in favour of cultural studies, reception theory and other empirical discourses. He describes the result as 'a peculiar, and particularly fashionable, absence of debate – about what film is, about its difference from other arts, about its effect on thought, about the way its images can be distinguished – in which a set of traditional assumptions quietly cement themselves' (2000: 7). Whether or not we concur with the details of such a thesis, this chapter has defended the tradition of continental European philosophizing about film: addressing cinema as a philosophically significant, potentially radical form; exploring the challenging implications of its bodies and worlds as rendered on screen for those in spectatorial engagement and critically assessing its role as the originary moving image form in a consumer culture. What emerges from the nexus between film and philosophy provided by this tradition is a striking exploration and analysis of cinema's destabilizing, elusive yet forever affective impact at the heart of contemporary experience.

NOTES

1 Adorno (1964) himself always acknowledged Kracauer's intellectual influence, dating from a teenage friendship shared reading Kant, even if this recognition was often expressed in the form of backhanded compliments (Jay, 1985).

2 Benjamin's hybrid materialist/Messianic utopian thought was forged through the idea of play and an aesthetics that sought to free objects from instrumental use. This led to critiques from other Marxist figures of the day, such as his friend Bertolt Brecht, for espousing materialism while yearning for 'mysticism in spite of an anti-mystical attitude' (Brecht, quoted in Bronner, 1998).

3 Even so, *Composing for the Films* (1994), Adorno's collaborative book with Hanns Eisler, published in 1947, suggests that only three years after *Dialectic of Enlightenment* Adorno could sound more hopeful about cinema's radical possibilities.

4 Paisley Livingston (1982) provides a rarely expansive example of a Film Studies scholar seeking to engage with Adorno's late aesthetics and radically anti-ontological philosophy in his study of Ingmar Bergman's modernism.

5 In *The Phenomenology of Perception* we read: 'A novel, poem, picture or musical work are individuals, that is, beings in which the expression is indistinguishable from the thing expressed, their meaning accessible only through direct contact ...' (1989: 15).

6 The closeness of their approach on this score can also be seen in cognitivist critiques of Deleuze's philosophy of cinema that would surely also be levelled at film theory inspired by Merleau-Ponty such as Sobchack's. Codruta Morari recounts that French film theorist Patrice Chateau critiques the concepts Deleuze reads in cinema as excessively 'autopoetic' – too close to perceptions, sensations and affect (2006: 95).

7 On 'becoming', see Deleuze (1983; 1990: 1–4; 1994) and Deleuze and Guattari (1983); also Grosz (1999: 3, 6) and Kaufman (1999: 154–6). On the 'eternal return', see Deleuze (1994: 28, 41, 136); also Colebrook (1999: 118, 129, 131) and Grosz (1999: 5).

8 While Deleuze's project ought not to be treated as a mid-twentieth-century museum piece, its historical groundedness – especially the importance of World War Two for his movement/time distinction – can easily be effaced in the process of contemporary adaptation, when used to address the work of filmmakers outside the cultural and historical context of Deleuze's purview. The risk is in underplaying Deleuze's positioning of the particular time-image cinema he addresses as engaged with, and emanating from, a very particular set of (largely European) socio-political conditions. If the difference between the films and their cultural context and those of the present era are bracketed (those pertaining to Godard's 1960s Paris and Wong Kar-Wai's 1990s Hong Kong, for example), Cubitt and other critics of the time-image can seem to have a point when it comes to ahistorical utopianism.

REFERENCES

Adorno, Theodor W. (1964) 'The Curious Realist: On Siegfried Kracauer', *NL*, 2: 58–75.

Adorno, Theodor W. (1973) *Negative Dialectics*. Tr. E.B. Ashton. London: Routledge & Kegan Paul.

Adorno, Theodor W. (1983) *Aesthetic Theory*. Ed. Gretel Adorno and Rolf Tiedemann. Tr. C. Lenhardt. London: Routledge & Kegan Paul.

Adorno, Theodor W. (1991) 'Transparencies on Film', in *The Culture Industry*. Ed. J.M. Bernstein. Tr. Thomas Y. Levin. London: Routledge & Kegan Paul. pp. 154–61.

Adorno, Theodor and Eisler, Hanns (1994) *Composing for the Films*. London: Athlone.

Adorno, Theodor and Horkheimer, Max (1979) *The Dialectic of Enlightenment*. Tr. John Cumming. London: Verso.

Andrae, Thomas (1979) 'Adorno on Film and Mass Culture: The Culture Industry Reconsidered'. *Jump Cut*, 20: 34–7.

Bazin, André (1967) 'The Evolution of the Language of Cinema', in *What is Cinema? Vol.1*. Ed. and tr. Hugh Gray. Berkeley: University of California Press. pp. 23–40.

Benjamin, Walter (1972) 'A Small History of Photography', *Screen*, 13(1): 5–26.

Benjamin, Walter (1973) *Charles Baudelaire: A Lyric Poet in the Era of High Capitalism*. Tr. Harry Zohn. London: New Left Books.

Benjamin, Walter (1992) 'The Work of Art in the Age of Mechanical Reproduction', in Gerald Mast, Marshall Cohen and Leo Braudy (eds), *Film Theory and Criticism*. 4th edn. Tr. Harry Zohn. New York: Oxford University Press. pp. 665–81.

Benjamin, Walter (1999) *The Arcades Project*. Tr. Howard Eiland and Kevin McLaughlin. Cambridge: Belknap Press.

Brecht, Bertolt (1964) *Brecht on Theatre: The Development of an Aesthetic*. Ed. and tr. John Willett. New York: Hill and Wang.

Bronner, Stephen (1998) 'Reclaiming the Fragments: On the Messianic Materialism of Walter Benjamin', *Illuminations: The Critical Theory Website*. Available at: http://www.uta.edu/huma/illuminations/bron3.htm.

Buck-Morss, Susan (1991) *The Dialectics of Seeing: Walter Benjamin and the Arcades Project*. Cambridge, MA: MIT Press.

Colebrook, Claire (1999) 'A Grammar of Becoming: Strategy, Subjectivism and Style', in Elizabeth Grosz (ed.), *Becomings: Explorations in Time, Memory, and Futures*. Ithaca, NY: Cornell University Press. pp. 117–40.

Cubitt, Sean (2004) *The Cinema Effect*. Boston: MIT Press.

Deleuze, Gilles (1983) *Nietzsche and Philosophy*. Tr. Hugh Tomlinson. New York: Columbia University Press.

Deleuze, Gilles (1986) *Cinema 1: The Movement-Image*. Tr. Hugh Tomlinson and Barbara Habberjam. Minneapolis: University of Minnesota Press.

Deleuze, Gilles (1989) *Cinema 2: The Time-Image*. Tr. Hugh Tomlinson and Robert Galeta. Minneapolis: University of Minnesota Press.

Deleuze, Gilles (1990) *The Logic of Sense*. Ed. Constantin V. Boundas. Tr. Mark Lester. New York: Columbia University Press.

Deleuze, Gilles (1994) *Difference and Repetition*. Tr. Paul Patton. New York: Columbia University Press.

Deleuze, Gilles and Guattari, Félix (1983) *Anti-Oedipus: Capitalism and Shitzophrenia*. Tr. Robert Hurley, Mark Seem and Helen R. Lane. Minneapolis: University of Minessota Press.

Flaxman, Gregory (2000) *The Brain is the Screen: Deleuze and the Philosophy of Cinema*. Minneapolis: University of Minnesota Press.

Grene, Margorie (1994) 'The Aesthetic Dialogue of Sartre and Merleau-Ponty', in Galen A. Johnson and M.B. Smith (eds), *The Merleau-Ponty Aesthetics Reader: Philosophy and Painting*. Evanston, IL: Northwestern University Press. pp. 212–32.

Grosz, Elizabeth (ed.) (1999) *Becomings: Explorations in Time, Memory, and Futures*. Ithaca, NY: Cornell University Press.

Hansen, Miriam B. (1981-82) 'Introduction to Adorno, "Transparencies on Film" (1966)', *New German Critique*, 24–5: 186–98.

Hansen, Miriam (1992) 'Mass Culture as Hieroglyphic Writing: Adorno, Derrida, Kracauer', *New German Critique*, 56: 43–73.

Hansen, Miriam (1993) ' "With Skin and Hair": Kracauer's Theory of Film, Marseille 1940', *Critical Inquiry*, 19(3): 437–69.

Hansen, Miriam (1995) 'America, Paris, The Alps: Kracauer (and Benjamin) on Cinema and Modernity', in Leo Charney and Vanessa Schwartz (eds), *Cinema and the Invention of Modern Life*. Berkeley: University of California Press. pp. 362–402.

Hansen, Miriam (1997) 'Introduction', in Siegfried Kracauer, *Theory of Film: The Redemption of Physical Reality*. Princeton, NJ: Princeton University Press. pp. vii–xlv.

Hansen, Miriam (1999) 'The Mass Production of the Senses: Classical Cinema as Vernacular Modernism', *Modernism/Modernity*, 6(2): 59–77.

Jay, Martin (1985) 'Adorno and Kracauer: Notes on a Troubled Friendship', in *Permanent Exiles: Essays* on the Intellectual Migration from Germany to America. New York: Columbia University Press. pp. 217–36.

Kaufman, Eleanor (1999) 'Klossowski or Thoughts-Becoming', in Elizabeth Grosz (ed.), Becomings: Explorations in Time, Memory, and Futures. Ithaca, NY: Cornell University Press. pp. 141–58.

Koch, Gertrud (1991) ' "Not Yet Accepted Anywhere": Exile, Memory, and Image in Kracauer's Conception of History', New German Critique, 54: 95–109.

Koch, Gertrud (2000) Siegfried Kracauer: An Introduction. Tr. Jeremy Gaines. Princeton, NJ: Princeton University Press.

Kracauer, Siegfried (1987) 'Cult of Distraction: On Berlin's Picture Palaces', New German Critique, 40: 91–6.

Kracauer, Siegfried (1995) 'The Mass Ornament', in The Mass Ornament: Weimer Essays. Tr. Thomas Y. Levin. Cambridge, MA: Harvard University Press. pp. 74–86.

Kracauer, Siegfried (1997) Theory of Film: The Redemption of Physical Reality. Princeton, NJ: Princeton University Press.

Krauss, Rosalind (1994) The Optical Unconscious. Boston, MA: MIT Press.

Livingston, Paisley (1982) Ingmar Bergman and the Rituals of Art. New York: Cornell University Press.

Merleau-Ponty, Maurice (1964a) 'Eye and Mind', in The Primacy of Perception and Other Essays. Ed. James M. Edie. Tr. Carleton Dallery. Evanston, IL: Northwestern University Press. pp. 159–90.

Merleau-Ponty, Maurice (1964b) 'The Film and the New Psychology', in Sense and Non-Sense. Tr. Herbert L. Dreyfuss and Patricia Allen Dreyfuss. Evanston, IL: Northwestern University Press. pp. 48–59.

Merleau-Ponty, Maurice (1964c) 'The Primacy of Perception and its Philosophical Consequences', in The Primacy of Perception and Other Essays. Ed. James M. Edie. Tr. James M. Edie. Evanston, IL: Northwestern University Press. pp. 12–42.

Merleau-Ponty, Maurice (1989) The Phenomenology of Perception. Tr. Colin Smith. London: Routledge.

Morari, Codruta (2006) 'The Paradoxes of Rationality', Film-Philosophy, 10(2): 87–98.

Rodowick, D.N. (1997) Gilles Deleuze's Time Machine. Durham, NC: Duke University Press.

Schlüpmann, Heide (1987) 'Phenomenology of Film: On Siegfried Kracauer's Writings of the 1920s', New German Critique, 40: 97–114.

Schwab, Martin (2000) 'Escape from the Image: Deleuze's Image-Ontology', in Gregory Flaxman (ed.), The Brain is the Screen. Minneapolis: University of Minnesota Press. pp. 141–52.

Sobchack, Vivian (1992) The Address of the Eye: A Phenomenology of Film Experience. Princeton, NJ: Princeton University Press.

Sobchack, Vivian (2000) 'What My Fingers Knew: The Cinesthetic Subject, or Vision in the Flesh', Senses of Cinema, 5. Available at: http://www.sensesofcinema.com/contents/00/5/fingers.html.

Weber, Max (1946) 'Science as a Vocation', in From Max Weber: Essays in Sociology. Ed. and tr. H.H. Gerth and C. Wright Mills. New York: Oxford University Press. pp. 129–56.

Weber, Max (1958) The Protestant Ethic and the Spirit of Capitalism. Tr. Talcott Parsons. New York: Charles Scribner's Sons.

Wollen, Peter (1976) 'Ontology and Materialism in Film', Screen, 17(1): 7–23.

12

Cinema and Art History:
Film has Two Eyes

Angela Dalle Vacche

During the 1970s and 1980s, Film Studies used models derived from literary theory, psychoanalysis, and Marxist criticism. By the 1990s, it had become apparent that these methods privileged a literary/verbal/textual- over a perceptual/visual/object-based train- ing. One brief example might illustrate the point: whereas a film analyst or a literary theorist would teach about film narrative as a system of differences and repetitions, an art historian may require students to hold a textile in their hands to assess its weight, or to look at an image for hours to decide about the quality of lighting. Thus, for art historians, storytelling does count, but equally important, if not more so, are the visual forms of narrative, namely all the various ways of seeing based on style, authorship, period, philosophical stance, ideology, genre, and so forth. To make things even more complicated, cinema is about perceiving, absence, distance, and projecting, while art history, which also involves looking, is built around solid, concrete entities.

In the wake of the emergence of cul- tural semiotics (cultural studies), usually

in literature departments, Film Studies has demonstrated the usefulness of popular sources, on the one hand, and the value of critical theory (Louis Althusser, Jacques Lacan, Michel Foucault) on the other. This is why art historians such as Norman Bryson, Michael Ann Holly and Keith Moxey (Bryson, 1983; 1988; Bryson et al., 1994), Jonathan Crary (1990; 2000) and Carol Armstrong (1999), have broadened the horizons of art history into the 'new' art history (see also Mitchell, 1994). A second group, led by Nicholas Mirzoeff (1995; 1999), have tackled the study of visual culture in the wake of British cultural studies (Stuart Hall, Fredric Jameson) by defying the traditional separation of high and low registers and by discussing territories such as advertisements, gender roles, and ethnographic images next to historical painting or the nude. Both the visual culture group and the new art history have inspired the psychoanalytic and semiotic breakthrough achieved by Film Studies. More specifically, visual culture in relation to film counts illustrious precursors, for this kind of multimedia research has been practised as early as the 1960s and 1970s by British critics such as John Berger and Peter Wollen. To this day, regardless of any trend, their two books, *Signs and Meaning* (Wollen, 1969–72) and *Ways of Seeing* (Berger, 1977), hold up and have become classic texts.

Such a shared appreciation of popular culture across Film Studies and art history, however, has focused on formulaic, mainstream examples. Much work in Film Studies, for example, has denounced Hollywood cinema by underlining its strategies of rhetorical persuasion for the sake of social consensus. Again, some art historians find this way of reading below the surface of the filmic text – a veritable hermeneutic of suspicion – difficult especially when they have been trained in areas such as minimalism or abstract expressionism. These kinds of specialist cherish tactile, kinetic, chromatic, and experiential variables whose common feature is to challenge verbal discourse. A recent exception to this dichotomy between phenomenological art and predictable Hollywood films is *Chromophobia* (2000) by David Batchelor.

In this book, Batchelor's history of colour pokes fun at the minimalist obsession with white, while it also charts the weight of ancient and canonical manuals celebrating the crisp pencil of drawing over the painter's volatile brush dripping on and mixing the world in unpredictable ways. Significantly, Batchelor includes a whole section about colour in *Victor Fleming's The Wizard of Oz (US, 1939)* next to a discussion of *Kenneth Anger's The Inauguration of the Pleasure Dome (US, 1954; re-cut 1966)*, an avantgarde film which well illustrates all the fears associated with chromatic power. Short, beautifully illustrated, and easy to understand, *Chromophobia* is the kind of book that proves the advantage of shuttling between an art historical training and Film Studies scholarship.

It is well known that art historians who teach the Renaissance period or nineteenth-century Impressionism are very interested in narrative. And yet, even these two groups appear to value the visual dimension through art theory. In fact, they spend a lot of time distinguishing many kinds of perspectival systems: one-point perspective, two-point perspective, and three-point perspective. In contrast, film specialists worry about Leon Battista Alberti's monocular model discussed by Jean-Louis Baudry (1985). Thus, while Renaissance painting often refers to Biblical or mythological tales, spatial diagrams about perspective techniques loom large in the art curriculum. Likewise specialists of Impressionism are well aware that their images narrate the stories of modernity, yet they nevertheless place great emphasis on the history of colour theory or on the development of motion studies in order to teach students how to discern a landscape by Alfred Sisley from one by J.M.W. Turner.

All this classroom effort about two- or three-point perspectives and about colour theory confirms that drawing and painting are not mechanical activities, but the result of highly manual skills which have been painstakingly acquired. No wonder that even art historians open to popular culture and mechanical reproduction are, in the end, unwilling to let the word 'art' (meaning artistry) completely disappear. To be sure, they fear that their artefacts' peculiarities will disappear as soon as they are overwhelmed by broad and, worst of all, vague terms such as ideology and representation. This fear is especially real because, in contrast to film analysts, they are not working with projected, but intangible, moving images on screen.

In short, the state of affairs regarding the interdisciplinary dialogue between Art History and Film Studies is more and more promising, but still hugely unresolved. This is why it is worth noting that during the annual conference sponsored by College Art Association (CAA), it is difficult to find many panels where Film Studies specialists present their work. This sense of separation, however, is mutual, since at the annual meeting of the Society of Cinema and Media Studies (SCMS), few participants work across film and art history, and if they do, they are likely to be on a panel about early cinema or the avant-garde.

SCHOLARLY EXAMPLES AND FILM PARADIGMS

And yet, the possibility of a more structured interdisciplinary dialogue is becoming more and more of a reality. Let us now look at some examples where individual scholarship overrides institutional constraints. The attempt to link early cinema to art theory characterizes one recent contribution to the intersection of Film Studies with Art History: Philippe-Alain Michaud's *Aby Warburg and the Image in Motion* (2004). In the footsteps of Aby Warburg, Michaud takes the reader through boxing and dancing scenes shot in W.K.L. Dickson and Thomas Edison's laboratory in West Orange, New Jersey. This first section is followed by Warburg's meditation on movement in regard to the use of the serpentine line in Sandro Botticelli's Florentine paintings. Warburg's inquiry into motion, and especially its corporeal choreography, concludes with an analysis of mystical writing systems, snake iconography and ritualistic dancing among the Pueblo Indians of New Mexico. Michaud's final argument is that Warburg's fascination with the depiction of movement finds a sort of proto-cinematic framework through his lifelong project *Mnemosyne*. There, the montage of a wide range of iconographic sources triggers an undeniable kinetic energy in the shift from picture to picture, while it also anticipates Sergei Eisenstein's use of the frame as a combinatorial unit in the wake of his research on Japanese ideograms and haiku poetry in *Film Form* (1949).

In my view Michaud's book is courageous, but scattered across loosely linked areas of inquiry. Whether we deal with Warburg's *Mnemosyne* or with André Malraux's 'museum without walls', a sort of history of art in several volumes based on his own sequencing of photographs (1949), the mystery of what happens perceptually and emotionally in the interval or interstice from one image to the next remains unresolved. Is it collage, montage or assemblage? And which ones of these constructs lean towards an allegorical direction instead of an analogical one? And what are the implications of Eisenstein's allegorical montage versus Jean-Luc Godard's analogical, collagist impulse? How do these filmic examples relate to Warburg's mnemonic atlas or to Malraux's eccentric, historiographical rethinking of art history through his extensive use of the humble medium of photography? The answers are not easy to reach.

Museums are beginning to rethink their whole installation practices in order to accommodate exhibitions on the interconnectedness of art and film. In this respect, the two most famous exhibitions have been *Hall of Mirrors* (1995), curated by Kerry Brougher and Russell Ferguson at the Museum of Contemporary Art (MOCA) in Los Angeles, and *Fatal Coincidences: Hitchcock and Art* (2001), a project begun by Guy Cogeval at the Montreal Museum of Fine Arts and continued by Dominique Paini at the Centre Georges Pompidou in Paris (see Brougher and Ferguson, 1996; Cogeval, 2000). For a reading list on art and film, I especially recommend the MOCA catalogue (Brougher and Ferguson, 1996), because the various essays cover a wide range of visual artists who have commented on the cinema in their works. This co-edited catalogue from MOCA is precious because a whole course on contemporary art is not always included in film graduate programmes. The same could be said of classes on the intersection of film and photography, another possible point of encounter between Art History departments and the Film Studies curriculum.

Having thus outlined the institutional constraints which Film Studies (a fifty-year-old discipline) experiences in relation to the History of Art (a one-hundred-year-old enterprise) I shall now list the most important paradigms of intersection between these two domains of study. The first can be called 'The Famous Citation' and it concerns films which have faithfully restaged a famous painting: for instance, Pier Paolo Pasolini's use of Andrea Mantegna's *Dead Christ* (1480–90) at the very end of *Mamma Roma* (Italy, 1962), or Bernardo Bertolucci's reliance on Giuseppe Pellizza Da Volpedo's *The Fourth State*

(1898–1901) in *Novecento* (France/Italy/West Germany/US, 1975). The second paradigm concerns 'Historical Films' which use art historical sources to bring back to life a whole epoch through a particular period's atmosphere. In this group, we can mention Stanley Kubrick's *Barry Lyndon* (UK, 1975) with his extensive references to John Constable and Sir Joshua Reynolds, or Federico Fellini's *Casanova* (Italy/US, 1976) replete with allusions to eighteenth-century Venetian painters such as Rosalba Carriera, Pietro Longhi, Francesco Guardi, and Antonio Canaletto. The third paradigm concerns the 'Biographical Mode', adopted whenever the lives of famous painters are recreated on the screen. Albert Lewin structured *The Moon and Sixpence* (US, 1942) around Paul Gauguin's adventures in Southern France and Polynesia, for example; Jacques Becker devoted his *Montparnasse* (France/Italy) to Amedeo Modigliani in 1958, and American painter-turned-filmmaker, Julian Schnabel, reconstructed Jean Michele Basquiat's career in *Basquiat* (US, 1996). The list could be extended, but I shall stop here by pointing out that Vincent Van Gogh's biography has a special status having been the subject of at least three films: Vincente Minnelli's *Lust for Life* (US, 1956); Robert Altman's *Vincent & Theo* (Netherlands/UK/France, 1990); and *Van Gogh* (France, 1991) by Maurice Pialat.

Painting in film can also become a 'Hypertext Device' in relation to the rest of the narrative, whenever it provides a commentary on the difference between two media. I am thinking, here, about the disappearance of the pictorial frame in *Dreams* (Japan/US, 1990) by Akira Kurosawa. Another case in point is Bertolucci's emblematic use of Francis Bacon's portrait with a male figure in pain at the beginning of *Last Tango In Paris* (Italy/France, 1972). The 'Chromatic Paradigm' is worth mentioning because films which explore colour inevitably raise questions about the relation of film, painting, creativity, and femininity. The most famous titles in this category are: Michelangelo Antonioni's *Red Desert* (Italy/France, 1964),

Chen Kaige's *Yellow Earth* (China, 1984), and Krzysztof Kieslowski's *Three Colours* series, *Blue* (France/Poland/Switzerland/UK, 1993), *White* (France/Poland/Switzerland, 1994) and *Red* (Poland/France/Switzerland, 1994).

Besides these paradigms about direct citation, period-atmosphere, meta-cinematic commentary, history, biography, and colour, there are also modernist films about the limits of painting in the sense that cinema can show how this medium tied to mechanical reproduction refuses to deliver all the psychological comforts linked to the concept of pictorial aura: plenitude, beauty, aesthetic contemplation. This is why Godard's *Passion* (France/Switzerland, 1982) and Jacques Rivette's *La Belle Noiseuse* (France/Switzerland, 1991) demonstrate that the filmic reconstruction of a famous work by Jean-Auguste-Dominique Ingres, *L'Odalisque* (1839), or a nude portrait with a beautiful model, fail miserably. Thus, these modernist films about the arts fit in the 'Crisis Paradigm' to comment on the ruptures of modernity, and postmodernity, respectively at the beginning of the twentieth century and immediately after World War Two.

Historically one of the most obvious, but also most important, paradigms of the intersection between film and art has been the one devoted to 'Avant-Garde Movements'. Any serious film curriculum is likely to involve a class on German Expressionist film with all the appropriate readings and references in theatre, painting, and architecture. Likewise, Surrealism is often taught as a film class with plenty of slides to illustrate the variety of media (photography, painting, sculpture, and collage) used by Surrealist artists. But there are additional and more complicated paradigms that inform recent books of film and painting. Both Brigitte Peucker and David Pascoe rely on the 'Body Paradigm' and on a postmodern definition of cinematic representation. In *Museums and Moving Images* (1997), Pascoe argues that Peter Greenaway makes films about the human body being eventually destroyed by competing representational frameworks based on either mechanical or digital reproduction. In *The Belly of an Architect* (UK/Italy, 1987) the protagonist repeatedly photocopies his own stomach. Stourley Kracklite (Brian Dennehy), an architect from Chicago, visits Rome for the first time. There, Kracklite faces not only his terminal gastric disease, but also his failure to impregnate his wife. The film ends with the protagonist's suicide.

Like Pascoe, in *Incorporating Images* (1995) and, more recently, *The Material Image* (2007), Peucker argues that cinema neither incorporates life, nor is its lifelike simply because of its alleged ability to a show movement. In contrast to the live beings which it reproduces, cinema is really a machine for cutting and dismemberment. It is only through editing and piecing back together images from painting and stories from literature that cinema can simulate a moving body that does not exist in the first place. Put another way, for Pascoe and for Peucker, no matter which art forms are brought inside the boundaries of film, the moving body is the uncanniest of fictions and the most indispensable centrepiece for cinematic illusion to occur.

Undoubtedly this postmodern emphasis on a filmic body that functions as a surrogate self and ensures the pseudo-materiality of the filmic image itself is a powerful argument. In a sense, I have developed a similar approach to Pascoe and Peucker for the 'National Paradigm' in my own *The Body in the Mirror: Shapes of History in Italian Cinema* (1992), in which I argued that all sorts of art historical sources were used by Italian filmmakers to bring to life a body politic that would overcome internal divisions due to class, region, and gender.

For my second book on film and art history, *Cinema and Painting: How Art is Used in Film* (1996), I relied on 'The Ranking Paradigm': history, portraiture, landscape, and still life. According to Sir Joshua Reynolds, this canonical sequence is based on levels of authority so that the historical painting is the domain of male artists, while female painters should devote themselves to the more modest depiction of genre scenes or

even flowers (see also Dalle Vacche, 2002).[1] It was interesting for me to discover that film directors keen on innovation, such as F.W. Murnau with the European art film, and Vincente Minnelli in the Hollywood studio system, chose to embed within their narratives modes of painting heavily based on subjective or even visceral responses such as landscape painting or abstract expressionism. These two strategies of hiding art and private emotional issues inside cinematic storytelling, horror film like *Nosferatu* (Germany, 1922) or whether in a musical like *An American in Paris* (US, 1951), suggest a desire to reject the much more spectacle-bound and public cluster of figuration, body, and history that sits at the top of Reynolds' scheme for art historical genres.

Finally, any cultural based paradigm for the dialogue between film and painting, involves issues of visual form. Such an expanded definition of film style or, better, such a conceptual handling of the filmic image, summons into the discussion religious philosophies as traditions of thought shaping all kinds of image-systems. For example, icon painting with all its rules and peculiarities becomes Andrei Tarkovsky's inspiration for handling objects, architecture, the construction of character, and so forth, in *Andrei Rublev* (USSR, 1966). Structured around the life of a medieval monk and a famous Russian icon painter, this film achieves a great hypnotic power and spiritual energy, instead of falling into the category of the flat and secular Hollywood biopic.

LACUNAE

The 'Theoretical Interdisciplinary Paradigm' is probably the least developed and the one most needed at this juncture. This is the case because all the paradigms I have listed are helpful, but not pivotal in regard to the ontology and the epistemology of the filmic image as a visual form, as a storytelling agent and as a component of the cinematic apparatus. And this is really the time to ask the question quite clearly why bother with art history at all from the standpoint of the cinema? It is not so much because filmmakers cite paintings or have unconsciously appropriated images from the history of art. The reason is that without art history and its knowledge about the history of vision that pre-dates the nineteenth century, film specialists risk missing out on valuable arguments about *looking*. Art History should function for Film Studies as a database about the history of ideas on perception, word and image, style, genre, ideology, spectatorship, looking, and visual form. Film colleagues may want to pick and choose, criticize and expand on this body of knowledge, but a better dialogue between the two disciplines can only be enriching.

Within the dialogue of between Art History and Film Studies, this theoretical move is necessary in order to understand better how the ontology of the cinema is about both time and space, word and image, fantasy and reality, to such an extent that cinema can be said to have 'two eyes' that seem to combine into one singular, monocular source of vision from the projector to the screen. Whether these two eyes conspire to hide one another, so that they may seem only one, or whether they are antithetical to each other in certain films, or whether, again, they may produce an oxymoron, remains to be assessed case by case. The point here is that we have a range of representational possibilities which are assumed but not explained, and eventually forgotten in the language that we use to write about film.

The language of film theory is so rich, but also so dense, that it remains somewhat obscure. In 'Ideological Effects of the Basic Cinematographic Apparatus', for example, Baudry explains how vision in the cinema is the result of a combination of two ways of seeing, the eye of Renaissance perspective and the shadow-like images captured by the camera obscura:

Fabricated on the model of the camera obscura, it permits the construction of an image analogous to the perspective projections developed during the Italian Renaissance. Of course, the use of lenses of different focal lengths can alter the perspective of an image. But this much, at least, is clear in the history of cinema: it is the perspective construction of the Renaissance which originally served as model … The dimensions of the image itself, the ratio between height and width, seem clearly taken from an average drawn from Western easel painting.… [T]he painting of the Renaissance will elaborate a centered space. (1985: 288–9, my italics)

Originally published in 1970 by *Cinéthique*, Baudry's essay argues that the technological features of the medium are not neutral, but inherently biased. Considering that Baudry begins his first sentence with a reference to the camera obscura, he strangely downplays the fact that cinema is a medium characterized by a double perceptual lineage, namely that the cinema involves two equally active eyes. The reader goes along with the metaphor of 'centering', to the point of understanding less and less, especially when Baudry refers to the 'combined inertia of painting, theater and photography' (1985: 289).

The question Baudry does not ask is: granted that both the mobilization of space and the visualization of time produce movement in film, which is the more important to the specificity of the filmic medium, space or time? Whereas Eisenstein would answer space, André Bazin would choose time. Of course, both space and time are of paramount importance, but different kinds of cinemas emerge when one dimension tends to prevail over the other.

Within the framework of this dilemma, I shall try to explain how the collapse of Renaissance perspective with the camera obscura produces a tight marriage in which it is the photographic side that makes visible the invisible, namely time. The access to this fourth dimension is an unprecedented event in the history of vision, the central topic for avant-garde, modernist movements striving towards utopia beyond space and time, and the fundamental problem of modernity. But there is more. With photography and cinema, time does not only become visible for the first time, but it also displaces the humanist subject of Renaissance perspective from the role of artist. In other words, time in photography amounts to light, and thus nature becomes the artist. It is only in certain kinds of cinematic traditions and with specific filmmakers, that this humanist Renaissance subject manages to re-centre itself (hence Baudry's terminology, 'centering'), and risks misrepresenting a complex combination of technological features pulling in different directions.

According to Helen Gardner's, *Art through the Ages*, a standard text book on many introductory Art History survey courses, during the age of daguerreotypes, photographic images were lively and entropic (as seen in Figure 12.1): 'There was a view of Paris ... the minutest details, the interstices of pavement and the brickwork, the effect of humidity from falling rain – all were reproduced *as in nature*' (1959: 739). In contrast to Alberti's *perspectiva artificialis*, where nothing is left to chance, everything in photography, planned or random, controlled or left to chance, contributes to making visible time's richness, namely the passing moment.

In her ground-breaking book, *The Art of Describing* (1983), Svetlana Alpers explains that with Alberti, the painter is worthy of praise as long as *historia*, that is a Biblical, or mythological, or historical tale, emerges from the way the pictorial composition reorganizes the space. To some extent, the good painter must be a good storyteller in a spatial sense, so that position and scale, colour and posture, costume and objects, size and gesture will

Figure 12.1 Louis J.M. Daguerre (1787–1851), *Paris Boulevard* (1839). Perpignan Museum, Perpignan, France.

clearly convey the story to any viewer at one glance. In contrast to this spatial-narrative approach, the descriptive power of the camera obscura relies much more on the unpredictable intersections of light and time. Put another way, the temporal-descriptive power of the camera obscura is based on receiving inside the box the shadow of a slice of time, so that this mechanical – rather than manual – reproduction – will reappear on top of the box because an internal mirror reverses the upside-down-projection. The hustle and the bustle of lived experience going by in the world, outside the box, characterize the 'photographic' core of the reproduced image.

Yet there is even more to renegotiate between film and art history, photography and Renaissance perspective, as soon as we pay attention to the ways in which art historians use the metaphors of window and mirror when they differentiate between Johannes Kepler's proto-photographic way of seeing and the perspectival Albertian eye. In Film Studies, specialists have applied the window metaphor to the screen, when they describe the nineteenth-century realist style of classical Hollywood cinema. In contrast, they often turn to the analogy of mirror and screen in order to discuss European modernist filmmaking. Generally speaking, Hollywood's window is associated with a passive and yet highly involved spectator, while the modernist mirror of the European art film is linked to self-referentiality in the sense that the spectator is encouraged to think about how the film is not just a narrative, but also a meditation on the medium itself.

Switching again to the art historians' bookshelf, it is interesting to note that the mirror applies to the camera obscura, whereas a grid-like window fits the model of Renaissance perspective. But, the most important point, here, is that the comparison of the camera obscura to an uncharted mirror implies a certain degree of passivity in contrast to the geometrical virtuosity of Alberti's ideal painter. For example, Leonardo Da Vinci – who also worked on the camera obscura – implicitly criticized a certain kind of Northern painting that limits itself to describing, or recording, the world with incredible precision, but without narrating a story:

> The painter who draws merely by practice and the eye, without any reason, is like a *mirror* which copies everything placed in front of it, without being conscious of their existence. (quoted in Friday, 2001: 356)

Assuming that the students of the history of vision diligently consult books in the two separate disciplines of film and art history, the transition from Alpers to Bazin's famous statement in 'The Ontology of the Photographic Image' resonates with strong Keplerian implications. In fact, in contrast to Leonardo's parallel between mirroring something and lacking originality, Bazin celebrates the disappearance of the human hand, of style, resemblance, mapping and signature, for the sake of likeness, passivity, reception, and a photo-chemical process in which time and light, that is nature, are the new agents of creativity: 'By the power of photography … nature at last does more than imitate art: she imitates the artist' (1967a: 15).[2]

But there is more to my re-reading of Baudry in light of a re-balancing act between photography and painting. It is this kind of intertextuality between Alpers and Bazin that can help us understand how the French critic distinguishes between two kinds of realisms: one Albertian, addictive and illusionistic, and relevant to classical Hollywood cinema; the other Keplerian, with less individual control, and ultimately more improvisational and phenomenological. Worth noting, is the fact that nature, for Bazin, does not mean 'natural', in the sense of a status quo to struggle against, the way it does for Eisenstein. The Soviet theorist, in fact, speaks of 'non-indifferent nature', where the word 'nature' does not mean rivers and mountains, but society and class issues (Montani, 1981). Understandably, Eisenstein believes in the power of the revolution and cinematic activism to change a state of affairs that is taken for granted as 'natural' when it is instead a cultural construction.

For Bazin, nature is indifferent, because we are smaller than the environment we live in, in the sense that we shall never be able to control it completely. Cinema acts as a sort of special antenna or sounding mechanism that is meant to be in touch with our unconscious and with worlds beyond our temporal finitude. To be sure, something, somehow, will always escape, or remain impenetrable to us. Although subject to human control, of all media invented untill now cinema is the one that is best attuned to some cosmic mystery in daily life. In Bazin's words, cinema is 'the little flashlight of the usher, moving like an uncertain comet across the night of our waking dream, the diffuse space without shape or frontiers that surrounds the screen' (1967c: 107). Put another way, it is nature's indifference towards human control that guarantees the world's creative independence in an artistic sense. Hence Bazin compares photography to nature and nature, namely light during the photographic process, to a non-human kind of artist.

Neither Bazin in 1945 nor Baudry in 1970, forgets that the two different eyes of Alberti and Kepler always operate together in the case of narrative cinema, since description (time) goes hand in hand with narrative (space). In fact, at the very end of 'The Ontology of the Photographic Image', Bazin writes: 'On the other hand, of course, cinema is also a language' (1967a: 16). And, as a system of differences and repetitions, language requires the weave of space and time, I would add. Bazin's awareness of the linguistic nature of cinema takes us back to Alberti's stress on historia and storytelling. And this is necessary because cinema does involve the two eyes of the camera obscura and Renaissance perspective. The French critic distinguishes between the constructed realism of Renaissance perspective in which the director reshapes the world (Hollywood, Soviet montage), and a more phenomenological notion of realism in which the world uses the medium, while the director participates in this event.

While Leonardo Da Vinci speaks of Alberti's *historia* thinking about static scale, size, and composition, for Bazin, language means that the articulation of space and time involved in editing is at the heart of storytelling, especially in classical

Hollywood cinema. As such, the more Baudry's spectator is 'centered', in relation to narrative development, the more intense the experiences of illusionism, identification, suspension of disbelief and ideological consensus. There is, however, one more reason why, in relation to mainstream, commercial, mostly Hollywood cinema, Baudry's 'centering' is correct. Yet the word is too dense and broad; it needs to be further unpacked not only through art history, but also via art theory.

The philosopher Jonathan Friday observes that the Albertian window and the Keplerian mirror imply two kinds of spectatorships respectively. The Albertian spectator looks at the world as if all the space was *outside* the window frame and ready for mastery. In contrast, Friday continues, the Keplerian

spectator sees the world as if it were *around* the figure reflected inside the mirror (2001: 351–62). Ironically, the great claim of perspective is 'objectivity', even if the image is built on a mathematical grid that has nothing to do with the surprises of the world out there. On the contrary, the situation of the Keplerian eye involves 'subjectivity', because the viewer's figure is implied inside the image, so that becomes objectively part of the world's fabric.

Think, for instance, of Jan Van Eyck's *Arnolfini Wedding Portrait* (1434), as shown in Figure 12.2, where the entire room, including the bridal couple, is reflected on the surface of a convex mirror. Yet this looking-glass is positioned in such a way that were two ordinary viewers to peer into the pictorial space from the threshold, they would either displace

Figure 12.2   Jan Van Eyck (active 1422–44), *Arnolfini Wedding Portrait* (1434). National Gallery, London. (Photo credit: Alinari/Art Resource)

the painting's protagonists or superimpose their own reflections on them. Likewise, in Diego Velazquez's *Las Meninas* (1656–76), the mirror in the background of the painting, behind the painter painting and looking at us, contains the reflection of the royal couple, as seen in Figure 12.3. At the same time, the positioning of the king and the queen is such that it also matches the end of the eye-line-match trajectory leading from the painter's look to the viewer's on the threshold of that world looking in and about to join that whole scene.

How, therefore, can Baudry rely on the theme of 'centering', after Friday argues for such a contrast between external control leading to subjective mastery and peripheral involvement opening out to actual participation? My answer is that Baudry's metaphor of 'centering' is not really about the ontology of the cinema, but about its epistemology. In other words, it refers to the suspension of disbelief which any spectator is willing to activate, regardless of which kind of film unfolds on the screen. But this suspension of disbelief begins with seeing uninterrupted movement instead of separate frames going by, so that the two eyes of the cinematic apparatus are grafted together on the so-called phenomenon of persistence of vision at the level of the retina.

Let us now shift from this basic retinal illusion to a higher level of illusionism. We need to reflect further on Bazin's distinction between two different kinds of realism: on the one hand, nineteenth-century-based classical Hollywood realism, and, on the other, the twentieth-century-based approaches of French Poetic Realism in the 1930s the Italian neorealism of the 1940s, and the French Nouvelle Vague of the 1960s. It is now time to ask how these two completely different traditions of realism might be, in any way, compatible with art history's distinction between the Keplerian eye for movement and temporality, and the Albertian eye for space and narrative/

Figure 12.3   Diego Rodriguez Velazquez (1599–1660), *Las Meninas* **(1656–57). Detail of central group. Museo del Prado, Madrid. (Photo credit: Scala/Art Resource)**

The answer to this question comes from Anne Hollander's *Moving Pictures* (1989), a book surprisingly about the Keplerian lineage of Hollywood cinema which until now we have associated with Alberti's Renaissance perspective. The fact is that Hollander works in the footsteps of Robert Rosenblum's (1975) model of a continuum that runs from Caspar David Friedrich to Mark Rothko, from northern landscape painting and the sublime to abstract expressionism turning colour into a quasi-mystical experience. Considering that it is customary to discuss the realism of classical Hollywood cinema exclusively in the light of Alberti and Baudry's illusionist models, a short foray into Hollander's research fills another lacuna about the history of vision in film through the lens of art historical training. In fact, Hollander's thesis parallels Robert Rosenblum's argument that Dutch art resonates in American art. In Hollander's *Moving Pictures*, the links between Northern European art and the invention of the cinema do not only go through the camera obscura, but also through the diffusion of black-and-white illustrations in popular journalism. In her introduction, the art historian writes:

> Many of the artists I discuss here followed the original example set forth in the Northern Renaissance, directly or derivatively or obliquely. At the same time they seem to a modern, post-cinematic eye to have prefigured the way movies work as pictures in the modern world. I see the rise of film as a natural continuation of their special kind of illustrative impulse, which appeared in serious painting of all kinds as well as in less serious graphic work. (1989: 7)

Leonardo Da Vinci's statement, that a mirror is only a humble tool for mechanical reproduction with no storytelling power, falls short of Hollander's enthusiasm for Northern art's descriptive power. The missing link between Baudry and Hollander can be found, once again, in a footnote in Bazin's 'The Ontology of the Photographic Image'. Right after a sentence on 'the tortured immobility of baroque art', Bazin offers the perfect transition to Hollander's argument:

> It would be interesting from this point of view to study, in the illustrated magazines of 1890 and 1910, the rivalry between photographic reporting and the use of drawings. The latter, in particular, satisfied the baroque need for the dramatic. A feeling for the photographic document developed only gradually. (1967a: 11)

From the ancient Greek word 'drama' for action, 'dramatic' is key, here, because it invokes Alberti's narrative mobilization of theatrical space within the grid of Renaissance perspective. The word 'dramatic' also demonstrates that the emotions attached to *historia* need the graphic intensity of black-and-white illustrations in order to compensate for the fact that the nineteenth-century viewer felt that photography was optically precise, but somewhat too scientific or cold. As soon as we remind ourselves of the fact that the words 'dramatic' and 'theatrical' are closely related, we understand that the photographic eye of the cinema seeks help from the theatre, in order to warm up its traces and make them look believable or artificially 'objective' as much as the images of Renaissance perspective.[3]

Baudry talks about the combined 'inertia' of painting, theatre and photography, but I hope I have demonstrated there there is no inertia. On the contrary, each one of these media is energetically involved in the invention of the cinema. The problem is to shift from the collapse of camera obscura and Renaissance perspective to a choice about which one of these three media (painting, theatre, and photography) is most crucial to the specificity of the cinema. And the answer is photography, because of this medium's special kinship with capturing an otherwise unstoppable, death-bound, indifferent time in contrast to painting and theatre's man-made, artificial reconstruction of time.

All this goes to show that the history of cinematic vision is far more complicated than an overarching metaphor about a centred kind of spectatorship. There are many different kinds of films, but the answer to what is cinema, in a technological sense, has been found by Gilles Deleuze who calls it 'a spiritual automaton' (1989; see also Bogue, 2003: 177–8). In plain language, Deleuze's 'spiritual automaton' is a time-machine that reminds us not only of our temporally-finite status as humans, but also of our creative abilities to represent the unrepresentable or the unthinkable that surround us in daily life and in the cosmos alike. In summary, Hollander's claim that the cinema comes from Northern painting is too slanted towards that tradition, while Baudry (1985) leans too much towards what Alpers calls the Italianate mode of painting which was originally informed by Renaissance perspective.

Baudry's ideological take does not tell the full story of the historical past and future potential of the medium, were it to become a source of inspiration for young contemporary artists. Thus, my final example begins in the Church of the Gesuati in Venice. At the very centre of the church, under an amazing ceiling painted by Giambattista Tiepolo, the Australian-American artist, Andrew Huston, has found a sort of tourist-toy in the guise of a mobile mirror. The latter is framed in exactly the same way the Venetian painter has framed his own ceiling, as is shown in Figure 12.4. The purpose of this playful alignment between the frame of the mirror and the frame of the painted ceiling is to encourage the visitor in the church to position the mobile mirror exactly underneath the painting on the ceiling and look at it on the glass surface, without having to bend their head backward too much.

In line with Baudry's theme of 'centering', classical Hollywood cinema does not want viewers to make too much effort and provides them with images that seem to centre the floating chaos of events in the world. But there

Figure 12.4   Giambattista Tiepolo (1696–1770), *Saint Dominic Starts the Religious Cult of the Rosary* **(1737–39), Church of the Gesuati (1726–36), built by Giorgio Massobrio (1687–1766). (Photo credit: Andrew Huston, 2005)**

is more to the mirror at the centre of the Venetian church, because this object happens to be far more interactive and unpredictable than the Hollywood screen. In fact, trapped in their seats, film viewers cannot play around with a gadget in order to change their placement. They can only rely on editing and camera movement to mobilize their point of view. In contrast, the mobile mirror inside the church can be turned away from Tiepolo's work towards the corners of the building, as is demonstrated in Figure 12.5. In all these areas, there is a great deal of architectural ornamentation that sits there, in an off-centred, subordinate position.

While reflecting on his own projects torn between ornament and painting, architecture and colour, Huston begins to speculate about a possible story of rivalry between painting and

architecture, Tiepolo and Giorgio Massobrio, the builder of the church between 1726 and 36, whose finished work, in a sense, is challenged by Tiepolo taking over the ceiling's project in 1737. The mobile mirror seems to be there in an ambiguous way: on the one hand, to glorify the ceiling and the centre, and, on the other, to allow the corners with no painting to steal the show and enable a full appreciation of Massobrio's quasi-sculptural decoration on each side. Needless to say, the upside-down image reflected in the looking glass below the corner wall hitting the ceiling, strikes a note of similarity with the reversed orientation of the camera obscura's shadows in relation to their referent.

Why is this mobile mirror a helpful prop to rethink the history of the arts in relation to the birth of the cinema? All of a sudden,

Figure 12.5   Church of the Gesuati (1726–36), *Mobile Mirror*. (Photo credit: Andrew Huston, 2005)

the mirror's mobility brings architectural ornament under the spotlight, so that the idea that decoration is minor is turned upside down. In his essay Baudry has piled up major arts, theatre, and painting – all of them subservient to cinematic illusionism. In contrast, Bazin's phenomenological realism is not only comparable to the usher's little flashlight, but it is also in tune with minor and low arts such as photography and Hollander's black-and-white journalistic illustrations. The tourists' mirror at the Church of the Gesuati helps us to understand how cinema's humble origins have more to do with ornamental, that is, superfluous work in the margins, than with the search for heavenly transcendence and eternal power coming out of Tiepolo's dynamic figures. As a matter of fact, it is meaningful that Saint Dominic himself falls off the sky-bound frame back down onto the earth below. After receiving the rosary from the Virgin, his mission is to spread this tool for prayer among the masses, as seen in Figure 12.6.

Figure 12.6   Giambattista Tiepolo (1696–1770), *Saint Dominic Starts the Religious Cult of the Rosary* (1737–39), Church of the Gesuati (1726–36). (Photo credit: Andrew Huston, 2005)

Stimulated by his own visit to the Church of the Gesuati, Huston began working with a variety of mirrors. These are not mobile in and of themselves, but they can be used in such a way as to explore marginality, randomness and the ephemeral, by reversing architectural ornament into a quasi-camp practice of urban and rural landscape-installations. In the footsteps of innumerable tourists visiting one Venetian church after another and possibly inspired by Robert Smithson's *Incidents of Mirror Travel in the Yucatan* (1969), Huston's mirrors have made sudden appearances on a window-shop mannequin in Munich wearing a pair of short, leather hiking pants, the stereotypical *Lederhosen* of yodelling German tourists. Another mirror has sprung up unexpectedly in the middle of the Venetian lagoon.

It features a yellow band that does not match any functional traffic sign of the waterways. Hieratic and mysterious, the reflecting surface of this camera obscura-like object intercepts the lagoon's ever-shifting waves, while the boat traffic enters the labyrinthine canals of the historical centre. During an exhibition at Sydney Non-Objective (15–30 December 2006), an art gallery in Sydney, Australia, Huston came up with a mirror that sat in the corner of one room. Thus, Huston demonstrates that the predictable angle produced by the meeting of two blank walls can become so pivotal that it deserves a mirror of its own, as shown in Figure 12.7.

Finally, back in the United States and mindful of Tiepolo's earthbound protagonist, Huston has come the closest to Tarkovsky's

Figure 12.7   Andrew Huston, *Corner Tondo* (2005). Sydney Non-Objective Gallery, Sydney. (Photo credit: Andrew Huston)

idea that cinema is 'sculpting in time' (1989). Besides owning the Russian director's famous book on film theory, Huston has decided to continue his work on mirrors between painting and architecture, heaven and earth, by going to the Long Island countryside. Once the artist gets there, a series of installations begins to unfold. Planted in the mud, Huston's mirror mimics the moving image, it intercepts the ever-changing motion of the waves. For Tarkovsky, the filmic image itself is comparable to the reeds in a river, bending, disappearing and swelling up again, the way only the frailest vegetation can record the story of a flowing river – an idea demonstrated in Figure 12.8.

Of course, Baudry is well aware that neither the viewer nor the filmic image is ever static. The very intentional choice of the gerund 'centering' is all about process, tendency rather than result or product. But the point here is not to prove a brilliant French theorist wrong, but simply to unpack the system of the arts in film. By planting a mirror inside

Figure 12.8 Andrew Huston, *Tidal Marker (Low Tide) Mirror in Situ*, North Sea Harbor, Long Island, NY (2005). (Photo credit: Andrew Huston)

Figure 12.9   Andrew Huston, *Tidal Marker (Low and High Tide) Mirrors in Situ*, North Sea Harbor, Long Island, NY (2005). (Photo credit: Andrew Huston)

a riverbank filled with reeds and mud and by photographing this sort of re-sculpturing of the environment through its changing reflection, Huston has dramatized the camera obscura's keen awareness of existential temporality (as seen in Figure 12.9). The specialist in visual culture, the film historian, and the art critic are going to be in a better position to appreciate the historical implications of Huston's work and many other artists' creative gestures the more familiar they are with both film theory and the history of art. It is only through an interdisciplinary training that they can revisit and rekindle the explanatory power of a whole set of critical terms.[4]

NOTES

This essay is an early draft based on my book-in-progress, *André Bazin and the Visual Arts*: a monograph completely built around the art historical issues of 'The Ontology of The Photographic Image' (1945).

I wish to thank Professor James Donald and Dr Effie Rassos; the two anonymous evaluators who helped me revise the essay and my friend, art historian Cristelle Baskins; Ms. Karole Vail, Assistant Curator, Guggenheim Museum, New York and Andrew Huston, Artist, New York, and my assistant in New York, Ms. Nadine Covert. All these people have offered ideas and images, editorial help, and organizational support. I am also indebted to Prof. Lynn Nead, Prof. Laura Mulvey, and Prof. Ian Christie at Birkbeck College and The Leverhulme Trust for their hospitality in London, while I revised the text. The section titled 'Lacunae' has been presented as a Leverhulme Lecture chaired by Prof. Laura Mulvey at Birkbeck College, University of London on 26 January 2007.

1 Many other books have also emerged on Film Studies and art history: Susan Felleman's *Art and The Cinematic Imagination* (2006); the anthology *The Image in Dispute: Art and Cinema in the Age of Photography* (1997), edited by Dudley Andrew; Linda Ehrlich and David Desser's *Cinematic Landscapes: Observations on the Visual Arts and Cinema in China and Japan* (1997); and the Patrice Petro-edited

Fugitive Images: From Photography to Video (1995).

2 In his book *The World Viewed: Reflections on the Ontology of Film*, American philosopher Stanley Cavell remarks:

> You can always ask of, an area photographed, what lies adjacent to that area, beyond the frame. This generally makes no sense asked of painting ... . The world of a painting is not continuous with the world of its frame; at its frame, a world finds its limits. We might say: A painting *is* a world; a photograph is *of* the world. (1971: 23–4, my italics)

3 Bazin, however, distinguishes between 'dramatic' and 'theatrical' in 'Theater and Cinema: Part One' (1967b) and 'Theater and Cinema: Part Two' (1967c).

4 For additional works that address the connection between Film Studies and art history see: Aumont (1989); Bonitzer (1987); Bruno (2003); De Haas (1985); Lant (1995); Leutrat (1988); Levine (1978); Michael (1997); Murray (1993); Ndalianis (2004); Schrader (1988); Sorlin (2002); Tashiro (1998); Tupitsyn (2002).

REFERENCES

Alpers, Svetlana (1983) *The Art of Describing*. Chicago: University of Chicago Press.

Andrew, Dudley (ed.) (1997) *The Image in Dispute: Art and Cinema in the Age of Photography*. Austin: University of Texas Press.

Armstrong, Carol (1999) *Odd Man Out: Readings of the Work and Reputation of Edgar Degas*. Chicago: University of Chicago Press.

Aumont, Jacques (1989) *L'oeil interminable: cinéma et peinture*. Paris: Librairie Seguier.

Batchelor, David (2000) *Chromophobia*. London: Reaktion Press.

Baudry, Jean-Louis (1985) 'Ideological Effects of the Basic Cinematographic Apparatus', in Philip Rosen (ed.), *Narrative, Apparatus, Ideology: A Film Theory Reader*. New York: Columbia University Press. pp. 286–98.

Bazin, André (1967a) 'The Ontology of the Photographic Image', in *What is Cinema? Vol. 1*. Ed. and tr. Hugh Gray. Berkeley: University of California Press. pp. 9–16.

Bazin, André (1967b) 'Theater and Cinema: Part One', in *What is Cinema? Vol. 1*. Ed. and tr. Hugh Gray. Berkeley: University of California Press. pp. 76–94.

Bazin, André (1967c) 'Theater and Cinema: Part Two', in *What is Cinema? Vol. 1*. Ed. and tr. Hugh Gray. Berkeley: University of California Press. pp. 95–124.

Berger, John (1977) *Ways of Seeing*. London: Penguin.

Bogue, Ronald (2003) *Deleuze on Cinema*. New York: Routledge.

Bonitzer, Pascal (1987) *Peinture et cinéma: Décadrages*. Paris: Cahiers du Cinéma/Editions de l'Etoile.

Brougher, Kerry and Ferguson, Russell (eds) (1996) *Art and Film since 1945: Hall of Mirrors*. Los Angeles: Museum of Contemporary Art.

Bryson, Norman (1983) *Vision and Painting: The Logic of the Gaze*. New Haven, CT/London: Yale University Press/Macmillan.

Bryson, Norman (1988) *Calligram: Essays in the New Art History from France*. Cambridge: Cambridge University Press.

Bryson, Norman, Holly, Michael Ann and Moxey, Keith (eds) (1994) *Visual Culture: Images and Interpretations*. Hanover, NH: University Press of New England.

Bruno, Giuliana (2003) *Atlas of Emotion: Film, Art, Architecture*. New York: Verso.

Cavell, Stanley (1971) *The World Viewed: Reflections on the Ontology of Film*. New York: Viking.

Cogeval, Guy (ed.) (2000) *Fatal Coincidences: Hitchcock and Art*. Montreal: Museum of Fine Art.

Crary, Jonathan (1990) *Techniques of the Observer: On Vision and Modernity in the Nineteenth Century*. Cambridge, MA: MIT Press.

Crary, Jonathan (2000) *Suspensions of Perception: Attention, Spectacle, and Modern Culture*. Cambridge, MA: MIT Press.

Dalle Vacche, Angela (1992) *The Body in the Mirror: Shapes of History in Italian Cinema*. Princeton, NJ: Princeton University Press.

Dalle Vacche, Angela (1996) *Cinema and Painting: How Art is Used in Film*. Austin: University of Texas Press.

Dalle Vacche, Angela (ed.) (2002) *The Visual Turn: Classical Film Theory and Art History*. New Brunswick, NJ: Rutgers University Press.

De Haas, Patrick (1985) *Cinéma intégral: De la peinture au cinéma dans les Années Vingt*. Paris: Transedition.

Deleuze, Gilles (1989) *Cinema 2: The Time-Image*. Tr. Hugh Tomlinson and Robert Galeta. Minneapolis: University of Minnesota Press.

Ehrlich, Linda and Desser, David (1997) *Cinematic Landscapes: Observations on the Visual Arts and Cinema in China and Japan*. Austin: University of Texas Press.

Eisenstein, Sergei (1949) *Film Form: Essays in Film Theory*. New York: Harcourt, Brace and World.

Felleman, Susan (2006) *Art and The Cinematic Imagination*. Austin: University of Texas Press.

Friday, Jonathan (2001) 'Photography and the Representation of Vision', *Journal of Aesthetics and Art Criticism*, 59(4): 351–62.

Gardner, Helen (1959) *Art through the Ages*. 4th edn. London: G. Bell.

Hollander, Anne (1989) *Moving Pictures*. New York: Knopf.

Lant, Antonia (1995) 'Haptical Cinema', *October*, 74: 45–73.

Leutrat, Jean-Louis (1988) *Kaleidoscope*. Lyons: Presses Universitaires des Lyons.

Levine, Steven Z. (1978) 'Monet, Lumière, and Cinematic Time', *Journal of Aesthetics and Criticism*, 36(4): 441–47.

Malraux, André (1949) *The Psychology of Art*. Tr. Stuart Gilbert. 3 vols. New York: Pantheon Books.

Michael, Leja (1997) *Reframing Abstract Expressionism: Painting and Subjectivity in the 1940s*. New Haven, CT: Yale University Press.

Michaud, Philippe-Alain (2004) *Aby Warburg and The Image in Motion*. Cambridge, MA: MIT Press.

Mirzoeff, Nicholas (1995) *Bodyscape: Art, Modernity and the Ideal Figure*. London: Routledge.

Mirzoeff, Nicholas (1999) *Introduction to Visual Culture*. London: Routledge.

Mitchell, W.J.T. (1994) *Picture Theory: Essays on Verbal and Visual Representation*. Chicago: University of Chicago Press.

Montani, Pietro (ed.) (1981) *Ejzenstein: La natura non-indifferente, 1945–47*. Venice: Marsilio.

Murray, Timothy (1993) *Like a Film: Ideological Fantasy on Screen, Camera, and Canvas*. London: Routledge.

Ndalianis, Angela (2004) *Neo-Baroque Aesthetics and Contemporary Entertainment*. Cambridge, MA: MIT Press.

Pascoe, David (1997) *Museums and Moving Images*. London: Reaktion Press.

Petro, Patrice (ed.) (1995) *Fugitive Images: From Photography to Video*. Bloomington: Indiana University Press.

Peucker, Brigitte (1995) *Incorporating Images: Film and the Rival Arts*. Princeton, NJ: Princeton University Press.

Peucker, Brigitte (2007) *The Material Image: Art and the Real in Film*. Stanford, CA: Stanford University Press.

Rosenblum, Robert (1975) *Modern Painting and The Northern Romantic Tradition: From Friedrich to Rothko*. New York: Harper and Row.

Schrader, Paul (1988) *Transcendental Style in Film: Ozu, Bresson, Dreyer*. New York: Da Capo Press.

Sorlin, Pierre (2002) *Persona, Del ritratto in pittura*. Mantova: Tre Lune Edizioni.

Tarkovsky, Andrei (1989) *Sculpting in Time: Reflections on the Cinema*. Austin: University of Texas Press.

Tashiro, Charles (1998) *Pretty Pictures: Production Design and the History of Film*. Austin: University of Texas Press.

Tupitsyn, Margarita (2002) *Malevich and Film*. New Haven, CT: Yale University Press.

Wollen, Peter (1969–72) *Signs and Meaning*. London: Secker & Warburg / BFI.

13

Film and History

Vanessa R. Schwartz

How many vague descriptions we will abandon the day a class can watch, projected on precise and moving images, the calm or troubled faces of a deliberating assembly, the meeting of chiefs of state ready to sign an alliance, the departure of troops and squadrons, or even the mobile and changing physiognomy of cities.

Boleslas Matuszewski, Paris 1898 (1997)

The enthusiasm evinced by Boleslas Matuszewski about moving pictures as the basis of a vast historical image archive, dates back to the very early years of film's history. Although as an unemployed cameraman Matuszewski may have had self-interested reasons for promoting film, his 1898 description anticipates what has become a commonplace notion about the power of film. Rather than the vague descriptions fostered by the written word, film would show rather than tell. Underlying this attitude is a naïve faith that photographic images are somehow less ambiguous and more direct than words because they are indexical and thus bear a literal trace of a person or object that was present in the world. In that way, photography and film are thought not to represent but to bear witness. As a result, they fulfil the dream of every historian: somehow

to be present in the past. The past hundred years have also produced much discussion aimed at unsettling just such easy notions about the 'directness' of the photographic image. This perspective, by contrast, suggests that showing can be just as ambiguous as telling.

Few forms of narrative and documentation have simultaneously stirred as much utopian fantasy and eye-rolling dismissal as history on film. There are so many dimensions to any consideration of the connection between Film and History that to attempt to analyze this vexed relation is, in the end, to discuss several different and not always overlapping issues. Yet where film and history themselves overlap, it is because there is an ontological similarity between them. After all, both film and history claim to bear a reference or relation to the real world in somewhat literal ways; both are also fundamentally concerned with issues of temporality. History and film can be thought to share the common project of presenting us, as Philip Rosen put it, with 'an absence, namely that of the represented past' (1984: 31). But if there is an ontological relation, such questions have largely escaped the majority of historians who are more interested in the stories they tell than in the ways they tell stories.

But rather than stress the disciplinary divisions as the fundamental divide in considerations of film and history, this chapter maps four areas of intersection between film and history that transcend mere distinction in field of study. Just as this essay suggests it is time to move the discussion away from who has the 'right' to adjudicate representations of the past, it also suggests that anyone interested in the intersection of film and history is wasting their time by concentrating on the divergence between scholars trained in film and those in history. This position fails to respect the conventions in Film Studies that separate fiction from non-fiction film and those approaches to history that separate the study of the past and historiography. Instead, this chapter begins from the presumption that cinehistorians have hybrid methods and questions that thus cross traditional boundaries within and between fields. It lays out several areas of inquiry: film as an historical object; film as an archival record; historical storytelling on film; and finally, cinehistory, the cinematic representation of the past and the simultaneous thought about it in films. By outlining the different aspects of the connection between film and history, this chapter is meant to ready scholars to pose two of the most fundamental and unasked questions at their intersection: How have our notions of the past and its representation been influenced by filmmaking over the last hundred years? How have historical method and practice been shaped by film? While it is a commonplace assumption that political events and the political climate shape the methods, questions and problems of the historian and produce a certain optic on the past, there has been almost no consideration of the influence of mass culture and its media such as film on historians, historicity and the development of historical representation over the course of the cinematic century. This chapter cannot answer these questions but rather lays out the intersection between film and history in such a way as to make clear why these are the important questions to ask next.

FILM AS HISTORICAL OBJECT

The intersection of film and history by definition needs to account for a history *of* film and its institutions. The history of image-making itself stands as a fundamental part of the cultural history of many times and places. The modern period, however, can be defined by image-making and mechanical reproducibility in a way that perhaps makes photographs, film, and, more recently, video a central characteristic of modern cultural production in the way that chronicles and epic poems were for scholars concerned with the cultural history of earlier periods. Film is also a source for narrating the history of other aspects of life in the past.

From Robert Sklar's early and still valuable, *Movie-Made America* (originally published in 1975), academic film history began to develop along a social-historical and then a cultural-historical path, and thus towards an intersection and overlap with the discipline of history. By moving beyond earlier internalist accounts that focused on either transformations in film narrative and style (a sort of history modelled after the formal histories in the fields of Art History and Literature perhaps best defined by the work of David Bordwell), or on the development of Hollywood and the studio system mostly as a mode of industrial production (as typified by the work of such scholars as Tino Balio), film history has become part of a broader historical context (see Balio, 1987; Bordwell, 1998; Sklar, 1975).

Early cinema provided a particularly rich site for historians interested in working-class culture in turn-of-the-century America, where film fit into a story about industrialization, leisure and Americanization. Studies such as Lauren Rabinovitz's *For the Love of Pleasure* (1998) and Steve Ross' *Working-Class Hollywood* (1999) offer excellent examples of work steeped in social history and its questions of class and gender as reflected in and instantiated by practices of leisure culture and through which film played a central role. More recently, Shelly Stamp's *Movie-Struck Girls* (2000) and Lee Grieveson's

Policing Cinema (2004) demonstrate the ways that studying film history and controversies around films and film screenings are vital meals for understanding broad social anxieties and transformations at the dawn of the new century.

Rabinovitz also tied early cinema to changes in urban culture in the service of what has been called (in derogatory terms by Bordwell) the 'modernity thesis'. That argument located early films and their exhibition in a broader history of visual culture in which questions of changes in perception (notions of time and space, especially), ideas about the real, and notions of spectatorship have been studied as historical practices. This literature, from its more theoretical historicist position (Crary, 1992; Friedberg, 1993) to its articulation in cultural histories (Tom Gunning's many essays on modernity to Giuliana Bruno's *Street-Walking on a Ruined Map* [1992]; the essays in *Cinema and the Invention of Modern Life* [Charney and Schwartz, 1995]), led the way in situating film as part of cultural history. It should come as no surprise that this work concentrated on early film and society, as it is much easier to integrate the study of film into a broader story when there is a smaller body of films and a less developed institutional culture.

Since then, however, scholars have moved past the silent era and have successfully shown that by studying the history 'of' film culture we can better understand film in the context of both political and cultural life. Put otherwise, one might think of this as the study of film culture's influence 'on' history. Antoine de Baecque's *La Nouvelle Vague: portrait d'une jeunesse* (1998) and his more recent *La cinéphilie: Invention d'un regard, histoire d'une culture* (2003), Saverio Giovacchini's *Hollywood Modernism* (2001), Peter DeCherney's *Hollywood and the Culture Elite* (2005) and Haidee Wasson's *Museum Movies* (2005) in different ways suggest how film is a privileged arena through which to understand relatively recent history (see also de Baecque and Delage, 1998). What these works share is their commitment to a history 'of' film in

which both the medium and the institutions that constitute what we might think of as 'film culture' are connected to broader contexts such as visual culture, the nation, international trade and the like. In effect, this history 'of film' is methodologically indistinguishable at times from cultural and social history, although at its best it connects an interest in the specificity of film as a form with these contexts.

'CANNED ARCHIVES'

Wasson's book describes the establishment of the Museum of Modern Art (MoMA) Film Library in 1935 (simultaneously paralleled in France by Henri Langlois and his cinemathèque), which 'preserved' films and inscribed them into history in unprecedented ways since film was then experienced as an entirely ephemeral form. The establishment of the Film Library is also proof of the recognition of the potential archival value of films. The Library attempted to assemble a record of everyday life that would have been otherwise lost. More than twenty years earlier, Albert Kahn, French banker and utopian internationalist, had already begun a project that sought to assemble an Atlas of the world in images: the *Archives de la planète*. This non-fiction film image archive constituted one of the first projects to recognize that film would stand as historical documentation for future generations. Kahn's ambition suggests a positivist enthusiasm for the photographic image that positioned film as a conscious as opposed to incidental archival record.

As Kahn knew, everyday life since the advent of moving pictures in 1895 could be captured from that moment forward on film. On the surface, few would dispute that film, both fiction and non-fiction, offers the historian of the twentieth century an entirely idiosyncratic but nevertheless photographic record of the past. We have no systematic archive as Kahn had hoped we would but we do have much more information than we have the ability to use. At its most mundane and incidental, historians of material culture and such fields as urban culture and geography (when location shooting took place, for example) can use any film, regardless of its status as fiction or non-fiction, for the information its can convey about dress, such objects as cars and buildings that were changed or razed.

Historians have also begun to examine the photographed and filmed record of the past as evidence of something else. For instance, they can see how people dressed on the Lower East Side, what San Francisco looked like after the 1906 earthquake, what the streets of Paris looked like with Nazi soldiers marching through them. As in every use of film, the image is necessary but not sufficient since the more the researcher knows, the better they are able to determine where location shots are filmed, when and whether cars were built or bought.

But scholars have rightly argued that the presence of the cameras and, surely, the knowledge of the presence of the camera altered what is shown and how people behave. In the end, films represent a filmed or photographed encounter as much as they succeed in representing the event photographed as a record of the past. This troubling scenario led to hand-wringing about how world events would be misunderstood in the future because only filmed or photographed events would be remembered. Daniel Boorstin, in his now classic text, *The Image*, first published in 1961, called such visualized happenings 'pseudo-events' (Boorstin, 1992). There is a rich history of the mediation of political events by movie and television cameras; from the staging of events in Nazi Germany such as the Nuremberg Nazi Party rallies to the Olympic Games, self-consciously organized and orchestrated as 'history' that had become historical not only because it was filmed but also because it *was* a film.[1]

Although fears that films offer 'canned' history abound, films have nevertheless played a role in serving as evidence and as a visual form of testimony, especially in trials. In *La Vérité par l'image: de Nuremberg au procès Milosevic* (2006), Christian Delage recounts how during the trial of Nuremberg,

the American judge and lead prosecutor, Robert H. Jackson gave film a doubly starring role.[2] On the one hand, the trial was filmed in order to provide a lasting historical record of the event. On the other hand, the court charged the famous Hollywood director, John Ford, who had directed the American film unit during the war, to edit the Allied footage of the concentration camps into a film of the atrocities to be shown at Nuremberg. Not only were the films meant to prove the barbarity of the Nazi crimes, but the court also wanted the accused to watch the films to find out whether and how they would react to the charges through the visual evidence presented. Of course, it was not just the Allies who knew how important a role film would play in the retelling of what happened during the war. The Soviets presented a film mostly of Majdanek and Auschwitz and the prosecution also assembled a compilation film called *The Nazi Plan* (George Stevens, US, 1945) made out of Nazi newsreel footage. The tribunal, however, lacked films of the camps taken by the Nazis themselves. Not that they had never existed. The Allies immediately set out to find them during the Liberation. The Nazis knew to destroy the evidence and the Soviet troops in the advance found only cans of burned films. Thus, for all the limits on the transparent use of films as evidence that we grasp with clarity today, the history of the value of photographed and filmed images as evidence, the power they have, from the heights of a world tribunal to their most personal uses in everyday life, has only just begun to be written.

The explosion of image-making in the nineteenth century through lithography, photography and, eventually, film made visual experience and visual literacy an important part of many aspects of life. For any historian working today on problems and questions of modernity, the perils and promises of photographic reproduction are increasingly a central part of the historian's craft. Just as historians of earlier eras have always required sophisticated tools for decoding and understanding the meaning of documents, so too do historians today require additional methods for making sense of the profusion of images that are so essential to the record of modern life.

Anyone considering the relationship between film and history is also faced with the question of whether some topics and problems, such as evidence in trials, lend themselves to certain modes of representation and not others. Is there a peculiarly 'cinematic' film(ed) history? Let me suggest some examples. Any history of a place such as a city or an object (the Eiffel Tower) is more amenable to illustration than the history of a concept. Nevertheless, such constructs as 'the family' are instantiated through home movies or 'The Republic' concretized through newsreels of crowds gathered at a political event. More significantly, some stories can make great movies precisely because of the filmed 'historical footage' available. For example, it should come as no surprise that the history of mass visual entertainment has often been told through the use of footage such as films and filmed interviews.[3] Finding footage for such films becomes the research equivalent to unearthing rare written documents. Three recent historical documentaries are particularly striking in this way and suggest how historians working on the twentieth century might privilege the intersections of politics and culture because of the record from filmed archives. *Morning Sun* (Geremie Barmé, US, 2003) treats the very touchy subject of the Cultural Revolution in China and opens with a visually compelling clip from a filmed version of the Chinese operatic spectacle, *The East is Red* (Wang Ping) made in 1964 to commemorate fifteen years of Communism in China. The film also includes clips from Soviet films such as *The Gadfly* (Aleksandr Fajntsimmer, USSR, 1955) that were popular in China and television newscasts of various events during the Cultural Revolution. The footage suggests how central a role film played in the projects of Communist China.

If political programs can be understood better by looking at their relationship to film, the seemingly ephemeral performing arts, dance and theatre, have been given a different kind of historical archive as filmed

performances become unearthed. One of the most well-researched recent documentaries to take advantage of 'found footage' is *Ballets Russes* (Daniel Geller/Dayna Goldfine, US, 2005), a gripping history of the birth of modern ballet and its transatlantic tale in the fulcrum of two wars (first the Russian Revolution and then World War Two). The filmmakers did the usual scouring of existing archival collections. But, because they interviewed many of the aging dancers, they also discovered that many of them had old films of their performances. Aware that this is one of the film's major accomplishments, the narration begins with a conceit framing the problem of the study of dance – 'It is the nature of dance to exist but for a moment' – as if to underscore what the film itself is about to accomplish: to make dance exist for all time through film. Although it is inevitable that the footage functions as entertainment, it also instructs and offers a remarkable archive of the development of dance and its production.

Finally, the history of material culture has served as an excellent domain for historical documentaries, as a recent film *Tupperware!* (Laurie Kahn-Leavitt, US, 2004), about the history of Tupperware suggests. Using corporate archives, collections at the National Museum of American History and home movies taken by 'Tupperware ladies' themselves, the director is able to paint a rich social portrait of women in the workforce and technological and material developments that led to revolutionary changes in everyday life.

Filmmakers are doing more than 'finding' footage, they are also creating 'archives' in ways that oral historians have. For example, the many interviews they conduct with 'witnesses' of the past for their documentary projects and the paper archives of the film production must be considered as part of the historical record. The rise of DVD has encouraged the packaging of fiction films as historical objects of cultural patrimony and multiple DVD sets are often rich with materials relating to production histories. For instance, 'Collector's Editions' act as a kind of production archive and often supply a vast array of 'Bonus Features' including audio commentary by participants and scholars, original trailers, re-release trailers, retrospective 'The Making of …' documentaries, contemporary publicity materials such as short promotional films that were made at the time of the film's release as well as cut scenes and screen tests. A remarkable three-DVD set of *The Battle of Algiers* (Algeria/Italy, 1966; DVD 2004) by Criterion combines the history of the Algerian liberation movement (including interviews with scholars and French military officers discussing their use of torture) with the production history of Gillo Pontecorvo's docudrama about it, which was itself often mistaken for a documentary. The line between history and its visual and scholarly representation is blurred in such DVD packages in interesting and important ways.

Anyone who has written about the moving image knows that it is far more satisfying to show than to describe a segment of film before you analyze it. Whether the increased use of filmed images as archives will motivate historians to use visual media as the mode through which to deliver their historical narratives is still an open question. Surely the development of multimedia publication is bound to facilitate a transition beyond the book. While works of history designed for a popular audience are increasingly delivered via visual media in such places as museums and in films (both fiction and documentary), there is no reason why scholarship aimed at a smaller audience of specialists would not benefit from visual narration.

'CLIO AT THE MULTIPLEX'[4]

Cinema has to consider the viewer. There has to be a dimension that goes beyond historical context to dive into the human heart, to reach out to what moves us all, beyond our differences.[5]

The focus on 'canned history' has thus far only addressed how the filmed present becomes the record of the past for future generations. While the use of visual sources (whether photographed or filmed, documentary or fictional films) should be the most

fundamental arena of overlap between the fields of Film (which has a strongly developed method of reading the language of film and a rich body of knowledge about the social and institutional history of filmmaking) and History (a field which can use images as evidence for something else or can embed a history of image production in a broad cultural historical narrative), this discussion has remained underdeveloped while a very public battle about historical films – that is, films that take the past as the subject of their narratives – has raged. The tension and division between filmmakers and historians needs to be reconciled in order to get beyond the habitual turf battles that erupt when 'Clio' makes her appearance at the multiplex.

If D.W. Griffith's *Birth of a Nation* (US, 1915) serves as a milestone in the rise of narrative film, it is significant that cinema's first big leap forward in terms of storytelling represents a tale about the past. The same can be said for such innovative films as Abel Gance's *Napoléon* (France, 1927) or Sergei Eisenstein's *Potemkin* (USSR, 1925). The past has, after all, provided the present with many of its most compelling and gripping stories. Filmmakers are driven as much by the power of the narrative as they are by the idea that they are advancing greater historical understanding. But because most historical films (whether fictional or documentary) aspire to capture a large audience, they are, by definition, 'popular' stories. Academic historians have difficulty with such 'popular' stories as they have particular historiographic and problem-oriented reasons for selecting the stories they tell. Yet, when pressed, one would rarely find an historian that does not also believe their work might also merit great public interest – as either a story or as an analysis of the past. But for better and worse, academic historians direct their work to a different audience and its value is generally judged by an accordingly small group of people. This must not be an either/or proposition. Mostly historians need to go off to archives and discover or reinterpret the past as a matter of contributing to research and scholarship. But where and if they can, they might partner with filmmakers to 'write' in a different idiom – so long as they do not presume to impose their own way of doing things on filmmakers, suggesting that they are the true guardians of the past. Yet we are a long way from seeing these imagined partnerships bearing fruit.

Instead, historians spend too much time criticizing filmmakers who seek identification rather than distance when they make films. For example, even Rachid Bouchareb, whose film, *Indigènes* (France/Morocco/Algeria/Belgium, 2006), caused the French government to restore the pensions of World War Two veterans from the colonies, describes in the epigraph above, how he sought identification between the past and the present when he made his film. As a result of this conflation of 'their mission' with 'our mission', the release of almost every historical film becomes an occasion on which to unloose a turf battle in which academics assert themselves as the true keepers of history. The enthusiasm for this sort of gate-keeping also reveals an unconscious design on the part of academics to wrest hold of the audience that has already been captured by Hollywood. The filmmakers and studios, on the other hand, set out to persuade the audience that they have been diligent and responsible guardians of the past and portray historians as an unwelcomed tribunal. The cases are too numerous to name here but there has yet to be any systematic collection or interpretation of these controversies. In this struggle, professional historians often simply end up defending an outmoded erudition.

Yet historians have become invested in commercial films because they recognize that film and television offer the largest audience for historical narratives. As people who grew up watching films and television, they have naturally turned to all sorts of visual and material objects themselves for both research and instructional purposes. Volumes such as the entertaining but predictable *Past Imperfect* (Carnes et al., 1996) and *The Columbia Companion to American History on Film* (Rollins, 2004) pit the professors against the producers in order to set the record straight or applaud the few instances of laudable

historical re-presentation in commercial film. Oliver Stone's historical films have prompted historians to engage in a discussion of true versus false history on film (Toplin, 2003). The subtitle of one of Robert Brent Toplin's books, *History by Hollywood* (1996), 'The Use and Abuse of the American Past', encapsulates the attitude of most historians towards popular film since it assumes that the historian is in a position to assess whether the past is being abused. Toplin himself has urged historians to consider what he calls 'cinematic history' on its own terms but he does a better job of outlining the persistent limits of historical films than he does making the case for their value beyond the now-familiar notions about emotion, landscape, and communicating a feeling for the past.

But, like all narratives of history, Hollywood histories can tell us a great deal about the moment in which they were made. Fiction films are social documents that are especially articulate as they function to make what is hidden in a society speak. Siegfried Kracauer articulated that notion in *From Caligari to Hitler*. In that study, written in 1947 (although some portions were published earlier as a MoMA pamphlet in 1942), he suggested that the films of the Weimar era both embodied and even helped shape the emergence of authoritarian leadership that led to the rise of Adolf Hitler. Films also function as a kind of latter-day folklore, he showed, and thus they have contributed to national identity-formation. Although ideas about collective fantasy and the audience unconscious have fallen out of favour, films do continue to be read as purveyors of a national identity and ideology (Hjort and Mackenzie, 2000; see also Nadel, 1995; McAlister, 2001).

Historical films are especially interesting because they are often explicit as reinterpretations of the past as seen through the present in ways that academic histories rarely acknowledge. We all study the past through our own moment and, while anachronism may thus hover as a constant danger, 'presentism' can also make history matter. Filmmakers, on the other hand, are perhaps a bit more shameless in their presentism. For example, despite using Antonia Fraser's book about Marie Antoinette, Sofia Coppola, it appears, had no prior commitment to deepening our knowledge of the past when she made *Marie Antoinette* (Japan/France/US, 2006) – a beautiful confection of a film that cleverly latches on to the detachment of life at the court and its wild material indulgence in order to speak about Hollywood today. Historians working in whatever medium must somehow manage to strike a balance between letting the past be the past and connecting it to the present.

The 'uses' of history are genuinely different between historians and filmmakers. Natalie Davis has underscored this contrast: 'the historian wants first and foremost to let the past be the past. Strange before it is familiar, particular before it is universal ...' (1987: 460). Davis has been an advocate for cinematic history, suggesting ways that filmmakers could better adapt their films to reflect several key elements valued by academic historians such as the multiple points of view of different sources and historical actors. Of course, *Rashomon* (Akira Kurosawa, Japan, 1950) did this as well as any written history and possibly before academic historians thought that way. She also urges filmmakers to find a way for viewers to gain knowledge of the evidentiary basis of their screen history. These suggestions, however, focus on applying the 'conventions' of written scholarly history to the production of visual history. After all, as Anthony Grafton has shown in *The Footnote: A Curious History* (1999), even such fundamental aspects of 'good history' as footnotes are merely conventions (see also Champion, 2003). How and why what we take to be the 'standards' of good history are in themselves historical effects and it seems hard to enforce such elements as the footnote as a 'golden' one.

Robert Rosenstone has taken a different approach to visual history. He argues that it is a mistake for historians to use the rules of written history to critique visual history (1995: 49). He also suggests that

film history neither replaces written history nor supplements it but rather stands adjacent to history, as do memory and oral tradition (2006: 65). Yet he shares with most historians a lack of appreciation for history by Hollywood. Instead, he identifies other filmmaking modes, which he calls postmodern, as models for cinematic history. These films share a mode of distancing the viewer from the narrative to reveal the notion of the partiality of historical interpretation. Rosenstone suggests that experimental films such as *Walker* (Alanis Obomsawin, Canada, 1992) and *Sans Soleil* (Chris Marker, France, 1983) are better because they are not tied to the 'realism' that has preoccupied historians and filmmaker-historians, both of whom are indebted to nineteenth-century narrative structures.[6] Yet the problem with this perspective is that it replaces the simplicity of unambiguous traditional historical narratives with a preference for a meta-critical approach to the past. Avant-garde films are better simply because they are more self-conscious about their status as constructed narratives. Rosenstone distinguishes between film as a window onto the past and film as a medium through which to consider a way of thinking about the past and 'past-ness' (2006: 54). But that window can and should act as both view and provocation to thought simultaneously. Learning about the past, with the understanding that to study history is to interpret it, is at the heart of every history. We should not abandon that practice, which is as old as Thucydides, and which also transcends the issue of written versus visual history. History cannot simply be about the construction of history nor can good histories avoid the fact that they are, indeed, narrative representations.

Simon Schama, in both word and deed, has taken up the idea that the future of historical 'writing' will be in visual form. Schama was already a well-respected scholar when he became something of a household name because of his appearance on fifteen episodes of the BBC's *A History of Britain* (Clare Beavan et al., UK, 2000), a series that he also wrote. In it, Schama takes us to monuments, tombs and archives to look at documents and inside palaces, prisons and caves. The immediacy of the past and its sources are beautifully orchestrated in this history. The series itself, and what Schama has also written in several articles dedicated to discussing film and history, argues for the role that imagination has always played in our understanding of the past and suggests that cinematic history, aside from the immediacy it offers, can emphasize issues of empathy between viewer and film. In addition, he points to film as possibly providing a form of moral engagement with the past by asking both why and what it means to us. Finally, he endorses the stirring of a sort of poetic connection between the present and the past that films provide for today's audiences (see Champion, 2003; Schama, 1998). By consciously contemplating fiction films, in fact, we might develop a better purchase on the imagination and so, he suggests, become better historians since without imagination it is, indeed, hard to invoke the past. Despite its material traces, the past is no longer here, but elsewhere, and has to be invoked by the power of the human imagination.

GENRE AND CINEMATIC HISTORY

When academic historians take up visual storytelling themselves, they might begin to practice the poetry Schama preaches by virtue of the demands placed on them by filmmaking. At that point they might also begin to reflect upon the extent to which their own sense of history and even scholarly historiography has already been shaped by the popular cinematic history of the last century. For example, we might look at works of history such as James Goodman's *Stories of Scottsboro* (1995) (which self-consciously sought the *Rashomon* effect) and Richard Fox's *Trials of Intimacy* (1999) with its reverse chronology and multiple perspectives, and consider how these works of scholarship testify to a scholarly history that, consciously or not, is being written under the influence of cinema.

For now, however, the study of the relation between most historians and fiction film is stuck in the face of our realization that history in fiction film is neither better nor worse than the work of professional historians and instead is simply a different matter altogether. Toplin, for example, has asked whether there are visual conventions of history-film storytelling that are archetypical. He notes that films about the Roman Empire 'often feature imposing classical buildings with huge columns and chambers' (2002: 12–13). But, of course, many years before this observation, Roland Barthes' very clever essay, 'The Romans in Films' (1997), contemplated the way that a sign as incidental as the 'fringe' of the hair could somehow have the power to denote 'Romanness' (see also Sobchack, 1997). Toplin appears to consider genre a safety valve that filmmakers employ in order to minimize the risk of their large-scale investments with a public that demands familiarity. Barthes, however, understood that such signs and symbols functioned as fundamental elements in the process of meaning-making, even if, as Vivian Sobchack has rightly noted, he dismissed their complicity in bourgeois culture as 'mythology' too quickly (1990; 1998; 2000; 2002). In other words, there is no storytelling without reference to convention or genre. What needs better understanding is how visual symbols, objects and 'signs' work in relation to broader conventions of verbal storytelling since film integrates symbols and narrative structures and more so in historical films where the physical environment can show the power of a political regime rather than having it 'told'.

The focus on genre shows that historical films are not only reinterpreting the past, but they are also reinterpreting other visual narratives. One avenue for research would be to ask how and why certain aspects of visual historical storytelling become conventionalized. Stanley Kubrick's *Barry Lyndon* (UK, 1975) is an historical film based on the mid-nineteenth-century novel by William Makepeace Thackeray. It seems 'authentic' because it refers to what have become iconic period visual representations such as paintings by Thomas Gainsborough and drawings by William Hogarth. But how and why those images and not others are iconic may tell us about both the original period of their production and its ongoing reinterpretation. In other words, as images from a moment become images 'of' a moment to later generations, we never entirely lose the original images. They are not, however, all the possible images from the past. So, those images, in their iconic reinterpretation, allow us to trace a long history of what becomes a legend at most.

If academic historians might develop a greater interest in visual historical story-telling, film scholars have long specialized in this issue. Yet, beginning famously with Kracauer, they too have ridiculed and dismissed historical films as invariably stagey and unrealistic because the camera's realism always reveals the reality of actors dressed in costume rather than a genuine representation of the past, no matter how high the level of directorial skill and production values (Kracauer, 1960: 77–81). Yet, from early silent films to widescreen epics, historical films have also been imagined as quality films because of their educational aspirations and their debuts have often served as occasions in which to foreground cinematic virtuosity and to celebrate the potentials of cinematic production wrought on a grand scale. Such scholars as George Custen (1992), Sue Harper (1994), Leger Grindon (1994) and Andrew Higson (1999) have approached the history film through genre by attempting to describe the conventions of the historical film into sub-genres such as the biopic, the costume drama and heritage film. Most often, these studies show the way that popular history functions within the national context to contribute to memory and serve the ends of national heritage.

Sobchack's work on historical films stands apart from other considerations of the historical film genre as she has attempted to understand the way historical films embody historicity phenomenologically through the viewer's experience. In particular, her essay on the epic is a bold departure from mere genre analysis because it asks about the connection between the epic and the phenomenological problem of comprehending ourselves in time. The effect, she suggests, that the scale and length of the epic (almost always a three- to four-hour film) is to make viewers feel the passage of time. Sobchack has also argued that mainstream historical films (and not simply recent self-consciously postmodern ones) never claimed to offer a naive and transparent history. Instead, she argues that they are rife with stylization, opacity and star power in order to deliver their message about history's magnitude and importance. She argues, thus, that epics function as stimulants for the desire for history and that their complex production histories and their scale simulate the 'bigness' of history (1990: 24).

From both fields, History and Film Studies, scholars have failed to interrogate the relation between a moment's scholarly historiography and its cinematic history. For example, one could try to understand the connection between the release of a film like *McCabe & Mrs. Miller* (Robert Altman, US) in 1971 and the simultaneous rise of social history. The film is a demythologization of the West, in which the hero is an everyman typical of the characters that peopled the accounts of social histories (see Appleby et al., 1995). The film's landscape of wet rot, nights of card-playing and drink designed to fend off boredom; the simple-minded and physically unappealing prostitutes (made bearable to viewers by offering a beautiful Julie Christie as their madame) may or may not accurately represent the development of a Western mining-town around the turn of the century. Its view of the past, however, is decidedly from the bottom up and would have been quite familiar to scholars grappling to rewrite history in the wake of the social changes of the 1960s. If we try to understand how and whether historical films, despite their structural repetition associated with generic convention, relate to the historiographic fashions and think through the changing generic conventions of scholarly historiography, we may observe more of a relationship between filmmakers and historians than we have previously grasped.

CINEHISTORY

By establishing a relationship between film and history, we can imagine a field called 'cinehistory'. Hayden White has tried to name this connection in identifying 'historiophoty' – that is, the cinematic representation of the past and the thought about it. 'Historiophoty' results from two intersecting forces. On the one hand, White sees history on film as emerging from a long lineage of historical storytelling and conventions, many of which he described in *Metahistory* (1975). On the other hand, he is aware that visual sources themselves have their own ways of making meaning and we have been made aware (again) of the many visual sources for history precisely because of the influence of photography and film. To grasp the purpose of defining such a thing as 'historiophoty', we need to consider film's value-added qualities that have shaped our ideas about how to think about the past and imagine the past, whether in visual or written form. Films rather easily encode multiple points of view (the *Rashomon* effect). Landscape and space not only evoke but also make arguments about the past (think about the uses of the desert in *Lawrence of Arabia* [David Lean, UK, 1962] or even Salzburg in *The Sound of Music* [Robert Wise, US, 1965] to depict a 'golden age'). The flashback gives film the power to narrate multiple temporalities in ways far more difficult to achieve in written histories (perhaps *The Godfather: Part II* [Francis Ford Coppola, US, 1974] is the quintessential example). The materiality of depictions of the past (consider the importance of cars and music in *American Graffiti* [George Lucas, US, 1973]) suggest both the importance of visual style in all historical eras and also privilege the history of material culture in ways that written histories have not. This incomplete list of what we might consider cinematic 'time-effects' has never been studied in a systematic way nor has their development been considered over the course of the history of film.

Cinehistory also returns us to a deeper reconsideration of the epistemological bases of history, especially concerning how and whether film reframes historicity and temporality. While it may seem commonplace now to imagine the past as a series of representations and images, this is the result of historically specific transformations, at once social, cultural and technological, that define modernity, which for Walter Benjamin was equivalent to the era of mechanical reproduction. Temporality and subjectivity have a particular shape in modernity and analyzing the changes in historical thinking wrought by modernity's visual culture must be part of the agenda in thinking about film and history. As Benjamin observed, 'the photograph inaugurates history itself and what takes place in this history is the emergence of the image' (see Cadava, 1998: 63). Benjamin argued that the indexical technologies of representation would forever change our notions of the past and our access to it. At stake in this understanding of representation is the difference in narrative quality and mode of a medium that seems to be fundamentally about an insistent presence – both of objects that are represented (the iconic figuration of a car is achieved through filming a real car) and a perceptual presence that seems resistant to the passage of time itself.

Film, it has been argued by Benjamin and others, has transformed our notions of time and space, has showed us life as the naked eye cannot perceive it and created an unconscious optics. Early critics of film such as Georges Duhamel complained about the overwhelming sense of the epistemological transformations wrought by film: 'I can no longer think what I want to think. My thoughts have been replaced by moving images' (quoted in Benjamin, 1969: 238). Early on Benjamin identified the way cinema would come to dominate the modern imagination in which people began to speak of certain experiences 'as if they were a movie' (see Boorstin, 1992; Gabler, 2000).

If the question of the image is essential to Benjamin's thoughts about modernity, it later became the core of his avant-garde notions for the foundations of a materialist history. His idea of history was shaped, most of all, by the cinematic, and he insisted on thinking about 'the materialist presentation of history as imagistic in a higher sense than in the traditional presentation' (1999: 463, n.3). Benjamin's cinematic history was achieved through the decomposition of cinema into its elements, particularly as still photographs and through the seemingly exclusively cinematic means of narration which had recently been extensively discussed in avant-garde aesthetic circles: montage. 'History decays into images, not stories', he pronounced, offering the means to recompose it through the technique of montage; 'the first stage in this undertaking will be to carry over the principle of montage into history' (1999: 461, n.2).

Extending the Benjaminian approach, and working hard to distinguish between photography and film, Mary Ann Doane, in *The Emergence of Cinematic Time* (2002), has argued that such technologies are fundamentally concerned with temporality itself. In film, she suggests, time itself is conceptualized as what is storable and representable. The cinema, she argues, is at once about the illusion of continuous time but also a medium that would, by recording images, 'appear impervious to the passage of time' as opposed to photography's assertion of pastness (2002: 103). As one late-nineteenth century-newspaper announced in relation to the invention of film, 'Death will have ceased to be absolute' (Doane, 2002: 62). By logical extension, historical thinking, which feeds off the finality of death and the pastness of the past, will either be eradicated or transformed into an eternal present – as many postmodernists have pondered.

In *Change Mummified*, Philip Rosen has taken up the problem of temporality, in which he identifies André Bazin's 'mummy complex' as a meditation on the ways in which moving images preserve and stop concrete reality in time (2001: 27). Others have suggested ways in which film might help us rethink the philosophy of history, replacing chronology and narratives of origins, causes and conclusions with 'becoming' as Gilles Deleuze (1986; 2001) and Paul Ricoeur (1998) suggest (see also

Delage and Guigueno, 2004; Flaxman, 2000; Rodowick, 1997). I would like to propose that films themselves are articulate instances of cinehistory rather than texts that can suggest an external theory or philosophy of either film or history. Not all films are equally articulate on this matter, just as not all philosophers are equally interesting. I want to turn to a brief example of how one might use a rather canonical Film Studies' fiction film not previously considered as an 'historical film' (outside its status as a 'Hollywood' film) to think about film as cinehistory.

Sunset Boulevard (Billy Wilder, US, 1950) is a revealing text of cinehistory. Like its later shinier musical cousin, *Singin' in the Rain* (Stanley Donen/Gene Kelly, US, 1952), *Sunset Boulevard* looks at the transition from silent to sound film, surely one of the greatest historical transformations in the industry's, by then approximately fifty-years-long, history. But Norma Desmond (Gloria Swanson) is not Lina Lamont (Jean Hagen). We see no actual reason why she failed to make the transition in terms of a voice problem, an over-acting problem etc. Norma has not failed to make the transition and keep up with the times. She, like every star, is actually evidence of Hollywood's strange relationship to history and the passage of time. Norma, a symbol of Hollywood film culture itself, is emblematic of a cinematic construction of time in which the past is figured as an eternalized present. *Sunset Boulevard*, rather than being simply the straightforward narrative of the history of the transition from silent to sound, is also a film about Hollywood's relationship to history, its construction of the past and the passage of time.

Like many an historical film, *Sunset Boulevard* begins with a voice-over narration verbally establishing the time and place that the camera's establishing shot visually narrates. The film opens with a curb sign reading 'Sunset Boulevard' and the voice of a man, engaging our identification of the place – 'yes, this is *SUNSET BOULEVARD*' – with added information about time – 'it is about 5:00 a.m., a murder has been reported'. We see a dead body floating in the pool.

It is the narrator's, but that is not entirely clear until the flashback sequence that follows the scene. He then promises the historical film's conceit that 'Maybe you'd like to hear the facts, the whole truth'. Again, he manages our temporal awareness: 'Let's go back, six months … I was living …'. We transition to flashback and understand that the narrator is not a neutral omniscient 'voice of history' but rather a part of the story. He is, of course, Joe Gillis (William Holden), who impossibly narrates the scene of his own death and its investigation, and who serves as the film's guardian of time and reality.

Rather than understand Joe as the representative of contemporary Hollywood – he is washed up and headed back to Ohio – Norma, Max (Erich von Stroheim), and Cecil B. DeMille represent Hollywood's bizarre and delusional resistance to the passage of time. For example, DeMille is introduced in the film to perpetuate Norma's fantasy about the eternal present. When they reunite, DeMille indulges in a nostalgic discussion with her about the time they shared the celebration of Lindbergh landing in Paris. But, he warns, pictures have changed since then, as if to remind her they are not living in those good ol' days. If DeMille thus seems not to suffer from Norma's delusions, the setting suggests otherwise. He is, after all, on the set of *Samson and Delilah* making one of his usual epic costume films and he is wearing his director's jodhpurs – both of which went out of fashion at the same time as Norma Desmond did. The film's other 'Hollywood'-identified character in the film is Norma's fancy Italian car, the Isotta-Franschini, whose 1932 license plate reassured Joe early in the film that the house on Sunset Boulevard must be unoccupied. They begin riding around town in a twenty-year-old car without Norma having any sense of its datedness. It is the car, of course, not Norma, that Paramount wants for a film – presumably one set in the 1930s. Film's realism necessitates the use of contemporaneous objects in a way that highlights the temporal consistency needed to create a believable present, even of a moment in the past. Often films set in the past use real

objects like the car. But the logic of using real past objects is also repeated by the film's casting – of Gloria Swanson, the ageing film star as the ageing film star, directors DeMille and Erich von Stroheim, even Buster Keaton as one of her friends, referred to by Joe as the 'waxworks'.

Joe and Norma's relationship anchors the film. Within it, the distant, detached and ironic Joe constantly summons the past and remarks on the passage of time. His acute awareness of temporality corresponds, I would suggest, to his failure in Hollywood. He simply does not grasp that history, Hollywood-style, resists the passage of time and is figured, as is Norma, in an enduring present. Joe's interaction with Norma is riddled with his insistence about the passage of time coupled with her denial of its pastness. For example, when he realizes who she is, he says in the past tense, 'You used to be big'. She responds with the present tense: 'I am big'. He later tells her that the audience left twenty years ago and that 'there is nothing tragic about being fifty unless you try to be twenty-five', suggesting that neither the passage of time nor history is tragic – only the denial of them. Norma does not seem to agree.

From the start, the film suggests that Norma's present is somewhere in the past. From her house, replete with a pipe organ that can only be associated in this context with silent film, she is, as Joe complains, a 'sleepwalker' and her friends are the 'waxworks'. What these both share is a sense of being frozen in a moment without the possibility of historical transition. Her New Year's Eve party even resists the passage from one year to the next, as she invites no guests to witness this passage and attempts to kill herself before the band plays 'Auld Lang Syne'. When she is not screening her old films, she performs her old roles live – what Joe sarcastically calls 'the Norma Desmond Follies'. She acts the bathing beauty and coquettishly twirls an umbrella, repeating her role as a Mack Sennett bathing beauty, exclaiming, 'I can still see myself in the line'. Rather than have a vivid memory, Norma instead seems to be running a film in her mind.

Norma, I would like to suggest, is not simply mad because she is living in the past. The film suggests that technologies of photographic reproduction and film as a medium, rather than Hollywood as an institution, perpetuate Norma's status as trapped in the past with no sense that it is anything but the present. We grasp this early in the film when we see the living room littered with pictures of Norma, all of them taken when she was a young star. This notion is graphically highlighted in the scene of Norma watching her old films. Norma rises to her feet and is caught in the projector's light as if to be re-framed as part of the image on the screen, creating an illusion of continuity of the past with the present and this is precisely the delusion she is playing out. There she sits in the dark, watching herself as if it were live. I would suggest that film's realism only underscored the presentness of the reproduced image, arrested and endlessly repeated in the past as if it were the present as in Norma's nocturnal screenings.

The film's final confrontation between Joe and Norma reiterates the film's gloss on cinematic notions of historicity as the eternal present. Joe attempts to jolt Norma out of her delusional state. He tells her the audience left twenty years ago. He reveals that Max writes her fan mail (to which he replies, in the present tense, 'Madame is the greatest star of them all'.) And he explains that Paramount wanted to use her car. Her vengeful tirade that ends in a shooting spree begins with a re-articulation of her sense of temporality: 'No one ever leaves a star'. This statement is both a plea to affirm she is in charge but also reveals her temporal thinking. If no one leaves, then a narrative sequence cannot unfold and instead the players become frozen in time. After shooting Joe, she says, 'The stars are ageless'. The film emphasizes Norma's perspective here by reintroducing Joe's voice-over, which we now know is the corpse talking, re-situating us in time: 'This is where you came in'. In a final rush to counter Norma's temporality, newsreel cameras arrive: what better time machine is there? However, their historical function is trumped by Max's appropriation of the setting

as he pretends to direct Norma's performance and thus return her (and us) to Norma's eternal present. Joe rushes to reassert his sense of history by anticipating the headlines about his death, all with adjectives that suggest the passage of time: 'Forgotten star of yesteryear, aging actress, yesterday's glamour queen'. Yet Norma has the final word because the viewer loses the frame of the film, *Sunset Boulevard*, and is confronted instead with a different Norma Desmond film, one directed by Max. Without Joe's framing (he is dead), the viewer is now trapped in Norma's sense of time and space. She enlists us and reaches out to us with her version of temporality: 'This is my life and it always will be', she insists. The blurring and disintegration of this final image suggests that Norma is somehow entering the camera and becoming part of the film itself. The film ends in an unrealistic blur into Norma's eternal present.

Not all films, of course, offer the same quality of reflection concerning cinematic historicity and time as *Sunset Boulevard*. But by reading what a particular film might tell us about such basic elements as temporality, we can begin to explore how and whether not only film as a form but also individual films have shaped ideas about history and historicity in ways that far transcend debates about true and false history up on the screen. By thinking more systematically about the accumulation of filmed images as the record of the past, we will better understand our own notions of temporality and historicity.

Film is like history, it has been the archive of history since 1895, and it helps us think about history. But even more suggestive, history is best imagined as an image, which is what Benjamin famously described. With that in mind, I end with a final citation, not from the well-known German philosopher but from a Hollywood royal: Liza Minnelli in the 1974 documentary, *That's Entertainment!* (Jack Haley Jr, US). That compilation documentary, made in celebration of MGM's fiftieth anniversary, was the last film to be shot on the back lot at MGM's Culver City Studio and it is an important text for cinehistory. Minnelli appears in order to discuss her mother, Judy Garland, but makes a wonderfully telling comment after the segment that celebrates the career of Garland at MGM. After a medley of clips that summarizes Garland's career in reverse, beginning and ending with 'Get Happy' from *Summer Stock* (Charles Walters, US, 1950), her last MGM film, the frame first freezes and then fades completely to black. Seated on a dilapidated lot, Minnelli utters: 'Thank God for film. It can capture a performance and hold it right there forever. And if anyone says to you, "Who was he or who was she and what made them so good?", I think a piece of film answers that question better than any words I know of'. As this essay has suggested in multiple ways: me too.

Film's hold on the twentieth century has changed the kind of documents historians have at their disposal, has enriched historiography, and has redefined such elemental historical notions as temporality. Whatever the twenty-first century may have in store, film and its allied new media will be essential to its history and to our historical imaginations.

NOTES

1 See *The Wonderful, Horrible Life of Leni Riefenstahl* (Ray Müller, France/UK/Germany/Belgium, 1993).

2 Also see the film *The Nazi Plan*.

3 See the Public Broadcasting Service television series *American Masters* (Susan Steinberg et al., US, 1983). Another television documentary that manages to breathe new interpretive life into familiar images is the American Broadcasting Company's *Life with Judy Garland: Me and My Shadows* (Robert Allan Ackerman, Canada/US, 2001).

4 See Schama's 'Clio at the Multiplex' (1998).

5 Press materials provided by Weinstein Company, 'Days of Glory'. Rachid Bouchareb: Director's statement.

6 Rosenstone draws on Hayden White's *Metahistory: The Historical Imagination in Nineteenth-Century Europe* (1975).

REFERENCES

Appleby, Joyce, Hunt, Lynn and Jacob, Margaret (1995) *Telling the Truth About History*. New York: Norton.

Balio, Tino (1987) *United Artists: The Company That Changed the Film Industry*. Madison: University of Wisconsin Press.

Barthes, Roland (1997) 'The Romans in Films', in *Mythologies*. Tr. Annette Lavers. New York: Hill and Wang. pp. 26–8.

Benjamin, Walter (1969) 'The Work of Art in the Age of Mechanical Reproduction', in Hannah Arendt (ed.), *Illuminations*. Tr. Harry Zohn. New York: Schocken. pp. 217–51.

Benjamin, Walter (1999) *The Arcades Project*. Tr. Howard Eiland and Kevin McLaughlin. Cambridge: Belknap Press.

Boorstin, Daniel (1992) *The Image: A Guide to Pseudo-Events in America*. New York: Vintage.

Bordwell, David (1998) *On the History of Film Style*. Cambridge, MA: Harvard University Press.

Bruno, Giuliana (1992) *Streetwalking on a Ruined Map*. Princeton, NJ: Princeton University Press.

Cadava, Eduardo (1998) *Words of Light: Theses on the Photography of History*. New York: Princeton University Press.

Carnes, Mark C., Mico, Ted, Miller-Monzon, John and Rubel, David (eds) (1996) *Past Imperfect: History According to the Movies*. New York: Henry Holt.

Champion, Justin (2003) 'Simon Schama's *A History of Britain* and Public History', *History Workshop Journal*, 56(1): 153–74.

Charney, Leo and Schwartz, Vanessa (eds) (1995) *Cinema and the Invention of Modern Life*. Berkeley: University of California Press.

Crary, Jonathan (1992) *Techniques of the Observer: On Vision and Modernity in the Nineteenth Century*. Cambridge: MIT Press.

Custen, George (1992) *Bio/pics: How Hollywood Constructed Public History*. New Jersey: Rutgers University Press.

Davis, Natalie Zemon (1987) 'Any Resemblance to Persons Living or Dead: Film and the Challenge of Authenticity', *Yale Review*, 76: 460.

de Baecque, Antoine (1998) *La Nouvelle Vague: Portrait d'une jeunesse*. Paris: Flammarion.

de Baecque, Antoine (2003) *La Cinéphilie: Invention d'un regard, histoire d'une culture*. Paris: Fayard.

de Baecque, Antoine and Delage, Christian (eds) (1998) *De l'histoire au cinéma*. Paris: Éditions Complexe.

DeCherney, Peter (2005) *Hollywood and the Culture Elite: How the Movies Became American*. New York: Columbia University Press.

Delage, Christian (2006) *La Vérité par l'image: de Nuremberg au procès Milosevic*. Paris: Éditions Denoël.

Delage, Christian and Guigueno, Vincent (2004) *L'Historien et le film*. Paris: Gallimard.

Deleuze, Gilles (1986) *Cinema 1: Movement-Image*. Tr. Hugh Tomlinson and Barbara Habberjam. Minneapolis: University of Minnesota Press.

Deleuze, Gilles (2001) *Cinema 2: The Time-Image*. Tr. Hugh Tomlinson and Robert Galeta. Minneapolis: University of Minnesota Press.

Doane, Mary Ann (2002) *The Emergence of Cinematic Time: Modernity, Contingency, the Archive*. Cambridge, MA: Harvard University Press.

Flaxman, Gregory (2000) *The Brain Is the Screen: Deleuze and the Philosophy of Cinema*. Minneapolis: University of Minnesota Press.

Fox, Richard (1999) *Trials of Intimacy*. Chicago: University of Chicago Press.

Friedberg, Anne (1993) *Window Shopping: Cinema and the Postmodern*. Berkeley: University of California Press.

Gabler, Neal (2000) *Life: The Movie: How Entertainment Conquered Reality*. New York: Vintage.

Giovacchini, Saverio (2001) *Hollywood Modernism: Film and Politics in the Age of the New Deal*. Philadelphia: Temple University Press.

Goodman, James (1995) *Stories of Scottsboro*. New York: Vintage Press.

Grafton, Anthony (1999) *The Footnote: A Curious History*. Cambridge, MA: Harvard University Press.

Grieveson, Lee (2004) *Policing Cinema: Movies and Censorship in Early-Twentieth-Century America*. Berkeley: University of California Press.

Grindon, Leger (1994) *Shadows on the Past: Studies in the Historical Fiction Film*. Philadelphia: Temple University Press.

Harper, Sue (1994) *Picturing the Past*. London: BFI.

Higson, Andrew (1999) *Film Europe and Film America: Cinema, Commerce, and Cultural Exchange 1920–1939*. Exeter: University of Exeter Press.

Hjort, Mette and Mackenzie, Scott (eds) (2000) *Cinema and Nation*. London: Routledge.

Kracauer, Siegfried (1947) *From Caligari to Hitler: A Psychological History of the German Film*. London: Dobson.

Kracauer, Siegfried (1960) *Theory of Film: The Redemption of Physical Reality*. New York: Oxford University Press.

Matuszewski, Bolesas (1997) 'A New Source For History: The Creation of a Depository for Historical Cinematography (Paris 1898)', *Screening The Past*, 1. Available at: http://www.latrobe.edu.au/screeningthepast/classics/clasjul/mat.html.

McAlister, Melani (2001) *Epic Encounters: Culture, Media and U.S. Interests in the Middle East, 1945–2000*. Berkeley: University of California Press.

Nadel, Alan (1995) *Containment Culture: American Narratives, Postmodernism, and the Atomic Age*. Durham, NC: Duke University Press.

Rabinovitz, Lauren (1998) *For the Love of Pleasure: Women, Movies and Culture in Turn-Of-The Century*. Chicago. New Jersey: Rutgers University Press.

Ricoeur, Paul (1998) 'Histoire et mémoire', in Antoine de Baecque and Christian Delage (eds), *De l'histoire au cinéma*. Paris: Éditions Complexe. pp. 17–28.

Rodowick, D.N. (1997) *Gilles Deleuze's Time Machine*. Durham, NC: Duke University Press.

Rollins, Peter C. (2004) *The Columbia Companion to American History on Film*. New York: Columbia University Press.

Rosen, Philip (1984) 'Securing the Historical: Historiography and The Classical Cinema', in Patricia Mellencamp and Philip Rosen (eds), *Cinema Histories, Cinema Practices*. Los Angeles: AFI. p. 31.

Rosen, Philip (2001) *Change Mummified: Cinema, Historicity, Theory*. Minneapolis: University of Minnesota Press.

Rosenstone, Robert A. (1995) *Visions of the Past: The Challenge of Film to Our Idea of History*. Cambridge, MA: Harvard University Press.

Rosenstone, Robert A. (2006) *History on Film, Film on History*. Harlow: Pearson Education Ltd.

Ross, Steve (1999) *Working-Class Hollywood*. Princeton, NJ: Princeton University Press.

Schama, Simon (1998) 'Clio at the Multiplex', *New Yorker*, 19 January: 38–43.

Sklar, Robert (1975) *Movie Made America*. New York: Vintage.

Sobchack, Vivian (1990) '"Surge and Splendor": A Phenomenology of the Cinematic Historical Epic', *Representations*, 29: 24–49.

Sobchack, Vivian (1997) 'The Insistent Fringe: Moving Images and the Palimpsest of Historical Consciousness', *History and Theory: Studies in the Philosophy of History*, 36(4): 4–20.

Sobchack, Vivian (1998) '"Lounge Time": Post-War Crises and the Chronotope of Film Noir', in Nick Browne (ed.), *Refiguring American Film Genres: History and Theory*. Berkeley: University of California Press. pp. 129–70.

Sobchack, Vivian (2000) 'What is Film History? Or the Riddle of the Sphinxes', in Christine Gledhill and Linda Williams (ed.), *Reinventing Film Studies*. London: Arnold Press. pp. 300–15.

Sobchack, Vivian (2002) '"Happy New Year/Auld Lang Syne": On Televisual Montage and Historical Consciousness', in James Friedman (ed.), *Reality Squared: Televisual Discourse on the Real*. New Brunswick, NJ: Rutgers University Press. pp. 92–116.

Stamp, Shelly (2000) *Movie Struck Girls*. New Jersey: Princeton University Press.

Toplin, Robert Brent (1996) *History By Hollywood: The Use and Abuse of the American Past*. Urbana: University of Illinois Press.

Toplin, Robert Brent (2002) *Reel History: In Defense of Hollywood*. Lawrence: University Press of Kansas.

Toplin, Robert Brent (2003) *Oliver Stone's USA*. Lawrence: University of Kansas Press.

Wasson, Haidee (2005) *Museum Movies: The Museum of Modern Art and the Birth of Art Cinema*. Berkeley: University of California Press.

White, Hayden (1975) *Metahistory: The Historical Imagination in Nineteenth-Century Europe*. Baltimore, MD: John Hopkins University Press.

14

Mass Media, Anthropology and Ethnography

Faye Ginsburg

In 1993, in a comprehensive review essay, Debra Spitulnik invoked the insights of Stuart Hall and other sociologically-grounded media scholars to call for more engagement by anthropologists with 'mass media as vehicles of culture, as modes of imagining and imaging communities' (1993: 295).[1] Years later, a fertile domain of study – the anthropology of media – has emerged along with a general reconceptualization of anthropology that addresses our changing relationship with informants as our cultural worlds grow ever closer (Marcus, 1996). The social domains we need in order to track to understand contemporary lives are increasingly shaped by processes of late capitalism, requiring multi-sited research strategies (Gupta and Ferguson, 1997; Hannerz, 1996). Anthropologists studying media – from their political economy to their presence in everyday lives – are developing research that will help us understand the way these forms are affecting people around the globe, part of a larger effort to create an 'anthropology of the present' (Fox, 1991).

For many years mass media were seen as almost a taboo topic for anthropology, too redolent of Western modernity and cultural imperialism for a field identified with tradition, the non-Western and the vitality of the local. As media are becoming more ubiquitous even in remote locales, an increasing number of anthropologists have recognized not only the necessity of attending to their presence, but also their significance. As anthropologists attempt to account for the growing importance of the presence of film, television, video, and radio as part of the everyday life of people throughout the world, we have taken up with new interest the study of the production, circulation, and consumption of mass mediated forms (Abu-Lughod, 1993; 1997; Appadurai, 1991; Dickey, 1993; Dornfeld, 1998; Himpele, 1996; Mankekar, 1999; Marcus, 1996; Michaels, 1994; Pedelty, 1995; Rofel, 1994; Spitulnick, 2002) as well as visual culture, broadly conceived (Edwards, 2001; MacDougall, 1998; Marcus and Myers, 1995; Pinney, 1998; Ruby, 2000). People who are studying these forms as vehicles for the mediation and expression of social processes and cultural meanings, are working in field sites as diverse as BBC boardrooms (Born, 1998), to villages in upper Egypt (Abu-Lughod, 2002), to fan clubs in south India (Dickey, 1993), to radio stations in Zambia (Spitulnick, 2002), to popular talk shows in Bolivia (Himpele, 2002).

The anthropology of mass media is informed by several intertwined legacies of thought within anthropology and media studies. Studies of feature films and propaganda were carried out during and following World War Two, for example (Bateson, 1943; Mead and Metraux, 1953; Powdermaker, 1950) within the American culture and personality paradigm, and later as part of a developing field of studies in visual communication.[2] Following that lineage, a number of scholars link their work on media to the field of visual anthropology (Banks and Morphy, 1997; Ginsburg, 1998; Hughes-Freeland, 1997; Pinney, 1998), often bringing a critical revision of that field through the lens of postcolonial scholarship, especially on ethnographic, documentary, and popular film practices, past and present (Rony, 1996; Shohat and Stam, 1994). Others focus on its empirical counterpart in the production of a variety of alternative (Downmunt, 1993; Juhasz, 1995; Riggins, 1992), diasporic (Gillespie, 1995; Cunningham and Sinclair, 2000; McLagan, 2002; Naficy, 1993) and small media practices (Haynes, 1997; Manuel, 1993; Sreberny-Mohammadi and Mohammadi, 1994), made by people who until recently were only objects and never producers in the enterprise of cross-cultural representation.

Another related strand of thought, closely identified with the journal *Public Culture*, emerges from those interested in how processes of modernity, postmodernity, and globalization actually work on the ground, tracking the cultural effects of transnational flows of people, ideas and objects – in some cases mediated by film, video, and television – that are instrumental in creating a sense of a social world that is rapidly 'respatializing' culture and power in ways that characterize fin-de-siècle cultural life (Marcus, 1997;

Larkin, 1997). This scholarship builds, in particular, on the work of two key scholars whose work addresses the mediation of the structures and processes of nationalism and consciousness: Benedict Anderson's ground-breaking insights into the role of print (1991) – and now other – media in the creation of the 'imagined communities' of nation states, and the extension of Anderson's Durkheimian frame to a broader notion of the social imaginary[3]; and Jurgen Habermas' articulation of the historical emergence of the public sphere (1989) (and the ensuing debates and critiques of that model articulated by Robbins [1993], Fraser [1993], Calhoun [1992], and others). The work of Arjun Appadurai (1996), has been particularly influenced by these thinkers, and in turn has been influential in synthesizing their frameworks with anthropological concerns and methods. In his model, media is a central part of public culture, particularly important to the articulation of national and transnational with local processes. His influential essay on 'global ethnoscapes' points to the significance of the spread of film, television, video, and photography throughout the world. Attending to the ways in which satellite and video technologies transcend nation-state boundaries that were sustained more easily through print and terrestrial television, he argues for the increasing significance of 'the imagination' in the production of culture and identity in the contemporary world as:

> more persons in more parts of the world consider a wider set of 'possible' lives than they ever did before. One important source of this change is the mass media, which present a rich, ever-changing store of possible lives, some of which enter the lived imaginations of ordinary people more successfully than others. Important also are contact with, news of, and rumors about others in one's social neighborhood who have become inhabitants of these faraway worlds. The importance of media is not so much as direct sources of new images and scenarios for life possibilities but as semiotic diacritics of great power, which also inflect social contact with the metropolitan world facilitated by other channels. (1991: 198)

In his 1996 edited volume *Connected: Engagements with Media*, George Marcus also focuses on electronic and visual media of various kinds and how they operate increasingly as 'a direct and intimate complement to the self and self-capacity' (1996: 10).

The significance of media as a hermeneutic for entering and comprehending the contemporary social world is especially clear in a number of recent groundbreaking projects that provide models for how programmatic claims about media can actually guide research. Lila Abu-Lughod's work on the production, circulation and impact of Egyptian television melodrama serials is exemplary, tracking how these are intended to operate (if not always successfully) as social technologies through which modern citizens are produced and subjectivities are partially constituted (Abu-Lughod 2004). In one of her articles on the social life of these narrative forms as they move from producers to audiences, she demonstrates how, by staging interiorities through heightened emotional display, they encourage the embrace of individuality over kinship, a key transformation in the making of modern subjects (1998).

Finally, Pierre Bourdieu's framing of the field of cultural production (1993) – the system of relations (and struggles for power) among agents or institutions engaged in generating the value of works of art, while creating cultural capital for themselves – has been especially influential for those whose emphasis is on the institutional sites for the production of media work. For example, in his innovative ethnography, Barry Dornfeld draws on Bourdieu's model to understand the production of a public television series as a 'cultural field' in which producers are also always prefiguring audiences in their work. This position, he argues, calls more generally for 'rethinking and bridging the theoretical dichotomy between production and consumption, between producers' intentional meanings and audience members' interpreted meanings and between production studies and reception studies' (1998: 12–13).

One might think of these linked processes of the cultural production of media, media circulation as a social technology, and the relationship of mediated worlds to

self-fabrication as existing on a continuum. At one end is the more self-conscious cultural activism in which cultural material is used and strategically deployed as part of a broader project of political empowerment, providing a 'third space' (Bhabha, 1989) for indigenous and minoritized groups as well as what some have called 'Third Cinema' (Pines and Willemen, 1989), often created in circumstances in which choices are heavily constrained and political mobilization is incipient (Downmunt, 1993; Juhasz, 1995; McLagan, 1996; Riggins, 1992).[4] In the middle range are reflexive but less strategic processes in which the imaginative encounter with cinematic or televisual images and narratives may be expressive and/or constitutive of a variety of social worlds such as the transnational links that video, television shows, films, and computer networks provide for diasporic communities (Gillespie, 1995; McLagan, 1996; Schein, 2002). At the other end of the continuum are the more classic formations of mass media which require institutional framings and imply some dimension of social segregation between producers and audiences. Anthropological research on these mediations focuses on the complex and divergent ways in which national cinemas (Bikales, 1997; Faraday, 2000; Ganti, 1998 and 2002) and television in Third World settings operate, tracking the often unstable relationship between intention and effect as these media are put to the service of constituting modern citizens, through a variety of forms, notably in popular soap operas, telenovelas, melodramatic serials (Abu-Lughod, 2002; Mankekar, 2002; Miller, 1992; Rofel, 1994; Salamandra, 1998; Yang, 2002), cultural programming (Hobart, 2002; Hughes-Freeland, 1997), talk shows (Gordon, 1998; Himpele, 2002), and how these are intended and understood in relation to larger conjunctures and in a variety of settings from production to distribution to consumption.

Because anthropologists so frequently locate themselves in non-Western and 'out of the way' places, the research offers not only a thick, vertically integrated, and multi-sited sense of the social life of media, but also engages with how this occurs outside the circuits of first world settings which have provided an ethnocentric frame for much academic discussion of media until quite recently. Ironically, even those arguing about and against cultural imperialism (Schiller, 1991) or researching the exporting of American culture through the circulation of popular film and television programs (Ang, 1985; Liebes and Katz, 1990; Silj, 1988), nonetheless presume the centrality of American media. In an effort to correct that, ethnographers and scholars in media studies are attending increasingly to the circulation of media in settings not dependent on Western hegemonic practices, such as the export of Hindi cinema (Pendakur and Subramanyam, 1996) or of Mexican telenovelas (Sinclair, 1996).

At the same time, anthropological research on mass media reiterates the insufficiency of bounded concepts of culture as a way of understanding contemporary lives in our own or other societies. As Abu-Lughod argued in considering the impact of Egyptian serials in the life of Zaynab, an older peasant woman living in a peasant village in Upper Egypt:

> Television is an extraordinary technology for breaching boundaries and intensifying and multiplying encounters among life worlds, sensibilities, and ideas ... It brings into Zaynab's home, her conversations and her imagination a range of visions and experiences that originated outside her community ... hardly unusual produced elsewhere and consumed in a variety of localities. Even if it ultimately helps create something of a 'national habitus' or hints of a transnational habitus, television is most interesting because of the way it provides material which is then inserted into, interpreted with, and mixed up with local but themselves socially differentiated knowledges, discourses and meaning systems ... Television, in short, renders more and more problematic a concept of cultures as localized communities of people suspended in shared webs of meaning. (1997: 122)

Scholars developing ethnographies of media usually begin with an interest in understanding questions generated by the phenomenon itself, often motivated by a desire to comprehend the popularity, power, and/or passion attached to certain kinds of media production and viewing (for example,

why is Indian cinema so popular among Hausa men in northern Nigeria?). It quickly becomes apparent in almost every case that answering these questions leads to an appreciation of the complexity of how people interact with media in a variety of social spaces and the resulting shifts in the sense of the local as its relationship to broader social worlds becomes almost a routine part of everyday life. Understanding the social relations of media production, circulation, and reception in this way entails a grounded focus on the everyday practices and consciousness of social actors as producers and consumers of different forms of media. Their interests and responses shape and are shaped by a variety of possible subject positions: cultural, generational, gendered, local, national, regional and transnational communities of identity requiring an increasingly complex and plural notion of audience. Indeed, these multiple identities may be part of a single social subject's repertoire of cultural resources, as is clear in this hypothetical example:

> An Egyptian immigrant in Britain, for example, might think of herself as a Glaswegian when she watches her local Scottish channel, a British resident when she switches over to the BBC, an Islamic Arab expatriate in Europe when she tunes in to the satellite service from the Middle East and a world citizen when she channel surfs on CNN. (Sinclair et al., 1996: 25)

While our work is distinguished by an effort to track qualitatively and with the kind of cultural knowledge that enables what Clifford Geertz calls 'thick description', the practices, consciousness and distinctions that emerge for people out of their quotidian encounters with media are also always situated within the context of a broader social universe.[5] To comprehend that reality, studies are increasingly multi-sited, tracking the various social players engaged when one follows the object – a television serial or film as it moves from elite directors to consumers (Dickey, 1993; Mankekar, 1999), or the object itself such as a cassette recorder (Manuel, 1993), radio (Spitulnick, 2002), or even radio sound (Tacchi, 1998 and 2002) as it circulates through a variety of milieux.

Whether in our own societies (Dornfeld, 2002; McLagan, 2002) or elsewhere, ethnographers look at media as cultural artefacts enmeshed in daily lives, to see how they are imperfectly articulated with (and sometimes created as a counter to) larger hegemonic processes of modernity, assimilation, nation-building, commercialization, and globalization, but in terms that draw attention to how those processes are being localized.

Perhaps because of the intensity and self-consciousness of the concern with media's possible deleterious effects as well its utopian possibilities, most of us carrying out research on media with indigenous or other subaltern groups have an activist engagement with this work as well (Philipsen and Markussen, 1995), as supporters and even catalyzers of activity, bringing cameras to communities and assisting in the logistics of projects (Asch, 1991; Carelli, 1988; Gallois and Carelli, 1993/4; Ginsburg, 2002; Michaels, 1994; Prins, 1997 and 2002; Turner, 2002) or helping to develop visibility, funding, and circulation systems for the work (Berger, 1995; Fleming, 1991; Ginsburg, 2003; Meadows and Molnar, 2001; Wortham, 2000). In a less direct but equally engaged concern, Abu-Lughod points out that studying popular television 'is particularly useful for writing against the grain [of global inequalities] because it forces us to represent people in distant villages as part of the same cultural worlds we inhabit – worlds of mass media, consumption, and dispersed communities of the imagination' (1997: 128). Some have argued that these projects go beyond advocacy as authorial relations are reversed and 'the anthropologist's voice supplements that of indigenous people' (Marcus, quoted in Palattella, 1998: 50–7), underscoring the ways in which we are increasingly 'complicit' with our subjects when engaged with such material (Marcus, 1997), as we find ourselves jointly engaged in the project of objectifying and representing culture. This relationship grows even more complex as anthropologists (and fellow travellers) are beginning to study cyberspace (see Kirshenblatt-Gimblett, 1996; Lotfalian, 1996; McLagan, 1996; Miller and Slater, 2000; Pound, 1996), a site of sociality in which the research takes place (in part) through the medium of study itself.

One can see a trajectory in the theorizing of the relationship between culture and media over the last half-century as the objectification of the category of culture becomes evermore widespread and the observer becomes increasingly implicated as a participant. In the early work on mass media, culture operated as a kind of unconscious Durkheimian indicator of the national which was interpreted in metaphors of personality types in the work of Margaret Mead, Gregory Bateson, John Weakland, Martha Wolfenstein, and others in the 1950s. When, in the 1990s, anthropologists began to turn their attention to film and television once again, they looked at media, not so much as a reductive mirror, but rather as a social force in which culture is a resource in struggles for political and/or economic hegemony over the representation of society in mass media, from efforts to shore up state control over television to the development of the Third Cinema movement that was part of a global anti-colonial project. Most recently, scholars are developing research that will help us rethink abstract notions such as globalization, to see how new technologies and economies of late modernity are being framed both by 'the new international division of cultural labor' (Miller, 1995) as well as practices on the ground (or rooftops as satellite dishes proliferate!) as people at every end of the social spectrum – from Rupert Murdoch's STAR TV to the videographers in Hmong communities dispersed across the globe – are engaging with mediascapes that increasingly escape the control of national political structures and economies, rearranging the ways in which cultural formations are spatialized and imagined in the process. For many social theorists interested in media as a site for either social possibilities or cultural decay, the question is still open as to whether even alternative media practices inevitably 'eat their young' because of the impossibility of escaping the discursive and institutional structures that even small media require. While the lack of resolution is undoubtedly healthy for intellectual debate, an unanticipated dimension of continued research during an era of ever-widening penetration and availability of media is the way in which we are increasingly implicated in the representational practices of those we study, a social fact that brings absolute and welcome closure to the allochronic tendencies of the field that Fabian warned against.

Anthropologists are at last coming to terms with the inescapable presence of media as a contemporary cultural force engaged with the mediation of hegemonic forms and resistance to them; the growth and transnational circulation of public culture; the creation of national and activist social imaginaries with the development of media as new arenas for political expression and the production of identity. Such research offers a salutary effect on anthropology as well as media studies, opening up new questions regarding the production and circulation of film and electronic media throughout the world, in non-Western as well as Western societies, potentially resituating the 'looking relations' that take place between and among cultures and across boundaries of inequality (Gaines, 1988).

NOTES

1 Hall argues that as the mass media 'have progressively *colonized* the cultural and ideological sphere' they increasingly provide 'a basis on which groups construct an image of the lives, and accomplishment meanings, practices, and values of *other* groups and classes' as well as 'the images, representations, and ideas around which the social totality can be coherently grasped as a *whole*' (1997: 47).

2 Sol Worth's approach, developed in the 1970s, reflected the theoretical preoccupations of that time with structural semiotics and ethnoscience (see Worth, Adair and Chalfen, [1972] 1997.) Although he also developed a interest in the political economy and global reach of media, Worth's focus on the anthropology of visual communication looked primarily at how films made by any group of people could provide visual maps of worldviews and cognitive categories, serving as a kind of window onto the native's point of view. Later, influenced by Worth's ideas and efforts, Jay Ruby, along with Worth's student Richard Chalfen, initiated the first Masters in Visual Anthropology in the US at Temple University with a focus on culture and communication which included the social uses and cultural meanings of film, television, video, and photography, for example, Chalfen's study of snapshot photography (1987) or Michael Intintoli's ethnographic study of the production of American soap operas, *Taking Soaps Seriously* (1984).

3 Fredric Jameson, in his discussion of the imaginary (1991: 48), appropriates the Althusserian (and Lacanian) redefinition of ideology as 'the representation of the subject's *imaginary* relationship to his or her *real* conditions of existence' (quoted in Jameson, 1991: 51). See a useful discussion of the concept of the imaginary in Lilley (1993).

4 As Jeremy MacClancy noted in his discussion of the contemporary uses of art, 'Many peoples, bent on self-determination and unhappy with the way they are represented by others, wish to represent themselves to others, and art is one of the most powerful media by which to do so' (1997: 2).

5 For an excellent discussion of how the notion of 'thick description' enters into ethnographies of mass media, see Abu-Lughod (1997).

REFERENCES

Abu-Lughod, Lila (1993) 'Finding a Place for Islam: Egyptian Television Serials and the National Interest', *Public Culture*, 5(3): 493–514.

Abu-Lughod, Lila (1997) 'The Interpretation of Culture(s) after Television', *Representations*, 59: 109–33.

Abu-Lughod, Lila (1998) 'Television and the Virtues of Education', in Nicholas Hopkins and Kirsten Westergaard (eds), *Directions of Change in Rural Egypt.* Cairo: American University in Cairo Press. pp. 147–65.

Abu-Lughod, Lila (2002) 'Egyptian Melodrama, Technology of the Modern Subject?', in Faye Ginsburg, Lila Abu-Lughod and Brian Larkin (eds), *Media Worlds: Anthropology on New Terrain.* Berkeley: University of California Press. pp. 115–33.

Abu-Lughod, Lila (2004) *Dramas of Nationhood: The Politics of Television in Egypt.* Chicago: University of Chicago Press.

Anderson, Benedict (1991) *Imagined Communities: Reflections on the Origins and Spread of Nationalism.* London: Verso.

Ang, Ien (1985) *Watching Dallas: Soap Opera and the Melodramatic Imagination.* London: Methuen.

Appadurai, Arjun (1991) 'Global Ethnoscapes: Notes and Queries for a Transnational Anthropology', in Richard Fox (ed.), *Recapturing Anthropology.*

Santa Fe, NM: School of American Research Press. pp. 191–210.

Appadurai, Arjun (1996) *Modernity at Large: Cultural Dimensions of Globalization*. Minneapolis: University of Minnesota Press.

Asch, Timothy (1991) 'The Story We Now Want to Hear is Not Ours to Tell – Relinquishing Control over Representation: Toward Sharing Visual Communication Skills with the Yanomamo', *Visual Anthropology Review*, 7(2): 102–6.

Banks, Marcus and Morphy, Howard (eds) (1997) *Rethinking Visual Anthropology*. New Haven, CT: Yale University Press.

Bateson, Gregory (1943) 'Cultural and Thematic Analysis of Fictional Films', in *Transactions of the New York Academy of Sciences*. New York: New York Academy of Sciences. pp. 72–8.

Berger, Sally (1995) 'Move Over Nanook', *Wide Angle*, 17(1–4): 177–92.

Bhabha, Homi (1989) 'The Commitment to Theory', in Jim Pines and Paul Willemen (eds), *Questions of Third Cinema*. London: BFI. pp. 111–32.

Bikales, Tom (1997) 'From "Culture" to "Commercialization": The Production and Packaging of an African Cinema in Ougadougou, Burkina Faso'. PhD dissertation, New York University.

Born, Georgina (1998) 'Between Aesthetics, Ethics and Audit: Reflexivities and Disciplines in the BBC'. Unpublished paper presented at the Department of Anthropology, New York University, 28 April.

Bourdieu, Pierre (1993) *The Field of Cultural Production*. New York: Columbia University Press.

Calhoun, Craig (ed.) (1992) *Habermas and the Public Sphere*. Cambridge, MA: MIT Press.

Carelli, Vincent (1988) 'Video in the Villages', *Commission on Visual Anthropology Bulletin*, 4(2): 10–15.

Chalfen, Richard (1987) *Snapshot Versions of Life*. Columbus, OH: Bowling Green State University Press.

Cunningham, Stuart and Sinclair, John (eds) (2000) *Floating Lives: The Media and Asian Diasporas*. St. Lucia, Queensland: University of Queensland Press.

Dickey, Sara (1993) *Cinema and the Urban Poor in South India*. Cambridge: Cambridge University Press.

Dornfeld, Barry (1998) *Producing Public Television*. Princeton, NJ: Princeton University Press.

Dornfeld, Barry (2002) 'Putting American Public Television Documentary in its Places', in Faye Ginsburg, Lila Abu-Lughod and Brian Larkin (eds), *Media Worlds: Anthropology on New Terrain*. Berkeley: University of California Press. pp. 247–63.

Downmunt, Tony (ed.) (1993) *Channels of Resistance: Global Television and Local Empowerment*. London: BFI.

Edwards, Elizabeth (2001) *Raw Histories: Photographs, Anthropology, and Museums*. Oxford: Berg.

Faraday, George (2000) *Revolt of the Filmmakers: The Struggle for Artistic Autonomy and the Fall of the Soviet Film Industry*. Philadelphia: Penn State University Press.

Fleming, Kathleen (1991) 'Zacharias Kunuk: Videomaker and Inuit Historian', *Inuit Art Quarterly*, 6(3): 24–8.

Fox, Richard (ed.) (1991) *Recapturing Anthropology: Working in the Present*. Santa Fe, NM: School of American Research Press.

Fraser, Nancy (1993) 'Rethinking the Public Sphere: A Contribution to the Critique of Actually Existing Democracy', in Bruce Robbins (ed.), *The Phantom Public Sphere*. Minneapolis: University of Minnesota Press. pp. 1–32.

Gaines, Jane M. (1988) 'White Privilege and Looking Relations: Race and Gender in Feminist Film Theory', *Screen* 29(4). pp. 12–27.

Gallois, Dominique and Carelli, Vincent (1993/4) 'Video in the Villages:The Waipani Experience', *CVA Newsletter*. pp. 7–11.

Ganti, Tejaswini (1998) 'Centenary Commemorations or Centenary Contestations? Celebrating Hundred Years of Cinema in Bombay', *Visual Anthropology*, 11(4): 399–419.

Ganti, Tejaswini (2002) 'The (H)Indianization of Hollywood by the Bombay Film Industry', in Faye Ginsburg, Lila Abu-Lughod and Brian Larkin (eds), *Media Worlds: Anthropology on New Terrain*. Berkeley: University of California Press. pp. 281–300.

Gillespie, Marie (1995) *Television, Ethnicity, and Cultural Change*. London: Routledge.

Ginsburg, Faye (1998) 'Institutionalizing the Unruly: Charting a Future for Visual Anthroplogy', *Ethnos*, 63(2): 173–201.

Ginsburg, Faye (2002) 'Screen Memories: Resignifying the Traditional in Indigenous Media', in Faye Ginsburg, Lila Abu-Lughod and Brian Larkin (eds), *Media Worlds: Anthropology on New Terrain*. Berkeley: University of California Press. pp. 77–104.

Ginsburg, Faye (2003) 'Atanarjuat Off-Screen: From "Media Reservations" to the World Stage', *American Anthropologist*, 105(1): 822–6.

Gordon, Joel (1998) 'Becoming the Image: Words of Gold, Talk Television, and Ramadan Nights on the Little Screen', *Visual Anthropology*, 10(2–4): 247–64.

Gupta, Akhil and Ferguson, James (1997) 'Discipline and Practice: "The Field" as Site, Method, and Location in Anthropology', in Akhil Gupta and James Ferguson (eds), *Anthropological Locations*. Berkeley: University of California Press. pp. 1–46.

Habermas, Jurgen (1989) *The Structural Transformation of the Public Sphere*. Tr. Thomas Burger and Frederick Lawrence. Cambridge, MA: MIT Press.

Hall, Stuart (1997) *Representation: Cultural Representations and Signifying Practices*. London: Sage.

Hannerz, Ulf (1996) *Transnational Connections*. New York: Routlege.

Haynes, Jonathan (ed.) (1997) *Nigerian Video Film*. Rev. edn. Ohio: Ohio University Press.

Himpele, Jeff (1996) 'Film Distribution as Media: Mapping Difference in the Bolivian Cinemascape', *Visual Anthropology Review*, 12(1): 47–66.

Himpele, Jeff (2002) 'Arrival Scenes: Complicity and Media Ethnography in the Bolivian Public Sphere', in Faye Ginsburg, Lila Abu-Lughod and Brian Larkin (eds), *Media Worlds: Anthropology on New Terrain*. Berkeley: University of California Press. pp. 476–500.

Hobart, Mark (2002) 'Live or Dead? Transforming Balinese Theater into Television', in Faye Ginsburg, Lila Abu-Lughod and Brian Larkin (eds), *Media Worlds: Anthropology on New Terrain*. Berkeley: University of California Press. pp. 548–603.

Hughes-Freeland, Felicia (1997) 'Consciousness and performance', *Social Anthropology*, 5(1), pp. 55–68.

Intintoli, Michael (1984) *Taking Soaps Seriously*. New York: Praeger.

Jameson, Fredric (1991) *Postmodernism, or the Cultural Logic of Late Capitalism*. Durham, NC: Duke University Press.

Juhasz, Alexandra (1995) *Aids TV: Identity, Community, and Alternative Video*. Durham, NC: Duke University Press.

Kirshenblatt-Gimblett, Barbara (1996) 'The Electronic Vernacular', in George Marcus (ed.), *Connected: Engagements with Media*. Vol.3, Late Editions Series. Chicago: University of Chicago Press. pp. 21–66.

Larkin, Brian (1997) 'Indian Films and Nigerian Lovers: Media and the Creation of Parallel Modernities', *Africa*, 67(3): 406–439.

Liebes, Tamar and Katz, Elihu (1990) *The Export of Meaning: Cross-Cultural Readings of 'Dallas'*. New York: Oxford University Press.

Lilley, Roseanne (1993) 'Claiming Identity: Film and Television in Hong Kong', *History and Anthropology*, 6(2–3): 261–92.

Lotfalian, Mazyar (1996) 'A Tale of an Electronic Community, in Connected. Engagements' in George Marcus (ed.), *Connected: Engagements with*

Media. Vol.3, Late Editions Series. Chicago: University of Chicago Press.pp. 117–56.

MacClancy, Jeremy (1997) *Contesting Art: Art, Politics and Identity in the Modern World*. London: Berg.

MacDougall, David (1998) *Transcultural Cinema*. Princeton, NJ: Princeton University Press.

Mankekar, Purnima (1999) *Screening Culture, Viewing Politics: An Ethnography of Television, Womanhood, and Nation in Postcolonial India*. Durham, NC: Duke University Press.

Mankekar, P. (2002) Epic Contests. Television and religious identity in India. in Faye Ginsburg, Lila Abu-Lughod and Brian Larkin (eds), *Media Worlds: Anthropology on New Terrain*. Berkeley: University of California Press.

Manuel, Peter (1993) *Cassette Culture: Popular Music and Technology in North India*. Chicago: University of Chicago Press.

Marcus, George (1996) 'Introduction', in George Marcus (ed.), *Connected: Engagements with Media*. Vol.3, Late Editions Series. Chicago: University of Chicago Press. pp. 1–18.

Marcus, George (ed.) (1997) *Cultural Producers in Perilous States*. Vol.4, Late Editions Series. Chicago: University of Chicago Press.

Marcus, George and Myers, Fred (1995) 'Introduction', in George Marcus and Fred Myers (eds), *The Traffic in Culture: Refiguring Anthropology and Art*. Berkeley: University of California Press. pp. 1–51.

McLagan, Meg (1996) 'Computing for Tibet: Virtual Politics in the Post-Cold War Era', in George Marcus (ed.), *Connected: Engagements With Media*. Vol.3, Late Editions Series. Chicago: University of Chicago Press. pp. 159–94.

McLagan, Meg (2002) 'Spectacles of Difference: Cultural Activism and the Mass Mediation of Tibet', in Faye Ginsburg, Lila Abu-Lughod and Brian Larkin (eds), *Media Worlds: Anthropology on New Terrain*. Berkeley: University of California Press. pp. 90–112.

Mead, Margaret and Metraux, Rhoda (1953) *The Study of Culture at a Distance*. Chicago: University of Chicago Press.

Meadows, Micheal and Molnar, Helen (2001) *Songlines to Satellites: Indigenous Communications in Australia, the South Pacific, and Canada*. Leichhardt, New South Wales: Pluto Press.

Michaels, Eric (1994) *Bad Aboriginal Art: Tradition, Media, and Technological Horizons*. Minneapolis: University of Minnesota Press.

Miller, Daniel (1992) 'The young and the restless in Trinidad: A case of the local and the global in mass consumption', in R. Silverstone and E. Hirsch (eds), *Consuming Technology*. London: Routledge. pp. 163–82.

Miller, Daniel (1995) 'Introduction: Anthropology, Modernity, Consumption', in Daniel Miller (ed.), *Worlds Apart: Modernity through the Prism of the Local*. London: Routledge. pp. 1–23.

Miller, Daniel and Slater, Don (2000) *The Internet: An Ethnographic Approach*. London: Berg.

Naficy, Hamid (1993) *The Making of Exile Cultures: Iranian Television in Los Angeles*. Minneapolis: University of Minnesota Press.

Palattella, John (1998) 'Pictures of Us', *Lingua Franca*, 8(5): 50–7.

Pedelty, Mark (1995) *War Stories: The Culture of Foreign Correspondents*. New York: Routledge.

Pendakur, Manjunath and Subramanyam, Radha (1996) 'Indian Cinema beyond National Borders', in John Sinclair, Elizabeth Jacka and Stuart Cunningham (eds), *New Patterns in Global Television: Peripheral Vision*. London: Oxford University Press. pp. 69–82.

Philipsen, Hans Henrik and Markussen, Birgitte (eds) (1995) *Advocacy and Indigenous Film-making*. Aarhaus, Denmark: Intervention Press.

Pines, Jim and Willemen, Paul (eds) (1989) *Questions of Third Cinema*. London: BFI.

Pinney, Chris (1998) *The Social Life of Photographs*. London: Blackwell.

Pound, Christopher (1996) 'Framed, or How the Internet Set Me Up', Engagements', in George Marcus (ed.), *Connected: Engagements with Media*. Vol.3, Late Editions Series. Chicago: University of Chicago Press. pp. 99–116.

Powdermaker, Hortense (1950) *Hollywood, The Dream Factory*. Boston: Grosset & Dunlap.

Prins, Harold (1997) 'The Paradox of Primitivism: Native Rights and the Problem of Imagery in Cultural Survival Films', *Visual Anthropology*, 9(3–4): 243–66.

Prins, Harold (2002) 'Visual Media and the Primitivist Perplex: Colonial Fantasies and Indigenous Imagination in the Decolonization of the Fourth World', in Faye Ginsburg, Lila Abu-Lughod and Brian Larkin (eds), *Media Worlds: Anthropology on New Terrain*. Berkeley: University of California Press. pp. 105–30.

Riggins, Stephen Harold (1992) *Ethnic Minority Media: An International Perspective*. London: Sage.

Robbins, Bruce (ed.) (1993) *The Phantom Public Sphere*. Minneapolis: University of Minnesota Press.

Rofel, Lisa (1994) 'Yearnings: Televisual Love and Melodramatic Politics in Contemporary China', *American Ethnologist*, 21(4): 700–22.

Rony, Fatima (1996) *The Third Eye: Race, Cinema, and Ethnographic Spectacle*. Durham, NC: Duke University Press.

Ruby, Jay (2000) *Picturing Culture: Explorations of Film and Anthropology*. Chicago: University of Chicago Press.

Salamandra, Christa (1998) 'Moustache Hairs Lost: Ramadan Television Serials and the Construction of Identity in Damascus, Syria', *Visual Anthropology*, 10(2–4): 227–46.

Schein, Louisa (2002) 'Mapping Hmong Media in Diasporic Space', in Faye Ginsburg, Lila Abu-Lughod and Brian Larkin (eds), *Media Worlds: Anthropology on New Terrain*. Berkeley: University of California Press. pp. 229–45.

Schiller, Herbert (1991) 'Not Yet the Post-Imperialist Era', *Critical Studies in Mass Communication*, 8: 13–28.

Shohat, Ella and Stam, Robert (1994) *Unthinking Eurocentrism: Multiculturalism and the Media*. New York: Routledge.

Silj, Alessandro (1988) *East of Dallas: The European Challenge to American Television*. London: BFI.

Sinclair, John (1996) 'Mexico, Brazil, and the Latin World', in John Sinclair, Elizabeth Jacka and Stuart Cunningham (eds), *New Patterns in Global Television: Peripheral Vision*. London: Oxford University Press. pp. 33–66.

Sinclair, John, Jacka, Elizabeth and Cunningham, Stuart (eds) (1996) *New Patterns in Global Television: Peripheral Vision*. London: Oxford University Press.

Spitulnik, Debra (1993) 'Anthropology and the Mass Media', in *Annual Review of Anthropology*. Vol. 22. Palo Alto, CA: Annual Reviews Inc.

Spitulnik, Debra (2002) 'Mobile Machines and Fluid Audiences: Rethinking Reception through Zambian Radio Culture', in Faye Ginsburg, Lila Abu-Lughod and Brian Larkin (eds), *Media Worlds: Anthropology on New Terrain*. Berkeley: University of California Press. pp. 532–60.

Sreberny-Mohammadi, Annabelle and Mohammadi, Ali (1994) *Small Media, Big Revolution: Communication, Culture, and the Iranian Revolution*. Minneapolis: University of Minneapolis Press.

Tacchi, Jo (1998) 'Radio Texture: Between Self and Others', in Daniel Miller (ed.), *Material Cultures: Why Some Things Matter*. Chicago: University of Chicago Press. pp. 39–60.

Tacchi, Jo (2002) 'Radio Texture: Between Self and Others', in Kelly Askew and Richard Wilk (eds), *The Anthropology of Media: A Reader*. London: Blackwell. pp. 241–57.

Turner, Terence (2002) 'Representation, Politics and Cultural Imagination in Indigenous Video: General Points and Kayapo Examples', in Faye Ginsburg, Lila Abu-Lughod and Brian Larkin (eds), *Media Worlds: Anthropology on New Terrain*. Berkeley: University of California Press. pp. 131–53.

Worth, Sol, Adair, John and Chalfen, Richard [1972] (1997) *Through Navajo Eyes*. Albuquerque: University of New Mexico Press.

Wortham, Erica Cusi (2000) 'News from the Mountains: Redefining the Televisual Borders of Oaxaca', in *Sphere 2000*. New York: World Studio Foundation.

Yang, Mayfair Mei-hui (2002) 'Mass Media and Transnational Subjectivity in Shanghai: Notes on (Re)Cosmopolitanism in a Chinese Metropolis', in Faye Ginsburg, Lila Abu-Lughod and Brian Larkin (eds), *Media Worlds: Anthropology on New Terrain*. Berkeley: University of California Press. pp. 302–38.

15

Psychoanalysis and Cinema

Patrick Fuery

That psychoanalysis and cinema share a great deal has almost become a conceptual and historical (indeed teleological) given. But one of the key attributes they share is hardly, if ever, mentioned. This is the idea of resistances – resistances to psychoanalysis and cinema as cultural processes, as analytic modes (indeed, as something worthy of analysis), their status within their fields, and even a questioning of their legitimacy to exist within the academy. Jacques Derrida, in a series of essays on psychoanalysis and resistance, commences with this idea that for its entire history psychoanalysis has always had to engage with the resistances to it, with its internal resistances, and through such engagements justify its existence. As Derrida puts it: '[T]here is a return, once again, of a resistance *to* psychoanalysis. There are countless signs that this resistance is growing and often novel in its social and institutional forms. It is as if, once assimilated or domesticated, psychoanalysis could be forgotten' (1998: vii). Note that Derrida stops short of saying that such resistances could banish psychoanalysis altogether; but, like its most fundamental materiality, psychoanalysis risks becoming repressed through its analytic

assimilation and domestication. Derrida then companions this resistance to psychoanalysis (as a methodology, as a culture of ideas) to another form of resistance, that of the resistances within analysis itself – an issue in which psychoanalysis is well versed in both theory and practice. What is suggested here is that cinema has experienced a similar history of resistance in both senses – to its existence as aesthetic object and for its analysis as critical worth. It may seem a little disingenuous to say that cinema has faced the same sorts of questions about its legitimacy, and yet there are comparisons to be found. For the greater part of its history cinema has had to 'prove' its aesthetic worth, to demonstrate that it should be taken seriously. The parallel histories run with resistances making not simply their uses an issue, but also the discourses that surround and commentate on them. How we might read psychoanalysis and cinema in such a way focuses part of the discussion here.

Rather than take up the relatively straightforward line that the relationship between psychoanalysis and cinema[1] is one of theoretical approach to textual object, the main issue here is to consider how these two discourses operate in similar ways. Always present in such concerns, sometimes as a stumbling block and sometimes the offspring of a fecund marriage, is the fact that psychoanalysis never set out to become a theory of cinema. Which is, of course an issue not unique to cinema and psychoanalysis. Jean Laplanche argued against the type of psychoanalytic approaches to forms of textuality (for our concerns here this is cinema) that are perhaps the most seductive – of applying the terms to the texts. As he put it: 'Applied is merely derivative, but what I call "extra-mural psychoanalysis", psychoanalysis "outside the walls" or outside the cure, should have the ambition to have findings of its own …' (1992: 35). The idea of psychoanalysis with something like cinema having its own findings is what makes the relationship still one of great promise.

What is at hand here is the common ground of the cultural intentionality of both cinema and psychoanalysis. This can be addressed in the rather innocent sounding statement that what both discourses share are a cultural relationship, and a relationship to culture. Sigmund Freud asserts often, and with vigour, that psychoanalysis has a cultural intent – it needs to understand cultural processes in order to understand the psyche. Similarly, it is impossible to imagine a cinema outside culture. Clearly this is too large a project to be dealt with here so the approach will be one of focus and illustration. Even though there is a long and detailed historical relationship between cinema and psychoanalysis, there is still much work to be done and many ideas to be developed. One of the key aspects is how cinema might be employed to understand psychoanalysis (and psychoanalytic concepts). This in itself is not especially new. Indeed, Freud was well aware of how texts drawn from literature, painting, and sculpture could be employed to explore psychoanalytic ideas. What we are particularly interested in here is the idea that cinema produces ideas that can be measured against psychoanalytic theory in the analysis of culture.

Freud most often located psychoanalysis and its cultural contexts and contents within quite specific modes. He would, for example, return to the ideas of childhood and early histories of cultures, or speak of the comparisons between neurosis and what he termed 'primitive cultures'. For him, these were rich sources of comparison which allowed him to make fruitful points of connection. However, Freud also spoke about the analytic capacity of psychoanalysis to examine 'our great cultural institutions – on religion, morality, justice and philosophy' (2001f: 185). Psychoanalysis, he argues, emphasizes that the individual psyche and cultural organization share the same dynamic forces. In this way Freud asserts the close connection between psychoanalysis and culture, revealing an expansive project that would cover all aspects of cultural life. His comments on aesthetics are far more guarded than other cultural modes (ethnicity and anthropological issues, for example), even though he clearly enjoyed the arts a and employed them extensively throughout his works. A good example of this acknowledged difficulty is the following: 'Psychoanalysis throws a satisfactory light upon some of the problems concerning the arts and artists; but others escape it entirely' (2001d: 187).[2] The escaping others occur at various points in his works, and Freud was never afraid to admit when he did not understand something. One of the recurring motifs in Freud's works was the issue of aesthetic objects and their relationship to the unconscious. But at every moment Freud is more interested in turning the artistic text into something that supports his development of psychoanalysis as a methodology.[3] In other words, psychoanalysis commences with (that is, its historical origins determine) the idea that the arts can be employed in the service of psychoanalysis, rather than the other way around. One of the greatest developments in terms of psychoanalysis and textuality has been to shift Freud's 'uses' so that the emphasis falls on how to employ psychoanalytic concepts outside the context of the cure.

Before we turn to an all too brief consideration of psychoanalysis and cinema as a viable theoretical model it may prove useful to review the series of discourses (some historically marked) that bring us to the point of asking, why psychoanalysis? Although some of this material is well known it would seem that each generational moment has tended to offer revision and review in terms of how psychoanalytic approaches to cinema might be, or even should be, devised. Let us begin with some of the key moments in these developments.

1   The trajectory into cinema by psychoanalysis does not follow what might have seemed to be the most direct and obvious route. Whilst literary criticism played around with the possibility of such approaches in the 1940s (some directly out of Freudian theory, others from Carl Jung), the key moment for cinema takes place in the late 1960s and the 1970s through what starts out as a type of quasi-structuralist and linguistic/discourse analysis approach. The key figure is, of course, Christian Metz and, for all of the problems and questions that one might see in his work, the influence was undeniably powerful. Metz shapes a great deal of film theory during this time through his key work *The Imaginary Signifier: Psychoanalysis and the Cinema* (1985). (The title is a give-away – a strong and uncompromising move towards Lacanian theory is found here.) It is noteworthy that Metz's earlier works, *Film Language: A Semiotics of Cinema* (1974) demonstrated a semiotic approach and this is a pattern that we see emerging from almost all forms of psychoanalytic theory of cinema. It is psychoanalysis' capacity to combine with other theoretical approaches that makes it successful – and perhaps the one attribute that undercuts its status as a theory that can stand alone. From the early period of combinations with language theory, and then ideology (via Louis Althusser), psychoanalysis subsequently combines with feminism, gender and sexuality, queer theory, theories of the body. Even the most recent manifestation, psychoanalysis and new media, shows how it combines to produce new ways of examining the material.

2   Metz provided a sustained approach to cinema and was keen to prove the practical potential of the approach. His work utilizes detailed analysis, applying the legacy of his previous

structuralist approach. Jean-Louis Baudry, who was a contemporary of Metz, contributed a key interpretation by arguing that a psychoanalytic approach needed to consider the whole institution (including both production and reception of the cinematic text). He termed this 'the cinematic apparatus' (1986a; 1986b) and it is significant that much of the attention of this approach was directed at ideological aspects. Baudry, like Metz, saw Jacques Lacan as an increasingly important figure in developing a cinematic psychoanalytic approach. Lacan's appeal to these two theorists lay in a number of factors, notably: Lacan's introduction of Freud into the French intellectual scene paved the way for psychoanalysis to have an analytic rigour; Lacan demonstrated the diversity of psychoanalysis, particularly in the ways in which it could account for cultural processes, hermeneutic systems, issues of ethics, interpretations of subjectivity, and the possibility of discourse analysis; Lacan's philosophical inflections allowed both Baudry and Metz to explore a much wider terrain than might have been done within a closed model of psychoanalysis.

3   Crucial to Baudry's apparatus theory and Metz's Imaginary Signifier was the Lacanian (via Freud, of course) theory of desire premised on lack. This is found in many different guises in both Freud (such as repression, sublimation, the drive, the very sense of the unconscious, and so on) and Lacan (such as the Other and the *objet petit a*, alienation and aphanisis, *jouissance*, and so on) and can be seen as a crucial aspect of their theories. It became the linchpin for utilizing psychoanalysis in the interpretation of cinema because it allowed for a radical project on spectatorship. For all the possible laws of such an approach, it is difficult to deny that the theories of spectatorship that emerged at this time offered something quite new and profound.

4   Just after these developments there occurred an Anglicized model of psychoanalytic film theory taking off from the highly influential essay by Laura Mulvey entitled 'Visual Pleasure and Narrative Cinema' (1975). What Mulvey's essay did was to realign the landscape and open up the debate between feminism and psychoanalysis. Taking up the concepts of scopophilia, castration, and fetishism, Mulvey inscribed gender as a key marker in film spectatorship. Both Baudry and Metz were reread in terms of the politics of feminism and the masculine/feminine subject positions in terms of the gaze and pleasure. The ensuing debates and arguments led to a paradigmatic series of articles

that dominated the journal *Screen* and in many ways shaped the development of film theory in this period.

5 One trajectory out of this set of debates was feminist film theory, arguing for and against psychoanalysis as a viable methodology. Theorists posited both positive and negative views on how psychoanalysis might be used, or why it should be refused, in film theory: among them were Jacqueline Rose (1980), Teresa de Lauretis (1984), Annette Kuhn (1985), Mary Ann Doane (1987), Tania Modleski (1988), Kaja Silverman (1988), E. Ann Kaplan (1990), Constance Penley (1989) and Joan Copjec (1994). Interestingly, some of these debates followed a line very similar to the larger feminist theory paradigm, that is, a split between an Anglo-American 'refusal' (although that might be too strong a term) and a Continental 'acceptance' of psychoanalysis. Julia Kristeva (1982; 1984), who is clearly a key figure in the latter camp, demonstrates her desire to use and develop psychoanalysis in a variety of textual approaches, including film.

6 The resistances to psychoanalysis in these terms falls roughly into two orders – those who argue against the ways in which the theory has been employed (for example, discussions around Mulvey's interpretations on the gaze), and those who argue against the psychoanalytic approach entirely. Of this second order the key figures are David Bordwell and Noël Carroll who, in their edited book, *Post-Theory: Reconstructing Film Studies* (appearing in 1996) attempted to address what they perceived as a theory imbalance. They posed cognitive psychology as a more viable method to understand spectatorship. One of the difficulties of what they proposed, however, is that it is not as far removed from the original project set out by Freud, as they appear to think. The possibility of combining the two models is something that remains on the table as a distinct possibility in the future. Many of the issues that the cognitive psychology approach suggests (and the subsequent difficulties) are not that far removed from the 'classical' psychoanalytic model. Indeed, the potential answers would seem to lie within both Freud and Lacan. Not the least of these is the distinction between ideal and real/actual spectators. The same points can be made for the other alternative, that of the works of Gilles Deleuze and Félix Guattari. Again, a careful reading of a text such as *Anti-Oedipus* (1985) reveals that Deleuze and Guattari are far more interested in

exploring both Freud and Lacan than rejecting them. This is particularly significant, as Deleuze has become such a central figure in the theorizing of new media, and so potentially in the reshaping of film theory and the issues of the digital form.

This all too brief overview reveals at least a number of recurring themes. First psychoanalytic theory gained its strength (both historically and textually) and its potential weaknesses through its capacity to combine with other theoretical models. Second, the splits for and against this approach rarely (perhaps never?) amounted to a total rejection of psychoanalysis. Third, the paradigm shifts that took place in terms of sexuality, subjectivity, hermeneutics, and ideology, went far beyond the confines of psychoanalytic approaches. And finally, the debates are still continuing and look to be sustained for some time to come. Keeping all this in mind, it is now time to return to the issue at hand, which is essentially how we might map out the relationship of film to psychoanalysis through a reflection on the cultural intent of the two. To this end we now turn to the notion of the symptom.

CINEMA AS SYMPTOM

A further set of related issues to this involves reading cinema as a type of intervention in the cultural order. This is where psychoanalysis can play a decisive hand, for this intervention can best be described in terms of cinema as symptom. This can be understood in a number of different ways, and we should be reticent to rule any of them out. The most straightforward interpretation is that cinema is a symptom of various cultural processes and issues. An almost literal example of this would be the rise of science-fiction films in Hollywood in the 1950s and 1960s dealing with invasion and threats of domination from outsiders: the fear of the other. These films can be read as a cinematic symptom of cultural paranoia produced through the political tensions between the US and Communism during the Cold War. A true Freudian reading would stress that such a manifestation is not unique in itself, but renders attitudes towards the other in a manner that has found a mode of representation that is foregrounded by its political agendas. Just as the dream work relies on condensation and displacement to form modes of representation (what Freud sees as part of the *Vorstellungrepräsentanz* – the representative of representation, and Lacan argues is the determining force of the unconscious) that become crucial to the dream as it is evoked, so this rendering of cinema relies on a mix of cinematic, aesthetic, and ideological discourses to produce the films. Another example would be the representation of masculinity in the 1980s and 1990s, once more in Hollywood, as one of excessive muscles and force, of subjectivity made of flesh and fluids. This could be read as a symptom of masculine resistance to the rise of feminism, or as a symptom of the right-wing politics of the Reagan administration. However, to move the idea of the cinematic symptom beyond what is an interesting but ultimately limited discussion along these lines, it is important to return to the ways in which psychoanalysis figures the symptom. This will allow us to locate cinema as a different sort of cultural intervention – one that is seen as less responsive and reactive, and more catalytic. (And here we recall the etymology of *catalyst*: to dissolve and to loosen; a term that will prove its worth later in the discussion.) To do so we can take up a number of propositions around the idea of cinema as symptom. The driving rationale behind these points is to locate cinema within its cultural interventions: in other words, if cinema is a symptom, it is so within the sense of culture.

Before we attend to this a number of questions should be addressed concerning such an approach, namely: What is gained in determining the notion of cinema as symptom? What is gained in reading cinema as symptom and not, say, ideological consequence? (Althusser could well be evoked here.) Would we not be better off reading the above examples through their (relatively obvious)

ideological determinations rather than wade into the murky waters of psychoanalysis and symptom? Of course, one of the strategies here is to employ the notion of symptom to analyse the connections between cinema and psychoanalysis, and in doing so to avoid some of the methodologies that film theory articulated in the 1970s and 1980s when it examined issues of the gaze and sexuality. That is, psychoanalysis as an analytic tool for exploring cinema. But more than this, the concept of the symptom allows us to consider cinema and psychoanalysis on a more equal footing. Psychoanalytic theory opens up the possibilities of reading cinema as a symptom; and cinema allows us to consider the cultural significance of psychoanalysis because it can be seen as a cultural symptom and a symptom of psychoanalytic theory. It may seem a grand claim to say that the cinema we have today exists in its forms because of the influences of psychoanalysis. However, if psychoanalysis is acknowledged as one of the key forces in shaping, at the very least, Western culture's attitudes to sexuality, desire, subjectivity, death, childhood and repression, then perhaps there is something in the claim after all, for much of this material is also the core material of cinema. Whether we love or loathe psychoanalysis, there can be little doubt that Freud radically shifted Western attitudes and ideas on these issues, and cinema has become one of the dominant textual systems for dealing with them.

The following overview proceeds by initially considering the idea of psychoanalysis' reading of the symptom and the role of cinema in quite a specific fashion, focussing on the relationship between symptom and repression – one of the key aspects of psychoanalysis in this area. Two sections follow this, one on the relationship between cinema, anxiety and symptom formation, and the other on the relationship between symptom and signification. To locate these ideas even more firmly within culture the issue of desire and ethics is then addressed. Once more, the idea is to consider how cinema and psychoanalysis operate in terms of these (culturally derived) issues, and to note in particular how they can be read as engaging in the same sorts of issues in an analytic way.

SYMPTOM AND REPRESSION

Psychoanalysis invariably ties the symptom to repression, but the relationship is far from direct. The most overt manifestation of this is that the symptom exists because repression denies the expression of a wish or desire that is not 'acceptable' to the superego. For Freud this leads to a compromise – that is, the symptom is a compromise between absolute repression and complete expression.[4] Reading cinema in this way yields the idea that films, like other creative practices according to psychoanalysis, act as a release for the repressed material or just for the act of repression itself. Seen in this way cinema is located within the economic model – a playing out of psychical energies in order to keep the 'system' in balance. The problem with such a reading is that it demands a consensual view of the repressed material. In other words, we would need to believe that the cultural order is characterized by a set of repressed materials and issues and that various institutions (such as cinema) function to allow this to be manifested. We should be apprehensive of such an interpretation because it implies too strong a sense of homogeneity within the culture. Can we really argue that all parts of a culture's repressed material are worked through the cinematic apparatus? Clearly not, but the relationship between repression and cinema as symptom can still produce useful ideas.

This expands the Freudian model of the dream to a broader cultural order. In fact, Freud discusses the relations between dreams and symptoms at length in *The Interpretation of Dreams* (2001a; 2001b). When he comes to the revision of his theories later in his life he maintains this line, and summarizes with great clarity how he sees the two: 'You have realised that the dream is a pathological product, the first member of the class which includes hysterical symptoms, obsessions and delusions' (2001g: 15–16). Lacan describes

this as a family resemblance, adding: 'The dream is only part of the activity of the subject, while the symptom is spread out over several domains' (1988: 122). To extend this to the cinematic would be to suggest that the symptom is spread over several domains of the cinematic field – films of a particular type, or from a particular director, or of a specific period, and so on. This is also the moment of confluence that locates cinema within a wider aesthetic and cultural set of contexts. Lacan's sense of the symptomatic spread means that cinema as symptom necessarily locates it across a number of domains; cinema is spread across cultural domains because of this attribute of the symptom. Let us take up a number of indicative propositions to see if these ideas can be developed into a sustainable approach to films.

Cinema, anxiety, and symptom formation

For psychoanalysis, one of the ways symptoms arise is through anxiety. However, more than this, Freud argued that the relationship between the two extends beyond that of a causal relationship, and in fact the productive agency of each can be seen as interchangeable: '[O]ur attention was drawn to a highly significant relation between the generation of anxiety and the formation of symptoms – namely, that these two represent and replace each other' (2001e: 83). The replacement function here can be read as one of the principal factors in the formation and continuation of symptoms because they allow psychical processes to continue, and the subject to avoid even greater repression (and so neurosis and even psychosis). The fact that Freud sees them as essentially interchangeable indicates how closely he interpreted their bond. In this sense if cinema is a symptom, then at times it functions in terms of cultural anxiety, replacing and operating in its stead. The implication is that not all films can be read in terms of this (cultural) anxiety, and that some may lend themselves to this category more readily than others. (Or, to paraphrase the words of perhaps one of Freud's most lucrative escape clauses, sometime a cigar is just a cigar, and a film is just a film and not necessarily a manifestation of some cultural anxiety.)

There are a number of ways that we could approach this idea of a paradigm of films as cultural anxiety[5]: the repetition of certain themes or forms at specific periods in time could be read as symptoms of anxiety (such as the example given above in terms of versions of excessive masculinity and the rise of feminism). This would often rely on the modes of metaphor/metonymy and condensation/displacement (thus linking this idea even more closely to the interpretation of dreams given by Freud), as well as seeing certain film forms as knitting together, reacting against the others. So, to continue with the example of excessive masculinity, the subsequent rise of female buddy films could be seen as a symptom formation to the hyper-masculinity of the male films of the 1980s. These films are positioned as antimony, as well as an anxious response, to masculine isolationalism, pairing women as close friends, supportive and almost without need of men. Such a pattern fits with the psychoanalytic reading of symptoms and anxiety; Freud stresses the importance of being to able to read symptoms almost as a language in order to understand their origin and function.[6] Such an idea does not run counter to Lacan's assertion that 'the symptom is the inverse side of a discourse' because Lacan wants us to see the symptom not as that which exists outside of discourse, but alongside it (1988: 320). The inversion that Lacan designates for the symptom does not deny its discursive capacity, but emphasizes its otherness to those discourses it is attached to. It is a parallel discourse in effect. Such a relationship can be described as one based on a structure of *Aufhebung* – the dialectical process whereby the thesis and antithesis produce a third order that merges certain attributes, denies others, and elevates the new order. In this way the cinematic symptom carries with it a different order of cultural anxiety and subsequent responses.

Another way of reading the relationship between symptoms and anxiety (within this attribute of exchange and culture) would be to locate the manifestations within a directorial context.[7] How far a reading of films by, for example, David Lynch or Martin Scorsese would produce a sense of anxiety about suburbia in the former and guilt in the latter is perhaps contentious. We would always be left with the inherent problems of the auteurist approach (the intentional fallacy, for example) and probably satisfy little else. However, there is something critically valid to be said in taking up these recurring motifs as symptoms, if not to explain the psychical motivations of the director, but rather to better understand how cinema functions as symptom. There can be little doubt that Scorsese returns to the issue of guilt in a number of different ways, and it does perform a textual function in his films (motivating characters, devising the narrative developments, explaining events, and so on). But what we are dealing with in this sense is different from an auteur-driven exercise and to understand the reason for this we can turn to a second proposition on symptoms and cinema.

Symptoms and signification

Psychoanalysis necessarily treats psychical manifestations – and in particular symptoms – as meaningful utterances. Whilst their meanings may be obscure and perhaps even impossible to decipher, psychoanalysis never questions that they mean something. This status of meaning given to symptoms is important because it provides much of the interpretative energy of psychoanalysis. If we symptom (and leaving what cinema might be symptomatic of as an open question), then we must also consider that cinema has this same sense of meaningfulness. On the surface, this seems self-evident. Films are meaningful, and we don't need psychoanalysis to tell us so. However, there is more to the idea that films are meaningful than first appears. At one level there must be a sense of phenomenological intentionality: that is, meaningful of what? There must also be the idea that it is not just individual films that are meaningful, but the institution of cinema must have meaning, which is inevitably embedded in the heterogeneity of cultural contexts. What we are concerned with here is the idea that cinema's meaningfulness can be read in the same manner as the symptom, and to do so we must keep in mind the interplay between the individual and the collective (or, put another way, between spectator and culture). This also suggests that to read the significations of cinema (as institution, cultural product, as well as the individual film), we can employ a methodology forged out of psychoanalysis' efforts to understand and decipher symptoms. If this is the case, we must ask, how does psychoanalysis see the relationship between the symptom and meaning? According to Lacan, it does so within an almost absolute sense of truth: '[T]he symptom is in itself, through and through, signification, that is to say, truth, truth taking shape' (1988: 320). What Lacan is arguing here is no less than the idea that symptoms reveal the truth because they operate within the discourse of truth (for the unconscious, which for a psychoanalyst is the repository of truth, and so the reason that Lacan attaches it to the Real). It would be an impossible claim to defend that cinema as symptom is truth, cultural or otherwise. However, something can be gleaned from this Lacanian approach that will help us understand the relationship between cinema and psychoanalysis further. If it is at all possible to speak of a cinematic truth, then this can be best explained and articulated in terms of the symptom. And this idea of cinematic signification as truth makes further connections to the cultural basis of cinema.

Just as psychoanalysis must ask, and constantly return to, the question 'this is a symptom of what?' (which is really a way of asking, what is the truth of the symptom?), so we may ask: 'What is the truth that is to be found in cinema? What is cinema's truth?' Note that this is not the truth of cinema (that is, the understanding of cinema as some truth-giving process), or even the meaning of a film, but rather the

negotiation of cinema as versions of truth and meaningfulness as it operates within a cultural sphere. Cinema's truth lies in its symptomatic attributes because at the very least it can stand in for truth and look like meaning. In other words, when cinema means something (that is, has relevance to the spectator and/or the culture) it does so in the same way as psychoanalysis reads and utilizes the symptom. Not as some shared and universal absolute, but as a set of meaningful utterances, signification, which can be read and interpreted beyond its own contexts. In doing so, meaningfulness in cinema becomes located outside the films and within an almost unending chain of discourses. This can be seen in, for example, the Eisensteinian conflation of ideology and montage (thus collision as symptom of political and psychical effect); of representations of male groups in Howard Hawks' films (thus homosocial groupings as symptom of homoerotic repression in both the films and the cultural production[8]); in the connecting of active female sexuality and hysteria in *Betty Blue* (Jean-Jacques Beineix, France, 1986). (This last example is complex because once something like hysteria is brought into play in such a context the function and operation of the symptom exceeds cinematic form and reveals a much longer history.) The examples can continue, but the unifying idea is that how films are made sense of, rendered as having meaning, relies on more than the films themselves can hold. Cinema's truth is one that exceeds its form.

To illustrate this idea further we can take up another point from Lacan's interpretation of the symptom:

[For Freud there is the] necessary requirement that for a symptom to occur there must be at least a duality, at least two conflicts at work, one current and one old.... The material linked to the old conflict is preserved in the unconscious as a potential signifier, as a virtual signifier, and then captured in the signified of the current conflict and used by it as language, that is, as a symptom. (1993: 119–20)

This is a rich set of ideas and deserves to be taken slowly. We can begin by translating this directly onto the cinematic equivalent. It can thus be read, bit by bit, as: for cinema to occur there must be a duality, at least two conflicts at work, one current and one old. These conflictual dualities can be seen in any number of ways (limitless in effect, just as is the conflict in the production of symptoms), but some suggestive possibilities include: the specific film against the cinematic tradition; form against theme; *mise en scène* against montage; representation against resistance (which also necessarily includes the sorts of resistances spoken of at the beginning of this chapter). The conflict is necessary because it is how cinema continues to produce new ideas and forms. The paradigm shift (again, used here very much within Thomas Kuhn's sense of the term [1974][9]) of depth of field in *Citizen Kane* (Orson Welles, 1941), for example, holds the conflict between montage and *mise en scène* to be an integral part of the narrative. In this way duality is not a by-product or something to be laboured through, but an essential and vital aspect of the cinematic process.

Beyond this dimension of the symptomatic dualities within cinema, there are also those that exist and operate through the relationships between cinema and culture. Taking up the Lacanian line, cinematic material is the domain of the potential signifier (it is too much to devise this as part of the unconscious, no matter how much support we may find in Freud to do so) that gets taken up by the current cultural issues and concerns and re-used to explore them. (This aspect of the recycling of material is quite within keeping of Freud's idea of the dream work.) It is fortuitous that Lacan adds that this is a virtual signifier – so much in keeping with the cinematic form. The fact that the symptom for Lacan can only exist within such an operation strengthens the reading of cinema as symptom because it embeds the two discourses within one another. In other words, cinema gains much of its cultural relevance through this status of the symptom with all of these issues of duality and conflict. This is the cultural underpinning of cinema as well as its interpellation of the spectator.

ETHICS *CONTRA* DESIRE: THE IDEA OF THE CINEMA OF *ENTFREMDET*

Reading the cinematic symptom is a difficult and complex process, not least because, like all symptoms within the psychoanalytic context, there is a protracted system of disguise at work. Ultimately there can be little resolution, in part because so many of the elements under scrutiny exist beyond the issues at hand – hence cinematic truth as excess. One can never be fully aware of all that is at play in reading a film as symptom, if for no other reason that the symptomatic basis may be located in any number of different sources (the spread through discourses as Lacan [1993] puts it). As with the resistances of and to psychoanalysis, the point of solution of the cinematic symptom is rarely, if ever, invested in an unscrambling of a meaning. This is why a psychoanalytic approach to cinema is far less about what a film means and much more about the processes of constructing meaning. There are very, very few analytic systems that are as comfortable with the prospect of non-resolution as psychoanalysis is. This is because the starting-point of psychoanalysis is the impossibility of resolution, almost the denial of the end cure. Perhaps the most famous of such acknowledgments is Freud's idea of the navel of a dream – that core element that can never be resolved, never be totally disentangled and understood (2001a). This forms part of the resistance to analysis that psychoanalysis deals with so well to the point where it embraces the processes as a necessary part of its operation. The Freudian exemplar of this is the analysis of the dream of Irma's injection, in *The Interpretation of Dreams* (2001a), but it is fulfilled many times over in the psychoanalytic approach. It is worth recalling that a key focus of Freud's work in *The Interpretation of Dreams* is not just dreams, but interpretation itself. Freud is setting up what become the foundations for understanding processes of interpretation, specifically for psychoanalysis, but the implications far exceed that discipline. He even establishes a type of category of instances where interpretation is impossible and must give ground to resistances – these are *Widerstände* – and recognizing them becomes essential to the analytic process. Like dreams, cinema also produces elements that are resistances to interpretation, and this is part of the symptomatic force. We must be clear here that these are not simply made up of those films that appear excessively polysemic or ambiguous. Luis Buñuel's *Un Chien andalou* (1929) comes to mind as an example of this type of film, as do David Lynch's *Mulholland Drive* (2001), and perhaps Michael Haneke's *Caché* (2005) – even though all them do offer resistances of their own in quite different ways. True resistances – those of the order of *Widerstände* – will be far less obvious in their relation to seeming meaninglessness. Or, put another way, the type of resistances to interpretation that are revealed in certain forms of cinema only become apparent when we turn to psychoanalysis; and one of the key aspects here is how this can also be seen as symptom and intervention. For at the heart of this is the formation of the symptom through desire.

In order to limit this difficulty, this section pursues the idea that cinema and psychoanalysis as cultural intervention share a common project related to *desire* and *ethics*. Simply put, there is a constant tension between the need to express individual desires and the compulsion imposed on the individual to conform to social laws, and this tension creates symptoms of conflict. Cinema thus becomes one of the primary manifestations and negotiations of this conflict as much as an analytic discourse or a textualization. In other words, cinema, in all its plurality, is the domain of these tensions in much the same way as psychoanalysis figures phantasy as a domain.[10] Seen in this way, cinema is both one of the sources of the conflict (through its discourses of desire) and at the same time one of the attempts to alleviate the tensions. However, the caveat must always be that the relationship is founded on negotiating resistances, and the particular example here is to be the operation of ethics. To understand this we need briefly to consider the relationship between psychoanalysis and

ethics, and then we may be better positioned to understand cinema's function in all this.

Of course, the relationship between psychoanalysis and ethics is an impossible one to summarize. In many ways it is still being worked out. What is clear is that the relationship is not based solely on the issue of the ethical behaviour of psychoanalysts, although this is something at the heart of the analytic process – transference is embedded in issues of ethics. The relationship has more to do with the way that psychoanalysis can be used to analyse and understand ethical codes and processes. This is the line of investigation that keeps us close to the issues of cinema, culture, and the symptom. Once we acknowledge that one of the analytic forces of psychoanalysis is the ethics of a cultural order, then we are also able to position cinema within this context. This contextualisation can range from the idea that cinema is a manifestation (read 'symptom') of the ethical issues of a culture through to the identification of cinema as a potential site of resistance to such ethics. This is played out in a multiplicity of ways, but the focus here is that of desire. Thus we are led to the proposition that cinematic desire is the field of cultural ethics, and psychoanalysis allows an investigation of this exchange.

One of the most interesting facets of this relationship between psychoanalysis and ethics is that there appears to be an almost consistent resistance to the binarisms that can plague discussions of ethics. The defining aspect of psychoanalysis' relationship to ethics (to risk oversimplification) is that of oppositional conflict. Psychoanalysis sees the struggle of ethics as embedded in the necessary tensions of desire. In Freud this can be mapped out as part of his notion of *entfremdet* – that which is strange and yet an essential feature of the subject.[11] Here we find echoes of the uncanny (the familiar and the strange) and of Lacan's idea of *extimacy* (that which is a defining part of us and yet appears to be strange – a perversion of intimacy as it were) (1992). At the heart of the psychoanalytic field lie these conflicts and tensions, where the opposition is contained within itself. If ever we were to seek a cinematic articulation, we need look no further than the first few minutes of Terrence Malick's *The Thin Red Line* (1998), where the dialectic of ethical tension is seen as the core of nature itself. Psychoanalysis requires us to acknowledge the dangerous interplay that this ethical dialectic performs within us and within the cultural order. It is dangerous because it constantly threatens to exceed the tenuous repressions that keep it in check. And rather than see cinema as a sublimating process to aid this checking, it can be seen as a symptom of the tensions and even a provocation of them. Once more we must acknowledge that different aspects of cinema perform differently in this regard. The sublimating effect – of keeping the dialectic of ethics in balance – would see cinema as performing a sort of ethical certainty. Or, put another way, some strands of cinema act out the issues of ethics in order to assert or deny the cultural order of things. What must be avoided, however, is the sense that films can be categorized – fixed in their position, as it were – in such a manner. Romantic comedies act out such cultural ethics because their interpretation of sexual relations is clearly spelt out in generic conventions. In doing so they reinforce certain ideologies of sexuality. Yet the same can be said of something like Pier Paolo Pasolini's *Salò* (1975), not because it is part of the same order as romantic comedies, but because it demonstrates without compromise an ethical interpretation of sexuality and power. Malick's cinema, on the other hand, can be seen as less ethically certain or stable. *Badlands* (1973), for example, continually plays out an ambiguity of ethics, and not just in its representation. Kit (Martin Sheen) and Holly (Sissy Spacek) demonstrate precisely the consequences, both individual and social, when people do what Lacan asks when he poses the question, 'Have you acted in conformity with your desires today?' (1992).

What in fact we are approaching here is not the narrativization of ethics, or even the cultural representation of them. (One of the key aspects of this strangeness at the heart of the self – *entfremdet* – is its resistance to representation.) We can take overtly ethically themed films such as Fred Zinneman's McCarthy-era western *High Noon* (1952) and compare them to those that perform a similar task not in the representation, but in the demands they place on the spectator. So, for example, how does *Irreversible* (Gaspar Noé, France, 2002) read in terms of ethics? It violently confronts the spectator with the tension between masculinity conforming to its desires (sexual and violent) and the breakdown of cultural order specifically in terms of ethics. The revenge film, and in particular the rape-revenge film, is premised on giving the spectator the pleasure of acting out violence that is directly antithetical to the social order's investment in law. In many ways it presents a highly encoded moral stance that runs counter to the social order. How do we resolve the ethical issues of Leni Riefenstahl's celebration of Hitler and Nazism in *Triumph of the Will* (Germany, 1935)? Here is a film that is seen as aesthetically significant, and yet depicts the most abhorrent ideology of the twentieth century (the same may be said of the racial politics in D.W. Griffith's *The Birth of a Nation* [US, 1915]). To attempt to perform a sort of phenomenological epoché of the ethical issues in such films only causes more problems in the analysis. What is happening in films such as *The Godfather* (Francis Ford Coppola, 1972), when the spectator's sympathies are so directly constructed around an immoral gangster? How does Travis Bickle (Robert De Niro), in *Taxi Driver* (Martin Scorsese, 1976), become a symbol of defiance rather than psychotic rage? What these questions share is the idea that the ethical dialectic – the conflict and oppositional tensions carried within an ethical or unethical utterance – stems from *emfremdet*: that is, the conflict within the spectating self and his/her social conditions. The cinematic realization of this *emfremdet* is more than a manifestation of textually realized ethical issues. It can be seen as a particular contribution to cultural symptoms of anxiety. We may even suggest that this is a particular category of films that become accessible only once psychoanalysis has been employed. Further to this, psychoanalysis would not attempt a resolution of the cinema of *emfremdet* because it would recognize that as an impossibility. This is part of the resistances of cinema in its ethical dimensions.

Psychoanalysis proves its worth here, not because it can resolve issues of this sort, but precisely because it cannot. It cannot, and that inability demonstrates that no system of thought can. One of the resistances to psychoanalysis is its confession that the analysis is without end; and yet a similar line of argument has been posited for the text.[12] These are not issues to be resolved. The ethical conflict is, for psychoanalysis, an essential and unyielding part of our psyche. And the fact that so many (perhaps all) films can be seen as dealing with such an issue indicates that it is an essential part of the cinematic material as well. This is not to suggest that cinema exists (that is, is a symptom) for the ethical tensions of the psyche and subsequent cultural order. However, the relationship between cinema and psychoanalysis is heavily invested in this issue. As a consequence, it is possible to confront the idea that cinematic spectatorship is a perversion – and that it is a perversion born out of ethical conflict and *emfremdet*. Before doing so, however, we require at least one further point on the interaction between cinema and psychoanalysis through the agency of ethics.

We can take our starting-point for this attempt to understand cinema's cultural function from Immanuel Kant. As Lacan pointed out (1992), Kantian philosophy continues to shape not just the discourse and production of ethics in general,[13] but a great deal of psychoanalysis' orientation towards ethics in particular. It is possible to identify a number of resonances between Freudian theory and *The Critique of Practical Reason* (2002), for example. In the section entitled 'On the Concept of an Object of Pure Practical Reason', there is a sustained analysis of ethics, desire, good, and evil that hinges on the tension between the notion of the good for the self and the good for the social order – and the acknowledgment that the two are often

in conflict with one another. Consider the following:

> The subject's property in reference to which alone he can engage in this experience is the *feeling* of pleasure and displeasure, which is a receptivity belonging to inner sense; thus the concept of what is directly good would apply only to that with which the sensation (*Empfindung*) of *gratification* is directly linked, and the concept of absolutely evil would have to be referred only to what directly gives rise to *pain*. (Kant, 2002: 80–1)[14]

Here we see in embryo the psychoanalytic idea of the pleasure principle and the psychoanalytic theorisation of desire. There are also echoes here of the tension between desires from the unconscious (the dark, repressed material that constantly threatens to become manifest and disturb the social order), the need to expiate them, and the compulsion to retain the moral order. It is interesting to note that for Kant the objects of desire are not stable and the categories of good and evil are determined through the law of reason. The cinematic intervention in all of this is that, although it necessarily exists in the domain of pleasure and unpleasure, determined through cultural coding (the moral fabric of a social order as it is determined at that moment in time), it also continually attempts to exceed those restrictions, and so acts out a challenge to notions of good and evil, pleasure and unpleasure. This does not deny the hegemonic underpinning of a great many films, especially in terms of their repetition of the ethical order of society. But even in such films there is always the potential to resist and subvert this very order. This is why it is described here as the cinematic intervention rather than presented as some sort of doxa of cinema itself. In this sense the intervention is part of the cinema of *emfremdet*. To understand this better we can turn to the issue of spectatorship and pleasure/unpleasure.

SPECTATORSHIP AS PERVERSION

Apart from sexuality/gender and subjectivity, one of the most fertile grounds of psychoanalytic examinations of cinema has been in the role of the spectator. The tradition is not as pure (if we can trust such a word) as it sometimes appears to assert, and a great deal of spectatorship theory relies on the semiotic developments of Roland Barthes and the version of reception theory emerging out of phenomenology that flourished in the 1960s. Our concern here is not this history, however. We can sustain the issue at hand by taking up the idea of the spectator, not simply in terms of pleasure and gender (two of the themes in psychoanalytic film theory), but instead through *perversion* (although as will be noted later, neither of these topics is excluded from such a reading).

We are, of course, drawing on a heavily loaded term here. Perversion defines itself as standing outside the norm (whatever that may be) and beyond any sort of cultural redemption. Quite simply, at first appearance anyway, it would seem that if something conforms to a social requirement or modality then it could hardly be considered a perversion. Yet time and again this is the position that Freud starts from in order to argue against it, and in doing so to define and understand what perversion and the perverse are. It is one of the strengths of Freud's approach that he consistently argues that everyone necessarily (and healthily) commits acts of perversion, and that the true struggle lies in the definition and purpose of such perversions.[15] One of his favourite points of illustration of this (in terms of sexuality) is the kiss. Freud argues that if the 'normal' sexual function is reproduction, then all aspects that are not involved in this can be seen as perversions. The kiss, he posits, belongs to that category of acts that provides a link between perversion and normal sexual life; it exists in both camps, as it were. The cinematic kiss works exceedingly well in this sense, for it is firmly located within this liminal space of both the film and beyond it, which necessarily includes the space of the spectator. The cinematic kiss is almost always invested with a force to involve the spectator, and this force renders these representations particularly open to a psychoanalytic reading of perversion. Consider, for example, the following kisses and how they mark profound narrative moments, character definition, and an invitation for the spectator to complete the lacunae of what is taking place and the consequences within the narrative:

(a) The kiss given by Ethan (John Wayne) to his brother's wife Martha (Dorothy Jordan) in John Ford's *The Searchers* (1956). This is a kiss imbued with past (and possibly future) complications, with repressed love, with sacrifice for the sake of the family; in short, the dominant themes of the entire narrative. It is a kiss that explains the obsessive quest of Ethan not just for the daughters, but also for the preservation of the family unit over passion. In this sense it exemplifies a type of Freudian perversion that allows for the family romance to exist as a type of unconscious struggle.

(b) The unrepressed kiss in the alley beside the house between Jack (Jake Gyllenhaal) and Ennis (Heath Ledger) in Ang Lee's *Brokeback Mountain* (2005). The moment is caught by Ennis' wife, Alma (Michelle Williams), which leads to the unravelling of the marriage. Once more the family as a social and romantic formation is under threat from the kiss. Thus the perversion is not the homosexuality of the act (as may appear within the heteronormative context), but, like Ethan's kiss in *The Searchers*, it is a signifier of repression and the act of sacrifice. Even though the spectator has been aware of the love between the two men for some time, they are positioned at this moment through the spectating gaze of the wife. The kiss takes the relationship out of the mountainous wilderness and into the urban, thus exposing it to the ethics of a different order.

(c) Almost any of the kisses to be found in Jean-Luc Godard's political romances, including *A bout de souffle* (1960), *Weekend* (1967), *Passion* (1982) and *Hail Mary* (1985), or Federico Fellini's sexual-political manifestos like *City of Women* (1980), yield evidence of a perversion of social values. These are usually kisses that underscore the turbulent relations between men and women as they are fixed within gendered positions. The kiss here becomes political first and romantic/loving second. This is the perversion of politics in a space where it matters most.

All three 'types' of kisses – the repressed in terms of family romances, the ethically transitional, and the politicized – offer a perversion of a perversion. Each takes the initial perversity of the kiss (in Freudian ironic terms) and plays out this potential into a 'true' perversion; that is, repression, ethical uncertainty, and ideological investment.[16]

A lucid and compact definition of perversion is given in *Three Essays on the Theory of Sexuality*: 'Perversions are sexual activities which either (a) extend, in an anatomical sense, beyond the regions of the body that are designed for sexual union, or (b) *linger* over the immediate relations to the sexual object which should normally be traversed rapidly on the path towards the final sexual aim' (Freud, 2001c: 118). Freud then goes on to list and explicate versions of these perversions. The sexual object becoming invested with greater value, the sexual use of the mouth, sexual use of the anus, erotic readings of other parts of the body, and fetishism are all seen as examples of type (a); investments in new aims of sexuality, touching and looking, sadism and masochism are seen as examples of type (b). The contention here is that cinema requires the spectator to become perverse in order to function (that is, to fulfil the role of agency within the narrative), and these perversions are an essential aspect of the pleasure of the gaze.[17] Without such a perversion, cinema and its spectators would become impossible.

Perhaps the most transparent link here is between Freud's idea that the perversion of looking as it lingers over, and therefore sexualizes, the object and the formation of the spectator in his/her relationship to the film. Freud's point is that the pleasure of looking is 'normal' but the sustained gaze, or one that ultimately replaces the sexual act, can be seen as a perversion. A great deal of film theory has circled around this idea; so much so that it has become a relatively secure critical reading of film from a psychoanalytic perspective and thus we can move quickly on from it. It is, however, worth recalling that the perversion of the spectator operates here because this is what cinema does best: the sustained lingering over the eroticized object. This eroticization does not necessarily have to be sexual. The body in cinema demands the lingering gaze even when it is not being sexual. Its very form

is produced for the gaze. Freud makes just this point, in terms of art, when he argues that the function of art is to beautify and sexualize the body. (Interestingly, he argues that the beautiful has its origins in sexual excitation. The German *Reitz* carries connotations of both stimulation and attraction, but there does not seem to be an English equivalent.) As Freud puts it: 'This curiosity seeks to complete the sexual object by revealing its hidden parts. It can, however, be diverted ('sublimated') in the direction of art, if its interest can be shifted away from the genitals on to the shape of the body as a whole' (2001c: 122). This, it is argued here, is an underlying pleasure of cinema and what attracts us to the role of spectator. This perverse erotic curiosity can sometimes be seen almost literally: Krzysztof Kiéslowski's lingering camera on the Irene Jacobs' characters in *Three Colours: Red* (1994) and *The Double Life of Véronique* (1991); the way Scorsese films the body of Robert De Niro in *Raging Bull* (1980); the hours of slow examination of Emmanuelle Béart's body in Jacques Rivette's *La Belle Noiseuse* (1991). In other examples it becomes more abstract: the lingering camera of Lynch on suburbia in *Blue Velvet* (1986) and *The Straight Story* (1999), and Malick's sustained representations of nature in *The Thin Red Line* and *The New World* (2005). In this way the body, objects, landscapes, urban spaces and so on, are eroticized because we, as spectators, are exposed to them in a manner beyond the normal. These are perversions of a particular order, for their eroticized nature is culturally sanctioned through the textualities of cinema, just as the body is portrayed in sculpture. In these examples it is the body (and parts of the body, such as the face), the suburban, and nature that become perversions of themselves through this cinematic intervention. This is the second order of perversion that is at work in cinema, the rendering of one order to itself as a beyond, an other.

This sense of the gaze and the 'looking at' is, as noted above, firmly established as a nexus of film and psychoanalysis. The acts of the spectator as perversions are closely linked to the issue of cinema as symptom and the idea of intervention; for what is implied here is that cinema as symptom is a sort of sanctioned (which necessarily includes an ethical dimension) cultural perversion. There is space for just a single example here, and this should be taken as no more than that – a single moment in a range of possible readings.

In some ways Lacan's take on perversion both complicates the subject and makes it more pliable for the concerns here. If we were to trace the use of the term throughout Lacan's seminars, we would note an almost 'classical' Freudian use at the beginnings, ending with a much more idiosyncratic version in the latter seminars. This final version is no more clearly demonstrated in the 1975 *Conférences aux Etats-Unis*, in which he argues for art to be seen as symptom, and in the 1975–76 seminar *Le Sinthome* (an archaic term for 'symptom'), where Lacan seems to be heading towards the idea that almost anything can operate as a symptom (including women, art) (Lacan, 2005). Perhaps what is most striking about Lacan's theorizing of the symptom here is that he sees it as the fourth component in a 'knot' also made up of the Imaginary, Symbolic, and Real – those most archetypal of Lacanian concepts. The symptom becomes part of the perversion through its connection to the Other and *jouissance*.

A single cinematic example to conclude, then: two brief moments in a long and complicated history of film that can satisfy very little, but will hopefully indicate how cinema as symptom and spectatorship as perversion contribute to the uses of psychoanalysis beyond its own walls. It is impossible to represent either the Other (in Lacan's terms here, but the same could be said of a great many uses of the concept) or *jouissance* – that is, after all, part of their nature. But there is a way to approach them through this idea of the fourth component of the knot, and in doing so draw psychoanalysis and cinema closer together. There is a scene in David Lynch's *Lost Highway* (1997) where, after the brutal slaying of a man, Alice (Patricia Arquette) takes Peter Dayton (Bill Pullman) out into the desert and there, in a strange mix of light and dark, begins the seduction so often

found at the heart of Lynch's films. But as this seduction envelopes Dayton he turns to her and asks: 'Why me, Alice? Why me?' There is no answer, of course. The universe of such narratives excludes answers within itself, but the perversion of the spectator is complete here as we are forced to acknowledge the question and subsequent seduction. There is *jouissance* here, within the narrative and the suturing of the spectator, but the real symptom lies in this question of 'Why me?' The layers are complex. Alice acts not only as a symptom of the Lynchian world order, but as a symptom of a certain form of phallocentric constructions of the woman as *femme fatale* (the threat of castration is never far away in this symptom) and also as symptom of the beyond of the pleasure principle. This is the moment when sexuality exceeds ethics and any form of investment by the spectator becomes perverse.

As Dayton asks 'Why me?', he is effectively evoking what Lacan concludes with in *Seminar XX: On Feminine Sexuality, The Limits of Love and Knowledge*: 'There is no such thing as a sexual relationship because one's *jouissance* of the Other taken as a body is always inadequate – perverse, on the one hand, insofar as the Other is reduced to object *a*, and crazy and enigmatic' (1998: 145). For Dayton, this is Alice and all that she leads him into, but for the spectator it is everything within the film, and everything that the films leads us to. And this necessarily includes not just the narrative (with its perverse twists and turns) and the characters (with their perverse sexualities and violent acts), but also the settings (such as the desert in this scene), constructions of time, light, music, and so on. But the connection between what Lacan wants us to take away from *Seminar XX* and this psychoanalytic approach to *Lost Highway* does not end there. The concluding points on love have resonance in this film, and a great many others:

Doesn't the extreme of love, true love, reside in the approach to being? And true love – analytic experience assuredly didn't make this discovery, borne witness to by the eternal modulation of themes on love – true love gives way to hatred....

[T]o know what your partner will do is not a proof of love. (Lacan, 1998: 146)

Read in these terms, cinema's intervention is part of these eternal modulations and thus part of the question of not just 'Why me?' but also 'Why this?' Such questions are constantly evoked in cinema – it is part of the cinematic drive – and they are at the core of how psychoanalysis interprets the act of spectating and, by extension, the function of cinema in culture.

THE ILLUSION OF A FUTURE?

It is a rare moment when someone predicts the trajectory of a theoretical movement and comes off unscathed. What has been suggested here is the viability of psychoanalysis with cinema as it has emerged out of its own convoluted past. The implication has always been that the cultural resonance of both institutions (the textualities of cinema and the practices of psychoanalysis) will prove to be vital for such a combination to survive. Anyone who favours, supports, or quite simply acknowledges a psychoanalytic approach to film will have seen a revival of sorts, and will have taken heart in the fact that even the harshest critics tend to give credit to what this approach has achieved. For all the flaws, stutters and difficulties, there is almost always the sense that psychoanalysis' relationship to film has been a significant and worthwhile one. Part of this stems from the Freudian model, which always promotes interdisciplinarity and resists the compartmentalizing of knowledge. Psychoanalysis has a 'natural' (if such a word may be dared here) connection to cinema, not simply because of the common issues such as desire and subjectivity (leading to theories of spectatorship) or image and language (leading to a semiotic inflection); the connection comes from the more fundamental aspects of hermeneutics and cultural theory. Both offer the chance to interpret meaning and locate such gestures within cultural concerns. The revival of psychoanalysis as a theoretical

model for cinema studies has come not from primary sources of psychoanalytic theorists, but from philosophers such as Slavoj Žižek and Deleuze. Here the common ground is the question of how cinema and psychoanalysis act as investigations into the ways in which things come to mean, and how we understand things within a theory of culture – a true philosophical aim. This is one possible future direction; a second is for psychoanalysis to attend to cinema once more as a source for analytic production. Once this happens, then the future of psychoanalytic Film Studies becomes even less of an illusion.

NOTES

1 Cinema is a more difficult term than is perhaps usually acknowledged. The heterogeneity of the material it refers to makes the assumption that there is anything like a unified discourse of cinema deeply problematic. It would seem overly complicated to refer to something like 'cinemas', but throughout this piece the idea that there exists such a thing as cinema needs to be set in parenthesis. A similar point could be made regarding psychoanalysis – but the 'school' of most concern here is the Freudian/Lacanian.

2 In a perspicacious note Freud adds later: '[M]ost of the problems of artistic creation and appreciation await further study' (2001d: 187). The beauty of this comment is that Freud anticipates, at the very least, the emergence of postmodern studies of reception theory.

3 See, for example, Freud's analysis of Jensen's short story 'Gradiva' where he is primarily concerned with examining the idea that dreams are meaningful; or the study of Hoffman's 'The Sandman', which is ultimately about the castration complex (2001d).

4 See, for example, Freud's 'Delusions and Dreams in Jensen's Gradiva' (2001d), 'Hysterical Phantasies and their Relation to Bisexuality' (2001c), and 'Inhibitions, Symptoms and Anxiety' (2001e). Here Freud speaks of compromise-formation, where the symptom is an attempt to diffuse some of the repression of a wish or desire.

5 The term 'paradigm' is used here in Thomas Kuhn's sense in *The Structure of Scientific Revolutions* (1974) because it necessarily involves hermeneutic work.

6 To continue this line further, it could be argued that the continued success of the female buddy film beyond the death of the masculine excess of the 1980s is that it is now acting as a counter position to the representation of male teen fantasies in sexual comedies. Such films invariably represent the urgency

of the male sexual drive and the division of women into the sexually active and the virginal.

7 The idea of reading texts as psychical products, and thus performing a sort of analysis of the author, has fallen out of favour since the 1950s. Whilst not advocating a return here, it is noteworthy that Freud saw great promise in such an approach. See, for example, his preface to Marie Bonaparte's work on Edgar Allan Poe, where he speaks of the fruitfulness of looking at the works to understand the mind of the author (2001g).

8 This invites the idea that *Brokeback Mountain* is part of a lineage set up in Hawks' westerns. Read in this way we return to a film like *Rio Bravo* (US, 1959) and see the real struggle not as one of the law against threatening lawlessness, but of one type of masculinity (the Burdette family) in conflict with the homoerotic undertones of another (represented in the four characters of the law, but especially those of Sheriff John T. Chance [John Wayne] and Dude [Dean Martin]). As cinematic symptom this revision of such westerns works because of the agencies of repression and sexuality. It is part of the homoerotic/masculine space of nature that invites revisitations; in *Brokeback Mountain* this is the return of Jack and Ennis to the mountain; in wider generic concerns it is quite simply the return to the 'West'.

9 Here the 'highly cumulative enterprise' of puzzle-solving activities as, Kuhn puts it in terms of science, can be read in terms of how the analysis of cinema proceeds from its own inventions such as those that we witness in a film like *Citizen Kane* (1974: 52).

10 See in particular Laplanche and J.B. Pontalis' famous essay 'Fantasy and the Origins of Sexuality' (1986).

11 As Lacan puts it: that which is 'something strange to me, although it is at the heart of me' (1992: 71).

12 Consider, for example, Umberto Eco's idea of unlimited semiosis – that the sign continually produces more and more layers of meaning (1976); or Barthes' reading of the literary text as an unending business (1975).

13 Lacan's seminar *The Ethics of Psychoanalysis* (1992) is one of the best readings of ethics from a psychoanalytic perspective. In it he also engages extensively with Kant; this forms part of a larger engagement with Kant, mostly in *The Ethics of Psychoanalysis* (delivered in1959), *Séminaire VIII: Le Transfert dans sa disparité subjective, 1960–1* (1981), the short paper for *Les Temps modernes'* tribute to Maurice Merleau-Ponty (1961), and in *Kant avec Sade* (1966). Interestingly, some fifteen years later, in *Seminar XX: Encore: On Feminine Sexuality, The Limits of Love and Knowledge*, Lacan singles out *The Ethics of Psychoanalysis* as the only seminar of his worthy of rewriting, and even of being written: '[I]t is perhaps the only one I will rewrite myself and make into a written text' (1998: 53).

14 And later: '*Well-being* or *bad* always signifies only a reference to our state of *agreeableness* or *disagreeableness*, of gratification or pain; and if we desire or loathe an object on that account then we do so only insofar as it is referred to our sensibility and the feeling of pleasure and displeasure that it brings about. But *good* and *evil* always signifies a reference to the *will*' (Kant, 2002: 81).

15 'Consistently' is used with intent here; from the early letters to Fliess (in the late 1800s) right through to the revisions in the *Introductory Lectures* (2001g) and onto *Civilization and its Discontents* (2001f), Freud maintained a remarkably uniform position on the idea of perversion. It was almost always read within this context of the cultural inscription of perversion and the tensions that arise from the individual's pursuit of unconscious desires.

16 It should be noted that such examples should not be seen as fixed within their categories. The fantasized kiss of Lester Burnham (Kevin Spacey) in *American Beauty* (Sam Mendes, 1999) fulfils all three agendas; the fought-over kisses in a great many Buñuel films, such as *That Obscure Object of Desire* (1977) and *Belle de jour* (1967) move across the divisions in similar ways.

17 I have argued elsewhere along these lines that film spectatorship shares a great deal with the cultural construction of madness (see Fuery, 2004).

REFERENCES

Barthes, Roland (1975) *The Pleasure of the Text.* Tr. A. Lavers. London: Jonathan Cape.

Baudry, Jean-Louis (1986a) 'Ideological Effects of the Basic Cinematographic Apparatus', in Philip Rosen (ed.), *Narrative, Apparatus, Ideology: A Film Theory Reader.* New York: Columbia University Press. pp. 286–98.

Baudry, Jean-Louis (1986b) 'The Apparatus: Meta-physical Approaches to Ideology', in Philip Rosen (ed.), *Narrative, Apparatus, Ideology: A Film Theory Reader.* New York: Columbia University Press. pp. 299–318.

Bordwell, David and Carroll, Noël (eds) (1996) *Post-Theory: Reconstructing Film Studies.* Wisconsin: University of Wisconsin Press.

Copjec, Joan (1994) *Read My Desire: Lacan against the Historicists.* Boston: MIT Press.

de Lauretis, Teresa (1984) *Alice Doesn't: Feminism, Semiotics, Cinema.* Bloomington: Indiana University Press.

Deleuze, Gilles and Guattari, Félix (1985) *Anti-Oedipus: Capitalism and Schizophrenia.* Tr. Robert Hurley, Mark Seem and Helen R. Lane. London: Athlone Press.

Derrida, Jacques (1998) *Resistances of Psychoanalysis*. Tr. Peggy Kampf, Pascale-Anne Brault and Michael Nass. Stanford, CA: Stanford University Press.

Doane, Mary Ann (1987) *The Desire to Desire: The Woman's Film of the 1940s*. Bloomington: Indiana University Press.

Eco, Umberto (1976) *A Theory of Semiotics*. Bloomington: Indiana University Press.

Freud, Sigmund (2001a) *The Interpretation of Dreams (I)*. Vol.4, *The Standard Edition of the Complete Psychological Works*. Tr. James Strachey. London: Hogarth Press.

Freud, Sigmund (2001b) *The Interpretation of Dreams (II) and On Dreams*. Vol.5, *The Standard Edition of the Complete Psychological Works*. Tr. James Strachey. London: Hogarth Press.

Freud, Sigmund (2001c) *A Case of Hysteria, Three Essays On Sexuality and Other Works*. Vol.7, *The Standard Edition of the Complete Psychological Works*. Tr. James Strachey. London: Hogarth Press.

Freud, Sigmund (2001d) *Jensen's 'Gradiva' and Other Works*. Vol. 9, *The Standard Edition of the Complete Psychological Works*. Tr. James Strachey. London: Hogarth Press.

Freud, Sigmund (2001e) *An Autobiographical Study, Inhibitions, Symptoms and Anxiety, Lay Analysis and Other Works* Vol.20, *The Standard Edition of the Complete Psychological Works*. Tr. James Strachey. London: Hogarth Press.

Freud, Sigmund (2001f) *The Future of an Illusion, Civilization and its Discontents, and Other Works*. Vol.21, *The Standard Edition of the Complete Psychological Works*. Tr. James Strachey. London: Hogarth Press.

Freud, Sigmund (2001g) *New Introductory Lectures on Psycho-analysis and Other Works*. Vol.22, *The Standard Edition of the Complete Psychological Works*. Tr. James Strachey. London: Hogarth Press.

Fuery, Patrick (2004) *Madness and Cinema: Psychoanalysis, Spectatorship and Culture*. London: Palgrave.

Kant, Immanuel (2002) *Critique of Practical Reason*. Tr. Werner Pluhar. Indianapolis: Hackett.

Kaplan, E. Ann (ed.) (1990) *Psychoanalysis and the Cinema*. New York: Routledge.

Kristeva, Julia (1982) *Powers of Horror: An Essay on Abjection*. Tr. Leon S. Roudiez. New York: Columbia University Press.

Kristeva, Julia (1984) *Desire in Language: A Semiotic Approach to Literature and Art*. Tr. Thomas Gora, Alice Jardine and Leon S. Roudiez. Oxford: Blackwell.

Kuhn, Annette (1985) *The Power of the Image: Essays on Representation and Sexuality*. London: Routledge.

Kuhn, Thomas (1974) *The Structure of Scientific Revolutions*. Chicago: University of Chicago Press.

Lacan, Jacques (1961) 'Maurice Merleau-Ponty', *Les Temps modernes*, 184–85: 245–54.

Lacan, Jacques (1966) 'Kant avec Sade', in *Écrits*. Paris: Seuil. pp. 765–90.

Lacan, Jacques (1981) *Séminaire VIII: Le Transfert dans sa disparité subjective (1960–1)*. Paris: Seuil.

Lacan, Jacques (1988) *The Ego In Freud's Theory and in the Technique of Psychoanalysis*. Tr. S. Tomaselli and J.A. Miller. Cambridge: Cambridge University Press.

Lacan, Jacques (1992) *The Ethics of Psychoanalysis*. Tr. D. Porter. London: Routledge.

Lacan, Jacques (1993) *The Psychoses*. Tr. R. Grigg. London: Routledge.

Lacan, Jacques (1998) *Seminar XX: Encore: On Feminine Sexuality, The Limits of Love and Knowledge*. Tr. Bruce Fink. New York: Norton.

Lacan, Jacques (2005) *Le Sinthome: Séminaire XXIII, 1975–6*. Paris: Seuil.

Laplanche, Jean (1992) *Seduction, Translation, Drives*. London: ICA.

Laplanche, Jean and Pontalis, J.B. (1986) 'Fantasy and the Origins of Sexuality', in Victor Burgin, James Donald and Cora Kaplin (eds), *Formations of Fantasy*. London: Methuen. pp. 5–34.

Metz, Christian (1974) *Film Language: A Semiotics of Cinema*. T. Michael Taylor. Oxford: Oxford University Press.

Metz, Christian (1985) *The Imaginary Signifier: Psychoanalysis and the Cinema*. Tr. Celia Britton, Annwyl Williams, Ben Brewster, and Alfred Guzzetti. Bloomington: Indiana University Press.

Modleski, Tania (1988) *The Women Who Knew Too Much: Hitchcock and Feminist Theory*. New York: Methuen.

Mulvey, Laura (1975) 'Visual Pleasure and Narrative Cinema', *Screen*, 16(3): 6–18.

Penley, Constance (1989) *The Future of an Illusion: Film, Feminism and Psychoanalysis*. Minneapolis: University of Minnesota Press,

Rose, Jacqueline (1980) 'The Cinematic Apparatus: Problems in Current Theory', in Teresa de Lauretis and Stephen Heath (eds), *The Cinematic Apparatus*. New York: St Martin's Press. pp. 172–86.

Silverman, Kaja (1988) *The Acoustic Mirror: The Female Voice in Psychoanalysis and Cinema*. Bloomington: Indiana University Press.

16

The Political Economy of Film

Tom O'Regan

The rubric of a 'political economy of cinema' has proved attractive to generations of film scholars. Few writers on cinema or its close relations of television and new media have not at one time or another turned their attention to the way that politics and economics, whether separately or together, have shaped the production, circulation and social uptake of film. It is not hard to see why. By virtue of its public visibility and industrial character, politics and government tend to exercise a defining influence upon filmmaking by helping to establish the formal and informal 'rules of the game' under which cinema operates.

Equally, the changing structures of the industry both globally and nationally have been determined in large part by film production costs, the complex infrastructures required for both production and screening, the ongoing reliance upon technology and innovation, and the sheer scale of the finance involved at all stages of the cycle from production to exhibition. Furthermore, the interaction of political and economic considerations are pivotal not only in giving cultural and economic regulation of the cinema its characteristic shape in film classification and urban zoning of cinemas, but also in informing cultural and industry policies such as incentives for the production of films and even the building of cinemas. The combination of politics and economics is also writ large in the actions of media corporations and industry associations and agencies – especially the Hollywood majors and the Motion Picture Association of America (MPAA) – in securing friendly operating conditions both at home and abroad for their operations (Guback, 1969; Miller et al., 2005; Pendakur, 1990; Thompson, 1985).

Cinema, then, is at one and the same time a textual and aesthetic system, an economic institution, an object of government and a social institution. Having recognized the institution's multiple dimensions, it is a small step to conclude with Graham Murdock that our ways of organizing and financing cultural production have 'traceable consequences for the range of discourses and representations in the public domain and accessibility to audiences' (1989: 46), or, to put this more precisely, the way that films are conceived, planned, produced, funded and circulated 'leave their marks upon the films – not only directly, in telltale details, but structurally as well' (Bordwell et al., 1985: xiv). Film Studies is therefore full of examples like Kevin Heffernan's study of Hollywood's 1950s horror cycle, which demonstrates the relation between, on the one hand, form and content and, on the other, the changing industrial circumstances associated with exhibition, distribution and production (2004). For Heffernan this horror cycle stemmed from the economic imperatives of the cinema industry faced with the 'double whammy' of the advent of television and the break-up of the vertical integration that had placed not only production but also cinema exhibition and distribution under the control of the big studios. These provided the conditions for the emergence of the horror movie screened at drive-ins aimed at youth audiences escaping the strictures of family life and television's family orientation.

These varying specifications of the cinema – as a textual and aesthetic system, an economic institution, an object of government and a social institution – help to explain the organization of the field of scholarship surrounding film and television. We have, first, approaches which seek to stitch these various 'orders' together into multifaceted accounts of the cinema institution – whether it be the Classical Hollywood style, the studio system in the classical period (Schatz, 1988; 1996), Hollywood in the information age (Wasko, 1994), the French New Wave of the 1950s and 1960s (Marie, 2003) or the New German cinema of the 1960s and 1970s (Elsaesser, 1989). Within this body of scholarship we can distinguish between weaker and stronger versions of political economy, depending on the accent given and purpose behind the explanations. Film historians and cultural analysts usually undertake weaker versions. Typically, they investigate particular political and economic aspects of the film phenomenon being studied in order to explain the impacts of government policy, the interaction of style and mode of production, and the shaping influence of

consumption upon the production, circulation and uptake of particular kinds of films and filmmaking. Stronger versions of political economy are generally undertaken within communication or related social science disciplines. Here the emphasis is more likely to be on political economy, using the approach to insist upon the genesis of the system (cinema) or object (films) in the capitalist mode of production and in the institutions and circuits of commodified production, distribution and consumption (see Garnham, 2000; Hesmondhalgh, 2002). What both the weaker and stronger variants have in common is the attempt to integrate political and economic aspects of the cinema into broad explanations about the nature and character of the cinema, its films, its institutions, its politics and its markets.

Besides the weaker and stronger versions of political economy we have an increasing number of approaches which tend to concentrate on one of these dimensions, typically relegating consideration of others to a more incidental basis. Some perspectives, dealt with extensively elsewhere in this Handbook, concentrate upon either textual or aesthetic dimensions of the cinema or upon cinema as a social and cultural institution. Of particular interest at this moment, however, is the growing number of approaches which foreground political, economic and geographical explanations in their examination of the film and media industries. This emerging focus has been prompted in large part by significant changes both within the media industries and in governmental priorities for those industries. It is in this new context that film has become an object of government in new ways and so increasingly an object of study for policy and political studies (Cunningham, 2002; Dyson and Humphreys, 1990; Venturelli, 1998). In this emerging perspective, film becomes one facet of broader audio-visual industries, including the broadcasting, information and creative industries. At the same time, media and cultural economists concerned with the formation of audio-visual markets, and within these the economics of the film and television industries, have variously sought to understand these industries and to frame, query or legitimate existing political interventions and cultural support systems (Noam, 1985; Siwek and Wildman, 1988; Throsby, 2001). For their part, economic and cultural geographers in an era with increased focus and policy attention towards regional economic development have been exploring the formation of film and television industries focusing upon their local and extra-local networks, the formation of particular industrial districts and the development of cities (see notably Christopherson, 2003; 2006; Coe, 2000; Coe and Johns, 2004; Scott, 2000; Scott and Storper, 2003). These developments ensure that overviews of the political economy of film need to increasingly consider perspectives developed out of a variety of disciplinary domains which are less oriented to film in itself than to broader processes and larger concerns.

This chapter is organized as follows. It examines weaker and stronger versions of political economy, first separately and then together, before turning to accounts of the political and economic aspects of the cinema being developed outside the disciplinary nexus of these familiar film, media and communication approaches. The chapter ends with a brief consideration of the interaction and significance of this field for future research and scholarship.

THE WEAK VERSION OF POLITICAL ECONOMY: FILM STUDIES

Despite the widely recognized importance of political economic aspects of production and circulation to the cinema and to film scholarship, there are comparatively few Film Studies scholars who would describe themselves first and foremost as political economists. Eileen Bowser (1990) is typical of a tendency – particularly evident among film historians, national cinema analysts and cultural studies practitioners – to integrate political and economic perspectives

with other kinds of explanation in order to produce multiple and intersecting perspectives on film. Film and the cinema necessarily emerge from such studies as complex sociocultural, aesthetic and economic phenomena. In *The Transformation of Cinema: 1907–1915*, for example, Bowser writes:

> This volume is an effort to understand, through a better knowledge of how films were seen and experienced at the time they first appeared to their audiences and of the surrounding circumstances of their production, distribution, and exhibition, and the prevalent cultural and social ideas at the time, just how it was films and filmmaking were transformed in this period. (1990: xi)

In such an analysis both political and economic perspectives on the circumstances of production, distribution and exhibition are present. They exist, however, only alongside other perspectives drawn from social, cultural and intellectual history, textual analysis, histories of acting, performance and staging and so on. A focus on the political economy of film is here one component among several components needing to be mobilized by the researcher as historian and analyst of a complex, multifaceted cultural institution.

Such a mixing of elements characterizes much of the analysis of national cinemas and many analyses seeking to illuminate the intersecting and diverse aspects of the cinema – whether to explain the Hollywood studio system of the 1930s and 1940s (Schatz, 1996) or the Australian cinema after 1960 (O'Regan, 1996). Such scholars are animated by the multiple and diverse points of view required to reconstruct and explain particular film milieu, filmmaking trajectories or aspects thereof. Typically, they are concerned with how and why particular films came to be made, why these films looked the way they did, and why they mattered to historical audiences and critics. The object of analysis here is the history and disposition of an art and/or cultural form. Their collective concern is for the 'cultural politics' of cinema – with cinema as a cultural institution. Often, work in this tradition sees film as a combination of cultural-aesthetic meanings and/or politics that, to an extent, confers its own end and set of interests.

This is an inevitably 'messy' approach (O'Regan, 1996). Varying factors are seen as influencing film production. These can range from a particular mode of production with specific stylistic entailments (Bordwell et al., 1985) to the structuring influence of marketing upon the selection and investment in the contemporary high-budget block-buster (Wyatt, 1994), from the centrality of film and television policy to European film production (Elsaesser, 2005; Nowell-Smith and Ricci, 1998) to the role of key creative personnel in constructing a studio and its slate of films (Balio, 1987; Schatz, 1996). As John Downing, whose work has always combined film with wider media deliberations, observed, 'for many purposes political economy is more a question of insistence on the impact of economic vectors as a matter of empirical observation than of having a developed ... acknowledged theory which illuminates their interaction with other sets of factors' (1996: 27). For Downing, the selection of determinations is made on a case-by-case basis and is usually based upon what the empirical record reveals. Writers within this tradition tend to worry away at creating a 'monolithic determining status' (Bordwell et al., 1985: xv) for any explanatory grid and particularly political economic notions such as mode of production or capitalism in its varying guises (mercantile, monopoly or information). David Bordwell, Janet Staiger and Kristin Thompson are typical in arguing in their landmark study, *The Classical Hollywood Cinema: Film Style and Mode of Production to 1960*, that 'film style and mode of production are ... reciprocal and mutually influencing', rather than one creating the other (1985: xiv). This characteristic reluctance to accord the political and economic privileged status distinguishes these scholars from avowed political economists of film who place these economic systems at the centre of their analysis (Garnham, 2000; Hozic, 2001; Wasko, 1994).

THE STRONG VERSION OF POLITICAL ECONOMY: A CRITICAL POLITICAL ECONOMY

The familiar complaint of our next group, the critical political economists, against the first group is that this kind of piecemeal approach is only ever designed to answer particular and limited mid-range questions. It lacks the holistic view political economy perspectives purport to provide. As David Hesmondhalgh puts it, it is only when such studies are 'synthesized into a more comprehensive vision of how cultural production and consumption fit into wider, economic, political and cultural contexts that an analysis of specific conditions of cultural production really produces its explanatory pay-off' (2002: 36). Political economy is here a theory and a perspective upon how these various messy bits might be (permanently) arranged into a coherent pattern of analysis persisting across multiple studies and suited to a variety of different contexts.

Political economy claims, first, to answer how the various aspects and circumstances of production and circulation may be optimally arranged. Secondly, it claims to recognize in diverse phenomena so many shared generating mechanisms and determinants organizing the conditions and circumstances under study. It finds a stabilizing and common set of features organizing production and its circulation in capitalism and its modes of production. For Nicholas Garnham, the capitalist mode of production brings 'into a specific historically constructed set of relations the means and forces of production, capital and labour to produce and exchange commodities (whether goods or services) on competitive markets' (2000: 41).

According to critical political economists, the problem with our first group of scholars is that they fail to attend systemically to the determining consequences of commodified production. For Garnham:

political economists find it hard to understand how, within a capitalist social formation, one can study cultural practices and their political effectivity – the ways in which people make sense of their lives

and then act in the light of that understanding –
without focusing attention on how the resources
for cultural practice, both material and symbolic …
are made available in structurally determined ways
through the institutions and circuits of commodified
cultural production, distribution and consumption.
(1990: 72)

They therefore tend to treat the cultural
object – here the filmic object – as 'isolated systems cut off from political and
socio-economic conflict', and so sideline
'issues of power and domination' stemming
from the circumstances of the capitalist
mode of production itself (Hesmondhalgh,
2002: 36).

The defining characteristics of the capitalist
mode of production are, first, the evident
'competition between capitals in search of
accumulation which drives innovation and
the search for efficiency and thus growth
in productivity for the system as a whole'.
Second, there is the 'separation of labour from
the means of production', which produces
an 'increasingly deep division of labour, and
thus the provision and allocation of labour
through a labour market based on wages'
(Hesmondhalgh, 2002: 41). And, third, it has
an inescapable character in that '[n]either
individual capitals nor workers have any
choice but to participate in the system'
(Hesmondhalgh, 2002: 42).

Given this focus, the central preoccupation
of this 'strong' approach is to uncover
'the dynamics of capitalism' (Wasko, 1999:
222). The political economist focuses upon
the study of 'the relationships among commodities, institutions, social relations and
hegemony'. They want to discuss 'the policy
problems and moral issues which arise'.
And they want to 'transcend the distinction
between research and policy' and instead to
orient 'work towards actual social change'
(Wasko, 1999: 222–223). To Janet Wasko's
list we can add the concern of Garnham (2001)
and Toby Miller et al. (2005) to chart the 'deep'
division of labour within film production
itself. For Miller et al. this is the distinction
between above-the-line and below-the-line
film workers in a new cultural division of
labour within Hollywood and now extending

beyond the US to a global scale with the
advent of geographically dispersed film and
television production in so-called 'runaway'
productions. This work shares a concern for
cultural workers including film workers not in
the elite and highly paid zones having greater
access to the means of production and control
over their often exploitative labour conditions.

CONNECTING AND DISTINGUISHING WEAK AND STRONG VERSIONS OF POLITICAL ECONOMY

What fundamentally distinguishes those
approaches that avowedly, and centrally, focus
on political economy from those that to
varying degrees investigate political and economic aspects of the film phenomenon being
investigated? The first point of difference
turns on critical political economy's insistence
upon the genesis of the system or object
in the capitalist mode of production and
the institutions and circuits of commodified
production, distribution and consumption.
By contrast, much more diverse purposes
are associated with the weaker versions
of political economy evident in the work
of the film historian and cultural analysts
who variously emphasize the influence of
government policy, the interaction of style and
mode of production, and the shaping influence
of consumption.

A second major point of distinction is that
critical political economists do not as a rule see
themselves as primarily concerned with the
political economy of films and filmmaking.
For such scholars a critical political economy
of communication is at the centre of their
work, superintending both their own methods
of research and any other perspectives they
may incorporate. Wasko is typical here. In
a series of books on Hollywood and its
corporations, beginning with *Movies and
Money* in 1982 and including *Understanding
Disney: The Manufacture of Fantasy* (2001),
Hollywood in the Age of Information (1994)
and more recently *How Hollywood Works*
(2003), she has situated her work as part of

a broader contribution, not so much to Cinema and Film Studies, but to, as her website puts it, 'the political economy of communications, its structure and policies'.[1] Her focus on the 'United States film industry' provides a good vantage-point from which to observe the operations of the contemporary globalizing and diversified media corporation operating across multiple media and with interests in production, exhibition, distribution and exhibition in cinema, pay-TV and television. By contrast, our Film Studies theorist and historian concerned with the interplay of the films, their circumstances of production and circulation and their uptake by audiences is likely to take the cinema, and therefore Film Studies including film history, as their principal disciplinary domain.

But while positioning themselves within critical political economy, the actual studies undertaken routinely intersect with other work. *Understanding Disney* and Miller et al.'s *Global Hollywood* (2001, 2005) draw on more than political economy to explore cinema and filmmaking's work as an economic and ideological institution suggesting significant points of continuity between these two approaches. As Wasko observes:

> Political economy draws upon several disciplines – specifically history, economics, sociology and political science .... [It] draws on a wide variety of techniques and methods, including not only Marxist economics, but methods used in history and sociology, especially power-structure research and institutional analysis. (1999: 224)

The adoption of multiple perspectives here is seen as being ordered and coherent in that, as with Wasko's analysis of the continued expansion and popularity of the Disney group, her object of study calls 'for the deliberate integration of political economic analysis with insights drawn from cultural analysis and audience studies or reception analysis, or, in other words, analysis emphasizing the economic as well as the ideological, or production as well as consumption' (2001: 5). Miller et al. explicitly draw upon cultural studies and cultural policy analysis to bolster political economy in their attempt to

explain Hollywood's continuing hegemony in a globalizing era. This disciplinary spread is similarly justified as a means of throwing explanatory light onto the material factors underlining Hollywood's global success.

Characteristically, both approaches are connected in that they recognize the importance of thinking through possible ways of incorporating economic and political forces and processes into social analysis – (to paraphrase Downing (1996: 27). They are also drawn from a family of related disciplines – the Media/Communication and Film/Cultural Studies nexus – which are dedicated to analyzing cultural and media production and associated cultural meanings through a mix of film and media history, sociology and political economy. Where they differ lies in the attention critical political economists give to the determining impact of the economic in capitalism recognized predominantly through a Marxist lens, and its associated ownership and control features over and against the more fragmented and diverse perspectives adapted by the weaker versions of political economy found in Film Studies traditions.

The film scholar Kristin Thompson's book *Exporting Entertainment: America in the World Film Market, 1907–1934* (1985) can be taken as one index of this difference. At one level this study is almost exclusively concerned with political and economic developments. She shows how America achieved hegemony in international film markets through a combination of innovations in film distribution, opportunities the First World War presented for Hollywood export with weakened European competitors, and a concerted business strategy of 'eroding' the base of support for the European film industry abroad by targeting key international territories in Australia and South America (1985: x). But her purpose in doing so is not to uncover an underlying dynamic of monopoly capitalism and trends towards concentration of ownerships and increasing divisions of labour (critical political economist ends) – although she certainly shows these things in action. Rather, it is to help the 'historian of style' establish 'the norms of cinematic practice to which audiences (including filmmakers) would have been accustomed' (1985: xi). That is, she is drawn to establish the dynamics of filmmaking so as to establish what it is that audiences were watching and how this product was being distributed. She wanted to use this to understand better the practice and options of European filmmakers in the inter-war period. This different agenda no doubts accounts for the way that Miller et al. (2001) dismiss Thompson's study as 'archival empiricism', drawing attention to its failure to draw out the larger significance and implications of its research.

What is loosely being played out here is a broader distinction between two approaches. One tends to see 'culture' and its distinctive forms of media, such as the cinema, as an unusual domain of social, institutional and public life and government worthy of attention in its own right. The other perspective recognizes in such media just another institutional, public and governmental domain. The first, more humanities-oriented version of Film Studies grows out of a longer history of the aesthetic consideration of culture and individual art forms. It reflexively sees cultural institutions and forms as having developed in their own, *sui generis*, fashion with their own sense of themselves, their own particular domain of interventions, their own rules and procedures, their protocols of public commentary and interpretation, their own policy processes that have made the cultural domain quite unlike other domains of social, public and economic life and from each other. This research tradition takes its cue from what immediately relates to the filmic object being examined for the analysis undertaken – whether the study of filmmakers and their careers, film movements, or particular national cinemas. This humanities orientation licences attention to the media form and makes this attention in turn a self-justifying end in itself authorizing attention to film and the cinema as a pre-eminently cultural institution with economic and political aspects.

On the other hand, for the critical political economist the cinema is self-evidently and increasingly part of broader capital formations and policy networks which are so insistent in their impact as to warrant greater attention to them. Film is connected here with other national governmental programs, wider projects of state and inexorable market forces. Critical political economy is therefore strongly associated with media communication scholarship and stresses the cinema as part of, rather than apart from, other, larger communications, cultural, creative or copyright industries. It further stresses the communication industries' relation with larger dynamics of capitalism, its strategies and its facilitatory and regulatory orientations. This perspective tends to turn Hollywood film and television industries into a case study of, in Garnham's words, 'key problems within the general project of the social sciences', and as exemplary vantage-points from which to witness the dynamics of capitalism in operation (1990: 3).

Such a division of scholarly labour would certainly appear to hold true if one were to take Herb Schiller's 1969 *Mass Communication and the American Empire* as the point of departure for the development of a critical political economy. Schiller's influential thesis was that a project of American cultural imperialism was forged from connections between the US military industrial complex and US media industries, including Hollywood. In a European counterpart to Schiller's approach, Armand Mattelart's early work elaborated an explanation of 'international image markets' (1979; Mattelart et al., 1984). This critical perspective still broadly informs the work of Garnham (1990), Peter Golding and Murdock (1997) on media concentration and control, and much of Wasko's work. And, if one set against this body of work studies of French (Hayward, 1993), Italian (Sorlin, 1996) or Australian national cinemas (O'Regan, 1996), studies of the studio system incorporating diverse aspects including but not privileging the economic and political (Schatz, 1988; Staiger, 1995), and studies of individual production-distribution companies such as the 'artist's studio', Universal Studios (Balio, 1987), then it would be easy enough to support the characteristic patterns of perspective and orientation that differentiate weaker versions of political economy from the stronger.

There are immediate problems with doing so, however. After all, one of the seminal works in the political economy of communications is Thomas Guback's *The International Film Industry* (1969), which was concerned with the nexus of politics and economics as it related to Western European film policy, domestic production industries and Hollywood's intersection and strategic shaping of these in the immediate post-war period as it sought to (re)gain market entry and assert a degree of control. Part political science and policy studies, part economic analysis and part assessment of the impact of these conditions on both Hollywood and European films, Guback's book helped frame later trajectories of film scholarship – and indeed film activism outside the US. I was first lent the book to read by Australian film activist Sylvia Lawson in the 1970s. I noticed it had the Australian film director, producer and fellow activist Ken Quinnell's name inside its front cover. Lawson and Quinnell were using Guback to help them understand their own Australian predicament and think through how they could use cultural arguments to lobby (ultimately successfully) for state support for a local film industry whose products would be insulated, to some extent, from the full pressure of the market through subsidy mechanisms analogous to those beginning to be available in the performing arts.

The International Film Industry is notable for its attention to the specific characteristics of each of the major Western European cinemas. Here two major traditions of filmmaking – Hollywood and European art cinema – were thought together in an integrated analysis with political and economic imperatives given due weight.[2] Guback's subsequent work could have gone in two directions. He could have become a specialist on the European film industries or he could have focused on international (now named 'global') Hollywood. He chose the latter path, situating this work variously within critical

political economy traditions, and towards the end of his career with 'institutional analysis' (Wasko, 1999: 221). His attention became less focused on European film policy development then on the changing dimensions of Hollywood's international market and its control of international territories, including its capacity to get governments to do its bidding (Guback, 1985a; 1985b).

If Guback had chosen the European film policy path, he probably would not have been so closely identified with critical political economy. This is because the close relation of the state to domestic film production in Western Europe and beyond would have likely required some moderation of the straightforward calculus of concentration and control by transnational Hollywood majors that is obtained when considering the activity of Hollywood corporations. Indeed, when we compare the role of the nation state in the US to its international counterparts, we see a different, more defensive, role being assumed by other nation states. In Europe, Canada and Australia, for instance, the state acts as facilitator, creating favourable investment conditions for private investment in film. It often acts as a patron by selectively funding film projects through arm's-length decision-making processes in various film commissions and other bodies like the Australian Film Finance Corporation (FFC) modelled initially on arts funding bodies (see Craik, 1996). These measures ensure the underwriting of production levels beyond a minimal level and ensure a national presence to 'dream our own dreams and tell our own stories', just as they also introduce the possibility of producers being more interested in 'obtaining financial subsidies than they are with actually attracting audiences' (Scott, 2000: 110). The nation state is typically dealing here with a considerably weaker, more disorganized and fragmented production sector – something of a cottage industry with undeveloped links with distribution and exhibition. By contrast, Hollywood's relation with the American state is that of a co-participant. The state is dealing here with one of its major economic institutions – and one that brings together production, distribution and, increasingly, exhibition interests and has important export markets and operations abroad to protect (Siwek, 2002). This is, crudely, the difference between two types of film policy. One sees cinema as an issue primarily for cultural policy and therefore focuses on providing support for local film production and local filmmakers and relies on subsidy as the policy instrument to provide that support. The other sees cinema as an industry, incorporating the mix of filmmaking, distribution and exhibition, and therefore sees it as an issue for economic and international trade policy.

From the perspective of the researcher, these structural differences largely determine the relationship between film scholarship and the film industry. People working on non-Hollywood film making often find it easier to get close to the local film industry, as it is more socially accessible and practitioners are often ready to talk. Indeed, the close proximity of the state means that there is another public reason – a sense of public entitlement, obligation and ownership stemming from governmental largesse – to grease the wheels of conversation and controversy. For such scholars there is also a David-versus-Goliath factor. 'Our' smaller, locally accented, independent, more 'cottage industry'-like and, above all, non-Hollywood producers and filmmakers can be seen as taking on the corporate and soulless Hollywood Goliath. Undeniably, the prospect of scholarship mattering not just to government but also to the film industry has coloured the cultural and critical presuppositions of many national cinema scholars and influenced the type of research questions they ask. Unsurprisingly, they often register notions of cultural imperialism, cultural erosion and loss of cultural diversity in their scholarship (see O'Regan, 1996: 115–21).

Michael Dorland's study of the emergence of Canadian feature film policy, *So Close to the State/s* (1998), hints at the particular dynamic in operation outside the US in its very title, with its ambiguous play on the Canadian state and the US stressing the inter-relation between them. Dorland is concerned with the

story of how it became in the (Canadian) national interest to fund Canadian feature films. He emphasizes the 'decisive role' of what he calls 'state knowledge or governmentality' in the emergence of Canadian feature film (1998: 148). Operating within a 'national cinemas' rubric there is a strong sense that economic and political considerations are simply one among a number of conditions under which a filmmaking milieu emerges and is sustained. This recognizes the fact that the market for domestic production in national cinemas is informed – even generated – by dynamics that are not ruled by simple economic supply-and-demand equations. Indeed, sometimes the opposite is the case. Film production support mechanisms can be explicitly designed to cushion local production from the full operation of the market. Such considerations can, at times, partially suspend supply-and-demand dynamics, leading to the overproduction and supply of films and to levels of filmmaking greater than the trivial levels on its own would support the 'market'. The taxation incentives period in Australian cinema of the 1980s and the 'quota quickies' of British and Canadian cinema in the 1930s spring to mind. Film support mechanisms can also, as Allen J. Scott observes for the contemporary French film industry, lead to 'propping up domestic market share by dramatically reducing entrepreneurial risk', with the consequence that 'new competitive strategies' or 'new synergies of a type that might promote superior levels of economic performance' have not emerged (2000: 107). The close involvement of the state in its film policy for the film production sector ensures a role for the film scholar as a public intellectual, industry analyst and commentator – and even, on occasion, policy advisor.

By contrast, the researcher of mainstream Hollywood will usually experience the film industry as being both more distant and also far less dependent upon film scholarship to provide it with needed cultural and social capital or political and cultural ballast. Hollywood can be in a corporate sense unreachable. It exists as its own world – impervious, even imperious, with regard to criticism and research. Here corporate economic orientations towards profits and returns dominate with supply closely related to demand. Corporate economic interests that drive political agendas and concerns dominate interaction between the economic and the political and governmental. There is no 'cottage industry' with fraught relations to exhibition and distribution for the researcher to identify with and no situation of film as an integral part of a nation's cultural policy. Rather, there is a complex and integrated machinery directly and seamlessly connecting production to distribution and exhibition. The resulting distance between the film and media scholar and a Hollywood corporate machine helps explain two distinct aspects of scholarship on Hollywood. For scholars of contemporary Hollywood, their information and data archive will be largely made up of 'outsider', publicly-available sources of information in the form of newspaper and magazine journals, annual company reports and occasional business and industry reports – theirs is a relationship marked by distance. Whereas for the historical scholar with access to company archives and personal papers of significant individuals, Hollywood strategy and practice can be readily accessed allowing for a greater 'insider' contribution to the understanding of developments in the film industry, its circulation and uptake. This creates a significant mismatch between historical and contemporary accounts of Hollywood, and suggests that the generalist and generalizing orientation of the political economist may stem in part from the lack of meaningful dialogue between scholar and industry. By contrast, national cinema and historical analyses of Hollywood tend to be under pressure to pull together the textual and the economic, the sociocultural and the organizational into an explanatory framework which is unlikely to privilege, save on a case-by-case basis, the economic determinants of the film and related sectors.

Having made this point, it is important to register that Miller et al.'s *Global Hollywood*

books are not just an important restatement of critical political economy, but are also in their own ways instances of a rapprochement between political economy and other perspectives, particularly cultural policy studies. Many aspects of *Global Hollywood* echo Guback's earlier study, including its fine-grained concern for the particular countries participating in Hollywood film and television production. Furthermore, the very domain which, on my line of argument above, would be least susceptible to a rigorous political economy – the analysis of a national cinema – has been the subject of sustained and rigorous political economy scrutiny. Manjuneth Pendakur's *Canadian Dreams and American Control: The Political Economy of the Canadian Film Industry* (1990) explains how other cinemas (mainly the US but also Britain) have maintained their dominance of the Canadian film industry, principally through their long-term stranglehold of local distribution and exhibition and their capacity to shape successive Canadian government policies seeking to aid the Canadian industry into supporting continuing US control. The study is notable for its consideration of films not in cultural and aesthetic terms but as 'little more than commodities' (Straw, 1993). Pendakur's analysis is centred on the terms and conditions required for a national film industry to generate and reinvest the revenues upon which its film production depends. The focus is therefore upon distribution and exhibition – a focus often neglected in production studies (Thompson, 1992: 152). Characteristically, what unites the weaker and stronger versions of political economy is a movement towards integration and holistic analysis, but achieved through different points of intersection and identifiably distinct though overlapping orientations.

The continuing practice of both versions of political economy is anchored in the very circumstances of the film and media industries themselves. As a result, which perspective is adopted turns significantly on which aspects of cinema and the film industry are being investigated. This is not only a question of the nature and character of the object, but also a matter of what questions we are asking of the object. Our variants of political economy might best be seen as responses to changes over time in the audience, the industry, and filmmaker's intelligence and knowledge of these. For instance, the high concept blockbuster that is the subject of Justin Wyatt's analysis (1994) is unthinkable without more extended and systematized pre-testing regimes and the widespread acceptance in business and academic circles of marketing as not only both selling a finished product but as shaping its very construction (Levitt, 1986). In Wyatt's analysis the demands of marketing are, in an unprecedented fashion, superintending and informing the kind of films that get made.

Similarly, Hesmondhalgh's analysis of the cultural industries and film and cinema's place within them is anchored in moves in the film and broader cultural industries from the 1950s towards

> ... a labour market in which some creative workers are vastly rewarded but most are underemployed and underpaid, the increasing presence of large corporations, often in the form of vertically integrated conglomerates; significant international-ization, dominated by the US cultural industries; and associated regimes of technology, consumption and policy. (2002: 256)

In the 1980s and 1990s these developments have been accompanied by the 'marketization' of government communication policies with the consequence that 'the view that the production and exchange of cultural goods and services for profit is the best way to achieve efficiency and fairness in the production and consumption of texts' (2002: 257). This not only led to the attack on 'various rationales for high degrees of state intervention', but also had the consequence of privatizing 'public telecommunications organizations and some public broadcasting institutions; the opening up of television systems to other terrestrial, commercial broadcasters and to cable and satellite companies; the watering down of regulatory walls between different industries; plus significant changes in laws and rules on content, media ownership and subsidies'

(2002: 257). Hesmondhalgh calls this a move towards 'neoliberalism'.

CONCENTRATING ON POLITICS, ECONOMY AND THEIR GEOGRAPHICAL ENTAILMENTS

This same mix of developments, which not only includes the transformation and growth of audio-visual media but also the transformation of instruments for regulating and facilitating its production and circulation, helps explain the growing attention to the cinema and the film and media industry more generally by a range of both disciplinary perspectives and governmental and private sector agencies. Their interest in the intersection of politics and economics in the film and media industries is not based so much on a sudden interest in political and economic aspects of film, but is instead a consequence of broader policy, analytical and industrial attentions which include, but are not limited to, film production, circulation and consumption.

Most immediately, wider attention has been pulled towards the film and film-related industries by their evident transformation. Previous settlements between cinema and television, between media and telecommunications have become unsettled and blurred. Privatization, the entry of new players, regulation for competition and technological change associated with digitization and convergence have all altered the relationships between different media and between media and telecommunications. In a more fragmented, diverse and internationalized film milieu, problems are posed for 'business as usual' in both national cinemas and Hollywood alike. Time-honoured private-sector strategies and public policy choices seem to be creaking under the strain of change and require adjustment. Additionally, new forms of audio-visual entertainment, particularly, computer games, are emerging to challenge film and television's dominance of the audio-visual economy and the thinking about it.

Such circumstances have made film and media policy-making a much more challenging (and interesting) area for political scientists, economists and geographers, just as they have generated new strategic issues for film producers, media and telecommunications companies, industry associations and for international, national, state and city governments.

Film as a domain of government initially came onto the horizon of policy and political studies in the late 1980s as a by-product of broader attentions to the media industries – particularly the television industries – in the context of the opening up of broadcasting to new commercial television operators beyond public broadcasters in Europe, the emergence of pay and subscription television and cross-border satellite and cable television systems globally, and the increasing policy reach of the European Union in this area (Collins and Murroni, 1996). While primarily affecting television, its regulations and its place on governmental horizons, these developments also materially affected the film industry and the policy horizons within which it operated. As convergence between telecommunications and broadcasting developed with the rolling out of fixed and wireless broadband networks from the 1990s, attention to the film industry became more direct as it was increasingly seen as a prime instance of an industry and production system being reshaped by convergence and digitization. It was a sector strategically needing to adopt new horizons and exploit new opportunities for 'content creation'. Both developments encouraged scholarship to make sensible these new orderings and offer policy and regulatory solutions and diagnosis.

In these circumstances, film production and film policy became part of the tapestry of a desired 'efficient communication system' (Collins and Murroni, 1996: 2), of a coherent information policy covering information technology and communications (Venturelli, 1998), of the copyright (Siwek, 2002) and creative industries which share critical features and scope for development (Caves, 2000; Cunningham, 2004). The resulting policy

studies have allowed us, in an unprecedented fashion, to think about film policy in its continuities and commonalities with other sectors and as an integral component in policy-making and development, as they relate to cultural industries more broadly. On an international level there is the political statecraft of national governments, as they use their film and media policies to order their relations among each other, whether to seek national competitive advantage (Dyson, 1988) or to protect their perceived cultural patrimony, particularly through the use of 'cultural exceptions' in international trade agreements and the development of a Convention on Cultural Diversity to safeguard their film and television industries (Grantham 2000; Smiers, 2004). When combined with cultural policy studies, orientations towards film policy in the vein of Albert Moran and his collaborators (1996) have ensured a wide variety of approaches towards film policy-making which are cross-fertilizing each other.

These attentions also signal the perceived importance to national, regional and even city competitiveness of the 'new economy' and its industries – variously the 'copyright', 'creative' or 'information' industries. Characterized by and important for their networks, dependence upon information and trajectories of globalization (Castells, 1996; Caves, 2000; Cunningham, 2004), these industries include film, but film neither dominates nor is it important in itself. Rather, film production is significant for component parts like digital postproduction which have the capacity to contribute to broader economic and industrial transformations. For policy makers, politicians, analysts and lobbyists, new analysis and research into production systems are required to fill out the new opportunities and problems that the 'cultural economy' and 'knowledge society' create. This need has provided the impetus to consider the diverse sectors, companies and infrastructures making up and providing inputs into the film and television industries and to ascertain how these relate to each other and to other industries. In the process the lines between industries have become blurred and the synergies and connections between them have been emphasized. This policy and research orientation has led to more place-based considerations of film industry development and its relation to other cognate industries. Proactive strategies such as 'cluster development' (that is, the benefits of industrial co-location) have become as a consequence increasingly important means to facilitate industry growth (Pratt, 2004). There have been a variety of initiatives mapping the location and distribution of creative and digital-content industries (DCITA and NOIE, 2002; DCMS, 1998; 2001; Jeffcutt, 2004) and these in turn have led to a sustained engagement with economic and cultural geography both as a discipline and in terms of the perspectives and orientations being developed. Useful research has also been done on media cities (Curtin, 2004; Scott, 2005) and the spread of globally dispersed infrastructures for, and involvements in, film and television production (Elmer and Gasher, 2005; Gasher, 2002; Goldsmith and O'Regan, 2004; 2005; Tinic, 2005).

Economic and cultural geographers are particularly suited to these tasks (see notably Christopherson, 2003 and 2006; Coe, 2000; Coe and Johns, 2004; Scott, 2000 and 2005). They now regularly explore the formation of film and television industries focusing upon their spatial logics – their local and extra-local networks, their forms of locational concentration in particular industrial districts and urban conurbations and their labour dynamics. Importantly, place enters into consideration not only because cities owe 'their genesis to basic economic processes', but also because 'they play a critical role in the social reproduction of economic systems and are an essential element in the formation of competitive advantage' (Scott, 2005: xi). While it is still unexceptionable to show how 'the cultural is embedded in the economic', the pay-off comes with the attention to the 'spatial logic of the cultural economy' and the ways in which 'locational concentration enhances both its competitive performance and its creative potentials' (Scott, 2000: ix). The impacts of these developments are

'especially evident in a number of giant cities representing the flagships of a new global capitalist cultural economy' (Scott, 2000: 3).

Allen J. Scott sees a trend for the production of culture to 'become more and more concentrated in a privileged set of localized clusters of firms and workers' in global media cities. Yet the cultural products are now 'channeled into ever more spatially extended networks of consumption' (Scott, 2000: 4). Such globalizing dynamics clearly have an impact upon regional economic development and upon the structure of a variety of industries. While Scott (2000; 2005) and Susan Christopherson (2003; 2006) cover the global media cities of Los Angeles, Paris and New York respectively, Neil Coe (2000; Coe and Johns, 2004) has looked at 'satellite' production centres such as Vancouver and Manchester. The result is a fine-grained analysis of film production industries, the industry clusters and networks involved in creating production and the linkages to the broader urban environment in which they are produced. In *On Hollywood: The Place, The Industry* (2005), Scott offers perhaps the most powerful contemporary re-description of Hollywood and its history. Hollywood is seen as 'a dense, multifaceted agglomeration of capital and labour whose organizational dynamics and socially constructed competitive advantages, in combination with massive capabilities in distribution and marketing, have enabled it to rise to virtually absolute mastery of global film and television markets' (2005: 159).

Media and cultural economists are also concerned with the formation of audio-visual markets and within these the economics of the film and television industries (see Picard, 1989; 2003; Siwek and Wildman, 1988; Throsby, 2001). This set of approaches is likely to understand and frame political interventions and cultural aspects of film and television as either remedying market failure and seeking sustainability (Throsby, 2001) – or as performing market-forming or distorting functions (see Noam, 1985; Siwek and Wildman, 1988). The same elements, which Hesmondhalgh lamented as 'marketization', are regarded neutrally and even positively by economists such as Robert Picard. They diagnose the 'worldwide realignment and expansion of existing markets and the breakdown of traditional national markets' as leading to the increasing 'establishment of *natural markets* based on regional, continental and global communications, with less emphasis on the role of the nation-state in markets' (Picard, 2003: 303, my italics). Indeed, the resulting disturbance to 'traditional public policy approaches' and 'traditional organizational analysis' are seen as an opportunity for economists to participate in the development of appropriate responses and strategies for firms and governments 'to use in controlling or responding to the changes in the economy and consumer behaviour' (Picard, 2003: 302–3). In these circumstances the 'need to understand media economics is growing rapidly' (Picard, 2003: 304).

Picard goes on to make a useful distinction between cultural economic and media economic perspectives as they overlap in the area of film production and circulation. He suggests that media economics is more 'content-neutral' and 'less normative on issues of culture and the role of media in cultural development and maintenance' than is cultural economics (2003: 301). Cultural economics' normative orientation may have to do with its close relation to the not-for-profit sector and with arts-based funding and policy regimes. In an era when arts funding, including funding made available for feature filmmaking and for public broadcasters, needs to be justified, economic notions of value, market failure, public and merit goods and cost-benefit and economic impact have been enlisted to argue for continued public support for culture including film (Throsby, 2001). We can see something of this impetus to shore up a case, for instance, with the commissioning of Simon Molloy and Barry Burgan in 1993 to survey *The Economics of Film and Television in Australia*. The resulting analysis helped the sector answer trenchant criticisms by economic commentators of continued support for Australian film

and television production both through film production support mechanisms and content quotas.

Mainstream media economics, by contrast, has tended to take its cue from the study of newspapers, commercial broadcasting and telecommunication systems. This has resulted in the 'study of the way economic and financial pressures affect a variety of communications activities, systems, and organizations and enterprises, including media and telecommunications'. Such financial and economic concerns are not only central to understanding media systems and firms operating within media markets, but are also important to the 'formulation of public policies regarding communications' (Picard, 2003: 301). This last aspect helps explain the role that economists have played in the 'forecast' industry of industry policy-making, stock market broker analysis (Vogel, 1990; 2004), and the debate over the direction of regulatory settings for the media industries including film. The aim here is often 'to theoretically identify optimal choices' for businesses operating in a sector or to explore 'optimal outcomes for policy choices' (Picard, 2003: 302). Picard cites Bruce Owen and Steven Wildman's *Video Economics* (1992) as an important contribution in this vein; while Colin Hoskins et al.'s *Global Television and Film* explicitly provides a 'mainstream microeconomic perspective on a subject area which has long been dominated by academics of other disciplines' (1997: vi).

These disciplinary perspectives on the political economy of film and of the audio-visual media more generally have developed without any significant connection to the media and communication, and film and cultural studies nexus examined earlier. Scholars here do not see themselves as carrying out a political economy of film – instead they may be economists, cultural and economic geographers, urban studies and regional development specialists, and political scientists – drawn to the film and film-related industries for a wide variety of disciplinary purposes.

CONCLUSION

The range of perspectives dealing with what we might call 'political economy' matters are likely to increase further as media markets become more internationalized, as fragmentation increases, and as digitization, broadband and DVD reshapes the cinema, the film industry and audio-visual markets more generally, leading to new forms of production, delivery, consumption and marketing – and the decline of older forms. This suggests that our weaker and stronger versions of the political economy of film are likely to be increasingly inflected by, and interested in, the considerations of film and television generated within economics, politics and policy studies and geography. It also suggests that we shall see the continuing proliferation of forms of analysis which conceptualize the 'film industry' as a component of larger 'industry' agglomerations. This combination of developments suggests that future overviews of the political economy of film will need both to consider perspectives developed across a variety of disciplinary domains and to integrate perspectives in which film exists less and less seen as a discrete domain.

This then is the force field within which a contemporary political economy of cinema is operating. One group uses the perspectives but not all its entailments, preferring a 'messy' approach. Another situates its work explicitly within a critical political economy perspective. A third, diverse, group produces analyses which centrally address the conjunction of culture, politics and economics but from different disciplinary angles. The political economy of film emerges here as fundamentally fragmented. For the Film scholar and Cultural Studies practitioner it is a label to illuminate the interface between industry and policy, market and government, organization and film meaning from Film, Media and Cultural Studies perspectives. For the critical political economists, it is a tradition of scholarship, a scholarly project with its roots in the emergence of economics and Marxism. Finally, for the economist, political scientist

or economic geographer, it is an analysis of the conjunction of politics and economics in the film and television industries, but undertaken from the disciplinary perspectives of each.

This chapter has been concerned with each perspective and their intersections. Each has its value, although none seems satisfactory for all circumstances. Driven by dramatic growth in media industries including filmmaking and even a resurgent cinema, governments are attending to media as 'just another industry' over which the slide-rule of competition policy, industry development, economic analyses and the needs of the new economy may be placed; and a still special area of government given their connections to the state, identity and a reflexive sense that works of culture need to be treated differently, as in the new impetus to preserve and promote cultural diversity internationally in a knowledge society. There is a mix of policy-making here which looks like business as usual in film policy; and another mix which might suggest its significant reshaping. Within each discipline, moreover, our understanding of the film industry and the cinema are being reshaped in light of these changing industry and governmental emphases. This makes the political economy of film a continually fascinating and permanently unfinished business.

NOTES

1 Available at: http://jcomm.uoregon.edu/facstaff/Profile.php?id=316.

2 For a contemporary 'version' of Guback's seminal work, see Geoffrey Nowell-Smith and Steven Ricci (1998).

REFERENCES

Balio, Tino (1987) *United Artists: The Company that Changed the Film Industry*. Madison: University of Wisconsin Press.

Bordwell, David, Staiger, Janet and Thompson, Kristin (1985) *The Classical Hollywood Cinema: Film Style and Mode of Production to 1960*. London: Routledge & Kegan Paul.

Bowser, Eileen (1990) *The Transformation of Cinema: 1907–1915.* Vol. 2. *History of the American Cinema.* New York/Berkeley: Charles Scribner's Sons/University of California Press.

Castells, Manuel (1996) *The Rise of the Network Society.* Malden, MA: Blackwell.

Caves, Richard (2000) *Creative Industries.* Cambridge, MA: Harvard University Press.

Christopherson, Susan (2003) 'The limits to "New Regionalism": (Re)Learning from the media industries', *Geoforum,* 34: 413–15.

Christopherson, Susan (2006) 'Behind the Scenes: How transnational firms are constructing a new international division of labor in media work', *Geoforum,* 37: 739–51.

Coe, Neil M. (2000) 'The view from out West: embeddedness, inter-personal relations and the development of an indigenous film industry in Vancouver', *Geoforum,* 31: 391–407.

Coe, Neil M. and Johns, Jennifer (2004) 'Beyond Production Clusters: Towards a Critical Political Economy of Networks in the Film and Television Industries', in Dominic Power and Allen J. Scott (eds), *Cultural Industries and the Production of Culture.* London: Routledge. pp. 188–204.

Collins, Richard and Murroni, Cristina (1996) *New Media, New Policies: Media and Communications Strategies for the Future.* Cambridge: Polity Press.

Craik, Jennifer (1996) 'The Potential and Limits of Cultural Policy Strategies', *Culture and Policy,* 7(1): 177–204.

Cunningham, Stuart (2002) 'From Cultural to Creative Industries: Theory, Industry, and Policy Implications', *Media International Australia, Incorporating Culture and Policy,* 102: 54–65.

Cunningham, Stuart (2004) 'The creative industries after cultural policy: A genealogy and some possible preferred futures', *International Journal of Cultural Studies,* 7(1): 105–15.

Curtin, Michael (2004) 'Media Capitals: Cultural Geographies of Global TV', in Lynn Spigel and Jan Olsson (eds), *Television after TV: Essays on a Medium in Transition.* Durham, NC: Duke University Press. pp. 270–302.

Department of Communications Information Technology and the Arts and National Office for the Information Economy (DCITA and NOIE) (2002) *Creative Industries Cluster Study, Stage One Report.* Canberra: DCITA.

Department of Culture, Media and Sport (DCMS) (1998) *The Creative Industries Mapping Report.* London: HMSO.

Department of Culture, Media and Sport (DCMS) (2001) *The Creative Industries Mapping Report.* London: HMSO.

Dorland, Michael (1998) *So Close to the State/s: The Emergence of Canadian Feature Film Policy.* Toronto: Toronto University Press.

Downing, John (1996) *Internationalizing Media Theory.* London: Sage.

Dyson, Kenneth (1988) 'Conclusions: Patterns of Regulatory Change in Western Europe', in Kenneth Dyson and Peter Humphreys (eds), *Broadcasting and New Media Policies in Western Europe.* London: Routledge & Kegan Paul. pp. 305–37.

Dyson, Kenneth and Humphreys, Peter (eds) (1990) *The Political Economy of Communication: International and European Dimensions.* London: Routledge.

Elmer, Greg and Gasher, Mike (eds) (2005) *Contracting out Hollywood: Runaway Productions and Foreign Location Shooting.* Lanham, MD: Rowman and Littlefield.

Elsaesser, Thomas (1989) *New German Cinema: A History.* New Brunswick, NJ: Rutgers University Press.

Elsaesser, Thomas (2005) *European Cinema: Face to Face with Hollywood.* Amsterdam: Amsterdam University Press.

Garnham, Nicholas (1990) 'Contribution to a political economy of mass communication', in Fred Englis (ed.), *Capitalism and Communication: Global, Culture and the Economics of Information.* London: Sage. pp. 20–55.

Garnham, Nicholas (2000) *Emancipation, the Media and Modernity: Arguments about the Media and Social Theory.* Oxford: Oxford University Press.

Gasher, Mike (2002) *Hollywood North: The Feature Film Industry in British Columbia.* Vancouver: University of British Columbia Press.

Golding, Peter and Murdock, Graham (eds) (1997) *The Political Economy of the Media.* Cheltenham: Edward Elgar.

Goldsmith, Ben and O'Regan, Tom (2004) 'Locomotives and Stargates: Inner-city Studio Complexes in Sydney, Melbourne and Toronto', *International Journal of Cultural Policy,* 10(1): 29–46.

Goldsmith, Ben and O'Regan, Tom (2005) *The Film Studio: Film Production in the Global Economy.* Lanham, MD: Rowman and Littlefield.

Grantham, Bill (2000) *'Some Big Bourgeois Brothel': Contexts for France's Culture Wars with Hollywood.* Luton: University of Luton Press.

Guback, Thomas (1969) *The International Film Industry: Western Europe and America since 1945.* Bloomington: Indiana University Press.

Guback, Thomas (1985a) 'Hollywood's International Market', in Tino Balio (ed.), *The American Film Industry.* Madison: University of Wisconsin Press. pp. 463–86.

Guback, Thomas (1985b) 'Non-Market Factors in the International Distribution of American Films', in Bruce A. Austin (ed.), *Current Research in Film: Audiences, Economics and Law.* Vol.1. Norwood: Ablex. pp. 111–26.

Hayward, Susan (1993) *French National Cinema.* London: Routledge.

Heffernan, Kevin (2004) *Ghouls, Gimmicks and Gold: Horror Films and the American Movie Business, 1953–1968.* Durham, NC: Duke University Press.

Hesmondhalgh, David (2002) *The Cultural Industries.* London: Sage.

Hoskins, Colin, McFayden, Stuart and Finn, Adam (1997) *Global Television and Film: An Introduction to the Economics of the Business.* Oxford: Clarendon Press.

Hozic, Aida (2001) *Hollyworld: Space, Power, and Fantasy in the American Economy.* Ithaca, NY: Cornell University Press.

Jeffcutt, Paul (2004) 'Knowledge Relationships and Transactions in a Cultural Economy: Analysing the Creative Industries Ecosystem', *Media International Australia, Incorporating Culture and Policy*, 112: 67–82.

Levitt, Theodore (1986) *The Marketing Imagination.* New York: The Free Press.

Marie, Michel (2003) *The French New Wave: An Artistic School.* Tr. Richard Neupert. Oxford: Blackwell Publishing.

Mattelart, Armand (1979) *Multinational Corporations and the Control of Culture: The Ideological Apparatuses of Imperialism.* Tr. Michael Chanan. Sussex: Harvester Press.

Mattelart, Armand, Delcourt, Xavier and Mattelart, Michele (1984) *International Image Markets: in Search of an Alternative Perspective.* Tr. David Buxton. London: Comedia Publishing Group/Marion Boyars.

Miller, Toby, Govil, Nitin, McMurria, John and Maxwell, Richard (2001) *Global Hollywood.* London: BFI.

Miller, Toby, Govil, Nitin, McMurria, John, Maxwell, Richard, and Wang, Ting (2005) *Global Hollywood 2.* London: BFI.

Molloy, Simon and Burgan, Barry (1993) *The Economics of Film and Television in Australia.* Sydney: Australian Film Commission.

Moran, Albert (ed.) (1996) *Film Policy: International, National and Regional Perspectives.* London: Routledge.

Murdock, Graham (1989) 'Cultural Studies at the Crossroads', *Australian Journal of Communication*, 16: 37–49.

Noam, Eli (ed.) (1985) *Video Media Competition: Regulation, Economics and Technology.* New York: Columbia University Press.

Nowell-Smith, Geoffrey and Ricci, Steven (eds) (1998) *Hollywood and Europe: Economics, Culture, National Identity, 1946–95.* London: BFI.

O'Regan, Tom (1996) *Australian National Cinema.* London: Routledge.

Owen, Bruce and Wildman, Steven (1992) *Video Economics.* Boston: Harvard University Press.

Pendakur, Manjuneth (1990) *Canadian Dreams and American Control: The Political Economy of the Canadian Film Industry.* Detroit: Wayne State University Press.

Picard, Robert G. (1989) *Media Economics: Concepts and Issues.* Newbury Park, CA: Sage.

Picard, Robert G. (2003) 'Media Economics', in Ruth Towse (ed.), *A Handbook of Cultural Economics.* Cheltenham: Edward Elgar. pp 301–05.

Pratt, Andy C. (2004) 'Creative Clusters: Towards the Governance of the Creative Industries Production System?', *Media International Australia, Incorporating Culture and Policy*, 112: 50–66.

Schatz, Thomas (1988) *Hollywood Genres: Formulas, Filmmaking, and the Studio System.* New York: Pantheon Books.

Schatz, Thomas (1996) *The Genius of the System: Hollywood Filmmaking in the Studio Era.* New York: Henry Holt.

Schiller, Herbert (1969) *Mass Communication and the American Empire.* Boston: Beacon Press.

Scott, Allen J. (2000) *The Cultural Economy of Cities.* London: Sage.

Scott, Allen J. (2005) *On Hollywood: The Place, The Industry.* Princeton, NJ: Princeton University Press.

Scott, Allen J. and Storper, Michael (2003) 'Regions, Globalization, Development', *Regional Studies*, 37(6–7): 579–93.

Siwek, Stephen E. (2002) *Copyright Industries in the US Economy: The 2002 Report.* Washington: International Intellectual Property Alliance.

Siwek, Stephen and Wildman, Steven (1988) *International Trade in Films and Television Programs.* Cambridge, MA: American Enterprise Institute/Ballinger.

Smiers, Joost (2004) 'A Convention on Cultural Diversity: From WTO to UNESCO', *Media International Australia, Incorporating Culture and Policy*, 111: 81–96.

Sorlin, Pierre (1996) *Italian National Cinema, 1896–1996.* London: Routledge.

Staiger, Janet (ed.) (1995) *The Studio System.* New Brunswick, NJ: Rutgers University Press.

Straw, Will (1993) Review of *Canadian Dreams and American Control: The Political Economy of the Canadian Film Industry* by Manjuneth Pendakur, *Canadian Journal of Communication*, 18(1). Available at: http://www.cjc-online.ca/viewarticle.php? id=159 & layout=html.

Thompson, Kristin (1985) *Exporting Entertainment: America in the World Film Market, 1907–1934.* London: BFI.

Thompson, Kristin (1992) Review of *Canadian Dreams and American Control* by Manjuneth Pendakur, *Journal of Communication*, 42(1): 152.

Throsby, David (2001) *Economics and Culture.* Cambridge: Cambridge University Press.

Tinic, Serra (2005) *On Location: Canada's Television Industry in a Global Market.* Toronto: University of Toronto Press.

Venturelli, Shalini (1998) *Liberalizing the European Media: Politics, Regulation and the Public Sphere.* Oxford: Clarendon Press.

Vogel, Harold (1990) *Entertainment Industry Economics: A Guide for Financial Analysis.* 2nd edn. New York: Cambridge University Press.

Vogel, Harold (2004) *Entertainment Industry Economics: A Guide for Financial Analysis.* 6th edn. New York: Cambridge University Press.

Wasko, Janet (1982) *Movies and Money: Financing the American Film Industry.* Norwood, NJ: Ablex.

Wasko, Janet (1994) *Hollywood in the Information Age: Beyond the Silver Screen.* Cambridge: Polity Press.

Wasko, Janet (1999) 'The Political Economy of Film', in Toby Miller and Robert Stam (eds), *A Companion to Film Theory.* Oxford: Blackwell. pp. 221–33.

Wasko, Janet (2001) *Understanding Disney: The Manufacture of Fantasy.* Cambridge: Polity.

Wasko, Janet (2003) *How Hollywood Works.* London: Sage.

Wyatt, Justin (1994) *High Concept: Movies and Marketing in Hollywood.* Austin: University of Texas Press.

17

TV's Next Season?

Lynn Spigel

For those of us who attended the Second International Television Studies Conference (ITSC) in London in 1986, the 2005 Society for Cinema and Media Studies (SCMS) conference (held in the same building at the University of London, Institute of Education) evoked an eerie wave of déjà vu. Talking with friends I met at the ITSC, I recalled how formative that gathering was for TV and cultural studies. The sense of TV ghosts lurking at the 2005 SCMS conference was palpable. Although I admit to some personal nostalgia for that 'Golden Age' of TV studies, I think the earlier moment of television scholarship did its work, and now there are different things to do.

In one respect, television scholarship is changing because TV itself is so different from what it was in the past. The demise of the US three-network system, the increasing commercialization of public-service/state-run systems, the rise of multi-channel cable and global satellite delivery, multinational conglomerates, Internet convergence, changes in regulatory policies and ownership rules, the advent of high-definition TV, technological changes in screen design,

digital video recorders, and new forms of media competition – as well as new forms of programming (for example, reality TV) and scheduling practices (year-long seasons or multiplexing, for instance) – have all transformed the practice we call watching TV. This does not mean all of television is suddenly unrecognizable – indeed, familiarity and habit continue to be central to the TV experience – but it does mean that television's past is recognizably distinct from its present.

In the wake of these changes, much of the literature in television studies now seems out of sync with the object it aims to describe. When teaching the seminal books and essays of television studies, I often notice that my students object to aesthetic/cultural theories that were developed to explain terrestrial broadcast systems and pre-VCR TV sets. Although classic texts such as Raymond William's *Television: Technology and Cultural Form* (1975) still have great explanatory value, today's television systems demand new inquiries and theories.

To be sure, television studies in the humanities has always been a hybrid, inter-disciplinary venture, drawing on fields of inquiry that were often at odds with one another. As it developed in the 1970s and 1980s in the Anglophone university and publishing industry, television studies drew upon at least five critical paradigms: (1) the 'mass society' critique associated with the Frankfurt School and post-war intellectuals such as Dwight MacDonald; (2) a textual tradition (to borrow John Hartley's term [1999: Ch. 6]) associated with literary and film theory and, by the late 1970s, with feminist theories of spectatorship; (3) a journalistic tradition associated especially with theatre criticism (in the United States, this tradition formed a canon of Golden Age programming); (4) quantitative and qualitative mass communications research on audiences and content; and (5) cultural studies approaches to media and their audiences. Although these traditions developed differently in different national contexts, they all formed a discursive field – a set of interrelated ways of speaking about TV – that continues to affect the way we frame television as an object of study.

Television studies in the humanities in the 1970s through the 1990s accompanied the rise of cultural studies and the general move away from thinking about TV through top-down models of effects to thinking of television as culture. What followed were a flurry of essays, books, and anthologies that dealt with subjects ranging from institutional history to television aesthetics to genre to spectator theory to audiences and fans. People still study these subjects, and there is still important work to do in these areas. Nevertheless, the field is shifting.

So where is TV studies headed? Honestly, I am not sure, and I do not know if I am going with it. The field – like the object itself – is in a moment of uncertainty. Nonetheless, some trends or shifts seem identifiable.

Insofar as television has always been studied under several disciplinary protocols, it is not surprising that TV is now studied under umbrella terms like new media studies and visual culture studies (which – to make matters more messy – are sometimes both the same field). What is to be gained from studying TV under the rubric of new media? On the one hand, it is true that media forms are merging, and to study them in isolation often overlooks not only the technological/industrial convergences, but also the cultural convergences that take place among film, television, literature, music, and fine arts. On the other hand, insofar as TV has always been denigrated in universities, and at best existed as a poor relation to film, it is not entirely clear that television will fare better if television and new media are linked.

Often, it seems, the term 'new media' works to reinvest television in yet another set of cultural hierarchies because the term suggests something avant-garde, high-tech, revolutionary, utopian, and fundamentally 'other' than ordinary TV. Today's universities tend to value anything called new media (or sometimes just media) as a somehow more high-end field of culture, and thus worthy of study. Moreover, the political/moral debates about the Internet, the military applications of new media, and our culture's general love affair with new technologies make government grants more available and the pursuit of new media more lucrative and prestigious for universities. Despite the fact that the new media are technologies of mass distribution, studying anything that comes over the Internet (including TV shows) has somehow become more legitimate than studying television itself.

That said, there are, of course, important reasons to study new media (and sometimes to study television within this rubric). Scholars have shown how Internet culture rearticulates (and at times replicates) gender, sexual, class, and racial struggles; how it provides alternative modes of 'gathering' as communities and political bodies; and how it reconstructs the politics of national borders and our sense of place (Berry et al., 2003; Couldry, 2003; Gomez-Pena, 2001; Hill, 2001; Jones, 1997; Kolko et al., 2000; Nakamura, 2002; Shohat, 1999; Sundaram, 2000; Wakeford, 1997). Insofar as television studies has been centrally concerned with similar issues, and insofar as television now converges with digital platforms, it seems only right that people who study television would also study the Internet and other digital devices.[1]

Visual culture studies serves more broadly to organize media studies across traditionally separate disciplines or topics and thus to create new dialogues among them. Recently, art historians have explored the intersections between psychedelic art, Andy Warhol, McLuhanism, the Yippies, and TV/video in the 1960s (Joselit, 2002; Joseph, 2002), while television historians have looked at the relation of television to post-war art and theatre movements (Caughie, 2000; Spigel, 1996; 2004b).[2] However, apart from these specific histories, work in visual culture studies has tended to gravitate towards the study of either very old technologies (nineteenth-century photography or visual toys up through early cinema) or new digital media. When television is studied at all, it is usually in relation to video art and/or digital media, or as a technological apparatus (rather than as a medium consisting of individual programs) (see Fullerton and Olsson, 2005; Mirzoeff, 2002; Rabinovitz and Geil, 2004).

Within visual cultural studies, W.J.T. Mitchell has called for a new kind of 'medium theory' that attempts to theorize media in Marshall McLuhan's wake (although Mitchell claims that his project differs from a general theory of media by eschewing universalizing claims). Along these lines, Mitchell calls for 'hybrid disciplinary formations such as visual culture and iconology to address the widely reported phenomenon of a pictorial turn in culture' and speaks to 'a media revolution that exceeds the categories of cinema, television, and the mass media' (2003: 4). It is too early to evaluate this project, but it is clear (at least from the talks I have heard) that Mitchell's 'medium theory' is still pretty general, lacking the thick description, context, historicity, and situatedness that have propelled much of the most significant media scholarship. Indeed, one of the great achievements of film and television research over the past thirty years has been the move away from 'grand'- or even 'medium'-scale abstractions

(which is not the same as a move away from theory) toward questions about how film and television intersect with the textures and rhythms of everyday life (the early feminist work that situated the media in relation to women's time and space is seminal in this respect).

There is a similar 'waning of the TV object' in *Echographies of Television* (2002), Bernard Stiegler's book-length dialogue with Jacques Derrida, which is ultimately only occasionally about TV and instead a more general dialogue on theoretical issues pertaining to recording technologies, from photography to digital media, and their implications for democracy, citizenship, history, and the state. The discussion is staged and performed televisually (Derrida and Stiegler talk to each other in Derrida's home while being recorded on camera). Although the discussion is often interesting, it lacks any engagement with work in film or television studies – in fact, ironically, the dialogue 'records' this absence.

It is, of course, easy to see all these absences as affronts on 'our' TV studies. Given that TV scholars were never exactly welcomed in traditional academic departments (or for that matter in the old Society for Cinema Studies), it is easy to feel annoyed, as I am. I wish people who talk about TV would take TV more seriously, actually watch it, and read the scholarship about it.

But my point here isn't simply to indulge a melodramatic tale of exclusions and humiliations. Rather, it is important to note that the new interest in media across the disciplines is not exactly a cross-disciplinary romance where doors fly open and graduate students with TV dissertations land jobs in art history or comparative literature departments. Despite calls for interdisciplinary mergers, disciplinary boundaries still exist and the familiar canons, mentor networks, and specialized dialogues still reassert themselves. Insofar as I am currently working on projects that merge television with interests in architecture and the visual arts, I am all too aware of my own lack of knowledge in these fields. The goal, I hope, is not to master all disciplines but to be willing to ask questions from another point of view.

Meanwhile, although it is increasingly interdisciplinary in nature, a more site-specific project called television studies has been made visible through book series (such as those published by Duke, Wayne State, and Oxford University Press), journals such as *TV and New Media*, new online forums such as *Flow*, and conferences (SCMS and Consoleing Passions). Some of the most interesting work presented in these forums is still formed out of a cultural materialist project.

TV scholarship spans a diverse set of subjects. Since the 1990s, critical geography, national and globalization studies, and ethnographic methods have informed what is now a growing body of TV/media scholarship on nationhood, mobility, global flows, satellites, and diaspora (Naficy, 1993; Gillespie, 1995; Morley and Robins, 1995; Mankekar, 1999; Morley, 2000; Aksoy and Robins, 2000; Yoshimi, 2003; Curtin, 2003; Abu-Lughod, 2004; Parks, 2005; Kumar, 2005; Hadj-Moussa, 2008; Ermi and Chua, 2005). Scholars are also writing in new ways about television, education, citizenship, and cultural policy (Banet-Weiser, 2004a, 2004b; Classen, 2004; Hartley, 1999; Miller, 1998; Noriega, 2000; Ouellette, 2002; Streeter, 1996). In increasingly interdisciplinary ways, scholars continue to consider television – as well as computers, cell phones, and other everyday media – in relation to the social place, use, and meanings of media in domestic and public contexts (Couldry and McCarthy, 2004; Fyfe and Bannister, 1998; Klinger, 2006; Lally, 2002; McCarthy, 2001; Morley, 2000; Turow and Kavanaugh, 2003). Recent industry studies offer new insights into contemporary TV/media production practices (Caldwell, 2008; Ellis, 2000; Hartley, 2005; Zook, 1999), and there is a continuing and large body of work on gender, feminism, postfeminism, girls, and/or sexual difference/queer theory (Abu-Lughod, 2004; Acosta-Alzuru, 2003; Akass and McGabe, 2004; Arthurs, 2003; Banet-Weiser, 2004a

and 2004b; Brunsdon, 2000; Dow, 2001; Haralovich and Rabinovitz, 1999; Hollows, 2003; Jermyn, 2003; Lentz, 2000; Mankekar, 1999; Salo, 2003; Smith-Shomade, 2002; Thomas, 2002).

There is also a sustained interest in fans and audiences (Coleman, 2002; Hills, 2002) and a welcome reinvestment in underexplored issues of television genre, narrative, aesthetics, and program forms/schedules (Andrejevic, 2004; Brunsdon, 2003; Friedman, 2002; Geraghty, 2003; Lury, 2001; Mittell, 2004; Murray and Ouellette, 2004; Sconce, 2004; White, 2004). So too, television historians are rethinking the 'discursive series' into which television might be placed so that TV history may be explored in relation to historical events and cultural practices that previously seemed separate or distinct.[3] Finally, there is a good deal of speculation about the future (or end) of television and television scholarship – both in casual conversation and in the literature (see Corner, 1999; Ellis, 2000).[4]

Paradoxically, the recent interest in the future of television also has a history. Looking back on the history of TV scholarship, we see that television has seemed perpetually on the verge of transformation. In 1986, when Phillip Drummond and Richard Paterson published papers from the First International Television Studies Conference (held in 1984), they titled their book *Television in Transition* (1986). A final chapter on 'the future' (exploring topics ranging from educational TV and UHF to video to convergence) is somewhat of a convention of the TV book. This 'future chapter' runs through such classic texts as Erik Barnouw's *Tube of Plenty* (1975), Raymond Williams' *Television: Technology and Cultural Form* (1974), and John Ellis' *Visible Fictions* (1982). It is also found in less well-known studies on television written over the past fifty years.

Indeed, even as television promises to deliver a 'live', instantaneous sense of the present, the future – as a mental construct – has been consistently necessary to the secondary (critical) elaboration of the socio-political import and meaning of television in culture.

In this respect, the *Cinema Journal* forum in which this chapter first appeared was a symptom of the television scholar's endless projection of her/himself into the speculative realm of what media will be. Meanwhile, television's 'present' (its sheer density and dissonance of material) is harder to see, even when – or perhaps because – you can now record it, edit it, and maybe even watch it later on your PC.

NOTES

1 Issues of media convergence are taken up, for example, in *New Media: Theories and Practices of Digitextuality* (Everett and Caldwell, 2003); *New Media and Popular Imagination: Launching Radio, Television, and Digital Media in the United States* (Boddy, 2004); and *Television after TV: Essays on a Medium in Transition* (Spigel and Olsson, 2004).

2 Museum exhibits have also considered TV in relation to the fine arts. 'The New Frontier: Art and Television, 1960–65', curated by John Alan Farmer and mounted in 2000 at the Austin Museum of Art, showed works by artists who used television as a subject, medium, or found object/inspiration, and the show (as well as the exhibition catalogue) more generally considered the intersections between popular and fine arts.

3 John Caughie's *Television Drama* (2000) explores television within a larger history of post-war British theatre movements; Steven Classen's *Watching Jim Crow* (2004) studies television within the oral history of the black leaders and citizens engaged in the famous legal battle against TV station WLBT (in Jackson, Mississippi) during the civil rights era; Jeffrey Sconce's *Haunted Media: Electronic Presence from Telegraphy to Television* (2000) studies television in relation to the history of spiritualism and telepresence; Chon Noriega's *Shot in America* (2000) studies television within a larger history of Latino independent filmmaking and PBS; Jeffrey S. Miller's *Something Completely Different: British Television and American Culture* (2000) studies the history of convergences between British and US television; and Aniko Bodroghkozy (following Todd Gitlin's work on news) in *Groove Tube: Sixties Television and the Youth Rebellion* (2001) studies entertainment television in the context of 1960s radical youth movements.

4 Paddy Scannell and Elihu Katz are currently preparing a conference/project on the idea that television has come to an end. We shall see. The title of my own recent co-edited collection, *Television after TV*, suggests something less final, as does my introduction to that collection, which elaborates in more detail on some of the issues I have raised here (Spigel, 2004a).

REFERENCES

Abu-Lughod, Lila (2004) *Dramas of Nationhood: The Politics of Television in Egypt*. Chicago: University of Chicago Press.

Acosta-Alzuru, Carolina (2003) "'I'm Not a Feminist... I Only Defend Women as Human Beings": The Production, Representation, and Consumption of Feminism in a Telenovela', *Critical Studies in Media Communication*, 20(3): 269–94.

Akass, Kim and McGabe, Janet (2004) *Reading 'Sex and the City'*. London: I.B. Tauris.

Aksoy, Asu and Robins, Kevin (2000) 'Thinking across Spaces: Transnational Television from Turkey', *European Journal of Cultural Studies*, 3: 343–65.

Andrejevic, Mark (2004) *Reality TV: The Work of Being Watched*. New York: Rowman and Littlefield.

Arthurs, Jane (2003) '*Sex and the City* and Consumer Culture: Remediating Postfeminist Drama', *Feminist Media Studies*, 3(1): 83–98.

Banet-Weiser, Sarah (2004a) 'Girls Rule! Gender, Feminism, and Nickelodeon', *Critical Studies in Media Communication*, 21(2): 119–39.

Banet-Weiser, Sarah (2004b) 'We Pledge Allegiance to Kids: Nickelodeon and Citizenship', in Heather Hendershot (ed.), *Nickelodeon Nation: The History, Politics, and Economics of America's Only TV Channel for Kids*. New York: New York University Press. pp. 209–37.

Barnouw, Erik (1975) *Tube of Plenty: The Evolution of American Television*. New York: Oxford University Press.

Berry, Chris, Martin, Fran and Yue, Audrey (2003) *Mobile Cultures: New Media in Queer Asia*. Durham, NC: Duke University Press.

Boddy, William (2004) *New Media and Popular Imagination: Launching Radio, Television, and Digital Media in the United States*. London: Oxford University Press.

Bodroghkozy, Aniko (2001) *Groove Tube: Sixties Television and the Youth Rebellion*. Durham, NC: Duke University Press.

Brunsdon, Charlotte (2000) *The Feminist, the Housewife, and the Soap Opera*. Oxford: Oxford University Press.

Brunsdon, Charlotte (2003) 'Lifestyling Britain', *International Journal of Cultural Studies*, 6(1): 5–23.

Caldwell, John T. (2008) *Production Cultures: Industrial Reflexivity and Critical Practice in Film/Television*. Durham, NC: Duke University Press.

Caughie, John (2000) *Television Drama: Realism, Modernism, and British Culture*. Oxford: Oxford University Press.

Classen, Steven (2004) *Watching Jim Crow*. Durham, NC: Duke University Press.

Coleman, Robin R. (ed.) (2002) *Say It Loud! African American Audiences, Media, and Identity*. New York: Routledge.

Corner, John (1999) 'Television 2000', in *Critical Ideas in Television Studies*. London: Oxford University Press. pp. 120–28.

Couldry, Nick (2003) *Contesting Media Power: Alternative Media in a Networked World*. New York: Rowman and Littlefield.

Couldry, Nick and McCarthy, Anna (eds) (2004) *Mediaspace: Place, Scale, and Culture in a Media Age*. London: Routledge.

Curtin, Michael (2003) 'Media Capitals: Towards the Study of Spatial Flows', *International Journal of Cultural Studies*, 6: 202–8.

Derrida, Jacques and Stiegler, Bernard (2002) *Echographies of Television*. Tr. Jennifer Bajorek. Cambridge: Polity Press.

Dow, Bonnie (2001) 'Ellen, Television, and the Politics of Gay and Lesbian Visibility', *Critical Studies in Media Communication*, 18(2): 123–40.

Drummond, Phillip and Richard Paterson (eds) (1986) *Television in Transition: Papers from the First International Television Studies Conference*. London: BFI.

Ellis, John (1982) *Visible Fictions: Cinema, Television, Video*. London: Routledge & Kegan Paul.

Ellis, John (2000) *Seeing Things: Television in the Age of Uncertainty*. London: I.B. Tauris.

Erni, John Nguyet and Chua, Siew Keng (eds) (2005) *Asian Media Studies*. London: Blackwell.

Everett, Anna and Caldwell, John T. (eds) (2003) *New Media: Theories and Practices of Digitextuality*. New York: Routledge.

Friedman, James (ed.) (2002) *Reality Squared: Televisual Discourse on the Real*. New Brunswick, NJ: Rutgers University Press.

Fullerton, John and Olsson, Jan (eds) (2005) *Allegories of Communication: Intermedial Concerns from Cinema to the Digital*. London: John Libbey.

Fyfe, Nicholas R. and Bannister, Jon (1998) 'The "Eyes upon the Street": Closed Circuit Television Surveillance and the City', in Nicholas R. Fyfe (ed.), *Images of the Street: Planning, Identity, and Control in Public Space*. London: Routledge. pp. 254–67.

Geraghty, Christine (2003) 'Aesthetics and Quality in Popular Television Drama', *International Journal of Cultural Studies*, 6: 25–45.

Gillespie, Marie (1995) *Television, Ethnicity, and Cultural Change*. London: Routledge.

Gomez-Pena, Guillermo (2001) 'The Virtual Barrio @ the Other Frontier: (or the Chicano Interneta)', in Alondra Nelson and Thuy Linh N. Tu (eds), *Technicolor: Race, Technology, and Everyday Life*. New York: New York University Press. pp. 191–98.

Hadj-Moussa, Ratiba (2008) 'The Slippery Road: The Maghreb and the New Media', in Chris Berry, Soyoung Kim and Lynn Spigel (eds), *Electronic Elsewheres: Media and Social Space*. Minneapolis: University of Minnesota Press.

Haralovich, Marybeth and Rabinovitz, Lauren (eds) (1999) *Television, History, and American Culture: Feminist Critical Essays*. Durham, NC: Duke University Press.

Hartley, John (1999) *Uses of Television*. London: Routledge.

Hartley, John (ed.) (2005) *Creative Industries*. London: Blackwell.

Hill, Logan (2001) 'Beyond Access: Race, Technology, Community', in Alondra Nelson and Thuy Linh N. Tu (eds), *Technicolor: Race, Technology, and Everyday Life*. New York: New York University Press. pp. 13–33.

Hills, Matt (2002) *Fan Cultures*. London: Routledge.

Hollows, Joanne (2003) 'Feeling Like a Domestic Goddess: Postfeminism and Cooking', *European Journal of Cultural Studies*, 6(2): 179–202.

Jermyn, Deborah (2003) 'Women with a Mission', *International Journal of Cultural Studies*, 6(1): 46–63.

Jones, Steven G. (ed.) (1997) *Virtual Culture: Identity and Communication in Cybersociety*. London: Sage.

Joselit, David (2002) 'Yippie Pop: Abbie Hofman, Andy Warhol, and Sixties Media Politics', *Grey Room*, 8: 62–79.

Joseph, Branden W. (2002) '"My Mind Split Open": Andy Warhol's Exploding Plastic Inevitable', *Grey Room*, 8: 80–107.

Klinger, Barbara (2006) *Beyond the Multiplex: Cinema, New Technologies, and the Home*. Berkeley: University of California Press.

Kolko, Beth E., Nakamura, Lisa and Rodman, Gilbert B. (eds) (2000) *Race and Cyberspace*. New York: Routledge.

Kumar, Shanti (2005) *Gandhi Meets Primetime: Globalization and Nationalism in Indian Television*. Urbana: University of Illinois Press.

Lally, Elaine (2002) *At Home with Computers*. Oxford: Berg.

Lentz, Kirsten Marthe (2000) 'Quality versus Relevance: Feminism, Race, and the Politics of the Sign in 1970s Television', *Camera Obscura*, 43: 45–93.

Lury, Karen (2001) *British Youth Television: Cynicism and Enchantment*. London: Oxford University Press.

Mankekar, Purnima (1999) *Screening Culture, Viewing Politics: An Ethnography of Television, Womanhood, and Nation in Postcolonial India*. Durham, NC: Duke University Press.

McCarthy, Anna (2001) *Ambient Television*. Durham, NC: Duke University Press.

Miller, Jeffrey S. (2000) *Something Completely Different: British Television and American Culture*. Minneapolis: University of Minnesota Press.

Miller, Toby (1998) *Technologies of Truth: Cultural Citizenship and the Popular Media*. Minneapolis: University of Minnesota Press.

Mirzoeff, Nicholas (ed.) (2002) *The Visual Culture Reader*. 2nd edn. New York: Routledge.

Mitchell, W.J.T. (2003) 'Medium Theory', *Critical Inquiry*, 30(2): 4. Available at: http://www.uchicago.edu/research/jnl-crit-inq.

Mittell, Jason (2004) *Genre and Television: From Cop Shows to Cartoons in American Culture*. New York: Routledge.

Morley, David (2000) *Home Territories: Media, Mobility, and Identity*. London: Routledge.

Morley, David and Robins, Kevin (1995) *Spaces of Identity: Global Media, Electronic Landscapes, and Global Boundaries*. London: Routledge.

Murray, Susan and Ouellette, Laurie (eds) (2004) *Reality TV: Remaking Television Culture*. New York: New York University Press.

Naficy, Hamid (1993) *The Making of Exile Cultures: Iranian Television in Los Angeles*. Minneapolis: University of Minnesota Press.

Nakamura, Lisa (2002) *Cybertypes: Race, Ethnicity, and Identity on the Internet*. London: Routledge.

Noriega, Chon A. (2000) *Shot in America: Television, the State, and the Rise of Chicano Cinema*. Minneapolis: University of Minnesota Press.

Ouellette, Laurie (2002) *Viewers Like You? How Public TV Failed the People*. New York: Columbia University Press.

Parks, Lisa (2005) *Cultures in Orbit*. Durham, NC: Duke University Press.

Rabinovitz, Lauren and Geil, Abraham (eds) (2004) *Memory Bytes: History, Technology, and Digital Culture*. Durham, NC: Duke University Press.

Salo, Elaine (2003) 'Negotiating Gender and Personhood in the New South Africa: Adolescent Women and Gangsters in Manenberg Township on the Cape Flats', *European Journal of Cultural Studies*, 6: 345–65.

Sconce, Jeffrey (2000) *Haunted Media: Electronic Presence from Telegraphy to Television*. Durham, NC: Duke University Press.

Sconce, Jeffrey (2004) 'What If? Charting Television's New Textual Boundaries', in Lynn Spigel and Jan Olsson (eds), *Television after TV: Essays on a Medium in Transition*. Durham, NC: Duke University Press. pp. 93–112.

Shohat, Ella (1999) 'By the Bitstream of Babylon: Cyberfrontiers and Diasporic Vistas', in Hamid Naficy (ed.), *Home, Exile, Homeland: Film, Media, and the Politics of Place*. New York: Routledge. pp. 213–32.

Smith-Shomade, Beretta E. (2002) *Shaded Lives: African American Women and Television*. New Brunswick, NJ: Rutgers University Press.

Spigel, Lynn (1996) 'High Culture in Low Places: Television and Modern Art, 1950-1970', in Cary Nelson and Dilip Gaonkar (eds), *Disciplinarity and Dissent in Cultural Studies*. New York: Routledge. pp. 313–45.

Spigel, Lynn (2004a) 'Introduction', in Lynn Spigel and Jan Olsson (eds), *Television after TV: Essays on a Medium in Transition*. Durham, NC: Duke University Press. pp. 1–34.

Spigel, Lynn (2004b) 'Television, the Housewife, and the Museum of Modern Art', in Lynn Spigel and Jan Olsson (eds), *Television after TV: Essays on a Medium in Transition*. Durham, NC: Duke University Press. pp. 349–85.

Spigel, Lynn and Olsson, Jan (eds) (2004) *Television after TV: Essays on a Medium in Transition*. Durham, NC: Duke University Press.

Streeter, Thomas (1996) *Selling the Air: A Critique of the Policy of Commercial Broadcasting in the United States*. Chicago: University of Chicago Press.

Sundaram, Ravi (2000) 'Beyond the Nationalist Panopticon: The Experience of Cyberpublics in India', in John T. Caldwell (ed.), *Electronic Media and Technoculture*. New Brunswick, NJ: Rutgers University Press. pp. 270–94.

Thomas, Lyn (2002) *Fans, Feminisms, and 'Quality' Media*. London: Routledge.

Turow, Joseph and Kavanaugh, Andrea L. (2003) *The Wired Homestead: An MIT Sourcebook on the Internet and the Family*. Cambridge, MA: MIT Press.

Wakeford, Nina (1997) 'Networking Women and Grrrls with Information/Communication Technology: Surfing Tales of the World Wide Web', in Jennifer Terry and Melodie Calvert (eds), *Processed Lives: Gender and Technology in Everyday Life*. London: Routledge. pp. 51–66.

White, Mimi (2004) 'The Attractions of Television: Reconsidering Liveness', in Nick Couldry and Anna McCarthy (eds), *Mediaspace: Place, Scale, and Culture in a Media Age*. London: Routledge. pp. 75–91.

Williams, Raymond (1975) *Television: Technology, and Cultural Form*. New York: Schocken Books.

Yoshimi, Shunya (2003) 'Television and Nationalism: Historical Change in the National Domestic TV Formation of Postwar Japan', *European Journal of Cultural Studies*, 6: 459–87.

Zook, Kristal Brent (1999) *Color by Fox: The Fox Network and the Revolution in Black Television*. New York: Oxford University Press.

18

Film and Cultural Studies

Graeme Turner

Writing about 'Film Studies' as if it were a singular object requires a level of invention at the best of times; the disciplinary transnationalism it implies bears very little inspection before it falls apart. In relation to my topic here, this is especially the case. The relationships between Film Studies and cultural studies have varied significantly from one national location to another over the last several decades. Even if we only address the Anglo-American tradition, which is after all where the influences are most direct and significant, important differences come to light.

It is in the US where Film Studies has had the strongest institutional presence, although in many cases it has been located in schools or departments of literary studies. From the 1960s onwards, Film Studies in the US developed its own identity as a discipline, proving a little resistant to influences from outside; from mass communications studies and the social sciences early on, and from cultural and media studies later. Literary studies, with its increasingly sophisticated mode of textual analysis and canon formation, proved a congenial disciplinary ally for American Film Studies; certainly, it was the most prominent

of very few disciplines given their due within the field over the years. Cultural studies, of course, developed much later in the US than in the UK, and its early proponents in America were not particularly interested in film: instead, you would have to say, television and popular music were the preferred sites of examination. All of this has changed over time – particularly over the last decade – and, while American Film Studies has largely maintained its focus upon film texts and the processes through which we understand and interpret them, it has certainly begun to conceptualize these texts and processes within a wider context – social and cultural as well as canonical. The relatively recent renaming of the Society for Cinema Studies in the US (becoming the Society for Cinema and Media Studies) is a significant step, marking the formal resolution of a very long debate. However, the length of that debate, and the determination it reflects among some sections of the association to resist the inclusion of popular media such as television within their disciplinary field, indicates how doggedly American Film Studies has protected an exclusivist disciplinary identity. Nonetheless, as we will see, there are significant areas of research and theory within American Film Studies, that have prospered in recent years, which reveal the influence of work from within cultural, media, and communications studies and which move us away from a text-centred aesthetic model of contemporary Film Studies.

In the UK it was quite different. Film Studies took longer to establish itself in the university system and, when it did gain a foothold there, film theory and cultural theory developed more or less in tandem. During the 1970s and 1980s, proponents of both traditions participated enthusiastically in many of the same debates – albeit often from competing points of view. In the late 1970s, for instance, the Birmingham Centre for Contemporary Cultural Studies devoted a whole research project to debating and refining the textual approaches identified with the editorial position articulated in the pages of the journal, *Screen* (for example see Hall, 1980; Morley, 1980). The popular success and broadly cross-disciplinary application of an early outcome of such debates, John Berger's *Ways of Seeing* (1972), indicates something of the contemporary consensus around the problems to be addressed – and the methodologies available – within cultural, representational, and film theory at that time. Unlike its American counterpart, British Film Studies did not exclude the consideration of television, although it had its own way of dealing with it. As was the case with their interest in the feature film, British Film Studies maintained an aesthetic and political agenda which privileged those television texts seen to be challenging, avant-garde or politically 'progressive'. While not discounting them, British Film Studies was never as focused on generic or canonical questions as its counterpart in the US. Much of the debate during the 1970s and early 1980s was about the politics of specific film texts, but from this distance it is clear that the overarching interest at the time was inherently theoretical – participating in the elaboration of a grand theory which might explain the workings of the medium as a signifying practice and as ideology.

The cross-disciplinary take-up of recently translated French theorists such as Roland Barthes (1975) and Louis Althusser (1971) helped to construct the debates which connected Film Studies to related theoretical developments in literary, cultural and media studies.

It would be some years, however, before British Film Studies took a serious interest in actual film audiences, in the cinema as a form of mass entertainment (rather than as a reproducer of ideologies), or in researching the historical contexts within which popular cinema was actually produced and consumed. The mainstream developments in British cultural studies during the 1980s – the shift from the text to the audience, and the increasingly contextualized accounts of cultural production – did not immediately filter through into work being done in film. During the 1990s, however, a number of important books which worked comfortably across both theoretical traditions began to appear – Yvonne Tasker's *Spectacular Bodies* (1993), for instance. These could not be confidently pigeonholed as definitively either film or cultural studies and indeed were warmly welcomed by readers from both traditions.

Of course, there were many other formations of the Film Studies-cultural studies relationship in other national locations. In Australia, Film Studies began in a particularly close partnership with interdisciplinary developments in communications, media and cultural studies. The grounds for exchange were there from the beginning and many would argue that the broadly contextualized version of Film Studies which grew up around the revival of the Australian film industry led the way into cultural theory – rather than the other way around (Turner, 1993). Given such different histories, then, it would be unrealistic to expect the following account of the relationship between Film Studies and cultural studies to compel assent from everyone, no matter where they were located. In some cases, as well, there is a danger of considerable overlap in the account of the influence from cultural studies and that from, say, television studies, which is dealt with elsewhere in this book.

This account will speak primarily to the Anglo-American traditions which have dominated theoretical debate and peda-gogic practice in the Western take-up of Film Studies. Inevitably, it will present a generalized account of these traditions that will to some extent elide national and theoretical differences in order to make the argument in the space available. The reader of what follows might also require a little tolerance for the precise arrangement of the definitional boundaries chosen to configure the structure of the trade between these two intellectual fields. Whereas it might be true that Film Studies has been historically quite intent on maintaining its disciplinary boundaries, cultural studies and some of its cognate fields – media studies, television studies, communications studies – have not necessarily been that way inclined. These more intrinsically interdisciplinary fields have often regarded a disciplinary boundary merely as a challenge to be overcome – certainly, if it is a boundary demarcating territory as belonging to someone else. Cultural studies is renowned for performing methodological smash-and-grab raids on its more traditional colleagues.

Nonetheless, this account of the rela-tionship between film and cultural studies highlights what I suggest are genuinely significant developments in Film Studies over the last two decades – and developments which cultural studies has helped to generate. I would also suggest that it is precisely these changes which are most fundamentally impor-tant now as Film Studies must position itself to deal with the dramatic expansion of screen cultures across many media and entertainment formats and systems of delivery.

DOES FILM STUDIES NEED CULTURAL STUDIES?

Let us ask this question: why might Film Studies *need* cultural studies? My short answer to this is that cultural studies has proved valuable in helping Film Studies deal with the understanding of film as a social practice. I want to flesh out some of the arguments behind that answer in this section.

The dominant focus for the broad field of Film Studies for most of its history, and in most of its locations, has been upon the privileged film text. A canon of texts was developed through which film history was discussed, and through which arguments were elaborated about the nature of the film experience for the ideal spectator. Until relatively recently, that is probably until the late 1980s, there was little interest within Film Studies in interrogating the film experience of the *actual* audience sitting in an actual cinema. The film texts selected were analyzed as artistic expression rather than as popular entertainments. Popular cinema did figure at times, but largely through the lens of an enquiry into the workings of genre or of the director as auteur. Both of these categories enabled the retrieval of certain popular film forms and many mainstream cinema texts; however, that retrieval did not easily extend to a consideration of what it was that made these films specifically *popular* entertainments.

It is not hard to see why that might look like a disciplinary formation in need of cultural studies. In its early days in the UK, cultural studies cut its teeth on defining the popular, on rescuing mass cultural forms from elitist disregard in order to understand the meaningfulness of the practices of everyday life. Over the 1980s, in particular, cultural studies had been especially interested in television, and had found ways of deal-ing with the television text that explicitly set aside the consideration of its aesthetic dimensions. Cultural studies had also engaged in vigorous debates with scholars in Film Studies about the processes through which all kinds of texts were both produced and understood. Cultural studies' characteristic move at that time was to contextualize both sets of processes, implying a high degree of determination behind both the composition and the reading of the text. Film Studies had a similarly deterministic view of the operation of texts, seeing them as able to position the reader in ways that appeared, at certain points in the debate, virtually irresistible. However, as cultural studies, over time, shifted its interests from the text to the audience, and as it modified its assumptions about the agency of that audience over the determinations of the text, cultural studies and screen theory started to move apart.

I would locate this moment in the early 1990s, and I would suggest that as the two fields begin to define their differences, interestingly, cultural studies' usefulness to Film Studies increased. The fact that the two fields had fallen out of step with each other seemed to enable a clearer focus on the value of the differences that were revealed. This, in turn, seems to have highlighted the value of the more contextual or 'cultural' approaches to film. As I said earlier, one needs to be cautious about generalizing comments here, but I think Film Studies experienced something of its own 'cultural turn' over the 1990s as it became more receptive to the approaches and bodies of knowledge from related disciplinary fields – not only cultural studies, but also media studies, communications studies, cultural history, and the group of approaches to design, architecture and art history usually gathered under the label of visual culture.

As a result, it is now possible to suggest, Film Studies has experienced a series of pluralizing shifts that better reflects the social and cultural resonance of the locations of its objects of study. Importantly, these locations have not remained static; the range of options for cinema audiences has multiplied dramatically in recent years. There is now a proliferation of screen cultures and it would be hard to argue that film is any longer the dominant one. The shape of the film industry has been restructured as it has become entangled in the global shift towards convergence that suddenly makes Internet service provision as important as home theatre formats. Film Studies has had to respond to these developments. As Toby Miller puts it in a provocative contribution to the collection, *Keyframes*:

> The brief moment when cinema could be viewed as a fairly unitary phenomenon in terms of exhibition (say, 1920 to 1950) set up the *conceptual* prospect of its textual fetishisation in academia... Now that viewing environments, audiences, technologies and genres are so multiple, the cinema is restored to a mixed-medium mode. At this crucial juncture, the division between the text and context must be broken up. The who, what, when, where, and how of screen culture – its occasionality – must become central to our work. (2001: 306)

In such an industrial context, cultural studies' focus upon the culture that surrounds film's production and consumption now makes more sense than ever. As a result, it was only a matter of time before scholars and departments using a literature-based model of Film Studies – concerned only, really, with the film text and its presentation in cinemas – had to decide in what way and on whose terms it must accommodate these shifts.

Speaking from the position of someone working in cultural studies but with a longstanding interest in negotiating ways of dealing with film – as text, as industry, and as popular culture – my view is that the need for such an accommodation has been apparent for a long time. My own film textbook, *Film as Social Practice*, first published back in 1988, was explicitly designed as a cultural studies intervention into Film Studies. It focused upon popular cinema rather than canonical texts, upon the cinema as a site of consumption, and upon the full range of social practices connected with going to the movies. The strategy of dealing with film as a social practice was employed as a means of disconnecting film from discourses of the aesthetic and reconnecting it with the practices of its popular audiences. Others had developed the notion in more sophisticated ways before me, however, and still more were able to think about what that might mean for the study of film in the future. James Hay, for instance, writing from a background in film, cultural studies and communications studies, saw its potential in this way:

> What is necessary, I would argue, is a way of discussing film as a social practice that begins by considering how social relations are spatially organized – through sites of production and consumption – and how film is practiced from and across particular sites and always in relation to other sites. In this respect, cinema is not seen in a dichotomous relation with the social, but as dispersed within an *environment* of sites that *defines* (in spatial terms) the meanings, uses and places of 'the cinematic'. (1997: 216)

This is the kind of suggestion that now tends to be routinely embedded in contemporary writing about cinema. Those who have directly advocated this kind of approach to Film Studies – just in the last few years – include many of the contributors to Christine Gledhill and Linda Williams' reader *Reinventing Film Studies* (2000), Gill Branston in *Cinema and Cultural Modernity* (2000), Matthew Tinkcom and Amy Villarejo in their reader *Keyframes: Popular Cinema and Cultural Studies* (2001), Janet Harbord's *Film Cultures* (2002), Janet Staiger's *Perverse Spectators* (2000), and my own *Film Cultures Reader* (2002), to name a few. If we were to add to these the range of books which deal with popular cinema genres from a cultural studies point of view – from the early mix of cultural history and cultural studies in Thomas Doherty's (1988) study of teenpics to the amalgam of industry, cultural and textual analysis in Will Brooker's (2000) study of the *Batman* franchise – we would build up quite a significant body of work.

In the classroom, the study of film has already been redefined over the last decade. Most film programs today not only deal with the film text and the processes through which we make sense of film as a discrete medium, but they also – in some cases, even primarily – focus upon the cultural contexts in which the consumption of film takes place, as well as the industrial contexts within which it is produced. Although there are still complaints about the residual disciplinary insularity of contemporary American Film

Studies, specifically its failure to interest itself in the more empirical material that has come from research into political economy, technology and policy studies (Miller, 2001), this situation has improved significantly in recent years.

In what follows, then, I want to review four areas where the multilateral trade between film and cultural studies has been most active, and productive – for both sides. It is not always easy to pick up the precise pattern of such trade. Rarely is it a simple transaction, where one body of work directly and explicitly influences another. In many instances, what we are dealing with is a categoric conceptual shift – such as the turn to audiences – which affects work on television, on film, on computer games, on the developing theorization of cultural consumption in general. To argue that such a shift is an effect solely of cultural studies is to grossly oversimplify. So, I want to pick out those areas where it seems to me the influence of cultural studies upon Film Studies has been, if not unilateral nor unalloyed by influences from other disciplines, certainly highly significant over the last decade or so.

FROM AESTHETIC OBJECT TO SOCIAL PRACTICE

I have argued elsewhere (Turner, 2002) that the contemporary academic study of film has moved away, decisively, from a predominantly aesthetic interest in the text as well as from the enterprise of 'grand theory' – the elaboration of an overarching theoretical model for Film Studies. Significantly, an increasing number of the studies of contemporary cinema focus upon the meanings and pleasures popular films provide for their audiences. While the interest remains in the film text – they tend to look at specific genres or groups of texts, the nature of the meanings and pleasures examined as the products of these texts is social, political or cultural rather than aesthetic. Increasingly, it would seem to me, the default motivation for research into popular cinema is to understand the cultural function of the feature film as a form of popular entertainment in contemporary Western societies.

Among the outcomes of such work is a large critical literature on film genres that have little aesthetic cachet at all: the 'trashier' end of popular cinema – horror films, action movies, slasher/teen flicks. What this kind of work does is to reintegrate previously denigrated genres with the field of study in order to more adequately acknowledge their centrality to the production industry, as well as to the cinema's commercial audience. Interestingly, while many of those working on such topics may have chosen not to identify their projects exclusively with the discipline of Film Studies, they have tended to present an insider's critique of the positions which had excluded such texts from analysis in the past. Tania Modleski's important early study of horror films is aimed at puncturing what she describes as the 'postmodern' dismissal of all popular culture as inherently complacent, bourgeois and beneath consideration (1986). Carol Clover's highly influential study of slasher/horror films directly confronts screen theory's 'male gaze' orthodoxy to argue for a more flexible positioning of the spectator through the analysis of such trash-culture texts as *I Spit on Your Grave* (Meir Zarchi, US, 1978) (1992). Tasker's account of the 'action heroine' in *Spectacular Bodies* (1993) sets out to recover the positive political potential of the films she examines (*The Terminator* [James Cameron, US, 1984], *The Long Kiss Goodnight* [Renny Harlin, US, 1996] and *G.I. Jane* [Ridley Scott, US, 1997], for example): their contribution to expanding the range of female identities represented in popular film. Tasker's objective is not to reconcile these films with a traditional aesthetic, but rather to draw attention to the elite prejudices that would exclude their consideration from the field of Film Studies. Drawing on cultural studies as well as screen theory, Tasker provides an analysis of these films' cultural functions and their spectacular pleasures in a way that also helps to explain their popular success.

It is important to recognize the usefulness of the examples set by those who have worked on television with similar aims in mind. A remarkable number of scholars and researchers who have participated in the shift I am describing work across the two media and carry over into their film analysis the benefits of being able to deal with television texts as popular cultural forms that generate meaning and pleasure. Among the writers I have in mind here are Mark Jancovich, Jane Feuer, Steve Neale, Ed Buscombe, Miller, Modleski, and Staiger; there are many others. Television studies, in particular that part of it connected with cultural studies, has become (if anything, too) comfortable with its deferral of issues of aesthetics and quality, but its application to the renovation of a Film Studies hitherto ill-equipped to deal with mainstream cinema as popular entertainment has been extremely useful.

Tinkcom and Villarejo represent this shift as a reflection of cultural studies' emphasis on 'the specificity of the cultural commodity to the formation of social identities and practices' (2001: 2). It is certainly true that much of what you might call this 'revisionist' account of popular cinema is concerned with examining popular cinema's participation in the construction of social and cultural identity. In some cases, such as Richard Dyer's *White* (1997), the discussion is about how the naturalization of particular production practices assists in the reproduction of whole ideological categories within the field of representation developed in the Western cinema. More often, though, the focus is upon how particular cultural communities make use of film texts through the manner of their consumption. There is a growing literature on the appropriation of popular cinema by queer sexualities, by racial minorities, and by other marginalized communities (see Straayer, 1996, on queer readings, for example). Larger still, however, is that literature which examines how cinema works to construct, deconstruct and problematize mainstream cultural identities as well. Examples of the work I have in mind include Susan Jeffords' work on masculinity (1994), Barbara Creed (1993) on the 'monstrous-feminine', and John Hill (1997) on national cinema.

These approaches still centre on the film text, however, and so it is important to point to another way of dealing with film as a social practice: by examining the cinema as a social space, as a specific site of consumption, offering pleasures in its own right and confirming the social identities implicated in the choice to go there in the first place. Some of this work has an historical dimension. Miriam Hansen (1991) argues that the early cinema presented women with an 'alternate public sphere', a public social space where they were entitled to inhabit on their own, and which was separate from the world of family to which they were otherwise tied. Jackie Stacey's account of British women's experience of the picture palaces of the 1940s and 1950s uncovers the cinema's capacity to provide an alternative space that was magically and consolingly different to the everyday world of post-war Britain (1993). The material conditions of the cinema – what Stacey describes as the sensuous experience of the luxury of the cinema space – contrasted dramatically with the material conditions of these women's daily lives and Stacey demonstrates how important this was to their experience. Coming to the idea of the cinema as a social space from quite a different direction, Harbord (2002) examines the way particular sites of exhibition – the multiplex, the art house, the film festival – differently construct the experience of cinema-going, and how this difference influences the production of 'the value of the film'. Rather than focusing upon the film text exhibited, however, her analysis of these sites deals with them as domains of circulation: the multiplex is folded into the experience of shopping, for instance, whereas the film festival becomes incorporated into, among other things, the spatial practices of tourism. Such approaches move us away from focusing upon the film text as aesthetic object towards a much broader approach to the movies that attempts to better understand the industrial conditions which enable its production and the cultural conditions which support its consumption.

FROM THE SPECTATOR TO THE AUDIENCE

This is the area where cultural studies' influences have been most significant to the development of the contemporary practice of Film Studies. Drawing upon its work with television audiences, in particular, cultural studies has assisted Film Studies' shift from an almost exclusive focus upon a spectator who was almost entirely a theoretical proposition to a more empirical engagement with histories and quasi-ethnographies of actual film audiences.

Theoretical development in the early years of Film Studies was confined largely to theorizing the processes thought to structure audiences' understanding of the screened text. Psychoanalytic accounts were favoured, examining film's participation in the production of subjectivities. Dominant, though, was the practice of interrogating film's political function – which was largely, it has to be said, 'read off' the specific text. Mostly, the film critic in these early years outlined the reading they argued was generated by the text and relied on the explanatory power of the interpretation they could present as a means of defending their reading. During the heyday of what came to be called 'screen theory', the 1970s and 1980s, there was little consideration of attempting to capture and analyze the processes of consumption employed by actual viewers inside the cinema. Similarly, as a result of the dismissal of what was regarded as the regressive and complacent politics of popular cinema, there was very little serious investigation of the appeal of popular film to its viewers. To some extent, it was taken for granted that the film text's capacity to position its reader provided us with all the explanation we needed; that these films reproduced dominant ideological positions and that this was confirmatory and pleasurable for its audiences.

The history of Film Studies from the early 1990s onward changes much of this, however. A crucial factor seems to have been the gradual building of the critique of the Laura Mulvey argument about the dominance of the male gaze, which resulted in a series of modifications and qualifications – in which Mulvey herself, of course, was a significant participant. As I have put it elsewhere:

> The modification of theories of what [Mulvey] called 'the male gaze'... are part of a progressive renovation of the claims made by screen theory as it responded to the competing claims from other traditions of research. In particular, the recovery of a sense of agency for the individual viewer and the acceptance that the process of viewing must be historically contingent, as well as a renewed interest in the social and economic history of the commercial production industry, has displaced the universalizing implications of screen theory. The need to account for the pleasures of popular cinema audiences, in ways that acknowledge at least the theoretical possibility that they may not be ideological dupes, has become irresistible. (2002: 4)

Cultural studies was not the only competing research tradition, of course, that helped provoke this shift. Social history, for one, has been particularly significant; as noted earlier, Hansen's important history of the audiences for silent cinema demonstrates the usefulness of archival research for establishing the meanings and pleasures contemporary audiences found in this body of film. In such accounts, popular cinema remains in the centre of the frame, the notion of the historical audience replaces the theoretical category of the spectator, and cultural studies, social history, and television audience studies become increasingly relevant. In Melvyn Stokes and Richard Maltby's *Hollywood Spectatorship* (2001), the comparison of the two models of the spectator/audience is explicit: the theoretical, text-based construction of the spectator is placed against the historical evidence of actual audience consumption and viewing patterns.

Among the provocations from within cultural studies, Tony Bennett and Janet Woollacott's study of the James Bond phenomenon has been particularly influential in its proposition that the film text must be understood as the product of a specific set of conditions of reception – industrial, discursive, ideological, cultural – which they call 'reading formations' (1987). While there are textual determinants that limit the extent to which this happens, they argue, in general the particular 'reading' of the text at any one point in time is overdetermined by details of the reading formation at that time. The text is provisionalized by such a move, and the focus of study shifts onto the conditions of reception. It is a shift endorsed by Staiger in her review of reception studies, *Interpreting Films* (1992), where she recommends what she calls British cultural studies as a means of recovering the importance of the historical context in which film is consumed in order to affirm the role of the audience in generating meaning. Similarly, Barbara Klinger's book on Douglas Sirk makes the point that, as films 'pass through culture and history, they are subject to systems of signification that lie outside textual boundaries, systems largely responsible for negotiating their public identity' (1994: xvi). Klinger acknowledges Staiger's work on reception and singles out Bennett and Woollacott's influence in 'demonstrating the importance of analyzing contextual factors in discussions of the social meaning of texts' (1994: xvii). By the time the next instalment of Staiger's project appears, *Perverse Spectators* (2000), she is in no doubt that 'contextual factors, more than textual ones, account for the experiences [audiences] have watching films and television and for the uses to which those experiences are put in navigating our everyday lives. These contextual factors are social formations and constructed identities of the self in relation to historical conditions' (2000: 1).

Other attempts to find a way to make the move from the spectator to the audience have turned explicitly to work within cultural studies analyses of television as a model for future practice. Annette Kuhn (1984) does this very early on, for instance, pointing to the work of Charlotte Brunsdon and Dorothy Hobson on the British soap opera, *Crossroads* (1964–88). The most obvious connection to cultural studies work on television has occurred in the borrowing of television studies' ethnographic or quasi-ethnographic accounts of the experience of audiences. In her research for *Star-Gazing* (1993), which included archival and historical study, Stacey sought the contribution of women who wished to share their memories from the 1940s and 1950s of the function of the cinema and of cinema stars in their lives. The letters sent by these women became the sources for a rich study of the audience's experience of cinema during this time. Jaqueline Bobo's interviews with black women about their response to the film *The Color Purple* (Steven Spielberg, US, 1985), are aimed at using the evidence drawn from these audience members in order to challenge the interpretation of the film presented by white, liberal, readers: as a negative representation of black culture (1995). The study reveals how actively and contingently these audience members read their texts – a study of agency in practice. Jancovich's response to what he calls 'the turn to audiences' examines fan discussion sites on the web, developing insights provided by work on subcultures and their construction of distinction, in order to better understand how audiences participate in the construction and defence of film genres (2000: 24).

Finally, in this section, it is worth returning to the aspect of Stacey's work the previous brief description has elided – the function of the star, an object of identification and desire, as among the pleasures available to audiences in the cinema and as one of the key variables in audiences' choice of what films to see in the first place. Stacey's book is primarily about the classic Hollywood star's function for her correspondents, and it is contextualized within a strong tradition in Film Studies – initiated primarily by Dyer's *Stars* (1979), but carried on as an area of research ever since (see, for instance, Gledhill, 1991). While the film star remains a discrete category which it makes sense to retain, it has been displaced somewhat by cultural studies and other disciplines' growing interest in celebrity. Celebrity is the larger category, spanning a range of industries from television through to high-profile sports, and there is a danger of the specificity of the film star being submerged within it. On the other hand, the growth of celebrity culture, within the media and within the sports and entertainment industries generally, has accelerated the cycle of fame, developed new formats through which it can be produced, and blurred some of the distinctions used to differentiate the film star from the celebrity. As a result, cultural studies' work on celebrity has become increasingly relevant to understanding the cultural function of the film star in the age of the celebrity (Marshall, 1997; Turner, 2004).

NEW TECHNOLOGIES AND THE RETURN OF SPECTACLE

There are at least three dimensions to this topic: the challenge presented by the convergence of screen cultures enabled by new digital technologies, the influence of computer generated imagery on commercial cinema production, and the high profile now afforded to special effects as a means of marketing new cinema releases.

The rapid development of new formats of delivery for the film text, and of the media cultures which are building up around related screen cultures – computer games, computer graphics and design, for instance – give, urgency to the need to find ways of understanding film which accept that it can no longer be regarded as a free-standing, autonomous technology. The development of new visual media has outstripped existing models of analysis and so we must pay close attention to the practices of consumption or performance that have grown up around them. The digitized text has the capacity to be far more plastic than its predecessors – celluloid, videotape, and so on – and the exploitation of this potential enables an active conversation between producers and consumers, or between the user and the text. We need to investigate the practices involved in these conversations. Such work has begun, although much of it is speculative and highly theoretical – that is, without a large evidentiary base. Nonetheless, it is clearly possible that the relations developed through new media may differ greatly from those which structure the use of 'old' media such as television. Angela Ndalianis (2000) is representative of such a view when she argues that 'computergraphics' – used as a term to pick up the whole range of pc-based screen technologies – creates an illusory magical environment in which the audiences act and spectate at the same time. Such a proposition significantly revises the orthodox understandings of the agency available to audiences within screen cultures. It has become almost an alternative orthodoxy within the discussion of new media cultures that new forms of interaction – even, in some cases, new forms of subjectivity – are generated by new media technologies, and that these new forms dramatically shift the balance of power from the text towards 'the user'.

This takes us a considerable distance from the positioning text of post-Althusserian screen theory and from 1980s theories of the cinematic apparatus and so on. It is not at all clear, yet, what might be agreed about what we understand from such a distance, however. I don't think the contemporary formations of Film Studies are particularly well equipped to deal with these issues at the moment. Film Studies has had to look to other locations for developed accounts of new media technologies, their modality, and the relationships constructed around them by their users. There is some useful work in cultural and new media studies which focuses upon investigating pleasure, upon what it is that audiences derive from their use of these technologies or from their attendance at these spectacular events (for instance, Gauntlett and Horsley, 2004; Marshall, 2004). It is still a slim and undeveloped literature, however. Ironically, this is an instance where cultural and media studies need to do what they had earlier suggested Film Studies should do to renovate its understandings of the cinema audience: that is, to defer some of the more speculative theorizing until they can draw on a larger body of basic research which examines what actually happens between the user and the screen. While there has been a great deal of speculation about the potential of new media technologies which offer greater interactivity than conventional film or television, there is still very little examination of what actual users do with that interactivity. Consequently, it is premature to suggest that we are looking at a paradigm shift in which digital media radically democratizes the processes of media consumption.

The second issue I want to deal with here relates to what many would argue is a particular consequence of developments in computer-generated special effects in the cinema. It has become commonplace to suggest that Hollywood cinema now depends on the production of spectacle, rather than narrative, as a means of generating an audience for mass-marketed movies. Some, such as Geoff King (2000), take a counter view and argue that narrative remains dominant: in his account of *Jurassic Park* (Steven Spielberg, US, 1993), for instance, King argues that even the most spectacular of special effects are still contained with 'the arc' of the narrative. Whatever the resolution of this debate, it is commonly acknowledged that the development of CGI technologies has dramatically expanded the potential for, and reduced the cost of, the integration of CGI into the representation of setting, action, special effects – even of character – in the movies. Therefore, it is argued that the marketing of Hollywood cinema has been dominated by the presentation of the spectacular rather than the meaningful: by the promotion of the visual effects available in the film concerned rather than the narrative concept which structures it or, even, the stars who appear in it. It is not necessary to see all these as mutually exclusive categories, of course, and neither are such distinctions particularly novel. There have been previous instances in the history of film when new technologies exercised a similar, apparently magical, attraction. Tom Gunning's account of early cinema as 'a cinema of attractions' has been reprised recently by a number of writers as a means of reminding the field that the importance of spectacle to the contemporary popular cinema does have its historical antecedents (1986). Gunning's account of cinema's early history, when it was part of a vaudeville bill and when its performance was surrounded by other kinds of entertainment, is useful in nudging Film Studies slightly aside from its privileging of narrative as the necessary hook to consumption and from overstating the novelty of current trends.

Michele Pierson's study of special effects usefully places contemporary cinema's exploitation of the spectacle within a larger and much longer historical context (2002). Drawing upon a wide range of research traditions and theoretical insights (film theory, film history, cultural history, cultural studies, and new media technologies), Pierson writes a cultural history of the public visual spectacle – not merely spectacle in the cinema – from the nineteenth century to the present. This provides the perspective that enables Pierson to warn her readers about the historical shortsightedness of the contemporary enthusiasm for CGI in particular and notions of convergence in general. Spectacle, she argues, has always been there, and it has been integrated into screen cultures from the beginning. A benefit of Pierson's approach is its focus upon the specificity of the pleasures generated by the spectacle and thus implicated in the contemporary development of the spectacular potentials of CGI. So far, she argues, there has been very little scholarly treatment of special effects and thus very little information about 'the patterns of production and consumption governing the use of new technologies in relation to older cultural forms' (2002: 59). As a result, the narratives of convergence which have overwhelmed much media and academic discussion in recent years have received greater, and less critical, acceptance than they deserve. Her book sets out to address this by relating very different stories about how CGI has been used and what functions it has served.

What is most interesting about Pierson's project in this context is its refusal to simply jump on the new technologies bandwagon and argue that, once CGI and digitization arrives, everything has changed. While in many ways driven by the imperatives of cultural studies and essentially a work of

media or cultural history, Pierson's book is also clearly situated within a longstanding, continuing project for both Film Studies and cultural studies: that of understanding the specific pleasures of cinema as they shift and mutate in response to new systems of delivery and new formats of exhibition. This means we must acknowledge contemporary cinema's reliance on 'the novelty of its attractions to capture and sustain the attention of viewers', and thus its inevitable investment in new technologies which can produce new spectacular experiences to sell to its audiences (2002: 122). On the other hand, we must also recognize the audience's continuing 'emotional and intellectual attachment to the cinema – to the particular kind of experience it offers – that has continued to lure them away from the television set, the video or DVD player, the game console, and the computer screen' (2002: 122). There is still enough which is specific to this medium and its classic locations of consumption to require attention and explanation. Even if these locations have multiplied in ways that blur the boundaries between the cinema and 'the other spaces of consumption that surround it', the experience of cinema shows no signs of disappearing altogether (2002: 122). Rather, we need to understand these new locations, and these new experiences *as well as* those we have hitherto regarded as those of cinema. As a task for Film Studies that looks quite a tall order, but one that needs to be acknowledged, nonetheless.

CULTURAL HISTORY, FILM HISTORY AND POLITICAL ECONOMY

Among the dominant themes in screen theory over the 1970s and 1980s was the importance of psychoanalytic approaches to understanding spectatorship. While it was never uncontroversial, it did operate as an orthodoxy for some time and became the reference point for discussions of screen theory (or 'grand theory'). Since that time, there has been something of a backlash against the ambitions of grand theory (and not only in its application of psychoanalysis) in favour of a more modest but more empirically-based approach to understanding film (see Bordwell and Carroll, 1996). As we saw earlier, collections such as *Reinventing Film Studies*, *Keyframes*, and my own *Film Cultures Reader* constructed the subject of Film Studies differently, not only in terms of its integration into the analysis of popular culture, but also in terms of what kind of research and debate was seen as useful. Much of the writing referred to throughout this chapter (such as that of Staiger, Branston, or Miller), as well as that coming from quite different perspectives – such as David Bordwell's cognitivist approach – expresses an impatience with the dominance of 'grand theory' over the last few decades of Anglo-American Film Studies. In its place, there is frequently a defence of the usefulness of more instantiated, or what has been called 'middle level', research that seeks to contextualize film historically within the structures of consumption and production before focusing on more specific and conjunctural, rather than overarching and universalizing, issues.

Cultural studies has played a crucial role here, not only in the shift of focus, but also in the way that work responding to that shift has been pitched and framed. Klinger observes that one consequence of the 'growing importance of cultural studies to Film Studies in the 1980s' was that film criticism 'often shed the abstract language of the previous decade to embrace popular culture and make media analysis more responsive to concrete historical and social contexts, as well as the audience' (1994: 28). An increasing interest in cultural history within cultural studies has been reflected by a similar turn to cultural histories of film. The development of cultural policy studies has reinforced, in addition, what Miller has called a 'radical historicisation of context',

such that the analysis of textual properties and spectatorial processes must now be supplemented by an account of *occasionality* that details the conditions under which a text is made, circulated, received, interpreted, and criticized, taking seriously the conditions of existence of cultural production.' (2001: 306)

This expansion of context more directly acknowledges the parts played by cultural institutions and government policy environments as well as the globalizing political economies of the cultural and entertainment industries.

While, strictly speaking, there is little that we might call political economy in this tradition yet, Miller et al.'s *Global Hollywood* (2001) does indicate what that might look like, down the track. At the moment, however, it is certainly possible to point to related developments, such as the renewed interest in the histories of film economics or industrial analysis by such as that published by Tino Balio over the 1990s. If there has been a turn to audiences, as well as a cultural turn, and if it is increasingly common now to think of film as a social practice that involves more than just the interpretation of a text, it is probably also true to say that there is a growing academic interest in the workings of the film industry – an 'industrial turn', if you like. Hence, we have work such as Justin Wyatt's diagnosis of the high-concept film (1994), which blends industry economics, textual and genre analysis, and marketing to produce a detailed account of the generic preferences structuring the economic behaviour of the industry (and vice versa). More recently, we have Janet Wasko's thoroughly contextualized and empirically detailed analysis of the Hollywood film industry, *How Hollywood Works* (2003). There are more disciplinary influences involved in such work than cultural studies, of course, which has itself only relatively recently acknowledged the need for a properly economic or industrial analysis of the cultural sector. Indeed, what I am describing here is probably a multidisciplinary response to a growing realignment between some of the 'new humanities' with some of the social sciences that may have affected cultural studies before Film Studies. The effect of this general realignment on film history has been significant in that contextual, economic and industry matters now figure larger than ever before.

The study of film as a cultural industry, and as a component of the political economy of the media and entertainment industries, moves us in different directions from those outlined in my account of the beginning of Film Studies early in this chapter. When it becomes the object of this sort of examination, film no longer stands as a body of textual material or as a particular signifying practice. It stands instead as a locus of sociocultural history or as a site for the examination of sociocultural change.

CONCLUSION

Cultural studies has influenced what the study of film now looks like, and it has hastened the modification of the dominant paradigms under which the field was established. The cultural turn across the new humanities over the 1980s and the 1990s may suggest that this was something that was in the air at the time which effected an homologous series of shifts of focus within, rather than a direct intellectual transaction between, these two disciplinary formations. However, my argument is for a more dynamic relationship than this: that cultural studies has had a direct and important influence in several specific areas of development in contemporary Film Studies. These include the embracing and developing of research into the cultural function of popular film genres, into the audience's reception and consumption of the movies, and into a version of film history that is more interested in industry economics than the formation of a canon. These are significant shifts in focus for the field. Nevertheless, this does not constitute a sea change, but rather an expansion or diversification, a plurality of approaches to Film Studies that may help it deal with the changing media environment in which it must now situate itself.

REFERENCES

Althusser, Louis (1971) *Lenin and Philosophy and other essays*. Tr. Ben Brewster. New York: Monthly Review Press.

Barthes, Roland (1975) *Image, Music, Text*. Tr. Richard Miller. New York: Hill and Wang.

Bennett, Tony and Woollacott, Janet (1987) *Bond and Beyond: The Political Career of a Popular Hero*. London: Methuen.

Berger, John (1972) *Ways of Seeing*. London: BBC/Penguin.

Bobo, Jaqueline (1995) *Black Women as Cultural Readers*. New York: Columbia University Press.

Bordwell, David and Carroll, Noël (eds) (1996) *Post-Theory: Reconstructing Film Studies*. Madison: University of Wisconsin Press.

Branston, Gill (2000) *Cinema and Cultural Modernity*. Buckingham: Open University Press.

Brooker, Will (2000) *Batman Unmasked: Analysing a Cultural Icon*. London: Continuum.

Clover, Carol (1992) *Men, Women and Chainsaws: Gender in the Modern Horror Film*. Princeton, NJ: Princeton University Press.

Creed, Barbara (1993) *The Monstrous-Feminine: Film, Feminism, Psychoanalysis*. London: Routledge.

Doherty, Thomas (1988) *Teenagers and Teenpics: The Juvenilization of American Movies in the 1950s*. Boston: Unwin Hyman.

Dyer, Richard (1979) *Stars*. London: BFI.

Dyer, Richard (1997) *White*. London: Routledge.

Gauntlett, David and Horsley, Ross (eds) (2004) *Web.Studies*. London: Arnold.

Gledhill, Christine (ed.) (1991) *Stardom: Industry of Desire*. London: Routledge.

Gledhill, Christine and Williams, Linda (eds) (2000) *Reinventing Film Studies*. London: Arnold.

Gunning, Tom (1986) 'The Cinema of Attractions: Early Film, Its Spectator and The Avant-Garde', *Wide Angle*, 8 (3–4): 630–70.

Hall, Stuart (1980) 'Recent developments in theories of language and ideology: a critical note', in Stuart Hall, Dorothy Hobson, Andrew Lowe and Paul Willis (eds), *Culture, Media, Language*. London: Hutchison. pp. 156–62.

Hansen, Miriam (1991) *Babel and Babylon: Spectatorship in American Silent Film*. Cambridge, MA: Harvard University Press.

Harbord, Janet (2002) *Film Cultures*. London: Sage.

Hay, James (1997) 'Piecing Together What Remains of the Cinematic City', in David B. Clarke (ed.), *The Cinematic City*. London: Routledge. pp. 209–29.

Hill, John (1997) 'British Cinema as National Cinema: Production, Audience and Representation', in R. Murphy (ed.), *The British Cinema Book*. London: BFI. pp. 244–54.

Jancovich, Mark (2000) 'A real shocker: authenticity, genre and the struggle for distinction', *Continuum*, 14(1): 23–34.

Jeffords, Susan (1994) *Hard Bodies: Hollywood Masculinity in the Reagan Era*. New Brunswick, NJ: Rutgers University Press.

King, Geoff (2000) *Spectacular Narratives: Hollywood in the Age of the Blockbuster*. London: I.B. Taurus.

Klinger, Barbara (1994) *Melodrama and Meaning: History, Culture and the Films of Douglas Sirk*. Bloomington: Indiana University Press.

Kuhn, Annette (1984) 'Women's genres', *Screen*, 25(1): 18–28.

Marshall, P. David (1997) *Celebrity and Power*. Minneapolis: University of Minnesota Press.

Marshall, P. David (2004) *New Media Cultures*. London: Arnold.

Miller, Toby (2001) 'Cinema studies doesn't matter; or, I know what you did last semester', in Matthew Tinkcom and Amy Villarejo (eds), *Keyframes: Popular Cinema and Cultural Studies*. London: Routledge. pp. 303–11.

Miller, Toby, Govil, Nitin, Maxwell, Richard, and Murria, John (2001) *Global Hollywood*. London: BFI.

Modleski, Tania (1986) *Studies in Entertainment*. Bloomington: Indiana University Press.

Morley, Dave (1980) 'Texts, readers, subjects', in Stuart Hall, Dorothy Hobson, Andrew Lowe and Paul Willis (eds), *Culture, Media, Language*. London: Hutchison. pp. 163–73.

Ndalianis, Angela (2000) 'Special Effects, Morphing Magic and the 1990s Cinema of Attractions', in Vivian Sobchack (ed.), *Meta-Morphing: Visual Transformation and the Culture of Quick-Change*. Minneapolis: University of Minnesota Press. pp. 251–73.

Pierson, Michele (2002) *Special Effects: Still in Search of Wonder*. New York: Columbia University Press.

Stacey, Jackie (1993) *Star Gazing: Hollywood Cinema and Female Spectatorship*. London: Routledge.

Staiger, Janet (1992) *Interpreting Films*. Princeton, NJ: Princeton University Press.

Staiger, Janet (2000) *Perverse Spectators: The Practices of Film Reception*. New York: New York University Press.

Stokes, Melvyn and Maltby, Richard (2001) *Hollywood Spectatorship: Changing Perceptions of Cinema Audiences*. London: BFI.

Straayer, Chris (1996) *Deviant Eyes, Deviant Bodies*. New York: Columbia University Press.

Tasker, Yvonne (1993) *Spectacular Bodies*. London: Routledge.

Tinkcom, Matthew and Villarejo, Amy (eds) (2001) *Keyframes: Popular Cinema and Cultural Studies*. London: Routledge.

Turner, Graeme (1993) *Nation, Culture, Text: Australian Cultural and Media Studies*. London: Routledge.

Turner, Graeme ([1988] 1999) *Film as Social Practice*. 3rd edn. London: Routledge.

Turner, Graeme (ed.) (2002) *The Film Cultures Reader*. London: Routledge.

Turner, Graeme (2004) *Understanding Celebrity*. London: Sage.

Wasko, Janet (2003) *How Hollywood Works*. London: Sage.

Wyatt, Justin (1994) *High Concept: Movies and Marketing in Hollywood*. Austin: University of Texas Press.

Paradigms in Perspective

Having mapped the field in terms of geographical traditions and disciplinary boundaries, this final section projects a third way of surveying the discipline of Film Studies. By charting some of the dominant conceptual features of its landscape, this approach not only provides a record of how that landscape has evolved and taken on its familiar contours, but also offers some pointers to possible future developments.

Although the landmarks may be familiar, looking at them again in the context of a sustained self-reflection on Film Studies as an academic discipline and an intellectual field may offer new angles of vision and so shed new light on them. The question of Hollywood, for example, cannot and should not be avoided. Now, however, it becomes possible to ask what role the historical and social fact of Hollywood has played in shaping Film Studies as a discipline. In part, looking closely and seriously at Hollywood films has challenged old aesthetic hierarchies. In part, the concern to explain and understand spectatorship, stardom and celebrity has taught us a great deal about the social education of fantasies and desires. In part, the international reach and worldwide embrace of Hollywood movies has been key to understanding the shifting alignments of global and local in twentieth-century culture. And, again in part, the history

of the Hollywood industry has offered a paradigmatic and prophetic case of capitalism's adaptability to changing circumstances as well as one of the century's great melodramas.

Hollywood, or mainstream cinema, has not been the only pole in the magnetic field of Film Studies. Equally important have been the defining ambivalence of academic Film Studies towards Hollywood – the desire to bury as well as praise – and also an enthusiasm to champion alternatives, whether national cinemas, exotic cinemas or various kinds of avant-garde or experimental filmmaking and film cultures. These other impulses are a reminder that an education in watching films both sympathetically and critically might itself best be understood as part of the attempt to create the space for alternatives to Hollywood. Film Studies courses have been important not least because they have continued to expose students to films from a wider variety of different places and a wider variety of different eras than they would normally experience, and, in doing so, they have helped, or at least attempted to foster, more generous modes of consumption and more aesthetically open minds. In other words, Film Studies has not just offered a commentary on the game. It has itself been a player, and sometimes a more effective one than it has realized.

The foci of the critical and academic debates about film have varied from time to time – sometimes in response to what has been happening in the cinema industry, often in response to developments in the Humanities and the Social Sciences. In revisiting such once-hot topics as authorship, genre, realism and audiences, some of the contributions to this section take the opportunity not only to reflect on their past importance and current salience, but also to demonstrate their resilience and their continuing relevance not only to the study of film and cinema, but also to an understanding of emerging new audio-visual media.

Overall, then, the lesson seems to be this. Film Studies represents a restless and inquisitive search to find effective ways of thinking about cinema as one of the most important symbolic forms and global industries of modern times. In pursuing that objective, the discipline has come up with concepts, perspectives and methods that transcend its founding object of study, and have had a rejuvenating effect on many disciplines across the Humanities. To put that another way, and to adapt a phrase from Claude Lévi-Strauss, film and cinema have turned out to be things unexpectedly good to think with.

19

The Hollywood Industry Paradigm

Ruth Vasey

While there are countless ways of interrogating Hollywood, the industry's intrinsically commercial nature is necessarily at the heart of most of them, if only as something to elide or evade. The traditional critical approaches to Hollywood – studies of authorship, genre or ideology – have all provided systems of ordering, categorizing and analyzing movies as textual artefacts in ways that avoid or ignore the blunt commercial purpose of their production, distribution and exhibition. Constructing their critical practice from the methods and rationale of literary criticism, these approaches have tended to render Hollywood aesthetically respectable by ignoring or consciously discounting its commercial intent. Yet it is precisely Hollywood's enduring status as the world's most popular and financially successful cinema that requires analysis and explication.

Hollywood's dichotomous nature as 'show business' has long presented a methodological quandary to scholars seeking to articulate the creative and financial relationship between movie and audience. Where should one begin – with the hard-nosed financial imperatives of the 'business' or with the intangible attractions of the 'show'? While many studies have opted to concentrate on one of these factors to the exclusion of the other, the fact is that in relation to Hollywood the two have always been so thoroughly interdependent that it is impossible satisfactorily to account for the business of the movies without taking into account their aesthetic characteristics, and vice versa. To understand Hollywood is to understand the many interrelated strategies – some industrial and some aesthetic – that it has used to find acceptance amongst its diverse audiences. The extraordinary international success of the industry is testimony to the fact that many of these strategies have been sophisticated, inventive and responsive to historical change, despite the fact that the industry's products themselves have regularly been characterized by its critics as crude and repetitive. Hollywood's 'formula' for commercial success, far from being transparent, is sufficiently complex to ensure that, although the industry has been with us for the best part of a century, scholars are still searching for adequate ways to account for both its popularity and its influence.

In seeking to identify a 'Hollywood paradigm' of Film Studies, perhaps the first issue to confront is whether the object of study has been sufficiently coherent over time to be understood in relation to any single industrial or aesthetic model. There has been considerable debate as to whether the 'Classical Hollywood' that evolved until roughly World War Two can be meaningfully bracketed with the 'Post-Classical' cinema that followed the War, or indeed with the 'Contemporary Hollywood' that reoriented itself in the 1980s to pay TV, video and ultimately DVD and other digital formats.

At its height, 'Classical Hollywood' was dominated by a small, stable group of vertically integrated companies managing each stage of production, distribution and exhibition. The major companies excluded competition by cooperating closely with each other with respect to matters in which they had a mutual and non-competitive interest. Moviemaking within each company was characterized by highly efficient and concentrated production, with a permanent staff of specialized workers based in Los Angeles bringing out approximately a movie per major studio per week when the system was at its height in the late 1930s. The movies themselves were differentiated by budget and by their generic elements, but they were also subject to a high degree of centralized regulation, and were designed primarily to be consumed by general audiences in conventional cinemas.

Fifty years later, Hollywood's industrial landscape and the cultural status of its products had undergone a radical overhaul. The direct connection between production and exhibition constituted by vertical integration had been disrupted: in 1948, at the culmination of a legal case known as the 'Paramount Suit', the Supreme Court required production/distribution companies to divest themselves of their exhibition chains. As a result of the industrial instability that followed, by the end of the 1960s all the major companies had been acquired by larger diversified conglomerates; and by the 1980s they had been positioned, to greater or lesser degrees, at the heart of gigantic media corporations. In this new era, movie production was largely outsourced to external creative teams, many of which came together for a single production and subsequently disbanded. Filming and post-production increasingly moved away from its Los Angeles base, and the old studio facilities were largely sold off or given over to television production or theme parks. Since then, movies have been designed to be classified for viewing by targeted groups of consumers in cinemas or at home instead of by general audiences; now the majority of a movie's profits are realized in its video and television release and in many cases in merchandising. The 'aftermarket' of sales beyond the original cinematic release increasingly determines the nature of cinematic product rather than the other way around.

This bald overview may seem to suggest that Hollywood's history has been characterized by clear points of rupture that have transformed it from one industrial state to the next. On closer inspection, however, it appears that this type of periodization is unnecessarily reductive, and that the changes that have been wrought upon Hollywood have been more incremental than catastrophic. Technological changes, so often trumpeted as 'revolutionizing' the industry, have typically disturbed the fundamentals of the movie business very little (see Enticknap, 2005).

When Douglas Gomery asks in *The Coming of Sound*, 'How did the industry change as a new technology was innovated?' (2004: xv), he is shaping his argument around essentially the same question that John Belton (1992) asks of widescreen technology and Gianluca Sergi asks of the second 'sound revolution' in *The Dolby Era* (2004). Gomery's response – that a change driven by rational business decisions ultimately produced not chaos or revolution, but long-term growth and greater control for Hollywood over its global markets – demonstrates the rationality and coherence of the major companies' transition from the provision of silent cinema to 'talkies'. Gomery's industrial and economic analysis provides a significant corrective to other accounts of the introduction of sound, which have been more concerned with the history and aesthetic consequences of technological change (Lastra, 2000; O'Brien, 2005), and have most commonly presented sound as causing a complete break with Hollywood's past. Gomery's own account is itself informed and nuanced by Donald Crafton's emphasis, in *The Talkies* (1997), on the audience's enthusiastic acceptance of sound and on the overriding economic impact of the Depression on the industry's activities. Crafton's conclusion that, 'sound definitely changed cinema, but not across the board, and not as a radical overthrow of film convention … [whereby] in the long run, the social experience of going to the movies was remarkably unaffected' (1997: 543–4), might stand as a plausible summary for the effects that the major changes in production technology (sound, colour, widescreen) have had on the industry as a whole. The history of technology itself demonstrates film history's preoccupation with production and its techniques, rather than commerce. As Gomery also argues, 'the greatest technological change in the movie industry in the United States during the 1930s came with the installation of air conditioning into theatres' (2004: 148).

It is arguable that other pivotal moments of change were connected with the expansion of the foreign market in 1918; with the formulation of the Production Code in 1930, or perhaps its affirmation in 1934; with the filing of the Paramount Suit in 1938 or its resolution in 1948; with the reorientation of the foreign market during World War Two or changes in audience demographics following the war; with the widespread take-up of television in the 1950s or the abandonment of the Production Code and the adoption of movie ratings in 1968; with the experimentation with new profit-making strategies, including both new cinematic styles and new release patterns, in the 1970s; with the diffusion of cable and satellite delivery systems and video-cassette recorders in the 1980s; with the horizontal integration of the industry within multinational media companies or the rise of digital convergence; or with innumerable other factors that have impinged on the industry over time. There is no clear academic consensus about which of these 'moments' signals a clear point of departure for Hollywood. More fundamentally, there is as yet no clear academic consensus as to the basis for any periodization of the American cinema industry's history – whether, that is, its periodization should be determined by technological change, by changes in the structure or viewing practices of the audience, by changes in corporate management or on the basis of legal or legislative change.

Even during periods of supposed stability, the Hollywood industry has been obliged to evolve continuously in response to its changing business environment. Remarkably, of the eight companies that dominated the industry by the end of the 1920s, only one, RKO, has been officially wound up. The others – Paramount, MGM, Warner Bros Fox, United Artists, Columbia and Universal – have all survived to the present day, despite bouts of asset-stripping, merger, acquisition, divestment and the occasional near-death experience. Mostly they have thrived, with many of these companies now amongst the most powerful corporations in the world, along with the Walt Disney Company, that also had its roots in the late 1920s and 1930s. Throughout the industry's melodramatic history, audiences have not, on the whole, experienced Hollywood as a discontinuous phenomenon. Indeed, although the industry has constantly reshaped itself in order to profit from changing demographics, political climates and technologies, the nature of Hollywood's attraction to audiences has remained remarkably stable throughout its history. It has remained an essentially erotic, star-centred, generic cinema; it has kept a close association with wider consumerist trends, especially fashion; and it has maintained its global prestige with high production values, typically expressed through action and spectacle. Most importantly, it has continued to engage audiences on an emotional level, with promotional campaigns consistently built around the promise of tears, laughter, thrills, suspense and horror.

The tension between industrial change and aesthetic persistence in Hollywood has been reflected in commentaries on the industry, which have commonly tended to emphasize either the fluctuating and contingent mechanics of the industry's operations, or the more persistent ways in which movies have sought to engage and seduce audiences. The former perspective encompasses industrial, economic, institutional and cultural histories, including censorship practices and political economies. The second approach emphasizes factors such as stardom, film style, narrative construction and genre. There is clearly a good deal of overlap between these perspectives, and situated between the two is research, which seeks to integrate these two areas, by conceiving of Hollywood's output as an intrinsically commercially-based set of aesthetic practices. Indeed, in relation to contemporary Hollywood, advances in digital convergence make it increasingly difficult to identify a 'text' that is independent of the multiple circumstances under which it is consumed, whether as movie, DVD, electronic game or content for a mobile phone.

This chapter will consider some of the ways in which scholars working in these disparate traditions have sought to illuminate the Hollywood phenomenon.

INDUSTRIAL HISTORIES

Since Hollywood's inception, audiences have evinced an insatiable curiosity about the mechanics of movie production. The motion-picture medium itself was a sufficient novelty in the early twentieth century for audiences to be intrigued by the process by which fictions were produced for the screen. Short movie subjects depicting apparently candid behind-the-scenes action on the studio lot were popular in the silent period, in an early harbinger of today's obligatory *The Making of ...* television specials. Far from demystifying the process

of production, these shorts only served to emphasize Hollywood's allure by cultivating a sense of casual intimacy between audiences and players. The desire to be involved in the 'real' lives of moviemakers was additionally fed by fan magazines such as *Photoplay*, and from the 1910s onwards Hollywood supported a publishing sub-industry dedicated to the circulation of 'insider' accounts of the motion-picture business, including memoirs, biographies and blow-by-blow descriptions of individual productions. In the 1920s movie companies began to capitalize on the public's fetishization of Hollywood through advertising tie-ins, which encouraged moviegoers – especially women – to emulate the stars through their choice of fashion, hairstyles, cosmetics and homewares. In 1955 Walt Disney created Disneyland as a fictional movie Mecca which tantalised audiences with the promise of an 'authentic' behind-the-scenes experience.[1] Throughout, these vicarious experiences and accounts of the industry presented the 'story of the movies' in terms of entertaining narratives replete with casts of glamorous and/or endearingly dissolute and eccentric characters, and they concentrated almost exclusively on production.

Any serious industrial history of Hollywood is faced with the problem of how to provide a rational account of the operations of the movie business when a myriad of these attractive and entertaining 'histories' of the industry are already in circulation, many of which have sprung fully formed from the public relations offices of the industry itself. Moreover, since popular interest in all things Hollywood is as intense as ever, the temptation persists to play to the crossover market between serious enquiry and popular potboiler, especially in areas such as censorship and biography; the 'film' sections of bookshops have long been stocked with well-researched books spiced up to be widely consumable in paperback. This tendency, while often profitable and mostly harmless, perpetuates the impression that Hollywood has always operated as a maverick industry governed by passion, whim and individual desire, rather than as the kind of stable and securely profitable business that it has been for most of its history. First-hand accounts of Classical studio practice, such as Leo Rosten's *Hollywood: The Movie Colony, The Movie Makers* (1941) and Hortense Powdermaker's *Hollywood the Dream Factory* (1950), equally emphasize the melodramatic and entertaining aspects of the industry despite their evident seriousness of intent, setting the tone for many of the 'insider' works that would follow. Nevertheless, these were pioneering works that contained material observations and descriptions that still make them useful sources today.

Despite the reading public's demonstrated obsession with life on the set, production constitutes only the highest-profile aspect of Hollywood's business. Indeed, from a commercial point of view the industry's support and perpetuation of production might best be seen as an inconvenient necessity, occasioned by the fact that a regular supply of cinematic product is required to service the much more profitable areas of exhibition and (especially) distribution. In many ways, the changing relationship between production, distribution and exhibition has determined the behaviour of the industry over the years, including many of the fundamental characteristics of the movies themselves. In the Classical period up to World War Two, the fact that the five largest companies were vertically integrated, with each distribution company owning both a production studio and an important chain of cinemas, meant that there was a guaranteed pipeline between the point of production and their own places of exhibition. Packages or 'blocks' of movies were also bundled for sale to independent exhibitors or to chains controlled by other companies. Production schedules could therefore be geared towards regular output – a movie per week – with a standard ratio between low-and medium-budget production, and more prestigious headlining movies. Regular production meant that large, stable labour forces could be maintained in the employ of the studios, and the continuity of both on-screen and

off-screen personnel explains the close generic similarities between the bodies of work produced by the studios during the 1920s and 1930s.

It is remarkable how resistant film scholarship in general has been to acknowledging the importance of distribution and exhibition to an understanding of the 'whole equation of pictures' (Fitzgerald, 1974: 6) including an understanding of the production process itself. As early as 1927, *The Story of the Films*, written by industry insiders such as Sidney Kent and edited by Joseph P. Kennedy (1927), made it clear that Hollywood's operations were geared unequivocally towards the immediate exigencies of the marketplace, and industry trade journals such as *Variety* have consistently stressed the importance of marketplace fluctuations and 'the numbers' in determining company policy in Hollywood. Tino Balio's research on United Artists and the perspectives outlined in his *The American Film Industry* (1985) demonstrated the importance of looking beyond the limited perspective of production. In 1985 David Bordwell, Janet Staiger and Kristin Thompson brought out *The Classical Hollywood Cinema: Film Style and Mode of Production to 1960*, which emphasized the links between industrial context and film style, and 1986 saw the publication of Gomery's *The Hollywood Studio System,* which straightforwardly explained the interconnectedness of production, distribution and exhibition.[2] The ten-volume *History of the American Cinema* was brought out by Scribners and the University of California Press between 1990 and 2006, covering American cinema from its origins until the end of the 1980s. Each of these works engages with Hollywood's industrial history, but apart from them there has been only a trickle of industrial studies, and we still lack authoritative, well-documented accounts of most of the major studios or exhibition chains, or any book-length study of distribution practice.[3] The lack of romance attached to the financial end of the business has ensured that it is still generally underestimated, especially in relation to early Hollywood.

For example, standard histories of the industry relate how there was a broad relocation of movie production facilities from the eastern states to California in the 1910s, motivated by cheaper real estate and labour, plentiful sunshine and spectacular scenery for location shooting; but far less attention is paid to the fact that the financial headquarters of the companies remained in New York City in order to facilitate movie distribution to both the large population centres of the East, and after 1918 to Europe. This created a geographical separation between the creative and the fiscal hubs of the industry which ultimately worked to the advantage of both. The production work of the 'movie colony' at the studios in Los Angeles could be carried out relatively autonomously; yet its creative excesses were counterbalanced by the more hard-headed directives that were issued by company heads, who determined budgets and overall production slates as well as managing more general aspects of the companies' businesses. As Gomery insists,

> Historians have too long been distracted by the supposed chaos on the studio lots and the tales of woe told by old timers. The heads of these corporations – led by Adolph Zukor – saw correctly the movie making process as one part of the system – which also included distribution and exhibition. (2005: xvii)

From their position in New York, the company heads were well placed to assess the relationship of expenditure to box-office returns, exhibitor feedback and public relations, while being free of the day-to-day concerns of production. This balance and tension between these two centres of power help to explain why 'art' and 'industry' have always equally characterized Hollywood. They also suggests why attempts by other countries' film industries to imitate Hollywood's 'formula' for motion picture entertainment during the Classical period were mostly exercises in futility: the finely-tuned checks and balances involved in determining Hollywood's system of production were rooted in the very structure

of the industry, and were essentially incapable of reproduction in other national contexts.

A consideration of distribution and exhibition can also help to identify the underlying aspects of Hollywood which set it apart from potential international rivals and contributed to its global success. Most obviously, the Hollywood industry benefited from the size and economic strength of the domestic American market, which accounted for about 35 per cent of box-office revenues worldwide. This enabled the major costs associated even with most high-budget productions to be amortized before they entered international circulation; thus Hollywood producers could undercut any competition they encountered in the foreign field, and regard most income derived there as pure profit. Aided by the impact of World War One on Europe's incipient film industries, Hollywood's products occupied the vast majority of the world's screens by the early 1920s, and their high capitalization guaranteed that they maintained their market share by allowing for production standards that easily exceeded those of other national cinemas. In turn, the industry's global reach encouraged Hollywood to recruit moviemaking talent from around the world, helping to influence the development of a sophisticated style of entertainment that travelled without difficulty across improbably broad geographical territories. Thompson's meticulous analysis of Hollywood's early expansion into international markets in *Exporting Entertainment: America in the World Film Market, 1907–1934* (1985) has laid the foundation for future work in this area, which has long been neglected. My own study, *The World According to Hollywood 1918–1939* (1997) looks at the extent to which Hollywood's products were influenced by considerations of international distribution. Ian Jarvie (1992) and John Trumpbour (2002) have studied the Canadian, French and English markets in depth, while Thomas J. Saunders has looked at factors affecting Germany in *Hollywood in Berlin* (1994). So far, most work examining the influence of European immigrant filmmakers has concentrated on biography and production history (see Baxter, 1976; Giovacchini, 2001; Petrie, 1985; Thompson, 2006).

While production remains by far the most visible element of the Hollywood industry in literature relating to its 'Golden Years', questions of distribution and exhibition come into stronger focus in histories of the industry after World War Two, most immediately because of the way in which the industry and its products changed in the wake of the Paramount Suit. When the Supreme Court found that the vertical integration of the major companies was in effect monopolistic and constituted a restraint of trade under the Sherman Anti-Trust Act, they were obliged to divest themselves of their chains of cinemas and to desist from block booking (Muscio, 1997). This meant that movies had to be sold to exhibitors on their individual merits, a reorganization that had wide-ranging consequences for the structure of the industry and the nature of its products. The established studios gradually made fewer, more high-budget productions designed to reap ever higher profits, while the shortfall in production was made up by new 'independent' production houses, often playing to specific audience segments (typically teenagers, whose iconoclastic attitudes turned amateurish, shoestring production standards into cult virtues) rather than to a more generalized audience. As Thomas Doherty observes,

The courtship of the teenage audience began in earnest in 1955; by 1960, the romance was in full bloom. That shift in marketing strategy and production initiated a progressive 'juvenilization' of film content and the film audience that is today the operative reality of the American motion picture business. (1988: 3)

Although the major companies maintained their overall control of the movie business through their grip on distribution, the 'Classical' production-line system ceased and their large workforces were dispersed to form more transient alliances around individual productions. Tax changes, demographic shifts after the War, the impact of McCarthyism, and the rise of television all accelerated the rate

of change in Hollywood in the 1950s. The appearance of a degree of experimentation in style and content, the entry of new players into the business and an acceleration of technological innovation have helped to make this one of the most studied periods in Hollywood's history (see Belton, 1992; Biskind, 1983). Recent scholarship has seized on Hollywood's attitude to television, countering previously accepted accounts of early hostility between the two media with studies that suggest a far more complex and mutually accommodating relationship (Anderson, 1994).

Starting in the 1960s, Hollywood went through its first series of corporate takeovers, when large diversified conglomerates acquired the major companies. This was a period of industrial instability for the industry, during which its existing profit-making strategies proved unreliable. Hollywood's quest to attract new regular audiences with more successful movie formulae led the studios to experiment with a range of different approaches, from the conservative family film (*The Sound of Music*, Robert Wise, US, 1965) to products for 'hip' young adults (*Easy Rider*, Dennis Hopper, US, 1969; *Zabriskie Point,* Michelangelo Antonioni, US, 1970). Because some of these approaches were characterized by 'personal' or 'artistic' styles, this period has been dubbed the 'Hollywood Renaissance', and much of the commentary on it has taken an auteurist perspective (see Gilbey, 2003; Horwath et al, 2004). By contrast, David A. Cook's *Lost Illusions: American Cinema in the Shadow of Watergate and Vietnam, 1970–1979* (2000) in the *History of the American Cinema* series, provides a detailed account of the industry's history during this period; and Thomas Schatz offers a more condensed perspective in his essay 'The New Hollywood' (1993). Peter Biskind's *Easy Riders, Raging Bulls: How the Sex Drugs and Rock 'n' Roll Generation Saved Hollywood* (1998) is a more anecdotal, interior account. Ironically, while the director may have been hailed as a 'superstar' in the 1970s, the most radical and influential innovations of the decade were both off screen: Lew Wasserman's extraordinarily successful promotional and exhibition strategies for *Jaws* (Steven Spielberg, US, 1975), and George Lucas' demonstration of the virtually limitless profitability of ancillary products in the hype surrounding *Star Wars* (US, 1977).

As these developments suggest, if the importance of distribution and exhibition tended to be understated in accounts of Hollywood for most of the twentieth century – despite the fact that the largest investment in the industry was always in the real estate represented by cinemas, and that the greatest bargaining power in the industry was always controlled by distributors – by the 1980s their influence was inescapable. With the introduction of pay-TV systems, video technologies and the expansion of free markets and television networks across Europe, it became apparent that motion picture companies could form the nuclei of hugely profitable, horizontally integrated media systems, and 'Hollywood' companies began to be repositioned at the centre of some of the largest multinational corporations in the world. Instead of generating the majority of a movie's earnings, by this time a motion picture release essentially functioned to fix the price of subsequent sales into the 'aftermarket' of TV sales and video rentals, where the real money was to be made, especially for a high-budget production: a movie that did well in its cinematic release could command higher prices in negotiations over its subsequent release rights. The major companies' re-acquisition of theatre chains after 1980 was, as a result, much less significant to their overall structure and well-being. As Thomas Austin puts it, 'The heart of the Majors' business is software – the production of feature films – but the bulk of profits are earned further down the value chain in distribution and retail' (2002: 85), in the consumer products, soundtracks, books, videogames and TV spin-offs. All these ancillary products have lower costs, lower risks and higher returns, and a major company can control costs and stabilize its cash flow by controlling each stage of this value chain, but feature films remain the key component in this 'synergistic brand

extension' (Allen, 1999: 120–1; see also Dale, 1997: 5).

Barbara Klinger discusses this process in terms of 'repurposing':

> Providing a way to offset the high production costs of blockbusters, repurposing refers generally to the media industry's attempt to gain as much revenue as possible from a given property. For film, this may mean marketing tie-ins across a range of businesses and media, from fast-food franchise promotions and T-shirts to cartoon series spin-offs based on a film's original characters. (2006: 7–8)

Another form of repurposing is repackaging media for sale in as many different incarnations as possible; thus, the original movie reappears in the form of a Director's Cut, or repackaged as a video or DVD (followed by the Special Edition, the Collector's Edition and, perhaps finally, as part of a Nostalgia Series). With these multiple profit-making strategies integrated under a single corporate banner (such as Disney or AOL-Time Warner), the opportunities for exploiting a successful property are virtually limitless. At the same time, the institutional links between these avenues of exploitation amount to a reappearance of the vertical integration that was targeted in the Paramount Suit, albeit in much more complex corporate and technological forms. As Jennifer Holt argues, this situation is in fact very similar to the business conditions of Classical Hollywood (2001–2: 22–9). Five companies now own all the US broadcast networks, four of the major movie companies, 45 of the top 50 US cable channels, and provide 75 per cent of all US prime-time programming. It is arguable that the re-establishment of vertical integration, and the present sequential arrangement of distribution, has been of much greater economic – and therefore cultural – significance than the much more vaunted pursuit of synergy through mergers and convergence.

One notable difference between current conditions and those that pertained in Classical Hollywood is that in the Classical period a movie made the bulk of its profits in its first-release window. Now this balance has been reversed to the extent that a movie's initial release effectively acts as promotion for its more profitable 'afterlife'. The ballyhoo surrounding the theatrical release and the release itself is designed to create 'buzz' – public awareness of the product – that will fix its subsequent value. This is why a poor public response in a single opening weekend can spell the 'failure' of a movie costing hundreds of millions of dollars (see Bart, 1999).

Obviously, these developments have consequences for the style and content of motion pictures, but, as Robert C. Allen (1999) has argued, they also constitute a substantial case that a reconsideration of what constitutes the 'movie' industry's principal output is well overdue. With the rise of home theatre systems on the one hand, and portable entertainment devices (formerly 'telephones') on the other, academic discourse has yet to come to terms with the extent to which the object of study has been transformed in response to changes in modes of exploitation and consumption.

Although Hollywood has been oriented to an international market since the 1920s, the transformation of the industry into a more comprehensively global phenomenon – and with ownership and financing of the major media corporations sometimes being based outside the United States – the extent to which 'Hollywood' should continue to be conceived as an 'American' phenomenon remains the subject of debate. There is a case to be made on several grounds that the industry is becoming increasingly international in orientation. The international market has occasionally outstripped the American domestic sphere as a generator of profits since the 1990s, and production is frequently outsourced to international enterprises to take advantage of tax breaks, favourable exchange rates, cheaper labour costs and international centres of expertise. Britain, Canada, Ireland, Australia, New Zealand and most recently Indian animation studios have all provided attractive conditions for high-budget Hollywood production. Nevertheless, as Ben Goldsmith and Tom O'Regan have shown, production in these dispersed locations is typically controlled and coordinated from a nerve centre located in Los Angeles, and this

chain of command tends to reinforce the status of southern California as the capital – the 'design centre', if no longer necessarily the 'production centre' – of global film:

> There can be little doubt that Hollywood remains the vortex, the point in the circuit through which every project must pass on its path to global audiences, and where every project, however subtly, is transformed. (2005: 18)[4]

The cultural provenance of movies made in dispersed locations is complex, since, even if they are made by a preponderance of local or international talent, they are likely to conform to recognizable 'American' norms, especially with regard to American-accented English. This continues to make sense as long as the United States constitutes the largest single market for motion-picture fare. While it is possible that a continuing rise in the importance of the Indian and/or Chinese markets may destabilize such norms, it is also the case that a traditional association with an American Hollywood has become the hallmark of highly-capitalized product designed for global consumption, in an association that is now arguably independent of the United States itself. As Aida Hozic discusses in *Hollyworld* (2001), the converse is also true. The extent to which 'Hollywood's America' is identified as being meaningfully geographically located in the US is questionable, as it always has been. In this respect, production mirrors exhibition, where the revamping of exhibition venues and the development of multiplexes in Europe, Latin America and parts of Asia in particular, has frequently resulted from partnerships between local developers and major distribution companies. What Charles R. Acland (2003) has called the contemporary cinema's global 'screen traffic' does, at a superficial level, suggest the dismantling of local culture and an aesthetic of 'placelessness', as Roman tenements or Toronto streets provide chameleon-like locations for stories set in New York or Chicago, and movies are simultaneously released to thousands of near-identical screens across the northern hemisphere. Such a perspective, however, ignores the local context, and the collection of local interests, in which both production and reception occur.

From a different perspective, Hollywood's dominance in the area of popular film is, however, demonstrated by the fact that European 'national' filmmakers have themselves largely abandoned the attempt to make high-budget crowd-pleasing commercial cinema, conceding that ground to the international production arena that everyone has agreed to call 'Hollywood', while themselves concentrating on smaller-scale 'artistic' productions that define themselves in contradistinction to Hollywood's norms. Hollywood's high-budget productions are generally constructed according to risk-averse formulae and are characterized by stock situations, action and special effects, stars, heterosexuality, happy or heroic outcomes, emotion and spectacle. Meanwhile, lower-budget productions necessarily make a virtue of their distance from the commercial mainstream by declaring their allegiance to Art, localism and the politics of the 'real'.

It is ironic, therefore, that it is in this area of 'art cinema' that Hollywood's truly global dimensions are best understood, especially if we concede that the major companies' greatest power lies in their control of distribution, rather than in the area of production. During the 1990s all the major studios either acquired or created boutique distribution subsidiaries specifically to handle products that offered themselves as alternatives to cinema's more formulaic staple fare. The extent to which the products of the subsidiary can actually achieve any kind of formal or thematic radicalism when bonded so closely to a conservative Hollywood multinational is moot, but the intention to differentiate this product as having an alternative status in the mind of the consuming public is clear. The advantages of broader market control and the financial lure of a low-budget personal film that could prove to be the next breakout hit, mean that it makes good economic sense for these two differently labelled, differently expressive streams of cinema to be structurally combined under the control of the major media companies (King, 2005: 11–57; Wyatt, 1998: 74–90).

While Hollywood has been outsourcing its 'alternative' production to American low-to medium-budget 'independent' production companies since the 1950s, this sector of production has suffered in recent years by the change to wide-scale release patterns that have favoured expensively-hyped movies at the expense of more modest productions. 'Foreign' products offer an alternative source of material. Historically, Hollywood's rate of acquisition of international products has been low, although they have long been a feature of the art cinema circuit (Balio, 1998: 58–73). More recently, with the proportionate increase of the box-office revenues provided by the international market, more foreign-sourced product has been in demand, and Hollywood has profited from the output of 'national cinemas' around the world.

National cinemas are typically government protected and supported; they nurture new talent, underwrite training programmes, and virtually enforce creativity by expecting projects to be realized on a shoestring. They promote 'personal vision' by structurally favouring writer/directors to an extent not possible in the Hollywood system. In effect, they behave like 'independent' production companies, with the difference that they are typically willing to bear extraordinary levels of risk, even allowing for the normal bargaining advantage adhering to the large global companies. Unsurprisingly then, in the 1990s, Miramax, Fox and Fine Line set up strategic offices in film-producing nations around the world, with a view to tracking production, acquiring potentially profitable low-budget material, and securing key creative personnel. The shopfronts that we call 'film festivals' are neatly integrated into this arrangement, as they efficiently showcase what global cinema has to offer to the collected buying agents of the major media companies, as Biskind shows in *Down and Dirty Pictures: Miramax, Sundance, and the Rise of Independent Film* (2004). The understandable enthusiasm with which filmmakers around the world pursue film festival recognition (followed by a major distribution contract) is the most striking evidence of their complicity in the perpetuation of a global system of cinema, managed and controlled by 'Hollywood' multinational media companies.

ECONOMIC HISTORIES

A great deal of cinema history remains to be written about the practical operations of the distribution and exhibition industries, and about how many people actually saw different types of film. Until recently, the industry has attracted relatively little attention from economic historians, who bring distinctly different methodological practices and ask substantially different questions from those asked by aesthetic, cultural or social historians of cinema. For example, In the absence of detailed box-office information, John Sedgwick (2000) has developed a statistical analysis of the relative commercial status of a sample of cinema venues to examine audiences' consumption choices and preferences in 1930s Britain. Against the view of some social historians that audiences were principally drawn to the occasion of cinema, and that, as Allen puts it, 'in the 1920s in America, for example, many viewers were not particularly interested in what film was playing' (1990: 352–3), Sedgwick argues that the cinema environment was not by itself 'sufficiently important to override the influence of any particular film on any particular box-office take … . Different films attracted different sizes of audience at the same cinema' (2000: 6–7).

More generally, economists and economic historians bring their particular disciplinary methods and concerns to an understanding of Hollywood as an industry, using microeconomic tools of analysis to explain Hollywood's business practices: for example, to quantify how risky a business film production and distribution is, or to measure whether stars or marketing alter a movie's revenue. Some economic analyses supply an elaborated vocabulary and mathematical modelling to confirm the industry's public presentation of itself as unstable and unpredictable; movie revenue patterns are,

according to economist Arthur De Vany, 'so complex that they are nearly chaotic' (2004: 2). Other analyses, including those of Sedgwick and Michael Pokorny (2004), have argued convincingly that the major Hollywood studios have consistently treated the movies they distribute as a portfolio: in order to contain the uncertainty attached to the box-office performance of an individual movie, the company's risk is distributed across the whole product range. Decisions about story formats, budgets, genres and stars can, in this perspective, be seen as decisions about managing the risk of the unpredictability of audience taste, taken in the context of a studio's annual output:

> Films are not randomly different from one another. Highly successful films send back signals of audience preferences, as revealed through the box-office, to the originating studio and also to its rivals. Box-office success has regularly engendered clusters of films with similar story and aesthetic characteristics, forming, over time, lineages that are subject to life-cycle tendencies. (Sedgwick and Pokorny, 2004: 304)

Such analyses explain why Hollywood has continued to be dominated by a small number of large distributors, because risk can only be effectively spread across a relatively large portfolio of movies. They also provide underlying explanations of why movies are so often so similar to each other (as a form of risk minimization) and why audiences are only rarely inclined to see a movie more than once (for economic reasons, they are made to be fully accessible on a first viewing, so that a second viewing would add little to a viewer's pleasurable appreciation).

In *Hollywood's Road to Riches* (2005), David Waterman explains the history of post-Classical Hollywood as a consequence of its capacity to segment its market effectively. In the Classical system, the audience was segmented by time: movies would open first in the large city-centre cinemas charging the highest admission prices, and often take months to reach the neighbourhood, suburban and country venues where admission was much cheaper. Television eroded the lower tiers of the Classical exhibition system by flattening its system of price discrimination: by 1970, you either saw a movie in a first- or second-run cinema, or else you waited four years until you could see it for free on television. 'Low-value' customers simply lost the moviegoing habit, and Hollywood's market share, both domestically and internationally, reached its nadir while it was competing with European and Japanese production industries still protected from the impact of television on their domestic markets. Beginning with cable TV in the US in the mid-1970s, however, the development of pay media has greatly enhanced the movie industry's capacity to segment the market, and the faster growth of a home market for movie products in the US – from home video, to DVD, Video on Demand and direct downloads – has increased the economic resources of American movie producers in comparison to their foreign counterparts. New domestic technologies have given Hollywood a seemingly ever-expanding range of price points at which it can sell its products to everyone, from the avid first-night aficionado to the most recalcitrant couch potato. Hollywood's exponential profitability in the last twenty years comes from the fact that the revenue streams from these proliferating new media 'windows' have 'stacked' on top of each other: you see the movie in the cinema or pay cable, *and* you buy the DVD:

> The diffusion of pay media has transformed the revenue earning power of theatrical films not only by expanding markets to new consumers, like small children, but by allowing the studios to segment markets and extract far more of the demand that essentially had lain dormant within the queue of consumers waiting in a theater line of the 1940s. (Waterman, 2005: 116–17)

The industry has embraced Digital Rights Management technologies so enthusiastically not simply because it fears loss of revenue to 'piracy', but, more importantly, because it provides new levels of control for segmenting the market and discriminating prices, between, for example, the low-value customer who downloads for a single viewing and the higher-value customer who downloads a higher-resolution version for multiple viewings.

Waterman's is one of several recent attempts to explain the global success and the global decentralization of post-Classical Hollywood. These examinations of the contemporary industry range from populist celebrations of entertainment as 'the driving wheel of the new world economy' (Wolf, 1999: 4), and upmarket journalism (Epstein, 2005) through descriptive primers for film-school production courses (Daniels et al., 1998; Moore, 2000) marketing or commerce programs (Litman, 1998; Marich, 2005) to works of financial analysis ostensibly aimed at potential industry investors (Vogel, 2001). Their explanations broadly divide according to their analytical and ideological perspective between neoclassical economic endorsements of the 'free market' (De Vany, 2004; Waterman, 2005) and a broadly Marxist tradition of political economy (Hozic, 2001; Miller et al., 2005; Scott, 2005; Wasko, 2003). Econometric market analyses can to some extent explain post-Classical Hollywood's success, but the account cannot be complete without an examination of the level of state support that the 'copyright industries' have received from all levels of the State Department. In these considerations, an examination of the industry, particularly the contemporary industry, becomes inseparable from the analysis of the political economy of communications media (see O'Regan, Chapter 16). These are frequently attached to an engaged critique of existing systems of ownership and control, and advocacy for changes in public policy in relation to a range of issues from copyright, or 'cultural exemption', to labour practices.

The movie industry is now probably most important economically for its contribution to the US balance of payments, because of the extreme imbalance in the ratio of its exports to its imports. Incidentally, this may also be of some consequence to our perception of American culture, which makes much the same contradictory claims for its simultaneous exceptionalism and universality as are made for its political institutions and 'values'. Market analyses generally have little truck with attempts to explain Hollywood's international popularity on the grounds of its universal appeal, its immigrant heritage or some other element of cultural inheritance. Equally worthy of contemplation, however, is the inverse perspective. If Hollywood's dominance of the world's screens is explicable simply by force of numbers, where does that leave cultural accounts of Hollywood's power, whether those of the proselytizers of its 'soft power' in purveying American cultural values or the anti-American jeremiads of bourgeois cultural nationalists that American movies 'literally poison the souls of our children' turning them 'into the docile slaves of the American multi-millionaires' (Maurice Thorez, quoted in Jeancolas, 1998: 51)?

INTERPRETIVE HISTORIES

As an academic discipline, Film Studies was formed primarily in the image of literary studies. Its earliest academic practice was, and predominantly still is, textual interpretation. Methodologies of textual interpretation have also dominated most attempts to construct cultural histories of the movies, including most historians' use of film as a form of symptomatic evidence of a social or cultural condition pertaining at the time of their production. Social and political historians have, in the main, borrowed from film historians, and thus incorporated back into their histories the expectation that the artefacts of popular culture somehow reflect the culture of which they are a part. One historian of the 1930s, for instance, has described *I Am a Fugitive from a Chain Gang* (Mervyn Le Roy, US) as 'the perfect expression of the national mood in 1932: despair, suffering, hopelessness ... [The] film *was* 1932' (McElvane, 1984: 208, 213). How this relationship functions is seldom articulated, but while the word 'reflection' is itself often avoided, the talismanic powers of the term 'ideology' have been frequently invoked. The terminology of ideological analysis has, however, often done little more than complicate and obfuscate what is usually a fairly straightforward analytical procedure

by which critical interpretation substitutes for empirical research into how audiences might have understood and interpreted a movie at the time of its release.

These interpretive strategies nevertheless have a strongly seductive appeal, offering critics of popular culture the opportunity to make their objects of study meaningful by demonstrating their utility as surfaces reflecting the spirit of the times – the *Zeitgeist*. But as Mike Chopra-Gant has argued over what is perhaps the paradigmatic case of this interpretative history,

> There is no evidence to suggest that Hollywood filmmakers in the forties and fifties thought they were producing a 'film noir' or that American audiences of the period were ever conscious that a 'film noir' was what they were going to see ... . The use of a retrospectively constructed class such as 'film noir' as a lens through which the cinema and culture of the past might be examined is an inherently ahistorical endeavour that offers little prospect for producing a reliable impression of the period in question. (2006: 178)

Equally importantly, these interpretive strategies pay little attention to the popularity of the movies on which they concentrate on. Film historian Robert Ray has asserted that in the post-war period there was 'an enormous discrepancy ... between the most commercially successful movies and those that have ultimately been seen as significant' (1985: 140–1). Ray exaggerates only the uniqueness of this period: film history has, in almost its entirety, been written without regard to and often with deliberate disregard of the box office. Much has been omitted in the attempt to construct American film history as a story its historians want to tell and their audiences want to hear: a story of crisis, innovation, anxiety, subversion and turbulence. This conventional film history omits the great majority of Hollywood's most commercially successful products – Janet Gaynor, Nelson Eddy, Betty Grable, Shirley Temple – because, perhaps, no one wants to write the history of a cinema of complacency.

In much the same way as some stars and some films have acquired a cult critical status unrelated to their box-office earnings, some periods of Hollywood's history have come to be understood as more reflective of their cultural moment than others. Curiously, these tend to be periods of economic uncertainty, declining audiences and 'turbulence' in Hollywood's conventions of representation. While it is difficult to see why movies produced during such periods should be regarded as more *zeitgeistig* than those produced in periods of larger, more stable audiences and under more secure representational regimes, one of the attractions that periods of relative commercial instability have for critics is that they are often seen as giving rise to new forms. With their convoluted narratives and evident use of lighting codes and camera techniques to signify emotional states, *noir* films have an obvious appeal as objects of critical study, and a similar case can be made for many of the movies of Hollywood's 'Golden Age of Turbulence' in the early 1930s or the Hollywood Renaissance of the early 1970s.

Historical accounts that seek in the movies symptoms of social anxiety and disintegration almost inevitably become self-fulfilling, since they treat the movie-as-text as their primary historical source and, not surprisingly, select the most compelling examples as the evidence they present. In the process, an orthodox cultural history is constructed from a critically-prescribed canon of films. Film history is much more likely to view the *Zeitgeist* of 1953, for example, through the mirror of *The Big Heat* (Fritz Lang, US), distributed and received as 'a modest picture', than through *The Robe* (Henry Koster, US), the first CinemaScope production adapted from the year's best-selling novel, and one of a sustained cycle of lavishly-budgeted and commercially successful Biblical epics addressed to the 60 per cent of Americans who affirmed the American Way of Life through church membership. Although Cecil B. DeMille explained to his audiences in the prologue to *The Ten Commandments* (US, 1956) that 'the theme of this picture is whether men are to be ruled by God's law – or whether they are to be ruled by the whims of a dictator', explicitly paralleling it to the crusade against 'godless' Communism, the

Biblical blockbusters of the 1950s have been subject to even less critical examination as artefacts of ideology or of the popular mood than have the period's musicals. One reason for this may be that critics have failed to discover anything subversive in these movies. Ironically, much contemporary criticism is as concerned to investigate the subversive potential of Hollywood cinema as were the anti-Communists of the period, and although they come to praise the authors' subversion, not to incarcerate them, their methodology is also strikingly similar – and perhaps the comparison provides a salutary warning about the potent excesses of interpretation.

More generally, these interpretive cultural histories reveal the historiographical problems attached to critical approaches to Hollywood that fail to address its commercial core. As the case of film noir indicates, perhaps the most egregious of these approaches has been the belief that genre criticism provides a means of historically understanding the relationship between Hollywood movies and American culture. As Steve Neale has argued, this idea has 'in practice nearly always used the concept of genre as a way of avoiding detailed study of anything other than selective samples of Hollywood's art' (2000: 252). In reality, as both Neale and Rick Altman have cogently argued, critical presumptions about the coherence of generic taxonomies are challenged at every turn by historical examinations of production and reception, which demonstrate that while Hollywood's movies have consistently deployed generic conventions in their dialogue with their audiences, they have seldom if ever arranged themselves into a cinema of clearly differentiated genres (Altman, 1999: 16, 20).[5]

INSTITUTIONAL HISTORIES

In dramatic contrast to the creative speculation involved in the interpretive approach, institutional histories of Hollywood are grounded in the minutiae of memos, letters, the minutes of board meetings, financial records and the proceedings of court cases and Congressional hearings. A model for this kind of work is Balio's history of United Artists, comprising *United Artists: The Company Built by the Stars* (1976), based on the pre-1951 corporate records of United Artists that the company donated to the Wisconsin Center for Theater Research in 1969, and *United Artists: The Company that Changed the Film Industry* (1987). This research counters melodramatic histories founded on memory and anecdote with solid data that enables Balio to place the company in its corporate and social contexts.[6]

A further aspect of institutional history that has come under the spotlight in the last twenty years involves the operations of the industry's trade associations, principally the Motion Picture Producers and Distributors of America, Inc. (MPPDA), and its successor after 1945, the Motion Picture Association of America (MPAA). These studies reveal the ways in which the major studios have jointly represented their interests in the corporate, political and legal spheres, and the extent to which they have functioned as a cartel in the international market. They also reveal industry-wide responses to censorship problems and public relations crises, which resulted in the centralized regulation of Hollywood's motion-picture content over a period of nearly forty years, and are complemented by other studies that delve into the operations of state and international censorship boards themselves.

Classical Hollywood's most prominent mechanism for regulating on-screen material was the Production Code of 1930. Administered successively by the MPPDA and the MPAA, the Code has been the focus of several studies since its archive became available to researchers in 1983 (Bernstein, 1999; Couvares, 1996). The Production Code Administration (PCA) archive contains a file on most movies produced in Hollywood between 1930 and 1968, and consists of negotiations between the PCA and the studios over the representation of sensitive issues on the screen. The Code contained a list of subjects and treatments that producers were required to avoid (such as illegal drug traffic, 'white-slavery', 'sex perversion', and total

nudity), and a further list that they were advised to treat non-explicitly or with caution (such as seduction, rape, methods of crime and cruelty to animals). Although the MPPDA wielded the Code as a public relations weapon designed to reassure Hollywood's critics about the moral rectitude of the industry, in fact it also had a rational economic basis. All its strictures were based upon a thorough analysis of past censorship excisions, and so they formed a practical guide to producers about how to avoid shooting scenes that would be subject to expensive re-takes and re-editing. Seen from this point of view, the Code was a document designed to allow sex and violence onto the screen – albeit in a suggestive and non-explicit manner – rather than a method of keeping it off.

Some commentators have chosen to emphasize the PCA's role as 'industry censor', revealing details of negotiations around notorious movies which highlight the Administration's 'repressive' function in handling details of sex and violence under the Code. Gerald Gardner, for example, writing in *The Censorship Papers: Movie Censorship Letters from the Hays Office, 1934–1968* straightforwardly characterizes the work of the PCA as censorship, and expresses his sense of outrage:

> Behind closed doors, a group of men had the power to lay their hands on the creations of artists, to twist them this way and that, to satisfy the mandates and morals of a pious little group who feared for the souls of their fellow men. (1987: xiii)

More nuanced commentaries, such as those by Lea Jacobs (1991) and Richard Maltby (2003), have seen the operations of the PCA as a complex site of reconciliation between the desires of multiple diverse audiences, the demands of official cultural guardians represented by censors, the pressures exerted by powerful special-interest groups including the churches and the diplomatic requirements of both the State Department and foreign powers. These commentaries recognize that the Code itself cannot simply be taken at face value, but is underpinned by several competing agendas, some concerned with industry 'spin' and some purely utilitarian, which affect both its content and its rhetorical style. Jacobs, for example, writing in *The Wages of Sin: Censorship and the Fallen Woman Film, 1928–1942*, concludes:

> To study the process of self-regulation … is to restore some sense of the difficulties which the representation of sexuality posed within the institutional matrix defined by the relations between external agencies, film producers, and industry censors. In the face of the continual process of dispute and negotiation which the fallen woman cycle brought into play, we can begin to envision femininity as a construct that was at once tenuous and overdetermined in highly complicated ways. (1991: 153)

While the administration of the Production Code was the PCA's most widely-publicized role, the regulation of sex and violence was only one aspect of its function. Equally important, although never advertised to the public, was its administration of a second set of strictures known within the organization as 'industry policy'. Based, like the Production Code, on an analysis of past material that had caused public relations problems during distribution, industry policy identified and proscribed sensitive political subjects (such as themes that critiqued capitalism) and racial subjects (such as race relations in the American South). It also stipulated the ways in which prominent professional groups, such as politicians, judges, social workers and members of the press, could be treated on-screen: although individual members of these groups could be portrayed as villainous, drunk or incompetent, this had to be portrayed as atypical, rogue behaviour in the context of highly ethical professions. Similarly, industry policy required great care to be exercised in the portrayal of foreign nationals – a ruling which became sufficiently restrictive in the mid-1930s to encourage scriptwriters to set their scenarios in fictional mythical kingdoms rather than risk causing international offence (Vasey, 1997).

One of the most influential special-interest groups in Hollywood was the Catholic Church. The PCA's files demonstrate that Catholicism's interest in the movies did result in the direct modification of some aspects of motion picture representation, principally in the industry's representation of priests and of the Church itself. Much attention has been paid to the Catholic Legion of Decency campaign in 1933, during which branches of the Church distributed motion picture blacklists to their congregations (Black, 1994). It is arguable, however, that the effect of the Legion of Decency campaign, like that of the Code itself, was to reinforce the limits of acceptable representation that was possible under state and international censorship provisions; thus it ultimately served to assist Hollywood financially rather than penalizing it. The main lesson to be learnt from an examination of the PCA's archives is that the process of adapting a property to the screen involved an exhaustive process of compromise, transformation and negotiation, mainly to remove any causes of offence that might ultimately hinder its distribution through censorship or protest.

The PCA archive, together with the various studio archives that are now available to researchers, is amongst the best nuts-and-bolts evidence we have about how movies were put together in Classical Hollywood, particularly because they record how a variety of competing interests argued and negotiated over the final form of the movies. An appreciation of this process helps to explain why Hollywood narratives often appear incoherent, compromised or conventionalized, even while their central attractions function as powerfully as ever. The production process described in the archives should also lead us to be sceptical about claims that certain bodies of work take the form that they do because of the influence of individuals such as Jewish production executives, or Catholic PCA functionaries (see Gabler, 1988). There was little or no room within Hollywood's system of production for personal attitudes to find expression in this way. In this commercial cinema, the elements that stayed in were those that had found recent favour with audiences, and it was the job of production executives to ensure this in rapid time, regardless of their personal persuasions. The requirements of both censors and pressure groups were, by contrast, accommodated through the gaps, elisions and transformations in the cinema 'text' that often rendered it unrecognizable from its original source. Hollywood's capacity to respond quickly to both audience trends and conservative pressures – aided by the close links between production, distribution and exhibition that came about through vertical integration – helped it refine a formula for entertainment that was simultaneously normative and inventive. Schatz discusses something of the intricacy and complexity of this formula in *The Genius of the System* (1988), in which he argues against auteurist approaches to Hollywood in favour of the institutionally-based craftsmanship and creativity of the studio system.

Since the 1950s, when production first began to be outsourced to companies with looser links to the studios, the centralized checks and balances of Classical Hollywood have been eroded, and movies have become more diversely expressive. The abandonment of the Production Code in 1966 and the introduction of ratings in 1968 (still under the auspices of the MPAA) accelerated this trend, and in the quest for new markers of quality in the absence of the studio insignia the promotion of the 'director as star' has introduced 'personal' filmmaking styles to Hollywood's repertoire, and has established much broader parameters for the expression of sex and violence. Ironically, however, the consolidation of movie distribution at the centre of major media companies in the 1980s and 1990s has resulted in a new tension between artistic license and conservatism. As Justin Wyatt has observed, the formerly independent distributor Miramax became 'somewhat constrained' after it was acquired in 1993 by Disney, which has an inestimable investment in its historically family-friendly image. In 1995 a deliberately controversial advertising campaign for Antonia Bird's *Priest* (UK, 1994), for example, not only caused the film to attain the notoriety that was intended, but also resulted in a number of high-profile investors, including Senator

Bob Dole's wife Elizabeth, disposing of their Disney stock:

> The Knights of Columbus, selling $3 million of Disney stock, cited the company's ties to Miramax and *Priest*, while a Dole spokesman commented, 'Mrs Dole was surprised to learn that Disney owned Miramax and Hollywood Records and has decided to sell her stock'. (Wyatt, 1998: 85)

Public relations difficulties have also arisen in relation to the juvenile-sex movie *kids* (Larry Clark, US, 1995), Spike Lee's project *Summer of Sam* (US, 1999), Michael Moore's *Fahrenheit 9/11* (US, 2004) and others. While none of the Code and Ratings Administration's records have been made as publicly available as the Production Code Administration's, recent research into its operation has demonstrated a continuity of concern and, indeed, practice with the previous system, ensuring that the products of the MPAA member companies move freely through their markets. The major companies have consistently avoided releasing 'X' or 'NC-17' movies, from which minors are prohibited, and the borders between the other ratings are carefully patrolled and negotiated (Lewis, 2000; Lyons, 1997; Sandler, 2007; Vaughn, 2006). Self-regulation and self-censorship clearly remain in Hollywood's broad corporate interests, and the popular cinema remains a site where the limits of public taste and tolerance are negotiated and defined.

AESTHETIC ANALYSES

The aesthetics of Classical Hollywood film had little in common with European notions of high art, although occasionally the major studios brought out movies that were self-consciously serious in intent or formally experimental, in order to generate prestige for the studio and the American industry as a whole – for example, *Sunrise* (F.W. Murnau, US, 1927), *The Crowd* (King Vidor, US, 1928), *A Midsummer Night's Dream* (William Dieterle and Max Reinhardt, US, 1935). More routine production concentrated, instead, upon providing 'entertainment' that was sufficiently attractive and diverting to general audiences both within the United States and internationally to keep them turning up to the box office week in and week out. Defining and refining a general formula for a slate of productions with such enormously widespread appeal was Hollywood's grand, enduring and improbable achievement, part aesthetic and part commercial – what André Bazin famously called 'the genius of the system' (1968: 154). Despite the incorporation of cinematic expression of all kinds into the distribution apparatus of modern Hollywood, it is still the industry's most popular and widely consumed products that underpin its economics, and the most appealing elements of these products have varied little since the Classical era.

From an economic point of view, the remarkably consistent nature of Hollywood's attractions has resulted from the necessity of stabilizing audience demand and minimizing financial risk. It is largely for these reasons that Hollywood's output has been consistently star-centred and generically based: the appeal of a star or genre persists beyond the end of the film and invites the provision of similar, if reconfigured, pleasures in future productions. This begs the question, however, of exactly what it is about stardom and genre that proves so compelling to audiences, and commentators on Hollywood have written extensively on both areas in an attempt to analyse the pleasures they provide.[7]

On many levels Hollywood is an erotic cinema, and the audience's intimate association with the stars on screen are at the heart of this eroticism. From movie to movie, audiences become acquainted with the physical fascination, stylistic assurance, moral strength (or amoral insouciance) and emotional vulnerability of the star. Interviews, advertising tie-ins, magazine articles and 'candid' observations of the star work teasingly to suggest that they are sometimes to be found in the prosaic world inhabited by their fans, despite the fact that their glamorous personae are evidently dependent upon the rarefied oxygen of the hyperreal world on screen.

While the erotics of Hollywood are most obviously expressed through the vehicle of the star, equally persistent attractions are provided through Hollywood's employment of spectacle. This has several different but related dimensions. Exoticism is one, perhaps most obviously expressed in the James Bond franchise, which has taken its audiences to every conceivable extreme of exotic location. Science fiction and historical settings have also long been staples of exotic spectacle, with the locales themselves imaginatively engaging audiences to an extent that can rival or exceed the attractions of the characters and narrative. The offering of these exotic locations to the audience, in tandem with more generic elements of adventure, heroism or romance, constitutes a way in which Hollywood flaunts its ability to put money on the screen. From the point of view of the potential moviegoer seeking a good night out, a Hollywood movie may constitute a sound investment of their entertainment dollar precisely because it can deliver highly expensive art direction, effects and stars, at the same time as delivering the reliable staples of story and characterization with a guaranteed level of technical competence. The Busby Berkeley movies that Warner Bros brought out during the Depression were extravagant examples of this syndrome, offering moviegoers spectacular sets, costumes, choreography and dancing girls as a bonus on top of the basic love story, all for the small price of admission to the cinema during an era of material deprivation. While these were musicals, the broader spectrum of 'action' in movies – including increasingly elaborate chases, fights, explosions, monsters, cities collapsing and so on – also allows Hollywood to demonstrate its capacity for financial and technical excess in the production of audience pleasure. Hollywood literally delivers more bang for the moviegoer's buck, and in so doing maintains its differentiation from less highly capitalized forms of cinematic entertainment.

Given that they have constituted such a conspicuous and strongly promoted element of Hollywood's output, it is surprising that work on the spectacular elements of the cinema has not featured more strongly in scholarly writing on the movies – another hangover from film literature's early debt to literary criticism. Some useful early work was laid out by A. Nicholas Vardac in *From Stage to Screen* (1947), which traces some of early cinema's debt to the aesthetics of the spectacular popular stage. More recent work has concentrated on the visceral impact of action-based special effects, which toss the audience vicariously into the centre of the cinematic experience through the use of fast-paced editing, computer-generated imagery and energetic musical scoring. Following the example of *Star Wars*, which was successfully spun off into the theme-park ride Star Tours and a succession of computer games, action-based movies are increasingly designed with future exploitation options in mind, with the potential for rides, games and 'action figurines' influencing the style and form of the original cinematic production (King, 2000; Stringer, 2003).

Mainstream Hollywood movies are designed more to draw audiences into their imaginative worlds than to distance them and invite contemplation, with action-based movies being only the most extreme example. Continuity editing was devised in Hollywood, partly for reasons involved with streamlining production, but more fundamentally in order to provide audiences with a seamless, intimate and unobstructed perspective upon the action. Within this system the audience is normally positioned so as to see and hear the salient details of the movie's narration with a minimum of disruption and frustration; the camera/screen provides a perspective upon the action that rarely draws attention to its own mediating function. A paradigm for Hollywood's 'classical' approach to narration was elaborated by Bordwell in *Narration in the Fiction Film* (1985). Bordwell describes the mainstream Hollywood film as unified around 'psychologically defined individuals who struggle to solve a clear-cut problem or to attain specific goals'; the movies' style of narration is determined by this central line of action, and is structured as a series

of causal relations. Citing Eugene Vale's *The Technique of Screenplay Writing* (1972: 135–60), Bordwell points out that the basic features of this paradigm are supported by industry practice, in which screenplays are constructed along the classical lines of 'the well-made play, the popular romance, and, crucially, the late-nineteenth-century short story':

> Hollywood screenplay-writing manuals have long insisted on a formula which has been revived in recent structural analysis: the plot consists of an undisturbed stage, the disturbance, the struggle, and the elimination of the disturbance. (1985: 157)

Departures from the cause-and-effect structure of classical narrative can be motivated by a number of intrinsic factors: for example, displays of technical virtuosity or spectacle may be the result of artistic motivation, while characters suddenly bursting into song may result from generic motivation. Through Bordwell and Thompson's influential text *Film Art* (2003), this approach to Hollywood narration has become widely accepted: Thompson has since demonstrated its application to contemporary Hollywood in *Storytelling in the New Hollywood* (1999), and Bordwell has elaborated his ideas in relation to contemporary Hollywood in *The Way Hollywood Tells It* (2006).

While not necessarily challenging the details of Bordwell's analysis, some scholars, including Maltby (2003: 15), Elizabeth Cowie (1998: 178–90) and Geoff King, have questioned the primacy of classical narrational forms in the construction of Hollywood movies. King comments,

> The overriding aim of the studio system was not to produce 'classically' balanced and harmonious compositions, but to make money. The industry was, and remains, governed by what Maltby terms a 'commercial aesthetic, essentially opportunistic in its economic motivation', in which a variety of ingredients are used to increase the potential profitability of a film … . The star might be consumed as a form of spectacle: an audio-visual presence to be enjoyed in its own right. Films featuring favourite stars might be experienced in terms of the star presence as much as their

place within, and helping to shape, a developing narrative. The point, as Maltby suggests, is that viewers can pick and choose among different elements as the principal sources of pleasure. Seamless narrative might be more important to some viewers than to others. It might figure more centrally in some types of films, such as mystery or suspense, in which the complexity or resolution of plot elements is heavily foregrounded. Elsewhere, or for other viewers, the quality of narrative might be of less importance, subordinated to or combined with the display of star presence, action, locations, or whatever. (2002: 180–1)

The implication here is that in explaining the pleasures offered by the movies – which is to say, in accounting for the form, content and, indeed, continuing existence of the commercial cinema – the contribution of the scriptwriter need not necessarily be seen as being more determining than the presence of the star or the contribution of the special effects team. In *High Concept* (1994), Wyatt relates the aesthetic pleasures in the cinema of the 1980s and 1990s to the positioning at the centre of wider marketing and merchandising campaigns, which he sees as resulting in narrative disruptions that are motivated extrinsically to the movie 'text', in contradistinction to Bordwell's intrinsic motivations. Spin-off music videos, for example, account for 'detachable' and otherwise unmotivated musical sequences in movies such as *Flashdance* (Adrian Lyne, US, 1983), *Footloose* (Herbert Ross, US, 1984) and *Purple Rain* (Albert Magnoli, US, 1984).

In *Hollywood Cinema* (2003), Maltby introduces the idea of 'commercial aesthetics', cited above by King, as the basis for a revised understanding of the form and operations of the movies. He sees the construction of Hollywood movies as being motivated by the aim of 'providing the maximum pleasure for the maximum number, to ensure a maximum profit' (2003: 60). This leads him to ask 'how Hollywood movies are organized to deliver pleasure to their audiences', as well as to question how movies relate to their broader cultural, commercial and industrial contexts (2003: 16). The logic of commercial aesthetics sees the

evaluative criteria that are commonly brought to high culture as irrelevant to Hollywood's products, which are designed as much more open texts, available for pleasurable consumption at many different levels by their diverse audiences. Maltby sees the fundamental shape, rhythm and segmentation of commercial cinema as proceeding from the psychology of the audience, employing narrational strategies for continually engaging the audience's interest and – especially – their emotions.

There is a case to be made that, in Hollywood cinema, every element presented on-screen and in the soundtrack is designed to provide the audience with a structured emotional experience. The language of Western aesthetics deals poorly with nuanced descriptions of affect, in contrast of some Eastern cultures such as Japan and India. However, the elicitation of emotional responses, in a complex variety of combinations, evidently underlies much of the art and craft of Hollywood, including scriptwriting, lighting and cinematography, art direction and – most obviously – musical scoring. An emphasis on the audience's emotional experience can also add to our current understanding of how generic elements work in Hollywood cinema. Altman, for instance, argues that the obligation to arrive at a happy ending leads classical narrative to 'reason backward', 'retrofitting' the beginning so that it may lead logically to the predetermined happy ending (1992: 32). The use of generic classifications by movie publicists, video stores and reviewers operates as a way in which to advise potential consumers of movies about what kinds of emotional rewards to expect in specific productions. Thrillers, romances and horror movies are all self-explanatory in this regard, while westerns, detective stories, gangster movies, teenpics and science fiction are all characterized by widely-known emotional signatures, achieved through atmosphere (locations and art direction), characterization (actors/stars admixed with stereotypes of heroism, villainy, desirability and/or eccentricity), narrative and music.

If audiences go to the popular cinema to feel while they go to the art cinema to think, then placing the elicitation and management of emotion at the centre of the organization of the Hollywood 'text' may throw new light on such disparate, but perennial, elements of the commercial cinema already discussed above, including stardom, spectacle, erotic or comic plots and subplots, and narratives that appear, according to more rational criteria, to be incoherent or nonsensical. This approach seems to be particularly productive if 'emotion' or 'feeling' is defined sufficiently broadly to include comic, thrilling, awe-inspiring and sensational impacts. Since 1995, a number of publications have appeared in this area, including work by Murray Smith (1995), Ed S. Tan (1996), Greg M. Smith (2003) and Carl Plantinga (Plantinga and Smith, 1999). Some related work has also begun in the area of cognitive psychology (see Hogan, 2003). Models based upon the idea of popular film as a complex, structured emotional experience promise to prove more nuanced and productive than has the application of psychoanalytic theory to the cinema, with its globalizing notion of 'desire'.

In the end, what the question of Hollywood has brought to Film Studies has been less a conceptual paradigm than a provocation to explain and understand a complex and endlessly self-reinventing object of analysis. Because its products are so beguiling, so easily and so pleasurably consumed, 'Hollywood' remains a popular byword for a not quite serious industry, run by people who do not quite live in the real world. The challenge for the scholar is to find ways to take Hollywood seriously, despite itself (Maltby, 2003: 5–31). Hollywood is a phenomenon that demands our attention, not only for its status as a (very real) multi-billion industry, but also for its remarkable capacity to obscure its financial operations with a smokescreen of anecdote, biography and gossip, with the willing collusion of the popular and critical cultures it inhabits. Most of all, far from warranting dismissal for its commercial basis, Hollywood cinema uniquely expresses a complex formula for entertainment which, if not 'universal', demonstrates extraordinarily diverse cultural and demographic appeal. Apparently at its most guileless and open-hearted when it manages to appeal simultaneously to the emotions of its many audiences, this is also when Hollywood reveals its most sophisticated and highly developed industrial strategy.

NOTES

I wish to acknowledge the invaluable support that I received from Richard Maltby during the writing of this paper – practical (especially in the section on Interpretive Histories), inspirational, conceptual, emotional and most of all culinary.

1 There is an extensive literature on Disney, ranging from hagiographies to character assassinations and essays on cultural imperialism. For informative overviews of Disney company history, see Nicholas Sammond's *Babes in Tomorrowland: Walt Disney and the Making of the American Child, 1930–1960*(2005), Steven Watts' *The Magic Kingdom: Walt Disney and the American Way of Life* (1997), and Janet Wasko's *Understanding Disney: The Manufacture of Fantasy* (2001). Kerry Segrave provides a history of the symbiotic relationship between product advertising and the movies in *Product Placement in Hollywood Films: A History* (2004).

2 A revised edition of Gomery's book, *The Hollywood Studio System: A History* (2005), extends his summary account of the economic and institutional individual major companies beyond his original description of the Classical system to cover post-Paramount and contemporary Hollywood.

3 The *History of the American Cinema* series is edited by Charles Harpole and published by Charles Scribner's Sons (New York) and the University of California Press. Individual volumes, in volume order, are: Vol. 1: Charles Musser, *The Emergence of Cinema: The American Screen to 1907* (1990); Vol. 2: Eileen Bowser, *The Transformation of Cinema: 1907–1915* (1990); Vol. 3: Richard Koszarski, *An Evening's Entertainment: The Age of the Silent Feature Picture, 1915–1928* (1990); Vol. 4: Donald Crafton, *The Talkies: American Cinema's Transition to Sound, 1926–1931* (1997); Vol. 5: Tino Balio, *Grand Design: Hollywood as a Modern Business Enterprise, 1930–1939* (1993); Vol. 6: Thomas Schatz, *Boom and Bust: American Cinema in the 1940s* (1997); Vol. 7: Peter Lev, *The Fifties: Transforming the Screen, 1950–1959* (2006); Vol. 8: Paul Monaco, *The Sixties, 1960–1969* (2001); Vol. 9: David A. Cook, *Lost Illusions: American Cinema in the Shadow of Watergate and Vietnam, 1970–1979* (2000); Vol. 10: Stephen Prince, *A New Pot of Gold: Hollywood under the Electronic Rainbow, 1980–1989* (2000).

4 See also Allen J. Scott's *On Hollywood: The Place, the Industry* (2005).

5 Recent studies of film genres that have incorporated this criticism include Barry Langford's *Film Genre: Hollywood and Beyond* (2005); Kevin Heffernan's *Ghouls, Gimmicks, and Gold: Horror Films and the American Movie Business, 1953–1968* (2004); Peter Stanfield's *Hollywood, Westerns and the 1930s: The Lost Trail* (2001); and essays in *Genre and Contemporary Hollywood* (2002) by Neale.

6 Other studies based on comparable access to company archives include Matthew Bernstein's *Walter Wanger: Hollywood Independent* (1994) and *Inside Warner Bros. 1935–1951* (1986) edited by Rudy Behlmer.

7 On genre, see Altman's *Film/Genre* (1999); Neale's *Genre and Hollywood* (2000); Linda Williams' *Playing the Race Card: Melodramas of Black and White from Uncle Tom to O.J. Simpson* (2001). On stars, see Richard deCordova's *Picture Personalities: The Emergence of the Star System in America* (1990); *Stardom: Industry of Desire* (1991), edited by Christine Gledhill; Richard Dyer's *Stars* (1979) and *Heavenly Bodies: Film Stars and Society* (1987); Thomas Austin and Martin Barker's *Contemporary Hollywood Stardom* (2003); and Karen Hollinger's *The Actress: Hollywood Acting and the Female Star* (2006).

REFERENCES

Acland, Charles R. (2003) *Screen Traffic: Movies, Multiplexes, and Global Culture.* Durham, NC: Duke University Press.

Allen, Robert C. (1990) 'From Exhibition to Reception: Reflections on the Audience in Film History', *Screen,* 31(4): 352–53.

Allen, Robert C. (1999) 'Home alone Together: Hollywood and the Family Film', in Melvyn Stokes and Richard Maltby (eds), *Identifying Hollywood's Audiences: Cultural Identity and the Movies.* London: British Film Institute. pp. 109–31.

Altman, Rick (1992) 'Dickens, Griffith, and Film Theory Today', in Jane Gaines (ed.), *Classical Hollywood Narrative: The Paradigm Wars.* Durham, NC: Duke University Press.

Altman, Rick (1999) *Film/Genre.* London: British Film Institute.

Anderson, Christopher (1994) *Hollywood TV: The Studio System in the Fifties.* Austin: University of Texas Press.

Austin, Thomas (2002) *Hollywood, Hype and Audiences: Selling and Watching Popular Film in the 1990s.* Manchester: Manchester University Press.

Austin, Thomas and Barker, Martin (2003) *Contemporary Hollywood Stardom.* London: Arnold.

Balio, Tino (1976) *United Artists: The Company Built by the Stars.* Madison: University of Wisconsin Press.

Balio, Tino (ed.) (1985) *The American Film Industry.* Rev. edn. Madison: University of Wisconsin Press.

Balio, Tino (1987) *United Artists: The Company That Changed the Film Industry.* Madison: University of Wisconsin Press.

Balio, Tino (1993) *Grand Design: Hollywood as a Modern Business Enterprise, 1930–1939.* Vol.5, *History of the American Cinema.* New York/Berkeley: Charles Scribner's Sons/University of California Press.

Balio, Tino (1998) '"A Major Presence in All of the World's Important Markets": The Globalization of Hollywood in the 1990s', in Steve Neale and Murray Smith (eds), *Contemporary Hollywood Cinema.* London: Routledge. pp. 58–73.

Bart, Peter (1999) *The Gross: The Hits, the Flops – The Summer that Ate Hollywood.* New York: St Martin's Press.

Baxter, John (1976) *The Hollywood Exiles.* London: Grumbacher.

Bazin, André (1968) 'La Politique des auteurs', in Peter Graham (ed.), *The New Wave.* London: Secker and Warburg. pp. 137–55.

Behlmer, Rudy (ed.) (1986) *Inside Warner Bros. (1935–1951).* London: Weidenfeld and Nicolson.

Belton, John (1992) *Widescreen Cinema.* Cambridge, MA: Harvard University Press.

Bernstein, Matthew (1994) *Walter Wanger: Hollywood Independent.* Berkeley: University of California Press.

Bernstein, Matthew (ed.) (1999) *Controlling Hollywood: Censorship and Regulation in the Studio Era.* New Brunswick, NJ: Rutgers University Press.

Biskind, Peter (1983) *Seeing is Believing: How Hollywood Taught Us to Stop Worrying and Love the Fifties.* London: Pluto Press.

Biskind, Peter (1998) *Easy Riders, Raging Bulls: How the Sex Drugs and Rock 'n' Roll Generation Saved Hollywood.* New York: Simon & Schuster.

Biskind, Peter (2004) *Down and Dirty Pictures: Miramax, Sundance, and the Rise of Independent Film.* New York: Simon & Schuster.

Black, Gregory D. (1994) *Hollywood Censored: Morality Codes, Catholics, and the Movies.* Cambridge: Cambridge University Press.

Bordwell, David (1985) *Narration in the Fiction Film.* London: Methuen.

Bordwell, David (2006) *The Way Hollywood Tells It: Story and Style in Modern Movies.* Berkeley: University of California Press.

Bordwell, David, Staiger, Janet and Thompson, Kristin (1985) *The Classical Hollywood Cinema: Film*

Style and Mode of Production to 1960. London: Routledge & Kegan Paul.

Bordwell, David and Thompson, Kristin (2003) *Film Art: An Introduction*. 7th edn. New York: McGraw-Hill.

Bowser, Eileen (1990) *The Transformation of Cinema: 1907–1915*. Vol.2, *History of the American Cinema*. New York/Berkeley: Charles Scribner's Sons/University of California Press.

Chopra-Gant, Mike (2006) *Hollywood Genres and Postwar America: Masculinity, Family and Nation in Popular Movies and Film Noir*. London: I.B. Tauris.

Cook, David A. (2000) *Lost Illusions: American Cinema in the Shadow of Watergate and Vietnam, 1970–1979*. Vol.9, *History of the American Cinema*. New York/Berkeley: Charles Scribner's Sons/University of California Press.

Couvares, Francis G. (ed.) (1996) *Movie Censorship and American Culture*. Washington: Smithsonian Institution Press.

Cowie, Elizabeth (1998) 'Storytelling: Classical Hollywood Cinema and Classical Narrative', in Steve Neale and Murray Smith (eds), *Contemporary Hollywood Cinema*. London: Routledge. pp. 178–90.

Crafton, Donald (1997) *The Talkies: American Cinema's Transition to Sound, 1926–1931*. Vol.4, *History of the American Cinema*. New York/Berkeley: Charles Scribner's Sons/University of California Press.

Dale, Martin (1997) *The Movie Game: The Film Business in Britain, Europe and America*. London: Cassell.

Daniels, Bill, Leedy, David and Sills, Steven D. (1998) *Movie Money: Understanding Hollywood's (Creative) Accounting Practices*. Los Angeles: Silman-James Press.

deCordova, Richard (1990) *Picture Personalities: The Emergence of the Star System in America*. Urbana: University of Illinois Press.

De Vany, Arthur S. (2004) *Hollywood Economics: How Extreme Uncertainty Shapes the Film Industry*. London: Routledge.

Doherty, Thomas (1988) *Teenagers and Teenpics: The Juvenilization of American Movies in the 1950s*. Boston: Unwin Hyman.

Dyer, Richard (1979) *Stars*. London: BFI.

Dyer, Richard (1987) *Heavenly Bodies: Film Stars and Society*. London: Macmillan.

Enticknap, Leo (2005) *Moving Image Technology*. London: Wallflower.

Epstein, Edward Jay (2005) *The Big Picture: The New Logic of Money and Power in Hollywood*. New York: Random House.

Fitzgerald, F. Scott (1974) *The Last Tycoon*. Harmondsworth: Penguin.

Gabler, Neale (1988) *An Empire of Their Own: How the Jews Invented Hollywood*. New York: Crown Publishers.

Gardner, Gerald (1987) *The Censorship Papers: Movie Censorship Letters from the Hays Office, 1934–1968*. New York: Dodd, Mead and Company.

Gilbey, Ryan (2003) *It Don't Worry Me: The Revolutionary American Films of the Seventies*. New York: Faber & Faber.

Giovacchini, Saverio (2001) *Hollywood Modernism: Film and Politics in the Age of the New Deal*. Philadelphia: Temple University Press.

Gledhill, Christine (ed.) (1991) *Stardom: Industry of Desire*. London: Routledge.

Goldsmith, Ben and O'Regan, Tom (2005) *The Film Studio: Film Production in the Global Economy*. Lanham, MD: Rowman and Littlefield.

Gomery, Douglas (1986) *The Hollywood Studio System*. London: Macmillan.

Gomery, Douglas (2004) *The Coming of Sound: A History*. New York: Routledge.

Gomery, Douglas (2005) *The Hollywood Studio System: A History*. London: BFI.

Heffernan, Kevin (2004) *Ghouls, Gimmicks, and Gold: Horror Films and the American Movie Business, 1953–1968*. Durham, NC: Duke University Press.

Hogan, Patrick Colm (2003) *Cognitive Science, Literature and the Arts: A Guide for Humanists*. New York: Routledge.

Hollinger, Karen (2006) *The Actress: Hollywood Acting and the Female Star*. New York: Routledge.

Holt, Jennifer (2001–2002) 'In Deregulation We Trust: The Synergy of Politics and Industry in Reagan-Era Hollywood', *Film Quarterly*, 55(2): 22–9.

Horwath, Alexander, King, Noel and Elsaesser, Thomas (2004) *The Last Great American Picture Show: New Hollywood Cinema in the 1970s*. Amsterdam: Amsterdam University Press.

Hozic, Aida (2001) *Hollyworld: Space, Power, and Fantasy in the American Economy*. Ithaca, NY: Cornell University Press.

Jacobs, Lea (1991) *The Wages of Sin: Censorship and the Fallen Woman Film, 1928–1942*. Madison: University of Wisconsin Press.

Jarvie, Ian (1992) *Hollywood's Overseas Campaign: The North Atlantic Movie Trade, 1920–1950*. Cambridge: Cambridge University Press.

Jeancolas, Jean-Pierre (1998) 'From the Blum-Byrnes Agreement to the GATT Affair', in Geoffrey Nowell-Smith and Steven Ricci (eds), *Hollywood & Europe: Economics, Culture, National Identity, 1945–1995*. London: BFI. pp. 47–60.

Kennedy, Joseph P. (ed.) (1927) *The Story of the Films*. Chicago: A.W. Shaw.

King, Geoff (2000) *Spectacular Narratives: Hollywood in the Age of the Blockbuster.* London: I.B. Tauris.

King, Geoff (2002) *New Hollywood Cinema: An Introduction.* New York: Columbia University Press.

King, Geoff (2005) *American Independent Cinema.* Bloomington: Indiana University Press.

Klinger, Barbara (2006) *Beyond the Multiplex: Cinema, New Technologies, and the Home.* Berkeley: University of California Press.

Koszarski, Richard (1990) *An Evening's Entertainment: The Age of the Silent Feature Picture, 1915–1928.* Vol.3, *History of the American Cinema.* New York/Berkeley: Charles Scribner's Sons/University of California Press.

Langford, Barry (2005) *Film Genre: Hollywood and Beyond.* Edinburgh: Edinburgh University Press.

Lastra, James (2000) *Sound Technology and the American Cinema: Perception, Representation, Modernity.* New York: Columbia University Press.

Lev, Peter (2006) *The Fifties: Transforming the Screen, 1950–59.* Vol.7, *History of the American Cinema.* New York/Berkeley: Charles Scribner's Sons/University of California Press.

Lewis, Jon (2000) *Hollywood V. Hard Core: How the Struggle over Censorship Saved the Modern Film Industry.* New York: New York University Press.

Litman, Barry R. (1998) *The Motion Picture Mega-Industry.* Boston: Allyn and Bacon.

Lyons, Charles (1997) *The New Censors: Movies and the Culture Wars.* Philadelphia: Temple University Press.

Maltby, Richard (2003) *Hollywood Cinema.* 2nd edn. Malden, MA: Blackwell.

Marich, Robert (2005) *Marketing to Moviegoers: A Handbook of Strategies Used by Major Studios and Independents.* Boston: Focal Press.

McElvane, Robert (1984) *The Great Depression: America, 1929–1941.* New York: Times Books.

Miller, Toby, Govil, Nitin, McMurria, John, Maxwell, Richard and Wang, Ting (2005) *Global Hollywood 2.* London: BFI.

Monaco, Paul (2001) *The Sixties, 1960–1969.* Vol.8, *History of the American Cinema.* New York/Berkeley: Charles Scribner's Sons/University of California Press.

Moore, Schuyler M. (2000) *The Biz: The Basic Business, Legal and Financial Aspects of the Film Industry.* Los Angeles: Silman-James Press.

Muscio, Giuliana (1997) *Hollywood's New Deal.* Philadelphia: Temple University Press.

Musser, Charles (1990*) The Emergence of Cinema: The American Screen to 1907.* Vol.1, *History of the American Cinema.* New York/Berkeley: Charles Scribner's Sons/University of California Press.

Neale, Steve (2000) *Genre and Hollywood.* London: Routledge.

Neale, Steve (2002) *Genre and Contemporary Hollywood.* London: BFI.

O'Brien, Charles (2005) *Cinema's Conversion to Sound: Technology and Film Style in France and the U.S.* Bloomington: Indiana University Press.

Petrie, Graham (1985) *Hollywood Destinies:European Directors in America, 1922–1931.* London: Routledge.

Plantinga, Carl and Smith, Greg M. (eds) (1999) *Passionate Views: Film, Cognition and Emotion.* Baltimore, MD: Johns Hopkins University Press.

Powdermaker, Hortense (1950) *Hollywood the Dream Factory: An Anthropologist Looks at the Movie-Makers.* Boston: Little, Brown.

Prince, Stephen (2000) *A New Pot of Gold: Hollywood under the Electronic Rainbow, 1980–1989.* Vol.10, *History of the American Cinema.* New York/Berkeley: Charles Scribner's Sons/University of California Press.

Ray, Robert (1985) *A Certain Tendency of the Hollywood Cinema, 1930–1980.* Princeton, NJ: Princeton University Press.

Rosten, Leo (1941) *Hollywood: The Movie Colony, The Movie Makers.* New York: Harcourt, Brace.

Sammond, Nicholas (2005) *Babes in Tomorrowland: Walt Disney and the Making of the American Child, 1930–1960.* Durham, NC: Duke University Press.

Sandler, Kevin (2007) *The Naked Truth: Why Hollywood Does Not Make NC-17 Films.* New Brunswick, NJ: Rutgers University Press.

Saunders, Thomas J. (1994) *Hollywood in Berlin: American Cinema and Weimar Germany.* Berkeley: University of California Press.

Schatz, Thomas (1988) *The Genius of the System: Hollywood Filmmaking in the Studio Era.* New York: Pantheon Books.

Schatz, Thomas (1993) 'The New Hollywood', in Jim Collins, Hilary Radner and Ava Preacher (eds), *Film Theory Goes to the Movies.* New York: Routledge. pp. 8–36.

Schatz, Thomas (1997) *Boom and Bust: American Cinema in the 1940s.* Vol.6, *History of the American Cinema.* New York/Berkeley: Charles Scribner's Sons/University of California Press.

Scott, Allen J. (2005) *On Hollywood: The Place, the Industry.* Princeton, NJ: Princeton University Press.

Sedgwick, John (2000) *Popular Filmgoing in 1930s Britain: A Choice of Pleasures.* Exeter: University of Exeter Press.

Sedgwick, John and Pokorny, Michael (2004) *An Economic History of Film.* London: Routledge.

Segrave, Kerry (2004) *Product Placement in Hollywood Films: A History.* Jefferson, NC: McFarland.

Sergi, Gianluca (2004) *The Dolby Era: Film Sound in Contemporary Hollywood*. Manchester: Manchester University Press.

Smith, Greg M. (2003) *Film Structure and the Emotion System*. Cambridge: Cambridge University Press.

Smith, Murray (1995) *Engaging Characters: Fiction, Emotion and the Cinema*. Oxford: Clarendon Press.

Stanfield, Peter (2001) *Hollywood, Westerns and the 1930s: The Lost Trail*. Exeter: University of Exeter Press.

Stringer, Julian (ed.) (2003) *Movie Blockbusters*. London: Routledge.

Tan, Ed S. (1996) *Emotion and the Structure of Narrative Film: Film as an Emotion Machine*. Tr. Barbara Fasting. Mahwah, NJ: Lawrence Erlbaum Associates.

Thompson, Kristin (1985) *Exporting Entertainment: America in the World Film Market, 1907–1934*. London: BFI.

Thompson, Kristin (1999) *Storytelling in the New Hollywood: Understanding Classical Narrative Technique*. Cambridge, MA: Harvard University Press.

Thompson, Kristin (2006) *Herr Lubitsch Goes to Hollywood: German and American Film after World War I*. Amsterdam: Amsterdam University Press.

Trumpbour, John (2002) *Selling Hollywood to the World: U.S. and European Struggles for Mastery of the Global Film Industry, 1920–1950*. Cambridge: Cambridge University Press.

Vale, Eugene (1972) *The Technique of Screenplay Writing*. New York: Grosset and Dunlap.

Vardac, A. Nicholas (1947) *Stage to Screen: Theatrical Origins of Early Film: David Garrick to D.W. Griffith*. Cambridge, MA: Harvard University Press.

Vasey, Ruth (1997) *The World According to Hollywood, 1919–1939*. Exeter: University of Exeter Press.

Vaughn, Stephen (2006) *Freedom and Entertainment: Rating the Movies in an Age of New Media*. New York: Cambridge University Press.

Vogel, Harold L. (2001) *Entertainment Industry Economics: A Guide for Financial Analysis*. 5th edn. Cambridge: Cambridge University Press.

Wasko, Janet (2001) *Understanding Disney: The Manufacture of Fantasy*. Cambridge: Polity Press.

Wasko, Janet (2003) *How Hollywood Works*. London: Sage.

Waterman, David (2005) *Hollywood's Road to Riches*. Cambridge, MA: Harvard University Press.

Watts, Steven (1997) *The Magic Kingdom: Walt Disney and the American Way of Life*. Boston: Houghton Mifflin.

Williams, Linda (2001) *Playing the Race Card: Melodramas of Black and White from Uncle Tom to O. J. Simpson*. Princeton, NJ: Princeton University Press.

Wolf, Michael J. (1999) *The Entertainment Economy: How Mega-Media Forces Are Transforming Our Lives*. London: Penguin Books.

Wyatt, Justin (1994) *High Concept: Movies and Marketing in Hollywood*. Austin: University of Texas Press.

Wyatt, Justin (1998) 'The Formation of the "Major Independents": Miramax, New Line and the New Hollywood', in Steve Neale and Murray Smith (eds), *Contemporary Hollywood Cinema*. London: Routledge. pp. 74–90.

20

Formalist Tendencies in Film Studies

Warren Buckland

Formalism, both inside and outside Film Studies, is a rich and variegated paradigm. In Film Studies, the formalist tradition covers everything from the Russian formalists (see Eagle, 1981) to Rudolf Arnheim's pioneering *Film as Art* (1957), Christian Metz's film semiotics (1974a; 1974b; Buckland, 1999); Noël Burch's study of film's formal principles (1981); Edward Branigan's description of point of view in narrative cinema (1984); Raymond Bellour's shot-by-shot analyses of film segments (2000); Barry Salt's statistical style analysis (1974; 1992; 2004); David Bordwell's film poetics (1981; 1988a; 1989: ch.11; 1993; 1998; 2000); Kristin Thompson's neoformalism (1981; 1988); Noël Carroll's functional analysis of film form (1998); plus the productive tradition of *mise en scène* and auteur criticism (*Cahiers du cinéma* [Hillier, 1985; Hillier, 1986], *Movie* magazine [Cameron, 1972; Perkins, 1972], Andrew Sarris [1968]). Some researchers use formalist theory in a purely descriptive manner, constructing meticulously precise taxonomies; others, influenced by poetics, examine how a film is put together; while formalist critics use their formal descriptions to evaluate film style.

Other variations of formal criticism also exist. Art theorist Nick Zangwill (2001: ch. 4) identifies three conceptions of form: extreme formalism, moderate formalism, and anti-formalism. For extreme formalists such as the early-twentieth-century art critics Clive Bell (1928) and Roger Fry (1924), form is coterminous with aesthetics. Art appreciation, they argue, only requires a sustained attention to an artwork's internal properties – its arrangement of lines, shapes, and colours – to the exclusion of external properties such as its making or its representational function. Anti-formalists such as art theorists George Dickie (1974) and Arthur Danto (1964) argue from the opposite position: that aesthetic values are not formal, are not internal or intrinsic to a work of art, but are contextual and institutional. Zangwill attempts to defend a moderate aesthetic formalism, an intuitive notion in which some aesthetic properties are internal to a work of art, while others are external. Zangwill argues that form is not autonomous or independent, as extreme formalists argue, but always serves or is dependent on external properties, including an artwork's representation of content, and its process of making, or its poetics. We shall examine how and why moderate formalism in particular has dominated Film Studies, and consider two fundamental evaluative concepts which have had a strong and decisive influence on film criticism: the moderate formalist concept of organic unity and the extreme formalist concept of significant form.

In the final section, I extend the formalist tradition – especially poetics – by supplementing it with the decision-making processes of film production, as codified in filmmaking manuals. On reading these manuals, I discovered to my surprise that they advocate the same principles found in film criticism: they encourage filmmakers to achieve organic unity and significant form in their films. My extension of the formalist tradition signifies a possible rapprochement between film criticism and filmmaking, and therefore the continuing value of formalism in Film Studies.

INNER LOGIC

The project of modernity formulated in the 18th century by the philosophers of the Enlightenment consisted in their efforts to develop objective science, universal morality and law, and autonomous art according to their inner logic. (Habermas, 1983: 9)

Formalism emerged from the modernist project of the Enlightenment. The unified, cosmological world-view (informed by metaphysics, religion and myth) that held sway over everyday life and beliefs in pre-modern Western society was challenged during the Renaissance, and was eventually transformed by the time of the Enlightenment and the French Revolution. From the transformed cosmological world-view emerged three differentiated secular world-views (or value spheres) – those of science (study of nature), morality (study of social norms), and aesthetics (study of art, the self, and human freedom). Moreover, each value sphere had its

own type of validity – namely, truth, justice, and judgements of taste respectively. This tripartite distinction between value spheres was concretized in the seminal works of Immanuel Kant – his *Critique of Pure Reason* ([1787] 2003) (the study of scientific knowledge), his *Critique of Practical Reason* ([1788] 1997) (the study of morality), and his *Critique of the Power of Judgement* ([1790] 2001) (the study of aesthetics). These three value spheres bring to the fore the autonomy of specialized knowledge; together, they constitute the dominant characteristic of the Enlightenment project and cultural modernity.

For example, aesthetic experience became progressively liberated (or differentiated) from everyday perception and, by the nineteenth century, it had been transformed, in the *l'art pour l'art* movement, into an autonomous realm of self-validating experience. In the twentieth century, this 'aesthetic modernity' (as Jürgen Habermas calls it) has been manifest in various avant-garde movements which, through a series of self-reflexive practices, create a form of radical experience that criticizes the ideology of everyday life – or criticizes the constraints imposed upon everyday life by the other two value spheres, science and morality.

Parallel to this aesthetic modernity is the formalist study of art, an examination of what is unique and irreducible to each medium. For the formalists, although an artwork may be representational, what makes it art is its formal properties, not its representational features (which simply motivate the form) (Carroll, 1999: 110–11). 'Form' designates the inner logic of each art, the essential set of features that delimit and shape amorphous matter. Out of form emerges a range of options regarding how to shape matter and create a particular work of art. In pictorial art, 'form' refers to the essential features that render something visible. For example, all pictorial art arranges its parts in relation to a surface. Numerous options exist: either the parts can be arranged planimetrically (across the surface) or recessionally (receding into depth), or somewhere in between. The systematic choices made by an individual artist, or school, or period, in the making of artworks, names the preferred style of that artist, school, or period.

In other words, form is the essential set of features internal to each medium. From these features emerge a set of options concerning how to shape, arrange, or compose an individual artwork. Making choices from the formal options is an expressive activity that creates style. (Form is therefore 'impersonal' and exists prior to style and expression.) The analysis of style involves examining the range of formal options available to artists, and the choices they make in constructing an individual artwork. In pictorial art, choosing to organize a visual surface planimetrically, for example, creates an image in the 'classical' style, whereas a recessional choice creates a 'baroque' style of image.

ORGANIC UNITY AND SIGNIFICANT FORM

The term 'organic unity' is central to philosophy (especially to Plato, Aristotle, and G.E. Moore) and aesthetics – including film aesthetics (*mise en scène* and auteur criticism). Organic unity refers to the way the parts of a whole relate to one another, how they relate to the whole, and how the whole relates to external properties such as content. An organic unity is a whole that is more than the sum of its parts, for the whole possesses an intrinsic value not contained in any of its parts. This new value emerges from or is realized in the parts, but is not contained in any of them. It is not a property that exists by itself, but depends on other properties. It is an emergent value that lies only in the whole, although it is reflected back in the parts.

The concept of organic unity is an evaluative concept aimed at praising one style of art: Classicism. In classical art – meaning Classical Antiquity, the Italian Renaissance, and the various Neoclassical styles that imitate them – each work reaches a state of harmony and equilibrium, for an organic unity is the best possible (the most efficient and optimal) way to organize the parts. All the parts of an organic unity are necessary and sufficient to its status as a unity. Each part has an intrinsic value, and additional intrinsic values arise solely from the combination of all the parts. Any addition or diminution will destroy the intrinsic value of the whole, because the parts are so closely connected and interdependent that it is impossible to think of the whole otherwise. In an organic unity, the parts have reached their highest degree or best possible level of integration. Zangwill comments that '[t]he appellation "organic" is fitting in that the unity in question is like that of a living system where parts have a purpose with respect to each other and with respect to the whole' (2001: 62, n.16).

The extreme formalist Clive Bell came up with the term 'significant form' to designate a concept similar to 'organic unity':

> What quality is shared by all objects that provoke our aesthetic emotions? What quality is common to Sta. Sophia and the windows at Chartres, Mexican sculpture, a Persian bowl, Chinese carpets, Giotto's frescoes at Padua, and the masterpieces of Poussin, Piero della Francesca, and Cézanne? Only one answer seems possible – significant form. In each, lines and colours combined in a particular way, certain forms and relations of forms, stir our aesthetic emotions. These relations and combinations of lines and colours, these aesthetically moving forms, I shall call 'Significant Form'; and 'Significant Form' is the one quality common to all works of visual art. (1928: 8)

The main difference between organic unity and significant form is that significant form only refers to the relation between the different formal components of an artwork, for it excludes external properties such as the making of an artwork and its representation of content.

The concepts of organic unity and significant form are nonetheless related. To claim that an artwork has significant form similarly argues that the whole is more than the sum of its parts. For Stefan Sharff, who has applied the concept of significant form to film, in some films the parts add up to create a new entity that does not exist in each part: 'Significant form is the opposite of pedestrian rendition … Images fit together so magnificently that they ascend to a higher level of visual meaning' (1982: 7). Above I noted that each part of an organic unity has an intrinsic value, and additional intrinsic values arise solely from the combination of all the parts. The value of the individual parts may be very small. What defines an organic unity is the emergent value of the whole. In Sharff's terms, each individual part of a film may be pedestrian. A film with significant form is one that combines these pedestrian parts into an elevated form, in which the parts are strongly linked in a particular order. In contrast, a pedestrian film is one that is not more than the sum of its parts. The parts of a pedestrian film, when joined together, do not attain 'a higher level of visual meaning', but remain an aggregate collection of isolated pedestrian parts. Only a well-made film will manifest 'significant form' (and organic unity).

But how do we recognize significant form and organic unity? All filmmakers use the same standard parts – the same formal features, or 'film language'. The key to their success is the way they combine these features into an expressive style. This is the thinking behind the *mise en scène* and auteur criticism of *Cahiers du cinéma*, *Movie* magazine, and Andrew Sarris. In the next section I examine the film criticism of V.F. Perkins, a prominent member of the *Movie* group, and Noël Carroll's practice of film analyses.

STYLISTIC FILM CRITICISM

A fundamental characteristic of moderate formalism, in its argument against the autonomy of form, is that form is both appropriate to and dependent on an external property – namely, content, or what is represented. From a moderate formalist perspective, all aesthetic properties stand in a dependence relationship to non-aesthetic properties – including representational properties.

In Chapter Six of *Film as Film* (1972) Perkins outlines his analytical criteria for evaluating films from a moderate formalist perspective. Although he does not use the terms, he seeks 'significant form' and

especially 'organic unity'. The terms he uses are 'balance', 'coherence', 'relatedness' (the 'interaction' and 'integration' of filmic elements), 'productive tension', and 'intensity of cohesion'. 'Coherence', he writes 'is the means by which the film-maker creates significance' and the means by which the spectator 'recognize[s] meaning at all levels' (1972: 116). Moreover, coherence is not given in advance, is not part of the film's pre-existing content, but is an emergent value formed through the activity of constructing a film, through the creation of relationships that organize the various elements of film into a coherent synthesis:

> Useful criteria [for film analysis and evaluation] take account of relatedness by directing us not to single aspects but to the value of their interaction and the extent of their integration. The formal disciplines of balance and coherence embrace the effort to maintain the various elements in productive tension. (1972: 120)

What does Perkins mean by the effort to maintain a productive tension? He means two things – the identification of film's 'essence', and the organization of an individual film's *mise en scène*.

Classical film theorists in the realist camp, such as André Bazin, argued that film is essentially a realist medium due to its photographic capacity, while classical film theorists in the expressionist camp, such as Rudolf Arnheim, argued that film is essentially a new form of expression that defamiliarizes experience by creating a distinct view of the world. Perkins argues that film has no single essence, since it is a hybrid of two conflicting tendencies – realism, which creates credibility, and expressionism, which creates significance.[1] One of the primary skills of being a filmmaker is to find a balance between these two tendencies:

> The movie is committed to finding a balance between equally insistent pulls, one towards credibility [realism] and the other towards shape and significance [expressionism]. And it is threatened by collapse on both sides. It may shatter illusion in straining after expression. It may subside into meaningless reproduction presenting a world which is credible but without significance. (1972: 120)

The skilled filmmaker reconciles film's conflicting tendencies by maintaining a credible world and, at the same time, employing film's expressive capacities to achieve heightened coherence – or organic unity. An unbalanced, incoherent film is one that either pulls too much towards realism and credibility and does not exploit film's expressive capacity, or one that overuses its expressive capacity at the expense of realism and credibility: 'The great film approaches an intensity of cohesion such that its elements do not operate solely to maintain or further the reality of the fictional world, nor solely to decorative, affective or rhetorical effect' (1972: 131).

A coherent film creates an intensity of cohesion between realism and expressionism. More particularly, at the level of detail, each coherent film creates an intensity of cohesion between the particular elements of *mise en scène* it combines – action, image, décor, gesture, speech, camera movement and placement, cutting, and lighting. Perkins' examples throughout *Film as Film* each demonstrate a tight correspondence, plus novel and inventive relationships, between these elements: for example, speech-gesture-décor in *The Courtship of Eddie's Father* (Vincente Minnelli, US, 1963), or action-image-cutting in *Carmen Jones* (Otto Preminger, US, 1954) (1972: 76, 79–82).

At the other extreme, an imbalance is created in sentimental and pretentious films. A sentimental film, for Perkins, creates an imbalance between 'pathos asserted (in music, say, or image or gesture) and pathos achieved, in the action' (1972: 132), while a pretentious film creates imbalance by giving an elevated, unjustified emphasis and significance to particular elements of *mise en scène*.

Perkins' analytical criteria are geared towards one type of filmmaking – classical Hollywood films – and just one dimension of those films – *mise en scène* – and evaluates films positively if they conform to a classical style of *mise en scène*, negatively if the *mise en scène* becomes too ornate.

Adrian Martin's threefold distinction between classical, expressionist, and mannerist *mise en scène* is valuable in contextualizing Perkins' preferred style of filmmaking (Martin, 1992). In classical *mise en scène* the film style is unobtrusive, for it is motivated by the film's themes and dramatic developments. These films maintain a balance between showing and narrating, since style is linked to function, rather than being autonomous; the *mise en scène* functions as unobtrusive symbolism that confers upon the film heightened significance. In expressionist *mise en scène*, a broad or loose fit exists between style and theme. Finally, in mannerist *mise en scène*, style is autonomous; it is not linked to function, but draws attention to itself. In other words, style is not motivated or justified by the subject matter, but is its own justification.

Perkins argues that mannerist *mise en scène* is pretentious because it creates a disunity or imbalance between style and theme, and accuses the director of 'over-directing' the film: 'What happens on the screen must not emerge as a directorial "touch" detached from the dramatic situation; otherwise the spectator's belief in the action will decrease or disappear. The director's guiding hand is obvious only when it is too heavy' (1972: 77). Perkins prefers classical *mise en scène* because it creates what he calls 'an intensity of cohesion', and what we are calling organic unity and significant form. Mannerist *mise en scène*, by contrast, is simply decoration that lacks form and creates imbalance and disunity.

Additional aspects of classical *mise en scène* that may lead to organic unity and significant form include: foreground-background relations; productive use of the frame; and the tension between the choice of long takes or cutting. Filmmakers can choose to establish a productive and significant relationship between foreground and background in an image, as in the use of deep focus cinematography in the work of Jean Renoir, Orson Welles, and William Wyler, where several planes of action remain in play and in focus in the same frame. Another common *mise en scène* strategy involves using the frame to isolate characters in their own shot, or bring characters together in the same shot. If characters appear in the same frame (either a static frame or linked by camera movement), they are united; but if they are separated by cutting, then they are in conflict, or isolated from each other. William Paul writes that: 'Where the cutting is used to isolate the individual and his responses, the camera movement, as it reintegrates space, reunites the individual with his group to establish a sense of wholeness' (quoted in Bordwell, 1989: 179). Finally, filmmakers can choose to shoot a scene in one continuous take, where the camera is left rolling while the whole of the action takes place, or shoot the same scene with several shots. The first option involves the filmmaker filming the action as it unfolds, uninterrupted. The second option involves breaking the action down into individual shots. Each new shot will include a change in camera position, camera angle, shot scale, and so on. Film-makers have to weigh up the advantages and disadvantages in choosing one technique over another for each scene, since the choice of technique will influence whether the resulting scene will manifest unity or disunity.[2]

Significant form and organic unity can be created in film by combining various *mise en scène* strategies. However, these techniques should not be analyzed in a mechanical, numerical manner (as they typically are in Film Studies and film production classes), not should one automatically assume a film has significant form because it contains some of these techniques. Each technique needs to be evaluated according to how it is used to represent content, and how it works (or does not work) in relation to other *mise en scène* strategies.

Like Perkins, Noël Carroll is also a moderate formalist critic. In *Interpreting the Moving Image*, he carries out a series of film analyses – which he calls interpretations – and privileges organic unity. He aims to explain the presence of features (or parts) in a film and their interrelationships:

[M]y practice of interpretation … tends to be holistic or organic or functional. I interpret features of films, for the most part, in light of their relation to hypotheses about the *unity* of the works in question. In this, I do not imagine that my interpretations account for every detail of the films I discuss (I am talking about *relative* unity, not totalized unity), nor do I claim that there may be other (compatible) interpretations of the works I examine. (1998: 10)

In this statement Carroll does not sufficiently distinguish a functional analysis from a holistic-organic analysis, even though such a distinction is necessary to understand the difference between a totalized unity and a relative unity. In an organic unity, as we have already seen, all the parts interrelate to create the whole. This is a totalized unity, and involves examining all the relations between the parts, regardless of function. For Carroll, only those parts that perform the artwork's intended function need to be examined (relative unity). Carroll develops the concept of relative unity in Chapter Three of *Philosophy of Art*, in which he advocates examining only those relations that carry out the artwork's intended purpose or function: 'According to the functional account, the form of an artwork is correlative to its purpose' (1999: 146). In a functional analysis, one examines the purpose an artwork is intended to fulfil. If it successfully fulfils its function, it is designated as good art, and if it is unsuccessful, it is labelled bad art. The most important functions are representational and expressive. Carroll's emphasis on functionalism aligns him to a moderate formalist position, since he examines formal, expressive, and representational features in individual films.

FORMALIST FILM THEORY

In this section I review key descriptive studies of film form, those that give minimal attention to style or evaluation. The work of these researchers (Christian Metz, Noël Burch, Edward Branigan, Raymond Bellour, Barry Salt, David Bordwell, and Kristin Thompson) is marked by the same qualities: it is systematic, rigorous, methodical, and meticulous in its description of film form. It raises Film Studies to a higher level of precision and clarity – sometimes attempting to reach an axiomatic level, where it endeavours to present its findings as a series of unambiguous postulates.

Christian Metz's film semiotics

In 'Problems of Denotation in the Fiction Film' (1974a) Christian Metz identified a finite set of sequence (or syntagmatic) types operative in classical narrative cinema, a paradigm of syntagmas from which a filmmaker can choose to represent events in a particular order. Metz identifies each syntagma from a moderate formalist perspective, that is, by the particular way film form organizes the spatio-temporal relationship between the events it depicts. Syntagmas are distinct because the same events depicted by means of a different syntagma will have a different meaning. These spatio-temporal relationships between the images constitute cinematic language for Metz because they articulate the filmed events in terms of a specific cinematic space and time. In other words, this cinematic space and time confers upon these events a meaning that transcends their analogical relationship to the image.

Metz detected eight different spatio-temporal relationships in total, which constitute eight different forms of image ordering (syntagmas). Metz called the resulting 'paradigm of syntagmas' the 'grande syntagmatique' of the image track. The grande syntagmatique identifies syntagmatic units only when a change in shot produces a change in meaning – that is, when a spatio-temporal transition (the cut, etc.) on the level of the filmic signifier correlates with a change in meaning on the level of the signified (= the spatio-temporal relationship between the events). Each filmic syntagma is constituted by the same spatio-temporal relationship between its images. As long as the same relationship holds across cuts, there is no change in meaning. A change in meaning

therefore occurs when a spatio-temporal transition on the level of the filmic signifier is correlated with a *new* spatio-temporal relationship between filmed events, for a new relationship signals the end of one syntagma and the beginning of another.[3]

Noël Burch's study of film's formal principles

Noël Burch's formalist theory of film is presented in his book *Theory of Film Practice*. In a fashion similar to Metz, although edging towards extreme formalism, Burch created a formal taxonomy of all the possible spatio-temporal relationship that can exist between two shots (1981: 3–16). He identified five different temporal relationship (temporal continuity, measurable ellipsis, indefinite ellipsis, reversal in time, and flashback) and three types of spatial relationship (spatial continuity, discontinuity, and proximity). He then studied the techniques that work to create the last type of spatial relationship (spatial proximity), such as the eye-line match.

Burch supplemented this taxonomy of spatio-temporal relationship by examining the opposition between on-screen and off-screen space (1981: 17–31). On-screen space names the space inside the film frame, and off-screen space lies beyond the film frame. Off-screen space is divided into six segments: the four spaces beyond each frame line, a fifth space – the space behind the camera, and a sixth space – space hidden within the film frame. With the exception of the analytical cut-in, which shows a detail of the previous shot, a cut materializes one area of off-screen space, and consigns the on-screen space to the status of off-screen space. Furthermore, with any given shot, attention can be drawn to any off-screen space via an entrance to and exit from on-screen space, or via the use of off-screen sound. Burch notes that 'off-screen space has only an intermittent or, rather, *fluctuating* existence during any film, and structuring this fluctuation can become a powerful tool in a film-maker's hands' (1981: 21).

Edward Branigan's formal description of the point-of-view structure

Edward Branigan delineates the formal permutations of the point-of-view (POV) structure, which he defines as one 'in which the camera assumes the position of a subject in order to show us what the subject sees' (1984: 103). Taking his cue from Burch's study of the techniques that create spatial proximity between two shots, Branigan identifies the necessary and sufficient conditions for defining the POV structure: two shots in proximate relation, and six elements. Shot A (Point/Glance) is made up of (1) Origin: a point in space, and (2) Vision: the glance from the point. Between shots A and B there is (3) Time: a transition that suggests temporal continuity or simultaneity. Shot B (Point/Object) consists of (4) Frame: from the point in space defined in (1), the camera locates (5) the Object of the glance. Lastly, the viewer links shots A and B through the construction of (6) Mind: the presence of a character or subject (1984: 103).

Branigan identifies variations of this taxonomy that may produce deviant POV structures (for example, no point or several points may be given; there may be uncertainty as to whether a glance has actually occurred, etc.). Also, shot A may be repeated to create a closed, stable structure. Or shot B may occur before shot A, creating a retrospective POV structure. A and B can be separated, delaying the object of the glance; or the object may never be revealed, creating an open POV structure. A continuing POV, in which one character looks at several objects, rendered in several shot Bs or in a subjective travelling shot. A cheated POV occurs when the camera in shot B does not take the point in space identified in shot A (the camera may be placed closer to the object to give the spectator a better view). A multiple POV structure refers to more than one character glancing at the same object (the characters may be in the same shot, or shot B is linked to two separate A shots, one before and one after). An embedded POV structure names the nesting of one POV structure within another character's POV: 'For example, in *Psycho* we see Marion inside her car glance (shot A) at a policeman outside the car who then glances (shot B) at her licence plate (shot C)' (Branigan, 1984: 117). Finally, the reciprocal POV structure names moments when the object revealed by the glance is another person who returns the glance, which is common in conversation sequences.

Raymond Bellour's shot-by-shot analyses

Raymond Bellour is well known for his meticulous shot-by-shot analyses of key segments from classical Hollywood films. He usually combines his moderate formalist perspective with interpretation, in which he identifies a film's symptomatic meanings using psychoanalysis. In his predominantly formalist analysis of *The Big Sleep* (Howard Hawks, US, 1946) in 'The Obvious and the Code' (2000: 69–76), Bellour takes a seemingly innocuous, self-contained scene towards the end of the film, in which Marlowe (Humphrey Bogart) and Vivian (Lauren Bacall) drive from Eddy Mars' (John Ridgely) country home to Geiger's (Theodore von Eltz) home. Hawks uses 12 shots in this classically constructed economical scene that simply represents the characters' transition between two spaces. Bellour examines the formal relations that exist between these 12 shots to determine how they are integrated into the film, how their obviousness is constructed by codes. His analysis is based on the semiotic hierarchy between the finite, underlying (latent, non-observable) reality and potentially infinite surface (manifest, observable) reality. The underlying reality is 'an imperceptible content lending structure to the perceptible insofar as it signifies and conveys precisely the historical experience of the individual and group' (Deely et al., 1986: xiv). Semioticians call this finite, non-perceptible, underlying system, which lends structure to the perceptible, a 'system of codes'. Bellour incorporates this opposition into his analysis – and, indeed, into the title of his essay – in which the surface, perceptible reality is designated the 'obvious' and the underlying system that confers meaning on the surface reality is called a system of 'codes'. Bellour analyzes the action of six codes in this scene: differences in framing, static/moving camera, camera angle, characters in the frame, presence/absence of speech, and the relative duration of each shot.[4]

Using a table summarizing his analysis, plus 12 frame enlargements, Bellour enumerates the similarities and differences between the six codes from shot to shot. For example, between shots 1 and 2 he notes the following similarities: identity of duration, presence of the same two characters, and same camera angle; and the following differences: shot 1 – moving camera, shot 2 – static camera; no dialogue/dialogue; outside the car/inside the car. Between shots 2 and 3 he notes the following differences: shot 2 – long take, shot 3 – short take; two characters in the frame/one character (Marlowe); medium shot/close up; centring of dialogue on one character (Marlowe, on screen). From shots 3 to 4 he notices the following differences: in shot 4 Vivian (rather than Marlowe) is depicted; the angle has changed; and dialogue comes from both characters (that is, it comes from on- and off-screen).

At this stage of the analysis Bellour comments on the distribution of characters, dialogue, and time. In terms of characters, shots 3, 4, 5, 6, 8, 9, and 11 focus on individual characters, while 1, 2, 7, 10, and 12 unite the couple in the same frame. In the transition from the two-shot to the one-shot (which happens 3 times), Vivian is privileged twice and Marlowe once. Bellour concludes that Vivian is privileged in terms of the image (she appears on her own 4 times, Marlowe only 3 times). In terms of dialogue, Vivian speaks only when on-screen, whereas Marlowe speaks both when on- and off-screen. Bellour concludes that Marlowe is privileged in terms of dialogue. In terms of duration, the middle of the scene (shot 7) lasts almost as long as the other shots combined.

From this analysis Bellour draws a number of general conclusions regarding the formal structure of classical Hollywood films. His main conclusion is that a balance is maintained between symmetry (a repetition) and dissymmetry (variation) of codes. That is, the high number of shots allows for a huge variation of changes, but this potential is limited by means of the repetition and alternation of codes.

Barry Salt's statistical style analysis

Statistical style analysis (or stylometry) belongs to the extreme formalist tradition (and does not maintain a strict distinction between form and style). It analyses style numerically, by measuring and quantifying a film's formal parameters. At its simplest, the process of measuring involves counting elements, or variables, that reflect a text's style, and applying statistical tests to the data.

Statistical style analysis has three standard aims: (1) to offer a quantitative analysis of style, usually for the purpose of recognizing patterns, a task now made feasible by the use of computer technology. In language texts, the quantitative analysis of style and pattern recognition is usually conducted in the numerical analysis of the following variables: word length, or syllables per word, sentence length, the distribution of parts of speech (the different percentage of nouns, pronouns, verbs, adjectives, and so on in a text), calculating the ratio of parts of speech (for example, the ratio of verbs to adjectives), or by analyzing word order, syntax, rhythm, or metre; (2) for the purposes of authorship attribution, in cases of disputed authorship of anonymous or pseudonymous texts; and (3) for purposes of identifying the chronology of works, when the sequence of composition is unknown or disputed (for example, Plato, Shakespeare's plays).

The first aim, the quantitative analysis of style, involves descriptive statistics. The second and third aims (authorship attribution and chronology) involve both descriptive and inferential statistics. As its name implies, descriptive statistics simply describes a text as it is, by measuring and quantifying it in terms of its numerical characteristics. The result is a detailed, internal, molecular description of a text's (or group of texts') formal variables.

Inferential statistics then employs this formal description to make predictions – it uses this data as an index, primarily an index of an author's style, or to put the author's work into chronological order on the basis of measured changes in style of their work over time. Whereas descriptive statistics produces data with complete certainty, inferential statistics is based on assumptions the statistician makes on the basis of the descriptive data. The assumptions the inferential statistician extrapolates only have degrees of probability rather than certainty.

In film analysis, the descriptive statistics can be used to quantify the formal parameters of the shot in a film or group of films. It is primarily a systematic version of *mise en scène* criticism, and is more credible and valid because it downplays the critic's subjective impressions of a film in favour of a more detached, systematic, and explicit mode of analysis. One disadvantage is that it borders on extreme formalism. In 'Statistical Style Analysis of Motion Pictures' (1974), in his book *Film Style and Technology* (1992), and his study of the films of 1999 (2004), Salt describes the individual style of directors by systematically collecting data on the formal parameters of their films, particularly those formal parameters that are most directly under the director's control, including: duration of the shot (which involves the calculation of average shot length); shot scale; camera movement; angle of shot; and strength of the cut.

Salt then represents the quantity and frequency of these formal parameters in bar graphs, percentages, and 'Average Shot Lengths'. When he compares and contrasts the form of the films of different directors, he moves into the realm of stylistic analysis rather than simply formal description. Style in this sense designates a set of measurable patterns that significantly deviate from contextual norms. As just one example, Salt calculated that the average shot length of a Hollywood film between 1940–5 is 9.5 seconds (1992: 231). An early 1940s film with an average shot significantly higher than 9.5 seconds deviates from the norm, and is therefore a significant indicator of style. Salt (1992: 231) mentions Vincente Minnelli's *The Clock* (US, 1945), which has an average shot length of 19 seconds.

Historical poetics and Neoformalism

For more than two decades David Bordwell and Kristin Thompson (the latter under the name 'neoformalism') have been formulating and practicing historical poetics of film.

Since Aristotle, the term 'poetics' has designated the process of 'making', the activities and techniques involved in producing a (well-made) work of art. In its turn, poetics presupposes 'know-how', a set of skills or procedures in making a work of art. As such, poetics is sharply distinguished from aesthetics. Whereas poetics names the activity of making, aesthetics refers to the reception of art, including its contemplation and evaluation.

The process of making is an external property of an artwork because it refers to the decision-making activity – the choices an artist makes – prior to the artwork's completion, or final form. The form of an artwork is not autonomous but the end result of purposeful activity. As the art historian Michael Baxandall argues:

> The maker of a picture or other historical artefact is a man [*sic*] addressing a problem of which his product is a finished and concrete solution. To understand it we try to reconstruct both the specific problem it was designed to solve and the specific circumstances out of which he was addressing it. (1985: 14–15)

For Baxandall, artists use their know-how and knowledge of a medium to solve a problem. To analyze an artwork from this perspective entails explaining why the artwork has the form it does, rather than simply describing form as an autonomous entity. Explanation identifies the *function* formal parts play in relation to one another and in relation to the whole artwork.

Only the solution (the artwork) is pre-given. The art historian needs to work backwards from the solution and reconstruct the problems it is addressing, together with the artist's intentions. Baxandall is well aware of the problems surrounding the concept of intentionality, together with the difficulties in reconstructing the particular problem an artwork was designed to solve and the specific circumstances out of which the artist addressed the problem: 'We cannot reconstruct the serial action, the thinking and manipulation of pigments that ended in Piero della Francesca's *Baptism of Christ*, with sufficient precision to explain it as an action. We address the finished deposit of an activity we are not in a position to narrate' (1985: 13–14). Referring to the philosopher Karl Popper, Baxandall continues: 'we do not re-construct the actor's thought but produce an "idealized and reasoned reconstruction" of an objective problem and objective situation on a level different from [the artist's] actual reasoning' (1985: 14). The art historian's account of an artist's activity in making a work of art is not an actual representation of that activity, but is a simplified, albeit rational reconstruction of it.

For Bordwell, film poetics answers two basic questions: 'First, how are particular films put together? Call this the problem of films' *composition*. Second, what *effects* and *functions* do particular films have?' (1989: 263). Bordwell adds: 'At this moment I believe that the most promising avenues for poetic analysis are those opening onto compositional processes of form and style' (1989: 270–1). The study of composition is central to film poetics because it entails examining both the concrete activities involved in filmmaking plus the fundamental principles and conventions which guide that activity. The poetician looks for the options available to filmmakers at a specific historical period, and studies the preferred set of choices they make in putting together an individual film. As with Baxandall's model of art history, Bordwell's film poetics conceives a film as the end result of purposeful activity, and attempts to rationally reconstruct that activity from historical data. In studying the aesthetic effects achieved by a particular choice of options, Bordwell (1985) has primarily examined perceptual-cognitive effects, and has concluded that

spectators are active when watching a film.[5] Finally, in relation to determining how films serve specific functions in particular historical contexts, Bordwell writes: 'To analyze a film's composition and function requires us to consider what processes brought it into being (for example, to what problems does its composition represent an attempted solution?) and what forces have mobilized it for various purposes' (1989: 265). Again, the first part mirrors Baxandall's study of artworks as concrete solutions to problems.

Kristin Thompson makes explicit and clarifies many of the assumptions implicit in formalism and poetics. Neoformalist film analysis, she argues, closely adheres to and is guided by the film. It does not impose theoretical doctrines onto a film simply to illustrate the theory in a self-confirming manner. Instead, it treats each film individually, viewing it as an artificial construct formed by filmmakers choosing from and reinventing filmmaking strategies, norms, conventions and techniques. Two key terms for recognizing a film's individuality include 'function' and the 'dominant'. Thompson uses the concept of 'function' differently from Bordwell. For Thompson, function 'is crucial to understanding the unique qualities of a given artwork, for, while many works may use the same device, that device's function may be different in each work' (1988: 15). The neoformalist does not assume a particular device or technique has a fixed function from film to film. For example: 'Bar-like shadows do not always symbolize that a character is "imprisoned", and verticals in a composition do not automatically suggest that characters on either side are isolated from each other' (1988: 15). Given devices do not always or automatically signify a fixed meaning, for 'they can serve different functions according to the context of the work, and one of the analyst's main jobs is to find the device's function in this or that context' (1988: 15).

The dominant names 'the main formal principle a work or group of works uses to organize devices into a whole … The dominant will pervade the work, governing and linking small-scale ones; through the dominant, the stylistic, narrative, and thematic levels will relate to each other' (Thompson, 1988: 43). In a standard film, the dominant names the most typical devices and techniques, together with their organization, while in a highly original film, it names the most unusual devices.

The dominant is an important concept for rethinking organic unity. It is a principle of organization that does not simply involve all the elements of a film co-existing and mutually relating to one another. Instead, it involves a small number of elements organizing the remaining elements of a film. A hierarchy is set up between these more important organizing elements (the dominant) and the less important subordinate elements. Thompson notes that, without a concept such as the dominant, 'we would be condemned to study every device in a film with equal attention, for we would have no way of deciding which were the more relevant' (1988: 92). The concept of the dominant is closely related to Carroll's concept of relative unity, for both avoid the need to study a film as a totalized unity by setting up a hierarchy between each film's more important and less important elements. One of the skills of film analysis is to identify and privilege these dominant elements.

FILMMAKING MANUALS

At present, Film Studies only engages superficially (if at all) with filmmaking procedures. In this section I aim to overcome this superficial engagement by grounding Film Studies in filmmaking, but without compromising the integrity of Film Studies. In fact, I aim to reinvigorate Film Studies by expanding its disciplinary boundaries, and by making it more relevant to *both* Film Studies and film production students.

The essence of this expansion involves the combination of two types of knowledge – the declarative knowledge of Film Studies (the propositions of film aesthetics and film theory), and the procedural knowledge (technical know-how) of filmmaking. To bring into effect this expansion, Film Studies needs to be supplemented with the technical knowledge of filmmaking as embodied in filmmaking manuals.

Filmmaking manuals identify at least three fundamental skills at the core of filmmaking:

1. Visualization and shot flow (shot plans and storyboarding)
2. Blocking the action (staging the 'zones of action'[6])
3. Filming the action (not simply recording the action, but using visual rhetoric to create dramatic emphasis of action points).

1. Visualization and shot flow. Steven D. Katz has codified the director's tacit knowledge in his two books *Film Directing: Shot by Shot* (1991) and *Film Directing: Cinematic Motion* (1992). He argues that the two key terms for the working director are 'visualization' and 'shot flow'. Visualization involves hands-on pictorial design to work out the content of the shots, plus their sequencing; and a moment-by-moment evaluation of the images as they are shaped, making different choices from the many options available.

According to Katz, the visualization of options available and revising the choices made should be enabled and constrained by the content of the screenplay. The problem for the director to solve is the representation of the screenplay's content in visual and narrational terms, and his or her solutions are initially worked out in storyboards. This stage of filmmaking can be creative and imaginative, because 'the filmmaker is confronted with a variety of visual decisions that the screenplay does not address' (1991: 5).

An unimaginative or novice director may see his or her task as simply filling the frame with the content of the screenplay, and will not try out the most effective and efficient options for narrating the story in a particular scene. Such a film will be merely pedestrian and under-directed, and will create what Perkins calls an imbalance between credibility and coherence, by privileging credibility and not exploiting film's expressive capacity. Such a film will lack organic unity and significant form. Other directors may over-direct by imposing pretentious decorative flourishes on the screenplay, leading to a mannerist *mise en scène*. The ideal balance, as practitioners like Katz and critics like Perkins argue, is for the director to choose to intensify part of the script's possibilities, to visualize it in terms of significant form or organic unity.

The film director Edward Dmytryk agrees: 'If there is one rule that should hold for film it is that the techniques of filmmaking *must* be at the service of the material filmed rather than the other way around' (1988: 62).[7] Michael Rabiger holds the same opinion in his manual on film directing: 'Good camerawork, composition, and blocking [are] always trying to show *relatedness*. This helps to intensify meanings and ironies, and reduces obvious signification through editing' (1997: 53). His comments parallel those of Perkins, who also argues that films should show 'relatedness', and that film techniques need to intensify meanings without drawing attention to themselves.

Katz recommends visualization via storyboarding because the storyboard conveys the shot flow of a scene. 'Shot flow' is the name Katz gives to the kinetic effect of a sequence of shots, which is largely determined by the physical transformations brought about by shot size, camera angle, and the timing of cutting points. He uses the metaphor of a river to characterize shot flow, for an effective shot flow links together shots in a single, uninterrupted process. With the concept of 'shot flow' Katz has invented a powerful metaphor because it suggests a series of shots forming an organic unity.

2. Blocking the action. Much of Daniel Arijon's directing manual *Grammar of the Film Language* (1991) is taken up with outlining an elaborate set of options for blocking action and rendering it on film. His overwhelming number of countless variations can be reduced to a simple series of variables:

Blocking:

(a) Change the position of actors within the six different sectors of the image[8]
(b) Change the position of actors from zone to zone

(c) Change the actor's body level (standing, sitting, lying down).

Filming:

(a) Render on film using a static or moving camera
(b) Render on film using cutting or a long take.

In relation to zone changing, he writes:

> With changes of zone the group can move from zone to zone, expand to several zones or contract from several to only one zone. There is no limit to the number of areas that can be employed but three to five is generally enough since each area can be used several times if the development of the story so requires. (1991: 542)

Arijon develops his last point ('if the story so requires') further ahead when he writes: 'A pattern of movement that expands and contracts periodically during the sequence should be at the service of the story and not arbitrarily imposed on a scene' (1991: 554). Arijon clearly favours classical over mannerist *mise en scène*.

3. Filming the action. Finally, guided by visualization and blocking decisions, a director commits the scene to film. Directors who use the camera simply to record a scene are 'under-directing', for they end up producing a static, passive film that does not exploit the expressive capacities of film. Directors who use flashy camera movements and an excessive number of shot transitions (that is, unmotivated by and not serving the story) can be accused of 'over-directing' their film.

For Katz, a well-directed film uses film techniques to add dramatic emphasis to the story. Katz's comments parallel Perkins' discussion of classical *mise en scène*, in which the director uses the expressive elements of film to intensify the significance of the credible image without drawing attention to the expressive elements themselves.

Of course, a director can decide to film the entire scene with a fixed master shot keeping both subjects immobile while talking to one another. This is an instance of under-directing, although as an option it cannot be ruled out entirely, for its under-stated nature may reinforce the nature of the conversation, or the dramatic relationship between the characters, which is the case for example with Jim Jarmusch's early films *Stranger than Paradise* (US/West Germany, 1984) and *Down by Law* (US/West Germany, 1986). In analyzing and evaluating a film, each scene needs to be considered on its own terms. Film analysis and evaluation needs to be inductive, bottom up, and empirical, privileging perception of the work itself as a material object, rather than deductive, top down, and idealistic, which is dogmatic, reductionist and makes generalizations that are easily refutable through the close analysis of individual shots and scenes.

All three stages of directing – visualization, blocking, and filming – should be planned together to create a coherent film, a film unified by a clear vision and design. Katz's codification of the director's tacit knowledge is premised on the same principles as Perkins' guideline for film evaluation: a classically constructed film demonstrating organic unity and significant form.

In *Directed by Steven Spielberg* (2006), I analyze Spielberg's filmmaking practice through this combination of film aesthetics and technical know-how. I examine Spielberg's day-to-day decision-making process in solving filmmaking problems, and analyze the blocking and filming options available to him, especially those relating to style and narration. From the available filming options, Spielberg frequently makes a small number of habitual choices in the visualization and technical execution of each shot and scene in his films. I argue that a formalist analysis, informed by filmmaking procedures, is ideally equipped to examine in detail the structure and unity of a filmmaker's oeuvre.

CONCLUSION

In his defence of modernity, Habermas takes to task those who conflate cultural modernity with what Habermas calls 'societal modernization' (including Daniel Bell, Friedrich Nietzsche, Martin Heidegger, Gilles Deleuze, Michel Foucault, Jacques Derrida and other neoconservative, postmodern theorists). Although the idea of cultural modernity emerged from the eighteenth-century Enlightenment project, during the nineteenth century, modernity became equated with industrialism and the social reorganization it entails – particularly reification and alienation (the defining characteristics of societal modernization). In their discussion of modernity, neoconservative theorists concentrate exclusively on societal modernization, which accounts for their negative evaluation of the whole of the modernist/Enlightenment project. They argue that modernity *necessarily* leads to reification and alienation because it has simply resulted in the production of technologically exploitable knowledge. Stephen White succinctly expresses this negative side of modernity when he writes: 'Modernization in the West has thus generated a pathology: an unbalanced development of its potential' (1995: 8). However, following Habermas, White argues that this imbalance can be resisted, that modernity is not an 'iron cage', as Weber suggested. For Habermas, the rationality of cultural modernity (which emphasizes the process of communicative rationalism and the concrete realization of universal freedom) must be kept separate from the *Zweckrationalitat* (bureaucratic rationality and instrumental reason) that merely informs the economy and polity. However, postmodernists fail to make this distinction, and thereby fail to understand the value of modernity, including the achievements resulting from the formalist analysis of film's inner logic.

NOTES

1 The word 'credibility' is more appropriate than 'realism' because Perkins is referring to the fact that the actions and events in a film are not necessarily literal or true to life. Instead, the actions and events are plausible or believable within the world of the film's fiction: '[C]inematic credibility … depends on the inner consistency of the created world ….

[T]he created world must obey its own logic' (1972: 121). Kristin Thompson makes a similar point: 'Most actions are justified not, primarily, by an appeal to cultural beliefs about the real world, but by a seemingly necessary causal relationship to other actions within the film' (1988: 53).

2 See Chapter Three in Elsaesser and Buckland (2002) for a more detailed discussion.

3 See Metz for an outline of the eight syntagmatic types (1974a: 124–33), and Buckland (1999) for a broader examination of Metz's film semiotics.

4 These technical devices constitute a system of codes because each gains its meaning from a paradigm of choices (close up, medium shot, long shot, etc.).

5 Formalist film theory also extends to the study of narrative and narration, of which Bordwell's *Narration in the Fiction Film* (1985) and Branigan's *Narrative Comprehension and Film* (1992) are exemplary. Vladimir Propp's study of Russian folktales, written in 1927 but first published in English in 1968, also influenced film theorists such as Peter Wollen who developed a morphological analysis of Hitchcock's *North by Northwest* (US, 1959) (1982: 17–33). Bordwell questioned the applicability of Propp's work to film analysis in 'ApProppriations and ImProppfrieties: Problems in the Morphology of Film Narrative' (1988b). Structuralism also influenced film scholars, such as Seymour Chatman (1978; 1990).

6 Steven Katz (1992) states that in zone staging, the scene consists of separate groups of characters occupying their own space, and the camera moves from one zone (or space) to the next. This is in contrast to man-on-man staging, in which the camera follows characters as they move around the scene. The advantage of both types of staging is that they allow the director to vary the background of a scene – especially one scripted as a static dialogue. A large group of characters can be split into several zones in each scene. The scene is developed by moving the camera or cutting from zone to zone. Or the characters in one zone can expand into several zones before moving back to one zone.

7 Edward Dmytryk also writes: 'Nuances are as important in a setup as they are in a line of dialogue or in a performance, but if the audience sees them as such the director has failed. Like properly used symbols, nuances should enrich the scene as a whole, and not be seen as an exercise in theory or technique. A director's touch should be recognized only in postviewing analysis' (1984: 68).

8 Daniel Arijon divides the image into six sectors: vertically, the image is divided into thirds (left screen, middle screen, right screen); the image is also divided horizontally into a top half and a bottom half (1991: 37–45).

REFERENCES

Arijon, Daniel (1991) *Grammar of the Film Language*. Los Angeles: Silman-James Press.

Arnheim, Rudolf (1957) *Film as Art*. Berkeley: University of California Press.

Baxandall, Michael (1985) *Patterns of Intention: On the Historical Explanation of Pictures*. New Haven, CT: Yale University Press.

Bell, Clive (1928) *Art*. London: Chatto and Windus.

Bellour, Raymond (2000) *The Analysis of Film*. Bloomington: Indiana University Press.

Bordwell, David (1981) *The Films of Carl-Theodor Dreyer*. Berkeley: University of California Press.

Bordwell, David (1985) *Narration in the Fiction Film*. Madison: University of Wisconsin Press.

Bordwell, David (1988a) *Ozu and the Poetics of Cinema*. London/Princeton, NJ: BFI/Princeton University Press.

Bordwell, David (1988b) 'ApProppriations and ImProppfrieties: Problems in the Morphology of Film Narrative', *Cinema Journal*, 27(3): 5–20.

Bordwell, David (1989) *Making Meaning: Inference and Rhetoric in the Interpretation of Cinema*. Cambridge, MA: Harvard University Press.

Bordwell, David (1993) *The Cinema of Eisenstein*. Cambridge, MA: Harvard University Press.

Bordwell, David (1998) *On the History of Film Style*. Cambridge, MA: Harvard University Press.

Bordwell, David (2000) *Planet Hong Kong: Popular Cinema and the Art of Entertainment*. Cambridge, MA: Harvard University Press.

Branigan, Edward (1984) *Point of View in the Cinema: A Theory of Narration and Subjectivity in Classical Film*. Berlin: Mouton.

Branigan, Edward (1992) *Narrative Comprehension and Film*. London: Routledge.

Buckland, Warren (1999) 'Film Semiotics', in Toby Miller and Robert Stam (eds), *A Companion to Film Theory*. Oxford: Blackwell. pp. 84–104.

Buckland, Warren (2006) *Directed by Steven Spielberg: Poetics of the Contemporary Hollywood Blockbuster*. New York: Continuum.

Burch, Noël (1981) *Theory of Film Practice*. Princeton, NJ: Princeton University Press.

Cameron, Ian (ed.) (1972) *Movie Reader*. New York: Praeger.

Carroll, Noël (1998) *Interpreting the Moving Image*. New York: Cambridge University Press.

Carroll, Noël (1999) *Philosophy of Art: A Contemporary Introduction*. London: Routledge.

Chatman, Seymour (1978) *Story and Discourse: Narrative Structure in Fiction and Film*. Ithaca, NY: Cornell University Press.

Chatman, Seymour (1990) *Coming to Terms: The Rhetoric of Narrative in Fiction and Film.* Ithaca, NY: Cornell University Press.

Danto, Arthur (1964) 'The Art World', *Journal of Philosophy*, 61: 571–84.

Deely, John, Williams, Brooke and Kruse, Felicia E. (eds) (1986*) Frontiers in Semiotics*. Bloomington: Indiana University Press.

Dickie, George (1974) *Art and the Aesthetic: An Institutional Analysis.* Ithaca, NY: Cornell University Press.

Dmytryk, Edward (1984) *On Screen Directing.* Boston: Focal Press.

Dmytryk, Edward (1988) *Cinema: Concept and Practice.* Boston: Focal Press.

Eagle, Herbert (ed.) (1981) *Russian Formalist Film Theory.* Ann Arbor: University of Michigan.

Elsaesser, Thomas and Buckland, Warren (2002) *Studying Contemporary American Film: A Guide to Movie Analysis.* London/New York: Arnold/Oxford University Press.

Fry, Roger (1924) *Vision and Design.* London: Chatto and Windus.

Habermas, Jürgen (1983) 'Modernity – An Incomplete Project', in Hal Foster (ed.), *Postmodern Culture.* London: Pluto Press. pp. 3–15.

Hillier, Jim (ed.) (1985*) Cahiers du cinéma: The 1950s: Neo-Realism, Hollywood, New Wave.* Cambridge, MA: Harvard University Press.

Hillier, Jim (ed.) (1986) *Cahiers du cinéma: 1960–1968: New Wave, New Cinema, Re-evaluating Hollywood.* Cambridge, MA: Harvard University Press.

Kant, Immanuel [1787] (2003) *Critique of Pure Reason.* 2nd edn. Tr. Norman Kemp Smith. New York: Palgrave Macmillan.

Kant, Immanuel [1788] (1997) *Critique of Practical Reason.* Tr. Mary Gregor. Cambridge: Cambridge University Press.

Kant, Immanuel [1790] (2001) *Critique of the Power of Judgement.* Tr. Eric Matthews. Cambridge: Cambridge University Press.

Katz, Steven D. (1991) *Film Directing: Shot by Shot.* Studio City: Michael Weise Productions.

Katz, Steven D. (1992) *Film Directing: Cinematic Motion.* Studio City: Michael Weise Productions.

Martin, Adrian (1992) '*Mise en scène* is Dead, or the Expressive, the Excessive, the Technical and the Stylish', *Continuum*, 5(2): 87–140.

Metz, Christian (1974a) *Film Language: A Semiotics of the Cinema.* Tr. Michael Taylor. New York: Oxford University Press.

Metz, Christian (1974b) *Language and Cinema.* Tr. Donna Jean Umiker-Sebeok. The Hague: Mouton.

Perkins, V.F. (1972) *Film as Film: Understanding and Judging Movies.* Harmondsworth: Penguin.

Propp, Vladimir ([1927]1968) *Morphology of the Folktale.* Austin: University of Texas Press.

Rabiger, Michael (1997) *Directing: Film Techniques and Aesthetics.* 2nd edn. Boston: Focal Press.

Salt, Barry (1974) 'Statistical style analysis of Motion Pictures', *Film Quarterly*, 28(1): 13–22.

Salt, Barry (1992) *Film Style and Technology: History and Analysis.* London: Starword.

Salt, Barry (2004) 'The Shape of 1999', *New Review of Film and Television Studies*, 2(1): 61–85.

Sarris, Andrew (1968) *The American Cinema: Directors and Directions, 1929–1968.* New York: E.P. Dutton.

Sharff, Stefan (1982) *The Elements of Cinema: Toward a Theory of Cinesthetic Impact.* New York: Columbia University Press.

Thompson, Kristin (1981) *Eisenstein's Ivan the Terrible: A Neoformalist Analysis.* Princeton, NJ: Princeton University Press.

Thompson, Kristin (1988) *Breaking the Glass Armor: Neoformalist Film Analysis.* Princeton, NJ: Princeton University Press.

White, Stephen (1995) 'Introduction: Reason, Modernity, Democracy', in Stephen White (ed.), *The Cambridge Companion to Habermas.* Cambridge: Cambridge University Press. pp. 3–16.

Wollen, Peter (1982) 'Hitchcock's *North by Northwest*: A Morphological Analysis', in *Readings and Writings: Semiotic Counter-Strategies.* London: Verso. pp. 17–33.

Zangwill, Nick (2001) *The Metaphysics of Beauty.* Ithaca, NY: Cornell University Press.

21

The Persistence of the Avant-Garde

Michael O'Pray

Not only has the film avant-garde persisted, if at times by the skin of its teeth, since its inception in the post-World War One years, but it has burgeoned over the past decade. In doing so, it has become a more complex terrain. Revolutionary changes in media digital technology have coincided with a massive blooming of moving-image art in the galleries, since the mid-1990s. Whether this emerging moving-image art constitutes a new area of study or is simply a development of the historical avant-gardes is not clear. There seems little evidence that these new artists are building on the older tradition. On the contrary, there is often what seems to be an ignorance of and indifference to the avant-garde film canon or, to be more charitable, an attempt at a tabula rasa by the younger artists and the critical and art world establishment that supports them. At the same time, critics and academics and, inevitably, an older generation often level the charge of not knowing their tradition, against the artists usually. The relationship has also been clouded by the scale of commercial success achieved

by many of these gallery artist filmmakers, when set against the meagre financial gains of the traditional avant-garde artist. It is therefore, I believe, no accident that the common term used now to denote the practice is not 'avant-garde' but either 'experimental', as A.L. Rees (1999) and Jackie Hatfield (2006) use in the titles of their respective books, or 'artists film and video', as David Curtis (2007) uses for his book (O'Pray, 2003: 1–7). In what follows I eschew discussion of competing nomenclatures, fascinating as they are, and persist in using 'avant-garde' as a generic term, though well aware that it can carry important assumptions about its referent.

This enormous shift of status of film in the art world has had profound repercussions for avant-garde film study as an intellectual field.[1] The notion of 'avant-garde' that some of us have used so blithely for decades is now under severe strain. Used often as an umbrella term to cover the work of film and video artists who remained firmly at the margins of the mainstream, the concept of the 'avant-garde' was confronted by moving image artists who very much comprised part of the art-world mainstream, with dealers, shows in major galleries and critical appraisal from the traditional art-world journals and magazines. It is a scenario of poignant ironies and seeming paradoxes. For example, it is ironic that when the museums and galleries finally opened their doors to film, it was not in the form of the most art-based practices of the tradition of, say, Stan Brakhage, Malcolm Le Grice or Kurt Kren, but rather work that pillages the Hollywood mainstream, as in the pastiches of Sam Taylor-Wood (Hayward, 2002) or popular television as in the 'documentaries' of Gillian Wearing (Ferguson, 1999). But there is one figure who does connect these latter artists to the avant-garde tradition. That is Andy Warhol, whose early films influenced Taylor-Wood and seem to be precursors of Wearing's. Warhol's remarkable and continuing ability to kick-start new generations of filmmakers is a phenomenon that deserves analysis.

This seismic shift of the moving-image finding a central place in the gallery promises to dominate research in this area for years to come, especially as the transformation is still taking place and its shadow falls over this chapter. One result has been a separation between the mainstream gallery artists working with the moving image and the more artisanal traditional ones. Jackie Hatfield's recent collection of essays on experimental film and video artists does not include Taylor-Wood or Wearing, for example, but focuses on the older generation of artists – Peter Gidal, Jayne Parker, David Larcher, Le Grice, Chris Welsby, William Raban and others (2006). Hatfield returns to the avant-garde film upsurge of the 1970s in Britain to reassess its critical and philosophical debates in the light of contemporary practice.

THE ROLE OF INSTITUTIONS IN AVANT-GARDE FILM STUDIES

Avant-garde Film Studies has survived in British art schools by becoming part of the academic curriculum during and after the 1970s at the same time as film and video were being incorporated into the fine-art practice curriculum alongside the traditional disciplines of painting, sculpture and print-making. Many of the older-generation of avant-garde historians and theorists like Rees, David Curtis, Simon Field, Nicky Hamlyn and myself worked, and in most part still do, in art schools and not in university Film Studies departments. In Britain at least, the study of avant-garde film has been housed as much, if not more, in art school departments as it has in Film Studies itself. This historical arrangement has led to theory and criticism being practised alongside filmmaking. Most practitioners have taught in art schools at some time or other: for example, Steve Dwoskin and Gidal at the Royal School of Art, Le Grice and William Raban at St Martin's School of Art; Lis Rhodes and Chris Welsby at the Slade School of Art and Jayne Parker at Goldsmiths School of Art. The impact of this intimate relationship between practice and theory has not been negligible. This has not necessarily been a bad thing. In fact, it could be argued that the arrangement often brought a critical sensitivity to the actual processes of avant-garde filmmaking. Academics untouched by these connections are a recent phenomenon. It needs to be remembered that many of the major avant-garde artists have been theorists too – from Sergei Eisenstein (1949), Hans Richter (1986) through to Maya Deren (2001) and Hollis Frampton (1983) and on to Dwoskin (1975), Le Grice (1977; 2001) and Gidal (1976; 1989).

The beginnings of a serious intellectual discussion of avant-garde film occurred in the 1970s, when Film Studies courses first appeared in British universities. Issues around structural and formal film dominated these debates as they emanated from the London Filmmakers' Co-op (Gidal, 1976; Le Grice, 1977). They were part and parcel of *Screen*'s theoretical project based mainly on the writings of Louis Althusser, Jacques Lacan and Christian Metz, even though, interestingly, neither Gidal nor Le Grice subscribed to their theories. It was in this period that avant-garde film was most prominent in *Screen*, with essays published by Le Grice, Gidal, Rees, Peter Wollen, Laura Mulvey, Stephen Heath, Ben Brewster, Deke Dusinberre, Pam Cook and others. It is also often forgotten that Mulvey's seminal essay 'Visual Pleasure and Narrative Cinema', first published in *Screen* in 1975, was at root a polemic for an avant-garde film practice (Mulvey, 1989). *Screen* in these years was attempting to define the historical film avant-garde through the journal's engagement with Bertolt Brecht, FEKS and the Soviet experiments, especially those of Dziga Vertov. This project developed in tandem with an analysis of a particular Hollywood canon. The general collapse of the intellectual Left in Britain in the late seventies led to a less political stance in *Screen* and so also to the marginalization of the avant-garde film that had been understood as intrinsically political in its commitment to co-operative organization and its critique of the traditional illusionist forms of spectatorship and cinematic meaning (Gidal, 1976; Heath, 1981).

Avant-garde film remains marginal to Film Studies. A glance at the 1999 edition of Leo Braudy and Marshall Cohen's *Film Theory and Criticism* reveals a sorry state of affairs. The avant-garde is presented as academically undigested, with two extracts from the writings of Deren and Brakhage, and Wollen's essay on counter-cinema! Of course, Eisenstein is there, but more in terms of issues of film form rather than as an avant-gardist. There is no major contemporary writing: where is P. Adams Sitney? Study of avant-garde film persists in the academy, nonetheless, even if it now crops up now in less likely places such as Lev Manovich's *The Language of the New Media* (2002), where it is celebrated as a forerunner of the new digital media, or Garrett Stewart's *Between Film and Screen: Modernism's Photo Synthesis* (1999).

Academic research into the inter-war European film avant-gardes is also being carried out in departments of European languages and studies, while art school theory departments (where they still exist) and art history departments are applying recent art history concepts to gallery film and video

artists. Both these tendencies are more like consolidations of longstanding threads of interest running parallel to Film Studies, rather than being a part of the discipline of Film Studies as such. One problem has been a tendency in Film Studies, which is even more pronounced in media studies, to perceive art in general as deeply problematic. In this context, art cinema and the avant-garde are regarded as less convivial forms than popular culture and its visual manifestations.

HISTORIES

The avant-garde academic tradition can be divided very broadly into two approaches: one historical and the other theoretical. Under theory one would include critical and conceptual approaches that may not be full-blooded theories but do apply broad notions like Romanticism, Modernism or more formal concepts like space, time, structure and so forth. Fundamental to academic writing around the avant-garde has been the almost continual desire to establish and assert its identity. It is endemic in the idea of an avant-garde that there is much dispute as to what it actually comprises (Christie, 1998; Smith, 1998). No other area in Film Studies would seem to have the same need. It is by definition a highly contestable term, as its application implies a particular relationship to the world or at least its tradition which lies beyond simply a generic entitlement. To this end it is interesting to note how many key texts in the area have been polemics of sorts, for instance, Richter (1986), Dwoskin (1975), Mulvey ([1975] 1989), Sitney (1975), Gidal (1976), Wollen (1982a), and various writings in Sitney's reader on the avant-garde film (1987).

Broad histories of the avant-garde film are few and far between. Sitney, Le Grice and Rees have attempted fairly comprehensive ones, and there are others on national avant-gardes in particular large periods, like David E. James' work on the 1960s American avant-garde that reaches back into the 1950s (1989) and Paul Arthur's collection of essays covering the American scene post-1965 (2005). James' book can be seen as an antidote to Sitney's *Visionary Film* ([1979] 2002), providing a more socio-political context for the avant-garde and in many ways broadening its definition to include more political documentary films. James' book has also been seen as more theoretically based, more systematic. This is of course to misunderstand Sitney's project, which is a rich, complex and monumental study of Romanticism in American film influenced by the literary writing of Harold Bloom and Paul de Man. It also derives from an internal account of the American avant-garde film in so far as it engages with a Romanticism drawn from Kenneth Anger, Deren and Brakhage's own work and, most importantly, writings (Anger, 1989; Deren, 2001).

James' most recent book on American West Coast alternative filmmaking consolidates his position as the leading film historian of the American avant-garde film (2005). (His book is subtitled 'History and Geography of Minor Cinemas in Los Angeles'.) James' 'cultural history and theory' approach to avant-garde cinema is a model set against Sitney's developmental history of forms and styles. In his own words James states that 'almost always avant-garde films emerge from social movements, from identity groups, sub-cultures, and the like' (2005: 15). A critique of Sitney's book is also found in collections of essays edited by Jan-Christopher Horak and by Bruce Posner (Horak, 1995; Posner, 2001). They both attempt to date the origin of the American film avant-garde earlier than Sitney's time-frame of the early 1940s with Deren and Anger. This body of work represents a genuine debate in the historical writings on American film avant-garde.

In comparison, Le Grice's history of *Abstract Film and Beyond* (1977) is more rooted in European traditions. He provides an aesthetic rationale for what he calls the 'formal' film, identifying its foundations in modernist painting and especially cubism and its culmination in the centrality of duration as an essential qualification for an avant-garde film practice. Of course, Le Grice, unlike

Sitney, is addressing a film practice that has only been established since the sixties in Britain and the fifties in Europe. Against this, David Curtis (2007), taking a broader view by looking not simply at an avant-garde but at artists' films and videos, identifies an avant-garde tendency in British cinema much earlier as did either Le Grice or Dusinberre (1980). Although, like Sitney, Curtis uses genre as an organizing device, he draws less on Sitney's literary genres than on those associated with art history; his book contains chapters on landscape films and portraiture, for example.

Writing on the film avant-garde goes back to the 1920s especially among the French Impressionist filmmakers who are sometimes called the First Avant-Garde. The research and translations of Richard Abel (1988) have shown how the earliest 'art cinema' of Jean Epstein, Germaine Dulac, Marcel L'Herbier and others was perceived by some as 'avant-garde'. In contrast, the abstract cinema of the Germans in the 1920s seems more like a parallel movement and not one that attempts to lead cinema in the same way. It could be argued that the French Impressionist project was more akin to the Soviet one in its relationship to cinema in general and in its ambitions for a wide audience and its embrace of narrative forms. The early film journals (and the French were the first to produce one) often reflect this rather more eclectic or broader notion. The editing of essays from the influential film journal *Close Up* (1927-33) betrays a support of directors from Hollywood to which its feelings were often ambivalent (see Donald et al., 1998). Abel and James Donald et al.'s publications denote a move in the 1990s towards historical recovery in the avant-garde. This had usually been done in the service of embedded aesthetic approaches as in Le Grice's alignment of the formal European avant-garde with Paul Cezanne and early modernist painting (1977: 10). Interestingly, the early French avant-garde rooted itself, to some degree at least, in the nineteenth-century impressionist painting movement with its emphasis on artistic expression, poetic form and a relationship to nature.

For British avant-garde film research the inter-war period, and especially the 1930s (Macpherson, 1980), has held a strong fascination. The discovery of films from that period thought lost has already led to work on Len Lye and on the documentary movement in relation to the British mainstream cinema; it promises future research, particularly around its relationship to the culture in general. Central questions such as why, alone among the European countries, Britain's visual art modernists did not establish a relationship to film, remain to be answered. There were a few exceptions. Paul Nash and, of course, Lye (a definite modernist), Humphrey Jennings (a surrealist) and William Coldstream (a realist) were all painters involved in varying degrees with film. Work is proliferating around Jennings, but what is lacking is a fully-fledged study of film in relation to the other arts of that period in Britain. Even so, the period is also a rich one for understanding the relationship between the experimental film area and government and commercial production. It is also an early point of contact between the avant-garde and animation and the latter's role in advertising and government propaganda. The writings of John Grierson (1946; 1998), Jennings, Paul Rotha, Basil Wright (1974), and Nash are a rich source to be tapped. Ian Aitken's work on Cavalcanti signals the complexities of the period and highlights a further aspect; that is, the cosmopolitan flavour of the thirties as figures like Laszlo Moholy-Nagy, Naum Gabo and the German animator Lotte Reininger made themselves felt in Britain, albeit fleetingly (2000).

Debates about avant-garde film during the inter-war period can be seen essentially as a three-sided discussion between realists, abstractionists and surrealists, with politics and social progress being the prize. The ontological implications of these three broad positions have political and social consequences. Aesthetic alliances with the Left are not arbitrary, but reveal something about the way that realism, abstraction and surrealism conceived of themselves outside their manifestos, writings and more public pronouncements.

The other phenomenon concerns alliances and cross-movement between these aesthetic positions, Richter being exemplary. To some degree this is the alliance between dada and constructivism that is still being played out in different aesthetic guises.

THEORIES AND CRITICAL WRITINGS

The strongest impulse governing theories of film in the inter-war period was the new medium's visual essence. In Eisenstein (1949) and Rudolf Arnheim (1957), for instance, this assumes at times the direction of a taxonomy of possible forms. Whereas Arnheim took a cooler look at cinema in general, Eisenstein wanted to forge a narrower, but what he saw as a more progressive account, of cinematic forms to serve quite specific ends. Neither of them identified with the more abstract avant-garde, with Eisenstein in particular being dismissive of experimentalism both at home (Vertov) and abroad (Richter et al.). It is worth remembering, however, that it was the work of Eisenstein that a young Anger drew upon in the 1940s in the US (Pilling, 1989). Is Eisenstein avant-garde? In the strict sense the answer must be, yes, simply because he fulfils the sense of the avant-garde as being in the vanguard of the main army where the latter is taken to be cinema in general. His influence on the mainstream has been felt far more than Vertov's, a relatively obscure figure by comparison. If Vertov proposed a reform of perception as a prerequisite of authentic radical social change, then Eisenstein was a more pragmatic and fundamentally realist propagandist for the Communist cause (Petric, 1987; Bordwell, 1993; Taylor and Christie, 1991; 1993). He believed that political power was everything, or at least prime, and that without it all the rest was talk and formalist tricks. (This perceived division between these two filmmakers often ignores Vertov's more Party-inclined work as a documentarist.)

The tension between experimental documentary as an exploration of ideological forms and that of the historical and revolutionary drama is perhaps more pertinent to filmmakers working in colonial and struggling nationalist scenarios (see Willemen, 1994). It would seem that Eisenstein informs Isaac Julien's black cinema more than Vertov, as Julien like Eisenstein is interested in historical recovery and *à propos* Eisenstein in the body as a possibly subversive dramatic representation. It may also be true that it is in Eisenstein that the conflict between modernism, with its sometimes machine aesthetic, and the demands of symbolic gesture are most felt. The same issues are apparent in Brecht and best articulated in Roland Barthes' crucial essay (1977). With the recent return of the avant-garde film as dramatic form Eisenstein's pertinence is once more being felt.

In different ways, both Eisenstein and Vertov encapsulate and originally figured one model of a film avant-garde as politically revolutionary, a conception that was to reappear again in the 1960s and 1970s. The affiliation of avant-gardism with revolutionary politics lies at the very roots of avant-gardism, figuring in its original use in early-nineteenth-century French painting (Nochlin, 1967). The collapse of the Left and the rise of postmodernism for some inevitably spelt the end for an avant-garde as an historical practice as well as viable theory (Huyssen, 1986).

A neglected text translated and published only in the late eighties was Richter's *The Struggle for the Film* (1986), which was one of the few texts of the period to address the issue of avant-gardism, modernism and film as political practice. It is interestingly lodged in the same period as the great European literary debates of Brecht, Ernst Bloch, Georg Lukács, Walter Benjamin and Theodor Adorno around Socialist realism and modernism (Bloch et al., 1977). The limits set by the availability of texts by these thinkers and their English translations suggest that other academic disciplines are now more likely to develop future research. Kazimir Malevich too has recently attracted more attention in relation to his ideas on film, for he is known to have supported the abstractionists like Richter against his own theatrical-narrative-inclined comrades (Tupitsyn, 2002). Two aspects need

to be separated here, namely studies of the practitioners and protagonists of the inter-war period, from the research into the theoretical positions offered up during the same period. Of course, they are interleaved to some degree, but they remain distinct domains of inquiry.

A.L. Rees' major study of the history of the film avant-garde (1999) is exceptional in its attempt to disentangle the mess of practices and ideas that comprise the inter-wars European avant-garde *Kamfplatz*. He offers a modernist approach that accepts the canon as it stands while acknowledging the various back roads and minor detours endemic to this prolific period when artists crossed media at a bewildering rate and with blithe nonchalance. Adding a totally different perspective is surrealism. Its British historians like Robert Short and Paul Hammond have tended to be partisan apologists, which is not to underestimate what they have brought to research especially Hammond's key collection *The Shadow and its Shadow* (1991) (now in its third edition and always collecting new essays). Famously anti-avant-garde, surrealist films, scant in number, remain within the academic purview largely though research by art historians such as Dawn Ades. (Hammond himself is a freelance in the true sense.) Rudolf Kuenzli's collection (1987) was also a crucial academic intervention in the 1980s, bringing film historians like Thomas Elsaesser to bear on dada and surrealist film. Seen as a precursor of postmodernism, surrealism has attracted enormous interest, especially through the photography exhibition *L'Amour fou* and its influential catalogue with key essays by Rosalind Krauss, very much identified with the high-culture New York-based journal *October* (Krauss, 1985).

In many ways surrealism is understood too readily as hermetically sealed from its immediate context. Of course, its fairly tight organization as a movement with members, purges and official approvals and denunciations do seem to invite such an approach, even though figures like Luis Buñuel and Man Ray in their film work reveal how misleading it can be. Both have produced autobiographies which have helped to muddy the waters for researchers (Buñuel, 1984; Man Ray, 1988). Buñuel's allegiance to Spanish culture as an aesthetic inspiration and his own ambivalent relation to Catholicism raise serious issues for research into surrealist film. In recent years another surrealist, the Czech Jan Svankmajer, has been marginalized by the avant-garde domain and finds most academic support in animation studies (Hames, 1995). Svankmajer's official support by his State studios, like the Russian Yuri Norstein's, situates him beyond the avant-garde trajectory. But this begs the question confronted also in the case of Lye's adverts in the 1930s. That is, quite simply, what are the defining characteristics of an avant-garde?

This period of the 1970s witnessed a relatively large output of writing around the avant-garde that had a precursor in the Europe of the 1920s and 1930s but which has not been matched since. In recent years a new generation of younger researchers has started to look again at the 1970s with the benefits of hindsight and using new methodological and theoretical models – especially postmodernism and theories deriving from Gilles Deleuze and others. At the same time, there has been some growth in empirical historical research, with attempts to unpick the mythological aspects of this golden age of the film avant-garde. Some of this has arisen through writings on artists active and influential then, and a massive amount of research on Warhol has been generated since his death in 1987 that gives a more thorough account of the complex cultural milieu. Callie Angell's *catalogue raisonné* is probably the most thorough catalogue of any avant-garde filmmaker (2006; see also 1994). Reva Wolf's work has been enormously successful in placing Warhol within the New York literary circuit of the sixties (1997). At the same time postmodernists have reclaimed him as someone in a tradition of popular culture (Suarez, 1996) or of American gay culture (Grundmann, 2003). This has been a double-edged blade for avant-garde studies, as the postmodernist framework absorbs that strand of the avant-garde which includes Anger and Jack Smith while simultaneously denying the avant-garde itself.

Theoretical muscles have been flexed around the avant-garde in James Peterson's cognitivist account of the American avant-garde film tradition (1994) and Noël Carroll's more analytical-philosophy-inclined essays on avant-garde aesthetics (1996). Cognitivism, often allied to analytical philosophy, in its American form has been the emergent aesthetic view since the 1990s with the writings of David Bordwell (1996), Carroll and others like Greg Currie (1995) at the fore. Peterson's book applies these ideas to American avant-garde film within the problematic of spectatorship. It is one of the reasons for the avant-garde's persistence. By its nature, avant-garde film is often difficult to understand and for students often difficult to watch. Peterson interestingly takes this common scenario and attempts to demystify the theoretical notion of 'difficulty' frequently used by structural film theorists. Whether cognitivism resolves such a problem is arguable, but spectatorship as a theoretical issue finds a more recalcitrant object in avant-garde work. Much of the recent debate around this issue has been in relation to the classic surrealist film especially Buñuel's *Un Chien andalou* (France, 1929). If this is a response to the dominance of psychoanalytic views of spectatorship, then it is to be welcomed as another model of understanding. That the avant-garde should be the location of such a central issue in film theory is not surprising. After all, the horizon view of avant-garde film left the latter rather under-analyzed and seen as a functional outpost of the main theoretical body.

The interest in spectatorship in relationship to avant-garde film found in William Wees and Peterson elaborates on the experimental aspect of the tradition in which, at least implicitly, the spectator has occupied a problematic space so to speak. Both writers eschew the semiotic and psychoanalytically derived work found in Film Studies. In Wees' case his ideas evolve from a study of Brakhage's films with their exploration of various forms of perception and vision (1992). Unlike Sitney, who used vision in the

Romantic sense, Wees aligns his work with a more scientific conception of perception, though the Romantic paradigm is never far away. Wees is also interested in delineating what he sees as an important strand of the avant-garde which owes much to conceptions of 'seeing' in its broadest sense. The impact of science in recent years on brain studies has filtered through to the cultural arena, leading to the rise of cognitivism and a reassessment, if not total rejection, of Freudian-inspired notions of perception. There is an important issue of what is true here. Which theory – Freudian-semiotic or scientific-cognitivist – is true outside the domain of the humanities? It is no surprise that the Americans by and large should quickly dump the cultural and politically inflected Freudian approach in favour of the neutrality of 'science'. This is another fault-line that goes back to early modernism.

AUTEURS

The so-called theories of 'film authorship' have never sat easily in the avant-garde. The individual artist has always been a significant aspect of such work and remains so to this day. The literature on individual avant-garde artists has expanded with major studies of, for example, Brakhage (Elder, 1998; Wees, 1992), Deren (Nichols, 2001), Oskar Fischinger (Moritz, 2004), Derek Jarman (O'Pray, 1996a) and Jack Smith (Leffingwell, 1997). The avant-garde has been dominated by the single artist, sometimes working with a few friends or co-artists (for example, Smith, Warhol). Yet it is only in recent years that monographs on single artists have begun to appear in any number, largely due (one assumes) to the long period of style-dominance, namely the formal-structural school. The attraction of the single artist is obvious in so far as a particular theme within that person's oeuvre provides a point of analysis. Roy Grundbaum's book on a single minimal film, Warhol's *Blow Job* (US, 1963), is a case in point: it is a brilliant analysis of queerness in post-war American

society, posed in terms of a wild analysis of Warhol's provocative, short, silent black-and-white film (2003). This would seem to be a common trend as the avant-garde has long shed any broad political and social utopianism in favour of either the merits of single issues – whether it be from a gay, female or ethnic perspective – or an agenda outside the avant-garde. An example of the latter option might appear to be Esther Leslie's study of the relationship between the film avant-garde of the 1920s and the Hollywood cartoon under the methodological umbrella of critical theory, especially that of Benjamin (2002). But Leslie's book also represents the historical recovery of a particular cultural moment, driven by a refreshing Leftist political perspective, dividing American and European traditions. Similarly, a collection of essays on Lye, edited by Jean-Michel Bouhours and Roger Horrocks, shows how political agendas determined filmic ones in Britain in the 1930s (2000). The inter-War years in Europe await their chronicler of the film avant-gardes. While the American avant-garde has received two enormous histories of different kinds – Sitney's and James' – none has emerged for the European avant-garde as a whole. Substantial individual studies do exist – of Fischinger, for example, thanks to the late American animation historian William Moritz (2004) – but there are none of Richter, Walter Ruttman, Viking Eggeling, Ray or Fernand Léger.

Of course, these figures did not have extensive careers in the film avant-garde. Death, mainstream ambitions and the temptations of other art forms touch them with a certain insubstantiality when compared to figures like Brakhage, Frampton or Warhol. Wollen's 'two avant-gardes' these is relevant here, here for the European avant-gardes always worked in close proximity to, or in the shadow of, art cinema (Wollen, 1982b; 1982c). It is art-house directors who have attracted the studies – Jean Renoir, F.W. Murnau, Fritz Lang, Jean-Luc Godard, François Truffaut et al. – though gaps remain, such as G.W. Pabst. Some of these directors are treated as more 'avant-garde' than others – Godard,

Jean-Marie Straub and Daniele Huillet, and Michelangelo Antonioni are the obvious cases (on Straub and Huillet, see Byg, 1995). The historical moment of this debate was in the 1970s and it was very much propelled by essays by Wollen and Mulvey, who were intent on grasping the avant-garde baton from the Godardian and Vertovian tradition and rejecting the formalism of the British co-op movement.

Oddly, this remains a theoretical stumbling block and perhaps accounts for a reluctance to provide a history of the European avant-garde tradition, at least from the older generation. Another obvious difficulty remains that of accessing documentation in a wide array of European languages, although this has been alleviated somewhat by the end of the Cold War. Yuri Tsivian's impact on Soviet and Russian Film Studies is significant in that his exceptional film analyses are rooted in the very culture he researches (2002). Furthermore, the European history or analysis would necessarily be complex, comprising as it does separate nation states with long socio-political and cultural histories like Germany, France, Britain, Russia and so on. This is not to underestimate the power of early modernism to create international communities in European along particular city axes – Berlin, Paris, Moscow, London (see, for example, Williams, 1989). Wollen has contributed enormously to tracing the cultural trading routes between these capitals and their product and synthesizing movements – his essay (1987) on the impact of Sergei Diaghilev on a particular strand of modernism related to the body stemming from Matisse, an often neglected modernist figure, and passing through Paul Poiret and 1920s fashion, is exemplary of this kind of foray into European cultural history. The other great enforcer of European communality was, of course, the Great War of 1914–18, the impact on the of which avant-garde is usually restricted to that of the dada movement.

It is no accident that on some film study courses both 'avant-garde' film traditions, whether old or new, are neglected for Hollywood. Their association with high culture remains problematic, especially for some postmodernists who have come to dominate many film study departments. Books on British cinema still remain awkward in their treatment of the avant-garde tradition, except where it shades into art cinema. Derek Jarman and Peter Greenaway, for example, seem to be treated as British Godards – experimental, but working within the art-cinema institution of exhibition, production and distribution. This relationship remains very much a lacuna in contemporary research.

Although avant-garde film has often been approached through the concept of genre, the fit is not a happy one. A true set of genres for the avant-garde, following the example of Sitney's *Visionary Film*, would include the dramatic narrative, the lyrical, the abstract (perhaps) and so on. Instead, key traditions marking historical moments have been hijacked as genres: categories such as 'underground', 'beats', or 'structural'. Wees' book is a form of genre creation or study, for example, while Jack Sargeant's collection on the Beats focuses on a movement which has not inspired a fully-fledged genre (1997). Some of these so-called genres may better be understood as *modes*, as in the literary use of the concept. Steven Dillon's book on Jarman reflects on the latter's films using the notion of the lyric (2004). Scott MacDonald's book *The Garden in the Machine* (2001) seems to be an ambitious attempt to identify a mode-like strand in the American avant-garde; this draws on some diffuse notion of the pastoral or landscape in an advanced capitalist industrial society which still locates key cultural values in 'nature' and 'the countryside'.

In an additional chapter to his classic book *Visionary Film*, Sitney has brilliantly elaborated a further moment in the stylistic development of the American avant-garde film, what he calls the Menippean, derived from the classical Greek literary mode of satirical discourse in which characters represent ideas and is a 'dialogue of forms and ideas, open to narrative elaborations but not requiring them' ([1979] 2002: 410). For Sitney, the Menippean ousts postmodernism as a heuristic device for explaining new avant-garde forms emerging in the 1970s and persisting to the present. Yvonne Rainer, Frampton, James Benning and late Brakhage are key practitioners of this mode or genre. In recent years the 'found-footage' film has received much critical attention as a vibrant method in contemporary film art practice – although it is hardly a genre (Sjoberg, 2001; Wees, 1993).

There would seem to be a strong resistance to postmodernism by the older generation of historians like Sitney, Rees, Le Grice, Arthur (2005) and others. The reduction of avant-garde films to ideology and to a general cultural climate offends Sitney's sense of American avant-garde artists' loyalty to and awareness of their own film tradition. Their working-through of problems leads to solutions within the tradition. And, as Sitney points out, much of the theorizing within the avant-garde came from artists themselves: Deren, Brakhage, Mekas (1972), Frampton and Kubelka.

Parker Tyler's book *Underground Film* (1974) is an eccentric and sceptical but quintessentially underground text on the American avant-garde or underground as it tended to be signified at the time and since. An inspiration to Sitney, Tyler's writings are sublimely critical and his near relations are Manny Farber or Ray Durgnat in Britain. Their almost *belles lettres* approach to film is anathema to a generation of theorists dedicated to expunging the self and the insights of subjecthood from analytical and theoretical practice. The idea of the critic as a source of humane values in the arts is now identified with the eighteenth- and nineteenth-century tradition of writers like Samuel Coleridge, Matthew Arnold, and T.S. Eliot, and in America perhaps Clement Greenberg (1992), who hammered out his views in critical reviews. But Tyler et al. are now associated with the 'underground' with its connotations of social subversion, style and gesture, and forms of sexuality and gender that act as a radicalism preferable to the political focus found in much structural and formal work of the 1960s and 1970s.

The rise of the women's and gay film-making avant-garde in the late seventies and eighties latched on to the underground of Warhol, Jack Smith and Ron Rice, not to mention Deren and Anger, whose psychodramas were similarly resonant with a post-Left postmodernist generation. In Britain, Lis Rhodes' *Light Reading* (UK, 1978) has been seen as a watershed piece, marking the end of the structural film project as a dynamic form and the opening up of the British avant-garde film to voice and narrative albeit in her fragmentary and elusive work. Yet form is strongly felt in the film as it was in other formal-voice women filmmakers like Lucy Panteli, whose work had auto-biographical tones. But personal biography, portraiture and voice were to be brilliantly expressed in Jayne Parker's films emerging in the early eighties and resonating with an underground feel in which performance and the body (Parker's) was critically central (Rees, 2000). But Parker's aloof classical framing and minimal aesthetic ran parallel for some years with the Super 8-based New Romantic movement that openly denounced structural film and embraced the underground of Warhol, Smith, Rice and Anger as well as art cinema directors like Godard and Rosa von Praunheim. In John Maybury and Cerith Wyn Evan irony was *de rigueur* as was the strong use of popular cultural and sub-cultural images (O'Pray, 2001). In America the punk filmmakers, who also used Super 8, were more hard-edged, and drew on an aesthetic that mixed B-movie style and Warholian 'documentary' with a Smith-like celebration of Lower East Side detritus and druglife. In Britain there was a more stylized decadence of high theatricals, opera soundtracks and heavy use, at times, of superimposition and video effects. Jarman's Super 8 work was crucial here, with its swirling slow-motion poetics influenced by Carl Jung. *The Angelic Conversation* (UK, 1985) was a symbolic journey of gay male sexual initiation underpinned and distanced by Shakespeare's sonnets. Subjectivism was held at bay by voice-over, text and a self-conscious performativity.

In this context, Warhol's performance-based work, only fully seen after his death with the release of long forgotten and non-distributed films like *Horse* (US, 1965), *Kitchen* (US, 1965), *Vinyl* (US, 1965) in the early 1990s, established his reputation for a second time with queer theorists and cultural studies-based academics such as Juan Suarez, who could celebrate films that played with signifiers and did not try to erase them. There was also in the work a seeming neglect of high-art craft and style so apparent in the classicism of the structural films. Notions of the body, identity and authenticity were perceived in the films of Smith and Warhol that chimed with the theoretical proclivities of orthodox film and cultural studies lending it a much needed air of radicalism. The status of Jarman, especially in the American academy, is a case in point (Dillon, 2004; Pencak, 2002; Wymer, 2005). Snubbed by the traditional avant-garde throughout most of his career, he has attracted three major books and a long essay from Leo Bersani and Ulysse Dutoit (1999).

Unlike Tyler, Gene Youngblood's book *Expanded Cinema* (1970) has returned to favour with a younger generation, who now find its theories and prophecies less eccentric and more germane than they seemed to be in the 1960s. Expanded cinema has received much more attention with the wealth of film and video installation work in contemporary art (Iles, 2001; Michalka, 2003). The ubiquitous web and new media has meant some radical rethinking of the avant-garde, placing his work alongside another rediscovery from the sixties – Marshall MacLuhan. Le Grice's collection of essays on film, video and computer experimentation similarly chimes in with those for whom film purism associated with the formalists is no longer attractive (2001). With the growth of computer-generated imagery (CGI), the avant-garde has found a new role as a model for approaching new media. But typically there is also a groundswell of interest in old technologies, in the cheap, amateur and outdated, so that 8 mm (gauge), once thought virtually extinct, has found a new life. 16 mm (Tacita Dean) and even 35 mm (McQueen)

have found their way into the gallery almost perversely against the use of the DVD as common projection means. This raises an interesting and barely addressed question about medium specificity, as the medium is not simply the means of recording or projection, but is itself what constitutes the medium, now lamely called the 'moving image'.

What has always separated the American and European traditions remains in place. The most strident and theoreticized form of structuralism dominated until the 1980s and remains a touchstone for the European sensibility emanating from pre-war Europe of the German abstract movement and later of the Viennese formalists of Kren, Dieter Rot and Kubelka (Barber, 2004), and erupting in the work of Gidal, Le Grice, the Heins and so on (Curtis, 1971; 1979). The *Film as Film* exhibition of 1979 still casts a long shadow, as is witnessed by the successful *Shoot Shoot Shoot* exhibition of 2003, where a new generation packed the Tate Modern film theatre to rediscover the structural or formal film movement of the seventies. Sitney's grand genres of the mythopaeic, the lyric and the Menippean do not fit the European experience, which by and large stays wedded to formalism and the documentary shot through with socio-political experience. Patrick Keiller and Andrew Kotting returned to the poetic documentary form in the 1980s (last seen in the Free Cinema of the 1950s) with its class-based Leftist response to the industrial collapse of Britain and the finance economy of Thatcherism symbolized by the protean miner's strike of 1985 – an event that finds no parallel in America. The black cinema of the eighties also took a sophisticated look at the empire and, in Julien's feature film *Young Soul Rebels* (UK/France/Germany/Spain, 1991), at race and sexuality as a fictionalized social documentary of British working class life in the seventies.

If the avant-garde film seems to have found a more secure base in the academy in recent years, it is in a dispersed condition, existing in myriad contexts from art schools and university Film Studies programmes to art history and language departments. This seems to be a healthy state of affairs, bringing with it different ideas, approaches, methodologies and not least sensibilities, and thus providing a rich and promiscuous research landscape. For the future, no doubt historical research will carry on growing, especially in Europe, where political and linguistic barriers were for so long in force. As far as theory is concerned, the avant-garde by its nature has been eccentric and eclectic with odd periods of dogmatism, as was evident in the 1970s. To some degree, the museums are coming to dictate the theoretical agenda as they do in the traditional arts. Curatorship, with its obligatory theoretical baggage, plays an enormously powerful role in artists' film and moving image in general (see Iles, 2001; Michalka, 2003). Equally, the cognitive approaches found in Film Studies have found the experimental condition of film, with its emphasis on optical and perceptual strategies, a fertile area for research. With its new credibility in the international art market over the past decade, film lies at a juncture in which prediction as to how it is taken up in the academy is dangerous. It is probably safe to say at least that it is here to stay, and that it no longer holds the precarious position it once did.

NOTES

1 Some of the key texts that have helped to define the sub-field of avant-garde Film Studies, and which are not referred to elsewhere in this chapter, are: Danino and Maziere; (2003); Darke (1996); Dusinberre (1970); Gidal (1980; 1996); Hamlyn (1982–83; 2003); Hanhardt (1976); Hoberman (1997; 2001); James (1992); Keller (1986); Koestenbaum (2001); MacDonald (1988; 1993; 2002); Manvell (1949); Miller (1994); Moritz (1997); O'Pray (1996b; 1996c); Rees (1993–94); Renan (1967); Roberts and Steeds (eds) (2001).

REFERENCES

Abel, Richard (ed.) (1988) *French Film Theory and Criticism, 1907–1929*. Vol. 11. Princeton, NJ: Princeton University Press.

Aitken, Ian (2000) *Alberto Cavalcanti: Realism, Surrealism and National Cinemas*. Trowbridge: Flicks Books.

Angell, Callie (1994) *The Films of Andy Warhol Pt II*. New York: Whitney Museum of American Art.

Angell, Callie (2006) *Andy Warhol Screen Tests: The Films of Andy Warhol Catalogue Raisonné*. New York: Abrams/Whitney Museum of American Art.

Anger, Kenneth (1989) 'Modesty and the Art of Film', in Jayne Pilling and Michael O'Pray (eds), *Into the Pleasure Dome: The Films of Kenneth Anger*. London: British Film Institute. pp. 18–21.

Arnheim, Rudolf (1957) *Film as Art*. London: University of California Press.

Arthur, Paul (2005) *A Line of Sight: American Avant-Garde Film since 1965*. London: University of Minnesota Press.

Barber, Stephen (2004) *The Art of Destruction: The Film of the Vienna Action Group*. London: Creation Books.

Barthes, Roland (1977) *Image, Music, Text*. Glasgow: Fontana/Collins.

Bersani, Leo and Dutoit, Ulysse (1999) *Caravaggio's Secrets*. Cambridge, Mass.: MIT Press.

Bloch, Ernst, Lukács, Georg, Brecht, Bertolt, Benjamin, Walter and Adorno, Theodor (1977) *Aesthetics and Politics*. Tr. R. Taylor. London: New Left Books.

Bordwell, David (1993) *The Cinema of Eisenstein*. London: Harvard University Press.

Bordwell, David and Carroll, Noël (eds) (1996) *Post-Theory: Reconstructing Film Studies*. London: University of Wisconsin Press.

Bouhours, Jean-Michel and Horrocks, Roger (eds) (2000) *Len Lye*. Paris: Centre Pompidou.

Braudy, Leo and Cohen, Marshall (eds) (1999) *Film Theory and Criticism: Introductory Readings*. 5th edn. New York: Oxford University Press.

Buñuel, Luis (1984) *My Last Breath*. London: Cape.

Byg, Barton (1995) *Landscapes of Resistance: The German Films of Daniéle Huillet and Jean-Marie Straub*. London: University of California Press.

Carroll, Noël (1996) *Theorizing the Moving Image*. Cambridge: Cambridge University Press.

Christie, Ian (1998) 'The avant-gardes and European cinema before 1930', in John Hill and Pamela Church Gibson (eds), *Oxford Guide to Film Studies*. London: Oxford University Press. pp. 449–54.

Currie, Gregory (1995) *Image and Mind: Film, Philosophy and Cognitive Science*. Cambridge: Cambridge University Press.

Curtis, David (1971) *Experimental Film*. London: Studio Vista.

Curtis, David (ed.) (1979) *Film as Film: Formal Experiment in Film, 1910–1975*. London: Hayward Gallery.

Curtis, David (2007) *A History of Artists' Film and Video, 1897–2004*. London: BFI.

Danino, Nina and Maziere, Michael (2003) *The Undercut Reader: Critical Writings on Artists' Film and Video*. London: Wallflower Press.

Darke, Chris (1996) 'Avant-Garde Cinema in Europe', in John Caughie and Kevin Rockett (eds), *The Companion to British and Irish Cinema*. London: BFI/Cassell. pp. 167–69.

Deren, Maya (2001) 'An Anagram of Ideas on Art, Form and Film', in Bill Nichols (ed.), *Maya Deren and the American Avant-Garde*. London: University of California Press. pp. 267–322.

Dillon, Steven (2004) *Derek Jarman and the Lyric Film: The Mirror and the Sea*. Austin: University of Texas Press.

Donald, James, Friedberg, Anne and Marcus, Laura (eds) (1998) *Close Up, 1927–1933: Cinema and Modernism*. London: Cassell.

Dusinberre, Deke (1979) 'The Other Avant-gardes', in David Curtis (ed.), *Film as Film*. London: Hayward Gallery. pp. 53–8.

Dusinberre, Deke (1980) 'The Avant-Garde Attitude in the Thirties', in Donald Macpherson (ed.), *Traditions of Independence: British Cinema in the Thirties*. London: British Film Institute. pp. 34–50.

Dwoskin, Steve (1975) *Film Is... The International Free Cinema*. London: Peter Owen.

Eisenstein, Sergei (1949) *Film Form*. London: Faber & Faber.

Elder, R. Bruce (1998) *The Films of Stan Brakhage in the American Tradition of Ezra Pound, Gertrude Stein and Charles Olson*. Waterloo, Ontario: Wilfrid Laurier University Press.

Ferguson, Russell, De Salvo, Donna and Slyce, John (1999) *Gillian Wearing*. London: Phaidon.

Frampton, Hollis (1983) *Circles of Confusion: Film, Photography, Video Texts, 1968–1980*. Rochester, NY: Visual Studies Workshop Press.

Gidal, Peter (ed.) (1976) *Structural Film Anthology*. London: BFI.

Gidal, Peter (1980) 'Technology and Ideology in/through/and Avant-Garde Film: An Instance', in Teresa de Lauretis and Stephen Heath (eds), *The Cinematic Apparatus*. London: Macmillan. pp. 151–71.

Gidal, Peter (1989) *Materialist Film*. London: Routledge.

Gidal, Peter (1996) 'Theory and Definition of Structural/Materialist Film', in Michael O'Pray (ed.), *The British Avant-Garde Film, 1926–1995: An Anthology of Writings*. Luton: University of Luton/Arts Council of England. pp. 145–70.

Greenberg, Clement (1992) 'Avant-Garde and Kitsch', in Charles Harrison and Paul Wood (eds), *Art in Theory,* *1900–1990: An Anthology of Changing Ideas*. Oxford: Blackwell. pp. 529–41.

Grierson, John (1946) *Grierson on Documentary*. Ed. Forsyth Hardy. London: Collins.

Grierson, John (1998) 'Preface to Paul Rotha's *Documentary Film* (1952)', in Ian Aitken (ed.), *The Documentary Film Movement: An Anthology*. Edinburgh: Edinburgh University Press. pp. 115–22.

Grundmann, Roy (2003) *Andy Warhol's Blow Job*. Philadelphia: Temple University Press.

Hames, Peter (1995) 'The film experiment', in Peter Hames (ed.), *Dark Alchemy: The Films of Jan Svankmajer*. Trowbridge: Flicks Books. pp. 7–47.

Hamlyn, Nicky (1982–3) 'Seeing Is Believing: *Wavelength* Reconsidered', *Afterimage*, 11: 22–30.

Hamlyn, Nicky (2003) *Film Art Phenomena*. London: BFI.

Hammond, Paul (ed.) (1991) *The Shadow and Its Shadow: Surrealist Writings on the Cinema*. 2nd edn. Edinburgh: Polyglon.

Hanhardt, John (1976) 'The Medium Viewed: The American Avant-Garde Film', in *A History of the American Avant-Garde Cinema*. New York: American Film Association. pp. 19–47.

Hatfield, Jackie (ed.) (2006) *Experimental Film and Video: An Anthology*. London: John Libbey.

Hayward Gallery (2002) *Sam Taylor-Wood*. London: Steidl/Hayward Gallery.

Heath, Stephen (1981) *Questions of Cinema*. London: Macmillan.

Hoberman, Jim (1997) 'The Big Heat: Making and Unmaking Flaming Creatures', in Edward Leffingwell, Carole Kismaric and Marvin Heiferman (eds), *Jack Smith: Flaming Creatures: His Amazing Life and Times*. London: Serpent's Tail. pp. 152–67.

Hoberman, Jim (2001) *On Jack Smith's Flaming Creatures and Other Secret Flix of Cinemaroc*. New York: Granary Books.

Horak, Jan-Christopher (ed.) (1995) *Lovers of Cinema: The First American Film Avant-Garde, 1919–1945*. London: University of Wisconsin Press.

Huyssen, Andreas (1986) *After the Great Divide: Modernism, Mass Culture and Postmodernism*. London: Macmillan.

Iles, Chrissie (ed.) (2001) *Into the Light: The Projected Image in American Art 1964–1977*. New York: Whitney Museum of American Art.

James, David E. (1989) *Allegories of Cinema: American Film in the 1960s*. Princeton, NJ: Princeton University Press.

James, David E. (ed.) (1992) *To Free the Cinema: Jonas Mekas and the New York Underground*. Princeton, NJ: Princeton University Press.

James, David E. (2005) *The Most Typical Avant-garde: History and Geography of Minor Cinemas in Los Angeles*. London: University of California Press.

Keller, Marjorie (1986) *The Untutored Eye: Childhood in the Films of Cocteau, Cornell, and Brakhage*. London: Fairleigh Dickenson Press.

Koestenbaum, Wayne (2001) *Andy Warhol*. London: Weidenfeld and Nicolson.

Krauss, Rosalind (1985) *L'Amour fou: Photography and Surrealism*. New York: Abbeville Press.

Kuenzli, Rudolf E. (ed.) (1987) *Dada and Surrealist Film*. New York: Willis, Cocker and Owens.

Leffingwell, Edward, Kismaric, Carole and Heiferman, Marvin (eds) (1997) *Jack Smith: Flaming Creatures: His Amazing Life and Times*. London: Serpent's Tail.

Le Grice, Malcolm (1977) *Abstract Film and Beyond*. London: Studio Vista.

Le Grice, Malcolm (2001) *Experimental Cinema in the Digital Age*. London: BFI.

Leslie, Esther (2002) *Hollywood Flatlands: Animation, Critical Theory and the Avant-Garde*. London: Pluto.

MacDonald, Scott (1988) *A Critical Cinema: Interviews with Independent Filmmakers*. London: University of California Press.

MacDonald, Scott (1993) *Avant-Garde Film*. Cambridge: Cambridge University Press.

MacDonald, Scott (2001) *The Garden in the Machine: A Field Guide to Independent Films about Place*. London: University of California Press.

MacDonald, Scott (2002) *Cinema 16: Documents Toward a History of the Film Society*. Philadelphia: Temple University Press.

Macpherson, Donald (ed.) (1980) *Traditions of Independence: British Cinema in the Thirties*. London: BFI.

Manovich, Lev (2002) *The Language of New Media*. London: MIT Press.

Man Ray (1988) *Self Portrait*. London: Bloomsbury.

Manvell, Roger (ed.) (1949) *Experiment in the Film*. London: Grey Walls Press.

Mekas, Jonas (1972) *Movie Journal: The Rise of the New American Cinema, 1959–1971*. New York: Collier Books.

Michalka, Matthias (2003) *X-Screen Film Installations and Actions in the 1960s and 1970s*. Wien: Museum Moderner Kunst Stiftung Ludwig Wien.

Miller, Debra (1994) *Billy Name: Stills from the Warhol Films*. New York: Prestel.

Moritz, William (1997) 'Restoring the aesthetics of early abstract films', in Jayne Pilling (ed.), *A Reader in Animation Studies*. Eastleigh: John Libbey. pp. 221–7.

Moritz, William (2004) *Optical Poetry: The Life and Work of Oskar Fischinger*. Eastleigh: John Libbey.

Mulvey, Laura ([1975] 1989) 'Visual Pleasure and Narrative Cinema', in *Visual and Other Pleasures*. London: Macmillan. pp. 14–26.

Nichols, Bill (ed.) (2001) *Maya Deren and the American Avant-Garde*. London: University of California Press.

Nochlin, Linda (1967) 'The Invention of the Avant-Garde: France, 1830–80', in Thomas B. Hess and John Ashbery (eds), *Avant-Garde Art*. New York: Collier Books. pp. 3–24.

O'Pray, Michael (1996a) *Derek Jarman: Dreams of England*. London: British Film Institute.

O'Pray, Michael (ed.) (1996b) *The British Avant-Garde Film 1926–1995: An Anthology of Writings*. Luton: University of Luton/Arts Council of England.

O'Pray, Michael (1996c) 'The British Avant-Garde and Art Cinema from the 1970s to the 1990s', in Andrew Higson (ed.), *Dissolving Views: Key Issues in British Cinema*. London: Cassell. pp. 178–90.

O'Pray, Michael (2001) ' "New Romanticism" and the British Avant-Garde Film in the Early 80s', in Robert Murphy (ed.), *The British Cinema Book*. 2nd edn. London: British Film Institute. pp. 256–62.

O'Pray, Michael (2003) *Avant-Garde Film: Forms, Themes and Passions*. London: Wallflower Press.

Pencak, William (2002) *The Films of Derek Jarman*. London: McFarland.

Peterson, James (1994) *Dreams of Chaos, Visions of Order: Understanding the American Avant-garde Cinema*. Detroit: Wayne State University Press.

Petric, Vlada (1987) *Constructivism in Film: The Man with a Movie Camera: A Cinematic Analysis*. Cambridge: Cambridge University Press.

Pilling, Jayne and O'Pray, Mike (eds) (1989) *Into the Pleasure Dome: The Films of Kenneth Anger*. London: BFI.

Posner, Bruce (2001) *Unseen Cinema: Early American Avant-Garde Filmmaking, 1893–1941*. New York: Anthology Film Archives.

Rees, A.L. (1993-4) 'The Themersons and the Polish Avant-Garde: Warsaw-Paris-London', *PIX*, 1: 86–101.

Rees, A.L. (1999) *A History of Experimental Film and Video*. London: BFI.

Rees, A.L. (2000) 'The Artist as Filmmaker: Films by Jayne Parker 1979–2000', in *Jayne Parker Filmworks 79–00*. Exeter: Spacex Gallery. pp. 9–30.

Renan, Sheldon (1967) *The Underground Film: An Introduction to Its Development in America*. London: Studio Vista.

Richter, Hans (1986) *The Struggle for the Film*. London: Scolar Press.

Roberts, Catsou and Steeds, Lucy (eds) (2001) *Michael Snow almost Cover to Cover*. London/Bristol: Black Dog Publishing/Arnolfini.

Sargeant, Jack (1997) *Naked Lens: Beat Cinema*. London: Creation Books.

Sitney, P. Adams (ed.) (1975) *The Essential Cinema*. New York: Anthology Film Archives/New York University Press.

Sitney, P. Adams [1979] (2002) *Visionary Film: The American Avant-Garde, 1943–2000*. 3rd edn. London: Oxford University Press.

Sitney, P. Adams (ed.) (1987) *The Avant-Garde Film: A Reader of Theory and Criticism*. New York: Anthology Film Archives.

Sjöberg, Patrik (2001) *The World in Pieces: A Study of Compilation Film*. Stockholm: Aura forlag.

Smith, Murray (1998) 'Modernism and the avant-gardes', in John Hill and Pamela Church Gibson (eds), *Oxford Guide to Film Studies*. Oxford: Oxford University Press. pp. 395–412.

Stewart, Garrett (1999) *Between Film and Screen: Modernism's Photo Synthesis*. Chicago: University of Chicago Press.

Suarez, Juan A. (1996) *Bike Boys, Drag Queens and Superstars: Avant-Garde, Mass Culture, and Gay Identities in the 1960s Underground Cinema*. Bloomington: Indiana University Press.

Taylor, Richard and Christie, Ian (eds) (1991) *Inside the Film Factory: New Approaches to Russian and Soviet Cinema*. London: Routledge.

Taylor, Richard and Christie, Ian (eds) (1993) *Eisenstein Rediscovered*. London: Routledge.

Tsivian, Yuri (2002) *Ivan the Terrible*. London: BFI.

Tupitsyn, Margarita (2002) *Malevich and Film*. London: Yale University Press.

Tyler, Parker (1974) *Underground Film: A Critical Inquiry*. Harmondsworth: Penguin.

Wees, William C. (1992) *Light Moving in Time: Studies in the Visual Aesthetics of Avant-garde Film*. Berkeley: University of California Press.

Wees, William C. (1993) *Recycled Images*. New York: Anthology Film Archives.

Willemen, Paul (1994) 'An Avant-garde for the 90s', in *Looks and Frictions: Essays in Cultural Studies and Film Theory*. London: BFI. pp. 141–61.

Williams, Raymond (1989) 'The Politics of the Avant-Garde', in *The Politics of Modernism*. London: Verso. pp. 49–63.

Wolf, Reva (1997) *Andy Warhol, Poetry, and Gossip in the 1960s*. London: University of Chicago Press.

Wollen, Peter (1982a) 'Godard and Counter Cinema: *Vent d'est*', in *Readings and Writings: Semiotic Counter-Strategies*. London: Verso. pp. 79–91.

Wollen, Peter (1982b) 'The Two Avant-Gardes', in *Readings and Writings: Semiotic Counter-Strategies*. London: Verso. pp. 92–104.

Wollen, Peter (1982c) '"Ontology" and "Materialism" in Film', in *Readings and Writings: Semiotic Counter-Strategies*. London: Verso. pp. 189–207.

Wollen, Peter (1987) 'Fashion/orientalism/the body', *New Formations*, 1: 5–33.

Wright, Basil (1974) *The Long View*. London: Secker and Warburg.

Wymer, Rowland (2005) *Derek Jarman*. Manchester: Manchester University Press.

22

Film and (as) Modernity

Julian Murphet

Perhaps the most characteristic *bête noire* of 1970s 'materialist' film theory was that stalwart stereotype, the 'classic realist text' (MacCabe, 1980: 152–62). Though the more astute of the *Screen* gang were perfectly aware how 'resistant' such a film text could be, nevertheless a pervasive supposition of the era was that films constructed along industrial, 'Hollywood' lines could not 'deal with the real as contradictory', and moreover reinscribed the subject 'in a relation of dominant specularity' (MacCabe, 1980: 157). Which was not going quite so far as to say, with Michael Fried, that 'the cinema is not, even at its most experimental, a modernist art' (1998: 164); but it *was* to reserve the noble epithet –'modernist' – only for those properly experimental, avant-gardist film texts that eschewed everything 'realist'. It is a measure of the distance travelled since Fried's 1967 intervention that not only his purist notion of modernism, but also the more ambivalent and dialectical version of it promulgated by Stephen Heath and Colin MacCabe, seem equally dated, equally quaint and impossible to resurrect today. Now, indeed, it seems far more correct to feel with Laura Mulvey that cinema per se

is 'an emblem of modernity, both as popular entertainment and as modernist avant-garde' (2006: 37). The very idea that one might quibble about which films were, and which weren't, 'modernist' has about it the dusty scholastic air of arguments over angels and pinheads; for as Mulvey's formula has it, the broad church of modernity houses both the 'modernist avant-garde' *and* the classic realist text – both are emblems and icons of their age, an age which has, for better or worse, come to an end. And I want to insist up front that historical *coming to an end* of modernity is a vital precondition of the flowering in scholarship and academic debate of what will here be called 'cinematic modernism studies' – the subject of this chapter.

The notion that postmodernism might be the first condition of possibility of cinematic modernism studies is not quite as perverse as it sounds. After all, it is written into the conceptual architecture of the term that *coming after* modernism might dispose the latter to heightened levels of inspection and knowledge-production. Since the beginning of the 1980s, the academy has seen a veritable explosion of new intellectual interest in modernity, a flocking of scholarly labour towards an earlier twentieth-century canon whose new respectability reactively 'rebuke[d] the frivolities of the postmodern by returning to the truly serious older texts of a more wholesome past', as Fredric Jameson has argued (1998: 98–9). As far as cinema was concerned, a 'return to the cinema's past constitute[d] a gesture towards a truncated history, to those aspects of modernist thought, politics and aesthetics that seemed to end prematurely before their use or relevance could be internalised or exhausted' (Mulvey, 2006: 8). It is in the eddies and swirls created by these two postmodern biases toward the modern – piety and respect for the 'unfinished project' – that cinematic modernism studies has prospered and secured its remarkable achievements. But more immediate and pressing circumstances also conspired to propel the vanguard of contemporary Film Studies back toward the question of origins. The incipient demise of the medium of film itself was one such. When, in 1995, cinema's centenary was being blazoned around the globe, the simultaneous threat of a fully digitalized movie (*Toy Story*, John Lasseter, US, 1995) and the launch of the fledgling DVD market seriously dampened the jubilee's mood. The signs had long been in the wind: Jean-Luc Godard had complained for decades about the creeping undeath of cinema, and the crisis triggered by television had never fully been resolved. But now that film's literal death was imminent, and as the whole corpus of film history was migrating into binary code, the question of its emergence could be posed anew, as every obituary circles around origins and heydays. Cinematic modernism studies was, in a way, a flight from the perils of extinction into the glamour of parturition, infancy and adolescence.

At any rate, this movement in Film Studies was driven back upon the founding paradoxes and contradictions of its medium, a medium born the bastard child of photographic 'realism' and constructivist, editorial 'modernism'. The pivotal move here was precisely to disarm the *bête noire* of the 'classic realist text' by fully admitting the basis of its 'realism' in photography ('the very

standard of the reproduction of the real' [Heath, 1981: 26]), whilst nonetheless demonstrating how ineluctably 'modern' was the *modus operandi* of the apparatus that took the photographs, strung them together in illusions of motion, and assembled these illusions (shots) into larger narrative sequences. This wasn't to be the only, or even the dominant, antinomial fascination of the cinematic modernist scholars – more potent still was the dialectic between a pitiless and surgeon-like laying bare of the real, and a 'whole occult life' of ambulant ghosts and shadows (Artaud, 1972: 66); between, in a word, science and magic – but this most basic, constitutive contradiction of cinema (photography versus montage) could be seen openly to perform the agon between realism and modernism that had once defined modernity's cultural space. Photographic realism intersects directly with the inherent modernism of montage in cinematic experience, in a way that tends to invalidate the possibility of a choice between them. For us postmoderns, this choice is always and already a false one:

> [B]oth alternatives of realism and modernism seem intolerable to us: realism because its forms revive an older experience of a kind of life that is no longer with us in the already decayed future of a consumer society; modernism because its contradictions have in practice proved more acute than those of realism. (Jameson, 1977: 211)

Within the parameters of historical cinema studies, this paradox could assume hard and material form as a contradiction inherent in the apparatus itself. In an ideal solution for a postmodern initiative, the fusion of realism and modernism in cinema could at a stroke cancel the necessity of making the vexing choice between them: they were, all along, two sides of the same coin, and at any rate, no longer our own problem.

PROFESSIONALIZATION AND TRAINING

Henceforth, as far as cinema goes, modernism was not something that happened 'after realism', but these two things were never more than shadow images of one another in the machine that conjoined them. Something like this seems to have been the basic conceptual foundation for this illustrious academic trend, whose other efficient disciplinary cause was the tremendous upsurge in archival activity geared towards the earliest cinematic texts: 'Revisionism is a product of the professionalization of film research' (Bordwell, 1997: 139). There had been nothing previous to match the prodigious historical enterprises represented by Tom Gunning's *D.W. Griffith and the Origins of American Narrative Film* (1991), Eileen Bowser's *The Transformation of Cinema* (1990), Charles Musser's *The Emergence of Cinema* (1990), Thomas Elsaesser's *Early Cinema* (1990) and, standing behind all of this, the monument of David Bordwell, Janet Staiger and Kristin Thompson's *The Classical Hollywood Cinema* (1985), whose third part is surely the fountainhead of this fertile scholarly Nile. After such labour, never again could it be said that early cinema had striven clumsily towards a cultural modernism which it had actually (as Sergei Eisenstein had long ago insisted) absorbed involuntarily in the sideshows, music-halls and other 'low' venues where it first set up shop as one among many attractions vying for the attention of patrons (see Eisenstein, 1988: 39–58). Gunning's remarkable and far-reaching article 'The Cinema of Attraction' (1986) looms large here as well, setting the scene for a full-blooded reappraisal of the earliest conditions of cinematic possibility in a physiological assault on the motor-sensory system, rather than any representational aesthetic. As Gunning followed Walter Benjamin in insisting, what was first of all 'modernist' about cinema was the technical shock therapy it had administered to prevailing standards of perception and taste.

The retrieval of a vast reservoir of hitherto lost one-reelers, that vertiginous sense of discovery which Gunning recreates in his tale of the apocryphal filing clerk in the Library of Congress who first discovered the 'neglected vault' in which the bromide paper stills of all the earliest Biograph,

Mutoscope and Edison films were stored (1991: 1), also sets in play a series of more philosophical speculations. The then governing trend, established by the work of Bordwell, Staiger and Thompson, was historicist and evolutionary. The implicit logic of their classic study was that, as Miriam Hansen argued, the success of the system of classical narration established in Hollywood during the 1920s was 'attributed to the optimal engagement of *mental* structures and perceptual capacities' (1999: 66) that are, in Bordwell's words, 'an intricate mesh of hard-wired anatomical, physiological, optical, and psychological mechanisms produced by millions of years of biological selection' (1997: 142). The classical narration of the Studio Age was thus supposed to have led cinema (that ungainly machine) toward a conservative *rapprochement* with deeply embedded biological structures of apperception: a formal stability inimical to aesthetic modernism and more or less outside of history.

This unsatisfactory reaction against the excesses of 1970s film theory nevertheless prepared the way for what cinematic modernism studies would urge in response: namely, that far from being the incubation-stage of cinema's classical maturity, the earliest forms of cinema extended and developed the prototypically cinematic visual culture of the late nineteenth century, and did so by intensifying the new sorts of perceptual training begun by magic lanterns, phantasmagoria, phrenology, posters, music halls and other media of commercial Victoriana. This gravitational pull of cinema studies toward the nineteenth century, following the lead of Jonathan Crary's *Techniques of the Observer* (1992) and enshrined in the emblematic volume *Cinema and the Invention of Modern Life* (Charney and Schwartz, 1995), probed for the roots of cinematic modernity in the tentacles of nascent instrumental reason, the growth of technological culture and the urbanization of everyday life. On this view, early cinema (up to 1915) was a curiously ambivalent but genealogically unique mode of cultural production: straddling the gap between a persistent Victorian matrix of sensibility and manners, and a brash new world of commodities, speed and shocks.

The theoretical guru of this effort to relocate cinema's origins within the cultural web of Baron Hausmann's Paris was, of course, Benjamin, whose 1936 essay on the 'The Work of Art in the Age of Mechanical Reproduction' is still the most cited and discussed of all founding contributions to the field. Peter Wollen's 1993 account is one of the first to focus on the essay's affirmative reappraisal of the notion of 'distraction':

> Benjamin turned the concept of 'distraction' upside down. Instead of seeing it as antagonistic to thought and reason, he argued that it was supportive of reason. He did this in two ways. First, he argued that film, through its technique of shocks, instilled new habits in the masses, new modes of apperception. These, in turn, were necessary to the masses at the present turning point in history, when the human apparatus of perception was confronted with a multitude of new demands and new tasks. Thus cinema, in a sense, was fulfilling the role of fitting the masses for the new and progressive forms of production that were being introduced.... Shock... had become a form of training and film a form of training manual. (1993: 51)

Such a dramatic reversal of the generally dismissive accounts of mass-cultural distraction signalled open season, all these years later, for a revisionist assault on the fortress of classical cinema as an *a priori* modernist institution. Jameson's model of 'cultural revolution' (1981: 95–8), with its functionalist account of culture's role in reshaping collective social subjects, lurked in the wings of Wollen's excellent condensation of Benjamin's essay. The stage was set for some decisive historical analyses to follow. With scintillating historical contributions from such scholars as Crary (1992; 1999) and Martin Jay (1993; Jay and Brennan, 1996), one might thus have anticipated a major initiative of the emergent cinematic modernism studies to be the extension of this basic thesis into comprehensive demonstrations of cinema's power to 'retrain' the human body for the new rigours and speeds of the conveyor belt and commuter train. Works such as Tim

Armstrong's *Modernism, Technology and the Body* (1998) certainly leaned heavily on the central pillar of this argument, but by and large what is most surprising here is the absence of any major, sustained investigation into this conception of cinema as a 'training manual' for the habitus of modernity. Bordwell's scepticism – 'we do not have good reasons to believe that particular changes in film style can be traced to a new way of seeing produced by modernity' (1997: 146) – remains curiously unanswered by concrete analyses.

KRACAUER AND RECEPTION

Instead, the peerless reputation of Benjamin's 'Artwork' essay, with its emphasis on the medium's capacity both to 'ward off' and to adapt the body to modernity's circumambient shocks, was surprisingly outflanked by the revaluation and publication in English of the early work of Benjamin's contemporary, Siegfried Kracauer. Where Benjamin had accentuated the destructive-constructive consequences of film on the body, the senses and the psyche, Kracauer tended to the social and political dimensions of the medium. In the words of his most ardent proponent, Hansen,

> Kracauer saw in film and cinema the matrix of a specifically modern episteme, at once an expression of and a medium for the experience of a 'disintegrating' world. For much as the cinema participated in and advanced the process of modernization (mechanization, standardization, disembedding of social relations), it also emerged as the single most accessible institution in which the effects of modernization on human experience could be acknowledged, recognized, negotiated, and perhaps reconfigured and transformed. (1997: xi)

The Weimar essays of this intrepid theoretical journalist, assembled in the volume *The Mass Ornament* (1995), speak to an intensely paradoxical sense of how mass culture's grim reifications reverberate with Utopian, collective overtones. The 'mass subject' emerging into being around the institution of cinema was not simply a ruse of instrumental reason; rather, it groped and stumbled, blindly, towards the unrealized goal of a genuine public sphere. Again in Hansen's words: 'The cinema is a signature of modernity for Kracauer not simply because it attracts and represents the masses, but because it constitutes the most advanced cultural institution in which the masses, as a relatively heterogeneous, undefined, and unknown form of collectivity, can represent themselves as a *public*' (1995: 377). Thus, in the work that would follow in the wake of this considerable revaluation of a 'lost' theorist, a politicized awareness was sharpened by the contradictory collective dynamics of cinema-going as a cultural institution not to be dismissed with a wave of the hand and the charge of manipulation. Hansen's great work, *Babel and Babylon* (1991), perhaps the bible and certainly the masterpiece of this whole movement, deserves closer attention.

While Hansen's text abounds in provocative insights into the social life of the medium (not least, as we shall see later, the suggestion that cinema's capacity to incorporate and refract other media is essentially Darwinian[1]), its core thesis concerns the partial and stuttering establishment, through the spread and consolidation of cinema, of an alternative public sphere in the interstices of the hegemonic one built around bourgeois and patriarchal property relations. The essential anonymity and invisibility of cinematic reception, as it evolved into its institutionalized form (isolated bodies congregated in a darkened theatre), allowed for significant porosity at the spreading edges of a commercial medium officially oriented toward a WASP, male, middle-class public. Such porosity (absorbing immigrants, working-class Americans and, above all, women), and the augmented profits to be reaped from it by a canny double-consciousness on the part of producers, drove a wedge into what Theodor Adorno and Max Horkheimer would too hastily decry as a monolithic and imperturbable Culture Industry: 'if an alternative formation of spectatorship can be claimed, it existed both *because of* and *despite* the economic mechanisms upon which the cinema was founded, its status as an industrial-commercial public sphere' (quoted in Hansen, 1991: 92). The conditions for this intriguing counter-current within the maelstrom of uniformity and imbecility emanating from Hollywood were accidental and fleeting, emerging from the 'seams and fissures of institutional development' (Hansen, 1991: 93), rather than any stable location.

Indeed, what we could then say is specifically 'postmodern' about this discovered interstitial space is its ultimate unlocatability within the positivist grid-work of modernity's rationalizations. As a Foucauldian 'heterotopia' (neither here nor there, real-and-imagined, essentially dislocated), the cinema allowed room for groups such as immigrants and women to 'organize their [disjunct daily] experience on the basis of their own context of living, its specific needs, conflicts, and anxieties' (Hansen, 1991: 108). It was a zone that provided non-hegemonic collectives with opportunities to navigate the treacherous dynamics of urban modernity within an institutional framework (reeling from shot to shot, film to film, in a placeless space bombarded with the visually heteroclite, but surrounded by similar bodies) geared towards their management and conjunctural inflection. This alternative and local inflection (class-, ethnic-, or sex-based) nonetheless depended upon a form increasingly global in reach; indeed, it is as though the very universalism of cinema's nascent stature as a world language were the guarantee of such local acts of tactical organization. In a later development, Hansen argued that cinema 'played a key role in mediating competing cultural discourses on modernity and modernization, because it articulated, multiplied and globalized a particular historical experience' (1999: 68): namely, the experience of urban America. But just as the imperial arm of American cultural hegemony extended over the prostrate geography of war-torn Europe and Asia, so too the displaced European and Asian peasants taking up residence in the tenement cities of the New World, and the disenfranchised women and working populations of those cities, adapted those very films 'in locally quite specific, and unequally developed, contexts and conditions of *reception*' (Hansen, 1999: 68). This crucial dialectic triggered the birth of an entirely new concept in cultural theory: 'vernacular modernism'.

Hansen's notional and profoundly postmodern oxymoron strikes at the very heart of prevailing conceptualizations of modernism as an artistic vocation to wrestle against the fallen material of urban speech with a formal perfectionism that would, in T.S. Eliot's great Mallarméan phrase, 'purify the dialect of the tribe' (1974: 218). That the redoubtably realist classical Hollywood cinema should so unexpectedly have been revealed as 'an international modernist idiom' (Hansen, 1999: 68) does, however, reverberate strongly with Jameson's contemporary claims for art deco as 'something like the secret modernism or subordinated formalism of a whole new global "realism"' (1992a: 183), which is, ineluctably, 'a historical phenomenon, rather than an eternal formal possibility, and has it in it to come to an end, as well as to emerge' (1992a: 185). We here rejoin that earlier recursiveness whereby, in cinema, 'realism' and 'modernism' each effectively serves as the other's precondition. Indeed, the very historicity of which Jameson writes here is deeply ingrained in the economic and technological developments according to which a given style could be simultaneously classical and progressive. So it is that Hansen can mount her case that the

> juncture of classical cinema and modernity reminds us, finally, that the cinema was not only part and symptom of modernity's experience and perception of crisis and upheaval; it was also most importantly, the single most inclusive cultural horizon in which the traumatic effects of modernity were reflected, rejected or disavowed, transmuted or negotiated…. Neither simply a medium for realistic representation…, nor particularly concerned with formalist self-reflexivity, commercial cinema appeared to realise Johann Gottlieb Fichte's troping of reflection as 'seeing with an added eye' in an almost literal sense, and it did so not just on the level of individual, philosophical cognition but on a mass scale. (1999: 69)

'Modernity' here includes modernism not as its elitist auto-critique, but as the cultural means by which, at all levels, the reflexivity necessary to the consolidation and growth of a capitalist industrial economy was installed in the biomass of a human population still standing, as it were, with one foot in the Middle Ages. The installation of modernity via cultural modernism, however, precisely because of this reflexivity, was both variable and open to tactical misappropriation by interstitial 'alternative public spheres' in the exhibition venues where early cinema began its sentimental education of millions upon millions of viewers. This tremendous rediscovery of the neglected public realm of cinematic reception and spectatorship led Elsaesser to remark, as early as 1987, that the 'main theoretical thrust [of German film theory] today is in the direction not of textual analysis, but in illuminating the historical conditions of spectatorship and identification, both within and outside Freudian terms in which these questions are usually posed' (1987: 67). What was 'modern' about this was how it displaced the centre of scholarly gravity away from the 'classic realist text', and toward the assemblage of new forms of collective consciousness in the 'situation of reception' (Hansen, 1991: 93) – against the grain of the diegesis proper and the mode of its production. But such a reorientation was also decidedly postmodern in its demotion and displacement of the problematics of the 'subject' itself. Indeed, as those Freudian concerns of 1970s and 1980s apparatus theory gave way to sociologically grounded studies of historical spectatorial experience, the very notion of the subject was scattered to the four winds of a scrupulous archival reconstruction of the real, social processes of cinematic engagement.

BRITISH ECHOES

Meanwhile, in a parallel development on British ground, the film journal *Close Up* (1927-33) was revaluated as a site of theoretical and aesthetic intersection between modernism and cinema. The editors of a 1998 anthology of articles written for this journal argued specifically that the ruminations of frequent contributor Dorothy

Richardson 'offer an account of the novelty and modernity of the *experience* of cinema which is comparable in its scope to the pioneering essays being written by Siegfried Kracauer in the same period, and which also prefigures in intriguing and suggestive ways recent scholarship on cinema and modernity' (Donald et al., 1997: viii). Allowing for the inflated claim about 'scope' here (Kracauer wrote 1,900 articles [Quaresima, 2004: xv, n.2], to Richardson's 19), we can discern an identical move being made to establish a legitimating toehold in the annals of 'modernism' proper for the revisionist work being undertaken by Hansen, Leo Charney, Vanessa Schwartz and others. Indeed, in a striking anticipation of Hansen's deployment of Kracauer, Richardson's concern too was with the paradoxical effects of cinematic experience upon the subjects of a modernity that too often 'massified' them abstractly: they 'find in the cinema … their only escape from ceaseless association, their only solitude, the solitude that is said to be possible only in cities. They become for a while citizens of a world whose every face is that of a stranger' (1928: 55). In a dialectical leapfrogging of the urban alienation thesis, here cinema is adduced as a passport into a meta- or hyper-alienated public sphere where the psychological monad is released into collective anonymity and a consequent absolution from all social responsibility. Richardson's version of the cinematic 'alternative public sphere', then, is something like Oscar Wilde's vision of the soul of man under socialism, where, infamously, 'Socialism would relieve us from that sordid necessity of living for others which, in the present condition of things, presses so hardly upon almost everybody. In fact, scarcely any one at all escapes' (1975: 257). Richardson's cinema allows for momentary escape, and thus for the intermittent flourishing of something like Wilde's 'true, beautiful, healthy Individualism' (1975: 263) that meddles with nobody and is preoccupied only with its own nurturing. It is a Utopian alternative public sphere where, because each member of the audience is implacably isolated and anonymous, they come out the other

side of alienation into a new confraternity of free souls.[2] Laura Marcus aptly orchestrates the pith and pitch of Richardson's generous interventions:

> Whereas the 'utopian' aspirations of dreams of many of the journal's other contributors were of attaining a mass audience for minority culture, Richardson more often conjures up a community of spectators becoming educated for modernity, 'Everyman [made] at home in a new world' by 'the movies': 'They are there in their millions, the front rowers, a vast audience born and made in the last few years, initiated, disciplined, and waiting'; 'The only anything and everything. And here we all are, as never before. What will it do with us?' (1997: 152)

Unmistakable here, of course, as it is in Hansen's more rigorous formulations in the same vein, is the resonance of this Utopian populism with the work of postmodern film and media studies undertaken in the 1980s (by scholars such as John Fiske [1991], E. Ann Kaplan [1987] and Anne Friedberg [1993] herself): a reclamation of the viewing habits of the 'community of spectators' against the unforgiving grain of the Culture Industry thesis mounted by the mandarins of modernism. The modernism of this new field of cinema studies is, as Hansen's 'vernacular' emphasis clearly shows, anything but an elite preserve of cultural practices rather, it is a widely diffused, collective and anonymous popular front against both rural idiocy *and* dreary urban mechanization. It is a participatory crusade against everything culturally 'backward', mounted under the banner of the commodity, to be sure, yet possessed of a momentous public pathos that is not (exactly) hostile to the high aesthetics of Modernism proper, but collaborates clandestinely with its ulterior purposes: cultural modernization in the broadest sense. Postmodern in its essence, this initiative in cinema studies gamely reclaims the populist, spectatorial elements of early cinematic experience in order to flatten out any vestigial hierarchy within the corpus of film works themselves. It is, to borrow the phraseology of Marshall McLuhan (1994), the modernizing medium itself that is the message of any given film; the specific formal properties of individual films are a sacrifice worth making to the prodigious gains in cultural theory thereby attained. Or, as Bordwell among others has duly worried, *are they?*

AESTHETICS AND TEMPORALITY

It is a dilemma that can be brought into dramatic focus by suggesting that it once again, like so many debates in this period, stages the irresolvable dialectic between Adorno's *Aesthetic Theory* (1997) and Pierre Bourdieu's *Distinction: A Social Critique of the Judgment of Taste* (1984): the shift of the locus of cultural meaning toward the patterns and habits of social reception, and away from the formal integrity of the works themselves, suspends the question of aesthetics for only so long as the specific structural differences between the various texts consumed are not felt to compromise the hasty generalizations made in the name of the historical spectator. At some point, however, the sheer depth of the formal divide between, say, Dziga Vertov's *Man with a Movie Camera* (USSR, 1929) and Mack Sennett's *The New Halfback* (US, 1929), must present the bill and dictate some confrontation with the lingering question of aesthetic specificity; or, more pertinently, with the question of 'modernism' as precisely a formal sublation of 'realism' into a new self-consciousness, irony and depth. The most typical and arresting solution of cinematic modernism studies to this dilemma has been to 'transcode' the very question of aesthetics into the language of time and temporality; not only because these all-too familiar trademarks of aesthetic modernism are thus secretly a code for the aesthetic *tout court*, but also because here the very differences between aesthetics and philosophy, sociology and biology, can be tactically dismantled – time being, to say the least, only very partially an aesthetic dimension (since Gotthold Lessing's canonical distinction, indeed, 'space' had always been felt to be the 'more aesthetic' of the transcendental categories [1953]).

At any rate, it is entirely characteristic of the school of which it is a member to

read Mary Ann Doane's opening justification of her work *The Emergence of Cinematic Time*: 'the emerging cinema participated in a more general cultural imperative, the structuring of time and contingency in capitalist modernity. Although the rupture here is not technologically determined, new technologies of representation, such as photography, phonography, and the cinema, are crucial to modernity's reconceptualization of time and its representability' (2002: 3–4). Here, of course, the aesthetic is collapsed into an overarching 'more general cultural imperative' in which it can be strategically repositioned as a matter of the representability of time itself. Why the cinema should now be revealed to have been so critical in this regard is that, in the very technical properties of its apparatus, at an involuntary level quite divorced from the 'merely aesthetic' intention of this or that filmmaker, the motion picture machine 'represented' time via the artificial animation of inert visual cells into mobile segments of movement itself. At play here in the very mechanics of the medium is a technical prestidigitation of movement out of stasis, an excellent reason why cinematic presentation could be claimed as the *sine qua non* of modern culture itself – as no less a critic than Benjamin long ago discerned:

> The formula in which the dialectical structure of film – film considered in its technological dimension – finds expression runs as follows. Discontinuous images replace one another in a continuous sequence. A theory of film would need to take account of both these facts, first of all, with regard to continuity, it cannot be overlooked that the assembly line, which plays such a fundamental role in the process of production, is in a sense represented by the filmstrip in the process of consumption. Both came into being at roughly the same time. The social significance of the one cannot be fully understood without that of the other. ([1935] 2002: 94)

Thus, technically if not yet properly aesthetically, film as the quintessential cultural representation of the conveyor belt itself may well be said to have been the standard-bearer of modernism in all the arts, to which forms in other media could only dimly and more or less consciously aspire. It was in this spirit that Gertrude Stein declared, in a lecture from the 1930s, that in her earlier experimental fictions, she was 'doing what the cinema was doing'; 'any one is of one's period', she insisted, 'and this our period was undoubtedly the period of the cinema and series production. And each of us in our own way are bound to express what the world in which we are living is doing' (1998: 294). What the cinema and the conveyor belt of Henry Ford's epochal Highland Park plant in Detroit were 'doing' was nothing less than allowing the *ratio* of modernity – the quantification of every last atom of the social domain, the reification of the smallest quanta of movement – to remodel industry and culture both, simultaneously, in the name of instrumental reason.

SUR/REALISM?

On one view, that of Stein and any number of others in the period (like the Futurists, the dadaists, Adolf Loos and much of the Bauhaus), this was exhilarating and enabling; while for another important cadre, it was threatening and foreboding. For the vitalist philosopher Henri Bergson, one of the most influential of his day with artists, the degree to which knowledge and perception had been infiltrated by the reifying *ratio* was deleterious indeed. He castigated the modern instrumental intellect for the way it 'always starts from immobility, as if this were the ultimate reality: when it tries to form an idea of movement, it does so by constructing movement out of immobilities put together' (1911: 155). This artificial approach of the 'mechanism of our ordinary knowledge', which Bergson compared explicitly to a 'cinematograph' – 'abstract, uniform, and invisible', situated 'at the back of the apparatus of knowledge' (1911: 306) – is, as Benjamin also showed, intimately related to the modernity of the second industrial revolution: 'The causality it seeks and finds everywhere expresses the very mechanism of our industry, in which we go on recomposing the same whole with the

same parts, repeating the same movements to obtain the same results' (1911: 164).

Thus, what is most modern about the cinema and industrialism is also, on this view, what is most hostile to the truth of human experience; 'real becoming' being fluid and continuous, the rational, artificial and technological reduction of it to equivalent sections is a traducement of everything organic and authentic in human experience. Cinema is a piece of equipment that is, in Bergson's analogy, now internal to each of us, virtually a new cyborg-organ in its own right, installed 'at the back of the apparatus of knowledge' and carving up our manifold sensory experience into static negations of the genuine *poesis* of felt duration. This cinematic prosthesis that we all bear within us is inimical to real time, because it is predicated on the abstract measurement of temporal intervals: 1/24th of a second, the rate at which the frames of a standardized industrial film strip are exposed to the lit matter before the camera, and again to the light of the projector that casts their celluloid shadows on the screens of consciousness. Cinema's modernity, like Ford's assembly line, is what artistic modernism must on this account *resist*, by recoiling into irrational and sensuous modes of experience and finding durable figurative means for their notation. Surrealism is, if nothing else, to be explained by this inevitable reaction against artificial, cinematic reifications of time, its embrace of chthonic, irrational upsurges deep beneath a subjectivity not yet fully colonized by the 'cinematographic apparatus'.

The paradox here, of course, is how readily the film medium itself was adapted to these selfsame surrealist ends. In the hands of Luis Buñuel and Salvador Dali, or of René Clair or Germaine Dulac, the early cinematic avant-garde discovered that the new medium was far from incompatible with the irrational and subversive temporal energies unleashed by the unconscious; indeed, film was paradoxically the medium most perfectly equipped to furnish an aesthetic experience adequate to the uncanny and surreal economy of perception propounded in their manifestoes. 'For the Surrealists, it was above all the cinema that possessed the uncanny ability to penetrate the surface of the world and encapsulate in moments of shocking insight the nature of the physical and sensual universe', as Charney has argued in his book *Empty Moments*, summarizing the reflections of Antonin Artaud, Jean Epstein and Dulac (1998: 124). 'Because, in the mechanically reproduced image, we resee something familiar, the re-production allows for us to focus on new qualities; re-presentation elicits something that our habituated perceptions could not discover on their own' (Charney, 1998: 125). It is this curious ambivalence of the medium's tendency on the one hand to regulate, represent and discipline social time, and on the other to detonate strange, non-synchronous bundles of temporal energy in the humblest of everyday objects, that we will want to return to shortly under the rubric of the 'contingent' and the 'archive'.

More immediately, it is clear that this critical and theoretical return to the temporal paradoxes inherent to the cinematic medium brings to light some profound ambiguities within the various initial aesthetic manifestoes of modernism; since nothing is less clear than how to read off 'value' from the technical fact of what Bergson briskly summarized as cinema's 'immobile sections + abstract time' (Deleuze, 1992: 11). If the discovery of Surrealist uncanniness within this mechanical re-presentation of everyday temporality was one possibility and source of value, then just as surely Vertov could pronounce value on the ground of a new 'documentary' awareness of reality itself, in much the same spirit as Benjamin's famous metaphor of the surgeon slicing into the reified appearances of the quotidian domain. Benjamin had written:

> By close-ups of the things around us, by focusing on hidden details of familiar objects, by exploring commonplace milieus under the ingenious guidance of the camera, the film, on the one hand, extends our comprehension of the necessities which rule our lives; on the other hand, it manages to assure us of an immense and unexpected field of action. (1969: 236)

In an allied sense, Vertov committed his dynamic aesthetics of the Camera Eye to a merciless penetration of every encrusted bourgeois 'way of seeing', in order to liberate revolutionary potential from flashes of epistemological insight into such ephemera as the kicking of a football, the blinking of an eye, or the splicing of film strips. The accent on an aesthetic dedicated to epistemology could not be further removed from the vitalist wellsprings of the Bergsonians, with their accent on the irrational and more deeply ontological roots of the universe. The film medium was argued for by adherents of either vision as the single greatest instrument for aesthetic penetration into the mysteries (or mystifications) of time and being.

THINKING TIME

Gilles Deleuze, taking Bergson as his point of departure, but effectively reversing the latter's valuations of cinema, proposed the most startling thesis of all advanced so far under the rubric of cinema and temporality: that cinema was nothing less than a way, indeed *the* way, of 'thinking' time adequately in the modern period. The philosophic strategy lying behind the first of his two volumes on film-philosophy was breathtaking in its audacity. Bergson was not exactly wrong to suggest that the cinema redoubles the essential illusion of rational knowledge (approaching movement by way of static reifications), but what is involved in this redoubling is a 'negation of the negation' in a strangely Hegelian sense: 'is not the reproduction of an illusion in a certain sense also its correction?' (1992: 2). If this were the case, then cinema would be a critical correction of the false knowledges of bourgeois science and positivist empiricism. D.N. Rodowick, in his book *Gilles Deleuze's Time Machine* (1997), summed up the implications here economically:

> Deleuze argues that the selective, discontinuous images of natural perception are corrected cognitively 'above' perception by a mental apparatus that is part of perception itself.

Natural perception and cinematographic perception are therefore qualitatively different because the projector automates movement, immediately correcting the illusion separate from any human presence. (1997: 22)

This qualitative difference, the superaddition of an asubjective process of auto-correction to an all-too human and susceptible mental apparatus, brings into the world something new and definitive of the modern experience of time: mobile images which augur 'a new conception of movement and duration' (Rodowick, 1997: 33), an openness of any moment whatsoever to a potentially limitless futurity. Cinema inaugurates this conception; it does not merely train social subjects in the rhythms of Capital, or penetrate the reified surfaces of that lifeword, it essentially liberates moments from history. Time would thus, in the great sequence of works following the Second World War by those filmmakers whom we now feel comfortable describing as the 'sound-film modernists' (Akira Kurosawa, Roberto Rossellini, Ingmar Bergman, François Truffaut and so on), attain something like its own image, divorced from the compulsive logics of history and of action. Here, in modern cinema proper, 'the essence of the art, though it has always been active in the art's previous manifestations, has now gained its autonomy by breaking free of the chains of mimesis that has always fettered it' (Rancière, 2006: 108). As Jacques Rancière has pointed out of this, the least postmodern of all the interventions of this period, the 'division between movement-image and time-image doesn't escape the general circularity of modernist theory' (2006: 108); indeed, what Deleuze posits as an historical break is far better conceived of as a dialectic *built into* the nature of cinematic production itself. Rancière's far more satisfying, postmodern solution to the problem of the final indiscernibility between 'sensory-motor' articulations of the cut, and the Deleuzian 'time-image' proper, once again reaffirms the absence of any border between 'classical' and 'modern' cinema, and propels us toward an encounter with the medium's radical and volatile aesthetic impurity (2006: 114–22).

ARCHIVAL CONTINGENCIES

Meanwhile, for Doane, what most allures about the cinematic medium is its constitutive contradiction between a mechanical predisposition towards the rational regulation and segmentation of time, and the inscription on the celluloid strips themselves of fleeting and purely contingent indexical information about a vanished world. Of course, this mechanical capacity of the medium to record chance is something that Benjamin had long since detected in the art of photography itself, in the experience of which

the spectator feels an irresistible compulsion to look for the tiny spark of chance, of the here and now, with which reality has, as it were, seared the character in the picture; to find that imperceptible point at which, in the immediacy of that long-past moment, the future so persuasively inserts itself, that, looking back we may discover it. (1972: 7)

Putting this arrested dialectic into the mobile segments of cinematic photography only aggravates the pertinence of chance. The contingency preserved by film has, for Doane and the theorists she inducts into her argument (Charles Baudelaire, Georg Lukács, Benjamin, Kracauer), prodigious implications for modernity as a whole – modernity being both the ceaseless generation of the 'new', and the forcible confinement of it within immutable social and perceptual relations. Urbanization, industrialization, the giddy expansion of the market, faster and more efficient modes of travel and communication: what do these processes do but bombard their participants with shocks and collisions with the contingent, which must then be rationalized into abstraction and statistical homogeneity? Cinema is the medium in which these temporal dialectics of modernity come to an acute reflexivity. As the end result of a rapid evolution of technologies whose function would be to 'store' and make legible the infinity of contingent facts thrown off by modernity ('all that is solid melts into air'), cinema would 'correct' that immanent resistance to experiential durability by creating modernity's legitimate archive: permanent ephemera. By reconciling the fleeting with the homogeneous, cinema spontaneously enacted a crucial 'fix' within modernity's social reflexivity. For at the moment when time itself became fully representable in both of these dimensions simultaneously, an epistemological shift was also effected, whose reverberations in the domains of physiology, psychoanalysis, aesthetics, logic, thermodynamics, evolutionary theory and statistics Doane charts with extraordinary felicity. Yet always lurking in the background of her analyses is that open threat of the medium not to be circumscribed by the mechanics of closure within which its indices of contingency were confined by the 'classic realist text': 'The specific technology of the cinema – its apparent ability to represent the contingent without limit – posed the threat of an overwhelming detail, a denial of representation itself' (2002: 31). This threat is the poisoned chalice delivered by cinema to the society that looked to it as the ultimate reconciliation of fragment and whole. Friedrich Kittler's technological musings on Jacques Lacan's concept of the Real have direct relevance here (though Kittler himself wanted to associate it with phonography rather than the 'imaginary' screens of cinema): 'of the real nothing more can be brought to light than what Lacan presupposed – that is, nothing. It forms the waste or residue that neither the mirror of the imaginary nor the grid of the symbolic can catch: the physiological accidents and stochastic disorder of bodies' (1999: 15–16). Against the rationalist grain of the machine's analysis of time, then, this indiscriminate, more or less excremental tracing of the 'real' of human bodies endows their durations, their unpredictable motions and auratic details, with a spectral and even spiritual afterlife.

That afterlife is of quite recent date, according to Mulvey, who associates it with a third stage in the human relationship with film. When we return to the earliest of films today, she suggests, 'every gesture, expression, movement of wind or water is touched with mystery' (2006: 36). This is no longer the mystery (as it once was) of 'how they did that' – achieved that miraculous effect

of 'change mummified', in André Bazin's great formulation (1967: 15) – but of 'what is that?' The 'very reality' of filmic documents of the contingent 'has become the source of uncanniness. The phantom-like quality observed by Gorky and his contemporaries returns in force. The inanimate objects of the filmstrip not only come alive in projection, but are the ghostly images of the now-dead resurrected into the appearance of life' (Mulvey, 2006: 36). Cinema's stupid preservation of the real, its unblinking storage of indexical detail, is now a kind of haunting of the postmodern, deathless present by a legion of spectres. Jacques Derrida's point about the inherent capacity of the iterations of script to thrive well beyond the biological life of the author – 'Death by writing also inaugurates life' (1992: 80) – is ramified by a medium that spirits the 'real' of bodies away from their all-too mortal supports in biological matter, and allows it to drift in relative perpetuity through the cinematic archive.

ANIMATION

Whatever this spectral accompaniment to, and archiving of, modernity might have to tell us about our own ontological rootlessness and mediatic free-fall into digital hyperreality, it is worth pausing for a moment to reflect upon that other, neglected but equally modernistic capacity of the cinema, namely, animation. In one of the most striking lateral additions to cinematic modernism studies, Esther Leslie's book *Hollywood Flatlands* (2002) settles the account left open by the rush to actualities, nascent narrative cinema, and even the more fantastical strands of early film elsewhere in the field. The decisive move here was to associate the mechanics of animation with the social dialectics of commodity fetishism. Animated cartoons and avant-gardist experiments in a similar vein could be grasped as allegories, conscious or not, of the social spell of reification, and trial runs on a collective demystification. The obdurate resistance to animated films in the annals of classical film theory attests to a significant blockage in that theory's ability to think reification through to the ends of the medium itself. Leslie's welcome entry into the terrain recognizes the centrality to an understanding of modernity of animation as a concept:

> The coming to life of inanimate objects, through the action of commodity fetishism as well as in Marx's rhetoric ... is an illusion.... [B]ut it seems, to reified consciousness, that the things themselves propel their own movement. It seems as if sign-things acquire an occult power over producers and consumers. The sign-things are fetishized, invested with powers that make them animate, more animated than us, who, in relation to them, become mere things, lifeless. And so it seems in animation too, whether drawn frame by frame or photographed, then brought to life in projection. (2002: 7–8)

Thus, whether in the commercial shorts of Disney or in the experimental films of Viking Eggeling and Hans Richter, the exploitation of cinema's illusion of movement, making coherent and unlikely actions out of thousands of hand-drawn cells, could cast critical light upon the generalized illusion of commodity culture itself. This redoubled artificiality, a dogged refusal of the medium's indexical and realist capacities, might actually give rise to a heightened realism. That is to say, a *realism of modernity*, taking it at its own word, homeopathically participates in its own ritual of enchantment, while subtly and wittily exposing it to second-order reflection. That the 'Critical Theorists' themselves had long had a wary eye upon the animated spectacle of the Toons only seems to confirm Leslie's suspicion that Mickey Mouse may have been closer to the 'truth' of capitalist modernity than Jean Renoir or Orson Welles. Certainly, the principle that, in these films, '[a]nimation, the giving of life, battles with annihilation, and always overcomes, always reasserts the principle of motion, of continuation and renewal' (Leslie, 2002: 2), stands as a powerful counterstatement to the melancholic intonations of Doane, Mulvey and other witnesses to the spectral modernity preserved in the actualities and narrative films of the period. In any event, perhaps the most dynamic argument of the book has less to do with animation in a limited sense, and more

with the avant-garde's provocative seizure of the new mechanical medium as a medium of 'Art' itself:

> Avant-garde film surfaced out of the extension of problems posed in the fine arts: how to represent rhythmic processes not just in space and on a flat surface but also in time. And, once film-literate, they hoped to create a pure language of cinema, a cinematic specificity, labelled by Louis Delluc, in 1920, after Daguerre, *photogénie*. While some saw the move of art into film as anti-art, others saw it as art's fulfilment, an absolute art, evading psychologistic experience, in favour of pure willed forms, non-referential, loaded with metaphysical significance. (Leslie, 2002: 37)

It is this question, after all, that has most salience for any final assessment of the situation of cinema within a general conception of the modernism we so commonly associate with the 'most advanced' cultural product of the period. Whether or not cinema belongs in any canonical categorization of the arts of modernity is still not a question we can consider to have been settled by the various tactical manoeuvres surveyed so far in this chapter.

BACK TO BAZIN

For Bazin (1967), what was most modernist about cinema was its ontological openness to phenomena, its wide-eyed receptivity to things, which, as it is disconnected from any particular purposive subjectivity, attained at some outer limit to the very question of being itself. This ontological capacity of the medium was felt by Bazin (and Kracauer) to be properly trans-subjective, and allowed for the opacity and ambiguities of nature (the World itself) to resonate clearly within deep focus sequence shots. The fewer technical interventions the director brought to bear on this rich material, the more a film could be said to function the way James Joyce or Dos Passos' fictions did in the literary sphere – paradoxically, film could 'catch up' with the fifty-year jump-start of the modernist novel precisely by negating its apparently modernistic technical capacities (such as montage), and simply allowing the visual illusion of time passing in space, and of objects like human bodies moving within that space along a temporal vector, to *take place*.

Indeed, *pace* such early film theorists as Béla Balázs and Rudolf Arnheim, it was the originality of Bazin to have argued that the film medium met no criteria of artistic specificity as such – a fact which according to the dominant strains of late modernist aesthetic ideology would disqualify it immediately from the vicinity of Art. To revisit the cautionary words of Fried, '*The concepts of quality and value* – and to the extent that these are central to art, the concept of art itself – are meaningful, or wholly meaningful, only within the individual arts. *What lies between the arts is theater*' (1998: 164). This mainstay of high modernist criticism is directly resisted by Bazin's insistence on the inherent 'impurity' or 'mixed' aesthetic nature of film, and above all on its proximity and essential relation with the theatre (see MacCabe, 2003: 15–28). In a similar way, although much later, the philosopher Alain Badiou has argued that what marks film out among the various arts and media of modernity is its lack of any particular aesthetic vocation, its absence of a clear-cut medial mission. For Badiou, in a radical extension of Bazin's pioneering hypothesis:

> It is effectively impossible to think cinema outside of something like a general space in which we could grasp its connection to the other arts. Cinema is the seventh art in a very particular sense. It does not add itself to the other six while remaining on the same level as them. Rather, it implies them – cinema is the 'plus-one' of the arts. It operates on the other arts, using them as its starting point, in a movement that subtracts them from themselves. (2005: 79)

On this view, cinema would again be the medium par excellence of the modern period (the period of the second industrial revolution), both because of its sudden and unexpected addition to the hallowed and Academic realm of the six fine arts, and the fact that its addition is precisely 'subtractive', forcing each of these to surrender part of its significance and purpose to the brash industrial newcomer. Cultural modernity may then be said to be the general aesthetic condition of this 'plus-one', wherein each fine art is driven back on itself by the subtractive operation upon it of cinematic 'implication': 'The allusive quotation of the other arts, which is constitutive of cinema, wrests these arts away from themselves. What remains is precisely the breached frontier where an idea will have passed, an idea whose visitation the cinema, and it alone, allows' (Badiou, 2005: 82).

What Fried bemoaned as inauthentic 'theatricality', the deadly space between the arts, is here celebrated as the venue of a properly cinematic idea – the idea, that is, of impossible movements across the prophylactic frontiers between the fine arts. Dance, music and painting, for instance, are fused in Disney's *Fantasia* (James Algar/Samuel Armstrong, US, 1940) into a dizzying hybrid of 'inaesthetic' impurity, a cinematic idea of giddy transposition; a film it would be as meaningless to dismiss with the highbrow aesthetic ideology of late modernism as it would be to laud for any putative democratization of high culture itself. It is neither, but the contaminated pulse of an idea *between* the arts. Just like Bazin before him, Badiou would bear witness to such breaches and inaesthetic moments of subtraction – moments in which not 'purity', not artistic 'essence', but rather film's capacity to trouble and overturn strict aesthetic categories is indelibly enshrined.

MEDIA ECOLOGY

These reflections return us at once to a hint dropped in the bristling erudition of Hansen's *Babel and Babylon*, to the effect that, in its re-presentation of the medium of writing in a variety of scripts, discourses, and languages, a film like D.W. Griffith's *Intolerance* (US, 1916) actively incorporates the rival medium of the printed word the better to secure its own ontological status as a medium of mechanical storage. In McLuhan's great words, 'the "content" of any medium is always another medium' (1994: 8). What some of us like to call a 'media ecology' is that cultural environment in which this underlying competitive ecological dynamic is unconsciously re-inscribed in the content of any given media message – in the very drive to advertise and perpetuate its own medial DNA, every medium necessarily devours and exploits as content some other medium. Thus is set in chain a properly delirious set of transpositions across and between media, a chain in which the underlying Darwinian logic is never far from the surface. In a startling footnote from his *The Geopolitical Aesthetic*, Jameson adduces what is veritably a new aesthetic law from the work in cinematic modernism studies of Hansen and her nemesis, Bordwell: it is 'the general hypothesis that whenever other media appear within film, their deeper function is to set off and demonstrate the latter's ontological primacy' (1992b: 83–4, n.19). An extension of this 'Hansen-Bordwell hypothesis' (Jameson, 1992b: 140),[3] has far-reaching ramifications for media theory, and for the theory of modernism.[4] 'Media have always been advertising themselves', writes Kittler, and they do so through a parasitic incorporation of others (1999: 155). This process is perhaps nowhere more emblematically at work than in Joyce's *Ulysses* (1922), that colossal effort of the book-as-medium to reframe and cancel the prodigious successes of newer media in colonizing mass attention. As a book 'whose modes of representation ultimately declare themselves superior to such modes of storytelling as journalism', for instance, 'Joyce's epic excels in the reproduction of other modes of mimesis, ultimately aiming at creating a radically new literary artifact that incorporates within itself the various modes of reproduction with which it competes' (Danius, 2002: 180,185).

If cinematic modernism studies has pulled back from the brink of these radical realizations, it is doubtless due to the fact that a fully-fledged engagement with the congeries of overlapping, cannibalizing and mutually adapting media of modernity is well beyond the disciplinary capacities of all but the most advanced media theorists today. The place of the cinema within this mix, however, may prove to be more than merely 'emblematic'. Badiou's point that, as the 'plus-one' of the arts, the cinema was less a rival on the same terrain as the other fine arts than it was a kind of gravitational pull of all of them towards another cultural space altogether, an open invitation to a theatrical 'space between' where transpositions, subtractions, pulses and secret attractions would ultimately reconfigure the very name of 'Art', remains of signal importance. In such works as Paul Young's recent *The Cinema Dreams its Rivals* (2006), we are beginning to see the fruits of a reconceived approach to modernism, based within and springing from cinema studies, but not to be confined to it or any other disciplinary straitjacket, which would understand the formal revolutions of modernism as the aesthetic effects of a complex series of encounters and adjustments between new and old media. Modernism would thus be understood not only as the cultural expression of a gaping series of uneven developments between the country and the city, the developed and the colonized worlds, and the various metropolitan sites of its most typical phenomena, but moreover as the necessary cultural shape taken by an uneven development between new mechanical media capable of a swifter and more efficient cultural revolution at the superficial aesthetic level of the senses and habitus, and those older ones with residual powers of command over the deeper strata of modern subjectivity itself. That such a momentous redefinition of the very meaning and logic of modernism should have been generated from within the disciplinary initiative of cinematic modernism studies will stand as not the least of its many critical contributions to contemporary debate on the topic.

NOTES

1 This comes from the magnificent eighth chapter, a discussion of how writing is represented in the new medium (Hansen, 1991: 188–98).

2 Arguably this new collective is glimpsed as in a mirror passingly in the stream of characters in Robert Altman's *Popeye* (US, 1980) who, as Jameson tells us, 'no longer fettered by the constraints of a now oppressive sociality, blossom into the neurotics, compulsives, obsessives, paranoids and schizophrenics whom our society considers sick but who, in a world of true freedom, may make up the flora and the fauna of "human nature" itself' (1996: 102).

3 Of course it is needless to add that this hypothesis is itself purely synthetic – one could scarcely imagine two less likely collaborators on a pseudo-scientific speculation such as this. Bordwell's dismissal, in *On the History of Film Style*, of 'the modernity thesis' per se, is as inimical as can be imagined to the spirit of *Babel and Babylon* (Hansen herself is disparagingly referred to as 'another writer in this vein') (1997: 143). Ben Singer made an attempt to mediate between the two parties in his *Melodrama and Modernity: Early Sensational Cinema and its Contexts* (2001).

4 But it is still most gloriously to be seen at work in the film medium. Witness the extraordinary efforts of Oliver Stone's *Natural Born Killers* (US, 1994), which manages the 'categorical threat to cinematic sovereignty' posed by the dispersion of 'newly minted gadgetry' by embedding 'a rosy prospectus for cinema as *the* medium capable of co-opting, or merely reformatting, the technical options of every competitor' (Arthur, 2002: 344).

REFERENCES

Adorno, Theodor (1997) *Aesthetic Theory*. Tr. Robert Hullot-Kentor. London: Athlone.

Armstrong, Tim (1998) *Modernism, Technology and the Body: A Cultural Study*. Cambridge: Cambridge University Press.

Artaud, Antonin (1972) 'Witchcraft and the Cinema', in *Collected Works*. Vol.3. Tr. Alastair Hamilton. London: Calder and Boyars. pp. 65–7.

Arthur, Paul (2002) 'The Four Last Things', in Jon Lewis (ed.), *The End of Cinema as We Know It: American Film in the Nineties*. London: Pluto. pp. 342–55.

Badiou, Alain (2005) *Handbook of Inaesthetics*. Tr. Alberto Toscano. Stanford, CA: Stanford University Press.

Bazin, André (1967) 'The Ontology of the Photographic Image', in *What is Cinema? Vol.1*. Ed. and Tr. Hugh Gray. Berkeley: University of California Press. pp. 9–16.

Benjamin, Walter (1969) 'The Work of Art in the Age of Mechanical Reproduction', in Hannah Arendt (ed.), *Illuminations: Essays and Reflections*. Tr. Harry Zohn. New York: Schocken Books. pp. 217–51.

Benjamin, Walter (1972) 'A Short History of Photography', *Screen*, 13(1): 5–26.

Benjamin, Walter (2002) 'The Formula in which the Dialectical Structure of Film Finds Expression', in Howard Eiland and Michael W. Jennings (eds), *Selected Writings, Volume 3: 1935–1938*. Tr. Edmund Jephcott and Howard Eiland. Cambridge, MA: Belknap Press of Harvard University Press. pp. 94–5.

Bergson, Henri (1911) *Creative Evolution*. Tr. Arthur Mitchell. New York: Henry Holt.

Bordwell, David (1997) *On the History of Film Style*. Cambridge, MA: Harvard University Press.

Bordwell, David, Staiger, Janet and Thompson, Kristin (1985) *The Classical Hollywood Cinema: Film Style and Mode of Production to 1960*. London: Routledge.

Bourdieu, Pierre (1984) *Distinction: A Social Critique of the Judgment of Taste*. Tr. Richard Nice. Cambridge, MA: Harvard University Press.

Bowser, Eileen (1990) *The Transformation of Cinema: 1907-1915. Vol.2, History of the American Cinema*. New York/Berkeley: Charles Scribner's/University of California Press.

Charney, Leo (1998) *Empty Moments: Cinema, Modernity, and Drift*. Durham, NC: Duke University Press.

Charney, Leo and Schwartz Vanessa (eds) (1995) *Cinema and the Invention of Modern Life*. Berkeley: University of California Press.

Crary, Jonathan (1992) *Techniques of the Observer: On Vision and Modernity in the Nineteenth Century*. Cambridge, MA: MIT Press.

Crary, Jonathan (1999) *Suspensions of Perception: Attention, Spectacle and Modern Culture*. Cambridge, MA: MIT Press.

Danius, Sara (2002) *The Senses of Modernism: Technology, Perception, and Aesthetics*. Ithaca, NY: Cornell University Press.

Deleuze, Gilles (1992) *Cinema 1: The Movement-Image*. Tr. Hugh Tomlinson and Barabara Habberjam. London: Athlone.

Derrida, Jacques (1992) *Acts of Literature*. Ed. Derek Attridge. New York: Routledge.

Doane, Mary Ann (2002) *The Emergence of Cinematic Time: Modernity, Contingency, the Archive*. Cambridge, MA: Harvard University Press.

Donald, James, Friedberg, Anne and Marcus, Laura (eds) (1997) *Close Up, 1927–1933: Cinema and Modernity*. London: Cassell.

Eisenstein, Sergei M. (1988) *Selected Works, Volume 1: Writings, 1922–34*. Tr. Richard Taylor. London: BFI.

Eliot, T.S. (1974) 'Little Gidding', *Four Quartets*, in *Collected Poems, 1909–1962*. London: Faber & Faber. pp. 214–23.

Elsaesser, Thomas (1987) 'Cinema – The Irresponsible Signifier or "The Gamble with History": Film Theory or Cinema Theory', *New German Critique*, 40:65–89.

Elsaesser, Thomas (1990) *Early Cinema: Space, Frame, Narrative*. London: BFI.

Fiske, John (1991) *Reading the Popular*. London: Routledge.

Fried, Michael (1998) 'Art and Objecthood', in *Art and Objecthood: Essays and Reviews*. Chicago: University of Chicago Press. pp. 148–68.

Friedberg, Anne (1993) *Window Shopping: Cinema and the Postmodern*. Berkeley: University of California Press.

Gunning, Tom (1986) 'The Cinema of Attraction: Early Film, Its Spectator and the Avant-Garde', *Wide Angle*, 8(3–4): 1–14.

Gunning, Tom (1991) *D.W. Griffith and the Origins of American Narrative Film: The Early Years at Biograph*. Urbana: University of Illinois Press.

Hansen, Miriam (1991) *Babel and Babylon: Spectatorship in American Silent Film*. Cambridge, MA: Harvard University Press.

Hansen, Miriam Bratu (1995) 'America, Paris, the Alps: Kracauer (and Benjamin) on Cinema and Modernity', in Leo Charney and Vanessa Schwartz (eds), *Cinema and the Invention of Modern Life*. Berkeley: University of California Press. pp. 362–402.

Hansen, Miriam Bratu (1997) 'Introduction', in Siegfried Kracauer, *Theory of Film: The Redemption of Physical Reality*. Princeton, NJ: Princeton University Press. pp.vii–xlv.

Hansen, Miriam (1999) 'The Mass Production of the Senses: Classical Cinema as Vernacular Modernism', *Modernism/Modernity*, 6(2): 59–77.

Heath, Stephen (1981) 'Narrative Space', in *Questions of Cinema*. London: Macmillan. pp. 19–75.

Jameson, Fredric (1977) 'Reflections in Conclusion', in Ernst Bloch et al., *Aesthetics and Politics*. London: Verso. pp. 196–213.

Jameson, Fredric (1981) *The Political Unconscious: Literature as a Socially Symbolic Act*. Ithaca, NY: Cornell University Press.

Jameson, Fredric (1992a) 'The Existence of Italy', in *Signatures of the Visible*. London: Routlegde. pp. 155–229.

Jameson, Fredric (1992b) *The Geopolitical Aesthetic: Cinema and Space in the World System*. London: BFI.

Jameson, Fredric (1996) *Late Marxism: Adorno, or The Persistence of the Dialectic*. London: Verso.

Jameson, Fredric (1998) 'Transformations of the Image', in *The Cultural Turn: Selected Writings on the Postmodern 1983–1998*. London: Verso. pp. 93–135.

Jay, Martin (1993) *Downcast Eyes: The Denigration of Vision in Twentieth-Century French Thought*. Berkeley: University of California Press.

Jay, Martin and Brennan, Teresa (eds) (1996) *Vision in Context: Historical and Contemporary Perspectives on Sight*. New York: Routledge.

Joyce, James (1922) *Ulysses*. Paris: Shakespeare and Co.

Kaplan, E. Ann (1987) *Rocking Around the Clock: Music Television, Postmodernism, and Consumer Culture*. New York: Methuen.

Kittler, Friedrich A. (1999) *Gramophone, Film, Typewriter*. Tr. Geoffrey Winthrop-Young and Michael Wutz. Stanford, CA: Stanford University Press.

Kracauer, Siegfried (1995) *The Mass Ornament: Weimar Essays*. Tr. Thomas Y. Levin. Cambridge, MA: Harvard University Press.

Leslie, Esther (2002) *Hollywood Flatlands: Animation, Critical Theory and the Avant-Garde*. London: Verso.

Lessing, Gotthold Ephraim (1953) *Laocoon: An Essay on the Limits of Painting and Poetry*. Tr. E.C. Beasley. Bowling Green: Longman.

MacCabe, Colin (1980) 'The Classic Realist Text', in Christopher Williams (ed.), *Realism and the Cinema: A Reader*. London: Routledge & Kegan Paul. pp. 15–28.

MacCabe, Colin (2003) 'On Impurity', in Julian Murphet and Lydia Rainford (eds), *Literature and Visual Technologies: Writing after Cinema*. Houndmills: Palgrave. pp. 152–62.

Marcus, Laura (1997) 'Continuous Performance: Dorothy Richardson', in James Donald, Anne Friedberg and Laura Marcus (eds), *Close Up, 1927–1933: Cinema and Modernity*. London: Cassell. pp. 150–59.

McLuhan, Marshall (1994) *Understanding Media: The Extensions of Man*. Cambridge, MA: MIT Press.

Mulvey, Laura (2006) *Death 24x a Second*. London: Reaktion Books.

Musser, Charles (1990) *The Emergence of Cinema: The American Screen to 1907. Vol.1, History of the American Cinema*. New York/Berkeley: Charles Scribner's/University of California Press.

Quaresima, Leonardo (2004) 'Introduction to the 2004 Edition', in Siegfried Kracauer, *From Caligari to Hitler: A Psychological History of the German Film*. Princeton, NJ: Princeton University Press. pp. xv–l.

Rancière, Jacques (2006) *Film Fables*. Tr. Emiliano Battista. Oxford: Berg.

Richardson, Dorothy (1928) 'Continuous Performance XII: The Cinema in Arcady', *Close Up*, 3(1): 52–7.

Rodowick, D.N. (1997) *Gilles Deleuze's Time Machine*. Durham, NC: Duke University Press.

Singer, Ben (2001) *Melodrama and Modernity: Early Sensational Cinema and its Contexts*. New York: Columbia University Press.

Stein, Gertrude (1998) 'Portraits and Repetition', in *Writings 1932–1946*. New York: Library of America.

Wilde, Oscar (1975) 'The Soul of Man Under Socialism', in *Plays, Prose Writings and Poems*. London: Dent. pp. 255–88.

Wollen, Peter (1993) 'Modern Times', in *Raiding the Icebox: Reflections on Twentieth-Century Culture*. London: Verso. pp. 35–71.

Young, Paul (2006) *The Cinema Dreams Its Rivals: Media Fantasy Films from Radio to the Internet*. Minneapolis: University of Minnesota Press.

23

Cinema/Ideology/Society: The Political Expectations of Film Theory

Jane Gaines

Reality is what actually happens in a factory, in a school, in the barracks, in a prison, in a police station.

Gilles Deleuze (quoted in Foucault, 1977: 212)

The assumed link between cinema and social criticism begins with the fact that moving pictures, a nineteenth-century invention, exhibited such an amazing similarity to the social world, not as it was but as it appeared to its observers. This likeness was remarked upon again and again at the inception of the cinematograph. Certainly, the case has often been made that cinema is able to bring social realities to visibility more effectively than any other form of art or culture. Encapsulating the political anticipation attached to the new moving image machine, German experimental film-maker Hans Richter exclaimed in the 1930s: 'Our age demands the documented fact ... The modern reproductive technology of the cinematograph was uniquely responsive to

the need for factual sustenance' (1986: 43). This is one way of saying that political hopes and expectations in the first several decades of the century became attached to the invention that could deliver such a lifelike image-in-motion (through modern theatrical exhibition) to masses of urban viewers. Thus, it is nearly impossible to speak about the social in the cinema century, 1900 to 2000, without reference to the problem of aesthetic realism and its correspondence with historical realities. By convention, such correspondence anticipates correlation along a continuum from social reform to the cataclysmic utopianism of revolutionary change.

Correspondence would be the case complexly made for Dziga Vertov's revolutionary Soviet *kino pravda* films in the 1920s (Vertov, 1984) and later more problematically made for post-World War Two Italian neorealism (Bazin, 1971; Kracauer, 1997). By the 1970s, however, the very hallmark of neorealism, the apparent capacity of the camera to effortlessly render the social realm, became politically questionable.[1] The cinema institution, it was argued, could only bring us that which we already knew, not the new knowledge required to change social conditions. The political expectations that characterized 1970s film theory were French in origin, an outgrowth of the socially transformative events of May 1968, that culminated in the general strike in which workers joined students critical of the Vietnam War and authoritarian university structures (Harvey, 1978). That film theory, translated and exported to the English-speaking academy, now detached from its radical moment, stirred another generation.

How film theory moved from understanding the relationship between the moving image and the social world as privileged and toward seeing this automatic relation as politically suspect may be understood in retrospect with reference to a great world divide. The old antagonism between the Communist bloc and the capitalist West, mapped in recent memory by the Cold War, is one way of staging the central aesthetic polarity of the past century: globally dominating Hollywood narrative fiction film as countered and challenged by alternatives. Yet, as we will see, shifts in the political realm do not correlate with adjustments in the social realm, telling us that these realms will always be out of alignment, this disjuncture itself the great challenge to a politicized aesthetics. Indeed, it is the philosophical problem of non-correspondence, understood as the disjuncture between the economic base and the cultural superstructure, that has been a core question, with implications for what would be understood as a politically radical film theory.

Contemporary film theory's passionate interest in working conditions and social hierarchies owes all to a confluence of events that began with the success of the 1917 Russian Revolution and the later test to which Marxist utopianism was submitted, first in Germany in the 1930s and later in the post-World War Two world. Here, it would be the Russian experiments, the legacy of the Futurists as well as the Formalists that would underwrite the

challenge to a too easy, mirror-like art-reality relationship in favour of artistic practice as a transformative production in oblique relation to social conditions. The very terms of the social, however, would be as fraught as the question of how to re-present existing conditions. Since the expectation placed on the working class as the engine of revolution and author of proletarian culture, based first on the Russian experiments and later pinned to the Chinese Cultural Revolution, was not borne out historically, 'class' as theoretical category and historical structure was under review. As a constant, from the point of view of revolutionary Russia and later the post-World War Two European New Left, world strife was the legacy of medieval ownership and colonial rule, and the industrialization that had promised liberation depended upon new inequities, best grasped as class difference. Just as in the contemporary moment 'class' is translated into yet another set of inequities, the theory and practice of political cinema born of post-revolutionary circumstances has been translated into political cinema within and for the capitalist West. Here, motion pictures as the art form of the second industrial age has been seen as uniquely able to represent social imbalance as well as to agitate for its rectification. But whether the mode this new form took should be documentary, narrative fiction, or an avant-garde alternative to either of these has been hotly debated, certainly because of the persistence of the expectation we are tracking – the expectation that cinema can be powerfully political[2].

The degree of politics is thus crucial, as seen in the difference between reform and revolution organized around the legacy of two figures, producer John Grierson and filmmaker Sergei Eisenstein. Standing for moderate British social policy and revolutionary Russian ideals respectively, these figures continue to define the line between classical documentary and radical cinematic avant-gardism, even when that line is blurred. Griersonianism has been kept alive worldwide in the 'social problem' approach to television as well as theatrical film and low-budget video and now digital documentary

(Winston, 1995). Eisensteinian avant-gardism (supplemented with the distanciation devices associated with German playwright and theorist Bertolt Brecht [1974]) has been periodically invoked since the 1970s in the imagination of vanguard cinemas for the present (Godmilow, 2002). Here is where the question of class returns, as we remember that Eisenstein's theory of dialectical film form was originally derived from post-revolutionary Soviet theorizations of class antagonism and the critique of capitalism, and was intended to contribute to the education of a new citizenry according to Marxist-Leninist principles by an artistic elite (Eisenstein, 1988; 1992). Although in the development of a socially conscious film theory, Eisenstein has remained the centrepiece, legitimating the question of working conditions as well as checks on the power of the ruling class, over the last part of the cinema century, these questions have been reformulated, made moderate, safe, and academic.

To review, the twentieth was a century in which political alignments did not stay in the same place for long. To read the political expectations of the theory of the moving image is to follow capitalism as it spread, socialism as it grew and shrank, Marxist-Leninism as it migrated from Russia, colonialism as it lingered in Africa and Latin America, and finally Chinese Communism as it inspired and then betrayed revolutionary hope. Beginning in the 1970s, other movements substituted class for new ways of understanding oppression, best exemplified by the First World woman's movement as it swelled, levelled off, and gave way to other vanguards such as the gay rights movement (Bad Object Choices, 1991). Over this terrain, patterns emerge and recede, but it is possible to perceive large shapes in the approaches taken by filmmakers as well as critics, which might be summarized tentatively as follows: going with realism as opposed to going against it, form as political or apolitical, film language as illusionism or disruptive montage, critique as the work of the film as opposed to the work of the critic, opposition as outside or inside the text, and the popular narrative as utopian

or hegemonic, progressive or reactionary. No sooner have we set up these familiar critical oppositions, however, than the objects and terms of analysis begin to change sides. No concept has migrated more than 'reality' and the attendant aesthetic of 'realism', which was so thoroughly discredited by 1970s film theory, as we will see, but also utilized by major figures whose political sympathies were in alignment, but whose stated positions here seem at odds. André Bazin, for instance, praised director Eric von Stroheim because 'in his films reality lays itself bare like a suspect confessing under the relentless examination of the commissioner of police' (1967: 27). Bertolt Brecht instead defined realism as 'laying bare society's causal network/showing up the dominant viewpoint as the viewpoint of the dominators/writing from the stand point of the class which has prepared the broadest solutions for the most pressing problems afflicting human society' (1964: 109). One could contrast here the difference in investment in reality formed (into cinema) as opposed to reality unformed (or as it was said, appearing 'unmediated'), except that the social world in Bazin only yields its meaning under the gruelling analysis of cinema. Quite apart from the philosophical problem of 'reality as signified' is the historically recurring need for any socially aware cinema to invoke if not refer to a world 'reality' outside the cinema, if nothing other than as a sign of political commitment. Thus emerges the need for caution about the slipperiness of reality as a critical category, a concept which in the same century has been associated with truth, illusionism, deception, class difference, gender inequity, marginality, historical materialism, *and* bourgeois capitalism.

Despite these critical shifts, at least where filmmaking as social criticism has been concerned, over the last century a canon has emerged, comprised of films privileging the existence of 'real historical conditions'. What if we were to look at a cross-section of this international film canon, at works understood as unflinchingly social, or films that take peoples' life conditions as a starting point? Let us, for instance, consider films about labour strife, workers' societies, wage struggles, housing conditions, the aftermath of war, gender as well as race and sexuality as sources of oppression, and the struggle for socialism against its corruption and social justice against colonial rule. Finally, if we add films in which voice is given to the sexually abjected as well as to the traditionally poor and dispossessed, we might have the following list: *Strike* (Sergei Eisenstein, USSR, 1924), *Misère au Borinage* (Joris Ivens/Henri Storck, Belgium, 1929), *Las Hurdes* (*Land Without Bread*, Luis Buñuel, Spain, 1932), *Housing Problems* (Arthur Elton/Edgar Anstey, Britain, 1935), *Roma città aperta* (*Rome, Open City*, Roberto Rossellini, Italy, 1945), *Battle of Algiers* (Gillo Pontecorvco, Algeria/Italy, 1960), *The Brickmakers* (Marta Rodriquez/Jorge Silva, Columbia, 1972), *Memorias del subdesarrallo* (*Memories of Underdevelopment*, Thomas Gutierrez Alea, Cuba, 1973), *Czlowiek z Marmuru* (*Man of Marble*, Andrej Wayda, Poland, 1977), *Union Maids* (Julia Reichert/Miles Mogulescu/Jim Klein, US, 1976), *Tongues Untied* (Marlon Riggs, US, 1999). What this mix of documentary and fiction films from divergent moments and traditions share is not only a critical but a 'revealing' approach to social conditions. Yet even the conceptualization of 'revealed social conditions' raises a crucial problem, since the issue for film theory has never exactly been the conditions themselves, the conditions in front of, but irrespective of, the camera.

If the question had ever been people's experience of social conditions, then we might be satisfied with Gilles Deleuze's casual definition of 'reality' made in an interview with himself and Michel Foucault in the 1970s: 'Reality is what actually happens in a factory, in a school, in the barracks, in a prison, in a police station' (Foucault, 1977: 212). But Gayatri Spivak, who critiques this interview, reminds us of the traps that intellectuals continue to fall into in their invocation of the Other, as well as their recourse to a desire for 'what actually happens'. First, Deleuze and Foucault here exemplify what she calls 'empirical desire', expressed in the 'empirical register of resistance-talk', which

cannot help but shore up the positivism that is the underpinning of advanced capitalist neocolonialism (1999: 252, 255–6). Second, these two 'activist philosophers of history', she argues, appear oblivious to the function of ideology most significantly as they ignore the way they themselves are positioned (1999: 249). The double bind of social critique is that the intellectual defers to what the masses know but ventriloquizes the 'speaking subaltern' (1999: 255). In one move, Spivak both updates and criticizes Deleuze and Foucault's post-1968 French Leftism in an eerie rehearsal of the questions that defined thirty years of film theory, tribute to the longevity of the legacy of post-structuralism and testimony to what film scholars would call an impasse. The impasse – the 'no way out' for film theory – centred on the question of the empirical real (the factory, the school, the barracks, the prison, the police station). Called into question would be all of the canonical films listed above. Here, following post-structuralist theory, cinema would represent a special signifying problem, as it has been understood as doubly ideological: existing ideologies are reproduced by another ideology – the film form that delivered the exquisite 'impression of reality'. For the issue decidedly following poststructuralists Jacques Derrida, Roland Barthes, and especially Louis Althusser has been one of *what* language, and, by analogy, *what* film form and style is finally innocent. The point would be that the very cinematic carriers of meaning, and especially those that receded into an unseen stylistic realism, were not innocently neutral but invested in the society that produced them. The question of what we have come to understand as the ideology of film form has been *the* theoretical question of the last decades of the cinema century.

In order to see how social critique became ideological critique in the history of Western film theory, one begins after World War Two. At that time, it could be said, models for film theory as having a special relation to the political world began to announce themselves as just that. Early preparation for the approach to 'reading' society by studying the cinematic *mise en scène* can be found in Siegfried Kracauer's *From Caligari to Hitler* (1947). As it anticipates psychoanalysis, Kracauer's study of *The Cabinet of Dr Caligari* (Robert Weine, Germany, 1921), which understands the cinema of the Weimar Republic (1919 to 1933) as a 'premonition' of Adolf Hitler, is itself a 'premonition' of a later criticism. The very ambition of the reading that would locate the political unconscious of the historical moment in the visual style of the film looks ahead to the ideological analysis of the film as text that would appear two decades later. In another part of Europe, Italian film theory responded to the starkly different look of neorealism and the urban sociology of films such as *Roma città aperta*, but immediately interpreted this in relation to a new mobility of cinema production outside the corrupted Italian studio. Here, praise for the unscripted use of non-actors opened up the question of how some films might have a more proximate relation to real historical moments than others. Filmmaker Cesare Zavattini's reaction exemplifies the claim, reiterated by Bazin, that a cinema about social reality was (almost) social reality itself: 'It is not a question of making imaginary things become "reality" (making them look true, real), but of making things as they really are most significant, almost as if they were telling their story by themselves' (quoted in Casetti, 1999: 25; see also Zavattini, 1970; 1979). At the same time that critics were struck by the black-and-white treatment that appeared to perfectly match the film's interest in the heroism of a Communist former member of the Resistance (*Roma città aperta*), the easy equation of a new style ('realism') with a bold approach to uncensored subject matter ('reality') did not go unnoticed, even then. Guido Aristarco would caution that: 'There are many degrees of realism, just as there are many degrees of reality (reality as it is perceived)' (quoted in Casetti, 1999: 28).

So here we are confronted with one of the most compelling questions for a theory of film, brought on, in part, by the tendency to use the same vocabulary in reference to the world itself as is used to refer to the cinematic images

of that world. But cinematic reality's reality is only apparently an inadvertent or a mistaken conflation of the world with the image of it, and more certainly an ontological and philosophical question of larger proportions. There is another possibility. Perhaps the case for seeing neorealism as a breakthrough for the post-war conditions themselves was overstated. In French theorist Bazin's open letter to Guido Aristarco he would write, 'Rossellini directs facts' (1971: 100). Later, this paradox of self-effacing cinema aesthetics would be starkly seen in Peter Wollen's paraphrase of Bazin: 'No more actors, no more plot, no more *mise en scène*: the perfect illusion of reality. In fact, no more cinema' (1969: 131).[3] Neorealism appeared to be prized as a vehicle for social awareness only because it downplayed cinematic technique in favour of the untouched object before the camera. A return to Bazin, however, has found in him a much more complicated theorization of what has been recently addressed as the 'indexicality' of the photographic image, seen even in the same essay in which he praises Rossellini for directing facts where he would assert the 'ontological identity between the object and its photographic image' (1971: 98). Bazin's interest in a photographic privilege vis-à-vis the event before the camera's shot of it would be echoed in the truth claims made in the 1960s by *cinéma vérité* and yet again in the 1990s with the opposition between 'true' photographic and 'false' or falsified digital imagery (Rosen, 2001).

A later generation wonders where to place Bazin, the theorist who saw the 'total representation of reality' as both a 'myth' guiding the invention of photography, phonography and cinema and, in his terms, a 'reality' finally achieved by some select directors (1967: 20–1). Bazin might here have been writing as much about the guiding 'ideology of realism' as he was about the 'myth' of total reality that inspired inventors such as Thomas Edison to try to attach his kinetoscope to a phonograph to give sound to the image in approximation of the complete human sensorium. A second consideration of Bazin's defense of neorealism might find within it a struggle to think through a film theory adequate to a newly engaged post-war cinema. At the centre of this theory was a conception of realism that was unlike earlier realisms, and unlike literary naturalism, in that it was not satisfied to let the subject matter (in an objective way) define the aesthetic. It was based on the premise that 'reality' requires filtering, analysis, and, in Bazin's word, 'presentation' (1971: 97). And such a reconsideration of the theory gives a new perspective on what for a time was thought to be a 'revolt against the father' – a rejection of Bazin's position of intellectual dominance – staged in the French journal *Cahiers du cinéma* in the late 1960s and early 1970s (Browne, 1990). Another reading of Bazin's *Cahiers* writings from the 1950s against the seminal editorial 'Cinema/Ideology/Criticism' (1976), from October 1969, suggests the continuity with his thinking and that of co-authors Jean-Louis Comolli and Jean Narboni. However, at the same time that we would note Comolli and Narboni's debt to Bazin, we should also stress the distinct break and consequent breakthrough for film theory represented by this editorial which, in conjunction with key essays by Jean-Louis Baudry, served as a 1970s political manifesto for criticism (1974; 1986a; 1986b).

The field may now be cycling back to Bazin (see Chapter 25 in this volume), although not necessarily to 'Cinema/Ideology/Criticism', and a fuller discussion of this polemical piece is essential since it is here that the methodology of the ideological critique, the standard for close text analysis, is first laid out. Another way of putting this would be to say that after 'Cinema/Ideology/Criticism', film analysis has continued to be ideological critique, even when that analysis does not begin from the Leftist standpoint of the authors of the original article. Film production was originally another matter, which meant that the ramifications of realism as equated with ideology were dealt with on two different fronts, political filmmaking practice and film text analysis, with *Cahiers* invested in the latter. Returning to the *Cahiers* editorial is important if for

nothing more than to study the development of the influential argument that cinema's apparent 'reproduction' of reality (sometimes its successful 'impression of reality') is highly ideological. This would be understood against the historical function of realism (as a literary, pictorial, and finally photographic aesthetic) as support for the argument that the image that most closely resembles the world faithfully mirrors the world. But the post-1968 theorists went further. Here, the re-reading of 'Cinema/Ideology/Criticism', along with French Marxist Althusser's theorization of ideology as a system of representation that conditions necessary social hierarchies, dramatizes the comprehensiveness of this view of society as well as of cinema (Althusser, 1969; Comolli and Narboni (1969; 1971; 1976). In French capitalist bourgeois society, the *Cahiers* editorial argues, 'reality' advances bourgeois interests, interests not shared by groups not in power, most importantly the working class: 'Clearly, the cinema "reproduces" reality: this is what a camera and film stock are for – so says the ideology. But the tools and techniques of film-making are a part of "reality" themselves, and furthermore "reality" is nothing but an expression of the prevailing ideology' (Comolli and Narboni, 1976: 25).

Around the same time, the editor of *Tel Quel*, Marcellin Pleynet, in an interview with editors of the new radical journal *Cinéthique*, would make a connection that reinforced this understanding of the camera's reality as 'entirely caught in empiricism'. Tautologically, the empiricism of the camera lens itself was empirically verifiable: 'the camera is carefully built so as to "rectify" any anomaly of perspective, so as to reproduce in its full authority the code of specular vision as it was defined by Renaissance humanism' (Pleynet and Thibaudeau, 1979: 159). The camera, never a neutral instrument, appears to simulate the workings of the human eye, but it actually returns us to a perspective as old as the fifteenth century. Thus, the camera is so invested in the project of an emerging bourgeois class that it is impossible to use it to advance a working-class cinema, or to further the stated goal of so much of post-1968 film theory – to change the world.

The implications of this argument about the camera lens are staggering since all films, whether low-budget alternatives or mainstream studio productions, would use the lenses into which this perspective was ground; therefore all films would be reactionary, regardless of subject matter. The *Cahiers* solution to this filmmaking problem, part of a post-1968 political project, was to advocate films that might be able to 'disrupt' or 'sever' the connection to ideology with the use of techniques refined along the lines of Eisensteinian-Brechtian models to which I referred earlier. But some confusion may arise here since the implications for oppositional filmmaking practice were implicit in the *Cahiers* editorial, as I have said, leaving a more explicit imagination of a new practice to *Cinéthique*. And it would be there that the program for transforming the world through direct threats to bourgeois cinema, opposing the smooth cinema that erased the conditions of its production with a cinema that revealed everything about itself was developed (see Rodowick, 1988). Was such a project either possible or sufficient? In a Brechtian move, Paper Tiger Television, the New York City cable and low-budget video-tape phenomenon of the 1980s, listed the costs of each production in the credits. Politically astute as this move was, it was not exactly what 'revealing the conditions of production' originally meant. The French were advocating modernism, not popular mass culture nor even feisty experimental work.

The post-1968 radical project had its most lasting impact on filmmaking as Eisenstein's pattern of formal anti-realism was refined by filmmaker Jean-Luc Godard, giving 'revolutionary' film form a second historical moment in films like *Vent d'est* (France/Italy/West Germany, 1972) and *Week End* (Italy/France, 1967). For the English-speaking West, Peter Wollen (1972) formulated Godard's filmmaking practice as Brechtian 'counter-cinema'. Claire Johnston (1976) and Laura Mulvey (1975) soon advocated a new feminist counter-cinema following similar practices as the antidote to Hollywood's capitalist but also patriarchal narrative film form and its visual dangers: identification, gendered looking patterns, and realistic illusionism or the illusion of reality. In theory, Eisensteinian-Brechtian film practice was not only a set of aesthetic options but also came to involve prohibitions against making films and later videotapes about people's struggles using the illusionistic devices of narrative realism seen as embodying the world view of the social class in power, the bourgeois. Here, aligned with a historical modernism in high art, the film that aspired to the highest degree of politics had to foreground its own production conditions, eventually formulated as a self-reflexive approach to showing *that* it was made as well as *how* it was made. Yet, in retrospect, it is certain that only a handful of films met the standard: *Thriller* (Sally Potter, UK, 1979), *Far From Poland* (Jill Godmilow, US, 1984), *What Farouki Taught* (Jill Godmilow, US, 1998) and other films by Harun Farocki (from West Germany). Thus, in the US, the Black British *Looking for Langston* (Isaac Julien, UK, 1988) was preferred on political-aesthetic grounds to the African-American realist narrative fiction *Do the Right Thing* (Spike Lee, US, 1989). But a turning point was *Daughters of the Dust* (Julie Dash, US/UK, 1993), a film that, despite its glossy Hollywood 'look' and narrative realist construction, was an independent feature, produced and directed by an African-American woman. Who the film was by and who it was 'about' trumped all other oppositionalities, rendering 1970s political film form orthodoxy moot. Although *Daughters of the Dust* took some experimental licence with film form, using exquisite dissolves in fantasy sequences, it did not seriously disturb the realist aesthetic. In other words, a narrative film about a tight matriarchal culture of the descendants of South Carolina slaves, transcending the conditions into which they were born, but connecting them to the rituals of their African home, would be politically oppositional and recalcitrant enough in content to render a political analysis of its cinematic realism irrelevant.

Daughters of the Dust is particularly difficult to analyze ideologically given the stated political expectations of the 'Cinema/Ideology/Criticism' editorial, which divides films into seven categories according to their relationship to ideology, whether complicit or critical, and as manifest in their 'form' as well as in their 'content'. In the editorial, films with 'political content' are dismissed, and 'live cinema' or *cinéma direct* (direct cinema) films are deemed problematic because, even if they 'arise out of' social events, these events cannot on their own produce knowledge, or theory, since theory must be produced *out of* rather than *by* events (Comolli and Narboni, 1976: 28). The critical mission of the journal as defined by the *Cahiers* collective was work on the textual strategies of a category of films that might just as well be mainstream mass entertainment. This highly influential category (e) defined what came to be known as the progressive text, and sometimes the contradictory text. For over thirty years, the approach illustrated by the analyses of two American popular films, Josef von Sternberg's *Morocco* (1930) and *Young Mr. Lincoln* (John Ford, US, 1939) defined the methodology of the ideological critique, the most evolved form of social criticism (*Cahiers du cinéma*, 1980). The genre in which the ideological critique was most thoroughly developed, not surprisingly, was melodrama, for this would be where the 'internal criticism' of the category (e) was first tested on the films of Douglas Sirk. As a companion model, Thomas Elsaesser's 'Tales of Sound and Fury' (1992), first appearing in 1972, demonstrated how in films such as *Written on the Wind* (Douglas Sirk, US, 1957) and *Imitation of Life* (Douglas Sirk, US, 1959), the auteur director was able to use cinematic stylistics against the ideological message (see also Fischer, 1991). On the surface, Sirk's films performed a kind of criticism that, in the words of Comolli and Narboni, 'cracks the film apart at the seams' (1976: 27). But how these films are different from films in the largest group, the category (a) of films imbued

with the dominant ideology, has never been adequately demonstrated, particularly since a case for being ideologically oppositional or progressive could be made for any film, whether 'explicitly political' and seemingly not commercial, or blatantly commercial and 'blissfully' ideological (Comolli and Narboni, 1976: 25–6).

Sorting out the legacy of the ideological critique also requires recalling the development of the concept of ideology from Karl Marx and Friedrich Engels and following it through Althusserian Marxism as it met Lacanian psychoanalysis as well as Derridian deconstruction (Marx and Engels, 1970; Althusser, 1969; 1979; Derrida, 1980). The methodology of reading the unconscious of the text for the 'noticeable gap', after all, was evolving in French literary criticism and philosophy at around the time of the publication of the *Cahiers* editorial (Macherey, 1978). Derrida's epistemology of dismantlement had been developed in essays published in France in the 1950s and 1960s, so the critical ideal of 'partially dismantling the system from within' seems an echo of that tradition (1980: 27). Finally, the question of progressiveness, contradictoriness, or textual resistance to the ideological dominant still needs to be referred back to Frankfurt School utopianism, but without forgetting that Theodor Adorno and Max Horkheimer's analysis of the domination of the American capitalist culture industry was informed by their experience of European Fascism (see Adorno and Horkheimer, 1979; Gaines, 2000).

Heir to this confluence of traditions would be the analysis of melodrama as supremely social, the depository of all the imaginable scenarios of suffering and misery and readable in terms of what Linda Williams calls the 'destabilizing effects of the modern world' (2001: 22). Popular melodrama narrativizes the pathologies of wife and child abuse, racial and ethnic discrimination, gender inequity, marital infidelity, poverty, illegitimacy, mental illness, physical handicap, and financial ruin. But again, following the contours of the category (e) methodology, aesthetics can go one way and the overall ideology of the film another, and here feminist theory has powerfully demonstrated the generosity of melodrama as a genre which may deliver the ideology of male superiority while privileging the female victim and idealizing her domestic realm. Useful here is Christine Gledhill's assessment that realisms 'assume the world is capable of both adequate explanation and representation'. Melodrama, in contrast, 'has no such confidence ...' (1987, 31). Importantly, it is the most despised and denigrated popular forms that have been considered the richest territory to mine for insights into contemporary social relations. I would single out as particularly exemplary several ideological readings of the horror film genre such as Patricia White (1999) on *The Haunting* (Robert Wise, US, 1963), Carol Clover (1992) on *Halloween* (John Carpenter, US, 1978), and Richard Dyer (1997) on *Night of the Living Dead* (George Romero, US, 1968). The critics here illustrate how popular genre films tell us more about the fear of lesbianism, young male gender ambivalence, and white suburbia's racial nightmares than any sociology could hope to uncover. With the English translation of 'Cinema/Ideology/Criticism' appearing in *Screen* in 1971, the door was opened for exhaustive analysis of the most popular of narrative forms. Yet again we encounter the Cold War division not only of world territory, but also of intellectual tradition. How do we place, for instance, Cuban Leftist film criticism of the 1970s, then part of the Soviet bloc? One might assume a political continuity between Enrique Colina and Daniel Díaz Torres writing in 1972 in the Leftist journal *Cine Cubano* and the Marxist-Leninism of the 1970s *Cahiers du cinéma* collective. However, as the Soviet revolutionaries before them had denounced the decadence of pre-revolutionary czarist melodrama, the Cubans would reject the melodrama of an earlier Latin American cinema, this time by association with Hollywood's cultural imperialism. The dismissal of the Latin American melodrama of the 1930s and 1950s, than places *Cine Cubano* at odds with *Cahiers*, where a political criticism at the same moment might have

been interested in seeing how these decadent melodramas challenged the Hollywood dominance of Latin American markets as well as how the genre could be read as internally contradictory (López, 2000: 429–30).

There may be no more dramatic challenge posed to 1970s Western film theory, its world view, and its understanding of the political ideology of cinematic realism, than the case of the Chinese Fifth Generation cinema.[4] Eastern as well as Western legend locates talented youth, disillusioned with the 1970s Chinese Cultural Revolution after universities had been disbanded and students sent to the country for a decade of service. A gifted few of them are recruited as filmmakers and charged with making feature films for the Communist state at a relatively tolerant moment. One of the earliest films completed by the graduates of the first class of the Beijing Film Academy (1978–82) was the now-canonical *Yellow Earth* (China, 1984), directed by Chen Kaige with cinematography by Zhang Yimou. And it is with this film that the political expectations of 1970s film theory fall dramatically out of alignment with aesthetics. Here we see that Western capitalism is not the only antagonistic dominant, anti-realism is no longer the default oppositional form and classical narrative realism is not constitutionally unfit to produce political critique.

Young filmmakers with their first opportunity to write and direct rejected not European or American capitalist, but the Communist Chinese mainstream film ideology that historically glorified the party. *Yellow Earth* uses a young female peasant, Cuiqiao (Xue Bai), as an image of the readiness of the peasant classes to be rescued from the prison of arranged marriages and servitude to the hard land, a readiness to be recruited into a new society by the Red Army. Set in 1932 against the historical background of the growth of the Chinese Communist Party in Yan'an, where Chairman Mao built his organization, the film uses a lush cinematographic style, long horizontal pans and languid dissolves over the landscape of the Yellow River. But the narrative dares to be critical of the party's methods of recruitment, casting the soldier as travelling to Cuiqiao's village to collect folk songs that will then be turned into revolutionary songs used in the recruitment of the very people from whom the music has been taken. The soldier effectively betrays the hopes of the people when he fails to take Cuiqiao with him when he leaves, condemning her to a marriage from which the mere child finally flees. Taking the options held out by the Communists, Cuiqiao attempts to follow the soldier, but drowns in the river. *Yellow Earth* received immediate critical acclaim outside the People's Republic but not within China, where it offended the hardline Communists then in power.

With *Yellow Earth*, the filmmakers strike two orthodoxies in one blow – the Chinese Communist historical party ideology as well as the Western film theory party line. But while the first target may have been hit strategically, the second was hit inadvertently. By all accounts, following the political tenets of 1970s film theory, *Yellow Earth* should be formally at odds with Hollywood continuity techniques because it was aligned with socialism, capitalism's opposition. The first wave of Western criticism (Yau, 1991; McDougall, 1991), following these principles, described the film as aesthetically antithetical to Hollywood style as well as critical of the party. But for *Yellow Earth* and its Chinese dissident makers, Hollywood was not the enemy, nor was bourgeois capitalism an ideological opponent and realist aesthetics were not exclusively bourgeois aesthetics. In the end, what the case of *Yellow Earth* demonstrates is the ultimate impossibility of lining up political aims with cinematic devices. According to the political expectations of 1970s film theory, the young Chinese Communists should have followed the Soviet model, and their films should have looked like Eisenstein's. After all, as Ni Zhen tells us in *Memoirs of the Beijing Academy*, students in the class of 1978-82 were taught editing by Russian teachers schooled in the Soviet montage method (2004: 66). But, he says, the class rejected this style in favour of the Soviet Socialist Realism

of the late 1950s and 1960s. The students preferred films about disillusionment with Communism, such as *The Cranes are Flying* (Mikheil Kalatozishvili, USSR, 1957) and *Ivan's Children* (Andrei Tarkovsky, USSR, 1962). In championing the Socialist Realism of the Russians, they were paradoxically reproducing the Russian-inspired Socialist Realism of the Chinese mainstream films that they sought to reject not emulate. Since *Yellow Earth* is more a work of epic narrative realism than anything else, it is thus an anomaly for 1970s Western film theory – a revolutionary realist film for Communist dissidents and a counter-revolutionary film from the point of view of Chinese Communist Party tradition (see also Donald and Donald, 2000).

It is safe to say that, since the cataclysmic event of the Tiananmen Square Massacre in 1989, all earlier political as well as aesthetic alignments are off. As Rey Chow has argued, since China no longer represents anti-imperialism for Third World nations and Left intellectuals, it can no longer be seen as 'oppositional' in relation to the West. Instead, China is on a course to becoming the capitalist 'equal' of the West (Chow, 2000: 406). Film theory as it considers globalization has not yet fully come to terms either with China as culturally dominant or with the international stardom of former Chinese dissidents, the producers of *Yellow Earth*, who now make epic fictional narrative films financed by international co-production arrangements, best exemplified by *Farewell, My Concubine* (Chen Kaige, China/Hong Kong, 1993) and *Hero* (Zhang Yimou, Hong Kong/China, 2004).

Perhaps the point is that despite the concern that politically committed filmmakers have had historically for world events, despite the way that cinema itself traversed the world in translation, the cinema century did not produce one world film theory. People's struggles throughout many parts of the world were depicted in moving images entirely without the benefit of Eisenstein and Brecht. But just as we might now look for exceptions to the rule that narrative realism is politically bankrupt (Latin American melodramas and Chinese dissident epics), we might also consider more examples of historical styles, thus opening up the category of political aesthetics by looking, for instance, at stylistic variation within regions of the world. This project might begin, not with the First World, but with the so-called 'postcolonial' world where a social cinema has been interested in residual oppression, but also look at 'post-third-world' spaces where liberation narratives have been updated (Stam and Shohat, 1994).[5] Thus, we might consider the revolutionary rhetoric of the Brazilian experimental short *Ilha das Flores* (*Isle of Flowers*, Jorge Furtado, 1989) alongside the epic Chilean three-part traditionally shot documentary *La batalla de Chile* (*The Battle of Chile*, Patricio Guzmán 1975; 1977; 1979) (López, 1990). The most experimental and loose Francophone African film *Touki-Bouki* (Djibril Diop Mambéty, Senegal, 1973) could be considered in relation to the classically constructed and tight *Black Girl* (Ousmane Sembene, France/Senegal, 1965). As for the premises of Western counter-cinema, this approach still needs to be explored and tested on such forgotten anti-realist and anti-continuity editing experiments as Peter Watkins' *Culloden* (UK, 1964) or the newer work of Austrian dismantler Martin Arnold such as *Alone: Life Wastes Andy Hardy* (Austria, 1998) and *Deanimated* (Austria, 2000), which erases the images in the 1941 Hollywood horror film, *Invisible Ghost* (Joseph H. Lewis, US).

'Reality is what happens in a factory, in a school, in the barracks, in a prison, in a police station', is of course not an answer to the question of cinema and the visibility of social reality, but it does lead us back to the historical origins of 'Cinema/Ideology/Criticism' with which we are still engaged. Whether we argue that reality produces or is made to produce its own critique, with or without cinema, the question of which class 'can' and will be responsible for social transformation stands behind this philosophical issue. But the legacy of Marxist theory we hear echoed in the French philosopher's

statement from the moment following May 1968, is under review. We now ask, for instance, how 'class' has been differently theorized in China and Russia, and in Western Marxism before and after 1989, since the most comprehensive way to grasp 'lived realities' in any given social formation has been to ask the question of class. Perhaps in the post-1989 moment we can argue with more confidence, following Stanley Aronowitz, that classes are always historical. And thus, with him, start again from the standpoint that: 'Saying classes are historical means that their composition changes at every level of the social structure – ruling groups as well as subordinate groups. *Classes form when they make historical difference*' (2003: 38, my italics; see also James and Berg, 1995).

The mandate for reviewing and renewing the political expectations of film theory comes from a radically revised post-Cold War world historical picture. Perhaps today, in the interests of a one-world film theory, we are called upon to ask more about historically situated classes as we ask about the political reality of, for instance, the police station as the site of social upheaval. The international circulation of popular genres challenges the earlier approach to reading texts for what they say about historical ideologies, where historical situation was local rather than global. Once we might have analyzed *Fort Apache, the Bronx* (Daniel Petrie, US, 1981) in relation to an ideology of racism, the western genre and its Native American genocide displaced onto a modern New York City police station under siege. In contrast, analyzing a Hong Kong police thriller film such as *Die xue shuang xiong* (*The Killer*, John Woo, 1989), might require an understanding of the ideology of chivalry and the Chinese martial arts tradition with reference to *wu xia* fiction (see Bordwell, 2000). But also a political reading would look for the figuration of existing Hong Kong capitalism and anxiety about Communism before the 1997 handover of the former Crown colony to the People's Republic of China. But this approach is taxed when the international mixture of genres and traditions, once an implicit widely-practiced borrowing, becomes explicit, and now a travelling from East to West rather than via the old route in which Hollywood 'exported' popular ideologies to the world. Consider, for instance, how *The Departed* (Martin Scorsese, US/Hong Kong, 2006), an American adaptation of the Hong Kong thriller, *Infernal Affairs* (Andrew Lau and Alan Wak, 2002), won Academy awards in so many categories, the most important of which was best adaptation from existing material. Thus, the earlier question of the gangster genre structure, the critique of capitalism as family business and ethnicized class mobility does not tell us enough about *The Departed* with its undeniable Hong Kong origins, which are themselves already both Chinese and American. *The Departed*, this pronounced cultural composite, owes its narrative structure as much to an older Chinese understanding of honour and the violent dance of two mutually admiring, perfectly matched heroes, as it does to the familial obligations of American capitalism via the gangster genre. The striking structural difference between the two is in the figuration of the vertical hierarchy and strict loyalties of the Hong Kong police force which, transported to Boston, is both instituted and broken down, crossed by familial loyalties and challenged by entrepreneurial survivalism.

But film theory must now, and is now following, as it must, a phenomenon that outdistances it – the traffic in film titles over the World Wide Web. So the question of social structures mixed and modified is speeded up as these ideologies embedded in genres are trafficked. Back and forth and back and forth, the vertical Chinese relationships of respect are exported, but broken down in translation, built up in the West only to be broken down as the new narrative is returned to Asia, but the Hong Kong thriller and the American gangster film now travel together, their two capitalisms intertwined. If there is a new political expectation placed on the critique, it would be the imperative to follow the ideological traffic.

NOTES

1 Critiques of various aspects of realism first published the 1970s, and texts that influenced them at the time, include; Barthes (1977); Brecht (1974); Hall (1981); Heath (1975–76); Jameson (1990); MacCabe (1978–79); Wollen (1972; 1976). Already rethinking the critique in the 1980s were Klinger (1984); MacCabe (1985); Ryan and Kellner (1988); Sklar (1988). For a more recent review, see Williams (2000).

2 Relevant writing on documentary includes Juhasz (1999); López (1990); Nichols (1991; 1995); Renov (2004).

3 Wollen has almost 'lifted' the quotation but also managed to change the original description of *The Bicycle Thief*: 'No more actors, no more story, no more sets, which is to say that in the perfect illusion of reality there is no more cinema' (Bazin, 1971: 60).

4 On the Fifth Generation and Chinese cinema, see Berry (ed.) (1991); Chow (1995); Pickowicz (1993); Yau (1995); Zhen (2004).

5 Also relevant here is the debate about 'Third Cinema', inspired in part by the work of Frantz Fanon (1963) and Wallerstein (1995) as well as filmmaker-theorists like Solanas and Getino (1976) (see also Burton, 1986). The term 'Third Cinema' was coined by Jim Pines and Paul Willemen (1989).

REFERENCES

Adorno, Theodor and Horkheimer, Max (1979) *Dialectic of Enlightenment*. London: Verso.

Aronowitz, Stanley (2003) *How Class Works: Power and Social Movements*. New Haven, CT: Yale University Press.

Althusser, Louis (1969) *For Marx*. Tr. Ben Brewster. London: Verso.

Althusser, Louis (1979) *Reading Capital*. Tr. Ben Brewster. London: Verso.

Bad Object Choices (1991) *How Do I Look? Queer Film and Video*. Seattle: Bay Press.

Barthes, Roland (1977) *Image, Music, Text*. Tr. Stephen Heath. New York: Hill and Wang.

Baudry, Jean-Louis (1974) 'Writing/Fiction/Ideology', *Afterimage*, 5: 22–39.

Baudry, Jean-Louis (1986a) 'Ideological Effects of the Basic Apparatus', in Philip Rosen, (ed.), *Narrative, Apparatus, Ideology: A Film Theory Reader*. New York: Columbia University Press. pp. 286–98.

Baudry, Jean-Louis (1986b) 'The Apparatus', in Philip Rosen (ed.), *Narrative, Apparatus, Ideology: A Film Theory Reader*. New York: Columbia University Press. pp. 299–318.

Bazin, André (1967) *What is Cinema? Vol.1*. Ed. and tr. Hugh Gray. Berkeley: University of California Press.

Bazin, André (1971) *What is Cinema? Vol.2.* Ed. and tr. Hugh Gray. Berkeley: University of California Press.

Berry, Chris (ed.) (1991) *Perspectives on Chinese Cinema.* London: BFI.

Bordwell, David (2000) *Planet Hong Kong.* Cambridge, MA: Harvard University Press.

Brecht, Bertolt (1964) *Brecht on Theatre.* Tr. John Willett. New York: Hill and Wang.

Brecht, Bertolt (1974) 'A Small Contribution to the Theme of Realism', Screen, 15(2): 45–8.

Browne, Nick (ed.) (1990) *Cahiers du cinéma, 1969–72: The Politics of Representation.* Cambridge, MA: Harvard University Press.

Burton, Julianne (ed.) (1986) *Cinema and Social Change in Latin America: Conversations with Filmmakers.* Austin: University of Texas Press.

Cahiers du Cinéma (1980) '*Morocco*', in Peter Baxter (ed.), *Sternberg*. London: BFI. pp. 81–93.

Casetti, Francesco (1999) *Theories of Cinema, 1945–1995.* Tr. Francesca Chiostri, Elizabeth Gard Bartolini-Salimbeni and Thomas Kelso. Austin: University of Texas Press.

Chow, Rey (1995) *Primitive Passions: Visuality, Sexuality, Ethnography, and Contemporary Chinese Cinema.* New York: Columbia University Press.

Chow, Rey (2000) 'Digging an Old Well: The Labor of Social Fantasy in a Contemporary Chinese Film', in Christine Gledhill and Linda Williams (eds), *Reinventing Film Studies.* London: Arnold. pp. 402–18.

Clover, Carol (1992) *Men, Women, and Chainsaws.* Princeton, NJ: Princeton University Press.

Comolli, Jean-Louis and Narboni, Jean (1969) 'Cinéma, idéologie, critique', *Cahiers du cinéma,* 216: 11–15.

Comolli, Jean-Louis and Narboni, Jean (1971) 'Cinema/Ideology/Criticism', Screen, 12(1): 131–144.

Comolli, Jean-Louis and Narboni, Jean (1976) 'Cinema/Ideology/Criticism', in Bill Nichols (ed.), *Movies and Methods, Vol.1.* Berkeley: University of California Press. pp. 22–30.

Derrida, Jacques (1980) *Writing and Difference.* Tr. Alan Bass. Chicago: University of Chicago Press.

Donald, James and Donald, Stephanie Hemelryk (2000) 'The Publicness of Cinema', in Christine Gledhill and Linda Williams (eds), *Reinventing Film Studies.* London: Arnold. pp. 114–29.

Dyer, Richard (1997) *White.* London: Routledge.

Eisenstein, Sergei (1988) *Selected Works, Vol. I: Writings, 1922–1934.* Tr. Richard Taylor. Bloomington: Indiana University Press.

Eisenstein, Sergei (1992) *Selected Works, Vol. II: Towards a Theory of Montage.* Ed. Richard Taylor and Michael Glenny. Tr. Michael Glenny. Bloomington: Indiana University Press.

Elsaesser, Thomas (1992) 'Tales of Sound and Fury: Observations on the Family Melodrama', in Gerald Mast, Marshall Cohen and Leo Braudy (eds), *Film Theory and Criticism.* 4th edn. New York: Oxford University Press. pp. 512–35.

Fanon, Franz (1963) *The Wretched of the Earth.* New York: Grove Press.

Fischer, Lucy (ed.) (1991) *Imitation of Life.* New Brunswick, NJ: Rutgers University Press.

Foucault, Michel (1977) 'Intellectuals and Power: A Conversation between Michel Foucault and Gilles Deleuze', in *Language, Counter-Memory, Practice.* Tr. Donald Bouchard and Sherry Simon. Ithaca, NY: Cornell University Press. pp. 205–17.

Gaines, Jane M. (2000) 'Dream/Factory', in Christine Gledhill and Linda Williams (eds), *Reinventing Film Studies.* London: Arnold. pp. 100–13.

Gledhill, Christine (1987) 'The Melodramatic Field: An Investigation', in Christine Gledhill (ed.), *Home is Where the Heart Is.* London: British Film Institute. pp. 5–39.

Godmilow, Jill (2002) 'Kill the Documentary as We Know It', *Journal of Film and Video,* 54(2–3): 3–10.

Hall, Stuart (1981) 'Notes on Deconstructing "The Popular"', in Raphael Samuel (ed.), *People's History and Socialist Theory.* Boston: Routledge & Kegan Paul. pp. 227–49.

Harvey, Sylvia (1979) *May '68 and Film Culture.* London: BFI.

Heath, Stephen (1975–6) 'From Brecht to Film: Theses, Problems', Screen, 16(4): 34–5.

James, David and Berg, Rick (eds) (1995) *The Hidden Foundation: Film and the Question of Class.* Minneapolis: University of Minnesota Press.

Jameson, Fredric (1990) 'Class and Allegory in Contemporary Mass Culture: *Dog Day Afternoon* as a Political Film', in *Signatures of the Visible.* New York: Routledge. pp. 35–54.

Johnston, Claire (1976) 'Notes on Women's Cinema', in Bill Nichols (ed.), *Movies and Methods, Vol.1.* Berkeley: University of California Press. pp. 208–17.

Juhasz, Alexandra (1999) 'They Said We Were Trying to Show Reality – All I Want to Show is My Video: The Politics of Realist Feminist Documentary', in Jane Gaines and Michael Renov (eds), *Collecting Visible Evidence.* Minneapolis: University of Minnesota Press. pp. 190–215.

Klinger, Barbara (1984) 'Cinema/Ideology/Criticism Revisited: The Progressive Text', Screen, 25(1): 36–41.

Kracauer, Siegfried (1947) *From Caligari to Hitler: A Psychological History of the German Film.* Princeton, NJ: Princeton University Press.

Kracauer, Siegfried (1997) *Theory of Film: The Redemption of Physical Reality.* Princeton, NJ: Princeton University Press.

López, Ana (1990) '*The Battle of Chile*: Documentary, Political Process, and Representation', in Julianne Burton (ed.), *The Social Documentary in Latin America.* Pittsburgh: University of Pittsburgh Press. pp. 267–87.

López, Ana (2000) 'Facing Up to Hollywood', in Christine Gledhill and Linda Williams (eds), *Reinventing Film Studies.* London: Arnold. pp. 419–37.

MacCabe, Colin (1978-9) 'The Discursive and the Ideological in Film: Notes on the Condition of Political Intervention', *Screen*, 19(4): 29–44.

MacCabe, Colin (1985) 'Class of '68: Elements of an Intellectual Autobiography, 1967-1981', in *Tracking the Signifier: Theoretical Essays: Film, Linguistics, Literature.* Minneapolis: University of Minnesota Press. pp. 1–32.

Macherey, Pierre (1978) *A Theory of Literary Production.* Tr. Geoffrey Wall. London: Routledge & Kegan Paul.

Marx, Karl and Engels, Friedrich (1970) *The German Ideology.* Ed. C.J. Arthur. New York: International Publishers.

McDougall, Bonnie S. (ed.) (1991) *The Yellow Earth.* Hong Kong: Chinese University Press.

Mulvey, Laura (1975) 'Visual Pleasure and Narrative Cinema', *Screen*, 16(3): 6–18.

Nichols, Bill (1991) *Representing Reality: Issues and Concepts in Documentary.* Bloomington: Indiana University Press.

Nichols, Bill (1995) '*Strike*', in David James and Rick Berg (eds), *The Hidden Foundation: Film and the Question of Class.* Minneapolis: University of Minnesota Press. pp. 72–89.

Pickowicz, Paul (1993) 'Melodramatic Representation and the "May Fourth" Tradition of Chinese Cinema', in Ellen Widmer and David Der-Wei Wang (eds), *From May Fourth to June Fourth – Fiction and Film in Twentieth Century China.* Cambridge, MA: Harvard University Press. pp. 295–326.

Pines, Jim and Willeman, Paul (eds) (1989) *Questions of Third Cinema.* London: BFI.

Pleynet, Marcellin and Thibaudeau, Jean (1979) 'Economical – Ideological – Formal', interview by Gérard Leblanc, in Sylvia Harvey, *May '68 and Film Culture.* Tr. Elias Noujaim. London: BFI. pp. 149–70.

Renov, Michael (2004) *The Subject of Documentary.* Minneapolis: University of Minnesota Press.

Richter, Hans (1986) *The Struggle for the Film.* Tr. Ben Brewster. New York: St. Martin's Press.

Rodowick, D.N. (1988) *The Crisis of Political Modernism: Criticism and Ideology in Contemporary Film Theory.* Urbana: University of Illinois Press.

Rosen, Philip (2001) *Change Mummified: Cinema, Historicity, Theory.* Minneapolis: University of Minnesota Press.

Ryan, Michael and Kellner, Douglas (1988) *Camera Politica: The Politics and Ideology of Contemporary Cinema and History.* Bloomington: Indiana University Press.

Sklar, Robert (1988) 'Oh! Althusser! Historiography and the Rise of Cinema Studies', *Radical History Review*, 41: 10–35.

Solanas, Ferdinand and Getino, Octavio (1976) 'Towards a Third Cinema', in Bill Nichols (ed.), *Movies and Methods, Vol.1.* Berkeley: University of California Press. pp. 44–64.

Spivak, Gayatri (1999) *A Critique of Postcolonial Reason.* Cambridge, MA: Harvard University Press.

Stam, Robert and Shohat, Ella (1994) *Unthinking Eurocentrism: Multiculturalism and the Media.* London: Routledge.

Vertov, Dziga (1984) *Kino-Eye: The Writings of Dziga Vertov.* Ed. Annette Michelson. Tr. Kevin O'Brien. Berkeley: University of California Press.

Wallerstein, Immanuel (1995) 'Revolution as Strategy', in *After Liberalism.* New York: The New Press. pp. 210–8.

Waugh, Tom (ed.) *'Show Us Life': Toward a History and Aesthetics of the Committed Documentary.* Metuchen, NJ: Scarecrow Press.

White, Patricia (1999) *UnInvited: Classical Hollywood Cinema and Lesbian Representability.* Bloomington: Indiana University Press.

Willeman, Paul (1989) 'The Third Cinema Question: Notes and Reflections', in Jim Pines and Paul Willeman (eds), *Questions of Third Cinema.* London: BFI. pp. 1–29.

Williams, Christopher (2000) 'After the Classic, the Classical and Ideology: The Differences of Realism', in Christine Gledhill and Linda Williams (eds), *Reinventing Film Studies.* London: Arnold. pp. 206–20.

Williams, Linda (2001) *Playing the Race Card.* Berkeley: University of California Press.

Winston, Brian (1995) *Claiming the Real: The Documentary Film Revisited.* London: British Film Institute.

Wollen, Peter (1969) *Signs and Meaning in the Cinema.* Bloomington: Indiana University Press.

Wollen, Peter (1972) 'Godard and Counter Cinema: *Vent D'Est*', *Afterimage*, 4: 6–16.

Wollen, Peter (1976) 'Two Avant-Gardes', *Edinburgh 76 Magazine*, 1: 77–85.

Yau, Esther C. (1991) '*Yellow Earth*: Western Analysis and a Non-Western Text', in Chris Berry (ed.), *Perspectives on Chinese Cinema*. London: BFI. pp. 62–79.

Yau, Esther C. (1995) 'Compromised Liberation: The Politics of Class in Chinese Cinema of the Early 1950s', in David James and Rick Berg (eds), *The Hidden Foundation: Film and the Question of Class*. Minneapolis: University of Minnesota Press. pp. 138–71.

Zavattini, Cesare (1970) *Zavattini: Sequences from Cinematic Life*. Tr. William Weaver. Englewood Cliffs, NJ: Prentice-Hall.

Zavattini, Cesare (1979) *Neorealismo ecc.* Milan: Bompiani.

Zhen, Ni (2004) *Memoirs from the Beijing Film Academy: The Genesis of China's Fifth Generation*. Tr. Chris Berry. Durham, NC: Duke University Press.

24

'We Do Not Die Twice': Realism and Cinema

George Kouvaros

In her introduction to the anthology *Rites of Realism*, Ivone Margulies begins by posing a difficult set of questions: 'How can one recall an event's concrete peculiarity or reproduce its original urgency through a medium that so clearly defers? ... How is one to grant a corporeal weight to faces, places, and events through a medium that can imply but lacks depth?' (2003: 1). The difficult thing about these questions, Margulies adds, is the way they open up a set of issues that constitute a defining moment for Film Studies, the debates on realism and cinema that occurred during the 1970s. In these debates, realism came to stand for something both more and less than a set of aesthetic styles or filmmaking traditions. It served as shorthand for a range of approaches in which the mediating role of the filmmaking process was ignored for the sake of an ideologically inflected view of cinema as a 'window on the world'. In their 1969 editorial statement, 'Cinéma, idéologie, critique' (1999), the editors of *Cahiers du cinéma*, Jean-Louis Comolli and Jean Narboni, drew on the work of the French Marxist philosopher, Louis

Althusser, to frame the argument against realism. ' "[R]eality" ', they declare,

> is nothing but an expression of the prevailing ideology. Seen in this light, the classic theory of cinema that the camera is an impartial instrument which grasps, or rather is impregnated by, the world in its 'concrete reality' is an eminently reactionary one. What the camera in fact registers is the vague, unformulated, untheorized, unthought-out world of the dominant ideology. (1999: 755)[1]

These comments served both to ignite discussions on the ideological implications of different styles of filmic representation and, at the same time, marginalize a tradition of writing on cinema focusing on its realist dimensions. Referring to such diverse figures as John Grierson, Béla Balázs, Siegfried Kracauer and André Bazin as part of a tradition may be implying too direct an affiliation between differing positions; yet what links this group is their belief in cinema's unique ability to provide us with access to a pro-filmic event *and* a fundamental rejection of that – ideologically tainted notion identified by Comolli and Narboni of the camera as an impartial instrument. The coexistence of these principles highlights how far their work differs from the characterization of classic theory provided by Comolli and Narboni. It also explains why the recent reconsideration of their work has coincided with a rejection of one of the most canonical distinctions of 1970s film theory, the opposition between realism and modernism. Ian Aitken, for example, frames the work of Grierson, Kracauer and Bazin in terms of an 'intuitionist modernist and realist tradition' influenced by German idealist philosophy, romanticism, phenomenology and the work of the Frankfurt School writers (2001: 1). The common strand of this tradition is not a naïve belief in the impartiality of cinematic representation, but rather a concern with cinema's ability to reveal underlying aspects, things hidden from view or unavailable otherwise. While this does not constitute a new agenda for art, it does serve as a useful starting-point for questioning the distinction between realism and modernism, a debate taken up also in Chapter 22 and Chapter 23 of this volume.

More synoptic in its intentions than the work of Aitken, this chapter also seeks to play a part in the return to realism. It will do so by, first, reviewing how the discussion of realism came to be figured in such negative terms. As I shall show, this negative characterization was the result not of a misreading of a particular body of work but rather a situating of realism within larger critical and institutional agendas. The other thing I want to do is give a sense of the way current writing on realism has been shaped by work done in other fields, most notably, that of nineteenth-century visual culture and modernity. The work of writers such as Linda Nochlin, Jonathan Crary and Mary Ann Doane has helped form an approach to realism defined not as an attempt to show 'things as they are', but rather grounded in moments of sensory experience in which the contingency and finitude of everyday life is brought to the fore. I will highlight how this emphasis plays a central part in the writings of film realism's most influential exemplar, André Bazin. The decision to focus on Bazin is based on both his totemic status in discussions of film and the way his various critical texts on post-war cinema helped set the terms for the return to realism. More generally, a focus on Bazin can illustrate the value of examining theoretical concepts through a close engagement with a range of different film texts.

FILM AND IDEOLOGY

One reason why 'Cinéma, idéologie, critique' has been so influential is that the authors go beyond stating positions concerning the link between film and ideology. More important in terms of the activity of criticism, they also outline seven filmic categories that can be used to distinguish and make sense of the various relationships between cinema and its ideological functions. The first and by far the largest of these categories consists of films that Comolli and Narboni claim 'are imbued through and through with the dominant ideology in pure and unadulterated form, and give no indication that their makers were even aware of the fact' (1999: 755). The authors clarify they 'are not just talking about so-called "commercial" films. The *majority* of films in all categories are the unconscious instruments of the ideology which produces them' (1999: 755). These unself-conscious transmitters of ideology are grouped together under the category of 'bourgeois realism': 'Nothing in these films jars against the ideology or the audience's mystification by it. They are very reassuring for audiences for there is no difference between the ideology they meet every day and the ideology on the screen' (1999: 756). Rather than explaining exactly how such films serve as vessels for ideology, Comolli and Narboni end their discussion by flagging the need 'for film critics to look into the way the ideological system and its products merge at all levels' (1999: 756).

During the early 1970s, a number of film scholars writing in the journal *Screen* and its sister publication at the Society for Education in Film and Television, *Screen Education*, built on the work of Comolli and Narboni by examining the connection between dominant cinematic forms and broader political issues. At stake was both an understanding of realism's ideological functioning and a larger issue concerning the possibility of a progressive form of cinematic critique involving both theorists and filmmakers. As well as drawing inspiration from the work of Comolli and Narboni, these writings were informed by a close reading of the work of the German playwright Bertolt Brecht, in particular, his account of the aesthetic and political implications of realism as a literary practice. In 'Against Georg Lukács' Brecht writes: 'Realism is an issue not only for literature: it is a major political, philosophical and practical issue and must be handled and explained as such' (1974: 45). Colin MacCabe echoes Brecht's estimation when he notes: 'The problems of realism occur in an acute and critical form in the cinema and perhaps no single topic concentrates so many of the developments that have taken place in film theory' (1976: 7–8). The outcome of this endeavour by a number of film scholars was that critical object of attraction and repulsion *par excellence*, the 'classic realist text'. And, for a time, the possibilities and scope of a radical film theory seemed to hinge on the way this term was understood and theorized. As well as the work of MacCabe, mention should also be made of the work of Stephen Heath, Thierry Kuntzel and Raymond Bellour. For these writers, the fascination of Hollywood cinema is based on its articulation of a textual system in which psychic processes find expression through the structuring devices and repetitions of classical narrative film. For these writers, also, it is only by stopping the flow of the narrative and carefully unpacking how these devices and repetitions affirm a particular type of subject position that an understanding of classical Hollywood realism can be achieved.[2]

Despite the differences in approach, a common point of reference across the work on classical Hollywood film is an explicit connection between the structuring principles of narrative cinema and the operation

of the nineteenth-century novel. Using the nineteenth-century novel as a point of reference, MacCabe defines the classic realist text 'as one in which there is a hierarchy amongst the discourses which compose the text and this hierarchy is defined in terms of an empirical notion of truth' (1974: 8). MacCabe takes as his example the novels of George Eliot, in which an authorial metalanguage works to explain and arbitrate between the various discourses that make up the narrative: 'Transparent in the sense that the metalanguage is not regarded as material; it is dematerialised to achieve perfect representation – to let the identity of things shine through the window of words' (1974: 8). MacCabe believes that this claim to 'direct access to a final reality' is also one of the great lures of realist cinema (1974: 10). In the case of film, however, the establishment of a position of knowledge is less likely to occur through a form of authorial commentary than through the camera's tendency to align itself with the point of view of certain characters:

> Through the knowledge we gain from the narrative we can split the discourses of the various characters from their situation and compare what is said in these discourses with what has been revealed to us through narration. The camera shows us what happens – it tells the truth against which we can measure the discourses. (MacCabe, 1974: 10)

Using Alan J. Pakula's film *Klute* (US, 1971) as an example, McCabe shows how a rigid hierarchy of discourses underpins the film's patriarchal logic and locates the spectator in a position of knowledge. McCabe claims that, while the narrative tracks the gradual awareness of the central female character, Bree Daniels (Jane Fonda), the dominant source of narrative knowledge and authority is the male detective, John Klute (Donald Sutherland):

> Far from being a film which goes any way to portraying a woman liberated from male definition (a common critical response), *Klute* exactly guarantees that the real essence of a woman can only be discovered and defined by a man. (1974: 11)

This guarantee rests on the film's ability to align its own processes and structures with the point of view of the central male character while also making this process invisible – turning it into simply a matter of showing things as they are. Despite the synoptic nature of MacCabe's discussion of the film, he goes on to extrapolate a fundamental principle: 'The unquestioned nature of the narrative discourse entails that the only problem that reality poses is to go and look and see what *Things* there *are*. The relationship between the reading subject and the real is placed as one of pure specularity. The real is not articulated – it is' (1974: 12).

For MacCabe and a number of other writers engaged in the discussions on realism, the necessary next step in the process of critique was to identify alternative strategies for filmmakers to follow that could circumvent, redirect or question the ideological functioning of bourgeois realism. This involved marrying progressive content with a model of narration in which the spectator is no longer inscribed in a privileged position of knowledge, but is made aware of their place in the production of meaning. 'It is this emphasis on the reader as producer', notes MacCabe in relation to *Tout va bien* (Jean-Luc Godard/Jean-Pierre Gorin, Italy/France, 1972), 'which suggests that these films do not just offer a different representation for the subject but a different set of relations to both the fictional material and "reality"' (1974: 25). In a slightly later piece, MacCabe expands on the implication of this shift in the spectator's relation to represented content:

> The film-maker must draw the viewer's attention to his or her relation to the screen in order to make him or her 'realise' the social relations that are being portrayed. Inversely one could say that it is the 'strangeness' of the social relations displayed which draws the viewer's attention to the fact that he or she is watching a film. (1976: 25)

REALISM OF THE BODY

Since the mid-1970s, a number of writers, including MacCabe himself, have sought to address some of the problems associated with the critique of realism.[3] Central to this

process has been a re-examination of the opposition between modernism and realism. The outcome of this heavily loaded opposition was a highly prescriptive account of the relationship between ideology and aesthetic form. In their overview of the debates on cinematic realism, Dick Hebdige and Geoff Hurd criticize the implication that certain narrative structures are intrinsically progressive or reactionary, as both essentialist and bound to a formalism in which 'the only cinematic practices which can be endorsed … are avant-garde ones' (1978: 72). In her own reading of the debates on realism, Margulies reiterates this general complaint.

> [I]t was only in the 1970s that formal strategies such as the foregrounding of surface flatness, the visible integrity of the shot, and breaks with cinematic verisimilitude … gained an overblown critical (and moral) valence. Conversely, any reading attentive to the reality in front of the camera, to the materiality shared by actor and individual, by a specific place and a dramatic setting, was somehow compromised by the illusory pull of verisimilitude. (2003: 8)

It is important to understand the nature of Margulies' complaint and her desire to look again at issues of realism and film. Margulies wants to re-prioritize cinema's ability to give weight to a world of bodies and things – in other words, its complex referential function rather than just its capacity for formal reflection. Hence, the essays collected in *Rites of Realism* tend to focus on films that have a documentary element – not because this makes the films more truthful, but rather because such films have a tendency to bring the encounter between film and what it represents more clearly into view. As Margulies explains in relation to the first part of the book's title, '[T]he title word *rites* is meant to invoke the ritual connotation of representations that have actual effects on reality and in particular the reality of profilmic bodies' (2003: 1–2).

In defining the project of cinematic realism around issues of corporeality, Margulies pays tribute to a, by now, long history of scholarship concerned with issues of bodily engagement. In Film Studies, this work on the body occurred in close proximity to a number of other theoretical investigations concerning film form, spectatorship and gender. More than anything else, this work put paid to the notion of a disembodied spectator-subject who is guaranteed a position of mastery through their interpolation in the narrative. In place of this discredited notion, Margulies prioritizes a realist aesthetic based on a 'shared physicality' linking actor and spectator (2003: 4). It is this emphasis that runs through the various essays collected in Margulies' anthology. Taken as a whole, these essays give a good indication of the range of topics that, in one way or another, constitute the emerging paradigm of film realism.

The work on the body in cinema also serves as a meeting-point for another area of scholarly research closely linked to the current reinvestment of realism, namely, the study of nineteenth-century visual culture. In her overview of the visual arts during the nineteenth century, Linda Nochlin offers a reading of realism quite different from the way this term operated in film debates in the early 1970s. For Nochlin, realism's organizing principle was not a search for a 'transparent style ... or mirror image of visual reality', but rather the prioritizing of phenomena over and above the dictates of pre-existing schemata (1971: 14). She quotes Edgar Degas' invocation in his notebooks regarding potential subjects:

> Do every kind of worn object ... corsets which have just been taken off ... series on instruments and instrumentalists .... On the bakery, the bread: series on journeyman bakers, seen in the cellar itself or through the air vents from the street .... No one has ever done monuments or houses from below, from beneath, up close, as one sees them going by in the streets. (1971: 19)

Degas' comments capture the sense of a new range of subjects opening up to the artist and also a new way of representing these subjects 'from below, from beneath, up close, as one sees them going by in the streets'. For Degas, the task of art is to render the activities and places of everyday life disturbed from their traditional sureties – everyday life as fleeting, caught on the run, impermanent.

As Nochlin writes about the representation of movement in Degas' *Dancer on the Stage* (1878):

> Realist motion is always motion captured as it is 'now', as it is perceived in a flash of vision.... Degas showed no interest in conveying any ideal image of movement but concentrated on creating the equivalent of a concrete instant of perceived temporal fact – an isolated moment.... The appearance of a single moment is painted from a viewpoint which makes its discreteness, its lack of significant compositional or psychological focus most apparent. (1971: 29–31)

Nochlin notes that in Degas' work, '[t]ime is seen as the arrester of significance not – as in traditional art – the medium in which it unfolds' (1971: 31).

In Nochlin's account of realism, the viewer is brought face-to-face with the instability of a world caught on the run. She traces a direct link between realism's concern with the flow of life and the later work of the Impressionists. 'The "instantaneity" of the Impressionists', she writes,

> is 'contemporaneity' taken to its ultimate limits .... No doubt photography helped to create this identification of the contemporary with the instantaneous. But, in a deeper sense, the image of the random, the changing, the impermanent and unstable seemed closer to the experienced qualities of present-day reality than the imagery of the stable, the balanced, the harmonious. (1971: 28)

This account of changes in the perception and representation of everyday life during the nineteenth century is taken further in the work of Jonathan Crary. In a number of separate studies, Crary uses developments in the visual arts to track broader shifts in models of subjective vision. According to Crary, it was during the first half of the nineteenth century that a new set of discourses and practices of vision emerged that 'effectively broke with a classical regime of visuality and grounded the truth of vision in the density and materiality of the body' (1994: 21). He goes on to observe: 'One of the consequences of this shift was that the functioning of vision became dependent on the contingent physiological makeup of the observer, thus rendering vision faulty, unreliable, and even, it was argued, arbitrary' (1994: 21). Crary's exemplar of this new type of vision is the French Impressionist painter, Edouard Manet. For Crary manet's importance is based less on his status 'as an emblematic figure supporting some of the most dominant accounts of modernism, and more as one of a number of thinkers about vision in the late 1870s' (1994: 27).

The cumulative effect of the work done on nineteenth-century visual culture by scholars such as Nochlin and Crary, as well as others working more directly in the field of Film Studies, has been the development of a sophisticated understanding of the impact of modernity's emergence in a number of different contexts. It now seems clear that cinema's appearance at the end of the nineteenth century was less a bold new development than the crystallization of a range of developments and ideas about time, contingency and everyday life already at work elsewhere. In order to understand the way this work helped reshape debates on realism, we need to look more closely at how these notions connect with the capacity of the cinematic image not simply to represent a sense of material contingency, but to make it present on screen.

One writer whose work has been central to forging this connection is Mary Ann Doane. Referring to a range of different developments occurring at the end of the nineteenth century, Doane identifies a fundamental change in the conception of time. The diffusion of watches, the development of assembly-line practices and the demands for a greater synchronization of labour provide evidence of a drive to abstract and control time: 'No longer a medium in which the human subject is situated (it is no longer *lived* or experienced in quite the same way), time is externalized and must be consulted' (2002: 7). This pressure to rationalize and control time had the inevitable consequence of a growing fascination with instances that escape or undermine this effort. Doane points to Impressionism as 'the concerted attempt to fix a moment, to grasp it as, precisely, fugitive' (2002: 10).

Another area where this drive to fix a moment is evident is in the field of photography. Doane describes photography as 'the culmination of a tendency in the history of art that rejects the general, the ideal, and the schematic and focuses upon the particular, the singular, the unique, the contingent. Photography is allied with a "thisness", a certainty in the absolute representability of things and moments' (2002: 10). Photography's unique relationship to the singular stems from its indexicality. Referring to the work of Charles Sanders Peirce on different sign systems, Doane explains how indexical signs manifest a particular relation to their referents:

> Unlike icons and symbols, which rely upon association by resemblance or intellectual operations, the work of the index depends upon association by contiguity (the foot touches the ground and leaves a trace, the wind pushes the weathercock, the pointing finger indicates an adjoining site, the light rays reflected from the object 'touch' the film). The object is made 'present' to the addressee. (2002: 92)

This ability to make the object 'present' underpins not just the history of photography, but also the early history of motion pictures. As testified by the dominance of the 'actualities' during the first decades of production, cinema revelled in its capacity to make the most ephemeral and passing aspects of everyday life the subject of a show. 'While photography could fix a moment, the cinema made archievable duration itself. In that sense, it was perceived as a prophylactic against death, ensuring the ability to "see one's loved ones" gesture and smile long after their deaths' (Doane, 2002: 22). Yet, this unique ability also brought with it an experience of time that implied a negation of the subject. The image of the past that returns and is brought back to life in film comes to us as 'past'. Hence, rather than defeating time's passing, the indexical nature of film reaffirms a notion of time as fleeting and non-essential. Referring to the key arguments in Kracauer's 1927 essay on photography, Doane concludes that 'film makes visible not a knowledge of the original but a certain passing temporal configuration' (2002: 23).

In her introduction to Kracauer's *Theory of Film* (1997), Miriam Hansen also gives due weight to the implications of indexicality. For Hansen, rather than leading to 'a naively realist' theory of film, Kracauer's insistence on the cinema's photographic dimension emphasizes film's capacity to displace the world it depicts. She goes on to explain:

> [T]he same indexicality that allows photographic film to record and figure the world also inscribes the image with moments of temporality and contingency that *dis*figure the representation. If Kracauer seeks to ground his film aesthetics in the medium of photography, it is because photographic representation has the perplexing ability not only to resemble the world it depicts but also to render it strange, to destroy habitual fictions of self-identity and familiarity. (1997: xxv)

By highlighting the disturbing implications of indexicality, both Doane and Hansen make important contributions to the rehabilitation of classic film theory and debates on realism more generally. Both writers offer a way of understanding the realist impulse that traverses the work of Kracauer and others not in terms of an affirmation of cinema's fidelity to the world, but rather its capacity to bring forth an encounter with temporal finitude and mortality – what Hansen evocatively terms 'an awareness of a history that does not include us' (1997: xxvi). It is this difficult awareness that provides the best clue yet as to both the specific type of realism that has dominated recent debates on film and why realism, more generally, continues to play a crucial role in Film Studies. As much as it may confuse, alienate and bring back questions we'd rather forget, realism stubbornly insists that we understand cinema not simply in terms of its capacity to reflect on its own internal processes but to also provide us with experience grounded in the uncertainties and impermanence of everyday life.

CHANGE MUMMIFIED

In *Rites of Realism* the figure who clears a path for the possibilities of a newly-defined notion of realism is the influential French critic and co-founder of *Cahiers du cinéma*, André Bazin. Margulies attributes the value of Bazin's work to 'a heightened sense of the eclectic materiality of film' (2003: 2–3). She clarifies the combination of factors central to this approach: 'Images that bear the marks of two heterogeneous realities, the filmmaking process and the filmed event, perfectly illuminate his search for visceral signifiers for the real. And the registered clash of different material orders best defines for him, in turn, that which is specifically cinematic' (2003: 3). For Margulies, it is not just the image's formal qualities, but also its relation to bodies, faces and histories that hold sway in Bazin's writings. She sums up her case thus: 'What interests Bazin are precisely the rough edges of representation, the moment of encounter and productive maladjustment between representation and the actuality of filmmaking' (2003: 4). Margulies' focus on Bazin is linked to a sustained consideration of his work carried on since the writer's early death in 1958. Along with the return to critical favour of Kracauer's *Theory of Film*, the interest in Bazin's writings is the most telling indication of realism's re-emergence as a topic worthy of critical discussion. In the remarks that follow, I want to trace the way his writings hinge upon that ultimate marker of material contingency and human finitude, death. Such an examination can reveal important aspects of Bazin's work and why his work still serves as a touchstone for film theorists engaging with the limits and possibilities of cinematic realism.

As well as containing a number of essays that take Bazin's writings as starting-points, *Rites of Realism* includes a translation of Bazin's 'Death Every Afternoon' (2003), a short but telling account of the ontological implications of Pierre Braunberger's *The Bullfight* (*La Course de taureaux*, France, 1951). Bazin's interest in the film centres on its capacity to engage with the bullfight's 'essential quality, its metaphysical kernel: death'. Bazin goes on to explain: 'The tragic ballet of the bullfight turns around the presence and permanent possibility of death (that of the animal and the man). That is what makes the ring into something more than a theater stage: death is played on it' (2003: 29–30). In Bazin's discussions of cinematic specificity, death claims a special place. Better than anything else, it marks the limit of what cinema can make re-presentable:

> Art of time, cinema has the exorbitant privilege of repeating it, a privilege common to all mechanical arts, but one that it can use with infinitely greater potential than records or radio. Let us be even more precise since there are other temporal arts, like music. But musical time is immediately and by definition aesthetic time, whereas the cinema only attains and constructs its aesthetic time based on lived time, Bergsonian 'durée', which is in essence irreversible and qualitative. The reality that cinema reproduces at will and organizes is the same worldly reality of which we are a part, the sensible continuum out of which the celluloid makes a mold both spatial and temporal. I cannot repeat a single moment of my life, but cinema can repeat any one of these moments indefinitely before my eyes. (Bazin, 2003: 30)

Two moments escape this infinite repeatability and thereby reveal cinema's limiting conditions: 'Like death, love must be experienced and cannot be represented (it is not called the little death for nothing) without violating its nature. This violation is called obscenity. The representation of a real death is also an obscenity, no longer a moral one, as in love, but metaphysical. We do not die twice' (Bazin, 2003: 30). As the ultimate moment of singularity, the passage from life to death is, for Bazin, the event that defines cinema's limit as an art of time. It cannot be re-presented, only experienced. But death has another role to play – not just as limit point, but also as the basis of a preservative obsession. In 'The Ontology of the Photographic Image', Bazin traces this preservative obsession back to the ancient tradition of embalming the dead: 'The religion of ancient Egypt, aimed against death, saw survival as depending on the continued existence of the corporeal body. Thus, by providing a defense against the passage of time it satisfied a basic psychological need in man, for death is but the victory of time' (1967a: 9). This need for a defence against the passage of time underpins the history of

the plastic arts. In contemporary times, it is manifested in the role played by images in practices of memorialization:

> No one believes any longer in the ontological identity of model and image, but all are agreed that the image helps us to remember the subject and to preserve him from a second spiritual death .... It is no longer a question of survival after death, but of a larger concept, the creation of an ideal world in the likeness of the real, with its own temporal destiny. (Bazin, 1967a: 10)

By helping us to remember the subject, representational art forms part of what Bazin describes as a 'primitive need to have the last word in the argument with death by means of the form that endures' (1967a: 10). It is the satisfaction of this need that guides the emergence of photography. The discovery of perspectival representation that allowed artists to create the illusion of three-dimensional space was essentially a distraction. It fed an appetite for illusion that 'bit by bit ... consumed the plastic arts' (1967a: 11). Photography and cinema redeem this fascination with likeness – not because they offer an image that looks more real than a painting, but rather because of the special credibility afforded automatically-produced images:

> The objective nature of photography confers on it a quality of credibility absent from all other picture-making. In spite of any objections our critical spirit may offer, we are forced to accept as real the existence of the object reproduced, actually re-presented, set before us, that is to say, in time and space. Photography enjoys a certain advantage in virtue of this transference of reality from the thing to its reproduction. (Bazin, 1967a: 13–14)

At the end of this paragraph, Bazin inserts an explanatory note, connecting our response to photographs to 'the psychology of relics and souvenirs which likewise enjoy the advantages of a transfer of reality stemming from the "mummy-complex"' (1967a: 14). We need to be clear about what Bazin is proposing. He is not proposing that the photographic image is the thing itself. Rather, he sees in the conditions of its creation the trigger for an ambivalent response. In front of a photograph our knowledge that the image is not the person or thing occurs simultaneously with irrefutable proof of their existence: 'Only a photographic lens can give us the kind of image of the object that is capable of satisfying the deep need man has to substitute for it something more than a mere approximation, a kind of decal or transfer' (Bazin, 1967a: 14). This 'deep need' for something more than an approximation lies at the heart of our attachment to family albums. Bazin describes the fading snapshots gathered in family albums as 'the disturbing presence of lives halted at a set moment in their duration, freed from their destiny; not, however, by the prestige of art but by the power of an impassive mechanical process: for photography does not create eternity, as art does, it embalms time, rescuing it simply from its proper corruption' (1967a: 14).

These last lines are crucial for under-standing Bazin's discussion of the photo-graphic image. While photographs help quell the anxiety caused by time's passing, the temporality of these images actually affirms our helplessness in time. Like the Egyptian mummies that form the basis of a trans-historical obsession, the photographic image gives rise to the realization that the world it preserves is a world that has passed, a world of the dead. It is at this point that Bazin's ontol-ogy of the photographic image most closely resembles Kracauer's position in his essay on photography. Describing the 'blizzard of pho-tographs' found in the illustrated magazines, Kracauer claims that what these photographs 'attempt to banish is the recollection of death, which is part and parcel of every memory image. In the illustrated magazines the world has become a photographable present, and the photographed present has been entirely eternalized' (1995: 59). The downside of this process is an affirmation of time as non-essential. For Kracauer, the reality grasped in the photograph

consists of elements in space whose configuration is so far from necessary that one could just as well imagine a different organization of these elements. Those things once clung to us like our skin, and this is how our property still clings to us today.

Nothing of these contain us, and the photograph gathers fragments around a nothing. (1995: 56)

Bazin does not share Kracauer's interest in exploring the implications of photography for history and memory, nor the way that photography might redeem the abstraction of human experience. Yet, in the work of both writers, we find a subject engaged in a struggle for security and knowledge in the face of a real that includes the threat of time. Philip Rosen draws out the implications of this view of the subject:

Time passing, duration, and change, are exactly what Bazin's ontological subject is driven to dis-avow, for they raise the problem of death. The lure of automatically, produced images is attributable to subjective obsession precisely because time is a threat to the stable existence of the subject as well as the object. Hence, the paradox: automatically produced images are founded from a desire that the concrete be preserved, stopped in time, and this desire leads to the special appeal of cinema, when the subject is led to open itself to a revelatory experience of reality; *but* reality itself evolves in time and is even perceived in time. (2003: 56)

The cinema adds another layer to the ambivalent appeal of automatically-produced images by conferring movement on the image of the past: 'Now, for the first time, the image of things is likewise the image of their duration, change mummified as it were' (Bazin, 1967a: 15). It is on the basis of cinema's ability to enable (and safeguard against) this encounter with time that we can understand both its special appeal and the way issues of textuality and style function in Bazin's writings. The choices and decisions made by the filmmaker serve as the basis of his or her style *and* the mark of a particular encounter with time. As Rosen and others have noted, questions of style for Bazin hinge not on absolutes, but on the myriad ways the cinema renders and abstracts a concrete objective realm that includes time. As Bazin himself puts it in 'An Aesthetic of Reality':

The same event, the same object, can be repre-sented in various ways. Each representation discards or retains various of the qualities that permit us to recognize the object on the screen. Each introduces, for didactic or aesthetic reasons, abstractions that operate more or less corrosively and thus do not permit the original to subsist in its entirety. At the conclusion of this inevitable and necessary 'chemical' action, for the initial reality there has been substituted an illusion of reality composed of a complex of abstraction (black and white, place surface), of conventions (the rules of montage, for example), and of authentic reality. (1971a: 27)

The interlinking of this inevitable abstraction with the deep need for an image of time lies at the heart of Bazin's understanding of cinema's fundamental attraction and his writings on filmic styles. Over and above any fictional subject, it is the inevitably abstract relationship of the filmmaker to (once) living matter that, for Bazin, is the true subject of a film. This is why, in his discussions of Vittorio de Sica's films, Bazin is adamant that in order to explain the films 'we must go back to the source of [De Sica's] art, namely to his tenderness, his love. The quality shared in common by *Miracolo a Milano* [Italy, 1951] and *Ladri di Biciclette* [Italy, 1948], in spite of differences more apparent than real, is De Sica's inexhaustible affection for his characters' (1971b: 69). Affection is what binds the filmmaker to his actors and the characters they perform. In front of the screen, we do not encounter this affection directly, but filtered through an inevitable abstraction. It is how this abstraction incorporates or seeks to deny the implications of the image's temporality that is crucial for assessing both the filmmaker's approach and the spectator's response to the image. In the following remarks, I want to consider how this principle can be applied to other aspects of film practice – aspects such as film performance, for instance. How does Bazin's discussion of film acting relate to his views on realism more generally?

TEMPORAL AVATARS

In his discussion of Roberto Rossellini's treatment of actors, Bazin urges us to understand acting as not simply the simulations of feelings and identities, but as something more direct: that is, acting as the physical manifestation of being.

Rossellini does not make his actors *act*, he doesn't make them express this or that feeling; he compels them only to be a certain way before the camera. In such a *mise en scène*, the respective places of the characters, their ways of walking, their movements on the set, and their gestures have much more importance than the feelings they show on their faces, or even than the words they say. (1997: 138–9)

Bazin underscores this proposition often-quoted claim that, in neorealism, '[i]t is from appearance only, the simple appearance of beings and of the world, that it knows how to deduce the ideas that it unearths. It is a phenomenology' (1971b: 64–5). Neorealism thus affirms a world revealed through the actions and behaviour of individual subjects rather than the exposition of underlying truths. It follows that the task of acting in such an approach is not about linking behaviour to inner truths, but rather about the presentation of states of being. This difference is developed in Bazin's discussion of what he terms 'classic' acting:

According to the classic understanding of this function, inherited from the theater, the actor expresses something: a feeling, a passion, a desire, an idea. From this attitude and his miming the spectator can read his face like an open book. In this perspective, it is agreed implicitly between spectator and actor that the same psychological causes produce the same physical effect and that one can without any ambiguity pass backwards and forwards from one to the other. This is, strictly speaking, what is called acting. (1971b: 65)

The continuity between internal psychological causes and external gesture is central to the readability and coherence of classic acting. The inner world of the character determines the nature of the external gesture; but each determines and legitimates the other. It is from this principle that the structures of the *mise en scène*, shooting and editing are elaborated:

[D]ecor, lighting, the angle and framing of the shots, will be more or less expressionistic in their relation to the behavior of the actor. They contribute for their part to confirm the meaning of the action. Finally, the breaking up of the scenes into shots and their assemblage is the equivalent of an expressionism in time, a reconstruction of the event according to an artificial and abstract duration: dramatic duration. (Bazin, 1971b: 65)

Bazin finishes his exposition by affirming: 'There is not a single one of these commonly accepted assumptions of the film spectacle that is not challenged by neorealism' (1971b: 65). This challenge is first registered on the level of performance. The imperative for the actor to be rather than to express an emotion places an emphasis on external manifestations of comportment, faciality and ways of walking that suggest an existence prior to the commencement of filming. This emphasis on the making present of something pre-existent safeguards against the tendency to expressionistic acting. It also links Bazin's comments on acting to his claims concerning the basis of cinema's special attraction, its ability to give us an image of time.

In Bazin's writings, a key indicator of the consequences of cinema's ambivalent temporality is the body of the actor. Not only does it age before our eyes, but its liveness in the past also affirms death in the future. This is what emerges in Bazin's description of Charlie Chaplin's final speech in *The Great Dictator* (Charles Chaplin, US, 1940):

> In this interminable, yet (in my view) too short scene I remember only the spellbinding tone of a voice and the most disconcerting of metamorphoses. Charlie's lunar mask disappears little by little, corroded by the gradations of the panchromatic stock and betrayed by the nearness of the camera, which intensifies the telescopic effect of the wide screen. Underneath, as if it were a superimposition, appears the face of an already aging man, furrowed here and there by grief, his hair sprinkled with white, the face of Charles Spencer Chaplin. (1971c: 110–111)

For Bazin, the cinematic actor is not simply an imitator but also a temporal avatar whose existence points the way to a future already determined by death.[4] It follows that in a genuinely realist cinema the work of acting would be judged not by its capacity to re-create character, but in terms of its ability to transpose affective states and durations fundamentally different from those which characterize classic acting, in other words, affective states and durations that highlight the contingency and finitude of human existence. Again, death enters Bazin's discussions of cinema's essential qualities as

both an ever-present lure and the thing that marks the limits of what it can show. Serge Daney lists the following as examples of other events that have a similar function: 'Death as rupture, passage par excellence. But just as much everything that simulates death: the sexual act, metamorphosis. More generally, the main nodes of a story, the decisive moments when, under the impassive eye of the camera, something is unraveled, someone changes. Irreversibly' (2003: 38–9). The questions that exercise Bazin's writings and the strand of film criticism that followed in his wake are: How are these limit points registered? What effects do they have on the film in which they occur?

In Bazin's discussion of De Sica's *Umberto D* (Italy, 1952), two scenes stand out as examples of affective states and durations that test the limits of cinema: the scene of Umberto D (Carlo Battisti) going to bed thinking he has a fever and the one immediately following, when Maria (Maria Pia Casilio), the young housemaid, awakens and begins the day's chores. At stake in both scenes is a new kind of drama and a new kind of time made visible through the work of the actor. Bazin begins his account of the first scene by noting that: '[E]xperiments in continuous time are not new in cinema' (1971b: 76). The classic example of such an experiment is Alfred Hitchcock's *Rope* (US, 1948), which runs for eighty minutes without a single visible edit. The presentation of continuous time in *Rope*, however, is subject to a process of segmentation imposed not externally through the editing, but through the segmentations inherent in what Bazin terms 'theatrical time': '*Rope* could be filmed without a change of focus, without any break in the shots, and still provide a dramatic spectacle, because in the original play the incidents were already set in order dramatically according to an artificial time – theatrical time – just as there is musical time and dance time' (1971b: 76).

By replacing the abstract logic of theatrical time with another type of temporal logic, the two scenes from *Umberto D* mark a breakthrough in the presentation of duration in film. 'In these instances it is a matter of making "life time" – the simple continuing to be of a person to whom nothing in particular happens – take on the quality of a spectacle, of a drama' (Bazin, 1971b: 76). In other words, the logic of the drama is determined not by the traditional dramatic requirements of suspense and eventual resolution, but by the durations of the characters' actions wrested free of a larger narrative purpose:

> To put it another way, the subject exists before the working scenario, but it does not exist afterward. Only the 'fact' exists which the subject had itself forecast. If I try to recount the film to someone who has not seen it – for example what Umberto D is doing in his room or the little servant Maria in the kitchen, what is there left for me to describe? An impalpable show of gestures without meaning, from which the person I am talking to cannot derive the slightest idea of the emotion that gripped the viewer. (Bazin, 1971b: 77)

The long scene of *Umberto D* preparing for bed is structured around a number of incidents and encounters that give shape to the drama: his conversation with Maria about his health; the revelation of her pregnancy; the keyhole glimpse of the two adulterers in the room next door; the landlady's threat to evict him; her rejection of partial payment of his rent; the selling of his books to the trader near the building; the accidental intrusion of the landlady's fiancé; the noisy goodbyes of her guests; the closing of the roof of the neighbourhood cinema located just beneath *Umberto D*'s window; and, finally, his failed attempt to set the alarm clock. These events follow one another both logically and temporally. Yet, the attention De Sica pays to each event undercuts our attempt to extract a sense of the story's determining agenda. As Bazin sees it, in De Sica's films 'the real time of the narrative is not that of the drama but the concrete duration of the character' (1971b: 77). Bazin illustrates this notion of 'concrete duration' in his discussion of Maria in the kitchen:

> The camera confines itself to watching her doing her little chores: moving around the kitchen still half asleep, drowning the ants that have invaded the sink, grinding the coffee. The cinema here is conceived as the exact opposite of that 'art of ellipsis' to which we are much too ready to believe

it devoted. Ellipsis is a narrative process; it is logical in nature and so it is abstract as well; it presupposes analysis and choice; it organizes the facts in accord with the general dramatic direction to which it forces them to submit. On the contrary, De Sica and [Cesare] Zavattini attempt to divide the event up into still smaller events and these into events smaller still, to the extreme limits of our capacity to perceive them in time. (1971d: 81)

Bazin notes that whereas 'in a classical film' the narrative event of Maria getting out of bed would take two or three shots, De Sica breaks this basic event into a series of micro-events or actions: '[S]he wakes up; she crosses the hall; she drowns the ants; and so on' (1971d: 81). But these micro-events or actions are subjected to further division:

> We see how the grinding of the coffee is divided in turn into a series of independent moments; for example, when she shuts the door with the tip of her outstretched foot. As it goes in on her the camera follows the movement of her leg so that the image finally concentrates on her toes feeling the surface of the door. (Bazin, 1971d: 82)

De Sica's insistence on enclosing the actor's performance within a series of smaller and smaller gestures and tasks allows us to grasp something fundamental about the circumstances and lives of the people depicted on screen. It does so not through a detailed exposition of their state of mind, but through an engagement with a set of actions in which the laws of traditional drama give way to another set of imperatives. Bazin describes these guiding principles as 'the succession of concrete instants of life, no one of which can be said to be more important than another, for their ontological equality destroys drama at its very basis' (1971d: 81).

In *Umberto D*, the attention paid to these concrete instants poses a challenge to traditional drama: How long should an action last? What is important to show and what can be elided? It also brings the spectator into contact with a duration whose lack of dramatic purpose seems to unravel our claims to subjective mastery. This is what Rosen means when he describes the type of realism promoted in Bazin's writings as 'an act of heroism': 'In the genuine realist attitude the impulse to control time is both exploited and checked. That is, the desire to master reality is achieved yet somehow sublimated so that the self-protective mechanisms motivating the projection toward the real are diverted from their defensive stance' (2003: 56).

THE ASSUMPTION OF THE IMAGE

Bazin's response to *Umberto D* highlights how easily realism crosses paths with the critical suppositions and terminology of modernist inquiry. An overturning of classical standards of drama and editing; an emphasis on the ontological equality of people and things; a privileging of gesture over psychological explication; a sensitivity to everyday alienation. In the years after Bazin's death, these features became hallmarks of the discussions on modernist cinema and the type of realist cinema tracked in Margulies' anthology. Bazin's role in these discussions is not surprising given his insistence that a realist cinema does not simply defend against the anxiety generated by an encounter with time, but also acknowledges its force on the present. Likewise, it is the manner in which those limit points of representation – of which death is the most prominent example – find a place in the image that, for Bazin, defines a realist impulse.

It is this concern with the limits of representation that drives one of Bazin's most important expositions of realist aesthetics, his discussion of Robert Bresson's adaptation of Georges Bernanos' novel *Diary of a County Priest* (*Le Journal d'un curé de campagne*, France, 1950). In this film, the approach of death occurs within a fictional context, but one marked by a fundamental disturbance in the relationship between sound and image. Bazin notes that Bresson's use of sound in *Diary of a Country Priest* 'never serves simply to fill out what we see. It strengthens it and multiplies it just as the echo chamber of a violin echoes and multiplies the vibrations of the strings' (1967b: 140). He clarifies the meaning of this metaphor by affirming that the relationship between image and sound is

not one of resonance but rather of mismatch, 'as when a color is not properly superimposed on a drawing' (1967b: 140).

Over the course of the film, this disturbance in the relationship between image and sound creates the sense of a world both tangibly present yet more and more out of synch. This disturbance reaches its climax with the death of the young priest (Claude Laydu). In the lead-up to this event, the young priest's worst fears are confirmed when he is told that the reason for his ill health is advanced cancer. Rather than returning to his vicarage, the priest seeks out a former friend from his days at the seminary, Louis Dufrety (Bernard Hubrenne). While listening to his friend's justifications for abandoning his vocation, the young priest collapses. When he revives, he finds himself laid out on a cot in a dusty attic room. It is here that he spends his last days writing in his diary and worrying about his friend's spiritual torment. The penultimate shot of the film is a close-up of a typed envelope being opened by the priest's mentor, the Vicar of Torcy (André Guibert). On the soundtrack, we hear Dufrety reading the letter that we see in front of us. After a few seconds, a slow dissolve substitutes the typed letter with a shot of a simple black cross on a white screen. For what seems an eternity, Bresson fixes on this unadorned shot as Dufrety's voice recounts the priest's final hours. His account ends with the last words spoken by the young priest: 'What does it matter? Everything is grace'.

For Bazin, the gruelling final moments of *Diary of a Country Priest* mark the culmination of Bresson's attempt to grant the words of Bernanos' novel a presence in the film and the desire to represent something that by its nature is unrepresentable, what Bazin terms 'the transcendence of grace' (1967b: 134). Both these endeavours end up at the same place:

Just as the blank page of [Stéphane] Mallarmé and the silence of [Arthur] Rimbaud is language at the highest state, the screen, free of images and handed back to literature, is the triumph of cinematographic realism. The black cross on the white screen, as awkwardly drawn as on the average memorial card, the only trace left by the 'assumption' of the image, is a witness to something the reality of which is itself but a sign. (Bazin, 1967b: 141)

The simple black cross at the end of *Diary of a Country Priest* stands in for the physical presence of Bernanos' novel and signals the inevitable elision of the grace sought by the young priest. Both have found their place through a process of textual disturbance that culminates with an image hovering between graphic inscription and religious symbol. For Bazin, this awkward image is an embodiment of the limit of what cinema is capable of representing. Like his comments on Braunberger's *The Bullfight*, Bazin's discussion of the final moments of *Diary of a Country Priest* affirms how much his writings on cinema are drawn to instances that highlight its limits as a representational medium. We can go further and say that it is around this question of limits – both of the subject and cinema itself – that we can begin to understand the special appeal of Bazin's realism and its influence on contemporary debates.

NOTES

1 'Cinéma, idéologie, critique' was originally published in *Cahiers du cinéma* in 1969, and translated in *Screen* two years later (Comolli and Narboni, 1971).

2 See Thierry Kuntzel, 'The Film-Work' (1978) and Stephen Heath, *Questions of Cinema* (1981). An important overview of Bellour's work on classical Hollywood cinema is provided in Bergstrom (1979: 71–103).

3 See Colin MacCabe, *Tracking the Signifier: Theoretical Essays: Film, Linguistics, Literature* (1985).

4 See also Bazin's admiring reference to the comments by Robert Lachenay (François Truffaut's pseudonym) in his commemoration, 'The Death of Humphrey Bogart': 'Each time he began a sentence he revealed a wayward set of teeth. The set of his jaw irresistibly evoked the rictus of a spirited cadaver, the final expression of a melancholy man who would fade away with a smile. That is indeed the smile of death' (quoted in Bazin, 1985: 98).

REFERENCES

Aitken, Ian (2001) *European Film Theory and Cinema: A Critical Introduction*. Edinburgh: Edinburgh University Press.

Bazin, André (1967a) 'The Ontology of the Photographic Image', in *What is Cinema? Vol.1*. Ed. and tr. Hugh Gray. Berkeley: University of California Press. pp. 9–16.

Bazin, André (1967b) '*Le Journal d'un curé de campagne* and the Stylistics of Robert Bresson', in *What is Cinema? Vol.1*. Ed. and tr. Hugh Gray. Berkeley: University of California Press. pp. 125–43.

Bazin, André (1971a) 'An Aesthetic of Reality: Cinematic Realism and the Italian School of Liberation', in *What is Cinema? Vol.2*. Ed. and tr. Hugh Gray. Berkeley: University of California Press. pp. 16–40.

Bazin, André (1971b) 'De Sica: Metteur en scène', in *What is Cinema? Vol.2*. Ed. and tr. Hugh Gray. Berkeley: University of California Press. pp. 61–78.

Bazin, André (1971c) 'The Myth of Monsieur Verdoux', in *What is Cinema? Vol.2*. Ed. and tr. Hugh Gray. Berkeley: University of California Press. pp. 102–23.

Bazin, André (1971d) '*Umberto D*: A Great Work', in *What is Cinema? Vol.2*. Ed. and tr. Hugh Gray. Berkeley: University of California Press. pp. 79–82.

Bazin, André (1985) 'The Death of Humphrey Bogart', in Jim Hillier (ed.), *Cahiers du cinéma: The 1950s: Neo-Realism, Hollywood, New Wave*. Cambridge, MA: Harvard University Press. pp. 98–101.

Bazin, André (1997) 'Europe 51', in *Bazin at Work: Major Essays and Reviews from the Forties and Fifties*. Tr. Alain Piette and Bert Cardullo. New York: Routledge. pp. 137–39.

Bazin, André (2003) 'Death Every Afternoon', in Ivone Margulies (ed.), *Rites of Realism: Essays on Corporeal Cinema*. Tr. Mark A. Cohen. Durham, NC: Duke University Press. pp. 27–31.

Bergstrom, Janet (1979) 'Alternation, Segmentation, Hypnosis: Interview with Raymond Bellour', *Camera Obscura*, 3–4: 71–103.

Brecht, Bertolt (1974) 'Against Georg Lukács', *New Left Review*, 84: 39–54.

Comolli, Jean-Louis and Narboni, Jean (1969) 'Cinéma, idéologie, critique', *Cahiers du cinéma*, 216: 11–15.

Comolli, Jean-Louis and Narboni, Jean (1971) 'Cinema/Ideology/Criticism', *Screen*, 12(1): 131–44.

Comolli, Jean-Louis and Narboni, Jean (1999) 'Cinema, Ideology, Criticism', in Leo Braudy and Marshall Cohen (eds), *Film Theory and Criticism: Introductory Readings*. New York: Oxford University Press. pp. 752–9.

Crary, Jonathan (1994) 'Unbinding Vision', *October*, 68: 21–44.

Daney, Serge (2003) 'The Screen of Fantasy (Bazin and Animals)', in Ivone Margulies (ed.), *Rites of Realism: Essays on Corporeal Cinema*. Durham, NC: Duke University Press. pp. 32–41.

Doane, Mary Ann (2002) *The Emergence of Cinematic Time: Modernity, Contingency, the Archive.* Cambridge, MA: Harvard University Press.

Hansen, Miriam Bratu (1997) 'Introduction', in Siegfried Kracauer, *Theory of Film: The Redemption of Physical Reality.* Princeton, NJ: Princeton University Press. pp. vii–xiv.

Heath, Stephen (1981) *Questions of Cinema.* London: Macmillan Press.

Hebdige, Dick and Hurd, Geoff (1978) 'Reading and Realism', *Screen Education*, 28: 68–78.

Kracauer, Siegfried (1995) 'Photography', in *The Mass Ornament: Weimer Essays.* Tr. Thomas Y. Levin. Cambridge, MA: Harvard University Press. pp. 47–63.

Kracauer, Siegfried (1997) *Theory of Film: The Redemption of Physical Reality.* Princeton, NJ: Princeton University Press.

Kuntzel, Thierry (1978) 'The Film-Work', *Enclitic* 2(1): 38–61.

MacCabe, Colin (1974) 'Realism and the Cinema: Notes on Some Brechtian Theses', *Screen*, 15(2): 7–27.

MacCabe, Colin (1976) 'Theory and Film: Principles of Realism and Pleasure', *Screen*, 17(3): 7–27.

MacCabe, Colin (1985) *Tracking the Signifier: Theoretical Essays: Film, Linguistics, Literature.* Minneapolis: University of Minnesota Press.

Margulies, Ivone (2003) 'Bodies Too Much', in Ivone Margulies (ed.), *Rites of Realism: Essays on Corporeal Cinema.* Durham, NC: Duke University Press. pp. 1–23.

Nochlin, Linda (1971) *Realism.* Harmondsworth: Penguin.

Rosen, Philip (2003) 'History of Image, Image of History: Subject and Ontology in Bazin', in Ivone Margulies (ed.), *Rites of Realism: Essays on Corporeal Cinema.* Durham, NC: Duke University Press. pp. 42–79.

25

Feminist Perspectives in Film Studies

Alison Butler

Feminist Film Studies emerged from the dialogue between the women's movement and progressive film theory in the early 1970s. It is tempting to cast this as an encounter between the pleasures of cinephilia and the politics of feminism, but more accurate to point to the tensions and contradictions between pleasure and politics within film theory as well as within feminist thinking at that time. In the 1970s and 1980s, feminism contained a spectrum of views on sexuality, ranging from sexual libertarianism to radical separatism. In everyday feminist debate, the critique of female objectification often lapsed from political analysis into puritan outrage. At the same time, progressive Film Studies was turning from the pleasures of cinephilia towards the strictures of Althusserian ideological analysis. In this context, feminist film theorists struggled to reconcile the negative conclusions of their theoretical inquiry with the love of cinema which had inspired their work. This conflict was sharpened by the fact that most of these activist writers were located outside institutionalized academia at this time, and saw their work as a contribution to alternative film culture and particularly to the aesthetics of radical counter-cinema, in which the reconciliation of pleasure and politics was a pressing and practical issue.

Two ground-breaking essays inaugurated feminist film theory: Claire Johnston's 'Women's Cinema as Counter-Cinema' (1973b) and Laura Mulvey's 'Visual Pleasure and Narrative Cinema' (1975). The intellectual background to these essays was a wave of new theories from France: Louis Althusser's theory of ideology, Roland Barthes' semiotics, Michel Foucault's analyses of institutional power, Jacques Lacan's neo-Freudian psychoanalysis and, within film theory, the work of Christian Metz and Jean-Louis Baudry on the metapsychology of the cinematic apparatus. Johnston and Mulvey dismissed what they saw as the sociological stance of previous feminist critics such as Molly Haskell (1975) and Marjorie Rosen (1973) in favour of the analysis of the cinematic apparatus, film form and film texts from the perspective of these new methodologies. Embracing Althusser's conception of the all-pervasiveness of ideology, they rejected the popular feminist notion of replacing distorted images of women with accurate ones, on the grounds that there could be no position outside patriarchal ideology from which this task might be accomplished. In common with other feminist intellectuals of the time, they understood gender as an ideological effect, distinct from biological sex. Their anti-essentialist arguments aimed to reveal the ways in which gender ideology was mediated and produced by cinema. Questions about women's 'positive or negative', 'true or false' representation were thus displaced by theoretical inquiry into the nature and ideological effects of the medium.

In her introduction to *Notes on Women's Cinema*, the pamphlet in which her best-known essay first appeared, Johnston attacks feminist film criticism that 'takes as its starting point the manipulation of women as sexual objects by the media' (1973a: 3). This view, she claims, articulates a puritanical distrust of entertainment and spectacle in general and overlooks the specificity and sophistication of cinema as a medium. Allying herself with the critics of *Cahiers du cinéma* in its post-1968 phase, she argues for Marxist ideological analysis, but also for entertainment and fantasy, because to achieve its aims, political cinema needs to generate pleasure. Women's cinema, she argues, should learn from the successes of Hollywood: 'In order to counter our objectification in the cinema, our collective fantasies must be released: women's cinema must embody the working through of desire: such an objective demands the use of the entertainment film' (1973b: 31). (The tension between pleasure and politics in Johnston's theory is expressed forcefully in her almost oxymoronic rhetoric, in which fantasy and desire become the objects of collective work.)

Johnston argues for the possibility of the progressive text within Hollywood cinema, in the existence of films that appear superficially to conform to the prevailing ideology, but which contain within themselves ideological contradictions that subvert their ostensible meanings. Drawing on Barthes' *Mythologies*,

she suggests that Hollywood's reliance on stereotypes renders it particularly liable to subversion: '[M]yth uses icons, but the icon is its weakest point' (1973b: 25). The less realistic the icon, the better, as verisimilitude naturalizes iconography, whereas obvious stereotypicality is always in some sense reflexive. It points to textuality, and to the place of the text in a cultural tradition: 'In fact, because iconography offers in some ways a greater resistance to the realist characterisations, the mythic qualities of certain stereotypes become far more easily detachable and can be used as a short-hand for referring to an ideological tradition in order to provide a critique of it' (1973b: 25). Johnston suggests that, to combat sexist ideology, feminist films and film criticism should operate reflexively to foreground its working within texts, through the conventions of the medium.

Although Johnston's argument is not substantially underpinned by psychoanalytic theory, it is shored up by it at one crucial point. Her anti-realist position is reinforced by the claim that in mainstream cinema: 'Woman represents not herself, but by a process of displacement, the male phallus', so that, 'despite the enormous emphasis placed on woman as spectacle in the cinema, woman as woman is largely absent' (1973b: 25–6). This striking statement complicates her argument somewhat, burdening her proposal for a progressive reworking of mainstream cinematic conventions with the challenging aim of transforming patriarchal values at the deep structural level, which Lacanians term 'the symbolic'. Johnston's thought is consistently concerned with an aesthetic of reworking, but this is re-inflected by the incorporation of Lacanian psychoanalysis, so that positive – and pleasurable – appropriation gives way to negation and problematization.

A psychoanalytic perspective is embedded more deeply in Mulvey's 'Visual Pleasure and Narrative Cinema', perhaps the most influential and contentious essay in the history of Film Studies. Like Johnston, Mulvey writes in the tradition of textual analysis, but she extends this to encompass the spectator – not the actual viewer, but the spectator implied or anticipated by the text. Mulvey's argument is premised on the metapsychology of cinema elaborated by Metz and Baudry, who theorize the spectator's relationship to the cinema screen as a revisitation of formative infantile fantasies about vision and power. Mulvey argues that the looking relations which structure the spectator's relationship to the screen are also gender relations. In mainstream cinema, she contends, there is a gendered division of labour which allies the male hero with the movement of the narrative and the female figure with pleasurable spectacle. The cinematic apparatus aligns the look of the spectator with that of the camera, and editing conventions subsume the look of the camera into that of the protagonist. This 'system of looks' assumes narcissistic identification with the male protagonist of the narrative and voyeuristic enjoyment of the female object of the gaze. This enjoyment is, however, ambivalent because of the castration anxiety engendered by the sight of the woman. The two forms of pleasure associated with the female image are also defences against this threat: sadism, which acknowledges sexual difference and takes pleasure in investigating woman's guilt; and fetishism, which disavows sexual difference and worships woman (or a particular body part or item of clothing) as phallic substitute. Less sanguine about the progressive possibilities of Hollywood than Johnston, Mulvey concludes her devastating polemic against mainstream narrative film by advocating the creation of 'a new language of desire' to 'free the look of the camera into its materiality in time and space and the look of the audience into dialectics, passionate detachment' (1975: 8). Women, she argues, should view the decline of traditional film form with nothing more than 'sentimental regret' (1975: 18).

Mulvey's avant-gardism, which was allied to her own practice as a filmmaker, places her in the tradition of feminist modernism from Virginia Woolf to Julia Kristeva. In an essay on melodrama, Mulvey comments on the betrayal of cinema's modernity, specifically by D.W. Griffith, who brought the spectacle and sentiment of late Victorian theatre into silent cinema, and with them 'a conscious political stance that was already conservative and nostalgic': 'There seems, in Griffith's work, to be a desperate refusal to acknowledge the modernity of the cinema, the contemporary world and its aesthetics and, particularly, a new and changing concept of womanhood' (1986: 86). Writing in 1926, Woolf is similarly critical of the predominance of melodrama and stereotype in silent film, and imagines an alternative future for the medium as '[s]omething abstract, something which moves with controlled and conscious art …' in which 'we should be able to see thought in its wildness, in its beauty, in its oddity …' (1996: 36). However, while Woolf represents the positive projects of feminism and modernism, seeking new forms for modern consciousness, Mulvey's 1970s stance is closer to Kristeva's assertion, in the context of second-wave feminism and psychoanalysis, that 'feminist practice can only be negative, at odds with what already exists' (1981: 137).

This argument contributed to the formation of a feminist canon in the 1970s and 1980s that was dominated by cinematic counterparts of the theory in the work of formalist filmmakers such as Chantal Akerman, Marguerite Duras, Bette Gordon, Sally Potter, Yvonne Rainer and Helke Sander. At the same time, this tendency has been questioned and opposed by critics who have disputed its political effectiveness and its artistic inclusiveness. Christine Gledhill notes that negative aesthetics risk postponing indefinitely the production of meaning which is essential to political art, 'dissolving the subject in an endless play of radical difference' (1994: 117). Anneke Smelik complains of the 'largely unjustified acclaim of experimental women's cinema among the elected few who get to see it', and points out the paradox of requiring female spectators to renounce visual pleasures already denied to them (1998: 12). Mulvey concedes that negation was a strategy of its time never intended as an end in itself, but rather, designed to facilitate a decisive break: 'Counter-aesthetics, too, can harden into a system of dualistic opposition' (1987: 8).

MIMESIS AND ONTOLOGY

Underlying this debate is perhaps the most problematic issue in feminist Film Studies, the question of mimesis. Annette Kuhn summarizes the feminist critique of mimesis as follows: 'To the extent that a signification process is effaced in realist representations, it is argued, realism perpetuates illusionism, the notion that, in the case of cinema, what is on the screen is an uncoded reflection of the "real world"' (1982: 156–7). Illusionism, she explains, is ideological because it conceals its own operations and those of the spectator in making meaning, which is then displaced onto a purportedly objective reality 'out there'. However, she also concedes that the appropriation of realist strategies 'can in certain circumstances be productive' (1982: 134), implicitly acknowledging the need for feminist film theory to reconcile its anti-realist principles with political demands for engagement with concrete and worldly realities.

The rejection of mimetic signification narrowed the scope of feminist aesthetics to only one of film's expressive modalities, the cinematic codes, excluding from consideration some of the richest communicative potentialities of the medium. The abandonment of the reflectionist model of representation which Johnston termed 'sociological' also left open the question of how – and even whether – texts relate to society. Johnston recognized this herself, pointing out that 'work on text/subject relations which aims to transform the relationship between text and viewer cannot be seen as a goal in itself' (1980: 29) and advocating 'a move away from the notion of "text" and "spectator" conceptualised in abstract and a-historical terms and towards a more interventionist conception of textual practice seen within specific historical conjunctures' (1981: 55).

Mary Ann Doane has recently suggested that the issue of mimesis has never really been adequately resolved by feminist Film Studies, perhaps because the 1980s deflected debate into other areas:

> The negativity subtending the feminist avant-garde was an attempt to avoid the dangers of essentialism attendant on mimetic procedures, but it simply relocated mimesis at another level – that of the codes subject to critique. The reflected entity – woman – has anyway begun to shatter into a spectrum of identities, which were contingent themselves on assumptions about mimesis. Is feminist criticism one of the final abodes of a reflection theory of art? Must its underlying theory of the relation between aesthetics and politics hinge on mimesis? (2004: 1234)

A feminist re-evaluation of the relationship of the cinematic image to reality would have interesting and significant effects, given that feminist Film Studies was founded on the rejection of Bazinian realism and the acceptance of a linguistic semiology. This process may perhaps already be under way, in a discontinuous and oblique manner, for example in Ivone Margulies' work on hyperreality in the films of Akerman (1996), in Mulvey's recent writing on cinematic ontology and time (2000) and, above all, in the engagement of some feminist film scholars with the film theory of philosopher Gilles Deleuze. Laleen Jayamanne, for example, makes the notion of mimesis central to her critical project (1995; 2000; 2004). Her use of the term is influenced by Walter Benjamin's modernist conception of mimesis and anthropologist Michael Taussig's notion of cross-cultural mimesis. In order to grasp and describe the mimetic effects of films, Jayamanne adopts Deleuze's film semiotics rather than the linguistic and psychoanalytic semiotics of most feminist film theory, which she dismisses as reductive and narrow: 'It seems to me that, without an interest in cinematic ontology or its mimetic nature, the intellect tends to instrumentalize the image, and we only see "gender" and "genre" and not the movements that constitute these categories' (2004: 1253). For Jayamanne, mimesis is a rich and fluid concept which crosses divisions between abstract categories such as aesthetics and politics or reality and representation. The musical and rhythmic concept of modulation which she adopts from Deleuze, instead of the linguistic concept of difference normally invoked in feminist film theory, allows new thought to emerge from film analysis, rather than repeated illustrations of the same ideas (the phallus, castration, etc): 'Gesture is not seen simply as the expression of a fully formed subject but rather as having the power to create an unknown body or to render a known one unfamiliar' (2004: 1251).

SPECTATORSHIP AND FANTASY

In its first two decades, feminist Film Studies was less concerned with confronting the question of mimesis at the level of signification than with elaborating its sublated effects on the film spectator. Mulvey and Johnston's interventions sparked a debate that continued for several decades. The crucial issues are succinctly summarized by film critic B. Ruby Rich:

> According to Mulvey, the woman is not visible in the audience which is perceived as male; according to Johnston, the woman is not visible on the screen. She is merely a surrogate for the phallus, a signifier for something else, etc. As a woman going into the movie theater, you are faced with a context that is coded wholly for your invisibility, and yet, obviously, you are sitting there and bringing along a certain coding from outside the theatre. (Citron et al., 1978: 87)

The difficulty of accounting for the pleasure of the female spectator within the constraints imposed by feminist apparatus theory in any way other than through the crudest conception of false consciousness became the central issue in the feminist film theory of the 1980s.

Mulvey's own hypothesis about female spectatorship is elaborated through a reading of King Vidor's western melodrama, *Duel in the Sun* (US, 1946), in which the central character's oscillation between 'boyish' and 'ladylike' behaviour invites the female spectator to draw on the repressed masculinity of her own pre-Oedipal history, thus identifying with both active and passive narrative positions in

the film (1981). Teresa de Lauretis (1984) modifies this thesis by claiming that the two forms of identification are continuously engaged rather than alternating, and that the tension between them plays on the contradictions inherent in Oedipal femininity and the contradiction between women as historical subjects and Woman as sign. Doane's work on female spectatorship centres on the psychoanalytic problem of theorizing female desire within a conceptual framework that specifies femininity as passive object (a conceptual framework which, it is assumed, mainstream cinema shares). Her book *The Desire to Desire* (1987) theorizes the Hollywood woman's film of the 1940s in relation to the problem of female spectatorship. She identifies four main sub-genres, each of which constructs its own specific ways of mediating between the apparently irreconcilable categories of femininity and desire. These mediating fantasies are characterized by masochistic tendencies (as one would expect, given that women's films were also known as 'weepies'). However, Doane stresses that the spectator positions she describes are functions of the text rather than of actual female viewers, who may have other ways of mediating the rather stressful pleasures of the woman's film. In an earlier essay, Doane (1982) offers a more general hypothesis on female spectatorship. Drawing on the work of psychoanalyst Joan Rivière, she suggests that the female spectator, like the patients described by Rivière, performs femininity. In doing so, she establishes enough distance between herself and the image for meaningful looking to take place (voyeurism depends on distance), thus avoiding the perils of masochistic or narcissistic over-identification.

Without underestimating the complexity of theories of spectatorial identification, most of these analyses concentrate on the female spectator's relationship with female characters and femininity. Elizabeth Cowie's article 'Fantasia' (1984) usefully shifts emphasis away from the individual character and towards the text as a whole. Citing Jean Laplanche and J.B. Pontalis' definition of fantasy as a '*mise en scène* of desire',

Cowie argues that film texts are a form of public fantasy in which the staging of desire creates shifting patterns of identification with multiple entry points for the spectator. Through analyses of *Now, Voyager* (Irving Rapper, US, 1942) and *The Reckless Moment* (Max Ophuls, US, 1949), Cowie concludes that, '[w]hile the terms of sexual difference are fixed, the places of characters and spectators in relation to those terms are not' (1984: 102).

Carol J. Clover's *Men, Women and Chainsaws* (1992), develops the implications of this thesis further in relation to a less respectable genre, the horror film. Overturning the common-sense view that horror films in which female characters are terrorized by male killers encourage male spectators to take sadistic pleasure in violence against women, Clover argues that the predominantly adolescent male audience of slasher-films actually identifies with the female victim-hero (the Final Girl) who eventually, after a terrifying ordeal, overcomes the villain. Clover observes that both of the principal characters in the genre may be ambiguously gendered, the killer taking on aspects of a monstrous phallic femininity, for example, while the Final Girl is often a tomboy. She distinguishes between the actual gender of the characters and their figurative gender; that is, the ways their significant attributes can be correlated to gendered subject positions. On this basis, she argues that the Final Girl is figuratively a boy whose suffering allows the majority audience to explore castration anxiety in the relative safety of vicariousness. Clover is reluctant to make any claims for the progressiveness of horror films on the basis of these insights, but her approach does highlight the mobility of cinematic identification and the (relative) permeability of the boundary between genders.

The growth of cultural studies and media studies in the 1970s and 1980s influenced debates about gender and film spectatorship, offering alternative models which drew on sociological methodologies rather than – or as well as – textual analysis and apparatus theory (Stacey, 1994). Kuhn has stressed the importance of distinguishing between spectators as textual subjects and actual audience members as social subjects:

> A film may, through the modes of address it constructs, privilege a certain kind of spectator-text relationship. This, however, is no guarantee that every member of every audience for that film will react to it in precisely this way. 'Audience' may have a broad range of connotations, which may include – but is not necessarily limited to – a notion of the spectator as a component of the cinematic apparatus. (1982: 191)

Gledhill adopts from cultural studies theorist Stuart Hall the distinction between 'preferred readings' and 'negotiated readings', in order to argue that meaning is not a given in the text, but 'arises out of a struggle or negotiation between competing frames of reference, motivation and experience' (1988: 68). Gledhill's argument moves away from the totalizing conception of ideology associated with Althusser and assimilated by 1970s film theory, and towards a Gramscian conception of ideology as a process of hegemony and resistance. Jacqueline Bobo uses cultural studies methodologies to research the practices of Black women as cultural readers. Her study of Black women's responses to Steven Spielberg's adaptation of *The Color Purple* (US, 1985), a film which Black critics accused of perpetuating stereotypes, draws on the concept of negotiated reading to argue that Black women have learned, from force of habit, 'to ferret out the beneficial and put up blinders against the rest' (1988: 96).

Bobo's work on Black female spectators was part of a wave of criticism in the mid-1980s that drew attention to the inadequacy of early feminist film theory's formulation of looking relations and female spectatorship in relation to non-white subjects. bell hooks (1992) criticizes white feminist theorists for assuming the universality of their own experiences, and describes the 'oppositional gaze' of the resistant black female spectator. Jane Gaines (1988) points out that the inability of early feminist film theory to deal adequately with issues of race arises from its almost exclusive reliance on universalizing psychoanalytic concepts. These, she claims, cannot account for the changing historical forms of looking relations, which in the US have been shaped by white privilege as well as patriarchal prerogative. Gaines argues powerfully for historical materialist analysis to supersede psychoanalytic discourse analysis, which she regards as resolutely ahistorical. The reconciliation of these two approaches is precisely what E. Ann Kaplan attempts in *Looking for the Other* (1997), in which she articulates feminist gaze theory with theories of colonial and postcolonial subjectivity in an attempt to bridge the gap between the analyses of two radically different and incommensurate forms of oppression.

Like the 'male gaze', the concept of the 'female spectator' has fallen from favour because of its lack of historical and cultural specificity or mutability. The publication of Judith Butler's hugely influential *Gender Trouble* (1990), which reconceives gender in relation to the concept of discursive performativity, effectively broke the stranglehold of Lacanian psychoanalysis on feminist theory by suggesting that the mobility of subjects in relation to sexual difference might, in fact, have the capacity to change the terms of sexual difference itself. As Butler states, '[A]ny claim to establish the rules that "regulate desire" in an inalterable and eternal realm of law has limited use for a theory that seeks to understand the conditions under which the social transformation of gender is possible' (2004: 44). Butler's reconceptualization of gender regulation has enabled lesbian and queer film theory to reconfigure sexual difference and looking relations in more flexible and varied ways. Judith Halberstam's article on *Boys Don't Cry* (Kimberly Peirce, US, 1999), for instance, argues for the possibility of a transgender gaze divided between a self that accepts castration and one that disavows it (2001). Chris Straayer's research on deviant looking relations (1996) and Patricia White's work on lesbian representability in classical Hollywood cinema (1999) both emphasize the capacity of spectators to turn the erotic and Oedipal structures of cinematic looking against the heterosexual disposition of the apparatus. The queer and lesbian theory of the 1990s added considerably to the complexity of thinking about the permutations of spectatorial possibilities in cinema, but it was the resurgence of film history in that decade that really transformed feminist film scholarship.

THE TURN TO HISTORY

Feminist film theory and academic Film Studies developed in tandem during the 1970s and 1980s, so that the concerns of the former seemed securely embedded in the foundations of the latter. The turn away from theory and towards history in the early 1990s, coupled with explicit attacks on 'theory' by neoformalist film scholars, therefore seemed to pose a particular threat to feminist Film Studies, as Patrice Petro commented in 1991:

> It would appear that a certain division of labor has come to characterize Film Studies as a discipline in which 'historians' pursue the realm of the empirical, the quantifiable, the concretely known (the realm of history proper), and 'feminists' explore the more intangible realm of theoretical speculation (the realm of interpretation). (2002: 31–2)

In the long run, however, the turn to history has greatly benefited feminist Film Studies, as the challenges of thinking historically have enabled feminist film scholars to move beyond the conceptual blockages of apparatus and gaze theory.

In the late 1980s and early 1990s, feminist scholars began to forge connections between film theory, film history and cultural studies in order to explore the diverse and specific configurations of female subjectivity in modernity. Petro's historical study of women and melodramatic representation in Weimar cinema, *Joyless Streets* (1989), draws on the approaches of Benjamin and Siegfried Kracauer to argue that, rather than being excluded from modernity, women were engaged by it as gendered subjects. In *Babel and Babylon* (1991), Miriam Hansen extends the Frankfurt School's debates on mass culture and the public sphere to argue that, during the silent period, cinema may have functioned as an alternative public sphere for women by providing an intersubjective context, in which they could recognize aspects of their own experience. Giuliana Bruno's *Streetwalking on a Ruined Map* (1993) echoes Benjamin's great, unfinished project on arcades and urban modernity in its emphasis on the relations between cinema and metropolitan topography. Bruno's book is a reclamation not only of the prolific but neglected early Italian filmmaker, Elvira Notari, but also of the city streets which early cinema rendered newly accessible to the female spectator. Bruno argues that early cinema 'triggered a liberation of the woman's gaze, enabling her to renegotiate, on a new terrain of intersubjectivity, the configuration of public/private' (1993: 51). These accounts of women's engagement with cinema during the silent period displace historical assumptions about women's absence and silence in cinematic tradition and refocus debate around more nuanced understandings of the articulation of femininity and modernity in and around cinema.

A number of studies employing methodologies more typical of film history reinforce the findings of these cultural theorists and historians, including Janet Staiger's *Bad Women* (1995), Lauren Rabinovitz's *For the Love of Pleasure* (1998) and Shelley Stamp's *Movie-Struck Girls* (2000). All three books contextualize representations of women and female spectatorship in the practices and discourses of the emerging consumerism of the early twentieth century, and more widely in the context of modernity. Stamp's examination of the women's genres and cinema-going behaviour in the 1910s, Staiger's study of representations of women in the same period and Rabinovitz's research on cinema-going in turn-of-the-century Chicago, all use historical data to show how cinema participated in debates about women's public and private behaviour and helped to redefine their role in modern society. The concentration of a significant amount of feminist historical scholarship on cinema's first two or three decades is notable, resulting in part from an ingrained tendency in Film Studies to associate the stabilization of forms and conventions generally termed 'classical' with

ideological stabilization, but also undoubtedly influenced by the richness of historical and theoretical scholarship on early modernity. Moreover, within early cinema scholarship, the displacement of Mulvey's famous thesis on visual pleasure by Tom Gunning's conception of a 'cinema of attractions' has freed analysts of early films to conceptualize the relationships between image culture and sexual difference in more diverse ways.

The empirical turn taken by Film Studies in the 1990s and the privileged status assumed by research into early cinema also revived interest in 'lost' women filmmakers after a twenty-year lull. In the early 1970s, feminists had rediscovered pioneers such as Alice Guy-Blaché, Lois Weber and Germaine Dulac, but this work of recovery and celebration abated in the 1970s and 1980s. The forceful arguments mounted against essentialist notions of female identity and humanist conceptions of authorship had made the idea of a feminine aesthetic or a suppressed tradition waiting to be unearthed, 'like a gold mine in a garden', in Mulvey's elegant phrase (1979: 4), seem more or less untenable. In the 1990s, however, the general climate of interest in historical research on early cinema and the appearance of key publications, including Anthony Slide's *The Silent Feminists* (1996a), which documents the existence of over a dozen female filmmakers in the silent era, encouraged feminist scholars to question assumptions about the exclusion of women from early and silent cinema. This new mood led to the recovery of several dozen other female pioneers. (Information on this research is coordinated by the Women Film Pioneers project, hosted by Duke University in the US.) Jennifer M. Bean has described the present moment as 'an age of discovery' for feminist historians of women in early cinema (Bean and Negra, 2002: 2). As a result of this historical research, it has become clear that before the coming of sound and the institutionalization of the film industry, women were present in key creative roles in far greater numbers than feminist film scholars had previously supposed. Although the disappearance of many small companies and the professionalization of production in the 1920s seem to have driven these women out of the industry, for a time they occupied positions of power and prestige. This is shown by Alison McMahan's extensive research on Guy-Blaché (2002), who headed her own company, produced over a thousand feature films and shorts and directed many hundreds herself, possibly including – though it is a matter of some contention – the first fiction film.

FEMALE AUTHORSHIP REVISITED

The rediscovery of a generation of women directors in early cinema, in tandem with the small but significant increase in the number of women directors in contemporary cinema, has revived interest in the issue of female authorship. Since the early 1990s, the body of scholarship on contemporary and historical women filmmakers has increased, including dictionaries and encyclopedias (Acker, 1991; Foster, 1995), studies of women directors within particular film traditions (Flitterman-Lewis, 1990; Lane, 2000; Rabinovitz, 1991) and monographs on single directors such as Akerman (Foster, 1999; Margulies, 1996), Dorothy Arzner (Mayne, 1994), Claire Denis (Beugnet, 2004; Mayne, 2005), Maya Deren (Jackson, 2002), Valie Export (Mueller, 1994), Diane Kurys (Tarr, 1999), Ida Lupino (Kuhn, 1995), Nell Shipman (Armatage, 2003), Agnès Varda (Smith, 1998) and Weber (Slide, 1996b).

The emphasis on issues of spectatorship and reception in 1980s feminist Film Studies can be explained not only by assumptions of women's absence, as makers of meaning, from film history, but also by the problematization of authorship as a concept in Film Studies. Barthes' influential pronouncement of the 'death of the author' and the 'birth of the reader' in 1973 foreclosed auteurism as a critical project in Film Studies, which shifted its attention from the 'writerly' text to the 'readerly' text, just as feminists began to demand equal access to the means of cultural production. For feminist film theory, this

created an impossible dilemma, which is well-explained by Judith Mayne. She argues that any unproblematic assumption of female authorship 'risks appropriating, for women, an extremely patriarchal notion of cinematic creation', but also that, at the same time, female authorship, as well as being a useful political strategy, 'is crucial to the reinvention of the cinema as it has been undertaken by women filmmakers and feminist spectators' (1990: 95; 97). Mayne's theory of feminist authorship has little in common with auteur theory, functioning not to express an original and coherent vision, but rather to disarticulate and revise masculinist cinematic conventions:

> The analysis of female authorship in the cinema raises somewhat different questions than does the analysis of male authorship, not only for the obvious reason that women have not had the same relationship to the institutions of cinema as men have, but also because the articulation of female authorship threatens to upset the erasure of 'women' which is central to the articulation of 'woman' in the cinema. (1990: 97)

The distinction between 'women' and 'woman' here echoes de Lauretis' call for feminist films to enact the disjunction between women and Woman, as well as harking back to Johnston's conception of women's counter-cinema. The idea of female authors as 'mistresses of discrepancy', in Mayne's phrase, rewriting the conventions of mainstream cinema, also animates Lucy Fischer's *Shot/Countershot* (1989), which theorizes women's cinema as an intertextual counter-tradition in dialogue with the mainstream, and Patricia Mellencamp's *A Fine Romance* (1995), which reads film feminism as a concerted riposte to the fiction of romance.

The rediscovery of women film pioneers has reinvigorated debates about female authorship from a historical (and historiographical) perspective. McMahan is careful to state that she does not treat Guy-Blaché as an auteur, but points out simply that 'we cannot build on the work women before us have done unless we know their work' (2002: 245). Gaines writes eloquently about the importance, in her view, of holding to anti-auteurist positions, and argues that the recovery of Guy-Blaché's history may serve to problematize authorship and its attendant concepts, including originality and 'first times' (2002; 2004). Gaines cites Bruno on Notari and Mayne on Arzner as models of revisionist engagement with questions of authorship. Bruno self-consciously constructs the female author as a retrospective effect of feminist criticism, a projection of her own desire, while Mayne in effect does the opposite, carefully sifting historical evidence in order to determine, with impartial accuracy, the extent to which the influence of Arzner's lesbianism can be discerned at a textual level in the films she made in Hollywood between the late 1920s and the early 1940s. Methodological issues raised by this historical work have influenced the approaches taken by researchers into contemporary women's filmmaking. For example, in *Feminist Hollywood*, Christina Lane uses interviews with directors as primary sources, alongside textual analyses, on the grounds that 'discussion of authors (and spectators for that matter) as constructions of projections cannot fully exclude their existence as flesh-and-blood individuals' and aims to 'hold these two positions in tension' (2000: 45). At the same time, feminist scholars have remained interested in finding ways of looking at women's cultural production that do not privilege the figure of the director as maker of meaning. Books by Lizzie Francke (1994) and Martha MacCreadie (1994) have emphasized the importance of women's authorial contribution to cinema as scriptwriters, and Sue Harper's *Women in British Cinema* (2000) includes chapters on women producers, writers, costume designers, art directors and editors as well as directors, underlining the collaborative nature of film production. The ambivalence and equivocation which surround questions of authorship in feminist Film Studies are a clear indication of the continuing need to theorize women's activities as cultural producers, as well as consumers. This may be especially so, given that change in film production has taken place at a much slower pace than in academic Film Studies, so that the women's filmmaking practices (and practitioners) anticipated by the

theorists of the 1970s have emerged later, more sporadically, and in more varied forms, than the theorists anticipated.

FILM FEMINISM AND GEOPOLITICS

The tendency to historical specificity in feminist film theory has been accompanied by a tendency to cultural particularity. A number of books on women in national cinemas have explored the ways in which national cultures mediate gender ideology through cinematic images (Harper, 2000; Knight, 1992; Rollet and Tarr, 2001), and the popularization of a multiculturalist notion of 'world cinema' has generated interest in cultural identity and difference within the cinema. In recent years, the new Iranian cinema has provided the most striking example of a national cinema with its own distinct mediations of gender. After the Iranian revolution, new regulations rigorously imposed 'Islamic values' on film production, paying particular attention to modesty conventions governing the veiling of women and contact between the sexes. In effect, these regulations created a new formal language in Iranian cinema. As Hamid Naficy explains:

> A new grammar for filming developed, involving shot composition, acting, touching and relay of the gaze between male and female actors. In essence, this grammar encouraged a 'modesty of looking and acting' and instituted an 'averted look' instead of the direct gaze, particularly one imbued with desire. (1996: 676–7)

Although this 'purification' of cinema reduced the visibility of women on the screen, it did make filmmaking into a suitable profession for women. As a result, Iran probably now has more female film directors than most other countries in the world, with the exception of France. In several essays on the veil and the veiling of meaning in Iranian cinema, Naficy (1999; 2001) argues that veiling is a dynamic social practice, dialectically related to unveiling, and capable of empowering as well as oppressing women. Certainly, the acknowledgement of the spectator's gaze, implicit in the cinematic codification of hijab, challenges basic categories, such as fetishism and voyeurism, in feminist film theory.

Beyond simple recognition of the national and cultural specificity of cinematic constructions of gender, feminist film theory also faces the challenge of conceptualizing the effects of these constructions, as they circulate transnationally through the international film industry and through globalized culture. Feminist film theory first began to engage with such issues in relation to postcolonial criticism. Ella Shohat's essay, 'Gender and Culture of Empire: Toward a Feminist Ethnography of the Cinema' (2000), examines the interrelations between constructions of the subaltern and constructions of the feminine in (post)colonial discourse and cinema. She identifies gendered metaphors in colonial discourse, examines contradictions between national and sexual narrative hierarchies in a variety of films, and looks at the sexual ambiguity of orientalist tropes in American cinema. As well as showing how national identity can confer positional superiority on white female characters in films, Shohat offers several examples of resistant counter-narratives that subvert patriarchal colonial discourse, including Nelson Pereira dos Santos' *How Tasty Was My Frenchman* (*Como Era Gostoso o Meu Francês*, Brazil, 1970) and Tracey Moffatt's *Nice Coloured Girls* (Australia, 1987). In the essay, 'Framing Post-Third-Worldist Culture: Gender and Nation in Middle Eastern/North African Film and Video' (1997), Shohat argues for the use of the term 'post-Third-Worldist' rather than postcolonial as a way of moving beyond the unifying exigencies of anti-colonial nationalist ideology and Third-Worldist ideology, and beginning to address the gendered divisions within postcolonial nations. As well as discussing revisionist histories of women's roles in and after national liberation struggles, including Lebanese director Heiny Srour's *Leila and the Wolves* (*Leile wal dhiab*, Belgium/Netherlands, 1984) and Tunisian Moufida Tlatli's *Silences of the Palace* (*Samt al Qusur*, France/Tunisia, 1994), Shohat considers the deterritorialized

critique of gendered national identities implicit in transnational works, such as Mona Hatoum's experimental video piece *Measures of Distance* (UK, 1988).

Although there are instances of postcolonial film feminisms that embrace notions of authentic and resistant identity – most notably, Julie Dash's *Daughters of the Dust* (US/UK, 1991) and Toni Cade Bambara's writing on this 'unabashedly Afrocentric' film (1993: 129) – for the most part, film feminism has carried the anti-essentialist critique of identity over into its engagement with geopolitics. Vietnamese filmmaker and theorist Trinh T. Minh-ha, a key thinker in this area, introduces the concept of the 'Inappropriate Other' as a way of challenging essentialist and colonial constructions of self and other. She offers a deconstruction of ethnographic ways of viewing 'the Other', and of participant observation in particular. Drawing on Zora Neale Hurston's idea of the 'pet negro system', Trinh argues that white liberal demands for postcolonial 'others' to represent themselves is always in effect repressive tokenism:

[A] non-white view is desirable because it would help to fill a hole that whites are now *willing* to leave more or less empty so as to lessen the critical pressure and to give the illusion of a certain incompleteness that needs the native's input to be more complete, but is ultimately dependent on white authority to attain any form of 'real' completion. (1991: 72)

Trinh argues that the only way to escape the logic by which (neo)colonial discursive mastery is continually reasserted is to undercut conceptions of authentic identity and essential difference:

Essential difference allows those who rely on it to rest reassuringly on its gamut of fixed notions. Any mutation in identity, in essence, in regularity, and even in physical place poses a problem, if not a threat, in terms of classification and control. If you can't locate the other, how are you to locate yourself? (1991: 73)

The strategy of the Inappropriate(d) other informs Trinh's films, especially her first film, *Reassemblage* (US, 1982). In this experimental documentary on Senegalese women, a reflexive soundtrack repeatedly comments that her aim is not to speak 'about' the women, but to 'speak nearby'. The very fact of a Vietnamese filmmaker based in the US making a documentary in Africa is enough to unsettle ethnographic assumptions about who speaks for and about whom, and Trinh reinforces this through formal strategies, which continually undercut the film's authority and objectivity. Trinh argues that it is not only her experience as an exiled intellectual which is cross-cultural, but the heterogeneous reality of postmodern times, in which hybrid and hyphenated identities are becoming the norm.

Such anti-essentialist arguments about cultural and gender identity are now taken for granted in feminist theory, but their real significance is only just beginning to be understood, as the economics of globalization intensify the material inequalities that underpin cultural and national differences. Inderpal Grewal and Caren Kaplan outline an agenda for transnational feminism capable of articulating the relationship of gender to 'scattered hegemonies such as global economic structures, patriarchal nationalisms, "authentic" forms of tradition, local structures of domination and legal-juridical oppression on multiple levels' (1994: 17). In their critique of Prathiba Parmar and Alice Walker's *Warrior Marks* (UK, 1993), a documentary about female genital surgery/mutilation in Africa, Grewal and Kaplan claim that the film's 'global womanism' inadvertently reasserts the power of colonial discourse over its subjects. In support of this claim, they argue that the diversity of views of such surgery is suppressed, that first-world conceptions of sexual health and personal freedom are universalized, that a neocolonial assumption of the superiority of modernity is made, and that the film uses discredited ethnographic tropes to organize its material. Distinguishing between transnational feminism and global womanism, Grewal and Kaplan argue that the 'global woman' exists only as a projection, an affirmation of the subject of metropolitan feminism: 'The multicultural subject, as it is constituted through such a globalized practice of feminism, may be part of an anti-racist

strategy but its only space of negotiation is a modern nation-state' (2003: 272). Grewal and Kaplan's argument reflects the difficulty of constructing – within film, Film Studies or any other medium or discipline – a discourse which genuinely recognizes cross-cultural differences and which accomplishes something more useful than ventriloquizing the transnational Other. At the same time, it draws attention to the most pressing conceptual problem for feminism: how, in the face of all this difference and anti-essentialism, to define the terms on which women might constitute any kind of category, group or collectivity capable of acts and expressions of effective solidarity. Moreover, the charge that Parmar and Walker universalize the subject of feminist modernity opens onto complex debates about the universality of human rights and the interrelated histories of human rights and feminism.

The difficulty of constructing transnational feminist arguments that do not rely on the reductive antinomy of global (bad) and local (good) is negotiated more successfully by Sujata Moorti's discussion of globalization and modernity in her study of Indian media responses to *Fire* (India/Canada, 1996). This melodrama about arranged marriage in the Hindu middle class, directed by Indian-Canadian Deepa Mehta, provoked controversy on its release in India, and in other countries with substantial Hindu populations, by its depiction of a sexual relationship which develops between two women trapped in loveless arranged marriages to brothers. The film was defended by the liberal intelligentsia, by feminists, and by some gay/lesbian activists (although others criticized its lack of commitment to the depiction of lesbian sexual identity and social subjectivity). Moorti argues that the controversy demonstrates the complex and conjunctural relationships between global 'modernity' and local 'tradition'. Those who attacked the film from the right did so for its alleged lack of cultural authenticity, its 'Westernized' depictions of sexuality (lesbianism) and its Muslim star (Shabana Azmi), in the process defining national cultural authenticity through xenophobia, homophobia, sexism and religious bigotry. According to Moorti, anxieties regarding the social transformations brought by globalization coalesced in the hostile responses to the film:

> [L]ocal resistance to the global is manifested in a series of practices that invoke religion to regulate women; control over female bodies becomes a crucial strategy for rejecting the global. Issues pertaining to female identity, sexuality and social location are repeatedly reworked in the context of global flows. The female body … becomes a central site where discourses of power and regulation come to bear. (2000)

Although the protests against *Fire* were not primarily about women, but more about cultural authenticity, ideas about female identity and propriety became caught up in the debate. The context for this was a major reinvention of Indian womanhood: 'The controversy over *Fire* occurred at a historical moment when Indian woman was being reconstituted as a diacritic of Hindu nationalism, a specific religious nationalism' (Moorti, 2000). The debate around the film reinstates a well-worn paradigm which maps the opposition between authentic tradition and corrosive modernity onto that between the local (national) and the global, inventing tradition as a focus for imagined community.

Moorti's depiction of local hostility to the modernizing forces of transnational, media, not as popular resistance to the manipulations of global capital, but as an opportunistic extension of local ideological control, casts an interesting sidelight on Grewal and Kaplan's rejection of 'global womanism'. Unlike Grewal and Kaplan, who state categorically that, by supporting the agendas of modernity, feminists misrecognize or fail to recognize Western hegemonies, Moorti argues that the politics of the antinomies global/local and tradition/modernity are purely conjunctural. They have particular meaning or value prior to their emergence at a specific time and place. Moreover, since irreversible modernization, of one kind or another, has already taken place throughout the world, and since anti-modernism is itself a modern ideology, the question for feminists is not whether women should be modern, but how.

FEMALE ACTION AND AGENCY

Since the beginning of the 1990s, questions of representation that had been bracketed by the psychoanalytic and semiotic feminist film theory of the 1970s and 1980s have reappeared in critical discussions of the female action hero. Strong women, such as Howard Hawks' female characters, were a feature of early feminist film criticism, but were read as 'phallic women' within the psychoanalytic paradigm. Psychoanalytic film theorists Barbara Creed (1986), writing on horror, and Tania Modleski (1988), writing on Hitchcock's heroines, questioned assumptions about the passivity of female characters in mainstream fiction film, though they did so by developing, rather than departing from, the psychoanalytic model. Feminist criticism's return to the question of the active female protagonist was prompted by the emergence of a new breed of female action hero in contemporary Hollywood films, as exemplified by the *Alien* films (Ridley Scott, UK, 1979; James Cameron, US/UK, 1986; David Fincher, US, 1992; Jean-Pierre Jeunet, US, 1997), the first two *Terminator* films (James Cameron, US, 1984; James Cameron, France/US, 1991), *Blue Steel* (Kathryn Bigelow, US, 1990), *The Silence of the Lambs* (Jonathan Demme, US, 1991), *The Long Kiss Goodnight* (Renny Harlin, US, 1996) and the *Kill Bill* films (Quentin Tarantino, US, 2003; 2004). Along with these new cinematic images of female agency, the feminist and queer theory of the 1990s developed new models of female identity and subjectivity. Butler's work is central to these developments. Her construction of gender as performative and citational shares with earlier feminist theory the notion that gender identity is regulated by social norms, but departs from them in that it allows for the possibility that these norms can be shifted or eroded by deviant or parodic performances or citations (1990; 2004). In Film Studies, Yvonne Tasker's work on gender in action cinema makes a congruent argument, that the meanings of bodies in contemporary action films are 'very far from being the transparent signifiers of a simplistic sexual and racial hierarchy that some critics take them to be' (1993: 165). Tasker examines representations of male and female corporeal identity through the interplay of power and powerlessness, strength and vulnerability that characterizes action genres. Far from simply confirming gender norms, Tasker concludes that contemporary action cinema articulates profound ambivalences about them. As a fantasy space in which identities and identifications can be negotiated, according to Tasker, popular cinema not only affirms gender norms, but also destabilizes them.

The figure of the female action hero is associated with a theoretical shift in feminist Film Studies, as Elizabeth Hills (1999) has explained. Feminist criticism that works within the classical Freudian paradigm equates femininity with passivity and masculinity with activity, with the consequence that active female heroes can only be understood as 'figuratively male' at some level, as Clover argues in the case of the Final Girl. Hills contends that female action heroes confound this binary logic by selectively appropriating masculine prerogatives and attributes, whilst retaining certain conventionally feminine characteristics. She suggests that an alternative critical framework could be derived from certain concepts in the philosophy of Deleuze and Félix Guattari. Hills sees the Body without Organs, assemblages, and becoming as particularly appropriate to the body of the female action hero, transformed by prosthetic weaponry. This argument is not entirely convincing, given that the female action hero seems to be constructed by an interplay between masculinity and femininity, activity and passivity, which, however complex, remains within binary gender terms, unlike the radical rhetoric of Deleuze and Guattari. Films which feature female action heroes, especially the *Alien* films, tend to be organized around the proliferation and ever-more complex recombination of binaries rather than alternative logics. As such, they are better described in the theoretical vocabulary of Butler than that of Deleuze and Guattari.

Writing on the female action hero is revisionist in several senses. It revises the psychoanalytic presuppositions of feminist film theory, and it also revises the radical project of film feminism. Instead of locating feminist resistance in alterity and oppositionality, it finds resistances within mainstream systems. These resistances tend to be cast in the form of individual character agency that, more often than not, is equated with an escape from the straitjacket of femininity. The female action hero thus embodies certain aspects of feminist politics. but not others: empowerment rather than an end to power structures, equality rather than difference. In short, the female action hero represents a selective, and elective, appropriation of feminist values that is post-feminist rather than feminist. Evidence for this view can be seen with particular clarity in glamorous, ironic variants such as *Charlie's Angels* (McG, US/Germany, 2000) or *Lara Croft: Tomb Raider* (Simon West, UK/Germany/US/Japan, 2001).

The burgeoning critical debate on female action heroes has displaced psychoanalytic feminism's theory of representation without, as yet, producing an account of spectatorship capable of replacing psychoanalytic feminism's sophisticated theorization of the spectator's relationship to cinematic images of gendered bodies. This theoretical challenge is complicated by the use of digital technology in much recent action cinema, which turns the film-theoretical truism that the image is always artificially constructed into a literal fact. Despite the initial enthusiasm of cyberfeminists for new media technologies, it has now become evident that digital imagery, freed from the constraints and resistances of reality, is often more profoundly permeated by ideology as a consequence, as has been seen in the iconography of computer games. Feminist Film Studies has always been a self-reflective discourse, constantly rethinking itself. The task now confronting feminist – or post-feminist – Film Studies is to rethink itself in relation to new technologies of gender and new transnational gender politics.

REFERENCES

Acker, Ally (1991) *Reel Women: Pioneers of the Cinema, 1896 to the Present*. London: Continuum.

Armatage, Kay (2003) *The Girl from God's Country: Nell Shipman and the Silent Cinema*. Toronto: University of Toronto Press.

Bambara, Toni Cade (1993) 'Reading the Signs, Empowering the Eye: *Daughters of the Dust* and the Black Independent Cinema Movement', in Manthia Diawara (ed.), *Black American Cinema*. London: Routledge. pp. 118–44.

Bean, Jennifer M. and Negra, Diane (eds) (2002) *A Feminist Reader in Early Cinema*. Durham, NC: Duke University Press.

Beugnet, Martine (2004) *Claire Denis*. Manchester: Manchester University Press.

Bobo, Jacqueline (1988) '*The Color Purple*: Black Women as Cultural Readers', in E. Deirdre Pribram (ed.), *Female Spectators: Looking at Film and Television*. London: Verso. pp. 90–109.

Bruno, Giuliana (1993) *Streetwalking on a Ruined Map: Cultural Theory and the City Films of Elvira Notari*. Princeton, NJ: Princeton University Press.

Butler, Judith (1990) *Gender Trouble: Feminism and the Subversion of Identity*. New York: Routledge.

Butler, Judith (2004) *Undoing Gender*. New York: Routledge.

Citron, Michelle, Lesage, Julia, Mayne, Judith, Rich, B. Ruby and Taylor, Anna Marie (1978) 'Women and Film: A Discussion of Feminist Aesthetics', *New German Critique*, 13: 83–107.

Clover, Carol J. (1992) *Men, Women and Chainsaws*. London: BFI.

Cowie, Elizabeth (1984) 'Fantasia', *m/f*, 9: 71–105.

Creed, Barbara (1986) 'Horror and the Monstrous-Feminine', *Screen*, 27(1): 44–70.

de Lauretis, Teresa (1984) *Alice Doesn't: Feminism, Semiotics, Cinema*. London: MacMillan.

Doane, Mary Ann (1982) 'Film and the Masquerade: Theorising the Female Spectator', *Screen*, 23(3–4): 74–87.

Doane, Mary Ann (1987) *The Desire to Desire: The Woman's Film of the 1940s*. Bloomington: Indiana University Press.

Doane, Mary Ann (2004) 'Aesthetics and Politics', *Signs*, 30(1): 1229–35.

Fischer, Lucy (1989) *Shot/countershot: Film Tradition and Women's Cinema*. Princeton, NJ: Princeton University Press.

Flitterman-Lewis, Sandy (1990) *To Desire Differently: Feminism and the French Cinema*. Urbana: University of Illinois Press.

Foster, Gwendolyn Audrey (1995) *Women Film Directors: An International Bio-Critical Dictionary*. Westport, CT: Greenwood Press.

Foster, Gwendolyn Audrey (ed.) (1999) *Identity and Memory: The Films of Chantal Akerman*. Trowbridge: Flicks.

Francke, Lizzie (1994) *Script Girls: Women Screenwriters in Hollywood*. London: BFI.

Gaines, Jane (1988) 'White Privilege and Looking Relations: Race and Gender in Feminist Film Theory', *Screen*, 29(4): 12–27.

Gaines, Jane (2002) 'Of Cabbages and Authors', in Jennifer M. Bean and Diane Negra (eds), *A Feminist Reader in Early Cinema*. Durham, NC: Duke University Press. pp. 88–118.

Gaines, Jane (2004) 'First Fictions', *Signs*, 30(1): 1293–317.

Gledhill, Christine (1988) 'Pleasurable Negotiations', in E. Deirdre Pribram (ed.), *Female Spectators: Looking at Film and Television*. London: Verso. pp. 64–89.

Gledhill, Christine (1994) 'Image and Voice', in D. Carson, L. Dittmar and J.R. Welsch (eds), *Multiple Voices in Feminist Film Criticism*. Minneapolis: University of Minnesota Press. pp. 109–23.

Grewal, Inderpal and Kaplan, Caren (1994) *Scattered Hegemonies: Postmodernity and Transnational Feminist Practices*. Minneapolis: University of Minnesota Press.

Grewal, Inderpal and Kaplan, Caren (2003) '*Warrior Marks*: Global Womanism's Neo-Colonial Discourse in a Multicultural Context', in Ella Shohat and Robert Stam (eds), *Multiculturalism, Postcoloniality, and Transnational Media*. New Brunswick, NJ: Rutgers University Press. pp. 256–78.

Halberstam, Judith (2001) 'The Transgender Gaze in *Boys Don't Cry*', *Screen*, 42(3): 294–98.

Hansen, Miriam (1991) *Babel and Babylon: Spectatorship in American Silent Film*. Cambridge, MA: Harvard University Press.

Harper, Sue (2000) *Women in British Cinema: Mad, Bad and Dangerous to Know*. London: Continuum.

Haskell, Molly ([1975] 1987) *From Reverence to Rape: The Treatment of Women in the Movies*. 2nd edn. Chicago: University of Chicago Press.

Hills, Elizabeth (1999) 'From "figurative males" to action heroines: further thoughts on active women in the cinema', *Screen*, 40(1): 38–51.

hooks, bell (1992) *Black Looks: Race and Representation*. London: Turnaround.

Jackson, Renata (2002) *The Modernist Poetics and Experimental Film Practice of Maya Deren, 1917–1961*. Lewiston, Queenston: Edwin Mellen Press.

Jayamanne, Laleen (1995) *Kiss Me Deadly: Feminism and Cinema for the Moment.* Sydney: Power Publications.

Jayamanne, Laleen (2000) *Toward Cinema and Its Double: Cross-Cultural Mimesis.* Bloomington: Indiana University Press.

Jayamanne, Laleen (2004) 'Pursuing Micromovements in Room 202', *Signs*, 30(1): 1248–56.

Johnston, Claire (ed.) (1973a) *Notes on Women's Cinema.* London: Society for Education in Film and Television.

Johnston, Claire (1973b) 'Women's Cinema as Counter-Cinema', in Claire Johnston (ed.), *Notes on Women's Cinema.* London: Society for Education in Film and Television. pp. 24–31.

Johnston, Claire (1980) 'The Subject of Feminist Film Theory/Practice', *Screen*, 21(2): 27–34.

Johnston, Claire (1981) '*Maeve*', *Screen*, 22(4): 54–63.

Kaplan, E. Ann (1997) *Looking for the Other: Feminism, Film and the Imperial Gaze.* New York: Routledge.

Knight, Julia (1992) *Women and the New German Cinema.* London: Verso.

Kristeva, Julia (1981) 'Woman Can Never Be Defined', in Elaine Marks and Isabelle de Courtivron (eds), *New French Feminisms: An Anthology.* Brighton: Harvester Press. pp. 137–41.

Kuhn, Annette (1982) *Women's Pictures: Feminism and Cinema.* London: Routledge.

Kuhn, Annette (ed.) (1995) *Queen of the B's: Ida Lupino Behind the Camera.* Trowbridge: Flicks.

Lane, Christina (2000) *Feminist Hollywood From Born in Flames to Point Break.* Detroit: Wayne State University Press.

MacCreadie, Marsha (1994) *The Women who Write the Movies: From Frances Marion to Nora Ephron.* Seacaucus, NJ: Birch Lane Press.

Margulies, Ivone (1996) *Nothing Happens: Chantal Akerman's Hyperrealist Everyday.* Durham, NC: Duke University Press.

Mayne, Judith (1990) *The Woman at the Keyhole: Feminism and Women's Cinema.* Bloomington: Indiana University Press.

Mayne, Judith (1994) *Directed by Dorothy Arzner.* Bloomington: Indiana University Press.

Mayne, Judith (2005) *Claire Denis.* Urbana: University of Illinois.

McMahan, Alison (2002) *Alice Guy-Blaché: Lost Visionary of the Cinema.* New York: Continuum.

Mellencamp, Patricia (1995) *A Fine Romance: Five Ages of Film Feminism.* Philadelphia: Temple University Press.

Modleski, Tania (1988) *The Women Who Knew Too Much: Hitchcock and Feminist Theory.* New York: Methuen.

Moorti, Sujata (2000) 'Inflamed Passions: *Fire*, the Woman Question, and the Policing of Cultural Borders', *Genders*, 32. Available at: http://www.genders.org/g32/g32_moorti.html.

Mueller, Roswitha (1994) *Valie Export: Fragments of the Imagination.* Bloomington: Indiana University Press.

Mulvey, Laura (1975) 'Visual Pleasure and Narrative Cinema', *Screen*, 16(3): 6–18.

Mulvey, Laura (1979) 'Feminism, Film and the Avant-Garde', *Framework*, 10: 3–10.

Mulvey, Laura (1981) 'Afterthoughts on "Visual Pleasure and Narrative Cinema" inspired by *Duel in the Sun*', *Framework*, 15/16/17: 12–15.

Mulvey, Laura (1986) 'Melodrama in and out of the home', in Colin MacCabe (ed.), *High Theory/Low Culture: Analysing Popular Television and Film.* Manchester: Manchester University Press. pp. 80–100.

Mulvey, Laura (1987) 'Changes: Thoughts on Myth, Narrative and Historical Experience', *History Workshop Journal*, 23: 3–19.

Mulvey, Laura (2000) 'The Index and the Uncanny', in Carolyn Bailey Gill (ed.), *Time and the Image.* Manchester: Manchester University Press. pp. 139–48.

Naficy, Hamid (1996) 'Iranian Cinema', in Geoffrey Nowell-Smith (ed.), *The Oxford History of World Cinema.* Oxford: Oxford University Press. pp. 672–8.

Naficy, Hamid (1999) 'Veiled Visions/Powerful Presences: Women in Postrevolutionary Iranian Cinema', in Rose Issa and Sheila Whitaker (eds), *Life and Art: The New Iranian Cinema.* London: National Film Theatre. pp. 43–65.

Naficy, Hamid (2001) 'Veiled Voice and Vision in Iranian Cinema: The Evolution of Rakhshan Banietemad's Films', in Murray Pomerance (ed.), *Ladies and Gentlemen, Boys and Girls: Gender in Film at the End of the Twentieth Century.* Albany, NY: State University of New York Press. pp. 37–53.

Petro, Patrice (1989) *Joyless Streets: Women and Melodramatic Representation in Weimar Germany.* Princeton, NJ: Princeton University Press.

Petro, Patrice (2002) *Aftershocks of the New: Feminism and Film History.* New Brunswick, NJ: Rutgers University Press.

Rabinovitz, Lauren (1991) *Points of Resistance: Women, Power and Politics in the New York Avant-Garde, 1943–1971.* Urbana: University of Illinois Press.

Rabinovitz, Lauren (1998) *For the Love of Pleasure: Women, Movies, and Culture in Turn-of-the-Century Chicago.* New Brunswick, NJ: Rutgers University Press.

Rollet, Brigitte and Tarr, Carrie (2001) *Cinema and the Second Sex: Women's Filmmaking in France in the 1980s and 1990s*. London: Continuum.

Rosen, Marjorie (1973) *Popcorn Venus: Women, Movies and the American Dream*. New York: Coward, Mcann and Geoghegan.

Shohat, Ella (1997) 'Framing Post-Third-Worldist Culture: Gender and Nation in Middle Eastern/North African Film and Video', *Jouvert: A Journal of Postcolonial Studies,* 1(1). Available at: http://152.1.96.5/jouvert/v1i1/shohat.htm.

Shohat, Ella (2000) 'Gender and Culture of Empire: Toward a Feminist Ethnography of the Cinema', in Robert Stam and Toby Miller (eds), *Film and Theory: An Anthology*. Oxford: Blackwell. pp. 669–96.

Slide, Anthony (1996a) *The Silent Feminists*. Lanham, MD: Scarecrow Press.

Slide, Anthony (1996b) *Lois Weber: The Director Who Lost Her Way in History*. Westport, CT: Greenwood Press.

Smelik, Anneke (1998) *And the Mirror Crack'd: Feminist Cinema and Film Theory*. Basingstoke: Palgrave.

Smith, Alison (1998) *Agnès Varda*. Manchester: Manchester University Press.

Stacey, Jackie (1994) *Star Gazing: Hollywood Cinema and Female Spectatorship*. New York: Routledge.

Staiger, Janet (1995) *Bad Women: Regulating Sexuality in Early American Cinema*. Minneapolis: University of Minnesota Press.

Stamp, Shelley (2000) *Movie-Struck Girls: Women and Motion Picture Culture After the Nickelodeon*. Princeton, NJ: Princeton University Press.

Straayer, Chris (1996) *Deviant Eyes, Deviant Bodies: Sexual Re-Orientations in Film and Video*. New York: Columbia University Press.

Tarr, Carrie (1999) *Diane Kurys*. Manchester:Manchester University Press.

Tasker, Yvonne (1993) *Spectacular Bodies: Gender, Genre and the Action Cinema*. London: Routledge.

Trinh, T. Minh-ha (1991) *When the Moon Waxes Red: Representation, Gender and Cultural Politics*. New York: Routledge.

White, Patricia (1999) *UnInvited: Classical Hollywood Cinema and Lesbian Representability*. Bloomington: Indiana University Press.

Woolf, Virginia (1996) 'The Cinema', in Mike O'Pray (ed.), *The British Avant-Garde Film, 1926–1995: An Anthology of Writings*. London/Luton: The Arts Council of England/John Libbey Media/University of Luton. pp. 33–6.

26

Authors and Auteurs: The Uses of Theory

John Caughie

You know there's a lot of detail in this movie; it's absolutely essential because these little nuances enrich the over-all impact and strengthen the picture ... At the beginning of the film we show Rod Taylor in the bird shop. He catches the canary that has escaped from its cage, and after putting it back, he says to Tippi Hedren, 'I'm putting you back in your gilded cage, Melanie Daniels'. I added that sentence during the shooting because I felt it added to her characterization as a wealthy, shallow playgirl. And later on, when the gulls attack the village, Melanie Daniels takes refuge in a glass telephone booth and I show her as a bird in a cage. This time it isn't a gilded cage, but a cage of misery, and it's also the beginning of her ordeal by fire, so to speak. It's a reversal of the age-old conflict between men and birds. Here the humans are in cages, and the birds are on the outside. When I shoot something like that, I hardly think the public is likely to notice it.

Alfred Hitchcock on *The Birds* (quoted in Truffaut, 1985: 285)

Returning to auteurism and authorship after a decent interval, I am struck by two contradictory perceptions: first, that the auteur seems to have disappeared from the centre of theoretical debate in Film Studies; second, that this disappearance may in fact be an illusion and that the grave to which we consigned him – and, by implication, her – is, in fact, empty.

Reading the academic literature diagnostically, it seems that the delirium of auteurism has been sanitized by common sense. First, there is a select body of 'postscripts', 'retrospects' and 'revisitations' which permit writers associated with 'first-generation' auteurism (Peter Wollen [2003], Geoffrey Nowell-Smith [2003], Robin Wood [2002], for example) to temper their affiliations, qualify their claims, and complicate their positions. Second, and perhaps more importantly, in a number of areas – gender, sexuality, nationality, ethnicity – there is a very pointed recognition that it may have been irresponsible or arrogant to declare the author dead just at the point at which previously 'un-authorized' constituencies began to speak with authority. And, third, there is now a more scholarly and empirical understanding of the actual conditions of production which permitted and constrained the creativity and self-expression of the auteur; an understanding which, in fact, no longer needs the concept of an 'auteur' and is content to write about directors within 'director-centred criticism'. 'The death of the *auteur*', says Victor Perkins, 'is without the drastic consequences that some have imagined for the theory and practice of director-centred criticism' (1990: 63).

There is, then, a retreat both from the wilder shores of critical ecstasy ('If anyone persists in thinking *Party Girl* an imbecility, 'wrote Fereydoun Hoveyda', I will cry out: Long live the imbecility which dazzles my eyes, fascinates my heart, and give me a glimpse of the kingdom of heaven!' [1986a: 127]) and from the opposite, but equally wild, shore of the closing sentence of Roland Barthes' inescapable essay, in which he dramatically – or melodramatically – sentences the Author to death:

> We are now beginning to let ourselves be fooled no longer by the arrogant, antiphrastical recriminations of good society in favour of the very thing it sets aside, ignores, smothers or destroys; we know that to give writing its future, it is necessary to overthrow the myth: the birth of the reader must be at the cost of the death of the Author. (1977: 148)

Avoiding the opposite extremes of beatification and damnation, academic discourse about authorship has become properly 'academic': measured, sceptical and open. Generations of students have learned not to be auteurist ('I'm not being auteurist, but …'), and that authorship is a critical problem, whose history they must learn in order to avoid temptations which they may never have felt. While the virtues of a measured, sceptical and open discourse are undoubtedly the ones we should be teaching and practising, they do not wholly encompass the place which auteurism and authorship have occupied in Film Studies. Approached 'commonsensically', authorship as an area of engagement and debate seems to have lost its energizing force, its function as an irritant soothed by knowing hindsight.

Meanwhile, slowly vanishing from academic debate, the auteur appears everywhere else – in publicity, in journalistic reviews, in television programmes, in film retrospectives, in the marketing of cinema. Sometime around the point at which Film Studies began to be embarrassed by its affiliation to the author, the film industry and its subsidiaries began to discover with renewed enthusiasm the value of authorial branding for both marketing and reputation. It was already apparent by the late 1960s that auteurism was capacious and could accommodate even those who had first poured scorn on the *politique des auteurs* as Gallic intellectual hooliganism. Now, it has become the air we breathe. A *auteurism* has become ideology; 'it *really* represents something without representing something real' (Marx and Engels, 1974: 52).

I should acknowledge at the outset my own contribution to this process. In the first paragraph of an article on homosexuality and authorship in *Screen* in 1991, Andy Medhurst paid waspish tribute to the Reader, *Theories of Authorship* (Caughie, 1981), which I edited for the British Film Institute in 1981:

> Authorship is hardly a hot issue these days. The very word itself conjures up ancient dusty battles over the cultural legitimacy of cinema, battles that were fought, won and forgotten long ago. The idea that a film's director is the primary, shaping force of its meaning is simultaneously inscribed as middlebrow commonsense … and dismissed as hopelessly outmoded by every branch of recent critical theory. It is a dead debate, and its tombstone was the BFI Reader, *Theories of Authorship*, which offered an inbuilt teleology, a narrative trajectory which led me, as a postgraduate student, away from the embarrassments of romantic individualism to the chastening rigours of poststructuralist thought. (1991: 197–8)

It would be hard to miss the double-edge. On the one hand, the collection of articles was indeed intended to do more than simply summarize positions. It was conceived as a theoretical intervention and it did have the narrative strategy which Medhurst experienced. On the other hand, I know irony when I see it, and I have some sympathy for its object. I have always had the suspicion that the success of the Reader – and, twenty-five years later, it is still in print – was that it made authorship teachable by making it orderly. More than I would have thought at the time or would now welcome, a book that was intended to undermine the certainties of creative authority became authoritative. Such is the fate of authorial intention.

In his *Theories of Cinema*, Francesco Casetti argues for an approach to theory which leaves open a space for debate, and he insists on the productivity of theoretical knowledge. 'It is the *productivity* of a knowledge', he says, 'that ensures, perhaps more than anything else, its theoretical status' (1999: 3). In his conclusion, he argues that it is not scientific rationality that defines a theory, but its '*cognitive* capacity, in the broadest sense of the word' (1999: 315). Rather than an achieved knowledge, theory is a means of achieving knowledge. Like experimental science itself, its methods can no longer be reduced to formalized 'scientific' constructs, but are drawn to such nuanced forms as metaphor, analogy or parallelism. Furthermore, he says,

> a theory is knowledge that circulates among those working in a given field and through them reaches broader audiences, producing discussion, loyalties, and dissent. In this respect, it is a social device, something that is diffused and shared within a community. Finally, a theory is also a historical event: it is a discourse that comes on the scene at a given time, in a given place, and by its very presence is capable of defining the ambience in which it appears. In this sense, it is a historical reality, something that reflects the path (or even the error) of thought. (1999: 315)

Theory, then, 'institutionalizes' knowledge, but as a dynamic field constantly under review and revision that is always open to debate and dissent.

In Casetti's sense, then, authorship is a theory: '*a set of assumptions, more or less organized, explicit, and binding, which serves as a reference for scholars so that they can understand and explain the nature of the phenomenon under investigation*' (1999: 2). While recognizing its origins in the editorial *policy* (the so-called '*politique des auteurs*') of *Cahiers du cinéma* in the 1950s, the significance of authorship *theory* for Film Studies lies in its productivity: its production and institutionalization not simply of a 'knowledge field', but also of a community within which that field could be shared and contested; a field on which sides could be taken, theoretical

battles fought, and solidarities formed and reformed. It was a field of debate in which the members of an emerging community began to identify themselves and define their studies and their terms of engagement. The practical and experiential importance of debate – not just in articles and books, but, in Britain, in BFI summer schools, Edinburgh Film Festival seminars, SEFT weekend schools, the foyers of cinemas – to an emerging field of academic study cannot be overemphasized. In the United States, the vituperative denunciation of Andrew Sarris' 'Notes on the auteur theory in 1962' (1962–3) by Pauline Kael gave a polemical edge to auteurism that reverberated across the Atlantic ('the *Movie* group', she says, 'is like an intellectual club for the intellectually handicapped' [1963: 22]) and inflected the partisan ways in which auteurism was taken up by criticism and, in turn, by academic Film Studies. 'A spark was ignited', said Sarris famously, 'in far-off San Francisco by a lady critic with a lively sense of outrage' (1968: 26). Just as the lines of battle had been drawn in Paris between *Cahiers du cinéma* and *Positif*, so in Britain they were drawn between *Sight and Sound*, *Movie* and *Screen* and in the United States between the west-coast *Film Quarterly* and the east-coast *Film Culture*. The fact that the emerging field of study felt itself to be academically marginalized only intensified the debates, reinforced the solidarities and drew the wagons into a tighter circle. The 'historical reality' of the various engagements with authorship was formative for many of us, and has left its mark on Film Studies – both the path of thought *and* the errors that went with it.

It is customary for 'historical realities' to be so by forgetting the histories and realities that went before them, and the period from the 1950s to the 1970s was fertile ground for both 'new waves' and for amnesia. It is easy to form the impression that film theory – like teenagers and sex – was invented in that period, and that before the polemics of *Cahiers* in the 1950s, and its skirmishes with *Positif*, there was no debate about the art of film, or that before the meeting of auteurism and structuralism in the 1970s there was no theory of the artist. To get the measure of authorship theory and its particular impact, it seems important to have some sense of the theoretical field which preceded it and into which it burst.

In 1948, Alexandre Astruc had already proclaimed the 'new age of cinema' to be 'the age of the *caméra stylo*', in which, using the camera as his pen, 'an artist can express his thoughts, however abstract they may be, or translate his obsessions exactly as he does in the contemporary essay or novel' (1981: 9). Astruc was referring specifically to an avant-garde cinema, and in the Anglophone world he can be placed most clearly in the tradition of *Close Up* and the group around Kenneth MacPherson, where the role of the director/artist as poet of the cinema was implicit in the criticism and explicit in the filmmaking practice (Donald et al., 1998). The assumption of the artist applied to the avant-garde, however, was only more explicit than the insistence on film as an art form which can be found in a number of the theoretical discussions of cinema from the silent period onwards. In Rudolf Arnheim's *Film as Art* (1932; 1933; 1957), the 'film artist' appears almost interchangeably with the director in the application of creative technique to expression. Arnheim argues that, in the earliest film, the intention was simply to capture objective reality without mediation or 'distortion':

> Only gradually, and at first probably without conscious intention, the possibility of using the differences between film and real life for the purpose of making formally significant images was realized. What before had been ignored or simply accepted was now intelligently developed, displayed, and made into a tool to serve the desire for artistic creation. The object as such was no longer the first consideration. Its place in importance was taken by the pictorial representation of its properties, the making apparent of an inherent idea, and so forth. (1957: 41–2)

Here, the film artist 'distorts' the unmediated photographic reality through representation in order to bring forth an inherent idea, a concept of expressiveness which would be comfortable with both Russian montage theory and German expressionism.

For Béla Balázs, whose *Theory of Film* was first published in Moscow in 1945 as *Iskusstvo Kino* (*The Art of Cinema*), the story was one of

> the transformation of cinematography from a technique into an art, the transformation of a moving picture industry, which merely reproduced stage performances, into an autonomous, independent, utterly novel art-producer .... (1970: 155)

Sharing a distrust of the avant-garde with Georg Lukács, his compatriot and fellow-member of the Budapest Sunday Circle – 'a hangover from the psychotic conditions following the first world war; it was one of the ways in which bourgeois consciousness sought to escape reality' (Balázs, 1970: 158) – Balázs found no difficulty in conceptualizing an art form which was both popular and industrial. With Siegfried Kracauer and André Bazin, however, he shared an insistence on an artist/director whose subjectivity was to be subjugated in the service of reality:

> [T]he artist may see any however unusual and strange physiognomy in his object, but as long as he sees it *in* the object and cuts it *out* of it, as Michelangelo cuts the figures he saw in his mind out of the block of marble, so long as he derives the physiognomy of the work of art *from* his object and does not project it *into* the object, so long is his art realistic. The artist is a realist as long as he does not change the structure and meaning of his object by subjectively drawn outlines. (1970: 101)

What emerges most clearly from these early theorists is an explication of the evolutionary development of techniques, which allow cinema to move from the photographic reproduction of reality to its creative representation, from a technology to an art. This is not to suggest that there was a consensus about film authorship before the debates of the 1950s and 1960s. With Kracauer's insistence that an art of representation is defined by the technology of reproduction (1960), one can see the debate opening up between those who held that the artist/director is defined by the creative use of the techniques available to him, and those for whom the business of the artist was to reshape the world or construct a new one. While Eisenstein and the Soviet theorists, would have taken the latter view, they would probably have agreed about the subjugation of the individual personality in the face of a revolutionary reality. It was the reality that was different, rather than the role of the artist. In this respect, these theorists of cinema can be located in a critical tradition of impersonality, a tradition that stretches from the socialist pragmatism of Friedrich Engels ('The more the opinions of the author remain hidden, the better for the work of art' [1976: 91]) to the literary modernism of T.S. Eliot ('Poetry is not a turning loose of emotion, but an escape from emotion; it is not the expression of personality, but an escape from personality' [1960: 58]).

This suggests at least one part of the theoretical context for the offensive of *Cahiers* and the significance of the debates and arguments about authorship which followed. When Sarris proclaims 'the distinguishable personality of the director as a criterion of value' (1981: 64), he is out of harmony not only with Kael and the assumptions of established film criticism and theory, but also with a dominant current of modernist thought about intention, impersonality and the artist. It is a commonplace that auteurism is a romanticism and can be traced to the aesthetic theories of the nineteenth-century Romantics. In fact, however, its antecedents may be found more clearly in the agonism of the early-twentieth-century avant-garde, and it is appropriate that the journal in which Sarris published his 'Notes and the auteur theory in 1962' was *Film Culture*, founded by Jonas Mekas in 1954 as the critical and theoretical voice of New York 'underground' film. In this respect, the criticism of *Cahiers* may have constituted an even more radical break than Bazin suspected from the prewar hostility to the aesthetic or revolutionary avant-garde of the 1920s and 1930s, which he shared with Balázs and Kracauer. The line between auteurism and the avant-garde is in no sense straightforward, and it is complicated by *Cahiers'* skirmishes over auteurism with *Positif*, the journal more usually linked with the politics of surrealism in France. Nevertheless, it is worth establishing some lines of connection between auteurism and the

agonistic aesthetic of the avant-garde, if only to rescue it from automatic association with a simple and infantile romanticism.

Even more contentious for film criticism than the assertion of personality as a criterion of value was the assertion that the value of the auteur was guaranteed not by the seriousness or moral purpose of the film's content, but by the audacity of its style. 'Morality', said Luc Moullet infamously, 'is a question of tracking shots' (1985: 148). This opened the way for a criticism that had little to say about 'important' films like *Lawrence of Arabia* (David Lean, UK, 1962) or *The Red Badge of Courage* (John Huston, US, 1951), but which could find the kingdom of heaven in *Party Girl* (Nicholas Ray, US, 1958) or *The Girl Can't Help It* (Frank Tashlin, US, 1956). The claim which brought down the greatest contempt from their contemporaries on both sides of the English Channel, and even won an indulgent finger-wagging from their *paterfamilias*, Bazin, was that the best film of a *metteur en scène*, a director without a consistent signature, was less interesting than the worst film of an auteur. Emblematically, *Casablanca* (Michael Curtiz, US, 1942) was less interesting than *Wee Willie Winkie* (John Ford, US, 1937). Furthermore, since, as Eric Rohmer argued (scandalously invoking Titian, Rembrandt and Beethoven), 'The history of art ... contains no example of an authentic genius who has experienced, at the end of his career, a period of decline' (1981: 38), then it follows that *Casablanca* must be considerably less interesting than *Red Line 7000* (Howard Hawks, US, 1965). Reviewing *Red Line 7000* in *Cahiers* in 1966, Jean Narboni finds in it the mark of 'someone ageless' for whom 'everything ... was being presented once and for all in a unique present'. 'What we have here', he says,

is a cinema that has to be taken in its entirety, a vast nervous system, a magnetic field, a multi-layered network. It conjures up the belief voiced by Edward G. Robinson in *Tiger Shark* that a man can only enter heaven whole (repeated in *The Big Sky*). So it is with Hawks's films, which posterity and our own rather remotely connected generation will have to accept as a totality, a whole *oeuvre*, and not as a series of films. (1986: 217)

The 'effrontery' of *Cahiers* is well documented, its enthusiasms on occasion masking a political insouciance which toppled over into reaction. However, following Casetti – 'a theory is also a historical event' – it was precisely this effrontery that effected a paradigm shift in thinking and writing about cinema. Theoretical and critical writing about cinema from the 1920s, 1930s and 1940s, exactly anticipating writing about television from the 1980s and 1990s, was concerned to 'take film seriously': for Balázs, 'the question of educating the public to a better, more critical appreciation of the films is a question of the mental health of nations' (1970: 17). The concept of a *popular* art was by no means widely accepted, and there was still work to be done to establish 'in the consciousness of our generation this most important artistic development of our century' (Balázs, 1970: 17). Film theory, like film education, was bound up in film appreciation. It was important that the public understood the techniques which the film artist had at his or her disposal in order that it could appreciate the good and shun the bad.

Cahiers, by contrast, in its sensibility and its rhetoric, begins from the premise that cinema is – self-evidently – an art that can be discussed in the same way as the great monuments of European culture, applying to Nicholas Ray the same criteria as might be applied to Goethe ('It would mean little enough to say that *Bitter Victory* is the most Goethian of films' [Godard, 1985: 119]) or comparing Luchino Visconti to Vermeer (Ayfre, 1985: 185).

If Domarchi, for example, quotes Hegel and Kant in discussing Minnelli, he does so neither out of pedantry nor a love of paradox, but simply because cinema is at least as important as theatre, literature or painting! (Hoveyda, 1986b: 139)

Differing both from its predecessors and from its contemporaries in England, where the engagement with popular culture was always pulled between cultural advocacy and political inoculation, *Cahiers*, in a critical language unfamiliar to the empirical traditions of Anglo-Saxon protestantism, celebrated

the mysteries of its chosen auteurs, whose personalities broke through the routines of industry, commerce and small-mindedness. The first achievement of the *Cahiers* writers was to develop, almost by accident, a critical 'style' which, rather than 'educating the public to a better, more critical appreciation of the films', created a field of debate within a community of interest, the kind of field out of which theory develops. Their writing was the first step towards the institutionalization of a knowledge, the formation of a critical community which really cared whether Minnelli was an auteur or a *metteur en scène*.

Their second achievement, of course, was to establish some of the terms in which that debate might be conducted. While it may have been self-evident that film was an art, and that directors were its primary artists, it was not self-evident which directors were artists, the true auteurs; which were *metteurs en scène*, the craftsmen capable of producing meritorious films but without a consistent personality; and which were mere tradesmen, more or less competent but seldom rising about the meretricious. To place directors in this hierarchy, later formalized in a finer grain by Sarris (1968), and particularly to settle boundary disputes both within their own ranks and with their favourite adversaries in *Positif*, required both a knowledge and a method. It required a knowledge of a very large corpus of films: not simply a sampling along an already approved crest line, but a kind of profligate intemperance of viewing, in which nothing could be left out in case that were where the key lay, and in which, as Narboni says, the auteur's work can be grasped as a whole, an oeuvre, rather than as a series of films. And it required a method of *reading* films, a reading which, somewhat curiously, resonates with F.R. Leavis' definition of the critic's task as being 'to determine what is actually *there* in the work of art', sensitive to 'the difference between that which has been willed and put there, or represents no profound integration, and that which grows from a deep centre of life' (1963: 224–5).

However, far current film scholars might wish to distance themselves from the impressionistic agonism of *Cahiers*' judgements in the 1950s, the journal's footprint can still be seen in the sand: a legacy of debate, of reading and of the omnivorous appetite of the cinephile. Two pathways opened up from the *politique d'auteurs* which determined the direction of authorship theory and marked out routes for film theory more generally. First, and most indelibly, there was an attention to *mise en scène*, not simply as a set of techniques for the representation of reality, but as a language of creativity with which an auteur transformed material.

> When I say that everything is expressed on the screen through *mise en scène*, I in no way contest the existence or the importance of the subject matter. I simply want to point out that the distinguishing feature of a great author is precisely his ability to metamorphose the stupidest plot through his technique. It is obvious that if we tried to summarize the plot of *Time Without Pity* [Joseph Losey, UK, 1957], we would end up with a very weak melodrama. But do we go to the cinema to translate images into words? (Hoveyda, 1986b: 139)

Mise en scène was the language – the 'specific signifying practice' – of cinema, and the analysis of *mise en scène* was a method of detection, finding there rather than in subject matter the signature of the director. Though the object of detection may have shifted in later theory away from the creative subject (the auteur) towards the 'positioned subject' (the spectator), the methods of decipherment or decoding through an investigation of the language and signification of *mise en scène* provided the foundation for the textual analysis that secured for Film Studies a place of grudging respect in the humanities and the academy.

If the first pathway led towards language and the significations of the image, the second pathway led towards narrative and the themes which structured narrative. In his 'Autocritique' in *Cahiers* in 1961, Fereydoun Hoveyda anticipates the figure who will later move to the centre of the theoretical stage, the psychoanalyst.

> This leads me to clarify my ideas on the critic's function. In many respects, it resembles that of

the psychoanalyst. Does he not, in effect, have to reconstruct through the film the discourse of the auteur (subject) in its continuity, bring to light the unconscious that underpins it and explain the particular way it is articulated? (Hoveyda, 1986c: 261)

What came to be known as auteur structuralism or cine-structuralism, identified in Britain in the late 1960s and early 1970s with the work of Peter Wollen and Geoffrey Nowell-Smith, followed from the insistence of the *politique* on thematic consistency and wholeness as a mark of the auteur's signature. While for *Cahiers* much of the attention focused on *mise en scène* as the scene of personality, it was a relatively short step, following the success of structuralism in the social sciences, to seek out thematic structures across the work of an auteur, and crucially, as Hoveyda implies, to seek structures of which the auteur himself may be unconscious. Increasingly in the 1960s, the writers of *Cahiers*, in step with a growing body of theory in both Britain and the US, moved away from the auteur as creator of varying degrees of genius, and towards an author-subject who is written by the text, and can be read out of its signs and structures. Wollen's famous distinction between 'Fuller or Hawks or Hitchcock, the directors' and ' "Fuller" or "Hawks" or "Hitchcock", the structures named after them' (1972: 168) appears again in Jean-Pierre Oudart's identification of John Ford as an 'inscription' (1981: 185) in the influential reading of Ford's *Young Mr Lincoln* (US, 1939) which the editors of *Cahiers* undertook collectively in 1970 (1970: 29–47). The beneficiary of this devaluation of the authorial currency and the depreciation in the dignity of the auteur from artist to structure, from inscriber to inscription, was 'ideology'. It was not the author who spoke, but ideology, an ideology which could be detected in the gaps, ruptures and contradictions of the text. The method inherited from auteurism remained the same, a detailed reading to uncover the text's hidden places, but it was no longer the personality of the author which was hidden there, but ideology – of which the author was the bearer rather than the creator. It is at this point that the author becomes, almost literally, a shadow of his or her former self, leaving traces in the text rather than dominating it with a unique signature; shading into structure, inscription or function; an object of desire for the cinephile, a subject whose subjectivity is an effect of the text.

In this account, I am giving particular weight to the contribution of the early writing of *Cahiers du cinéma* because, revisiting earlier teleologies, including my own (1981), I am struck by the impression they give that the *theory* of authorship does not really start until the arrival of structuralism, bringing with it 'science' to rescue us from 'ideology'. I would argue now that it was in that earlier period that the field of knowledge and a method to define it began to be defined, and that theory as a field of debate and contestation became both formative and animating, generating an engagement which was quite distinct from the educative impulse of the pioneers and an intellectual excitement, which was symptom and cause of a paradigm shift in the study of film and cinema.

It was a short step from the author as an 'unconscious' effect of the text to the theoretical death of the author. Barthes' short essay, 'The Death of the Author' (1977), first published in France in 1968, is one of those texts which has reverberated through the whole field of criticism and critical theory, echoing the 'death of God', causing similar forms of perturbation and consternation, and leaving behind similar gaps and possibilities in the hermeneutics of meaning and the determination of value. In many spheres, the death of the author has become so much a commonplace that it has become a barrier to further thought, a knowing wink which can be shared as a mark of distinction between people who know better than to think anything else. And yet, as Wollen notes in his essay on Michael Curtiz, returning to his yellowing copy of the original in *Manteia*, 'although written in Barthes's most provocative style (shades of Truffaut), it is not quite as earthshaking as I had remembered' (2003: 69). Stripped of the rhetorical flourish of his final resounding (and infinitely repeatable)

phrase – 'the birth of the reader must be at the cost of the death of the Author' (Barthes, 1977: 148) – the essay appears to be itself the condensed trace of positions already elaborated in Barthes' writing and in a tradition of modernist writing stretching back to the nineteenth century. (Barthes himself appeals to Mallarmé and Proust.) The 'scandal' of 'The Death of the Author' is the tip of a more complex historical argument turned into a rhetorical *coup de grâce*.

Again, it is worth establishing the context into which Barthes' essay intervened. He was reacting against an interpretative criticism, which seeks in the personality of the author the truth of the fiction and the guarantee of the interpretation.

> The *explanation* of a work is always sought in the man or woman who produced it, as if it were always in the end, through the more or less transparent allegory of the fiction, the voice of a single person, the *author* 'confiding' in us. (1977: 143)

The tyranny of the author is attributed to an 'ordinary culture', hungry for the biographical and psychological background which *fleshes out* the 'image of literature', and to a tradition of criticism which finds in Baudelaire's work 'the failure of Baudelaire the man', in Van Gogh's 'his madness' and in Tchaikovsky's 'his vice' (1977: 143). These are powerful traditions in both the academy and the public sphere. The strength of their appeal cannot be ignored, particularly in the present moment, when a culture of celebrity obsessed with the biography and psychology of the artist seeps into any discussion of contemporary authorship. Indeed, the tradition which finds in the life of the author the meaning of the work is so embedded that it could not, even in 1968, simply be extirpated by a theoretical intervention, however persuasive. Rather, in Film Studies as in other branches of the humanities, it was driven underground for a fairly brief period to the place where unfashionable ideas regroup. In more recent writing, there is a palpable sense of relief that the proscription against auteurism has been lifted: witness Dudley Andrew's sharp irony in 1993: 'Breathe easily. *Épuration* has ended.

After a dozen years of clandestine whispering we are permitted to mention, even to discuss, the auteur again' (1993: 77).[1]

These are the terms of engagement governing the skirmishes by which we mark out territory and keep debate alive. But before we exhume the author and bury Barthes, it is worth recalling what was at stake. For Barthes, the author – or 'modern scriptor' – does not precede the text, but is 'born simultaneously' with it (1977: 145). He or she does not stand behind the text as its truth, authorizing a correct reading, but is written in the text, identical with the writing. 'Writing', says Barthes,

> is the destruction of every voice, of every point of origin. Writing is that neutral, composite, oblique space where our subject slips away, the negative where all identity is lost, starting with the very identity of the body writing. (1977: 142)

While we might legitimately wish to draw back from the absolutism of Barthes' decree, particularly in respect of film, where the moment of 'writing' becomes a process of corporate and industrial production, there is a challenge here to the authority of 'origins' and 'intentions' which is liberating for criticism and enabling for the critical reader. In the context of current debate, it may not be necessary to insist on the death of the author, but it is still worth contesting her or his authority as the determinant of meaning.

One of the effects of the challenge to the centrality of the author was a challenge to the centrality of interpretation as the primary purpose of criticism. The business of a textual criticism focused on writing, rather than meaning, is to engage with the work and play of language and signification, rather than to fix meaning. Interestingly, it becomes easier to see the importance of Susan Sontag (a writer who often plays leapfrog with Barthes) and her key, similarly manifesto-like essay, 'Against interpretation' (1969), written in 1964, four years before 'The Death of the Author':

> The aim of all commentary on art now should be to make works of art – and by analogy, our own experience – more, rather than less, real to us. The function of criticism should be to show *how it is what it is*, even *that it is what it is*, rather than to show *what it means* ... In place of a hermeneutics we need an erotics of art. (1969: 23)

Interestingly also, an erotics of art seems to rescue auteur criticism from the reductive structuralism which reduced films and oeuvres to a pattern of meanings identified, *post facto*, with an 'unconscious' auteur and returns it to the exuberance of *Cahiers*, its attention to film as a 'writing' – a '*caméra stylo*' – and the kingdom of heaven found in a tracking shot. It is just such an erotics of art that Laura Mulvey wrestles with in her much-cited 1975 article, 'Visual pleasure and narrative cinema'. It also forms the basis for a body of criticism across the arts which tries to understand the complex interplay of textuality and subjectivity, an interplay which frequently invokes, if not the personality or biography of the author, at least the figure of the author as, in Michel Foucault's terms, a 'function' of the text (1977). Such a criticism still seems to me to form a central, if not an exclusive, focus of the film theory with which a critical Film Studies still needs to engage.

However unfashionable Barthes in his turn may become – or may already have become – the debt to him is considerable. In many ways, his argument in its more nuanced forms gives a centrality to the development of a rigorous and robust film analysis, the kind of reading of films which has been one of the jewels in Film Studies' crown. In the absence of an authorizing voice, the critic or the student seeks support for her reading in the authority of her analysis, opening up how the text works rather than closing it down to what it means. Without the author as the ultimate guarantee, the analysis is never final and complete, but always remains partial. In the retreat from extremes, this is one of the things we hold on to. It is one of the terms of engagement that the pendulum does not swing all the way back.

While Barthes' impact on *auteurism* and authorship theory was direct, apparent and tangible, an indirect, but probably more pervasive, impact can be identified in the development of a body of film scholarship which questioned, in the name of empirical evidence and historical enquiry, what it believed to be the inflated claims of 'Grand Theory'. This body of work is most clearly associated with David Bordwell, who has provided – most particularly in *The Classical Hollywood Cinema* (1985), written with Kristin Thomson and Janet Staiger – a scholarly account of a particular period of Hollywood cinema which, among other things, replaces the 'genius' of the author with 'the genius of the system', a familiar phrase appropriated from André Bazin's comradely critique in 1957 of the auteurism of his younger colleagues at *Cahiers du cinéma*:

> The American cinema is a classical art, but why not then admire in it what is most admirable, i.e. not only the talent of this or that filmmaker, but the genius of the system, the richness of its ever-vigorous tradition, and its fertility when it comes into contact with new elements. (1985: 258)

Though Bordwell (1996) has confronted 'Grand Theory' more directly and more tendentiously elsewhere, it is in the historical scholarship of his and his colleagues' development of Bazin's 'classical art' that the work has been most persuasive, leaving its mark on the teaching and writing even of those of us who would not align ourselves with his philosophical position. Bordwell uses the term 'classical' precisely, not to assign value or consign a film or filmmaker to a particular place in the memory of cinema, but to define a system. In the opening section of the book, he justifies the use of the term thus:

> [T]he principles which Hollywood claims as its own rely on notions of decorum, proportion, formal harmony, respect for tradition, mimesis, self-effacing craftsmanship, and cool control of the perceiver's response – canons which critics in any medium usually call 'classical'. (1985: 3–4)

He goes on to describe the components of this classical narrative system in terms of 'devices' (pan, dissolve, field reverse-field), 'systems' (time, space, narrative causation), and crucially, 'relations between systems': 'In the Hollywood style, the systems do not play equal roles: space and time are almost always made vehicles for narrative causality' (Bordwell, 1985: 6).

A classical cinema, then, like any classical art, is rule-bound and systematic, and the strengths and limitations of Bordwell's approach lie in its system building, a scholarly rationality that is both explanatory and oppressively totalizing. The artist is one insofar as he or she articulates the rules with a proper balance of originality and deference, imagination and propriety. It is an art not of unbridled expression, but of articulation. It articulates the conventions and expectations in a way that gives the audience enough repetition to ensure recognition and familiarity, and enough difference to make it new and singular. Among the factors which might motivate the components of the filmic system (genre, verisimilitude, narrative causality), Bordwell includes 'artistic motivation'. This permitted individual artistic flourish as a signature of variation, but discouraged – or punished – it when it threatened the integrity of the classical narration: 'Overt narration, the presence of a self-conscious "author" not motivated by realism or genre or story causality, can only be intermittent and fluctuating in the classical film' (1985: 79). A classical art, at its most classical, acknowledges the presence of an artist, but as a component of the system, articulating its conventions, enlivening its rules, refreshing it but never dominating it with his or her personality or self-expression. It is worth quoting Bordwell at length to trace his delimitation of the auteur:

> In Western music, the classical style creates dynamism by departing from and returning to a stable tonal center. Something like this dynamism appears in the Hollywood auteur film. The auteur film draws its sustenance from the classical base, which is visible in the film. The film mixes narrational modes – some systems operating according to classical probabilities, others intermittently foregrounded as less probable and more distinctive. Far from being a fault or flaw, this mixture can be a source of aesthetic value to those prepared to perceive it. Most often, an idiosyncratic exploration of causality, time, or space works to reaffirm the norm by revealing the suppleness and range of the paradigm. At rarer moments, a deviant narrational process can be glimpsed.

We see the norm afresh, understand its functions better, recognize previously untapped possibilities in it, and – on a few occasions – reflect upon how our trust in the norm can mislead us. The Hollywood auteur film offers a particular pleasure and knowledge: the spectator comes to recognize norm and deviation oscillating, perhaps wrestling, within the same art work, that work being actively contained by the pressures of tradition. (1985: 82)

Such common sense makes sense of the auteur in the classical system in a way which is hard to contest, and in their closing chapter, Bordwell, Staiger and Thompson make explicit their recognition of alternative – and post-1960 – modes of film practice, which do not conform to the classical system and in which the auteur functions differently – though nonetheless systematically. As well as being apparently flexible, the approach is eminently teachable, because susceptible to historical evidence and to demonstration through the close analysis of what is actually there on the screen. It avoids the mysteries of intention and expressive personality, on the one hand, and of an abstract 'writing without origin', on the other.

To pause for a moment, however, on the concept of the classical, and to push a little Bordwell's analogy with Western music, both confirming it and qualifying it, I want to quote – again at length – from an essay in the *Times Literary Supplement*. Stephen Brown's 'Mozart, Classical form, and the rescue from equanimity' was one of a number of articles associated with Mozart's two-hundred-and-fiftieth anniversary in 2006. Like Bordwell, Brown begins by sketching the outlines of the classical system:

A formula for producing a convincing Classical piece of music might look like this: start with an axiomatic idea, one so simple and basic that it is hard to imagine reducing it further. You're in the key of C? Then create an outline of a C major chord. (A little more than half of Mozart's piano sonatas start with an outline of the home-key chord.) That's a little angular; balance it with a softer turn of phrase. Now balance those two bars with two other bars. Where the first used chords I and V, the balancing phrase could start with IV and work its way back to I. Now we have four bars without much flow; balance them with another four bars of running scales. Keep in mind that everything must be clear

and distinct: no thick textures, just melody and accompaniment. Continue along this path, follow the rules of sonata form, and you too can create a bad – but realistic – example of Classical-sounding music. (2006: 18)

He then proceeds to cases:

I recently attended a concert where I heard a lovely performance of the Concerto for Two Clarinets by Franz Krommer, born in 1759, just three years after Mozart. It followed the kind of Classical formula described above and bored me nearly senseless with its predictability. But I have heard Mozart's Piano Sonata No. 11 on A Major (K331), the one that ends with the famous 'Rondo alla Turca', countless times; at one time in my youth I could play the piece from memory, and even today I do not find it boring. How can Krommer be boring on a first hearing and Mozart not boring on the 500th? (2006: 18)

The analogy helps to illuminate and illustrate the functioning of the classical analogy, but, more importantly, Brown's simple question – how can Krommer be boring and Mozart not boring? – seems to me to lie at the heart of the question of authorship in a classical system, limiting the explanatory reach of a purely systematic approach. The displacement of the auteur onto the system and the systematization of motivation within the rules of the game, however appealingly common sense they may be, leave some nagging questions about creativity, imagination and the artist which apply even within – or particularly within – a classical art. What is it that makes the difference, and what difference does difference make? Or as Samuel Beckett, appropriated by Foucault, asked: 'What matters who's speaking, someone said, what matter's who's speaking?' (Beckett, 1974: 16).[2]

The work of Bordwell – and his colleagues and associates – has been hugely influential. (With irresistible irony, Bordwell himself has suffered the fate of the structuralist's auteur: an apostrophization in which Bordwell, the scholar, must often be rescued from 'Bordwell', the structure named after him.) Most particularly in his essay, 'Contemporary Film Studies and the vicissitudes of Grand Theory', in the collection which he edited with Noël Carroll in 1996, Bordwell challenges what he identifies as 'Grand Theories', such as 'subject-position theory' and 'culturalism'. These are defined as 'Grand Theories' because 'their discussions of cinema are framed within schemes which seek to describe or explain very broad features of society, history, language and psyche' (1996: 3). Bordwell diagnoses what he depicts as a pathological attachment to Parisian theory, offering an account of its 'vicissitudes' supported by evidence based on quotation – quotation which is, of course, selected to support the diagnosis. 'Why this reliance on Parisian sources?' he asks (1996: 19). He turns back to the process of self-definition as a discipline which Film Studies was going through in the 1970s and 1980s, and he takes auteurism as an exemplary instance:

> [I]n the effort to win academic respectability, film scholars could best show their work to have significance if there were a powerful theory backing it up. Auteurism was a connoisseurship that required a staggering knowledge of particular films. In an academic context, such knowledge could seem mere buffery, so auteur studies could not justify studying movies 'seriously'. An analysis of Hitchcock that purported to demonstrate a theory of signification or the unconscious was more worthy of academic attention than an analysis of recurring authorial motifs. (1996: 19)

In place of 'Grand Theory', Bordwell supports the emergence in the 1980s of what he calls 'middle-level research', pre-empting accusations of being 'anti-theory' with the argument that such research addresses questions that have both 'empirical and theoretical import' (1996: 27), and insisting, in his own italics, '*you do not need to have a Theory of Everything to do enlightening work in a field of study*'. Or, with fewer italics but more persuasively:

> Contrary to what many believe, a study of United Artists' business practices or the standardization of continuity editing or the activities of women in early film audiences need carry *no* determining philosophical assumptions about subjectivity and culture, *no* univocal metaphysical or epistemological or political presumption – in short, no commitment to a Grand Theory. (1996: 29)

Like the influence of Barthes in his time, the influence of Bordwell and his associates has been emancipatory in certain ways, freeing up the citation list from the usual suspects (Foucault, Barthes, Lacan), and realigning theory with empirical research in a way that has been productive for Film Studies in the academy. Since the 1980s, the growth of historical research and the increased respect for empirical evidence have been formative for Film Studies as an academic discipline. For example, there is now a greater willingness to recognize a study of the activities of women in early film audiences, that even if not theoretical in itself becomes a building-block in a theory that appeals to evidence rather than to avatars. For work on authorship, this change has led to a diversity of approaches which is embodied in a collection such as that of David Gerstner and Janet Staiger, *Authorship and Film* (2003). Perhaps most emblematic, in that collection, is Wollen's revisitation of his early auteurism in a study of Michael Curtiz, which now brings together empirical evidence, textual analysis and theory.

The change has also permitted those questions to be re-opened that were shamefully closed by the 'death of the author' thesis: questions of agency in areas in which authority was socially and critically neglected. There were always degrees of death, and Hitchcock was always likely to be more dead than Jean-Luc Godard. Raised from the dead, can a single theory of authorship deal with Hitchcock, Godard, Abbas Kiarostami, Sally Potter and Bill Viola? And how does a 'high theory' of authorship deal with the intention expressed in the quotation which forms the epigraph to this essay?

As this essay was being written, *Good Night, and Good Luck* (George Clooney, US, 2005) was released in the UK, and it seemed to me to crystallize some of the variables which now open up in front of authorship. There is George Clooney, directing and co-writing an openly 'political' film – in black and white and at a very precise political moment in both Britain and the US, when issues of freedom of speech are at the top of the agenda. The moment gives particular sharpness to questions of agency and intention, an intention which is made explicit as it is repeated in interview after interview. The power of agency which is required to direct a political film in black and white is conferred by celebrity, a celebrity which is conferred, in its turn, through acting – and not only through acting, but through acting on television (and not only on television but on hospital melodrama). The power of this agency is confirmed, rather than denied, by Clooney's own self-effacing performance as supporting actor in 'his' film – a self-effacement which only real power can aspire to. And, as Barthes correctly claims, 'ordinary culture' is hungry for the biography which precedes and explains the motive behind the film. In interviews, reviews, articles and television programmes, Clooney's authorship is attributed to his respect for his father and for his father's history of engagement. It is his family biography, his inheritance of political integrity from his father, which is called into play to define and explain his authorship. And behind the biographies of father and son, there is the historical agency of Ed Murrow, 'a principled journalist who took a stand against a malignant demagogue and helped bring him down' (Kemp, 2006: 58).

There is also a production company, Participant Productions, replete with agency and intention, a company, operating in Hollywood, whose website bears the strap line and mission statement:

Changing the world
one story at a time
Participant believes in the power of media to create great social change. Our goal is to deliver compelling entertainment that will inspire audiences to get involved in the issues that affect us all.[3]

We did not expect that in the days of Hollywood-Mosfilm. While analysis would, of course, complicate all of this, the play of agency is fertile ground for thinking through the pragmatics of contemporary authorship.

And yet, none of this quite answers Beckett's question – 'What matters who's speaking …?' – or even decides whether it is a question of indifference or of making a difference. Is there something more to the difference between Krommer and Mozart than dexterity in articulating the classical norms? Within the genius of the system, is there still room for the genius of the artist?

While our engagement with authorship – and the attendant issues of agency, authority, intention and creativity – is greatly enriched and complicated by an empirical understanding of its historical and contemporary conditions of existence, an accumulation of interesting facts without a theory seems to me to lead by a different route to the 'buffery' which Bordwell tries so hard to avoid: that is, a knowledge-based appropriation of film, which is impressive without being fully satisfying as an account of our experience of cinema. It is theory that defines the questions which research asks and confounds the easy answers, which assume the sufficiency of empirical knowledge. The beneficiary is a more complex and more appropriate theory. There may be no Theory of Everything, and the 'Grand Theory' which Bordwell characterizes and caricatures, if it ever existed, has probably now gone the way of the Grand Narrative of Progress. There still remain fields, however, which require a more sophisticated theoretical, as well as historical, understanding. One of these is the constantly shifting field of imagination and creativity, raising issues of art and authorship which the anti-humanism of earlier film theory has constantly avoided, and for which Bordwell's systematic rationality has not delivered satisfactory answers. A theory of creativity and the creative imagination in film and cinema is complicated, of course, by technology, industry, commerce and collective production. But without it, film and cinema are impoverished and it is difficult to account for those cinephilic moments which give us glimpses of the 'kingdom of heaven' and which make studying film an 'affair of the heart' as well as a quest for knowledge.

In his book, *The Singularity of Literature*, Derek Attridge concludes that:

the attempt to do justice to literary works as *events*, welcoming alterity, countersigning the singular signature of the artist, inventively responding to invention, combined with a suspicion of all those terms that constitute the work as an object, is the best way to enhance the chances of achieving a vital critical practice. (2004: 137)

In Film Studies, similarly, a criticism informed by empirical research but motivated by theory – including a theory which engages in new ways with authorship, creativity and invention – seems to me to be the only way of establishing a vital critical practice which avoids constituting the work as an object.

Finally, then, the continuing work of theory is to keep alive debate and engagement, not simply applying institutionalized theories and knowledges, but re-discovering fields in which contesting theories of authorship and their conflicting desires and demands have historically played a key role. It is for this reason that I believe the writing in *Cahiers du cinéma* in the 1950s and 1960s still resonates, if not as a model of scholarship, at least as a confirmation that critical excitement and a love of films and cinema still has a role to play. In his book, *Literature, Theory, and Common Sense* (whose chapter on authorship and intention in literature repays attention) Antoine Compagnon describes a familiar scenario:

> The theorists often give us the impression of raising very sensible criticisms against the positions of their adversaries; but as those adversaries, comforted by their ever clear conscience, refuse to give up and continue to hold forth, the theorists too begin to hold forth and push their own theses, or antitheses, to absurd lengths, and as a result annihilate themselves before their rivals, who are delighted to see themselves justified by the extravagance of their opponents' position. (2004: 5)

Despite the apparent absurdity of the ritual, Compagnon shares Casetti's belief (and mine) in the importance of the productivity of theory, producing knowledge not only through research and the accumulation of information and understanding, but also by constituting a field of discussion and debate – the field, in fact, of dialectics. Theory is important in the 'rejuvenating struggle it led against received ideas in literary studies, and in the equally determined resistance with which those received ideas

opposed it' (2004: 5). In the end, for Compagnon:

> The aim of theory is in effect the defeat of common sense. It contests it, criticizes it, denounces it as a series of fallacies – the author, the world, the reader, style, history, value; theory makes it seem indispensable to begin by freeing oneself from these fallacies in order to talk about literature. But the resistance of common sense to theory is unimaginable. (2004: 193)

The history of Film Studies charts a narrative in which the common sense of authorship has been contested time after time. Each common sense has been vanquished and each theory institutionalized so effectively that the victor has become the new received idea; contested again, vanquished again; and a new common sense installed, waiting for the challenge of new theories. Beckett again: 'Ever tried. Ever failed. No matter. Try Again. Fail again. Fail better' (1974: 1). At each stage, something is lost and something gained. The work of theory is still contestatory, moving forward dialectically, rather like Walter Benjamin's Angel of History, continually looking backwards to pick up any fragments which may have been lost in the rubble of earlier encounters. The questions of art and authorship, creativity and imagination, may still prove an irritant in our attempts to come to terms with our complex engagements with cinema.

NOTES

1 'Epuration', Andrew tells us, was the period in post-war France when certain individuals, suspected of collaboration, were prohibited from working in the film industry (1993: 77).

2 This line is quoted by Foucault in 'What is an author?' (1977) and abbreviated as the final line of the essay.

3 Available at: http://www.participantproductions.com.

REFERENCES

Andrew, Dudley (1993) 'The unauthorized auteur today', in Jim Collins, Hilary Radner and Ava Preacher Collins (eds), *Film Theory Goes to the Movies*. New York: Routledge. pp. 77–85.

Arnheim, Rudolf (1932) *Film als Kunst*. Berlin: Ernst Rowohlt.

Arnheim, Rudolf (1933) *Film*. Tr. L.M. Sieveking and Ian F.D. Morrow. London: Faber & Faber.

Arnheim, Rudolf (1957) *Film as Art*. Berkeley: University of California Press.

Astruc, Alexandre (1948) 'The birth of a new avant-garde: *la caméra stylo*', *Ecran français*, 144: n.p.

Astruc, Alexandre (1981) 'The birth of a new avant-garde: *la caméra stylo*', in John Caughie (ed.), *Theories of Authorship*. London: Routledge & Kegan Paul/BFI. p.9.

Attridge, Derek (2004) *The Singularity of Literature*. London: Routledge.

Ayfre, Amédeé (1985) 'Neorealism and phenomenology', in Jim Hillier (ed.), *Cahiers du cinéma: The 1950s: Neo-Realism, Hollywood, New Wave*. Tr. Diana Matias. London: BFI/Routledge & Kegan Paul. pp. 182–91.

Balázs, Béla (1970) *Theory of the Film: Character and Growth of a New Art*. Tr. Edith Bone. New York: Dover Publications.

Barthes, Roland (1968) '*La Mort de l'auteur*', *Mantéia*, 5: 12–16.

Barthes, Roland (1977) 'The Death of the Author', in *Image, Music, Text*. Tr. Stephen Heath. London: Fontana. pp. 142–48.

Bazin, André (1985) 'On the *politique des auteurs*', in Jim Hillier (ed.), *Cahiers du cinéma: The 1950s: Neo-Realism, Hollywood, New Wave*. Tr. Peter Graham. London: BFI/Routledge & Kegan Paul. pp. 248–59.

Beckett, Samuel (1974) *Texts for Nothing*. London: Calder and Boyars.

Bordwell, David (1985) 'Part One: The classical Hollywood style, 1917–60', in David Bordwell, Janet Staiger and Kristin Thompson, *The Classical Hollywood Cinema: Film Style and Mode of Production to 1960*. London: Routledge & Kegan Paul. pp. 1–84.

Bordwell, David (1996) 'Contemporary Film Studies and the vicissitudes of Grand Theory', in David Bordwell and Noël Carroll (eds), *Post-Theory: Reconstructing Film Studies*. Madison: University of Wisconsin Press. pp. 3–36.

Bordwell, David, Staiger, Janet and Thompson, Kristin (1985) *The Classical Hollywood Cinema: Film Style and Mode of Production to 1960*. London: Routledge & Kegan Paul.

Brown, Stephen (2006) 'Mozart, Classical form, and the rescue from equanimity', *Times Literary Supplement*, 27 January: 18–19.

Cahiers du cinéma editors (1970) 'John Ford's *Young Mr. Lincoln*', *Cahiers du Cinéma*, 223: 29–47.

Cahiers du cinéma editors (1972) 'John Ford's *Young Mr. Lincoln*', Screen, 13(3): 5–44.

Casetti, Francesco (1999) *Theories of Cinema, 1945–1995*. Tr. Francesca Chiostri, Elizabeth Gard Bartolini-Salimbeni and Thomas Kelso. Austin: University of Texas Press.

Caughie, John (ed.) (1981) *Theories of Authorship*. London: Routledge & Kegan Paul/BFI.

Compagnon, Antoine (2004) *Literature, Theory and Common Sense*. Tr. Carol Cosman. Princeton, NJ: Princeton University Press.

Donald, James, Friedberg, Anne and Marcus, Laura (eds) (1998) *Close Up, 1927–1933: Cinema and Modernism*. London: Cassell.

Eliot, T.S. (1960) 'Tradition and the individual talent', in *The Sacred Wood: Essays on poetry and criticism*. London: Methuen. pp. 47–59.

Engels, Friedrich (1976) 'Letter to Margaret Harkness', in Karl Marx and Friedrich Engels, *On Literature and Art*. Moscow: Progress Publishers. pp. 89–92.

Foucault, Michel (1977) 'What is an author?', in *Language, Counter-Memory, Practice: Selected Essays and Interviews*. Tr. Donald F. Bouchard and Sherry Simon. Oxford: Basil Blackwell. pp. 1114–38.

Gerstner, David A. and Staiger, Janet (eds) (2003) *Authorship and Film*. New York: Routledge.

Godard, Jean-Luc (1985) 'Beyond the Stars: *Bitter Victory*', in Jim Hillier (ed.), *Cahiers du cinéma: The 1950s: Neo-Realism, Hollywood, New Wave*. Tr. Tom Milne. London: BFI/Routledge & Kegan Paul. pp. 118–20.

Hoveyda, Fereydoun (1986a) 'Nicholas Ray's Reply: *Party Girl*', in Jim Hillier (ed.), *Cahiers du cinéma: 1960–1968: New Wave, New Cinema, Re-evaluating Hollywood*. Tr. Norman King. London: BFI/Routledge & Kegan Paul. pp. 122–31.

Hoveyda, Fereydoun (1986b) 'Sunspots', in Jim Hillier (ed.), *Cahiers du cinéma: 1960–1968: New Wave, New Cinema, Re-evaluating Hollywood*. Tr. Jill Forbes. London: BFI/Routledge & Kegan Paul. pp. 135–46.

Hoveyda, Fereydoun (1986c) 'Self-criticism', in Jim Hillier (ed.), *Cahiers du cinéma: 1960–1968: New Wave, New Cinema, Re-evaluating Hollywood*. Tr. Norman King. London: BFI/Routledge & Kegan Paul. pp. 257–63.

Kael, Pauline (1963) 'Circles and Squares', *Film Quarterly*, 16(3): 12–26.

Kemp, Philip (2006) Review of *Good Night, and Good Luck, Sight and Sound*, 16(3): 58, 60.

Kracauer, Siegfried (1960) *Theory of Film: The Redemption of Physical Reality*. Oxford: Oxford University Press.

Leavis, F.R. (1963) 'Henry James and the function of criticism', in *The Common Pursuit*. Harmondsworth: Penguin. pp. 223–32.

Marx, Karl and Engels, Friedrich (1974) *The German Ideology*. London: Lawrence and Wishart.

Medhurst, Andy (1991) ' "That special thrill": *Brief Encounter*, homosexuality and authorship', *Screen*, 32(2): 197–208.

Moullet, Luc (1985) 'Sam Fuller: In the Footsteps of Marlow', in Jim Hillier (ed.), *Cahiers du cinéma: The 1950s: Neo-Realism, Hollywood, New Wave*. Tr. Norman King. London: BFI/Routledge & Kegan Paul. pp. 145–55.

Mulvey, Laura (1975) 'Visual Pleasure and Narrative Cinema', *Screen*, 16(3): 6–18.

Narboni, Jean (1986) 'Against the clock: *Red Line 7000*', in Jim Hillier (ed.), *Cahiers du cinéma: 1960–1968: New Wave, New Cinema, Re-evaluating Hollywood*. Tr. Diana Matias. London: BFI/Routledge & Kegan Paul. pp. 216–19.

Nowell-Smith, Geoffrey (2003) *Luchino Visconti*. 3rd edn. London: BFI.

Oudart, Jean-Pierre (1981) 'Conclusion to *Cahiers du cinéma* editors' "John Ford's *Young Mr. Lincoln*"', in John Caughie (ed.), *Theories of Authorship*. London: Routledge & Kegan Paul/BFI. pp. 183–90.

Perkins, V.F. (1990) 'Film authorship: The premature burial', *CineAction!*, 21–2: 57–64.

Rohmer, Eric [Schérer, Maurice] (1952) 'Renoir Américain', *Cahiers du cinéma*, 8: 33–40.

Rohmer, Eric [Schérer, Maurice] (1981) 'Renoir Américain', in John Caughie (ed.), *Theories of Authorship*. London: Routledge & Kegan Paul/BFI. p. 38.

Sarris, Andrew (1962–3) 'Notes on the auteur theory in 1962', *Film Culture*, 27: 1–8.

Sarris, Andrew (1968) *The American Cinema: Directors and Directions, 1929–1968*. New York: E.P. Dutton.

Sarris, Andrew (1981) 'Notes on the auteur theory in 1962', in John Caughie (ed.), *Theories of Authorship*. London: Routledge & Kegan Paul/BFI. pp. 61–5.

Sontag, Susan (1969) 'Against interpretation', in *Against Interpretation and Other Essays*. New York: Dell. pp. 13–23.

Truffaut, François (1985) *Hitchcock*. New York: Simon & Schuster.

Wollen, Peter (1972) *Signs and Meaning in the Cinema*. London: Secker and Warburg.

Wollen, Peter (2003) 'The auteur theory: Michael Curtiz and *Casablanca*', in David A. Gerstner and Janet Staiger (eds), *Authorship and Film*. New York: Routledge. pp. 61–76.

Wood, Robin (2002) *Hitchcock's Films Revisited*. New York: Columbia University Press.

27

Where Sound Is: Locating the Absent Aural in Film Theory

Philip Brophy

Was there ever such a thing as silence? Surely, only the mind could project such an existence – a mind with shrunken ears and swollen brain, cloistered in the concert hall, the opera house, the theatre, the library. That brainiac never experienced the rowdy din of consumption that defined the 'sound of the crowd' excited by the multi-media explosiveness that follows the morphological slip across two centuries from slide lantern lectures to carnival phantasmagoria to silent movies with live accompaniment of all kinds to that thing people finally call 'the cinema'. No, there was never silence; there has only been the deluded desire for silence. That wish for wisting the masses, their machines and their mania cordoned off the cinema to welcome authors, librettists, playwrights – respected soloists of silence – and disallow any noisemakers during cinema's so-called formative era. Thus, silence was born as a denial of the audience and the auditorium – words whose etymology need only be pointed out to the dumb.

This is the true abject silence of 'so-called silent cinema': a silence held by the mute repression of describing these multi-media maelstroms at the time which no sophisticated writer would bother to note in any way save for pretending it didn't exist; a silence framed by the problematized historiography that places Eadweard Muybridge and Edwin S. Porter in a mime puppet show to demonstrate the magical ocular invention of cinema. It's the same silence that researchers have progressively been impelled to 'sound out' by piecing together mood-music cue folios, hyperbolic trade-magazine ads, faded photos of piano players. But despite the irrefutable evidence provided by historians like Rick Altman in his ultimate summation of the genesis of cinematic audiovisuality, *Silent Film Sound* (2004), it is a sound-world we will never experience, let alone hear.

This impossible reverie and the *fait accompli* of its a-sonic reality have created a gravitational pull back to the silent cinema again and again. Maybe there we can rewrite film history and get it right this time; maybe there we can find some Darwinian proof to bring back to the Society of Film Scholars to expose their silence as fundamentally flawed in its false inscripture of the audiovisual medium of cinema; maybe, if we keep mounting 'authentically verifiable' versions of ye olde musical accompaniment to faded and restored film prints, this history will come to life for everyone. Maybe, maybe, maybe. For all the amazing research published and presentations made in the field of silent film sound/music over the last twenty years, one can't help feeling it falls mostly on deaf ears. Film sound/music is still treated as a 'special issue', as if its destabilized reprioritization of the aural is a disability, requiring a special ramp way up into the heads of film theorists, historians, academics and editors. The point many are likely to miss in Altman's exhaustive *Silent Film Sound* is that his tome's intention for cinema to be 'reconfigured through sound' invites its manual to be used for extending all possibilities of sono-musicality in the cinema from the silent period onwards (2004: 7). I prefer that 'silent cinema' be renamed 'Live Cinema' and that the advent of sound cinema be regarded as the birth of 'Dead Cinema' (more on this notion later). For some, history is a virtual time machine, cosy and baroque, just like the chair Rod Taylor rides in *The Time Machine* (George Pal, US, 1960). For me, history is a giant metallic mobile-suit with internal psycho-neural fluids, just like Shinji rides in *Neon Genesis Evangelion* (Hideaki Anno, Japan, 1997).

Let's take a trip.

OUTSIDE THE MOVIE THEATRE ...

I was once transported to the Nickelodeon of Neverland. It was winter 1983. I took in my first triple bill at Times Square, New York City: *Piranha II: Flying Killers* (James Cameron, US/Italy, 1981), *Cannibal Holocaust* (Ruggero Deodato, Italy/Colombia, 1980) and *Pieces* (Juan Piquer Simón, US/Spain/Puerto Rico, 1982). The audience yelled through the whole picture, men and women shrieking

'muthafucka!' a million times over. The movie was turned up so loud to get over the crowd noise that any gun shots (or chainsaw sounds) were even more distorted and gut-punching. Come intermission, the lights went up, murky early-1970s slide advertisements were projected onto the screen, and about twenty ghetto blasters were instantly cranked up high. Humongous security guards idly paced the downstairs aisles, slapping baseball bats in their fat hands. The air smelt of rancid butter. I was in heaven – and it was as noisy as hell.

For the intelligentsia, early-twentieth-century cinema was nothing but noise. The possessed patrons, the infernal machinery, the diabolical din of it all were everything the angels in the wings of theatre had strived to obliterate. The baseness of cinema would have been as attractive to theatre critics then as death metal mega-bill concerts would be to the concert music critics of today. The noise of production and consumption is a hallmark of twentieth-century exchange, typifying industrialization as a cacophonic manifestation of the warping of time and speed that increased manufacture brought to bear on a modernist economy. Audio-visual entertainment of the originating milieu was bound to be similarly 'noisy' through its hybridity, malleability, compaction and condensation of all traditional art forms. The modernist tropes of collage, fusion and rupture quite organically increased the aural and the sonic primarily through a 'live multi-tracking' of events and occurrences. Voice, sound effects, music, atmosphere and a mix of controlled and unplanned circumstances fuelled equally post-vaudevillian and proto-cinematic monstrosities, creating audiovisual chimera whose sensational effects and spectacularized presentations embraced the essential quality of noise.

While noise today instantly evokes some kind of aural sandpaper on the ear or fingernails on the blackboard, the automatic presumption that it is merely irritating and aggravating clouds clarity of its defining attributes. Irritation and aggravation are only effects on the auditor; they do not describe the cause or identify its circumstance. Furthermore, negative response to noise is mere cultural conditioning: lots of people love noise – but they're not writing books about it. Most writers of any persuasion (but especially film theorists) label anything as 'noise' that does not conform to their pre-fab sound world, rendering their consequent arguments thin, due to the dismissal of a wide range of sound and music purely on aesthetic terms. Beyond aesthetics, three key characteristics can be used to discuss noise in fuller terms:

(a) Noise is an interruption to some pre-stabilized continuum so as to produce an *interference* (for example, an industrial garbage truck collecting bins in the middle of the night while you try to sleep).
(b) Noise is the disproportionate, unbalanced and/or emphasized conveyance of sound so as to produce *distortion* (for example, a voice as heard on a security guard's walky-talky weakly receiving the broadcast signal).
(c) Noise is the multiple voicing of discrete contents, thereby overloading communication so as to produce *incomprehension* (for example, a restaurant with wooden floors and high ceiling full of people talking over background music).

All three modalities of noise might be irritating and aggravating, but their 'voicing' as noise is determined by entirely different modes of production, acousmatic factors, psychoacoustic parameters and environmental conditions. To not hear difference in these voices clinically impairs one to then talk about film sound specifically, and cinematic realism generally.

'Interference' is a ploy used on the film soundtrack to agitate and induce anxiety directly within the psychological corpus of the audience, in preference of having a character express dialogued angst about how 'anxious' they feel: from the slamming cupboard doors of *Patty Hearst* (Paul Schrader, UK/US, 1988) to the rattling aircon ducts of *Resident Evil* (Paul W.S. Anderson, UK/Germany/France/US, 2002). 'Distortion' is the prime operational method for orchestrating shifts between subjective and objective perspectives on the film

soundtrack, in preference to voice-over narrating and 'cut-to-thinking-close-up' signage that acinematically directs audiences into reading shifts of perspective: from the screeching aviary of *The Birds* (Alfred Hitchcock, US, 1963) to the smashed-up toilet of *Punch Drunk Love* (Paul Thomas Anderson, US, 2002). And 'incomprehension' is the bold tack taken in having overlapping dialogue, densely mixed location sound and/or surround-sound spatialization bombard the audience, creating an excess of information that renders the audience incapable of discerning singularity and distinction: from the pathological yabber of *California Split* (Robert Altman, US, 1974) to the vocalized schizophrenia of *Doctor Doolittle* (Betty Thomas, US, 1998). The innumerable film soundtracks from around the world – mostly modern, some postmodern, none classical – that use these ploys have progressively been outweighing those quaint, humble chamber dramas of the human spirit which quietly whisper to the intelligent cultured film critic: cover your ears and they'll go away.

Wake up: they won't.

OUTSIDE THE CONCERT HALL …

When John Cage calmly noted from his anechoic chamber in the 1950s that silence does not exist, he intended to welcome all sound through the liberating act of listening. But prior to his 'soft-core sonica', the Futurists in the 1910s ferociously forbade silence to exist. Their 'hard-core sonica' in the form of *intonarumori* – literally, 'noise-makers' – were designed to celebrate and symbolize the pervasiveness of noise in the then-recently-advanced push of the industrial era. Cage adopted the stance of the Buddhist monk whom you still find standing at intersections of central Tokyo, engulfed by more scurrying people than there are ants in a sugar mill. Peer carefully at those monks and you can see their lips barely move: they're chanting a mantra of silence that erases them from their surroundings. Cage's idea of silence evokes the calm in the storm as a means to be at ease with the world of noise that encases any modern metropolis. The Futurists wanted to both be embattled by noise and to bombard with noise. Tonal terrorists, they heard *leitmotifs* in industry, symphonies in war. Opposed yet conjoined, Cage and the Futurists were engaged in profound acts of listening. Though they never directly addressed the cinema, their poems and polemics concurred and coincided with the transition from noisy silent cinema to noisy sound cinema. Their wild ideas and notions are exceedingly more applicable and relevant than the ear-muffed sensibilities of critics like André Bazin, whose contemporaneous writing on cinema was and remains entirely out-of-synch with the cinesonic.

The polarities of soft-core sonica and hard-core sonica are continually marked on the film soundtrack as states of existence within which one perceives audiovisual modulation. Some films attack with their soundtrack in order to corporeally, viscerally and materially 'unsound' the audience and shock them (the hard-core sonica of *Electric Dragon 80,000 Volts* [Sogo Ishii, Japan, 2001], *The Texas Chainsaw Massacre* [Tobe Hooper, US, 1974] and *Hail Mary* [Jean-Luc Godard, France/Switzerland/UK, 1985]). Other films generate an aural excess through their sound-tracks in order to create a detached, divorced or existential state that 'disquiets' the audience and freezes them (the soft-core sonica of *Kaidan* [Masaki Kobayashi, Japan, 1964], *The Convent* [Manuel Olivera, Portugal, 1998] and *Taxi Driver* [Martin Scorsese, US, 1976]). And, of course, some films shift between these polarities, or start at one end to progressively move to the other. These distinctions are not evidence of a simplistic binary of passive/aggressive stratagems employed in cinema, as both deal with notions of noise. Rather, the hard-core/soft-core turbulence of aurality can be parlayed as variable ranges within key dynamic forces of audiovisuality in cinema:

(a) *Score production and music phonology*: between the live encoding of an acoustic time-space continuum, and the fractal fragmented multi-tracking of post-musical detailing

(b) *Sound design and spatialization*: between the multi-miced on-location mix and capture of actual sound-spaces, and the post-produced highly-processed remix and rendering of artificial surround-sound zones

(c) *Sound-image conflation*: between the synchronous/plausible/compatible spectre of 'naturalism', and the desynchronous/irrespective/incohate manifestation of audiovisual simultaneity

(d) *Psychological audition*: between the symbolic/linguistic coding of musical themes to represent a character's emotional state, and the sono-musical atomization of musical substantia that externalizes the interiority of a character's disequilibrium.

But music, you might offer, has been doing all this and more throughout the cross-wired narrative histories of opera and cinema. True, it has. But we also have a century's worth of composed sound and folk musics that have rejected the harmonic dogma, linguistic system, authorial manuscript and conducted control of music as it had been defined by the end of the eighteenth century. The Futurists took to the factories to score sirens and machinery to 'sing' the praises of their acoustic reality. Cage placed mics on the street outside the concert hall and 'mixed' his acoustic reality into the musical decorum inside. The twentieth century witnessed a lapse in faith of music as stricture and scripture: its written word was deemed incapable of even poetically and metaphorically evoking the complex frequencies, saturated timbres and dense orchestrations of the world of sound which were transforming the act of listening and the boundaries of the acoustic with far greater acceleration than any preceding epoch.

Music has become Latin – a dead language.

OUTSIDE THE SONG …

Much writing on Live Cinema (so-called 'silent cinema') emanates from the American multi-mediarization of Tin Pan Alley's (circa World War One) advent of pop music commodification, and from there traces notions of formalized, codified and pre-designed 'musical accompaniment' into the 'classical American film' so as to site a penultimate cine-text for music in Dead Cinema (so-called 'sound cinema'). It's a great place to start, but an awful place to end. It traces the noisy birth of Tin Pan Alley – where tune hucksters beat tins to drown out the noise of their competitors – to the induction of that 'song noise' into the live eventfulness of the Nickelodeon and dramatic shorts – where rowdy undisciplined ad hoc connections of over-communication were fostered – to its education and maturation in silent, dual-format and synch-sound features – where music became the 'film score' authorially inscribed by departmental authority of the studio system's logistics. This is a life cycle of song more than a song-cycle of life. It ends on a flat note: Dead Cinema is the successful erasure of serendipity, simultaneity and sono-musicality in the narrowed name of art, craft and language. The growth from 'song noise' to 'film score' is for many the attainment of great sophistication. But maybe a lot was lost in the transition from purchasing sheet music to purchasing a movie ticket. The movie experience of music come World War Two amounted to a museographic display of the skeletal remains of musical ingestion – relabelled 'musical accompaniment' – that signposts the regime of Dead Cinema.

This is not to territorially embrace the arch-conservatism that clutches theatre's 'living art' as a means of denigrating cinema's tech-nological power of representation. Moreso, it is to point out that music – that 'sound of Latin' – as analyzed within the classical Hollywood film text is bound never to venture into the twentieth-century expulsion of musical language as a practice ill-equipped to signify the times. Plenty of pianists write about cinema and music. But where are the trumpet improvisers? The electric guitarists? The drum machine programmers? Where are their critical voices and their counter-texts to the classical texts? What is cinema to their ears? Nor is this to denigrate the canonical findings of audiovisual narrative complexity

in American films up to and beyond World War Two. The critical problem that persists – and is seemingly forever side-stepped with incredible deftness – is how does one move from Dead Cinema into, well, whatever happens after that?

The answer is not so difficult to supply. Cinema, as we speak, is a machine of transcendence. It has so thoroughly mutated that it bears little relation to its genetic origins, despite the coding, clothing and costumery it salaciously wears. Only a fool today would connect a kid with scraggly long hair and beard to the counter-cultured delirium of the 1960s. Only a fool would think that *The Lord Of The Rings* (Peter Jackson, New Zealand/US, 2001) is grand cinema, or that Iranian cinema is the hope for global cinematic humanism. In defiance of all semiological appearance, cinema has become a choral coven of Otherness: its audiovisual miasma of form and style is a completely reanimated corpus of Frankensteinian design. In *100 Modern Soundtracks* (2004), I used this notion to demarcate the Modern Soundtrack as a means of hearing the death-rattle and raspy breath of Dead Cinema and its attempt to breathe through the soundtrack. The Modern Soundtrack is the triumph over the colonization of music and its striated utterance in the classically mixed film in Dead Cinema, celebrating the collapse of music back into the noise from where it came. And it is this rebirth as a Possessed Cinema (so called 'modern cinema', sometimes labelled 'contemporary cinema') wherein sound – that's anything that quivers on the soundtrack, irrespective of its nature – dynamizes and energizes audiovisuality beyond structural, categorical and ontological paradigms, and into dimensions of illegibility, irreducibility and confoundability.

You know something's really dead when you proclaim, 'It's alive!'

OUTSIDE THE MUSICAL ...

Just as the possessed speak with voices 'from beyond' both themselves and their terrain, so does Possessed Cinema import, receive and attract music from beyond the film score. This is where music pre-exists and counter-exists cinema, defining 'musicality' not simply as the figuring of notes to express music, but as the source from where music comes and the place where it arrives. Key modes of musicality would be:

(a) The *phonological* – where music is transformed through its rendering and afforded repeatable listening and consumption
(b) The *radiophonic* – where music is conducted and replayed in open absence of visuality, in order to narrate rather than describe or evoke
(c) The *broadcast* – where music enters multiple and contrasted spaces simultaneously to instigate random and previously undefined presences
(d) The *ambienced* – where music is filtered and combined with existing environment acoustics, so as to create states of distracted listening.

A composer cannot simply 'write' music and have it convey the effect of these modes of musicality. Such authorial acts would be delusional – as is most film music that attempts to be something (to voice a musicality) it isn't. To hear the precise aura of these modes of musicality requires displacing the composer and the film score, and welcoming all the zones and realms from which music emanates. Possessed Cinema's soundtrack necessitates tracing how music bleeds into spaces and places outside of its origination. Hence, pop songs are welcomed for their infection of the soundtrack and their shredding of the film score. From *American Graffiti* (George Lucas, US, 1973) to *Amar Akbar Anthony* (Manmohan Desai, India, 1977) to *An Independent Life* (Vitaly Kanevski, Russia, 1991) to *Sign 'O' The Times* (Prince, US, 1987) to *Furi Kuri* (Kazuya Tsurumaki, Japan, 2001), this is precisely where we can hear cinema 'reconfigured through sound', as Altman dreams (2005: 7) – and it is not surprising that these importations of music and song 'from outside' echo the same mechanisms inherent in the Nickelodeon phenomenon.

It is equally unsurprising that in the quest to sanctify the film score during Hollywood's 'golden era' as the fundamentalist writing of music for cinema, the Musical was consequently left to wither and wander destitute, demeaned and defrocked throughout the 1960s. The Musical then gets pathetically recouped as realism (the *Cabaret* effect) or dressed in drag (*The Rocky Horror Picture Show* effect). Yet both tendencies return to the Broadway Musical in a desperate cling to the 'song-writing craftsmanship' of the theatrical musical – the former in sway with a Jewish excavation of Berlin decadence during the 1930s, the latter in an embrace of a Gay adoration of the B-Grade American serial from the same era. Either way, the Musical is acknowledged as a hulk of its former self, now emptied and ripe to be transfigured as camp in reinforcement of its voice as 'untrue'. Like old clothes in a second-hand store, the Broadway Musical is the dressing-up of musicality from the past. The ultimate irony is how dated it is to buy old clothes that look new and well-kept, when all major global fashion companies are selling distressed denim that is brand new, but made to look like it's from a second-hand store.

More in synch with the times are the many films of Possessed Cinema that are boldly emblazoned with the afore-mentioned modes of musicality. A 'phonological' musical is *O Brother, Where Art Thou?* (Joel Coen, UK/France/US, 2000), in which the soundtrack inter-textually depicts music, anthropologically sifting through palimpsestual recordings to locate the film's setting in a bygone era of technology. A 'radiophonic' musical is *Pulp Fiction* (Quentin Tarantino, US, 1994), in which songs are plucked from the radio of the mind, and freewheelingly distributed throughout and without the diegesis and its multiple stages. A 'broadcast' musical is *Stand By Me* (Rob Reiner, US, 1986), in which memories of songs return to haunt unexpected locations, transporting one back to lost moments of song consumption and enjoyment. And an 'ambienced' musical is *Heat* (Michael Mann, US, 1995) in which no songs are sung, yet they are 'sounded' through their tonal backgrounding of existential drama, creating scrims of instrumental song to metre character. All these films, and many more, place pop music – its recording, its distribution, its consumption, its archiving – centre-stage on the soundtrack. Score composers like Ennio Morricone, Henry Mancini, Michel Legrand, Quincy Jones, John Carpenter, Ryuchi Sakamoto and John Brion in fact don't do 'film scores'. Rather, they respond to how music beyond the cinema conducts them into sounding their scores as documents of song noise and in doing so they openly foreground how film music is produced in this Possessed Cinema era.

It is neither composed nor experienced in silence.

OUTSIDE THE BODY ...

I mentioned earlier that cinema now is a machine of transcendence. From being live, to being dead, to being possessed, its trajectory is one typical of most art forms. Although this model is not dissimilar from the common notion that the arts move through primitive/classical/modern phases, the transcendent aspect of cinema is a salient difference. Recorded media upset the notions of art forms which reach their apotheosis purely through form, because rendered representations simulate form to then repeat the pre-rendered cycles of form. Cinema is a fractal network of such renderings – its time-line of plastic developments in cinematography, production design, acting technique, film score and sound design is not singular and synchronous, but multiple and asynchronous. Peaks and troughs of each plastic art in cinema rarely coincide, characterizing its development as transhistorical (hence the ongoing problem in cinema's historiography). This innate multiplicity of plasticity constitutes the metabolism of cinema: the calculable rate at which it digests and recycles its own internal energies. Being merogenetic (comprised by segmented arts and disciplines uniting to form a complex aggregated form), cinema is bound to reinvent itself through the sheer dynamic principles of its existence. It will always be becoming something other than itself.

Pertinent to our discussion here, the transcendent state of cinema due to its merogenetic structure and its metabolic momentum is particularly – possibly fundamentally – governed by how sound and music exist within the cinema as a plasmatic energy. This assertion is less a concoction of mystical biology than it appears. Some prime distinctions between sight and sound need to be recalled here:

(a) The act of seeing involves the self witnessing that which is before one's eyes, requiring the viewer to direct and control this act so as to see what is in front of one, thereby always qualifying 'the seen' as something outside of the self.

(b) The act of hearing involves the self auditing that which is *around* one's complete body, *not* requiring the auditor to direct and control this act so as to hear what is around one, thereby always qualifying 'the heard' as something *in which the self is immersed.*

Put bluntly, I can only see what's in front of me; yet I can hear everything in front, behind, underneath and above me. This means that the complete lexicon of scopic procedure that has been used ad nauseum in film theory is severely problematic, if not basically useless. The facile binary notions of on-screen/off-screen, sync/non-sync, compatible/incompatible, naturalistic/stylized, to name but a few, which have been used to fix the aural to the visual as if they were structurally dependent on each other, reduce the compound interactivity of cinema and negate the immersivity crucial to our inhabitation of acoustic reality. How a film theory can even begin to address identity, psychology and spectatorship without distinguishing between sight 'displacing' the self and hearing 'incorporating' the self is a frightful indication of the ocular fascism that strangles audiovisual discourse. Just as the written word 'cat' and the spoken word 'cat' have no correlating semblance bar their abstract attachment, so too do sound and image entail no essential co-determining relationship in cinema. They have simply been placed there, and once placed, they coexist.

Live Cinema knew this – formally, conventionally and technologically. Dead Cinema denies it and attempts to neutrally unify sound and image, as if the creation of the soundtrack dictated audiovisuality as locked, tied and bound as the optical printing on the side of the film strip. Possessed Cinema unleashes sound from image, returning it to unpredictable apparitions of ethereal, fluid, porous and transparent coincidences. A full awareness of audovisuality's capacity to generate serendipity, simultaneity and sono-musicality is virtually absent from film theory as we know it. Comb the canon of film theory from the last half-century to try and find mention of how cinema reconstructs the act of seeing-in-front while hearing-behind – an activity in which we are engaged every waking moment of our existence.

Not a single strand comes up, because film theory is bald.

OUTSIDE THE MICROPHONE ...

Just about every film theorist has seen the inside of a film camera. They've also been in a bio-box and witnessed the mechanisms of film projection. These revelations of the mechanical corpus of cinema would likely have taken on a near-mystical aura, reminding one of how these clunky, clacketty technological apparati are the ungainly means by which the magical moving imagery of cinema comes to life. But I wonder how many film theorists have seen the inside of a microphone. The collected writing on film sound in authoritative 'books on cinema' implicates film theorists and historians as somehow imagining that the microphone is a sonic camera: a directional, navigational torpedo of encoding. This is not to mock the technically uniformed. The incorporation of microphones in video cameras is a designed reinforcement of this principle. Lay movie consumers and professional film critics equally presume vaguely that film sound 'happens' when the camera is pointed and turned on – a doctrine French cinema has polemically advanced under the banner of 'direct sound'.

Industry-bound sound editors, designers and mixers (in America particularly) join sound to image with fundamentalist zeal, as if to move things slightly beyond, beside or between their 'logical' assignation would cause the depicted world on screen to apocalyptically cave in and traumatize the audience. The mania for matching sound to image understandably indoctrinates those unknowing of audio post-production to presume that sound always 'happens with the image'.

This is all easily debunked. Coming from radio drama and creating landmark radiophonic texts in the preceding five years before he made *Citizen Kane* (US, 1941), Orson Welles structured the whole film around the microphone, contrary to what history tells us about this 'hyper-visual' mythic grail of American cinema. In an early scene, we have a single shot: Kane (Welles) is in the background; Bernstein (Everett Sloane) is right in extreme close-up; Thatcher (George Coulouris) is left in mid-shot. They are now old men, deciding how to foreclose on parts of Kane's crumbling media empire. They speak in hushed, halted tones, weary with age, too tired to battle their opinions between each other as they had done for so many years. It's a classic 'film-as-art' shot historians love – perfect for teaching students (who have watched a million video clips and ads and played a thousand computer games) about the dynamics of visual framing and its effect on filmic narrative. But this scene's arch framing is there for one reason alone: Kane has deliberately been placed off-mic. In the shadowed distance he speaks. He sounds displaced, distanced, disenfranchised. The radiophonic inscripture of Kane's voice symbolizes his weariness and his fading existential self, as he is framed and mixed between the close-miced close-ups of his two colleagues. Kane then moves forward while talking. As he makes his decision final, to sell off shares and foreclose the newspaper of his long lost dreams, his voice becomes clearer. His aural blend into the room's resonance has now morphed into a distinctly clear voice that intimates that Kane is accepting his actions.

This moment is one of an astounding number that reveal *Citizen Kane* to be filmed radio drama – counter to the film's grand status as a cinematographic text, redolent with visual flourishes that evoke the signature of that thing called 'Orson Welles'. Welles' modus operandi was to centralize the microphone: to work with it, around it, beyond it. The fact that this scene uses a single microphone, when most other scenes are using multiple microphones to map the scenography aurally as what I would term 'spatialized sound in motion', indicates that Welles considered something as sacrilegious as 'off-mic' as part of the sonic palette for the depiction of his cine-world. But perhaps the ultimate irony of how deaf film theory is to the so-called visuals of *Citizen Kane* is the oft-cited use of low-angled camera angles – the famous 'shooting into the ceiling' stylization that typifies much of *Citizen Kane*'s *mise en scène*. Those ceilings are scrims, stretched lightweight linen lit to appear like plaster ceilings. And behind them are a strategically placed network of microphones that return the recorded space back into a theatrical space, allowing actors to move in complex configurations in open counterpoint to the camera, rather than being forced to 'block' their movements for the camera alone.

This use of scrims is an uncanny recall of the movie-theatre screen which hides something we do not see but undoubtedly hear: the speakers. Welles hid his microphones on-screen, as opposed to sending them off-screen. In effect, throughout *Citizen Kane*, the microphone is always in shot, surreptitiously bending the penultimate law of cinematic form: you can't have the microphone in shot. Yet Welles is one of many similarly silenced voices who explored how the cinema sets up dialogues with the microphonic. Busby Berkeley musicals have their share of 'shooting into the ceiling', but just as Welles literally jack-hammered pits in the Hollywood sound stage in order to angle his camera up, Berkeley just as famously issued his familiar command: '[R]aise the roof'. That was the only way he could get up and above the reverse anthropomorphic

'human kaleidoscopes' below. Not once did Berkeley's spectacular musicals accept that song and music were sited within the cinema – upon its sound-stage, hidden off-camera, cabled to the camera. Song was the meta-shell for Berkeley's movies during the 1930s, within which he architecturally sculpted staged analogues of the music's patterns, shapes and rhythms. Everyone, everybody and everything moved in-time to music. Celebrated as uniquely cinematic sound musicals, they in fact wholly disregard the instrument which is meant to have created sound cinema: the microphone. This is not through ignorance or rejection; it signifies an acceptance of the greater expansiveness of sound into which the camera could only ever peer, rove, track and traverse.

There is much silenced cinema that knows that the microphone need not be treated as a camera.

OUTSIDE THE READER ...

The tone poem that emerged in nineteenth-century Romantic music (also referred to as programme music, scene painting and image folios) represents a form of musical narration that is proto-cinematic in its emphasis on evocation, pastoralisation and pictorialism – key devices employed through the narrational functions of the film score. When Franz Liszt's impressionist tone poem *At the Lake of Wallenstadt* (*Au Lac de Wallenstadt*, 1848–54) unfurls flurries of chordal trilling of blurred and overlaid tonal keys, so as to simulate harmonically the overlapping and self-dissolving shimmering of light-sparkles flitting across the undulating surface of water, it only partially uses harmony's linguistic scripture and readability to effect a state of water-play. Fundamentally, Liszt's piece is an intuitive and organic algorithmic configuration of frequencies and proportionate patterning that are not dissimilar to the acoustic sound of lapping water, as heard near and far from the lakeside vantage point. It's not as if there are certain notes or collections of notes that referentially signify 'water' in the way that utterance of the word 'water' would abstractly connect our mind to the idea, memory or experience of 'water'. Sound's physical manifestation overwhelms any linguistic analogue, for sound (in which I include music as a subset) becomes language only through abstract metaphor. Music doesn't 'become' sound: it *is* sound, and the means by which it references, replicates and represents a physical reality will be through a reconstruction of scale, ratio, mass, volume and frequency.

Tone poems of the nineteenth century invite one less to 'read' music than to 'hear' it. This infection of musical composition by the poetic – in opposition to classicism's crypto-rational 'argumentative positions' on harmony and tonality – has been embraced mostly as a celebration of the humanist voice encodable within musical composition; hence the 'heroicism' of impressionist and expressionist modes of musical communication. Yet tone poems and their poetic denouement are more interesting in their narrational grasp of a space, environment or world within which the listener is situated. The hidden irony – in both musical and cinematic historiography – is that while tone poems were adapted as film scores to describe spaces and places, they ended up becoming 'stages': artificial frames, backdrops and cycloramas. Perceived this way, film scores linked to this tradition (and that's a lot of film scores) empty the immersive sensational evocation of the tone poem form and flatten its sono-musical attributes into a coded linguistic system. Images of glinting lakes, overlaid with trilled piano chords appropriating Liszt's tone poem, over-communicate and audiovisually saturate the spatial realm depicted. It's not dissimilar from zooming in hard on a reproduction of an oil painting of the Swiss Alps in a Swiss restaurant in Nebraska: you're there, but you're not there.

Film music as delivered by the film score promotes an act of reading: of recognizing, identifying and comprehending music as a 'post-titled' layer of signification in the audiovisual text. Hearing is treated essentially as the motor-neurological means to activate the reading. Hence, an arpeggiated octave-run

on piano in the pentatonic mode 'means' light-on-water vis-à-vis the musical etymology strung through Debussy, Sibelius and Liszt among others. It is not surprising that so many analyses of film music reproduce the score's sheet notation as evidence of the reading required. These are indications of how 'a-sonic' the film score is in its formulation and promulgation both as composed art and critical analysis. On the one hand, the recourse to 'read music' within the cinematic object via the film score is a well-aimed strategy to dig deep into the film's intertextual layering. On the other hand, musicological analysis of this type, while it works great for classical film texts that clearly demarcate where the film score resides, doesn't help us once the film score vanishes – when it is rejected, doesn't exist or has been deliberately lambasted from the film. This shortcoming of 'score reading' laterally enforces a segregation of song, sound and noise from the quasi-literary modes of signification, contributing to the critical silencing of the more abjectly sonic and materially aural soundtracks.

Film music makes plenty of sound, but writing on it makes hardly a sound.

OUTSIDE THE LISTENER ...

Am I really speaking an incomprehensible language here? If you think that what you've read is an oppositional polemic of unscholarly dyspeptic compulsion, a terse radical diatribe that accuses cinema of being ontologically unfulfilled, you've misread and misheard this text. The above-detailed notions of *noise*, *musicality* and *audiovisuality* are not intended to foreground sound as the overpowering of image, as if, just because one discusses sound, one is throwing down the gauntlet for a territorial duel to defend a definition of cinema. These notions are offered as additional, additive and ancillary textual operations for *listening* to cinema, so as to incorporate such perspectives into the existing and multifarious Babel of critical theory, all of which has some substantive relevance to this thing we call 'the cinema'.

Italian neorealism, French *Nouvelle Roman* cinema, American Blaxploitation movies, German early-sound operettas, Russian hard-core porno, Mandarin *Huangmei* (yellow plum) musicals, Japanese sci-fi *anime* – they're all waiting to let you hear their soundtracks. (Even David Lynch, Martin Scorsese, Francis Ford Coppola, Robert Altman and Orson Welles wouldn't mind if you actually talked *about* their sound rather than through it.) These and so many more moments, movements and mavericks in cinema have been platformed into critical compatibility via the standard respected politicized discursive practices – but they may as well be silent movies for the amount of critical insight afforded their soundtracks. The 'absent aural' in film theory is likely the most pervasive, unifying and interconnected critical voice in what has been written on cinema. The positive push of this text is to suggest that next time you get the pang to ideologically dissect a film and hold up your forensic findings for the intelligentsia's musing, try also listening to the patient you just cut up: their groans could be meaningful and relevant.

Find me a book on cinema that somewhere doesn't have film frames referenced in its cover design – or eyes, screens, viewers, cameras, projectors. Then find me a book on film sound or music that doesn't reference ears, sheet music, pianos, orchestras. If there were audiovisual balance in film theory, a book could simply be called 'Cinema' – and its cover would be a close-up photo of a microphone. This chapter is not called 'where sound should be', 'where sound can be found', 'where sound is defined' or 'where sound can be researched'. The 'is' is the important marker – a statement of the prescience, presence and presentness of sound as a phenomenological occurrence.

The answer to the query where sound is? It's while image is.

SUGGESTED READING

The reading indicated in the following sections collects most key writings on film sound and film music which investigate myriad ways in which cinematic audiovisuality can be textually constituted according to a wide range of critical methodologies. Appended to this are selected works for those seeking some primary grounding in the broader terrain of sound culture and attendant sonic practices. Collectively, these writings – despite their individual orientation and chosen fields of enquiry – contribute to an understanding of cinema as not only an essentially audiovisual medium, but also as a form shaped by modern and modernist relations to culture and technology. Taken holistically, they forward ways in which to consider both the phenomenological aspects of the full cinematic experience, and the broader implications of cinema's malleable ontological status as determined by modulating technological factors.

Film sound and film music theory

Altman, Rick (2004) *Silent Film Sound*. New York: Columbia University Press.

Brophy, Philip (2004) *100 Modern Soundtracks*. London: BFI.

Brown, Royal S. (1994) *Overtones and Undertones: Reading Film Music*. Berkeley: University of California Press.

Chion, Michel (1994) *Audio-vision Sound on Screen*. Tr. Claudia Gorbman. New York: Columbia University Press.

Chion, Michel (1999) *The Voice in Cinema*. Tr. Claudia Gorbman. New York: Columbia University Press.

Egorova, Tatiana K. (1997) *Soviet Film Music: An Historical Survey*. Tr. Tatiana A. Ganf and Natalia A. Egunova. Amsterdam: Harwood Academic Publishers.

Flynn, Caryl (1992) *Strains of Utopia: Gender, Nostalgia and Hollywood Film Music*. Princeton, NJ: Princeton University Press.

Flynn, Caryl (2004) *The New German Cinema*. Berkeley: University of California Press.

Gabbard, Krin (1996) *Jammin' at the Margins: Jazz and the American Cinema*. Chicago: Chicago University Press.

Gorbman, Claudia (1987) *Unheard Melodies: Narrative Film Music*. Bloomington: Indiana University Press.

Kalinak, Kathryn (1992) *Settling the Score*. Madison: *Music and the Classical Hollywood Film*. University of Wisconsin Press.

Kassabian, Anahid (2001) *Hearing Film: Tracking Identifications in Contemporary Hollywood Film Music*. New York: Routledge.

Kozloff, Sarah (1988) *Invisible Storytellers. Voice-Over Narration in American Fiction Film*. University of California Press.

Kozloff, Sarah (2000) *Overhearing Film Dialogue*. Berkeley: University of California Press.

Lastra, James (2000) *Sound Technology and the American Cinema*. New York: Columbia University Press.

Smith, Jeff (1998) *The Sounds of Commerce: Marketing Popular Film Music*. New York: Columbia University Press.

Walker, Alexander (1978) *The Shattered Silents: How the Talkies Came to Stay*. London: Elm Tree.

Weis, Elisabeth (1982) *The Silent Scream: Alfred Hitchcock's Sound Track*. Rutherford Fairleigh: Dickinson University Press.

Weis, Elisabeth and Belton, John (eds) (1985) *Film Sound*. New York: Columbia University Press.

Film sound and film music theory: critical anthologies

Altman, Rick (ed.) (1992) *Sound Theory, Sound Practice*. New York: Routledge.

Brophy, Philip (1999) *Cinesonic: The World of Sound in Film*. Sydney: AFTRS Publishing.

Brophy, Philip (2000) *Cinesonic: Cinema and the Sound of Music*. Sydney: AFTRS Publishing.

Brophy, Philip (2001) *Cinesonic: Experiencing the Soundtrack*. Sydney: AFTRS Publishing.

Buhler, James, Flynn, Caryl and Neumeyer, David (eds) (2000) *Music And Cinema*. Hanover, NM: University Press of New England.

Dickinson, Kay (ed.) (2003) *Movie Music: The Film Reader*. London: Routledge.

Goldmark, Daniel, Kramer, Lawrence and Leppert, Richard (eds) (2007) *Beyond The Soundtrack: Representing Music in Cinema*. Berkeley: University of California Press.

Film sound technique

LoBrutto, Vincent (1994) *Sound-On-Film: Interviews with Creators of Film Music*. Westport, CT: Praeger.

Pasquariello, Nicholas (1996) *Sounds of Movies: Interviews with the Creators of Feature Sound Tracks*. San Francisco: Port Bridge.

Sound culture

Eisenberg, Evan (1987) *The Recording Angel: Explorations in Phonography*. New York: Penguin.

Lanza, Joseph (1994) *Elevator Music*. New York: Picador.

Picker, John M. (2003) *Victorian Soundscapes*. New York: Oxford University Press.

Toop, David (1995) *Ocean of Sound: Aether Talk, Ambient Sound and Imaginary Worlds*. London: Serpent's Tail.

Thompson, Emily (2002) *The Soundscape of Modernity*. Cambridge, MA: MIT Press.

Sound culture: critical anthologies

Bull, Michael and Back, Les (2003) *The Auditory Culture Reader*. Oxford: Berg.

Cox, Christopher and Warner, Daniel (2004) *Audio Culture*. New York: Continuum.

Young, Rob (2004) *Under-Currents*. London: Continuum.

28

The Question of Genre in Cult Film and Fandom: Between Contract and Discourse

Matt Hills

Compared with concepts such as authorship, genre has had a more stolid and reliable presence in Film Studies. Various writers have returned to the idea after many years, even if in a revisionist spirit (see Altman, 1999; Neale, 1980; 2000). The meanings and processes associated with genre have thus been the objects of fairly constant debate in film theory: 'Genre is a French word meaning "type" or "kind"', observes Stephen Neale; 'it has occupied an important place in the study of the cinema for over thirty years' (2000: 9).

Although other master-narratives are certainly possible – Sarah Berry-Flint (2004) offers a four-part model and Barry Langford (2005) a three-phase history – I want to suggest that there have really only been two major phases of work on film genre from the 1970s onward. The first dealt with genre as a 'contract' between film producers and consumers, the text itself being evidence of this. Assuming that genre operated like a contract fitted with a range of structuralist ideas, this work on genre invariably started and ended with close textual analysis.

The shift towards a post-structuralist perspective on genre – occurring predominantly from the 1990s on – generated a second phase of more audience-based work in Film Studies. Rather than the film text being treated as a stable source, or evidential base, from which producers' and consumers' views of genre could be inferred, the text was decentred within this more discursive frame. No longer a source of genre attributions, instead the film text became one cultural site which competing genre discourses could circle around. Taking this approach to genre meant that it was not enough to carry out textual analysis; at the very least, marketing materials and audience receptions also required study. Conceptualized as a discourse rather than a contract, the genre-identity of any one text became more fluid and multiple (Derrida, 1992). Different moments in a film's marketing and reception may see its genre category being shifted by producers and sections of the audience, and different sub-groups within the audience may also disagree over the genre-identity of a particular film.

In the next section, I unpack this binary distinction between genre-as-contract and genre-as-discourse a little more. I chart a specific course through these debates, focusing on how the category of 'cult film' can shed light on arguments surrounding genre. Though a category used to make sense of and organize films' receptions and cultural identities, can 'cult' be thought of as a genre? And if not, what can this tell us about the possible limits to the concept? Cult film may provoke further consideration of the theoretical dogmas of structuralist and post-structuralist views on genre. Rather than marginalizing agents' discourses of genre (in favour of focusing on the text-as-contract), or marginalizing textual structures (in favour of focusing on audience discourses of genre), the actions of cult film fans may call for a structuration theory of genre, that is, treating it as a recurrent process of text-audience interactions in which neither text nor audience is prioritized. I focus on this in the chapter's closing section.

FILM GENRE 'IN' (CULT) TEXTS AND (CULT) AUDIENCES: FROM CONTRACT TO DISCOURSE

Though it is certainly reasonable to say that 'the study of film genre is no more than an extension of literary genre study' (Altman, 1999: 13), any such expression of continuity surely plays down the extent to which film scholars have attempted to transfer general theories of genre into a distinctively cinematic register, hence creating ruptures, discontinuities, and new beginnings in genre theory. Stephen Neale's *Genre* (1980) represents one such rupture. Reacting against the 'visual' or iconographic emphasis of earlier work, Neale strives instead for a stance on film genre which acknowledges that visual conventions gain

their meanings from being positioned within narrative and semiotic structures. He also points out that any examination of the purely visual aspects of, say, the Western or the film noir would actually 'fail in its aim of engaging the specificity of film' precisely because these genres rely as much on film sound, titles, and other graphic elements, as they do on the merely 'visual' (1980: 12). *Genre* is hence concerned with articulating a cinema-specific theory of genre.

Given its major debts to structuralism, Neale's work at this point tends to view genre as a way of fixing meaning between text and audience, and thus as a regulative system of differences:

> As well as providing a means of regulating desire across a series of textual instances, and of offering an ordered variety of the discursive possibilities of cinema itself, genres also provide a means of regulating memory and expectation, a means of containing the possibilities of reading. Overall, they offer the industry a means of controlling demand, and the institution a means of containing coherently the effects that its products produce. (1980: 54–5)

However, Neale does not construct genre simply as a reaffirmation of audiences' expectations. He was careful to note that the system of film genre could also operate by excess – in other words, redefining prior expectations (1980: 54). Despite this, the rhetorical thrust of the booklet *Genre* was one that largely favoured repetition over difference, setting out a notion of genre as 'limiting the danger in difference' (1980: 54). The driving metaphor was one of limitation or 'containment'. Genre worked to contain audiences' pleasures and meanings, like a cage of industrial-textual rationality.

Neale was far from alone in offering this kind of structuralist-indebted accounts of film genre in the 1970s and 1980s. Another major contributor to film genre theory, Rick Altman, first published his article 'A Semantic/Syntactic Approach to Film Genre' (reprinted as part of *Film/Genre* [1999]) in the mid-80s. Taking as its starting point the 'heavy influence of semiotics on generic theory', Altman's analysis proceeded to posit a series of binaries in genre study which needed to be overcome (1999: 217). These included 'semantic' versus 'syntactic' and 'inclusive' versus 'exclusive' approaches to genre. Semantic/syntactic approaches had been investigated by Neale (1980). This was an opposition between approaches to genre which focused on repeated signs or units of meaning, and those which focused on characteristic syntax; that is, the structural relations between iconographic elements. Altman used 'inclusive' versus 'exclusive' to loosely overlap with this first binary, arguing that some genre critics included vast swathes of films in a given genre category because they were using a purely semantic definition, whilst theorists exploring a syntax of the same genre excluded many of the same examples: 'Because there are two competing notions of generic corpus ... it is perfectly possible for a film to be simultaneously included in a particular generic corpus [by one critic] and excluded from that same corpus [by another]' (1999: 217).

What was most interesting about Altman's work here was its 'to-do' list. Altman explicitly recognized the possibility of a post-structuralist theory of film genre, which would be able to tackle the fact that different critics/theorists tended to place given films within different genres (1999: 219). And Altman noted that further consideration of audience activity was called for: '[T]he agency of the spectator clearly deserves further study' (1999: 225). Whereas Neale emphasized the structuralist workings of genre – containing meanings and pleasures on behalf of audiences, and so regulating their film consumption – Altman was already beginning to unravel the fixity and fixations of this school of thought by highlighting how genre categories were very much open to contestation, debate, and audience disagreement.

Another scholar whose work on film genre has marked the field is media-sociologist Andrew Tudor. Examining the 'critical methodology' of genre criticism, Tudor observed that film scholars acted as if their examinations of genre refined or identified genre categories, yet this process actually depended on scholars recognizing in advance, and so *a priori*, which films ought to be placed in given genre categories:

> Almost all writers using the term genre ... are caught in a dilemma. They are *defining* a 'Western' on the basis of analysing a body of films which cannot possibly be said to be 'Westerns' until after the analysis ... [Therefore] we are caught in a circle which first requires that the films are isolated, for which purposes a criterion is necessary, but the criterion is, in turn, meant to emerge from empirically established common characteristics of the films. (1976: 120–1)

Tudor dubbed this the 'empiricist dilemma' (1976: 121). In effect, he demonstrated that there had been a kind of 'chicken and egg' problem in film genre criticism; that is, which comes first, the texts analyzed (giving rise to a genre category), or the genre category (giving rise to the texts under analysis)? Tudor's solution to this puzzle was to argue that most genre study has no choice other than 'to lean on a common cultural consensus as to what constitutes a "Western" [where this is the genre being studied], and then go on to analyse it in detail' (1976: 121).

Like Altman's early-eighties work, Tudor critically reflects on the limits to genre study. However, where Altman flags the need for later genre criticism to focus on social disagreements and audience dissensus over genre categories, Tudor assumes that genre scholarship must start from cultural consensus. Tudor comes close to viewing genre as a kind of structuralist contract between film producers and consumers: it is supposedly a tacit agreement, embedded in film culture – and culture more generally – about which films belong in which categories. And it is a regulative agreement, more importantly, over what kinds of pleasures and meanings genre categories should be expected to proffer. By contrast, even in his 'Semantic/Syntactic' paper, Altman (1999) begins to sketch out a post-structuralist perspective on genre, where audience interpretations of a film can lead to different genre categories being mobilized, and where critics might disagree over which genre a film 'belongs' to.

This alternative – genre as disseminated discourse rather than implied contract – has been very much picked up on by genre study across the past decade or so. Contributors to this body of work have included Altman in his book *Film/Genre*, Thomas Austin (2002) and Mark Jancovich (2000), with Jason Mittell (2004) examining television genres in a similar manner. Altman proposes a new manifesto for genre theory based around dissensus:

> Instead of a word or a category capable of clear and stable definition … genre has here been presented as a multivalent term … variously valorized by diverse user groups … In fact, the moments of clear and stable sharing typically adduced as generic models represent special cases within a broader general situation of user competition. (1999: 214–15)

Far from being a type or kind of film – as if this category could be deduced from empirical textual attributes – 'genre' instead represents a competing set of discourses, with different audiences 'doing genre' differently in line with their own established social interests and cultural identities. Alluding to previous structuralist conceptions, Altman argues that 'while genres may make meaning by regulating and co-ordinating disparate users, they always do so in an arena where users with divergent interests compete to carry out their own programmes' (1999: 215).

This shift towards viewing genre as more than just a 'type' of text has been linked to a growth in empirical work on film audiences, since logically it calls for the study of how flesh-and-blood movie audiences (including theorists and professional film reviewers) actually 'do genre'. Jancovich and Austin are amongst those who have offered up useful examinations of how audiences use film genre categories. Drawing on the work of French sociologist Pierre Bourdieu (1984), Jancovich's study of fan audiences for the film *Scream* (Wes Craven, US, 1996) indicates how genre categories form part of audiences' bids for cultural distinction. Jancovich shows that sections of horror fandom, invested in subcultural ideals of 'authentic' and 'underground' horror, deny that *Scream* belongs in this genre category, instead positioning it as feminized and hyper-commercialized 'horror'

where 'quotation marks … qualify this term; [working] to suggest that it is not *real* horror' (2000: 29). Conflict over genre categories emerges between different factions of one fan culture – with fans of 'underground' and 'real' horror (likely to be older, male fans) attacking the tastes of fans more likely to be younger women, as well as positioning highly commercially-successful films outside 'their' beloved genre category. This kind of genre-policing is not one that occurs across radically different taste cultures, but is part of an intra-fan-cultural bid for subcultural distinction.

Austin's work on 1990s 'quality costume horror' looks similarly at competing genre discourses used by audiences in relation to *Bram Stoker's Dracula* (Francis Ford Coppola, US, 1992). Austin shows that, while some horror fans rejected this genre category because of the film's 'failure to frighten' and its 'mainstream mishandling of horror', others welcomed it as an atmospheric, romantic horror movie (2002: 135–7). Again, viewers used genre discourses to perform their cultural identities. Those who valued the film as horror were positioning themselves as 'discerning' genre fans not just interested in gore and violence, whereas those who rejected the film as horror were, like Jancovich's fans, constructing their fan identities subculturally against 'mainstream' film.

These audience studies suggest that genre discourses need to be examined not just in relation to textual attributes and marketing materials, but also via the genre 'rewriting' of audience interpretations (Austin, 2002: 143). Further to this, Austin's work on *Bram Stoker's Dracula* also argues for the need to factor academics' own practices of regenrification into genre study (2002: 118), as well as suggesting that institutionally-validated genre categories always co-exist in audiences' discourses with more 'privatised' or 'personal' quasi-genre labels 'yet to attain institutional consolidation', such as the organizing category of 'intelligent cool films', which was used by one of Austin's respondents to classify their cinematic tastes (2002: 142–3).

Having set out the characteristics of structuralist text-based and post-structuralist audience-based approaches to film genre, I want to consider how the category of 'cult' film may fit into these different phases. I have already referred to horror film fandom, which resembles what Altman calls a 'constellated community' defined in relation to certain genre-based tastes, discourses and knowledges, even if it may also be an internally stratified generic community (1999: 161). But what of cult film fandom? Is this also best thought of as a genre-based cultural identity and community? And if genre isn't the most useful term here, what can this tell us about the concept, and about structuralist/post-structuralist approaches to film genre?

Influential work on cult film, such as Umberto Eco's essay '*Casablanca*: Cult Movies and Intertextual Collage' (1995), has sought to define 'cult' in terms of shared textual qualities. This exercise, indebted to structuralism and semiotics, implies that 'cult' is a kind of genre: an organizing category of film which works to cue certain audience expectations, and is linked to a range of textual meanings and structures. Just as structuralist views of genre tended to marginalize audience interpretations, implying that genre categories could be read off from texts themselves, so too does Eco's account of cult film suppress the question of fan reception: '[T]he work must be loved, obviously, but this is not enough' (1995: 198). The activities of cult fan audiences are basically relegated to this acknowledgement in Eco's essay, which then proceeds to investigate cult status as if it is something 'in' the text. Eco isolates several candidates for semantic/syntactic qualities of 'cult':

- A cult film 'must provide a completely furnished world so that its fans can quote characters and episodes as if they were aspects of the fan's sectarian world' (1995: 198).
- A cult film must 'be already ramshackle, rickety, unhinged in itself' since for Eco 'only an unhinged movie survives as a disconnected series of images ... It should display not one central idea but many ... It must live on because of its glorious

ricketiness. However, it must have some quality' (1995: 198–9).
- Cult films must 'display certain textual features ... [The cult movie] becomes a sort of textual syllabus, a living example of living textuality ... proof that ... cinema comes from cinema' (1995: 199).

More recently, critics have challenged some of these criteria: for example, how can the idea of a 'completely furnished world' actually be understood (Gwenllian-Jones, 2000: 12–13), when by definition all narrative worlds extend beyond what audiences are actually shown on-screen, and are inevitably marked by gaps and absences? Furthermore, Eco's views on the cult movie as 'ramshackle' are derived from the notion that cult films cannot be dipped in and out of, nor controlled, in the manner in which a reader controls a book – an argument which video and DVD technology falsify. And his argument with regard to cult films as 'living textuality' may fit *Casablanca* (Michael Curtiz, US, 1942), but it fails to address auteurist cult films, for instance, Quentin Tarantino movies, or the cult *oeuvre* of the likes of Tim Burton, David Cronenberg, and David Lynch. Eco's attempt at a generic definition of 'cult' falls short of accounting for the diverse range of films which have attracted the label, especially since he appears to link 'cult' only to movie fictions, rather than also considering cult documentaries and mockumentaries which nevertheless draw on notions of documentary realism for their effects, such as *This Is Spinal Tap* (Rob Reiner, US, 1984) or more recently, *American Movie* (Chris Smith, US, 1999).

In fact, Eco's entire cult-as-genre project has been rejected *tout court* (see Hills, 2002: 131; Staiger, 2005: 125–6). Anne Jerslev says of cult film scholarship such as Eco's:

> The concept of cult film ... [should] ... not ... be understood as some fixed structure of meaning inherent in the film text. It is not a genre concept ... A cult film is only brought into existence in so far as one talks of an interaction between a text and an audience ... *The existing literature on cult films has, however, aimed at anchoring the understanding of the concept by focusing ... on aesthetic and thematic structures inherent in the films.* (1992: 186, my italics)

To an extent, J.P. Telotte's edited collection *The Cult Film Experience* (1991) marks one transitional point between structuralist cult-as-genre exercises, and later audience-based or discourse-based models of 'cult'. Several contributors, among them Bruce Kawin, Timothy Corrigan, and Gaylyn Studlar, attempt to offer vague thematics or textual qualities which can predispose a film to achieve 'cult' status, even while they begin to question the validity of this approach.

Kawin suggests that cult films can be subcategorized into those which are 'inadvertent', such as *Casablanca*, that is, created by audience activity, and those which are 'programmatic' or generically designed as cults (1991: 19), examples being *Evil Dead II* (Sam Raimi, US, 1987) and *The Texas Chainsaw Massacre 2* (Tobe Hooper, US, 1986). The latter (that is genre) category, Kawin characterizes as 'subversive … tasteless', and as working by 'violating shared values' (1991: 19–22). For his part, Corrigan begins by approvingly citing Eco's *Casablanca* essay before discussing the thematics of cult films: '[T]hese are often films about outsiders … they commonly dramatize a clash between different cultures or subcultures' (1991: 28). Corrigan argues that 'the most important motif in these movies is the debris and excess that define characters and environments, which never quite fit or relate to each other as natural' (1991: 28). In stressing the denaturalization of narrative worlds allegedly offered by cult movies, his account of cult status again positions it as inherently anti-mainstream and 'subversive', and his examples include *Pink Flamingos* (John Waters, US, 1972), *Repo Man* (Alex Cox, US, 1984), and perhaps the most academically discussed of all cult movies, *The Rocky Horror Picture Show* (Jim Sharman, UK/US, 1975). Also linking cult movies to a sense of the 'counter-cultural', and discussing titles such as *Liquid Sky* (Slava Tsukerman, US, 1982) and *Eraserhead* (David Lynch, US, 1977), Studlar argues for the distinctive presence of 'excess' in programmatic cult films, suggesting that they unconventionally explore issues of sexual difference (1991: 153).

However, despite reeling off sets of putative thematic connections across cult films, Corrigan's ultimate argument is that 'thematics are only slightly relevant' to cult status (1991: 28). He suggests that a film's mode of reception is more significant, singling out the VCR as a key technological facilitator of cult status due to the fact that it allowed audiences to manipulate and take symbolic possession of film texts. Making an argument similar in some ways to Kawin's, Corrigan enacts a kind of splitting: cult is both akin to genre and radically distinct from it. But where Kawin keeps these contradictions in play via the binary of inadvertent/programmatic cults, Corrigan finally characterizes genre/thematic analysis of the cult movie as futile.

In his introductory chapter to *The Cult Film Experience* (1991), Telotte further betrays an oscillatory attitude towards the question of cult-as-genre:

> [U]sing the term 'cult' to mark off a group of films for study … implies a kind of routine genre criticism, rooted in the idea that 'cult' marks off a reasonably distinguishable film genre. That is a notion that many would quickly and justifiably challenge … The cult film simply transgresses even the boundaries we usually associate with the very notion of genre. (1991: 6)

However, even in the moment that he theorizes cult as a transgression of genre boundaries, Telotte nevertheless suggests that this very transgression (along with a contained ideological transgression) is what defines 'cult'. In other words, he paradoxically enacts a gesture of generic categorization by positioning cult as a sort of transgressive 'meta-genre', assigning it an organizational category. Genre returns, in this instance, through its very disavowal.

One writer who has repeatedly sought to explore the question of cult-as-genre is Barry Keith Grant. Contributing to both *The Cult Film Experience* (Telotte, 1991) and *Unruly Pleasures: The Cult Film and Its Critics* (Mendik and Harper, 2000), Grant may have re-written and extended his examination of cult film to take in a wider range of examples, but he remains intent on analyzing how 'many cult movies share a common deep structure' (2000: 15). For Grant, the diversity of cult movies is not grounds for immediately dismissing genre arguments, and he follows Telotte in making 'transgression' central to his definition of cult qualities. More specifically, Grant suggests that 'cult films encourage viewers not to take very seriously the threat of the Other. At the same time, they prod us to laugh at representations of the normal' (1991: 135). This inversion of classical film ideology – where the Other is usually a threat to cultural and social norms – marks out the cult film's transgression. Again recalling Telotte's argument, Grant also suggests that cult movies' transgression is recuperated, this time through cult films' tendency to flatten into caricature and 'work in terms of clearly defined oppositions. Their conflicts invariably can be reduced to some version of white hats versus black hats' (1991: 134; 2000: 25). Grant (2000) suggests that cult movies such as Peter Jackson's *Bad Taste* (New Zealand, 1988), *Meet the Feebles* (New Zealand, 1990) and *Braindead* (New Zealand, 1992) can be thought of in this way, as can many of the films of Paul Verhoeven, but especially *Showgirls* (France/US, 1995).

Summarizing cult-as-genre work by Eco and Grant, Janet Staiger argues that 'none of them covers every movie ... that typically is thought of as able to produce repeat viewings or initiation gestures. Nor do the theories explain why only some individuals become cult viewers' (2005: 126). Staiger opposes any cult-as-genre argument on the basis that cult movies are defined through audience activities – in this case, repeated viewing and the desire to 'initiate others' into the film cult. However, the difficulty here is that Staiger relies on a cultural consensus as to which movies are 'cult' for audiences, that is to say only certain movies 'typically ... produce repeat viewings' (2005: 125). Even while pursuing a genre theory of cult, however, Grant notes that where 'cult' is concerned, the 'problem [of such consensus] is ... acute' because of the way in which cult status can intersect with a range of conventional genres (cult horror/cult sci-fi/cult comedy etc.), and because of the

lack of agreement in academic and journalistic work as to which films are indeed 'cult' (1991: 123) – some films may be deemed 'cultish', for instance, because they adapt cult novels for the screen (Jackson's *The Lord of the Rings* trilogy [New Zealand/US, 2001; US/New Zealand/Germany, 2002; 2003]) or feature cult comic book characters (very many superhero movies would fit into this category). Such 'residual' or inherently inter-textual cult movies are different in kind to film cults which emerge purely around entirely 'original' screenplays and performances. Staiger's first critique therefore relies on a notion of cult completeness – that there is a complete and stable corpus of cult texts – which itself is an unsustainable assumption. And her second critique, that cult-as-genre arguments don't account for the fact that some viewers are unaffected by a 'cult' film, implies that an audience-based definition of cult must invalidate text-based theorizations. Staiger contrasts text- and audience-based approaches to cult film as if these are an irreconcilable binary or zero-sum game.

Rather than dismissing various stances on cult-as-genre by adopting a post-structuralist or audience-based position, I'd argue that the category of 'cult' has actually played a significant role in problematizing structuralist accounts of genre. Even where he brackets out the cult fan audience, Eco shows some awareness of the need to consider fans' 'love' and 'worship' of the cult text. And later critics writing in *The Cult Film Experience* (Telotte, 1991) tended to vacillate between arguments which retained elements of the cult-as-genre view and critiqued it. Cult status, and its theorization in Film Studies, has exerted considerable, productive pressure on structuralist versions of genre theory.

Though it is tempting to suggest that some approaches to cult status can be dubbed purely 'structuralist' or 'post-structuralist' (for example, Eco is a cult structuralist and Staiger a cult post-structuralist), this misses the complexities posed to theoretical paradigms by cult film. For, even those critics who have turned to constructivist or discourse- and audience-based views of cult (Jancovich et al., 2003; Le Guern, 2004) still need to address the marketing take-up of 'cult' as an organizing film category, and thus the textual qualities which both film publicists *and* audiences have sought to articulate with 'cult' discourses: 'when any film can be marketed commercially as a cult film – i.e. labelled a cult film before it has even been shown in a cinema – then the public relation business has labelled a tidal change in media culture' (Jerslev, 1992: 182).

Considering 'cult' as a discourse used by audiences as well as by film publicists doesn't entirely remove the textual question. If anything, finding answers to this question remains especially pressing due to the fact that cult movies often mean so much to their fans. 'Cult' status recurrently raises the cult-as-genre question of 'why this group of texts?' even where 'cultification' is addressed as a matter of audience activity (see Hills, 2002; 2004). Treating cult as a matter of competing genre discourses deployed by different 'user groups' in Altman's phraseology can mean considering competing discourses used in marketing and by different audience fractions (1999: 214) – a film may be 'cult' to some audiences but not to others. (See Hills [2003] on George Lucas's *Star Wars* [US, 1977] as a 'cult blockbuster'.) Alternatively, a film may be 'cult' in multiple different ways to multiple audiences. In each case of 'cult' status, the question of why 'cult' is felt to be an appropriate category by specific user groups still calls for close textual analysis, as well as intertextual and audience study.

Though it may be possible to narrate genre's place in Film Studies through the consensus/dissensus phases of genre-as-contract and genre-as-discourse, cult film threatens to deconstruct this sequence. It is no longer possible – if it ever was – to clearly contrast a grassroots audience-led 'cultification' process (Jenkins, 1992: 40) with industry-led and 'programmatic' cults, as per the splitting enacted in Kawin's argument (1991). The possibility of this conceptual distinction has been overwritten by the fact that 'cult' as

a discourse and a category has itself now been semiotically fought over by different user groups such as producers, marketers and audiences. This means that 'cult' as a label has become 'multi-accentual', and shot-through with the inflections and residues of its many differently contextualized uses (Hills, 2002: 121). Marketing appropriations of the term thus co-opt and re-tool its audience-led connotations, whilst different audiences' uses of the term respond to its marketing take-up, as well as to its deployment by rival fan cultures or factions within one generic community.

Cult's multi-accentuality places it between contact and discourse, carrying aspects of an industrial-regulative category and an audience-defined discourse. This also makes it a genre-like category that has successfully moved between the 'public' genre-categories and 'private' quasi-genres such as 'intelligent cool films' analyzed by Austin (2002). Unlike categorizations such as 'smart cinema' (Sconce, 2002), 'cult' has by now achieved a fairly secure institutional validation, something which has rendered it conventionally more genre-like in terms of acting as a film-industry device to interpellate audiences. At the same time, however, it has also continually moved outside of, and beyond, its film-industry appropriations in a variety of fan discourses. As a term, it has arguably moved dialectically between structuralist and post-structuralist conceptions of genre, being framed as 'contractual' at certain moments, and then dissolving into a range of discourses which disseminate outside both the film industry and its marketing.

As such, cult's fluctuations indicate some of the limits to (post)structuralist concepts of genre. Cult status exists partly 'below' genre as one of Austin's 'privatised' quasi-genres, but it has also taken on the qualities of a meta- or supra-genre via its ability to transgress, transcend, and articulate other genres such as comedy, science-fiction, or horror. This discursive aspect of cult's functioning suggests that it is closer to being a modality than a genre. In 'Rethinking Genre', Christine Gledhill argues for the importance of investigating modality, this being an organizing textual quality or category operating above and across the level of genre:

> The notion of modality ... defines a specific mode of aesthetic articulation adaptable across a range of genres ... It provides the genre system with a mechanism of 'double articulation', capable of generating specific and distinctively different generic formulae in particular historical conjunctures, while also providing a medium of interchange and overlap between genres. (2000: 229)

Could cult status be thought of more usefully as a modality rather than a genre? Like modality (tragedy/romance/melodrama), cult cuts across conventional genres such as sci-fi or comedy, and like other modalities it is arguably linked to a particular tone or register – focusing on the fantastic and/or the denaturalized. Indeed, Catherine Johnson, writing about 'telefantasy', has noted the 'discursive association of fantasy with cult media' (2005: 3). Although Johnson observes that cult status moves across genre categories, operating like a modality, she ultimately concludes that cult is a 'mode of reception' rather than being amenable to any kind of textual definition (2005: 3). She does, however, accord textual-analytical status to 'telefantasy', which she notes is heavily associated with cult TV status:

> [B]etween the specific generic conventions and the tone of each programme, are shared concerns with representation, with the stability of the fictional world, with the role of seeing, and with the image that arise specifically through the representation of the fantastic. (2005: 6)

Johnson terms these 'production strategies' which are also analyzable as 'textual strategies' (2005: 6–7). It seems odd to separate 'cult media' as a category that cannot be subjected to definitional textual analysis from 'telefantasy', which can supposedly be subjected to textual analysis of its 'shared concerns'. I would argue that Johnson's move with regard to 'telefantasy' might in fact shed light on the modality-like operations of 'cult' media. By linking, mediating, and crossing genre categories, 'cult' may offer up shared

concerns which are not only or inevitably counter-cultural, such as:

- Self-reflexively interrogating genre conventions (which partly acts to denaturalize the cinematic representations concerned, but also displays inter-textual subcultural capital). Alejandro Amenabar's *Tesis* (Spain, 1996) does this, as do the likes of *The Texas Chainsaw Massacre* (Tobe Hooper, US, 1974) and, more recently, Joss Whedon's *Serenity* (US, 2005) via its fusion of the western with science-fiction conventions. Cult mockumentaries, whether dark or light comedies – *Man Bites Dog* (Remy Belvaux, Belgium, 1992), *Best in Show* (Christopher Guest, US, 2000) – also necessarily involve and invoke this genre-probing process.
- Self-reflexively interrogating the material construction of the filmic image, either through exaggerated/distorted *mise en scène*, the unusual use of camera movement and framing, or the deployment of special effects. Stanley Kubrick's work, such as the Steadicam unease of *The Shining* (US/UK, 1980) or the technicolour trippiness of *2001: A Space Odyssey* (UK/US, 1968) would be good examples of this. So too are films like *Requiem for a Dream* (Darren Aronofsky, US, 2000), and even John Carpenter's *The Thing* (US, 1982).
- More-or-less explicitly addressing questions of identity in a 'philosophical' or existential register (that is, cult film frequently intersects with specific forms of intertextual cultural capital). Spike Jonze's *Being John Malkovich* (US, 1999) and Michel Gondry's *Eternal Sunshine of the Spotless Mind* (US, 2004) work in this manner, as do many sci-fi-thriller films such as *Cube* (Vincenzo Natali, Canada, 1997) and *Open Your Eyes* (Alejandro Amenabar, Spain/France/Italy, 1997).
- Seeking to provoke moments of 'ontological shock' which cannot fully be articulated with suspense or horror, but which can be characterized either by plot twists reorienting the viewer's understanding of narrative events, or by moments of extreme visceral disgust which, again, though related to the affects or emotions of horror, are not coterminous with these (Carroll, 1990). The films of M. Night Shyamalan tend to work in this way, as well as incorporating 'philosophical' or existential questions, as does the reverse noir-ish narrative of *Memento* (Christopher Nolan, US, 2000).

What unites all these 'shared concerns' of cult film's modality is not a focus on the fantastic per se – though 'ontological shock' and identity-questioning are especially achievable through the genres of sci-fi and horror – but is, rather, a focus on the cultural value of popular genre cinema. Cult film, as a modality crossing conventional genres, appears to work rather unusually, and highly self-reflexively, in that it incorporates discourses and debates surrounding the cultural value of cinematic genres, and attempts to bid, more-or-less outrageously, for recognition of its own intertextual (sub)cultural capital (Hills, 2005a: 166–71). In a sense, 'art house' cinema is the closest cousin of cult film: relatively speaking, movies have a securely consecrated position in relation to their cultural value. By contrast, the modality of cult film is one whereby questions and discourses of cultural value are insecurely incorporated into the text, often operating in tension with a more conventional, pop-cultural generic identity. To give another example, *The Matrix* franchise (Andy and Larry Wachowski, US, 1999; 2003; 2003) may appear to be generically identifiable as a science-fiction blockbuster, but by incorporating philosophical discourses of identity and ontology (what is the essence of the 'real'?), it fuses its sci-fi semantics and syntax with a cult mode, and so bids for recognition as a 'cult blockbuster'. The film *Total Recall* (Paul Verhoeven, US, 1990) worked in a similar way, as did the cult canonical movie *Blade Runner* (Ridley Scott, US, 1982) (Hills, 2005b). Although neither would be understood as 'art house' films – they are very much 'genre' films – they nevertheless incorporate moments of ontological shock, and/or philosophical explorations of identity, and thus reflect on their value as 'intelligent cool' films.

The self-reflexive philosophizing which characterizes many cult films makes it perhaps unsurprising that cult movies have been well represented in textbooks that seek to introduce philosophy via film: for example, Mary M. Litch's *Philosophy through Film* begins with *Total Recall* and *The Matrix* (2002: 7–36), whilst Christopher Falzon's *Philosophy Goes to the Movies* ends with an

analysis of *Monty Python and the Holy Grail* (Terry Gilliam and Terry Jones, UK, 1975) (2002: 183–211), and philosopher Stephen Mulhall devotes his entire book *On Film* (2002) to an analysis of the *Alien* franchise (Ridley Scott, UK, 1979; James Cameron, US/UK, 1986; David Fincher, US, 1992; Jean-Pierre Jeunet, US, 1997). Some scholars of cult film have also recognized the modality's closeness to a philosophical register: David Lavery (1991) argues that cult films often display 'gnostic' intellectual interests in other-worldiness, and there is certainly a cult lineage here which runs from at least the sci-fi ethos of *The Man Who Fell to Earth* (Nicolas Roeg, UK, 1976) through to the lo-fi, geek-otherness of *Napoleon Dynamite* (Jared Hess, US, 2004).

To offer another example of cult modality – and hence the way in which 'cult' status can intersect with other genre categories – here is Staiger writing about teaching *The Texas Chainsaw Massacre* on 'a course in Cult Movies' (2000: 179). Far from being terrorized, Staiger found herself laughing at the film's intertextual references to Alfred Hitchcock's *Psycho* (US, 1960):

> One way to reassure oneself that one is not perverted is to find a community of others – a subculture of like-minded individuals who mirror one's own nature. In my case, I needed an interpretative community of fellow scholars who would also have the cultural capital to see the massive intertextual allusions to *Psycho* in *Texas Chainsaw Massacre*. (2000: 181)

Staiger's recognition of this intertextual frame reassures her that 'I am smart enough to see this', being 'complicit with Hooper in … a tendentious joke, rather than [being] the "average" viewer of the movie' (2000: 185). Her response fits perfectly with Kawin's argument that cult films such as *The Texas Chainsaw Massacre* allow fans to find 'in them … recognitions … of themselves; such films, they gratefully thought, knew they were there. Even as they selected each work as one of special value, they felt selected by it' (1991: 21; see also Mendik and Harper, 2000: 240, 249). The modality of *The Texas Chainsaw Massacre* is one where intertextual subcultural capital – cinephile knowledge about genre precedents – is coded into its inter-textuality (Hills, 2005a). Staiger's reading thus causes her to view the film as somewhat denaturalized, that is, its representations are not just realist, they are also meta-generic, being part of a 'smart' game in horror-genre reference-spotting. Again, the relationship of this cult text to questions of genre and cultural value forms part of its own self-reflexive construction.

Not properly fitting into the notion of cult film as 'insecure ' philosophizing occurring within popular 'genre' movies, but never-theless displaying denaturalized cinematic representations – usually through directors' or actors' incompetence – 'trash' movies can also be identified as a subset of cult film. Here, films such as *Plan 9 From Outer Space* (Edward D. Wood, Jr, US, 1959) are valorized – those whose shlock and exploitation identities place them at the furthest possible remove from secure conse-cration as 'film art'. Rather than insecurely incorporating discourses of cultural value into their textuality, this subcategory of cult film relies on a deliberate disjunction between their identities as 'trash' and audience discourses of cultural/aesthetic value (Sconce, 1995).

As a modality, cult film is significantly and self-reflexively imbricated with issues of cultural value. To view 'cult' status only as a strategy of 'anti-mainstream' cultural distinction which is audience-led, as do some post-structuralist writers drawing on Bourdieu (1984), downplays the extent to which many cult films invoke cross-generic 'textual strategies' aimed at displaying generic, cin-ematic and discursive sophistication within the terrain of popular film genre. Cult film implies, in part, an art of popular film genre (see Collins, 1989; 2002). And though the 'trash' subset of cult films may certainly be re-positioned as anti-mainstream and 'cult' through the mode of reception and audience activity, this properly remains an empirical matter rather than an *a priori* judgement on the processes underpinning all 'cult' films.

Addressing 'cult' as a modality means recognizing that there is a range of textual

attributes that can be meaningfully connected with audience and producer discourses of 'cult'. Arguments in Film Studies which oppose the notion of cult-as-genre on the basis that cult is a discourse fail to consider how cult can operate, as a category, both below and above the level of genre:

(a) as a 'privatised' genre used by audiences and thus open to industry validation or co-option, and
(b) as a modality which can intersect with and qualify genre conventions, as is the case with 'cult horror' or 'cult science-fiction'.

Apparently resting somewhere between genre-as-contract and genre-as-discourse, and thus dialectically mediating the two approaches, 'cult' status calls for a careful examination of both textual structures and audience agencies. Whereas structuralist notions of genre underplayed audience activity, post-structuralist approaches have downplayed textual and institutional structures working in relation to genre or associated concepts ('private' film categories/modalities). For instance, Tico Romao argues that Altman's *Film/Genre* (1999) 'can be seen to under-theorize structural conditions and overstate the determinative force of the film audience on the direction of genre production' (2003: 40). Romao pursues a relatively unusual theoretical approach to film genre – one indebted to sociological 'structuration theory' – and in the next section I want to apply this to cult film and fandom, given that previous scholarship has called into doubt whether text-based structures or audience agency are the 'proper' source of cult movie status.

CULT FILM AND FANDOM: A STRUCTURATION THEORY OF GENRE

Recent overviews of genre theory, such as John Frow's (2006) and Barry Langford's have stressed 'the realisation that genre, and genres, are inherently processual' (Langford,

2005: 278). As such, a branch of sociological theory called 'structuration', developed by Anthony Giddens (1984), is probably best suited to deal with this, as it aims to 'transcend the division between "structure and ... agency" [by analyzing] structural properties of social systems ... as "both medium and outcome of the practices they recursively organise"' (Giddens, quoted in Moores, 2005: 9; see also Tudor, 1999).

Romao (2003) has used a version of structuration theory – the work of Margaret Archer (1996) – in an attempt to link film genre theory to film history. The separation of 'theoretical' and 'historical' genres has been a recurrent difficulty in Film Studies (Todorov, 1975: 13–14; 1990), with scholars tending to focus either on historical and institutional processes of genre-formation (for instance, Tudor's cultural history of the horror movie [1989]), or on the theoretical definition and philosophical refinement of genre categories (for example, Noël Carroll's *The Philosophy of Horror* from 1990). Work on 'theoretical' genre – a critic's argument for the essential attributes of, say, the horror film – has therefore been accused of ahistoricism, whilst work on the cultural history of specific genres has tended to be more sociological in tone, focusing on the historicization of genre categories.

However, structuration theory represents one way of synthesizing genre 'theory' with genre 'history', since it inevitably deals with social and cultural structures as these emerge out of agents' activities, and then work to reframe later, recursive instances of agency. The system of film genre can be thought of as 'both medium and outcome' of practices of genrification. That is, interpretations and ascriptions of genre are carried out through the medium of 'genre discourse', forming a range of outcomes which can include 'genre contracts' holding, for a time, between film producers and audiences. These outcomes become the medium – the structure – that frames subsequent genre discourses, and hence can also be modified, disrupted, or amended by these.

Such an approach is actually consistent with Neale's structuralist conception of genre (1980), despite the fact that he overemphasizes genre-as-contract, and with Altman's post-structuralist concept of genre (1999), even though he arguably stresses audience discourses at the expense of industry practices of genre. Structuration theory introduces a new 'chicken and egg' dilemma into the study of film genre, since it suggests that genre categories can always be producer-(re)defined and audience-(re)defined, with neither necessarily taking priority over a text's generic identity. In fact, Romao's use of structuration theory problematically collapses this duality of (genre) structure into a more conventional, one-way causality:

> While it is beyond doubt that critics and genre fans are involved in the production and dissemination of generic concepts along with Hollywood marketing, it is more questionable to place this generation of ideas in the same theoretical camp as genre production, a process that is historically prior to such critical categorization. (2003: 40)

Romao exchanges structuration theory's emphasis on the dialectical duality of genre – that it is both constructed by the film industry and by film audiences – for an 'industry-first' approach which assumes, in advance of analysis, that film production and marketing take institutional, causal precedence over the interpretations of genre fans. These audience activities are represented as 'conditioned by' industry-defined film genres (2003: 41).

The adequate following of the precepts of structuration theory should rule out this sort of assumption. At some moments in film history, a specific genre identity may be more significantly producer-led than audience-led, whereas at other moments a genre category may be significantly audience-defined (film noir, for example). It is only when a genre category has been put forward by either producers or audiences that each cultural group – not to mention cultural intermediaries such as film journalists and publicists – can then symbolically modify, reject, or re-categorize films by appropriating this new genre discourse. In short, structuration theory requires that film genres are thought about not just historically and processually, but also in terms of recurrent producer-text-audience interactions:

> We can begin to build a more satisfying macro-account of a genre's history from the bottom up, by collecting micro-instances of generic discourses in historically-specific moments ... This bottom-up approach reflects how genres actually form and change over time – out of the specific cultural practices of industries and audiences. (Mittell, 2004: 14)

As Mittell argues, this type of genre scholarship may involve decentring 'the text as the primary site of genre', but it does not wholly write out the text in favour of audience-based discourses: '[M]edia texts function as important locales of generic discourses and must be examined on a par with other sites, such as audience and industrial practices' (2004: 14). Again, this involves drawing on elements of both structuralist and post-structuralist concepts of genre, where it is either 'in' the text or the audience. Structuration theory suggests that genre is 'in' both text and audience, though not necessarily in the same manner.

Arguments that view cult status purely as a matter of audience response (even Frow falls prey to this [2006: 140]) fail to consider the duality of cult: that is, 'cult' status can arise both through audiences' discourses and through production or textual strategies. Cult can, at certain moments in its discursive history, operate precisely like a generic contract, whilst at other moments it can singularly fail to unite producers and audiences, either because it is a textual strategy which audiences refute, or because it is a type of reading 'imposed' on a text by audiences. 'Cult' can move in and out of the cultural efficacy of genre-as-contract, sometimes operating above the level of genre (as a modality inflecting other genres, such as 'cult horror'), and sometimes remaining below it in relatively 'private' audience discourses. What requires study in each empirical instance is the extent to which any 'cult' film is actually designated a cult, by whom, and with what further cultural repercussions or appropriations. For, of course, it is these 'micro-instances' which generate the possibility of any 'macro' cultural history of cult film.

Indeed, a number of scholars have produced versions of this history, among them Jancovich (2002), Jeffrey Sconce (1995) and Greg Taylor (1999). Each has argued that the identity and identification of 'cult' movies emerges through a series of interactions between film audiences and the film industry. Sconce argues that the rise of what he terms 'paracinema' – effectively, 'trash' cinema in its many guises – has been accompanied by 'caustic rhetoric [which] suggests a pitched battle between a guerrilla band of cult film viewers and an elite cadre of would-be cinematic tastemakers' (1995: 372).

Jancovich takes issue with this depiction of a struggle over taste and aesthetics, arguing that the historical mainstreaming and emergence of 'cult' film as a category from the 1960s onward depended on 'a species of bourgeois aesthetics' being imported into cult viewers' appreciations of specific films (2002: 311). What Jancovich and Sconce both capture is the fact that cult and trash designations initially arose as a result of audience-based discourses and strategies of filmic valorization. Cult film was therefore, from its very inception as a category, concerned with the revaluation of popular genre film, and with the ascription of 'art' status to titles not directly marketed as 'film art', or greatly distant from this cultural identity in the case of 'trash' cult film. Jancovich notes that a key moment in the emergence of cult film criticism, and thus audience and filmmakers' use of this discourse, was Andrew Sarris' campaign to promote auteurism within the appreciation of American cinema – Sarris' 1970 collected volume of film criticism was entitled *Confessions of a Cultist* (Jancovich, 2002: 308–9).

In his book-length study of cultism's historical emergence, *Artists in the Audience* (1999), Taylor takes a further look at the role of US cult film criticism such as Manny Farber's writing in the 1940s and 1950s, and Sarris' work in the 1960s and 1970s. As Taylor puts it:

> Farber's taste was ... doubly oppositional. In displaying his affection for popular movies, he openly defied conventional highbrow taste. But in

attacking those films which Hollywood marketed as art, he was equally resisting middlebrow taste and asserting his own privileged authority over Hollywood's popular aesthetics. (1999: 37)

Taylor argues that Farber's cult criticism was relatively marginal, whereas Sarris'

rival film cultism was nothing if not easier to emulate … because at root it was merely a polemical assertion that at least the personalities of the most interesting movie directors managed to shine through their humdrum, generic material. (1999: 85, 87)

Sarris popularized 'auteur theory' in the US, but again, he did this in such a way as to suggest that film art could and should be discovered within the terrain of popular or 'generic' film, rather than within highbrow 'art film' or middlebrow film masquerading (or being marketed) as art. In a sense, then, Sarris worked to continue and develop the basic type of vanguardist film cultism pioneered by Farber, despite their doctrinal differences (for a discussion of Sarris and Farber's writings, see Taylor, 1999). As Jancovich has pointed out, 'like … cult movie fans after him, Sarris overtly used the apparently "low brow" rather than the "high brow" to beat the "middle brow"' (2002: 316).

Whether cultism shares or opposes bourgeois aesthetics is thus, in a sense, a moot point. Regardless of such debate, what it initially achieved, as a critic-led and audience-based discourse in the 1960s and 1970s, was to assail 'normative taste distinctions by refusing suitable taste objects, instead seeking out inappropriate objects from a lower taste culture, or from the lower recesses of one's own taste culture' (Taylor, 1999: 32). Thus, cult films emerging in this era frequently tended to be those screened as 'midnight movies' at US repertory cinemas (Jancovich, 2002: 317; Pribram, 2002: 21). However, this articulation of specific audiences and exhibition practices led to a problematic and unsustainable 'tendency to treat as … synonymous the post-1960s cult movie … and the midnight movie' (Waller, 1991: 167; see also Hoberman and Rosenbaum, 1991).

Without calling for an absolutely 'completist' account of cult status, it has to be noted that what can and has been counted as 'cult' film has far exceeded the phenomena of midnight movies such as *Rocky Horror* or the sing-along version of *The Sound of Music* (Robert Wise, US, 1965). This has been the case regardless of the privileged place that the midnight movie has held in the history of cult films, being a highly 'visible phenomenon' calling for scholarly explanation (Staiger, 2005: 125).

Although cultural histories of the cult movie demonstrate (*contra* Romao, 2003) that 'cult' emerged on the audience side, we still need to be very wary of moving from this historical fact to an *a priori* audience-based definition of 'cult', as many scholars seem wont to. Any such movement ignores and falsifies the historical development of cult: its commercial co-option as a category and discourse by filmmakers and publicists, as well as its wider circulation as a discourse in scholarly and journalistic work. What 'cult' demonstrates, rather well, is that a film category may emerge as an audience/critical discourse, but can then mutate into a form of generic contract, or a form of interpellative marketing, or a series of production/textual strategies. All of these historically-situated 'micro-instances' call for empirical study, rather than a blanket dismissal of cult's 'selling out' or its latter-day commercialized inauthenticity (Jancovich, 2002: 318; Sconce, 1995: 372–3). The shifting status of cult, as it has progressed from critical/audience discourse to textual or marketing strategy, also highlights the need for a structuration approach – that is, an awareness of the duality of genre structure, whereby a genre such as 'cult' can be simultaneously the 'medium' which filmmakers and marketers appropriate and deploy, as well as the 'outcome' of audience discourses (and vice versa).

I want to conclude by examining two further micro-instances of cult movie discourse. First, here is an anecdote recounted by British writer-director Philip Ridley. Ridley is discussing the premiere of his film,

The Reflecting Skin (UK/Canada, 1990), at the Cannes Film Festival:

> The frog explodes over Lindsay Duncan and – mass exodus. I attended that screening. I was so depressed ... But, you know, a strange thing happened: that night everyone was talking about it. The press gave it lead reviews next morning. All the subsequent shows sold out ... I talked to a French journalist ten minutes after that first screening. He said to me, 'Your film is already a cult'. And he was right. (1997: xx)

This poses an interesting question – is this use of 'cult' discourse audience-based, producer-based, or journalist-based? The French film critic is already responding to one specific audience reaction in one national, cultural context, but their use of 'cult' as a description is one which can then be circulated in publicity and other intertexts (for example, the published screenplay for the film). This deployment of cult discourse, and its endorsement by the film's writer-director, licenses its further circulation. Indeed, *Sight and Sound* also called *The Reflecting Skin* 'a cult classic' (Ridley, 1997: vi).

Cult status works, here, through self-reinforcing accretion and iteration: one journalist cites it, then perhaps the director self-interestedly adopts it as a label which might aid audience interpretation and understanding of his film, not to mention his later work (*The Passion of Darkly Noon* [Philip Ridley, UK/Germany/Belgium, 1995]). Finally, various other cultural sites and agencies iterate the ascription. Cult status, in other words, can be achieved over time, as various cultural agents – filmmakers, audiences and critics – assent to its supposedly 'accurate' use to describe a film. What is notable and unusual about *The Reflecting Skin* is that it allegedly took only ten minutes after its premiere for the film to 'already be a cult'! But even this rapid citation and circulation of cult status draws not only on the term's history, but also on judgements about the film's textual qualities. Its 'gratuitous' and excessive style and content mark it down as 'cult'; and again matters of taste and cultural value are linked into this: seemingly, the fact that certain audiences literally couldn't

stomach its opening also marks the film out as cult. *The Reflecting Skin* can be said to use the 'cult-as-modality' textual strategy referred to above, in that it provokes visceral disgust and/or a version of ontological shock. As a film, it self-reflexively seeks to offer a 'mythological' or culturally-valued reframing of generic tropes such as the vampire or the child-killer, displaying intertextual cultural capital in relation to its own uneasy identity as an 'arty' genre film, rather than an outright 'art house' title.

Another example that raises intriguing empirical questions over the emergence of 'cult' status is the more recent US film *Donnie Darko* (Richard Kelly, 2001). Freelance journalist Soren McCarthy includes it in his reference book *Cult Movies in Sixty Seconds*, suggesting that it 'seems to be a film constructed from a recipe of cult cinema elements ... Whether due to a fondness for its own cleverness ... the film is unbelievably self-referential' (2003: 48–9). And Sconce includes the film in his survey of 'smart' cinema, again suggesting that performed 'cleverness' is at the heart of *Donnie Darko*'s appeal: '[T]he suspense, such as there is, comes from seeing just how much shit any one character can endure and how clever the universe (or the filmmaker) can be in meting out its interconnected twists of fate' (2002: 364).

However, *Donnie Darko* goes beyond simply being a 'programmatic' cult which proclaims its own intertextual cultural capital through metaphysical and philosophizing elements such as 'a demonic rabbit ... [which] challenges Donnie with existential questions' (McCarthy, 2003: 49). For it also co-opts discourses of cult status back into its region 2 DVD extras, which include a UK documentary *They Made Me Do It Too – The Cult of Donnie Darko*. Here, cult audiences and academics such as Xavier Mendik, of Brunel University's Cult Film Archive, are portrayed as recognizing the 'artistic' and 'popular' merits of the film. This DVD extra literalizes the metaphorical mirroring which has been observed as occurring between smart, genre-literate cult filmmakers and cult audiences (Kawin, 1991; Staiger, 2000). This time, the cult audience are literally shown themselves – or at least, representatives of their tastes and practices – and hence are applauded for their own cleverness in perceiving *Donnie Darko*'s cinematic cleverness. Attempts at analyzing this cult discourse as either 'text' or 'audience'-based would, of course, fail to address the very fact that it appears as an audience-based category co-opted by the movie's publicists, being dialectically brought back into 'the text' in the guise of a DVD documentary. At the same time, the text of the film itself knowingly plays with discourses and histories of 'cult' as transgressive (it mocks religious and self-help discourses via a range of characters) and as seeking to confer value on genre films (it fuses horror and science-fictional elements with philosophy/metaphysics). Here, 'cult' operates as a modality which inflects the film's more conventionally generic elements, but it also seems to move closer to becoming an accepted genre contract between filmmaker and fans. Thus, multiple levels of filmmaker/publicist/journalist/audience cultification can be said to overlap and intersect around the filmic object of *Donnie Darko*.

CONCLUSION

Throughout this chapter, I have argued that structuralist and post-structuralist approaches to genre have, in their theoretical dogmas, failed to account for the complexities thrown up by questions of 'cult film' status. Structuralist views, dominant in the 1970s and early 1980s, viewed genre as a text-based contract between film producers and audiences, while later the post-structuralists reconstituted genre as an object of study by examining it as a matter of competing discourses performed by different 'user groups'. Relating these schools of film genre criticism to cult movies, I have suggested that although some scholars have pursued 'cult-as-genre' or 'cult-as-fan-discourse' arguments which draw on structuralist/post-structuralist paradigms, cult film has acted as an irritant and a provocation to such party-line thinking. In particular,

analysis of the historical emergence of cult film, and the way that the category has been adopted and applied by filmmakers, critics, and fans, have suggested the need for a structuration theory of genre – one which views this as an empirical, historicized question of recurring industry-audience interactions, rather than assuming in advance that genre is 'in' either the text or the audience.

Cult film, as I have argued, shows that film categories can emerge through audience/critical discourse before being co-opted by the film industry to act like a generic contract, ultimately becoming a matter of semiotic and discursive struggle between the entire range of agents involved in classifying and valuing contemporary cinema. No film is now 'cult' simply or singularly to one fan audience – instead, films are variously 'cultified' in coffee-table guides to cult film; in academic writings like this chapter, and talking-head DVD extras; in film reviews; in assorted marketing and promotion. It is hypothetically possible for a film to be labelled 'cult' in reviews and publicity, but for it not to have any identifiable fan audience. Audience-based theories would no doubt deem this an 'inauthentic' or PR cult, a failed bid for cult status. Viewed from a structuration theory point-of-view, the hypothesized title would still be a cult film, just one in which marketing discourses, deployed in relation to certain textual qualities and drawing on the history of the term 'cult', failed to be taken up by wider audiences. 'Cult' status is not just a nomination or label, however, but an empirical question. Shuttling between genre-as-contract and genre-as-discourse, it carries with it a multi-accentual history of struggles over taste and – most spectacularly and insistently – over the cultural value of popular genre cinema itself.

REFERENCES

Altman, Rick (1999) *Film/Genre*. London: BFI.
Archer, Margaret (1996) *Culture and Agency: The Place of Culture in Social Theory*. Rev. edn. Cambridge: Cambridge University Press.

Austin, Thomas (2002) *Hollywood, Hype and Audiences: Selling and Watching Popular Film in the 1990s.* Manchester: Manchester University Press.

Berry-Flint, Sarah (2004) 'Genre', in Toby Miller and Robert Stam (eds), *A Companion to Film Theory.* Oxford: Blackwell Publishing. pp. 25–44.

Bourdieu, Pierre (1984) *Distinction: A Social Critique of the Judgement of Taste.* London: Routledge.

Carroll, Noël (1990) *The Philosophy of Horror.* New York: Routledge.

Collins, Jim (1989) *Uncommon Cultures: Popular Culture and Post-modernism.* New York: Routledge.

Collins, Jim (2002) 'High-pop: An Introduction', in Jim Collins (ed.), *High-Pop.* London: Blackwell. pp. 1–31.

Corrigan, Timothy (1991) 'Film and the Culture of Cult', in J.P. Telotte (ed.), *The Cult Film Experience.* Austin: University of Texas Press. pp. 26–37.

Derrida, Jacques (1992) 'The Law of Genre', in *Acts of Literature.* New York: Routledge. pp. 221–52.

Eco, Umberto (1995) '*Casablanca*: Cult Movies and Intertextual Collage', in *Faith in Fakes.* London: Minerva. pp. 197–211.

Falzon, Christopher (2002) *Philosophy Goes to the Movies.* London: Routledge.

Frow, John (2006) *Genre.* Abingdon: Routledge.

Giddens, Anthony (1984) *The Constitution of Society: Outline of the Theory of Structuration.* Cambridge: Polity Press.

Gledhill, Christine (2000) 'Rethinking Genre', in Christine Gledhill and Linda Williams (eds), *Reinventing Film Studies.* London: Arnold. pp. 221–43.

Grant, Barry Keith (1991) 'Science Fiction Double Feature: Ideology in the Cult Film', in J.P. Telotte (ed.), *The Cult Film Experience.* Austin: University of Texas Press. pp. 122–37.

Grant, Barry Keith (2000) 'Second Thoughts on Double Features: Revisiting the Cult Film', in Xavier Mendik and Graeme Harper (eds), *Unruly Pleasures: The Cult Film and its Critics.* Guildford: FAB Press. pp. 13–27.

Gwenllian-Jones, Sara (2000) 'Starring Lucy Lawless?', *Continuum*, 14(1): 9–22.

Hills, Matt (2002) *Fan Cultures.* London: Routledge.

Hills, Matt (2003) '*Star Wars* in Fandom, Film Theory, and the Museum: The Cultural Status of the Cult Blockbuster', in Julian Stringer (ed.), *Movie Blockbusters.* London: Routledge. pp. 178–89.

Hills, Matt (2004) 'Defining cult TV: Texts, inter-texts and fan audiences', in Robert C. Allen and Annette Hill (eds), *The Television Studies Reader.* London: Routledge. pp. 509–23.

Hills, Matt (2005a) *The Pleasures of Horror.* London: Continuum.

Hills, Matt (2005b) 'Academic Textual Poachers: *Blade Runner* as Cult Canonical Movie', in Will Brooker (ed.), *The Blade Runner Experience: The Legacy of a Science Fiction Classic.* London: Wallflower Press. pp. 124–41.

Hoberman, J. and Rosenbaum, Jonathan (1991) *Midnight Movies.* New York: Da Capo Press.

Jancovich, Mark (2000) '"Real Shocker": authenticity, genre, and the struggle for distinction', *Continuum*, 14(1): 23–35.

Jancovich, Mark (2002) 'Cult Fictions: Cult Movies, Subcultural Capital and the Production of Cultural Distinctions', *Cultural Studies*, 16(2): 306–22.

Jancovich, Mark, Lazaro Reboll, Antonio, Stringer, Julian and Willis, Andy (2003) (eds) *Defining Cult Movies.* Manchester: Manchester University Press.

Jenkins, Henry (1992) *Textual Poachers: Television Fans and Participatory Culture.* New York: Routledge.

Jerslev, Anne (1992) 'Semiotics by instinct: "Cult film" as a signifying practice between audience and film', in Michael Skovmand and Kim Christian Schrøder (eds), *Media Cultures: Reappraising Transnational Media.* London: Routledge. pp. 181–98.

Johnson, Catherine (2005) *Telefantasy.* London: BFI.

Kawin, Bruce (1991) 'After Midnight', in J.P. Telotte (ed.), *The Cult Film Experience.* Austin: University of Texas Press. pp. 18–25.

Langford, Barry (2005) *Film Genre: Hollywood and Beyond.* Edinburgh: Edinburgh University Press.

Lavery, David (1991) 'Gnosticism and the cult film', in J.P. Telotte (ed.), *The Cult Film Experience.* Austin: University of Texas Press. pp. 187–99.

Le Guern, Philippe (2004) 'Toward a Constructivist Approach to Media Cults', in Sara Gwenllian-Jones and Roberta E. Pearson (eds), *Cult Television.* Minneapolis: University of Minnesota Press. pp. 3–25.

Litch, Mary M. (2002) *Philosophy Through Film.* New York: Routledge.

McCarthy, Soren (2003) *Cult Movies in Sixty Seconds.* London: Fusion Press.

Mendik, Xavier and Harper, Graeme (2000) 'The Chaotic Text and the Sadean Audience', in Xavier Mendik and Graeme Harper (eds), *Unruly Pleasures: The Cult Film and its Critics.* Guildford: FAB Press. pp. 235–249.

Mittell, Jason (2004) *Genre and Television: From Cop Shows to Cartoons in American Culture.* New York: Routledge.

Moores, Shaun (2005) *Media/Theory: Thinking about Media and Communications.* Abingdon: Routledge.

Mulhall, Stephen (2002) *On Film.* London: Routledge.

Neale, Stephen (1980) *Genre.* London: BFI Publishing.

Neale, Steve (2000) *Genre and Hollywood.* London: Routledge.

Pribram, E. Deidre (2002) *Cinema and Culture: Independent Film in the United States, 1980–2001.* New York: Peter Lang Publishing.

Ridley, Philip (1997) *The American Dreams: The Reflecting Skin and The Passion of Darkly Noon – Two Screenplays.* London: Methuen.

Romao, Tico (2003) 'Engines of Transformation: An Analytical History of the 1970s Car Chase Cycle', *New Review of Film and Television Studies*, 1(1): 31–54.

Sarris, Andrew (1970) *Confessions of a Cultist: On the Cinema, 1955–1969.* New York: Simon & Schuster.

Sconce, Jeffrey (1995) 'Trashing the Academy: taste, excess and an emerging politics of cinematic style', *Screen*, 36(4): 371–93.

Sconce, Jeffrey (2002) 'Irony, nihilism and the new American "smart" film', *Screen*, 43(4): 349–69.

Staiger, Janet (2000) *Perverse Spectators: The Practices of Film Reception.* New York: New York University Press.

Staiger, Janet (2005) *Media Reception Studies.* New York: New York University Press.

Studlar, Gaylyn (1991) 'Midnight S/Excess', in J.P. Telotte (ed.), *The Cult Film Experience.* Austin: University of Texas Press. pp. 138–55.

Taylor, Greg (1999) *Artists in the Audience: Cults, Camp and American Film Criticism.* Princeton, NJ: Princeton University Press.

Telotte, J.P. (1991) 'Beyond All Reason: The Nature of the Cult', in J.P. Telotte (ed.), *The Cult Film Experience.* Austin: University of Texas Press. pp. 5–17.

Todorov, Tzvetan (1975) *The Fantastic.* New York: Cornell University Press.

Todorov, Tzvetan (1990) *Genres in Discourse.* Cambridge: Cambridge University Press.

Tudor, Andrew (1976) 'Genre and Critical Methodology', in Bill Nichols (ed.), *Movies and Methods*, Vol.1. Berkeley: University of California Press. pp. 118–26.

Tudor, Andrew (1989) *Monsters and Mad Scientists: A Cultural History of the Horror Movie.* Oxford: Blackwells.

Tudor, Andrew (1999) *Decoding Culture.* London: Sage.

Waller, Gregory A. (1991) 'Midnight Movies 1980–1985: A Market Study', in J.P. Telotte (ed.), *The Cult Film Experience.* Austin: University of Texas Press. pp. 167–86.

29

Film Audiences

Jostein Gripsrud and Erlend Lavik

When the centenary of cinema was celebrated in 1995, 'cinema' was defined as the screening of moving images for a paying audience. The presence of an audience, in other words, is an essential part of the very definition of the medium. There are very different kinds of film scholarship concerned with film audiences or relations between film and its audiences. In quantitative terms, scholarly research and writing about film audiences or some dimension of film-audience relations clearly outnumber (and outweigh!) publications about other aspects of the film medium, such as film production or the aesthetics of film.

Film's early status as a paradigmatic mass medium is a major part of the explanation for this. Its colossal popularity with working-class people, women and children gave various 'responsible' people reasons to worry about the impact of the movies on the minds and behaviours of these social categories. Given the intense and pleasurable experiences that people seemed to get from the cinema, it appeared obvious that the influence on people's minds would also be intense. Modern, social-scientific mass communication research was to a considerable

extent developed in response to such fears through projects launched to document and substantiate them (though not necessarily delivering the expected results).

But film's enormous potential for influencing the masses was also central to seminal contributions to theories of film as a textual form. The leader of the Bolshevik Revolution in Russia, V.I. Lenin, proclaimed that film was the most important of all the arts, since it was the most efficient medium for propaganda, and Soviet film theory (Sergei Eisenstein, in particular) was very much about how to move the mass audience of film to perceive the world in certain ways – and act accordingly. The basis for a long tradition in film theory is precisely a Marxist conception of film as a medium for changing people's way of thinking in 'progressive' directions, or, on the contrary, for the reproduction and dissemination of ideology in the sense of 'false consciousness'. The abstract semiotic and psychoanalytic '*Screen* theory' of the 1970s represented a particular development of this tradition.

A more recent, quite heterogeneous body of work favours a more pragmatic theory of meaning, according to which determinate meaning is not inherent in the filmic signs or texts themselves, but is constructed by spectators in accordance with certain context-dependent conventions. This position can take a variety of forms, drawing on diverse theoretical traditions such as hermeneutics, phenomenology, the semiotic theory of C.S. Peirce or eclectic formations such as British cultural studies. Cognitivist approaches, focusing on the 'processing' of film in the human brain, have also gained prominence.

All of the above approaches to film audiences, and actual encounters between audiences and films, share the idea that it is through the existence of an audience that film acquires social and cultural importance. The production of a film provides the raw material which regulates the potential range of experiences and meanings to be associated with it, but it is through audiences that film becomes an 'input' to larger socio-cultural processes.

The following overview will concentrate on the tradition of research on actual film audiences as it has developed in response to the history of the medium. (For reasons of space, we have excluded the otherwise very interesting forms of audience studies conducted by or for the film industry. A good overview is provided by Bruce A. Austin [1989].) This emphasis is chosen partly because other entries in the present volume will cover the other, text-centred approaches, and partly because there has been a revived interest in empirical audience research since the early 1980s, not least in studies of film history. Much of the prehistory of such work is little known, however. There is a kind of amnesia operating in competitive academic communities that is akin to the market-driven shifts of fashion in other areas. Although knowledge is not built in a steady, cumulative fashion, this does not mean that we need to reinvent the wheel every ten years. Moreover, empirical audience research has often been regarded as an antagonist by scholars in text-oriented Film Studies – and vice versa. This is due to fundamental epistemological differences, but it also has more dubious

institutional reasons. Creative scholarship can only benefit from a broad knowledge of different traditions.

THE MOVIES AS A SOCIAL PROBLEM: THE FIRST AUDIENCE STUDIES IN CONTEXT

The first public complaints over the moral standards of films could already be heard in the 1890s both in the US (Jowett, 1976: 109) and the UK (Kuhn, 1988: 15), but there was no real force in public reactions against the medium until after 1905. It seems reasonable to assume that it was the explosive international growth in the number of more or less permanent movie theatres from about 1905 that really brought the cinema to the attention of public authorities and the social groups that actively participated in public debates. Importantly, the repertoire being offered in cinemas was also beginning to change at about the same time, with fiction formats becoming increasingly prominent, including formats drawn from other media of popular culture – including anarchic farces, crime stories and melodramatic love stories.

The introduction of censorship is an indication of how seriously the 'dangers' of the movies were perceived, and it was introduced in a number of different forms in most Western countries in the course of just six to seven years around 1910. All such measures were preceded by public debates which to a greater or lesser extent also involved forms of research on movie theatres and movie audiences. The first film audience research was, in other words, motivated by anxieties over the social consequences of the medium's immense popularity, especially with children and adolescents. As early as 1910, numerous attempts were made in many countries to estimate audience numbers and social patterns of attendance in methodologically crude surveys often conducted by teachers' associations, school authorities, social workers and the like (see Jowett, 1976: 45–6). Such efforts would also be combined with attempts to verify the intuitive feelings of educators, religious leaders and many social reformers that movies were for the most part detrimental to the psychological, moral and even physical health of those who regularly went to see them.

The themes and results of these early studies were to be repeated again and again in later and methodologically more sophisticated studies. A research tradition was formed in which the medium of film was (is) conceived primarily as a social problem. It was seen as an isolated, primary cause of a number of negative effects. This cause-effect or, rather, stimulus-response conception of the relations between movies and audiences was drawn from mechanistic and biologistic psychological theories in vogue in the early decades of the twentieth century. Seeing the movies as a social problem was also related to widespread theories of the mass as a characteristic social form in modern societies. Individuals who had moved to rapidly growing cities had been cut off from their traditional bonds, norms and authorities, and were now considered a basically unreliable and easily persuaded mass that was capable of all kinds of horrible things. As the first theorist of the mass, Gustave LeBon, put it in 1895: 'Crowds are everywhere distinguished by feminine characteristics', as they tended to move very easily into emotional extremes (quoted in Huyssen, 1986: 196). Thus one might well suspect that the cinema was conceived as a social problem, not least because central parts of its 'audiences' were experienced as a problem for teachers and other authorities. That the problem was in part conceived as 'feminine' is highly significant: the threat of the movies was not least about a loss of control and a tendency toward self-indulgence and weakness.

The cinema became a highly visible sign of social and cultural change that worried elites and thus played the role, that rational argument could do little to change, of a much-needed scapegoat. In 1917, the British National Council of Public Morals undertook an 'independent enquiry into the physical, social, moral and educational influence of the cinema, with special reference to young people' (quoted in Richards, 1984: 70). A 400-page report based on numerous sources of information was published in which the general conclusion was, on the one hand, that 'no social problem of the day demands more earnest attention', and that the cinema had 'potentialities for evil' which were 'manifold', while on the other, it could also become 'a powerful influence for good'. And on the question of links between movies and juvenile crime, the Commission of Enquiry concluded that 'while a connection between the cinema and crime has to a limited extent in special cases been shown,… it certainly has not been proved that the increase in juvenile crime generally has been consequent on the cinema, or has been independent of other factors more conducive to wrongdoing' (quoted in Richards, 1984: 71). Still, the issue was not settled, and the same anxieties motivated new enquiries well into the 1930s.

THE MOVIES AS SOCIAL FORCE: THE PAYNE FUND STUDIES

By the 1920s, the cinema was well established as the major form of entertainment for most of the population in all Western countries. An 'art' cinema was developed in Germany and France, and an increasing degree of respectability could also be seen to develop in many countries from the emergence of film criticism in major newspapers and magazines. In the US as much as anywhere, however, it seems that the earlier moral panic over the influence of the movies was still very much alive. Unlike many other countries, the US had not established forms of public censorship which could calm the nerves of those most worried. As the prohibition of alcohol from 1920 to 1933 shows, the so-called 'Roaring 20s' were in fact a period where puritan morality was particularly strong. Such social anxieties can perhaps be seen as a reaction to a number of social and cultural changes challenging traditional values: women's entry into the labour force, new relations between the sexes and the emergence and spread of consumerism (spending rather than saving), to name but a few.

In this situation, the movies were still very much suspected of being a primary source of inspiration for delinquency and general moral decay. This remained a strongly embedded idea even though a 1925 study of 4,000 'juvenile delinquency' cases showed that only one per cent of them could in any way be tied to the influence of movies.[1] Alice Miller Mitchell, who in 1929 published the first major scholarly survey entirely devoted to children and the movies, concluded that even if 'the delinquent does have a wider cinema experience than do the other children studied', the survey did not provide any conclusive evidence for a causal link between movies and delinquency (quoted in Jowett, 1976: 219). But such sensible reasoning was unable to deter activists, who perceived the movie repertoire as largely offensive and threatening.

The most comprehensive and probably also the most influential of all empirical research projects on film audiences – the so-called Payne Fund Studies – was organized in 1928 by the Reverend William H. Short, who was the executive director of the Motion Picture Research Council. A group of psychologists, sociologists and educators from a number of institutions, directed by Dr W.W. Charters from the Bureau of Educational Research, Ohio State University, started to work as soon as a grant of $200,000 was secured from the philanthropic foundation, The Payne Fund. Investigations took place between 1929 and 1932, and the results were published in at least 12 volumes – eight books in 1933, three in 1935 and one in 1937. In addition, a journalist by the name of Henry James Forman wrote a popularized summary of the studies, *Our Movie Made Children* (1933). This book focused exclusively on results which seemed to support the view that movies had detrimental effects, and it became very influential in the public debate which preceded the much stricter enforcement of Hollywood's Production Code from the summer of 1934 on. The actual studies themselves also had an undertone of anxiety or concern, but they were far more nuanced than Forman's outright attack on the movie industry.

The Payne Fund Studies employed all the research methods then available to 'scientific' studies of sociological and psychological phenomena, and further developed some of them. Methods included quantitative 'content analyses', large-scale surveys, laboratory experiments, participant observation and the collection of written 'movie autobiographies' from large numbers of people. The studies can be grouped in two categories. The first consists of studies which tried to determine the size and composition of movie audiences, and to assess the 'contents' of films. The second category of studies was an attempt to assess various 'effects' of viewing.

A series of studies by Ruth C. Peterson and L.I. Thurstone (1933) also attempted to assess various effects of viewing. They were interested in whether films influenced the general attitudes of children toward ethnic or racial groups and certain important social issues such as crime, the punishment of criminals, war, capital punishment and prohibition. The results were very clear: even the viewing of a single film seemed to have considerable influence on children's attitudes, and the cumulative effect of several films with a similar view of groups or issues were even more striking (Lowery and DeFleur, 1995). There are, of course, a number of severe theoretical and methodological problems with these studies, even if they were sophisticated for their time. The term 'attitude' is itself problematic and the methods for 'measuring' the phenomenon are debatable (no control groups as such were used). Still, the evidence presented could well be seen as quite convincing, particularly since the children had little or no experience with, or insight into, the respective areas under investigation. Very few, if any, of these small-town kids had ever, for example, known African-American or Chinese people; in fact, they had hardly encountered any. Films portraying these groups positively or negatively could be all the more influential. It is similarly unlikely that they had given much thought to the issues of war or the treatment of criminals. What was demonstrated, then, was the impact of films in a situation where other sources of information were more or less lacking, and opinions and attitudes therefore were relatively easy to influence.

Perhaps the most interesting of the Payne Fund Studies was, however, methodologically very different. Herbert Blumer collected 'motion-picture autobiographies' from over 1,100 university and college students, 583 high-school students, 67 office workers, and 58 factory workers who were instructed to 'write in as natural and truthful manner as possible accounts of their experiences with "movies" as far as they could recall them' (1933: 4). In addition, about 150 students and schoolchildren were interviewed, and accounts of conversations ('taken nearly as verbatim as possible' [Blumer, 1933: 11]) between students at different levels were collected. Finally, questionnaires were distributed to 1,200 children in the fifth and sixth grades of 12 public schools in different areas of Chicago, and the behaviour of children at neighbourhood movie theatres and in play after these visits was observed. The extraordinarily voluminous material gathered by these methods was not primarily intended for sophisticated statistical treatment. The point was rather to explore the ways in which cinema audiences themselves thought and felt about their movie-going, the films they saw and how they were influenced by them. The published report, *Movies and Conduct* (Blumer, 1933), is full of vivid descriptions of movie experiences and of how young people picked up tips on anything from play, kissing, fashion and table manners to attitudes and daydreams. The following is a random example from a female high-school student's contribution:

> I have imagined playing with a movie hero many times, though; that is while I'm watching the picture. I forget about it when I'm outside the theatre. Buddy Rogers and Rudy Valentino have kissed me oodles of times, but they don't know it. God bless 'em! – Yes, love scenes have thrilled me and made me more receptive to love. I was going with a fellow whom I liked as a playmate, so to speak; he was a little younger than me and he liked me a great deal. We went to the movie – Billie Dove in it. Oh, I can't recall the name but Antonio Moreno was the lead, and there were some lovely scenes which just got me all hot 'n' bothered. After the movie we went for a ride 'n' parked along the lake; it was a gorgeous night. Well, I just melted (as it were) in his arms, making him believe I loved him, which I didn't. I sort of came to, but I promised to go steady with him. I went with him 'til I couldn't bear the sight of him… I've wished many times that we'd never seen the movie. (1933: 223)

Blumer's conclusions were relatively careful. But the material had convinced him that 'the forte of motion pictures is in their emotional effect', 'their appeal and their success reside ultimately in the emotional agitation which they induce' (1933: 223). A successful production was one which managed to draw 'the observer' into the drama so that 'he loses himself', and in such a condition 'the observer becomes malleable to the touch of what is shown' and 'develops a readiness to certain forms of action which are foreign in some degree to his ordinary conduct' (1933: 198). Blumer also argued that the movies were so emotionally demanding that the audience could be left 'emotionally exhausted' and, instead of ordinary emotional responses, they would experience an emotional and moral confusion:

> In so far as one may seek to cover in a single proposition the more abiding effect of motion pictures upon the minds of movie-goers, it would be, in the judgement of the writer, in terms of a medley of vague and variable impressions – a disconnected assemblage of ideas, feelings, vagaries, and impulses. (1933: 199)

Blumer finally concluded that films could confuse people morally in various ways, for instance by presenting immoral behaviour as attractive, even if the film's overt moral 'message' was impeccable. In a methodologically similar study of inmates, ex-convicts and young people in various reform schools, he pointed to the obvious importance of social background both in the choice of films and in reactions to them. But he remained convinced that movies could 'lead… to misconduct', and so they raised the issue of 'social control' (Blumer and Hauser, 1933: 202).

The 'Chicago School' sociologist Blumer was thus no simplistic 'hypodermic needle' theorist, even though there are clearly traces of the stimulus-response model in his conclusion that movies had a powerful influence on young people's lives. His observations of strong emotional experiences, and identification as 'losing oneself', have links to both previous and later scholarship on film (and television). The first significant contribution to a theory of film as a specific aesthetic form, Hugo Münsterberg's *The Photoplay: A Psychological Study* (1916) has been called 'the first systematic attempt to theorize spectatorship' (Hansen, 1983: 153, n.14). Münsterberg's book provided some theoretical basis for ideas of film as a 'strong' medium, which could be used both for better and for worse. Films could be an 'incomparable power for remoulding and upbuilding the national soul' and even if '[t]he possibilities of psychical infection cannot be overlooked…no psychologist can determine exactly how much the general spirit of righteous honesty, of sexual cleanliness, may be weakened by the unbridled influence of plays which lower moral standards' (Münsterberg, quoted in May, 1980: 42). With somewhat different and more impressive theoretical underpinnings, the whole theorization of 'the spectator' in psychoanalytic Film Studies from Christian Metz on is also centred on the persuasive ideological functions of 'identification'. Blumer may well have been more alert to the importance of contextual factors in determining the 'effects' of cinema than some of the work in the *Screen* tradition appeared to be.

However socially aware some of them may have been, none of the Payne Fund Studies shows much sensitivity to film as a form of art. They chop up filmic texts into so many 'themes' and 'content elements', with a total lack of respect for a film's integrity or the interrelationships between a variety of aesthetic techniques and potential meanings. This provoked the neo-Aristotelian philosopher Mortimer Adler to formulate a fundamental critique of this whole approach; in his book *Art and Prudence* (1937), subsequently popularized in Raymond Moley's *Are We Movie Made?* (1938), he proposed an alternative model of

what he considered an art form to be. Despite their aesthetic shortcomings, however, at least some of the Payne Fund Studies were more nuanced and more theoretically reflexive than much post-war research. The sociologist Paul G. Cressey summarized the insights gained in the course of the project as follows:

> 'Going to the movies' is a unified experience involving always a specific film, a specific personality, a specific social situation and a specific time and mood; therefore, any program of research which does not recognize all essential phases of the motion picture experience can offer little more than conjecture as to the cinema's net 'effect' in actual settings and communities. (1938: 518)

It is worth reflecting on where such insights went in the following decades. Research along similarly intelligent lines had in fact been done almost 25 years earlier in Germany. But for a number of imaginable reasons, it remained unknown to Anglo-Americans until Miriam Hansen referred to it in a 1983 article in English.

THE CINEMA AS CULTURAL RESOURCE: EMILIE ALTENLOH

The German sociologist Emilie Altenloh's short doctoral dissertation, *Zur Soziologie des Kino* (1914), which she wrote at the age of 26, is in fact one of the most interesting contributions to empirical audience studies (see Petro, 1989). This is particularly so because of her general approach. Altenloh's dissertation is marked not only by a holistic sociological understanding of the cinema and its audiences, but also by an historical perspective. Almost half of its 102 pages are devoted to film production, including the product itself, distribution and the legal framework. The second half is about the audience, and their cinema attendance is understood both in relation to their other cultural preferences (theatre and music, for example) and in relation to their gender, class, professions and political interests. An historical perspective runs through the whole text: both social developments (industrialization/modernization) and the changes in the domain of popular culture are brought into her interpretive and explanatory reasoning. What also makes it strikingly different from, say, the Payne Fund Studies, is that worries over 'harmful effects' are hardly expressed at all. While the author explicitly distinguishes between 'primitive' movies and tastes (the genre preferences of many young male workers were expressed in answers that 'smell of blood and dead bodies' [Altenloh, 1914: 66]), the tone is generally sympathetic, rather than moralizing.

Altenloh's primary material for the audience study was movie-theatre statistics and 2,400 simple questionnaires which had been distributed through professional organizations, trade unions and schools of various kinds in the city of Mannheim and in parts of Heidelberg. The study provides quite a detailed picture not only of the social composition of audiences, but also of the differences between its various component parts in terms of genre preferences and the overall context of their cinema attendance, including their relations to other cultural forms and media. The survey demonstrated, for instance, that male audiences varied quite a lot in their generic preferences and general attitudes to the cinema, in ways clearly related to which social groups they belonged to, while female movie-goers seemed to be more homogenous in their tastes for music, melodrama and particular kinds of documentary material (such as waterfalls, waves, ice-floes). What was striking in all the questionnaires, however, was how difficult people found it to articulate why they were so drawn to the movie experience. Although the reasons were as many and various as there were individuals in the audience, they all shared the desire for something their everyday lives did not provide. Altenloh thought that 'the cinema succeeds in addressing just enough of those individuals' needs to provide a substitute for what could really be 'better', thus assuming a powerful reality in relation to which all questions as to whether the cinema

is good or evil or has any right to exist appear useless' (Hansen, 1983: 179).

Altenloh's study suggested that the cinema functioned as a social space for experiences and forms of communication that were largely excluded from other public arenas – not least because many in the audience were in practice excluded from these other arenas. It was to a degree a public sphere for the unspeakable, where those otherwise spoken *for*, without a voice of their own, felt at least spoken *to*. And whatever else one could say about her questionnaire methodology it did, in fact, even if within strict limitations, allow cinema's core audiences to speak for themselves through a sympathetic interpreter.

BRITISH OBSERVATIONS – AND TWO BLANK DECADES

In Britain, the early 1930s brought a series of local enquiries into the 'effects' of cinema, particularly on children and youth. Although most of them sought to find justification for the hostility to the movies which motivated their efforts, they were hardly in compliance with scholarly standards of research and argumentation. While reports like these played an important role in public debates, the more interesting work on cinema audiences was of a different nature. The statistician Simon Rowson conducted the first systematic survey of cinema attendance in 1934, and the impresario Sidney Bernstein organized questionnaire surveys of audiences at the Granada chain of cinemas in 1931, 1934 and 1937. But the most fascinating of British studies of film audiences in the 1930s and 1940s were of the kind now referred to as 'ethnographic', that is, study mainly based in forms of participant observation.

Sociological studies such as E.W. Bakke's *The Unemployed Man* (1933) and H. Llewellyn Smith's *The New Survey of London Life and Labour* (1935) included observations of the role of the cinema in the everyday lives of ordinary people in particular social milieus, as did a number of other books and articles written by scholarly and other kinds of authors (Richards, 1984: Ch. 1). The interest in an 'anthropological study of our own civilization' also lay behind the establishment of Mass-Observation in 1937. This was quite a unique organization devoted to the gathering of knowledge by the unpaid, volunteer observational work of ordinary (if, predominantly, middle-class) people about everyday life in British society. Mass-Observation actually had its origins in the intellectual milieu around the famous documentary filmmaker John Grierson. Cinema-going was first studied in what was known as the 'Worktown' project – a study of Bolton, Lancashire – which was obviously inspired by Robert Lynd and Helen Merrell's *Middletown: A Study in American Culture* (1929). Survey methodology, loosely structured interviews and participant observation were employed in this project, and the material collected provides a rich and detailed picture of movie-going in Bolton. Both before and during the war, Mass-Observation continued to collect information from its volunteers all over Britain about cinema-going (including that of the volunteers themselves), reactions to particular films during screenings (laughs, comments, etc.), favourite stars and films and so on. Material was also gathered through popular newspapers and the film magazine *Picturegoer*, the readers of which were asked to write letters about their cinema habits and preferences (Richards and Sheridan, 1987: 1–18). The Mass-Observation archives are now at the University of Sussex.

The latter procedure was also used by the sociologist J.P. Mayer when working on his *British Cinemas and their Audiences* (1948), which includes 60 of the letters Mayer received from readers of *Picturegoer*. This book seems, however, to be, the last of its kind to arrive for decades. From the early fifties on, television largely took over the cinema's role as the major source of popular entertainment and consequently also became the object of concerns similar to those previously directed at the movies. Social scientists simply seemed to have lost interest in film and its 'effects', also in part

because the individualistic and consumer-oriented 'uses and gratifications' approach now replaced the older 'effects' paradigm in mainstream communication research. When Film Studies finally became established as an academic discipline in its own right in the 1960s and 1970s, it was as a purely aesthetic discipline, devoted to studies of films as texts, of masterpieces and auteurs. For film to be accepted as an object worthy of study entailed re-evaluating it as Art. Sociological studies of the audience came to be regarded as irrelevant, philistine activities, interesting only to aesthetically insensitive social scientists, politicians, bureaucrats and the movie business. 'Audience' first reappeared in film theory around 1970, but only as a generalized textual construct. In 1978, however, at the Centre for Contemporary Cultural Studies in Birmingham, Tom Jeffrey published a paper entitled 'Mass-Observation: A Brief History'. Mass-Observation and empirical studies of actual audiences were thus 'rediscovered' in the context of the ethnographic studies of contemporary (youth) culture conducted by the so-called Birmingham School. The 1980s then brought a new wave of interest in film audiences.

SCREEN THEORY, CULTURAL STUDIES AND THE HISTORICAL MATERIALIST APPROACH

The politically-inflected theorization of spectatorship in the 1970s could, with a psychoanalytic metaphor, be seen as a 'return of the repressed' after a period of predominantly aesthetic approaches. But the political interest in film spectators could also be seen as a kind of 'displacement', in that the central audiovisual medium had by then been television for decades. From a political point of view, it was also striking that most of the films analyzed were made decades earlier – they were not what contemporary audiences went to the cinema to see. An interest in contemporary movie audiences is still relatively rare in Film Studies.

This is not at all to say that the theories in question were irrelevant or that all the efforts of 'Screen theory' were a waste of time and energy. Ideas about 'spectator positions' suggested by the filmic texts are in line with ancient rhetorical theory and also with more recent phenomenological and hermeneutic theories of literature. However problematically simplified, Laura Mulvey's 1975 article about the structural gendering of mainstream film was a highly influential attempt to ground a feminist theory of film in something more fundamental than the simple counting of stereotyped sex roles. On the whole, psychoanalytic theory in the tradition of Metz is still the only significant theory which seriously approaches the 'deeper' reasons for our desires for and pleasures in film experiences. It deals with phenomena we cannot expect to explain either through direct observation or through interviews, but which still remain essential. The tradition of empirical studies of actual audiences can only, like Emilie Altenloh in 1914, conclude that people have few and hardly satisfactory answers when asked why they go to the movies again and again. The problem of Screen theory was rather that the issue of 'real' audiences was either dismissed as 'empiricist' or postponed indefinitely. This contrasted with developments in literary studies (out of which Film Studies for the most part grew), where studies of historical, concrete instances of reception were booming in many countries in the 1970s – not least inspired by German reception theorists. Film Studies only took a similar turn after cultural studies of television demonstrated that textual analysis and audience studies could be intelligently and fruitfully combined. Charlotte Brunsdon and David Morley's work on the British program Nationwide was seminal here (1978; Morley 1980). It was later followed, for instance, by Ien Ang's influential study of the Dutch reception of Dallas (1985), and in the late 1980s the 'ethnographic' study of television audiences was generally recognized as the 'sexiest field within the field' in the increasingly interdisciplinary area where mass communication, communication,

media, cultural and Film Studies converged. This convergence also occurred when the previously, quite strictly, positivist 'number-crunching' disciplines of communication and mass communication experienced a 'ferment in the field' which opened the way for qualitative methods (as opposed to strictly quantitative, statistical methods) in both textual and audience analyses, and forms of critical theory.

Because of its focus on television, it is generally held that the influence of the cultural studies tradition on the study of film has been an indirect one (Mayne, 1993: 59–60). For example, there exist remarkably few studies that have adopted outright the 'archetypal' method of cultural studies, characterized by the combination of textual analysis and ethnography. But in a roundabout way, the cultural studies tradition has had several important consequences. First and foremost, its findings demonstrated the inadequacies of Screen theory. Consequently, psychoanalytic film scholars were provoked to develop models of spectatorship that offered audiences a greater variety of viewing positions.

Meanwhile, cultural studies' investigations of people's often unauthorized uses of so-called low culture flew in the face of the central tenet of political modernism: the opposition between the ideological conservatism of popular film and the political progressiveness of the avant-garde. In general, cultural studies has compelled all approaches to the study of film to adopt a greater sensitivity to the cultural, political and sociological contexts within which film viewing takes place.

But the cultural studies tradition has also exerted a more direct influence on some of the most interesting audience research that has been conducted on film audiences – even as that research swears allegiance to approaches that go by other names. Martin Barker and Kate Brooks' Knowing Audiences (1998), an investigation into the reception of Judge Dredd (Danny Cannon, US, 1995), is a case in point. One of the few ethnographic studies of contemporary viewers of contemporary films, it mines respondents' talk for 'signs and symptoms of the social relations in which they are caught up' (1998: 115). This clearly parallels key concerns of the cultural studies tradition, even though the authors identify their approach as discourse analysis.

Janet Staiger's historical materialist approach to reception studies is another example. In *Interpreting Films* (1992) and *Perverse Spectators* (2000) she traces the various interpretive strategies that have been available to historical audiences by examining such materials as film reviews, surveys, interviews, academic criticism and fanzines. There are a number of methodological problems with such an account and Staiger freely acknowledges most of them. Probably the greatest challenge for historical materialist reception studies is to establish a link between, for example, a series of newspaper reviews of a film and actual viewers' experience of it. Staiger clearly wishes to treat the reviews she investigates as somehow symptomatic of larger constituencies, but there can be little doubt that professional film writers are far from representative of the majority of cinema-goers. They are, for instance, likely to be more knowledgeable about the cinema, and they can probably bring into play more (or at least different) interpretive contexts than average viewers. The discourses that Staiger identifies – which are often highly specialized, like those on authorship or reflexivity – thus become something like ideal viewing positions. And to the extent that they are projected onto more sizeable audiences, it creates ideal viewers, which is just what Staiger criticizes in other approaches.

This should not detract from the contribution that a historical materialist approach makes. It might be helpful to think of this, too, as a kind of discourse analysis. But instead of analyzing spectator responses, as Barker and Brooks do, Staiger identifies the development and circulation of various public and critical discourses historically, and accounts for their change over time. This productively draws attention to key factors that dictate terms of response. Its limitations, however, seem to be tied to the kind of claims it is able to make about actual audiences. It is one thing to establish which interpretive strategies were available at a certain time in history; it is something else to determine which of these were actually taken up and by whom.

It could be said that Staiger's work illustrates how difficult it is to separate the study of audiences from other areas of Film Studies. Much of her work probably contributes more to our understanding of cultural history and film theory than to an understanding of film reception. And much like Barbara Klinger's *Melodrama and Meaning* (1994) – which chronicles how the reputation of director Douglas Sirk has changed historically depending on the interpretative grids through which his films have been read – the historical-materialist approach to reception studies is an alternative to film interpretation as much as an alternative to the study of film audiences. Both Staiger and Klinger contest the traditional view that textual meaning is an inherent quality that simply awaits discovery by the analyst, and insist instead on the importance of contextual determinants.

Staiger's work is also part of the historical turn in Film Studies which, from around 1980, saw a greater interest in archive-based research. Scholars increasingly studies primary sources – not just the films themselves, but also demographical statistics, economic documents, production records and so on – to build up a fuller understanding of early cinema. Inquiries into the class and gender composition of early film audiences, as well as the number and location of theatres, were vital parts of this project. The definitive work on film exhibition is Douglas Gomery's *Shared Pleasures* (1992). It tracks both mainstream and specialized operations, like art cinemas and segregated theatres, from the earliest peep shows to the age of home video, cable and pay-per-view.

The intersection between film aesthetics, film history and film reception has proved particularly fashionable. For example, Tom Gunning (1990) incorporates an account of spectators' experiences of film into his periodization of American cinema. Still, he arrives at his highly influential concept of a 'cinema of attractions' primarily through an examination of the films' formal features, specifically their mode of address. Miriam Hansen's *Babel and Babylon* of 1991 is similar in many respects. Arguing that early modern cinema constituted an oppositional public sphere for women, Hansen too constructs a large-scale account of American film history on the basis of an analysis of the cinema-going experience.[2]

Partly an offshoot of this research is the so-called 'modernity thesis', which developed in the late 1980s as several film scholars turned to figures such as Siegfried Kracauer and Walter Benjamin to investigate cinema's place and role in the modern metropolitan experience (Charney and Schwarz, 1995; Friedberg, 1993; Gunning, 1994; 1995; Hansen, 1987; 1991b). Ben Singer (2001) has identified three key components of the modernity thesis. The first is the observation that there are some significant similarities between the cinematic and the urban experience. The spatio-temporal fragmentation and aggressive display of spectacle in picture palaces resemble the commotion and transience of the visual environment in the period of urbanization and modernization. The second component is the idea that the cinema was an integral part of modernity, interacting with a range of phenomena that were either appearing or greatly intensifying around the turn of the nineteenth century. These included technological innovations such as the telegraph, the telephone and the railroad; new entertainments like the diorama and the wax museum; as well as new social spaces and practices, like the arcade and shopping. The final component of the modernity thesis is the assumption that there is a relationship of causality between the two: that is, cinema is somehow a consequence of modernity. This argument can take many forms, but in general the causal link is taken to be human perception: modernity produced a distinctive perceptual mode – restless, jittery, distracted – that was sustained by and/or fed into cinema (2001: 101–3).

The modernity thesis has proved enormously attractive, but also controversial, as the third conjecture is particularly contentious (see Bordwell, 1997: 141–9). In response to this criticism, Gunning, one of the chief proponents of the thesis, has agreed that key terms like 'experience' and 'perception' are in need of clarification, and that 'the relations drawn between the structures of modernity and those of early film frequently lack specificity and remain on the level of vague analogies' (2000: 268). While these are substantial objections, they certainly highlight the function and tremendous ambitiousness of the modernity thesis. The greatest promise it holds is the ability to bring together the traditionally conflicting, sometimes aggressively antagonistic, scholarly concerns of empirical, archive-based film history and high-level cultural theory.

STAR STUDIES AND FAN STUDIES

'Star studies' brings together a variety of approaches to investigate the cultural meanings of stars. The seminal works here are Richard Dyer's *Stars* (1979) and *Heavenly Bodies* (1986). Unlike most biographies and journalistic discourses, Dyer's ambition is not to uncover the real personality behind the public image. Rather, he conceives of stars as clusters of signs, made up of both cinematic and extra-cinematic materials. Dyer draws primarily on semiotics and ideological criticism to analyze stars as texts. He finds that the appeal of stars is tied to the ways in which they embody and symbolically resolve real cultural contradictions. While Dyer occasionally makes use of Freudian psychology, psychoanalytic theories of desire, such as John Ellis' *Visible Fictions* (1982) were far more prominent in other star studies of the 1970s and 1980s.

The trajectory of star studies since the 1990s was symptomatic of a broader reorientation in the field of Film Studies, often sloganistically described as a shift from an interest in (hypothetical) subjects to (real) viewers, or from text to context. Central to this change was a frustration with so-called Grand Theories, those explanatory frameworks that are broad in scope, quite abstract, and often difficult to verify. Although Dyer's work on stardom is far from the most obvious example of this approach, it does sometimes give the impression that his general idea – that stars need to be explained ideologically – informs his textual analyses as much as the other way round. So instead of arriving at a theory on the basis of an investigation of particular films and their reception, the theory becomes a guiding principle for readings of individual texts.

Research on actual social subjects is the self-evident antidote to the problems posed by monolithic theories. Jackie Stacey's *Star Gazing* (1994) was the first major work to combine film theory with audience research to investigate the relationship between spectators and stars. She draws on letters and questionnaires from hundreds of cinemagoers to explore the ways in which particular female Hollywood stars were meaningful for British women. Ethnographic methods are also adopted in Joshua Gamson's *Claims to Fame* (1994) and, more recently, in some of the entries in Thomas Austin and Barker's *Contemporary Hollywood Stardom* (2003) and Rachel Moseley's *Growing Up with Audrey Hepburn* (2002).

These books, as well as Samantha Barbas' *Movie Crazy: Fans, Stars, and the Cult of Celebrity* (2001), demonstrate the ways in which star studies overlaps with fan studies. But whereas the former has most frequently examined historical reception – thus relying on letters, journals and audiences' memories – the latter has usually tackled contemporary viewers. (Annette Kuhn's work on the memories of British recalling moviegoing in the 1930s is an important exception to this [2002].)

Fandom has been a vibrant area of research since it was recognized in the early 1990s in two groundbreaking books: Henry Jenkins' *Textual Poachers* (1992) and Camille Bacon-Smith's *Enterprising Women* (1992). One reason for the success of fan studies is probably that it is so perfectly placed to

maintain and expand on key issues within the cultural studies tradition. Cultural studies was based on a redefinition of culture in the 1950s and 1960s. Richard Hoggart (1958), Raymond Williams (1965) and E.P. Thompson (1963) challenged the conventional view that identified culture as a canon of extraordinary works, preferring instead to think of it as a way of life. From the very beginning, then, cultural studies sided with ordinary citizens, frequently examining how distinctions act to legitimate the tastes of dominant social groups while celebrating audience activity, particularly signs of resistant readings. And fans, of course, are the ultimate active audiences. Indeed, one criticism frequently levelled at fan studies is that it tends to adopt a too romanticized a view of fan behaviour (McGuigan, 1992). In their examination of how specific audiences understand and re-appropriate texts, researchers have perhaps too eagerly looked for signs of audience agency and too routinely deemed any instance of activity progressive and self-liberatory.

Furthermore, studies of fans have tended to focus on highly popular texts, often cult classics (see Chapter 28 for a discussion of cult films). Followers of such films (or, more often, television series) are apt to be particularly devoted and participatory, and thus are not typical of the majority of viewers. In fairness, though, researchers do not usually claim that their studies of particular fan groups are representative of other audiences, either fans or non-fans. However, this points to another difficulty: how to determine what conclusions can legitimately be drawn on the basis of ethnographic studies. Are the various case-studies simply discrete collections of viewer testimony unable to connect with anything beyond them? There seems to be an inevitable trade-off here: the merits of Grand Theory are the disadvantages of ethnography, and vice versa. Grand Theories make sweeping claims that apply to all viewers at the expense of empirical variety; by contrast, while an insistence on detail, diversity and local factors allows ethnographic case-studies to account for a much greater range of audience responses, they have a hard time making generalizations. There is nothing mysterious about this: when we are dealing with something as complex as audience-film relations, the most productive way to accumulate knowledge is probably to play empirical case-studies and more general hypotheses off each other.

COGNITIVISM

Cognitivism, too, investigates film spectator-ship with great theoretical sophistication, but comes at it from an angle different from that of the approaches considered so far. Like cultural studies, cognitivism is very interdis-ciplinary, drawing on cognitive psychology, artificial intelligence, philosophy of the mind, linguistics, anthropology, neuroscience and evolutionary biology. It began to be applied to the study of film, albeit to a very small extent, in the 1970s. However, it was only with the publication of David Bordwell's *Narration in the Fiction Film* in 1985 that it gained widespread recognition.

Even more explicitly than the cultural studies tradition, cognitivism highlighted spectator activity in order to challenge the textual determinism of psychoanalytic film theories. But rather than emphasizing audiences' freedom to negotiate resistant or oppositional readings, cognitivism has investigated issues related to viewers' active processing of audiovisual information, such as recognition, comprehension and inference-making.

To begin with, cognitivists concentrated exclusively on the mental activities of specta-tors, leaving the study of emotional responses to psychoanalytic film theory. However, Noël Carroll's 1990 book *The Philosophy of Horror* endeavours to explain the genre's paradox – that people enjoy being scared – from a cognitive perspective. The decision to study this particular genre was of great symbolic significance, since it was commonly held that the analysis of irrationality – like horror fans finding pleasure in the unpleasant – was

the exclusive province of psychoanalysis. Since the mid-1990s, a number of important works on film and emotion by cognitive scholars have appeared. Torben Grodal's *Moving Pictures* (1997), for example, brings together, among other things, neuroscience and narrative theory in a highly complex and ambitious effort to ground aesthetic experience in hard science. On the assumption that cognitive and perceptual processes are closely linked to emotional processes, Grodal argues that it is possible to study prototypical film genres based on the kinds of sentiments and sensations that they elicit. Carl Plantinga and Greg M. Smith's anthology *Passionate Views* (1999) continues this process by collecting the major cognitive theories on the emotional aspects of cinema.

Cognitivists stress that they promote a stance or a program, not a unified theory. Indeed, there are fundamental differences between various strands. In *Narration in the Fiction Film,* for example, Bordwell advances a constructivist theory of film perception, which is a moderate version of cognitivism. Another influential cognitivist work – Edward Branigan's *Narrative Comprehension and Film* (1992) – merges cognitive psychol-ogy with insights from narratology and linguistics. Consequently, these works have one foot firmly planted in the humanistic research tradition out of which Film Studies originally emerged. As such, they contrast with 'harder' versions of cognitivism more explicitly modelled on the natural sciences. The 'ecological approach' put forward in Joseph D. Anderson's *The Reality of Illusion* (1996), for example, is exclusively devoted to those aspects of film that engage spectator responses that are hardwired or genetically determined: motion perception, brightness, depth, perspective. Even though viewer activ-ity lies at the heart of cognitivism, it is often not thought of as audience research 'proper', since it has little to do with what we are apt to see as its core activity, the investigation of the cultural practices of actual cinema-goers and the kinds of meaning they glean from the films that they see.

Many cognitive studies are empirical in nature, but unlike ethnographic studies they may take the form of laboratory experiments, measuring eye movement or object recognition, for example. But even though such studies investigate real, flesh-and-blood viewers, they do not necessarily investigate actual cinema viewers. In investigations of aspects of film perception – the eyes' fixation point, say – it does not matter whether the test subject is an avid or an occasional film-goer: researchers seem to assume that any person with a functioning sensory apparatus will do. So, whereas ethnographic studies play up diversity, the particular, and the local, cognitivists focus on universal features of film viewing. And where Staiger's materialist approach emphasizes the historical contingency of textual interpretations, cognitivism stresses the evolutionary constancy of audio-visual processing.

There is no reason not to think of this kind of cognitive research as 'true' audience research; it is just that its research questions and interests are different from those of the cultural studies paradigm. One way to describe the difference would be to say that, in general, cognitive film scholars have pursued questions that have tended to pertain more exclusively to film theory and film philosophy than to film sociology.

It needs pointing out, though, that far from all cognitivists perform first-hand empirical research. Often an abstract, hypothetical spectator is made to stand in as a representative for all spectators, just as in *Screen* theory. The difference, however, at least from a cognitivist point of view, is that cognitivism draws on the best available theories that are most relevant to the task at hand at any time.

AUDIENCE RESEARCH FOR THE FUTURE

Although audience research has often been accused of ignoring film as an aesthetic entity, this criticism is in need of qualification.

Bordwell has promoted what he calls an historical poetics of cinema, for example, which focuses on film's formal features and spectator effects. Thus, in *Narration in the Fiction Film* he integrates cognitive psychology into an account of the historical development of stylistic and narrative conventions in various cinematic traditions.

By and large there is still no doubt that the artistic dimensions of cinema tend to disappear from view in audience research. Even so, this is a function of the kinds of questions that it pursues, and it would be a problem simply if audience studies were the only kind of research conducted today. That being said, traditional textual interpretation that, more or less, treats film as an autonomous aesthetic object is clearly not coming to an end either. If, then, textual interpretations acknowledge the work that has been done in the field of audience research, they can begin to suspend broad claims about the effects of films on audiences based solely on analyses of stylistic, ideological or narrative structures.

For audience researchers, though, the notion of the autonomous film text is rapidly becoming obsolete. Viewers' experiences clearly extend beyond the approximately two hours or so that most films last. They involve, for example, the anticipation created through promotional materials, or online discussions with fellow fans. In the last decade, the limits of the film text have been redefined through technological developments. For instance, the multitude of special features found on DVDs, or films becoming videogames, provide viewers with new ways of expanding their experience of film.

Of course, scholars primarily interested in film aesthetics might legitimately want to ignore these consequences of the digital revolution. The expansion of the borders of the filmic text only becomes an issue when we are asking questions that pertain to audiences. And it may well be that we are currently witnessing, at least accumulatively, the greatest ever transformation in the relationship between the moving image and its audience. For example, Wheeler Winston

Dixon believes that the digital revolution has compromised the veracity of film, since CGI (computer generated imagery) makes just about any effect possible, and as such the audience no longer believes in images (2001: 358–9). Furthermore, the World Wide Web offers everyone with an Internet connection the opportunity to publish film reviews that are, in principle, available to millions of people, or to download films, or to seek out fans with similar interests from all over the world. The explosion of DVD and Internet shopping has made huge parts of film history available and affordable so that, even as the repertoire of films at cinemas decreases, the range of films available today, from all periods and traditions, is immeasurably greater than just a decade ago. Cheaper and more advanced editing software has enabled 'everyone' to engage with film in a much more hands-on manner; for instance, one recent trend is the practice of re-editing footage from famous films to create comical trailers that change the generic status of the original. Meanwhile, new platforms like video iPod will likely change the relationship between the moving image and personal space. Film scholars have barely broached such developments. Audience research should be a busy and fruitful field in the years to come.

NOTES

1 The study was conducted by Healy and Brommer and referred to in Blanchard (1928: 204) and Jowett (1976: 216).

2 For a summary and critique of these positions, see Staiger (2000: 11–27).

REFERENCES

Adler, Mortimer (1937) *Art and Prudence*. New York: Longmans, Green and Co.

Altenloh, Emilie (1914) *Zur Soziologie des Kino: Die Kino-Unternehmung und die sozialen Schichten ihrer Besucher*. Leipzig: Spamerschen.

Anderson, Joseph D. (1996) *The Reality of Illusion: An Ecological Approach to Cognitive Film Theory*. Carbondale: Southern Illinois University Press.

Ang, Ien (1985) *Watching 'Dallas': Soap Opera and the Melodramatic Imagination*. London: Methuen.

Austin, Bruce A. (1989) *Immediate Seating: A Look at Movie Audiences*. Belmont, CA: Wadsworth.

Austin, Thomas and Barker, Martin (2003) *Contemporary Hollywood Stardom*. London: Arnold.

Bacon-Smith, Camille (1992) *Enterprising Women: Television Fandom and the Creation of Popular Myth*. Philadelphia: University of Pennsylvania Press.

Bakke, E.W. (1933) *The Unemployed Man*. London: Nisbet.

Barbas, Samantha (2001) *Movie Crazy: Fans, Stars, and the Cult of Celebrity*. New York: Palgrave.

Barker, Martin and Brooks Kate (1998) *Knowing Audiences: Judge Dredd, Its Friends, Fans and Foes*. Luton: University of Luton Press.

Blanchard, Phyllis (1928) *Child and Society*. New York: Longmans, Green and Co.

Blumer, Herbert (1933) *Movies and Conduct*. New York: The MacMillan Company.

Blumer, Herbert and Hauser, Philip M. (1933) *Movies, Delinquency and Crime*. New York: The MacMillan Company.

Bordwell, David (1985) *Narration in the Fiction Film*. London: Routledge.

Bordwell, David (1997) *On the History of Film Style*. Cambridge, MA: Harvard University Press.

Branigan, Edward (1992) *Narrative Comprehension and Film*. London: Routledge.

Brunsdon, Charlotte and Morley, David (1978) *Everyday Television: 'Nationwide'*. London: BFI.

Carroll, Noël (1990) *The Philosophy of Horror, or Paradoxes of the Heart*. New York: Routledge.

Charney, Leo and Schwarz, Vanessa (eds) (1995) *Cinema and the Invention of Modern Life*. Berkeley: University of California Press.

Cressey, Paul G. (1938) 'The Motion Picture Industry as Modified by Social Background and Personality', *American Sociological Review*, 3(4): 516–25.

Dixon, Wheeler Winston (2001) 'Twenty-five Reasons Why It's All Over', in Jon Lewis (ed.), *The End of Cinema as We Know It: American Film in the Nineties*. New York: New York University Press. pp. 356–66.

Dyer, Richard (1979) *Stars*. London: BFI.

Dyer, Richard (1986) *Heavenly Bodies: Film Stars and Society*. London: Macmillan.

Ellis, John (1982) *Visible Fictions: Cinema, Television, Video*. London: Routledge & Kegan Paul.

Forman, Henry James (1933) *Our Movie Made Children*. New York: Macmillan.

Friedberg, Anne (1993) *Window Shopping: Cinema and the Postmodern*. Berkeley: University of California Press.

Gamson, Joshua (1994) *Claims to Fame: Celebrity in Contemporary America*. Berkeley: University of California Press.

Gomery, Douglas (1992) *Shared Pleasures: A History of Movie Presentation in the United States*. Madison: University of Wisconsin Press.

Grodal, Torben (1997) *Moving Pictures: A New Theory of Film Genres, Feelings, and Cognition*. Oxford: Clarendon Press.

Gunning, Tom (1990) 'The Cinema of Attractions: Early Film, Its Spectator and the Avant-Garde', in Thomas Elsaesser (ed.), *Early Cinema: Space – Frame – Narrative*. London: BFI. pp. 56–62.

Gunning, Tom (1994) 'The Whole Town's Gawking: Early Cinema and the Visual Experience of Modernity', *Yale Journal of Criticism*, 7(2): 189–201.

Gunning, Tom (1995) 'An Aesthetics of Astonishment: Early Film and the (In)credulous Spectator', in Linda Williams (ed.), *Viewing Positions: Ways of Seeing Film*. New Brunswick, NJ: Rutgers University Press. pp. 114–33.

Gunning, Tom (2000) 'Early American Film', in John Hill and Pamela Church Gibson (eds), *Oxford Guide to Film Studies*. Oxford: Oxford University Press. pp. 255–71.

Hansen, Miriam (1983) 'Early Silent Cinema: Whose Public Sphere?', *New German Critique*, 29: 147–84.

Hansen, Miriam (1987) 'Benjamin, Cinema, and Experience: "The Blue Flower in the Land of Technology"', *New German Critique*, 40: 179–224.

Hansen, Miriam (1991a) *Babel and Babylon: Spectatorship in Silent American Film*. Cambridge, MA: Harvard University Press.

Hansen, Miriam (1991b) 'Decentric Perspectives: Kracauer's Early Writings on Film and Mass Culture', *New German Critique*, 54: 47–76.

Hoggart, Richard (1958) *The Uses of Literacy*. Harmondsworth: Penguin.

Huyssen, Andreas (1986) 'Mass Culture as Woman: Modernism's Other', in Tania Modleski (ed.), *Studies in Entertainment: Critical Approaches to Mass Culture*. Bloomington: Indiana University Press. pp. 188–207.

Jeffrey, Tom (1978) 'Mass-Observation: A Short History', CCCS Stencilled Occasional Paper 55. Birmingham: Centre for Contemporary Cultural Studies.

Jenkins, Henry (1992) *Textual Poachers: Television Fans and Participatory Culture*. New York: Routledge.

Jowett, Garth (1976) *Film: The Democratic Art*. Boston: Little, Brown.

Klinger, Barbara (1994) *Melodrama and Meaning: History, Culture, and the Films of Douglas Sirk*. Bloomington: Indiana University Press.

Kuhn, Annette (1988) *Cinema, Censorship and Sexuality 1909-1925*. London: Routledge.

Kuhn, Annette (2002) *An Everyday Magic*. London: I.B. Tauris.

Lowery, Shearon A. and DeFleur, Melvin L. (1995) *Milestones in Mass Communication Research: Media Effects*. New York: Longman.

Lynd, Robert and Merrell, Helen (1929) *Middletown: A Study in American Culture*. New York: Harcourt, Brace & World.

May, Lary (1980) *Screening Out the Past: The Birth of Mass Culture and the Motion Picture Industry*. Chicago: The University of Chicago Press.

Mayer, J.P. (1948) *British Cinemas and their Audiences*. London: Dennis Dobson.

Mayne, Judith (1993) *Cinema and Spectatorship*. London: Routledge.

McGuigan, Jim (1992) *Cultural Populism*. London: Routledge.

Moley, Raymond (1938) *Are We Movie Made?* New York: Macy-Masius.

Morley, David (1980) *The 'Nationwide' Audience*. London: BFI.

Moeley, Rachel (2002) *Growing up with Audrey Hepburn: Text, Audience, Resonance*. Manchester: Manchester University Press.

Mulvey, Laura (1975) 'Visual Pleasure and Narrative Cinema', *Screen*, 16(3): 6–18.

Münsterberg, Hugo (1916) *The Photoplay: A Psychological Study*. New York: Dover.

Peterson, Ruth C. and Thurstone, L.I. (1933) *Motion Pictures and the Social Attitudes of Children*. New York: MacMillan.

Petro, Patrice (1989) *Joyless Streets: Women and Melodramatic Representation in Weimar Germany*. Princeton, NJ: Princeton University Press.

Plantinga, Carl and Smith, Greg M. (eds) (1999) *Passionate Views: Film, Cognition, and Emotion*. Baltimore, MD: John Hopkins University Press.

Richards, Jeffrey (1984) *The Age of the Dream Palace: Cinema and Society in Britain. 1930–1939*. London: Routledge.

Richards, Jeffrey and Sheridan, Dorothy (1987) *Mass-Observation at the Movies*. London: Routledge & Kegan Paul.

Singer, Ben (2001) *Melodrama and Modernity: Early Sensational Cinema and Its Contexts*. New York: Columbia University Press.

Smith, H. Llewellyn (ed.) (1935) *The New Survey of London Life and Labour*. London: P.S. King.

Stacey, Jackie (1994) *Star Gazing: Hollywood Cinema and Female Spectatorship*. London: Routledge.

Staiger, Janet (1992) *Interpreting Films: Studies in the Historical Reception of American Cinema*. Princeton, NJ: Princeton University Press.

Staiger, Janet (2000) *Perverse Spectators: The Practices of Film Reception*. New York: New York University Press.

Thompson, E.P. (1963) *The Making of the English Working Class*. Harmondsworth: Penguin.

Williams, Raymond (1965) *The Long Revolution*. Harmondsworth: Penguin.

Draws in part on material previously published as 'Film Audiences' by Jostein Gripsrud, in John Hill and Pamela Church Gibson (eds), *Oxford Guide to Film Studies*, pp. 202–11. Copyright ©1998 Oxford University Press. Used by permission of Oxford University Press. Free permission author's own material.

30

Re-mapping Bollywood Cinema: A Postcolonial Case-Study

Vijay Mishra

'Bollywood' has finally made it into the *Oxford English Dictionary* (*OED*). The 2005 edition defines 'Bollywood' as: 'a name for the Indian popular film industry, based in Bombay. Origin 1970s. Blend of Bombay and Hollywood'. The incorporation of Bollywood in to the *OED* acknowledges the strength of a film industry that in 2006 produced 152 films and, since the coming of sound in 1931, has in fact produced some 10,000 films. (This must not be confused with the output of Indian cinema generally, which would be five times more.) According to a report in the *Economic Times* (Chennai), 1 January 2007, the total Indian film industry is 'close to Rs 7,900 crore (A$ 2,268,722,000) and growing at the rate of 20% per annum'. The *Economic Times* continues: 'It is expected to touch Rs 15,300 crore (A$4,393,854,000) by 2010 and nearly 10% of this market is expected to be contributed by overseas box office' (2007: 14). Proof of the latter trend is already there. Films such as *Salaam Namaste* (Siddharth Raj Anand,

India, 2005), *Veer-Zaara* (Yash Chopra, India, 2004), *Kal Ho Naa Ho* (*Even if Tomorrow Never Comes*, Nikil Advani, India, 2003), *Devdas* (Sanjay Leela Bhansali, India, 2003) and *Kabhi Khushi Kabhi Gam* (Sometimes Happiness, Sometimes Grief, Karan Johar, India/UK, 2001) had box-office collections of between 1.5 and 3 million dollars in the US, and between 1.5 and 2.5 million pounds in the UK.

The short-time spans of these figures indicate the exponential demand for Bollywood in the UK as well as US Indian diaspora at the turn of the twenty-first century. A little detachment, a little caution is, however, in order. 'India's share in the global film industry, valued in 2004 at $200 billion, was less than 0.2 per cent', writes Daya Kishan Thussu (2008, forthcoming). Even then one would have expected better returns from the UK, where, in fact, the Bollywood market 'accounted for just 1.1 per cent of gross box office in 2004' (Thussu, 2008).

Relative returns notwithstanding, the proliferation of Bollywood continues unabated. B4U (a British Bollywood round-the-clock movie channel launched in 1999) is now 'available on eight satellites in more than 100 countries' (Thussu, 2008). With fanzines such as *Cine Blitz, Filmfare, Movie* and *Stardust* available globally, online and in hardcopies, immediately after production, the Bollywood experience is growing into a worldwide phenomenon.

What is even less evident from the *OED* definition is the way in which the word has acquired its current meaning, displacing its earlier descriptors (Bombay Cinema, Indian Popular Cinema, Hindi Cinema) and functioning, perhaps even disconcertingly, as an 'empty signifier' that may be variously used for a reading of popular Indian cinema. The triumph of the term over earlier ones is nothing less than spectacular and indicates the growing global sweep of this cinema not just as cinema *qua* cinema, but as cinema *qua* social effects and national cultural coding.[1] As the closing ceremony of the Melbourne Commonwealth Games in March 2006 showed, Bollywood is the cultural practice through which Indian national culture will be projected when the games are held in Delhi in 2010. International games (the Olympics, the Asian Games, the Commonwealth Games, or the World Cup) often inspire expressions of a nation's own emerging modernity. For India that modernity, in the realm of culture, is increasingly being interpellated by Bollywood.

BOLLYWOOD, THE WORD, MODERNITY AND DIASPORA

What the *OED* does not tell us – not yet at any rate – is how 'Bollywood' works as a 'cultural logic', as a way of defining Indianness or conversely as an archive through which Indianness is defined. This is particularly true of the 12 million strong Indian diaspora to whom Bollywood supplies models for weddings, dances, parties and dress codes. In recent years high culture too gets filtered through

Bollywood. Two adaptations of Shakespeare may be briefly mentioned here: *Omkara* (India, 2006), Vishal Bhardwaj's Bollywood version of *Othello*, where, appropriately, an alluring Kareena Kapoor misplaces not her handkerchief but her waistband; and Bhardwaj's *Maqbool* (India, 2003), which treats key themes in *Macbeth* – self-fulfilling prophecy, ambition, power and sex – with reference to the Mumbai (Bombay) underworld of Jehangir or Abbaji (Pankaj Kapoor) (the Duncan-like godfather), his mistress Nimmi (Tabbu) (the Lady Macbeth figure) and Maqbool (Irfan Khan), Jehangir's Macbeth-like lieutenant, who is also Nimmi's lover. Knowledge of the Mahatma too, a sad and lonely figure in India these days, gets resurrected as the way of *Gāndhigiri* (the path of Gandhi, the high priest of non-violence) against *dādāgiri* (the path of extortion and bullying endemic among underworld figures) in *Lage Raho Munna Bhai* (*Carry on Munna Bhai,* India, 2006).[2] Such has been its impact that the film's maker, Rajkumar Hirani, was invited to screen *Lage Raho Munna Bhai* at the United Nations – the first Bollywood film to be granted this privilege (*Filmfare*, 2007: 111).

The *OED* entry misses another crucial point: as a term, Bollywood has a much older and, in fact, Indian origin. Film critic Madhava Prasad (2003) has located the first use of 'Tollywood' (after Tollygunge, the site of the Calcutta film industry) in a telegram that Wilford E. Deming, an American working on films, received in 1932 as he was about to leave India: 'Tollywood sends best wishes happy new year to Lubill film . . .'.

'Tollywood', the neologism, thus anticipates Bollywood which we may now, in an echo of Fredric Jameson (1991), recognize more precisely as the cultural logic of Indian late modernity. In his foundational essay (2003), Ashish Rajadhyaksha distinguishes between the *reality* of the Indian popular cinema based in Mumbai and its surrounding *hype* in order to explain the varied meanings of the word 'Bollywood'. This he sees at once as a fad, a taste, an Indian exotica, and a global phenomenon growing out of the cultural and political economy of a film industry based primarily in Mumbai. Both the hype and the reality come together in Sanjay Leela Bhansali's remake (India, 2003) of the classic film *Devdas* (P.C. Barua, India, 1935; Bimal Roy, India, 1955): here the postmodern digital image takes over from cinematic lyricism. Some precision is clearly in order, because, presented as hype, the claims made by both Indians and the Indian diaspora often do not tally with the evidence. Is Bollywood truly global? Does it mean more than a film industry? Is it a style that transcends its cultural origins, making cultural specificity inconsequential? If we bring these questions together, the fact of diaspora strikes us immediately and we may begin to see that the specific inflection given to Bollywood now reflects new kinds of global migration and links to the homeland. In this respect I want to suggest that although the Bombay/Mumbai film industry has been read both as a filmic style and as an artefact producing specific cultural effects, the present reception reflects a late modern entry of India into global capital, most notably via the IT and outsourcing industries and the accumulation of vast amounts of capital in the hands of diaspora Indians.

In terms of money earned, the Indian diaspora is now one of the largest markets for Indian cinema (Bollywood as well as regional cinemas), to the extent that, for film entrepreneurs, the 'Brown Atlantic' now constitutes a separate 'distribution territory' (Desai, 2003: 2–3). Indeed, if the Internet figures gathered by Rachel Dwyer are a guide, the diaspora collects almost as much money as India itself (2006: 231–2). By the end of July 2001, gross receipts for *Lagaan* (*Land Tax*, India, 2001) in India was US\$2,427,510, while the combined revenue in the US and UK was US\$1,546,734. If returns from the old Indian diaspora and the other markets for Bollywood are added to this figure, then the overall intake for the film outside India would have equalled that within India. Indeed, the film *Asoka* (Santosh Sivan, India, 2001) earned more money overseas in the first few months after its release than in India: \$900,000 against US\$1,430,000 in the US and the UK. In the UK it is not unusual to

come across figures indicating that Bollywood cinema productions are among the nation's top-grossing foreign films.

The hype mentioned by Rajadhyaksha, as taken up by Suketu Mehta's account of the making of *Veer-Zaara* in the *National Geographic* (2005) and manifest in box-office receipts, was seen in the phenomenal success (and aftermath) of what has been referred to as the 'Indian Summer of 2002'. In London, Bollywood was celebrated by the department store Selfridges' '23-and-a-Half Days of Bollywood', the Victoria and Albert Museum's 'Cinema India: The Art of Bollywood', and the British Film Institute's 'Imagine Asia', and in musicals such as the Tamasha Theatre Company's *Fourteen Songs, Two Weddings and a Funeral,* an adaptation of the well-known Bollywood film *Hum Aap ke Hain Koun* (*Who am I to you*, Sooraj R. Barjatya, India, 1994).[3] To these Andrew Lloyd Webber's *Bombay Dreams* (2002) may be added, although that production had been in the making for some years.[4] And so, when the Indian diaspora began to intervene in British cultural productions with an eye to its own distinctive artistic traditions, Bollywood became the indispensable form to imitate (Mira Nair's *Monsoon Wedding* in 2001), parody (Kaizad Gustad's *Bombay Boys* in 1998), deconstruct (Gurinder Chadha's *Bhaji on the Beach* in 1993) or creatively rewrite (Gurinder Chadha's *Bride & Prejudice* in 2004).

It is clear that, by contrast to the *OED* definition, Bollywood functions as something more than popular Indian cinema produced in Mumbai.[5] Although cinema is central, it is, as Rajadhyaksha says, 'a more diffuse cultural conglomeration involving a range of distribution and consumption activities from websites to music cassettes, from cable to radio' (2003: 27). The film industry now appears to be one part of a larger culture industry that gained official recognition only in 2000 and that has only recently had bank finance made available to it. The Bollywood industry is an early-nineties phenomenon distinct from Bombay cinema, which dates back at least to the 1930s and even, if one wishes to be fastidious, to D.G. Phalke's first silent movie in Hindi (*Raja Harishchandra*, India, 1913). Thus, the term Bollywood 'today refers to a reasonably specific narrative and a mode of representation' (Rajadhyaksha, 2003: 28). Its features, some of which are not as new as they are made out to be, include: love stories couched in traditional values (2005's *Viruddh* [Mahesh Manjrekar, India] carried the subtitle on screen of 'Family comes first') and presented as staged musicals; stories that do not unsettle cultural presumptions (although inter-religious marriages are condoned, provided a Muslim is not involved); representations that are framed within Hindu iconography; form that fetishizes high-tech values, even if it means distorting a realist 30s film such as *Devdas*; and cinema whose target audience is increasingly the Indian diaspora. As a word, 'Bollywood' is used to catch the flavour of whatever may be linked to Indian popular culture. In the pages of Sydney's *Sun Herald*, we find pop-culture journalist Clara Laccarino using Bollywood to make this link: Bollywood industry, Bollywood bonanza, a Bollywood fix, Bollywood Shakedown, Bollywood romp, Bollywood breaks, Bollywood dancing, Bollywood calendar and 'hot 'n' spicy Bollywood fever' (2005: S34). And then there are others: a Planet Bollywood (restaurant) and a Mauritius Bollywood to which characters (as in the film *Benares* [Pankuj Parashar, India, 2006]) disappear to preach enlightenment or where Bollywood is simply used as a locale for everything from a university (as in *Kuch Kuch Hota Hai* [Things do happen Karan Johar, India, 1998]) to palm-fringed beaches for a romantic backdrop (in any number of films).

Compared with 'Bollywood' as techno-sublime (websites and computer technology being its defining characteristics), Bombay fever is a lot older. So although (after Rajadhyaksha) a 'techno-nationalism' is now presented as '*the* Bollywood thematic' in response to the new Indian diasporic and nationalist modernity driven by non-resident Indians (NRI) and the IT industry,

Bombay cinema has always generated its 'Bollywood' hype (though not named as such). Salman Rushdie's use of this hype provides one piece of supporting evidence.[6] Another comes from Bollywood's niche market.

There has been an overseas market for Indian popular cinema from at least the early 1930s, well before the emergence of the non-resident Indian, largely in the old Indian diaspora, but also in the Middle East, parts of Africa, Southeast Asia and the Soviet Union. A further qualification is in order. Contrary to claims about the global sweep of this cinema, in the Western world, including white settler states, it is safe to say that for a long while Indian cinema did not exist and that the market for it was absent. Nor was there a 'Western' spectator within colonial India itself, as there is little, if any, evidence that the country's colonizers watched Indian films. The present situation, at least in settler states and in the metropolitan centres of Europe, is rather different and in the end has to be linked to the new global Indian diaspora of late capitalism. This, one could argue, has effectively produced Bollywood, the cultural phenomenon as we now understand it, in response to a dislocated diaspora youth culture's need for an accessible, unproblematic and sanitized India – the 'imaginary' India that they and their parents left behind.

A classic case of the crossover into cinema of 'the Bollywood thematic' referred to by Rajadhyaksha (and an instance of a diasporic nationalism based on homeland fantasies made possible through computer technology) is the film *Swades* (*We the People*, Ashutosh Gowariker, India, 2004), in which a highly successful NRI NASA scientist returns to an Indian village to generate hydro-electricity.[7] The kind of techno-nationalism undertaken in this act implies redressing the nation's own pre-modernity and its age-old traditions and prejudices through Western technology. The effective synthesis of ancient, unchanging values and Western technological reason brings Mohan Bhargava (Shah Rukh Khan), the scientist, back yet again to India after he had finished constructing a rudimentary hydroelectric machine. It is in America, in the diaspora, that the call of Mother India remains urgent; it is there that the sound of a word recalled and the opening of a box full of Indian seeds and soil confirms the eternal verities of the homeland, resulting in Mohan Bhargava 'returning' home for good. In other words, Mother India has a different resonance in the diaspora. There is, then, a strange form of cultural authentication taking shape, one that has been at the heart of the problem of cinematic representation all along. As part of the nationalist ethos, cinema has had to display civic virtues. Now Bollywood displays the same urge towards cultural authentication mediated through the diaspora. Rajadhyaksha Writes: 'In the Bollywood sense of the export of the Indian spectator to distant lands, I want to suggest another kind of export: the export of Indian nationalism itself, now commodified and globalized into a "feel good" version of "our culture"' (2003: 37). The question posed by Rajadhyaksha is (2003: 38): how is it that a sense of cultural insiderism (emphasizing 'indigenism'), which once existed in the Indian heartland, is now being energized by its transference elsewhere in the diaspora? Culture then goes elsewhere and returns (like the letter in Jacques Lacan) to its origins. In a double take, Baz Lurhmann's use of Bollywood songs in *Moulin Rouge!* (Australia/US, 2001) is returned to Calcutta's Moulin Rouge with an ageing but still glamorous Rekha taking on Nicole Kidman's dance in *Parineeta* (Pradeep Sarkar, India, 2005). What Bollywood exports comes back Bollywoodized! To now theorize what Bollywood is implies reading it against the diaspora, because it is the latter that now charges Bollywood with meanings it never had. These meanings, of course, cannot be decoupled from the march of technology itself.

The transition from Bombay/Hindi cinema to Bollywood in terms of cultural production and reproduction may be narrated through shifts in the kinds of texts produced in the popular media. Even before cable, satellite TV (which only appeared in India in 1992) and the Internet, there was, of course, popular print media, notably film posters and fanzines, which created what may be called a proto-Bollywood hype. In Divia Patel's chapters, in her jointly-authored work, *Cinema India*, she establishes a direct link between poster art and, in the broadest sense, a national ethos. Patel begins with a discussion of the impact of the work of Raja Ravi Varma, arguably colonial India's finest Indian artist, whose use of Western techniques to represent deeply-felt and sensuously achieved representations of people led to film art posters that glorified the physicality of the Gods (Dwyer and Patel, 2002: 105). Patel then shows how other film-poster painters, such as Baburao Painter, G.B. Walh, and D.G. Pradhan, who followed in Varma's footsteps, mapped a vision of modernity corresponding to the avowedly modern themes of cinema. The posters demonstrate the use of modern European styles, including Art Deco and even psychedelia, as in the remarkable poster for *Bobby* (Raj Kapoor, India, 1973), to capture this Indian modernity. The art of posters takes a new turn with computer technology, which extends the link between cinema and modernist 'expressionism', as photographs are fed directly into a computer and edited. Websites belonging to Yash Raj Films and Vinod Chopra Films create immediately accessible global advertising.[8] Patel cites the following passage from the Yash Raj site for the film *Mohabbatein* (Aditya Chopra, India, 2000), in which the publicity is created in-house:

> The countdown begins! The shooting is over... The publicity material has begun to take shape and we have decided to use the internet to give the first glimpses into *Mohabbatein* at the Yash Raj Film website. So we are gearing up for an extensive web-peek into the film – everything from the making of the film, behind the scenes, previews of the music to the first introduction of the characters and stars who play them and a chance to chat on-line! (Dwyer and Patel, 2002: 180–1)

Although 'Bollywood' reflects a dramatically altered scene informed by the Internet and the cultural needs of the diaspora, the claim I make about Bollywood as the cultural logic of Indian modernity may be supported by going back in time: posters, handbills, programmes and, latterly, magazines mediated a culture of engagement with Bombay Cinema. Film magazines in English and in the vernacular languages began to appear from the moment of the talkies in the early 1930s (Dwyer, 2001: 251). The important film monthly, *Filmindia,* edited, written and produced by the acerbic Baburao Patel between 1935 and 1961, marks this new engagement. Patel's film magazine was not simply about the Hindi cinema: it carried large amounts of critical commentary on politics (in later years Patel's magazine was a leading critic of Nehru's five-year plans); and it also established the art of serious film journalism.[9] Other important fanzines include *Filmfare,* which began in 1952 and is owned by the *Times of India* newspaper group; *Stardust,* founded by Bombay entrepreneur Nari Hira in 1971 and in the early years under the editorship of the popular writer and Bombay socialite Shobha De; *Movie* and *Cine Blitz.*[10] Under De's editorship both the language and content of *Stardust* changed. Glamour, gossip, sexual innuendo, star rivalry and stories that titillated the imagination soon made it the fanzine with the largest circulation in India and with a reputation as the 'most foul of the bitch fanzines' (Mishra, 2002: 129).[11] The international edition sells a further 40,000 copies in the Indian diaspora (UK, US, Canada, South Africa, the Gulf States) (Dwyer, 2001: 253). The evidence of the fanzines, and especially of *Filmindia* and *Filmfare,* suggests that Bombay Cinema as proto-Bollywood was already heterogeneous, in that it always included both films and its own apparatus of consumption. Advances in technology (DVD, the Internet, etc) simply relocate Bollywood in a late or postmodern mode of artistic consumption.[12]

BOLLYWOOD CINEMA AND THE EASTERN SUBLIME

In *Lagaan,* Aamir Khan returns to the very colonial game of cricket and offers a sly postcolonial take on it: its gentlemanly virtues

are used to disrupt the seamless narrative of empire, as the film reworks C.R.L. James' astute observation that 'the cricket field was a stage on which selected individuals played representative roles which were charged with social significance' (quoted in Lazarus, 1999: 147).[13] In this respect it is a more fully articulated postcolonial text. Indeed, the film uses the aesthetics of the popular to insert the silenced subaltern back into reconstructed (even if historically quirky) evidence. The thematic itself, though, is not peculiar to *Lagaan* (although the postcolonial resonance is), as the mode of inserting the local, the indigenous, the homeland into the other and the diaspora, has become the dominant narrative of many recent films. We may want to refer to the paradigmatic instance of *Kal Ho Naa Ho* to make this clear. Set in New York, the central family is inter-religious (Sikh father, now dead; Christian mother), its past not a little murky with the memory of the father's suicide, and the presence of an adopted girl, Gia (Jhanak Shukla) (who, as it turns out, is the father's illegitimate child), making extended family life (the husband's mother is part of the family) difficult. For the eldest daughter Naina Catherine Kapur (Preity Zinta), only some form of supernatural intervention can bring sanity to her home: '*Angel kab āyegā?*' ('When will the angel come?'), is her question to Christ. She does have a very close friend in Rohit Patel (Saif Ali Khan), who loves her, but he is not quite the helper she needs. Enter into this New York neighbourhood the Indian diaspora's favourite actor, Shah Rukh Khan, as the angelic Aman Mathur. This angelic figure not only sets up the family's restaurant business (Indian food, it seems, is what New Yorkers want from Indians, not Italian coffee!), but also gives new meaning to love and laughter to Naina. But there is a dark shadow: Aman is dying and has only a few months to live. So he makes the predictable melodramatic sacrifice and persuades Rohit to marry Naina but not without leaving him his dying wish: 'In future lives, though, Naina will be mine'. Despite the New York setting, the narrative is pure Bollywood, the story not too different from that of films from *Anmol Ghadi* (*A Priceless Watch*, Mehboob Khan, India, 1946) to *Anand* (Hrishikesh Mukherji, India, 1970) with their melancholic, sacrificial, angelic heroes.

Kal Ho Naa Ho's formal pattern (which again strengthens the argument for Bollywood as an interconnected grand syntagm) is, however, less interesting for us than Bollywood's reading of the Indian diaspora and the latter's considerable influence on the new Bollywood product. We may wish to isolate three significant items and critique them briefly. The three are: inter-communal, non-sectarian Indian diaspora (where the Indian Muslim only exists as the 'real' actors Shah Rukh Khan and Saif Ali Khan); a largely entrepreneurial society unmarked by class difference and a culturally hybrid community comfortable with both India and the West. On all three counts the reading is patently false, so what is the pay-off here for us as readers/spectators, and how do we address it? Recalling the title of one of Slavoj Žižek's best-known books, we can say that the father-and-son production team of this film (Yash Johar and Karan Johar) and Bollywood producers generally 'know not what they do'. In his lengthy foreword to the second edition of his work, Žižek refers to the art of inventing 'objects which are sublime' (sublime objects we must note are, after all, practically useless) and makes a distinction between Western and Eastern sublimes:

> The Western Sublime offers a practical solution to a problem which does not arise; while the Eastern Sublime offers a useless solution to a real problem. The underlying motto of the Eastern Sublime is: 'Why do it simply, when you can complicate it?' (2002: cvii, n.124)

Žižek has a tendency to go for the overkill, and is often captivated by the force of rhetoric over content, but even so, as in the quotation given above, a startling problematic is addressed. In the case of *Kal Ho Naa Ho* and its diasporic take, the useless solution to the real problems of the diaspora (which are linked to larger questions of distributive justice, tolerance and recognition – issues central to multiculturalism generally) is an ingratiatingly excessive techno-realism in which felt-life is

transformed into a spectacle. This is also true of the extremely popular *Kabhi Alvida Naa Kehna* (*Never Say Good Bye* [Karan Johar, India, 2006]) which had a four-week run in Perth and which, according to a report in the *Economic Times* (Chennai), 1 January 2007, made more money in its overseas market than at home (2007: 14). Made by the same family company (the Yash Johar/Karan Johar Dharma Productions) as produced *Kuch Kuch Hota Hai*, *Kabhi Khushi Kabhi Gam* and *Kal Ho Naa Ho*, *Kabhi Alvida Naa Kehna* again offers a useless solution to a very serious problem in the diaspora. Once again this is New York and Dev Saran (Shah Rukh Khan) is in an unhappy (though initially not loveless) marriage with Rhea (Preity Zinta). They have a young, extraordinarily geeky son Arjun (Ahsaan Channa), who would rather learn how to play the violin than kick a soccer ball, even though father Dev is a much coveted New York football star. They all live together as an extended family with Dev Saran's mother, but it is Rhea, the rising fashion expert, who is the family's success story. Unhappy as Dev is, he meets Maya (Rani Mukherjee) sitting alone, it seems, on a park bench in the grounds of the palatial home of her would-be husband, Rishi (Abhishek Bachchan). She confesses her unease to this stranger, who has had doubts about his own marriage to Rhea. Maya's parents are dead and as a result she's been brought up by Mr Talwar (Amitabh Bachchan), whose son Rishi – the audience is aware of Amitabh and Abhishek as real life father and son – she is about to marry.

On the bench there is a kind of recognition and relay of desire, coded in high romantic (that is, Urduized) Bollywood cinema discourse – a sure sign that they are destined to be lovers. This is evident in the use of poetic lines (an Urdu *śāyar* which always begins '*arz kiyā hai*' ['If I may say so']), casual comments ('*soc kar kaun śādi kartā hai*' ['Who marries after serious thinking?']) and dramatic lines such as '*zindagī ke jis makām par tum ho*' ('Where you have reached in the narrative of life'). The genre of the sentimental romance (the dominant genre of Bollywood) establishes itself here. As Dev walks away from Maya – she moving towards the house/wedding hall; he towards the gate – she corrects him: 'Never say goodbye' ('*kabhī alvidā nā kahnā*'). Maya's marriage to Rishi is disastrous from the start. Dev's own marriage goes from bad to worse after an accident on that near fatal day on the park bench – he is hit by a car outside the gate as he says goodbye to Maya and can no longer play soccer as a multi-million dollar star player – but in time he meets Maya yet again. They recall their fleeting moments on the park bench, and love blossoms, appropriately in New York rain, recalling all those Bollywood *barsāt* (rain drenched) scenes after Raj Kapoor's great *mise en scène* of love in *Shree 420* (India, 1955), a Salman Rushdie favourite.

But what is the social pay-off here? Why is this a useless solution to a serious problem? Part of the difficulty lies with the genre itself – a genre which must continue to rewrite its sentimental romance in high poetic prose. Second is the tyranny of Bollywood's own codes of sentimental romance: belief in a pre-destined pure love and unease about breaking the vows of marriage. Not surprisingly, Dev and Maya's love is couched in the *rasa* of *karunā*, of pity, and is marked by the excessive outpouring of grief. There is guilt too on the part of these lovers, and this guilt surfaces almost as congenital guilt, as if the Indian were congenitally indisposed towards divorce. Or is it a statement more astutely about Indians in the diaspora, cut adrift from their sources of strength, from a continuous and once-mighty civilization relapsing into discourses which for Indians back at home are of a bygone age? So when Dev decides to leave for Toronto (another important site of the NRI), he says to his ex-wife Rhea: '*mai māfī to nahīṃ māng saktā lekin duā to de saktā*' ('I can't ask for your forgiveness, but may I give you my blessing'), as he touches her face. And as the lovers Dev and Maya finally meet in a New York subway, after three years of estrangement from their partners in cold and dark Philadelphia (contrasted with the light autumnal rains in New York) and unaware

that both are now in the same city (he in his sports casuals, she in a pink sari which denotes both high culture and demureness, civilized and Hindu), their meeting connects with the meeting on the bench years before. The film ends, but not before a reminder on the screen, the auteur's own signature-line as regret: '*kāś is manzil ke rāste tute hue diloṃ se nā guzare hote*' ('I wish though that the road to this destination did not have to go through fragments of broken hearts').

Thus, Bollywood filmmakers 'know what they do', without actually knowing what they do. In other words, they know that the Indian diaspora (invariably the 'new' disapora of late capitalism) understands that Bollywood cannot function outside of global market forces and that it generates enough money to cover the cost of producing a Bollywood film. But, unknown to Bollywood filmmakers, the diasporic spectator also knows that Bollywood creates an ideal (or rather an ideologically skewed ideal) rather than a realist image of diaspora. A growing body of opinion now believes that diasporas are being weaned away from narratives of return that are based primarily on fantasies of homeland, due to the pressing issues of the realities of living as minorities in nation-states that are not necessarily sympathetic towards them. It is true that Bollywood carries, to some extent, but often as parody, the successes and traumas of the Indian diaspora. But this representation of diaspora life requires critical self-awareness and distancing, both of which are missing from *Kal Ho Naa Ho*, where Aman, the 'knight in shining armour', is in the end no more than a 'patriarchal purveyor' from the ancient homeland, whose presence reinforces a particular order: it is the homeland alone which can set the dharmik order right. Or, in Gayatri Gopinath's insightful observation, Bollywood cinema (she has *Kal Ho Naa Ho* in mind) simply 'repackages [diasporic] Indianness as a valuable commodity that can be "modernized" into a sure-fire recipe for success and upward mobility in capitalist America' without in any way addressing their often traumatized lives in precisely that capitalist America (2005: 189).

A critical self-awareness is, therefore, missing from *Kabhi Alvida Naa Kehna*, which very conveniently forgets that the fact of diaspora imposes different strains upon marriage. In these terms Bollywood, at the level of lived experience, either depicts the older version of diasporas as contaminated collectivities in need of redemption from homeland values – Aman Mathur, the angelic miracle worker, affirms this reading in a rather fulsome manner, as did Mohan Bhargava (also played by Shah Rukh Khan), who returned 'home' to retrieve the purity of his *āyā*h Kaveriamma (Kishori Balal) in *Swades* – or it couches the inter-personal (as when marriages collapse) in a Bollywood simulacrum of the sentimental romance. But, in the absence of another readily available signifier of Indian cultural modernity, the diaspora tenaciously holds on to Bollywood as texts that give them an anchor, and allows them to claim, in the cultural sphere, something which they alone understand, or pretend to understand.[14] It offers a useless solution to their sense of Indianness, but they feel it somehow touches an inner core, the raw real, which forever eludes representation in the primarily European settler countries that they inhabit.

How and why Bollywood with its paradoxical claims to and endorsement of Indian modernity[15] – a reading of modernity which collides with lived experience, as even the most modern of Bollywood stars, Amitabh Bachchan, rushes with his son Abhishek to the Vishwanath Temple in Varanasi to perform rituals which would ward off the powers of the planet Mars because Abhishek's betrothed, Aishwarya Rai, is a *mangalī* (one born under the influence of the planet Mars) and hence likely to cause death in the family (*Times of India*, 2007: 15) – arrived here requires a return to the genealogy of Bombay cinema, which remains, in spite of the open-ended heterogeneous definition of 'Bollywood', its central text.[16] There is then a genealogy of Bollywood Cinema which, however selectively, needs to be written down. I do this with reference to the legacy of Parsi theatre, Muslim courtesan drama, the legacy of the genre of the melodramatic novel and

the impossibility of Mother India in the age of late capitalism.

PARSI THEATRE

As founders of a particular kind of discursivity and cross-generic capaciousness, the great epic texts, the *Mahābhārata* and the *Rāmāyaṇa*, shadow Indian popular culture. This much is a pre-given, an article of faith. Yet the manner in which the epic texts get transformed in cinema is indebted to Parsi theatre, a dramatic form which has had a far-reaching impact on Bollywood. In an exceptionally informative essay, Hansen (2001; see also 2003) argues that the second half of the nineteenth century saw the growth in metropolitan centres of India of a theatre in which 'disparate, localized performance practices' were used to create a pan-Indian theatrical style. In a passage that is crucial to any genealogy of Bollywood, Hansen continues:

> With its emphasis on spectacle and song, it [Parsi theatre] fostered modes of visual and aural discrimination that were linked to pre-existing forms, yet afforded new pleasures by means of technological innovations that conveyed the feel of modernity. This performative grammar together with an evolved typology of narrative later infused into Indian cinema the character of a national idiom. The early modern theatre, both as a temporal link to deep sources of cultural authority, and as a spatial connector mediating scattered genres of poetry, music, and dance, laid the ground for a shared expressive life, playing a critical role in the history of public culture in India. (2001: 76)

As an exemplary test case Hansen selects *Indar Sabha*, a lengthy verse narrative in Urdu composed by Agha Hasan Amanat in 1853 at the court of Wajid Ali Shah in Lucknow, which was adapted for Parsi theatre as a standard item. In Amanat's work, the basic genres of the Persian romance (the *masnavī*, *qissā*, *dāstān*) were overlaid with Urdu ghazals and local folk songs and *ragas*. Although not a play in the strict sense, it is a text that was quickly transformed into a performance piece. Over the next few decades this foundational text became a staple narrative, first of Parsi theatre and then of early cinema: as 'standard item in the repertoire of the Parsi theatrical', it may even be seen as a decisive influence on Bollywood cinema (Hansen, 2001: 79). The story itself, although not divided into acts and scenes, has sufficient dramatic material, since characters are given dialogues, as in Indian epics generally, through which to express their feelings. These dialogues also involve songs which combine local dialects with high Urdu and standard Hindi. The dramatized versions of *Indar Sabha* thus introduce elements of spectatorial pleasure (as the spectator in an 'erotic complicity' positions him/herself as the eponymous Raja Indar) and a number of 'viewing relationships' (between the performers, between the actor and the audience, and among the spectators) (Hansen, 2001: 88). In particular, there is a mode of sly recognition (which goes back to Sanskrit dramaturgy) – the sly glance that is bestowed by women on the king, known as the *tircchī nigāhem* (sidelong glances) – popularized by Parsi theatre, which became the stock-in-trade of performance.

While within the fixed confines of theatrical performance Parsi theatre adopted the proscenium stage and performed a range of English and sometimes European plays, its use of '"operatic" singing and declamatory acting techniques' paved the way for the arrival of talkies in 1931 (Hansen, 2001: 89). Parsi theatre was clearly the dominant form of urban entertainment until the arrival of talkies in 1931, its influence going well beyond the metropolitan centres of Bombay and Calcutta and affecting performances such as the *Maharastrian Sangeet Natak* and the North Indian *Nautanki*, both significant folk dramas. The impact on the latter was two-way, as here an urban-influenced form (Parsi theatre) through its regional tours influenced a folk drama and was in turn influenced by it. A primarily urban art form thus became a key defining feature of Indian drama generally.

It is therefore unsurprising that, when cinema came to India, entrepreneurs such as J.F. Madan would make the transition from Parsi theatre to cinema halls, and from producing drama to producing films. In fact,

the first talkie version of *Indar Sabha* (India), the definitive play of Parsi theatre, was made by J.F. Madan's third son, J.J. Madan, in 1932. Another version was made in 1956 by the Parsi producer Nanubhai Vakil.

In *Teesri Kasam* (*The Third Vow*, Basu Bhattacharya, 1966), based on the Hindi novelist Phanishwar Nath Renu's *Māre Gaye Gulfām*, the connection with Parsi theatre is reworked to show cinema's indebtedness to that art form. Indeed, the entire film may be seen as paying homage to the earlier theatrical tradition. The story revolves around a naïve country bullock-cart driver Hiraman (Raj Kapoor), who takes a Nautanki dancer Hirabai (Waheeda Rehman) to join a troupe of dancers. Although noted by critics for its 'lyrical imagery' and commentary on the 'oppression of women', what is interesting to me is the title of Renu's novel on which this film is based. 'Gulfam' in the title is, of course, the name of the earthly prince in Amanat's *Indar Sabha*, whom the heavenly Emerald Fairy (Sabz Pari) loves. He is smuggled into Raja Indar's heavenly abode only to be condemned to die in a well once the affair between the two is discovered. Sabz Pari has her wings clipped and she is banished to earth. Chanting songs of love-longing, she finally gains re-admission into heaven. Gulfam is clearly the opposite of Indar – effeminate, passive, indolent, perhaps even sentimental. In *Teesri Kasam* these features of Amanat's tale (*dāstān*) are incorporated into the modern film: Hirabai, the courtesan, for instance, is not unlike Sabd Pari – forward, seductive, alluring, with a language which echoes the *zanāni bolī* 'that identifies her as a member of a particular stratum of Lucknow society' (Hansen, 2001: 84). Apart from the narrative of an impossible love between a buffoon (Hiraman) and a courtesan (Hirabai), the film's *mise en scène* centres on performances (by Hirabai, the courtesan) on the Nautanki/Parsi stage. The courtesan, the dancer, the desirable but ungraspable figure of the alluring seductress, finds its source in the Parsi theatre, and, although *Teesri Kasam* captures that theme in the modern film, the theme itself also finds expression in a rarely-addressed type of Bollywood film. This type may be referred to as the film of the Muslim courtesan, a figure of love and sacrifice; a figure at once tragic, fragile, poetic and desirable. Although the figure has its manifold avatars, even when under erasure, almost everywhere in Bollywood cinema, it is only in the decidedly 'Muslim films' that the figure is given a precise ontology and capacious expression.

THE DANCE OF THE TRAGIC COURTESAN

One of the more influential plays performed in Parsi theatre was *Laila Majnun*, an Urdu play derived from the Persian Sufi poet Nizami's poetic rewriting of an Arab tragic romance. The Arabic tale seems to have originated in the late seventh century and was reputedly based on a Romeo and Juliet-style tragic love of one Qays ibn al Mulawwaht for his beloved Layla. In Nizami's version, the story is overlaid with strong mystical symbolism and the relationship of the lovers is also rendered as an allegory between human love for the divine. Parsi theatre used the story in its more secular 'Shakespearian' form and Bollywood too emphasized its secularity, a point made in the film *Aaja Nachle* (come Let's Dance, Aditya Chopra, India, 2007) where the play functions as the film's subtext. The story, though, has deeper significance in that its narrative was often presented as the quintessentially Muslim story around which the tale of the tragic Muslim courtesan unfolded. This figure of the 'Muslim courtesan' remains pivotal to the Bollywood conception of the heroine, but also suggestively points to the, at once central and marginalized, Muslim in Bollywood.

Without the power of Urdu and Muslim culture, the distinctiveness of Bollywood cannot be fully grasped. Yet this power, pervasive and aesthetically dominant as it is, is nevertheless captured in a figure of cultural exclusion and erasure. A quick look at four films – *Anarkali* (Nandlal Jashwantlal, India, 1953), *Mughal-e-Azam* (K. Asif, India, 1960), *Pakeezah* (Kamal Amrohi, India, 1972) and

Umrao Jaan (Muzaffar Ali, India, 1981) – should make this ambivalence clear.

No one is certain of where and how the Anarkali legend began, but we do know that a silent film about her was made in 1928 by the Imperial Film Company (directed by R.S. Choudhury) and it is highly likely that a play of sorts pre-dated the film. We know that the Urdu dramatist Agha Hashra Kashmiri wrote a play on the subject early in the twentieth century, and the fact that the names of the characters and the storyline have remained unchanged tends to suggest that the origin of the legend was probably literary. It seems clear that whoever the original writer was felt that the great Arab-Persian love story should be given an Indian context, and what better way to do it than by locating it in the court of the great Mughal Emperor Akbar. The storyline then is about Akbar's son, the Mughal Prince Salim (later Emperor Jehangir), falling in love with the court dancer Nadira, named Anarkali by none other than Akbar himself. This leads to political and dynastic tensions, open warfare between father and son, the sentence of death on both Salim and Anarkali and a final reprieve to the son, but not to Anarkali, who is entombed alive. The 1928 silent version as well as the Imperial Company's talkie version of 1935 (with the same director and lead actors), adheres to this storyline (R.S. Choudhury, India, 1928; 1935). The same fidelity to the narrative is shown in the 1953 film version, perhaps the best rendition of the story. It is interesting that in this version it is Emperor Akbar (Mubarak) himself who enters into extensive dialogues with Anarkali (Bina Rai) on the question of love and the law, agreeing with her that perhaps love is higher than the law and the proof of the latter lay in the love of Anarkali herself (about which for a while he remains ignorant). Much of the performance is staged, but Marshall Braganza's cinematography is so effective that the film captures the fragility of Anarkali remarkably well. And then there is also the haunting use of song, especially '*yah zindagī usī kī hai jo kisī kā ho gayā pyār hi me kho gayā*' ('Life is for those who love, who get lost in it') with which the film more or less begins and ends, and a song, in both its original version and later avatar as '*pyār kiyā to ḍarnā kyā*' ('Why be afraid when in love?'), celebrated by postcolonial writers like M.G. Vassanji (in *The Book of Secrets* [1994]) and Rushdie (in *Shalimar the Clown* [2005]).

The establishing shots of *Anarkali* juxtapose a tomb and a song, one signifying death, the other transcendence over it. As a film of the Muslim courtesan, *Anarkali* lays claim to the soul of Bollywood cinema as a 'Muslim' soul of love and longing, of poetry and self-denial. It also lays claims to a central tension between law, justice, cultural norms and love. In this battle, love triumphs even if tragically. But the Muslim theme and the film's historical location also lays claim to a syncretic Indo-Muslim heritage and argues that the Muslim is crucial to Indian cultural identity, especially for those people who speak Hindi/Urdu, the language of Bollywood. In a much grander version of the Anarkali theme, K. Asif's *Mughal-e-Azam*, the centrality of the Muslim is given a retrospective legitimacy through the recasting of Akbar (Prithviraj Kapoor) in the codes of ancient Hindu dharma, so that justice is not simply a matter of jurisprudence, a philosophy of what is just and right, but relies on codes that pre-date the arrival of Muslims and into which the Muslim establishment also reinserts itself. So, in this epic remake K. Asif distorts the received narrative by letting Anarkali (Madhubala) escape death because Emperor Akbar has given his word to Anarkali's mother, who had brought good tidings to the King on the birth of his son, that if and when she asked for a favour of the king, her wish would be granted.[17] But what neither of the films erases is the centrality of the *mujrā*, the dance of the courtesan in Bollywood, whose definitive form is the '*pyār kiyā to ḍarnā kyā*' ('Why be afraid when in love?') dance of Anarkali in *Mughal-e-Azam*. At the same time, the presentation of the *mujrā* as a distinctly Muslim courtesan dance isolates the form itself, confines it within a specific genre so that, in effect, there is no type of recognizable Muslim film other than a version of *Anarkali*.

'Anarkali', as a sign as well as a theme, is the antecedent of two key courtesan filmic dramas: *Pakeezah* and *Umrao Jaan*. The first of these takes the figure of the *tavayaf* (courtesan) but presents her, not so much as a sign of absolute exclusion – in reality she is a figure of illicit desire but also a threat to normative family values – but as a symbol (precisely because of her otherness) through which values of high aestheticism and love may be expressed. Thus, for Muslim culture the courtesan becomes emblematic of an elusive, but aesthetically pure and culturally pivotal, formation without which the culture itself is emaciated and forlorn. At the same time, however, the culture cannot endorse or celebrate the courtesan in social practice: no courtesan can become a mother or a wife; she can only be the desirable Other, through whom love, often absent in arranged marriages within close endogamous structures, can be given felt expression. Indeed, the courtesan affirms a fact of Indo-Muslim culture generally (where cousin marriages are the norm): only in the courtesan outsider (who by definition cannot be part of a family) is desire fulfilled. So in the case of *Pakeezah*, the excluded courtesan (whom the respectable man marries but cannot bring into his family) must live her life twice over, once as herself, and again as her daughter before she is incorporated back into respectability by the nephew of precisely the man who had rejected his courtesan wife (it is the nephew who marries Nargis [Meena Kumari], the courtesan's, daughter Sahibjaan).

In *Pakeezah*, the courtesan enters the text fully formed; she is what she is and it is Shahabuddin's (Ashok Kumar) fate to fall in love with her. It is a love signified by both mother, and later by her daughter, through the symbolism of a caged wingless bird (*pinjre ki ciṛiyā*) and the torn kite (*katīpatang*) hanging from the branch of a tree (both established metaphors of loss in Indian art). In *Umrao Jaan*, the courtesan is complicit with patriarchal violence towards women, as men seeking revenge against her father abduct the young girl Amiran (Rekha) from her village and take her to the city of Lucknow in order to sell her. Poet Muzaffar Ali, the director of this film, however, uses the tragic history of rape, abduction and sexual slavery to extend the link between the aesthetic and the courtesan. It may be that Muslim poetic forms derive much of their strength from the figure of the courtesan, whose *koṭhā* (brothel) provides a space where dance and song, desire and passion and sex and poetry can fuse into one, uninhibited by either religion or family. The *koṭhā* is a space of romantic transformation, where reality is changed into fantasy. In *Umrao Jaan*, the poetic impulse itself is connected to the courtesan because it is she who writes poetry and who seduces as much through song as through the body. The film then becomes a vehicle for the transmission of high Urdu dialogue and verse, as the courtesan masters both music and literature, mastering the rules of both *khayāl* and *alfāz*, both poetic suggestiveness and sound combinations, as in the establishing song of the courtesan: '*dil cīz kyā hai āp merī jān lījiye*' ('Why stop at my heart, take my life away'). And yet in spite of lovers' trysts that fill the film with exquisite moments of romantic love, the exclusion of the courtesan from society is not negotiable. When she finally returns home, she is rejected as the *bāzārī aurat* (available woman of bazaars). The final shot of the film is of Umrao Jaan looking at herself in a mirror: the courtesan is only an image, a reflection, a sign into which is poured romantic meaning but of itself is only a mirage, unreal and, like poetry, in the end untranslatable.

Muslim courtesan films demonstrate at the same time the centrality of Muslim culture in Bollywood and its exclusiveness. For that culture can only exist as a source for poetry and dance, for expressions of that elusive desire that cinema, as the art of the imaginary, always endorses. Without that cultural input Bollywood cannot be what it is; and yet the texts through which that culture is signified also exhausts that very culture, confining it in expressive terms, to just one form. When the form is reinterpreted through what Rajadhyaksha had called a 'techno-realism', where the sites of the culture are 'simulacrally' displaced, as happens in the highly finessed 2006 remake of *Umrao Jaan* (J.P. Dutta, India), then the legacy of the genre itself is strained, its centrality misplaced. Where Muzaffar Ali's *Umrao Jaan* made a statement about the necessity as well as the tragedy of the courtesan in Muslim high culture, the 2006 version transforms her into a pious, uncontaminated figure of sentimental remorse, in effect replacing the character by the star Aishwarya Rai who, pending marriage to Abhishek Bachchan, must be 'pure' on- and off-screen. We need to keep in mind the 1981 version so as to remember that for a genealogy of Bollywood the Muslim as expressed in the canonical genre is pivotal: it is the Muslim and her language and culture that have mediated what has come to be known as Bollywood.

MELODRAMA: THE TEXTS OF *DEVDAS*

If Parsi theatre provided Bollywood with a narrative structure, a mode of representation, songs, dialogues, and a repertoire of cast, and Muslim culture provided poetry, a courtly language, and the figure of the dancer-courtesan, it was English/colonial melodrama, suitably indigenized with *rasas* (notably of love-longing and the tragic) that gave Bollywood its distinctive content. We can follow this through the singular achievement of *Devdas* (1935) and its later remakes. The person who was instrumental in giving a definitive form to the figure of the melodramatic hero was Pramathesh Chandra Barua, often referred to as Prince P.C. Barua, the son of a ruler of a tiny native state in Bengal-Assam. However, given that his father was, in fact, nothing more than a large landowner (Nandy, 2001: 140), the title of prince was not a little misplaced. His life, though, was anything but simple, expressing a mixture of oedipal longings (he had his first solid food at the age of nine – one imagines he survived on nothing but milk up to this time!) and guilt. At the age of 14, he married a girl of 11 (Madhurilata), had many unhappy affairs, married four times in total (the last of which remained secret to the end) and was struck by tuberculosis (seen then as very much the disease that affected artists, rich in a kind of Bloomsbury cultural excess). All these items added to his melodramatic persona and mystique. His visit to England in 1926, after his mother's death a year earlier, was clearly a defining moment in sharpening his sense of exile, and released his nascent nationalism. A key motif in his films therefore became the idea of the journey, and here Saratchandra Chattopadhyay's (Chatterjee's) 1917 novel *Devdas* (2002), the film's source, was the perfect text.[18]

The novel's success lay in the manner in which Chattopadhyay adapted the English/European 'man of feeling' novels, so popular in colonial Bengal, to local conditions. In this rewriting the sentimentalist Devdas is a man who cannot translate love into action, who cannot come to terms with the nature of commitment and passion, and, when his beloved, Paro, against all feudal decorum, seeks him out in his own bedroom in the quiet of the night, he can only respond like a helpless victim of the social order, alternating between a fear of what people would say and his own unease at the strength of this forthright woman. But here is the Indian melodramatic sublime: denial of love does not lead to its transfer to another; nor does it lead to an alternative act of compensation; rather it leads to a defiant death-wish, the oceanic feeling, as if the world order itself would come to an end in this act of self-sacrifice.

Barua himself played the role of the doomed lover Devdas in the original Bengali version of the film – indecisive, sentimental and flooded with a death-wish. As an actor Barua embodied the post-Parsi theatre idea of the hero – handsome, seemingly androgynous, romantic and extremely fair; he was the sort of actor who could cross-dress as a woman in Parsi *dāstāns* (which were often *dard bharī dāstāns*, 'tales imbued with sentimentality'). Barua's Devdas was immensely popular and quickly reached a pan-Indian audience through the almost simultaneous production of the 1935 Hindi version, in which the great singer K.L. Saigal replaced Barua as Devdas – unsatisfactorily, according to some.[19]

But the moment of *Devdas* also signals Bollywood's debt to the realist-sentimental novel. Indeed, what Barua did was bring Sarachandra Chattopadhyay's novel, a colonial literary form, self-evidently bourgeois and different from the texts of Parsi theatre, into cinema. Four films may be mentioned here before we return to Bollywood's take on *Devdas*. The first, *Andaz* (*A Matter of Style*, Mehboob Khan, India, 1949), expressing the first burst of postcolonial enthusiasm, explores the uneasy relationship between tradition and modernity and its incommensurability in a postcolonial world in transition. At the centre of the story once again is the theme of desire for a woman, Nina (Nargis), on the part of a sentimental hero, Dilip (Dilip Kumar), who is in fact an Indian from the diaspora in Africa. The latter is contrasted with the dandy-*flâneur* figure of Rajan (Raj Kapoor), who is the woman's lover and who returns from the imperial metropolis of London to claim her.

The second, *Sangdil* (*The Stone-hearted*, R.C. Talwar, India, 1952), indigenizes David O. Selznick and Robert Stevenson's *Jane Eyre* (US, 1944), while keeping a little *film noir* camerawork. In the Bollywood version, Jane/Kamla (Madhubala) ends up not at the Lowood correctional school, but in a school for temple dancers. She comes to 'Thornfield' as part of a group of temple dancers and meets Rochester/Shekhar (Dilip Kumar) in similar circumstances – he too falls off his horse. But, as Jeffrey Sconce has noted in his readings of the film versions of *Jane Eyre*, 'the re-articulations of the "work" [the novel] as a new "text" [the film], one consonant with the medium's dominant signifying practices, produced an adaptation that rejected the work's authoritative meaning and replaced it instead with an authoritative mode of narrativity' (2001: 516). And it is this authoritative mode of an incipient (Bollywood) narrativity that explains the location of Jane/Kamla not in Lowood School, but in a temple; it also explains, via Parsi theatre, the use of the Gypsy scene in which Rochester/Shekhar, in the novel, cross-dresses so as to suggest to Jane (as a *deus ex machina*) that she get out of her monotonous life. In the Hollywood version this scene is never filmed; in *Sangdil* it is, but with the difference that Rochester/Shekhar dresses up as a male fortune-teller (a fakir), a not uncommon subplot or device to advance the narrative in Parsi theatre and Bollywood generally. The form survives, in a displaced manner, even in pure Bollywood – in a slick, avowedly cosmopolitan and diaspora-targeted film such as *Kal Ho Naa Ho* where the disguised fortune-teller of *Sangdil* comes as the angelic figure Aman (Shah Rukh Khan) to bring joy into the life and family of the New York-based Jane Eyre, Naina Catherine Kapur, and her family. Yet, unlike the Selznick/Stevenson film and the Charlotte Brontë original, Jane/Kamla in *Sangdil* does not enter the patriarchal order, produce a son and witness Rochester regain his sight. In *Sangdil*, with the first Mrs Rochester dead and Thornfield burnt down, the final shot is of the blind Rochester/Shekhar in the arms of Jane/Kamla. In this indigenization of a canonical book and film, the prominent use of song and dance in the *mise en scène* also draws on the mobilization of these performative elements in Parsi theatre.

A third film is *Anhonee* (*The Impossible*, India, 1952). This explores director K.A. Abbas' interest in geneticism versus determinism, a theme which he had, as screenwriter, canvassed in Raj Kapoor's *Awara* (India, 1951). More crucially though, this film, as in the case of *Andaz*, is also a narrative of modernity. Here Roop (Nargis) inherits her father's empire but is torn between correcting her sister Mohini's (Nargis) depraved former life as a courtesan (which could have been her life as the babies were swapped at birth), by making her an equal partner, and her own desire for the lawyer Raj Kumar Saxena (Raj Kapoor), whom both sisters love. In *Andaz* the resolution deprives both Dilip (who is shot) and Nina (who is convicted of murder) of their freedom. In *Anhonee*, Mohini (the courtesan, who is, in fact, genetically the rightful heir, as she was born within wedlock) shoots herself with her father's pistol in a suggestively resonant reversal of Goethe's archetypal sentimentalist

Werther, who shoots himself with a pistol touched by the hands of his beloved Charlotte.

Our fourth film, *Chalti Ka Naam Gadi* (*That which Goes is Life*, Satyen Bose, India, 1958), Bollywood's finest comedy, again raises questions of modernity but this time within the genre of comedy. In an extended song sequence structured as a dream, Kishore Kumar parodies Parsi theatre, Nautanki and classical *ragas* to locate cinema in a longer tradition of performances, even as the film ambiguously struggles to create a specifically Indian middle-class modernity that continues to be marked by its colonial heritage. It is that transitional period between colonial and postcolonial modernities which energized the early works of Guru Dutt, Bombay cinema's finest auteur, notably *Aar Paar* (India, 1954) and *Mr and Mrs 55* (India, 1955).

We return to *Devdas*. For anyone with even a modicum of knowledge of Bollywood, there is always excitement when this film is mentioned. There are three pertinent versions of *Devdas* in any construction of a Bollywood genealogy. First, and as we have already indicated, there is the Hindi Barua version of *Devdas*, in which the lead role is played by K.L. Saigal, and Barua himself has a minor role as Paro's stepson. P.C. Barua's 1935 version is remembered because it has the merit of being the first. It also featured the inimitable singer K.L. Saigal as Devdas and if nothing else, this fact alone may explain why the 1935 version has a rather special aura. Then, twenty years later, Bimal Roy (who was Barua's cameraman) made another *Devdas* following the narrative of the novel even more closely and acknowledging the power of the precursor filmic text in his dedication: 'In memory of P.C. Barua and K.L. Saigal'. Although artistically the most accomplished, to this day this version does not have the Bollywood mythology that has grown around the original Hindi version: the aristocratic and sensitive director P.C. Barua, the near alcoholic K.L. Saigal, who, it was said, could only sing when drunk, the music of Timir Baran (who, many years later, also composed the music for *Baadbaan* [Phani Majumbar, India, 1954] best known for the classic song *kaise koi jiye*), and, if memory does not betray me, the background singing of the blind K.C. Dey. But the Bimal Roy version starred Dilip Kumar as Devdas. Over a short period of time, Dilip Kumar had created a persona out of the melodramatic hero – in films such as *Andaz*, *Babul* (S.U. Sunny, India, 1950), *Deedar* (Nitin Bose, India, 1951), *Daag* (Amiya Chakrabarty, India, 1952), all made between 1949 and 1952 – so much so that he was very much identified as the definitive melodramatic actor. In *Devdas*, he finally had the kind of material that was perfect for him, the sort of material where everything is contained within the self and where self-denial is both self-pity as well as the height of selfishness. The rough edges of Saigal's Devdas were reshaped and given final form. There could be no Devdas (at least not in Hindi cinema) after Dilip Kumar, although this has never been acknowledged, given the almost god-like status of Barua among Bengalis.[20] And then, finally, there is Sanjay Leela Bhansali's *Devdas* (India, 2003), a film which may be read as pure 'Bollywood' in terms of Rajadhyaksha's definition. It is a crucial text which may be critically examined via a central question: How does Hindi/Bombay cinema become Bollywood?

Devdas is the single most important narrative of the melodramatic hero in Bollywood: its success reflects both an Indian excess of sentimentality and the impact of the melodramatic Werther-figure on the colonial Bengali imagination, a sentiment captured so well in the classic Bollywood song of the sentimental hero: '*satāyegā kise tū āsmān jab ham nahīṃ homge*' ('Who will you torture, O ye gods, when I'm no longer around?'). Devdas seeks out death and, after what can only be called a melancholic journey of life, finds it at the doorstep of Paro, now married to a much older but immensely rich widower. But, of course, the feudal order cannot countenance a woman outside of the walls of the mansion and the doors close on her even as she rushes out to meet her one and only beloved. The world, we know, never changes, but the melodramatic hero always believes that it will after his own

death (as in the song cited above). Sigmund Freud would have called this an incomplete mourning, a mourning that seeks out the oceanic sublime because it is denied the law of reason. But Bollywood cinema would not be Bollywood without the Devdas figure. And while elsewhere the form is dead, in Bollywood it thrives, although not necessarily with the fulsome narrative of a *Devdas*.

Bansali's *Devdas* is Bollywood in the third millennium, inheritor of a more specialized, identifiable style that began to emerge in the final decade of the twentieth century. It required stars to dance and if there are two, both should come together in a competitive dance. Third-millennium Bollywood requires that matters are spelled out: metaphors are not restricted to a song; they must be demonstrated visually. So, whereas in *Aag* (*Fire/Desire*, Raj Kapoor, India, 1948) the melancholic hero sings '*jaltā huā diyā hūm magar rośnī nahīm*' ('I am a burning candle that sheds no light') and insinuates through metaphor an impossible love, Bhansali's Paro (Aishwarya Rai) must hold on to an everlasting flame to signify her equally tragic love for Devdas (Shah Rukh Khan). Visual splendour overtakes a poetics of suggestiveness, of *vyanga*, and dialogue displaces the glance (in the 1955 version Paro [Suchitra Sen] and Chandramukhi's [Vijayantimala] gaze meet and part without recognition). Bhansali, therefore, defers to Bollywood and the homage is not so much to *Devdas* (and to Saratchandra Chattopadhyay, P.C. Barua and Bimal Roy, as the credits declare), but to Bollywood, to what is circulating now as *Bombay Dreams*. This is the film's success: contemporary Bollywood comes to *Devdas* and takes it over, modelling it in its own image.

The 1955 Bimal Roy version demonstrated cinematic fidelity to the original. This was necessary given the politics of representing the Barua original, for which Bimal Roy was the cameraman. For Bollywood, the fidelity is not to an earlier form, but to its own postmodern, simulacral modes of representation. Nevertheless, the case of Bhansali's *Devdas* shows that, even as Bollywood grows out of the new cultural logic of late modernity and its diasporic investments, the old Bombay Cinema still stalks it: its grand syntagm casts a long shadow, its foundational narratives are never forgotten.

There is much else to tell in any discussion of the genealogy of Bollywood – mythologies, the epic tradition, theories of aesthetic response (especially *rasa*), the rise of the spectacle (in films like *Aan* [Mehboob Khan, India, 1952] and *Mughal-e-Azam*), the *A Thousand and One Nights*-inspired fantasies of Homi Wadia, the links between ideology and cinema, especially cinema's construction of the Indian nation – but space precludes. But I do want to comment on an ideological impossibility in Bollywood, even as we concede the power of tradition. I have suggested that the 'feel-good-about-the-nation' message of Bollywood is directed primarily towards the diaspora. However, India also faces the contradictions that capitalism has brought into the social sphere and this renders that message ambiguous. Even as Bollywood endorses the diasporic myths of uncontaminated homelands, it also situates the impossibility of one of its central motifs, the motif of Mother India. I want to conclude with this problematic.

BOLLYWOOD AND THE DEATH OF MOTHER INDIA: *CHANDNI BAR*

The great text of Bollywood cinema is Mehboob Khan's *Mother India* (India, 1957), which is really a text not in the singular, but in the plural as, in any retrospective reading of it, one is conscious of the director's original version *Aurat* (*Woman*, India, 1940) and, marginally, his *Son of India* (India, 1962) too. But we must also consider the iconic sign of Mother India, which is endlessly reprised in culture. We recall Rushdie's narrator in *The Moor's Last Sigh*, who says: 'In *Mother India*, a piece of Hindu myth-making directed by a Muslim socialist, Mehboob Khan, the Indian peasant woman is idealized as bride, mother and producer of sons; as long-suffering, stoical, loving, redemptive and conservatively wedded to the maintenance of the status

quo' (1995: 138–9). The triumph is not so straightforward, as any deconstruction of the film shows. Even without such a deconstruction, a contradiction is implicit in the text from the outset, as the Marxist logo of the Mehboob Khan film is framed by a voice-over that affirms the power of destiny: *'vohī hotā hai jo manzūr-e-khudā hotā hai'* ('In the end only that which is destined by God happens'). Nevertheless, the central dharmik ideology of the film as suggested by Rushdie's narrator has remained the centrepiece of popular Indian cinema, and the figure of the Mother looms large.

Late modernity in postcolonial India, though, tells a different story, as it blasts open the contradictions that were glossed over in *Mother India*, its precursors and avatars. Mehboob Khan himself alludes to them in the film he made five years after *Mother India*. This film, *Son of India*, has a contemporary setting. The congruence – missing from *Mother India*, which comes into the present only at the end – led Mehboob Khan to rethink many of the fixed categories of social behaviour at the heart of *Mother India* and its precursor *Aurat*. In *Son of India* the 'Mother India' figure is Kamla (Kumkum), the daughter of an extremely rich industrialist, who manages to combine tradition with modernity (*bharat natyam* plus rock 'n' roll), and marries for love Kishore (Kamaljeet), a modern man who is rejected by her father. Kishore has a shady background, but the power of love transforms him and he becomes a devoted father and husband. But the world is no longer ideal, as political chicanery and the power of underworld dons from Bombay separate Kishore from Kamla and their child Gopal (Sajjid). The narrative then shifts its centre from husband-wife domestic tensions to the function of a child in society. As the title of the film indicates it is the 'son of India', the young child Gopal, who becomes the figure around whom Mehboob Khan creates his new narrative of Indian modernity: the child carries the consciousness of the new nation in the interface of tradition and modernity. The child actor (now a little older) is none other than the boy of five who played the role of rebellious

Birju when young in *Mother India*. At ten he is now the promise of the future, and the film moves away from the centrality of the Mother in culture to the political and social role of the child in India. But to use the actor, Master Sajjid, who played the role of the adolescent Birju (who grows up to become the anti-dharmik revolutionary played by Sunil Dutt in *Mother India*) overcodes the narrative, as the spectator (who had taken the side of Birju in *Mother India* against his dharmik mother) now reads the erstwhile rebellious son as the sign of redemption. The claim is maintained tenuously as the historical time of *Son of India* does not lend itself to an absolutist representation of Mother India.

The film I wish to examine as an instance of the impossibility of 'Mother India' in terms of Bollywood is *Chandni Bar* (*Moonlit Bar*, Madhur Bhandarkar, India, 2001), a film which takes on the two narratives of redemption found in *Mother India* and *Son of India*. In both, the acts of the mother and the child, respectively, are presented as national allegories, the former declaring one kind of eternal dharma (which required a mother to shoot her rebellious son), the latter declaring, through the figure of a judge, the necessity of a just and democratic society built around children, albeit children who believe in the dharmik order as sanctioned by God. That these narratives remain illusions in capitalist India is shown with unusual force in the quite remarkable film, *Chandni Bar*. This film too has its origins in peasant India and is presented, as *Mother India* was, as a memorial reconstruction.

The voice-over here is that of Mumtaz (Tabbu), who has seen her family slaughtered in the communal Hindu-Muslim riots in Sitapur (Uttar Pradesh) in 1985. The film traces her history from that year to 2000, some sixteen years in all. Mumtaz and her uncle (her *māmu*) leave for Bombay and take shelter in one of the Muslim *bastis*, thanks to a relative, Iqbal Chamdi (Rajpal Yadav). In Bombay she is persuaded by her uncle to work as a dancing girl in Chandni Bar, an uninspiring drinking hole for shady money-changers, and one frequented by the thugs of underworld bosses. Raped by her uncle, Mumtaz gradually accepts her lot as a prostitute, ending up marrying Potya (Atul Kulkarni), an underworld functionary with a violent temper. Within a year or two of their marriage, just before the birth of their second child, Potya is killed by the police as part of a deal Potya's underworld boss cuts with them. Mumtaz is determined to ensure that her children, Abhay (Vishal Thakkar) and Payal (Minakshi Sahani), grow up to be respectable citizens, but they don't. Social pressures and Mumtaz's prior history give her no escape; indeed her boss at Chandni Bar, Anna (Abhay Bhargav), warns her against crossing class boundaries and reminds her that there can be neither return to the certainties of the village nor to a life of respectability. But Mumtaz, like the erstwhile Mother India, persists in her efforts in spite of hints all round her. Early in the film after she had joined Chandni Bar, one of the dancing girls, who is married and wishes to have a child, is told by her pimp-husband, '*mother india bhāṣan mat de; sālī mā bannā cāhti hai*' ('Don't give me the Mother India bullshit; the bitch wants to be a mother'). Mumtaz survives, her illusions remaining intact until 2000, by which time her son is 15, her daughter 13. The police charge Abhay with extortion and he is raped by two other juveniles while in custody. Although Abhay is innocent, the police have not forgiven his father Potya for killing one of their informants. Mumtaz has to bribe the police and must raise 75,000 rupees, a third of which is beyond her capacity. She sleeps with her former customers in an effort to get the money, while her barely adolescent daughter raises the difference by selling her virginity at Chandni Bar. Abhay is released, but recent events have traumatized him. With gun in hand and Mumtaz running after him, Abhay guns down his two rapists as his mother watches. And without pausing, the gun still in his hand, he walks away, as his mother cries a long unbroken cry of death, a primal scream. Payal becomes Mumtaz the dancer/call-girl of Chandni Bar; Abhay, the son, his father Potya. There can be no return to 'Mother India'.

The film has enormous power, the intensity is unrelieved, the narrative uncompromising; like *Othello*, it has very little subplot as such. The spectator undergoes an experience that is cathartic, for no theory of Sanskrit poetics (not even the *rasa* of *karunā*) provides an adequate theory for this kind of emotional reception. Apart from the obvious reference to the impossibility of recovering the past of *Mother India*, the diegesis in the film focuses on phallic power and the abuse of women's bodies. The call-girls have their own solidarity, but it is an ineffectual solidarity against the combined power of police brutality and the underworld. But the discourse of both patriarchy and police is no different from the discourse of India generally: the defiled woman cannot gain respectability, a call-girl can never be a wife (*patni*); she is always a concubine (a *rakhel*), the woman of the *koṭhā*, the Muslim courtesan; her children too must follow in the footsteps of their parents. At one point, a movie being shown at the Minerva Cinema is mentioned: Raj Kapoor's last film *Ram Teri Ganga Maili* (*Lord Rama, Your Ganges is Polluted*, India, 1985), an obsessive study of purity defiled by modernity, but a telling critique, in its title, of the Indian world order. The popular Bombay film is present in other ways too, principally as background songs to which the call-girls in Chandni Bar dance.

What takes me to *Chandni Bar* is the end of the myth of Mother India, which now functions as myth only in the diaspora; but it is a myth without a text, for if there are Bollywood texts of it (a theme that Bollywood eschews), they will have to take the form of *Chandni Bar*. Given its uncompromising portrayal of the end of the myth – Nargis' songs in *Mother India*, from '*duniyā me ham āyeṃ haiṃ to jīnā hi paṛegā*' to '*dharti pukārti hai laut ke ā*' ('In this world one has to live' to 'This earth calls you back'), once so redeeming and optimistic, can only exist as a narrative of loss and as a primal cry with which the film ends – *Chandni Bar* effectively plays out the impossibility of the original myth of the mother. So Bollywood can either make the anti-myth (as it does in *Chandni Bar*), or reformulate it as an absence in the diaspora to be remembered but without a (contemporary) text.

IN THE BEGINNING WAS MY END

In the beginning were the mythologies, which carried the narratives of the epics and *purānas* mediated through Parsi theatre. The codes of dharma that underpinned these myths persisted as cinema entered modernity and began to define the nation state. Even the texts that threw up the contradictions of the making of the nation within capitalism (*Awara* locating itself uncomfortably between Indian geneticism and socialist determinism; *Gumrah* [B.R. Chopra, India, 1963] trying to confront modernist sexual politics while keeping traditional family values intact) carried the idioms of the dharmik tradition and upheld its time-honoured values. The latter informed the spectacles too (*Aan, Mughal-e-Azam*). Now there is Bollywood, which clearly cannot exist outside of the genealogy I have outlined; neither, however, can it replicate the essence of its early forms in the way that the 1955 *Devdas* had repeated Barua's 1935 rendition. Rajadhyaksha is correct in locating Bollywood as an industry which has grown out of the logic of the forces of late capitalism, with aims which are primarily postmodern. My point is that Bollywood is both the earlier cinema and its impossibility; it cannot exist without the prior syntagm; but it cannot replicate it either. It cannot reproduce *Mother India* (except as *Chandni Bar*), even as it memorializes India via a diasporic eye. It is a contradiction that Bollywood cannot resolve, largely because it is now becoming pure form (we recall *Swades, Kal Ho Naa Ho, Parineeta* or, more narrowly, Aishwarya Rai's modernist '*kajarā re*' dance of the courtesan in *Bunty Aur Babli* [Shaad Ali Sahgal, India, 2005]) emptied of its contents. The computer image – the simulacral absolute – takes over from the image as ideology. To resolve that contradiction, Bollywood has to create its own impossibility in the shape of *Chandni Bar*: a film that both blasts open Bollywood's outward show of dharmik ideals and demonstrates fractures inherent in its form.

NOTES

1 The ascendancy of Bollywood has been such that in the Mauritian writer Dev Virahsawmy's Creole play *Toufann* (which premiered in Mauritius in 1995 and then again in an English version in December 1999), the writer names one of the characters, a junkie, Dammarro, and suggests via this naming the growing cultural pull of Bollywood Cinema in Indo-Mauritian culture. High on ganja, Dammarro relapses into the song, 'Dam marro dam! Hare Krishna, hare Ram' (Virahsawmy, 2001: 225). What Dammarro recalls are lines from a well-known song in the Bollywood film *Hare Rama Hare Krishna* (Dev Anand, India, 1971): 'dam māro dam mit jāyem ham bolo subha sām hare kṛiṣṇa hare rām'.

2 See, for instance, *Weekend Australian*, 28–9 October 2006:

'Gandhigiri is the latest magic mantra inspiring unusual protests and discussion with a difference', *The Hindu* noted. The BBC reported the film had inspired poor farmers in Maharashtra to garland a bank manager with flowers to persuade him to disperse loans. Reuters reported a girl breaking up with her boyfriend for making whistling noises at a waiter, considered disrespectful according to Gandhigiri. The *Gulf Times* said a university professor offered flowers to his vice-chancellor to prevent his suspension for having an affair with a young student. (2006: 32)

3 Formed in 1989 by Kristine Landon-Smith and Sudha Bhuchar, the Tamasha Theatre Company has produced a number of plays. Perhaps best known among them is their 1997 production, *East is East*, which was made into a film two years later (Damien O'Donnell, UK, 1999).

4 The *TimeOut* essay 'Hooray for Bollywood' by Tom Charity mentions that the film *Asoka* was released in mainstream cinema houses (2001: 14–18). The transformation of old cinema halls into multiple cinema complexes devoted exclusively to Bollywood cinema (Southall's 1920s *Liberty Cinema* into *Himalaya Palace*, is an example) is now a not-uncommon feature of the British cinemascape. *Inter alia, Asian Woman* (UK) claims to be the 'biggest Asian Magazine in the world' (see Biswas, 2000).

5 It should be noted that whereas Bombay can be renamed Mumbai, no one has made the suggestion that Bollywood (Bombay + Hollywood) should now be renamed Mollywood (Mumbai + Hollywood). In defence it may be argued that Tamil cinema styles

itself 'Mollywood' anyway (Madras + Hollywood), but here again the city's name has also been changed to Chennai.

6 As Ian Hamilton writes, 'It [the consumption of popular cultural texts] seems to have been much the same with films, if we can judge from Rushdie's habit of peppering books with allusions to American and to local "Bollywood" extravaganzas' (1995–6: 93). See also Rushdie (1991); Mishra (2007, pp. 11–28).

7 An Internet entry for this film tells us that the early scenes of this film were shot at Launch Pad 39A, Kennedy Space Center, Florida – a first for an Indian film. Available at: http://www.nasa.gov/missions/shuttle/f-swades.html.

8 Available at: http://www1.yashrajfilms.com; http://www.vinodchopra.com/chrono1.html.

9 Patel's own 1940 commentary on V. Shantaram's classic socialist-realist *Aadmi* (India, 1939), in which he drew connections between the film and Robert Sherwood's *Waterloo Bridge* (US, 1931) and another, written in 1957, on Mehboob Khan's *Mother India* are exemplary in this regard.

10 For *Filmfare*, see the fanzine's website, available at: http://www.filmfare.com.

11 The magazine's circulation in English is 125,000; in Gujarati (1987-), 75,000; in Hindi (1985-), 30,000.

12 In films such as *Viruddh* global labels (Pepsi, for instance) are prominently displayed.

13 This is the sort of challenge that the great Gary Sobers took when he declared on the final afternoon of the Fourth Test against England in the 1967–8 test series. Sobers knew that there was no way his team could dismiss England in 165 minutes, and miscalculated England's ability to make the required 215 runs to win, which they did. But the point is that the declaration was an act of defiance against conventional establishment logic; Sobers used cricket to make a counterstatement about West Indian postcolonial difference and self-confidence. He uncoupled cricket from its colonialist practices. He also brought life back into what had been, until then, three very dull and drawn-out Test matches.

14 For their children and grandchildren who, although born 'elsewhere', also consume Bollywood, its value is only as a reminder of the sublime otherness of their being.

15 A paradox most profoundly explored in many of Guru Dutt's masterpieces, in which a colonial modernity is inscribed within the body of postcolonial difference as in *Aar Paar* and *Mr and Mrs 55*.

16 Aishwarya Rai and Abhishek Bachchan were married, after more elaborate rituals which also involved the appeasement of various Gods and saints (both Hindu and Sufi), on 20 April 2007.

17 The granting of a boon, even at the expense of great personal loss, has its textual antecedent in the *Rāmāyaṇa*, where King Dasaratha gives his kingdom to Prince Bharata and banishes his eldest son and heir to the throne, Rama, because Keikeyi,

the mother of Prince Bharata and the king's prettiest wife, demanded that boons given to her by the King must be honoured.

18 Saratchandra Chattopadhyay was alive when P.C. Barua made both the Bengali and Hindi versions in 1935.

19 There is a direct link between the Bombay auteur Guru Dutt and Barua, for in Guru Dutt's films sensibility is also rendered impotent by urban modernity, from which escape is often sought in the arms of the courtesan-cum-mother figure, as in *Pyaasa* (*The Thirsty One*, India, 1957). In artistic terms, Guru Dutt's films may be seen as modern India entering the Parsi theatre, as identities are refashioned in response to new demands, consolidating cinema 'as a form of self-expression in Indian society' (Nandy, 2001: 148). But the country's subject cannot return home, as is made so painfully clear in *Devdas* and its later versions, including Raj Kapoor's original version of *Aah* (Raja Nawathe/Raj Kapoor, India, 1953).

20 Most Bengalis, however, have never accepted any version as being equal to the Barua original, since Barua himself came to be seen as the embodiment of the character Devdas, which in fact meant that no one could play that role except Barua himself. It is said that Bengali actors (Uttam Kumar, for one) have refused to act the part.

REFERENCES

Biswas, Moushumi (2000) 'Indian Popular cinema', *Sunday Pioneer*, 8 October: 13.

Charity, Tom (2001) 'Hooray for Bollywood', *TimeOut*, 10–17 October: 14–18.

Chattopadhyay (Chatterjee), Saratchandra (2002) *Devdas*. Tr. Sreejata Guha. New Delhi: Penguin.

Desai, Jigna (2003) *Beyond Bollywood: The Cultural Politics of South Asian Diasporic Film*. New York: Routledge.

Dwyer, Rachel (2001) 'Shooting Stars: The Indian Film Magazine, *Stardust*', in Rachel Dwyer and Christopher Pinney (eds), *Pleasure and the Nation: The History, Politics and Consumption of Public Culture in India*. Delhi: Oxford University Press. pp. 247–85.

Dwyer, Rachel (2006) 'Real and Imagined Audiences: *Lagaan* and the Hindi Film after the 1990s', in Martina Ghosh-Schellhorn and Vera Alexander (eds), *Peripheral Centres, Central Peripheries*. Berlin: Lit. pp. 223–41.

Dwyer, Rachel and Patel, Divia (2002) *Cinema India: The Visual Culture of Hindi Film*. London: Reaktion Books.

Economic Times (Chennai) (2007) 'Indian Film Industry', 1 January: 14.

Filmfare (2007) 'Lage Raho Munna Bhai', January: 111.

Gopinath, Gayatri (2005) *Impossible Desires: Queer Diasporas and South Asian Public Cultures*. Durham, NC: Duke University Press.

Hamilton, Ian (1995–96) 'The First Life of Salman Rushdie', *The New Yorker*, 25 December–1 January: 90–113.

Hansen, Kathryn (2001) 'The *Indar Sabha* Phenomenon: Public Theatre and Consumption in Greater India (1853–1956)', in Rachel Dwyer and Christopher Pinney (eds), *Pleasure and the Nation: The History, Politics and Consumption of Public Culture in India*. Delhi: Oxford University Press. pp. 76–114.

Hansen, Kathryn (2003) 'Languages on Stage: Linguistic Pluralism and Community Formation in the Nineteenth-Century Parsi Theatre', *Modern Asian Studies*, 37(2): 381–405.

Jameson, Fredric (1991) *Postmodernism, or, The Cultural Logic of Late Capitalism*. Durham, NC: Duke University Press.

Laccarino, Clara (2005) 'Bollywood', *Sun Herald*, 11 September: S34.

Lazarus, Neil (1999) *Nationalism and Cultural Practice in the Postcolonial World*. Cambridge: Cambridge University Press.

Mehta, Suketu (2004) *Maximum City: Bombay Lost and Found*. New York: Knopf.

Mishra, Vijay (2002) *Bollywood Cinema: Temples of Desire*. New York: Routledge.

Mishra, Vijay (2007) 'Salman Rushdie and Bollywood Cinema', in Abdulrazak Gurnah (ed.), *The Cambridge Companian to Salman Rushdie*. Cambridge: Cambridge University Press. pp. 11–28.

Nandy, Ashish (2001) 'Invitation to an Antique Death: The Journey of Pramathesh Barua as the Origin of the Terribly Effeminate, Maudlin, and Self-destructive Heroes of Indian Cinema', in Rachel Dwyer and Christopher Pinney (eds), *Pleasure and the Nation: The History, Politics and Consumption of Public Culture in India*. Delhi: Oxford University Press. pp. 139–60.

Prasad, Madhava (2003) 'The Name of a Desire: Why They Call It Bollywood', *Unsettling Cinema: A Symposium on the Place of Cinema in India*, 525. Available at: http://www.india-seminar.com/2003/525.

Rajadhyaksha, Ashish (2003) 'The "Bollywoodization" of the Indian Cinema: Cultural Nationalism in a Global Arena', *Inter-Asia Cultural Studies*, 4(1): 25–39.

Rushdie, Salman (1991) *Imaginary Homelands: Essays and Criticism 1981–1991*. London: Granta Books.

Rushdie, Salman (1995) *The Moor's Last Sigh*. London: Jonathan Cape.

Rushdie, Salman (2005) *Shalimar the Clown*. London: Jonathan Cape.

Sconce, Jeffrey (2001) 'The Cinematic Reconstruction of *Jane Eyre*', in Charlotte Brontë, *Jane Eyre*. Ed. Richard J. Dunn. New York: W.W. Norton. pp. 515–22.

Times of India (2007) 'Bollywood News', 16 January: 15.

Thussu, Daya Kishan (forthcoming, 2008) 'The Globalization of "Bollywood" – the Hype and the Hope', in Anandam P. Kavoori and Aswin Punathambekar (eds), *The Bollywood Reader*. New York: New York University Press.

Vassanji, M.G. (1994) *The Book of Secrets*. Toronto: McClelland & Stewart.

Virahsawmy, Dev (2001) *Toufann: A Mauritian Fantasy*, in Martin Banham, James Gibbs and Femi Osofisan (eds), *African Theatre: Playwrights and Politics*. Tr. Nisha Walling and Michael Walling. Oxford: James Currey. pp. 217–54.

Žižek, Slavoj (2002) *For They Know not What They Do: Enjoyment as a Political Factor*. London: Verso.

31

Film in the Context of Digital Media

Scott McQuire

In 1997, as the extended celebrations of the first centenary of cinema were winding down, I undertook a research project examining the impact of digital technology on Australian film production (see McQuire, 1997). One of the most striking features of the several dozen interviews I conducted that year was that everyone I talked to – from leading directors, cinematographers, editors and those involved in various aspects of post-production, to producers and film educators – was unanimous that future cinema would no longer depend on film. While the time-frame for such a transition varied, no one doubted the trajectory towards cinema without celluloid. A decade on, much has changed, but film is still with us. Recalling this is not to suggest that the prognosis about filmless cinema was wrong, but to acknowledge that the transition to digital cinema has proved far more complex than was initially imagined.

Digitizing cinema has demanded the reinvention of basic aspects of film production, while simultaneously altering the experience of watching film, both in terms of what

audiences see and hear, and how it might be delivered. It has also demanded a fundamental re-examination of the way the film industry functions as a business. The fact that the transition to digital cinema has occurred as part of a broader agenda of globalization manifested in accelerated transnational flows of cultural content and heightened conflict over intellectual property multiplies the dimensions at play. In the digital era of convergent media, film content is increasingly imbricated not only with television, video and DVD, but the Internet, video games and mobile devices. Add to this mix the way that online databases and new forms of storage and distribution are altering access to films as objects of both fan culture and scholarly analysis, and the full scope of current change becomes more apparent. Traditional Film Studies questions concerning authorship, narrative, style and subjectivity have increasingly been supplemented by analyses of the exigencies of transnational markets and global franchises, the logistics of new delivery systems and the politics of 'piracy', the emergence of new cultural forms and the promises of interactivity. Is it any wonder that a common lament within Film Studies over the last decade has been the 'disappearance of the object'?

From its inception, the film industry has been a site of constant technological innovation. Nevertheless, looking beyond the undoubted hype around what Vincent Mosco (2004) aptly calls the digital sublime, there is something distinctive in the magnitude of change affecting the film industry in the present. Many innovations in film technology, such as changes in film stock, lighting or lenses, have been incremental. Others, such as the introduction of colour film or 16mm cameras had a broader impact on film style and aesthetics. Prior to digitization, the most far-reaching technological transformation of the film industry was arguably the introduction of synchronized sound, which cut across various industry sectors including production and exhibition, producing a markedly different narrative style and audience experience, while short-circuiting the incipient internationalism of silent film in favour of the dominance of linguistically-based national cinemas. However, the impact of the digital threshold is demonstrably wider than all previous technological shifts. It not only affects all sectors of the industry simultaneously, from production through distribution to exhibition, but the broader context established by digital convergence means that the boundaries of film – its status as a distinctive cultural entity – is up for grabs in a new way.

In the following I want to examine the influences of digital technology on key changes occurring in the film industry. I begin with an overview of the way film production and post-production were digitized, and then discuss current moves in distribution and exhibition. I then focus on issues of security, intellectual property and piracy, before turning to debates over aesthetics and film scholarship in the digital era. Running through all these issues is the emergence of a new economic structure for the film industry in the digital era.

PRODUCTION

Prior to the 1980s, computers were largely ignored by the film industry. A few independent filmmakers such as Malcolm Le Grice (2001) conducted experiments in 'computer film art'. The mainstream uses were the relatively few images that fitted narrative demands (the 'Death Star' simulation in *Star Wars* [George Lucas, US, 1977], the ship's computer screen in *Alien* [Ridley Scott, UK, 1979]), and title sequences (beginning with *Superman* [Richard Donner, UK, 1978]) constructed by what was then called computer graphics. Nor were the first experiments in integrating computer-generated images (CGI) with live action such as *TRON* (Steven Lisberger, US/Taiwan, 1982) or *The Last Starfighter* (Nick Castle, US, 1984) particularly promising. As Brad Fisher put it, 'The problem was that digital technology was both comparatively slow and prohibitively expensive. In fact, workstations capable of performing at film resolution were driven by Cray supercomputers' (1993b: 52; see also 1993a).

However, even as the initial obituaries were being written, changes were underway which completely altered the situation. Exponential increases in computing speed coupled to decreases in the cost of processing not only launched the personal computer revolution of the mid-1980s, but put digital cinema on an entirely different footing. A second wave of CGI was signalled by *Terminator 2: Judgement Day* (James Cameron, France/US, 1991), which made morphing a household word.[1] Two years later, the runaway box-office success of *Jurassic Park* (Steven Spielberg, US, 1993), followed by Pixar's breakthrough digital animated feature *Toy Story* (John Lasseter, US, 1994), changed the question from whether computers could be effectively used in filmmaking to how soon this would occur. The subsequent decade, with its array of CGI-driven blockbusters led by the billion-dollars-plus worldwide theatrical gross of James Cameron's *Titanic* (US, 1997), seems to have confirmed the shift.

Nevertheless, it would be a mistake to assume a linear trajectory, or, for that matter, a neat break from analogue to digital processes. While CGI gained the most attention from critics and audiences, the transition to digital technology happened rather earlier and more rapidly in areas such as sound production and picture editing. Digital recording and processing of sound took off in the early 1980s, building directly on the radical changes to film sound initiated by the introduction of Dolby Stereo in 1975. Ease of sonic manipulation in the digital domain facilitated the growing complexity of film soundtracks. Rick Altman noted the way that the 'spatialization' of discrete sound elements in the cinema auditorium altered audience experience:

> Whereas Thirties film practice fostered unconscious visual and psychological spectator identification with characters who appear as a perfect amalgam of image and sound, the Eighties ushered in a new kind of visceral identification, dependent on the sound system's overt ability, through bone-rattling bass and unexpected surround effects, to cause spectators to vibrate – quite literally – with the entire narrative space. It is thus no longer the eyes, the ears and the brain that alone initiate identification and maintain contact with a sonic source; instead, it is the whole body that establishes a relationship, marching to the beat of a different woofer. Where sound was once hidden behind the image in order to allow more complete identification with the image, now the sound source is flaunted, fostering a separate sonic identification contesting the limited rational draw of the image and its characters. (1995)

The use of sound to produce a more visceral experience was soon complemented by changes in the image. One aspect was the shift to digital picture editing which became widespread following the introduction of the Mac-based Avid Media Composer Series in 1988.[2] Although it had been possible to finish films on video since the early 1970s, the advantage of video's range of cheap, instantly viewable visual effects was purchased only at the cost of reducing editing to a linear tape-based process. But once digital non-linear systems had sufficient image quality to enable editors to obtain accurate lip-synch, digital editing blossomed. By 1994,

the switchover for feature film production was near complete. In a paper presented at the 1994 SMPTE (Society of Motion Picture and Television Engineers) Conference, Dominic Case from leading film-services provider Atlab argued:

> Non-linear editing has been adopted in the film and video industry faster than any comparable innovation, and I believe that it has had a greater effect on production and post-production methods even than the introduction of video. (1994: 50)

The reason for the rapid acceptance of the digital pathway in picture editing echoed the experience with sound: by reducing the material labour and the potential degradation of source material in the editing process, digital systems enabled significantly greater creative experimentation. As leading Australian editor Nicholas Beauman commented during his edit of *Oscar and Lucinda* (Gillian Armstrong, US/Australia/UK, 1997):

> When you do a cut on film, it requires you to think about how you are actually going to construct a scene a lot more carefully than if you are cutting on a digital, non-linear system. I can throw something together on non-linear very quickly and then look at it and think 'well, no, that's not right'. I can just make a copy of that, or I can put that cut aside do another one and another one. And I can show them all to somebody else. You can't do that on film. Because of the time constraints, you have to think about it very carefully and say 'OK, I am going to go down that road, I think this is the way to go with this scene'. If it doesn't work, you have to peel all those splices apart again and start all over, and very few films can afford to do that. (1997)[3]

Digital workstations also enabled easier utilization of images from different sources. Directors such as Oliver Stone in *Natural Born Killers* (US, 1994) and Baz Luhrmann in *Romeo + Juliet* (US, 1996) soon incorporated a wide range of formats in feature film, including video Hi-8 and Super-8. While both *Natural Born Killers* and *Romeo + Juliet* were particularly complex edits, they belonged to a time when the pacing of films was accelerating. David Bordwell notes that the average shot-length in mainstream US films during the decades from 1930 to 1960 varied between eight to eleven seconds, while the average number of shots comprising a film over the same period was 300 to 700 (2006: 121–3). In contrast, films of the last decade regularly include 2,000–3,000 shots with average shot-lengths of two to four seconds, with the fastest paced films dipping below the two second threshold. The experienced Luhrmann editor Jill Bilcock concurs with Bordwell that this shift is conditioned by digital editing (2006: 155):

> *Romeo + Juliet* was such a big post-production job it wouldn't have been able to be done in the time on film... You can quickly see those results on the non-linear system, where if you were doing it on film, you would probably have to put in a request for extra money to get inter-pos and create a film optical. You just wouldn't get it done. It takes a lot more time to do ... You wouldn't cut like that on film. If I was cutting on film, I would be looking for two frames off the floor, I'd be scrounging around. It just wouldn't have that creative freedom. So, creatively, it's really good. (1997)

POST-PRODUCTION

All these changes were in progress prior to the headlines made by Steven Spielberg's 'digital dinosaurs' in 1993. Despite containing only about five to six minutes of CGI, *Jurassic Park* changed the industry's thinking about the use of digital technology in film. The ensuing decade saw rapid experimentation with digital effects, as successive blockbusters undertook pioneering R&D in their attempts to show audiences things they had never seen before. By 1996 Cameron could claim, 'anything is possible ... if you throw enough money at it, or enough time' (quoted in Parisi, 1996a). Nevertheless, CGI still remains one technique among a range of others, including stunts, models, animatronics, and motion control. The computer has not replaced other pathways so much as redefined their use.

Arguably the biggest effect the flexibility and speed of digital technology has had on post-production is the marked move away from the traditional linear process of film production, comprising relatively distinct phases of pre-production, shooting and post-production. Increasingly, these phases overlap. Pre-visualization involves planning not only the logistics of set construction and camera placement, but the relationship between live action cinematography and computer-generated effects, while sound and picture editing are often proceeding in tandem with principal photography. This shift to parallel processing represents less the disappearance of 'post-production' than its dispersal across all production phases. George Lucas highlighted this change during the making of *Star Wars* Episodes I–III (US, 1999; 2002; 2005):

> I have been writing it [the next *Star Wars* episode] for two years, but I've also been shooting and editing, exploring different kinds of actors for different kinds of parts, and shooting and figuring it out. It's not done sequentially at all. (quoted in Kelly and Parisi, 1997)

Pre-visualization has taken on an increasingly important role in the contemporary production process. While classical directors such as Alfred Hitchcock were fond of pre-planning scenes using model sets, digital technology has enabled far greater precision. Special effects supervisor Peter Doyle notes:

> In the major films now no-one will even attempt to make a film without doing pre-visualisation. The complexity with which that happens depends on the budget, and the type of director. If you look at a James Cameron or John McTiernan, who did the *Last Action Hero* and all the *Die Hard* films, for the big action sequences they will actually make the entire scene in a computer with little stick men and CGI animation and full camera moves and the whole bit, and that is what's signed off on. If that's signed off, then the DOPs and the art directors and everyone else is then brought in, and they can then dial up what they need to know. So the camera men will know, 'well this move is now on a 50 mm lens and I need to have lights here and I need to green screen here'. So that really changes the dynamics of the film. (1997)

Even though the majority of feature films are still shot on 35mm film, hybrid cameras provide a video split, enabling directors to instantly review shot coverage, as well as a data-stream that allows indicative sound and picture edits. Because of the increasing tendency for post-production to overlap with production, close communication between directors, producers and post-production houses assumes a premium. Different tasks need to be more tightly coordinated. Renowned sound mixer Roger Savage notes: 'Now, there's much more collaboration. There has to be … It's all running in parallel. So you have to not only communicate, but you have to be technically compatible' (1997).

As well as traditional horizontal editing, involving the sequential linking of images, films increasingly involve the 'vertical editing' of digital compositing, as individual picture elements are added or subtracted. Andrew Lesnie, who went on to win an Oscar in 2002 for his cinematography on *The Lord of the Rings: The Fellowship of the Ring* (Peter Jackson, New Zealand/US, 2001), comments:

> I think it hasn't changed the priority of my job which is to rationalise a project's intent onto an image. So the technology is basically just another tool. You have a camera, lenses, filters, you've got the lab, all of which provides you with a certain scope, and you have digital technology which I am more than happy to use because it offers you all sorts of exciting possibilities. I think that probably the biggest thing to bear in mind is that you could get a little lazy about it by saying that it can fix things. (1997)

As Lesnie warns, the increased flexibility of the digital pathway does not always lead to efficient production. The contemporary tendency towards multi-camera coverage and the multiplication of 'takes' to ensure options for fine-tuning films during editing can lead critics conditioned by the standard Hollywood practice of producer control over the final cut, such as Bordwell (2006), to complain of sloppy shooting practices. But flexibility also offers new creative possibilities. It has often been noted that digital texts are radically 'open', insofar as digital tools lower the threshold for remixing and re-editing. The culture of the technological 'mash-up' favours the proliferation of director's cuts on DVDs replete with out-takes and extra scenes, not to mention 'updates' of the sort that Lucas applied to the first three *Star Wars* films when he wanted to 'fix' their special effects for a re-released 'digital edition'. As the existence of different versions of the same film becomes increasingly commonplace, film enters more fully into the remix culture characteristic of contemporary music or hybrid forms such as machinima. In the longer term, this is likely to further undermine the unifying fiction of the singular and bounded text, with its correlate of a lodestone of stable meaning. Even in a post-structural interpretative milieu, with its emphasis on polysemy and situated audiences rather than the sovereignty of authorial intention, an article of faith is that audiences are seeing the same text. Perhaps this assumption was always suspect: the contingency of dodgy projectors, different protocols of censorship and other forms of rough handling means that films – particularly 'classic films' – have often been seen in quite different versions by different audiences. But such differences pale in comparison to Steven Soderbergh's proposal for remixing current releases:

> I'd like to do multiple versions of the same film. I often do very radical cuts of my own films just to experiment, shake things up and see if anything comes of it. I think it would be really interesting to have a movie out in release and then, just a few weeks later say, 'Here's version 2.0, recut, rescored'. The other version is still there – people can see either or both. (quoted in Jardin, 2005)

DISTRIBUTION AND EXHIBITION

Following the rapid transformation of film production in the 1990s, digital distribution and exhibition were the next steps in the seemingly irresistible march towards cinema without celluloid. In 1999 Lucas instigated the equipping of four US cinemas with digital projection systems for the premiere of *Star Wars: Episode I – The Phantom Menace*, and soon announced plans to capture and show *Episode II – Attack of the Clones* with a high-definition digital camera and to screen it only in digital format. Ambitious initiatives to fund the roll-out of digital projection systems across the United States were announced at ShoWest 2001 by Technicolor Digital Cinema (formed by film services group Technicolor and digital communications company Qualcomm), while new players such as aerospace giant Boeing expressed interest in entering satellite-based distribution. Advocates listed numerous benefits of digitizing distribution and exhibition: Lucas extolled the improved image quality for audiences over the whole of a film's run, while distributors focused on potentially substantial savings in distribution costs, and exhibitors were promised a range of rewards from increased programming flexibility to the generation of new revenue streams. However, in common with the experience of the production sector, the transition to digital distribution and exhibition has been significantly slower and proven far more complex than was first imagined. Although *Episode II* was captured on high-resolution digital cameras, the bulk of screens utilized film prints.[4]

One of the key issues affecting the transition to digital cinema has been the question of common standards of equipment and software, from projectors and servers to encryption systems. Speaking in 2002 Julian Levin (Executive Vice-President Digital Exhibition and Special Projects at Twentieth Century Fox) noted:

> [S]uddenly in the US about a year ago, we had 50 or 60 systems, three different compression technologies required, at least two forced distribution channels through Boeing and Technicolor, having to provide your content in three or four different forms, and being forced to go through certain players at an expense that exceeds film to get the digital content to destination. (2002)

While proprietary systems appealed to those trying to gain a Microsoft-like grip on digital cinema, they made less sense to an industry accustomed to the universality of its product. Unlike television and video, 35mm film can be shot, processed and projected on standard equipment made by different manufacturers all around the world. In order to protect this existent interoperability, the seven major Hollywood studios formed the Digital Cinema Initiatives (DCI) consortium chaired by Fox's Levin in March 2002. According to DCI CEO Chuck Goldwater:

> Digital cinema was beginning to develop in different, not compatible directions, depending on who was the manufacturer, or the integrator of the system. Theatre owners had been through the digital stereo development issue, which resulted in three different and not compatible digital stereo systems and nobody wanted to see that happen again. This was an opportunity for the studios to bring focus to what they believe were objectives that everybody would find desirable and that is to ultimately develop a system with specifications and standards that were consistent and uniform in what they would produce. (2002)

While the process took significantly longer than expected, DCI finally released its specifications for system architecture in August 2005.[5] However, having a common set of technical standards for manufacturers to adopt has not resolved all the issues. Alongside standards, the biggest question mark around digital exhibition has been its cost. High-definition digital projectors that comply with the DCI standard are significantly more expensive than 35mm projectors. While 2K resolution digital projectors cost between $70,000 and $100,000, a new 35mm projector might cost $20,000, or less if second hand. Film projectors that are well maintained can have a life span of decades, while digital projectors are likely to follow the pattern of computer equipment and need regular upgrades.

This question is complicated by the established industry structure. While the bulk of savings will accrue to distributors, who will no longer have to pay for the production and shipping of bulky film reels, the cost of re-equipping theatres would generally fall on exhibitors. The expectation, in the US at least, has been that the two parties would eventually arrive at a commercially negotiated cost-sharing arrangement.[6] However, despite a rise in the number of digital screens in 2005, US exhibitors remain cautious.[7] Michael Karagosian (2006), digital cinema consultant to the National Organization of Theatre Owners in the US, points to continuing exhibitor concerns about cost, content security and the need for a certification programme to give exhibitors greater confidence in the technology. Karagosian argues that the low take-up of high-end digital systems (less than 1 per cent of world screens) reflects the 'chasm' currently preventing 'early adopters' from coalescing into an 'early majority'.

The cost premium of the DCI-mandated standard does reflect the fact that it was designed to replicate or exceed 35mm projection, and thereby protect the theatrical experience from the emerging challenge of 'home cinema' technologies. However, the fact that the high-resolution systems mandated by DCI exceeded most of those already in operation around the world raises the real possibility that different regions may well adopt different technical standards. This is partly a question of fitting the technology to the context. In rural China, for instance, low-resolution digital projectors have been installed in settings which previously had no cinemas. Here the need to compete with the audio-visual quality of 35mm film does not arise. Similarly, many art house cinemas and non-traditional venues are utilizing low-resolution digital projectors to screen niche films in boutique spaces. The question of the cost of digital projection has to be balanced against potential savings and the creation of additional revenue streams, even in territories such as Australia, where mainstream screens are dominated by Hollywood products and where the quality of the theatrical experience is critical. Here considerable uncertainty still reigns.

Most observers agree that digital cinema will offer exhibitors advantages in terms of more flexible programming options. Exhibitors will be able to expand the number of screens devoted to a popular film without having to wait for extra prints to be shipped, and they will also be able to improve the quality and versatility of pre-feature advertising, as the practice of manually assembling platters is replaced by a computer-controlled playlist. However, this flexibility would come at a price, as theatres will be required to employ new IT specialists to service the networks and equipment.

Another major drawcard of digital cinema is that it should enable exhibitors to broaden their operations from exclusive reliance on feature films towards a more varied menu of attractions. Networked theatres able to display digital content delivered by cable or satellite can also use their screens for broadcasting live events. However, while isolated experiments with premium sporting events have been successful, there are significant hurdles to live content becoming a regular revenue stream. As Karagosian has pointed out:

> Sports would be really neat, except that sports has much better return for the buck on a satellite TV network. It's copyrighted and it's time valued … Sports seems so interesting, but it's probably not practical, except for very special occasions. (2002)

Moreover, increasingly those 'special occasions', such as World Cup football, are available on large screens which are located not in cinemas but in public spaces.[8] Other mooted alternative uses of digital cinemas are multiplayer interactive gaming and 3D projection. The advantage of gaming is that it could exploit the high-quality image and sound facilities of theatres, while potentially attracting audiences outside of peak times. Digital technology has also given 3D cinema – the perennial 'next-big-thing' – another lease of life. Following the strong support given to 3D films by leading directors such as Cameron and Lucas at trade convention ShoWest in 2005, 3D-equipped cinemas experienced rapid growth in 2006.[9]

However, alternative uses of theatres such as gaming and 3D remain in their infancy. Given the significant cost premium on high-resolution digital projection systems compared to 35mm projectors, the limited take-up in most territories is unsurprising. In mid-2006, Australian exhibitors were still expressing a high level of scepticism as to whether a roll-out of DCI-mandated facilities made economic sense, particularly given that 1.3K resolution projectors were now available for around $11,000.[10] In fact, low-end digital projection systems used for pre-show advertising have already made significant inroads into cinemas. The business case for low-end digital projectors has been far more compelling to exhibitors, with smaller upfront costs directly offset by increased revenues flowing from flexible content and more precise targeting of specific audiences.[11] Karagosian argues that cinema becomes proportionally more attractive to advertisers as viewers continue to drift away from network television:

> Electronics offers this whole level of interesting management of who you can target with your advertising. What that means to the exhibitor is more bucks for that ad, because of the higher quality of those eyeballs he can sell. (2002)

One of the long held dreams around digital distribution and exhibition is that it will enable a democratization of cinema as thresholds to market entry diminish. There are a number of different dimensions to the issue. Web-based distribution has clearly become an increasing presence for both legitimate (Atom Films, Movielink, CinemaNow, iTunes and so on), as well as for 'pirated' exchange using peer-to-peer software. However, access to theatrical screens is a different issue. Film distribution remains a highly concentrated industry, with the seven major Hollywood studios dominating global revenues.[12] Karagosian argues:

> Let's say you're a filmmaker and you have a great piece of art that you're proud of and you're not sure whether anybody else is. But you're proud of it and you want to distribute it. So let's say there's a network to 10,000 screens in the US, what's compelling to them? Why do they want to look at your movie? Why do they want to put it out there? What you will need is an enabler, a distributor of some kind who you cut your deal with and who is able to take your movie and put it out. I think it's going to be a well-controlled channel. It's not going to be open, not because the electronics won't allow it to be open, but because there isn't a compelling reason for people to just be able to play any kind of content. (2002)

Karagosian's analysis is confirmed by economists such as Abraham Ravid who argues that the major studios are currently undergoing an extensive functional shift as they morph into entities more akin to book publishers, less concerned with production than with marketing and distribution (2005: 54). Nevertheless, the rapid growth in networks of low-end digital projectors used to screen pre-show advertising in cinemas raises the possibility that, even in the absence of a broad shift to high-definition digital exhibition for mainstream feature films, there is new scope for screening alternative content such as films originated on DV.

This possibility is facilitated by another aspect of digitization: that is, databases. Karagosian highlights the role of companies such as Hollywood Software, which pioneered distribution software for breakout films like the Hi-8-shot *The Blair Witch Project* (Daniel Myrick/Eduardo Sánchez, US, 1999) and *My Big Fat Greek Wedding* (Joel Zwick, US/Canada, 2002):

> [Y]ou can go in with your movie and say it's a drama, it's this long, geared for this age group, what screens would this best show on in the US? This database can come back and say it's going to show best on these screens. I want to show it for about three months, what time base can I get?... And it goes on down the line. So these tools help you optimise where you're going to get your biggest bang for your buck historically from your class of movie in the theatre. Previously this task would've taken a large team of people to get on the phone and find out the availability of every cinema chain around. Suddenly you're learning all this information from databases and very smart software. (2002)

SECURITY, 'PIRACY' AND IP

Digital distribution of films immediately raises the contentious issue of content security. Because of the extremely high ratio between film development costs and digital reproduction costs, as well as the film industry's reliance on sequenced release windows cascading through different territories and across different platforms, film is peculiarly susceptible to 'piracy'.[13] For this reason, peak industry bodies such as the Motion Picture Association of America (MPAA) have taken a leading role in public debates and political lobbying around copyright protection. From former MPAA Chairman Jack Valenti's mantra, 'If you can't protect what you own, you don't own anything', to his successor Dan Glickman's assertion that 'Protecting intellectual property will become a resounding theme for our economy in the decades to come' (MPAA, 2005a), the MPAA has been active in promoting legislative, technological and behavioural change. Heightened concern with copyright protection and intellectual property (IP) reflects a broader economic shift away from trade in goods towards trade in services, knowledge and information. The emergence of new regulatory regimes since the 1980s also reflects a transition from what John Frow (2000) calls a 'development' framework for regulating transnational knowledge exchange to a 'trade'-based framework.

Copyright infringement has been a concern for the major studios at least since the arrival of the VCR in the 1980s.[14] However, digital technology has vastly increased the scale of copying. The MPAA put the direct worldwide cost of piracy to film producers at US$6.1b in 2005, and the worldwide loss to the motion-picture sector (producers, distributors, theatres, video stores, pay-per-view operators) at a staggering US$18.1b (see MPAA, 2005b).[15] Digital technology has also increased the complexity of the issues involved. The standard means of controlling the ability of users to modify traditional consumer goods has been to restrict physical access to them. Once someone has purchased (for example) a car, it is nearly impossible to prevent the user from 'tinkering' with it.[16] In the analogue past, when one purchased a book or musical recording, there were few restrictions on what one did with the physical object. Unauthorized republication of *content* could be dealt with through copyright law and private copying was generally so laborious and the results were of such dubious quality that there was little effort to police it except in exceptional cases.

However, the 'perfect' nature of today's digital copies, coupled with the increasing speeds of networks enabling widespread peer-to-peer distribution, has altered this situation radically and irrevocably.[17] Fear about the 'Napsterization' of film content has meant that the first line of defence against copyright infringement has moved from legal prohibitions to technical prophylactics. Since unrestricted access to digitally-stored information inevitably enables high-quality copying, embedded technical protection measures such as Digital Rights Management (DRM) schemes become 'logical' responses.

At a technical level, films released on DVD generally have encrypted content that requires a 'key' for access. In order to get the key from the content owner, DVD-player manufacturers are required to sign a license mandating design standards which specify limits to user interaction with the copyrighted work. In addition, manufacturers must also comply with 'robustness' requirements which make their technical mechanisms harder to circumvent.[18] Technical fixes have been supported by legislative changes such as Digital Millennium Copyright Act (enacted in the US in 1998), which made it illegal to break encryptions such as the Content Scramble System (CSS), and also outlawed devices designed to circumvent technical protection.[19]

Of course, effective operation of DRM schemes requires both technical and legislative implementation. Legislation remains essential to content owners since, despite their market power, it is difficult to get every manufacturer to agree to technical standards that restrict consumer rights. As digital television became an increasing reality, the same coalition of film studios and technology manufacturers which developed CSS proposed the 'broadcast flag' as a means of limiting the copying of broadcast material.[20] As Tarleton Gillespie notes, such mechanisms significantly limit user agency in relation to computer technology by excluding the operation of the technology from the users' scrutiny.[21] They also have major potential ramifications for the future of software design. In their response to the Federal Communications Commission concerning the proposed bill, the Electronic Frontier Foundation (EFF) argued that 'robustness' requirements would effectively lock Open Source designers out of the emerging market for digital television software:

> To the extent [that] the open source development model embraces the freedom to modify, however, this necessarily means that open source software cannot be made 'tamper-resistant' in the fashion contemplated by the broadcast flag mandate. (EFF, 2004)

As well as technical and legal measures, content owners have conducted sustained promotional campaigns to alter social behaviour.

The legal cases conducted against key peer-to-peer distribution sites and high-profile users have been supplemented by the widespread use of the rhetoric of 'piracy' to change perceptions about file sharing, and to legitimate the shift to a more common use of criminal sanctions.[22] The MPAA website now carries a wide range of material directed at parents, teachers, and students, arguing the case against 'piracy', as well as promoting 'legal' online distribution sites.

THEORIZING DIGITAL AESTHETICS

Alongside the transformation of production, distribution and exhibition, digital cinema represents a fundamental change in the nature of the film image. Trinh T. Minh-Ha argues:

> What is at stake is the difference that begins at the core, with the formation of the image itself. The film image is something well-defined, that one can touch: a still, a frame, a rectangle, a piece of celluloid. Whereas with video, there is no real stasis, no 'still' in other words; the image is in perpetual formation, thanks to a scanning mechanism. Such a distinction can radically impact the way we conceive images, which is bound to differ from one medium to another. Rather than experimenting with sequences of stills, one is here working, on both macro and micro levels, with the pulses of an ever-appearing and disappearing continuum of luminous images. (2005: 201)

Following hard on the heels of the 'death of photography', digital cinema was rapidly associated with the death of film narrative. In the special 'Digital Cinema' issue of *Screen*, Sean Cubitt noted a 'common intuition among reviewers, critics and scholars that something has changed in the nature of cinema – something to do with the decay of familiar narrative and performance values in favour of the qualities of the blockbuster' (1999: 123). Lev Manovich aligned the predominance of 'blockbusters' with 'digital cinema' by defining the latter almost entirely in terms of increased special effects: 'A visible sign of this shift is the new role which computer-generated special effects have come to play in the Hollywood industry in the last few years. Many recent blockbusters have been driven by special effects, feeding on their popularity' (1999). Paul Young discerned a 'reliance on digital technology to produce spectacle at the expense of narrative' (1999: 41), while filmmaker Jean Douchet expressed the shift in more extreme terms: '[Today] cinema has given up the purpose and the thinking behind individual shots [and narrative], in favour of images – rootless, textureless images – designed to violently impress by constantly inflating their spectacular qualities' (quoted in Buckland, 1999: 178). Other writers such as Geoff King (2000) and Andrew Darley (2000) elaborated the theme into book-length analyses.

How should such claims be evaluated? In terms of commercial success, it is undeniable that the highest grossing films of the last decade have been dominated by genres such as action, adventure, fantasy, horror and science fiction, which make copious use of special effects. However, it would be reductive to treat this trajectory as if it was simply *generated* by digital technology. As Scott Bukatman (1995) noted in a thoughtful essay focusing on the work of special-effects pioneer Doug Trumbull, the shift to effects-laden films capable of producing a technological 'sublime' predates digital technology. Most analysts date the rise of the 'blockbuster' from the 1970s, with films such as *Jaws* (Steven Spielberg, US, 1975), *Star Wars* and *Close Encounters of the Third Kind* (Steven Spielberg, US/UK, 1977). As Bordwell notes, never before had films made so much money so quickly (2006: 2). But none of these films employed digital effects, apart from Lucas' successful adoption of motion control. The dominance of the blockbuster in contemporary cinema must therefore be situated in relation to other shifts in the film industry, including the emergence of multiplexes and megaplexes (Acland 2003), the growing importance of international revenues to Hollywood production, and the fact that film faces increasing competition from other entertainment platforms.

Nevertheless, digital technology has played an important role in this trajectory. As David Waterman notes: 'While computer use in film making would seem to have real cost-saving potential, computer technology seems to have fuelled, not mitigated, rising film budgets' (2005: 234).[23] The average cost of Hollywood films, excluding marketing costs, has spiralled from US$3.1m in 1971 to US$60m in 2005.[24] While there are many factors contributing to increasing production costs, including burgeoning 'star' salaries for bankable actors, producers, writers and directors, the increasing scale and complexity of film production is a significant part of the story.

While the sort of morphing effects that made *T-2* an eye-opener in 1991 are now easily obtainable on PCs, Hollywood has consistently raised the bar, both in terms of the complexity and cost of individual effects, and the number of them packed into a single film. Stunts and special effects now regularly comprise 10–15 per cent of the budget of major studio films. Some far exceed this: *The Matrix Reloaded* (Andy Wachowski/Larry Wachowski, US, 2003) and *Matrix Revolutions* (Andy Wachowski/Larry Wachowski, US, 2003) devoted US$100m out of their joint US$300m budget to stunts and effects. Waterman contrasts the famous car chase in *The French Connection* (William Friedkin, US, 1971) to a comparable sequence in *The Matrix Reloaded* (2005: 216). Where the former involved a single stunt driver and the destruction of three or four vehicles, the latter included the construction of a six lane freeway at a cost of US$2.5m and the demolition of US$2m worth of cars. Another sign of this tendency is the rapid increase in the number of people involved in effects. Whereas the average number of end credits for special/visual effects for a major film in 1971 was 2.1, by 2001 this figure had risen to 150.[25]

This inflation of effects budgets and crews suggests that spectacle, manifested in the dominance of genres such as action, adventure, sci-fi and horror, has become the currency whereby Hollywood 'buys' its lion's share of the international film market, while also competing for audiences increasingly surrounded by options for their limited entertainment dollars, including mobile phones, iPods, subscription television and the Internet.[26] As *Independence Day* (Roland Emmerich, US, 1996) proved, spectacular effects can drive an advertising campaign and cut across cultural barriers, enabling an otherwise ordinary film to perform extraordinarily well at the box office. In this respect, it can be argued that, while effects-driven blockbusters are not the sole or necessary outcome of digital technology, they have been an economically dominant tendency. Cameron has gone so far as to suggest that digital technology freed filmmakers from the constraints of the old 'A' and 'B' picture hierarchy:

> [I]n the '40s you either had a movie star or you had a B-movie. Now you can create an A-level movie with some kind of visual spectacle, where you cast good actors, but you don't need an Arnold or a Sly or a Bruce or a Kevin to make it a viable film. (quoted in Parisi, 1996a)

If Cameron's claim is overblown – most major effects-laden films are so costly to produce they demand star presence if only to secure the free advertising space routinely available to star-driven film promotion – it serves to highlight another aspect of the changing economic structure of the film industry, the growing role of ancillaries. The much-remarked decline of the proportion of total revenues derived from theatrical box office is partly a result of the emergence of new release windows such as subscription television, and sell-through and rental video and DVD.[27] But it is also a function of the rising tide of new revenue streams, from toys, clothing and accessories to CDs, games, books and theme park rides. Ravid cites *The Lion King* (Roger Allers/Rob Minkoff, US, 1994) as a classic example of the ancillary tail wagging the cinematic dog (2005: 36). While it grossed a very respectable US$313m at the North American box office, US$454m abroad, and $520m in video, this billion-dollar-plus take was far outweighed by the US$3b it achieved in related merchandise sales. Such options multiply in the digital domain. As Lucie Fjeldstad, then head of IBM's multimedia division, remarked at the time: 'Digital content is a return-on-assets goldmine, because once you create Terminator 3, the character, it can be used in movies, in theme-park rides, videogames, books, educational products' (quoted in Parisi, 1995). As David Marshall (2004) has noted, the digital era is one of heightened intertexuality. Digital convergence means that the labour used in designing CG characters for a film can also be utilized on a promotional website, in a videogame, or in off-shore factories manufacturing plastic toys. The commercial reality which is creating pressure for global day and date releases to combat 'piracy' of high-budget films, coupled to the need for alliances with partners such as fast-food chains and department stores for promotional movie tie-ins and shelf space to sell toys, suggest that the criteria for evaluating the 'success' of a film have altered significantly.

But has it ever really been all that different? Presenting the issue in terms of an opposition between spectacle and narrative recycles positions which have been consistently articulated – and regularly reversed – throughout cinema history. Revisionist film history has successfully challenged the stereotyping of early cinema in terms of its narrative 'primitivism', arguing instead that it catered for a different mode of pleasure and spectatorship that Tom Gunning (1986) influentially dubbed the 'cinema of attractions'. In the 1920s, avant-garde filmmakers railed against 'narrative', because it was associated primarily with literary and theatrical scenarios at the expense of cinematic qualities. Similar concerns emerged with debates over auteur theory in France during the 1950s, when the 'literary' qualities of script were opposed to the 'properly cinematic' qualities of *mise en scène*. In the 1970s, the 'refusal of narrative' took on radical political connotations in publications such as *Screen, Cahiers du cinéma, Framework, Wide Angle* and *Camera Obscura*. In current debates there has been a widespread restoration of narrative as a filmic 'good object'. Rather than attempting to resolve the issue in favour of one side or the other, the more salient need is to recognize that narrative

and spectacle are inextricably intertwined. Attention then shifts to the examination of the sort of stories being told, and the sort of spectacles being deployed in their telling.

An early attempt to 'periodize' digital visual effects in science-fiction films was Michelle Pierson's argument that early effects sequences were designed to stand out from the narrative and temporal flow by displaying a 'hyperreal' electronic aesthetic. Pierson suggests that after *Jurassic Park* a higher premium was placed on the narrative integration of effects (1999: 169). While her argument was coherent from the spectator's point of view, it ignored the production side of the process. As CG effects guru Scott Billups recalls, filmmakers had to educate computer programmers in order to achieve a 'film' look:

> For years we were saying: 'Guys, you look out on the horizon and things get grayer and less crisp as they get farther away'. But those were the types of naturally occurring event structures that never got written into computer programs. They'd say 'Why do you want to reduce the resolution? Why do you want to blur it?' (quoted in Parisi, 1996b)

Digital tools such as Flame gradually introduced 'defects' such as film grain, lens flare, motion blur and edge halation to make images look *as if they might have been filmed*. This suggests that it is not so much the ambition for narrative integration of CGI which has changed, as the capacity to realize that ambition. In the process, as Michael Allen (2002) notes, special-effects shots have gradually got longer as they have become more able to withstand spectator scrutiny. Once 'live action' images become more or less indistinguishable from CG images, Stephen Prince's concept of 'perceptual realism' offers a useful refinement to the category of 'realism'. In the context of digital imaging, Prince suggested that the operative 'referent' is less the real world than our audio-visual experience:

> A perceptually realistic image is one which structurally corresponds to the viewer's *audio-visual experience* of three-dimensional space .... Such images display a nested hierarchy of cues which organise the display of light, colour, texture, movement and sound in ways that correspond

to the viewer's own understanding of these phenomena in daily life. Perceptual realism, therefore,
designates a relationship between the image on
film and the spectator, and it can encompass both
unreal images and those which are referentially
realistic. Because of this, unreal images may
be referentially fictional but perceptually realistic.
(1996: 32, my italics)

In other words, because of the extent to
which audiences have internalized the camera's qualities as the hallmark of credibility,
contemporary cinema no longer aims to mime
'reality', but 'camera-reality'. Recognizing
this shift underlines the ambivalence of
realism in the digital domain. A filmmaker's
ability to take the image apart at ever-
more-minute levels is counterpointed by the
spectator's desire to comprehend the resulting
image as 'realistic' – or, at least, equivalent
to other cine-images. This heightens the need
to understand the way in which images are
constructed into *texts* in order to achieve
credibility, whether this is a function of
'fiction' or 'documentary'.

One of the more interesting theses concerning the impact of digital technology on
film narrative is put forward by Cubitt, who
sees 'technological' cinema as an extension
of what he calls the shift to 'neo-baroque'
film (2004: 235). The neo-baroque is marked
by the exploration of increasingly detailed
diegetic worlds in which the temporal axis of
narrative progress and resolution is displaced
by spatialization:

Space succeeds time as organizing principle syn-
chronously with neo-baroque narratives' turn to
the database form, a spectacularization of plot in
an ironic mode in which mere coincidence satirizes
the classical working-through of causes and their
effects. As the lifeworld appears consistently more
random, so the mediascape becomes more scathing
at any pretence at order, mocking the revelations
and resolutions that once passed as realistic... In
the process, pattern is divorced from its old task of
establishing morality. (Cubitt, 2004: 249)

For Cubitt, this shift raises an ethical problem,
insomuch as the spatialized narrative 'worlds'
of contemporary effects-laden cinema promote a stunted intrapsychic narcissism which
forecloses the relation to the other on which
ethical communication is based.

Arguably the most influential attempt to
theorize 'digital cinema' has been the various
offerings of Manovich, which accumulated
into his *The Language of New Media* (2001).
Manovich describes an historical 'loop' in
which the growing control over the image
granted by digital technology has enabled the
once marginal cinematic practice of animation
to encompass the whole of cinema in the
digital era. In this context, live-action footage
and the 'reproduction of reality', proclaimed
as the essence of cinema by theorists such
as Siegfried Kracauer (1960) and Jean Mitry
(1963–5; 1998), is dethroned to become
simply another element in a general art of
animation:

In retrospect, we can see that 20th century
cinema's regime of visual realism, the result of
automatically recording visual reality, was only an
exception, an isolated accident in the history of
visual representation... (Manovich, 1999)

While the argument captures the way that
the digital threshold enhances the fluidity of
the film image, there are significant problems
with Manovich's formulation. One is that
his understanding of 'live action' cinema
in terms of its direct reliance on 'physical
reality' is extremely reductive. Cinema has
always involved the plastic transformation
of physical reality, not least through the
conventions of montage which became central
to film narrative nearly a century ago. Dziga
Vertov, whose Constructivist classic *Man with
a Movie Camera* (USSR, 1929) is converted
by Manovich into a precocious 'database
narrative' that provides the leitmotif for
his book, boasted that the film-eye could
decompose and recompose physical reality at
will. Yet Manovich ignores this long history
of plasticity to set up a neat contrast between
'automatic recording' and 'animation'. In
this respect, Manovich's position dovetails
neatly with the stance of filmmakers such as
Lucas, who has long proselytized the ability
of the new technology to realize directorial
vision:

I think cinematographers would love to have
ultimate control over the lighting; they'd like to be
able to say, 'OK, I want the sun to stop there on the

horizon and stay there for about six hours, and I want all of those clouds to go away'. Everybody wants that kind of control over the image and the storytelling process. Digital technology is just the ultimate version of that. (quoted in Magid, 1997: 52)

Ultimate control fits Lucas' aesthetic, which places little or no premium on the peculiar attractions of 'automatic recording', whether of complex locations such as city streets or equally complex psychological terrains such as an actor's face. (*Star Wars* lead Mark Hamill notes ruefully that, if Lucas could produce films without actors, he probably would [Seabrook, 1997: 53].) However, erecting 'film as animation' into the totality of cinema in the digital age underestimates the persistent attraction of the chance effects of 'live action'. Long ago Walter Benjamin eulogized the productive aspect of the encounter between the camera and the world in terms of the camera's registration of the 'spark of contingency' (1979: 243), a value Roland Barthes later ontologized as the photographic *punctum* (1984: 47). If Lucas' highly controlled cinema-as-animation is one dominant tendency of contemporary cinema, it finds various counter-tendencies in the continuing pull of location shooting and improvised performance, in the anti-interventionist stance of the Dogme movement, in the desire for 'authentic' social interactions in various 'reality TV' scenarios.

FILM STUDIES IN THE TWENTY-FIRST CENTURY

In one of my first teaching jobs in the mid-1980s, I well remember having to lug a 16mm projector across campus in order to screen films. On one memorable occasion during *Letter to Jane* (Jean-Luc Godard/Jean-Pierre Gorin, France, 1972), I belatedly realized the take-up reel wasn't functioning properly, and had to wind it by hand as metres of celluloid spooled across the floor. I was understandably nervous about potential damage, as it was probably the only copy of the film in Australia, sent by rail from the National Library in Canberra. Conditions of access are remarkably different today. DVDs and online databases have made it far easier to view certain texts, particularly current releases and 'classics'. But this easy availability raises its own issues for Film Studies. In a world of ubiquitous digital images, what incentive is there for students to take the trouble of searching out and accessing films? And, even if we are prepared to trade off the specific materiality of celluloid for the rewards of broader accessibility, are we utilizing digital technology in the most effective way?

Patricia Zimmerman has argued persuasively for the need to 're-imagine the borders of film history' to include a broader range of film production than the existing canon (2001: 111). While the number of DVD titles is expanding, the release of historical material with limited market appeal is inevitably selective. Writing in 2004, Kay Hoffmann noted that only 100 films from between 1920 and 1928 were available on DVD, most of them from the US (2004: 161). Jan-Christopher Horak asks:

If only a limited canon is available for such classroom use, then only the canon according to Blockbuster will indeed be taught and shown to students. How do you teach a course on Third World cinema, on American independent documentary, on classical documentaries from the 30s, on avant-garde films from any period, when at present virtually no one is willing to finance their digitalization? (2003: 21)

This is the 'dark side' of the undoubted potential for digital media to enrich Film Studies, not only by improving access to films, but supplementing them with a range of ephemeral materials such as posters, scripts, design sketches and stills, as well as critical voiceovers and alternative language tracks.

One productive way in which digital technology might contribute to a broadening of the film canon is by facilitating new modes of access to established archives. Projects such as Moving History in the UK involve the construction of an online catalogue and guide to archive collections in the UK with the aim of promoting archival resources to educational users.[28] Frank Gray and Eileen Sheppard express the hope that 'an expanding knowledge of film-archive collections will influence not only the production of new histories of film and television, but also interdisciplinary research across the arts and humanities' (2004: 116). They also point out that the viability of such projects depends on the allocation of scarce resources away from traditional tasks of archiving to educating end-users in negotiating technological differences, resolving copyright issues, and the like. Achieving best practice will depend on the extent to which film archives are able to gain wider recognition as a critical cultural resource.

The ambition for a broader array of disciplines to make more critical and systematic use of film resources is paralleled by the new range of pressures on Film Studies as a coherent discipline. Digital convergence brings film into close relation not only with television, but the Internet, video gaming, and mobile media. As well as the need to explore both the continuities and specificities of different platforms, there is an increasing need to recognize that globalization demands more situated analyses of specific audiences. Attempting to fence off a domain specific to Film Studies in the context of digital media strikes me as an exercise in nostalgia which risks irrelevance, particularly to future students born *after* the explosion of the Internet in 1993. As those such as Henry Jenkins (2006) point out, fan culture has been transformed by the Internet, and has established such a degree of influence that major film productions no longer take place 'in camera', but with the enthusiastic participation of extensive fan communities. And while the demand for audience-configured 'interactive' narrative pathways has never seriously threatened to alter mainstream theatrical releases, user navigation has nevertheless emerged as a major driver of contemporary entertainment culture. If the burgeoning field of games studies does not belong entirely to Film Studies, it cannot remain entirely separate. The shift to subscription-based models for online gaming offers a far steadier income stream than the notoriously volatile film industry, where mega-profits of one year can easily give way

to catastrophic losses in the next. No doubt the major studios are watching closely, as much as they are watching websites such as YouTube, CurrentTV and MySpace. In this time of transition, it is worth remembering that the productivity of Film Studies has historically been its willingness to embrace and develop interdisciplinary methodologies. Innovation in both empirical research and theoretical paradigms seems more necessary than ever.

NOTES

1 Cameron argues, convincingly in my opinion, that *Terminator 2* was the first film which made CGI pivotal to its outcome: '[O]n *The Abyss* the computer was really used to solve single sequences, and if that sequence had failed the film would still have succeeded dramatically. On *T*-2 the success or failure of the film was really predicated on the success or failure of the digital techniques' (quoted in Parisi, 1996a).

2 This was followed three years later by the PC-based Lightworks.

3 In relation to *Oscar and Lucinda*, Beauman noted: 'We are up to something like version five of the film at the moment now, but in fact it's probably like version seven, and there will be at least one other version after this. You just didn't have the time to go through the film that many times when you were cutting on film, and every time you do, you refine, refine, refine' (1997).

4 As Charles Schwarz points out, *Episode II* was also archived on film: 'I don't think there's anybody we've ever encountered in Hollywood who believes we're anywhere near where we want with using digital material as the archival master ... ' (2002). Schwarz is Executive Director and CEO of USC's Entertainment Technology Centre, which runs the Digital Cinema Laboratory, the major testing facility for digital exhibition systems in Hollywood.

5 The DCI press release, with supporting comments from a range of industry luminaries, can be found online at: http://www.dcimovies.com/press/07-27-05.tt2.

6 By contrast, the UK has adopted a publicly-funded rollout, using National Lottery revenues to fund the UK Film Council's Digital Screen Network project to install about 240 2K projectors in 200 locations. The aim is to improve access to specialized or non-mainstream film.

7 In March 2005 the MPAA put the number of digital screens worldwide at 849, up sharply from 335 the previous year. However, the figure does not specify the critical issue of projector resolution.

8 For instance, the 2006 World Cup in Germany was watched by audiences on large public screens in all host cities, including million-plus audiences in Berlin's Tiergarten. For more on public space broadcasting, see McQuire (2006).

9 There are two competing 3D processes. In-Three's 'Dimensionalization' process converts 2D film images to 3D, but requires expensive glasses which exhibitors will need to collect and clean. The 'Real D' 3D system Disney employed for its 2006 release of *Chicken Little* (Mark Dindal, US, 2005) involves a combination of pre-processing, and projector and screen modification. It will use cheap, give-away viewing glasses. Real D has about 300 screens in the US at the time of writing, with plans announced for a further 150 screens in partnership with exhibition chain Cinemark. However, this remains only a fraction of the approximately 30,000 screens in the US.

10 See the discussion of various stakeholders in 'Industry Panel: Digital Cinema: Why the delay?' (Hall and Williams, 2006). As Case argues: 'When you can put a screen in for less cost that putting a 35mm screen in, that's a threshold, I'd say' (quoted in Hall and Williams, 2006: 18).

11 This issue has greater potential significance in the US, where revenue from cinema advertising has historically been minimal, compared to territories such as Europe or Australia. Michael S. Katz et al. (2002) calculated advertising revenues at US$22,000 per screen in Europe compared to US$200 in the US.

12 Shujen Wang notes that the 'big seven' studios represent around 90 per cent of total global revenues (2003: 29).

13 As Majid Yar (2005) points out, using the term 'piracy' to describe copyright infringements carries an ideological connotation which belongs to the attempt to legitimate a shift from civil to criminal sanctions.

14 As Jack Valenti, President of the MPAA famously testified before the House Hearing on 'Home Recording of Copyrighted Works' in 1982: 'I say to you that the VCR is to the American film producer and the American public as the Boston strangler is to the woman home alone' (Valenti, 1982).

15 Yar (2005) analyzes the methodological assumptions which tend to inflate this figure, which is nevertheless widely accepted by governments.

16 In practice, guarantees and insurance policies function to restrict user modification.

17 In practice, the quality of a digital copy will depend on sampling frequency and file size.

18 The Content Scramble System (CSS) introduced for DVDs in 1996 combines compliance and robustness rules. Gillespie argues that the DeCSS case, which involved the prosecution of certain individuals who circulated anti-encryption software, in fact testifies to the effectiveness of the system. It was only the failure of one manufacturer (Real Networks) to adequately obscure the encryption key that enabled it to be broken (2006: 656).

19 The Digital Millennium Copyright Act (DMCA) is increasingly having a global effect as the US uses bi- and multi-lateral trade agreements to enforce similar protections in other markets such as Australia. Similarly, Article 6 of the EU Copyright Directive (2001), which is intended to implement the WIPO Copyright Treaty, provides protection for 'technological measures'.

20 Broadcast flag involves digitally watermarking television broadcasts. The Broadcast Protection Discussion Group included Fox, Sony, Matsushita/Panasonic, Intel, Toshiba and Hitachi.

21 Gillespie (2006: 661) argues, 'Technological design anticipates users and builds roles for them', adding that an important aspect of user agency is their perception of their right and ability to exercise agency'. One argument against emerging DRM mechanisms is that they overly restrict user agency in the name of content security.

22 Yar notes that between 1970 and 1980 there were less than 20 prosecutions for copyright offences in the UK, while there were more than 500 in the year 2000 alone, mostly in the area of music (2005: 686–7). As well as reflecting the criminalization of a range of previously legal practices, these figures reflect a symbolic shift in industry response.

23 The potential to use digital technology to lower production costs is certainly there, as witnessed by the recent growth of the low-budget production shot on DV and edited on domestic computers. Increasing processing speed and the availability of off-the-shelf software means there has also been a consistent decrease in the cost of special effects. For this reason, it is more accurate to say that Hollywood has *chosen* not to use digital technology to save money.

24 This is down slightly from a peak of US$63.8m in 2003 (MPAA, 2006). As Harold Vogel points out, this inflation of production costs means that, despite the rapid growth of new revenue streams including international theatrical markets, subscription television, video and DVD rental and sales, and ancillary merchandising, which contribute to huge grosses on successful films, the profitability of the film industry as a whole has in fact declined since the 1970s (2005: 78).

25 Similarly, credits for sound effects grew from 4.6 to 30.2 and for stunts from 0.2 to 43.7. Certain films – famously *Titanic* with its seven minutes of credits listing over 1,200 individuals and businesses – vastly exceed this.

26 International revenues have become increasingly important to Hollywood studios over the last decade and now regularly comprise around half of total revenues.

27 In 2004, for instance, DVD sale and rental worldwide more than doubled theatrical revenue (US$21b to US$9.5b) (see Bordwell, 2006: 2).

28 Available at: http://www.movinghistory.ac.uk.

REFERENCES

Acland, Charles (2003) *Screen Traffic: Movies, Multiplexes and Global Culture*. Durham, NC: Duke University Press.

Allen, Michael (2002) 'The impact of digital technology and film aesthetics', in Dan Harries (ed.), *The New Media Book*. London: BFI. pp. 109–18.

Altman, Rick (1995) 'The Sound of Sound: A Brief History of the Reproduction of Sound in Movie Theatres', *Cineaste*, 21(1–2). Available at: http://www.geocities.com/Hollywood/Academy/4394/altman.html.

Barthes, Roland (1984) *Camera Lucida*. Tr. Richard Howard. London: Fontana.

Beauman, Nicholas (1997) Interview by author. Audio recording. Sydney, 10 June.

Benajmin, Walter (1979) 'A Small History of Photography', in *One-Way Street and Other Writings*. Tr. Edmund Jephcott and Kinglsey Shorter. London: New Left Books. pp. 240–257.

Bilcock, Jill (1997) Interview by author. Audio recording. Melbourne, 17 June.

Bordwell, David (2006) *The Way Hollywood Tells It: Story and Style in Modern Movies*. Berkeley: University of California Press.

Buckland, Warren (1999) 'Between science fact and science fiction: Spielberg's digital dinosaurs, possible worlds and the new aesthetic realism', *Screen*, 40(2): 177–92.

Bukatman, Scott (1995) 'The artificial infinite: on special effects and the sublime', in Lynne Cooke and Peter Wollen (eds), *Visual display: Culture beyond appearances*. Seattle: Bay Press. pp. 254–89.

Case, Dominic (1994) 'Converging Technologies and Newton's Third Law of Motion, or: The Close-up, the cutaway and the freeze-frame', *Cinema Papers*, 101: 59.

Cubitt, Sean (1999) 'Le réel, c'est l'impossible: The sublime time of special effects', *Screen*, 40(2): 123–30.

Cubitt, Sean (2004) *The Cinema Effect*. Cambridge, MA: MIT Press.

Darley, Andrew (2000) *Visual Digital Culture: Surface Play and Spectacle in New Media Genres*. London: Routledge.

Doyle, Peter (1997) Interview by author. Audio recording. Sydney, 15 May.

Electronic Frontier Foundation (EFF) (2004) 'EFF Reply Comments re Broadcast Flag', 15 March. Available at: http://www.eff.org/IP/broadcastflag/EFF_FNPRM_Reply.pdf.

Fisher, Brad (1993a) '"Digital Cinematography": A Phrase of the Future? (Part 1)', *American Cinematographer*, 74(4): 31–2.

Fisher, Brad (1993b) '"Digital Cinematography": A Phrase of the Future? (Part 2)', *American Cinematographer*, 74(5): 50–2.

Frow, John (2000) 'Public Domain and the New World Order in Knowledge', *Social Semiotics* 19(2): 173–85.

Gillespie, Tarleton (2006) 'Designed to "effectively frustrate": copyright, technology and the agency of users', *New Media and Society*, 8(4): 651–69.

Goldwater, Chuck (2002) Interview by author. Audio recording. Hollywood, 22 June.

Gray, Frank and Sheppard, Eileen (2004) 'Promoting Moving Image Archive Collections in the Emerging Digital Age', *The Moving Image*, 4(2): 110–118.

Gunning, Tom (1986) 'The Cinema of Attraction: Early Film, Its Spectator and the Avant-Garde', *Wide Angle*, 8(3–4): 63–70.

Hall, David and Williams, Fiona (2006) 'Industry Panel: Digital Cinema: Why the Delay?', *Encore*, 24(8): 17–19, 62, 64.

Hoffmann, Kay (2004) 'Celluloid Goes Digital', *The Moving Image*, 4(1): 161–4.

Horak, Jan-Christopher (2003) 'Old Media become new', in Martin Loiperdinger (ed.), *Celluloid goes digital: Historical-critical editions of films on DVD and the internet*. Trier: Wissenschaftlicher. pp. 13–22.

Jardin, Xeni (2005) 'Thinking outside the box office', *Wired*, 13(12). Available at: http://www.wired.com/wired/archive/13.12/.

Jenkins, Henry (2006) *Fans, Bloggers, and Gamers: Exploring Participatory Culture*. New York: New York University Press.

Karagosian, Michael (2002) Interview by author. Audio recording. Hollywood, 19 November.

Karagosian, Michael (2006) 'Digital Cinema Progress?'. Available at: http://www.mkpe.com/publications/digital_cinema/presentations/2006–Sep%20IBC%20-%20Karagosian.pdf.

Katz, Michael, Frelinghuysen, John and Bhatia, Kristan (2002) *Digital Cinema: Breaking the Logjam*. Virginia: Booz Allen Hamilton.

Kelly, Kevin and Parisi, Paula (1997) 'Beyond *Star Wars*: What's Next For George Lucas', *Wired*, 5(2): 160–6. Available at: http://www.wired.com/5.02/features/fflucas.htm.

King, Geoff (2000) *Spectacular narratives: Hollywood in the age of the blockbuster*. London: I.B. Tauris.

Kracauer, Siegfried (1960) *Theory of Film: The Redemption of Physical Reality*. London: Oxford University Press.

Le Grice, Malcolm (2001) 'Computer as film art', in *Experimental Cinema in the Digital Age*. London: BFI Publishing. pp. 219–33.

Lesnie, Andrew (1997) Interview by author. Audio recording. Sydney, 12 May.

Levin, Julian (2002) Interview by author. Audio recording. Los Angeles, 19 November.

Magid, Ron (1997) 'George Lucas: Past, Present and Future', *American Cinematographer*, 78(2): 48–54.

Manovich, Lev (1999) 'What is Digital Cinema?'. Available at: http://jupiter.ucsd.edu/~manovich/text/digital-cinema.html.

Manovich, Lev (2001) *The Language of New Media*. Cambridge, MA: MIT Press.

Marshall, P. David (2004) *New Media Cultures*. London: Arnold.

McQuire, Scott (1997) *Crossing the Digital Threshold*. Brisbane/Sydney: Australian Key Centre for Culture and Media Policy/Australian Film Commission.

McQuire, Scott (2006) 'The Politics of Public Space in the Media City', *First Monday*, 4. Available at: http://www.firstmonday.org/issues/special11_2/mcquire/index.html.

Mitry, Jean (1963–5) *Esthétique et psychologie du cinema*. 2 vols. Paris: Editions universitaires.

Mitry, Jean (1998) *The Aesthetics and Psychology of the Cinéma*. Tr. Christopher King. Bloomington: Indiana University Press.

Mosco, Vincent (2004) *The Digital Sublime: Myth, Power, and Cyberspace*. Cambridge, MA: MIT Press.

Motion Picture Association of America (MPAA) (2005a) 'MPAA Chief Testifies in Front of House Judiciary Committee', 3 November. Available at: http://www.mpaa.org/PressReleases.asp.

Motion Picture Association of America (MPAA) (2005b) 'Piracy Data Summary'. Available at: http://www.mpaa.org/researchStatistics.asp.

Motion Picture Association of America (MPAA) (2006) '2006 U.S. Theatrical Market Statistics'. Available at: http://www.mpaa.org/researchStatistics.asp.

Parisi, Paula (1995) 'The New Hollywood', *Wired*, 3(12). Available at: http://www.wired.com/wired/archive/3.12/new.hollywood.html.

Parisi, Paula (1996a) 'Cameron Angle', *Wired*, 4(4). Available at: http://www.wired.com/archive/4.04/cameron/html.

Parisi, Paula (1996b) 'Shot by an Outlaw', *Wired*, 4(9). Available at: http://www.wired.com/wired/archive/4.09/billups.html.

Pierson, Michelle (1999) 'CGI Effects in Hollywood Science Fiction Cinema 1989–95', *Screen*, 40(2): 158–76.

Prince, Stephen (1996) 'True Lies: Perceptual Realism, Digital Images and Film Theory', *Film Quarterly*, 49(3): 27–38.

Ravid, S. Abraham (2005) 'Film Production in the Digital Age – What Do We Know about the Past and the Future?', in Charles Moul (ed.), *A Concise Handbook of Movie Industry Economics*. Cambridge: Cambridge University Press. pp. 32–58.

Savage, Roger (1997) Interview by author. Audio recording. Melbourne, 22 May.

Schwarz, Charles (2002) Interview by author. Audio recording. Los Angeles, 18 November.

Seabrook, John (1997) 'Why Is The Force Still With Us?', *New Yorker*, 6 January: 53.

Trinh, T. Minh-Ha (2005) *The Digital Film Event*. New York: Routledge.

Valenti, Jack (1982) 'Testimony at "Home Recording of Copyrighted Works"', Hearings before the Subcommittee of Courts, Civil Liberties, and the Administration of Justice of the Committee of the Judiciary of House of Representatives, Second Session, 12 April, US Government Printing Office. Available at: http://cryptome.org/hrcw-hear.htm.

Vogel, Harold (2005) 'Movie Industry Accounting', in Charles Moul (ed.), *A Concise Handbook of Movie Industry Economics*. Cambridge: Cambridge University Press. pp. 59–79.

Wang, Shujen (2003) 'Recontextualizing copyright: piracy, Hollywood, the state and globalization', *Cinema Journal*, 43(1): 25–43.

Waterman, David (2005) *Hollywood's Road to Riches*. Cambridge, MA: Harvard University Press.

Yar, Majid (2005) 'The global "epidemic" of movie "piracy": crime-wave or social construction', *Media, Culture and Society*, 27(5): 677–96.

Young, Paul (1999) 'The Negative Reinvention of Cinema: Late Hollywood in the Early Digital Age', *Convergence*, 5(2): 24–50.

Zimmerman, Patricia (2001) 'Morphing history into histories: from amateur film to the archive of the future', *Moving Image*, 1(1): 109–30.

Index